Constitutional Law for a Changing America

Eighth Edition

Constitutional Law for a Changing America
A Short Course
Eighth Edition

Lee Epstein
Washington University in St. Louis

Kevin T. McGuire
The University of North Carolina at Chapel Hill

Thomas G. Walker
Emory University

FOR INFORMATION:

CQ Press
An Imprint of SAGE Publications, Inc.
2455 Teller Road
Thousand Oaks, California 91320
E-mail: order@sagepub.com

SAGE Publications Ltd.
1 Oliver's Yard
55 City Road
London EC1Y 1SP
United Kingdom

SAGE Publications India Pvt. Ltd.
B 1/I 1 Mohan Cooperative Industrial Area
Mathura Road, New Delhi 110 044
India

SAGE Publications Asia-Pacific Pte. Ltd.
18 Cross Street #10-10/11/12
China Square Central
Singapore 048423

Acquisitions Editor: Scott Greenan
Content Development Editor: Jennifer Jovin-Bernstein
Editorial Assistant: Lauren Younker
Production Editor: Veronica Stapleton Hooper
Copy Editor: Colleen Brennan
Typesetter: C&M Digitals (P) Ltd.
Indexer: Integra
Cover Designer: Scott Van Atta
Marketing Manager: Erica DeLuca

Printed in the United States of America

Library of Congress Cataloging-in-Publication Data

Names: Epstein, Lee, 1958- author. | McGuire, Kevin T., author. | Walker, Thomas G., 1945- author.

Title: Constitutional law for a changing America : a short course / Lee J. Epstein, Washington University in St. Louis; Kevin T. McGuire, University of North Carolina at Chapel Hill; Thomas G. Walker, Emory University.

Description: Eighth edition. | Thousand Oaks, California : CQ Press, an Imprint of SAGE Publications, Inc., [2021] | Includes bibliographical references and index.

Identifiers: LCCN 2020018158 | ISBN 9781544390628 (paperback) | ISBN 9781544390635 (epub) | ISBN 9781544390642 (epub) | ISBN 9781544390659 (pdf)

Subjects: LCSH: Constitutional law—United States. | Civil rights—United States.

Classification: LCC KF4749 .E668 2021 | DDC 342.73—dc23
LC record available at https://lccn.loc.gov/2020018158

This book is printed on acid-free paper.

SUSTAINABLE FORESTRY INITIATIVE

Certified Chain of Custody
Promoting Sustainable Forestry
www.sfiprogram.org
SFI-01268

SFI label applies to text stock

20 21 22 23 24 10 9 8 7 6 5 4 3 2 1

BRIEF CONTENTS

DETAILED CONTENTS

CHRONOLOGICAL TABLE OF CASES

TABLES, FIGURES, AND BOXES

BOXES

PREFACE

OVER THE PAST two decades or so, constitutional law texts for political science courses have experienced a radical change. At one time, relatively short volumes, containing either excerpts from landmark cases or narratives of them, dominated the market. Now, large, almost mammoth books abound—some in single volumes, others in two volumes, but all designed for a two-semester sequence.

This trend, while fitting compatibly with the needs of many instructors, bypassed others, including those who teach institutional powers, civil liberties, rights, and justice in a single academic term and those who prefer a shorter core text. *Constitutional Law for a Changing America: A Short Course* was designed as an alternative text for these instructors. The first edition appeared in 1996. Its positive reception encouraged us to prepare subsequent editions—including this, the eighth edition.

Like its predecessors, this edition of *A Short Course* seeks to combine the best features of the traditional, concise volumes—it interweaves excerpts of the U.S. Supreme Court's most important decisions and narratives of major developments in the law. For example, our discussion of the right to counsel offers not only the landmark decision *Gideon v. Wainwright* (1963) but also an account of the critical cases preceding *Gideon*, such as **Powell v. Alabama** (1932), and those following it, such as **Scott v. Illinois** (1979). (*Note:* Boldface here and throughout the book indicates cases we analyze in the text and excerpt in the book's archive. More details on the archive follow.)

At the same time, we thought it important to move beyond the traditional texts and write a book that reflects the exciting nature of constitutional law. In doing so, we were not without guidance. For more than two decades we have been producing *Constitutional Law for a Changing America*, now moving into its eleventh edition. This two-volume book, we believe, provides an accessible yet sophisticated and contemporary take on the subject.

A Short Course, then, although presenting cases and other materials in ways quite distinct from our two-volume book, maintains some of its most desirable features. First, we approach constitutional law, as we do in the *Constitutional Law for a Changing America* series, from a social science perspective, demonstrating how many forces—not just legal factors—influence the development of the law. The justices carry out their duties in the context of the political, historical, economic, and social environment that surrounds them. Accordingly, throughout *A Short Course*, we highlight how relevant political, historical, economic, and social events; personnel changes on the Court; interest groups; and even public opinion may have affected the justices' decisions, in addition to traditional legal considerations, such as precedent, text, and history.

Second, just as our two-volume set seeks to animate the subject, so, too, does *A Short Course*. To us and, we suspect, most instructors, constitutional law is an exciting subject, but we realize that some students may not (at least initially) share our enthusiasm. To whet their appetites, we develop the human side of landmark litigation. Where possible, we include photographs of litigants and places that figured prominently in cases. For each excerpted case, we provide a detailed description, in accessible prose, of the dispute that gave rise to the suit. Students are spared the task of digging out facts from Court opinions and can plunge ahead to the ruling with the contours of the dispute firmly in mind. We also present information about the political environment surrounding various cases in tables, figures, and boxes that supplement the narrative and case excerpts.

Third, because many adopters of *Constitutional Law for a Changing America* commented favorably on the supporting material we provide in those volumes, we maintain that feature in *A Short Course*. Along these lines, chapter 2, "Understanding the U.S. Supreme Court," reviews not only the procedures the Court uses to decide cases but also the various legal and extralegal approaches scholars have invoked to understand and explain why the Court rules as it does. Fourth, *A Short Course* takes advantage of the expanding resources available to students of constitutional law that can be found on the Internet. With each excerpted opinion we provide locations online where students may read the full, unabridged decision. We also alert students whenever the oral arguments for a case have been made available on the Internet by the Oyez Project.

With each edition we attempt to enhance the coverage and accessibility of the material, and this eighth edition is no exception. The most significant changes are in the individual chapters. We have thoroughly updated each to include important opinions handed down during the Roberts Court era. Since Chief Justice John G. Roberts took office in 2005, the Court has taken up many pressing issues of the day, including, of course, health care; we've thus excerpted, in chapters 7 ("The Commerce Power") and 8 ("The Power to Tax and Spend"), the major dispute over the 2010 Patient Protection and Affordable Care Act (often referred to as Obamacare), *National Federation of Independent Business v. Sebelius* (2012). Then there's same-sex marriage, which we discuss in several chapters but especially in chapter 16 ("The Right to Privacy") where we excerpt *Obergefell v. Hodges* (2015), invalidating all existing state bans on the practice. We also excerpt other Roberts Court decisions of note, including *Carpenter v. United States* (2018), which addresses whether law enforcement's use of cell phone records without a warrant violates the Fourth Amendment; *Shelby County, Alabama v. Holder* (2013), which concerns the Voting Rights Act; and *Fisher v. the University of Texas* (2016), in which the justices consider the constitutionality of an affirmative action program. Other contemporary decisions have received less attention but are no less important for understanding constitutional law, including ***Zivotofsky v. Clinton*** (2012) (political question doctrine) and ***United States v. Comstock*** (2010) (the necessary and proper clause).

But readers will find more than just updating. We have tried to bring a fresh eye to each chapter, reconsidering all existing case excerpts and clarifying existing material. In the previous edition, we reworked some of the discussion relating to federalism (chapter 6) and the commerce clause (chapter 7) to highlight new developments. Here we continue along the same path, enhancing the Takings Clause chapter (chapter 11) to include a section on just compensation (along with an excerpt of *United States v. 564.54 Acres of Land*). Chapters 12 ("Religion") and 13 ("Freedom of Speech, Assembly, and Association") have received even more extensive facelifts. Recent decisions in the areas of legislative power (chapter 4), executive power (chapter 5), religion (chapter 12), privacy (chapter 16), and discrimination (chapter 19) also provided us

the opportunity to supplement and, we hope, further illuminate some important new and perennial topics. To provide one example, in chapter 4 we substituted *Gundy v. United States* (2019) for ***Mistretta v. United States*** (1989) to attend to debates among today's justices over the delegation of legislative powers.

These are but a few examples of the many changes we have made throughout the book. At the same time, we have retained and enhanced two innovative features from previous editions. The first is a series of "Aftermath" boxes sprinkled throughout the text. These boxes are a response to our own experiences in the classroom when confronted with questions such as "Whatever happened to Ernesto Miranda?" The Aftermath boxes discuss what occurred after the Supreme Court handed down its decision. In addition to providing human interest material, they lead to interesting discussions about the Court's impact on the lives of ordinary Americans. We hope these materials demonstrate to students that Supreme Court cases are more than merely legal names and citations; they involve real people involved in real disputes.

The second feature we have retained and expanded reflects our effort to respond to an inevitable question facing any author of a constitutional law text: Which Supreme Court cases should be included? Other than classic decisions such as *Marbury v. Madison*, instructors have differing ideas about which cases best illustrate the various points of constitutional law. Each has his or her list of personal favorites, but given the page limitations of a printed book, not every instructor's preferences can be satisfied.

We have attempted to overcome this problem by creating, and regularly updating, an electronic archive of more than three hundred supplemental Supreme Court decisions. These cases are excerpted using the same format as the case excerpts that appear in this printed volume. The archive allows instructors to use additional cases or to substitute favorite cases for those that appear in the printed text. The archive also provides an efficient source of material for students who want to read more deeply into the law and for instructors who wish to direct their students to an easily accessible information source for paper assignments. The cases included in the archive are identified in the text in bold italic type. The archive can be accessed online at http://edge.sagepub.com/conlaw.

We keep the electronic archive current between printed editions. Instructors and students no longer must wait until the next edition is published to have ready access to recent rulings presented in a format designed for classroom use.

WELCOMING A NEW COAUTHOR

After nearly five decades of teaching law-related courses to undergraduate and PhD students (including Lee Epstein), Tom Walker has taken on the much-deserved status as an emeritus professor. Although Professor Walker will always be a member of the *Constitutional Law for a Changing America* team, he has stepped back from the day-to-day responsibilities of producing the volumes.

It is with great pleasure then that we welcome Kevin T. McGuire of the University of North Carolina at Chapel Hill as a coauthor for the entire *Constitutional Law for a Changing America* series—beginning with this edition of *A Short Course*. If you are familiar with Professor McGuire's justifiably famous work on the U.S. Supreme Court, lawyers, and judicial-legislative relations, you know that he is a meticulous scholar and an excellent writer. He is also a superb teacher, with deep expertise in all topics covered in *Constitutional Law for a Changing America*. A better coauthor Epstein and Walker could not imagine!

Sara Miller McCune founded SAGE Publishing in 1965 to support the dissemination of usable knowledge and educate a global community. SAGE publishes more than 1000 journals and over 600 new books each year, spanning a wide range of subject areas. Our growing selection of library products includes archives, data, case studies and video. SAGE remains majority owned by our founder and after her lifetime will become owned by a charitable trust that secures the company's continued independence.

Los Angeles | London | New Delhi | Singapore | Washington DC | Melbourne

ACKNOWLEDGMENTS

The roots of this eighth edition of *A Short Course* extend back to our two-volume book. As a consequence, those who influenced the development of the original version of *Constitutional Law for a Changing America* influenced this project as well. We are particularly grateful to our four former editors, Joanne Daniels, Brenda Carter, Charisse Kiino, and Monica Eckman, as well as our current editor, Scott Greenan. Joanne conceived of a constitutional law book that would be accessible, sophisticated, and contemporary. She brought the concept to our attention and helped us develop it. Brenda guided us through the completion of the project and its subsequent editions and urged us to go forward with *A Short Course*. Her support for our projects was constant and strong, and her advice always wise. Charisse brought new enthusiasm and ideas to this book. Her responsiveness to our needs and requests was extraordinary. Working with her was a joy. Monica Eckman came aboard just as we were completing the seventh edition, and she provided us with terrific support and encouragement as we continued to develop the *Constitutional Law for a Changing America* books and supplementary materials.

Other members of the CQ Press team also deserve our thanks and praise. Neither of us is quite sure what we would have done without Carolyn Goldinger, our copy editor for many earlier editions of the *Constitutional Law for a Changing America* series. To call her "our copy editor" is true enough. But she did so much more than perfect our writing and check our facts. She contributed so many ideas for presentation and content that our books would have been far the worse without her. We'll never be able to thank her enough. Judy Selhorst and Gretchen Treadwell, who copyedited more recent versions of our books, more than filled Carolyn's shoes. After nearly three decades of producing this series, it might seem that a copy editor would be left with little to hone, query, or correct. Not so. Colleen Brennan, our most recent copy editor, has done a fabulous job improving this volume in ways big and small. We are very grateful for all her efforts on our behalf. We also owe a debt of gratitude to our content development editor, Jennifer Jovin-Bernstein; editorial assistant, Lauren Younker; and production editor, Veronica Stapleton Hooper. Finally, other members of the CQ Press family, too numerous to mention, brought ideas, enthusiasm, and efficiency to the project.

Over the years, we have also benefited from the suggestions of numerous scholars who read our manuscripts, offered suggestions, provided data, or shared their thoughts about constitutional law. We are especially grateful to Judith A. Baer, Ralph Baker, Lawrence Baum, Robert W. Bennett, John Brigham, Rebecca Brown, Gregory A. Caldeira, Bradley C. Canon, Robert A. Carp, Phillip J. Cooper, Sue Davis, Jolly Emrey, John Fliter, John B. Gates, Leslie Goldstein, Edward V. Heck, Dennis Hutchinson, Jack Knight, Joseph F. Kobylka, Adam Liptak, John A. Maltese, Wayne McIntosh, Susan Mezey, Richard L. Pacelle Jr., Martin H. Redish, C. K. Rowland, Jeffrey A. Segal, Donald Songer, Harold Spaeth, and Harry P. Stumpf. We would like to thank John Brigham of the University of Massachusetts, Paula A. Franzese of Barnard College, Lori Cox Han of Austin College, Gordon P. Henderson of Widener University, Susanna Peters of Michigan Technological University, Chris Edelson of American University, Marshall DeRosa of Florida Atlantic University, Donna Merrell of Kennesaw State University, Meg Hobday of Hamline University, Angela Narasimhan of Idaho State University, Joseph Ross of Florida Gulf Coast University, Andrew Trees of Roosevelt University, Laura Wing, of California State University East Bay, Wendy Brame of Briar Cliff University, Lara Schwartz of American University, Harold A. Young of Austin Peay State University, Eric Schwartz of Hagerstown Community College, Jennifer Woodward of Middle Tennessee State University, and Kristen Coopie of Duquesne University for their suggestions. We are also grateful to those instructors and students who have used *Constitutional Law for a Changing America* and sent us comments and suggestions, especially Akiba J. Covitz, Alec C. Ewald, Neil Snortland, and Melvin I. Urofsky.

Finally, we acknowledge the encouragement of our friends and families. We are forever grateful to our former professors for instilling in us their genuine interest in and curiosity about things judicial and legal and to our home institutions for providing substantial support of our efforts.

Any errors of omission or commission, of course, remain our sole responsibility. We encourage students and instructors alike to comment on the book and to inform us of any errors. Contact us at *epstein@wustl.edu* or *kmcguire@unc.edu*.

THE U.S. CONSTITUTION

EQUAL·JUSTICE·UNDER

ACCORDING TO James Madison, "The happy Union of these States is a wonder; their Constitution a miracle; their example the hope of Liberty throughout the world. Woe to the ambition that would meditate the destruction of either." In a very real sense, the U.S. Constitution is a marvel. It was crafted in an environment of political uncertainty, and its success was by no means certain. Not only has it survived, it has demonstrated its strength, as well, weathering challenges and change that its authors scarcely could have foreseen. Even after two and a quarter centuries, the document remains the foundation for the structure of American government; it is the world's oldest written constitution.[1] This is especially impressive, given that most constitutions hardly endure for a generation. Since the Constitution was ratified in 1789, national constitutions around the world have lasted an average of only seventeen years.[2]

In what follows, we provide a brief introduction to the U.S. Constitution—in particular, the circumstances under which it was written, the basic principles underlying it, and some controversies surrounding it. This material may not be new to you, but it is especially important to review, since these concerns frequently frame and inform how the Supreme Court interprets the Constitution.

THE ROAD TO THE U.S. CONSTITUTION

While the fledgling United States was fighting for its independence from England, it was being run (and the war conducted) by the Continental Congress. Although this body had no formal authority, it met in session from 1774 through the end of the war in 1781, establishing itself as a de facto government. But it may have been something more than that: About a year into the Revolutionary War, the Continental Congress took steps toward nationhood. On July 2, 1776, it passed a resolution declaring the "United Colonies free and independent states." Two days later, on July 4, it formalized this proclamation in the Declaration of Independence, in which the nation's founders used the term *United States of America* for the first time.[3] But even before the adoption of the Declaration of Independence, the Continental Congress had selected a group of delegates to make recommendations for the formation of a national government. Composed of representatives of each of the thirteen colonies, this committee labored for several months to produce a proposal for a national charter, the Articles of Confederation.[4] Congress passed the proposal and submitted it to the states for ratification in November 1777. Ratification was achieved in March 1781, when Maryland—a two-year holdout—gave its approval.

The Articles of Confederation, however, had little effect on the way the government operated; instead, the articles more or less institutionalized practices that had developed under the Continental Congress (1774–1781). Rather than provide for a compact between the people and the government, the 1781 charter institutionalized "a league of friendship" among the states, an agreement that rested on strong notions of state sovereignty. Having just fought successfully for independence from what they perceived as "repeated injuries and usurpations" by a distant, overbearing government, they were naturally wary of concentrating power. This is not to suggest that the charter failed to provide for a central government. As is apparent in Figure I-1, which depicts the structure and powers of government under the Articles of Confederation, the articles created a national governing apparatus, however simple and weak. The plan created a one-house legislature, with members appointed as the state legislatures directed, but with no formal federal executive or judiciary. And although the legislature had some power, most notably in foreign affairs, it derived its authority from the states that had created it and not from the people.

---

[1]Technically, the small microstate of San Marino, located completely within the nation of Italy, has the oldest constitution, but it is not a single document. It consists of a series of books that date to 1600.

[2]Zachary Elkins, Tom Ginsburg, and James Melton, *The Endurance of National Constitutions* (Cambridge: Cambridge University Press, 2009).

[3]The text of the Declaration of Independence is available at http://avalon.law.yale.edu/18th_century/declare.asp.

[4]The full text of the Articles of Confederation is available at http://avalon.law.yale.edu/18th_century/artconf.asp.

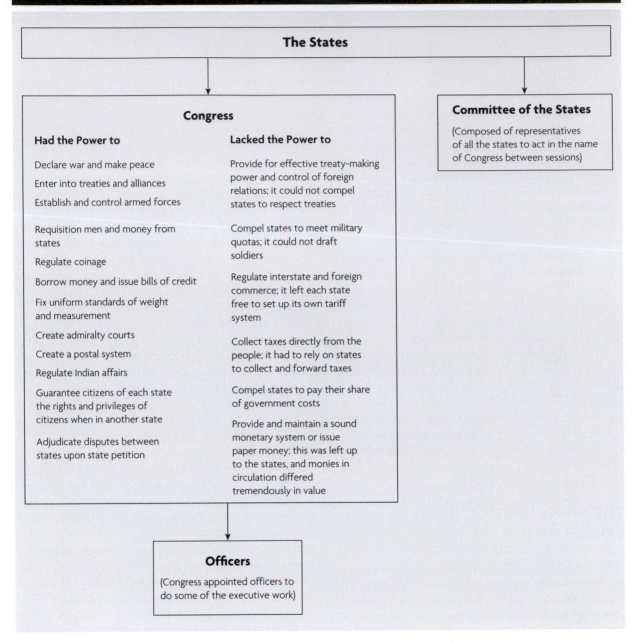

The States

Congress

Had the Power to

Declare war and make peace

Enter into treaties and alliances

Establish and control armed forces

Requisition men and money from states

Regulate coinage

Borrow money and issue bills of credit

Fix uniform standards of weight and measurement

Create admiralty courts

Create a postal system

Regulate Indian affairs

Guarantee citizens of each state the rights and privileges of citizens when in another state

Adjudicate disputes between states upon state petition

Lacked the Power to

Provide for effective treaty-making power and control of foreign relations; it could not compel states to respect treaties

Compel states to meet military quotas; it could not draft soldiers

Regulate interstate and foreign commerce; it left each state free to set up its own tariff system

Collect taxes directly from the people; it had to rely on states to collect and forward taxes

Compel states to pay their share of government costs

Provide and maintain a sound monetary system or issue paper money; this was left up to the states, and monies in circulation differed tremendously in value

Committee of the States

(Composed of representatives of all the states to act in the name of Congress between sessions)

Officers

(Congress appointed officers to do some of the executive work)

Source: Adapted from Steffen W. Schmidt, Mark C. Shelley II, and Barbara A. Bardes, *American Government and Politics Today,* 14th ed. (Boston: Wadsworth, 2008), 42.

The condition of the United States under the Articles of Confederation was less than satisfactory. Analysts have pointed out several weaknesses of the articles, including the following:

- Because it allowed Congress only to requisition funds and not to tax, the federal government was virtually broke. From 1781 to 1783 the national legislature requested $10 million from the states and received only $1.5 million. Given the foreign debts the United States had accumulated during the Revolution, this problem was particularly troublesome.

- Because Congress lacked any concrete way to regulate foreign commerce, treaties between the United States and other countries were of limited value. Some European nations (for example, England and Spain) took advantage by imposing restrictions on trade that made it difficult for America to export goods.

- Because the government lacked coercive power over the states, cooperation among them quickly dissipated. The states engaged in trading practices that hurt one another economically. In short, they acted more like thirteen separate countries than a union or even a confederation.

- Because the exercise of most national authority required the approval of nine states and because the passage of amendments required unanimity, the articles stymied Congress. Indeed, given the divisions among the states at the time, the approval of nine states for any action of substance was rare, and the required unanimity for amendment was never obtained.

Nevertheless, the government accomplished some notable objectives during the years the Articles of Confederation were in effect. Most critical among these, it brought the Revolutionary War to a successful end and paved the way for the 1783 Treaty of Paris, which helped make the United States a presence on the international scene. The charter served another important purpose: it prevented the states from going their separate ways until a better system could be put into place.

In the mid-1780s, as the articles' shortcomings were becoming more and more apparent, several dissidents, including James Madison of Virginia and Alexander Hamilton of New York, held a series of meetings to arouse interest in revising the system of government. At a session in Annapolis in September 1786, they urged the states to send delegations to another meeting scheduled for the following May in Philadelphia. Their plea could not have come at a more opportune time. Just the month before, a former Revolutionary War captain, Daniel Shays, had led disgruntled farmers in an armed rebellion in Massachusetts. They were protesting the poor state of the economy, particularly as it affected farmers.

Shays' Rebellion was suppressed by state forces, but it was seen as yet another sign that the Articles of Confederation needed amending. In February 1787 Congress issued a call for a convention to reevaluate the current national system. It was clear, however, that Congress did not want to scrap the articles; in fact, it stated that the delegates were to meet "for the sole and express purpose of revising the Articles of Confederation."

Despite these words, the convention's fifty-five delegates quickly realized that they would be doing more than "revising" the articles: they would be framing a new charter. We can attribute this change in purpose, at least in part, to the Virginia delegation. When the Virginians arrived in Philadelphia on May 14, the day the convention was supposed to start, only they and the Pennsylvania delegation were there. Although lacking a quorum, the Virginia contingent used the eleven days that elapsed before the rest of the delegates arrived to craft a series of proposals that called for a wholly new government structure composed of a strong three-branch national government empowered to lead the nation.

Known as the Virginia Plan, these proposals were formally introduced to all the delegates on May 29, just four days after the convention began. And although it was the target of a counterproposal submitted by the New Jersey delegation, the Virginia Plan set the tone for the convention. It served as the basis for many of the ensuing debates and, as we shall see, for the Constitution itself (see Table I-1). With the delegates now drafting an entirely new charter, they had to consider both the structure of the national government and its relationship to the states. Since the framers reflected competing political ideologies and represented diverse interests from across the states, one might well wonder how they were able to reach consensus—and do so in just four months.

A plausible explanation is that the Constitutional Convention was an assembly of very able men, the generation's leading lights of statecraft. According to historian Melvin I. Urofsky, "Few gatherings in the history of

Table I-1 The Virginia Plan, the New Jersey Plan, and the Constitution

Item	Virginia plan	New Jersey Plan	Constitution
Legislature	Two houses	One house	Two houses
Legislative representation	Both houses based on population	Equal for each state	One house based on population; one house with two votes from each state
Legislative power	Veto authority over state legislation	Authority to levy taxes and regulate commerce	Authority to levy taxes and regulate commerce; authority to compel state compliance with national policies
Executive	Single; elected by legislature for a single term	Plural; removable by majority of state legislatures	Single; chosen by Electoral College; removable by national legislature
Courts	National judiciary elected by legislature	No provision	Supreme Court appointed by executive, confirmed by Senate

this or any other country could boast such a concentration of talent." And, "despite [the framers'] average age of forty-two [they] had extensive experience in government and were fully conversant with political theories of the Enlightenment."[5] That certainly would have been apparent to observers at the time; Thomas Jefferson, who was serving as ambassador to France during the convention, observed that it was "an assembly of demigods." Indeed, they were an impressive group. Thirty-three had served in the Revolutionary War, forty-two had attended the Continental Congress, and two had signed the Declaration of Independence. Two would go on to serve as U.S. presidents, sixteen as governors, and two as chief justices of the United States.

Nevertheless, some commentators take issue with this rosy portrait of the framers. Because they were a relatively homogeneous lot—white men, well-educated, and affluent—skeptics suggest that the document the framers produced was biased in various ways. This point of view was expressed by historian Charles Beard in *An Economic Interpretation of the Constitution of the United States*, which depicts the framers as self-serving. Beard says the Constitution was an "economic document" devised to protect the "property interests" of those who wrote it.

Various scholars have refuted this view, and Beard's work, in particular, has been largely negated by other studies.[6] Still, *by today's standards*, it is impossible to deny that the original Constitution discriminated on the basis of race and sex or that the framers wrote it in a way that benefited their class. As Justice Thurgood Marshall once observed, the Constitution was "defective from the start"; despite its first words, "We the People," it excluded "the majority of American citizens" because it left out blacks and women. He further alleged that the framers "could not have imagined, nor would they have accepted, that the document they were drafting would one day be construed by a Supreme Court to which had been appointed a woman and the descendant of an African slave."[7] Over time, of course, Americans have revised the Constitution to make it substantially more egalitarian.

This is not to suggest that controversies surrounding the Constitution no longer exist. To the contrary,

---

[5]Melvin I. Urofsky and Paul Finkelman, *A March of Liberty*, 2nd ed. (New York: Oxford University Press, 2002), 94–95.

---

[6]See, for example, Robert E. Brown's *Charles Beard and the Constitution* (Princeton, NJ: Princeton University Press, 1956). Brown concludes, "[W]e would be doing a grave injustice to the political sagacity of the Founding Fathers if we assumed that property or personal gain was their only motive" (198).

[7]Quoted in *Washington Post*, May 7, 1987. See also Thurgood Marshall, "Reflections on the Bicentennial of the United States Constitution," *Harvard Law Review* 101 (1987): 1–5.

charges abound that the document has retained an elitist or otherwise biased flavor. Some argue that the amending process is too cumbersome, that it is too slanted toward the will of the majority. Others point to the Supreme Court as the culprit, asserting that its interpretation of the document—particularly at certain points in history—has reinforced the framers' biases.

Throughout this volume, you will have many opportunities to evaluate these claims. They will be especially evident in cases involving economic liberties—those that ask the Court, in some sense, to adjudicate claims between the privileged and the underdogs in society. For now, let us consider some of the basic features of that controversial document—the U.S. Constitution.

UNDERLYING PRINCIPLES OF THE CONSTITUTION

Table I-1 sets forth the basic proposals considered at the convention and how they got translated into the Constitution. What it does not show are the fundamental principles underlying, but not necessarily explicit in, the Constitution. Three are particularly important: the separation of powers, with checks and balances to govern relations among the branches of national government; federalism, which governs relations between the states and the national government; and the principle of individual rights and liberties, which governs relations between the government and the people.

Separation of Powers with Checks and Balances

One of the fundamental weaknesses of the Articles of Confederation was their failure to establish a strong and authoritative federal government. The articles created a national legislature, but that body had few powers, and those it did have were kept in check by the states. The new U.S. Constitution overcame this deficiency by creating a national government invested with a host of explicit powers and significant authority independent of the states. Despite their desire to invigorate national power, though, the framers were also aware that power could be abused, especially when it was concentrated. One guard against such abuse was to diffuse authority, to divide and disperse it rather than allow it to be centralized. By creating a national government with three branches—the legislature, the executive, and the judiciary—and providing each with its own set of responsibilities, the members of the convention sought to limit the possibility of arbitrary and oppressive policy making.

The framers did not consider the separation of powers sufficient protection, however. As depicted in Figure I-2, they allowed each branch to impose limits on the primary functions of the others through the use of checking powers. Before Congress could enact legislation, it would need the support of the president. The president could not make treaties without supervision from the Senate. If the president, as commander in chief, had designs on entering into foreign conflicts, the Congress retained the power to declare war as well as the fiscal authority to refuse to pay for the executive's ambitions. The Supreme Court may have been empowered to interpret federal law, but the president and Senate together limit the Court when selecting its members. In addition to these checking powers, the framers included a number of institutional balances: they made each element of the national government responsible to a different constituency and had them all selected on different timetables. This made it unlikely that the national government could be overwhelmed by the prevailing passions of the day.

These various institutional designs underscored the framers' pessimism about human nature. They were realists; as Madison observed, in steering the ship of government, "[e]lightened statesmen will not always be at the helm." The solution was to craft a government that incorporated their distrust. "Ambition must be made to counteract ambition."

Federalism

Another flaw in the Articles of Confederation was how the document envisioned the relationship between the national government and the states. As already noted, the Congress under the articles was not just weak—it was more or less an apparatus controlled by the states. Remember that, only a few years earlier, most Americans thought of themselves as residents of British colonies—the Connecticut Colony, the Delaware Colony, the Colony of Virginia, and so on. Now they were independent states, and their citizens did not necessarily have a "national" consciousness. The Articles of Confederation reflected that view; the states were the center of political life.

Some of the delegates at the convention—most notably, Alexander Hamilton—greatly preferred national power over state authority and proposed to place there as much control as possible. Under the articles, states had often pursued their own particular interests, attempting to raise revenue by charging tariffs on goods passing across their borders. These "rival, conflicting, and angry regulations," as Madison called them, hindered national economic growth.

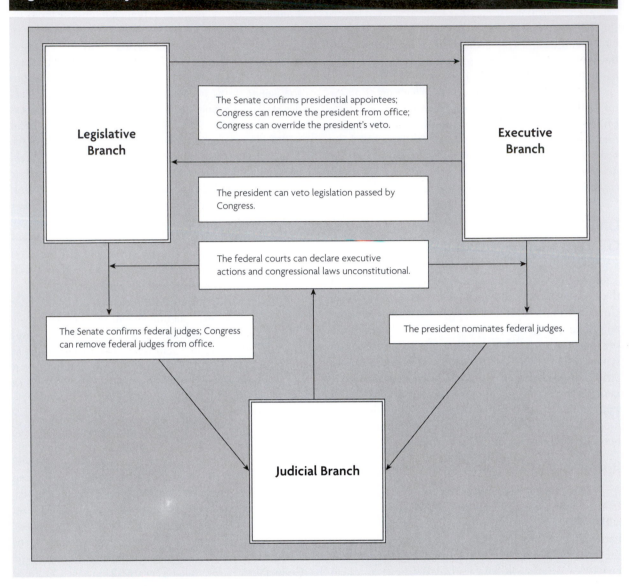

Legislative Branch

The Senate confirms presidential appointees; Congress can remove the president from office; Congress can override the president's veto.

Executive Branch

The president can veto legislation passed by Congress.

The federal courts can declare executive actions and congressional laws unconstitutional.

The Senate confirms federal judges; Congress can remove federal judges from office.

The president nominates federal judges.

Judicial Branch

Other delegates, by contrast, were quite worried about ceding any power to a new national government. After all, the states were sovereign entities. Skeptical of national authority, they believed that a republican government worked best on a localized level, where policy makers were more likely to be attuned to the needs and desires of those whom they represented. Fortunately, the framers were familiar with the political philosophies of Enlightenment thinkers, and one of the most prominent was Montesquieu. This French lawyer had written an influential book on democratic theory, *The Spirit of the Laws*, and it contained a number of ideas that appealed to the framers. Most notably, he proposed what he called a "confederate republic," a government that was composed of *both* a national government limited by the separation of powers and smaller individual governments. By his logic, the national government would provide strength and protect the nation in foreign affairs and the smaller, local governments could better reflect the interests of the people in crafting domestic policy. Although the delegates modified the specifics of Montesquieu's plan, they adopted its broad principles. Thus, federalism became a key element of the framers' design, one that was meant to appeal to both sides of the debate over national versus state power.

Under this framework, the states agreed to relinquish only some of their sovereignty. The national government would be one of limited authority, restricted to exercising only those powers that were enumerated in the Constitution. Although the Constitution and the laws written by Congress were to be "the supreme law of the land," the states retained all of the remaining power.

This strategy both enlarged and limited the power of the national government, but the Constitution still left unanswered many questions about federal-state relations. For example, would the national government be empowered to exercise other, non-explicit powers in order to carry out its explicit obligations? What would happen if Congress, in exercising one of its explicit powers, regulated something that might have been reserved to the states? Could states judge for themselves the meaning of national law? As you will see, the Supreme Court has played a prominent role in defining the boundaries of federal and state power by answering these questions. In so doing, it has helped shape the contours of American federalism.

Individual Rights and Liberties

The Constitutional Convention was called in response to conditions resulting from the ineffectiveness of government under the Articles of Confederation. For that reason, most of the efforts in Philadelphia were focused on the creation of a new governmental structure, with careful attention given to the powers the national government could wield and appropriate limitations to be placed on those powers. The document that emerged from the convention reflected that emphasis.

The prominence of issues of governmental powers and structure, however, did not mean that the framers had forgotten the purposes of the Revolution. The war for independence had ended only a few years before the convention met. The values of individual liberty and freedom, over which the war was fought, were still fresh in the framers' minds. There is no doubt that safeguarding those rights remained a high priority. In fact, records of the debates indicate that some of the delegates offered specific guarantees of individual rights. George Mason, Charles Pinckney, and Edmund Randolph, for example, all proposed to enumerate rights in the Constitution,

but their efforts could muster no support.[8] Mason, the author of the Virginia Declaration of Rights, refused to sign the Constitution because it failed to include explicit limits on the powers of the national government.

It is therefore a puzzle to many that the Constitution drafted in Philadelphia had only scant references to individual rights and liberties. Other than prohibiting government from passing ex post facto laws or bills of attainder—that is, laws that punish retroactively or legislative declarations that convict and punish—the framers included no explicit limitations. How could such a fundamental governing document produced by those who had led the nation to its independence fail to include a systematic statement of basic freedoms?

One explanation is that the central concern of the convention was increasing, not decreasing, the authority of the national government. In light of the failures of the Articles of Confederation, creating a government that had ample power to stabilize the economy and stimulate growth was the highest priority. There was no immediate civil liberties crisis; oppressive English rule had been overthrown. Moreover, the states all had their own bills of rights that protected individual liberties.

Another reason, according to some of the framers, was that the Constitution itself served to limit the power of the national government. Hamilton and Madison, for instance, pointed out that the national government was one of limited powers, granted by the states. By enumerating power—by explicitly stating what Congress *may* do—the Constitution, in fact, protected rights—by implicitly stating what Congress *may not* do. Not only that, Madison believed that abuses of individual rights were much more likely to take place at the state level, where local populations were more homogenous and thus more likely to be intolerant of political minorities. If national power was to be feared, he was optimistic that the checks and limitations the framers imposed would be sufficient to block abuses of personal liberty.

In addition, there was a more practical problem facing the delegates. By the time the convention had resolved matters of governmental structure and power, the delegates understandably were exhausted. Leaving behind their personal businesses and occupations, they had spent May through September confined together in a hot and humid room, engaged in intense debates and

---

[8]This information comes from Daniel A. Farber and Suzanna Sherry, *A History of the American Constitution*, 2nd ed. (St. Paul, MN: Thomson/West, 2005), 316–317. This book reprints verbatim debates over the Constitution and Bill of Rights.

negotiations. The prospect of spending additional time attempting to resolve questions of what liberties should be included in a bill of rights and how those rights should be stated was not an attractive one. Yet the question of a bill of rights would not go away. Once the states set about debating ratification of the proposed Constitution, one of the primary complaints was that it lacked a bill of rights. Many argued that despite the various restraints on governmental power placed in the document, the new government would have the potential to become a very powerful institution, and one that would be quite capable of depriving the people of their freedoms. This argument was particularly persuasive, and consequently ratification was placed in jeopardy. In response, supporters of the Constitution began to suggest a compromise: if the Constitution was ratified, one of the new government's first orders of business would be the drafting of a bill of rights to be added to the Constitution. That compromise took the form of the first ten amendments to the Constitution—the Bill of Rights. Since the ratification of the Bill of Rights, on December 15, 1791, those basic principles of the Constitution—separation of powers, federalism, and individual liberties and rights—have remained the defining features of American government. How the Constitution has been able to sustain those principles over time is a topic we consider in chapter 1.

CHAPTER ONE

THE LIVING CONSTITUTION

HOW HAS the Constitution of the United States endured as the oldest constitution on the earth? How has it survived the stresses of massive social, political, and economic upheaval? Constitutions are more likely to endure when they are flexible—that is, when "they provide reasonable mechanisms by which to amend and interpret the text to adjust to changing conditions."[1] Thus, part of the explanation for the long-lasting success of the American Constitution is that its meaning can be changed, either by constitutional amendment or by its interpretation by the members of the U.S. Supreme Court. It is, in a sense, a living constitution.

An important qualification, however, is that these changes reflect a genuine reconfiguration of fundamental values in society, not simply the regular movement of preferences that result from shifting political winds. One of the most revered figures in American legal history is Justice Joseph Story, whose *Commentaries on the Constitution of the United States* remains an indispensable analysis of the development of American law. Story spoke to precisely this issue—the need to balance stability and change—when he wrote:

> It is obvious that no human government can ever be perfect; and that it is impossible to foresee, or guard against all the exigencies which may, in different ages require different adaptations and modifications of powers to suit the various necessities of the people. A government, forever changing and changeable, is, indeed, in a state bordering upon anarchy and confusion. A government, which, in its own organization, provides no means of change, but assumes to be fixed and unalterable, must, after a while become wholly unsuited to the circumstances of the nation; and it will either degenerate into a despotism, or by the pressure of its inequalities bring on a revolution.[2]

As Story recognized, a Constitution too easily adjusted promotes chaos, and one that frustrates adaptation is too rigid. To that end, the framers required constitutional amendments to have overwhelming majority support across the nation. Likewise, by providing for life tenure for the members of the Supreme Court, they ensured that constitutional interpretation would not be in chronic flux, something that might well happen if the justices were subject to being replaced every few years.

In the following sections, we trace both means of effecting constitutional change. We examine how, through the amendment process and the Court's interpretation of the law, the Constitution has maintained its vitality over time.

THE AMENDMENT PROCESS

The framers were quite pleased with their handiwork; when the convention concluded, they "adjourned to City Tavern, dined together and took cordial leave of each other."[3] After the long, hot summer in Philadelphia,

---

[1]Tom Ginsburg, Zachary Elkins, and James Melton, "The Lifespan of Written Constitutions" (*UC Berkeley: Berkeley Program in Law and Economics*, 2007, retrieved from https://escholarship.org/uc/item/6jw9d0mf), 51.

[2]Joseph Story, *Commentaries on the Constitution of the United States*, 2nd ed. (Boston: Little, Brown, 1851), Book III, 564.

[3]*1787*, compiled by historians of the Independence National Historical Park (New York: Exeter Books, 1987), 191.

Table 1-1 The Ratification of the Constitution

State	Date of Action	Decision margin
Delaware	December 7, 1787	Ratified, 30–0
Pennsylvania	December 12, 1787	Ratified, 46–23
New Jersey	December 18, 1787	Ratified, 38–0
Georgia	December 31, 1787	Ratified, 26–0
Connecticut	January 8, 1788	Ratified, 128–40
Massachusetts	February 6, 1788	Ratified with amendments, 187–168
Maryland	April 26, 1788	Ratified, 63–11
South Carolina	May 23, 1788	Ratified with amendments, 149–73
New Hampshire	June 21, 1788	Ratified with amendments, 57–47
Virginia	June 25, 1788	Ratified with amendments, 89–79
New York	July 26, 1788	Ratified with amendments, 30–27
North Carolina	August 2, 1788	Rejected, 184–84
	November 21, 1789	Ratified with amendments, 194–77
Rhode Island	May 29, 1790	Ratified with amendments, 34–32

Sources: Ratifying documents in the Avalon Project at Yale Law School (http://www.yale.edu/lawweb/avalon/constpap.htm); Ralph Mitchell, *CQ's Guide to the U.S. Constitution,* 2nd ed. (Washington, DC: Congressional Quarterly, 1994), 28–30.

most of the delegates left for home, confident that the new document would receive speedy passage by the states. At first, it appeared as if their optimism was justified. As Table 1-1 depicts, before the year was out, four states had ratified the Constitution—three by unanimous votes. But after January 1788, the pace began to slow. By this time, a movement opposed to ratification was growing and marshaling arguments to deter delegates at state ratifying conventions. What these opponents, the Anti-Federalists, feared most was the Constitution's new balance of power. They believed that strong state governments provided the best defense against an inordinate concentration of power in the national government. The Constitution, they believed, tipped the scales too far in favor of federal authority.

These fears were countered by the Federalists, who supported ratification. Although their arguments and writings took many forms, among the most important was a series of eighty-five articles published in New York newspapers under the pen name "Publius." Written by John Jay, James Madison, and Alexander Hamilton, *The Federalist Papers* continue to provide insight into the objectives and intent of the founders.[4] Debates between the Federalists and their opponents often were highly philosophical in tone, with emphasis on the appropriate roles and powers of national institutions. In the states, however, ratification drives were full of the stuff of ordinary politics—deal making. Massachusetts provides a case in point. After three weeks of debate among the delegates, Federalist leaders there realized that they would never achieve victory without the support of Governor John Hancock. They went to his house and proposed that he endorse ratification on the condition that a series of amendments be tacked on for consideration by Congress. The governor agreed, but in return he wanted to become president of the United States if Virginia failed to ratify or if George Washington refused to serve. Or he would

[4]*The Federalist Papers* are available at http://thomas.loc.gov/home/histdox/fedpapers.html.

accept the vice presidency. With the deal cut, Hancock went to the state convention to propose the compromise—the ratification of the Constitution with amendments. The delegates agreed, making Massachusetts the sixth state to ratify.[5]

This compromise, the call for a bill of rights, caught on, and the Federalists used it wherever close votes were likely. As it turned out, they needed to do so quite often. As Table 1-1 indicates, of the nine states ratifying after January 1788, seven recommended that the new Congress consider amendments. Indeed, New York and Virginia probably would not have agreed to the Constitution without such an addition; Virginia actually called for a second constitutional convention for that purpose. Other states began devising their own wish lists—enumerations of specific rights they wanted put into the document.

Whatever their specific motives might have been, most were in general agreement with Thomas Jefferson, who in a letter to James Madison noted that, while "I like much the general idea of framing a government which should go on of itself peaceably," he remained uneasy because of the absence of explicit limits on the power of the national government. He argued that "a bill of rights is what the people are entitled to against every government on earth, general and particular, and what no just government should refuse, or rest on inference." What Jefferson's remark suggests is that many thought well of the new system of government but were troubled by the lack of a declaration of rights. Remember that at the time Americans clearly understood the concepts of *fundamental* and *inalienable* rights. They shared the views expressed by the English philosopher John Locke, who believed that government did not grant rights; instead, there were natural rights, those that inherently belonged to individuals and that no government could deny. Even England, the country they fought against to gain their freedom, had such guarantees. The Magna Carta of 1215 and the Bill of Rights of 1689 gave Britons the right to a jury trial, to protection against cruel and unusual punishment, and so forth. Moreover, after the Revolution, virtually every state constitution included a philosophical statement about the relationship between citizens and their government or a listing of fifteen to twenty inalienable rights, such as religious freedom and electoral independence. Small wonder that the call for such a statement or enumeration of rights in the federal Constitution became a battle cry.

The reality of the political environment caused many Federalists to change their views on including a bill of rights. They realized that if they did not accede to state demands, either the Constitution would not be ratified or a new convention would be necessary. Because neither alternative was particularly attractive, they agreed to amend the Constitution as soon as the new government came into power.

In May 1789, one month after the start of the new Congress, Madison announced to the House of Representatives that he would draft a bill of rights and submit it within the coming month. As it turned out, the task proved a bit more difficult than he had anticipated; the state conventions had submitted nearly two hundred amendments, some of which would have decreased significantly the power of the national government. After sifting through these lists, Madison at first thought it might be best to incorporate the amendments into the Constitution's text, but he soon changed his mind. Instead, he presented the House with the following statement, echoing the views expressed in the Declaration of Independence: "That there be prefixed to the Constitution a declaration, that all power is originally vested in, and consequently derived from, the people."[6]

The legislators rejected this proposal, preferring a listing of rights to a philosophical statement. Madison returned to his task, eventually fashioning a list of seventeen amendments. When he took it back to the House, however, the list was greeted with suspicion and opposition. Some members of Congress, even those who had argued for a bill of rights, now did not want to be bothered with the proposals, insisting that they had more important business to settle. One suggested that other nations would not see the United States "as a serious trading partner as long as it was still tinkering with its constitution instead of organizing its government."[7] Finally, in July 1789, after Madison had prodded and even begged, the House considered his proposals. A special committee scrutinized them and reported a few days later, and the House adopted, with some modification, Madison's seventeen amendments. The Senate approved some and rejected others, so that by the time the Bill of Rights was submitted to the states on October 2, 1789,

---

[5]J. T. Keenan, *The Constitution of the United States: An Unfolding Story*, 2nd ed. (Chicago: Dorsey Press, 1988).

[6]The full text of Madison's statement is available in Neil H. Cogan, *Contexts of the Constitution: A Documentary Collection on Principles of American Constitutional Law* (New York: Foundation Press, 1999), 813–815.

[7]Farber and Sherry, *A History of the American Constitution*, 330.

only twelve remained.[8] The states ended up ratifying ten of the twelve.[9]

Despite the somewhat disorderly process, the Bill of Rights became part of the U.S. Constitution when Virginia ratified it on December 15, 1791. So, very early in the history of the republic, Americans demonstrated a capacity for amending their fundamental charter. Rather than rejecting and replacing the document, they signaled their belief that the Constitution was an effective instrument for self-government. Once written, it was not beyond the reach of alteration; it could be transformed to embrace the shared values of those who sought to change it.

The actual mechanics of adding the Bill of Rights illustrated how the framers expected constitutional change to take place. They wanted to create a government that would have some permanence; they wanted a system that would resist easy alteration. At the same time, they recognized the need for flexibility; they were well aware that one of the major limitations of the Articles of Confederation was its amending process, which required the unanimous approval of all thirteen states. The Philadelphia convention imagined an amending procedure that would be "bendable but not trendable, tough but not insurmountable, responsive to genuine waves of popular desire, yet impervious to self-serving campaigns of factional groups."[10]

The specific mechanism they established in Article V was a two-stage process (see Table 1-2). Proposing a constitutional amendment is the first step. This may be done either by a two-thirds vote of both houses of Congress or by two-thirds of the states petitioning for a constitutional convention. To date, all proposed constitutional amendments have been the products of congressional action. A second constitutional convention has never been called.[11] The second step is ratification. Here, too, the framers allowed two options. Proposed amendments may be ratified by three-fourths of the state legislatures or by three-fourths of special state-ratifying conventions. Only the Twenty-first Amendment, which repealed Prohibition, was ratified by state conventions. The others were all ratified by the required number of state legislatures.

Responding to various political pressures, members of Congress have since proposed all manner of amendments—more than 11,000, in fact—but only thirty-three have been sent to the states for ratification. Among the six that did not receive the approval of enough states were the child labor amendment (proposed in 1924), which would have placed restraints on "the labor of persons under 18 years of age," and the equal rights amendment (ERA; proposed in 1972), which stated, "Equality of rights under law shall not be denied or abridged by the United States or any State on account of sex." Suggestions for new constitutional amendments, not surprisingly, continue to be advanced.

Unlike the Congress, the president and the Supreme Court are not participants in the process, but they can certainly have an influence. Presidents often instigate and support proposals for constitutional amendments. Indeed, from George Washington to Donald Trump, virtually every chief executive has wanted some alteration to the Constitution. In other instances, presidential politics have led to amendments. Prior to the presidential election of 1804, members of the Electoral College cast two votes, and the first- and second-place finishers became president and vice president, respectively. In 1796, that process resulted in John Adams, the candidate of the Federalist Party, being chosen as president and his opposition, the Democratic-Republican's Thomas Jefferson, being selected as his vice president. Four years later, that same procedure resulted in a tie that was broken by the House of Representatives in favor of Thomas Jefferson—after thirty-five votes. The Twelfth Amendment sought to avoid these complications by requiring electors to

---

[8]Among those rejected was the one Madison prized above all others: that the states would have to abide by many of the enumerated guarantees.

[9]The amendments that did not receive approval were the original Articles I and II. Article I dealt with the number of representatives in relation to state population. Article II prohibited changes in congressional salary from taking effect until after an election. Why the states originally refused to pass these amendments is something of a mystery, because few records of state ratification proceedings exist. Interestingly, the second proposal was ratified in 1992, more than two hundred years after it was first proposed, and it became the Twenty-seventh Amendment to the U.S. Constitution.

[10]Keenan, *The Constitution of the United States*, 41.

[11]This is not to say that attempts to call a constitutional convention have never been made. Perhaps the most widely reported was Senator Everett Dirksen's effort to get the states to request a national convention for the purpose of overturning *Reynolds v. Sims*, the Supreme Court's 1964 reapportionment decision. He failed, by one state, to do so. A later attempt by the states to initiate constitutional change was a proposed amendment to require a balanced federal budget. This effort stalled with just two additional states required to call a convention.

Table 1-2	Methods of Amending the Constitution		
Proposed by	**Ratified by**	**Used for**
Two-thirds vote in both houses of Congress	State legislatures in three-fourths of the states	Twenty-six amendments
Two-thirds vote in both houses of Congress	Ratifying conventions in three-fourths of the states	Twenty-first Amendment
Constitutional convention (called at the request of two-thirds of the states)	State legislatures in three-fourths of the states	Never used
Constitutional convention (called at the request of two-thirds of the states)	Ratifying conventions in three-fourths of the states	Never used

cast one vote for president and one for vice president. Similarly, after Franklin D. Roosevelt was elected to an unprecedented fourth term in 1944—and died shortly after his last inauguration—Congress introduced what became the Twenty-second Amendment, limiting presidential tenure to two terms.

For its part, the Supreme Court has played a role as an instigator of constitutional amendments. The Court's interpretation of laws enacted by Congress can be easily overcome by the passage of new legislation, but that is not the case when the justices interpret the meaning of the Constitution. Short of the justices changing their minds—or their replacement with new justices of a different mindset—the only way to overturn the Court's interpretation of the Constitution is by amending the Constitution itself. Occasionally, the Court's constitutional decisions have been sufficiently out of step with public preferences that they have resulted in amendments that overturned those decisions (*see Table 1-3*). Some of these amendments—prohibiting federal law suits against states by citizens of another state or guaranteeing the right to vote to eighteen-year-olds, for example—were aimed specifically at overturning a decision of the justices. Others, like the Civil War amendments, were not designed uniquely to reverse the Court but achieved that result, nonetheless.

Given the unpopularity of a number of the modern Court's rulings, there are continued campaigns within the halls of Congress to overturn some of the justices' more controversial policies. Congress has considered a number of proposed amendments, all of which target decisions of the Court: a human life amendment that would make abortion illegal (in response to *Roe v. Wade*, 1973), a school prayer amendment that would allow students in public schools to engage in prayer (in response to **Engel v. Vitale**, 1962, and *School District of Abington Township v. Schempp*, 1963), a flag desecration amendment that would prohibit mutilation of the American flag (in response to *Texas v. Johnson*, 1989), and a term limits amendment (to overturn the Supreme Court's ruling in *U.S. Term Limits v. Thornton*, 1995).[12]

CONSTITUTIONAL CHANGE AND THE SUPREME COURT

Quite apart from amending the nation's fundamental law, the meaning of the Constitution can also be changed through interpretation by the justices. As Chief Justice John Marshall famously noted, "It is emphatically the province and duty of the judicial department to say what the law is." When the justices issue decisions about the meaning of the Constitution, that is precisely what they are doing. Thus, when those decisions change, so, too, does the Constitution.

Part of what makes the Court's changing interpretations possible is the general language in which much of the Constitution is written. In a sense, the document contains more principles and structures than it does rules and procedures. One indicator of its lack of specificity is its length. The United States has one of the world's shorter constitutions, less than 8,000 words. The constitutions of Australia, Canada, and Ireland are twice as long. Germany has a constitution that is four times the length of its U.S. counterpart, and Mexico's is seven times longer. Even a casual inspection of the U.S.

---

[12]Boldface type indicates that the opinions in the case can be found in the online archive at http://edge.sagepub.com/conlaw. For a complete list of cases in the archive, see the Online Case Archive List (Appendix 4) at the end of this volume.

Table 1-3   Six Amendments That Overturned Supreme Court Decisions

Amendment	Date Ratified	Supreme Court Decision Overturned
Eleventh	February 7, 1795	*Chisholm v. Georgia* (1793). In its first major decision, the Court authorized citizens of one state to sue another state in the Supreme Court. The decision angered advocates of states' rights.
Thirteenth	December 6, 1865	*Scott v. Sandford* (1857). The Court ruled slaves are property with which Congress may not interfere, and that neither slaves nor their descendants are citizens under the Constitution. Ratified in the wake of the Civil War, the Thirteenth and Fourteenth Amendments rectified the Court's decision.
Fourteenth	July 9, 1868	*Scott v. Sandford* (1857).
Sixteenth	February 3, 1913	*Pollock v. Farmers' Loan & Trust* Co. (1895). The Court declared the federal income tax unconstitutional, occasioning the adoption of the Sixteenth Amendment eighteen years later.
Nineteenth	August 18, 1920	*Minor v. Happersett* (1875). The Court held that, because the right to vote was not among the "privileges or immunities" of U.S. citizenship protected against state infringement by the Fourteenth Amendment, states could limit the right to vote to men. The continued efforts of the women's suffrage movement eventually led to the passage of the Nineteenth Amendment.
Twenty-sixth	July 1, 1971	*Oregon v. Mitchell* (1970). The Court ruled that Congress has the power to lower the voting age to eighteen only for federal, not state and local, elections. At a period when eighteen-year-olds were drafted to serve in the Vietnam War, Congress quickly responded to *Mitchell*, proposing the Twenty-sixth Amendment in March 1971.

Source: Lee Epstein, Jeffrey A. Segal, Harold J. Spaeth, and Thomas G. Walker, *The Supreme Court Compendium: Data, Decisions, and Developments,* 6th ed. (Thousand Oaks, CA: CQ Press, 2015), Tables 1-1 and 7-1.

Constitution reveals that it contains provisions that can be reasonably understood in multiple ways. True, some language—such as the requirement that the president be thirty-five years old or the provision that senators serve six-year terms—is not open to widely varying interpretations, but the meaning of other elements is not as obvious; phrases such as "necessary and proper," "due process law," "cruel and unusual punishments," "establishment of religion," and "unreasonable searches and seizures" are quite open-ended. Because there are not straightforward answers to questions about how to apply such words to specific cases, their meaning, as understood by the justices, has changed over time.

Consider, for example, the Supreme Court's interpretation of the commerce clause. The inability of the national government to regulate interstate commerce was a deficiency of the Articles of Confederation, and thus the framers invested Congress with the "Power . . . To regulate Commerce . . . among the several States." What qualifies as "interstate commerce"? Early in the twentieth century, the Supreme Court made a distinction between the production and manufacturing of a good and its subsequent sale and distribution. The latter was "interstate commerce" and subject to congressional regulation, but the former was not. Given that interpretation, the justices ruled that Congress could not use its commerce power to limit manufacturing monopolies, such as the sugar industry.[13] Neither would

[13]*United States v. E.C. Knight* (1895).

the justices permit Congress to use the commerce clause to set minimum wages and maximum working hours for the coal industry.[14] Manufacturing and labor were not a part of interstate commerce and thus subject only to state regulation. Later, however, the Court reconsidered this approach. It brought to bear a new interpretation of interstate commerce, one that was sufficiently broad to permit Congress to regulate not only activities it had previously forbidden—such as labor activity—but also actions far removed from commercial activity, such as the growth of wheat that never leaves a farm.[15] Under this subsequent approach, whatever had a substantial relationship to interstate commerce was subject to regulation by Congress.

What changed? Not the text of the Constitution; it was instead how the members of the Court interpreted its words. By moving from an interpretation that confined congressional power to an alternative interpretation that took a more expansive view, the Supreme Court effectively altered the meaning of the Constitution.

More recently, the Court has brought about another revision of its understanding of the commerce clause, this time by reconsidering whether state and local governments must adhere to federal labor law. In 1976, the justices ruled that, while national wage and hours standards could be applied to private employers, Congress could not force its choices about labor policy on the states; the Tenth Amendment, which expressly reserves to the states the powers not delegated to national government, does not permit Congress to impair the policy making of states.[16] Less than ten years later, however, the justices reversed course, holding that the states were not impaired by having to abide by federal wage regulations.[17] In that short span of time, no amendments were made to the Constitution; the justices amended their interpretation of it.

We began this chapter by discussing the adoption of the Bill of Rights as an illustration of constitutional change. We end here by revisiting the Bill of Rights and its application to the states, one of the Court's most significant interpretive changes to the Constitution.

As we have noted, the Bill of Rights was designed to serve as a limitation on the power of the national government. The passage of the Fourteenth Amendment in 1868, however, introduced new provisions to the Constitution, including a stipulation that "[n]o state shall . . . deprive any person of life, liberty, or property, without due process of law." To some, this language meant that states would have to adhere to the Bill of Rights, just like the national government; if the due process clause protected "liberty" from infringement by the states, then that "liberty" should certainly include the basic protections already in the Constitution.

Initially, when those arguments came before the Court, the justices rejected them. They ruled, for instance, that the due process clause did not include the First Amendment's guarantee of freedom of assembly.[18] Nor did it include the Fifth Amendment's right to indictment by a grand jury.[19] The Court emphasized that the states were free to recognize those freedoms they deemed important and to develop their own guarantees against state violations of those rights.

Through a doctrine called selective incorporation, however, the justices have applied, one by one, virtually all of the provisions of the Bill of Rights to the states; when they concluded that a specific protection in one of the amendments was so fundamental that it was "implicit in the concept of ordered liberty," the states would be bound by its commands, no less than the national government (see Table 1-4). The result has been a considerable alteration in the nature of national-state relations and an expansion of the constitutional protection of liberties. Redrawing the scope of liberties protected by the Constitution has been a consequence of doctrinal shifts on the Supreme Court.

The ability of the Court to change doctrine in this fashion, combined with the possibility of formal amendments, ensure that the Constitution has the flexibility necessary to be adaptable from one generation to the next. The framers constructed a resilient framework for government, and its capacity for promoting both continuity and change is a key explanation for its longevity.

---

[14]*Carter v. Carter Coal Co.* (1936).

[15]*National Labor Relations Board v. Jones & Laughlin Steel Corp.* (1937) and *Wickard v. Filburn* (1942), respectively.

[16]*National League of Cities v. Usery* (1976).

[17]*Garcia v. San Antonio Metropolitan Transit Authority* (1985).

[18]*United States v. Cruikshank* (1876).

[19]*Hurtado v. California* (1884).

Table 1-4   Cases Incorporating Provisions of the Bill of Rights into the Due Process Clause of the Fourteenth Amendment

Constitutional Provision	Case	Year
First Amendment		
Freedom of speech and press	*Gitlow v. New York*	1925
Freedom of assembly	*De Jonge v. Oregon*	1937
Freedom of petition	*Hague v. CIO*	1939
Free exercise of religion	*Cantwell v. Connecticut*	1940
Establishment of religion	*Everson v. Board of Education*	1947
Second Amendment		
Right to bear arms	*McDonald v. Chicago*	2010
Fourth Amendment		
Unreasonable search and seizure	*Wolf v. Colorado*	1949
Exclusionary rule	*Mapp v. Ohio*	1961
Fifth Amendment		
Payment of compensation for the taking of private property	*Chicago, Burlington & Quincy Railroad v. Chicago*	1897
Self-incrimination	*Malloy v. Hogan*	1964
Double jeopardy	*Benton v. Maryland*	1969
When jeopardy attaches	*Crist v. Bretz*	1978
Sixth Amendment		
Public trial	*In re Oliver*	1948
Due notice	*Cole v. Arkansas*	1948
Right to counsel (felonies)	*Gideon v. Wainwright*	1963
Confrontation and cross-examination of adverse witnesses	*Pointer v. Texas*	1965
Speedy trial	*Klopfer v. North Carolina*	1967
Compulsory process to obtain witnesses	*Washington v. Texas*	1967
Jury trial	*Duncan v. Louisiana*	1968
Right to counsel (misdemeanor when jail is possible)	*Argersinger v. Hamlin*	1972
Eighth Amendment		
Cruel and unusual punishment	*Louisiana ex rel. Francis v. Resweber*	1947
Ninth Amendment		
Privacy[a]	*Griswold v. Connecticut*	1965

Note: Provisions the Court has not incorporated: Third Amendment right against quartering soldiers, Fifth Amendment right to a grand jury hearing, Seventh Amendment right to a jury trial in civil cases, and Eighth Amendment right against excessive bail and fines.

[a]The word *privacy* does not appear in the Ninth Amendment (nor anywhere in the text of the Constitution). In *Griswold* several members of the Court viewed the Ninth Amendment as guaranteeing (and incorporating) that right.

ANNOTATED READINGS

In the text and footnotes, we mention many interesting studies on the Supreme Court. Our goal in each chapter's "Annotated Readings" section is to highlight a few books for the interested reader.

Analyses of the framing of the Constitution include Michael Kammen, *A Machine That Would Go of Itself: The Constitution in American Culture* (New York: Routledge, 2017); Michael J. Klarman, *The Framers' Coup: The Making of the United States Constitution* (New York: Oxford University Press, 2016); Forrest McDonald, *Novus Ordo Seclorum: The Intellectual Origin of the Constitution* (Lawrence: University Press of Kansas, 1987); Jack N. Rakove, *Original Meanings: Politics and Ideas in the Making of the Constitution* (New York: Knopf, 1997); David Brian Robertson, *The Original Compromise: What the Constitution's Framers Were Really Thinking* (New York: Oxford University Press, 2013); and John R. Vile, *The Writing and Ratification of the U.S. Constitution: Practical Virtue in Action* (Lanham, MD: Rowman & Littlefield, 2012).

Books on the creation and ratification of the Bill of Rights include Akhil Reed Amar, *The Bill of Rights: Creation and Reconstruction* (New Haven, CT: Yale University Press, 1998); Neil Cogan, ed., *The Complete Bill of Rights: The Drafts, Debates, Sources, and Origins* (New York: Oxford University Press, 1997); Richard Labunksi, *James Madison and the Struggle for the Bill of Rights* (New York: Oxford University Press, 2006); Leonard W. Levy, *Origins of the Bill of Rights* (New Haven, CT: Yale University Press, 1999); Gerard Magliocca, *The Heart of the Constitution: How the Bill of Rights Became the Bill of Rights* (New York: Oxford University Press, 2018); and Robert Allen Rutland, *The Birth of the Bill of Rights, 1776–1791* (Boston: Northeastern University Press, 1997).

CHAPTER TWO

UNDERSTANDING THE U.S. SUPREME COURT

THIS BOOK IS DEVOTED to providing an overview of how the U.S. Supreme Court has interpreted the Constitution. It is organized around a discussion of the principal issues that the justices have confronted, with a primary focus on the text of the Court's opinions. Making sense of these opinions often requires a blend of different types of knowledge; depending upon the case, an understanding of some leading legal concepts, an awareness of history, a grasp of the mechanics of deliberative government, an appreciation of social conditions, and some familiarity with principles of economics can each offer insight into the justices' constitutional choices. One constant across all these opinions, however, is a set of procedures by which the Supreme Court makes decisions. Like any governmental institution, the Court is bound by formal rules and informal norms; they provide structure to the business of judicial policy making, and they channel and constrain how (and in some cases, whether) the Court exercises its power. Because the opinions that you will read are the product of the justices following an established set of rules and procedures, it is important to understand how those rules and procedures guide the Court to reaching its results. In what follows, we outline the basic features of Supreme Court decision making. We begin with a discussion of how the justices select their cases. We then consider how—and why—the justices make their most significant decisions, the resolution of disputes.

PROCESSING SUPREME COURT CASES

A great deal happens before the justices actually decide cases. As Figure 2-1 shows, the Court must first sort through a large number of potential candidates in order to identify which cases it will resolve on the merits. During the 2018–2019 term, a total of 6,442 cases arrived at the Supreme Court's doorstep, but the justices decided only sixty-six with signed opinions.[1] The disparity between the number of parties that want the Court to resolve their disputes and the number of disputes the Court agrees to resolve raises some important questions: How do the justices decide which cases to hear? What happens to the cases they reject? Those the Court agrees to resolve?

Deciding to Decide: The Supreme Court's Caseload

As the figures for the 2018–2019 term indicate, the Court heard and decided less than 1 percent of the cases it received. This percentage is quite low, but it follows the general trend in Supreme Court decision making: the number of requests for review increased dramatically during the twentieth century, but the number of cases the Court formally decided each year did not increase. For example, in 1930 the Court agreed to decide 159 of the 726 disputes sent to it. In 1990 the number of cases granted review fell to 141, but the sum total of petitions for review had risen to 6,302—nearly nine times greater than in 1930.[2]

---

[1]Chief Justice John Roberts, "2019 Year-End Report on the Federal Judiciary," https://www.supremecourt.gov/publicinfo/year-end/2019year-endreport.pdf.

[2]Data are from Lee Epstein, Jeffrey A. Segal, Harold J. Spaeth, and Thomas G. Walker, *The Supreme Court Compendium: Data, Decisions, and Developments*, 6th ed. (Thousand Oaks, CA: CQ Press, 2015), Tables 2-5 and 2-6.

Figure 2-1   The Processing of Cases

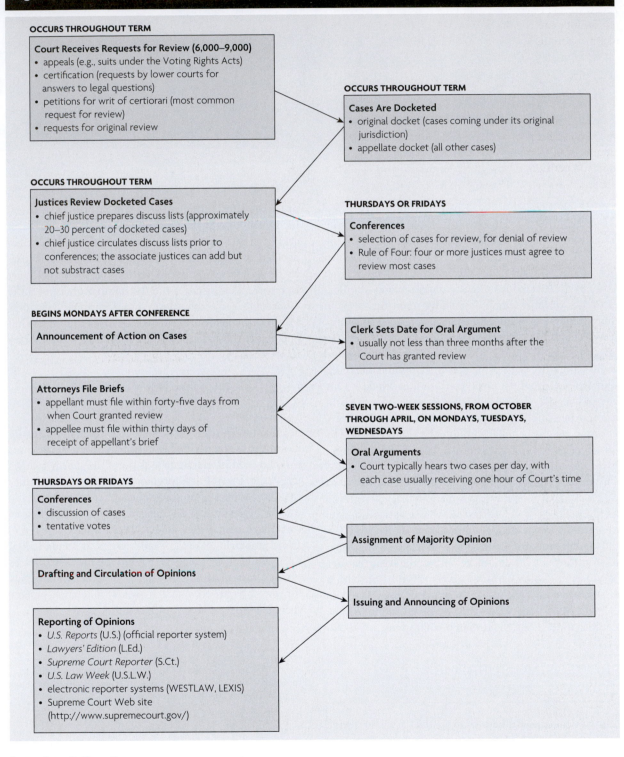

OCCURS THROUGHOUT TERM

Court Receives Requests for Review (6,000–9,000)
- appeals (e.g., suits under the Voting Rights Acts)
- certification (requests by lower courts for answers to legal questions)
- petitions for writ of certiorari (most common request for review)
- requests for original review

OCCURS THROUGHOUT TERM

Cases Are Docketed
- original docket (cases coming under its original jurisdiction)
- appellate docket (all other cases)

OCCURS THROUGHOUT TERM

Justices Review Docketed Cases
- chief justice prepares discuss lists (approximately 20–30 percent of docketed cases)
- chief justice circulates discuss lists prior to conferences; the associate justices can add but not substract cases

THURSDAYS OR FRIDAYS

Conferences
- selection of cases for review, for denial of review
- Rule of Four: four or more justices must agree to review most cases

BEGINS MONDAYS AFTER CONFERENCE

Announcement of Action on Cases

Clerk Sets Date for Oral Argument
- usually not less than three months after the Court has granted review

Attorneys File Briefs
- appellant must file within forty-five days from when Court granted review
- appellee must file within thirty days of receipt of appellant's brief

SEVEN TWO-WEEK SESSIONS, FROM OCTOBER THROUGH APRIL, ON MONDAYS, TUESDAYS, WEDNESDAYS

Oral Arguments
- Court typically hears two cases per day, with each case usually receiving one hour of Court's time

THURSDAYS OR FRIDAYS

Conferences
- discussion of cases
- tentative votes

Assignment of Majority Opinion

Drafting and Circulation of Opinions

Issuing and Announcing of Opinions

Reporting of Opinions
- *U.S. Reports* (U.S.) (official reporter system)
- *Lawyers' Edition* (L.Ed.)
- *Supreme Court Reporter* (S.Ct.)
- *U.S. Law Week* (U.S.L.W.)
- electronic reporter systems (WESTLAW, LEXIS)
- Supreme Court Web site (http://www.supremecourt.gov/)

Source: Compiled by authors.

How do cases get to the Supreme Court? How do the justices decide which will get a formal review and which will be rejected? What affects their choices? Let us consider each of these questions, for they are fundamental to an understanding of judicial decision making.

How Cases Get to the Court: Jurisdiction and the Routes of Appeal

Cases come to the Court in one of four ways: either by a request for review under the Court's original jurisdiction or by three appellate routes—appeals, certification, and petitions for writs of certiorari (*see Figure 2-2*). Chapter 3 explains more about the Court's original jurisdiction, as it is central to understanding the landmark case of *Marbury v. Madison* (1803). Here, it is sufficient to note that original cases are those that no other court has heard. Article III of the Constitution authorizes such suits in cases involving ambassadors from foreign countries and those to which a state is a party. But, because Congress has authorized lower courts to consider such

cases, as well, the Supreme Court does not have exclusive jurisdiction over them. Consequently, the Court normally reviews, under its original jurisdiction, only those cases in which one state is suing another (usually over a disputed boundary). In recent years, original jurisdiction cases have made up only a tiny fraction of the Court's overall docket—between one and five cases per term.

Almost all cases reach the Court under its appellate jurisdiction, meaning that a lower federal or state court has already rendered a decision and one of the parties is asking the Supreme Court to review that decision. As Figure 2-2 shows, such cases typically come from one of the U.S. courts of appeals or state supreme courts. The U.S. Supreme Court, the nation's highest tribunal, is the court of last resort.

To invoke the Court's appellate jurisdiction, litigants can take one of three routes, depending on the nature of their dispute: appeal as a matter of right, certification, or certiorari. Cases falling into the first category (normally called "on appeal") involve issues Congress has determined are so important that a ruling by the

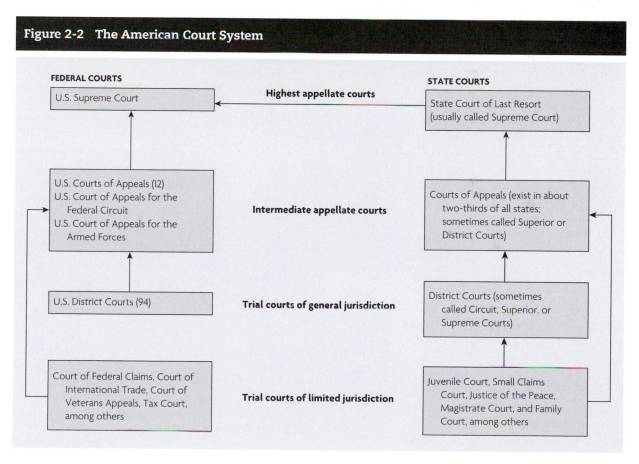

Figure 2-2   The American Court System

FEDERAL COURTS

U.S. Supreme Court

STATE COURTS

State Court of Last Resort (usually called Supreme Court)

Highest appellate courts

U.S. Courts of Appeals (12)
U.S. Court of Appeals for the Federal Circuit
U.S. Court of Appeals for the Armed Forces

Intermediate appellate courts

Courts of Appeals (exist in about two-thirds of all states; sometimes called Superior or District Courts)

U.S. District Courts (94)

Trial courts of general jurisdiction

District Courts (sometimes called Circuit, Superior, or Supreme Courts)

Court of Federal Claims, Court of International Trade, Court of Veterans Appeals, Tax Court, among others

Trial courts of limited jurisdiction

Juvenile Court, Small Claims Court, Justice of the Peace, Magistrate Court, and Family Court, among others

Source: Compiled by authors.

Supreme Court is necessary. Before 1988 these included cases in which a lower court declared a state or federal law unconstitutional or in which a state court upheld a state law challenged on the ground that it violated the U.S. Constitution. Although the justices were technically obligated to decide such appeals, they often found a more expedient way to deal with them—by either failing to consider them or issuing summary decisions (shorthand rulings). At the Court's urging, in 1988 Congress virtually eliminated "mandatory" appeals. Today, the Court is legally obliged to hear only those few cases (typically involving the Voting Rights Act) appealed from special three-judge district courts. When the Court agrees to hear such cases, it issues an order noting its "probable jurisdiction."

A second, but rarely used, route to the Court is certification. Under the Court's appellate jurisdiction and by an act of Congress, lower appellate courts can file writs of certification asking the justices to respond to questions aimed at clarifying federal law. Because only judges may use this route, very few cases come to the Court this way. The justices are free to accept a question certified to them or to dismiss it.

That leaves the third and most common appellate path, a request for a writ of certiorari (from the Latin meaning "to be informed"). In a petition for a writ of certiorari, the litigants seeking Supreme Court review ask the Court, literally, to become "informed" about their cases by requesting the lower court to send up the record. Most of the six thousand or more cases that arrive each year come as requests for certiorari. The Court, exercising its ability to choose which cases to review, grants "cert" to less than 1 percent of the petitions. A grant of cert means that the justices have decided to give the case full review; a denial means that the decision of the lower court remains in force.

How the Court Decides:
The Case Selection Process

Regardless of the specific design of a legal system, in many countries jurists must confront the task of "deciding to decide"—that is, choosing which cases among many hundreds or even thousands they will actually resolve. The U.S. Supreme Court is no exception; it, too, has the job of deciding to decide, or identifying those cases to which it will grant cert. This task presents something of a mixed blessing to the justices. Selecting cases to review—about 70 or so in recent terms—from the large number of requests is an arduous undertaking

that requires the justices or their law clerks to look over hundreds of thousands of pages of briefs and other memoranda. The ability to exercise discretion, however, frees the Court from one of the major constraints on judicial bodies: the lack of agenda control. The justices may not be able to reach out and propose cases for review the way members of Congress can propose legislation, but the enormous number of petitions ensures that they can resolve at least some issues important to them.

In selecting cases, the justices follow a set of protocols that they have established over time. The original pool of about six to seven thousand petitions faces several checkpoints (see Figure 2-1) that significantly reduce the amount of time the Court, acting as a collegial body, spends deciding what to decide. The staff members in the office of the Supreme Court clerk act as the first gatekeepers. When a petition for certiorari arrives, the clerk's office examines it to make sure it is in proper form and conforms to the Court's precise rules. Briefs must be "prepared in a 6 1/8- by 9 1/4-inch booklet, . . . typeset in a Century family 12-point type with 2-point or more leading between lines." Exceptions are made for litigants who cannot afford to pay the Court's administrative fees, currently $300. The rules governing these petitions, known as *in forma pauperis* briefs, are somewhat looser, allowing indigents to submit briefs on 8½-by-11-inch paper. The Court's major concern, or so it seems, is that the document "be legible."[3]

The clerk's office gives all acceptable petitions an identification number, called a "docket number," and forwards copies to the chambers of the individual justices. At present (2020), all the justices but Samuel Alito and Neil Gorsuch use the certiorari pool system, in which clerks from the different chambers collaborate by dividing, reading, and then writing memos on the petitions.[4] Upon receiving the preliminary or pool memos, the individual justices may ask their own clerks for their thoughts about the petitions. The justices then use the pool memos, along with their clerks' reports, as a basis for making their own independent determinations about which cases they believe are worthy of a full hearing.

---

[3]Rules 33 and 39 of the Rules of the Supreme Court of the United States. All Supreme Court rules are available at https://www.supremecourt.gov/filingandrules/2019RulesoftheCourt.pdf.

[4]Supreme Court justices are authorized to hire four law clerks each. Typically, these clerks are outstanding recent graduates of the nation's top law schools. Pool (or preliminary) memos, as well as other documents pertaining to the Court's case selection process, are available at http://epstein.wustl.edu/blackmun.php.

Figure 2-3   A Page from Justice Harry Blackmun's Docket Books

	HOLD FOR	DEFER		CERT.			JURISDICTIONAL STATEMENT				MERITS		MOTION		
		RELIST	CVSG	G	D	G&R	N	POST	DIS	AFF	REV	AFF	G	D	
Rehnquist, Ch. J.					✓							✓			
White, J.				3								✓			
Blackmun, J.				✓							✓				
Stevens, J.				✓							✓				
O'Connor, J.				3								✓			
Scalia, J.					✓							✓			
Kennedy, J.				✓							✓				
Souter, J.				✓								✓			
Thomas, J.					✓							✓			

Source: Dockets of Harry A. Blackmun, Manuscript Division, Library of Congress, Washington, D.C.

Note: As the docket sheet shows, the justices have a number of options when they meet to vote on cert. They can grant (G) the petition or deny (D) it. They also can cast a "Join 3" (3) vote. Justices may have different interpretations of a Join 3 but, at the very least, it tells the others that the justice agrees to supply a vote in favor of cert if three other justices support granting review. In the MERITS column, REV = reverse the decision of the court below; AFF = affirm the decision of the court below.

During this process, the chief justice plays a special role, serving as yet another checkpoint on petitions. Before the justices meet to make case selection decisions—which they do on Fridays when the Court is in session—the chief circulates a "discuss list" containing those cases he feels merit consideration; any justice may add cases to this list but may not remove any. About 20 percent to 30 percent of the cases that come to the Court make it to the list and are actually discussed by the justices in conference. The rest are automatically denied review, leaving the lower court decisions intact.[5]

This much we know. Because only the justices attend the Court's conferences, we cannot say precisely what transpires. We can offer only a rough picture based on scholarly writings, the comments of justices, and our examination of the private papers of a few retired justices. These sources tell us that the discussion of each petition begins with the chief justice presenting a short summary of the facts and, typically, stating his vote. The associate justices, who sit at a rectangular table in order of seniority, then comment on each petition, with the most senior justice speaking first and the newest member last. As Figure 2-3 shows, the justices record the certiorari votes—and, for cases they agree to decide on the merits, their subsequent votes on the outcome—in their personal records, called docket books. But, given the large number of petitions, the justices apparently discuss few cases in detail.

By tradition, the Court adheres to the so-called Rule of Four: it grants certiorari to those cases receiving the affirmative vote of at least four justices. The Court identifies the cases accepted and rejected on a "certified orders list," which is released to the public. For cases granted certiorari or in which probable jurisdiction is noted, the clerk informs participating attorneys, who then have specified time limits in which to submit their written legal arguments (briefs), and the case is scheduled for oral argument.

Considerations Affecting Case Selection Decisions

The process described here is how the Court considers petitions, but why do the justices make the decisions that they do? Scholars have developed

[5]For information on the discuss list, see Gregory A. Caldeira and John R. Wright, "The Discuss List: Agenda Building in the Supreme Court," *Law and Society Review* 24 (1990): 807–836.

several answers to this question. Two sets are worthy of our attention: legal considerations and political considerations.[6]

Legal considerations are listed in Rule 10, which the Court has established to govern the certiorari decision-making process. Many cases in the lower courts raise similar legal questions, and when judges reach different conclusions on those issues, there is conflict—disagreement among judges about the meaning of federal law. Under Rule 10, the Court considers "conflict," such as when a U.S. "court of appeals has entered a decision in conflict with the decision of another United States court of appeals on the same important matter" or when decisions of state courts of law collide with one another or the federal courts.[7]

To what extent do the considerations in Rule 10 affect the Court? The answer is mixed. On one hand, the Court seems to follow its dictates. The presence of actual conflict between or among federal courts substantially increases the likelihood of review; if actual conflict is present in a case, it has a 33 percent chance of gaining Court review, as compared with the usual 1 percent certiorari rate.[8] On the other hand, although the Court may look more closely at cases that present actual conflict, it does not accept all cases with conflict because there are too many.[9]

If cases that present genuine conflict are still rejected, then there must be additional criteria that the justices weigh in their decision making. That is why scholars have looked to *political* factors that may influence the Court's case selection process. Three are particularly important. The first is the U.S. solicitor general (SG), the attorney who represents the U.S. government before the Supreme Court. Simply stated, when the SG files a petition, the Court is very likely to grant certiorari. In fact, the Court accepts about 70 percent to 80 percent of the cases in which the federal government is the petitioning party, a staggeringly high success rate compared to other litigants.

Why is the solicitor general so successful? One reason is that the Court is well aware of the SG's special role. A presidential appointee whose decisions often reflect the administration's philosophy, the SG also represents the interests of the United States. As the nation's highest court, the Supreme Court cannot ignore these interests. In addition, the justices rely on the solicitor general to act as a filter—that is, they expect the SG to examine carefully the cases to which the government is a party and bring only the most important to their attention. Further, because solicitors general are involved in so much Supreme Court litigation, they acquire a great deal of knowledge about the Court that other litigants do not. They are "repeat players" who can use their knowledge of Supreme Court decision making to their advantage. For example, they know how to structure their petitions to attract the attention and interest of the justices. Finally, the professionalism of the SG and the lawyers working in that office is also beneficial; the justices know that these lawyers are invested in the Court's mission. They are, as some scholars have put it, "consummate legal professionals whose information justices can trust."[10]

The second political factor is the amicus curiae (friend of the court) brief. Interest groups and other third parties usually file these briefs after the Court makes its decision to hear a case, but they can also be filed at the certiorari stage (*see Box 2-1*). Research by political scientists shows that amicus briefs significantly enhance a case's chances of being heard, and multiple briefs have a greater effect.[11] An interesting finding of these studies is that, even when groups file *in opposition* to granting certiorari, they increase—rather than decrease—the probability that the Court will hear the case.

What can we make of these findings? Most important is this: the justices may not be strongly influenced by the arguments contained in these briefs

---

[6]Some scholars have noted a third set: procedural considerations. These emanate from Article III, which—under the Court's interpretation—places constraints on the ability of federal tribunals to hear and decide cases. Chapter 3 considers these constraints, which include justiciability (the case must be appropriate for judicial resolution by presenting a real "case" and "controversy") and standing (the appropriate person must bring the case). Unless these procedural criteria are met, the Court—at least theoretically—will deny review.

[7]Rule 10 also stresses the Court's interest in resolving "important" federal questions.

[8]See Gregory A. Caldeira and John R. Wright, "Organized Interests and Agenda Setting in the U.S. Supreme Court," *American Political Science Review* 82 (1988): 1109–1127.

[9]See Lawrence Baum, *The Supreme Court*, 12th ed. (Washington, DC: CQ Press, 2016), 91.

[10]Ryan C. Black and Ryan J. Owens, *The Solicitor General and the United States Supreme Court: Executive Branch Influence and Judicial Decisions* (Cambridge: Cambridge University Press, 2012), 71.

[11]Caldeira and Wright, "Organized Interests and Agenda Setting"; Ryan C. Black and Ryan J. Owens, "Agenda Setting in the Supreme Court: The Collision of Policy and Jurisprudence," *Journal of Politics* 71 (2009): 1062–1075.

(if they were, why would amicus briefs opposing certiorari have the opposite effect?), but they seem to use them as cues. In other words, because amicus curiae briefs filed at the certiorari stage are somewhat uncommon—less than 10 percent of all petitions are accompanied by amicus briefs—they do draw the justices' attention. If major organizations are sufficiently interested in an appeal to pay the cost of filing briefs in support of (or against) Court review, then the petition for certiorari is probably worth the justices' serious consideration.

In addition, we have strong reasons to suspect that a third political factor—the ideology of the justices—affects actions on certiorari petitions. Specifically, the members of the Court favor reviewing lower court decisions that run contrary to their preferences. Researchers tell us, for example, that the justices during the liberal period under Chief Justice Earl Warren (1953–1969) were more likely to grant review to cases in which the lower court reached a conservative decision so that they could reverse that legal policy, while those of the moderately conservative Court during the years of Chief Justice Warren Burger (1969–1986) took cases in order to undo the liberal decisions of lower courts. It would be difficult to believe that the current justices would be any less likely than their predecessors to vote based on their ideology. These ideological considerations are brought to bear in a collegial context, and the members of the Court consider not only their preferences but the preferences of their brethren, as well. Scholarly studies suggest that justices engage in strategic voting behavior at the cert stage. In other words, justices are forward thinking; they consider the implications of their cert vote for the later merits stage, asking themselves, If I vote to grant a particular petition, what are the odds of my position winning down the road? As one justice explained his calculations, "I might think the Nebraska Supreme Court made a horrible decision, but I wouldn't want to take the case, for if we take the case and affirm it, then it would become precedent."[12]

The Role of Attorneys

Once the Supreme Court agrees to decide a case, the clerk of the Court informs the parties. The parties present their side of the dispute to the justices in written and oral arguments.

Written Arguments

Written arguments, called briefs, are the major vehicles for parties to Supreme Court cases to document their positions. Under the Court's rules, the appealing party (known as the appellant or petitioner) must submit its brief within forty-five days of the time the Court grants certiorari; the opposing party (known as the appellee or respondent) has thirty days after receipt of the appellant's brief to respond with arguments urging affirmance of the lower court ruling.

As is the case for cert petitions, the Court maintains specific rules covering the presentation and format of merits briefs. For example, the briefs of both parties must be submitted in forty copies and may not exceed 15,000 words. Rule 24 outlines the material that briefs must contain, such as a description of the questions presented for review, a list of the parties, and a statement describing the Court's authority to hear the case. Also worth noting: the Court's rules now mandate electronic submission of all briefs (including amicus briefs) in addition to the normal hard copy submissions.

The clerk sends the briefs to the justices, who normally study them before oral argument. Written briefs are important because the justices may use them to formulate the questions they ask the lawyers representing the parties. The briefs also serve as a permanent record of the positions of the parties, available to the justices for consultation after oral argument when they decide the case outcome. A well-crafted brief can place into the hands of the justices arguments, legal references, and possible remedies that later may be incorporated into the opinion. Indeed, some research suggests that such briefs do exactly that.[13]

In addition to the briefs submitted by the parties to the suit, Court rules allow interested persons, organizations, and government units to participate as amici curiae on the merits—just as they are permitted to file such briefs at the review stage (see Box 2-1). Those wishing to submit friend of the court briefs must obtain the written permission of the parties or the Court. Only the federal government and state governments are exempt from this requirement.

---

[12]Quoted in H. W. Perry Jr., *Deciding to Decide: Agenda Setting in the United States Supreme Court* (Cambridge, MA: Harvard University Press, 1991), 200.

[13]Pamela C. Corley, "The Supreme Court and Opinion Content: The Influence of Parties' Briefs," *Political Research Quarterly* 61 (2008): 468–478.

BOX 2-1

The Amicus Curiae Brief

The amicus curiae practice probably originates in Roman law. A judge would often appoint a consilium (officer of the court) to advise him on points where the judge was in doubt. That may be why the term *amicus curiae* translates from the Latin as "friend of the court." But today it is the rare amicus who is a friend of the court. Instead, contemporary briefs almost always are a friend of a party, supporting one side over the other at the certiorari and merits stages. Consider one of the briefs filed in *United States v. Windsor* (2013), the cover of which is reprinted here. In that case, the American Psychological Association and other organizations filed in support of Edith Windsor. They, along with Windsor, asked the Court to invalidate the Defense of Marriage Act (DOMA), which defined marriage under federal law as a "legal union between one man and one woman." These groups were anything but neutral participants.

How does an organization become an amicus curiae participant in the Supreme Court of the United States? Under the Court's rules, groups wishing to file an amicus brief at the certiorari or merits stage must obtain the written consent of the parties to the litigation (the federal and state governments may file at their own discretion). If the parties refuse to give their consent, the group can file a motion with the Court asking for its permission. The Court today almost always grants these motions.

No. 12–307

IN THE

SUPREME COURT OF THE UNITED STATES

UNITED STATES OF AMERICA, *Petitioner*

—V.—

EDITH SCHLAIN WINDSOR, IN HER CAPACITY AS EXECUTOR OF THE ESTATE OF THEA CLARA SPYER, ET AL.,

ON WRIT OF CERTIORARI TO THE UNITED STATES COURT OF APPEALS FOR THE SECOND CIRCUIT

BRIEF OF THE AMERICAN PSYCHOLOGICAL ASSOCIATION, THE AMERICAN ACADEMY OF PEDIATRICS, THE AMERICAN MEDICAL ASSOCIATION, THE AMERICAN PSYCHIATRIC ASSOCIATION, THE AMERICAN PSYCHOANALYTIC ASSOCIATION, THE CALIFORNIA MEDICAL ASSOCIATION, THE NATIONAL ASSOCIATION OF SOCIAL WORKERS AND ITS NEW YORK CITY AND STATE CHAPTERS, AND THE NEW YORK STATE PSYCHOLOGICAL ASSOCIATION AS *AMICI CURIAE* ON THE MERITS IN SUPPORT OF AFFIRMANCE

NATHALIE F.P. GILFOYLE AMERICAN PSYCHOLOGICAL ASSOCIATION 750 First Street, N.E. Washington, DC 20002

WILLIAM F. SHEEHAN *Counsel of Record* ANDREW HUDSON GOODWIN | PROCTER LLP 901 New York Avenue, N.W. Washington, D.C. 20001 (202) 346–4000 wsheehan@goodwinprocter.com

PAUL M. SMITH JENNER & BLOCK LLP 1099 New York Avenue, N.W. Washington, DC 20001 Counsel for Amici Curiae

Oral Arguments

Attorneys also present their cases orally before the justices. Each side has thirty minutes to convince the Court of the merits of its position and to field questions from the justices, though sometimes the Court makes small exceptions to this rule. In the 2011 term, it made a particularly big one, hearing six hours of oral argument, over three days, on the Patient Protection and Affordable Care Act, the health care law passed in 2010. This was unprecedented in the modern era, but not in the Court's early years. In the past, because attorneys did not always prepare written briefs, the justices relied on oral arguments to learn about the cases and to help them marshal their arguments for the next stage. Orals were considered important public events, opportunities to see the most prominent attorneys of the day at work. Arguments often went on for days: *Gibbons v. Ogden* (1824), the landmark commerce clause case, was argued for five days, and *McCulloch v. Maryland* (1819), the litigation challenging the constitutionality of the national bank, took nine days to argue.

The justices can interrupt the attorneys at any time with comments and questions, as illustrated by the following exchange between Justice Byron White and Sarah Weddington, the attorney representing Jane Roe in *Roe v. Wade* (1973). White got the ball rolling when he asked Weddington to respond to an issue her brief had not addressed: whether abortions should be performed during all stages of pregnancy or should somehow be limited. The following discussion ensued:

WHITE: And the statute doesn't make any distinction based upon at what period of pregnancy the abortion is performed?

WEDDINGTON: No, Your Honor. There is no time limit or indication of time, whatsoever. So I think—

WHITE: What is your constitutional position there?

WEDDINGTON: As to a time limit . . . It is our position that the freedom involved is that of a woman to determine whether or not to continue a pregnancy. Obviously, I have a much more difficult time saying that the State has no interest in late pregnancy.

WHITE: Why? Why is that?

WEDDINGTON: I think that's more the emotional response to a late pregnancy, rather than it is any constitutional—

WHITE: Emotional response by whom?

WEDDINGTON: I guess by persons considering the issue outside the legal context, I think, as far as the State—

WHITE: Well, do you or don't you say that the constitutional—

WEDDINGTON: I would say constitutional—

WHITE: —right you insist on reaches up to the time of birth, or—

WEDDINGTON: The Constitution, as I read it . . . attaches protection to the person at the time of birth.

In the Court's early years, there was little doubt about the importance of such exchanges, and of oral arguments in general, because, as noted above, the justices did not always have the benefit of written briefs. Today, however, some have questioned the effectiveness of oral arguments and their role in decision making. Chief Justice Earl Warren contended that they made little difference to the outcome. Once the justices have read the briefs and studied related cases, most have relatively firm views on how the case should be decided, and so these arguments change few minds. Justice William J. Brennan Jr., however, maintained that they are extremely important because they help justices to clarify core arguments. Recent scholarly work seems to come down on Brennan's side. According to a study by Timothy Johnson and his colleagues, the justices are more likely to vote for the side that performs more effectively at oral argument. Along somewhat different lines, a study by Epstein, Landes, and Posner shows that orals may be a good predictor of the Court's final votes: the side that receives more questions tends to lose.[14] One possible explanation is that the

---

[14]Timothy R. Johnson, Paul J. Wahlbeck, and James F. Spriggs, II, "The Influence of Oral Arguments on the U.S. Supreme Court," *American Political Science Review* 100 (2006): 99–113; Lee Epstein, William Landes, and Richard A. Posner, "Inferring the Winning Party in the Supreme Court from the Pattern of Questioning at Oral Argument," *Journal of Legal Studies* 39 (2010): 433–467.

justices use oral argument as a way to express their opinions and attempt to influence their colleagues because formal deliberation (described below) is often limited and highly structured.

Even if oral arguments turn out to have little effect on the justices' decisions, we should not forget their symbolic importance: they are the only part of the Court's decision-making process that occurs in public and that you now have the opportunity to hear. Political scientist Jerry Goldman has made the oral arguments of many cases available online at www.oyez.org. Throughout this book, you will find references to this website, indicating that you can listen to the arguments in the case you are reading.

The Supreme Court Decides: Some Preliminaries

After the Court hears oral arguments, it meets in a private conference to discuss the case and to take a preliminary vote. Below, we describe the Court's conference procedures and the two stages that follow the conference: the assignment of the opinion of the Court and the opinion circulation period.

The Conference

Despite popular support for "government in the sunshine," the Supreme Court insists that its decisions take place in a private conference, with no one in attendance except the justices. Congress has agreed to this demand, exempting the federal courts from open government and freedom of information legislation. There are two basic reasons for the Court's insistence on the private conference. First, the Court—which, unlike Congress, lacks an electoral connection—is supposed to base its decisions on factors other than public opinion. Opening up deliberations to press scrutiny, for example, might encourage the justices to take notice of popular sentiment, which is not supposed to influence them. Or so the argument goes. Second, although in conference the Court reaches tentative decisions on cases, the opinions explaining the decisions remain to be written. This process can take many weeks or even months, and a decision is not final until the opinions have been written, circulated, and approved. Because the Court's decisions can have major impacts on politics and the economy, any party having advance knowledge of case outcomes could use that information for unfair business and political advantage.

The system works so well that, with only a few exceptions, the justices have not experienced information leaks—at least not prior to the public announcement of a decision. After that, clerks and even justices have sometimes thrown their own sunshine on the Court's deliberations. *National Federation of Independent Business v. Sebelius* (2012), involving the constitutionality of the health care law passed in 2010, provides a recent example. Based on information from reliable sources, Jan Crawford of CBS News reported that Chief Justice John G. Roberts initially voted to join the Court's four conservative justices to strike down the law but later changed his vote to join the four liberals to uphold it.[15]

So, although it can be difficult to know precisely what occurs in the deliberation of any particular case, from journalistic accounts and the papers of retired justices we can piece together the procedures and the general nature of the Court's discussions. We have learned the following. First, we know that the chief justice presides over the deliberations. He calls up the case for discussion and then presents his views about the issues and how the case should be decided. The remaining justices state their views and vote in order of seniority.

The level and intensity of discussion, as the justices' notes from conference deliberations reveal, differ from case to case. In some, it appears that the justices had very little to say. The chief presented his views, and the rest noted their agreement. In others, every Court member had something to add. Whether the discussion is subdued or lively, it is unclear to what extent conferences affect the final decisions. It would be unusual for a justice to enter the conference room without having reached a tentative position on the cases to be discussed; after all, he or she has read the briefs and listened to oral arguments. But the conference, in addition to oral arguments, provides an opportunity for the justices to size up the positions of their colleagues. This sort of information, as we shall see, may be important as the justices begin the process of crafting and circulating opinions.

Opinion Assignment and Circulation

The conference typically leads to a tentative outcome and vote. What happens at this point is critical because it determines who assigns the opinion of the Court—the Court's only authoritative policy statement, the only one that establishes precedent. Under Court norms, when the chief justice votes with the majority,

---

[15]Jan Crawford, "Roberts Switched Views to Uphold Health Care Law," CBS News, *Face the Nation*, July 2, 2012, https://www.cbsnews.com/news/roberts-switched-views-to-uphold-health-care-law/.

he or she assigns the writing of the opinion. The chief may decide to write the opinion or assign it to one of the other justices who voted with the majority. When the chief justice votes with the minority, the assignment task falls to the most senior member of the Court who voted with the majority.

In making these assignments, the chief justice (or the senior associate in the majority) takes a number of factors into account.[16] First and perhaps foremost, the chief tries to equalize the distribution of the Court's workload. This makes sense: The Court will not run efficiently, given the burdensome nature of opinion writing, if some justices are given many more assignments than others. The chief may also consider the justices' particular areas of expertise, recognizing that some justices are more knowledgeable about particular areas of the law than others. By encouraging specialization, the chief may also be trying to increase the quality of opinions and reduce the time required to write them.

Along similar lines, there has been a tendency among chief justices to self-assign especially important cases. Warren took this step in the famous case of *Brown v. Board of Education* (1954), and Roberts did the same in the health care case. Some scholars and even some justices have suggested that this is a smart strategy, if only for symbolic reasons. As Justice Felix Frankfurter put it, "[T]here are occasions when an opinion should carry extra weight which pronouncement by the Chief Justice gives."[17] Finally, for cases decided by a one-vote margin (usually 5–4), chiefs have been known to assign the opinion to a moderate member of the majority rather than to an extreme member. There is a strategic reason for this decision: if the writer in a close case drafts an opinion with which other members of the majority are uncomfortable, the opinion may drive justices to the other side, causing the majority to become a minority. A chief justice may try to minimize this risk by asking justices squarely in the middle of the majority coalition to write.

Regardless of the factors the chief considers in making assignments, one thing is clear: the opinion writer is a critical player in the opinion circulation phase, which eventually leads to the final decision of the Court. The writer begins the process by circulating an opinion draft to the others.

Once the justices receive the first draft of the opinion, they have many options. First, they can join the opinion, meaning that they agree with it and want no changes. Second, they can ask the opinion writer to make changes, that is, *bargain* with the writer over the content of and even the disposition—to reverse or affirm the lower court ruling—offered in the draft. The following memo sent from Brennan to White is exemplary: "I've mentioned to you that I favor your approach to this case and want if possible to join your opinion. If you find the following suggestions . . . acceptable, I can join you."[18]

Third, they can tell the opinion writer that they plan to circulate a dissenting or concurring opinion. A concurring opinion generally agrees with the disposition but not with the rationale; a dissenting opinion means that the writer disagrees with the disposition the majority opinion reaches and with the rationale it invokes. Finally, justices can tell the opinion writer that they await further writings, meaning that they want to study various dissents or concurrences before they decide what to do.

As justices circulate their opinions and revise them—the average majority opinion undergoes three to four revisions in response to colleagues' comments—many different opinions on the same case, at various stages of development, may be floating around the Court over the course of several months. Because this process is replicated for each case the Court decides with a formal written opinion, it is possible that scores of different opinions may be working their way from office to office at any point in time.

Eventually, the final version of the opinion is reached, and each justice expresses a position in writing or by signing an opinion of another justice. This is how the final vote is taken. When all of the justices have declared themselves, the only remaining step is for the Court to announce its decision and the vote to the public.

SUPREME COURT DECISION MAKING: LEGALISM

So far, we have examined the processes the justices follow to reach decisions on the disputes brought before them.

---

[16]See, for example, Forrest Maltzman and Paul J. Wahlbeck, "May It Please the Chief? Opinion Assignments in the Rehnquist Court," *American Journal of Political Science* 40 (1996): 421–443; Elliot E. Slotnick, "The Chief Justices and Self-Assignment of Majority Opinions," *Western Political Quarterly* 31 (1978): 219–225.

[17]Felix Frankfurter, "The Administrative Side of Chief Justice Hughes," *Harvard Law Review* 63 (1949): 4.

[18]Memorandum from Justice Brennan to Justice White, December 9, 1976, re: 75–104, **United Jewish Organizations of Williamsburgh v. Carey.**

We have answered basic questions about the institutional procedures the Court uses to carry out its responsibilities. The questions we have not addressed concern why the justices reach particular decisions and what forces play a role in determining their choices.

As you might imagine, the responses to these questions are many, but they can be categorized into two groups. One focuses on the role of law, broadly defined, and legal methods in determining how justices interpret the Constitution, emphasizing, among other things, the importance of its words, American history and tradition, and precedent (previously decided constitutional rulings). Judge Richard Posner and his coauthors have referred to this as a legalistic theory of judicial decision making.[19] The other—what Posner et al. call a realistic theory of judging—emphasizes nonlegalistic factors, including the role of politics. "Politics" can take many forms, such as the particular ideological views of the justices, the mood of the public, and the political preferences of the executive and legislative branches.

Commentators sometimes define these two sides as "should" versus "do." That is, they say the justices *should* interpret the Constitution in line with, say, the language of the text of the document or in accord with precedent. They reason that justices are supposed to shed all their personal biases, preferences, and partisan attachments when they take their seats on the bench. But, it is argued, justices *do not* shed these biases, preferences, and attachments; rather, their decisions often reflect the justices' own politics or the political views of those around them.

Although it may be tempting to assume that the justices use the law to camouflage their politics, there are several reasons to believe that they actually do seek to follow a legal approach. One reason is that the justices themselves often say they look to the founding period, the words of the Constitution, previously decided cases, and other legalistic approaches to resolve disputes because they consider them appropriate criteria for reaching decisions. Another is that some scholars express agreement with the justices, arguing that Court members cannot follow their own personal preferences, the whims of the public, or other non–legally relevant factors "if they are to have the continued respect of their colleagues, the wider legal community, citizens, and leaders." Rather, they "must be principled in their decision-making process."[20]

Whether they are principled in their decision making is for you to determine as you read the cases to come. For you to make this determination, it is of course necessary to develop some familiarity with both legalism and realism. In the next section we turn to realism; here we begin with legalism, which, in constitutional law, centers on the methods of constitutional interpretation that the justices frequently say they employ. We consider some of the most important methods and describe the rationale for their use. These methods include original intent, original meaning, textualism, structural analysis, stare decisis, pragmatism, and polling other jurisdictions.[21] Using the Second Amendment as an example, Table 2-1 provides a brief summary of these methods, after which we supply more details on each one.

The Second Amendment of the U.S. Constitution reads as follows: "A well regulated Militia, being necessary to the security of a free State, the right of the people to keep and bear Arms, shall not be infringed." In *District of Columbia v. Heller* (2008) *(excerpted in chapter 15)*, the U.S. Supreme Court ruled that the amendment protects the right of individuals who are not affiliated with any state-regulated militia to keep handguns and other firearms in their homes for their own private use.

Legal briefs filed with the Court, as well as media and academic commentary on the case, employed diverse methods of constitutional interpretation. Notice that no method seems to dictate a particular outcome; rather, lawyers for either side of the lawsuit could plausibly employ a variety of approaches to support their side.

Originalism

Originalism comes in several different forms, and we discuss two below—original intent and original understanding (or meaning)—but the basic idea is that

---

[19]Lee Epstein, William M. Landes, and Richard A. Posner, *The Behavior of Federal Judges: A Theoretical and Empirical Study of Rational Choice* (Cambridge, MA: Harvard University Press, 2013).

[20]Ronald Kahn, "Institutional Norms and Supreme Court Decision Making: The Rehnquist Court on Privacy and Religion," in *Supreme Court Decision-Making*, ed. Cornell W. Clayton and Howard Gillman (Chicago: University of Chicago Press, 1999), 176.

[21]For overviews (and critiques) of these and other approaches, see Eugene Volokh, "Using the Second Amendment as a Teaching Tool—Modalities of Constitutional Argument," *UCLA Law*, http://www2.law.ucla.edu/volokh/2amteach/interp.htm; Philip Bobbitt, *Constitutional Fate: Theory of the Constitution* (New York: Oxford University Press, 1982); and Lackland H. Bloom, *Methods of Constitutional Interpretation: How the Supreme Court Reads the Constitution* (New York: Oxford University Press, 2009).

Table 2-1 Methods of Constitutional Interpretation

Method	Example
Originalism *Original Intent.* Asks what the framers wanted to do.	"The framers would have been shocked by the notion of the government taking away our handguns." OR "The framers would have been shocked by the notion of people being entitled to own guns in a society where guns cause so much death and violence."
Original Meaning. Considers what a clause meant (or how it was understood) to those who enacted it.	"'Militia' meant 'armed adult male citizenry' when the Second Amendment was enacted, so that's how we should interpret it today." OR "'Arms' meant flintlocks and the like when the Second Amendment was enacted, so that's how we should interpret it today."
Textualism. Places emphasis on what the Constitution says.	"The Second Amendment says 'right of the people to keep and bear arms,' so the people have a right to keep and bear arms." OR "The Second Amendment says 'A well regulated militia . . . ,' so the right is limited only to the militia."
Structural Analysis. Suggests that interpretation of particular clauses should be consistent with or follow from overarching structures or governing principles established in the Constitution—for example, the democratic process, federalism, and the separation of powers.	"Article 1, Section 8, of the Constitution lists the powers of Congress. Included among them are the powers to provide for calling 'forth the militia to execute the laws of the union, suppress insurrections and repel invasions' and 'for organizing, arming, and disciplining, the militia.' Because these clauses suggest the federal government controls the militia, reading the Second Amendment as a grant of power to the states would be inconsistent with them." OR "The Constitution sets up a government run by constitutional democratic processes, with various democratic checks and balances, such as federalism and elections. To read the Second Amendment as facilitating violent revolution is inconsistent with this structure."
Stare Decisis. Looks to what courts have written about the clause.	"Courts have held that the Second Amendment protects weapons that are part of ordinary military equipment, and handguns certainly qualify." OR "Courts have held that the Second Amendment was meant to keep the militia as an effective force, and they can be nicely effective just with rifles."
Pragmatism. Considers the effect of various interpretations, suggesting that courts should adopt the one that avoids bad consequences.	"The Second Amendment should be interpreted as protecting the right to own handguns for self-defense because otherwise only criminals will have guns and crime will skyrocket." OR "The Second Amendment should be interpreted as not protecting the right to own handguns for self-defense because otherwise we'll never solve our crime problems."
Polling Jurisdictions. Examines practices in the United States and even abroad.	"The legislatures of all fifty states are united in their rejection of bans on private handgun ownership. Every state in the Union permits private citizens to own handguns. Practices in other countries are immaterial to the task of interpreting the U.S. Constitution." OR "The largest cities in the United States have local laws banning handguns or tightly regulating their possession and use, and many industrialized countries also ban handguns or grant permits in only exceptional cases."

Sources: We adapt much of the material in this table from Eugene Volokh, "Using the Second Amendment as a Teaching Tool—Modalities of Constitutional Argument," *UCLA Law,* http://www2.law.ucla.edu/volokh/2amteach/interp.htm. Other material comes from the briefs filed in *District of Columbia v. Heller.*

originalists attempt to interpret the Constitution in line with what it meant at the time of its drafting. One form of originalism emphasizes the intent of the Constitution's framers. The Supreme Court first invoked the term *intention of the framers* in 1796. In **Hylton v. United States**, the Court said, "It was . . . obviously the intention of the framers of the Constitution, that Congress should possess full power over every species of taxable property, except exports. The term taxes, is generical, and was made use of to vest in Congress plenary authority in all cases of taxation."[22] In *Hustler Magazine v. Falwell* (1988), the Court used the same grounds to find that cartoon parodies, however obnoxious, constitute expression protected by the First Amendment.

No doubt, justices over the years have looked to the intent of the framers to reach conclusions about the disputes before them.[23] But why? What possible relevance could the framers' intentions have for today's controversies? Advocates of this approach offer several answers. First, they assert that the framers acted in a calculated manner—that is, they knew what they were doing—so why should we disregard their precepts? One adherent said, "Those who framed the Constitution chose their words carefully; they debated at great length the most minute points. The language they chose meant something. It is incumbent upon the Court to determine what that meaning was."[24]

Second, it is argued that if they scrutinize the intent of the framers, justices can deduce "constitutional truths," which they can apply to cases. Doing so, proponents say, produces neutral principles of law and eliminates value-laden decisions.[25] Consider speech advocating the violent overthrow of the government. Suppose the government enacted a law prohibiting such expression and arrested members of a radical political party for violating it. Justices could scrutinize this law in several ways. A liberal might conclude, solely because of his or her liberal values, that the First Amendment prohibits a ban on such expression. Conservative jurists might reach the opposite conclusion. Neither would be proper jurisprudence in the opinion of those who advocate an original intent approach because both are value-laden and ideological preferences should not creep into the law. Rather, justices should examine the framers' intent as a way to keep the law value-free. Applying this approach to free speech, one adherent argues, leads to a clear, unbiased result:

> Speech advocating violent overthrow is . . . not [protected] "political speech" . . . as that term must be defined by a Madisonian system of government. It is not political speech because it violates constitutional truths about processes and because it is not aimed at a new definition of political truth by a legislative majority.[26]

Finally, supporters of this mode of analysis argue that it fosters stability in law. They maintain that, without originalism, the law becomes far too fluid, changing with the ideological whims of the justices and creating havoc for those who must interpret and implement Court decisions. Lower court judges, lawyers, and even ordinary citizens do not know if today's rights will still exist tomorrow. Following a jurisprudence of original intent would eliminate such confusion because it provides a principle that justices can consistently follow.

The last justification applies with equal force to a second form of originalism: *original meaning or understanding*. Justice Antonin Scalia explained the difference between this approach and intentionalism:

> The theory of originalism treats a constitution like a statute, and gives it the meaning that its words were understood to bear at the time they were promulgated. You will sometimes hear it described as the theory of original intent. You will never hear me refer to original intent, because as I say I am first of all a textualist, and secondly an originalist. If you are a textualist, you don't care about the intent, and I don't care if the framers of the Constitution had some secret meaning in mind when they adopted its words. I take the words as they were promulgated to the people of the United States, and what is the fairly understood meaning of those words.[27]

---

[22]Example cited by Boris I. Bittker in "The Bicentennial of the Jurisprudence of Original Intent: The Recent Past," *California Law Review* 77 (1989): 235.

[23]Given the subject of this volume, we deal here exclusively with the intent of the framers of the U.S. Constitution and its amendments, but one also could apply this approach to statutory construction by considering the intent of those who drafted and enacted the laws in question.

[24]Edwin Meese III, address before the American Bar Association, Washington, DC, July 9, 1983.

[25]See, for example, Robert Bork, "Neutral Principles and Some First Amendment Problems," *Indiana Law Journal* 47 (1971): 1–35.

[26]Ibid., 31.

[27]Antonin Scalia, "A Theory of Constitutional Interpretation," remarks at the Catholic University of America, Washington, DC, October 18, 1996.

By "textualist," Justice Scalia means that he looks at the words of whatever constitutional provision he is interpreting and then interprets them in line with what they would have ordinarily meant to the people of the time when they were written.[28] This is the "originalist" aspect of his method of interpreting the Constitution. So, while intentionalism focuses on the intent behind phrases, an original understanding approach would emphasize "the meaning a reasonable speaker of English would have attached to the words, phrases, sentences, etc. at the time the particular provision was adopted."[29]

Even so, as we suggested earlier, the merits of this approach are similar to those of intentionalism. By focusing on how the framers defined their own words and then applying their definitions to disputes over those constitutional provisions containing them, this approach seeks to generate value-free and ideology-free jurisprudence. Indeed, one of the most important developers of this approach, historian William W. Crosskey, specifically embraced it to counter "sophistries"—mostly, the idea that the Constitution is a living document whose meaning should evolve over time.[30]

Chief Justice William H. Rehnquist's opinion in *Nixon v. United States* (1993) provides an example. Here, the Court considered a challenge to the procedures the Senate used to impeach a federal judge, Walter L. Nixon Jr. Rather than the entire Senate trying the case, a special twelve-member committee heard evidence and reported to the full body, which in turn used that report to convict and remove him from office. Nixon argued that this procedure violated Article I of the Constitution, which states, "The Senate shall have the sole Power to try all Impeachments." But before addressing Nixon's claim, Rehnquist sought to determine whether courts had any business resolving such disputes. He used a meaning of the words approach to consider the word *try* in Article I:

> Petitioner argues that the word "try" in the first sentence imposes by implication an additional requirement on the Senate in that the proceedings must be in the nature of a judicial trial. . . . There are several difficulties

with this position which lead us ultimately to reject it. The word "try," both in 1787 and later, has considerably broader meanings than those to which petitioner would limit it. Older dictionaries define try as "[t]o examine" or "[t]o examine as a judge." See 2 S. Johnson, A Dictionary of the English Language (1785). In more modern usage the term has various meanings. For example, try can mean "to examine or investigate judicially," "to conduct the trial of," or "to put to the test by experiment, investigation. . . ." Webster's Third New International Dictionary (1971).

Nixon is far from the only example of originalism. Indeed, many Supreme Court opinions contemplate the original intent of the framers or the original meaning of the words, and at least one justice on the current Court—Clarence Thomas—regularly invokes forms of originalism to answer questions ranging from the appropriate balance of power between the states and the federal government to limits on campaign spending.

Such a jurisprudential course would have dismayed Thomas's predecessor, Thurgood Marshall, who did not believe that the Constitution's meaning was "forever 'fixed' at the Philadelphia Convention." And, considering the 1787 Constitution's treatment of women and blacks, Marshall did not find "the wisdom, foresight, and sense of justice exhibited by the framers particularly profound."[31]

Marshall has not been the only critic of originalism (whatever the form); the approach has generated many others over the years. One reason for the controversy is that originalism became highly politicized in the 1980s. Those who advocated it, particularly Edwin Meese, an attorney general in President Ronald Reagan's administration, and defeated Supreme Court nominee Robert Bork, were widely viewed as conservatives who were using the doctrine to promote their own ideological ends.

Others joined Marshall, however, in raising several more concrete objections to this jurisprudence. Justice Brennan in 1985 argued that if the justices employed only this approach, the Constitution would lose its applicability and be rendered useless:

> We current Justices read the Constitution in the only way that we can: as Twentieth

---

[28]See Scalia's "Originalism: The Lesser Evil," *University of Cincinnati Law Review* 57 (1989): 849–865.

[29]Randy E. Barnett, "The Original Meaning of the Commerce Clause," *University of Chicago Law Review* 68 (2001): 105.

[30]W. W. Crosskey, *Politics and the Constitution in the History of the United States* (Chicago: University of Chicago Press, 1953), 1172–1173.

[31]Thurgood Marshall, "Reflections on the Bicentennial of the United States Constitution," *Harvard Law Review* 101 (1987): 1.

Century Americans. We look to the history of the time of the framing and to the intervening history of interpretation. But the ultimate question must be, what do the words of the text mean in our time? For the genius of the Constitution rests not in any static meaning it might have had in a world that is dead and gone, but in the adaptability of its great principles to cope with current problems and current needs.[32]

Some scholars have echoed the sentiment. C. Herman Pritchett has noted that originalism can "make a nation the prisoner of its past, and reject any constitutional development save constitutional amendment."[33]

Another criticism often leveled at intentionalism is that the Constitution embodies not one intent but many. Jeffrey A. Segal and Harold J. Spaeth pose some interesting questions: "Who were the Framers? All fifty-five of the delegates who showed up at one time or another in Philadelphia during the summer of 1787? Some came and went. . . . Some probably had not read [the Constitution]. Assuredly, they were not all of a single mind."[34] Then there is the question of what sources the justices should use to divine the original intentions of the framers. They could look at the records of the constitutional debates and at the founders' journals and papers, but some of the documents that pass for "records" of the Philadelphia convention are jumbled, and some are even forged. During the debates, the secretary became confused and thoroughly botched the minutes. James Madison, who took the most complete and probably the most reliable notes on what was said, edited them after the convention adjourned. And then there are other writings of the period, such as the enormous number of pamphlets in circulation that argued for and against ratification of the new Constitution. Perhaps this is why in 1952 Justice Robert H. Jackson wrote:

> Just what our forefathers did envision, or would have envisioned had they foreseen modern

conditions, must be divined from materials almost as enigmatic as the dreams Joseph was called upon to interpret for Pharaoh. A century and a half of partisan debate and scholarly specification yields no net result but only supplies more or less apt quotations from respected sources on each side of any question. They largely cancel each other.[35]

As hard as it may be to ascertain the intention of the framers, it may be just as difficult for the Court to determine the original meaning of their words. There were a variety of dictionaries that were available during the founding era—some general and some legal, sometimes with contrary definitions. Even conscientious efforts to divine the meaning of a word or phrase as it was used in the late eighteenth century could yield inconclusive results.

Textualism

On the surface, textualism resembles originalism: it values the Constitution itself as a guide above all else. But this is where the similarity ends. In an effort to prevent the infusion of new meanings from sources outside the text of the Constitution, adherents of original intent seek to deduce constitutional truths by examining the *intended* meanings behind the words. Textualists look no further than the words of the Constitution to reach decisions.

This may seem similar to the original meaning approach we just considered, and there is certainly a commonality between the two approaches: both place emphasis on the words of the Constitution. But under the original meaning approach (Scalia's brand of textualism), it is fair game for justices to go beyond the literal meanings of the words and consider what they would have ordinarily meant to the people of that time. Other textualists, those we might call pure textualists or *literalists*, believe that justices ought to consider only the words in the constitutional text, and the words alone.

And it is these distinctions—between original intent and even meaning versus pure textualism—that can lead to some radically different results. To use the example of speech aimed at overthrowing the U.S. government, originalists would hold that the meaning or intent behind the First Amendment prohibits such expression. Those who consider themselves *pure* literalists, on the other hand, might scrutinize the words of the First

[32]William J. Brennan Jr., address to the Text and Teaching Symposium, Georgetown University, Washington, DC, October 12, 1985.

[33]C. Herman Pritchett, *Constitutional Law of the Federal System* (Englewood Cliffs, NJ: Prentice Hall, 1984), 37.

[34]Jeffrey A. Segal and Harold J. Spaeth, *The Supreme Court and the Attitudinal Model Revisited* (New York: Cambridge University Press, 2002), 68. See also William Anderson, "The Intention of the Framers: A Note on Constitutional Interpretation," *American Political Science Review* 49 (1955): 340–352.

[35]*Youngstown Sheet & Tube Co. v. Sawyer* (1952).

Amendment—"Congress shall make no law . . . abridging the freedom of speech"—and construe them literally: *no law* means *no law*. Therefore, any statute infringing on speech, even a law that prohibits expression advocating the overthrow of the government, would violate the First Amendment.

Originalism and pure textualism sometimes overlap. When it comes to the right to privacy, particularly where it is leveraged to create other rights, such as legalized abortion, *some* originalists and literalists would reach the same conclusion: it does not exist. The former would argue that it was not the intent of the framers to confer privacy; the latter, that because the Constitution does not expressly mention this right, it does not exist.

Textual analysis is quite common in Supreme Court opinions. Many, if not most, opinions interpreting the Constitution look to its words in one way or another, but Justice Hugo Black is most closely associated with this view—at least in its pure form. During his thirty-four-year tenure on the Court, Black continually emphasized his literalist philosophy. His own words best describe his position:

> My view is, without deviation, without exception, without any ifs, buts, or whereases, that freedom of speech means that government shall not do anything to people . . . either for the views they have or the views they express or the words they speak or write. Some people would have you believe that this is a very radical position, and maybe it is. But all I am doing is following what to me is the clear wording of the First Amendment. . . . As I have said innumerable times before I simply believe that "Congress shall make no law" means Congress shall make no law. . . . Thus we have the absolute command of the First Amendment that no law shall be passed by Congress abridging freedom of speech or the press.[36]

Why did Black advocate literalism? Like originalists, he viewed it as a value-free form of jurisprudence. If justices looked only at the words of the Constitution, their decisions would not reflect ideological or political values, but rather those of the document. Black's opinions provide good illustrations. Although he almost always supported claims of free *speech* against government challenges, he

refused to extend constitutional protection to *expression* that was not strictly speech. He believed, for example, that symbolic activities—such as wearing armbands or burning a draft card or the American flag—even if calculated to express political views, fell outside the protections of the First Amendment. Speech is protected; conduct is not.

Despite the seeming logic of his justifications and the high regard many scholars have for Black, his brand of jurisprudence has been vulnerable to attack. Some assert that it led him to take some rather odd positions, particularly in cases involving the First Amendment. Most analysts and justices—even those considered liberal—agree that obscene materials fall outside of First Amendment protection and that states can prohibit the dissemination of such materials. But in opinion after opinion, Black clung to the view that no publication could be banned because it was obscene.

A second objection is that literalism can result in inconsistent outcomes. Is it really sensible for Black to hold that obscenity is constitutionally protected while other types of expression, such as desecration of the flag, are not?

Segal and Spaeth raise yet a third problem with literalism: it presupposes a precision in the English language that does not exist. Not only may words, including those used by the framers, have multiple meanings,[37] but also the meanings themselves may be contrary. For example, the common legal word *sanction*, as Segal and Spaeth note, means both to punish *and* to approve.[38] How, then, would a literalist construe it?

Finally, even when the words are crystal clear, pure textualism may not be on firm ground. Despite the precision of some constitutional provisions—such as minimum age of the thirty-five for the president—they are loaded with "reasons, goals, values, and the like."[39] Law professor Frank Easterbrook notes that the framers might have imposed the presidential age limit "as a percentage of average life expectancy" (to ensure that presidents have a

---

[36]Hugo L. Black, *A Constitutional Faith* (New York: Knopf, 1969), 45–46.

[37]Anyone who has ever seen Shakespeare's *The Merchant of Venice* has seen this illustrated when the clever Portia, posing as judge, saves Antonio from forfeiting a "pound of flesh" for his failure to repay a loan. While other characters assume a commonly understood meaning of the word "flesh," Portia interprets the word more strictly—to exclude "blood"—and thus makes it impossible for the bargain to be fulfilled.

[38]Segal and Spaeth, *The Supreme Court and the Attitudinal Model Revisited*, 54.

[39]Frank Easterbrook, "Statutes' Domains," *University of Chicago Law Review* 50 (1983): 536.

good deal of practical political experience before ascending to the presidency and little opportunity to engage in politicking after they leave) or "as a minimum number of years after puberty" (to guarantee that they are sufficiently mature while not unduly limiting the pool of eligible candidates). Seen in this way, the words "thirty-five Years" in the Constitution may not have much value: they may be "simply the framers' shorthand for their more complex policies, and we could replace them by 'fifty years' or 'thirty years' without impairing the integrity of the constitutional structure."[40] More generally, as Justice Oliver Wendell Holmes Jr. once put it, "A word is not a crystal, transparent and unchanged, it is the skin of a living thought and may vary greatly in color and content according to the circumstances and the time in which it is used."[41]

Structural Analysis

Textualist and originalist approaches tend to focus on particular words or clauses in the Constitution. Structural reasoning suggests that interpretation of these clauses should follow from, or at least be consistent with, over-arching structures or governing principles established in the Constitution—most notably, federalism and the separation of powers. Interestingly enough, these terms do not appear in the Constitution, but they "are familiar to any student of constitutional law,"[42] and they will become second nature to you, too, as you work your way through the material in the pages to follow. The idea behind structuralism is that these structures or relationships are so important that judges and lawyers should read the Constitution with an eye toward preserving them.

There are many famous examples of structural analyses, especially, as you would expect, in separation of powers and federalism cases. Charles Black, a leading proponent of structuralism, for example, points to *McCulloch v. Maryland* (1819). Among the questions the Court addressed was whether a state could tax a federal entity—the Bank of the United States. Even though states have the power to tax, Chief Justice John Marshall for the Court said it could not be taxed because the states could use this power to extinguish the bank. If states could do this, they would damage what Marshall believed

to be "the warranted relational properties between the national government and the government of the states, with the structural corollaries of national supremacy."[43]

Here, Marshall invalidated a state action aimed at the federal government. Throughout this book, you will see the reverse, as well: the justices invoking structural-federalism arguments to defend state laws against attack by individuals. You will also spot structural arguments relating to the democratic process. We provide an example in Table 2-1, and there are many others in the pages to follow.

Despite their frequent appearance, structural arguments have their weaknesses. Primarily, as Philip Bobbitt notes, "while we all can agree on the presence of the various structures, we [bicker] when called upon to decide whether a particular result is necessarily inferred from their relationship."[44] What this means is that structural reasoning does not necessarily lead to a single answer in each and every case. *INS v. Chadha* (1983), involving the constitutionality of the legislative veto (used by Congress to veto decisions made by the executive branch), provides an example. Writing for the majority, Chief Justice Burger held that such a veto violated the constitutional doctrine of separation of powers; it eroded the "carefully defined limits of the power of each Branch" established by the framers. Writing in dissent, Justice White, too, relied in part on structural analysis but came to a very different conclusion: the legislative veto fit compatibly with the separation of powers system because it ensured that Congress could continue to play "its role as the Nation's lawmaker" in the wake of the growth in the size of the executive branch.

The gap between Burger and White reflects disagreement over the very nature of the separation of powers system, and similar disagreements arise over federalism and the democratic process. Hence, even when justices reason from structure, it is possible, even likely, that they will reach different conclusions.

Stare Decisis

Translated from Latin, the term *stare decisis* means "let the decision stand." What this concept suggests is that, as a general rule, jurists should decide cases on the basis of previously established rulings, or precedent. In shorthand terms, judicial tribunals should honor prior rulings.

---

[40]Tushnet, "A Note on the Revival of Textualism," 686.

[41]*Towne v. Eisner* (1918).

[42]Michael J. Gerhardt, Stephen M. Griffin, and Thomas D. Rowe Jr., *Constitutional Theory: Arguments and Perspectives*, 3rd ed. (Newark, NJ: LexisNexis, 2007), 321.

[43]Charles L. Black Jr., *Structure and Relationship in Constitutional Law* (Baton Rouge: Louisiana State University Press, 1969), 15.

[44]Bobbitt, *Constitutional Fate*, 84.

The benefits of this approach are fairly evident. If justices rely on past cases to resolve current cases, the law they generate becomes predictable and stable. Justice Harlan F. Stone acknowledged the value of precedent in a somewhat more ironic way: "The rule of stare decisis embodies a wise policy because it is often more important that a rule of law be settled than that it be settled right."[45] The message, however, is the same: if the Court adheres to past decisions, it provides some direction to all who labor in the legal enterprise. Lower court judges know how they should and should not decide cases, lawyers can frame their arguments in accord with the lessons of past cases, legislators understand what they can and cannot enact or regulate, and so forth.

Precedent, then, can be an important and useful factor in Supreme Court decision making. It certainly seems important to the justices; the Court rarely reverses itself, having done so fewer than three hundred times over its entire history. Even modern-day Courts, as Table 2-2 shows, have been loath to overrule precedents. In the seven decades covered in the table, the Court overturned only 168 precedents, or, on average, about 2.5 per term. What is more, the justices almost always cite previous rulings in their decisions; indeed, it is the rare Court opinion that does not mention other cases.[46] Finally, several scholars have verified that precedent helps to explain Court decisions in some areas of the law. In one study, analysts found that the Court reacted quite consistently to legal doctrine presented in more than fifteen years of death penalty litigation. Put differently, using precedent from past cases, the researchers could correctly categorize the outcomes (for or against the death penalty) in 75 percent of sixty-four cases decided since 1972.[47] Scholarly work considering precedent in search and seizure litigation has produced similar findings.[48]

Despite these data, we should not conclude that the justices necessarily follow this approach. Many allege that judicial appeal to precedent often is mere window dressing, used to hide ideologies and values, rather than

Table 2-2	Precedents Overruled, 1953–2018 Terms		
Court Era (Terms)	Number of Terms	Number of Overruled Precedents	Average Number of Overrulings Per Term
Warren Court (1953–1968)	16	46	2.9
Burger Court (1969–1985)	17	56	3.3
Rehnquist Court (1986–2004)	19	45	2.4
Roberts Court (2005–2018)	14	21	1.5

Source: Calculated by the authors from data in the U.S. Supreme Court Database (http://supremecourtdatabase.org).

a substantive form of analysis. There are several reasons for this allegation.

First, the Supreme Court has generated so much precedent that it is usually possible for justices to find support for any conclusion. By way of proof, turn to almost any page of any opinion excerpted in this book and you probably will find the writers—both for the majority and the dissenters—citing precedent.

Second, it may be difficult to locate the rule of law emerging in a majority opinion. That conflict is an important determinant of case selection is an indicator that the lines drawn by precedent can be difficult to discern; if lower courts, doing their level best, end up reaching different conclusions on the same legal question, a clear command of stare decisis may not exist. To decide whether a previous decision qualifies as a precedent, judges and commentators often say, one must strip away the nonessentials of the case and expose the basic reasons for the Supreme Court's decision. This process is generally referred to as "establishing the principle of the case," or the ratio decidendi. Other points made in a given opinion—obiter dicta (any expression in an opinion that is unnecessary to the decision reached in the case or that relates to a factual situation other than the one actually before the court)—have no legal weight and do not bind judges. It is up to courts to separate the ratio decidendi from dicta. Not only is this task difficult but

---

[45]*United States v. Underwriters Association* (1944).

[46]See Jack Knight and Lee Epstein, "The Norm of Stare Decisis," *American Journal of Political Science* 40 (1996): 1018–1035.

[47]Tracey E. George and Lee Epstein, "On the Nature of Supreme Court Decision Making," *American Political Science Review* 86 (1992): 323–337.

[48]Jeffrey A. Segal, "Predicting Supreme Court Cases Probabilistically: The Search and Seizure Cases, 1962–1984," *American Political Science Review* 78 (1984): 891–900.

it also provides a way for justices to skirt precedent with which they do not agree. All they need to do is declare parts of it to be dicta. Or justices can brush aside even the ratio decidendi when it suits their interests. What this means is that justices can always deal with "problematic" ratio decidendi by distinguishing a case from those already been decided (or, alternatively, by refusing to decide such cases).

A scholarly study of the role of precedent in Supreme Court decision making offers a third reason. Two political scientists hypothesized that if precedent matters, it ought to affect the subsequent decisions of at least some members of the Court: if a justice dissented from a decision establishing a particular precedent, the same justice would not dissent from a subsequent application of the precedent. But that, it turned out, was not the case. Of the eighteen justices included in the study, only two occasionally subjugated their preferences to precedent.[49]

Finally, many justices recognize the limits of stare decisis in cases involving constitutional interpretation. Indeed, the justices often say that when constitutional issues are involved, stare decisis is a less rigid rule than it might normally be. This view strikes some as prudent, for the Constitution is difficult to amend, and judges make mistakes or they come to see problems quite differently as their perspectives change. As Justice Lewis Powell wrote:

> Where the Court errs in its construction of a statute, correction may always be accomplished by legislative action. Revision of a constitutional interpretation, on the other hand, is often impossible as a practical matter, for it requires the cumbersome route of constitutional amendment. It is thus not only our prerogative, but also our duty, to reexamine a precedent where its reasoning or understanding of the Constitution is fairly called into question. And if the precedent or its rationale is of doubtful validity, then it should not stand.[50]

[49]Jeffrey A. Segal and Harold J. Spaeth, "The Influence of Stare Decisis on the Votes of U.S. Supreme Court Justices," *American Journal of Political Science* 40 (1996): 971–1003.

[50]Justice Powell, concurring in *Mitchell v. W. T. Grant Co.*, 416 U.S. 600 (1974). Whether the justices follow this idea—that stare decisis policy is more flexible in constitutional cases—is a matter of debate. See Lee Epstein, William M. Landes, and Adam Liptak, "The Decision to Depart (or Not) from Constitutional Precedent," *NYU Law Review* 90 (2015): 1115–1159.

Pragmatism

Justices often look to the future, appraising alternative rulings and forecasting their consequences. This means that, quite apart from legal principle, the members of the Court often consider the effects of a decision for different segments of society—agriculture, airlines, banks, churches, energy producers, financial institutions, physicians, railroads, retirees, technology companies, among others. The Court is not necessarily interested in abstract doctrine alone; it often wants to know how its doctrines will work when put into practice.

This interpretive approach often takes the form of a balancing exercise: How should one weigh the president's interest in confidentiality against the need for information in a criminal proceeding? Which demands greater consideration—a state's safety interest in banning certain trucks from its highways or the national interest in eliminating burdens on interstate commerce? What is the appropriate balance between the state's interest in compulsory education and a religious claim to be exempt from such laws? In answering such questions, a justice will select from among plausible constitutional interpretations the one that has the best consequences and reject the ones that have the worst.

Thus, when pragmatism makes an appearance in the Supreme Court opinions, justices may attempt to create rules, or analyze existing ones, so that they maximize benefits and minimize costs. Consider the exclusionary rule, which forbids use in criminal proceedings of evidence obtained in violation of the Fourth Amendment. Claims that the rule hampers the conviction of criminals have affected judicial attitudes, as Justice White frankly admitted in *United States v. Leon* (1984): "The substantial social costs exacted by the exclusionary rule for the vindication of Fourth Amendment rights have long been a source of concern." In *Leon* a majority of the justices applied a "cost-benefit" calculus to justify a "good faith" seizure by police on an invalid search warrant.

When you encounter cases that engage in this sort of analysis, you might ask the same questions some critics of the approach raise: By what account of values should judges weigh costs and benefits? How do they take into account the different people whom a decision may simultaneously punish and reward?

Polls of Other Jurisdictions

Aside from turning to originalism, textualism, or other historical approaches, a justice might probe English traditions or early colonial or state practices to determine how public officials of the times—or of contemporary times—interpreted similar words or phrases.[51] The Supreme Court has frequently used such evidence. When **Wolf v. Colorado** (1949) presented the Court with the question whether the Fourth Amendment barred use in state courts of evidence obtained through an unconstitutional search, Justice Felix Frankfurter surveyed the law in all the states and in ten jurisdictions within the British Commonwealth. He used the information to bolster a conclusion that, although the Constitution forbade unreasonable searches and seizures, it did not prohibit state officials from using such questionably obtained evidence against a defendant. In 1952, however, when *Rochin v. California* asked the justices whether a state could use evidence it had obtained from a defendant by pumping his stomach—evidence admissible in the overwhelming majority of states at that time—Frankfurter declined to call the roll. Instead, he declared that gathering evidence by a stomach pump was "conduct that shocks the conscience" whose fruits could not be used in either state or federal courts.

When *Mapp v. Ohio* overruled *Wolf* a few years later and held that state courts must *exclude* all unconstitutionally obtained evidence, the justices again returned to survey the field. For the Court, Justice Tom C. Clark said, "While in 1949 almost two-thirds of the States were opposed to the exclusionary rule, now, despite the *Wolf* case, more than half of those since passing upon it, by their own legislative or judicial decision, have wholly or partly adopted or adhered to the [rule]."

The point of this set of examples is not that Frankfurter or the Court was inconsistent but that the method itself—although it offers insights—is, according to some commentators, far from foolproof. First of all, the Constitution of 1787 as it initially stood and has since been amended rejects many English and some colonial and state practices. Second, even a steady stream of precedents from the states may signify nothing more than the fact that judges, too busy to give the issue much thought, imitated each other under the rubric of stare decisis. Third, if justices are searching for original intent or understanding, it is difficult to imagine the relevance of what was in the minds of people in the eighteenth century to government practices in the twentieth and twenty-first centuries. Polls are useful if we want to know what other judges, now and in the recent past, have thought about the Constitution, writ large or small. Nevertheless, they say nothing about the correctness of those thoughts—and the correctness of a lower court's interpretation may be precisely the issue before the Supreme Court.

Despite these criticisms, the Supreme Court continues to consider the practices of other U.S. jurisdictions, just as courts in other societies occasionally look to their counterparts elsewhere—including the U.S. Supreme Court—for guidance. The South African ruling in *The State v. Makwanyane* (1995) provides a vivid example. To determine whether the death penalty violated its nation's constitution, South Africa's Constitutional Court surveyed practices elsewhere, including those in the United States. Ultimately, the justices decided not to follow the path taken by the U.S. Supreme Court, ruling instead that their constitution prohibited the state from imposing capital punishment. Rejection of U.S. practice was made all the more interesting in light of a speech Justice Harry Blackmun delivered only a year before *Makwanyane*.[52] In that address, Blackmun chastised his colleagues for failing to take into account a decision of South Africa's court to dismiss a prosecution against a person kidnapped from a neighboring country. This ruling, Blackmun argued, was far more faithful to international conventions than the one his court had reached in *United States v. Alvarez-Machain* (1992), which permitted U.S. agents to abduct a Mexican national.

Alvarez-Machain aside, the tendency seems to be growing for American justices to consider the rulings of courts abroad and practices elsewhere as they interpret the U.S. Constitution. This trend is particularly evident in opinions regarding capital punishment; justices opposed to this form of retribution often point to the nearly one hundred countries that have abolished the death penalty.

Whether this practice will become more widespread or filter into other legal areas is an intriguing question, and one that has caused debate among the justices. In his book, *The Court and the World*,[53] Justice Stephen Breyer contends that the cases before his Court increasingly raise questions that, like it or not, force the justices to confront "foreign realities." He suggests that in response the justices should and must expand their horizons beyond U.S. borders. Others, though, apparently agree with Justice Antonin Scalia, who argued "the views of

---

[51]We adapt the material in this section from Walter F. Murphy, C. Herman Pritchett, Lee Epstein, and Jack Knight, *Courts, Judges, and Politics*, 6th ed. (New York: McGraw-Hill, 2006).

[52]"Justice Blackmun Addresses the ASIL Annual Dinner," *American Society of International Law Newsletter*, March 1994.

[53]Stephen Breyer, *The Court and the World* (New York: Knopf, 2016).

other nations, however enlightened the Justices of this court may think them to be, cannot be imposed upon Americans through the Constitution."[54]

SUPREME COURT DECISION MAKING: REALISM

So far in our discussion we have not mentioned the justices' ideologies, their political party affiliations, or their personal views on various public policy issues. The reason is that legal approaches to Supreme Court decision making do not admit that these factors figure into the way the Court arrives at its decisions. Instead, they suggest that justices divorce themselves from their personal and political biases and settle disputes based upon the law. The approaches we consider below—recall, what some call more realistic or nonlegalistic approaches—posit a quite different vision of Supreme Court decision making. They argue that the forces that drive the justices are anything but legal in orientation and that it is unrealistic to expect justices to shed all their preferences and values or to ignore public opinion when they put on their black robes. Indeed, the justices are people and, like all people, tend to have strong and pervasive political biases and partisan attachments.

Because justices usually do not admit that they are swayed by the public or that they vote according to their ideologies, our discussion of realism is distinct from that of legalism. Here you will find little in the way of supporting statements from Court members, for it is an unusual justice indeed who admits to following anything but, say, precedent, history, the text of the Constitution, in deciding cases. Instead, we offer the results of decades of research by scholars who think that political and other extralegal forces shape judicial decisions. We organize these nonlegalistic approaches into three categories: preference-based, strategic, and external forces. See if you think these scholarly accounts are persuasive.

Preference-Based Approaches

Preference-based approaches see the justices as rational decision makers who hold certain values they would like to see reflected in the outcomes of Court cases. Two prevalent preference-based approaches stress the importance of judicial attitudes and the judicial role.

Judicial Attitudes

Attitudinal approaches emphasize the centrality of the justices' political ideologies. Typically, scholars examining the ideologies of the justices discuss the degree to which a justice is conservative or liberal—as in "Justice X holds conservative views on issues of criminal law" or "Justice Y holds liberal views on free speech." This school of thought maintains that when a case comes before the Court, each justice evaluates the facts of the dispute and arrives at a decision consistent with his or her personal ideology.

C. Herman Pritchett was one of the first scholars to study systematically the relevance of the justices' personal attitudes.[55] Examining the Court during the 1930s and 1940s, Pritchett observed that dissent had become an institutionalized feature of judicial decisions. During the early 1900s, in no more than 20 percent of the cases did one or more justices file a dissenting opinion; by the 1940s, that figure was more than 60 percent. If precedent and other legal factors drove Court rulings, why did various justices interpreting the same legal provisions frequently reach different results? Not only that, why did the same sets of justices consistently vote together? Perhaps the justices might disagree, but why did they disagree so systematically? Pritchett concluded that the justices were not following precedent but were "motivated by their own preferences."[56]

Pritchett's findings touched off an explosion of research on the influence of attitudes on Supreme Court decision making.[57] Much of this scholarship describes how liberal or conservative the various justices have been and attempts to predict their voting behavior based on their ideological preferences. To understand some of these differences, consider Figure 2-4, which presents the voting records of the present chief justice, John G. Roberts, and his three immediate predecessors: Earl Warren, Warren Burger, and William Rehnquist. The data report the percentage of times each voted in the liberal direction in two different issue areas: civil liberties and economic liberties.

---

[54]*Thompson v. Oklahoma* (1987); see also his dissent in *Atkins v. Virginia* (2002).

[55]C. Herman Pritchett, *The Roosevelt Court* (New York: Macmillan, 1948); and Pritchett, "Divisions of Opinion among Justices of the U.S. Supreme Court, 1939–1941," *American Political Science Review* 35 (1941): 890–898.

[56]Pritchett, *The Roosevelt Court*, xiii.

[57]The classic works in this area are Glendon Schubert, *The Judicial Mind* (Evanston, IL: Northwestern University Press, 1965), and Rohde and Spaeth, *Supreme Court Decision Making*. For a lucid modern-day treatment, see Segal and Spaeth, *The Supreme Court and the Attitudinal Model Revisited*, chaps. 3 and 8.

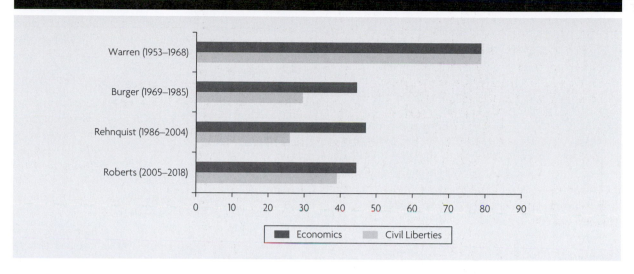

Figure 2-4 Percentage of Cases in which Each Chief Justice Voted in the Liberal Direction, 1953–2018 Terms

Source: Calculated by the authors from data in the U.S. Supreme Court Database (http://supremecourtdatabase.org).

The data show dramatic differences among these four important jurists, especially in cases involving civil liberties. Cases in this category include disputes over issues such as the First Amendment freedoms of religion, speech, and press; the right to privacy; the rights of the criminally accused; and illegal discrimination. The liberal position is a vote in favor of the individual who is claiming a denial of these basic rights. Warren supported the liberal side almost 80 percent of the time, but Burger and Rehnquist did so in about one-third (or less) of such cases. Roberts has voted for the liberal position a bit more often but still only 40 percent of the time.

Economics cases involve challenges to the government's authority to regulate the economy. The liberal position supports an active role by the government in controlling business and economic activity. Here, too, the four justices show different ideological positions. Warren is the most liberal of the four, ruling in favor of government regulatory activity in more than 80 percent of the cases, while Burger, Rehnquist, and Roberts supported such government activity in less than half. The data depicted in Figure 2-4 are typical of the findings of most attitudinal studies: within given issue areas, individual justices tend to show consistent ideological predispositions.

Moreover, we often hear that a particular Court is ideologically predisposed toward one side or the other. For example, on May 29, 2002, the *New York Times* ran

a story claiming that "Chief Justice William Rehnquist and his fellow conservatives have made no secret of their desire to alter the balance of federalism, shifting power from Washington to the states." Three years later, in September 2005, it titled the chief justice's obituary "William H. Rehnquist, Architect of Conservative Court, Dies at 80." After President George W. Bush appointed Rehnquist's replacement, John G. Roberts, and a new associate justice, Samuel Alito, the press was quick to label both "reliable members of the conservative bloc." And now Sonia Sotomayor and Elena Kagan, President Obama's appointees, are often deemed "liberal." Sometimes an entire Court era is described in terms of its political preferences, such as the "liberal" Warren Court or the "conservative" Rehnquist Court. The data in Figure 2-5 confirm that these labels have some basis in fact. Looking at the two lines from left to right, from the 1950s through the early 2000s, note the mostly downward trend, indicating the increased conservatism of the Court in economics and civil liberties cases.

How valuable are the ideological terms used to describe particular justices or Courts in helping us understand judicial decision making? On one hand, knowledge of justices' ideologies can lead to fairly accurate predictions about their voting behavior. Suppose that the Roberts Court (prior to Justice Scalia's death) handed down a decision dealing with the death penalty and that

Figure 2-5 Court Decisions on Economics and Civil Liberties, 1953–2018 Terms

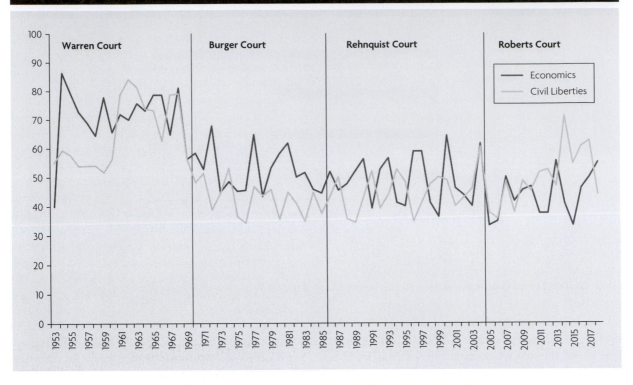

Source: Calculated by the authors from data in the U.S. Supreme Court Database (http://supremecourtdatabase.org).

the vote was 5–4 in favor of the criminal defendant. The most conservative members of that Court on death penalty cases are Chief Justice Roberts and Justices Antonin Scalia, Clarence Thomas, and Samuel Alito—they almost always vote against the defendant in death penalty cases. If we predicted that Roberts, Scalia, Thomas, and Alito cast the dissenting votes in our hypothetical death penalty case, we would almost certainly be right.[58]

On the other hand, preference-based approaches are not foolproof. First, how do we know if a particular justice is liberal or conservative? The answer typically is that we know a justice is liberal or conservative because he or she casts liberal or conservative votes. Scalia favored conservative positions on the Court because he was a conservative, and we know he was a conservative because he favored conservative positions in the cases he decided. This is circular reasoning indeed. Second, knowing that a

justice is liberal or conservative or that the Court decided a case in a liberal or conservative way does not tell us much about the Court's (or the country's) actual policy positions. To say that *Roe v. Wade* is a liberal decision is to say little about the policies governing abortion in the United States. If it did, this book would be nothing more than a list of cases labeled liberal or conservative—such labels would give us no sense of more than two hundred years of constitutional interpretation.

Finally, we must understand that ideological labels are occasionally time dependent, that they are bound to particular historical eras. In ***Muller v. Oregon*** (1908), the Supreme Court upheld a state law that set a maximum number on the hours women (but not men) could work. How would you, as a student in the twenty-first century, view such an opinion? You might well classify it as conservative because it seems to patronize and protect women. But when it was decided, most considered *Muller* a liberal ruling because it allowed the government to regulate business.

A related problem is that some decisions do not fall neatly on a single conservative-liberal dimension. In

---

[58]We take this example from Jeffrey A. Segal and Harold J. Spaeth, *The Supreme Court and the Attitudinal Model* (New York: Cambridge University Press, 1993), 223.

Wisconsin v. Mitchell (1993), the Court upheld a state law that increased the sentence for crimes if the defendant "intentionally selects the person against whom the crime is committed" on the basis of race, religion, national origin, sexual orientation, and other similar criteria. Is this ruling liberal or conservative? If you view the law as penalizing racial or ethnic hatred, you would likely see it as a liberal decision. If, however, you see the law as treating criminal defendants more harshly and penalizing a person because of what he or she believes or says, the ruling is conservative.

Judicial Role

Another concept within the preference-based category is the judicial role, which scholars have defined as norms that constrain the behavior of jurists.[59] Students of the Court sometimes argue that each justice has a view of his or her role, a view that is based far less on political ideology and far more on fundamental beliefs of what a good judge should do or what the proper role of the Court should be. Some scholars claim that jurists vote in accordance with these role conceptions.

Analysts typically discuss judicial roles in terms of activism and restraint. An activist justice believes that the proper role of the Court is to assert independent positions in deciding cases, to review the actions of the other branches vigorously, to be willing to strike down acts the justice believes are unconstitutional, and to impose far-reaching remedies for legal wrongs whenever necessary. Restraint-oriented justices take the opposite position. Courts should not become involved in the operations of the other branches unless absolutely necessary. The benefit of the doubt should be given to actions taken by elected officials. Courts should impose remedies that are narrowly tailored to correct a specific legal wrong.

Based on these definitions, we might expect to find activist justices more willing than their opposites to strike down legislation. Therefore, a natural question to ask is this: To what extent have specific jurists practiced judicial activism or restraint? The data in Table 2-3 address this question by reporting the votes of justices serving on the Court for the period between the 1994 and 2018 terms (and who are still on the Court) in cases in which the majority declared federal, state, or local legislation unconstitutional. Note that the two justices most willing to invalidate federal laws are Thomas and Kagan, justices of quite different ideological orientation.

Likewise, those most reluctant to strike federal laws are both liberal (Breyer and Ginsburg) and conservative (Alito). Most of the justices, regardless of where they might fall on the ideological spectrum, have about the same affinity for invalidating state and local laws; they join their colleagues in exercising judicial review in about 75 percent of those cases (with the exceptions of Alito and Thomas, who join a bit less often).

These patterns are suggestive: judicial activism and restraint do not necessarily equal judicial liberalism and conservatism. An activist judge need not be liberal, and a judge who practices restraint need not be conservative. In the aggregate, it is also true that so-called liberal Courts are no more likely to strike down legislation than are conservative Courts. During the liberal Warren era, the Court invalidated 156 laws—or about 9.8 per term. During the more conservative Rehnquist years, the Court struck 158 laws—or about 8.3 per term, which was less than during the equally conservative Burger Court (240 laws or about 14 per term). Data such as these may call into question a strong relationship between ideology and judicial role.

Table 2-3 Percentage of Votes to Invalidate Laws as Unconstitutional, 1994–2018 Terms		
Justice	Federal Laws	State and Local Laws
Thomas	75.4	59.0
Kagan	75.0	72.0
Roberts	70.8	73.0
Sotomayor	61.9	70.4
Alito	58.3	61.1
Breyer	57.9	76.2
Ginsburg	56.1	73.8

Source: Calculated by the authors from data in the U.S. Supreme Court Database (http://supremecourtdatabase.org).

Note: The figures shown indicate the percentage of cases in which each justice voted with the majority to invalidate laws as unconstitutional. Fifty-seven cases struck down federal laws and eighty-four cases struck state and local laws. Some justices may not have participated in all cases. We include only justices currently on the Court, though we exclude Gorsuch and Kavanaugh because they each participated in fewer than ten of the cases. Roberts, Alito, and Sotomayor all joined the Court after the 1994 term.

[59]See James L. Gibson, "Judges' Role Orientations, Attitudes, and Decisions," *American Political Science Review* 72 (1978): 911–924.

Although scholars have used the number of laws struck down to assess the extent to which the justices practice judicial activism or restraint, the question arises: To what extent does this information help us understand Supreme Court decision making? This is difficult to answer because few scholars have studied the relationship between roles and voting in a systematic way. One obstacle to undertaking such research is the challenge of separating roles from attitudes. When Thomas (the most conservative justice on the Roberts Court) votes to uphold a law restricting access to abortions, can we conclude that he is practicing restraint? The answer is probably no. It may be his attitude toward abortion, not restraint, that guides him. Another limitation of the role approach is that it tells us very little about the resulting policy in a case, just as was true for attitudinal studies. To say that *Roe v. Wade* was an activist decision because it struck down abortion laws nationwide is to say nothing about the policy content of the opinion.

Strategic Approaches

Strategic accounts of judicial decisions rest on a few simple propositions: justices may be primarily seekers of legal policy (as the attitudinal adherents claim) or they may be motivated by jurisprudential principles (as approaches grounded in law suggest), but they are not unconstrained actors who make decisions based solely on their own ideological attitudes or jurisprudential desires. Rather, justices are strategic actors who realize that their ability to achieve their goals—whatever those goals might be—depends on a consideration of the preferences of other relevant actors (such as their colleagues and members of other political institutions), the choices they expect others to make, and the institutional context in which they act. Scholars term this approach "strategic" because the ideas it contains are derived from the rational choice paradigm, on which strategic analysis is based and as it has been advanced by economists and political scientists working in other fields. Accordingly, we can restate the strategic argument in this way: we can best explain the choices of justices as strategic behavior and not merely as responses to ideological or jurisprudential values.[60]

Such arguments about Supreme Court decision making seem to be sensible: a justice can do very little alone. It takes a majority vote to decide a case and a majority agreeing on a single opinion to set precedent. Under such conditions, human interaction is important, and case outcomes—not to mention the rationale of decisions—can be influenced by the nature of relations among the members of the group.

Although scholars have not considered strategic approaches to the same degree that they have studied judicial attitudes, a number of influential works point to their importance. Research started in the 1960s and continuing today into the private papers of former justices consistently has shown that through intellectual persuasion, effective bargaining over opinion writing, informal lobbying, and so forth, justices have influenced the actions of their colleagues.[61]

How does strategic behavior manifest itself? One way is in the frequency of vote changes. During the conference deliberations that take place after oral arguments, the justices discuss the case and vote on it. These votes do not become final until the opinions are completed and the decision is made public *(see Figure 2-1)*. Research has shown that between the initial vote on the merits of cases and the official announcement of the decision, at least one vote switch occurs more than 50 percent of the time.[62]

A very recent example, as we already noted, is Chief Justice Roberts's change of heart over the constitutionality of the health care law. Because of his (purported) vote switch, the Court upheld key parts of the law by a vote of 5–4 rather than striking them down by a vote of 5–4. This episode, along with the figure of 50 percent, indicates that justices change their minds—perhaps reevaluating their initial positions or succumbing to the persuasion of their colleagues—which seems inexplicable if we believe that justices are simply liberals or conservatives and always vote their preferences.

Vote shifts are just one manifestation of the interdependence of the Court's decision-making process.

[60]For more details on this approach, see Lee Epstein and Jack Knight, *The Choices Justices Make* (Washington, DC: CQ Press, 1998).

[61]Walter F. Murphy, *Elements of Judicial Strategy* (Chicago: University of Chicago Press, 1964); David J. Danelski, "The Influence of the Chief Justice in the Decisional Process of the Supreme Court," in *The Federal Judicial System*, ed. Thomas P. Jahnige and Sheldon Goldman (New York: Holt, Rinehart & Winston, 1968); J. Woodford Howard, "On the Fluidity of Judicial Choice," *American Political Science Review* 62 (1968): 43–56; Epstein and Knight, *The Choices Justices Make*; Forrest Maltzman, Paul J. Wahlbeck, and James Spriggs, *Crafting Law on the Supreme Court: The Collegial Game* (New York: Cambridge University Press, 2000).

[62]Forrest Maltzman and Paul J. Wahlbeck, "Strategic Considerations and Vote Fluidity on the Burger Court," *American Political Science Review* 90 (1996): 581–592.

Another is the revision of opinions that occurs in almost every Court case.[63] As opinion writers try to accommodate their colleagues' wishes, their drafts may undergo five, ten, even fifteen revisions. Bargaining over the content of an opinion is important because it can significantly alter the policy ultimately expressed. A clear example is *Griswold v. Connecticut* (1965), in which the Court considered the constitutionality of a state law that prohibited the dissemination of birth control information and devices, even to married couples. In his initial draft of the majority opinion, Justice William O. Douglas struck down the law on the ground that it interfered with the First Amendment's right of association. A memorandum from Brennan convinced Douglas to alter his rationale and to establish the foundation for a right to privacy. "Had the Douglas draft been issued as the *Griswold* opinion of the Court, the case would stand as a precedent on the freedom of association," rather than serve as the landmark ruling it became.[64]

External Factors

In addition to internal bargaining, strategic approaches (as well as others) also take account of political pressures that come from outside the Court. We consider three sources of such influence: public opinion, partisan politics, and interest groups. While reading about these sources of influence, keep in mind that one of the fundamental differences between the Supreme Court and the political branches is the lack of a direct electoral connection between the justices and the public. Once appointed, justices may serve for life. They are not accountable to the public and are not required to undergo any periodic reevaluation of their decisions. So why would they let the stuff of ordinary partisan politics, such as public opinion and interest groups, influence their opinions?

Public Opinion

To address this question, let us first look at public opinion as a source of influence on the Court. We know that the president and members of Congress are always trying to find out what the people are thinking. Conducting and analyzing public opinion polls is a never-ending task, and those who commission the polls have a good reason for this activity. The political branches are supposed to represent the people, and incumbents can jeopardize their reelection prospects by straying too far from what the public wants. But federal judges—including Supreme Court justices—are not dependent upon pleasing the public to stay in office, and they do not serve in the same kind of representative capacity that legislators do.

Does that mean that the justices are not affected by public opinion? Some scholars say they are, and offer three reasons for this claim.[65] First, because justices are political appointees, nominated and approved by popularly elected officials, it is logical that they should reflect, however subtly, the views of the majority. It is probably true that an individual radically out of step with either the president or the Senate would not be nominated, much less confirmed. Second, the Court, at least occasionally, views public opinion as a legitimate guide for decisions. It has even gone so far as to incorporate that consideration into some of its jurisprudential standards. For example, in evaluating whether certain kinds of punishments violate the Eighth Amendment's prohibition against cruel and unusual punishment, the Court announced that it would look toward "evolving standards of decency," as defined by public sentiment.[66] The third reason relates to the Court as an institution. Put simply, the justices have no mechanism for enforcing their decisions. Instead, they depend on other political officials to support their positions and on general public compliance, especially when controversial Court opinions have ramifications beyond the particular concerns of the parties to the suit.

Certainly, we can think of cases that lend support to these claims—cases in which the Court seems to have embraced public opinion, especially under conditions of extreme national stress. One example occurred during World War II. In *Korematsu v. United States* (1944) the justices endorsed the government's program to remove all Japanese Americans from the Pacific Coast states and relocate them to inland detention centers. It seems clear that the justices were swept up in the same wartime apprehensions as the rest of the nation. But it is equally easy to summon examples of the Court handing down rulings that fly

---

[63]Epstein and Knight, *The Choices Justices Make*, chap. 3.

[64]See Bernard Schwartz, *The Unpublished Opinions of the Warren Court* (New York: Oxford University Press, 1985), chap. 7.

[65]See, for example, Barry Friedman, *The Will of the People* (New York: Farrar, Straus & Giroux, 2009); William Mishler and Reginald S. Sheehan, "The Supreme Court as a Counter-majoritarian Institution? The Impact of Public Opinion on Supreme Court Decisions," *American Political Science Review* 87 (1993): 89.

[66]*Trop v. Dulles* (1958).

in the face of what the public wants. The most obvious example occurred after Franklin D. Roosevelt's 1932 election to the presidency. By choosing Roosevelt and electing many Democrats to Congress, the voters sent a clear signal that they wanted the government to take vigorous action to end the Great Depression. The president and Congress responded with many laws—the so-called New Deal legislation—but the Court remained unmoved by the public's endorsement of Roosevelt and his legislation. In case after case, at least until 1937, the justices struck down many of the laws and administrative programs designed to get the nation's economy moving again.

In fact, some scholars doubt that public opinion affects the Court's decision making. After systematically analyzing the data, Helmut Norpoth and Jeffrey A. Segal concluded: "Does public opinion influence Supreme Court decisions? If the model of influence is of the sort where the justices set aside their own (ideological) preferences and abide by what they divine as the vox populi, our answer is a resounding no."[67] What Norpoth and Segal find instead is that Court appointments made by Richard Nixon in the early 1970s caused a "sizable ideological shift" in the direction of Court decisions *(see Figure 2-5)*. The entry of conservative justices, they argue, created the illusion that the Court was echoing public opinion; it was not that sitting justices modified their voting patterns to conform to the changing views of the public.

This finding reinforces yet another criticism of this approach: that public opinion affects the Court only indirectly through presidential appointments, not through the justices' reading of public opinion polls. This distinction is important, for if justices were truly influenced by the public, their decisions would change with the ebb and flow of opinion. But if they merely share their appointing president's ideology, which must mirror the majority of the citizens *at the time of the president's election*, their decisions would remain constant over time. They would not fluctuate, as public opinion often does.

The question of whether public opinion affects Supreme Court decision making is still open for discussion, as illustrated by a more recent article, "Does Public Opinion Influence the Supreme Court? Possibly Yes (But We're Not Sure Why)."[68] The authors find that

when the "mood" is liberal (or conservative), the Court is significantly more likely to issue liberal (or conservative) decisions. But why, as the article's title suggests, is anyone's guess. It could be that the justices bend to the will of the people because the Court requires public support to remain an efficacious branch of government. Or it could be that "the people" include the justices; the justices do not respond to public opinion directly but rather respond to the same events or forces that affect the opinions of other members of the public. As Justice Benjamin Cardozo once put it, "The great tides and currents which engulf the rest of men do not turn aside in their course and pass the judge by."[69]

Partisan Politics

Public opinion is not the only political factor that allegedly influences the justices. As political scientist Jonathan Casper wrote, we cannot overestimate "the importance of the political context in which the Court does its work." In his view, the statement that the Court follows the election returns "recognizes that the choices the Court makes are related to developments in the broader political system."[70] In other words, the political environment has an effect on Court behavior. In fact, many assert that the Court is responsive to the influence of partisan politics, both internally and externally.

On the inner workings of the Court, social scientists long have argued that political creatures inhabit the Court, that justices are not simply neutral arbiters of the law. Since 1789, the beginning of constitutional government in the United States, those who have ascended to the bench have come from the political institutions of government or, at the very least, have affiliated with particular political parties. Judicial scholars recognize that justices bring with them the philosophies of those partisan attachments. Just as the members of the present Court tend to reflect the views of the Republican Party or Democratic Party, so, too, did the justices who came from the ranks of the Federalists and Jeffersonians. As one might expect, justices who affiliate with the Democratic Party tend to be more liberal in their decision making than those who are Republicans. Some commentators say that *Bush v. Gore* (2000), in which the Supreme Court issued a ruling that virtually ensured that George W.

[67]Helmut Norpoth and Jeffrey A. Segal, "Popular Influence in Supreme Court Decisions," *American Political Science Review* 88 (1994): 711–716.

[68]Lee Epstein and Andrew D. Martin, "Does Public Opinion Influence the Supreme Court? Possibly Yes (But We're Not Sure Why)," *University of Pennsylvania Journal of Constitutional Law* 13 (2010): 263–281.

[69]Benjamin Cardozo, *The Nature of the Judicial Process* (New Haven, CT: Yale University Press, 1921), 168.

[70]Jonathan Casper, *The Politics of Civil Liberties* (New York: Harper & Row, 1972), 293.

Bush would become president, provides an example. In that case, five of the Court's seven Republicans "voted" for Bush, and its two Democrats "voted" for Gore.

Political pressures from the outside also can affect the Court. Although the justices have no electoral connection or mandate of responsiveness, the other institutions of government have some influence on judicial behavior, and, naturally, the direction of that influence reflects the partisan composition of those branches. The president has some direct links with the Court, including obviously the power to nominate justices and shape the Court. Historically, presidents have even had personal friendships with sitting justices, such as Franklin Roosevelt's with James Byrnes, Lyndon Johnson's with Abe Fortas, and Richard Nixon's with Warren Burger. In addition, when presidents are buoyed by high levels of public support, their political capital is enhanced, and that may be hard for the Court to ignore.

A less direct source of influence is the executive branch, which operates under the president's command. The bureaucracy can assist the Court in implementing its policies, or it can hinder the Court by refusing to do so, a fact of which the justices are well aware. As a judicial body, the Supreme Court cannot implement or execute its own decisions. It often must depend on the executive branch to give its decisions legitimacy through action. The Court, therefore, may act strategically, anticipate the wishes of the executive branch, and respond accordingly to avoid a confrontation that could threaten its legitimacy. *Marbury v. Madison*, in which the Court enunciated the doctrine of judicial review, is the classic example *(see chapter 3 for an excerpt)*. Some scholars suggest that Chief Justice John Marshall, aware that the Jefferson administration might spurn any direct order from the Court, crafted an opinion that expressed disagreement with Jefferson, without risking a costly rebuff from the president. Another indirect source of presidential influence is the U.S. solicitor general. In addition to the SG's success as a petitioning party, the office can have an equally pronounced effect at the merits stage. In fact, data indicate that whether acting as an amicus curiae or as a party to a suit, the SG's office is generally able to convince the justices to adopt the position advocated by the SG.[71]

Presidential influence is also demonstrated in the kinds of arguments an SG brings into the Court. That is, SGs representing Democratic administrations tend to present more liberal arguments; those from the ranks of the Republican Party, more conservative arguments. The transition from George H. W. Bush's administration to Bill Clinton's administration provides an interesting illustration. Bush's SG had filed amicus curiae briefs—many of which took a conservative position—in a number of cases the Court heard during the 1993–1994 term. Drew S. Days III, Clinton's first SG, rewrote at least four of those briefs to reflect the new administration's more liberal posture. Thus, for example, Days argued that the Civil Rights Act of 1991 should be applied retroactively, whereas the Bush administration had suggested that it should not be. In another case, Days claimed trial attorneys could not systematically challenge prospective jurors on the basis of sex; his predecessor had argued that such dismissals were constitutional.

Congress, too—or so some argue—can influence Supreme Court decision making. Like the president, the legislature has many powers over the Court the justices cannot ignore.[72] Some of these resemble presidential powers—the Senate's role in confirmation proceedings, the implementation of judicial decisions—but there are others. Congress can restrict the Court's jurisdiction to hear cases, enact legislation or propose constitutional amendments to recast Court decisions, and hold judicial salaries constant. To forestall a congressional attack, the Court might accede to legislative wishes. Often-cited examples include the Court's willingness to defer to the Radical Republican Congress after the Civil War and to approve New Deal legislation after Roosevelt proposed his Court-packing plan in 1937. Of course, these examples could represent anomalies, not the rule. The Court, one might argue, has no reason to respond strategically to Congress because it is so rare that the legislature threatens, much less takes action against, the judiciary. Only infrequently has Congress taken away the jurisdiction of the Supreme Court to hear particular kinds of cases, most prominently just after the Civil War and more recently in response to the war on terrorism *(see chapter 3 for more details)*. Still, there is good evidence that the justices are close students of how they are regarded by the Congress and are sensitive to legislative displeasure.[73] You should keep this argument in mind as you read the cases that pit the Court against Congress and the president.

---

[71]See Epstein et al., *Supreme Court Compendium*, Tables 7-15 and 7-16.

[72]See Gerald N. Rosenberg, "Judicial Independence and the Reality of Political Power," *Review of Politics* 54 (1992): 369–398.

[73]Tom S. Clark, *The Limits of Judicial Independence* (New York: Cambridge University Press, 2010).

Interest Groups

In *Federalist* No. 78, Alexander Hamilton wrote that the U.S. Supreme Court was "to declare the sense of the law" through "inflexible and uniform adherence to the rights of the constitution and individuals." Despite this expectation, Supreme Court litigation has become political over time. We see manifestations of politics in virtually every aspect of the Court's work, from the nomination and confirmation of justices to the factors that influence their decisions, but perhaps the most striking example of this politicization is the incursion of organized interest groups into the judicial process.

Naturally, interest groups may not attempt to persuade the Supreme Court the same way lobbyists deal with Congress. It would be grossly improper for the representatives of an interest group to approach a Supreme Court justice directly. Instead, interest groups try to influence Court decisions by submitting amicus curiae briefs *(see Box 2-1)*. Presenting a written legal argument to the Court allows interest groups to make their views known to the justices, even when the group is not a direct party to the litigation.

These days, it is a rare case before the U.S. Supreme Court that does not attract such submissions.[74] In recent years, organized interests have filed at least one amicus brief in over 90 percent of all cases decided by full opinion between 2000 and 2015, on average.[75] Some cases, particularly those involving controversial issues such as abortion and affirmative action, are especially attractive to interest groups. In **Regents of the University of California v. Bakke** (1978), involving admission of minority students to medical school, more than one hundred organizations filed fifty-eight amici briefs: forty-two backed the university's admissions policy and sixteen supported Allan Bakke. A more recent affirmative action case, **Grutter v. Bollinger** (2003), drew eighty-four briefs from a wide range of interests—colleges and universities, Fortune 500 companies, and retired military officers, to name just a few.[76] And eighty-eight amicus briefs were submitted in **Fisher v. University of Texas**, the affirmative action case in the 2012 term. But it is not only cases of civil liberties and rights that attract interest group

attention. In the 2012 challenge to the constitutionality of the Patient Protection and Affordable Care Act ("Obamacare"), the Court received more than one hundred amicus briefs. In addition to participating as amici, groups in record numbers are sponsoring cases—that is, providing litigants with attorneys and the money necessary to pursue their cases.

The explosion of interest group participation in Supreme Court litigation raises two questions. First, why do groups go to the Court? One answer is obvious: they want to influence the Court's decisions. But groups also go to the Supreme Court to achieve other, subtler, ends. One is the setting of institutional agendas: by filing amicus curiae briefs at the case selection stage or by bringing cases to the Court's attention, organizations seek to influence the justices' decisions on which disputes to hear. Group participation also may serve as a counterbalance to other interests that have competing goals. So if Planned Parenthood, a pro-choice group, knows that Life Legal Defense Foundation, a pro-life group, is filing an amicus curiae brief in an abortion case (or vice versa), it, too, may enter the dispute to ensure that its side is represented in the proceedings. Finally, groups go to the Court to publicize their causes and their organizations. The National Association for the Advancement of Colored People (NAACP) Legal Defense Fund's legendary litigation campaign to end school segregation provides an excellent example. It not only resulted in a favorable policy decision in *Brown v. Board of Education* (1954) but also established the Legal Defense Fund as the foremost organizational litigant of this issue *(excerpted in chapter 19)*.

The second question is this: Can groups influence the outcomes of Supreme Court decisions?[77] This question has no simple answer. When interest groups participate on both sides, it is reasonable to speculate that one or more exerted some intellectual influence—or at least that the intervention of groups on the winning side neutralized the arguments of those who lost. In some instances, the Court's opinion may cite directly an argument advanced in an amicus brief, but that might indicate merely that a justice is citing the brief to support a conclusion he or she had already reached.

What we can say is that attorneys for some groups, such as the Women's Rights Project of the American Civil Liberties Union and the NAACP, are often more experienced and their staffs more adept at research than

---

[74] See Paul M. Collins Jr., *Friends of the Supreme Court: Interest Groups and Judicial Decision Making* (New York: Oxford University Press, 2008).

[75] See Epstein et al., *The Supreme Court Compendium*, Table 7-22.

[76] We adapt some of this material from Pritchett et al., *Courts, Judges, and Politics*, chap. 6.

[77] We adapt some of this material from Murphy et al., *Courts, Judges, and Politics*, chap. 6.

counsel for what law professor Marc Galanter called "one-shotters."[78] When he was chief counsel for the NAACP, Thurgood Marshall would solicit help from allied groups and orchestrate their cooperation on a case, dividing the labor among them by assigning specific arguments to each while enlisting sympathetic social scientists to muster supporting data. Before going to the Supreme Court for oral argument, he would sometimes have a practice session with friendly law professors, each one playing the role of a particular justice and trying to pose the sorts of questions that justice would be likely to ask. Such preparation can pay off, but it need not be decisive. In oral argument, Allan Bakke's attorney displayed a surprising ignorance of constitutional law and curtly told one justice who tried to help him that he would like to argue the case his own way. Despite this poor performance, Bakke won.

Some evidence, however, suggests that attorneys working for interest groups are no more successful than private counsel. One study paired two similar cases decided by the same district court judge in the same year, with the only major difference being that one case was sponsored by a group and the other was brought by attorneys unaffiliated with an organized interest. Despite Galanter's contentions about the obstacles confronting one-shotters, the study found no major differences between the two.[79]

The debate over the influence of interest groups is one that you will have ample opportunity to consider. With the case excerpts in this volume, we often provide information on the arguments of amici and attorneys so that you can compare these points with the justices' opinions.

CONDUCTING RESEARCH ON THE SUPREME COURT

As you can see, considerable disagreement exists in the scholarly and legal communities about how justices should interpret the Constitution, and even why they decide cases the way they do. These approaches show up in many of the Court's opinions in this book.

Keep in mind, however, that the opinions are not presented here in full; the excerpts included in the text are intended to highlight the most important points of the various majority, dissenting, and concurring opinions. Occasionally you may want to read the decisions in their entirety. Following is an explanation of how to find opinions and other kinds of information on the Court and its members.

Locating Supreme Court Decisions

U.S. Supreme Court decisions are published by various reporters. The four major reporters are *U.S. Reports*, *Lawyers' Edition*, *Supreme Court Reporter*, and *U.S. Law Week*. All contain the opinions of the Court, but they vary in the kinds of ancillary material they provide. For example, as Table 2-4 shows, the *Lawyers' Edition* contains excerpts of the briefs of attorneys submitted in orally argued cases, *U.S. Law Week* provides a topical index of cases on the Court's docket, and so forth.

Locating cases within these reporters is easy if you know the case *citation*. Case citations, as the table shows, take different forms, but they all work in roughly the same way. To see how, turn to the excerpt of *Texas v. Johnson* (1989) in chapter 13. Directly under the case name is a citation: 491 U.S. 397, which means that *Texas v. Johnson* appears in volume 491, page 397, of *U.S. Reports*.[80] The first set of numbers is the volume number; the U.S. is the form of citation for *U.S. Reports*; and the second set of numbers is the starting page of the case.

Texas v. Johnson also can be found in the three other reporters. The citations are as follows:

Lawyers' Edition: 105 L. Ed. 2d 342 (1989)

Supreme Court Reporter: 109 S. Ct. 2533 (1989)

U.S. Law Week: 57 U.S.L.W. 4770 (1989)

Note that the abbreviations vary by reporter, but in form the citations parallel *U.S. Reports* in that the first set of numbers is the volume number and the second set is the starting page number.

---

[78]Marc Galanter, "Why the 'Haves' Come out Ahead: Speculations on the Limits of Legal Change," *Law and Society Review* 9 (1974): 95–160.

[79]Lee Epstein and C. K. Rowland, "Debunking the Myth of Interest Group Invincibility in the Court," *American Political Science Review* 85 (1991): 205–217.

[80]In this book, we list only the *U.S. Reports* cite for each case citation because *U.S. Reports* is the official record of Supreme Court decisions. It is the only reporter published by the federal government; the other three are privately printed. Almost every law library has *U.S. Reports*. If your college or university does not have a law school, check with your librarians. If they have any Court reporter, it is probably *U.S. Reports*.

Table 2-4 Reporting Systems

Reporter/Publisher	Form of Citation (Terms)	Description
United States Reports, Government Printing Office	Dall. 1–4 (1790–1800) Cr. 1–15 (1801–1815) Wheat. 1–12 (1816–1827) Pet. 1–16 (1828–1843) How. 1–24 (1843–1861) Bl. 1–2 (1861–1862) Wall. 1–23 (1863–1875) U.S. 91–(1875–)	Contains official text of opinions of the Court. Includes tables of cases reported, cases and statutes cited, miscellaneous materials, and subject index. Includes most of the Court's decisions. Court opinions prior to 1875 are cited by the name of the reporter of the Court. For example, Dall. stands for Alexander J. Dallas, the first reporter.
United States Supreme Court Reports, Lawyers' Edition, Lawyers' Cooperative Publishing Company	L. Ed. L. Ed. 2d	Contains official reports of opinions of the Court. Additionally, provides per curiam and other decisions not found elsewhere. Summarizes individual majority and dissenting opinions and counsel briefs.
Supreme Court Reporter, West Publishing Company	S. Ct.	Contains official reports of opinions of the Court. Contains annotated reports and indexes of case names. Includes opinions of justices in chambers. Appears semimonthly.
United States Law Week, Bureau of National Affairs	U.S.L.W.	Weekly periodical service contains full text of Court decisions. Includes four indexes: topical, table of cases, docket number table, and proceedings section. Contains summary of cases filed recently, journal of proceedings, summary of orders, arguments before the Court, argued cases awaiting decisions, review of Court's work, and review of Court's docket.

Sources: Lee Epstein, Jeffrey A. Segal, Harold J. Spaeth, and Thomas G. Walker, *The Supreme Court Compendium: Data, Decisions, and Developments,* 6th ed. (Thousand Oaks, CA: CQ Press, 2015), table 2.9. Dates of reporters are from David Savage, *Guide to the U.S. Supreme Court,* 5th ed. (Washington, DC: CQ Press, 2010).

These days, however, many students turn to electronic sources to locate Supreme Court decisions. Several companies maintain databases of the decisions of federal and state courts, along with a wealth of other information. In some institutions these services—Lexis and Westlaw—are available only to law school students. If you are in another academic unit, check with your librarians to see if your school provides access to other students, perhaps through Nexis Uni (a subset of the LexisNexis service and formerly known as Academic Universe). Also, the Legal Information Institute (LII) at Cornell Law School (https://www.law.cornell.edu/supremecourt/text), FindLaw (https://caselaw.findlaw.com/court/us-supreme-court), and now the Supreme Court itself (http://www.supremecourt.gov)—to name just three—house Supreme Court opinions and offer an array of search capabilities. You can read the opinions online, have them e-mailed to you, or download them immediately.

Locating Other Information on the Supreme Court and Its Members

As you might imagine, there is no shortage of reference material on the Court. Three (print) starting points are the following:

1. *The Supreme Court Compendium: Data, Decisions, and Developments,* 6th edition, contains

information on the following dimensions of Court activity: the Court's development, review process, opinions and decisions, judicial background, voting patterns, and impact.[81] You will find data as varied as the number of cases the Court decided during a particular term, the votes in the Senate on Supreme Court nominees, and the law schools the justices attended.

2. *Guide to the U.S. Supreme Court*, 5th edition, provides a fairly detailed history of the Court. It also summarizes the holdings in landmark cases and provides brief biographies of the justices.[82]

3. *The Oxford Companion to the Supreme Court of the United States*, 2nd edition, is an encyclopedia containing entries on the justices, important Court cases, the amendments to the Constitution, and the like.[83]

The U.S. Supreme Court also gets a great deal of attention on the Internet. The Legal Information Institute (http://www.law.cornell.edu) is particularly useful. In addition to Supreme Court decisions, the LII contains links to various documents (such as the U.S. Code and state statutes) and to a vast array of legal indexes and libraries. If you are unable to find the material you are looking for on the LII site, you may locate it by clicking on one of the links.

[81]Epstein et al., *Supreme Court Compendium*.

[82]David Savage, *Guide to the U.S. Supreme Court*, 5th ed. (Washington, DC: CQ Press, 2010).

[83]Kermit Hall, ed., *The Oxford Companion to the Supreme Court of the United States*, 2nd ed. (New York: Oxford University Press, 2005).

Another worthwhile site is SCOTUSblog, a project of a law firm (http://www.scotusblog.com). This site provides extensive summaries of pending Court cases, as well as links to briefs filed by the parties and amici.

As already mentioned, you can listen to selected oral arguments of the Court at the Oyez Project site (http://www.oyez.org). Oyez contains audio files of Supreme Court oral arguments for selected constitutional cases decided since the 1950s.

These are just a few of the many sites—perhaps hundreds—that contain information on the federal courts. But there is at least one other important electronic source of information on the Court worthy of mention: the U.S. Supreme Court Database, developed by Harold J. Spaeth, a political scientist and lawyer. This resource provides a wealth of data from the time of the Vinson Court (1946 term) to the present. Among the many attributes of Court decisions it includes are the names of the courts that made the original decisions, the identities of the parties to the cases, the policy contexts of the cases, and the votes of each justice. Indeed, we deployed this database to create many of the charts and tables you have just read. You can obtain all the data and accompanying documentation, free of charge, at http://supremecourtdatabase.org.

In this chapter, we have examined Supreme Court procedures and attempted to shed some light on how and why justices make the choices they do. Our consideration of preference-based factors, for example, highlighted the role ideology plays in Court decision making, and our discussion of political explanations emphasized public opinion and interest groups. After reading this chapter, you may have concluded that the justices are relatively free to go about their business as they please. But, as you shall see in the next chapter, that is not necessarily so. Although Court members have a good deal of power and the freedom to exercise it, they also face considerable institutional obstacles. It is to the subjects of judicial power and constraints that we now turn.

ANNOTATED READINGS

Lawrence Baum's *The Supreme Court*, 13th ed. (Washington, DC: CQ Press, 2018), and Linda Greenhouse's *The Supreme Court: A Very Short Introduction* (New York: Oxford University Press, 2012) provide modern-day introductions to the Court and its work. For insightful historical-political analyses, see Robert G. McCloskey's *The American Supreme Court* (Chicago: University of Chicago Press, 2004) and Barry Friedman's *The Will of the People* (New York: Farrar,

Straus & Giroux, 2009). Several justices have written books outlining their approaches to interpreting the Constitution. See Stephen Breyer's *Active Liberty: Interpreting Our Democratic Constitution* (New York: Knopf, 2005) and his *The Court and the World* (New York: Knopf, 2016) and Antonin Scalia's *A Matter of Interpretation: Federal Courts and the Law* (Princeton, NJ: Princeton University Press, 1997), which includes responses from prominent legal scholars. For other studies of approaches to constitutional interpretation, see Philip Bobbitt, *Constitutional Fate: Theory of the Constitution* (New York: Oxford University Press, 1982); Leslie Friedman Goldstein, *In Defense of the Text* (Savage, MD: Rowman & Littlefield, 1991); Pamela S. Karlan, *A Constitution for All Times* (Cambridge, MA: MIT Press, 2013); Jack N. Rakove, *Original Meanings: Politics and Ideas in the Making of the Constitution* (New York: Vintage Books, 1996); Keith E. Whittington, *Constitutional Interpretation: Textual Meaning, Original Intent, and Judicial Review* (Lawrence: University Press of Kansas, 1999); Richard H. Fallon Jr., *Implementing the Constitution* (Cambridge, MA: Harvard University Press, 2001); Michael J. Gerhardt, *The Power of Precedent* (New York: Oxford University Press, 2008); and Gary L. McDowell, *The Language of Law and the Foundations of American Constitutionalism* (New York: Cambridge University Press, 2010).

Noteworthy political science studies of judicial decision making (including case selection) are C. Herman Pritchett, *The Roosevelt Court* (New York: Macmillan, 1948); Glendon Schubert, *The Judicial Mind* (Evanston, IL: Northwestern University Press, 1965); Walter J. Murphy, *Elements of Judicial Strategy* (Chicago: University of Chicago Press, 1964); H. W. Perry Jr., *Deciding to Decide: Agenda Setting in the United States Supreme Court* (Cambridge, MA: Harvard University Press, 1991); Lee Epstein and Jack Knight, *The Choices Justices Make* (Washington, DC: CQ Press, 1998); Forrest Maltzman, James F. Spriggs II, and Paul J. Wahlbeck, *Crafting Law on the Supreme Court: The Collegial Game* (New York: Cambridge University Press, 2000); Jeffrey A. Segal and Harold J. Spaeth, *The Supreme Court and the Attitudinal Model Revisited* (New York: Cambridge University Press, 2002); Stefanie A. Lindquist and Frank B. Cross, *Measuring Judicial Activism* (New York: Oxford University Press, 2009); Michael A. Bailey and Forrest Maltzman, *The Constrained Court: Law, Politics, and the Decisions Justices Make* (Princeton, NJ: Princeton University Press, 2011); Richard L. Pacelle Jr., Brett W. Curry, and Bryan W. Marshall, *Decision Making by the Modern Supreme Court* (New York: Cambridge University Press, 2011); and Lee Epstein, William M. Landes, and Richard A. Posner, *The Behavior of Federal Judges: A Theoretical and Empirical Study of Rational Choice* (Cambridge, MA: Harvard University Press, 2013).

On the work of interest groups and attorneys (including the solicitor general), see Ryan C. Black and Ryan J. Owens, *The Solicitor General and the United States Supreme Court: Executive Branch Influence and Judicial Decisions* (Cambridge: Cambridge University Press, 2012); Kevin T. McGuire, *The Supreme Court Bar: Legal Elites in the Washington Community* (Charlottesville: University Press of Virginia, 1993); Timothy R. Johnson, *Oral Arguments and the United States Supreme Court* (Albany: State University of New York Press, 2004); and Paul M. Collins Jr., *Friends of the Supreme Court: Interest Groups and Judicial Decision Making* (New York: Oxford University Press, 2008).

INSTITUTIONAL AUTHORITY

ONE OF THE FIRST THINGS everyone learns in an American government course is that two concepts undergird the U.S. constitutional system. The first is the separation of powers doctrine, under which each of the branches has a distinct function: the legislature makes the laws, the executive implements those laws, and the judiciary interprets them. The second concept is the notion of checks and balances: each branch of government imposes limits on the primary functions of the others. The Supreme Court may interpret laws, but Congress can introduce legislation to override the Court's interpretation. If Congress takes action, then the president has the option of vetoing the proposed law. If that happens, Congress must decide whether to override the president's veto. Seen in this way, the rule of checks and balances inherent in the system of separation of powers suggests that policy in the United States emanates not from the separate actions of the branches of government but from the interaction among them.

A full understanding of the basics of institutional powers and constraints therefore requires a consideration of two important subjects. First, we must investigate the separation of powers system and why the framers adopted it; we take up this subject in the following pages. Second, because of the unique role the judiciary plays in the American government system, we need to understand how the Court has interpreted its own powers (located in Article III of the Constitution) and the constraints on those powers, as well as the powers of Congress (Article I) and the president (Article II). We consider these matters in chapters 3, 4, and 5.

ORIGINS OF THE SEPARATION OF POWERS/CHECKS AND BALANCES SYSTEM

Even a casual comparison of the Articles of Confederation and the U.S. Constitution reveals major differences in the way the two documents structured the national government (*see Figure I-1*). Under the articles, the powers of government were concentrated in the legislature, a unicameral Congress in which the states had equal voting powers. There was no executive or judicial branch separate and independent from the legislature. Issues of separation of powers and checks and balances were not particularly relevant to the articles, largely because the national government had almost no power to abuse. The states were capable of checking anything the central government proposed, and they provided whatever restraints the newly independent nation needed.

The government under the Articles of Confederation failed at least in part because it lacked sufficient power and authority to cope with the problems of the day. The requirements for amending the document were so restrictive that fundamental change within the articles proved impossible. When the Constitutional Convention met in Philadelphia in 1787, the delegates soon concluded that the articles had to be scrapped and replaced with a charter that would provide more effective power for the national government. The country had experienced conditions of economic decline, crippling taxation policies, interstate barriers to commerce, and isolated but alarming insurrections among the lower economic classes. The framers saw a newly structured national government as the only method of dealing with the problems besetting the nation in the aftermath of the Revolution.

But allocating significant power to the national government was not without its risks. Many of the framers feared the creation of a federal power capable of dominating the states and abusing individual liberties. It was apparent to all that the new government would have to be structured in a way that would minimize the potential for abuse and excess. The concept of the separation of powers and its twin, the idea of checks and balances, appealed to the framers as the best way to accomplish these necessary restraints.

The idea of separated powers was not new to the framers. They had been introduced to it by the political philosophy of the day and by their own political experiences. The theories of James Harrington and Charles de Montesquieu were particularly influential in this respect. Harrington (1611–1677) was an English political philosopher whose emphasis on the importance of property found a sympathetic audience among the former colonists. His primary work, *Oceana*, published in 1656, was a widely read description of a model government. Incorporated into Harrington's ideal state was the notion that government powers ought to be divided into three parts. A Senate made up of the intellectual elite would propose laws; the people, guided by the Senate's wisdom, would enact the laws; and a magistrate would execute the laws. This system, Harrington argued, would impose an important balance that would maintain a stable government and protect property rights.

Harrington's concept of a separation of powers was less well developed than that later proposed by Montesquieu (1689–1755), a French political theorist. Many scholars consider his *Spirit of the Laws* (published as *De l'Esprit des Loix* in 1748), which was widely circulated during the last half of the eighteenth century, to be the classic treatise on the separation of powers philosophy. Montesquieu was concerned about government abuse of liberty. In his estimation, liberty could not long prevail if too much power accrued to a single ruler or a single branch of government. He warned, "When the legislative and executive powers are united in the same person, or the same body of magistrates, there can be no liberty. . . . Again, there is no liberty if the judicial power be not separated from the legislative and executive." Although Montesquieu's message was directed to the citizens of his own country, he found a more receptive audience in the United States.

The influence of these political thinkers was reinforced by the framers' political experiences. The settlers had come to the New World largely to escape the abuses of European governments. George III's treatment of the colonies taught them that executives were not to be trusted with too much power. The colonists also feared an independent and powerful judiciary, especially one not answerable to the people. The framers undoubtedly had more confidence in the legislature, but they knew it, too, had the potential of exceeding its proper bounds. The English experience during the reign of Oliver Cromwell was lesson enough that muting the power of the king did not necessarily lead to the elimination of government abuse. What the framers sought was balance, a system in which each branch of government would be strong enough to keep excessive power from flowing into the hands of any other single branch. This necessary balance, as John Adams pointed out in his *Defence of the Constitutions of Government of the United States of America* (1787–1788), would also have the advantage of keeping the power-hungry aristocracy

in check and preventing the majority from taking rights away from the minority.

SEPARATION OF POWERS AND THE CONSTITUTION

The debates at the Constitutional Convention and the various plans the delegates considered all focused on the issue of dividing government power among the three branches as well as between the national government and the states. A general fear of a concentration of power permeated all the discussions. James Madison noted, "The truth is, all men having power ought to be distrusted to a certain degree." Separated powers turned out to be the framers' solution to the difficult problem of expanding government power and, at the same time, reducing the probability of abuse.

Although the term *separation of powers* is nowhere to be found in the document, the Constitution plainly adopts the central principles of the theory. A reading of the first lines of each of the first three articles—the vesting clauses—makes this point clearly:

> All legislative Powers herein granted shall be vested in a Congress of the United States, which shall consist of a Senate and House of Representatives. [Article I]

> The executive Power shall be vested in a President of the United States of America. [Article II]

> The judicial Power of the United States, shall be vested in one supreme Court, and in such inferior Courts as the Congress may from time to time ordain and establish. [Article III]

In the scheme of government incorporated into the Constitution, the legislative, executive, and judicial powers resided in separate branches of government. Unless otherwise specified in the document, each branch presumably was limited to the political function granted to it, and that function could not be exercised by either of the other two branches.

In addition to the separation of powers, which reserves certain functions to specific branches, the framers placed into the Constitution a number of mixed powers. That is, the document reserves certain functions for specific branches, but it also provides explicit checks on the exercise of those powers. As a consequence, each branch of government imposes limits on the primary functions of the others. A few examples illustrate this point:

- Congress has the right to pass legislation, but the president may veto the bills passed by Congress.

- The president may veto bills Congress passes, but the legislature may override the president's veto.

- The president may make treaties with foreign powers, but the Senate must vote its approval of those treaties.

- The president is commander in chief of the army and navy, but Congress must pass legislation to raise armies, regulate the military, and declare war.

- The president may nominate federal judges, but the Senate must confirm them.

- The judiciary may interpret the law and even strike down laws as being in violation of the Constitution—a power the Court asserted for itself—but Congress may pass new legislation or propose constitutional amendments.

- Congress may pass laws, but the executive must enforce them.

The framers also structured the branches so that the criteria and procedures for selecting the officials of the institutions differed, as did their tenures. Consequently, the branches all have slightly different sources of political power.

In the original scheme these differences were even more pronounced than they are today. Back then the two houses of Congress were politically dependent on different selection processes. Members of the House were, as they are today, directly elected by the people, and the seats were apportioned among the states on the basis of population. With terms of only two years, the representatives were required to go back to the people for review on a frequent and regular basis. Senators, in contrast, were, and still are, representatives of whole states, with each state, regardless of size, having two members in the upper chamber. But state legislatures originally selected their senators, a system that was not changed until 1913, when the Seventeenth Amendment, which imposed popular election of senators, was ratified. The six-year, staggered terms of senators were intended to make the upper house less immediately responsive to the volatile nature of public opinion.

The Constitution dictated that the president be selected by the Electoral College, a group of political elites chosen by the people or their representatives who would exercise judgment in casting their ballots among presidential candidates. Although the electors over time have ceased to perform any truly independent selection function, presidential selection remains a step away from direct popular election. The president's four-year term places the office squarely between the tenures conferred on representatives and senators. The original Constitution placed no limit on the number of terms a president could serve, but a two-term limit was observed by tradition until 1940 and was then imposed by constitutional amendment in 1951.

Differing altogether from the other two branches is the judiciary, which was assigned the least democratic selection system. The people have no direct role in the selection or retention of federal judges. Instead, the president nominates individuals for the federal bench, and the Senate confirms or rejects them. Once in office, federal judges serve for life, removable against their will only through impeachment. The intent of the framers was to make the judiciary independent. To do so, they created a system in which judges would not depend on the mood of the masses or on a single appointing power. Furthermore, judges would be accountable only to their own philosophies and consciences, with no periodic review or reassessment required.

Through a division of powers, an imposition of checks, and a variation in selection and tenure requirements, the framers hoped to achieve the balanced government they desired. This structure, they thought, would be the greatest protection against abuses of power and government violations of personal liberties and property rights. Many delegates to the Constitutional Convention considered this system of separation of powers a more effective method of protecting civil liberties than the formal pronouncements of a bill of rights.

Most political observers would conclude that the framers' invention has worked remarkably well. Through the years, the relative strengths of the branches have fluctuated. At certain times, the judiciary has been exceptionally weak, such as immediately after the Civil War. At other times, the judiciary has been criticized as being too powerful, such as when it repeatedly blocked New Deal legislation in the 1930s or when it expanded civil liberties during the Warren Court era. The executive also has led the other branches in political power. Beginning with the tenure of Franklin Roosevelt and extending into the 1970s, references were often made to the "imperial presidency." But when one branch gains too much power and abuses occur, as in the case of Richard Nixon and the Watergate crisis, the system tends to reimpose the balance sought by the framers.

As you read the next three chapters, consider the Supreme Court's decisions against the framers' original understandings of the separation of powers. What powers does each branch have? What are the sources of those powers? How do the powers of one branch offset those of the other two? How has the balance of power among the branches evolved since the Constitution was drafted in 1787?

In addition to assessing their powers, look for areas of conflict among the branches. American political history has been marked with interbranch disputes. The resolution of those disputes, often through Supreme Court decisions, has determined how political power is allocated and exercised. Undoubtedly, the ongoing and inevitable tensions among the branches will continue to spawn constitutional controversies. To the Supreme Court will be left the task of settling such disputes in a manner that is both true to the principles of the founders and responsive to the needs of our times.

CHAPTER THREE

THE JUDICIARY

CONCERNED ABOUT THE GROWTH of child pornography, especially on the Internet, Congress passed the Child Pornography Prevention Act of 1996. The law prohibited "any visual depiction, including any photograph, film, video, picture, or computer generated image or picture" that "is or appears to be of a minor engaging in sexually explicit conduct."

In *Ashcroft v. Free Speech Coalition* (2002) the U.S. Supreme Court struck down the law for violating the First Amendment's freedom of expression guarantees. The justices found that the law went beyond a valid regulation of obscenity. Not only did the statute fail to conform to the standards set by the Court in previous obscenity decisions, but also its overbroad provisions prohibited legitimate accounts of the sexual behavior of minors.

In many ways, the Court's action was less than startling. For two centuries federal courts have exerted the power of judicial review—that is, the power to review acts of government to determine their compatibility with the U.S. Constitution. And even though the Constitution does not explicitly give them such power, the courts' authority to do so has been challenged only occasionally. Today we take for granted the notion that federal courts may review government actions and strike them down if they violate constitutional mandates.

Nevertheless, when courts exert this power, as the U.S. Supreme Court did in *Ashcroft v. Free Speech Coalition*, they provoke controversy. Look at it from this perspective: Congress, composed of officials we *elect*, passed the Child Pornography Prevention Act, which was then rendered invalid by a Supreme Court of nine *unelected* justices. Such an occurrence strikes some people as quite odd, perhaps even antidemocratic. Why should we Americans allow a branch of government over which we have no electoral control to review and nullify the actions of the government officials we elect to represent us? This chapter attempts to answer that question and further our understanding of the federal judiciary and its powers.

We first explore the circumstances leading to the adoption of Article III of the Constitution, which outlines the contours of judicial power. Next, we turn to the development of judicial review in the United States. Judicial review is the primary weapon available to the federal courts, the check the judiciary has on other branches of government. Because this power can be awesome in scope, many tend to emphasize it but overlook the factors that constrain its use, as well as other checks on the power of the Court. Therefore, in the final section of this chapter, we explore the limits on judicial power.

ESTABLISHMENT OF THE FEDERAL JUDICIARY

The federal judicial system is built on a foundation created by two major statements of the 1780s: Article III of the U.S. Constitution and the Judiciary Act of 1789. In this section, we consider both, with an emphasis on their content and the debates they provoked. Note, in particular, the degree to which the major controversies reflect more general concerns about federalism. Designing and fine-tuning the U.S. system of government required many compromises over the balance of power between the federal government and the states, and Article III and the Judiciary Act are no exceptions.

Article III

The framers of the Constitution spent days upon days debating the contents of Article I (the legislature) and Article II (the executive), but they had comparatively little trouble drafting Article III. Indeed, it caused the least controversy of any major constitutional provision. Why? One reason is that the states and Great Britain had well-entrenched court systems, and the founders had firsthand knowledge of the workings of courts—knowledge they lacked about the other political institutions they were establishing. Second, thirty-four of the fifty-five delegates to the Constitutional Convention were lawyers or had some training in the law. They held a common vision of the *general* role courts should play in the new polity.[1]

Alexander Hamilton expressed that vision in *Federalist* No. 78, one of a series of papers designed to generate support for the ratification of the Constitution. Hamilton specifically referred to the judiciary as the "least dangerous branch" of government; he (and virtually all the founders) saw the courts as legal, not political, bodies. He wrote, "If [judges] should be disposed to exercise *will* instead of *judgment*, the consequence would equally be the substitution of their pleasure to that of the legislative body." To that end, the framers agreed on the need for judicial independence. They accomplished this goal by allowing judges to "hold their offices during good behavior"—that is, giving them life tenure—rather than subjecting them to periodic public checks through the electoral process. The framers also concurred on the need to block Congress from reducing a federal judge's compensation during terms of continuous service. The compensation clause, located in Article III, implies judicial independence: the framers hoped to prevent members of the legislature upset with court decisions from punishing judges by cutting their pay.

Federal judges continue to enjoy these protections, but many state court judges do not. In only three states do judges hold their jobs for life or until they reach a specified retirement age. In the remaining states judges must periodically face the electorate. In some states the voters decide whether to retain judges; in other states judges must be elected (or reelected), just as any other officials are. Either way, the practice of retaining or reelecting has raised interesting constitutional questions. In ***Caperton v. A. T. Massey Coal Co.*** (2009), for example, the Court considered whether a judge should recuse himself from a case in which he has received substantial campaign contributions from a person with an interest in the outcome. The majority held that when there is a "serious risk of actual bias"—as it seemed clear in *Caperton*—failure to recuse amounts to a violation of the due process clause, which requires a "fair trial in a fair tribunal."

That the framers settled on life tenure for federal judges, and not some form of electoral or legislative check, and more generally shared a fundamental view of the role of the federal judiciary does not mean that they agreed on all the specifics. For example, although they agreed that federal judges would serve for "good behavior," the delegates debated how the judges would get their jobs—that is, who appoints them. The Virginia Plan, which served as the basis for many of the proposals debated at the convention, suggested that Congress should appoint these judges. Some of the delegates backed this idea, while others proposed that the Senate should make the appointments. Benjamin Franklin argued that perhaps lawyers should decide who would sit on the courts. After all, Franklin joked, the lawyers would select "the ablest of the profession in order to get rid of him, and share his practice among themselves."[2] Finally, the delegates decided that the appointment power should be given to the president, with the "advice and consent" of the Senate. Accordingly, the power to appoint federal judges is located in Article II, which lists the powers of the president. The Senate, however, has read the "advice and consent" phrase to mean that it must approve the president's nominees by a majority vote. And it has taken its part in the process quite seriously, rejecting outright 12 of the 163 nominations to the Supreme Court over the past two centuries—a greater number (proportionally speaking) than any other group of presidential appointees requiring senatorial approval.[3]

Other debates centered on the structure of the American legal system. The delegates agreed that there would be at least one federal court, the Supreme Court of the United States, but disagreed over the establishment of federal tribunals inferior to the Supreme Court. The Virginia Plan, which served as the basis for many of the proposals debated at the convention, suggested that Congress should establish lower federal courts. Delegates who favored a strong national government agreed with this plan, with some wanting to insert language in Article III to create such courts.

But delegates favoring states' rights over those of the national government vehemently objected to the

---

[1] See Daniel A. Farber and Suzanna Sherry, *A History of the American Constitution*, 2nd ed. (St. Paul, MN: Thomson/West, 2005), 65.

[2] Quoted in Farber and Sherry, *A History of the American Constitution*, 70.

[3] Data are from U.S. Senate's website, www.senate.gov/pagelayout/reference/nominations/Nominations.htm.

creation of any federal tribunals other than the U.S. Supreme Court. As one delegate, Pierce Butler of South Carolina, put it, "The people will not bear such an innovation. The states will revolt at such encroachments."[4] Instead of creating new federal courts, they proposed that the existing state courts should hear cases in the first instance, with an allowance for appeals to the U.S. Supreme Court. "This dispute," as Justice Hugo L. Black wrote in 1970, "resulted in compromise. One 'supreme Court' was created by the Constitution, and Congress was given the power to create other federal courts."[5] The first sentence of Article III—the vesting clause—reflects this compromise:

> The judicial power of the United States, shall be vested in one Supreme Court, and in such inferior courts as the Congress may from time to time ordain and establish.

In other words, Article III does not establish a system of lower federal courts; rather, it gives Congress the option of doing so.

Did the framers anticipate that Congress would take advantage of this language and create lower federal courts? The answer is likely yes because much of Article III—specifically Section 2, the longest part—defines the jurisdiction of federal courts that did not yet exist (or at least the jurisdiction that Congress could give them). In Section 2, the framers outlined two types of jurisdiction that the federal courts might exercise: over cases involving certain subjects or over cases brought by certain parties (see Box 3-1).

As Box 2-1 also indicates, Section 2 contains separate language on the authority of the U.S. Supreme Court, providing for original and appellate jurisdiction—both of which come into play in the cases we excerpt below. Note, though, that Article III is silent over whether the Court has judicial review power. It is not that the framers didn't consider some system for reviewing and invalidating government acts; they did. Several times over the course of the convention, they took up James Madison's proposal for the creation of a council of revision, made up of Supreme Court justices and the president, with the power to veto legislative acts. But each time proposal

came up, the delegates voted to defeat it. In *Marbury v. Madison* (1803), the first case we excerpt in this chapter, Chief Justice John Marshall in essence articulated such veto power for the Court. Those who take a dim view of Marshall's decision occasionally point to the delegates' rejection of the council of revision as proof that Marshall skirted the framers' intent.

Judiciary Act of 1789

Although Section 2 of Article III suggests that the framers likely anticipated the creation of lower federal courts, recall that Article III itself did not establish any courts other than the U.S. Supreme Court. It was left up to Congress to create (or not) additional federal courts. Dominated by Federalists, the First Congress did just that in the Judiciary Act of 1789, giving some "flesh" to the "skeleton" that was Article III.[6] The Judiciary Act of 1789 is a long and relatively complex law that, at its core, had two purposes. First, it sought to establish a federal court structure, which it accomplished by providing for the Supreme Court and circuit and district courts. Under the law, the Supreme Court was to have one chief justice and five associate justices. That the Court initially had six members illustrates an important point: Congress, not the U.S. Constitution, determines the number of justices on the Supreme Court. That number has been nine since 1869.

As Figure 3-1 shows, the act also created thirteen district courts. Each of the eleven states that had ratified the Constitution received a court, with separate tribunals created for Maine and Kentucky, which were then parts of Massachusetts and Virginia, respectively. District courts, then as now, were presided over by one judge. But the three newly established circuit courts were quite extraordinary in composition. Congress grouped the district courts—except those for Kentucky and Maine—geographically into the Eastern, Middle, and Southern Circuits and put one district court judge and two Supreme Court justices in charge of each. In other words, three judges would hear cases in the circuit courts. Today, appeals courts continue to hear cases in panels of three. However, these courts now have their own permanent judges, making regular participation by district court judges and Supreme Court justices unnecessary.

A second goal of the Judiciary Act was to specify the jurisdiction of the federal courts. Section 2 of Article III speaks broadly about the authority of federal courts,

---

[4]Quoted in Farber and Sherry, *A History of the American Constitution*, 70.

[5]*Atlantic Coast Line Railroad Co. v. Brotherhood of Locomotive Engineers* (1970).

[6]Russell R. Wheeler and Cynthia Harrison, *Creating the Federal Judicial System* (Washington, DC: Federal Judicial Center, 1989), 2.

BOX 3-1

Jurisdiction of the Federal Courts as Defined in Article III

Jurisdiction of the Lower Federal Courts

Subjects falling under their authority:

- Cases involving the U.S. Constitution, federal laws, and treaties

- Cases affecting ambassadors, public ministers, and consuls

- Cases of admiralty and maritime jurisdiction

Parties falling under their authority:

- United States

- Controversies between two or more states

- Controversies between a state and citizens of another state[a]

- Controversies between citizens of different states

- Controversies between citizens of the same state claiming lands under grants of different states

- Controversies between a state, or the citizens thereof, and foreign states, citizens, or subjects

Jurisdiction of the Supreme Court

Original jurisdiction:

- Cases affecting ambassadors, public ministers, and consuls

- Cases to which a state is a party

Appellate jurisdiction:

- Cases falling under the jurisdiction of the lower federal courts, "with such Exceptions, and under such Regulations as the Congress shall make."

[a]In 1795 this was modified by the Eleventh Amendment, which removed from federal jurisdiction those cases in which a state is sued by the citizens of another state.

---

potentially giving them jurisdiction over cases involving particular parties or subjects or, in the case of the Supreme Court, original and appellate jurisdiction (see Box 3-1). The Judiciary Act provided more specific information, defining the parameters of authority for each of the newly established courts and for the U.S. Supreme Court. The district courts were to serve as trial courts, hearing cases involving admiralty issues, forfeitures and penalties, and petty federal crimes, as well as minor U.S. civil cases. Congress recognized that some of these courts would be busier than others and fixed judicial salaries accordingly. Delaware judges received only $800 per year for their services, while their counterparts in South Carolina, a coastal state that would generate many admiralty disputes, earned $1,800.[7]

Unlike today, the circuit courts were trial courts with jurisdiction over cases involving citizens from different states and major federal criminal and civil cases. Congress also gave them limited appellate authority to hear major civil and admiralty disputes coming out of the district courts.

Finally, the 1789 act contained several provisions concerning the jurisdiction of the U.S. Supreme Court. Section 13 reiterated the Court's authority over suits in the first instance (its original jurisdiction) and gave the justices appellate jurisdiction over major civil disputes, those involving more than $2,000, which was a good deal of money back then. Section 13 also spoke about the Court's authority to issue writs of mandamus, which command a public official to carry out a particular act or duty: "The Supreme Court . . . shall have the power to issue . . . writs of mandamus, in cases warranted by the principles and usages of law, to any courts appointed, or persons holding office, under the authority of the United States." This matter may seem trivial, but, as we shall see, the Court's interpretation

---

[7]Ibid., 6.

Figure 3-1   The Federal Court System under the Judiciary Act of 1789

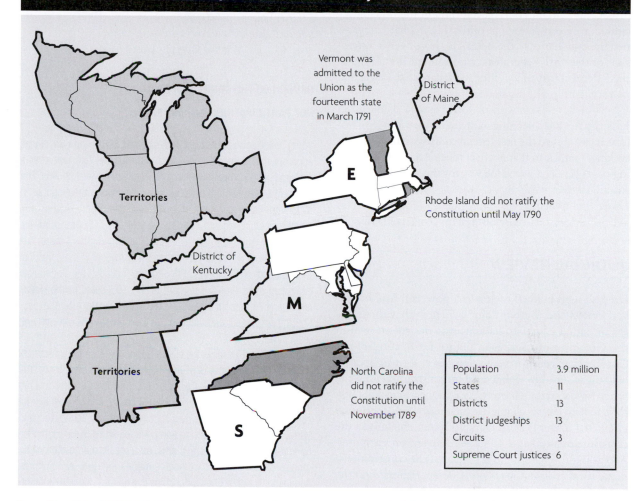

Vermont was admitted to the Union as the fourteenth state in March 1791

District of Maine

Territories

E

Rhode Island did not ratify the Constitution until May 1790

District of Kentucky

M

Territories

North Carolina did not ratify the Constitution until November 1789

S

Population	3.9 million
States	11
Districts	13
District judgeships	13
Circuits	3
Supreme Court justices	6

Source: Russell R. Wheeler and Cynthia Harrison, *Creating the Federal Judicial System,* 3rd ed. (Washington, DC: Federal Judicial Center, 2005), 5.

Note: The Judiciary Act of 1789 created thirteen districts and placed eleven of them in three circuits: the Eastern, Middle, and Southern. Each district had a district court, which was a trial court with a single district judge and primarily admiralty jurisdiction. A circuit court also met in each district of the circuit and was composed of the district judge and two Supreme Court justices. The circuit courts exercised primarily diversity and criminal jurisdiction and heard appeals from the district courts in some cases. The districts of Maine and Kentucky (parts of the states of Massachusetts and Virginia, respectively) were part of no circuit; their district courts exercised both district and circuit court jurisdiction.

of this particular provision formed the centerpiece of *Marbury v. Madison.*

Another part of the act, Section 25, authorized the Supreme Court to review certain kinds of cases coming out of the states. Specifically, the Court could now hear appeals from the highest state courts if those tribunals upheld state laws against claims that the laws violated the Constitution or denied claims based on the U.S. Constitution, federal laws, or treaties. This section moved to the fore in *Martin v. Hunter's Lessee,* which we discuss later in the chapter.

At first glance, the components of the 1789 act—its establishment of a federal court system and of rules governing that system—appear to favor the Federalists' position. Recall that Anti-Federalist delegates at the Constitutional Convention did not want the document even to mention lower federal tribunals, much less to give Congress the authority to establish them. The 1789 act did that and more: it gave the Supreme Court the power to review state supreme court cases—surely an Anti-Federalist's worst nightmare! But it would be a mistake to believe that the act did not take into account the position taken by states' rights advocates. For example, the 1789 act used state lines as the boundaries for the district and circuit courts, even though the boundaries could have been defined in other ways.[8] That Congress tied the boundaries to the states may have been a concession to the Anti-Federalists, who wanted the judges of the federal courts to feel they were part of the legal and political cultures of the states.

Whichever side won or lost, passage of the 1789 Judiciary Act was a defining moment in American legal history. It established the first federal court system, one that is strikingly similar to that in effect today. And, as the following pages reveal, it paved the way for three landmark constitutional cases—*Marbury v. Madison*, **Martin v. Hunter's Lessee**, and **Cohens v. Virginia**—all of which centered on judicial review, the major power of the federal judiciary.

JUDICIAL REVIEW

Even though judicial review is a powerful tool of federal courts and there is some evidence that the framers intended courts to have it, it is not mentioned in the Constitution. Yet, even before ratification of the Constitution, courts in seven states, in at least eight cases, held that a state law violated a state constitution (or some other fundamental charter).[9] So, too, early in U.S. history, federal courts claimed it for themselves. In **Hylton v. United States** (1796), Daniel Hylton challenged the constitutionality of a 1793 federal tax on carriages. According to Hylton, the act violated the constitutional mandate that direct taxes must be apportioned on the basis of population. With only three justices participating, the Court upheld the act. But even by considering the challenge, the Court in effect reviewed the constitutionality of an act of Congress.

Not until 1803, however, would the Court invoke judicial review to strike down legislation it deemed incompatible with the U.S. Constitution. That decision came in the landmark case *Marbury v. Madison*. How does Chief Justice Marshall justify the Court's power to strike down legislation in light of the failure of the newly framed Constitution to provide it?

---

[8]As Wheeler and Harrison note, "The creators of the federal judiciary might have established separate judicial administrative divisions that would ensure roughly equal allocation of workload and would be subject to realignment to maintain the allocation" (ibid.).

[9]Saikrishna B. Prakash and John C. Yoo, "The Origins of Judicial Review," *University of Chicago Law Review* 70 (2003): 887–982.

Marbury v. Madison

5 U.S. (1 Cranch) 137 (1803)
http://caselaw.findlaw.com/us-supreme-court/5/137.html
Vote: 4 (Chase, Marshall, Paterson, Washington)
    0

OPINION OF THE COURT: *Marshall*

NOT PARTICIPATING: *Cushing, Moore*

When voting in the presidential election of 1800 was over, it was apparent that Federalist president John Adams had lost after a long and bitter campaign, but it was not known who had won. The Electoral College voting resulted in a tie between the Republican candidate, Thomas Jefferson, and his running mate, Aaron Burr, and the election had to be settled in the House of Representatives. In February 1801 the House elected Jefferson. This meant that the Federalists no longer controlled the presidency; they also lost their majority in Congress. Prior to the election, the Federalists controlled more than 56 percent of the 106 seats in the House and nearly 70 percent of the 32 seats in the Senate. After the election, those percentages declined to 35 percent and 44 percent, respectively.[10]

With these losses in the elected branches, the Federalists took steps to maintain control of the third branch of government, the judiciary. The lame-duck Congress enacted the Circuit Court Act of 1801, which created six new circuit courts and several district courts to accommodate the new states of Kentucky, Tennessee, and Vermont. These new courts required judges and support staff such as attorneys, marshals, and clerks. As a result, during the last six months of his term in office Adams made more than two hundred nominations, with sixteen judgeships (called the "midnight appointments" because of the rush to complete them before Adams's term expired) approved by the Senate during his last two weeks in office.

An even more important opportunity had arisen in December 1800, when the third chief justice of the United States, Federalist Oliver Ellsworth, resigned so that Adams—not Jefferson—could name his replacement. Adams first offered the post to John Jay, who had served as the first chief justice before leaving the Court to take the then-more-prestigious office of governor of New York. When Jay refused, Adams turned to his secretary of state, John Marshall, an ardent Federalist. The Senate confirmed Marshall in January 1801, but he also continued to serve as secretary of state.

In addition, the Federalist Congress passed the Organic Act of 1801, which authorized Adams to appoint forty-two justices

---

[10]Data are from the House's and Senate's websites, http://artandhistory.house.gov/house_history/partyDiv.aspx and http://www.senate.gov/history/partydiv.htm.

William Marbury, whose suit against James Madison led to a landmark decision in 1803. John Marshall's opinion in *Marbury v. Madison* established the Court's authority to review the constitutionality of acts of Congress.

of the peace for the District of Columbia. It was this seemingly innocuous law that set the stage for the dramatic case of *Marbury v. Madison.* In the confusion of the Adams administration's last days in office, Marshall, the outgoing secretary of state, failed to deliver some of these commissions. When the new administration came into office, James Madison, the new secretary of state, acting under orders from Jefferson, refused to deliver at least five commissions.[11] Indeed, some years later, Jefferson explained the situation in this way:

> I found the commissions on the table of the Department of State, on my entrance into office, and I forbade their delivery. Whatever is in the Executive offices is certainly deemed to be in the hands of the President, and in this case, was actually in my hands,

because when I countermanded them, there was as yet no Secretary of State.[12]

As a result, in 1801 William Marbury and three others who were denied their commissions went directly to the Supreme Court and asked it to issue a writ of mandamus ordering Madison to deliver the commissions. Marbury thought he could take his case directly to the Court because Section 13 of the 1789 Judiciary Act gives the Court the power to issue writs of mandamus to anyone holding federal office. The relevant passage of Section 13 reads as follows:

> The Supreme Court shall . . . have appellate jurisdiction from the circuit courts and courts of the several states, in the cases herein after specifically provided for; and shall have power to issue . . . mandamus in cases warranted by the principles and usages of law, to any courts appointed, or persons holding office, under the authority of the United States.

In this volatile political climate, Marshall, now serving as chief justice, was perhaps in the most tenuous position of all. On one hand, he had been a supporter of the Federalist Party, which now looked to him to "scold" the Jefferson administration. On the other, Marshall wanted to avoid a confrontation between the Jefferson administration and the Supreme Court, which not only seemed imminent but also could end in disaster for the Court and the struggling nation. In fact, Jefferson and his party were so annoyed with the Court for agreeing to hear the *Marbury* dispute that they began to consider impeaching Federalist judges—with two justices (Samuel Chase and Marshall himself) high on their lists. Note, too, the year in which the Court handed down the decision in *Marbury;* the case was not decided until two years after Marbury filed suit because Congress and the Jefferson administration had abolished the 1802 term of the Court.

THE FOLLOWING OPINION OF THE COURT WAS DELIVERED BY THE CHIEF JUSTICE.

The peculiar delicacy of this case, the novelty of some of its circumstances, and the real difficulty attending the points which occur in it, require a complete exposition of the principles, on which the opinion to be given by the court, is founded.

In the order in which the court has viewed this subject, the following questions have been considered and decided.

1st. Has the applicant a right to the commission he demands?

2dly. If he has a right, and that right has been violated, do the laws of his country afford him a remedy?

[11]Historical accounts differ, but it seems that Jefferson decreased the number of Adams's appointments to justice of the peace positions to thirty from forty-two. Twenty-five of these thirty appointees received their commissions, but five, including William Marbury, did not. See Francis N. Stites, *John Marshall* (Boston: Little, Brown, 1981), 84.

[12]Quoted in Charles Warren, *The Supreme Court in United States History*, vol. 1 (Boston: Little, Brown, 1922), 244.

3dly. If they do afford him a remedy, is it a *mandamus* issuing from this court?

The first object of enquiry is,

1st. Has the applicant a right to the commission he demands?

. . .

In order to determine whether he is entitled to this commission, it becomes necessary to enquire whether he has been appointed to the office. For if he has been appointed, the law continues him in office for five years, and he is entitled to the possession of those evidences of office, which, being completed, became his property. . . .

These are the clauses of the constitution and laws of the United States, which affect this part of the case. They seem to contemplate three distinct operations:

1st. The nomination. This is the sole act of the President, and is completely voluntary.

2d. The appointment. This is also the act of the President, and is also a voluntary act, though it can only be performed by and with the advice and consent of the senate.

3d. The commission. To grant a commission to a person appointed, might perhaps be deemed a duty enjoined by the constitution. "He shall," says that instrument, "commission all the officers of the United States." . . .

The transmission of the commission, is a practice directed by convenience, but not by law. It cannot therefore be necessary to constitute the appointment which must precede it, and which is the mere act of the President. . . . A commission is transmitted to a person already appointed; not to a person to be appointed or not, as the letter enclosing the commission should happen to get into the post office and reach him in safety, or to miscarry. . . .

If the transmission of a commission be not considered as necessary to give validity to an appointment; still less is its acceptance. The appointment is the sole act of the President; the acceptance is the sole act of the officer, and is, in plain common sense, posterior to the appointment. . . .

Mr. Marbury, then, since his commission was signed by the President, and sealed by the secretary of state, was appointed; and as the law creating the office, gave the officer a right to hold for five years, independent of the Executive, the appointment was not revocable; but vested in the officer legal rights, which are protected by the laws of his country.

To withhold his commission, therefore, is an act deemed by the court not warranted by law, but violative of a vested legal right.

This brings us to the second enquiry; which is,

2dly. If he has a right, and that right has been violated, do the laws of his country afford him a remedy?

The very essence of civil liberty certainly consists in the right of every individual to claim the protection of the laws, whenever he receives an injury. One of the first duties of government is to afford that protection. In Great Britain, the King himself is sued in the respectful form of a petition, and he never fails to comply with the judgment of his court.

The government of the United States has been emphatically termed a government of laws, and not of men. It will certainly cease to deserve this high appellation, if the laws furnish no remedy for the violation of a vested legal right.

If this obloquy is to be cast on the jurisprudence of our country, it must arise from the peculiar character of the case. . . .

It behooves us, then, to inquire whether there be in its composition any ingredient which shall exempt from legal investigation or exclude the injured party from legal redress. . . .

Is it in the nature of the transaction? Is the act of delivering or withholding a commission to be considered as a mere political act belonging to the Executive department alone, for the performance of which entire confidence is placed by our Constitution in the Supreme Executive, and for any misconduct respecting which the injured individual has no remedy?

That there may be such cases is not to be questioned. But that every act of duty to be performed in any of the great departments of government constitutes such a case is not to be admitted. . . .

It follows, then, that the question whether the legality of an act of the head of a department be examinable in a court of justice or not must always depend on the nature of that act.

If some acts be examinable and others not, there must be some rule of law to guide the Court in the exercise of its jurisdiction.

In some instances, there may be difficulty in applying the rule to particular cases; but there cannot, it is believed, be much difficulty in laying down the rule.

By the Constitution of the United States, the President is invested with certain important political powers, in the exercise of which he is to use his own discretion, and is accountable only to his country in his political character and to his own conscience. To aid him in the performance of these duties, he is authorized to appoint certain officers, who act by his authority and in conformity with his orders.

In such cases, their acts are his acts; and whatever opinion may be entertained of the manner in which executive discretion may be used, still there exists, and can exist, no power to control that discretion. The subjects are political. They respect the nation, not individual rights, and, being entrusted to the Executive, the decision of the Executive is conclusive. . . .

But when the Legislature proceeds to impose on that officer other duties; when he is directed peremptorily to perform certain acts; when the rights of individuals are dependent on the performance of those acts; he is so far the officer of the law, is amenable to the laws for his conduct, and cannot at his discretion, sport away the vested rights of others.

The conclusion from this reasoning is, that where the heads of departments are the political or confidential agents of the Executive, merely to execute the will of the President, or rather to act in cases in which the Executive possesses a constitutional or legal discretion, nothing can be more perfectly clear than that their acts are only politically examinable. But where a specific duty is assigned by law, and individual rights depend upon the performance of that duty, it seems equally clear that the individual who considers himself injured, has a right to resort to the laws of his country for a remedy…

The question whether a right has vested or not, is, in its nature, judicial, and must be tried by the judicial authority. If, for example, Mr. Marbury had taken the oaths of a magistrate, and proceeded to act as one; in consequence of which a suit had been instituted against him, in which his defence had depended on his being a magistrate; the validity of his appointment must have been determined by judicial authority.

So, if he conceives that, by virtue of his appointment, he has a legal right, either to the commission which has been made out for him, or to a copy of that commission, it is equally a question examinable in a court, and the decision of the court upon it must depend on the opinion entertained of his appointment.

That question has been discussed, and the opinion is, that the latest point of time which can be taken as that at which the appointment was complete, and evidenced, was when, after the signature of the president, the seal of the United States was affixed to the commission.

It is then the opinion of the court,

1st. That by signing the commission of Mr. Marbury, the president of the United States appointed him a justice of peace, for the county of Washington in the district of Columbia; and that the seal of the United States, affixed thereto by the secretary of state, is conclusive testimony of the verity of the signature, and of the completion of the appointment; and that the appointment conferred on him a legal right to the office for the space of five years.

2dly. That, having this legal title to the office, he has a consequent right to the commission; a refusal to deliver which, is a plain violation of that right, for which the laws of his country afford him a remedy.

It remains to be enquired whether,

3dly. He is entitled to the remedy for which he applies.

The act to establish the judicial courts of the United States authorizes the supreme court "to issue writs of mandamus, in cases warranted by the principles and usages of law, to any courts appointed, or persons holding office, under the authority of the United States."

The secretary of state, being a person holding an office under the authority of the United States, is precisely within the letter of the description; and if this court is not authorized to issue a writ of mandamus to such an officer, it must be because the law is unconstitutional, and therefore absolutely incapable of conferring the authority, and assigning the duties which its words purport to confer and assign.

The constitution vests the whole judicial power of the United States in one supreme court, and such inferior courts as congress shall, from time to time, ordain and establish. This power is expressly extended to all cases arising under the laws of the United States; and consequently, in some form, may be exercised over the present case; because the right claimed is given by a law of the United States.

In the distribution of this power it is declared that "the supreme court shall have original jurisdiction in all cases affecting ambassadors, other public ministers and consuls, and those in which a state shall be a party. In all other cases, the supreme court shall have appellate jurisdiction."

It has been insisted, at the bar, that as the original grant of jurisdiction, to the supreme and inferior courts, is general, and the clause, assigning original jurisdiction to the supreme court, contains no negative or restrictive words; the power remains to the legislature, to assign original jurisdiction to that court in other cases than those specified in the article which has been recited; provided those cases belong to the judicial power of the United States.

If it had been intended to leave it in the discretion of the legislature to apportion the judicial power between the supreme and inferior courts according to the will of that body, it would certainly have been useless to have proceeded further than to have defined the judicial power, and the tribunals in which it should be vested. The subsequent part of the section is mere surplussage, is entirely without meaning, if such is to be the construction. If congress remains at liberty to give this court appellate jurisdiction, where the constitution has declared their jurisdiction shall be original; and original jurisdiction where the constitution has declared it shall be appellate; the distribution of jurisdiction, made in the constitution, is form without substance.

Affirmative words are often, in their operation, negative of other objects than those affirmed; and in this case, a negative or exclusive sense must be given to them or they have no operation at all.

It cannot be presumed that any clause in the constitution is intended to be without effect; and therefore such a construction is inadmissible, unless the words require it.

If the solicitude of the convention, respecting our peace with foreign powers, induced a provision that the supreme court should take original jurisdiction in cases which might be supposed to affect them; yet the clause would have proceeded no further than to provide for such cases, if no further restriction on the powers of congress had been intended. That they should have appellate jurisdiction in all other cases, with such exceptions as congress might make, is no restriction; unless the words be deemed exclusive of original jurisdiction.

When an instrument organizing fundamentally a judicial system, divides it into one supreme, and so many inferior courts as the legislature may ordain and establish; then enumerates its powers, and proceeds so far to distribute them, as to define the jurisdiction of the supreme court by declaring the cases in which it shall take original jurisdiction, and that in others it shall take appellate jurisdiction; the plain import of the words seems to be, that in one class of cases its jurisdiction is original, and not appellate; in the other it is appellate, and not original. If any other construction would render the clause inoperative, that is an additional reason for rejecting such other construction, and for adhering to their obvious meaning.

To enable this court then to issue a mandamus, it must be shewn [sic] to be an exercise of appellate jurisdiction, or to be necessary to enable them to exercise appellate jurisdiction.

It has been stated at the bar that the appellate jurisdiction may be exercised in a variety of forms, and that if it be the will of the legislature that a mandamus should be used for that purpose, that will must be obeyed. This is true, yet the jurisdiction must be appellate, not original.

It is the essential criterion of appellate jurisdiction, that it revises and corrects the proceedings in a cause already instituted, and does not create that cause. Although, therefore, a mandamus may be directed to courts, yet to issue such a writ to an officer for the delivery of a paper, is in effect the same as to sustain an original action for that paper, and therefore seems not to belong to appellate, but to original jurisdiction. Neither is it necessary in such a case as this, to enable the court to exercise its appellate jurisdiction.

The authority, therefore, given to the supreme court, by the act establishing the judicial courts of the United States, to issue writs of mandamus to public officers, appears not to be warranted by the constitution; and it becomes necessary to enquire whether a jurisdiction, so conferred, can be exercised.

The question, whether an act, repugnant to the constitution, can become the law of the land, is a question deeply interesting to the United States; but, happily, not of an intricacy proportioned to its interest. It seems only necessary to recognise certain principles, supposed to have been long and well established, to decide it.

That the people have an original right to establish, for their future government, such principles as, in their opinion, shall most conduce to their own happiness, is the basis, on which the whole American fabric has been erected. The exercise of this original right is a very great exertion; nor can it, nor ought it to be frequently repeated. The principles, therefore, so established, are deemed fundamental. And as the authority, from which they proceed, is supreme, and can seldom act, they are designed to be permanent.

This original and supreme will organizes the government, and assigns, to different departments, their respective powers. It may either stop here; or establish certain limits not to be transcended by those departments.

The government of the United States is of the latter description. The powers of the legislature are defined, and limited; and that those limits may not be mistaken, or forgotten, the constitution is written. To what purpose are powers limited, and to what purpose is that limitation committed to writing, if these limits may, at any time, be passed by those intended to be restrained? The distinction, between a government with limited and unlimited powers, is abolished, if those limits do not confine the persons on whom they are imposed,

and if acts prohibited and acts allowed, are of equal obligation. It is a proposition too plain to be contested, that the constitution controls any legislative act repugnant to it; or, that the legislature may alter the constitution by an ordinary act.

Between these alternatives there is no middle ground. The constitution is either a superior, paramount law, unchangeable by ordinary means, or it is on a level with ordinary legislative acts, and like other acts, is alterable when the legislature shall please to alter it.

If the former part of the alternative be true, then a legislative act contrary to the constitution is not law: if the latter part be true, then written constitutions are absurd attempts, on the part of the people, to limit a power, in its own nature illimitable.

Certainly all those who have framed written constitutions contemplate them as forming the fundamental and paramount law of the nation, and consequently the theory of every such government must be, that an act of the legislature, repugnant to the constitution, is void.

This theory is essentially attached to a written constitution, and is consequently to be considered, by this court, as one of the fundamental principles of our society. It is not therefore to be lost sight of in the further consideration of this subject.

If an act of the legislature, repugnant to the constitution, is void, does it, notwithstanding its invalidity, bind the courts, and oblige them to give it effect? Or, in other words, though it be not law, does it constitute a rule as operative as if it was a law? This would be to overthrow in fact what was established in theory; and would seem, at first view, an absurdity too gross to be insisted on. It shall, however, receive a more attentive consideration.

It is emphatically the province and duty of the judicial department to say what the law is. Those who apply the rule to particular cases, must of necessity expound and interpret that rule. If two laws conflict with each other, the courts must decide on the operation of each.

So if a law be in opposition to the constitution; if both the law and the constitution apply to a particular case, so that the court must either decide that case conformably to the law, disregarding the constitution; or conformably to the constitution, disregarding the law; the court must determine which of these conflicting rules governs the case. This is of the very essence of judicial duty.

If then the courts are to regard the constitution; and the constitution is superior to any ordinary act of the legislature; the constitution, and not such ordinary act, must govern the case to which they both apply.

Those then who controvert the principle that the constitution is to be considered, in court, as a paramount law, are reduced to the necessity of maintaining that courts must close their eyes on the constitution, and see only the law.

This doctrine would subvert the very foundation of all written constitutions. It would declare that an act, which, according to the principles and theory of our government, is entirely void; is yet, in practice, completely obligatory. It would declare, that if the legislature shall do what is expressly forbidden, such act, notwithstanding the express prohibition, is in reality effectual. It would be giving to the legislature a practical and real omnipotence, with the same breath which professes to restrict their powers within narrow limits. It is prescribing limits, and declaring that those limits may be passed at pleasure.

That it thus reduces to nothing what we have deemed the greatest improvement on political institutions—a written constitution—would of itself be sufficient, in America, where written constitutions have been viewed with so much reverence, for rejecting the construction. But the peculiar expressions of the constitution of the United States furnish additional arguments in favour of its rejection.

The judicial power of the United States is extended to all cases arising under the constitution.

Could it be the intention of those who gave this power, to say that, in using it, the constitution should not be looked into? That a case arising under the constitution should be decided without examining the instrument under which it arises?

This is too extravagant to be maintained.

In some cases then, the constitution must be looked into by the judges. And if they can open it at all, what part of it are they forbidden to read, or to obey?

There are many other parts of the constitution which serve to illustrate this subject.

It is declared that "no tax or duty shall be laid on articles exported from any state." Suppose a duty on the export of cotton, of tobacco, or of flour; and a suit instituted to recover it. Ought judgment to be rendered in such a case? Ought . . . the judges to close their eyes on the constitution, and only see the law?

The constitution declares that "no bill of attainder or *ex post facto* law shall be passed."

If, however, such a bill should be passed and a person should be prosecuted under it; must the court condemn to death those victims whom the constitution endeavours to preserve?

"No person," says the constitution, "shall be convicted of treason unless on the testimony of two witnesses to the same overt act, or on confession in open court."

Here the language of the constitution is addressed especially to the courts. It prescribes, directly for them, a rule of evidence not to be departed from. If the legislature should change that rule, and declare one witness, or a confession out of court, sufficient for conviction, must the constitutional principle yield to the legislative act?

From these, and many other selections which might be made, it is apparent, that the Framers of the constitution contemplated that instrument, as a rule for the government of *courts,* as well as of the legislature.

Why otherwise does it direct the judges to take an oath to support it? This oath certainly applies, in an especial manner, to

their conduct in their official character. How immoral to impose it on them, if they were to be used as the instruments, and the knowing instruments, for violating what they swear to support!

The oath of office, too, imposed by the legislature, is completely demonstrative of the legislative opinion on this subject. It is in these words, "I do solemnly swear that I will administer justice without respect to persons, and do equal right to the poor and to the rich; and that I will faithfully and impartially discharge all the duties incumbent on me as according to the best of my abilities and understanding, agreeably to *the constitution,* and laws of the United States."

Why does a judge swear to discharge his duties agreeably to the constitution of the United States, if that constitution forms no rule for his government? if it is closed upon him, and cannot be inspected by him?

If such be the real state of things, this is worse than solemn mockery. To prescribe, or to take this oath, becomes equally a crime.

It is also not entirely unworthy of observation, that in declaring what shall be the *supreme law* of the land, the *constitution* itself is first mentioned; and not the laws of the United States generally, but those only which shall be made in *pursuance* of the constitution, have that rank.

Thus, the particular phraseology of the constitution of the United States confirms and strengthens the principle, supposed to be essential to all written constitutions, that a law repugnant to the constitution is void; and that *courts,* as well as other departments, are bound by that instrument.

The rule must be discharged.

Scholars differ about Marshall's opinion in *Marbury,* but supporters and critics alike acknowledge Marshall's shrewdness. By ruling against Marbury—who never did receive his judicial appointment *(see Box 3-2)*—Marshall avoided a potentially devastating clash with Jefferson. But, by exerting the power of judicial review, Marshall sent the president a clear signal that the Court would be a major player in the American government.

The decision helped to establish Marshall's reputation as perhaps the greatest justice in Supreme Court history. *Marbury* was just the first in a long line of seminal Marshall decisions. Most important here, *Marbury* asserted the Court's authority to review and strike down government actions that were incompatible with the Constitution. In Marshall's view, such authority, although not explicit in the Constitution, was clearly intended by the framers of that document.

Note that in *Marbury* the Court addressed only the power to review acts of the federal government.

BOX 3-2

Aftermath . . . *Marbury v. Madison*

From meager beginnings, William Marbury gained political and economic influence in his home state of Maryland and became a strong supporter of John Adams and the Federalist Party. Unlike others of his day who rose in wealth through agriculture or trade, Marbury's path to prominence was banking and finance. At age thirty-eight he saw his appointment to be a justice of the peace as a public validation of his rising economic status and social prestige. Marbury never received his judicial position; instead, he returned to his financial activities, ultimately becoming the president of a bank in Georgetown. He died in 1835, the same year Chief Justice John Marshall died.

Other participants in the famous decision played major roles in the early history of our nation. Thomas Jefferson, who refused to honor Marbury's appointment, served two terms as chief executive, leaving office in 1809 as one of the nation's most revered presidents. James Madison, the secretary of state who carried out Jefferson's order depriving Marbury of his judgeship, became the nation's fourth president, serving from 1809 to 1817. Following the *Marbury* decision, Chief Justice Marshall led the Court for an additional thirty-two years. His tenure was marked with fundamental rulings expanding the power of the judiciary and enhancing the position of the federal government relative to the states. He is rightfully regarded as history's most influential chief justice.

Although *Marbury* established the power of judicial review, it is ironic that the Marshall Court never again used its authority to strike down a piece of congressional legislation. In fact, it was not until *Scott v. Sandford* (1857), more than two decades after Marshall's death, that the Court once again invalidated a congressional statute.

Sources: John A. Garraty, "The Case of the Missing Commissions," in *Quarrels That Have Shaped the Constitution,* rev. ed., ed. John A. Garraty (New York: Harper & Row, 1987); David F. Forte, "Marbury's Travail: Federalist Politics and William Marbury's Appointment as Justice of the Peace," *Catholic University Law Review* 45 (1996): 349–402.

Could the Court also exert judicial review over the states? Section 25 of the 1789 Judiciary Act suggested that it could. Recall from our discussion of the act that Congress authorized the Court to review appeals from the highest state courts, if those tribunals upheld state laws against challenges of unconstitutionality or denied claims based on the U.S. Constitution, federal laws, or treaties. But the mere existence of this statute did not necessarily mean that either state courts or the Supreme Court would follow it. After all, in *Marbury* the justices told Congress that it could not interpret Article III to expand the original jurisdiction of the Supreme Court—if that is, in fact, what Congress did. Would they say the same thing about Section 25, that Congress improperly read Article III to authorize the Court to review certain kinds of state court decisions?

Also to be considered was the potentially hostile reaction from the states, which in the 1780s and 1790s zealously guarded their power from federal encroachment. Even if the Court were to take advantage of its ability to review state court decisions, it was more than likely that the states would disregard its rulings. Still, threats from the states did not deter the Court. In a case coming from Virginia, **Martin v. Hunter's Lessee** (1816), the justices upheld Section 25, thereby sustaining the Court's power to review state court decisions that met the section's requirements (those upholding a state law against challenges of unconstitutionality or denying a claim based on the U.S. Constitution, federal laws, or treaties).

In so doing, they refuted claims that allowing the Court to review state court decisions would destroy the independence of state court judges. As Justice Joseph Story wrote in *Martin:*

> [S]uch a right [cannot be] deemed to impair the independence of state judges. It is assuming the very ground in controversy to assert that they possess an absolute independence of the United States. In respect to the powers granted to the United States, they are not independent; they are expressly bound to obedience by the letter of the

constitution; and if they should unintentionally transcend their authority, or misconstrue the constitution, there is no more reason for giving their judgments an absolute and irresistible force, than for giving it to the acts of the other coordinate departments of state sovereignty.

Marbury, *Martin*, and *Cohens* established the power of federal courts to exert judicial review over national and state actions. What they did not do, and perhaps could not do, was put an end to the controversies surrounding judicial review.

Some of the complaints about the Court's decisions were heard while Marshall was still on the bench. Jefferson griped about *Marbury* until his last days. In an 1823 letter, he wrote:

> This practice of Judge Marshall, of travelling out of his case to prescribe what the law would be in a moot case not before the court, is very irregular and very censurable. . . . [In *Marbury v. Madison*] the Court determined at once, that being an original process, they had no cognizance of it; and therefore the question before them was ended. But the Chief Justice went on to lay down what the law would be, had they jurisdiction of the case, to wit: that they should command the delivery. The object was clearly to instruct any other court having the jurisdiction, what they should do if Marbury should apply to them. Besides the impropriety of this gratuitous interference, could anything exceed the perversion of law? . . . *Yet this case of Marbury and Madison is continually cited by bench and bar, as if it were settled law, without any animadversion on its being merely an obiter dissertation of the Chief Justice* [emphasis added].[13]

Strong words from one of our nation's most revered presidents!

But Jefferson was not the last to complain about Marshall's opinion. Some critics have picked apart specific aspects of the ruling, as Jefferson did. He argued that once Marshall ruled that the Court did not have jurisdiction to hear the case, he should have dismissed it. Another criticism of Marshall's opinion is that Section 13 of the 1789 Judiciary Act—which *Marbury* held unconstitutional—did not actually expand the Supreme Court's original jurisdiction. If this is so, then Marshall "had nothing to declare unconstitutional"![14]

Other debates center on the Court's holding, in particular, on what legal scholar Alexander Bickel called the "countermajoritarian difficulty": Given our nation's fundamental commitment to a representative form of government, why should we allow a group of unelected officials to override the wishes of the people, as expressed by their elected officials?[15]

Supporters argue that the power of judicial review is necessary to keep the federal government and the states within proper constitutional bounds and to protect minority rights from infringement by political majorities. They claim, for example, that the exercise of judicial review was instrumental in ending racial segregation, protecting the rights of the criminally accused, and establishing a right to privacy.

Despite these debates, there is little doubt that judicial review has become an accepted power, and one that is exercised not infrequently. Between 1980 and 2019 the Court issued 75 decisions striking down all or parts of federal statutes and 221 invalidating state or local laws.[16]

CONSTRAINTS ON JUDICIAL POWER

Given all the attention paid to judicial review, it is easy to forget that the power of courts to exercise it and their judicial authority, more generally, has substantial limits. Article III—or the Court's interpretation of it—places three major constraints on the ability of federal tribunals to hear and decide cases: (1) courts must have authority to hear a case (jurisdiction), (2) the case must be appropriate for judicial resolution (justiciability), and (3) the

[13]Quoted in Andrew A. Lipscomb, *The Writings of Thomas Jefferson*, vol. 15 (Washington, DC: Thomas Jefferson Memorial Association, 1905), 447–448.

[14]Jeffrey A. Segal and Harold J. Spaeth, *The Supreme Court and the Attitudinal Model Revisited* (Cambridge: Cambridge University Press, 2002), 24. A counter to this argument is that people of the day must have considered Section 13 as expanding the Court's original jurisdiction, or else why did Marbury bring his suit directly to the Supreme Court?

[15]Alexander Bickel, *The Least Dangerous Branch of Government* (New York: Bobbs-Merrill, 1962).

[16]Calculated from data in the U.S. Supreme Court Database, http://supremecourtdatabase.org.

appropriate party must bring the case (standing to sue). In what follows, we review doctrine surrounding these constraints. As you read this discussion, consider not only the Court's interpretation of its own limits, but also the justifications it offers. Note, in particular, how fluid these can be: sometimes the Supreme Court has favored loose constructions of the rules, whereas during others it has interpreted them more strictly. What factors might explain these different tendencies? Or, to think about it another way, to what extent do these constraints limit the Court's authority?

Jurisdiction

According to Chief Justice Salmon P. Chase, "Without jurisdiction the court cannot proceed at all in any cause. Jurisdiction is power to declare the law, and when it ceases to exist, the only function remaining to the court is that of announcing the fact and dismissing the cause."[17] In other words, a court cannot hear a case unless it has the authority—the jurisdiction—to do so.

Article III, Section 2, defines the jurisdiction of U.S. federal courts. Lower courts have the authority to hear disputes involving particular parties and subject matter. The U.S. Supreme Court's jurisdiction is divided into original and appellate: the former are classes of cases that originate in the Court; the latter are those it hears after a lower court.

To what extent does jurisdiction actually constrain the federal courts? *Marbury v. Madison* provides some answers, although contradictory, to this question. Chief Justice Marshall informed Congress that it could not alter the original jurisdiction of the Court. Having reached this conclusion, perhaps Marshall should have merely dismissed the case on the ground that the Court lacked authority to hear it, but that is not what he did.

Marbury remains an authoritative ruling on original jurisdiction. The issue of appellate jurisdiction may be a bit more complex. Article III explicitly states that for those cases over which the Court does not have original jurisdiction, it "shall have appellate Jurisdiction . . . with such Exceptions, and under such Regulations as the Congress shall make." In other words, the exceptions clause seems to give Congress authority to alter the Court's appellate jurisdiction—including to subtract from it.

Would the justices agree? In *Ex parte McCardle* the Court addressed this question, examining whether

Congress can use its power under the exceptions clause to *remove* the Court's appellate jurisdiction over a particular category of cases.

Ex parte McCardle

74 U.S. (7 Wall.) 506 (1869)
http://caselaw.findlaw.com/us-supreme-court/74/506.html
Vote: 8 (Chase, Clifford, Davis, Field, Grier, Miller, Nelson, Swayne)
0

OPINION OF THE COURT: *Chase*

After the Civil War, the Radical Republican Congress imposed a series of restrictions on the South.[18] Known as the Reconstruction laws, they in effect placed the region under military rule. Journalist William McCardle opposed these measures and wrote editorials urging resistance to them. As a result, he was arrested for publishing allegedly "incendiary and libelous articles" and held for a trial before a military tribunal established under Reconstruction.

Because he was a civilian, not a member of any militia, McCardle claimed that he was being illegally held. He petitioned for a writ of habeas corpus under an 1867 act stipulating that federal courts had the power to grant writs of habeas corpus to all prisoners—state and federal—who were deprived of his or her liberty in violation of the Constitution, laws, or treaties of the United States. When this effort failed, McCardle appealed to the U.S. Supreme Court. Under the Judiciary Act of 1789, the Supreme Court already had appellate jurisdiction over federal habeas cases; the 1867 law extended appellate to state and federal prisoners. Even though McCardle was held by federal authorities, he brought his case to the Court under the 1867 law.

In early March 1868 *McCardle* "was very thoroughly and ably [presented] upon the merits" to the U.S. Supreme Court. It was clear to most observers that "no Justice was still making up his mind": the Court's sympathies, as was widely known, lay with McCardle.[19] But before the justices issued their decision, Congress, on March 27, 1868, enacted a law repealing the provision of the 1867 Habeas Corpus Act that gave the Supreme Court authority to hear appeals arising from it; that is, Congress removed the Court's jurisdiction to hear appeals in cases like McCardle's. This move was meant either to punish the Court or to send it a strong message. Two years before

---

[17]*Ex parte McCardle* (1869).

[18]See Lee Epstein and Thomas G. Walker, "The Role of the Supreme Court in American Society: Playing the Reconstruction Game," in *Contemplating Courts*, ed. Lee Epstein (Washington, DC: CQ Press, 1995), 315–346.

[19]Charles Fairman, *History of the Supreme Court of the United States*, vol. 7, *Reconstruction and Reunion* (New York: Macmillan, 1971), 456.

McCardle, in 1866, the Court had invalidated President Abraham Lincoln's use of military tribunals in certain areas, and Congress did not want to see the Court take similar action in this dispute.[20] The legislature felt so strongly on this issue that after President Andrew Johnson vetoed the 1868 repealer act, Congress overrode the veto.

The Court responded by redocketing the case for oral arguments in March 1869. During the arguments and in its briefs, the government made its position clear: when the jurisdiction of a court to determine a case or a class of cases depends upon a statute and that statute is repealed, the jurisdiction ceases absolutely. In short, the government contended that the Court no longer had authority to hear the case and should dismiss it.

THE CHIEF JUSTICE DELIVERED THE OPINION OF THE COURT.

The first question necessarily is that of jurisdiction, for if the act of March, 1868, takes away the jurisdiction defined by the act of February, 1867, it is useless, if not improper, to enter into any discussion of other questions.

It is quite true, as was argued by the counsel for the petitioner, that the appellate jurisdiction of this court is not derived from acts of Congress. It is, strictly speaking, conferred by the Constitution. But it is conferred "with such exceptions and under such regulations as Congress shall make."

It is unnecessary to consider whether, if Congress had made no exceptions and no regulations, this court might not have exercised general appellate jurisdiction under rules prescribed by itself. From among the earliest Acts of the first Congress, at its first session, was the Act of September 24th, 1789, to establish the judicial courts of the United States. That Act provided for the organization of this court, and prescribed regulations for the exercise of its jurisdiction. . . .

The principle that the affirmation of appellate jurisdiction implies the negation of all such jurisdiction not affirmed having been thus established, it was an almost necessary consequence that acts of Congress, providing for the exercise of jurisdiction, should come to be spoken of as acts granting jurisdiction, and not as acts making exceptions to the constitutional grant of it.

The exception to appellate jurisdiction in the case before us . . . is not an inference from the affirmation of other appellate jurisdiction. It is made in terms. The provision of the Act of 1867, affirming the appellate jurisdiction of this court in cases of habeas corpus, is expressly repealed. It is hardly possible to imagine a plainer instance of positive exception.

We are not at liberty to inquire into the motives of the Legislature. We can only examine into its power under the

Constitution; and the power to make exceptions to the appellate jurisdiction of this court is given by express words.

What, then, is the effect of the repealing Act upon the case before us? We cannot doubt as to this. Without jurisdiction the court cannot proceed at all in any cause. Jurisdiction is power to declare the law, and when it ceases to exist, the only function remaining to the court is that of announcing the fact and dismissing the cause. And this is not less clear upon authority than upon principle. . . .

It is quite clear, therefore, that this . . . court cannot proceed to pronounce judgment in this case, for it has no longer jurisdiction of the appeal; and judicial duty is not less fitly performed by declining ungranted jurisdiction than in exercising firmly that which the Constitution and the laws confer. . . .

Counsel seem to have supposed, if effect be given to the repealing act in question, that the whole appellate power of the court, in cases of habeas corpus, is denied. But this is an error. The act of 1868 does not except from that jurisdiction any cases but appeals from Circuit Courts under the act of 1867. It does not affect the jurisdiction which was previously exercised.

The appeal of the petitioner in this case must be dismissed for want of jurisdiction.

DISMISSED FOR WANT OF JURISDICTION

As we can see, the Court acceded and declined to hear the case. *McCardle* suggests that Congress has the authority to remove the Court's appellate jurisdiction as it deems necessary. As Justice Felix Frankfurter put it in 1949, "Congress need not give this Court any appellate power; it may withdraw appellate jurisdiction once conferred and it may do so even while a case is *sub judice* [before a judge]."[21] Former justice Owen J. Roberts, who apparently agreed with Frankfurter's assertion, proposed an amendment to the Constitution that would have deprived Congress of the ability to remove the Court's appellate jurisdiction.[22] To Frankfurter, Roberts, and others in their camp, the *McCardle* precedent, not to mention the text of the exceptions clause, makes it quite clear that Congress can remove the Court's appellate jurisdiction. In 1962, however, Justice William O. Douglas remarked, "There is a serious question whether the *McCardle* case could command a majority view today."[23] And even Chief Justice Chase himself suggested limits on congressional

---

[20]That action came in **Ex parte Milligan** (1866), discussed in chapter 5.

[21]*National Mutual Insurance Co. v. Tidewater Transfer Co.* (1949).

[22]See Owen J. Roberts, "Now Is the Time: Fortifying the Supreme Court's Independence," *American Bar Association Journal* 35 (1949): 1. The Senate approved the amendment in 1953, but the House tabled it. Cited in Gerald Gunther, *Constitutional Law*, 12th ed. (Westbury, NY: Foundation Press, 1991), 45.

power in this area. After *McCardle* was decided, he noted that use of the exceptions clause was "unusual and hardly to be justified except upon some imperious public exigency."[24]

To this day, then, *McCardle*'s status remains an open question.[25] To Frankfurter and others in his camp, the *McCardle* precedent, not to mention the text of the exceptions clause, makes it quite clear that Congress can remove the Court's appellate jurisdiction. To Douglas and other commentators, *McCardle* was something of an oddity that does not square with American traditions: before *McCardle*, Congress had never stripped the Court's jurisdiction, and since *McCardle*, Congress has only rarely taken this step, and did not take it in the wake of some of the Court's most controversial decisions, such as *Roe v. Wade* and *Brown v. Board of Education*. Then there is the related argument that, taken to its extreme, jurisdiction stripping could render the Court virtually powerless. Would the framers have created an institution only to allow Congress to destroy it? Many scholars say no.

Justiciability

According to Article III, the federal courts' judicial power is restricted to "cases" and "controversies." Taken together, these words mean that litigation must be justiciable—appropriate or suitable for a federal tribunal to hear or to solve. As Chief Justice Earl Warren asserted, cases and controversies

> are two complementary but somewhat different limitations. In part those words limit the business of federal courts to questions presented in an adversary context and in a form historically viewed as capable of resolution through the judicial process. And in part those words define the role assigned to the judiciary in a tripartite allocation of power to assure that the federal courts will not intrude into areas committed to the other branches of government. Justiciability

is the term of art employed to give expression to this dual limitation placed upon federal courts by the case-and-controversy doctrine.[26]

Although Warren also suggested that "justiciability is itself a concept of uncertain meaning and scope," he elucidated several characteristics of litigation that would render it nonjusticiable. In this section, we treat five: advisory opinions, collusive suits, mootness, ripeness, and political questions. In the following section we deal with another concept related to justiciability—standing to sue.

Advisory Opinions

A few states and some foreign countries require judges of the highest court to advise the executive or legislature, when so requested, as to their views on the constitutionality of a proposed policy. Since the time of Chief Justice John Jay, however, federal judges in the United States have refused to issue advisory opinions. They do not render advice in hypothetical suits because if litigation is abstract, it possesses no real controversy. The language of the Constitution does not prohibit advisory opinions as opinions, but the framers rejected a proposal that would have permitted the other branches of government to request judicial rulings "upon important questions of law, and upon solemn occasions." Madison was critical of this proposal on the ground that the judiciary should have jurisdiction only over "cases of a Judiciary Nature."[27]

The Supreme Court agreed. In July 1793, Secretary of State Thomas Jefferson asked the justices if they would be willing to address questions concerning the appropriate role America should play in the ongoing British–French war. Jefferson wrote that President George Washington "would be much relieved if he found himself free to refer questions [involving the war] to the opinions of the judges of the Supreme Court in the United States, whose knowledge . . . would secure us against errors dangerous to the peace of the United States."[28] Less than a month later the justices denied Jefferson's request, with a reply written directly to the president:

---

[23]*Glidden Co. v. Zdanok* (1962).

[24]*Ex parte Yerger* (1869).

[25]For a review of various answers, see Tara Leigh Grove, "The Structural Safeguards of Federal Jurisdiction," *Harvard Law Review* 124 (2011): 869–940. See also **Patchak v. Zinke** (2018), in which the justices agreed that Congress had stripped the Court's jurisdiction to hear disputes involving a particular piece of land but disagreed over whether Congress had acted constitutionally.

[26]**Flast v. Cohen** (1968).

[27]Quoted by Farber and Sherry, *A History of the American Constitution*, 65.

[28]The full text of Jefferson's letter is in Henry M. Hart Jr. and Albert M. Sacks, *The Legal Process*, ed. William N. Eskridge Jr. and Philip P. Frickey (Westbury, NY: Foundation Press, 1994), 630–632.

We have considered [the] letter written by your direction to us by the Secretary of State [regarding] the lines of separation drawn by the Constitution between the three departments of government. These being in certain respects checks upon each other, and our being judges of a court in the last resort, are considerations which afford strong arguments against the propriety of our extra-judicially deciding the questions alluded to, especially as the power given by the Constitution to the President, of calling on the heads of departments for opinions, seems to have been *purposely* as well as expressly united to the *executive* departments [italics provided].[29]

With these words, the justices sounded the death knell for advisory opinions: such opinions would violate the separation of powers principle embedded in the Constitution. The subject has resurfaced only a few times in U.S. history; in the 1930s, for example, President Franklin Roosevelt considered a proposal that would require the Court to issue advisory opinions on the constitutionality of federal laws. But Roosevelt quickly gave up on the idea, at least in part because of its dubious constitutionality.

Nevertheless, scholars still debate the Court's 1793 letter to Washington. Some agree with the justices' logic. Others assert that more institutional concerns were at work; perhaps the Court—out of concern for its institutional legitimacy—did not want to become embroiled in "political" disputes at this early phase in its development. Whatever the reason, all subsequent Courts have followed that 1793 precedent: requests for advisory opinions to the *U.S. Supreme Court* present nonjusticiable disputes.[30]

Collusive Suits

Justiciability also precludes collusive lawsuits. The Court will not decide cases in which the litigants (1) want the same outcome, (2) show no real adversariness between them, or (3) are merely testing the law. Why the Court deems collusive suits nonjusticiable is well illustrated in *Muskrat v. United States* (1911). At issue

here were several federal laws involving land distribution and appropriations to Native Americans. To determine whether these laws were constitutional, Congress enacted a statute authorizing David Muskrat and other Native Americans to challenge the land distribution law in court. This legislation also ordered the courts to give priority to Muskrat's suit and allowed the attorney general to defend his claim. Furthermore, Congress agreed to pay Muskrat's legal fees if his suit was successful. When the dispute reached the U.S. Supreme Court, the justices dismissed it. Justice William Day wrote:

This attempt to obtain a judicial declaration of the validity of the act of Congress is not presented in a "case" or "controversy," to which, under the Constitution of the United States, the judicial power alone extends. It is true the United States is made a defendant to this action, but it has no interest adverse to the claimants. The object is not to assert a property right as against the Government, or to demand compensation for alleged wrongs because of action upon its part. The whole purpose of the law is to determine the constitutional validity of this class of legislation, in a suit not arising between parties concerning a property right necessarily involved in the decision in question, but in a proceeding against the Government in its sovereign capacity, and concerning which the only judgment required is to settle the doubtful character of the legislation in question.

The Court, however, has not always followed the *Muskrat* precedent. Indeed, several collusive suits resulted in landmark decisions, including *Pollock v. Farmers' Loan and Trust Co.* (1895), in which the Court declared the federal income tax unconstitutional. The litigants in this dispute, a bank and a stockholder in the bank, both wanted the same outcome—the demise of the tax. *Carter v. Carter Coal Co.* (1936) is also exemplary. Here the Court agreed to resolve a dispute over a major piece of New Deal legislation even though the litigants, a company president and the company, which included the president's father, both wanted the same outcome—the legislation to be declared unconstitutional.

Why did the justices resolve these disputes? One answer is that the Court might overlook some element of collusion if the suit presents a real controversy or the potential for one. But some analysts see it differently. The temptation to set "good" public policy (or strike

---

[29]Quoted in ibid., 637.

[30]We emphasize the Supreme Court because some state courts do, in fact, issue advisory opinions.

down "bad" public policy), they say, is sometimes too strong for the justices to follow their own rules. Then again, some commentators argue that they should resist. In 1913 the country ratified the Sixteenth Amendment to overturn *Pollock*, and the Court itself limited *Carter Coal* in the 1941 case of *United States v. Darby*.

Mootness

In general, the Court will not decide cases in which the controversy is no longer live by the time it reaches the Court's doorstep. *DeFunis v. Odegaard* (1974) provides an example. Rejected for admission to the University of Washington Law School, Marco DeFunis Jr. sued the school, alleging that it had engaged in reverse discrimination because it had denied him a place but accepted statistically less qualified minority students. In 1971 a trial court found merit in his claim and ordered that the university admit him. While DeFunis was in his second year of law school, the state's high court reversed the trial judge's ruling. DeFunis then appealed to the U.S. Supreme Court. By that time, he had registered for his final quarter in school. In a per curiam opinion, the Court refused to rule on the merits of DeFunis's claim, asserting that it was moot:

> Because [DeFunis] will complete his law school studies at the end of the term for which he has now registered regardless of any decision this Court might reach on the merits of this litigation, we conclude that the Court cannot, consistently with the limitations of Art. III of the Constitution, consider the substantive constitutional issues tendered by the parties.

In his dissent, Justice William J. Brennan Jr. noted that DeFunis could conceivably not complete his studies that quarter, and so the issue was not necessarily moot. This suggests that the rules governing mootness are a bit fuzzier than the *DeFunis* majority opinion characterized them.

To see this possibility, consider another example: *Roe v. Wade* (1973), in which the Court legalized abortions performed during the first two trimesters of pregnancy. Norma McCorvey, also known as Roe, was pregnant when she filed suit in 1970, and by the time the Court handed down the decision in 1973, she had long since given birth and put her baby up for adoption. But the justices did not declare this case moot. Why not? What made *Roe* different from *DeFunis*?

The justices provided two legal justifications. First, DeFunis brought the litigation in his own behalf, but *Roe* was a class action—a lawsuit brought by one or more persons who represent themselves and all others similarly situated. Second, DeFunis had been admitted to law school, and he would "never again be required to run the gauntlet." Roe could become pregnant again; that is, pregnancy is a situation "capable of repetition, yet evading review." Are these reasonable points? Or is it possible, as some suspect, that the Court developed them to avoid particular legal issues? In either case, it is clear that the exceptions the Court has carved out can make mootness a rather slippery concept, open to interpretation by different justices and Courts.

Ripeness

Ripeness is the flip side of mootness. Whereas moot cases are brought too late, "unripe" cases are those that are brought too early. That is, under existing Court interpretation, a case is nonjusticiable if the controversy is premature—has insufficiently jelled—for review. *International Longshoreman's Union v. Boyd* (1954) provides an example. This case involved a 1952 federal law mandating that all aliens seeking admission into the United States from Alaska be "examined" as if they were entering from a foreign country. Believing that the law might affect seasonal American laborers working in Alaska temporarily, a union challenged the law. Writing for the Court, Justice Frankfurter dismissed the suit. In his view,

> Appellants in effect asked [the Court] to rule that a statute the sanctions of which had not been set in motion against individuals on whose behalf relief was sought, because an occasion for doing so had not arisen, would not be applied to them if in the future such a contingency should arise. That is not a lawsuit to enforce a right; it is an endeavor to obtain a court's assurance that a statute does not govern hypothetical situations that may or may not make the challenged statute applicable. Determination of the . . . constitutionality of the legislation in advance of its immediate adverse effect in the context of a concrete case involves too remote and abstract an inquiry for the proper exercise of the judicial function.

In addition, the ripeness requirement mandates that a party exhaust all available administrative and lower court remedies before seeking the Supreme Court's review. Until these opportunities have been fully explored, the case is not ready for the justices to hear.

Political Questions

Another type of nonjusticiable suit involves a political question. Chief Justice Marshall stated in *Marbury v. Madison*,

> The province of the court is, solely, to decide on the rights of individuals, not to inquire how the executive, or executive officers, perform duties in which they have a discretion. Questions in their nature political, or which are, by the constitution and laws, submitted to the executive, can never be made in this court.

In other words, the Court recognizes that there is a class of questions the Court will not address because they are better solved by other branches of government, even though they may be constitutional in nature. But what exactly constitutes a political question? When challenges to legislative malapportionment were first brought to the Court in the 1940s, the allegations were based on Article IV of the Constitution, which provides that the "United States shall guarantee to every State in this Union a Republican Form of Government." The justices were reluctant to address the issue, concluding that enforcement of this provision was better left to the political process; courts were not competent to evaluate whether a state's particular set of congressional district lines fulfilled the requirements of a representative system of government. In *Baker v. Carr* (1962), however, the legal challenge to malapportionment was based on the equal protection clause of the Fourteenth Amendment. This was an area, the Court explained, in which there were established judicial standards, and the Court could, therefore, evaluate whether legislative districts of different sizes were consistent with the constitutional requirements of equality. So initially, legislative districting was not justiciable, and later it was. What was the difference? In *Baker*, Justice Brennan set out the elements of a political question:

> Prominent on the surface of any case held to involve a political question is found a textually demonstrable constitutional commitment of the issue to a coordinate political department; or a lack of judicially discoverable and manageable standards for resolving it; or the impossibility of deciding without an initial policy determination of a kind clearly for nonjudicial discretion; or the impossibility of a court's undertaking independent resolution without expressing lack of the respect due coordinate branches of government; or an unusual need for unquestioning adherence to a political decision already made; or the potentiality of embarrassment from multifarious pronouncements by various departments on one question.

Note that Brennan's statement contains two major prongs. First, the Court will look to the Constitution to see if there is a "textually demonstrable commitment" to another branch of government. Second, the justices consider whether particular questions should be left to another branch of government as a matter of prudence. This is where factors such as the lack of judicially discoverable standards, embarrassment, and so forth come into play.

Nixon v. United States (1993) provides an example of both. In that case, a federal judge, who had been impeached by the House of Representatives, challenged the procedures the Senate used to convict him. But the Court held that impeachment procedures are not subject to judicial review because, first, Article I of the Constitution assigns the task of impeachment to Congress, and, second, judicial intrusion into impeachment proceedings could create confusion. Imagine the kinds of problems that would emerge if U.S. presidents could challenge their impeachment in the federal courts. Would they still be president as their case made its way through the courts or would their successor be the president? This is not a scenario for which the Court wanted to take responsibility.

Although *Baker* established a relatively clear doctrinal base for determining political questions, the doctrine itself remains controversial. Some commentators say that the Court has a responsibility to address constitutional questions; that failure to do so is antithetic to *Marbury v. Madison*–type review. Others, however, suggest that the federal courts should continue to avoid cases raising political questions, with *Nixon* a good example.[31]

---

[31]This debate played out most recently in ***Rucho v. Common Cause*** (2019), involving challenges to "highly partisan" districting plans.

Standing to Sue

Another constraint on federal judicial power is the requirement that the party bringing a lawsuit have standing to sue: if the party bringing the litigation is not the appropriate party, the courts will not resolve the dispute. Put in somewhat different terms, "not every person with the money to bring a lawsuit is entitled to litigate the legality or constitutionality of government action in the federal courts."[32]

According to the Court's interpretation of Article III, standing requires (1) that the party must have suffered a concrete injury or be in imminent danger of suffering such a loss, (2) that the injury must be "fairly traceable" to the challenged action of the defendant (usually the government in constitutional cases), and (3) that the party must show that a favorable court decision is likely to provide redress.[33] In general these three elements are designed, as Justice Brennan noted in *Baker*, "to assure . . . concrete adverseness which sharpens the presentation of issues upon which the Court so largely depends for illumination of difficult constitutional questions."

In many disputes, the litigants have little difficulty meeting the standing requirements mandated by Article III. A citizen who has been denied the right to vote on the basis of race, a criminal defendant sentenced to death, and a church member jailed for religious proselytizing would have sufficient standing to challenge the federal or state laws that may have deprived them of their rights. But what about parties who do not have an injury that affects them in a "personal and individual way." Rather they have a "generally available grievance about government," with the only real harm being to their (and every other citizen's) interest in applying appropriately the laws and constitution.[34] As such, should they win their case, they benefit no more directly or tangibly than all other citizens. Do these parties have standing to sue?

In general, the answer is no. In addition to the three constitutionally derived requirements, the Court has articulated several prudential considerations to govern standing. These do not strictly follow from Article III but rather from the Court's own view of the prudent administration of justice. Among the most prominent of these considerations are those that limit generalized grievance suits—especially taxpayer suits, which are brought by parties whose only injury is that they do not want the government to spend tax money in a particular way.

The Court first addressed this matter in *Frothingham v. Mellon* (1923), a lawsuit filed by Harriet Frothingham to challenge the constitutionality of the Sheppard-Towner Maternity Act. The statute provided federal aid to the states to fund programs designed to reduce infant mortality rates, to which Frothingham was opposed on the ground that the law was an unconstitutional intrusion into the rights of the states. She did not want her federal tax dollars to fund it, and her attorneys argued that as a taxpayer she had sufficient grounds to bring suit.

The Court refused to adopt this position, holding that Frothingham lacked standing to bring the litigation. Justice George Sutherland wrote for the majority:

> If one taxpayer may champion and litigate such a cause, then every other taxpayer may do the same, not only in respect of the statute here under review but also in respect of every other appropriation act and statute whose administration requires the outlay of public money, and whose validity may be questioned. The bare suggestion of such a result, with its attendant inconveniences, goes far to sustain the conclusion which we have reached, that a suit of this character cannot be maintained.

He also outlined an approach to standing:

> The party . . . must be able to show not only that the statute is invalid but that he has sustained or is immediately in danger of sustaining some direct injury as the result of its enforcement, and not merely that he suffers in some indefinite way in common with people generally.

For the next forty years, *Frothingham* served as a major bar to taxpayer suits. Unless litigants could demonstrate that a government program injured them or threatened to do so—beyond the mere expenditure of tax dollars—they could not bring suit. In *Flast v. Cohen* (1968), however, the Court carved out an exception to the rule. *Flast* involved seven taxpayers who sought to challenge federal expenditures made under the Elementary and Secondary Education Act of 1965. Under this law,

---

[32]C. Herman Pritchett, *The American Constitution* (New York: McGraw-Hill, 1959), 145.

[33]See *Lujan v. Defenders of Wildlife* (1992), which lays out these three elements.

[34]*Hollingsworth v. Perry* (2013).

states could apply to the federal government for grants to assist in the education of children from low-income families. They could obtain funds for the acquisition of textbooks, school library materials, and so forth. The taxpayers alleged that some of the funds disbursed under this act were used to finance "instruction in reading, arithmetic, and other subjects and for guidance in religious and sectarian schools." Such expenditures, they argued, violated the First Amendment's prohibition on religious establishment: "Congress shall make no law respecting an establishment of religion."

A three-judge district court dismissed their complaint. It reasoned that because the plaintiffs had suffered no real injury and because their only claim of standing rested "solely on their status as federal taxpayers," they failed to meet the criteria established in *Frothingham*.

Writing for the Court, Chief Justice Earl Warren disagreed. And, in so doing, he revamped the *Frothingham* standard. To determine whether a taxpayer has the requisite "personal stake" to bring suit, Warren wrote:

> [I]t is both appropriate and necessary to look to the substantive issues for another purpose, namely, to determine whether there is a logical nexus between the status asserted and the claim sought to be adjudicated. . . .
>
> The nexus demanded of federal taxpayers has two aspects to it. First, the taxpayer must establish a logical link between that status and the type of legislative enactment attacked. Thus, a taxpayer will be a proper party to allege the unconstitutionality only of exercises of congressional power under the taxing and spending clause of Art. I, §8, of the Constitution. It will not be sufficient to allege an incidental expenditure of tax funds in the administration of an essentially regulatory statute. . . . Secondly, the taxpayer must establish a nexus between that status and the precise nature of the constitutional infringement alleged. Under this requirement, the taxpayer must show that the challenged enactment exceeds specific constitutional limitations imposed upon the exercise of the congressional taxing and spending power and not simply that the enactment is generally beyond the powers delegated to Congress by Art. I, §8. When both nexuses are established, the litigant will have shown a taxpayer's stake

in the outcome of the controversy and will be a proper and appropriate party to invoke a federal court's jurisdiction.

Applying this standard to the dispute at hand, Warren found that the *Flast* taxpayers had standing:

> Their constitutional challenge is made to an exercise by Congress of its power under Art. I, §8, to spend for the general welfare, and the challenged program involves a substantial expenditure of federal tax funds. In addition, appellants have alleged that the challenged expenditures violate the Establishment and Free Exercise Clauses of the First Amendment.

Would Harriet Frothingham have met this new, more relaxed standard? To this question, Warren answered no:

> The allegations of the taxpayer in *Frothingham v. Mellon* were quite different from those made in this case, and the result in *Frothingham* is consistent with the test of taxpayer standing announced today. The taxpayer in *Frothingham* attacked a federal spending program and she, therefore, established the first nexus required. However, she lacked standing because her constitutional attack was not based on an allegation that Congress, in enacting the Maternity Act of 1921, had breached a specific limitation upon its taxing and spending power. . . . In essence, Mrs. Frothingham was attempting to assert the States' interest in their legislative prerogatives and not a federal taxpayer's interest in being free of taxing and spending in contravention of specific constitutional limitations imposed upon Congress' taxing and spending power.

In the end, *Flast* did not overrule *Frothingham*; in fact, as the above quotation indicates, the Court was careful to indicate that had the 1968 ruling been applied to *Frothingham*, the plaintiff still would have been unable to attain standing. Still, some thought that *Flast* substantially revised the 1923 precedent. It seemed that if taxpayers could indicate a logical link between their status and the legislation, and one between their status and a specific constitutional infringement, then they might have standing.

In the years since *Flast*, however, the Court has indicated that unless the suit is a virtual carbon copy of that case, it will maintain its ban against general grievance suits. Consider **Hein v. Freedom from Religion Foundation** (2007). During the George W. Bush administration, the Freedom from Religion Foundation brought this establishment clause suit to challenge activities associated with the White House Office of Faith-Based and Community Initiatives. It claimed it had standing because its individual members were federal taxpayers opposed to executive branch use of congressional appropriations for activities that allegedly promoted religious community groups over secular groups. The Supreme Court disagreed. Because these were executive branch programs, they did not meet the *Flast* standard. More broadly, Justice Samuel Alito noted in his judgment for the Court that "the payment of taxes is generally not enough to establish standing to challenge an action taken by the Federal Government." *Flast*, Alito wrote, was a "narrow exception."

Such a reading led some scholars to assert that current doctrine governing standing now resembles *Frothingham* rather than *Flast*. At the least, Justice Antonin Scalia suggested, in a concurring opinion (joined by Thomas) in *Hein*, that the Court's decision was inconsistent with *Flast*:

> Today's opinion is, in one significant respect, entirely consistent with our previous cases addressing taxpayer standing to raise Establishment Clause challenges to government expenditures. Unfortunately, the consistency lies in the creation of utterly meaningless distinctions which separate the case at hand from the precedents that have come out differently, but which cannot possibly be (in any sane world) the reason it comes out differently. If this Court is to decide cases by rule of law rather than show of hands, we must surrender to logic and choose sides: Either *Flast v. Cohen* (1968) should be applied to (at a minimum) all challenges to the governmental expenditure of general tax revenues in a manner alleged to violate a constitutional provision specifically limiting the taxing and spending power, or *Flast* should be repudiated. For me, the choice is easy. *Flast* is wholly irreconcilable with the Article III restrictions on federal-court jurisdiction that this Court has repeatedly confirmed are embodied in the doctrine of standing.

Whether this and other Roberts Court decisions render *Flast* on life support, we leave for you to determine. What does seem to be true is that standing, like the other "constraints" on judicial power—jurisdiction and justiciability—is open to interpretation.

CONSTRAINTS ON JUDICIAL POWER AND THE SEPARATION OF POWERS SYSTEM

The jurisdiction, justiciability, and standing requirements place considerable constraints on the exercise of judicial power. Yet it is important to note that these doctrines largely come from the Court's own interpretation of Article III and its view of the proper role of the judiciary—the constraints are largely self-imposed. In *Ashwander v. Tennessee Valley Authority* (1936) Justice Louis Brandeis took the opportunity in a concurring opinion to provide a summary of the principles of judicial self-restraint as they pertain to constitutional interpretation *(see Box 3-3)*. His goal was to delineate a set of rules that the Court should follow to avoid unnecessarily reaching decisions on the constitutionality of laws. In the course of outlining these "avoidance principles," he considered many of the constraints on judicial decision making we have reviewed in this section. More to the point, these "*Ashwander* Principles" serve as perhaps the best single statement of how the Court limits its own powers—and especially its exercise of judicial review.

Given the cases and materials you have just read, we wonder whether you think these are substantial constraints on the Court. Either way, it would be a mistake to conclude that the use of judicial power is limited only by self-imposed constraints. Rather, members of the executive and legislative branches also have expectations concerning the appropriate limits of judicial authority. If the justices are perceived as exceeding their role by failing to restrain the use of their own powers, a reaction from the political branches may occur. Congress could pass statutes or propose constitutional amendments to counteract decisions of the Court. The legislature might also alter the Court's appellate jurisdiction or fail to provide the Court with its requested levels of funding. The political branches might react by being slow to implement and enforce Court rulings. And the president and Senate could use their powers in the judicial selection process to fill Court vacancies with new justices whose views on judicial power are more consistent with their own.

BOX 3-3

Justice Brandeis, Concurring in *Ashwander v. Tennessee Valley Authority*

IN 1936 Justice Louis D. Brandeis delineated, in a concurring opinion in *Ashwander v. Tennessee Valley Authority,* a set of Court-formulated rules to avoid unnecessarily reaching decisions on the constitutionality of laws. A portion of his opinion setting forth those rules, minus case citations and footnotes, follows.

The Court developed, for its own governance in the cases confessedly within its jurisdiction, a series of rules under which it has avoided passing upon a large part of all the constitutional questions pressed upon it for decision. They are:

1. The Court will not pass upon the constitutionality of legislation in a friendly, nonadversary, proceeding, declining because to decide such questions "is legitimate only in the last resort, and as a necessity in the determination of real, earnest and vital controversy between individuals. It never was the thought that, by means of a friendly suit, a party beaten in the legislature could transfer to the courts an inquiry as to the constitutionality of the legislative act."

2. The Court will not "anticipate a question of constitutional law in advance of the necessity of deciding it." "It is not the habit of the Court to decide questions of a constitutional nature unless absolutely necessary to a decision of the case."

3. The Court will not "formulate a rule of constitutional law broader than is required by the precise facts to which it is to be applied."

4. The Court will not pass upon a constitutional question although properly presented by the record, if there is also present some other ground upon which the case may be disposed of. This rule has found most varied application. Thus, if a case can be decided on either of two grounds, one involving a constitutional question, the other a question of statutory construction or general law, the Court will decide only the latter. Appeals from the highest court of a state challenging its decision of a question under the Federal Constitution are frequently dismissed because the judgment can be sustained on an independent state ground.

5. The Court will not pass upon the validity of a statute upon complaint of one who fails to show that he is injured by its operation. Among the many applications of this rule, none is more striking than the denial of the right of challenge to one who lacks a personal or property right. Thus, the challenge by a public official interested only in the performance of his official duty will not be entertained. . . .

6. "The Court will not pass upon the constitutionality of a statute at the instance of one who has availed himself of its benefits."

7. "When the validity of an act of the Congress is drawn in question, and even if a serious doubt of constitutionality is raised, it is a cardinal principle that this Court will first ascertain whether a construction of the statute is fairly possible by which the question may be avoided."

The justices are fully aware that the president and Congress can impose such checks, and on occasion they may exercise their powers with at least some consideration of how other government actors may respond. Therefore, constraints on judicial power emanate not only from Article III and the Court's interpretation of it but also from the constitutional separation of powers—a system giving each governmental branch a role in keeping the other branches within their legitimate bounds.

ANNOTATED READINGS

For studies of judicial power, consult the citations in the footnotes in this chapter. Here we wish only to highlight several interesting books that explore the development of judicial power and how the Court interprets (or should interpret) its powers in Article III, along with the role the Court plays (or should play) in American society. These books include Alexander M. Bickel, *The Least Dangerous Branch* (New York: Bobbs-Merrill, 1962); Jesse H. Choper, *Judicial Review and the National Political Process* (Chicago: University of Chicago Press, 1980); Justin Crowe, *Building the Judiciary: Law, Courts, and the Politics of Institutional Development* (Princeton, NJ: Princeton University Press, 2012); John Hart Ely, *Democracy and Distrust* (Cambridge, MA: Harvard University Press, 1980); Thomas M. Franck, *Political Questions/Judicial Answers: Does the Rule of Law Apply in Foreign Affairs?* (Princeton, NJ: Princeton University Press, 2009); Scott Douglas Gerber, *A Distinct Judicial Power: The Origins of an Independent Judiciary* (New York: Oxford University Press, 2011); Larry D. Kramer, *The People Themselves: Popular Constitutionalism*

and Judicial Review (New York: Oxford University Press, 2004); William Lasser, *The Limits of Judicial Power* (Chapel Hill: University of North Carolina Press, 1988); Scott E. Lemieux and David J. Watkins, eds., *Judicial Review and Contemporary Democratic Theory* (New York: Routledge, 2017); Philippa Strum, *The Supreme Court and Political Questions* (Tuscaloosa: University of Alabama Press, 1974); and Cass R. Sunstein, *One Case at a Time: Judicial Minimalism on the Supreme Court* (Cambridge, MA: Harvard University Press, 1999).

To greater and lesser extents, these works cover *Marbury v. Madison*. Books more explicitly about the case include Robert Lowry Clinton, Marbury v. Madison *and Judicial Review* (Lawrence: University Press of Kansas, 1989); William E. Nelson, Marbury v. Madison: *The Origins and Legacy of Judicial Review* (Lawrence: University Press of Kansas, 2000); and Cliff Sloan and David McKean, *The Great Decision: Jefferson, Adams, Marshall, and the Battle for the Supreme Court* (New York: Public Affairs, 2009).

CHAPTER FOUR

THE LEGISLATURE

ARTICLE I OF THE U.S. CONSTITUTION is its longest and most explicit. The founders spelled out in great detail the powers Congress did and did not have over its own operations and its authority to make laws. Reading through Article I, we might conclude that it could not be the source of much litigation. After all, given its specificity, how much room for interpretation could there be?

For cases involving Congress's authority over its internal affairs, this assumption would be accurate. The Supreme Court has heard relatively few cases touching on the first seven sections of Article I, which deal with the various qualifications for membership in Congress, the ability of the chambers to punish members, and certain privileges the members enjoy. On the relatively few of those on which the Court has ruled, it generally, though not always, has given the legislature wide latitude over its own business.

That assumption, however, is incorrect when we consider cases that deal directly with Congress's most basic power, the enactment of laws, and with its position in American government. Article I, Section 8, enumerates specifically the substantive areas in which Congress may legislate. But is it too specific, failing to foresee how congressional powers might need to be exercised in areas it does not cover? Section 8 provides Congress with the power to borrow and coin money, but not with the authority to make paper money for the payment of debts. Since 1792 congressional committees have held investigations and hearings, but no clause in Section 8 authorizes them to do so. In general, the Supreme Court has had to determine whether legislative action that is not explicitly covered in Article I falls within Congress's authority, and that is why the Court so often has examined statutes passed by Congress.

There is another reason. As we saw earlier, and as we shall see throughout this book, basic (and purposeful) tensions were built into the design of the government. Disputes occur between the branches of the federal government, between the federal government and the states, and between governments and individuals. Arising from the basic principles underlying the structure of government—federalism, the separation of powers, and checks and balances—these conflicts have provided the stuff of myriad legal disputes, and the Court has been right in the middle of many of them.

This chapter examines how the justices have interpreted Article I of the Constitution. It is divided into four sections: the first provides a historical overview of Article I, the second explores cases involving Congress's authority over its own structure and operations, and the third looks at the sources and scope of its lawmaking power. We end with a discussion of Congress and its authority in relation to the other branches of government, especially the executive.

ARTICLE I: HISTORICAL OVERVIEW

Many issues led the colonists in America to rebel against England. An important one, sometimes neglected in treatments of the American Revolution, was the different ways the British and the colonists thought about legislative bodies such as Parliament. The British viewed legislatures as "deliberative bodies whose allegiance was to the nation rather than specific constituencies."[1] Underlying this view is the notion of "virtual" representation:

---

[1]We adopt the discussion in this paragraph from Daniel A. Farber and Suzanna Sherry, *A History of the American Constitution*, 2nd ed. (St. Paul, MN: Thompson/West, 2005), 153–157.

"[S]ince the *interests* of all British citizens were represented in Parliament, the *citizens* themselves did not need to be." Therefore, the British reasoned, it was unnecessary for the colonists to vote for members of Parliament because they were "virtually represented" within it. The Americans took quite a different stance. To them, legislators "were nothing more and nothing less than agents of their constituents." As John Adams wrote in 1776, the ideal legislature "should be in miniature an exact portrait of the people at large. It should think, feel, reason and act like them."

During the founding period, the American states created legislatures that reflected some of Adams's views of representation. Most states provided for short terms of office, with elections typically occurring every other year. They also mandated that legislatures have open sessions and publish their proceedings. Finally, many states actually gave their inhabitants the right to "instruct" their representatives on how to vote on certain issues. These and other measures were designed to keep legislators responsive to their constituents. Concerns about representation at the federal level also were present, as were suspicions about a national government that would be as powerful as England's. The unicameral Congress that the Articles of Confederation created had few important powers, and many of those it had it could not exercise without state compliance, which it seldom received *(see Figure I-1)*.

The problems Congress and the nation faced under the Articles of Confederation made it clear to the delegates attending the Constitutional Convention of 1787 that a very different kind of legislature was necessary if the United States was to endure. But what form would that legislature take? And what powers would it have? These questions produced a great deal of discussion during the convention; in fact, debates over the structure and powers of Congress occupied more than half of the framers' time.

Structure and Composition of Congress

The Virginia Plan set the tone for the Constitutional Convention and became the backbone for Article I. Essentially, the plan called for a bicameral legislature, with the number of representatives in each house apportioned on the basis of state population. Under this scheme, the lower house (now the House of Representatives) would be elected by the people; the upper house (the Senate) would be chosen by the lower house based on recommendations from state legislatures.

The framers dealt with two aspects of the Virginia Plan with relative ease. Almost all agreed on the need for a bicameral legislature. Accord on this point was not surprising: by 1787 only four states had one-house legislatures. The plan for selecting the upper house provoked more discussion. Some thought that having the lower house elect the upper would make the Senate subservient to the House and upset the delicate checks and balances system. Instead, the delegates agreed that state legislatures should select the senators. (The Seventeenth Amendment to the Constitution, ratified in 1913, changed the method of selection; senators, like representatives, are now elected by the people.)

The third aspect of the Virginia Plan—the composition of the houses of Congress—generated some of the most acrimonious debates of the convention. As historians Alfred Kelly, Winfred Harbison, and Herman Belz put it,

> Would the constituent units be the states, represented equally by delegates chosen by state legislatures, as the small-state group desired? Or would the constituent element be the people of the United States . . . with representation in both chambers apportioned according to population, as the large-state group wished?[2]

On one level, the answer to this question implicated the straightforward motivation of self-interest. Naturally, the large states wanted both chambers to be based on population because they would send more representatives to the new Congress. The smaller states thought all states should have equal representation in both houses and regarded their plan as the only way to avoid tyranny by the majority. On another level, the issue of composition went to the core of the Philadelphia enterprise. The approach the small states advocated would signify the importance of the states in the new system of government, while that put forth in the Virginia Plan would suggest that the federal government received its power directly from the people rather than from the states and was truly independent of the states.

It is no wonder, then, that the delegates had so much trouble resolving this issue: it defined the basic character of the new government. In the end they took the course of action that characterized many of their

---

[2]Alfred H. Kelly, Winfred A. Harbison, and Herman Belz, *The American Constitution: Its Origins and Development*, 7th ed. (New York: W. W. Norton, 1991), 90.

decisions—they agreed to disagree. Specifically, the delegates reached a compromise under which the House of Representatives would be constituted on the basis of population, and the Senate would have two delegates from each state.

Reaching this compromise was crucial to the success of the convention. Without it, the delegates may have disbanded without framing a constitution. But because the founders split the difference between the demands of the small and large states, they never fully dealt with the critical underlying issue: Do the people or the states empower the federal government? We address the impact of this lingering question on the development of the country in chapter 6. Here, we note that this question not only has been at the center of many disputes brought to the Supreme Court but also was a leading cause of the Civil War.

Powers of Congress

With the possible exceptions of reapportionment and term limits for members of Congress, Americans today rarely debate issues concerning the structure and composition of Congress: most of us simply accept the arrangements outlined in the Constitution. Instead, we tend to concern ourselves with what Congress does or does not do, with its ability to change our lives—sometimes dramatically—through the exercise of its lawmaking powers. Should Congress increase taxes? Provide aid for the homeless? Authorize military action? Such questions—not structural points—generate heated debate among Americans.

In 1787 the situation was reversed. The framers argued over the makeup of the legislature but generally agreed about the particular powers it would have. This consensus probably reflected their experience under the Articles of Confederation: severe economic problems due in no small part, as the framers knew, to "congressional impotence."[3]

To correct these problems, Article I, Section 8 lists seventeen specific powers the delegates gave to Congress (*see Box 4-1*)—six of which relate to the economy. Consider the problem of funding the government. Under the Articles of Confederation the legislature could not collect taxes from the people; instead, it had to rely on the less-than-dependable states to collect and forward taxes (from 1781 through 1783, the legislature requested $10 million from the states but received less than $2 million). In response, the first power given to

Congress in the newly minted Constitution was to "lay and collect taxes." In addition to the six specific powers dealing with economic issues, Section 8 gives Congress some authority over foreign relations, the military, and internal matters such as the establishment of post offices.

The framers obviously agreed that Congress should have these powers, but two others provoked controversy. The first concerned a proposal in the Virginia Plan to give Congress veto authority over state legislation. This idea had the strong support of James Madison, who argued that the states would put their own particular concerns above the general interest. Madison and others who supported this veto proposal were once again reacting to problems with the Articles of Confederation. Because the federal government lacked any coercive power over the states, cooperation among them was virtually nonexistent. They engaged in practices that harmed one another economically and, in general, acted more like thirteen separate countries than a union or even a confederation. But the majority of delegates thought that the states would oppose a congressional veto, jeopardizing ratification. Accordingly, they compromised with Article VI, the supremacy clause, which made the Constitution, U.S. laws, and treaties "the supreme law of the land," binding all judges in all the states to follow them.

The second source of controversy was over this question: Would Congress be able to exercise powers that were not listed in Article I, Section 8, or was it limited to those explicitly enumerated? Some analysts would argue that the last clause of Article I, Section 8, the necessary and proper clause, addressed this question by granting Congress the power "[t]o make all Laws which shall be necessary and proper for carrying into Execution the foregoing Powers." But is that interpretation correct? Even after they agreed on the wording of that clause (with little discussion), the delegates continued to debate the issue. Delegate James McHenry of Maryland wrote about a conversation that occurred on September 6: "Spoke to Gov. Morris Fitzsimmons . . . to insert a power . . . enabling the legislature to erect piers for protection of shipping in winter. . . . Mr. Gov. thinks it may be done under the words of [Article I]—'and provide for the common defense and general welfare.'"[4] In other words, Fitzsimmons was arguing that one of Congress's enumerated powers (to provide for the common defense and general welfare) implied the power to erect piers. Under this argument, then, Congress could assert powers connected to, but beyond, those that were enumerated.

---

[3]Farber and Sherry, *A History of the American Constitution*, 189.

[4]Quoted in ibid., 199.

BOX 4-1

The Powers of Congress

Article I, Section 8, of the Constitution grants Congress the following specific powers:

To lay and collect taxes, duties, imposts, and excises

To pay the debts and provide for the common defense and general welfare of the United States

To borrow money

To regulate commerce with foreign nations, among the states, and with the Indian tribes

To establish uniform rules for naturalization and bankruptcies

To coin money, regulate its value, and fix a standard for weights and measures

To provide for the punishment of counterfeiting

To establish a post office

To establish copyright and patent laws

To create lower courts

To define crimes on the high seas

To declare war

To raise and support armies

To establish and maintain a navy

To create rules regulating the land and naval forces

To call forth the militia to enforce the laws, suppress insurrections, and repel invasions

To organize, arm, and discipline the militia

To pass all legislation over the district that becomes the seat of government

To make all laws necessary and proper to the execution of the foregoing powers

---

A majority of the founders may have agreed with Fitzsimmons. Because the question of congressional power is central to an understanding of the role Congress plays in American society, we shall return to it. At this point, however, we consider the Court's interpretation of the first parts of Article I, which lay out the structure of Congress and its authority over its internal affairs.

MEMBERS OF CONGRESS: QUALIFICATIONS, IMMUNITY, AND DISCIPLINE

While the framers were debating Congress's structure and composition, they were also thinking about what qualifications legislators should have, how members could be punished if they failed to behave in accord with congressional norms, and how they might safeguard the independence and integrity of the institution. Each of these matters is addressed in Article I, but the Supreme Court occasionally has been called upon to resolve questions the framers did not anticipate.

Membership in Congress: Seating and Discipline

In addition to specifying the structure and composition of Congress, Article I contains the requirements that all prospective members of the institution must meet:

- A senator must be at least thirty years old and have been a citizen of the United States not less than nine years (Section 3, Clause 3).

- A representative must be at least twenty-five years old and have been a citizen not less than seven years (Section 2, Clause 2).

- Every member of Congress must be, when elected, an inhabitant of the state that he or she is to represent (Section 2, Clause 2; and Section 3, Clause 3).

- No one may be a member of Congress who holds any other "Office under the Authority of the United States" (Section 6, Clause 2).

Finally, Section 3 of the Fourteenth Amendment states that no person may be a senator or a representative who, having previously taken an oath as a member of Congress to support the Constitution, has engaged in rebellion against the United States or given aid or comfort to its enemies, unless Congress has removed such restriction by a two-thirds vote of both houses.

With only a few exceptions, these standards qua standards have not caused much controversy or litigation. Nor has there been much debate over whether Congress can censure or expel sitting members. The second paragraph of Article I, Section 5, is clear on this point: "Each House may determine the Rules of its Proceedings, punish its Members for disorderly Behaviour, and, with the Concurrence of two thirds, expel a member." The Court has not dealt directly with a dispute involving the punishment of members, such as censure or expulsion; rather, it has suggested that this is a broad privilege, best left to the judgment of the individual chambers.[5] Still "punishment of members" is rare; for example, since 1787 the House has expelled only four members and the Senate, 15.[6]

Where controversy has arisen is over another sentence in Article I, Section 5, which reads, "Each House shall be the Judge of the Elections, Returns and Qualifications of its own Members." Several interpretations of this clause are possible. One is that it ought to be read in conjunction with the Article I requirements for members. That is, Congress cannot deny a duly elected person a seat in the institution unless that person fails to meet the specified criteria, such as the age requirement. Another interpretation is that Congress is free to develop additional qualifications, independent of those specified elsewhere in Article I.

For the better part of the nation's history, the Court did not resolve this debate, even though Congress occasionally acted as if it could add qualifications or ignore them when they were not met. During the Civil War, Congress enacted the Test Oath Law of 1862, which required incoming members to "swear . . . that they had never voluntarily borne arms against the United States." Moreover, as shown in Table 4-1, both the House and the Senate have refused to seat properly elected individuals, sometimes on extraconstitutional grounds. The Senate excluded Philip Thomas of Maryland on loyalty grounds when it was discovered that he had given money to his son when he became a soldier in the Confederate Army. The House refused to seat Brigham H. Roberts of Utah because he had been convicted of violating an antipolygamy law.

In the course of investigating the Roberts case, a congressional committee concluded that the framers "had not foreclosed the right of Congress to establish qualifications for membership other than those mentioned in the Constitution."[7] As Table 4-1 shows, both

[5]See, for example, *In re Chapman* (1897).

[6]Calculated from the House (http://history.house.gov/Institution/Discipline/Expulsion-Censure-Reprimand/) and Senate's (https://www.senate.gov/reference/index_sub_items/Expulsion_vrd.htm) websites.

[7]Congressional Quarterly, *Guide to Congress*, 7th ed. (Washington, DC: CQ Press, 2013), 1132.

Table 4-1 Duly Elected Members of Congress Excluded

Chamber (Year)	Member-Elect (Party-State)	Grounds for Exclusion
Senate (1793)	Albert Gallatin (D-Pa.)	Citizenship
House (1823)	John Bailey (Ind.-Mass.)	Residence
Senate (1849)	James Shields (D-Ill.)	Citizenship
House (1867)	John Y. Brown (D-Ky.)	Loyalty
House (1867)	John D. Young (D-Ky.)	Loyalty
House (1867)	John A. Wimpy (Ind.-Ga.)	Loyalty
House (1867)	W. D. Simpson (Ind.-S.C.)	Loyalty
Senate (1867)	Philip F. Thomas (D-Md.)	Loyalty
House (1870)	Benjamin F. Whittemore (R-S.C.)	Malfeasance
House (1900)	Brigham H. Roberts (D-Utah)	Polygamy
House (1919)	Victor L. Berger (Socialist-Wis.)	Sedition
House (1920)	Victor L. Berger (Socialist-Wis.)	Sedition
House (1967)	Adam C. Powell Jr. (D-N.Y.)	Misconduct

Source: Congressional Quarterly, *Guide to Congress,* 7th ed. (Washington, DC: CQ Press, 2013).

houses subscribed to this theory. The question of whether the Supreme Court would follow suit remained largely unaddressed until 1969, when the Court decided **Powell v. McCormack**, a case in which it squarely responded to Congress's traditional approach to seating qualifications.

As pastor of the Abyssinian Baptist Church in Harlem, one of the nation's largest congregations,

Representative Adam Clayton Powell Jr. had been a force within that New York City community since the 1930s. His influence only increased when he was elected to the House in 1944 after receiving nominations from both the Democratic and Republican Parties (though he was elected as a Democrat). He continued to be reelected by wide margins for the next twenty-five years.

By the early 1960s Powell had acquired enough seniority to chair the House Committee on Education and Labor, but his relations with his colleagues were troubled. Some House members disliked his opulent, unconventional lifestyle, his unpredictable leadership, and his use of the media to suit his political ends. In addition, Powell became entangled in various legal controversies; for example, he refused to pay damages assessed against him in a defamation of character suit and actively sought to avert efforts to compel him to pay.

The Eighty-ninth Congress (1965–1966) launched an inquiry into Powell's activities, which yielded two major violations of House rules: Powell had used federal moneys to fly a woman staff member with him on trips to his vacation home in the Bahamas and to pay his former wife a salary of $20,000, even though she did not work in his district or Washington office, in accordance with law. Even though Powell was reelected in November 1966, the House refused to seat him pending further investigation.

In March 1967 a House investigating committee reached two conclusions: (1) from a constitutional standpoint, Powell met the requirements for office: he was older than twenty-five, had been a citizen of the United States for seven years, and was an inhabitant of New York; and (2) Powell had sought to evade the fine associated with the defamation of character offense, had misused public funds, and had filed false expenditure reports. The committee recommended "that Powell be sworn and seated as a member of . . . Congress but that he be censured by the House, fined $40,000 and be deprived of his seniority." The House, however, rejected that recommendation and instead adopted, by a vote of 307–116, a resolution that excluded Powell from the House and directed House Speaker John McCormack to notify the governor of New York that the seat was vacant.

Powell and thirteen of his constituents responded by filing a lawsuit against McCormack and other members of the House. They claimed that the House's refusal to seat him violated the qualifications clause of the Constitution. Because Powell met the requirements

Speaker of the House John McCormack, left, and Representative Adam Clayton Powell walk in separate directions after conferring during the 1967 controversy over proposed disciplinary action against Powell for violating House rules.

for office and was properly elected, they argued, the House had no choice but to seat him. Under this view, Article I, Section 5—"Each House shall be the judge of the Elections, Returns and Qualifications of its own Members"—does not give Congress authority to exclude members who met the constitutional standards for office. McCormack's attorneys thought otherwise. In their opinion and in accord with institutional tradition, the Court should read the qualifications clause and Section 5 separately. They argued that the House has the authority to exclude members, even if they meet constitutional standards.

The justices held for Powell. In his opinion for the majority, Chief Justice Earl Warren relied heavily on the records of the constitutional debates to conclude that the framers intended to "deny either branch of Congress the authority to add or to otherwise vary the membership qualifications expressly set forth in the Constitution." Warren also asserted that even if the intent of the framers had been less clear, the Court would "nevertheless have been compelled to resolve any ambiguity in favor of a narrow construction of the scope of Congress' power to exclude members-elect." Why? Warren put it this way:

A fundamental principle of our representative democracy is, in Hamilton's words, "that the people should choose whom they please to govern them." As Madison pointed out at the Convention, this principle is undermined as much by limiting whom the people can select as by limiting the franchise itself. In apparent agreement with this basic philosophy, the Convention adopted his suggestion limiting the power to expel. To allow essentially that same power to be exercised under the guise of judging qualifications, would be to ignore Madison's warning, against "vesting an improper & dangerous power in the Legislature." ... Unquestionably, Congress has an interest in preserving its institutional integrity, but in most cases that interest can be sufficiently safeguarded by the exercise of its power to punish its members for disorderly behavior and, in extreme cases, to expel a member with the concurrence of two thirds. In short, both the intention of the Framers, to the extent it can be determined, and an examination of the basic principles of our democratic system persuade us that the Constitution does not vest in the Congress a discretionary power to deny membership by a majority vote.

Chief Justice Warren's holding in *Powell* was clear: because Powell was duly elected and because he met the constitutional standards for membership, the House could not refuse to seat him. Or, as Warren emphatically noted, "Congress is limited to the standing qualifications prescribed in the Constitution."

An important question to ask yourself about *Powell* concerns its relevance to one of the more interesting debates about Article I: Does the U.S. Constitution give states the power to enact term limits for members of the U.S. Congress? In *U.S. Term Limits v. Thornton* (1995) the Court addressed this question. As you read Justice John Paul Stevens's opinion for the majority, compare it with Chief Justice Warren's position in *Powell v. McCormack:* Does the rationale the majority used in *Thornton* square with Warren's reasoning? Also pay close attention to how both the majority and dissenting opinions deal with arguments following from originalism. Is *Thornton* yet another example of the difficulty of applying these modes of analysis to actual cases? Finally, consider this question: Would the Court have arrived at a different answer had the U.S. House of Representatives mustered the votes to propose a term limits amendment?

U.S. Term Limits, Inc. v. Thornton

514 U.S. 779 (1995)
http://caselaw.findlaw.com/us-supreme-court/514/779.html
Oral arguments available at https://www.oyez.org/cases/1994/93-1456
Vote: 5 (Breyer, Ginsburg, Kennedy, Souter, Stevens)
    4 (O'Connor, Rehnquist, Scalia, Thomas)

OPINION OF THE COURT: *Stevens*

CONCURRING OPINION: *Kennedy*

DISSENTING OPINION: *Thomas*

In 1990 Colorado became the first state to limit terms for federal officeholders. Subsequently, twenty-three additional states passed term limit initiatives. *U.S. Term Limits* involved one of those initiatives. It originated in Arkansas, where in 1992 voters approved an amendment to the state constitution (Amendment 73) prohibiting from the ballot anyone seeking reelection who previously had served two terms in the U.S. Senate or three terms in the U.S. House of Representatives. It permitted anyone to be elected as a write-in candidate, presumably as a way of allowing for the reelection of a popular incumbent.

The amendment was to apply to all persons seeking reelection after January 1, 1993. About two months before that date, the League of Women Voters and various citizens of Arkansas, including U.S. Representative Ray Thornton, filed suit asking a state court to declare the amendment unconstitutional. Among the arguments they made in this court and later in the Arkansas Supreme Court was that Amendment 73 violated Article I of the U.S. Constitution. In particular, based on *Powell v. McCormack,* they claimed that the federal Constitution establishes the sole qualifications for federal office, and the states may not alter them. Arkansas and U.S. Term Limits, an organization supporting the amendment, responded by pointing to Section 4 of Article I: "The Times, Places and Manner of holding Elections for Senators and Representatives, shall be prescribed in each State by the Legislature thereof." In their view, this section—not the qualifications clauses—was applicable because term limits would regulate access to the ballot, not the qualifications for office. They further suggested that *Powell* spoke only about the ability of the U.S. House of Representatives, not the states, to set qualifications. Finally, because the Constitution does not explicitly prohibit the states from setting qualifications for office, it is a power reserved to them under the Tenth Amendment.

The Arkansas courts disagreed. The lower court struck down the amendment as a violation of Article I, and in 1994 the state supreme court affirmed. According to that court, "The qualifications clauses fix the sole requirement for congressional service. This is not a power left to the states." With this defeat in hand, amendment proponents appealed to the U.S. Supreme Court, which agreed to hear the case.

JUSTICE STEVENS DELIVERED THE OPINION OF THE COURT.

Today's cases present a challenge to an amendment to the Arkansas State Constitution that prohibits the name of an otherwise eligible candidate for Congress from appearing on the general election ballot if that candidate has already served three terms in the House of Representatives or two terms in the Senate. The Arkansas Supreme Court held that the amendment violates the Federal Constitution. We agree with that holding. Such a state-imposed restriction is contrary to the "fundamental principle of our representative democracy," embodied in the Constitution, that "the people should choose whom they please to govern them" *Powell v. McCormack* (1969). Allowing individual States to adopt their own qualifications for congressional service would be inconsistent with the Framers' vision of a uniform National Legislature representing the people of the United States. If the qualifications set forth in the text of the Constitution are to be changed, that text must be amended. . . .

As the opinions of the Arkansas Supreme Court suggest, the constitutionality of Amendment 73 depends critically on the resolution of two distinct issues. The first is whether the Constitution forbids States from adding to or altering the qualifications specifically enumerated in the Constitution. The second is, if the Constitution does so forbid, whether the fact that Amendment 73 is formulated as a ballot access restriction rather than as an outright disqualification is of constitutional significance. Our resolution of these issues draws upon our prior resolution of a related but distinct issue: whether Congress has the power to add to or alter the qualifications of its Members.

Twenty-six years ago . . . *Powell v. McCormack* . . . establishe[d] two important propositions: first, that the "relevant historical materials" compel the conclusion that, at least with respect to qualifications imposed by Congress, the Framers intended the qualifications listed in the Constitution to be exclusive; and second, that that conclusion is equally compelled by an understanding of the "fundamental principle of our representative democracy . . . 'that the people should choose whom they please to govern them.'" . . .

Unsurprisingly, the state courts and lower federal courts have similarly concluded that *Powell* conclusively resolved the issue whether Congress has the power to impose additional qualifications. [And] we reaffirm that the qualifications for service in Congress set forth in the text of the Constitution are "fixed," at least in the sense that they may not be supplemented by Congress.

Our reaffirmation of *Powell* does not necessarily resolve the specific questions presented in these cases. For petitioners argue that whatever the constitutionality of additional qualifications for membership imposed by Congress, the historical and textual materials discussed in *Powell* do not support the conclusion that the Constitution prohibits additional qualifications imposed by States. In the absence of such a constitutional prohibition, petitioners argue, the Tenth Amendment and the principle of reserved powers require that States be allowed to add such qualifications.

Before addressing these arguments, we find it appropriate to take note of the striking unanimity among the courts that have considered the issue. None of the overwhelming array of briefs submitted by the parties and amici has called to our attention even a single case in which a state court or federal court has approved of a State's addition of qualifications for a member of Congress. To the contrary, an impressive number of courts have determined that States lack the authority to add qualifications. . . . This impressive and uniform body of judicial decisions . . . indicates that the obstacles confronting petitioners are formidable indeed.

Petitioners argue that the Constitution contains no express prohibition against state-added qualifications, and that Amendment 73 is therefore an appropriate exercise of a State's reserved power to place additional restrictions on the choices that its own voters may make. We disagree for two independent reasons. First, we conclude that the power to add qualifications is not within the "original powers" of the States, and thus is not reserved to the States by the Tenth Amendment. Second, even if States possessed some original power in this area, we conclude that the Framers intended the Constitution to be the exclusive source of qualifications for members of Congress, and that the Framers thereby "divested" States of any power to add qualifications. . . .

Contrary to petitioners' assertions, the power to add qualifications is not part of the original powers of sovereignty that the Tenth Amendment reserved to the States. Petitioners' Tenth Amendment argument misconceives the nature of the right at issue because that Amendment could only "reserve" that which existed before. As Justice Story recognized, "the states can exercise no powers whatsoever, which exclusively spring out of the existence of the national government, which the Constitution does not delegate to them. . . . No state can say, that it has reserved, what it never possessed." . . .

With respect to setting qualifications for service in Congress, no such right existed before the Constitution was ratified. The contrary argument overlooks the revolutionary character of the government that the Framers conceived. Prior to the adoption of the Constitution, the States joined together under the Articles of Confederation. In that system, "the States retained most of their sovereignty, like independent nations bound together only by treaties." [When the Constitution's framers] decided "to create an entirely new government with a National Executive, National

Judiciary, and a National Legislature," [they] envisioned a uniform national system, rejecting the notion that the Nation was a collection of States, and instead creating a direct link between the National Government and the people of the United States. In that National Government, representatives owe primary allegiance not to the people of a State but to the people of a Nation. . . .

In short, as the Framers recognized, electing representatives to the National Legislature was a new right, arising from the Constitution itself. The Tenth Amendment thus provides no basis for concluding that the States possess reserved power to add qualifications to those that are fixed in the Constitution. Instead, any state power to set the qualifications for membership in Congress must derive not from the reserved powers of state sovereignty, but rather from the delegated powers of national sovereignty. In the absence of any constitutional delegation to the States of power to add qualifications to those enumerated in the Constitution, such a power does not exist.

Even if we believed that States possessed as part of their original powers some control over congressional qualifications, the text and structure of the Constitution, the relevant historical materials, and, most importantly, the "basic principles of our democratic system" all demonstrate that the Qualifications Clauses were intended to preclude the States from exercising any such power and to fix as exclusive the qualifications in the Constitution. . . .

The available affirmative evidence indicates the Framers' intent that States have no role in the setting of qualifications. . . .

We find compelling the complete absence in the ratification debates of any assertion that States had the power to add qualifications. In those debates, the question whether to require term limits, or "rotation," was a major source of controversy. The draft of the Constitution that was submitted for ratification contained no provision for rotation . . . At several ratification conventions, participants proposed amendments that would have required rotation.

The Federalists' responses to those criticisms and proposals addressed the merits of the issue, arguing that rotation was incompatible with the people's right to choose. . . . Hamilton argued that the representatives' need for reelection rather than mandatory rotation was the more effective way to keep representatives responsive to the people, because "when a man knows he must quit his station, let his merit be what it may, he will turn his attention chiefly to his own emolument."

Regardless of which side has the better of the debate over rotation, it is most striking that nowhere in the extensive ratification debates have we found any statement by either a proponent or an opponent of rotation that the draft constitution would permit States to require rotation for the representatives of their own citizens. . . .

Our conclusion that States lack the power to impose qualifications vindicates the same "fundamental principle of our representative democracy" that we recognized in *Powell,* namely that "the people should choose whom they please to govern them."

. . . [S]tate-imposed restrictions, unlike the congressionally imposed restrictions at issue in *Powell,* also violate [an] idea central to this basic principle: that the right to choose representatives belongs not to the States, but to the people. . . .

Petitioners attempt to overcome this . . . evidence against the States' power to impose qualifications by arguing that the practice of the States immediately after the adoption of the Constitution demonstrates their understanding that they possessed such power. One may properly question the extent to which the States' own practice is a reliable indicator of the contours of restrictions that the Constitution imposed on States, especially when no court has ever upheld a state-imposed qualification of any sort. . . . But petitioners' argument is unpersuasive even on its own terms. At the time of the Convention, "almost all the State Constitutions required members of their Legislatures to possess considerable property." Despite this near uniformity, only one State, Virginia, placed similar restrictions on members of Congress, requiring that a representative be . . . a "freeholder." Just 15 years after imposing a property qualification, Virginia replaced that requirement with a provision requiring that representatives be only "qualified according to the constitution of the United States." . . .

In sum, the available historical and textual evidence, read in light of the basic principles of democracy underlying the Constitution and recognized by this Court in *Powell,* reveal the Framers' intent that neither Congress nor the States should possess the power to supplement the exclusive qualifications set forth in the text of the Constitution.

Petitioners argue that, even if States may not add qualifications, Amendment 73 is constitutional because it is not such a qualification, and because Amendment 73 is a permissible exercise of state power to regulate the "Times, Places and Manner of Holding Elections." We reject these contentions.

Unlike §1 and §2 of Amendment 73, which create absolute bars to service for long-term incumbents running for state office, §3 merely provides that certain Senators and Representatives shall not be certified as candidates and shall not have their names appear on the ballot. They may run as write-in candidates and, if elected, they may serve. Petitioners contend that only a legal bar to service creates an impermissible qualification, and that Amendment 73 is therefore consistent with the Constitution. . . .

We need not decide whether petitioners' narrow understanding of qualifications is correct because, even if it is, Amendment 73 may not stand. As we have often noted, "'constitutional rights would be of little value if they could be . . . indirectly denied.'" The Constitution "nullifies sophisticated as well as simple-minded modes" of infringing on Constitutional protections.

In our view, Amendment 73 is an indirect attempt to accomplish what the Constitution prohibits Arkansas from accomplishing directly. . . . Indeed, it cannot be seriously contended that the intent behind Amendment 73 is other than to prevent the election of incumbents. The preamble of Amendment 73 states explicitly: "The people of Arkansas . . . herein limit the terms of elected officials." Sections 1 and 2 create absolute limits on the number of terms that may be served. There is no hint that §3 was intended to have any other purpose.

Petitioners do, however, contest the Arkansas Supreme Court's conclusion that the Amendment has the same practical effect as an absolute bar. They argue that the possibility of a write-in campaign creates a real possibility for victory, especially for an entrenched incumbent. One may reasonably question the merits of that contention. . . . But even if petitioners are correct that incumbents may occasionally win reelection as write-in candidates, there is no denying that the ballot restrictions will make it significantly more difficult for the barred candidate to win the election. In our view, an amendment with the avowed purpose and obvious effect of evading the requirements of the Qualifications Clauses by handicapping a class of candidates cannot stand. . . .

The merits of term limits, or "rotation," have been the subject of debate since the formation of our Constitution, when the Framers unanimously rejected a proposal to add such limits to the Constitution. The cogent arguments on both sides of the question that were articulated during the process of ratification largely retain their force today. . . . Term limits, like any other qualification for office, unquestionably restrict the ability of voters to vote for whom they wish. On the other hand, such limits may provide for the infusion of fresh ideas and new perspectives, and may decrease the likelihood that representatives will lose touch with their constituents. It is not our province to resolve this longstanding debate.

We are, however, firmly convinced that allowing the several States to adopt term limits for congressional service would effect a fundamental change in the constitutional framework. Any such change must come not by legislation adopted either by Congress or by an individual State, but rather—as have other important changes in the electoral process—through the Amendment procedures set forth in Article V. The Framers decided that the qualifications for service in the Congress of the United States be fixed in the Constitution and be uniform throughout the Nation. That decision reflects the Framers' understanding that Members of Congress are chosen by separate constituencies, but that they become, when elected, servants of the people of the United States. They are not merely delegates appointed by separate, sovereign States; they occupy offices that are integral and essential components of a single National Government. In the absence of a properly passed constitutional amendment, allowing individual States to craft their own qualifications for Congress would thus erode the structure envisioned by the Framers, a structure that was designed, in the words of the Preamble to our Constitution, to form a "more perfect Union."

The judgment is affirmed.

It is so ordered.

JUSTICE THOMAS, WITH WHOM THE CHIEF JUSTICE, JUSTICE O'CONNOR, AND JUSTICE SCALIA JOIN, DISSENTING.

It is ironic that the Court bases today's decision on the right of the people to "choose whom they please to govern them." Under our Constitution, there is only one State whose people have the right to "choose whom they please" to represent Arkansas in Congress. The Court holds, however, that neither the elected legislature of that State nor the people themselves (acting by ballot initiative) may prescribe any qualifications for those representatives. The majority therefore defends the right of the people of Arkansas to "choose whom they please to govern them" by invalidating a provision that won nearly 60% of the votes cast in a direct election and that carried every congressional district in the State.

I dissent. Nothing in the Constitution deprives the people of each State of the power to prescribe eligibility requirements for the candidates who seek to represent them in Congress. The Constitution is simply silent on this question. And where the Constitution is silent, it raises no bar to action by the States or the people.

Because the majority fundamentally misunderstands the notion of "reserved" powers, I start with some first principles. Contrary to the majority's suggestion, the people of the States need not point to any affirmative grant of power in the Constitution in order to prescribe qualifications for their representatives in Congress, or to authorize their elected state legislators to do so . . .

When they adopted the Federal Constitution, of course, the people of each State surrendered some of their authority to the United States (and hence to entities accountable to the people of other States as well as to themselves). They affirmatively deprived their States of certain powers and they affirmatively conferred certain powers upon the Federal Government. Because the people of the several States are the only true source of power, however, the Federal Government enjoys no authority beyond what the Constitution confers: the Federal Government's powers are limited and enumerated . . .

In each State, the remainder of the people's powers—"the powers not delegated to the United States by the Constitution, nor prohibited by it to the States,"—are either delegated to the state government or retained by the people. The Federal Constitution does not specify which of these two possibilities obtains; it is up to the various state constitutions to declare which powers the people of each State have delegated to their state government. As far as the Federal Constitution is concerned, then, the States can exercise all powers that the Constitution does not withhold from them. The Federal Government and the States thus face different default rules: where the Constitution is silent about the exercise of a particular power—that is, where the Constitution does not speak either expressly or by necessary implication—the Federal Government lacks that power and the States enjoy it.

These basic principles are enshrined in the Tenth Amendment, which declares that all powers neither delegated to the Federal Government nor prohibited to the States "are reserved to the States respectively, or to the people." With this careful last phrase, the Amendment avoids taking any position on the division of power between the state governments and the people of the States: it is up to the people of each State to determine which "reserved" powers their state government may exercise. . . .

The majority begins by announcing an enormous and untenable limitation on the principle expressed by the Tenth Amendment. According to the majority, the States possess only those powers that the Constitution affirmatively grants to them or that they enjoyed before the Constitution was adopted; the Tenth Amendment "could only 'reserve' that which existed before." From the fact that the States had not previously enjoyed any powers over the particular institutions of the Federal Government established by the Constitution, the majority derives a rule precisely opposite to the one that the Amendment actually prescribes: "The states can exercise no powers whatsoever, which exclusively spring out of the existence of the national government, which the constitution does not delegate to them."

. . . Given the fundamental principle that all governmental powers stem from the people of the States, it would simply be incoherent to assert that the people of the States could not reserve any powers that they had not previously controlled.

The Tenth Amendment's use of the word "reserved" does not help the majority's position. If someone says that the power to use a particular facility is reserved to some group, he is not saying anything about whether that group has previously used the facility. He is merely saying that the people who control the facility have designated that group as the entity with authority to use it. The Tenth Amendment is similar: the people of the States, from whom all governmental powers stem, have specified that all powers not prohibited to the States by the Federal Constitution are reserved "to the States respectively, or to the people."

The majority is therefore quite wrong to conclude that the people of the States cannot authorize their state governments to exercise any powers that were unknown to the States when the Federal Constitution was drafted. Indeed, the majority's position frustrates the apparent purpose of the Amendment's final phrase. The Amendment does not pre-empt any limitations on state power found in the state constitutions, as it might have done if it simply had said that the powers not delegated to the Federal Government are reserved to the States. But the Amendment also does not prevent the people of the States from amending their state constitutions to remove limitations that were in effect when the Federal Constitution and the Bill of Rights were ratified. . . .

I take it to be established, then, that the people of Arkansas do enjoy "reserved" powers over the selection of their representatives in Congress. . . . Whatever one might think of the wisdom of this arrangement, we may not override the decision of the people of Arkansas unless something in the Federal Constitution deprives them of the power to enact such measures.

The decision in *U.S. Term Limits v. Thornton*, coupled with the *Powell* ruling, authoritatively settled the issue of qualifications for congressional office. The Constitution's age, residency, and citizenship requirements are a complete statement of congressional eligibility standards. Neither Congress nor the states may add to or delete from those requirements. According to the Court, only a constitutional amendment could alter the requirements for membership in the federal legislature.

Speech or Debate Clause

The Court's reading of the Constitution in *Powell* protects those who have been duly elected to Congress and meet the qualifications of office from being excluded by members of their own branch; and *Thornton* says that the states cannot limit the terms of office of members of the House or Senate. The Constitution also contains a safeguard against harassment or intimidation by the executive branch. Article I, Section 6, specifies:

> The Senators and Representatives . . . shall in all Cases, except Treason, Felony, and Breach of the Peace, be privileged from Arrest during their Attendance at the Session of their respective Houses, and in going to and returning from the same; and for any Speech or Debate in either House, they shall not be questioned in any other Place.

Called the speech or debate clause, this privilege of membership derives from British practice. The English Parliament, during its struggles with the Crown, asserted that its members were immune from arrest during its sessions, and the English Bill of Rights embodies this guarantee. The importance of the speech or debate clause's protection is undeniable: without it, a president could order the arrest of, or otherwise intimidate, members of Congress who disagree publicly with the administration. The framers thought the statement was necessary "to protect the integrity of the legislative process by insuring the independence of individual legislators."[8]

---

[8]*United States v. Brewster* (1972).

The language of Article I, Section 6, of the U.S. Constitution has generated two kinds of constitutional questions: What is protected, and who is protected? The Court took a stab at addressing the first question in **Kilbourn v. Thompson** (1881). Though the justices dealt primarily with the scope of congressional investigations, they noted that the clause extends to

> written reports presented . . . by its committees, to resolutions offered, which, though in writing, must be reproduced in speech, and to the act of voting, whether it is done vocally or by passing between the tellers. In short, to things generally done in a session [of Congress] by one of its members in relation to the business before it.

With only some minor modifications, *Kilbourn* remained the Court's most significant statement on the clause until 1972, when **Gravel v. United States** was decided. This case had important implications for both questions arising out of Article I, Section 6: Who is protected, and what is protected?

Gravel began on June 29, 1971, when Senator Mike Gravel (D-Alas.) held a public meeting of the Subcommittee on Buildings and Grounds, which he chaired. Before the hearing began, Gravel made a statement about the Vietnam War, noting that it was "relevant to his subcommittee . . . because of its effects upon the domestic economy and . . . the lack of federal funds to provide for adequate public facilities." He then read portions of a classified government document, now known as the Pentagon Papers, that provided a history of U.S. involvement in the war. After he finished, Gravel introduced the forty-seven-volume document into the committee's record and later arranged for its publication by Beacon Press, a publishing division of the Unitarian Universalist Association.

The Justice Department began an investigation to determine how the classified Pentagon Papers were released. It requested a district court judge to convene a grand jury, which in turn subpoenaed, among others, Senator Gravel's aide, Dr. Leonard Rodberg. Gravel and Rodberg asked the court to quash the subpoena, claiming protection under the speech or debate clause.

When the case reached the Supreme Court, Gravel presented the justices with the two classic questions: Who is covered, and what is covered under the speech or debate clause? The government argued that the clause applied to Senator Gravel but not to his aide. Gravel countered with the argument that the job of a contemporary

legislator demanded a more expanded view of protection if the spirit and goals of the speech or debate clause were to be realized. In effect, forcing Rodberg to testify would be tantamount to requiring Gravel to do so.

As for who was protected, Justice Byron R. White, writing for the majority, held that the clause gave similar protection to both the senator and his aide. For

> it is literally impossible, in view of the complexities of the modern legislative process, . . . for Members of Congress to perform their legislative tasks without the help of aides and assistants; the day-to-day work of such aides is so critical to the Members' performance that they must be treated as the latter's alter egos; and that if they are not so recognized, the central role of the Speech or Debate Clause—to prevent intimidation of legislators by the Executive and accountability before a possibly hostile judiciary—will inevitably be diminished and frustrated.

At the same time, however, White asserted that speech or debate clause protection was not absolute. Both the senator and the aide could be questioned for activities that had no direct connection to or "impinged upon" the legislative process. Because "private publication by Senator Gravel through the cooperation of Beacon Press was in no way essential to the deliberations of the Senate," the speech or debate clause did not provide Rodberg with immunity from testifying before the grand jury about the publishing arrangement between Gravel and Beacon Press "or about his own participation, if any, in the alleged transaction, so long as legislative acts of the Senator are not impugned."

Despite the specificity of the Court's ruling in *Gravel*, it did not put an end to controversies under the speech or debate clause. Indeed, as illustrated in Table 4-2, in the 1970s the Court decided several important issues that were left open by *Gravel*. For the most part, these decisions supported congressional immunity. In *United States v. Helstoski* (1979) the justices refused to allow prosecutors to introduce evidence into a court proceeding against a former member of Congress involving legislative activities. *Hutchinson v. Proxmire* (1979), however, was a defeat for congressional authority. Here the Court examined a dispute arising when Senator William Proxmire, D-Wis., on the floor of the Senate and later in a newsletter and on television, labeled Ronald R. Hutchinson's federally funded research virtually worthless and a waste of taxpayers' money. Hutchinson brought a libel suit against Proxmire. When the case reached the Court, the justices addressed the issue of whether the speech or debate clause immunized the senator from a libel proceeding on the ground that he had first made the remarks on the chamber's floor. The Court held that it did not:

> A speech by Proxmire in the Senate would be wholly immune and would be available to other Members of Congress and the public in the Congressional Record. But neither the newsletters nor the press release was "essential to the deliberations of the Senate," and neither was part of the deliberative process.

Since *Proxmire*, speech or debate clause cases have not occupied much of the justices' attention, though exceptions occasionally arise. In 2008 the Justice Department asked the Court to review a decision by the U.S. Court of Appeals for the District of Columbia, holding that the speech or debate clause gave members of Congress some protection against searches—with warrants—of their congressional offices. The Justice Department was investigating Representative William Jefferson, D-La., for allegedly taking bribes and claimed that the D.C. court's ruling would impede its ability to enforce federal law against Jefferson and other lawmakers. The Supreme Court declined to hear the case, *United States v. Rayburn House Office Building, Room 2113*.

THE SOURCES AND SCOPE OF LEGISLATIVE POWERS

Section 8 of Article I contains a virtual laundry list of Congress's powers. These enumerated powers, covered in seventeen clauses, establish congressional authority to regulate commerce, to lay and collect taxes, to establish post offices, and so forth.

The enumerated powers qua powers pose few constitutional problems: because the Constitution names them, Congress clearly possesses them. It is when Congress exercises these powers that questions can emerge. Some questions hinge on how to define the power—for example, Congress has the power to "regulate commerce among the states," but what does "commerce" mean? Other questions focus on whether congressional use of an enumerated power violates other constitutional provisions—say, the First Amendment or, more relevant to this volume, structures underlying the

Constitution, such as the separation of powers system or federalism.

But what of other sources of legislative authority? For example, does the legislative branch have powers beyond those explicitly specified in the Constitution? Even though the framers may have left this question unaddressed, the Court has answered it affirmatively. As Table 4-3 shows, the Court has suggested that Congress possesses implied and inherent powers in addition to those explicitly mentioned in Article I. The Court has also acknowledged that Congress has the power to enforce certain constitutional amendments, but this power stems from language in the Constitution—though in specific amendments, not in Article I, Section 8. For example, the Thirteenth Amendment, which outlaws slavery, says that "Congress shall have power to enforce this article by appropriate legislation."

In this section, we examine the cases in which the Court has delineated and interpreted these powers. We also explore constraints on Congress's ability to exercise these powers. For example, the Court has permitted Congress to conduct hearings and investigations (an unenumerated power), but it also has asserted that the power is not unlimited, that certain restrictions apply.

As you read the next cases, keep in mind not only the sources of legislative power but also its scope. What limits has the Court placed on Congress and, more important, why? What pressures have been brought to bear on the justices in making their decisions?

Enumerated and Implied Powers

The Constitution's specific list of congressional powers leaves no doubt that Congress has these powers. Where debate has occurred is over the question of whether Congress has more powers, or was intended to have more powers, than those specifically granted. And if so, how broad should they be? Those who look to the plain language of the Constitution or to the intent of the framers would find few concrete answers, although both camps would point to the same clause. Article I, Section 8, Clause 18, provides that Congress shall have the power

> to make all Laws which shall be necessary and proper for carrying into Execution the foregoing Powers, and all other Powers vested by this Constitution in the Government of the United States, or in any Department or Officer thereof.

Called by various names—the necessary and proper clause, the elastic clause, the sweeping clause—this

Table 4-2   Speech or Debate Clause Cases after *Gravel v. United States*

Case	Legal Question	Court's Response
United States v. Brewster (1972)	Whether the speech or debate clause protect members of Congress from prosecution for alleged bribery to perform a legislative act?	The clause protects members from inquiry into legislative acts; it does not protect all conduct relating to the legislative process.
Doe v. McMillan (1973)	Whether the speech or debate clause protects members (and their staff) and other persons who were involved in creating and distributing a report on the D.C. school system that identified, by name, specific children and did so in a negative way?	The clause offers absolute immunity to members and staff but not to individuals who, acting under congressional authority, distributed the materials.
Eastland v. U.S. Servicemen's Fund (1975)	Whether the speech or debate clause protects members against a suit brought by an organization to stop the implementation of a subpoena ordering a bank to produce certain records?	The clause offers absolute protection because the activities fall within the "legitimate legislative" sphere.
Davis v. Passman (1979)	Whether the speech or debate clause protects a member against charges of sex discrimination?	The Court decided the case on Fifth Amendment grounds and reached no result on the member's claim that he was protected by the speech or debate clause.
United States v. Helstoski (1979)	Whether the speech or debate clause protects a member against prosecution (for accepting bribes) when evidence introduced in that action hinges on past legislative acts?	The clause does not permit the introduction of evidence involving past legislative acts.
Hutchinson v. Proxmire (1979)	Whether the speech or debate clause protects a member from a civil suit in response to negative statements made to the press and in newsletters about a government grant awardee's research?	The clause does not protect a member from a libel judgment when information is disseminated to the press and the public through newsletters.

provision was the subject of heated debate early in the nation's history. Many affiliated with the Federalist Party, which favored a strong national government, argued for a loose construction of the clause. In their view, the framers inserted it into the Constitution to provide Congress with some "flexibility"; in other words, Congress could exercise powers beyond those listed in the Constitution, those that were "necessary and proper" for implementing legislative activity. In contrast, the Jeffersonians asserted the need for a strict interpretation of the clause; in their view, it constricted rather than expanded congressional powers. In other words, Congress could exercise only those powers necessary to carry out its enumerated functions.

John Marshall and Implied Powers

Which view would the Supreme Court adopt? Would it interpret the necessary and proper clause strictly or loosely? This was one of two major questions at the core of *McCulloch v. Maryland* (1819),[9] which many consider the Court's most important explication of congressional powers, as well as Chief Justice John Marshall's finest. As you read this case, consider not only the Court's holding but also the language and logic of *McCulloch*.

Why is it regarded as such a landmark decision?

_____

[9]The other question involved federalism (*see chapter 6*).

Table 4-3 Sources of Congressional Power

Power[a]	Defined	Illustration
Enumerated powers	Those that the Constitution expressly grants	Article I, Section 8. Includes the powers to borrow money, raise armies, and regulate commerce among the states.
Implied powers	Those that may be inferred from power expressly granted	Article I, Section 8, Clauses 2–17, in conjunction with Clause 18, the necessary and proper clause. For example, the enumerated power of raising and supporting armies leads to the implied power of operating a draft.
Inherent powers	Those that do not depend on constitutional grants but grow out of national sovereignty	Foreign affairs. The national government would have foreign affairs powers even if the Constitution were silent, because these are powers that all nations have under international law. For example, the federal government can issue orders prohibiting U.S. businesses from selling arms to particular nations.
Amendment-enforcing powers	Those contained in some constitutional amendments that provide Congress with the ability to enforce them	Amendments 13, 14, and 15, for example, state that Congress shall have the power to enforce the article by "appropriate legislation."

Source: Adapted from Sue Davis and J. W. Peltason, *Corwin and Peltason's Understanding the Constitution,* 16th ed. (Belmont, CA: Wadsworth, 2004), 126.

[a]Some analysts suggest that Congress also possesses resulting powers (those that result when several enumerated powers are added together) and inherited powers (those that Congress inherited from the British Parliament, such as the power to investigate).

McCulloch v. Maryland

17 U.S. (4 Wheat.) 316 (1819)

http://caselaw.findlaw.com/us-supreme-court/17/316.html

Vote: 6 (Duvall, Johnson, Livingston, Marshall, Story, Washington)

0

OPINION OF THE COURT: *Marshall*

NOT PARTICIPATING: *Todd*

Although Americans take for granted the power of the federal government to operate a banking system—today called the Federal Reserve System—in the late eighteenth and early nineteenth centuries this topic was a political battleground. The first sign of controversy appeared in 1791 when George Washington's secretary of the Treasury, Alexander Hamilton, asked Congress to adopt a comprehensive economic plan for the new nation. Among the proposals was the creation of a Bank of the United States, which would receive deposits, disburse funds, and make loans; Congress responded with a bill authorizing the first federal bank.

When the bill arrived at President Washington's desk, however, he did not sign it immediately. He wanted to ascertain whether in fact Congress could create a bank, because it lacked explicit constitutional authority to do so. To this end he asked Hamilton, Secretary of State Thomas Jefferson, and Attorney General Edmund Randolph for their opinions on the bank's constitutionality.

Box 4-2 presents excerpts of Hamilton's and Jefferson's responses. We offer them not only because the two men reached different conclusions—Hamilton argued that the bank was constitutional, Jefferson that it was not—but also because the arguments represent the classic competing theories of congressional power. As historian Melvin I. Urofsky puts it, "Where Jefferson . . . argued that Congress could only do what the Constitution expressly permitted it do, Hamilton claims that Congress could do everything except what the Constitution specifically forbade."[10] The debates may also suggest the limits of originalism as a method of constitutional interpretation. Does it seem odd that just four years after the writing of the Constitution, two of the nation's foremost leaders could hold such different views? In his argument, Hamilton, in fact, noted that there was a "conflicting recollection" of a convention debate highly

---

[10]Melvin I. Urofsky, *Supreme Decisions: Great Constitutional Cases and Their Impact* (Boulder, CO: Westview Press, 2012), 19.

BOX 4-2

Jefferson and Hamilton on the Bank of the United States

Opinion on the Constitutionality of a National Bank (1791)

Thomas Jefferson

To take a single step beyond the boundaries . . . specially drawn around the powers of Congress, is to take possession of a boundless field of power, no longer susceptible of any definition.

The incorporation of a bank, and other powers assumed by this bill have not, in my opinion, been delegated to the U.S. by the Constitution.

I. They are not among the powers specially enumerated, for these are

1. A power to lay taxes for the purpose of paying the debts of the U.S. But no debt is paid by this bill, nor any tax laid. . . .

2. "to borrow money." But this bill neither borrows money, nor ensures the borrowing of it. . . .

3. "to regulate commerce with foreign nations, and among the states, and with the Indian tribes." To erect a bank, and to regulate commerce, are very different acts. . . ."

II. Nor are they within either of the general phrases, which are the two following.

1. "To lay taxes to provide for the general welfare of the U.S." that is to say "to lay taxes for the purpose of providing for the general welfare." For the laying of taxes is the power and the general welfare the purpose for which the power is to be exercised. They are not to lay taxes . . . for any purpose they please; but only to pay the debts or provide for the welfare of the Union. In like manner they are not to do anything they please to provide for the general welfare, but only to lay taxes for that purpose. . . .

2. The second general phrase is "to make all laws necessary and proper for carrying into execution the enumerated powers."

But they can all be carried into execution without a bank. A bank therefore is not necessary, and consequently not authorised by this phrase.

It has been much urged that a bank will give great facility, or convenience in the collection of taxes. Suppose this were true: yet the constitution allows only the means which are "necessary" not those which are merely "convenient" for effecting the enumerated powers. If such a latitude of construction be allowed to this phrase as to give any non-enumerated power, it will go to every one, for there is no one which ingenuity may not torture into a convenience, in some way or other, to some one of so long a list of enumerated powers. It would swallow up all the delegated powers, and reduce the whole to one phrase as before observed. Therefore it was that the constitution restrained them to the necessary means, that is to say, to those means without which the grant of the power would be nugatory.

Opinion as to the Constitutionality of the Bank of the United States (1791)

Alexander Hamilton

[It seems to me] [t]hat every power vested in a government is in its nature sovereign, and includes, by force of the term, a right to employ all the means requisite and fairly applicable to the attainment of the ends of such power, and which are not precluded by restrictions and exceptions specified in the Constitution, or not immoral, or not contrary to the essential ends of political society. . . .

This general and indisputable principle puts at once an end to the abstract question, whether the United States have power to erect a corporation. . . . [I]t is unquestionably incident to sovereign power to erect corporations, and consequently to that of the United States, in relation to the objects intrusted to the management of the government. . . .

It is not denied that there are implied [as] well as express powers, and that the . . . implied powers are to be considered as delegated equally with express ones. Then it follows, that as a power of erecting a corporation may as well be implied as any other thing, it may as well be employed as an instrument or mean of carrying into execution any of the specified powers, as any other instrument or mean whatever. The only question must be . . . whether the mean to be employed or in this instance, the corporation to be erected, has a natural relation to any of the acknowledged objects or lawful ends of the government. Thus a corporation may not be erected by Congress for superintending the police of the city of Philadelphia, because they are not authorized to regulate the police of that city. But one may be erected in relation to the collection of taxes, or to the trade with foreign countries, or to the trade between the States, or with the Indian tribes; because it is the province of the federal government to regulate those objects, and because it is incident to a general sovereign or legislative power to regulate a thing, to employ all the means which relate to its regulation to the best and greatest advantage. . . .

To this mode of reasoning respecting the right of employing all the means requisite to the execution of the specified powers of the government, it is objected, that none but necessary and proper means are to be employed; and the Secretary of State maintains, that no means are to be considered as necessary but those without which the grant of the power would be nugatory. . . .

It is essential to the being of the national government, that so erroneous a conception of the meaning of the word necessary should be exploded. Necessary often means no more than needful, requisite, incidental, useful, or conducive to. It is a common mode of expression to say, that it is necessary for a government or a person to do this or that thing, when nothing more is intended or understood, than that the interests of the government or person require, or will be promoted by, the doing of this or that thing.

The imagination can be at no loss for exemplifications of the use of the word in this sense. And it is the true one in which it is to be understood as used in the Constitution. The whole turn of the clause containing it indicates, that it was the intent of the Convention, by that clause, to give a liberal latitude to the exercise of the specified powers. The expressions have peculiar comprehensiveness. They are thought to make all laws necessary and proper for carrying into execution the foregoing powers. . . .

To understand the word as the Secretary of State does, would be to depart from its obvious and popular sense, and to give it a restrictive operation, an idea never before entertained. It would be to give it the same force as if the word absolutely or indispensably had been prefixed to it.

Such a construction would beget endless uncertainty and embarrassment. The cases must be palpable and extreme, in which it could be pronounced, with certainty, that a measure was absolutely necessary, or one, without which, the exercise of a given power would be nugatory. There are few measures of any government which would stand so severe a test. . . .

The only question is, whether [the government] has a right to [create the bank], in order to enable it the more effectually to accomplish ends which are in themselves lawful.

[A bank relates] to the power of collecting taxes, to that of borrowing money, to that of regulating trade between the States, and to those of raising and maintaining fleets and armies. To the two former the relation may be said to be immediate; . . . and that it is clearly within the provision which authorizes the making of all needful rules and regulations.

Source: Yale Law School, The Avalon Project, http://avalon.law.yale.edu/18th_century/bank-ah.asp.

relevant to the bank issue.[11] In the end, Hamilton persuaded the president to sign the bill. Congress then created the First Bank of the United States in 1791 and granted it a twenty-year charter.

Nevertheless, the bank controversy did not disappear. Among other factors, the bank became a symbol of the loose-construction, nationally oriented Federalist Party, which had lost considerable power from its heyday in the 1790s. Indeed, at the close of the eighteenth century, a strict-construction approach to congressional power was among the primary ideas endorsed by the Federalists' competitors, the Jeffersonian Republicans. Even though the bank had done an able job, to no one's surprise the Republican Congress refused to renew its charter in 1811.

After the War of 1812, it became apparent even to the Republicans that Congress should recharter the bank. During the war the lack of a national bank for purposes of borrowing money and transferring funds became a source of embarrassment to the administration. Moreover, with the absence of a federal bank, state-chartered institutions flooded the market with worthless notes, contributing to

---

[11]One scholar notes that the framers rejected a proposal that would have allowed Congress to establish corporations in part because of the possibility that Congress would create banks. See Jethro K. Lieberman, *Milestones!* (St. Paul, MN: West, 1976), 19. Still, Hamilton argued that the debate was unclear.

economic problems throughout the country. Amid renewed controversy and cries for strict constructionism, Congress in 1816 created the Second Bank of the United States, granting it a twenty-year charter and $35 million in capital (about $603 million today).

Some scholars have suggested that a challenge to the new bank was inevitable, primarily because the Supreme Court had never decided whether the first bank was constitutional. It is possible, however, that litigation would not have materialized had the second bank performed as well as its predecessor did, but it did not. It flourished during the postwar economic boom, mainly because it was fiscally aggressive and encouraged speculative investing. These practices caught up to bank officials when, in 1818, in anticipation of a recession, they began calling in the bank's outstanding loans. As a result, they caused overextended banks to fail throughout the South and West. To make matters worse, accusations of fraud and embezzlement were rampant in several of the bank's eighteen branches, particularly in Maryland, Pennsylvania, and Virginia. Among those most seriously implicated was James McCulloch, the cashier of the Baltimore branch bank and its main lobbyist in Washington. According to some accounts, his illegal financial schemes had cost the branch more than $1 million.

In response to these allegations, Congress began to hold hearings on the bank, and some states reacted by attempting to regulate branches located within their borders. Maryland mandated that branches of the bank in the state pay either a 2 percent tax on all banknotes or a fee of $15,000. When a state official came to collect from the Baltimore branch, McCulloch refused to pay and, by refusing, set the stage for a monumental confrontation between the United States and Maryland on not one but two major issues. The first involved the bank itself: whether Congress, in the absence of an explicit constitutional authorization, has the power to charter the bank (the subject of the excerpt below). The second question—whether the state exceeded its powers by seeking to tax a federal entity—we take up in chapter 6 (Federalism).

By the time the case reached the Supreme Court, it was clear that something significant was going to happen. The Court reporter noted that *McCulloch* involved "a constitutional question of great importance." The justices waived their rule that permitted only two attorneys per side "and allowed three each."[12] Oral arguments took nine days.

Both sides were ably represented. Some commentators praise Daniel Webster's oratory for the federal government's side as extraordinary. But it was former attorney general and U.S. Senator William Pinkney with whom the Court was most taken. Justice Joseph Story said later, "I never, in my whole life, heard a greater speech."[13] Even so, the gist of his arguments (and those of his colleagues) was familiar stuff: Pinkney largely reiterated Hamilton's original defense of the bank, particularly his interpretation of the necessary and proper clause.

Maryland's legal representation may have appeared less astute. According to one account, "[I]t has been rumored" that one of the state's lawyers, Attorney General Luther Martin, "was drunk when he made his two-day-long argument. If he was, it apparently did not affect his acuity." For his side, he reiterated parts of Jefferson's argument against the bank, added arguments on states' rights, and read some of the speeches John Marshall had delivered at the Virginia convention.[14] Another attorney for the state, Joseph Hopkinson, took a somewhat different tack. He claimed that the bank might have been useful when it was first created but that it is no longer necessary what with the existence of many other financial institutions.

CHIEF JUSTICE MARSHALL DELIVERED THE OPINION OF THE COURT.

The constitution of our country, in its most interesting and vital parts, is to be considered; the conflicting powers of the government of the Union and of its members, as marked in that constitution, are to be discussed; and an opinion given, which may essentially influence the great operations of the government. No tribunal can approach such a question without a deep sense of its importance, and of the awful responsibility involved in its decision. But it must be decided peacefully, or remain a source of hostile legislation, perhaps of hostility of a still more serious nature; and if it is to be so decided, by this tribunal alone can the decision be made. On the Supreme Court of the United States has the constitution of our country devolved this important duty.

The first question . . . is, has Congress power to incorporate a bank? . . .

This government is acknowledged by all to be one of enumerated powers. The principle, that it can exercise only the powers granted to it, would seem too apparent to have required to be enforced by all those arguments which its enlightened friends, while it was depending before the people, found it necessary to urge. That principle is now universally admitted. But the question respecting the extent of the powers actually granted, is perpetually arising, and will probably continue to arise, as long as our system shall exist. . . .

Among the enumerated powers, we do not find that of establishing a bank or creating a corporation. But there is no phrase in the instrument which, like the articles of confederation, excludes incidental or implied powers; and which requires that everything granted shall be expressly and minutely described. Even the

[12]Quoted in Fred W. Friendly and Martha J. H. Elliot, *The Constitution: That Delicate Balance* (New York: Random House, 1984), 256.

[13]Quoted in Lieberman, *Milestones!*, 122.

[14]Farber and Sherry, *A History of the American Constitution*, 357.

10th amendment, which was framed for the purpose of quieting the excessive jealousies which had been excited, omits the word "expressly," and declares only that the powers "not delegated to the United States, nor prohibited to the states, are reserved to the states or to the people;" thus leaving the question, whether the particular power which may become the subject of contest has been delegated to the one government, or prohibited to the other, to depend on a fair construction of the whole instrument. . . . A constitution, to contain an accurate detail of all the subdivisions of which its great powers will admit, and of all the means by which they may be carried into execution, would partake of a prolixity of a legal code, and could scarcely be embraced by the human mind. It would probably never be understood by the public. Its nature, therefore, requires, that only its great outlines should be marked, its important objects designated, and the minor ingredients which compose those objects be deduced from the nature of the objects themselves. That this idea was entertained by the framers of the American constitution, is not only to be inferred from the nature of the instrument, but from the language. Why else were some of the limitations, found in the ninth section of the 1st article, introduced? It is also, in some degree, warranted by their having omitted to use any restrictive term which might prevent its receiving a fair and just interpretation. In considering this question, then, we must never forget that it is a constitution we are expounding.

Although, among the enumerated powers of government, we do not find the word "bank" or "incorporation," we find the great powers to lay and collect taxes; to borrow money; to regulate commerce; to declare and conduct a war; and to raise and support armies and navies. The sword and the purse, all the external relations, and no inconsiderable portion of the industry of the nation, are entrusted to its government. It can never be pretended that these vast powers draw after them others of inferior importance, merely because they are inferior. Such an idea can never be advanced. But it may with great reason be contended, that a government, entrusted with such ample powers, on the due execution of which the happiness and prosperity of the nation so vitally depends, must also be entrusted with ample means for their execution. The power being given, it is the interest of the nation to facilitate its execution. It can never be their interest, and cannot be presumed to have been their intention, to clog and embarrass its execution, by withholding the most appropriate means.

Throughout this vast republic, from the St. Croix to the Gulf of Mexico, from the Atlantic to the Pacific, revenue is to be collected and expended, armies are to be marched and supported. The exigencies of the nation may require, that the treasure raised in the north should be transported to the south, that raised in the east, conveyed to the west, or that this order should be reversed. Is that construction of the constitution to be preferred, which would render these operations difficult, hazardous and expensive? Can we adopt that construction (unless the words imperiously require it), which would impute to the framers of that instrument, when granting these powers for the public good, the intention of impeding their exercise, by withholding a choice of means?

It is not denied, that the powers given to the government imply the ordinary means of execution. That, for example, of raising revenue, and applying it to national purposes, is admitted to imply the power of conveying money from place to place, as the exigencies of the nation may require, and of employing the usual means of conveyance. But it is denied, that the government has its choice of means; or, that it may employ the most convenient means, if, to employ them, it be necessary to erect a corporation. On what foundation does this argument rest? On this alone: the power of creating a corporation, is one appertaining to sovereignty, and is not expressly conferred on congress. This is true. But all legislative powers appertain to sovereignty.

The creation of a corporation, it is said, appertains to sovereignty. This is admitted. . . . The power of creating a corporation, though appertaining to sovereignty, is not, like the power of making war or levying taxes or of regulating commerce, a great substantive and independent power which cannot be implied as incidental to other powers or used as a means of executing them. It is never the end for which other powers are exercised, but a means by which other objects are accomplished. . . . The power of creating a corporation is never used for its own sake, but for the purpose of effecting something else. No sufficient reason is therefore perceived why it may not pass as incidental to those powers which are expressly given if it be a direct mode of executing them.

But the constitution of the United States has not left the right of Congress to employ the necessary means for the execution of the powers conferred on the government to general reasoning. To its enumeration of powers is added that of making "all laws which shall be necessary and proper, for carrying into execution the foregoing powers, and all other powers vested by this constitution, in the government of the United States, or in any department thereof."

The counsel for the State of Maryland have urged various arguments, to prove that this clause, though in terms a grant of power, is not so in effect; but is really restrictive of the general right, which might otherwise be implied, of selecting means for executing the enumerated powers. . . .

The word "necessary" is considered as controlling the whole sentence, and as limiting the right to pass laws for the execution of the granted powers, to such as are indispensable, and without which the power would be nugatory. That it excludes the choice of means, and leaves to Congress, in each case, that only which is most direct and simple.

Is it true that this is the sense in which the word "necessary" is always used? Does it always import an absolute physical necessity, so strong that one thing, to which another may be termed necessary, cannot exist without that other? We think it does not. If reference be had to its use, in the common affairs of the world, or in approved authors, we find that it frequently imports no more than that one thing is convenient, or useful, or essential to another. To employ the means necessary to an end, is generally understood as employing any means calculated to produce the end, and not as being confined to those single means, without which the end would be entirely unattainable. . . . Almost all compositions contain words which, taken in their rigorous sense, would convey a meaning different from that which is obviously intended. It is essential to just construction that many words which import something excessive should be understood in a more mitigated sense—in that sense which common usage justifies. The word "necessary" is of this description. It has not a fixed character peculiar to itself. It admits of all degrees of comparison, and is often connected with other words which increase or diminish the impression the mind receives of the urgency it imports. A thing may be necessary, very necessary, absolutely or indispensably necessary. To no mind would the same idea be conveyed by these several phrases. The comment on the word is well illustrated by the passage cited at the bar from the 10th section of the 1st article of the Constitution. It is, we think, impossible to compare the sentence which prohibits a State from laying "imposts, or duties on imports or exports, except what may be absolutely necessary for executing its inspection laws," with that which authorizes Congress "to make all laws which shall be necessary and proper for carrying into execution" the powers of the General Government without feeling a conviction that the convention understood itself to change materially the meaning of the word "necessary," by prefixing the word "absolutely." This word, then, like others, is used in various senses, and, in its construction, the subject, the context, the intention of the person using them are all to be taken into view.

Let this be done in the case under consideration. The subject is the execution of those great powers on which the welfare of a nation essentially depends. It must have been the intention of those who gave these powers, to insure, as far as human prudence could insure, their beneficial execution. This could not be done by confiding the choice of means to such narrow limits as not to leave it in the power of Congress to adopt any which might be appropriate, and which were conducive to the end. This provision is made in a constitution intended to endure for ages to come, and, consequently, to be adapted to the various crises of human affairs. To have prescribed the means by which government should, in all future time, execute its powers, would have been to change, entirely, the character of the instrument, and give it the properties of a legal code. It would have been an unwise attempt to provide, by immutable rules, for exigencies which, if foreseen at all, must have been seen dimly, and which can be best provided for as they occur. To have declared that the best means shall not be used, but those alone without which the power given would be nugatory, would have been to deprive the legislature of the capacity to avail itself of experience, to exercise its reason, and to accommodate its

legislation to circumstances. If we apply this principle of construction to any of the powers of the government, we shall find it so pernicious in its operation that we shall be compelled to discard it . . .

So, with respect to the whole penal code of the United States: whence arises the power to punish, in cases not prescribed by the constitution? All admit, that the government may, legitimately, punish any violation of its laws; and yet, this is not among the enumerated powers of congress. . . .

Take, for example, the power 'to establish post-offices and post-roads.' This power is executed, by the single act of making the establishment. But, from this has been inferred the power and duty of carrying the mail along the post-road, from one post-office to another. And from this implied power, has again been inferred the right to punish those who steal letters from the post-office, or rob the mail. It may be said, with some plausibility, that the right to carry the mail, and to punish those who rob it, is not indispensably necessary to the establishment of a post-office and post-road. This right is indeed essential to the beneficial exercise of the power, but not indispensably necessary to its existence. . . .

The baneful influence of this narrow construction on all the operations of the government, and the absolute impracticability of maintaining it without rendering the government incompetent to its great objects, might be illustrated by numerous examples drawn from the constitution, and from our laws. . . .

In ascertaining the sense in which the word "necessary" is used in this clause of the constitution, we may derive some aid from that with which it is associated. Congress shall have power "to make all laws which shall be necessary and proper to carry into execution" the powers of the government. If the word "necessary" was used in that strict and rigorous sense for which the counsel for the State of Maryland contend, it would be an extraordinary departure from the usual course of the human mind, as exhibited in composition, to add a word, the only possible effect of which is to qualify that strict and rigorous meaning; to present to the mind the idea of some choice of means of legislation not straightened and compressed within the narrow limits for which gentlemen contend. . . .

We admit, as all must admit, that the powers of the government are limited, and that its limits are not to be transcended. But we think the sound construction of the constitution must allow to the national legislature that discretion, with respect to the means by which the powers it confers are to be carried into execution, which will enable that body to perform the high duties assigned to it, in the manner most beneficial to the people. Let the end be legitimate, let it be within the scope of the constitution, and all means which are appropriate, which are plainly adapted to that end, which are not prohibited, but consist with the letter and spirit of the constitution, are constitutional.

That a corporation must be considered as a means not less usual, not of higher dignity, not more requiring a particular specification than other means, has been sufficiently proved. . . .

If a corporation may be employed indiscriminately with other means to carry into execution the powers of the government, no particular reason can be assigned for excluding the use of a bank, if required for its fiscal operations. To use one, must be within the discretion of Congress, if it be an appropriate mode of executing the powers of government. That it is a convenient, a useful, and essential instrument in the prosecution of its fiscal operations, is not now a subject of controversy. All those who have been concerned in the administration of our finances, have concurred in representing the importance and necessity; and so strongly have they been felt, that statesmen of the first class, whose previous opinions against it had been confirmed by every circumstance which can fix the human judgment, have yielded those opinions to the exigencies of the nation. Under the confederation, Congress, justifying the measure by its necessity, transcended perhaps its powers to obtain the advantage of a bank; and our own legislation attests the universal conviction of the utility of this measure. The time has passed away when it can be necessary to enter into any discussion in order to prove the importance of this instrument, as a means to effect the legitimate objects of the government.

But, were its necessity less apparent, none can deny its being an appropriate measure; and if it is, the degree of its necessity, as has been very justly observed, is to be discussed in another place. Should Congress, in the execution of its powers, adopt measures which are prohibited by the constitution; or should Congress, under the pretext of executing its powers, pass laws for the accomplishment of objects not entrusted to the government, it would become the painful duty of this tribunal, should a case requiring such a decision come before it, to say that such an act was not the law of the land. But where the law is not prohibited, and is really calculated to effect any of the objects entrusted to the government, to undertake here to inquire into the degree of its necessity, would be to pass the line which circumscribes the judicial department, and to tread on legislative ground. This court disclaims all pretensions to such a power. . . .

After the most deliberate consideration, it is the unanimous and decided opinion of this court that the act to incorporate the bank of the United States is a law made in pursuance of the constitution, and is a part of the supreme law of the land.

As we can see, Marshall adopted Hamilton's reasoning and the government's claims about the proper interpretation of the necessary and proper clause: "necessary" does not mean absolutely necessary or essential, as Jefferson argued, but rather convenient or useful, as Hamilton believed. Some even believed Marshall's opinion was a virtual transcript of the oral arguments presented by the federal attorneys. Given that Marshall issued *McCulloch* just three days after the case had been presented, it is more likely, as others suspect, that he had written the opinion the previous summer.

How did the public respond? Despite the Court's opinion upholding the bank, sentiment was decidedly against the cashier, James McCulloch (*see Box 4-3*). As for Marshall's opinion? Immediate reaction was interesting in that it focused less on the portion of the opinion we have dealt with here—congressional powers—and more on the federalism dimension, which we take up in chapter 6. Nevertheless, the long-term effect of Marshall's interpretation of the necessary and proper clause has been significant: Congress now exercises many powers not named in the Constitution but implied by it. In this way *McCulloch* is a landmark decision and one that might very well have accomplished Marshall's stated objective: to allow the Constitution "to endure for ages to come."

Before turning to one of those powers—the power to investigate—it is worth considering how contemporary justices interpret Marshall's version of congressional authority under the necessary and proper clause. First, virtually all justices continue the Hamilton–Marshall tradition of defining "necessary" not as *absolutely* necessary but as convenient, useful, or beneficial to the exercise of congressional authority.

Second, the Court is usually deferential to congressional determination that a law is "necessary." But it also has acknowledged that Congress's power is not unlimited, just as Marshall did. Recall the Chief's words:

> Let the end be legitimate, let it be within the scope of the constitution, and all means which are appropriate, which are plainly adapted to that end, which are not prohibited, but consist with the letter and spirit of the constitution, are constitutional.

The Court continues to use this means–ends approach but in a more specific form than Marshall put it. In recent cases the justices have asked "whether the law constitutes a means that is rationally related [or reasonably adapted] to the implementation of a constitutionally enumerated power." **United States v. Comstock** (2010) provides an example.

At issue in *Comstock* was a law allowing a federal court, on the recommendation of the government, to order the civil commitment of a mentally ill, sexually dangerous, federal prisoner beyond the date he would otherwise be released. Writing for a 7–2 Court, Justice Stephen Breyer acknowledged that beyond

BOX 4-3

Aftermath . . . James McCulloch and the Second National Bank

John Marshall's opinion for a unanimous Court in *McCulloch v. Maryland* (1819) resolved the constitutional questions surrounding the Second Bank of the United States. The decision, however, did not diminish the strong public sentiment against Baltimore branch cashier James McCulloch (also known as M'Culloch or McCulloh), who had been accused of engaging with others in corruption and unchecked financial speculation. Negative newspaper articles and a congressional investigation into the affairs of the national bank led to claims that large amounts of money were unaccounted for or mishandled. On March 6, 1819, the same day the Court handed down the *McCulloch* decision, Langdon Cheves was installed as the new president of the national bank. Two months later Cheves relieved McCulloch of his duties, claiming that the Baltimore branch cashier had defrauded the bank of $1,671,221.87.

In July 1819 McCulloch, former branch president James Buchanan, and Baltimore businessman George Williams were indicted for conspiracy to defraud the bank of an amount exceeding $1.5 million. The indictment, instigated by Maryland attorney general Luther Martin, accused the defendants of "wickedly devising, contriving and intending, falsely, unlawfully, fraudulently, craftily and unjustly, and by indirect means, to cheat and impoverish" the bank. One observer at the time labeled the three "destroyers of widows and orphans." Among other schemes, the three accused men had operated a company that speculated in the bank's stock and were in a position to manipulate its value to their own advantage.

In April 1821 the trial court dismissed the charges on the ground that conspiracy to commit fraud was not a crime under common law or one specified by Maryland statute. Later that year, however, the Maryland Court of Appeals reversed, ordering a full trial on the charges. All along, the three defendants argued that they might have committed certain indiscretions but that the bank's losses were the result of bad economic times rather than any criminal acts. In March 1823, McCulloch and Buchanan were found not guilty and the charges against Williams were dismissed.

Following his acquittal, James McCulloch began rebuilding his life and reputation. In 1825 he was elected to the state legislature representing Baltimore County, and the next year his legislative colleagues selected him to be Speaker of the Maryland House of Delegates. He was also active as a lobbyist for the city and county of Baltimore as well as for the Chesapeake and Ohio Canal Company. Ironically, McCulloch even served a term as director of the Maryland Penitentiary. In 1842 the Senate confirmed President John Tyler's nomination of McCulloch to be the first comptroller of the United States Treasury, a post he held for seven years. McCulloch died in 1861.

The Second Bank of the United States continued to do business after the *McCulloch* decision. In 1832 President Andrew Jackson, a fierce opponent of the bank, vetoed a congressional act extending the bank's charter. When its charter expired in 1836, the bank became a private institution under the laws of Pennsylvania. But it did not prosper. In 1839 it temporarily suspended payment on its obligations and then unsuccessfully fought a two-year battle for survival. Its assets were liquidated in 1841. From 1836 until 1913, when the Federal Reserve System was created, the United States operated without an effective central bank.

Sources: Bray Hammond, "Jackson, Biddle, and the Bank of the United States," *Journal of Economic History* 7 (May 1947): 1–23; Mark R. Killenbeck, *M'Culloch v. Maryland: Securing a Nation* (Lawrence: University Press of Kansas, 2006); Melvin I. Urofsky, *Supreme Decisions: Great Constitutional Cases and Their Impact* (Boulder, CO: Westview Press, 2012).

federal crimes relating to "counterfeiting," "treason," or "Piracies and Felonies committed on the high Seas" or "against the Law of Nations," the Constitution does not explicitly mention "Congress' power to criminalize conduct [or] its power to imprison individuals who engage in that conduct, nor its power to enact laws governing prisons and prisoners." Still, Breyer maintained, Congress has "broad authority to do each of those things in the course of 'carrying into Execution' the enumerated powers 'vested by' the 'Constitution in the Government of the United States,'—authority granted by the Necessary and Proper Clause." In other words, the law at issue is rationally related to congressional power "to help ensure the enforcement of federal criminal laws [which even the first Congress] enacted in furtherance of its enumerated powers."

Only Justice Clarence Thomas, joined by Justice Antonin Scalia, dissented in *Comstock*. To them the law, while accomplishing an important end—protecting society from violent sex offenders—does not seem to execute *any* enumerated power. It rather piles one implied power on another in a way that Marshall would not have approved. To Thomas and Scalia, *McCulloch* demands that any implied power must follow plainly from, and not simply be vaguely related to, an enumerated end. Under their interpretation,

> [F]ederal legislation is a valid exercise of Congress' authority under the [Necessary and Proper] Clause if it satisfies a two-part test: First, the law must be directed toward a "legitimate" end, which *McCulloch* defines as one "within the scope of the [C]onstitution"—that is, the powers expressly delegated to the Federal Government by some provision in the Constitution. Second, there must be a necessary and proper fit between the "means" (the federal law) and the "end" (the enumerated power or powers) it is designed to serve. *McCulloch* accords Congress a certain amount of discretion in assessing means-end fit under this second inquiry. The means Congress selects will be deemed "necessary" if they are "appropriate" and "plainly adapted" to the exercise of an enumerated power, and "proper" if they are not otherwise "prohibited" by the Constitution and not "[in]consistent" with its "letter and spirit."

Thomas did not believe that the law at issue in *Comstock* met this test. Because the federal government could identify "no specific enumerated power or powers as a constitutional predicate for [the law]," it was not "'necessary and proper for carrying into Execution' one or more of those federal powers actually enumerated in the Constitution."

In *Comstock* Chief Justice John G. Roberts was in the majority but, in *National Federation of Independent Business v. Sebelius* (2012), a case over the health care law ("Obamacare") passed in 2010, he seemed more sympathetic to limiting congressional power under the necessary and proper clause. We excerpt *National Federation of Independent Business* in chapters 7 and 8, so suffice it to note here that an important question in the case concerned the constitutionality of a provision in the law mandating that most people either buy health insurance or pay a penalty for not buying insurance. Among the government's arguments in defense of the provision was that it was "necessary," under the necessary and proper clause, because without it the government could not require insurance companies to cover people with preexisting conditions (a major goal of the health care law). People would wait until they were sick to obtain insurance, and, without healthy people contributing, the system would go bankrupt. Roberts understood that the mandate was probably necessary but he rejected the idea that it was "proper." Why not? One of his reasons[15]—and the one that has generated a good deal of legal commentary—takes us back to Marshall's opinion in *McCulloch*. Recall Marshall's words:

> The power of creating [the bank] is not, like the power of making war or levying taxes or of regulating commerce, a great substantive and independent power which cannot be implied as incidental to other powers or used as a means of executing them.

To Roberts, compelling people to buy insurance is, in fact, "a great substantive and independent power," not a power lesser than or incidental to an enumerated power. As a result, he concluded that the mandate was inconsistent with the "letter and spirit" of the Constitution, meaning it was not proper.

In so writing, Roberts did not overturn *Comstock*, which he continued to believe was warranted under the necessary and proper clause if only because the law was "narrow in scope" and pertained to those already in federal custody. On the other hand, he did not offer a specific rule to differentiate great and independent powers from lesser derivative powers. This caused Justice Ruth Bader Ginsburg to wonder, "How is a judge to decide, when ruling on the constitutionality of a federal statute, whether Congress employed an 'independent power' or merely a 'derivative' one. Whether the power used is 'substantive' or just 'incidental'? The instruction The

---

[15]As we will see in chapters 7 and 8, the government also argued that the individual mandate was a valid exercise of Congress's power to regulate commerce among the states and to tax. In making the necessary and proper clause argument, the government contended that the mandate was incident to the power to regulate commerce. Roberts rejected this argument on the ground that Congress was not regulating commercial activity; rather, it was compelling the uninsured to become active in a commercial market. And so, in addition to not being "proper," the mandate was not incident to the legitimate exercise of an enumerated power.

Chief Justice, in effect, provides lower courts: You will know it when you see it."

From the different approaches in *Comstock* and *National Federation of Independent Business*, you can probably tell that the necessary and proper clause jurisprudence is somewhat murky, with clarification sure to come in future cases. For now, consider whether the Thomas–Scalia and, possibly, Roberts approach squares with *McCulloch*. One way to think about this is to ask yourself whether Marshall would have upheld or struck the laws at issue in *Comstock* and *Sebelius*. You can return to this question also when we consider the health care case in more detail in the chapters to come.

Power to Investigate

Of all the implied powers that Congress asserts, the power to investigate merits close examination. Many think it is one of the major congressional powers. As Woodrow Wilson noted, "The informing function of Congress should be preferred even to its legislative function." Another president, Harry Truman, concurred: "The power of investigation is one of the most important powers of Congress. The manner in which that power is exercised will largely determine the position and prestige of the Congress in the future." In addition, the scope of congressional authority in this area has been the subject of some rather interesting, perhaps conflicting, and most definitely controversial Supreme Court opinions.

What has never been controversial, however, is that Congress has the ability to conduct investigations. After all, to legislate effectively, Congress must be able to gather information to determine whether new laws are necessary and, if so, how best to construct them. Although this is not an enumerated power, there is little question that legislatures can hold inquiries. We refer to it as an implied power; other analysts say that it is an inherent power that legislatures have by virtue of being legislatures. And still others call it an inherited power that the British Parliament willed to Congress. In any event, Congress took advantage of this power virtually from the beginning, holding its first investigation in 1792. In any event, Congress took advantage of this privilege virtually from the beginning, holding its first investigation in 1792. Since then no period in American history has been without congressional investigations.

If the power of Congress to investigate is so well entrenched, what is controversial about the practice? We can point to several areas of dispute. One is the scope of the power: Into what subjects may Congress inquire?

Courtesy of the Library of Congress, Prints & Photographs Division

Attorney General Harry M. Daugherty, whose brother Mally S. Daugherty refused to appear before the Senate to answer questions concerning the Teapot Dome scandal, in which both were implicated. In *McGrain v. Daugherty* the Court affirmed congressional power to investigate, even without an explicitly stated legislative purpose.

Another is subpoena power: May Congress summon witnesses and punish, by holding in contempt, those who do not cooperate with the investigating body? If so, what rights do witnesses have? In ***Kilbourn v. Thompson*** (1881), the justices attempted to provide some firm answers to these questions.

Kilbourn involved a House investigation into a private banking firm. An important witness, Hallett Kilbourn, refused to produce documents demanded by the inquiring committee. By a House order, he was held in contempt and jailed. When he was released, he sued various officials and representatives for false arrest. In his view, the investigation was not legitimate because, first, the House of Representatives "has no power whatever to punish for a contempt of its authority"; and second, the investigation concerned private, not public, matters. Kilbourn stated that he would resist "the naked, arbitrary power of the House to investigate private businesses in which nobody but me and my customers have concern."[16]

---

[16]Quoted in Congressional Quarterly, *Guide to Congress*, 5th ed. (Washington, DC: CQ Press, 2000), 252.

The House, in turn, claimed that power "undoubtedly exists, and when that body has formally exercised it, it must be presumed that it was rightfully exercised."[17]

On the one hand, the Supreme Court conceded that Congress can summon witnesses and punish for contempt, though this turned out to be not much of a concession. As early as 1795 Congress jailed for contempt a man who had tried to bribe a member of Congress, and the Supreme Court theoretically approved of the practice as early as 1821, in *Anderson v. Dunn*. These rulings seem to reflect the view that the power to call and punish witnesses can be implied from the inherent nature of legislative authority. Congress is, by definition, a lawmaking institution, and an inherent quality of such an institution is the power to investigate. To function, therefore, Congress must have the authority to summon witnesses and punish those who do not comply, and both chambers have always availed themselves of this authority.

On the other hand, the justices seemed to agree with Kilbourn's arguments about the limited scope of the investigatory power. In what some have called a rather narrow ruling on legislative powers, the justices said that Congress could punish witnesses only if the inquiry itself was within the "legitimate cognizance" of the institution. Inquiries (1) must not "invade areas constitutionally reserved to the courts or the executive," (2) must deal "with subjects on which Congress could validly legislate," and (3) must suggest, in the resolutions authorizing the investigation, a "congressional interest in legislating on that subject."[18]

Under these limitations, Congress could hold inquiries only into subjects that are specifically grounded within its constitutional purview and, in particular, that the "private affairs of individuals," where the inquiry could result in "no valid legislation," did not fall into that category. As a result, Kilbourn won his case because the House resolution authorizing the investigation exceeded Congress's constitutional authority.

Forty-six years later, in **McGrain v. Daugherty** (1927), the Court was once again called on to examine the scope of congressional investigative authority. In 1922 Congress began an investigation of a huge scandal known as Teapot Dome. It involved the alleged bribery of public officials by private companies to obtain leasing rights to government-held oil reserves, including the Teapot Dome reserves in Wyoming. Initial inquiries

centered on employees of the Department of the Interior, but Congress soon turned its attention to the Justice Department. It was thought that Attorney General Harry M. Daugherty was involved in fraudulent activities because he failed to prosecute wrongdoers. A Senate committee ordered the attorney general's brother, Mally S. Daugherty, to appear before it and to produce documents. Mally was a bank president, and the committee suspected that he was involved in the scandal.

This suspicion grew stronger with the resignation of the attorney general and the subsequent refusal of his brother to appear before the committee. The Senate had Mally Daugherty arrested. He, in turn, challenged the committee's authority to compel him—through arrest—to testify against his brother. Picking up on one of the limits of investigation emanating from *Kilbourn*, Mally's lawyer argued that "the arrest of Mr. Daugherty is the result of an attempt of the Senate to vest its committee with judicial power." The U.S. government's brief also used *Kilbourn* to frame its arguments: "The investigation ordered by the Senate, in the course of which the testimony of the Appellee [Daugherty] and the production of books and records of the bank of which he is President were required, was legislative in its character."

The Court agreed with the government. Writing for the majority, Justice Willis Van Devanter held that "the power of inquiry—with process to enforce it—is an essential and appropriate auxiliary to the legislative function." In other words, he firmly established Congress's power to inquire and to enforce that power with the ability to punish as an implied power. This was an important affirmation of a long-standing practice. Since 1795 congressional committees had often invoked their power to punish, issuing more than 380 contempt citations over the years. If a committee does so and the parent chamber approves the action by a simple majority, the case is forwarded to a U.S. attorney for possible prosecution.[19]

Still, in *McGrain* the justices were unwilling to allow a virtually limitless use of that power. Although they ruled for the government and backed away from the rigid stance of *Kilbourn*, they continued to assert that Congress could not inquire, generally speaking, into private affairs. In this case, however, "the object of the investigation and of the effort to secure the witness's testimony was to obtain information for legislative purposes."

---

[17]The quotes in this paragraph come from the Court's summary of the parties' arguments.

[18]See Pritchett, *Constitutional Law of the Federal System*, 191.

[19]The executive branch has a (theoretical) duty to prosecute these cases, but Congress cannot force the executive branch to do so. For more on this point, see the end of this section.

Members of the House Un-American Activities Committee, including Richard Nixon, R-Calif. (center, seated), review testimony with committee investigator Robert Stripling following a 1948 espionage hearing.

In addition to shedding light on Congress's ability to "inquire," *McGrain* provides some insight into a controversial area of congressional inquiries: the rights of witnesses. Even as it ruled against Daugherty, the Court held that witnesses may refuse to answer "where the bounds of the power are exceeded or the questions are not pertinent to the matter under inquiry."

This window of opportunity for witnesses to refuse to testify became quite important during World War II and in the postwar period when, out of fear of an influx of foreign ideologies into the United States, Congress embarked on a new type of investigation: the "inquisitorial panel." That is, the goal of these hearings on "subversive activities" was, according to many observers, exposure, not necessarily information.

Falling under this rubric were the investigations held in the 1930s by the House Special Committee to Investigate Un-American Activities and in the 1940s and 1950s by Senator Joseph McCarthy (R-Wis.), and by the House Un-American Activities Committee (HUAC). The hearings held by these committees were quite controversial. At that time, the fear of communism was so pervasive that individuals summoned to testify before them lost their jobs, were placed on blacklists, and suffered other negative consequences. Moreover, many witnesses were sufficiently frightened of being branded communist sympathizers or supporters that they refused

to testify or asserted a constitutional protection against so doing, which resulted in an unusually high number of contempt citations. Between 1792 and 1942, Congress had issued 108 contempt citations; from 1945 to 1957, fourteen committees presented 226 such citations to their respective chambers. HUAC alone held 144 "uncooperative" witnesses in contempt.[20]

In the late 1950s the Supreme Court decided two major cases involving the rights of witnesses to refuse to answer Congress's questions. In the first, ***Watkins v. United States*** (1957), the justices considered HUAC's efforts to secure information from John T. Watkins, a labor union organizer. In response to committee questions probing his knowledge of communist activities, Watkins agreed to talk about his own relationship with the Communist Party as well as the activities of those he knew still to be active in the party. But Watkins refused to answer questions about people who had separated themselves from the party. He claimed that these individuals were not relevant to the committee's legislative purpose. After he was convicted for contempt, Watkins appealed. The justices ruled in his favor, concluding that the committee's questions that had been challenged were not pertinent to its legislative function. Instead, the Court

---

[20]Congressional Quarterly, *Guide to Congress*, 3rd ed. (Washington, DC: Congressional Quarterly, 1982), 163.

described the actions of the committee to be nothing more than exposure for the sake of exposure.

Two years later, the Court issued its ruling in **Barenblatt v. United States** (1959), which seemingly ran counter to the *Watkins* precedent. A HUAC subcommittee subpoenaed Lloyd Barenblatt to appear before it. An earlier witness had implicated Barenblatt in communist activities while he was a graduate student at the University of Michigan several years before. The legislators asked Barenblatt a series of questions about his current or past involvement in the Communist Party or communist-oriented groups. When he refused to answer these questions, Barenblatt was found in contempt of Congress. On appeal, the Supreme Court ruled in favor of the congressional committee. The majority decided that the purpose of the inquiry was now, two years after *Watkins*, more clearly defined and that Barenblatt's personal activities were relevant to the committee's legislative purpose.

The different results in *Watkins* and *Barenblatt* have led scholars to ask whether the Court acted consistently. The majority in *Barenblatt* went to great lengths to indicate that it did—indeed, that *Barenblatt* amounted to nothing more or less than a "clarification" of *Watkins*. But many legal analysts, along with Justice Hugo Black, who wrote a dissenting opinion in *Barenblatt*, suggest that at minimum the justices backed away from *Watkins*, and others say that *Barenblatt* signaled a retreat of sorts from *Watkins*.

If it was a retreat, how can we explain the shift, which occurred within a two-year period? There are two possibilities. The first is that *Barenblatt* constituted "a strategic withdrawal" because at the time the Court was under a good deal of pressure from the public and Congress.[21] In particular, *Watkins* and other "liberal" decisions on subversive activity and on discrimination, such as *Brown v. Board of Education* (1954), made the Court the target of numerous congressional proposals. A few even sought to remove the Court's jurisdiction to hear cases involving subversive activities. According to some observers, the justices felt the heat and acceded to congressional pressure. Another explanation is that personnel changes produced a more conservative Court, that *Barenblatt* represented a move "back toward a more conservative position" ushered in by President Dwight Eisenhower's appointments of Charles Whittaker and Potter Stewart.

Either way, the explanations indicate the susceptibility of the Court to political influences outside and inside its chambers. As the dangers associated with the Cold War began to ebb, the justices again evinced a change of heart on the rights of witnesses. In case after case in the 1960s, they reversed the convictions of many whom Congress had cited for contempt. In so doing, the Court sought to strike a balance between the rights of individuals and those of legislatures, no easy task because of the substantive nature of the power to investigate.

This is not to say that controversies over congressional hearings have faded with time. Actually, quite the opposite: each session of Congress seems to bring new disputes—especially when committees call former or current members of the executive branch to testify or turnover evidence. If the president does not want these members to comply, he will sometimes assert "executive privilege." When presidents make this claim, they are asserting that certain documents, conversations, and records are so closely tied to the sensitive duties of the president that they should remain confidential.

Because we have more to say about executive privilege in chapter 5, suffice it to note that claims of executive privilege sometimes put Congress in a bind. It could hold the executive official in contempt but it is possible, even likely, that the Justice Department, which is in the executive branch, could decline to prosecute. Should the Justice Department refuse to prosecute, Congress could file a civil suit compelling prosecution, but these suits might face dismissal on political question grounds *(see chapter 3)*. In these situations, perhaps the best Congress can do is to strike a compromise with the executive branch; for example, having the witness testify behind closed doors.

Amendment-Enforcing Power

The enumerated and implied powers we have considered so far come from Article I, Section 8: either Section 8 explicitly mentions them or they derive from the necessary and proper clause. Another important and frequently used source of legislative authority, amendment-enforcing power, comes from amendments to the Constitution. Seven (another, the Eighteenth Amendment, was repealed in 1933) contain some variant of the following language: *Congress shall have power to enforce, by appropriate legislation, the provisions of this article.* For example, the first section of the Fifteenth Amendment says, "The right of citizens of the United States to vote shall not be denied . . . on account of race,"

---

[21]C. Herman Pritchett, *Congress versus the Supreme Court, 1957–1960* (Minneapolis: University of Minnesota Press, 1961), 12.

and this statement is followed by an enforcement provision: "The Congress shall have power to enforce this article by appropriate legislation."

Presumably, the writers of this Reconstruction amendment, which was ratified in 1870, intended, at the very least, to implement its mandate by allowing Congress to pass legislation forbidding states to deny blacks the right to vote. One result of this amendment-enforcing power was passage of the Voting Rights Act of 1965, the nation's most far-reaching and effective regulation of the electoral process. The act may never have come into being had the federal government lacked power to enforce the Fifteenth Amendment.

For the most part, the Supreme Court has given Congress wide latitude to legislate on the basis of these amendment-enforcing powers.[22] But it has not abdicated its role altogether. In accordance with the language of the enforcement provision, the Court must determine whether the congressional law is "appropriate." This means, first, that the enforcing statute must target the specific subject matter the constitutional amendment covers. For example, in the **Civil Rights Cases** (1883) the Court struck down federal legislation aimed at curbing racial discrimination by private parties. The justices concluded that this legislation could not be justified as an action enforcing the Fourteenth Amendment because the equal protection clause of that article governs racial discrimination by government, not private parties. Second, enforcement legislation must be based on rational criteria reasonably related to the problems targeted by the amendment. In *Shelby County, Alabama v. Holder* (2013) the Court found this principle to have been violated by Congress in 2006 when it extended the provisions of the 1965 Voting Rights Act for an additional twenty-five years. The justices concluded that the section of the law determining which states were covered by the act was based on 1965 racial discrimination data that no longer represented conditions in the affected states. Congress exceeded its powers when it imposed restrictions on specific states based on forty-year-old data that no longer reflected contemporary conditions. (For a detailed discussion of this case, *see chapter 20*.)

Inherent Powers

In his position paper to President Washington over the constitutionality of the bank, Hamilton wrote,

"[T]here are implied [as] well as express powers, and that the former are as effectually delegated as the latter." This much we have already discussed. But Hamilton also noted "another class of powers":

> It will not be doubted, that if the United States should make a conquest of any of the territories of its neighbors, they would possess sovereign jurisdiction over the conquered territory. This would be rather a result, from the whole mass of the powers of the government, and from the nature of political society, than a consequence of either of the powers specially enumerated.

Hamilton referred to these as "resulting powers." Justice Story thought they could be another sort of implied power; for example, possessing sovereign jurisdiction over a conquered territory "could be deemed, if an incident to any, an incident to the power to make war." But Story was also quick to agree with Hamilton: there are powers, "nowhere declared in the Constitution," that are "natural incident(s), resulting from the sovereignty and character of the national government."[23]

Some scholars continue to refer to "resulting powers," but in today's nomenclature we tend to think about Hamilton's and Story's versions as "inherent powers." The idea is that federal government has certain inherent powers that are neither explicit nor directly implied by the Constitution but that somehow attach themselves to sovereign states *(see Table 4-3)*.

Although theorists had long espoused this concept, the very notion of inherent powers is controversial. Some argue that inherent powers cannot possibly conform with the vision of a federal government limited to its enumerated powers or those that can be inferred from them. As Madison wrote in *Federalist* No. 45, "The powers delegated by the proposed Constitution to the Federal Government, are few and defined. Those which are to remain in the State Governments are numerous and indefinite." The Tenth Amendment seems to echo Madison's sentiment: "The powers not delegated to the United States by the Constitution, nor prohibited by it to the States, are reserved to the States respectively, or to the people." Allowing the federal government to claim powers that it cannot trace back to the Constitution, some argue, runs the risk of a tyranny—an end the Constitution was designed to prevent.

---

[22]See, for example, **South Carolina v. Katzenbach** (1966), which upheld the validity of the 1965 Voting Rights Act.

[23]Joseph Story, *Commentaries on the Constitution*, vol. 3, Chapter XXIV; available at http://constitution.org/js/js_324.htm.

And yet the Court has not rejected the idea that there are inherent powers, as *United States v. Curtiss-Wright Export Corp.* (1936) suggests. As you read this case, pay particular attention to Justice George Sutherland's explication of inherent powers. How does he define them? More important, how does he square the existence of inherent powers with the idea of a government based on enumeration? Keep in mind that during Warren G. Harding's presidency, Sutherland had gained substantial international policy-making experience: in 1921 he chaired the advisory committee of the U.S. delegation to the International Conference on the Limitation of Naval Armaments, and the following year he served as counsel in arbitration between the United States and Norway over shipping. How might this experience have affected his resolution of this dispute?

United States v. Curtiss-Wright Export Corp.

299 U.S. 304 (1936)
http://caselaw.findlaw.com/us-supreme-court/299/304.html
Vote: 7 (Brandeis, Butler, Cardozo, Hughes, Roberts,
    Sutherland, Van Devanter)
        1 (McReynolds)

OPINION OF THE COURT: *Sutherland*

NOT PARTICIPATING: *Stone*

After Charles Lindbergh's 1927 transatlantic flight, the aviation industry began to boom. Americans were convinced that air travel would become the new mode of transportation.[24] As a result, many new companies, including Curtiss-Wright, formed to build aircraft.

Although it started off on a strong footing, Curtiss-Wright soon fell prey to the Great Depression, and in 1930–1931 the company lost $13 million. To avoid going bankrupt, it looked beyond the United States into the foreign market, where money still could be made. Curtiss-Wright sold its wares not to other private companies but to foreign governments involved in military conflicts and in need of war planes.

The company found a ready buyer in Bolivia, which since 1932 had been at war with Paraguay over the Chaco, a region east of Bolivia. Landlocked Bolivia was determined to take control of the Chaco to gain access to the Atlantic Ocean. It became an excellent customer of Curtiss-Wright's, buying thirty-four planes in the

---

[24]We adapt what follows from Robert A. Divine, "The Case of the Smuggled Bombers," in *Quarrels That Have Shaped the Constitution,* rev. ed., ed. John A. Garraty (New York: Harper & Row, 1987).

early 1930s. The Chaco War enabled the company to survive the Depression.

Things began to turn sour in 1934. Books and articles appeared attacking companies like Curtiss-Wright as "merchants of death." More important, the League of Nations wanted to put an end to the Chaco War and asked the United States to help. In response, President Franklin D. Roosevelt asked Congress to pass a resolution enabling him to prohibit the sale of arms to the warring countries. It did so on May 28, 1934.

[I]f the President finds that the prohibition of the sale of arms and munitions of war in the United States to those countries now engaged in armed conflict in the Chaco may contribute to the reestablishment of peace between those countries, and if after consultation with the governments of other American Republics and with their cooperation, as well as that of such other governments as he may deem necessary, he makes proclamation to that effect, it shall be unlawful to sell, except under such limitations and exceptions as the President prescribes, any arms or munitions of war in any place in the United States to the countries now engaged in that armed conflict, or to any person, company, or association acting in the interest of either country, until otherwise ordered by the President or by Congress.

Whoever sells any arms or munitions of war . . . shall . . . be punished by a fine not exceeding $10,000 or by imprisonment not exceeding two years, or both.

Shortly after the resolution was enacted, Roosevelt issued an order embargoing weapon sales to Bolivia and Paraguay. Curtiss-Wright refused to comply with the order and tried to get around it by disguising bombers as passenger planes. Eventually, the company got caught and was charged with violating the order.

Curtiss-Wright challenged the government's action. Among its arguments when the case reached the Court, the most pertinent was the contention that the 1934 resolution was invalid because it gave "uncontrolled" lawmaking "discretion" to the president. On this score, the company's reasoning appeared strong: in **Panama Refining Company v. Ryan** (1935) the Court had struck down a congressional act on the ground that the legislature had delegated lawmaking authority to the president without sufficient guidelines. In Curtiss-Wright's view, the 1934 resolution was no different from the law struck down in *Panama Refining*.

The U.S. government tried to distinguish the facts in this case from those in the 1935 decision, saying that the congressional delegation of power in *Panama Refining* involved domestic, not international, affairs. This distinction was important, in the government's argument, because "from the beginning of the government, in the conduct of foreign affairs, Congress has followed the practice of conferring upon the President power similar to that conferred by the present resolution." By way of example, U.S. attorneys indicated that as early as 1794, Congress had given the president the "duty of determining" when embargoes should be laid "upon vessels in ports of the United States bound for foreign ports."

JUSTICE SUTHERLAND DELIVERED THE OPINION OF THE COURT.

[A]ppellees urge that Congress abdicated its essential functions and delegated them to the Executive.

Whether, if the Joint Resolution had related solely to internal affairs it would be open to the challenge that it constituted an unlawful delegation of legislative power to the Executive, we find it unnecessary to determine. The whole aim of the resolution is to affect a situation entirely external to the United States, and falling within the category of foreign affairs. The determination which we are called to make, therefore, is whether the Joint Resolution, as applied to that situation, is vulnerable to attack under the rule that forbids a delegation of the law-making power. In other words, assuming (but not deciding) that the challenged delegation, if it were confined to internal affairs, would be invalid, may it nevertheless be sustained on the ground that its exclusive aim is to afford a remedy for a hurtful condition within foreign territory?

It will contribute to the elucidation of the question if we first consider the differences between the powers of the Federal government in respect of foreign or external affairs and those in respect of domestic or internal affairs. That there are differences between them, and that these differences are fundamental, may not be doubted.

The two classes of powers are different, both in respect of their origin and their nature. The broad statement that the Federal government can exercise no powers except those specifically enumerated in the Constitution, and such implied powers as are necessary and proper to carry into effect the enumerated powers, is categorically true only in respect of our internal affairs. In that field, the primary purpose of the Constitution was to carve from the general mass of legislative powers *then possessed by the states* such portions as it was thought desirable to vest in the Federal government, leaving those not included in the enumeration still in the states. That this doctrine applies only to powers which the states had, is self-evident. And since the states severally never possessed international powers, such powers could not have been carved from the mass of state powers but obviously were transmitted to the United States from some other source. During the colonial period, those powers were possessed exclusively by and were entirely under the control of the Crown. By the Declaration of Independence, "the Representatives of the United States of America" declared the United [not the several] Colonies to be free and independent states, and as such to have "full Power to levy War, conclude Peace, contract Alliances, establish Commerce and to do all other Acts and Things which Independent States may of right do."

As a result of the separation from Great Britain by the colonies, acting as a unit, the powers of external sovereignty passed from the Crown not to the colonies severally, but to the colonies in their collective and corporate capacity as the United States of America. Even before the Declaration [of Independence], the colonies were a unit in foreign affairs, acting through a common agency—namely the Continental Congress, composed of delegates from the thirteen colonies. That agency exercised the powers of war and peace, raised an army, created a navy, and finally adopted the Declaration of Independence. Rulers come and go; governments end and forms of government change; but sovereignty survives. A political society cannot endure without a supreme will somewhere. Sovereignty is never held in suspense. When, therefore, the external sovereignty of Great Britain in respect of the colonies ceased, it immediately passed to the Union. . . .

The Union existed before the Constitution, which was ordained and established among other things to form "a more perfect Union." Prior to that event, it is clear that the Union, declared by the Articles of Confederation to be "perpetual," was the sole possessor of external sovereignty, and in the Union it remained without change save in so far as the Constitution in express terms qualified its exercise. The Framers' Convention was called and exerted its powers upon the irrefutable postulate that though the states were several their people in respect of foreign affairs were one. . . .

It results that the investment of the Federal government with the powers of external sovereignty did not depend upon the affirmative grants of the Constitution. The powers to declare and wage war, to conclude peace, to make treaties, to maintain diplomatic relations with other sovereignties, if they had never been mentioned in the Constitution, would have vested in the Federal government as necessary concomitants of nationality. Neither the Constitution nor the laws passed in pursuance of it have any force in foreign territory unless in respect of our own citizens . . . and operations of the nation in such territory must be governed by treaties, international understandings and compacts, and the principles of international law. As a member of the family of nations, the right and power of the United States in that field are equal to the right and power of the other members of the international family. Otherwise, the United States is not completely sovereign. . . .

Practically every volume of the United States Statutes contains one or more acts or joint resolutions of Congress authorizing action by the President in respect of subjects affecting foreign relations, which either leave the exercise of the power to his unrestricted judgment, or provide a standard far more general than that which has always been considered requisite with regard to domestic affairs. . . .

The result of holding that the joint resolution here under attack is void and unenforceable as constituting an unlawful delegation of legislative power would be to stamp this multitude of comparable acts and resolutions as likewise invalid. And while this court may not, and should not, hesitate to declare acts of Congress, however many times repeated, to be unconstitutional if beyond all rational doubt it finds them to be so, an impressive array of legislation such as we have just set forth, enacted by nearly every Congress from the beginning of our national existence to the present day, must be given unusual weight in the process of reaching a correct determination of the problem. A legislative practice such as we have here, evidenced not by only occasional instances, but marked by the movement of a steady stream for a century and a half of time, goes a long way in the direction of proving the presence of unassailable ground for the constitutionality of the practice, to be found in the origin and history of the power involved, or in its nature, or in both combined. . . .

The uniform, long-continued and undisputed legislative practice just disclosed rests upon an admissible view of the Constitution which, even if the practice found far less support in principle than we think it does, we should not feel at liberty at this late day to disturb.

We deem it unnecessary to consider . . . the unconstitutionality of the Joint Resolution as involving an unlawful delegation of legislative power. It is enough to summarize by saying that, both upon principle and in accordance with precedent, we conclude there is sufficient warrant for the broad discretion vested in the President to determine whether the enforcement of the statute will have a beneficial effect upon the reestablishment of peace in the affected countries; whether he shall make proclamation to bring the resolution into operation; whether and when the resolution shall cease to operate and to make proclamation accordingly; and to prescribe limitations and exceptions to which the enforcement of the resolution shall be subject.

Reversed.

Curtiss-Wright was an important ruling. As we shall see later in this chapter, the decision ran directly counter to what the Court was doing in other areas of the law. At the same time it was striking down many segments of Roosevelt's New Deal, saying that the laws were unconstitutional delegations of power, in *Curtiss-Wright* the Court upheld congressional authority to delegate power. Why it did so brings us to another important, and for present purposes more relevant, aspect of the decision: the distinction between foreign and domestic affairs. Sutherland justified the delegation of power on the ground that it involved external affairs, while the Court's rulings on the New Deal programs involved domestic programs.

In this dichotomy the majority found the concept of inherent powers. In its view, the U.S. Constitution transferred some domestic powers from the states to the federal government, leaving some with the states or the people. That is why Congress cannot exercise authority over internal affairs beyond those explicitly enumerated in the document or that can be implied from it. In contrast, no such transfer occurred or could have occurred for authority over foreign affairs. Because the states never had such power to begin with, they could not have bestowed it on the federal government. Rather, "authority over foreign affairs is an inherent power, which attaches automatically to the federal government as a sovereign entity, and derives from the Constitution only as the Constitution is the creator of that sovereign entity."[25] It is not Congress specifically but the federal government that enjoys complete authority over foreign relations, which is an inherent power of sovereign nations, one that is derived not from their charters but from their status. As constitutional law scholar Louis Henkin summarizes:

> Foreign affairs are national affairs. The United States is a single nation-state, and it is the United States (not the States of the Union, singly or together) that has relations with other nations, and the United States Government that conducts these relations and makes foreign policy.[26]

But *Curtiss-Wright* also has provoked criticism. Some historians and legal scholars assert that Sutherland's historical analysis was inaccurate: "There is evidence that, after independence, at least some of the erstwhile colonies . . . considered themselves sovereign, independent states."[27] More relevant here, as we pointed out earlier, are the risks with allowing the government— Congress, the president, or both—to exercise "inherent powers," whether in the domestic or the foreign realm. At the very least, can it be that the language of the Tenth Amendment, which limits the federal government to its delegated powers, applies only to domestic powers and not to foreign affairs? *Curtiss-Wright* seems to teach this lesson, and it makes some analysts squirm.

[25]Pritchett, *Constitutional Law of the Federal System*, 305.

[26]Louis Henkin, *Foreign Affairs and the Constitution* (New York: W. W. Norton, 1975), 15.

[27]Ibid., 23.

Finally, we might raise questions about whether Sutherland's opinion remains authoritative doctrine. Have more recent cases undercut its view that the federal government possesses extraconstitutional authority over foreign affairs that provide it with considerable leeway? You will have a chance to think about this when you read the next chapter.

CONGRESS AND THE SEPARATION OF POWERS

In our discussion so far, you may have noted a pattern in the Court's decisions dealing with the sources and scope of congressional power. Overall, the Court has allowed Congress a good deal of leeway in exercising enumerated and extraconstitutional power, especially in disputes involving that body's power to regulate its own affairs and to enact legislation. As we will see, it has also given Congress a good deal of freedom to delegate some of its lawmaking authority to another branch of government. Where the Court has sometimes wavered and at times reined in Congress is when Congress tries to assert powers assigned to the executive and judicial branches.

The Delegation of Powers

Almost all discussions of the ability of Congress to delegate its lawmaking power begin with the old Latin maxim *Delegata potestas non potest delegari*, which means "A power once delegated cannot be redelegated." We could apply this statement to Congress in the following way: because the Constitution vests in Congress all legislative powers—lawmaking authority—it cannot give such power to another body or person. No branch of government has, however, fully accepted the principle expressed in the maxim—what is now commonly called the nondelegation doctrine. From the First Congress on, the legislature has delegated its power to other branches or even to nongovernmental entities.

But why would Congress want to give away some of its power? One reason is that Congress is often busy with other matters and must delegate some authority if it is to fulfill all its responsibilities. Another is that Congress might be fully capable of formulating general policies but lacks the time and expertise needed to develop specific methods for carrying out those policies. As the job of governance grows increasingly technical and complex, this reason becomes even more valid. *Curtiss-Wright* provides yet another reason: the need for flexibility. In

Curtiss-Wright Congress gave the president authority to issue an arms embargo if such an action would help to bring peace to warring South American nations. Congress recognized that once it enacts legislation, it may have difficulty amending it with sufficient speed to keep up with rapidly changing events. Finally, Congress might want to delegate for political reasons. To avoid dealing with certain "hot potato" issues, Congress might hand them off to others.

Even from this brief discussion, you may be able to see that the delegation of powers issue is tricky: although, in theory, Congress should not dole out its lawmaking authority, as a matter of practical and reasonable politics, it does so.

Not surprisingly, the Supreme Court has found itself enmeshed in this debate. As we just saw in *Curtiss-Wright*, it has been asked to determine whether particular delegations of power are appropriate, constitutionally speaking, and, as in that case, the Court generally has upheld such delegations, even if they involve domestic issues. **Wayman v. Southard** (1825) was the Court's first major ruling on the delegation of domestic powers. This dispute involved a challenge to a provision of the Judiciary Act of 1789 in which Congress delegated to the courts authority to establish rules for the conduct of judicial business.

Writing for the Court in *Wayman*, Chief Justice Marshall responded pragmatically. He sought to balance the letter of the Constitution with the practical concerns facing Congress by formulating the following standard: the legislature must itself "entirely" regulate "important subjects," but for "those of less interest" it can enact a general provision and authorize "those who are to act under such general provisions to fill up the details." Put simply, Marshall established a set of rules for the delegation of power that varied by the importance of the subject under regulation. Applying this standard to the delegation of power contained in the 1789 Judiciary Act, he found that Congress could grant courts authority to promulgate their own rules.

Wayman—in theory—created an important precedent for subsequent Courts to follow. We say "in theory" because for the next century or so never once did the Supreme Court invalidate a congressional delegation of power, but neither did it quite follow Marshall's standard. Rather, it was even more generous to Congress, allowing delegations over matters big and small.

Perhaps recognizing that the Court's approach to delegation of powers problems required clarification, Chief Justice William Howard Taft—a former president of the United States—set out to do just that in **Hampton & Co. v. United States** (1928). At issue was the Fordney-McCumber Act of 1922, in which Congress established a tariff commission within the executive branch and permitted the president to increase or decrease tariffs on imported goods by as much as 50 percent. Because Congress gave the president (and the commission) so much discretion to adjust rates, an import company challenged the act as a violation of the separation of powers doctrine. The company argued that Congress had provided the president with what was lawmaking power, and immense, unfettered power at that. It went so far as to say that "All lines of demarcation between legislative and executive powers are forever removed" were the Court to uphold the delegation.

Writing for a unanimous Court, Chief Justice Taft disagreed: "In determining what [Congress] may do in seeking assistance from another branch, the extent and character of that assistance must be fixed according to common sense and the inherent necessities of the governmental coordination." So long as Congress "shall lay down by legislative act an intelligible principle to which the person or body authorized to [exercise the delegated authority] is directed to conform," Taft wrote, "such legislative action is not a forbidden delegation of legislative power."

For nearly a decade, the Court seemed to accept Taft's intelligible principle approach to congressional delegation. But in 1935 the Court dealt Congress and the president major blows when it struck down provisions of the National Industrial Recovery Act (NIRA) as excessive delegations of power. The NIRA was a major piece of New Deal legislation designed to pull the nation out of the Great Depression. In *Panama Refining* the focus was on Congress allowing the president to prohibit the shipment in interstate commerce of oil produced in excess of state quotas; in *Schechter Poultry v. United States* (1935) the issue was Congress authorizing the president to approve fair competition codes and standards if representatives of a particular industry recommended he do so. In both instances, the Court struck down the delegations of power as unconstitutional.

As we will see in chapter 7, these decisions were part of a larger pattern of judicial actions hostile to the economic proposals of the Roosevelt administration. The justices may well have been using the excessive delegation of powers argument as an excuse to strike down New Deal legislation that they fundamentally and ideologically opposed. In the long run, *Panama Refining* and *Schechter Poultry* proved to be anomalies. In 1937 the Court shifted to a more sympathetic view of the New Deal and soon returned to its traditional position of giving Congress a great deal of latitude to delegate authority. In fact, since 1936 the Court has not struck down a single federal law explicitly on excessive delegation grounds (although a few of the more suspect laws never reached the Court).

An interesting example is *Gundy v. United States* (2019), in which the Court considered a delegation of authority involving the treatment of sex offenders.[28] Justice Kagan's opinion for a divided court takes us back to *Wayman v. Southard* and *Hampton & Co. v. United States.* But note that several justices seem to take issue with the Court's approach to delegation of power disputes. What alternative do they propose?

Gundy v. United States

588 U.S. __ (2019)
https://caselaw.findlaw.com/us-supreme-court/17-6086.html
*Oral arguments available at https://www.oyez.org/
    cases/2018/17-6086*
*Vote: 5 (Alito, Breyer, Ginsburg, Kagan, Sotomayor)
    3 (Gorsuch, Roberts, Thomas)*

OPINION OF THE COURT: *Kagan*

CONCURRING OPINION: *Alito*

DISSENTING OPINION: *Gorsuch*

NOT PARTICIPATING: *Kavanaugh*

In 2006, Congress passed the Sex Offender Registration and Notification Act (SORNA), which requires sex offenders to register where they live or work before completing their prison sentence or face criminal penalties. The question in this case centered on the approximately 500,000 "pre-act" offenders: those individuals convicted of a sex offense before SORNA's enactment, many of whom are no longer in prison. For these offenders, SORNA delegates to the U.S. attorney general (who heads the Department of Justice) authority to "specify the applicability" of SORNA's registration requirements and to prescribe rules for their registration.

Six months after SORNA's enactment, in February 2007, the Department of Justice issued an interim rule specifying that SORNA's registration requirements apply in full to "sex offenders convicted of the offense for which registration is required prior to the enactment of that Act." The final rule, issued in December 2010, reiterated that SORNA applies to all pre-act offenders.

---

[28]For another modern-day example, see **Mistretta v. United States** (1989).

Herman Gundy was a pre-act offender. A year before SORNA's enactment, he pleaded guilty under Maryland law for sexually assaulting a minor. After his release from prison in 2012, Gundy moved to New York, but he never registered there as a sex offender. A few years later, he was convicted for failing to register.

In challenging his conviction, Gundy argued that Congress unconstitutionally delegated legislative power when it authorized the attorney general to "specify the applicability" of SORNA's registration requirements to pre-act offenders. After a federal trial court and court of appeals rejected his argument, Gundy asked the Supreme Court to hear his case.

JUSTICE KAGAN DELIVERED THE OPINION OF THE COURT.

The nondelegation doctrine bars Congress from transferring its legislative power to another branch of Government. This case requires us to decide whether 34 U.S.C. §20913(d), [which authorized the attorney general to "specify the applicability" of SORNA's registration requirements to pre-act offenders]enacted as part of the Sex Offender Registration and Notification Act (SORNA), violates that doctrine. We hold it does not. Under §20913(d), the Attorney General must apply SORNA's registration requirements as soon as feasible to offenders convicted before the statute's enactment. That delegation easily passes constitutional muster . . .

Article I of the Constitution provides that "[a]ll legislative Powers herein granted shall be vested in a Congress of the United States." Accompanying that assignment of power to Congress is a bar on its further delegation. Congress, this Court explained early on, may not transfer to another branch "powers which are strictly and exclusively legislative." *Wayman* v. *Southard* (1825). But the Constitution does not "deny to the Congress the necessary resources of flexibility and practicality [that enable it] to perform its function[s]." Congress may "obtain the assistance of its coordinate Branches"—and in particular, may confer substantial discretion on executive agencies to implement and enforce the laws. *Mistretta* v. *United States* (1989). "[I]n our increasingly complex society, replete with ever changing and more technical problems," this Court has understood that "Congress simply cannot do its job absent an ability to delegate power under broad general directives." So we have held, time and again, that a statutory delegation is constitutional as long as Congress "lay[s] down by legislative act an intelligible principle to which the person or body authorized to [exercise the delegated authority] is directed to conform." *J. W. Hampton, Jr., & Co.* v. *United States* (1928) . . .

Given that standard, a nondelegation inquiry always begins (and often almost ends) with statutory interpretation. The constitutional question is whether Congress has supplied an intelligible principle to guide the delegee's use of discretion. So the answer requires construing the challenged statute to figure out what task it delegates and what instructions it provides. . . .

[Section] 20913(d) does not give the Attorney General anything like the "unguided" and "unchecked" authority that Gundy says. The provision, in Gundy's view, "grants the Attorney General plenary power to determine SORNA's applicability to pre-Act offenders—to require them to register, or not, as she sees fit, and to change her policy for any reason and at any time." If that were so, we would face a nondelegation question. But it is not. . . . Gundy bases that argument on the first half of §20913(d), isolated from everything else—from the second half of the same section, from surrounding provisions in SORNA, and from any conception of the statute's history and purpose. . . .

So begin at the beginning, with the "[d]eclaration of purpose" that is SORNA's first sentence. §20901. There, Congress announced . . . that "to protect the public," it was "establish[ing] a comprehensive national system for the registration" of "sex offenders and offenders against children." The term "comprehensive" has a clear meaning—something that is all-encompassing or sweeping [citing Webster's Third New International Dictionary]. That description could not fit the system SORNA created if the Attorney General could decline, for any reason or no reason at all, to apply SORNA to all pre-Act offenders. . . .

The Act's legislative history backs up everything said above by showing that the need to register pre-Act offenders was front and center in Congress's thinking. . . . Congress designed SORNA to address "loopholes and deficiencies" in existing registration laws [quoting the House Report]. And no problem attracted greater attention than the large number of sex offenders who had slipped the system. According to the House Report, "[t]he most significant enforcement issue in the sex offender program is that over 100,000 sex offenders" are "'missing,' meaning that they have not complied with" then-current requirements. . . . Imagine how surprising those Members would have found Gundy's view that they had authorized the Attorney General to exempt the missing "predators" from registering at all.

With that context and background established, we may return to § 20913(d). . . . . Both the title and the remaining text of that section pinpoint one of the "practical problems": At the moment of SORNA's enactment, many pre-Act offenders were "unable to comply" with the Act's initial registration requirements. That was because, once again, the requirements assumed that offenders would be in prison, whereas many pre-Act offenders were on the streets. In identifying that issue, § 20913(d) itself reveals the nature of the delegation to the Attorney General. It was to give him the time needed (if any) to address the various implementation issues involved in getting pre-Act offenders into the registration system. "Specify the applicability" thus does not mean "specify *whether* to apply SORNA" to pre-Act offenders at all, even though everything else in the Act commands their coverage. The phrase instead means "specify *how* to apply SORNA" to pre-Act offenders if transitional difficulties require some delay. In that way, the whole of § 20913(d) joins the rest of SORNA in giving the Attorney General only time-limited latitude to excuse pre-Act offenders from the statute's requirements. Under the law, he had to order their registration as soon as feasible.

Now that we have determined what § 20913(d) means, we can consider whether it violates the Constitution. The question becomes: Did Congress make an impermissible delegation when it instructed the Attorney General to apply SORNA's registration requirements to pre-Act offenders as soon as feasible? Under this Court's long-established law, that question is easy. Its answer is no.

[The *Hampton* standard], the Court has made clear, [is] not demanding. "[W]e have 'almost never felt qualified to second-guess Congress regarding the permissible degree of policy judgment that can be left to those executing or applying the law.'" Only twice in this country's history (and that in a single year) have we found a delegation excessive—in each case because "Congress had failed to articulate *any* policy or standard" to confine discretion; see *A. L. A. Schechter Poultry Corp.* v. *United States* (1935);*Panama Refining Co.* v. *Ryan* (1935). By contrast, we have over and over upheld even very broad delegations. Here is a sample: We have approved delegations to various agencies to regulate in the "public interest." We have sustained authorizations for agencies to set "fair and equitable" prices and "just and reasonable" rates. . . . And so forth.

In that context, the delegation in SORNA easily passes muster (as all eleven circuit courts to have considered the question found). The statute conveyed Congress's policy that the Attorney General require pre-Act offenders to register as soon as feasible. Under the law, the feasibility issues he could address were administrative— and, more specifically, transitional—in nature . . . That statutory authority, as compared to the delegations we have upheld in the past, is distinctly small-bore. It falls well within constitutional bounds.

Indeed, if SORNA's delegation is unconstitutional, then most of Government is unconstitutional—dependent as Congress is on the need to give discretion to executive officials to implement its programs. Consider again this Court's long-time recognition: "Congress simply cannot do its job absent an ability to delegate power under broad general directives." *Mistretta.* Among the judgments often left to executive officials are ones involving feasibility. In fact, standards of that kind are ubiquitous in the U.S. Code. See,*e.g.,*12 U. S. C. §1701z–2(a) (providing that the Secretary of Housing and Urban Development "shall require, to the greatest extent feasible, the employment of new and improved technologies, methods, and materials in housing construction under [HUD] programs . . ."

It is wisdom and humility alike that this Court has always upheld such "necessities of government." . . .We therefore affirm the judgment of the Court of Appeals.

JUSTICE ALITO, CONCURRING.

The Constitution confers on Congress certain "legislative [p]owers," Art. I, §1, and does not permit Congress to delegate them to another branch of the Government. Nevertheless, since 1935, the Court has uniformly rejected nondelegation arguments and has upheld provisions that authorized agencies to adopt important rules pursuant to extraordinarily capacious standards.

If a majority of this Court were willing to reconsider the approach we have taken for the past 84 years, I would support that effort. But because a majority is not willing to do that, it would be freakish to single out the provision at issue here for special treatment.

Because I cannot say that the statute lacks a discernable standard that is adequate under the approach this Court has taken for many years, I vote to affirm.

JUSTICE GORSUCH, WITH WHOM THE CHIEF JUSTICE AND JUSTICE THOMAS JOIN, DISSENTING.

The Constitution promises that only the people's elected representatives may adopt new federal laws restricting liberty. Yet the statute before us scrambles that design. It purports to endow the nation's chief prosecutor with the power to write his own criminal code governing the lives of a half-million citizens. Yes, those affected are some of the least popular among us. But if a single executive branch official can write laws restricting the liberty of this group of persons, what does that mean for the next?

Today, a plurality of an eight-member Court endorses this extraconstitutional arrangement but resolves nothing. Working from an understanding of the Constitution at war with its text and history, the plurality reimagines the terms of the statute before us and insists there is nothing wrong with Congress handing off so much power to the Attorney General. But Justice Alito supplies the fifth vote for today's judgment and he does not join either the plurality's constitutional or statutory analysis, indicating instead that he remains willing, in a future case with a full Court, to revisit these matters. Respectfully, I would not wait . . . .

At the time of SORNA's enactment, the nation's population of sex offenders exceeded 500,000, and Congress concluded that something had to be done about these "pre-Act" offenders too. But it seems Congress couldn't agree what that should be . . .So Congress simply passed the problem to the Attorney General. For all half-million pre-Act offenders, the law says only this, in 34 U. S. C. §20913(d):

> The Attorney General shall have the authority to specify the applicability of the requirements of this subchapter to sex offenders convicted before the enactment of this chapter . . . and to prescribe rules for the registration of any such sex offender.

Yes, that's it. The breadth of the authority Congress granted to the Attorney General in these few words can only be described as vast. As the Department of Justice itself has acknowledged, SORNA "does not require the Attorney General" to impose registration requirements on pre-Act offenders "within a certain time frame or by a date certain; it does not require him to act at all." If the Attorney General does choose to act, he can require all pre-Act offenders to register, or he can "require some but not all to register." For those he requires to register, the Attorney General may impose "some but not all of [SORNA's] registration requirements," as he pleases . . .

These unbounded policy choices have profound consequences for the people they affect. Take our case. Before SORNA's enactment, Herman Gundy pleaded guilty in 2005 to a sexual offense. After his release from prison five years later, he was arrested again, this time for failing to register as a sex offender according to the rules the Attorney General had then prescribed for pre-Act offenders. As a result, Mr. Gundy faced an additional 10-year prison term—10 years more than if the Attorney General had, in his discretion, chosen to write the rules differently. . . .

In Article I [of "our founding document"], the Constitution entrusted all of the federal government's legislative power to Congress. In Article II, it assigned the executive power to the President. And in Article III, it gave independent judges the task of applying the laws to cases and controversies.

If Congress could pass off its legislative power to the executive branch, the "[v]esting [c]lauses, and indeed the entire structure of the Constitution," would "make no sense." Without the involvement of representatives from across the country or the demands of bicameralism and presentment, legislation would risk becoming nothing more than the will of the current President. And if laws could be simply declared by a single person, they would not be few in number, the product of widespread social consensus, likely to protect minority interests, or apt to provide stability and fair notice. Accountability would suffer too. Legislators might seek to take credit for addressing a pressing social problem by sending it to the executive for resolution, while at the same time blaming the executive for the problems that attend whatever measures he chooses to pursue. In turn, the executive might point to Congress as the source of the problem. These opportunities for finger-pointing might prove temptingly advantageous for the politicians involved, but they would also threaten to "'disguise . . . responsibility for . . . the decisions.' . . .

Accepting, then, that we have an obligation to decide whether Congress has unconstitutionally divested itself of its legislative responsibilities, the question follows: What's the test? [T]he framers took this responsibility seriously and offered us important guiding principles.

First, we know that as long as Congress makes the policy decisions when regulating private conduct, it may authorize another branch to "fill up the details." *[Wayman v. Southard.] [This means that]* Congress must set forth standards "sufficiently definite and precise to enable Congress, the courts, and the public to ascertain" whether Congress's guidance has been followed.

Second, once Congress prescribes the rule governing private conduct, it may make the application of that rule depend on executive fact-finding. [For example,] Congress . . . made the construction of the Brooklyn Bridge depend on a finding by the Secretary of War that "the bridge wouldn't interfere with navigation of the East River." The Court held that Congress "did not abdicate any of its authority" but "simply declared that, upon a certain fact being established, the bridge should be deemed a lawful structure, and employed the secretary of war as an agent to ascertain that fact." *Miller* v. *Mayor of New York* (1883).

Third, Congress may assign the executive and judicial branches certain non-legislative responsibilities. While the Constitution vests all federal legislative power in Congress alone, Congress's legislative authority sometimes overlaps with authority the Constitution separately vests in another branch. *[E.g.,] Wayman* itself might be explained by [this] principle as applied to the judiciary: Even in the absence of any statute, courts have the power under Article III "to regulate their practice." . . .

Returning to SORNA with this understanding of our charge in hand, problems quickly emerge. Start with this one: It's hard to see how SORNA leaves the Attorney General with only details to fill up. [It's] hard to see how the statute before us could be described as leaving the Attorney General with only details to dispatch . . . . SORNA leaves the Attorney General free to impose on 500,000 pre-Act offenders all of the statute's requirements, some of them, or none of them. The Attorney General may choose which pre-Act offenders to subject to the Act. And he is free to change his mind at any point or over the course of different political administrations. . . .

Nor can SORNA be described as an example of conditional legislation subject to executive fact-finding. To be sure, Congress could have easily written this law in that way. It might have required all pre-Act offenders to register, but then given the Attorney General the authority to make case-by-case exceptions for offenders who do not present an "'imminent hazard to the public safety'" comparable to that posed by newly released post-Act offenders. It could have set criteria to inform that determination, too, asking the executive to investigate, say, whether an offender's risk of recidivism correlates with the time since his last offense, or whether multiple lesser offenses indicate higher or lower risks than a single greater offense.

But SORNA did none of this. Instead, it gave the Attorney General unfettered discretion to decide which requirements to impose on which pre-Act offenders. . . .

Finally, SORNA does not involve an area of overlapping authority with the executive. Congress may assign the President broad authority regarding the conduct of foreign affairs or other matters where he enjoys his own inherent Article II powers. But SORNA stands far afield from any of that. It gives the Attorney General the authority to "prescrib[e] the rules by which the duties and rights" of citizens are determined, a quintessentially legislative power. . . .

In a future case with a full panel, I remain hopeful that the Court may yet recognize that, while Congress can enlist considerable assistance from the executive branch in filling up details and finding facts, it may never hand off to the nation's chief prosecutor the power to write his own criminal code. That "is delegation running riot."

Note that Justice Kavanaugh did not participate in *Gundy* because it was argued before his confirmation. Kavanaugh's absence prompted Justice Gorsuch, in the last paragraph of his dissent, to suggest that the Court might revise its approach to delegation of powers questions when all nine justices participate. If Gorsuch is right—and there are reasons to suspect he might be[29]— how does Gorsuch's approach differ from the "intelligible principle" doctrine the Court has used almost without exception since 1928?

Congress and the Exercise of Executive and Judicial Powers

The cases discussed in the preceding section have a common thread: they involved cooperative relations between Congress and another branch of government, usually the executive. Congress was delegating some of its lawmaking authority to an executive who wanted, perhaps even requested, such authority. But Congress is not always so eager to give away its powers; indeed, on many occasions and through different devices, it has sought to exercise authority over the judicial and executive branches.

With respect to the judicial branch, Congress on occasion has attempted to tell the courts how to interpret the Constitution. It should not come as a surprise that the justices have taken a dim view of such efforts. For example, Congress, upset with the Court's interpretation of the First Amendment's free exercise of religion clause, passed the Religious Freedom Restoration Act of 1993. This statute dictated that all government agencies, including the courts, apply an interpretation of the free exercise clause that ran contrary to the Supreme Court's decision in *Employment Division v. Smith* (1990). The

Court struck down the Religious Freedom Restoration Act in **City of Boerne v. Flores** (1997) largely on the ground that Congress had overstepped its authority and had infringed on the power of the judiciary to determine what the Constitution means. The Court took a similar action in **Dickerson v. United States** (2000) when it invalidated a federal law that defined "voluntary confessions" in a manner at odds with the Supreme Court's decision in *Miranda v. Arizona* (1966).

Have the justices extended such protection to the executive branch? To address this question, let us consider a device Congress developed to keep tabs on the executive: the so-called legislative veto. This kind of veto seems to flip the mandated lawmaking process. Rather than following Article I procedures, meaning that both houses of Congress pass bills (bicameralism) and the president either signs or vetoes them (presentment), under this practice the executive branch makes policies that Congress can veto by a vote of both houses, one house, or even a committee. It should come as no surprise that the legislative veto has been a source of contention between presidents and Congresses, with the former suggesting that it violates constitutional principles and the latter arguing that it represents a way to check all the lawmaking power Congress has delegated to the executive branch.

When it was first developed, the legislative veto was not all that contentious; to the contrary, it was part of a quid pro quo between Congress and President Herbert Hoover, who wanted authority to reorganize the executive branch without going through the normal legislative process. The legislature agreed to go along, but only on the condition that either house of Congress could block the president's reorganization plan by passing a resolution expressing opposition. When Congress passed the 1933 legislative appropriations bill with that condition attached to it, the legislative veto was born.

Although Hoover had agreed to it, he was less than pleased when Congress used it the following year to veto part of the reorganization plan. His attorney general, William D. Mitchell, decried the device as a violation of the separation of powers doctrine. That sort of sparring over the legislative veto continued through the early 1980s, but the patterns of debate were somewhat contradictory and confusing. On one hand, until 1972 Congress had used the device rather sparingly, attaching it to only fifty-one laws.[30] Furthermore, it did not seem to be a matter that either the president or Congress

---

[29]After Kavanaugh was confirmed, the Court received a cert petition on the same statutory issue as *Gundy*. The Court denied the petition, but Kavanaugh took the opportunity to write a short opinion, stating that Justice Gorsuch's "scholarly analysis of the Constitution's nondelegation doctrine in his *Gundy* dissent may warrant further consideration in future cases."

[30]Melvin I. Urofsky, *A March of Liberty* (New York: Knopf, 1988), 945.

took very seriously. Scholars have observed that presidents have rejected only a handful of laws solely because they contained legislative vetoes and that in those few instances Congress almost always repassed the bills without the veto provisions.

On the other hand, some of the laws providing Congress with a veto over executive action have been quite important. Under the War Powers Resolution of 1973, for example, Congress can direct the president to remove U.S. armed forces engaged in foreign hostilities when there is no declaration of war. Moreover, presidents have always complained about the legislative veto. Dwight D. Eisenhower loathed it, claiming that it violated "fundamental constitutional principles." Complaints grew louder after the presidency of Richard M. Nixon, when Congress sought to reassert itself over the executive and enacted sixty-two statutes with legislative vetoes between 1972 and 1979. In fact, in 1976 the House of Representatives came close to approving a proposal that would have made all rules enacted by all agencies subject to a legislative veto.

This issue came to a head during the Carter administration. Jimmy Carter, like Eisenhower, believed legislative vetoes violated the Constitution. For that reason, he had the Justice Department join *Immigration and Naturalization Service v. Chadha* as a test. The result was the first U.S. Supreme Court ruling centering specifically on the constitutionality of the legislative veto. On what grounds did the Court strike down the practice? Two justices dissented. Why did Justice White, in particular, believe that the Court had committed a grave error?

Immigration and Naturalization Service v. Chadha

462 U.S. 919 (1983)
http://caselaw.findlaw.com/us-supreme-court/462/919.html
*Oral arguments available at https://www.oyez.org/
    cases/1981/80-1832*
Vote: 7 (Blackmun, Brennan, Burger, Marshall, O'Connor, Powell,
    Stevens)
    2 (Rehnquist, White)

OPINION OF THE COURT: *Burger*

CONCURRING OPINION: *Powell*

DISSENTING OPINIONS: *Rehnquist, White*

Jagdish Rai Chadha, an East Indian born in Kenya and holder of a British passport, was admitted into the United States in 1966 on a six-year student visa. More than a year after his visa expired, in October 1973, the Immigration and Naturalization Service ordered Chadha to attend a deportation hearing and show cause why he should not be deported. After two hearings, an immigration judge in June 1974 ordered a suspension of Chadha's deportation, which meant that Chadha could stay in the United States, because he was of "good moral character" and would "suffer extreme hardship" if deported.

Acting under a provision of the Immigration and Nationality Act, the U.S. attorney general recommended to Congress that Chadha be allowed to remain in the United States in accordance with the judge's opinion. The act states:

> Upon application by any alien who is found by the Attorney General to meet the requirements of . . . this section the Attorney General may in his discretion suspend deportation of such alien. If the deportation of any alien is suspended . . . a complete and detailed statement of the facts and pertinent provisions of the law in the case shall be reported to the Congress with the reasons for such suspension. Such reports shall be submitted on the first day of each calendar month in which Congress is in session.

Congress, in turn, had the authority to veto—by a resolution passed in either house—the attorney general's decision. The act specifies:

> [I]f during the session of the Congress at which a case is reported, or prior to the close of the session of the Congress next following the session at which a case is reported, either the Senate or the House of Representatives passes a resolution stating in substance that it does not favor the suspension of such deportation, the Attorney General shall thereupon deport such alien or authorize the alien's voluntary departure at his own expense under the order of deportation in the manner provided by law. If, within the time above specified, neither the Senate nor the House of Representatives shall pass such a resolution, the Attorney General shall cancel deportation proceedings.

For a while it appeared as if Chadha's suspension of deportation was secure, but at the last moment Congress asserted its veto power. Congress had until December 19, 1975, to take action, and on December 12 the chair of a House committee introduced a resolution opposing the "granting of permanent residence in the United States to [six] aliens," including Chadha. Four days later the House of Representatives passed the motion.

No debate or recorded vote occurred; indeed, it was never really clear why the chamber took the action.

That vote set the stage for a major showdown between Congress and the executive branch. Chadha filed a suit, first with the immigration court and then with a federal court of appeals, asking that they declare the legislative veto unconstitutional. The Carter administration joined him to argue likewise. The president agreed with Chadha's basic position, and administration attorneys thought his suit provided a great test case because it "pointed up the worst features of the legislative veto—no debate, no recorded vote, no approval by the other chamber, and no chance for presidential review."[31] Given the importance of the dispute, the court of appeals asked both the House and the Senate to file amicus curiae briefs supporting the veto practice, but in 1980 it ruled against their position, finding that the device violated separation of powers principles.

By the time the case was first argued before the Supreme Court in February 1982, the Carter administration was out and the Reagan administration was in. During his 1980 campaign, Ronald Reagan claimed to support the legislative veto, but once in office he instructed the attorney general to go forward with the *Chadha* case.

CHIEF JUSTICE BURGER DELIVERED THE OPINION OF THE COURT.

We begin, of course, with the presumption that the challenged statute is valid. Its wisdom is not the concern of the courts; if a challenged action does not violate the Constitution, it must be sustained. . . .

By the same token, the fact that a given law or procedure is efficient, convenient, and useful in facilitating functions of government, standing alone, will not save it if it is contrary to the Constitution. Convenience and efficiency are not the primary objectives—the hallmarks—of democratic government and our inquiry is sharpened rather than blunted by the fact that congressional veto provisions are appearing with increasing frequency in statutes which delegate authority to executive and independent agencies. . . .

Explicit and unambiguous provisions of the Constitution prescribe and define the respective functions of the Congress and of the Executive in the legislative process. [Art. I, §7 says]: "Every Bill which shall have passed the House of Representatives and the Senate, shall, before it becomes a law, be presented to the President of the United States; if he approve he shall sign it, but if not he shall return it, with his Objections to that House in which it shall have originated . . . and proceed to reconsider it."

Jagdish Chadha successfully challenged the constitutionality of the legislative veto during his legal efforts to avoid deportation

The records of the Constitutional Convention reveal that the requirement that all legislation be presented to the President before becoming law was uniformly accepted by the Framers. Presentment to the President and the Presidential veto were considered so imperative that the draftsmen took special pains to assure that these requirements could not be circumvented. . . .

The decision to provide the President with a limited and qualified power to nullify proposed legislation by veto was based on the profound conviction of the Framers that the powers conferred on Congress were the powers to be most carefully circumscribed. It is beyond doubt that lawmaking was a power to be shared by both Houses and the President. . . .

The bicameral requirement of Art. I, §§1, 7, was of scarcely less concern to the Framers than was the Presidential veto and indeed the two concepts are interdependent. By providing that no law could take effect without the concurrence of the prescribed majority of the Members of both Houses, the Framers reemphasized their belief . . . that legislation should not be enacted unless it has been carefully and fully considered by the Nation's elected officials. . . .

We see therefore that the Framers were acutely conscious that the bicameral requirement and the Presentment Clauses would serve essential constitutional functions. . . . It emerges clearly that the prescription for legislative action in Art. I, §§1, 7, represents the Framers' decision that the legislative power of the Federal Government be exercised in accord with a single, finely wrought and exhaustively considered, procedure. . . .

Examination of the action taken here by one House . . . reveals that it was essentially legislative in purpose and effect. In purporting to exercise power defined in Art. I, §8 . . . to "establish an uniform Rule of Naturalization," the House took action that had the purpose and effect of altering the legal rights, duties, and relations of persons, including the Attorney General, Executive Branch officials and Chadha, all outside the Legislative Branch . . . . The one-House

---

[31]Ibid., 947.

veto operated in these cases to overrule the Attorney General and mandate Chadha's deportation; absent the House action, Chadha would remain in the United States. Congress has acted, and its action has altered Chadha's status.

The legislative character of the one-House veto in these cases is confirmed by the character of the congressional action it supplants. Neither the House of Representatives nor the Senate contends that, absent the veto provision, either one of them, or both of them acting together, could effectively require the Attorney General to deport an alien once the Attorney General, in the exercise of legislatively delegated authority, had determined the alien should remain in the United States. Without the challenged provision, this could have been achieved, if at all, only by legislation requiring deportation.

The nature of the decision implemented by the one-House veto in these cases further manifests its legislative character. After long experience with the clumsy, time-consuming private bill procedure, Congress made a deliberate choice to delegate to the Executive Branch, and specifically to the Attorney General, the authority to allow deportable aliens to remain in this country in certain specified circumstances. It is not disputed that this choice to delegate authority is precisely the kind of decision that can be implemented only in accordance with the procedures set out in Art. I. Disagreement with the Attorney General's decision on Chadha's deportation—that is, Congress' decision to deport Chadha—no less than Congress' original choice to delegate to the Attorney General the authority to make that decision, involves determinations of policy that Congress can implement in only one way; bicameral passage followed by presentment to the President. Congress must abide by its delegation of authority until that delegation is legislatively altered or revoked. . . .

Since it is clear that the action by the House was not within any of the express constitutional exceptions authorizing one House to act alone, and equally clear that it was an exercise of legislative power, that action was subject to the standards prescribed in Art. I. The bicameral requirement, the Presentment Clauses, the President's veto, and Congress' power to override a veto were intended to erect enduring checks on each Branch and to protect the people from the improvident exercise of power by mandating certain prescribed steps. To preserve those checks, and maintain the separation of powers, the carefully defined limits on the power of each Branch must not be eroded. To accomplish what has been attempted by one House of Congress in this case requires action in conformity with the express procedures of the Constitution's prescription for legislative action: passage by a majority of both Houses and presentment to the President. . . .

We hold that the congressional veto provision . . . is unconstitutional. Accordingly, the judgment of the Court of Appeals is

Affirmed.

JUSTICE WHITE, DISSENTING.

The prominence of the legislative veto mechanism in our contemporary political system and its importance to Congress can hardly be overstated. It has become a central means by which Congress secures the accountability of executive and independent agencies. Without the legislative veto, Congress is faced with a Hobson's choice: either to refrain from delegating the necessary authority, leaving itself with a hopeless task of writing laws with the requisite specificity to cover endless special circumstances across the entire policy landscape, or in the alternative, to abdicate its lawmaking function to the Executive Branch and independent agencies. To choose the former leaves major national problems unresolved; to opt for the latter risks unaccountable policymaking by those not elected to fill that role. Accordingly, over the past five decades, the legislative veto has been placed in nearly 200 statutes. The device is known in every field of governmental concern: reorganization, budgets, foreign affairs, war powers, and regulation of trade, safety, energy, the environment, and the economy. . . .

The Court's holding today that all legislative-type action must be enacted through the lawmaking process ignores that legislative authority is routinely delegated to the Executive Branch, to the independent regulatory agencies, and to private individuals and groups . . .

If Congress may delegate lawmaking power to independent and Executive agencies, it is most difficult to understand Art. I as prohibiting Congress from also reserving a check on legislative power for itself. Absent the veto, the agencies receiving delegations of legislative or quasi-legislative power may issue regulations having the force of law without bicameral approval and without the President's signature. It is thus not apparent why the reservation of a veto over the exercise of that legislative power must be subject to a more exacting test. In both cases, it is enough that the initial statutory authorizations comply with the Art. I requirements.

Under the Court's analysis, the Executive Branch and the independent agencies may make rules with the effect of law while Congress, in whom the Framers confided the legislative power . . . may not exercise a veto which precludes such rules from having operative force. If the effective functioning of a complex modern government requires the delegation of vast authority which, by virtue of its breadth, is legislative or "quasi-legislative" in character, I cannot accept that Art. I—which is, after all, the source of the nondelegation doctrine—should forbid Congress to qualify that grant with a legislative veto.

The Court of Appeals struck [the legislative veto] as violative of the constitutional principle of separation of powers. It is true that the purpose of separating the authority of Government is to prevent unnecessary and dangerous concentration of power in one branch. . . .

But the history of the separation of powers doctrine is also a history of accommodation and practicality. Apprehensions of an overly powerful branch have not led to undue prophylactic measures that handicap the effective working of the National Government as a whole. The Constitution does not contemplate total separation of the three branches of Government.

Our decisions reflect this judgment. [T]he Court, recognizing that modern government must address a formidable agenda of complex policy issues, countenanced the delegation of extensive legislative authority to Executive and independent agencies. *J. W. Hampton & Co. v. United States* (1928). The separation-of-powers doctrine has heretofore led to the invalidation of Government action only when the challenged action violated some express provision in the Constitution. [For example], in . . . *Myers v. United States* (1926), congressional action compromised the appointment power of the President . . . Because we must have a workable efficient Government, this is as it should be.

I regret that I am in disagreement with my colleagues on the fundamental questions that these cases present. But even more I regret the destructive scope of the Court's holding. It reflects a profoundly different conception of the Constitution than that held by the courts which sanctioned the modern administrative state. Today's decision strikes down in one fell swoop provisions in more laws enacted by Congress than the Court has cumulatively invalidated in its history. I fear it will now be more difficult to insur[e] that the fundamental policy decisions in our society will be made notby an appointed official, but by the body immediately responsible to the people.

In theory, the Court banished legislative vetoes from the government system because they undermined Article I, Section 7: Congress was making law without presenting the bill to the president or, in the case of the one-house legislative veto in *Chadha*, passage by both houses. (A two-house legislative veto would violate the presentment requirement and so would also be unconstitutional.) In practice, however, that's only partially true. Since *Chadha*, Congress has not exercised the legislative veto to overturn decisions of executive agencies but, apparently, Congress allows committees to veto agency requests to move funds from one program to another. This may be considered a type of a legislative veto because Congress is taking action without presenting a bill to the president.

In this particular instance, then, the U.S. Supreme Court may have been the loser: its decision settling the *Chadha* dispute was unacceptable to the political branches and, to some extent, was ignored by them. But resistance has not stopped the Court from continuing to rule on important separation of powers questions. In the next chapter we examine how the Court has settled disputes over the executive branch and its role in the separation of powers scheme.

ANNOTATED READINGS

For discussion of Congress's authority over its structure and operations and the sources and scope of lawmaking power, see David Gray Adler and Larry N. George, eds., *The Constitution and the Conduct of American Foreign Policy* (Lawrence: University Press of Kansas, 1996); Chandler Davidson and Bernard Grofman, eds., *Quiet Revolution in the South: The Impact of the Voting Rights Act, 1965–1990* (Princeton, NJ: Princeton University Press, 1994); Ward E. Y. Elliott, *The Rise of Guardian Democracy: The Supreme Court's Role in Voting Rights Disputes, 1845–1969* (Cambridge, MA: Harvard University Press, 1974); Richard E. Ellis, *Aggressive Nationalism: McCulloch v. Maryland and the Foundation of Federal Authority in the Young Republic* (New York: Oxford University Press, 2007); Gerald Gunther, ed., *John Marshall's Defense of McCulloch v. Maryland* (Stanford, CA: Stanford University Press, 1969); Louis Henkin, *Foreign Affairs and the United States Constitution* (New York: Oxford University Press, 1996); Mark R. Killenbeck, M'Culloch v. Maryland: *Securing a*

Nation (Lawrence: University Press of Kansas, 2006); Gary Lawson, Geoffrey P. Miller, Robert G. Natelson, and Guy I. Seidman, *The Origins of the Necessary and Proper Clause* (New York: Cambridge University Press, 2010); M. Nelson McGeary, *The Development of Congressional Investigative Power* (New York: Columbia University Press, 1940).

Books on Congress–Court relations and constitutional deliberations in Congress include Jeb Barnes, *Overruled? Legislative Overrides, Pluralism, and Contemporary Court–Congress Relations* (Stanford, CA: Stanford University Press, 2004); Campbell C. Colton and John F. Stack Jr., eds., *Congress Confronts the Court: The Struggle for Legitimacy and Authority in Lawmaking* (Lanham, MD: Rowman & Littlefield, 2001); David P. Currie, *The Constitution in Congress: The Federalist Period, 1789–1801* (Chicago: University of Chicago Press, 1997); Neal Devins and Keith E. Whittington, eds., *Congress and the Constitution* (Durham, NC: Duke

University Press, 2005); Louis Fisher, *The Supreme Court and Congress: Rival Interpretations* (Washington, DC: CQ Press, 2009); Robert A. Katzmann, *Courts and Congress* (Washington, DC: Brookings Institution, 1997); Robert A. Katzmann, *Judges and Legislators: Toward Institutional Comity* (Washington, DC: Brookings Institution, 1988); Walter F. Murphy, *Congress and the Court* (Chicago: University of Chicago Press, 1962); Mitchell Pickerill, *Constitutional Deliberation in Congress: The Impact of Judicial Review in a Separated System* (Durham, NC: Duke University Press, 2004); C. Herman Pritchett, *Congress versus the Supreme Court, 1957–1960* (Minneapolis: University of Minnesota Press, 1961); John R. Schmidhauser and Larry L. Berg, *The Supreme Court and Congress* (New York: Free Press, 1972); Charles Warren, *Congress, the Constitution, and the Supreme Court* (Boston: Little, Brown, 1935).

Books on the delegation of power include Sotirios A. Barber, *The Constitution and the Delegation of Congressional Power* (Chicago: University of Chicago Press, 1975); Barbara H. Craig, *Chadha: The Story of an Epic Constitutional Struggle* (New York: Oxford University Press, 1988); Jessica Korn, *The Power of Separation: American Constitutionalism and the Myth of Legislative Veto* (Princeton, NJ: Princeton University Press, 1998).

CHAPTER FIVE

THE EXECUTIVE

THE CONSTITUTION'S FRAMERS would have trouble recognizing today's presidency. To be sure, they believed that the Articles of Confederation were flawed because they did not provide for an executive, but many delegates had serious reservations about awarding too much authority to the executive branch after what they had suffered under the British monarchy. In fact, those who supported the New Jersey Plan envisioned a plural executive in which two individuals would share the chief executive position as insurance against excessive power accruing to a single person. With little doubt the framers would be amazed at the far-reaching domestic and foreign powers wielded by modern presidents, to say nothing of the hundreds of departments, agencies, and bureaus that constitute the executive branch.

Some of this growth likely traces to the rather loose wording of Article II. The article has neither the detail nor the precision of the framers' Article I description of the legislature; instead, it is dominated by issues of selection and removal and devotes less attention to powers and limitations. The wording is quite broad. Presidents are given the undefined "executive power" of the United States and are admonished to take care that the laws are "faithfully executed." Other grants of authority, such as the president's role as "Commander in Chief of the Army and Navy" and the preferential position given the chief executive in matters of foreign policy, allow for significant expansion.

The presidency also has grown in response to a changing world. As American society became more complex, the number of areas requiring government action mushroomed. Overwhelmed by these responsibilities, among other reasons, Congress delegated to the executive branch authority that the framers probably did not anticipate. In addition, the expanding importance of defense and foreign policy demanded a more powerful presidency.

As these changes took place, the Supreme Court was frequently called on to resolve disputes over the constitutional limits of executive authority. This chapter explores how the justices have interpreted Article II of the Constitution. It is divided into four sections. The first and second provide overviews of the structure of the presidency and the president's constitutional powers. The third considers the domestic powers of the president, and the fourth explores the role of the president in external relations.

THE STRUCTURE OF THE PRESIDENCY

When the framers met in Philadelphia in 1787, they were uncertain about how to create an executive for the new nation.[1] They knew all too well the dangers of a strong executive. Indeed, widespread dissatisfaction with the British system led states, during the period from 1776 to 1778, to adopt constitutions that established weak governorships. State executives were given short terms of office, with few powers, and those few often shared with a council. By 1787, however, some states had become sufficiently dissatisfied with their weak governorships that they strengthened them. During the war with Britain, it had become apparent that state executives were too inexperienced and politically constrained to maintain an

---

[1]We adopt some of this discussion from Farber and Sherry, *A History of the American Constitution*, 107–110. Farber and Sherry contains excerpts of the debates over Article II.

effective effort. Therefore, by the time the framers met, a range of executive systems existed in the states—from those that remained weak to those that were quite strong.

Which position would the founders take? Answers come in Article II of the Constitution, which outlines the structure and powers of the presidency. We begin here with structure of the institution, focusing on four topics: the president's selection, removal, tenure, and succession.

Selection of the President

The convention delegates considered several mechanisms for choosing the president, including, notably, selection by the national legislature. In the end they devised a novel solution: the Electoral College. Until then, the executives of most nations were chosen by bloodline, military power, or legislative selection. No other country had experimented with a system like the Electoral College apparatus created in Philadelphia. Perhaps because it had never been tried, the system, as we shall see, was plagued with defects that required correction over time.

The framers designed the Electoral College system to allow the general electorate to have some influence on the selection of the chief executive without resorting to direct popular election. Then, as now, the plan called for each state to select presidential electors equal in number to the state's delegates to the Senate and House of Representatives. The Constitution empowered the state legislatures to decide the method of choosing the electors. Popular election was always the most common method, but in the past some state legislatures voted for the electors. The Electoral College system was based on the theory that the states would select as electors their most qualified citizens, who would exercise their best judgment in the selection of the president. And perhaps for that reason Article II specifies no qualifications for electors (other than disqualifying those who hold federal office).

As for the president, the Constitution mentions only three qualifications. First, Article II requires that only individuals who are natural-born citizens may become president.[2] Naturalized citizens—those who attain citizenship after birth—are not eligible. Second, to be president a person must have reached the age of thirty-five. Third, the president must have been a resident of the United States for fourteen years. The Constitution made no mention of qualifications for vice president, but this oversight was corrected with the 1804 ratification of the Twelfth Amendment, which says that no person can serve as vice president who is not eligible to be president.

Under the original procedures detailed in Article II, the electors were to assemble in their respective state capitals on Election Day and cast votes for their presidential preferences. Each elector had two votes, only one of which could be cast for the candidate from the elector's home state. These ballots were then sent to the federal capital, where the president of the Senate opened them. The candidate receiving the most votes would be declared president if the number of votes received was a majority of the number of electors.

Article II anticipated two possible problems with this procedure: First, because the electors each cast two votes, it was possible for the balloting to result in a tie between two candidates. In this event, the Constitution stipulated that the House of Representatives should select one of the two. Second, if multiple candidates sought the presidency, it would be possible that no candidate would receive the required majority. In this case the House was to decide among the top five finishers in the Electoral College voting. In settling such disputed elections, each state delegation was to cast a single vote, rather than allowing the individual members to vote independently.

In the original scheme the vice president was selected right after the president. The formula for choosing the vice president was simple—the vice president was the presidential candidate who received the second-highest number of electoral votes. If two or more candidates tied for second in the Electoral College voting, the Senate would select the vice president from among them.

The first two elections took place with no difficulty. In 1789 George Washington received one ballot from each of the 69 electors who participated and was elected president. John Adams became vice president because he received the next-highest number of electoral votes (thirty-four). History repeated itself in the election of 1792, with Washington receiving one vote from each of the 132 electors. Adams again gathered the next-highest number of votes (seventy-seven) and returned to the vice presidency.

The defects in the electoral system first became apparent with the election of 1796. By this time political parties had begun to develop, and this election was a contest between the (incumbent) Federalists and the Democratic-Republicans. With Washington declining to

---

[2]The Constitution also allowed individuals who were citizens at the time the Constitution was adopted to be eligible to hold the presidency.

run for a third term, John Adams became the Federalist candidate, and Thomas Jefferson was the choice of those who wanted political change. Adams won the presidency with seventy-one electoral votes, and Jefferson, with sixty-eight, became vice president. The nation therefore had a divided executive branch, with a president and vice president from different political parties.

Matters grew even worse with the 1800 election. The Democratic-Republicans were now the more popular of the two major parties, and they backed Jefferson for president and Aaron Burr for vice president. Electors committed to the Democratic-Republican candidates each cast one ballot for Jefferson and one for Burr. Although it was clear who was running for which office, the method of selection did not allow for such distinctions. The result was that Jefferson and Burr each received seventy-three votes, and the election moved to the outgoing Federalist-dominated House of Representatives for settlement. Each of the sixteen states had a single vote, and a majority was required for election. On February 11, 1801, the first vote in the House was taken. Jefferson received eight votes and Burr six. Maryland and Vermont were unable to register a preference because their state delegations were evenly divided. The voting continued until the thirty-sixth ballot on February 17, when Jefferson received the support of ten state delegations and was named president, with Burr becoming vice president.

It was clear that the Constitution needed to be changed to avoid such situations. Congress proposed the Twelfth Amendment in 1803, and the states ratified it the next year. The amendment altered the selection system by separating the voting for president and vice president. Rather than casting two votes for president, electors would vote for a presidential candidate and then vote separately for a vice presidential candidate. The House and Senate continued to settle presidential and vice presidential elections in which no candidate received a majority, although the procedures for such elections also were modified by the amendment.

Although the evolution of political parties and the reduction in the degree of independence exercised by presidential electors have changed in the way the system operates, presidential and vice presidential elections are still governed by the Twelfth Amendment—and the Electoral College persists. Despite calls by some to replace it with direct popular election, proponents of this reform have never achieved enough strength to prompt Congress or the state legislatures to propose the necessary constitutional amendment. Historically, opposition to popular election has come from the smaller states, which enjoy more influence within the Electoral College system than they would under popular election reforms.

Removal of the President

Although the framers spent some time dealing with presidential selection, they apparently agreed rather quickly about removal. If an incumbent president (or vice president) abuses the office, the Constitution provides for impeachment as the method of removal. Impeachment is a two-stage process. First, the House of Representatives investigates the charges against the incumbent. The Constitution stipulates that the president (as well as the vice president and all civil officers of the United States) "shall be removed from Office on Impeachment for, and Conviction of, Treason, Bribery, or other High Crimes and Misdemeanors." Once convinced that there is sufficient evidence of such misconduct, the House passes articles of impeachment specifying the crimes charged and authorizing a trial.

The second stage, the trial, takes place in the Senate, with the chief justice of the United States presiding. Conviction requires the agreement of two-thirds of the voting senators. The Constitution specifies that the chief justice shall preside over the Senate if it tries the president, but not when the vice president is being impeached. Could this mean that a vice president, acting as president of the Senate, may preside over his or her own impeachment? That is unlikely, but the procedures are not altogether clear because no vice president has ever been impeached by the House of Representatives. Finally, Congress may impose no penalty on a convicted official other than removal from office. The former officeholder may, however, be subject to separate criminal prosecution in the courts.

Congress has never removed a president from office, but four came closer than most. Andrew Johnson was impeached by the House in 1868, and he survived his trial in the Senate by one vote. Richard Nixon was well on his way to being impeached in 1974 when he resigned from office. The House passed two articles of impeachment against Bill Clinton in 1998, and the Senate vote in February 1999 fell far short of the sixty-seven votes of guilt needed to convict. Like Clinton, Donald J. Trump was impeached by the House but less than a majority of senators voted to convict him.

Worth noting here, though, is that none of these episodes resolved the grounds for impeachment. The

Constitution specifies impeachment for "Treason, Bribery, or other high Crimes and Misdemeanors," as we just noted. But what do those words mean? Must the president violate a criminal law to be impeached, or is, say, slander—making false and damaging statements—enough even though slander is not a criminal offense? Can Congress impeach the president for actions he takes in his "private" life outside of his official duties, or must the offenses trace directly to his job?

Scholars and other commentators debate the answers to these other questions, with each side developing answers from various and rather murky historical material.[3] Perhaps, though, President Gerald Ford supplied the most *politically accurate* answer when he, as a member of House of Representatives, led the charge to impeach Justice William O. Douglas. In response to claims that the impeachment effort was driven by Douglas's liberal decisions and not judicial misconduct, Ford said:

> What, then, is an impeachable offense? The only honest answer is that an impeachable offense is whatever a majority of the House of Representatives considers it to be at a given moment in history; conviction results from whatever offense or offenses two-thirds of the [Senate] considers to be sufficiently serious to require removal of the accused from office . . . there are few fixed principles from among the handful of precedents.[4]

Tenure and Succession

The Constitution sets the presidential term at four years. Originally, it placed no restriction on the number of terms a president could serve; George Washington began the tradition of a two-term limit when he announced at the end of his second term that he would not run again. Every president honored this tradition until the Roosevelts. After serving two terms in office, Theodore Roosevelt decided against running for a third

term in the election of 1908. But four years later he had a change of heart and ran as a third party candidate; he lost to Woodrow Wilson. His cousin, Franklin Roosevelt, had better luck: he sought and won election to a third term in 1940 and to a fourth term in 1944. In reaction, Congress proposed the Twenty-second Amendment, which held that no person could run for president after having served more than six years in that office. The states ratified the amendment in 1951.

In Article II the framers provided a mechanism for the replacement of the president in the event of death, resignation, or disability: the vice president assumes the powers and responsibilities of the office.[5] The Constitution further authorizes Congress to determine presidential succession if there is no sitting vice president when a vacancy occurs.

In 1965 Congress recommended additional changes in the Constitution to govern presidential succession. The need became apparent after Lyndon Johnson assumed the presidency following John F. Kennedy's assassination in 1963. Johnson's ascension left the vice presidency vacant. If anything had happened to Johnson, the federal succession law dictated that next in line was the Speaker of the House, followed by the president pro tempore of the Senate (*see Box 5-1*). In 1965 the Speaker was John McCormack (D-Mass.) who was seventy-four years old, and the president pro tempore was Carl Hayden (D-Ariz.) who was eighty-eight. Neither would have been capable of handling the demands of the presidency. Congress proposed that the Constitution be amended to provide that when a vacancy occurs in the office of vice president, the president nominates a new vice president, who takes office upon confirmation by majority vote in both houses of Congress. The proposal also clarified procedures governing those times when a president is temporarily unable to carry out the duties of the office. The change was ratified by the states as the Twenty-fifth Amendment in 1967.

It was not long before the country used the procedures outlined in the Twenty-fifth Amendment. In 1973 Vice President Spiro Agnew resigned when he was charged with income tax evasion stemming from alleged corruption during his years as governor of

---

[3]For reviews and perspectives, see Raoul Berger, *Impeachment: The Constitutional Problems*, enlarged edition (Cambridge, MA: Harvard University Press, 1999); Michael J. Gerhardt, *Impeachment: What Everyone Needs to Know* (New York: Oxford University Press, 2018); Cass R. Sunstein, *Impeachment: A Citizen's Guide* (Cambridge, MA: Harvard University Press, 2017).

[4]From a speech in the House of Representatives on April 15, 1970.

[5]Nine sitting presidents have failed to complete their terms. Four (William Henry Harrison, Zachary Taylor, Warren G. Harding, and Franklin D. Roosevelt) died of natural causes, and four (Abraham Lincoln, James A. Garfield, William McKinley, and John F. Kennedy) were assassinated. One (Richard Nixon) resigned from office.

Although presidential approval is not required for amendments to be proposed or ratified, President Lyndon B. Johnson, surrounded by congressional leaders, signed the Twenty-fifth Amendment on February 23, 1967. The amendment authorized the president to nominate a new vice president when a vacancy in that office occurred.

Maryland. Nixon nominated, and Congress confirmed, Representative Gerald R. Ford of Michigan to become vice president. Just one year later, Nixon resigned the presidency, and Ford became the nation's first unelected chief executive. Ford selected Nelson Rockefeller, former governor of New York, to fill the new vacancy in the vice presidency.

CONSTITUTIONAL AUTHORITY OF THE PRESIDENT

Despite the constitutional changes dealing with presidential selection and succession, the president's formal powers are the same today as when the Philadelphia convention drafted them. The first section of Article II, the vesting clause, stipulates that "[t]he executive Power shall be vested in a President of the United States of America." After this general grant of authority, Sections 2 and 3 of Article II list specific, formal powers. Those formal grants of authority fall into four categories:

- General executive powers

  To execute and enforce the laws

  To appoint and remove executive branch officials

- Military and foreign policy powers

  To be commander in chief of the armed forces

  To appoint ambassadors

  To receive foreign ambassadors

  To make treaties

- Powers related to the legislative branch

  To veto bills passed by Congress

  To convene special sessions of Congress

  To advise Congress on the state of the nation

BOX 5-1

Line of Succession

On March 30, 1981, President Ronald Reagan was shot by would-be assassin John Hinckley outside a Washington hotel and rushed to an area hospital for surgery. Vice President George H. W. Bush was on a plane returning to Washington from Texas. Presidential aides and cabinet members gathered at the White House, where questions arose among them and the press corps about who was "in charge."[a] In the press briefing room Secretary of State Alexander M. Haig Jr. told the audience of reporters and live television cameras, "As of now, I am in control here in the White House, pending the return of the vice president. . . . Constitutionally, gentlemen, you have the president, the vice president, and the secretary of state."

Haig was, as many gleeful critics subsequently pointed out, wrong. The Constitution says nothing about who follows the vice president in the line of succession. The Succession Act of 1947 (later modified to reflect the creation of new departments) establishes congressional leaders and the heads of the departments, in the order the departments were created, as filling the line of succession that follows the vice president. The line of succession is as follows:

vice president	secretary of commerce
Speaker of the House of Representatives	secretary of labor
president pro tempore of the Senate	secretary of health and human services
secretary of state	secretary of housing and urban development
secretary of the Treasury	secretary of transportation
secretary of defense	secretary of energy
attorney general	secretary of education
secretary of the interior	secretary of veterans affairs
secretary of agriculture	secretary of homeland security

A different "line"—not of succession to the presidency but of National Command Authority in situations of wartime emergency—was created according to the National Security Act of 1947. The command rules are detailed in secret presidential orders that each new president signs at the beginning of the term.

Among other things, the orders authorize the secretary of defense to act as commander in chief in certain specific, limited situations in which neither the president nor the vice president is available. Presumably, such situations would follow a nuclear or terrorist attack on Washington, D.C.

Source: Michael Nelson, ed., *Guide to the Presidency*, 3rd ed. (Washington, DC: CQ Press, 2002), 409.

[a]"Confusion over Who Was in Charge Arose following Reagan Shooting," *Wall Street Journal*, April 1, 1981.

- Powers related to the judicial branch

  To nominate federal judges

  To grant pardons to those convicted of federal crimes

Many of the provisions conferring powers on the chief executive are vaguely worded and open to interpretation. For example, just what is included in the "executive power" that the Constitution grants to the president? The lack of precision in the wording of Article II has given rise to two opposing theories of presidential power. The first, called the "mere designation of office" theory, holds that the first sentence of Article II simply summarizes the powers listed later on. That is, the president is limited to those specific grants of power contained in Sections 2 and 3 of Article II. This was the position James Madison implied in *Federalist* No. 51 and that President William Howard Taft advocated:

> The true view of the Executive function is, as I conceive it, that the President can exercise no power which cannot be fairly and reasonably traced to some specific grant of power or justly implied and included within such express grant as proper and necessary to its exercise. Such specific grant must be either in the Federal Constitution or in an act of Congress passed in pursuance thereof. There is no undefined residuum of power which he can exercise because it seems to him to be in the public interest.[6]

The opposing viewpoint is called the "general grant of power" theory (sometimes called the stewardship theory, or the prerogative or inherent power approach, by modern-day scholars). This approach holds that the grant of executive power is a broad one, giving the president whatever is needed to run the country. President Theodore Roosevelt, a well-known adherent of this perspective, put it this way in his autobiography:

> [When immediate and vigorous executive action is necessary] it is the duty of the President to act upon the theory that he is the steward of the people, and that the proper attitude for him to take is that he is bound to assume that he has the legal right to do whatever the needs of the people demand, unless the Constitution or laws explicitly forbid him to do it.[7]

It should not be surprising that these two very different views of presidential power have given rise to legal conflicts that ultimately found their way to the Supreme Court's doorstep. In no small way, the presidency has been shaped by how the justices have responded to these important conflicts.

THE DOMESTIC POWERS OF THE PRESIDENT

To understand the powers of the executive more thoroughly, it is useful to consider the domestic and foreign

[6]William Howard Taft, *Our Chief Magistrate and His Powers* (New York: Columbia University, 1916), 139–140.

[7]Theodore Roosevelt, *An Autobiography* (New York: Scribner's, 1920), 464.

policy roles of the president separately. This division reflects the perspective of political scientists who suggest that there are actually two "presidencies": one for domestic affairs and one for foreign relations. Although it is often hard to separate the two at times when one affects the other, differences remain. The president is generally more constrained—by the public, Congress, and even the Supreme Court—in domestic affairs than in the realm of foreign policy. As you read the material to come, consider whether this division makes sense.

The Faithful Execution of the Laws

At the heart of executive power is the enforcement of the law; Article II, Section 3, states that the president shall be given the responsibility to "take Care that the Laws be faithfully executed." Undoubtedly, the take care clause means that the provisions of the Constitution and the laws Congress enacts are entrusted to the president for administration and enforcement. Presidents may use the substantial powers of the executive branch to see that the law is followed.

In *In re Neagle* (1890) the Court held that presidential enforcement powers were to be interpreted broadly. *Neagle* stemmed from a disappointed litigant's threat to kill Justice Stephen Field. President Benjamin Harrison authorized the Justice Department to appoint a bodyguard to protect Field, although such appointments were not authorized by law. The Supreme Court upheld the appointment, thus endorsing the "general grant of power" view of presidential authority.

The Constitution obliges the president to enforce all the laws, not just those the administration supports. Although a number of presidents have been criticized for failing to carry out certain laws with sufficient enthusiasm, it would be difficult to show that the chief executive had not satisfied the constitutional mandate of faithful execution. On rare occasions, however, a president has openly refused to execute a law validly passed by Congress. In such cases, court challenges are to be expected.

Train v. City of New York (1975) provides an example. At issue was the Federal Water Pollution Control Act Amendments of 1972, which Congress passed over President Nixon's veto. The act made billions of dollars in federal money available to local governments for sewers and clean water projects. After losing the legislative battle, the president instructed the administrator of the Environmental Protection Agency (EPA) not to allot to local governments the full funds authorized by Congress. For example, for fiscal year 1973 Nixon directed officials to spend no more than $2 billion when Congress authorized as much as $5 billion for that year.

New York City, which expected to be a recipient of some of these funds, filed suit against Train, head of the EPA, to force the administration to release the impounded money. In interpreting the legislation, the Supreme Court in *Train* found no congressional grant of discretion to the president that would allow him to decide how much of the appropriated money to allocate. In the absence of such a grant, the president's obligation was to carry out the terms of the statute: the funds, the Court held, must be distributed according to the intent of Congress.

Train has come to stand for the proposition that the president cannot "frustrate the will" of Congress by destroying a program through impoundment; he must enforce and administer the policies enacted by the legislature (even if he opposes them) to fulfill his constitutional requirement to execute the laws. But some commentators wonder about the reach of *Train* because of the facts surrounding it: Nixon had vetoed the bill, substantial amounts of money were at stake, and the law did not seem to give the president discretion to reduce the amount allocated. Whether a different set of facts would lead the Court to give the president more leeway remains an open question.

Failure to enforce the law is one thing. Quite another is when administrations have chosen not to defend the constitutionality of particular federal laws. For example, in *Myers v. United States* (1926), which we will consider soon, the administration's solicitor general not only refused to defend the law at issue (curtailing presidential authority to fire a postmaster) but also argued against its constitutionality. *Myers* is not all that unusual. Between 2004 and 2010 alone the Justice Department declined to defend statutes in nearly fifteen cases;[8] the Trump administration has followed suit, refusing to defend the constitutionality of provisions of the Affordable Care Act ("Obamacare").

When the administration takes this position, criticism usually follows, as it did when Barack Obama's attorney general announced that the president would not defend the constitutionality of the Defense of Marriage Act (DOMA), which defines marriage for federal purposes as the legal union between one man and one woman.[9] The critics contend that the government has a

duty to "take Care that the laws be faithfully Executed," even if the president disagrees with those laws as a matter of policy. On the other side, presidents have argued that they take an oath to "preserve, protect, and defend" the Constitution and so have an obligation to make their own independent assessments of the constitutionality of federal laws, especially if they encroach on executive authority. In such a circumstance, the administration notifies Congress that it is not defending the law in question; Congress can then seek its own defense. In the case of DOMA, for example, the House of Representatives hired a former solicitor general, Paul Clement, to defend it.

Still, it is important to emphasize, the Constitution unambiguously gives the president the responsibility and authority to enforce the laws. But is this power given exclusively to the president, or may the other branches also exercise enforcement? This question has been at the root of several important battles between Congress and the president. In most instances the Court has held that powers clearly executive in nature must be carried out by the executive branch.

Consider *Bowsher v. Synar* (1986) involving a challenge to the constitutionality of certain provisions of the Balanced Budget and Emergency Deficit Control Act of 1985, better known as the Gramm-Rudman-Hollings Act. The legislation attempted to control the federal budget deficit by imposing automatic budget cuts when members of Congress were unable or unwilling to exercise sufficient fiscal restraint. The law established maximum budget deficit levels for each year beginning in 1986. The size of the deficit was to decrease each year until fiscal 1991, when no deficit would be allowed. If the federal budget deficit in any year exceeded the maximum allowed, across-the-board budget cuts would automatically be imposed.

Triggering the cuts involved steps to be taken by several government officials, culminating in a final report by the U.S. comptroller general. If the comptroller general concluded that budget projections required spending cuts under the statute, the president would issue an order to curb spending. This provision gave the comptroller general an important role in the enforcement of the balanced budget law. But the comptroller general is an officer within the legislative branch, not the executive branch. The justices ruled in *Bowsher* that giving the comptroller general such authority violated the separation of powers principle. Executive authority is not to be exercised by the legislative branch.

The *Bowsher* decision supplied an authoritative declaration of the boundaries between legislative and

---

[8]Tony Mauro, "Government's 'Duty to Defend' Not a Given," *National Law Journal*, October 27, 2010.

[9]***United States v. Windsor*** (2013).

executive authority. Once Congress makes its choice in enacting laws, its participation ends. Thereafter, Congress can control the execution of the law only indirectly—by passing new legislation. The execution and enforcement of the law must be left to the executive branch.

The Veto Power

Section 7 of Article I of the Constitution contains what has become known as the presentment clause. By its terms, after Congress passes a piece of legislation, it is sent to the president, who then has three options: sign it, veto it, or do nothing. If the president signs it, the bill becomes law. If he vetoes it, Congress can attempt to override him by the required two-thirds vote. If he does nothing, the bill becomes law after ten days, provided that Congress is in session; if Congress adjourns during the ten-day period, the bill is "pocket vetoed." Congress cannot override a pocket veto, but it can reintroduce the bill in its next session. Although presidents do not often use the pocket veto (since 1789, only 1,066 times, or about five times a year) or, for that matter, their regular veto power (since 1789, 1,514 times, or about seven times a year), they typically regard their option to do so as important.[10] At the very least, a president can hold the veto out as a threat against a recalcitrant Congress, and Congress has generally been unwilling or unable to override a presidential veto. Of the 1,514 regular vetoes since 1789, only 111 have been overridden.

For much of American history, the veto power generated few constitutional disputes, but that is no longer true. Two issues relating to the veto have been the cause of major controversies. The first, which we discuss in some detail in chapter 4, is the legislative veto (when one or both houses of Congress attempt to veto decisions of the executive branch). The other is the line-item veto, which allowed the president to cancel particular taxing and spending provisions after they were signed into law. To understand why the line-item veto is controversial, think first about the way bills become laws: since the days of George Washington, Congress has passed laws and the president has had to decide whether to accept or reject them in their entirety. Most presidents have not been happy with this arrangement. Beginning with Ulysses S. Grant, virtually all have sought the ability to veto parts of a bill and accept others.

[10]Data in this paragraph are from "Summary of Bills Vetoed, 1789–Present," *United States Senate*, http://www.senate.gov/reference/Legislation/Vetoes/vetoCounts.htm.

Among the rationales presidents have offered for the line-item veto, a common one is this: members of Congress must face periodic electoral checks, and they often include in the federal budget "pork-barrel projects"—projects designed solely to appease constituents—even though such projects waste money. Because members of Congress are unwilling to take fiscal responsibility and omit unnecessary spending from the budget, the argument goes, the president should take on this responsibility by being able to veto or "cancel" particular expenditures.

In 1996 Congress finally agreed and enacted the Line Item Veto Act but, in *Clinton v. City of New York*, the Court invalidated it. Why? Does the majority make a compelling case for the act's unconstitutionality?

Clinton v. City of New York

524 U.S. 417 (1998)
http://caselaw.findlaw.com/us-supreme-court/524/417.html
Oral arguments are available at https://www.oyez.org/cases/1997/97-1374
Vote: 6 (Ginsburg, Kennedy, Rehnquist, Souter, Stevens, Thomas)
3 (Breyer, O'Connor, Scalia)

OPINION OF THE COURT: *Stevens*

CONCURRING OPINION: *Kennedy*

OPINION CONCURRING IN PART AND DISSENTING IN PART: *Scalia*

DISSENTING OPINION: *Breyer*

In 1996 passed the Line Item Veto Act, which stated:

> [T]he President may, with respect to any bill or joint resolution that has been signed into law pursuant to Article I, section 7, of the Constitution of the United States, cancel in whole—(1) any dollar amount of discretionary budget authority; (2) any item of new direct spending; or (3) any limited tax benefit; if the President—
>
> [A] determines that such cancellation will—(i) reduce the Federal budget deficit; (ii) not impair any essential Government functions; and (iii) not harm the national interest; and
>
> [B] notifies the Congress of such cancellation by transmitting a special message . . . within five calendar days (excluding Sundays) after the enactment of the law [to which the cancellation applies].

President Bill Clinton used new power under the Line Item Veto Act on August 11, 1997, to cancel two spending provisions and a special tax break. Groups challenging the law won a Supreme Court ruling declaring the act unconstitutional.

The act contained another important provision. Although it gave the president the power to rescind various expenditures, it established a check on the ability to do so: Congress may consider "disapproval bills" that would render the president's cancellation "null and void." In other words, Congress could restore appropriations cuts by the president; but, it is worth noting, new congressional legislation would be subject to a presidential veto.

On January 2, 1997, just one day after it went into effect, the Line Item Veto Act was challenged by six members of Congress who had voted against it. The Supreme Court dismissed this suit on standing to sue grounds (*Raines v. Byrd,* 1997) but then considered the constitutional merits of the line-item veto in *Clinton v. City of New York.*

Following the Court's decision in *Raines v. Byrd,* President Clinton began actively using his new power, canceling more than eighty provisions in taxing and spending bills passed by Congress. Among the canceled items were a provision of the Balanced Budget Act of 1997 that provided money for New York City hospitals and a section of the Taxpayer Relief Act of 1997 that gave a tax break to potato growers in Idaho. The affected parties immediately challenged the president's action in court. Those in the first case were New York City, two hospital associations, and two unions representing health care employees. The parties in the second were a farmers' cooperative and one of its members.

A federal district court consolidated the cases, determined that at least one party in each suit had standing to sue, and then ruled that the line-item veto law violated the presentment clause. The administration then appealed to the U.S. Supreme Court.

JUSTICE STEVENS DELIVERED THE OPINION OF THE COURT.

Less than two months after our decision in [*Raines*], the President exercised his authority to cancel one provision in the Balanced Budget Act of 1997 and two provisions in the Taxpayer Relief Act of 1997. Appellees, claiming that they had been injured by two of those cancellations, filed these cases in the District Court. That Court again held the statute invalid and we again expedited our review. We now hold that these appellees have standing to challenge the constitutionality of the Act and, reaching the merits, we agree that the cancellation procedures set forth in the Act violate the Presentment Clause, Art. I, Sec. 7, cl. 2, of the Constitution. . . .

In both legal and practical effect, the President has amended two Acts of Congress by repealing a portion of each. "[R]epeal of statutes, no less than enactment, must conform with Art. I." *INS v. Chadha* (1983). There is no provision in the Constitution that authorizes the President to enact, to amend, or to repeal statutes. Both Article I and Article II assign responsibilities to the President that directly relate to the lawmaking process, but neither addresses the issue presented by these cases. The President "shall from time to time give to the Congress Information on the State of the Union, and recommend to their Consideration such Measures as he shall judge necessary and expedient. . . ." Art. II, Sec. 3. Thus, he may initiate and influence legislative proposals. Moreover, after a bill has passed both Houses of Congress, but "before it become[s] a Law," it must be presented to the President. If he approves it, "he shall sign it, but if not he shall return it, with his Objections to that House in which it shall have originated, who shall enter the Objections at large on their Journal, and proceed to reconsider it." Art. I, Sec. 7, cl. 2. His "return" of a bill, which is usually described as a "veto," is subject to being overridden by a two-thirds vote in each House.

There are important differences between the President's "return" of a bill pursuant to Article I, Sec. 7, and the exercise of the President's cancellation authority pursuant to the Line Item Veto Act. The constitutional return takes place *before* the bill becomes law; the statutory cancellation occurs *after* the bill becomes law. The constitutional return is of the entire bill; the statutory cancellation is of only a part. Although the Constitution expressly authorizes the President to play a role in the process of enacting statutes, it is silent on the subject of unilateral Presidential action that either repeals or amends parts of duly enacted statutes.

There are powerful reasons for construing constitutional silence on this profoundly important issue as equivalent to an express prohibition. The procedures governing the enactment of statutes set forth in the text of Article I were the product of the great debates and compromises that produced the Constitution itself. Familiar historical materials provide abundant support for the conclusion that the power to enact statutes may only "be exercised in accord with a single, finely wrought and exhaustively considered, procedure." *Chadha.* Our first President understood the text of the Presentment Clause as requiring that he either "approve all the parts of a Bill, or reject it in toto." What has emerged in these cases from the President's exercise of his statutory cancellation powers, however, are truncated versions of two bills that passed both Houses of Congress. They are not the product of the "finely wrought" procedure that the Framers designed. . . .

. . . [O]ur decision rests on the narrow ground that the procedures authorized by the Line Item Veto Act are not authorized by the Constitution. The Balanced Budget Act of 1997 is a 500-page document that became "Public Law 105–33" after three procedural steps were taken: (1) a bill containing its exact text was approved by a majority of the Members of the House of Representatives; (2) the Senate approved precisely the same text; and (3) that text was signed into law by the President. The Constitution explicitly requires that each of those three steps be taken before a bill may "become a law." Art. I, Sec. 7. If one paragraph of that text had been omitted at any one of those three stages, Public Law 105–33 would not have been validly enacted. If the Line Item Veto Act were valid, it would authorize the President to create a different law—one whose text was not voted on by either House of Congress or presented to the President for signature. Something that might be known as "Public Law 105–33 as modified by the President" may or may not be desirable, but it is surely not a document that may "become a law" pursuant to the procedures designed by the Framers of Article I, Sec. 7, of the Constitution.

If there is to be a new procedure in which the President will play a different role in determining the final text of what may "become a law," such change must come not by legislation but through the amendment procedures set forth in Article V of the Constitution.

The judgment of the District Court is affirmed.

It is so ordered.

JUSTICE KENNEDY, CONCURRING.

A nation cannot plunder its own treasury without putting its Constitution and its survival in peril. The statute before us, then, is of first importance, for it seems undeniable the Act will tend to restrain persistent excessive spending. Nevertheless, for the reasons given by JUSTICE STEVENS in the opinion for the Court, the statute must be found invalid. Failure of political will does not justify unconstitutional remedies. . . .

The Constitution is not bereft of controls over improvident spending. Federalism is one safeguard, for political accountability is easier to enforce within the States than nationwide. The other principal mechanism, of course, is control of the political branches by an informed and responsible electorate. Whether or not federalism and control by the electorate are adequate for the problem at hand, they are two of the structures the Framers designed for the problem the statute strives to confront. The Framers of the Constitution could not command statesmanship. They could simply provide structures from which it might emerge. The fact that these mechanisms, plus the proper functioning of the separation of powers itself, are not employed, or that they prove insufficient, cannot validate an otherwise unconstitutional device. With these observations, I join the opinion of the Court.

JUSTICE SCALIA, WITH WHOM JUSTICE O'CONNOR JOINS, AND WITH WHOM JUSTICE BREYER JOINS [IN PART], CONCURRING IN PART AND DISSENTING IN PART.

Insofar as the degree of political, "law-making" power conferred upon the Executive is concerned, there is not a dime's worth of difference between Congress's authorizing the President to *cancel* a spending item, and Congress's authorizing money to be spent on a particular item at the President's discretion. And the latter has been done since the Founding of the Nation. From 1789–1791, the First Congress made lump-sum appropriations for the entire Government—"sum[s] not exceeding" specified amounts for broad purposes. From a very early date Congress also made permissive individual appropriations, leaving the decision whether to spend the money to the President's unfettered discretion. . . .

The short of the matter is this: Had the Line Item Veto Act authorized the President to "decline to spend" any item of spending contained in the Balanced Budget Act of 1997, there is not the slightest doubt that authorization would have been constitutional. What the Line Item Veto Act does instead—authorizing the President to "cancel" an item of spending—is technically different. But the technical difference does *not* relate to the technicalities of the Presentment Clause, which have been fully complied with; and the doctrine of unconstitutional delegation, which *is* at issue here, is preeminently *not* a doctrine of technicalities. The title of the Line Item Veto Act, which was perhaps designed to simplify for public comprehension, or perhaps merely to comply with the terms of a campaign pledge, has succeeded in faking out the Supreme Court. The President's action it authorizes in fact is not a line-item veto and thus does not offend Art. I, §7; and insofar as the substance of that action is concerned, it is no different from what Congress has permitted the President to do since the formation of the Union.

JUSTICE BREYER, WITH WHOM JUSTICE O'CONNOR AND JUSTICE SCALIA JOIN [IN PART], DISSENTING.

The Court believes that the Act violates the literal text of the Constitution. A simple syllogism captures its basic reasoning:

> Major Premise: The Constitution sets forth an exclusive method for enacting, repealing, or amending laws.

Minor Premise: The Act authorizes the President to "repeal[l] or amen[d]" laws in a different way, namely by announcing a cancellation of a portion of a previously enacted law.

Conclusion: The Act is inconsistent with the Constitution.

I find this syllogism unconvincing, however, because its Minor Premise is faulty. When the President "canceled" the two appropriation measures now before us, he did not *repeal* any law nor did he *amend* any law. He simply *followed* the law, leaving the statutes, as they are literally written, intact . . . .

. . . I recognize that the Act before us is novel. In a sense, it skirts a constitutional edge. But that edge has to do with means, not ends. The means chosen do not amount literally to the enactment, repeal, or amendment of a law. Nor, for that matter, do they amount literally to the "line item veto" that the Act's title announces. Those means do not violate any basic Separation of Powers principle. They do not improperly shift the constitutionally foreseen balance of power from Congress to the President. Nor, since they comply with Separation of Powers principles, do they threaten the liberties of individual citizens. They represent an experiment that may, or may not, help representative government work better. The Constitution, in my view, authorizes Congress and the President to try novel methods in this way. Consequently, with respect, I dissent.

When the opinion was announced, President Clinton said, "I am deeply disappointed with today's Supreme Court decision striking down the line-item veto. The decision is a defeat for all Americans—it deprives the President of a valuable tool for eliminating waste in the Federal budget and for enlivening the public debate over how to make the best use of public funds." Whether the Court will reverse course on this issue in the near future is open to speculation. Of the six justices in the majority on *Clinton v. City of New York*, only three remain on the Court.

The Powers of Appointment and Removal

For presidents to carry out the executive duties of the government effectively, they must be able to staff the various federal departments and offices with administrators who share their views and in whom they have confidence. This duty implies the power to appoint and the power to remove. The Constitution offers guidelines on the president's appointment power, but it is silent on the removal power.

Principal versus Inferior Officers

Article II, Section 2, contains what is known as the appointments clause. It specifies the president's authority to appoint major administrative and judicial officials, but it also allows Congress to allocate that authority to other bodies for minor administrative positions:

> [The president] shall nominate, and by and with the Advice and Consent of the Senate, shall appoint Ambassadors, other public Ministers and Consuls, Judges of the supreme Court, and all other Officers of the United States, whose Appointments are not herein otherwise provided for, and which shall be established by Law: but the Congress may by Law vest the Appointment of such inferior Officers, as they think proper, in the President alone, in the Courts of Law, or in the Heads of Departments.

Although this clause seems detailed and specific enough,[11] it has raised interesting questions, especially over the difference between major (or principal) officers and inferior officers. Principal positions, according to the appointments clause, must be filled by presidential nomination and Senate confirmation, but selections of personnel to fill inferior positions may be made by some other means as determined by Congress. The question becomes how to distinguish between the two.

This is an important question because from time to time Congress establishes government positions that, for various reasons, are to be filled by an appointing authority other than the president. And on occasion, someone objects to the procedure on the ground that the position is too important for anyone other than the president to fill. Courts then must determine whether the official holds a principal position as an officer of the United States or is an inferior official. If it is the former, then the president must make the appointment with the advice and consent of the Senate; if the latter, the power may be vested in the "President alone, in the Courts of Law, or in the Heads of Departments."

In *Morrison v. Olson* (1988), involving the creation of the Office of Independent Counsel, the Court attempted to delineate the difference between "inferior" and

---

[11]Article II, Section 2 concludes with what is known as the recess appointments clause. For background on the clause, as well as the Court's most recent interpretation, see **National Labor Relations Board v. Noel Canning** (2014).

"principal" officers. At issue in *Morrison* was the 1978 Ethics in Government Act, which included a provision for an independent counsel to investigate and, when necessary, to prosecute high-ranking officials of the government for violations of federal criminal laws.

Because the duties of the independent counsel involved the investigation of wrongdoing in the executive branch, Congress did not want the president to have a role in the appointment of that official. Instead, the law established the following selection procedures: If, after a preliminary investigation, the attorney general concluded that an independent counsel was needed, a "special division" was convened. The special division consisted of three federal judges appointed by the chief justice of the United States. The judges were empowered to appoint the independent counsel. The selection of the counsel and a description of the counsel's tasks and jurisdiction were the special division's only function.

Once appointed, the independent counsel could exercise all of the powers of the Justice Department. Counsel appointed under the act could be removed by the attorney general, but only for cause or disabilities that substantially impaired the counsel from completing the required duties. Such dismissals could be reviewed by the federal district court. The independent counsel's tenure otherwise ended when he or she declared the work to be completed or the special division concluded that the counsel's assigned tasks had been accomplished.

Theodore B. Olson and two other Justice Department officials suspected of presenting false information to Congress in 1985 challenged the authority of the independent counsel on the ground that independent counsel was a major official and, as such, could be appointed only by the president, not by a panel of judges.

In *Morrison* the Supreme Court upheld the law. The majority acknowledged that the line between inferior and principal officers is a blurred one, but found that the independent counsel clearly fell into the inferior officer category. Chief Justice William Rehnquist's opinion cited four reasons. First, the independent counsel could be removed by the attorney general. Second, the independent counsel was authorized to perform only certain limited duties. Third, the jurisdiction of the independent counsel was limited to the investigation of specified federal officials. And finally, the independent counsel tenure was temporary; once the investigation was completed, the special prosecutor left office. In addition, the Court could find no substantial reason to believe that the independent counsel in any way infringed on the rights and powers of the president; nor was the law an attempt by Congress to increase its power at the expense of the president. In dissent, Justice Antonin Scalia accused the majority of violating both the letter and the spirit of the separation of powers doctrine by depriving the president of all the executive powers vested in the office by the Constitution. This argument follows from a theory called the unitary executive, which claims to find support in the vesting clause. This power, according to proponents, implies that only the president is vested with the authority to carry out the laws in the executive branch, so only the president can appoint and remove officers exercising executive powers, including the independent counsel.

The independent counsel statute, upheld in *Morrison*, expired at the end of 1992. Because of partisan differences at that time, it was not reenacted. In June 1994, however, a new statute became law and was invoked almost immediately to appoint independent counsel Kenneth Starr to investigate various activities of President Clinton that ultimately led to the president's 1998 impeachment by the House of Representatives.

The revised law received even more criticism than the earlier version. The independent counsel's open-ended term of office, nearly unconstrained prosecutorial power, and expensive operation doomed the prospects for renewing the statute without significant reform. The legislation expired without reauthorization in 1999.

Still, we should keep in mind that *Morrison* remains today an important standard for determining whether an officer is an inferior officer. But it is not the only one. Less than a decade after *Morrison*, Justice Scalia attempted to devise a new approach in his majority opinion *Edmond v. United States* (1997). After contending that "*Morrison* did not purport to set forth a definitive test for whether an office is 'inferior' under the Appointments Clause," he wrote:

> Generally speaking, the term "inferior officer" connotes a relationship with some higher ranking officer or officers below the President: whether one is an "inferior" officer depends on whether he has a superior. It is not enough that other officers may be identified who formally maintain a higher rank, or possess responsibilities of a greater magnitude. If that were the intention, the Constitution might have used the phrase "lesser officer." Rather, in the context of a clause designed to preserve political accountability relative to important

government assignments, *we think it evident that "inferior officers" are officers whose work is directed and supervised at some level by others who were appointed by presidential nomination with the advice and consent of the Senate.*

Even though Scalia's approach is more general than Rehnquist's, *Edmond* did not overrule *Morrison* and so today both approaches coexist. Had he applied his *Edmond* definition of "inferior" to the special prosecutor, do you think Scalia would have reached a different conclusion in *Morrison*? Why or why not?

The Power of Removal

The president's need to have executive branch officials who support the administration's policy goals is only partially satisfied by the power to appoint. What presidents also say they require is the corollary —the discretionary right to remove administrative officials from office. This need may arise when a president's appointees do not carry out their duties in the way the president wishes, or when an official appointed by a previous administration will not voluntarily step aside to make way for a nominee of the new president's choosing.

Article II, Section 4, of the Constitution specifies that "[t]he President, Vice President and all civil officers of the United States, shall be removed from office on Impeachment for, and Conviction of, Treason, Bribery, or other high Crimes and Misdemeanors." Short of impeachment, however, the Constitution does not delineate procedures for removals. In the absence of constitutional guidelines, a lingering controversy has centered on whether administrative officials can be removed at the discretion of the president alone or whether Congress also must play a role.

The argument supporting presidential discretion holds that the chief executive must be free to remove those subordinates who fail to meet the president's expectations or who are not loyal to the administration's policy objectives. It would be unreasonable to require the approval of Congress before such officials could be dismissed. Such a requirement might well paralyze the executive branch, particularly when the legislature and the presidency are under the control of different political parties. Moreover, to proponents of the unitary executive, this argument, as noted, finds support in the vesting clause of Article II. Only the president, they contend, is vested with the authority to execute the laws in the executive branch, and only he can remove officers in "his" branch.

The argument for legislative participation in the process holds that the Constitution anticipates Senate action. If the president can appoint major executive department officials only with senatorial approval, it is reasonable to infer that the chief executive can remove administrators only by going through the same process and obtaining the advice and consent of the Senate. In *The Federalist Papers'* only reference to the removal powers, Alexander Hamilton supported this view. He flatly stated in *Federalist* No. 77, "The consent of that body [the Senate] would be necessary to displace as well as to appoint." Hamilton argued that if the president and the Senate agreed that an official should be removed, the decision would be much better accepted than if the president acted alone. Hamilton also asserted that a new president should be restrained from removing an experienced official who had conducted his duties satisfactorily just because the president preferred to have a different person in the position.

Historical practice generally has rejected Hamilton's position. From the very beginning, Congress allowed the chief executive to remove administrative officials without Senate consent. In the First Congress James Madison proposed that three executive departments be created: Foreign Affairs, Treasury, and War Departments. The creation of the Foreign Affairs (later State) Department received the most legislative attention. According to Madison's recommendation, the department was to have a secretary, to be appointed by the president with the approval of the Senate, who the president alone could remove. The House and the Senate held long comprehensive debates on the removal power at that time and passed legislation allowing the secretary of state to be removed at the president's discretion without Senate approval.

At times, however, the legislature has asserted a right to participate in the process. The most notable example occurred with the passage of the Tenure of Office Act in 1867. This statute was enacted to restrict the powers of President Andrew Johnson, who took office after Lincoln's assassination in 1865. Following the Civil War, the Radical Republicans dominated Congress and had little use for Johnson, a Democrat from Tennessee. Congress did not want Johnson to be able to remove Lincoln's appointees. The Tenure of Office Act stipulated that the president could not remove high-ranking executive department heads without first obtaining the approval of the Senate. Johnson blatantly defied the statute by dismissing Secretary of War Edwin M. Stanton in August 1867 and appointing Ulysses S. Grant as interim secretary. The Senate ordered Stanton reinstated. Grant left office and Stanton returned in January 1868. The next month Johnson fired Stanton again. The president's failure to comply with the Tenure of Office Act constituted one of the grounds for his impeachment by the House of Representatives.

The Tenure of Office Act never had a judicial test. Once Johnson's term expired, the statute was weakened by amendment and then repealed in 1887. Consequently, as the nation entered the twentieth century there had yet to be an authoritative declaration of the constitutional parameters of the removal power, although some other statutes still on the books asserted a role for the Senate in the dismissal of administrative officials.

It was well into the twentieth century before the Supreme Court resolved the confusion over the president's removal powers. Its first and most important ruling came in *Myers v. United States* (1926), a lawsuit challenging the authority of President Woodrow Wilson to fire Frank Myers, a Portland, Oregon, postmaster. In a strongly worded opinion, Chief Justice William Howard Taft, a former U.S. president, upheld Wilson's power to remove.

Taft's opinion stressed that the power to remove is an incident of the power to appoint. It is an executive power that resides with the president. That the Constitution limits the appointment power by senatorial consent does not necessarily mean that the removal power is also to be limited by Senate participation. The president is entrusted with taking care that the laws are faithfully executed. To accomplish this goal, the president must have an administration in which he has confidence. To allow the Senate to participate in the removal of administrative officials would severely limit the chief executive's ability to carry out the constitutional obligations of the office. As a result of this reasoning, the Court declared unconstitutional the Tenure of Office Act of 1867 and any subsequent legislation having the same purpose.

Later, the Court qualified the president's removal power, partially backing away from the strong position expressed in *Myers*. In **Humphrey's Executor v. United States** (1935) and *Wiener v. United States* (1958), the Court distinguished between officials with purely executive responsibilities and those who exercise quasi-legislative or quasi-judicial power. In *Humphrey's Executor* the justices upheld the right of Congress to restrict the president's authority to remove commissioners serving on independent administrative agencies, such as the Federal Trade Commission. These officials are involved in administrative rule making

and enforcement. Congress purposefully placed them outside the president's direct command. In *Wiener* the justices allowed the legislature to limit the president's power to remove members of a special war claims commission created to adjudicate war-related compensation claims. Because of its quasi-judicial responsibilities, the commission was not organized under the president's executive command. Consistent with *Myers*, however, officials that exercise purely executive power serve at the pleasure of the president and can be removed at the president's discretion.

Executive Privilege: Protecting Presidential Confidentiality

Article II is silent on two potentially important and related questions pertaining to the president's roles as chief executive and commander in chief. The first, executive privilege, asks whether the president can refuse to supply the other branches of government with information about his activities. The second (covered in the next section) is immunity—whether and to what extent the president is protected from lawsuits while in office.

The executive privilege argument asserts that certain conversations, documents, and records are so closely tied to the sensitive duties of the president that they should remain confidential. Neither the legislature nor the judiciary should be allowed access to these materials without presidential consent, nor should the other branches be empowered to compel the president to hand over such items, especially those related to matters concerning national security or foreign policy. Executive privilege, it is argued, is inherent to the office of the president.

Although infrequently invoked, the privilege doctrine has been part of American history since the beginning of the nation. In some early disputes between the president and Congress, chief executives refused to provide certain information to the legislature. George Washington balked at giving the House of Representatives documents and correspondence pertaining to the Jay Treaty—a controversial treaty between the United States and Great Britain. During the investigation and trial of Aaron Burr, Thomas Jefferson cooperated with congressional information requests, but only up to a point. He refused to produce some items and later declined to testify at the trial even though he was subpoenaed.

Other presidents through the years have also refused to comply with congressional requests for testimony. It is generally accepted that Congress does not have the power to compel the president to come before it to answer questions. Whether other executive department officials are covered by claims of privilege is a more open question.

The George W. Bush administration claimed the privilege a handful of times against congressional investigations—mostly after Democrats took control of both houses of Congress in 2006 and launched a series of investigations.[12] In 2012 President Obama asserted executive privilege in response to demands from House Republicans for information on a sting operation against Mexican drug cartel activities that had gone awry. Interestingly, when Obama came into office, he had to decide how to deal with a claim of executive privilege by his predecessor, President Bush, over the firing of U.S. attorneys in the face of a congressional subpoena. The Obama administration chose to negotiate an agreement whereby only some of the requested documents and testimony would be provided but only those from a specific period, and the testimony would not be in front of the public. Furthermore, the witnesses would not have to testify about communications to or from the president.

This is typical. In many instances, disputes over executive privilege are handled through negotiation between the executive branch and the institution requesting information. Only rarely have such disputes blown up into major court cases. When pushed to the limit, executive privilege claims may or may not prevail, but a president probably can increase his chances of success when sensitive military or diplomatic matters requiring secrecy are involved.

No case involving executive privilege has been more important than *United States v. Nixon* (1974). It occurred at a time of great constitutional stress, when all three branches were locked in a fight about fundamental separation of powers issues.

The conflict ultimately was resolved when President Nixon resigned. Much of the impetus for breaking the constitutional deadlock came from the justices' unanimous decision in the *Nixon* case. Chief Justice Warren Burger's opinion for the Court reviewed the issues surrounding the executive privilege controversy and then rejected Nixon's invocation of the doctrine.

---

[12]Martin Rosenberg, "Presidential Claims of Executive Privilege: History, Law, Practice and Recent Developments," *Congressional Research Service Report for Congress*, 2008, http://www.fas.org/sgp/crs/secrecy/RL30319.pdf.

United States v. Nixon

418 U.S. 683 (1974)
http://caselaw.findlaw.com/us-supreme-court/418/683.html
Oral arguments are available at https://www.oyez.org/
cases/1973/73-1766
Vote: 8 (Blackmun, Brennan, Burger, Douglas, Marshall, Powell, Stewart, White)
0

OPINION OF THE COURT: *Burger*

NOT PARTICIPATING: *Rehnquist*

This case was one of many court actions spawned by the Watergate scandal. The controversy began on June 17, 1972, when seven men broke into the Democratic National Committee headquarters located in the Watergate complex in Washington, D.C. The men were apprehended and charged with criminal offenses. All had ties either to the White House or to the Committee to Re-elect the President. Five of the seven pleaded guilty, and two were convicted. At the end of the trial, one of the defendants, James McCord Jr., claimed that he had been pressured to plead guilty and that other people involved in the break-in had not been prosecuted. Many suspected that the break-in was only the tip of a very large iceberg of shady dealings and cover-ups perpetrated by influential persons with close ties to the Nixon administration.

On May 17, 1973, the Senate began its investigation of the Watergate incident and the activities related to it. The star witness was John Dean III, special counsel to the president, who testified under a grant of immunity. Dean implicated high officials in the president's office, and he claimed that Nixon had known about the events and the subsequent cover-ups. As surprising as Dean's allegations were, the most shocking revelation came from Nixon adviser Alexander Butterfield, who testified that the president had installed a secret taping system that automatically recorded all conversations in the Oval Office. Obviously, the tape recordings held information that would settle the dispute between the witnesses claiming White House involvement in the Watergate affair and the administration officials who denied it.

In addition to the Senate investigation, a special prosecutor (today called a special counsel) was appointed to look into the Watergate affair. The first person to hold this position, Archibald Cox, asked the president to turn over the tapes. When Nixon declined, Cox went to court to get an order compelling him to deliver the materials. The district and appeals courts ruled in favor of Cox. Nixon then offered to release summaries of the recordings, but that did not satisfy Cox, who continued to pursue the tapes. In response, Nixon ordered that Cox be fired. When the two highest officials in the

GRAND JURY   SUBPOENA DUCES TECUM

Subpoena Duces Tecum   **United States District Court**

For the District of Columbia

Misc. #47-73

THE UNITED STATES

vs.

JOHN DOE

REPORT TO UNITED STATES DISTRICT COURT HOUSE

Between 3d Street and John Marshall Place and on Constitution Avenue NW.

Grand Jury Room 3

Washington, D.C.

To: Richard M. Nixon, The White House, Washington, D. C., or any subordinate officer, official, or employee with custody or control of the documents or objects hereinafter described on the attached schedule.

FILED

JUL 24 1973

JAMES F. DAVEY, Clerk

You are hereby commanded to attend before the Grand Jury of said Court on **Thursday** the **26th** day of **July**, 19**73**, at **10** o'clock **A. M.**, to testify and to bring with you the documents or objects listed on the attached sched- *WITNESS:* The Honorable **John J. Sirica** Chief Judge of said Court, this ule.

23rd day of **July**, 19**73**.

JAMES F. DAVEY, *Clerk.*

Archibald Cox

ARCHIBALD COX

Attorney for the United States

By *Robert L. Line*

Deputy Clerk.

Form No. USA-9x-184 (Rev. 7-1-71)

34

This subpoena duces tecum was issued July 23, 1973. It ordered President Nixon or his representatives to appear before the federal grand jury on July 26 and to bring taped conversations relevant to the investigation of the Watergate affair.

This drawing illustrates Richard Nixon's attorney, James St. Clair, arguing the president's case before the Supreme Court in *United States v. Nixon* (1974). The four justices are (left to right) Chief Justice Warren Burger, William J. Brennan Jr., Byron R. White, and Harry A. Blackmun. The empty chair at the far right belongs to Justice William Rehnquist, who recused himself because of his former duties as assistant attorney general in the Nixon administration.

Justice Department resigned rather than comply with Nixon's order, Solicitor General Robert Bork became the acting attorney general and dismissed Cox. The firing and the resignations, popularly known as the "Saturday night massacre," enraged the American people, and many began calling for the president's impeachment.

Leon Jaworski was appointed to take Cox's place. An attorney from Houston, Jaworski pursued the tapes with the same zeal as had Cox. Finally, Nixon relented and agreed to produce some of the materials. But when he did so, the prosecutor found that the tapes had been heavily edited. One contained eighteen and one-half minutes of mysterious buzzing at a crucial point, indicating that conversation had been erased.

Jaworski obtained criminal indictments against several Nixon aides. Although no criminal charges were brought against the president, he was named in the indictment as a coconspirator. At about the same time, the House Judiciary Committee began an investigation into whether the president should be impeached.

The Judiciary Committee and Jaworski sought more of the tapes to review, but Nixon steadfastly refused to comply, claiming that it was his right under executive privilege to decide what would be released and what would remain secret. The district court issued a final subpoena duces tecum (a judicial command to bring forth physical evidence); thus the president was ordered to produce the tapes and other documents. Both the United States and Nixon requested that the Supreme Court review the case, and the justices accepted the case on an expedited basis, bypassing the court of appeals.

CHIEF JUSTICE BURGER DELIVERED THE OPINION OF THE COURT.

[The President claims that] the subpoena should be quashed because it demands "confidential conversations between a President and his close advisors that it would be inconsistent with the public interest to produce." The first contention is a broad claim that the separation of powers doctrine precludes judicial review of a President's claim of privilege. The second contention is that if he does not prevail on the claim of absolute privilege, the court should hold as a matter of constitutional law that the privilege prevails over the subpoena *duces tecum*.

In the performance of assigned constitutional duties each branch of the Government must initially interpret the Constitution, and the interpretation of its powers by any branch is due great respect from the others. The President's counsel, as we have noted, reads the Constitution as providing an absolute privilege of confidentiality for all Presidential communications. Many decisions of this Court, however, have unequivocally reaffirmed the holding of *Marbury v. Madison* (1803) that "[i]t is emphatically the province and duty of the judicial department to say what the law is." . . .

Notwithstanding the deference each branch must accord the others, the "judicial Power of the United States" vested in the federal courts by Art. III, §1, of the Constitution can no more be shared with the Executive Branch than the Chief Executive, for example, can share with the Judiciary the veto power, or the Congress share with the Judiciary the power to override a Presidential veto. Any other conclusion would be contrary to the basic concept of separation of powers and the checks and balances that flow from the scheme of a tripartite government. We therefore reaffirm that it is the province and duty of this Court "to say what the law is" with respect to the claim of privilege presented in this case.

In support of his claim of absolute privilege, the President's counsel urges two grounds, one of which is common to all governments and one of which is peculiar to our system of separation of powers. The first ground is the valid need for protection of communications between high Government officials and those who advise and assist them in the performance of their manifold duties; the importance of this confidentiality is too plain to require further discussion. Human experience teaches that those who expect public dissemination of their remarks may well temper candor with a concern for appearances and for their own interests to the detriment of the decision making process. Whatever the nature of the privilege of confidentiality of Presidential communications in the exercise of Art. II powers, the privilege can be said to derive from the supremacy of each branch within its own assigned area of constitutional duties. Certain powers and privileges flow from the nature of enumerated powers; the protection of the confidentiality of Presidential communications has similar constitutional underpinnings.

The second ground asserted by the President's counsel in support of the claim of absolute privilege rests on the doctrine of separation of powers. Here it is argued that the independence of the Executive Branch within its own sphere insulates a President from a judicial subpoena in an ongoing criminal prosecution, and thereby protects confidential Presidential communications.

However, neither the doctrine of separation of powers, nor the need for confidentiality of high-level communications, without more, can sustain an absolute, unqualified Presidential privilege of immunity from judicial process under all circumstances. The President's need for complete candor and objectivity from advisers calls for great deference from the courts. However, when the privilege depends solely on the broad, undifferentiated claim of public interest in the confidentiality of such conversations, a confrontation with other values arises. Absent a claim of need to protect military, diplomatic, or sensitive national security secrets, we find it difficult to accept the argument that even the very important interest in confidentiality of Presidential communications is significantly diminished by production of such material for *in camera* inspection with all the protection that a district court will be obliged to provide.

The impediment that an absolute, unqualified privilege would place in the way of the primary constitutional duty of the Judicial Branch to do justice in criminal prosecutions would plainly conflict with the function of the courts under Art. III. In designing the structure of our Government and dividing and allocating the sovereign power among three co-equal branches, the Framers of the Constitution sought to provide a comprehensive system, but the separate powers were not intended to operate with absolute independence. . . . To read the Art. II powers of the President as providing an absolute privilege as against a subpoena essential to enforcement of criminal statutes on no more than a generalized claim of the public interest in confidentiality of nonmilitary and nondiplomatic discussions would upset the constitutional balance of "a workable government" and gravely impair the role of the courts under Art. III.

Since we conclude that the legitimate needs of the judicial process may outweigh Presidential privilege, it is necessary to resolve those competing interests in a manner that preserves the essential functions of each branch. The right and indeed the duty to resolve that question does not free the Judiciary from according high respect to the representations made on behalf of the President.

The expectation of a President to the confidentiality of his conversations and correspondence, like the claim of confidentiality of judicial deliberations, for example, has all the values to which we accord deference for the privacy of all citizens and, added to those values, is the necessity for protection of the public interest in candid, objective, and even blunt or harsh opinions in Presidential decisionmaking. A President and those who assist him must be free to explore alternatives in the process of shaping policies and making decisions and to do so in a way many would be unwilling to express except privately. These are the considerations justifying a presumptive privilege for Presidential communications. The privilege is fundamental to the operation of Government and inextricably rooted in the separation of powers under the Constitution. . . .

But this presumptive privilege must be considered in light of our historic commitment to the rule of law. This is nowhere more profoundly manifest than in our view that "the twofold aim [of criminal justice] is that guilt shall not escape or innocence suffer." We have elected to employ an adversary system of criminal justice in which the parties contest all issues before a court of law. The need to develop all relevant facts in the adversary system is both fundamental and comprehensive. The ends of criminal justice would be defeated if judgments were to be founded on a partial or speculative presentation of the facts. The very integrity of the judicial system and public confidence in the system depend on full disclosure of all the facts, within the framework of the rules of evidence. To ensure that justice is done, it is imperative to the function of courts that compulsory process be available for the production of evidence needed either by the prosecution or by the defense. . . .

In this case the President challenges a subpoena served on him as a third party requiring the production of materials for use in a criminal prosecution; he does so on the claim that he has a privilege against disclosure of confidential communications. He does not place his claim of privilege on the ground they are military or diplomatic secrets. As to these areas of Art. II duties the courts have traditionally shown the utmost deference to Presidential responsibilities. . . . No case of the Court, however, has extended this high degree of deference to a President's generalized interest in confidentiality. Nowhere in the Constitution, as we have noted earlier, is there any explicit reference to a privilege of confidentiality, yet to the extent this interest relates to the effective discharge of a President's powers, it is constitutionally based.

The right to the production of all evidence at a criminal trial similarly has constitutional dimensions. The Sixth Amendment explicitly confers upon every defendant in a criminal trial the right "to be confronted with the witnesses against him" and "to have compulsory process for obtaining witnesses in his favor." Moreover, the Fifth Amendment also guarantees that no person shall be deprived of liberty without due process of law. It is the manifest duty of the courts to vindicate those guarantees, and to accomplish that it is essential that all relevant and admissible evidence be produced.

In this case we must weigh the importance of the general privilege of confidentiality of Presidential communications in performance of the President's responsibilities against the inroads of such a privilege on the fair administration of criminal justice. The interest in preserving confidentiality is weighty indeed and entitled to great respect. However, we cannot conclude that advisers will be moved to temper the candor of their remarks by the infrequent occasions of disclosure because of the possibility that such conversations will be called for in the context of a criminal prosecution.

On the other hand, the allowance of the privilege to withhold evidence that is demonstrably relevant in a criminal trial would cut deeply into the guarantee of due process of law and gravely impair the basic function of the courts. A President's acknowledged need for confidentiality in the communications of his office is general in nature, whereas the constitutional need for production of relevant evidence in a criminal proceeding is specific and central to the fair adjudication of a particular criminal case in the administration of justice. Without access to specific facts a criminal prosecution may be totally frustrated. The President's broad interest in confidentiality of communications will not be vitiated by disclosure of a limited number of conversations preliminarily shown to have some bearing on the pending criminal cases.

We conclude that when the ground for asserting privilege as to subpoenaed materials sought for use in a criminal trial is based only on the generalized interest in confidentiality, it cannot prevail over the fundamental demands of due process of law in the fair administration of criminal justice. The generalized assertion of privilege must yield to the demonstrated, specific need for evidence in a pending criminal trial . . . .

Accordingly, we affirm the order of the District Court that subpoenaed materials be transmitted to that court. We now turn to the important question of the District Court's responsibilities in conducting the *in camera* [in private in the judge's chambers] examination of Presidential materials or communications delivered under the compulsion of the subpoena *duces tecum* . . .

[I]t is obvious that the District Court has a very heavy responsibility to see to it that Presidential conversations, which are either not relevant or not admissible, are accorded that high degree of respect due the President of the United States . . . [The] President is [not] above the law, but . . . [his] communications and activities encompass a vastly wider range of sensitive material than would be true of any "ordinary individual." It is therefore necessary in the public interest to afford Presidential confidentiality the greatest protection consistent with the fair administration of justice.

Since this matter came before the Court during the pendency of a criminal prosecution, and on representations that time is of the essence, the mandate shall issue forthwith.

Affirmed

The Court's ruling was clear. In this case, the people's interest in the fair administration of criminal justice outweighed the president's interest in confidentiality. Executive privilege was rejected as a justification for refusing to make the tapes available to the special prosecutor. The opinion, however, does not answer questions about exactly who can invoke executive privilege or how long the privilege would be in effect, if at all. Based on the majority's logic, do you think former presidents, high-ranking executive aides, or even the spouses of presidents could invoke executive privilege?

Nixon complied with the Court's ruling, knowing full well that it meant the end of his presidency. In obeying the Court order, he avoided provoking what many feared would be the most serious of all constitutional confrontations. What if Nixon had refused to comply? What if he had destroyed the tapes rather than turn them over? Who could have enforced sanctions on the president for doing so? Impeachment and conviction of the president probably would have been the only way to handle such a crisis. Whatever Nixon's culpability in Watergate and related matters, he spared the nation a crisis by bowing to the Supreme Court's interpretation of the Constitution. The Nixon tapes revealed substantial wrongdoing. It was clear that the House of Representatives would present articles of impeachment and the Senate would vote to remove Nixon from office. Rather than put himself and the nation through such an ordeal, Nixon resigned.

Immunity: Protecting the President from Lawsuits

Presidential immunity is a variation on the notion of executive privilege. It deals with the extent to which the president is protected from lawsuits while in office, and the subject raises many interesting questions. May a president be ordered by a court to carry out certain executive actions, which are discretionary, or ministerial actions, which are performed as a matter of legal duty? Or, conversely, may a court restrain a president from taking such actions? May a private party sue the president for damages that might have been suffered because of the president's actions or omissions? If so, may a court order the president to pay damages or provide some other restitution? If a doctrine of immunity exists, should it extend only to actions presidents take while in office? These questions place us in a quandary. To grant the president immunity from such legal actions may remove needed accountability. But to allow the chief executive to be subject to suit could make the execution of presidential duties impossible.

The Supreme Court's first significant venture into the area of executive immunity came in ***Mississippi v. Johnson*** (1867). Following the Civil War, Congress passed a number of laws "for the more efficient government of the rebel states." More commonly known as the Reconstruction Acts, they imposed military rule over the southern states until such time as loyal

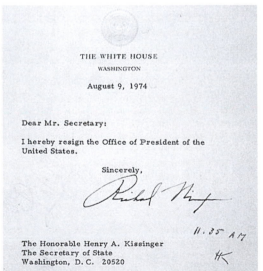

With this one-sentence letter, Richard Nixon became the first American president to resign from office.

Letters of Resignation and Declination of Federal Office, 1789–1974; General Records of the Department of State, 1756–1979; Record Group 59; National Archives and Records Administration.

republican governments could be established. Andrew Johnson, a southerner from Tennessee, who had assumed the presidency after Lincoln's assassination, vetoed the legislation, but the Radical Republicans in Congress had sufficient votes to override him. Once the acts were part of federal law, the president had little choice but to enforce them, despite his belief that they were unconstitutional.

The state of Mississippi joined the fray. Applying directly to the Supreme Court, Mississippi sued Johnson, asking the justices to issue an order prohibiting him from enforcing the laws, which the state argued were unconstitutional.

The Supreme Court rejected Mississippi's petition. The Court drew a distinction between ministerial and executive actions. A ministerial act is one over which there is no discretion. It occurs when a statute clearly directs the performance of a specific act. An executive act, by contrast, is one that allows discretion. The enforcement of a statute, such as the Reconstruction Act, is undoubtedly an executive action. A president enforces a law using judgment and discretion. It is not a simple ministerial act, but one that involves many political and administrative decisions. The judiciary is without power to enjoin the president in carrying out his "purely executive and political" functions. This stems from the separation of powers principle, but it is also a practical matter. If the courts enjoined the president and he refused to comply, how would the judiciary enforce its order? The Court concluded, as Chief Justice Salmon P. Chase wrote, "This court has no jurisdiction of a bill to enjoin the President in the performance of his official duties."

The decision in *Johnson* settles the issue of whether the president may be as a person or as president with respect to executive functions, but it did not answer the question of civil suits brought by private individuals who claim harm by a president's actions. If an incumbent president engages in unlawful activities that allegedly harm private individuals, can the president be held accountable in a court of law? Or is the president immune from such suits?

The Court answered these questions in **Nixon v. Fitzgerald** (1982). This legal action was initiated by A. Ernest Fitzgerald, who had been employed as a civilian management analyst for the U.S. Air Force. Fitzgerald blew the whistle in congressional testimony on some $2 billion in cost overruns for the development of the C-5A transport plane. His testimony was not well received by the Defense Department or military contractors.

Thirteen months later Fitzgerald lost his job in what Defense officials claimed was a necessary departmental reorganization. Fitzgerald, however, believed the elimination of his job was an illegal retaliation for his congressional testimony. He was able to gather some evidence to support his claim, including President Nixon's admission that he was aware of the firing and approved it. Fitzgerald sued several executive branch officials, including the president (who resigned during the early stages of the lower court proceedings). The former president's lawyers asserted that he should be removed from the suit on the ground of absolute executive immunity from legal actions based on his official conduct as president. The lower courts rejected the absolute immunity claim, and Nixon appealed.

By a 5–4 vote, the justices supported the president and extended immunity from lawsuit to cases such as this. Justice Powell explained:

> Because of the singular importance of the President's duties, diversion of his energies by concern with private lawsuits would raise unique risks to the effective functioning of government. . . . In view of the special nature of the President's constitutional office and functions, we think it appropriate to recognize absolute Presidential immunity from damages liability for acts within the "outer perimeter" of his official responsibility.

Decisions such as *Mississippi v. Johnson* and *Nixon v. Fitzgerald* speak to immunity from lawsuits based on the president's official conduct, but they do not consider the problem of lawsuits filed against the president for behavior unrelated to his office. This issue was raised in 1994 when Paula Corbin Jones, a former Arkansas state employee, filed a civil suit against President Clinton, claiming that while he was governor of Arkansas he had made improper and illegal sexual advances toward her in a Little Rock hotel room. There were heated public arguments over whether this was a case of inexcusable sexual harassment or a groundless, politically motivated lawsuit designed to undermine and embarrass the president. Political rhetoric aside, the case presented a major constitutional issue: Can a sitting president be required to stand trial on allegations concerning his unofficial conduct? Jones's supporters argued that the president is not immune from lawsuit and that Jones, like any other citizen, had the right to prompt judicial determination of her claims of being unlawfully treated. Clinton's supporters argued that the chief executive should not have to stand trial during his term of office. Allowing a trial to proceed would divert the president's attention from his official duties. Even worse, allowing such legal actions might encourage a rash of civil lawsuits instigated by political opponents of the president. The Supreme Court settled the issue on May 27, 1997.

Clinton v. Jones

520 U.S. 681 (1997)
http://caselaw.findlaw.com/us-supreme-court/520/681.html
Oral arguments are available at https://www.oyez.org/
  cases/1996/95-1853
Vote: 9 (Breyer, Ginsburg, Kennedy, O'Connor, Rehnquist, Scalia,
  Souter, Stevens, Thomas)
  0

OPINION OF THE COURT: Stevens

CONCURRING OPINION: Breyer

Bill Clinton was elected to the presidency in 1992 and reelected in 1996. Before becoming president, Clinton served as governor of Arkansas from 1979 to 1981 and from 1983 to 1992. In 1994 Paula Corbin Jones filed suit in federal district court in Arkansas against Clinton and Arkansas state trooper Danny Ferguson over an incident that was alleged to have occurred on May 8, 1991, at the Excelsior Hotel in Little Rock. On the day in question Jones, then an employee of the state Industrial Development Commission, was working at the registration desk for a management conference at which Governor Clinton had delivered a speech. According to her allegations, Trooper Ferguson approached Jones and indicated that the governor wanted to see her. Ferguson escorted her to Clinton's hotel suite where Jones and the governor were left alone in the room. The suit claimed that Clinton made "abhorrent" sexual advances to Jones, including exposing himself to her, touching her inappropriately, and making unwelcome sexual remarks. Jones said she rejected Clinton's suggestions, and the governor ceased his advances. As she was leaving the room, Jones alleged the governor told her, "You are smart. Let's keep this between ourselves."

Jones's suit claimed that after she returned to her state job, her superiors began treating her rudely; she was ultimately transferred to another position that had little potential for advancement. She attributed this harsh treatment to retaliation for her rejection of the governor. The suit asked for actual damages of $75,000 and punitive damages of $100,000 in compensation for Clinton's violations of state and federal civil rights and sexual harassment laws.

Paula Corbin Jones, shown here at a 1998 news conference, brought a sexual harassment lawsuit against President Bill Clinton. The suit led the Supreme Court to confront the question of whether a president can be tried while still in office for conduct unrelated to official executive duties.

Clinton denied the allegations and claimed the lawsuit was politically motivated. He filed motions asking the district court to dismiss the case on the ground of presidential immunity and to prohibit Jones from refiling the suit until after the end of his presidency. The district judge rejected the presidential immunity argument. Although she allowed pretrial discovery activities to proceed, the judge ordered that no trial would take place until Clinton was no longer president. Both Jones and Clinton appealed. Holding that "the President, like all other government officials, is subject to the same laws that apply to all other members of society," the court of appeals ruled that the trial should not be postponed. Clinton asked the Supreme Court to reverse the decision.

At the time, only three sitting presidents had been defendants in civil litigation involving their actions prior to taking office: Theodore Roosevelt, Harry Truman, and John F. Kennedy. In all three, the suits were dismissed or settled, and so, as the Court noted, they did not shed much "light on the constitutional issue" in this case.

JUSTICE STEVENS DELIVERED THE OPINION OF THE COURT.

This case raises a constitutional and a prudential question concerning the Office of the President of the United States. Respondent, a private citizen, seeks to recover damages from the current occupant of that office based on actions allegedly taken before his term began. The President submits that in all but the most exceptional cases the Constitution requires federal courts to defer such litigation until his term ends and that, in any event, respect for the office warrants such a stay. Despite the force of the arguments supporting the President's submissions, we conclude that they must be rejected. . . .

The principal rationale for affording certain public servants immunity from suits for money damages arising out of their official acts is inapplicable to unofficial conduct. In cases involving prosecutors, legislators, and judges we have repeatedly explained that the immunity serves the public interest in enabling such officials to perform their designated functions effectively without fear that a particular decision may give rise to personal liability. . . .

That rationale provided the principal basis for our holding that a former President of the United States was "entitled to absolute immunity from damages liability predicated on his official acts," [*Nixon v.*] *Fitzgerald* [1982]. Our central concern was to avoid rendering the President "unduly cautious in the discharge of his official duties."

This reasoning provides no support for an immunity for *unofficial* conduct. As we explained in *Fitzgerald,* "the sphere of protected action must be related closely to the immunity's justifying purposes." Because of the President's broad responsibilities, we recognized in that case an immunity from damages claims arising out of official acts extending to the "outer perimeter of his authority." But we have never suggested that the President, or any other official, has an immunity that extends beyond the scope of any action taken in an official capacity.

Moreover, when defining the scope of an immunity for acts clearly taken *within* an official capacity, we have applied a functional approach. "Frequently our decisions have held that an official's absolute immunity should extend only to acts in performance of particular functions of his office." Hence, for example, a judge's absolute immunity does not extend to actions performed in a purely administrative capacity. As our opinions have made clear, immunities are grounded in "the nature of the function performed, not the identity of the actor who performed it." . . .

Petitioner's strongest argument supporting his immunity claim is based on the text and structure of the Constitution. He does not contend that the occupant of the Office of the President is "above the law," in the sense that his conduct is entirely immune from judicial scrutiny. The President argues merely for a postponement of the judicial proceedings that will determine whether he violated any law. His argument is grounded in the character of the office that was created by Article II of the Constitution, and relies on separation of powers principles that have structured our constitutional arrangement since the founding.

As a starting premise, petitioner contends that he occupies a unique office with powers and responsibilities so vast and important that the public interest demands that he devote his undivided time and attention to his public duties. He submits that—given the nature of the office—the doctrine of separation of powers places limits on the authority of the Federal Judiciary to interfere with the Executive Branch that would be transgressed by allowing this action to proceed.

We have no dispute with the initial premise of the argument. Former presidents, from George Washington to George Bush, have consistently endorsed petitioner's characterization of the office. . . .

It does not follow, however, that separation of powers principles would be violated by allowing this action to proceed. The doctrine of separation of powers is concerned with the allocation of official power among the three coequal branches of our Government. . . .

Of course the lines between the powers of the three branches are not always neatly defined. But in this case there is no suggestion that the Federal Judiciary is being asked to perform any function that might in some way be described as "executive." Respondent is merely asking the courts to exercise their core Article III jurisdiction to decide cases and controversies. Whatever the outcome of this case, there is no possibility that the decision will curtail the scope of the official powers of the Executive Branch. The litigation of questions that relate entirely to the unofficial conduct of the individual who happens to be the President poses no perceptible risk of misallocation of either judicial power or executive power.

Rather than arguing that the decision of the case will produce either an aggrandizement of judicial power or a narrowing of executive power, petitioner contends that—as a by-product of an otherwise traditional exercise of judicial power—burdens will be placed on the President that will hamper the performance of his official duties. . . . As a factual matter, petitioner contends that this particular case—as well as the potential additional litigation that an affirmance of the Court of Appeals judgment might spawn—may impose an unacceptable burden on the President's time and energy, and thereby impair the effective performance of his office.

Petitioner's predictive judgment finds little support in either history or the relatively narrow compass of the issues raised in this particular case. [I]n the more than 200-year history of the Republic, only three sitting Presidents have been subjected to suits for their private actions. If the past is any indicator, it seems unlikely that a deluge of such litigation will ever engulf the Presidency. As for the case at hand, if properly managed by the District Court, it appears to us highly unlikely to occupy any substantial amount of petitioner's time.

Of greater significance, petitioner errs by presuming that interactions between the Judicial Branch and the Executive, even quite burdensome interactions, necessarily rise to the level of constitutionally forbidden impairment of the Executive's ability to perform its constitutionally mandated functions. . . . The fact that a federal court's exercise of its traditional Article III jurisdiction may significantly burden the time and attention of the Chief Executive is not sufficient to establish a violation of the Constitution. Two long-settled propositions, first announced by Chief Justice Marshall, support that conclusion.

First, we have long held that when the President takes official action, the Court has the authority to determine whether he has acted within the law. . . .

Second, it is also settled that the President is subject to judicial process in appropriate circumstances. Although Thomas Jefferson apparently thought otherwise, Chief Justice Marshall, when presiding in the treason trial of Aaron Burr, ruled that a subpoena *duces tecum* could be directed to the President. We unequivocally and emphatically endorsed Marshall's position when we held that President Nixon was obligated to comply with a subpoena commanding him to produce certain tape recordings of his conversations with his aides. *United States v. Nixon* (1974). As we explained, "neither the doctrine of separation of powers, nor the need for confidentiality of high-level communications, without more, can sustain an absolute, unqualified Presidential privilege of immunity from judicial process under all circumstances."

Sitting Presidents have responded to court orders to provide testimony and other information with sufficient frequency that such interactions between the Judicial and Executive Branches can scarcely be thought a novelty. President Monroe responded to written interrogatories, President Nixon—as noted above—produced tapes in response to a subpoena *duces tecum,* President Ford complied with an order to give a deposition in a criminal trial, and President Clinton has twice given videotaped testimony in criminal proceedings. Moreover, sitting Presidents have also voluntarily complied with judicial requests for testimony. . . .

In sum, "[i]t is settled law that the separation-of-powers doctrine does not bar every exercise of jurisdiction over the President of the United States." *Fitzgerald.* If the Judiciary may severely burden the Executive Branch by reviewing the legality of the President's official conduct, and if it may direct appropriate process to the President himself, it must follow that the federal courts have power to determine the legality of his unofficial conduct. The burden on the President's time and energy that is a mere by-product of such review surely cannot be considered as onerous as the direct burden imposed by judicial review and the occasional invalidation of his official actions. We therefore hold that the doctrine of separation of powers does not require federal courts to stay all private actions against the President until he leaves office. . . .

. . . [W]e are persuaded that it was an abuse of discretion for the District Court to defer the trial until after the President leaves office. Such a lengthy and categorical stay takes no account whatever of the respondent's interest in bringing the case to trial. The complaint was filed within the statutory limitations period—albeit near the end of that period—and delaying trial would increase the danger of prejudice resulting from the loss of evidence, including the inability of witnesses to recall specific facts, or the possible death of a party.

The decision to postpone the trial was, furthermore, premature. The proponent of a stay bears the burden of establishing its need. . . . We think the District Court may have given undue weight to the concern that a trial might generate unrelated civil actions that could conceivably hamper the President in conducting the duties of his office. If and when that should occur, the court's discretion would permit it to manage those actions in such fashion (including deferral of trial) that interference with the President's duties would not occur. But no such impingement upon the President's conduct of his office was shown here.

We add a final comment on two matters that are discussed at length in the briefs: the risk that our decision will generate a large volume of politically motivated harassing and frivolous litigation, and the danger that national security concerns might prevent the President from explaining a legitimate need for a continuance.

We are not persuaded that either of these risks is serious. Most frivolous and vexatious litigation is terminated at the pleading stage or on summary judgment, with little if any personal involvement by the defendant. Moreover, the availability of sanctions provides a significant deterrent to litigation directed at the President in his unofficial capacity for purposes of political gain or harassment. History indicates that the likelihood that a significant number of such cases will be filed is remote. Although scheduling problems may arise, there is no reason to assume that the District Courts will be either unable to accommodate the President's needs or unfaithful to the tradition—especially in matters involving national security—of giving "the utmost deference to Presidential responsibilities." Several Presidents, including petitioner, have given testimony without jeopardizing the Nation's security. In short, we have confidence in the ability of our federal judges to deal with both of these concerns.

If Congress deems it appropriate to afford the President stronger protection, it may respond with appropriate legislation. . . . If the Constitution embodied the rule that the President advocates, Congress, of course, could not repeal it. But our holding today raises no barrier to a statutory response to these concerns.

The Federal District Court has jurisdiction to decide this case. Like every other citizen who properly invokes that jurisdiction, respondent has a right to an orderly disposition of her claims. Accordingly, the judgment of the Court of Appeals is affirmed.

It is so ordered.

BOX 5-2

Aftermath . . . *Clinton v. Jones*

In *Clinton v. Jones* (1997) the Supreme Court rejected President Clinton's request to postpone a trial on Paula Jones's sexual harassment charges until his presidency ended. Thus began two years of intense legal difficulties for the president. Clinton was already under investigation by Independent Counsel Kenneth Starr for possible financial improprieties in the Whitewater matter, an Arkansas land deal that occurred prior to his presidency. That investigation coupled with the *Jones* lawsuit subjected Clinton to more intense scrutiny than any previous president had experienced.

While preparing their case, Jones's attorneys were made aware of a possible illicit relationship between Clinton and a young White House intern, Monica Lewinsky. Attempting to establish a pattern of wrongdoing, Jones's lawyers subpoenaed Lewinsky and the president. Lewinsky initially denied any sexual relationship with Clinton. On January 17, 1998, President Clinton gave a sworn deposition claiming that he had not had a sexual relationship with Lewinsky. Nine days later he made the same denial to the American people on national television. Taped telephone conversations between Lewinsky and her friend Linda Tripp, who had given the tapes to the independent counsel's office, revealed that a sexual relationship between Lewinsky and Clinton had occurred. Starr expanded his investigation to include an inquiry into the Lewinsky matter.

After receiving immunity from prosecution, Lewinsky changed her testimony, acknowledging a past relationship with the president. In August Clinton admitted to "a critical lapse of judgment" that had led to his affair with Lewinsky. By this time, other women had come forward claiming that Clinton had acted inappropriately with them. In November the president settled his legal dispute with Jones for $850,000 with no apology or admission of guilt.

Settling the *Jones* case, however, did not end Clinton's troubles. In December the House of Representatives considered four articles of impeachment its Judiciary Committee recommended. Two of the proposals passed: one charged Clinton with perjury, and the other alleged obstruction of justice. As a result, Bill Clinton became the second president in U.S. history to be impeached.

In January 1999, with Chief Justice William Rehnquist presiding and the senators acting as a jury, the U.S. Senate tried Clinton on the two articles of impeachment. On February 12 Clinton was acquitted on both counts. The senators voted 55–45 to acquit on the perjury charge and 50–50 on the obstruction of justice charge, both falling far short of the 67 guilty votes required to remove Clinton from office. Throughout the impeachment process, public opinion ran decidedly in Clinton's favor.

Clinton's legal problems continued. U.S. judge Susan Webber Wright, who presided over the *Jones* lawsuit, found Clinton in contempt and fined him $90,000 for undermining "the integrity of the judicial system" by giving "false, misleading, and evasive answers that were designed to obstruct justice." In May 2000, the Arkansas Supreme Court initiated disbarment proceedings against him. But on January 19, 2001, his last full day in office, Clinton reached an agreement with the independent counsel in which he admitted wrongdoing and accepted a $25,000 fine and a five-year suspension of his license to practice law, thereby settling the disbarment question.

Throughout all of these difficulties, Bill Clinton's presidency was surprisingly unaffected. Polls indicated that the public perceived Clinton as a man with serious personal character flaws but gave him historically high approval ratings for the job he was doing as president.

Sources: Los Angeles Times, May 23, 2000; *Omaha World-Herald*, February 13, 1999; *New York Times*, February 13, 1999, July 30, 1999; *San Francisco Chronicle*, February 13, 1999.

The Court's conclusion that Jones's sexual harassment suit could proceed was a blow to President Clinton, who was by that time heavily involved in other controversies that ultimately led to his impeachment (*see Box 5-2*). In the end, Clinton and Jones reached an out-of-court monetary settlement of the dispute. Although the *Jones* case never went to trial, the Supreme Court's ruling that presidents while in office may be sued for unofficial conduct is a meaningful addition to the law of presidential immunity. It also remains controversial.

Some scholars suggested that it would ultimately prove damaging to the presidency, while others argued that the Clinton episode was so anomalous that future plaintiffs would be unlikely to take advantage of the Court's ruling. The Trump presidency may supply more definitive answers about the importance of *Clinton v. Jones*, considering the number of civil suits now pending against Trump—including failure to pay hotel workers, misleading former students at Trump University, and defaming a former competitor on the television show *The Apprentice* (who had accused Trump of sexual assault).

POWERS OVER FOREIGN AFFAIRS

Americans have always looked to the president for leadership in foreign affairs, whether in the normal conduct of political and economic relationships with other countries or in times of war and national emergency. As with the exercise of power in other critical areas, the president's constitutional role in international affairs has occasionally required definition by the Supreme Court.

In the areas implicating the nation's external affairs—including foreign policy, militarized disputes, and war— the Constitution confers a good deal of authority on the president:

- Article II, Section 2, assigns to the president the role of commander in chief of the army and navy. Of course this role pertains mostly directly to military capability but also to foreign policy: military power not only enables a nation to deter hostile actions from other countries, but also can be used as a credible threat to persuade other nations to follow certain preferred courses of action. Armed interventions and full-scale wars can be major elements in executing a nation's foreign policy. Modern military actions, both small and large, taken by the United States in Grenada, Panama, Afghanistan, Kuwait, Kosovo, Libya, and Iraq demonstrate the use of this power.

- Article II gives the president the sole authority to make treaties on behalf of the United States. These international agreements may cover almost any area of interaction among nations, including defense pacts, economic understandings, and human rights accords.

- The president selects the individuals to represent the United States in contacts with other nations. The power to appoint ambassadors and ministers influences U.S. relations with the leaders of other states.

- Article II, Section 3, provides that the president is the appropriate official to receive ambassadors and ministers from foreign nations. When the president accepts the credentials of foreign emissaries, the act confers U.S. recognition on the governments they represent. This provision also suggests that when foreign diplomats communicate with the United States, they must do so through the president.

Considering this list of powers, it may come as no surprise that Supreme Court often reads the Constitution to give the president substantial authority for creating and implementing foreign policy. The broadest statement in this position comes in the case of **United States v. Curtiss-Wright Export Corp** (1936). We discussed this case in chapter 4 as an example of the Court endorsing the notion of inherent powers enjoyed by the federal government in the field of foreign relations. Justice George Sutherland's opinion for the Court also develops the president's constitutional position in these matters. Throughout the opinion he emphasizes the president's primacy: "In [the] external realm, with its important, complicated, delicate and manifold problems, the President alone has the power to speak or listen as a representative of the nation." Sutherland even contended that the president enjoys "plenary and exclusive power . . . as *the sole organ of the federal government in the field of international relations*—a power which does not require as a basis for its exercise an act of Congress, but [only] must be exercised in subordination to the applicable provisions of the Constitution (our emphasis)." Some of this language, as Sutherland noted in the opinion, comes from a speech that none other than John Marshall gave in the House of Representatives prior to his appointment as chief justice. Marshall said, "The President is the sole organ of the nation in its external relations, and its sole representative with foreign nations."

Why did Marshall and Sutherland characterize the president in this way? They both believed that more than Congress, the president has "the better opportunity of knowing the conditions which prevail in foreign countries, and especially is this true in time of war. He has his confidential sources of information. He has his agents in the form of diplomatic, consular and other officials. Secrecy in respect of information gathered by them may be highly necessary, and the premature disclosure of it productive of harmful results."

Have subsequent Courts agreed? Because we explore this question in the material to come, suffice it to say for now that the answer is both yes and no in part because the Constitution does not leave the president completely unfettered in the pursuit of the nation's external affairs. In fact, the framers were sufficiently concerned about the distribution of these foreign policy prerogatives that they gave the legislative branch certain powers to counterbalance those of the executive.

Although the president is commander in chief of the military, Congress has the power to raise and support the army and the navy, to make rules for the military, and to call up the militia. According to Article I, only Congress may declare war. The president has the constitutional authority to make treaties, but a treaty cannot take effect unless the Senate ratifies it by a two-thirds vote. The Senate must confirm the president's appointments of ambassadors and other foreign policy ministers.

For this reason, many cases about external relations center on the relationship between Congress and the president—and the powers they are trying to exercise. Often, the two elected branches will agree on a course of action, but that does not necessarily eliminate constitutional questions. When national survival is at stake or the country's relations with other nations are in jeopardy and emotions are running high, the elected branches may take action that skirts constitutional boundaries.[13] In these instances, the Court may be asked by affected individuals to determine what, if any, limits exist on the government's power.

Sometimes, though, Congress and the president disagree over the conduct of international relations, war, and other national emergencies. This is not especially surprising because the Constitution provides each elected branch with significant and potentially overlapping powers, it presents an "invitation to struggle" between the two.

This much you will see very soon, as the next section considers the Constitution's division over the power to wage war. As you will also see, though, disputes between the president and Congress do not begin and end with the war power; they also have done battle over matters of foreign policy. Either way, while reading the cases to come, consider the justices' responses: Have they tended to side with one branch over another? What bearing have they had on presidential efforts to combat terrorism and other threats to the nation's security? How far can the president go without obtaining approval from the legislature? And what steps can the president take to circumvent the courts altogether?

The Constitutional War Powers

The constitutional authority to send troops into combat has always sparked controversy. As we just suggested, the root of the problem is that the legislative and executive branches both have powers that can be interpreted as controlling the commitment of military forces to combat. The case for presidential control is based on the following passage in Article II, Section 2: "The President shall be Commander in Chief of the Army and Navy of the United States, and of the Militia of the several States, when called into the actual Service of the United States." Proponents of congressional dominance over the making of war rest their case on these words, all in Article I, Section 8, giving Congress the power:

> To declare War, grant Letters of Marque and Reprisal, and make Rules concerning Captures on Land and Water;

> To raise and support Armies, but no Appropriation of Money to that Use shall be for a longer Term than two Years;

> To provide and maintain a Navy;

> To make Rules for the Government and Regulation of the land and naval Forces;

> To provide for calling forth the Militia to execute the Laws of the Union, suppress Insurrections and repel Invasions.

The distribution of war-making powers as determined by the framers envisioned a situation in which Congress would raise and support military forces when necessary and provide the general rules governing those forces. By granting Congress the power to declare war, the Constitution anticipates that the legislature should

---

[13]Clinton L. Rossiter, *Constitutional Dictatorship: Crisis Government in the Modern Democracies* (Princeton, NJ: Princeton University Press, 1948).

determine when military force is to be used. Once the military is raised and war is declared, executive power becomes dominant, consistent with the philosophy that waging war successfully requires that a single official be in charge.

This allocation of powers was more realistic at the end of the eighteenth century than it is today. At the time the framers considered these issues, the United States was a remote nation far removed from the frequent wars in Europe. It took weeks for vessels to cross the Atlantic, allowing plenty of time for Congress to debate the question of initiating hostilities. Most delegates at the Constitutional Convention did not even anticipate the establishment of a standing military.

Today, with the rapid deployment of troops, airpower, and intercontinental missiles, hostile conditions demand quick and decisive actions. The nation expects the president to act immediately to repel an attack and to worry about congressional approval later.

In fact, Congress has taken the positive action of declaring a state of war only five times in the nation's history:[14]

1. The War of 1812 against Great Britain

2. The Mexican War in 1846

3. The Spanish-American War in 1898

4. World War I in 1917

5. World War II in 1941

But the president has initiated hundreds of military actions without declarations of war. President John Adams took the first such action when he authorized military strikes against French privateers. Some of these undeclared military actions begin and end so quickly that the president's move allows little time for congressional approval; an example is President Trump's authorization of airstrikes on targets in Syria in 2018. But two major long-term military efforts, the Korean War and the Vietnam War, were conducted without any formal declaration of war.

When military actions have extended over greater periods, Congress often has given approval through means other than a formal declaration of war. This approval may come in the form of a resolution authorizing the president to conduct military action, such as the 1964 Tonkin Gulf Resolution that granted President Lyndon Johnson authority to use force to repel attacks on U.S. forces and to forestall future aggression. Similarly, on January 12, 1991, Congress passed a joint resolution authorizing President George H. W. Bush to use force against Iraq, giving its approval to the Persian Gulf conflict in words just short of a formal declaration of war. Just days after the terrorist attacks on New York City and Washington, D.C., on September 11, 2001, the legislature passed a joint resolution authorizing President George W. Bush to use "United States Armed Forces against those responsible for the recent attacks launched against the United States." A little more than a year later, in October 2002, it voted in favor of a similar resolution, the Authorization for Use of Military Force (AUMF), enabling Bush to use military force against Iraq, although some suggest that the resolution did not authorize the war that later ensued. Finally, Congress can give indirect approval to the president in the form of continuing congressional appropriations to support military action. In the wake of September 11, Congress approved a bill authorizing $40 billion for various military operations and disaster relief.

But Congress has not abdicated its constitutional authority to approve war; in fact, the legislature has insisted that the president consult it on all military actions. In 1973 Congress passed the War Powers Resolution over Nixon's veto. This legislation acknowledges the right of the president to undertake limited military action without first obtaining formal approval from Congress but requires the president to file a formal report with Congress within forty-eight hours of initiating hostilities. Military action under this act is limited to sixty days with a possible thirty-day extension. If the president wishes to pursue military activity beyond these limits, prior congressional consent is required. Although the legislation was designed to impose restrictions on the president, most experts believe the law actually expands the chief executive's right to employ military force. The AUMF may provide an example. It contains language requiring the president to submit to Congress "a report on matters relevant to this joint resolution" at least "once every 60 days." But it also states, "The President is authorized to use the Armed Forces of the United States as he determines to be necessary and appropriate in order to—(1) defend the national security of the United States against the continuing threat posed by Iraq; and (2) enforce all relevant United Nations Security Council resolutions regarding Iraq."

---

[14]Congress also declared a state of war during the Civil War, but this conflict is technically classified as an internal rebellion rather than a true war between independent nations.

What role does the judiciary play in times of war? Because it must wait for an appropriate case to be filed before it can act, and because of its slow, deliberative procedures, the judicial branch is less capable than the other two branches of taking a leading role in matters of war and national emergency. Furthermore, the Constitution gives the courts no specified authority in these areas. The judiciary is, however, sometimes called on to decide if government power is being used legitimately or if constitutional limits have been exceeded. In times of war and national emergency, the government may find it necessary to take actions that would be unlawful at other times. The limits of the Constitution may be stretched to respond to the crisis. When legal disputes arise from such situations, the courts may become active participants in determining the government's legitimate authority. But it is also true, as we saw in chapter 3, that political actors have sometimes attempted to reduce or even eliminate the federal judiciary's participation in suits related to the crisis at hand.

In what follows, we consider the Court's responses to litigation arising in response to actions taken by the government during the Civil War, World War II, and the Korean conflict, as well foreign policy decisions related to the Mideast. In the last section, we look at the steps President George W. Bush and his administration took to combat terrorism and the Court's reactions. As you read the contemporary material, try to assess the justices' positions on presidential claims about the importance of strong executive authority in times of crisis. Did the justices' decisions support the administration? Or does the answer to that question depend on the particular actions at issue in the litigation, whether the president had support from Congress, or other factors?

Civil War Disputes

Fundamental questions about constitutional allocation of the war powers came to the Court early in the nation's history, in an 1863 dispute known as the **Prize Cases**. Among those the justices addressed were Who has power to initiate war? What war powers may the president pursue without a formal declaration from Congress?

Abraham Lincoln was elected president in November 1860. Before his inauguration on March 4, 1861, seven Southern states seceded from the Union, and Lincoln knew that he had to act quickly and decisively to restore the nation. Beginning in mid-April, shortly after the first shots were fired at Fort Sumter, Lincoln imposed a naval blockade of Southern ports. He took this action unilaterally without seeking the prior approval of Congress, which did not enact a formal declaration of hostilities until July 13 and did not ratify Lincoln's blockade until August 6. Before Congress could act, Union war vessels seized four ships trading with the Confederacy. The owners of the captured ships sued to recover their property, claiming that Lincoln had no authority to institute a blockade in the absence of a congressional declaration of war and that the seizures were illegal. Among other matters, the justices confronted this important constitutional issue: Did the president have the right to institute a blockade of ports under the control of persons in armed rebellion against the government before Congress had acted? Lincoln believed he did, on the grounds that a state of insurrection existed as a result of the shots at Fort Sumter and that he had the responsibility, under various constitutional provisions, to protect the country.

The Court upheld the president's actions. It ruled that the chief executive is bound to resist force or invasion from any hostile party without waiting to receive special authorization from the legislature. Regardless of whether a foreign nation or a rebelling state initiates the military action, a condition of war exists when hostilities are initiated. The lack of a formal declaration does not mean that a war has not begun. In fulfilling his duties, the president is bound to suppress insurrections. The commander in chief is the appropriate person to determine when a military response is necessary.

The blockade was only the first of Lincoln's acts that were questioned on constitutional grounds. In *Ex parte Milligan* (1866) the justices addressed another, this one concerning the president's actions suppressing civil liberties.[15]

During the Civil War, Lincoln was particularly worried about the presence of Confederate supporters in the Northern and border states. These individuals were capable of aiding the Southern forces without joining the Confederate Army. Of special concern were the large numbers of Southern sympathizers, known as Copperheads, who were especially active in Illinois, Indiana, Missouri, and Ohio. Combating these civilian enemies posed a difficult problem for the president. Lincoln decided that the Union was more important than the procedural rights of individuals.

---

[15]For a description of the events leading up to the Court's decision, see Allan Nevins, "The Case of the Copperhead Conspirator," in Garraty, *Quarrels That Have Shaped the Constitution*.

The *Prize Cases* examined the constitutionality of President Lincoln's orders to blockade Southern ports to disrupt trade between the Confederacy and foreign nations. As this map shows, the federal operation was divided into four regional blockading units: the North Atlantic Blocking Squadron based at Hampton Roads, Virginia; the South Atlantic Blocking Squadron at Port Royal, South Carolina; the East Gulf Blocking Squadron at Key West, Florida; and the West Gulf Blocking Squadron at Pensacola, Florida, and Ship Island, Mississippi.

Consequently, he gave his military commanders broad powers to arrest civilians suspected of engaging in traitorous activities. These suspects were to be tried in military courts.

In those parts of the country where hostilities were not occurring, however, the army had no legal authority to arrest and try civilians. State and federal courts were in full operation and were capable of trying civilians charged with treason or any other crime. Before civilians could be arrested and tried by military courts, a state of martial law had to be declared, and for that to happen, the right of habeas corpus had to be suspended. Habeas corpus is a legal procedure with roots extending far back into English legal history; it permits an arrested person to have a judge determine whether the detention is legal. If the court determines that there are no legal grounds for the arrest, it may order the release of the detained individual. Habeas corpus is essential to the doctrine of checks and balances because it gives the judiciary the right to intervene if the executive branch abuses the law enforcement power.

Article I, Section 9, of the Constitution provides for the suspension of habeas corpus in the following words: "The Privilege of the Writ of Habeas Corpus shall not be suspended, unless when in Cases of Rebellion or Invasion the public Safety may require it." This provision posed two problems for Lincoln. First, the suspension provision is found in Article I, which outlines legislative, not executive, powers. And second, if the civilian courts are in full operation and no armed hostilities are taking place in the area, the public safety probably does not demand a suspension of habeas corpus procedures.

These obstacles did not stop the president. Several times during the war he issued orders expanding military control over civilian areas, permitting military arrests and trials of civilians, and suspending habeas corpus. Congress later endorsed some of these actions. Arrests of suspected traitors and conspirators were common and often based on little evidence.

Lambdin P. Milligan, an attorney residing in northeastern Indiana, was among those arrested. As a member of the Democratic Party with strong states' rights beliefs, he was sympathetic toward the Confederate cause. He openly organized groups and gave speeches in support of the South. He also was involved in efforts to persuade men not to join the Union Army. At one point Milligan and his fellow Copperheads were suspected of hatching a plan to raid prisoner-of-war camps in Illinois, Indiana, and Ohio and to release the imprisoned Confederate soldiers, who would then take control of the three states. Federal military investigators followed Milligan closely and kept records of his activities and contacts.

On October 5, 1864, under orders from General Alvin Hovey, commander of the Union Army in Indiana, federal agents arrested Milligan at his home. Sixteen days later Hovey placed Milligan on trial before a military tribunal in Indianapolis. He was found guilty and sentenced to be hanged on May 19, 1865. On May 2, less than a month after the war ended with General Robert E. Lee's surrender at Appomattox, President Andrew Johnson, who had succeeded Lincoln, sustained the order that Milligan be executed. In response, Milligan's attorneys filed for a writ of habeas corpus in federal circuit court, claiming that Milligan should not have been tried by a military tribunal and that the president should not have suspended the writ of habeas corpus. Uncertain of how to apply the law, the circuit judges requested that the Supreme Court resolve certain questions regarding the legal authority of a military commission to try and sentence Milligan.

Nine months later, in March 1866, the Court heard the *Milligan* case. Oral arguments took place at a time of heightened political tension. Relations were strained between Johnson, who supported a moderate position toward the reintroduction of the Southern states into the Union, and the Radical Republicans in Congress, who demanded a stricter Reconstruction policy. A majority of the justices opposed the military trials at issue in *Milligan*, but there was concern about possible congressional retaliation if the justices struck a blow against military authority. The Court at this point was quite vulnerable, having suffered a decline in prestige because of the infamous decision in **Scott v. Sandford** (1857). But the justices had a potential ally in Johnson. The president opposed the use of military tribunals, and the Radicals had not yet gained sufficient strength to override a veto of a congressional act. The Court announced its decision in *Milligan* on April 3, 1866, but did not issue formal opinions until eight months later.

The Court condemned Lincoln's actions. It held that the military was without authority to try Milligan on the charges against him. The federal courts were in full operation in Indiana and open to adjudicate charges of criminal misconduct. Indiana was not in the theater of war, and Milligan was not a member of the military. Consequently, with the civilian courts in full operation and Milligan undeniably having civilian status, jurisdiction over his alleged misdeeds rested with the normal federal courts, not with a military tribunal. Milligan's constitutional rights had been violated.

Although the Court's decision was unanimous as to Milligan's claim of illegal imprisonment, the justices split on the power of the government to suspend habeas corpus under conditions presented in the case. A majority of five (Nathan Clifford, David Davis, Stephen Field, Robert Grier, and Samuel Nelson) held that neither the president nor Congress, acting separately or in agreement, could suspend the writ of habeas corpus as long as the civilian courts were operative and the area was not a combat zone. In a concurring opinion joined by Samuel Miller, Noah Swayne, and James Wayne, Chief Justice Salmon Chase argued that although the president did not have the power to suspend habeas corpus and establish these military tribunals, Congress did.

Before the Court handed down its ruling in this case, President Johnson commuted Milligan's sentence to life in prison, a sentence he was serving under General Hovey in an Ohio prison when the case was decided. Milligan was released from custody in April 1866 *(see Box 5-3)*.

World War II

As we already have seen, the restriction of civil liberties during time of war is not uncommon. Nations pressed for their very survival may feel compelled to deny basic liberties to insure against the efforts of traitors and saboteurs. World War II was no exception. During that period the government took many steps that amounted to suppressions of rights and liberties. The most infamous of such actions, which we discuss shortly, was the internment of Americans of Japanese descent.

Yet another action paralleled the one at issue in *Milligan*: the use of military tribunals. In 1941 federal authorities captured eight Nazi saboteurs who had illegally entered the country. All had previously lived in the United States, and one claimed to be a U.S. citizen. President Franklin D. Roosevelt, in his capacity as president and commander in chief of the army and navy, exercising what he believed to be authority granted to him by

BOX 5-3

Aftermath . . . Lambdin P. Milligan

Beginning with his October 1864 arrest for disloyal practices and continuing throughout the controversy over his activities, Lambdin Milligan claimed that the charges were a fantasy the Republicans created for political gain. By the time the Supreme Court reversed his conviction and death sentence, Milligan had spent eighteen months in prison. Upon his release, he returned to his hometown of Huntington, Indiana, where he was received as a local hero. Two decades earlier Milligan had moved with his family to the Indiana town from Ohio to farm and practice law. He had also been active in local Democratic Party politics, unsuccessfully running for Congress and the governorship.

Milligan immediately sought revenge for the treatment he had received at the hands of the military. He filed suit for trespass and false imprisonment against James Slack, a local attorney who had first urged that he be arrested; General Alvin Hovey, who had ordered his arrest; and twenty-two others involved in his prosecution. The jury decided in favor of Milligan, but the law placed a $5 ceiling on damages awarded in such cases, limiting the satisfaction he received from his judicial victory.

Milligan ran a successful legal practice in Huntington for an additional thirty years. He retired in 1897 at the age of eighty-five. He died two years later, only three months after the death of his second wife.

Source: American National Biography, vol. 15 (New York: Oxford University Press, 1999), 529–530.

Congress under the Articles of War,[16] ordered the saboteurs to be tried by a military tribunal. The Germans filed for a writ of habeas corpus, claiming that the president had no authority to subject them to military trial and that they, like Milligan, had the right to be tried in the civilian courts.

In *Ex parte Quirin* (1942), however, the justices unanimously upheld the government's authority to try these men by military tribunal. Why did the Court reach a decision seemingly inconsistent with the precedent set in *Milligan?* According to the justices, the Nazi saboteurs were unlawful combatants. Contrary to the laws of war, they secretly and illegally entered the country without uniform for the purpose of gathering military information or destroying life and property. As such, the saboteurs had no right to be treated as prisoners of war but could be subject to trial by military tribunal. Milligan, by comparison, was an American citizen, permanently residing in the United States, and not a military combatant in

service to the enemy. The *Quirin* Court also emphasized that Congress had explicitly approved of the use of military commissions in the Articles of War. In a case we mention later in this chapter, ***Hamdan v. Rumsfeld*** (2006), Justice John Paul Stevens took issue with the *Quirin* Court's conclusion that Congress gave its approval to the military commissions, deeming it "controversial."

Other commentators suggest that the circumstances surrounding the two earlier cases help explain the different result: *Milligan* was decided after the war was over, whereas *Quirin* came down "during the darkest days of World War II," as Chief Justice William H. Rehnquist wrote.[17]

Rehnquist is probably right: It did not help the Nazis that they, unlike Milligan, were captured and tried during one of the most desperate times of the war when public opinion toward Germany was especially hostile. Six of the eight saboteurs were sentenced to death, and the remaining two received long prison terms in return for their cooperation with federal authorities.

The government engaged in more infamous restrictions of civil liberties in its wartime treatment of Japanese Americans. The Japanese bombing of Pearl Harbor on December 7, 1941, touched off a wave of anti-Japanese

---

[16]Article I of the Constitution gives Congress the power to "make Rules for the Government and Regulation of the land and naval Force." Under this power, Congress enacted the Articles of War in 1806. The system of military justice continued to operate under the Articles of War (with revisions) until 1950, when Congress passed the Uniform Code of Military Justice, which went into effect in 1951 and replaced the Articles of War.

[17]William H. Rehnquist, *All the Laws but One: Civil Liberties in Wartime* (New York: Knopf, 1998), 221.

hysteria. In the early weeks of the Pacific war, the Japanese fleet showed remarkable strength and power, and the United States feared that Japanese forces were planning an invasion of the West Coast. Concern grew about the large numbers of people of Japanese ancestry who lived on the coast. Many thought that among the Japanese American population were significant numbers of people sympathetic to the Japanese war effort, people who might aid the enemy in an invasion of the United States.

To prevent such an occurrence President Roosevelt on February 19, 1942, issued the first of several orders affecting all people of Japanese background residing on the West Coast. His initial command placed all Japanese Americans under a tight curfew that required them to stay in their homes between 8:00 P.M. and 6:00 A.M. and to register for future relocation. In *Hirabayashi v. United States* (1943) the Supreme Court upheld the constitutionality of the curfew program. For the Court, Justice Harlan Stone explained that the war powers doctrine gave the government ample authority to impose the restrictions. The grave and threatening conditions of war made the racially based program constitutionally acceptable, he said.

The following year the Court heard *Korematsu v. United States* (1944), an appeal attacking the most serious denial of the civil liberties of Japanese Americans—the orders removing them to inland detention camps. Read Justice Black's decision carefully. Does he make a convincing case that the conditions of war stretch the Constitution to the point that exclusion orders based on race or national origin are permissible? How can you explain the fact that some of the justices who were the most sympathetic to civil liberties causes—Black, Harlan Fiske Stone, Douglas, and Wiley Rutledge—voted to approve the military orders? Compare Black's opinion with the dissents of Justice Frank Murphy, who emphasizes the racial foundations of the policy, and Justice Robert Jackson, who stresses the possible long-term consequences of construing the Constitution to uphold the government's actions.

Korematsu v. United States

323 U.S. 214 (1944)

http://caselaw.findlaw.com/us-supreme-court/323/214.html
Vote: 6 (Black, Douglas, Frankfurter, Reed, Rutledge, Stone)
  3 (Jackson, Murphy, Roberts)

OPINION OF THE COURT: *Black*

CONCURRING OPINION: *Frankfurter*

DISSENTING OPINIONS: *Jackson, Murphy, Roberts*

The origins of *Korematsu* lie in Japan's bombing of Pearl Harbor on December 7, 1941, which touched off a wave of anti-Japanese hysteria in the United States. In the early weeks of the Pacific war the Japanese fleet demonstrated remarkable strength and power, and the United States feared that Japanese forces were planning an invasion of the West Coast. The large numbers of people of Japanese ancestry living on the coast also became a matter of concern. Many thought that among the Japanese American population were significant numbers of people sympathetic to the Japanese war effort, people who might aid the enemy in an invasion of the United States.

To prevent such an occurrence, on February 19, 1942, President Roosevelt issued Executive Order 9066, which applied to all people of Japanese background residing on the West Coast. His initial command placed all Japanese Americans under a tight curfew that required them to stay in their homes between 8:00 P.M. and 6:00 A.M. and to register for future relocation. This order was followed by the much harsher orders to evacuate Japanese Americans from the Pacific Coast area and move them to inland detention centers. The first of these, Civilian Exclusion Order 34, came on May 3. It was not issued directly by Roosevelt, but by Lieutenant General John L. DeWitt, the commanding general of the Western Defense Command. The secretary of war had authorized DeWitt to issue the order pursuant to Roosevelt's executive order of February 19, which Congress had ratified in March.

The program made no attempt to distinguish the loyal from the disloyal or the citizen from the noncitizen—it affected all persons of Japanese ancestry. The government interned an estimated 110,000 Japanese American citizens and resident aliens, some for as long as four years.[18] These actions spawned a number of important lawsuits.

In 1943 the Supreme Court heard a challenge to the curfew regulations brought by Gordon Hirabayashi, an American citizen of Japanese descent. He was a native of Washington State and a pacifist of the Quaker faith. At the time he challenged the government actions, he was a senior at the University of Washington. In **Hirabayashi v. United States** (1943) the Supreme Court unanimously upheld the constitutionality of the curfew program. For the Court, Chief Justice Harlan Fiske Stone explained that the war powers doctrine gave the government ample authority to impose the restrictions. The grave and threatening conditions of war made the racially based program constitutionally acceptable.

The following year the Court heard *Korematsu v. United States* (1944), an appeal attacking the most serious denial of the civil liberties of Japanese Americans—the orders removing them to detention camps. Fred Korematsu was arrested May 30, 1942, by San Leandro, California, police for being on the public streets in

---

[18]See Peter H. Irons, *Justice at War: The Story of the Japanese American Internment Cases* (New York: Oxford University Press, 1983).

violation of the government's evacuation orders. Korematsu was a native-born American whose parents had immigrated to the United States from Japan. He grew up in the San Francisco area. Rejected for military service for health reasons, he worked in the defense industry as a welder. When arrested, he tried to convince police that he was of Spanish Hawaiian origin. He had undergone plastic surgery to make his racial characteristics less pronounced in an effort to avoid the anti-Japanese discrimination he feared because of his engagement to an Italian American woman.[19] After the arrest, representatives of the American Civil Liberties Union approached Korematsu and offered to defend him and challenge the validity of the evacuation program. The Japanese-American Citizens League also lent support.

MR. JUSTICE BLACK DELIVERED THE OPINION OF THE COURT.

It should be noted, to begin with, that all legal restrictions which curtail the civil rights of a single racial group are immediately suspect. That is not to say that all such restrictions are unconstitutional. It is to say that courts must subject them to the most rigid scrutiny. Pressing public necessity may sometimes justify the existence of such restrictions; racial antagonism never can. . . .

[I]n the *Hirabayashi* case . . . it was contended that the curfew order and other orders on which it rested were beyond the war powers of the Congress, the military authorities, and of the President, as Commander in Chief of the Army, and, finally, that to apply the curfew order against none but citizens of Japanese ancestry amounted to a constitutionally prohibited discrimination solely on account of race. To these questions, we gave the serious consideration which their importance justified. We upheld the curfew order as an exercise of the power of the government to take steps necessary to prevent espionage and sabotage in an area threatened by Japanese attack.

In the light of the principles we announced in the *Hirabayashi* case, we are unable to conclude that it was beyond the war power of Congress and the Executive to exclude those of Japanese ancestry from the West Coast war area at the time they did. True, exclusion from the area in which one's home is located is a far greater deprivation than constant confinement to the home from 8 P.M. to 6 A.M. Nothing short of apprehension by the proper military authorities of the gravest imminent danger to the public safety can constitutionally justify either. But exclusion from a threatened area, no less than curfew, has a definite and close relationship to the prevention of espionage and sabotage. The military authorities, charged with the primary responsibility of defending our shores, concluded that curfew provided inadequate protection and ordered

---

[19]Ibid., 93–99.

exclusion. They did so, as pointed out in our *Hirabayashi* opinion, in accordance with Congressional authority to the military to say who should, and who should not, remain in the threatened areas.

In this case the petitioner challenges the assumptions upon which we rested our conclusions in the *Hirabayashi* case. . . . After careful consideration of these contentions we are compelled to reject them.

Here, as in the *Hirabayashi* case, ". . . we cannot reject as unfounded the judgment of the military authorities and of Congress that there were disloyal members of that population, whose number and strength could not be precisely and quickly ascertained. We cannot say that the warmaking branches of the Government did not have ground for believing that in a critical hour such persons could not readily be isolated and separately dealt with, and constituted a menace to the national defense and safety, which demanded that prompt and adequate measures be taken to guard against it."

Like curfew, exclusion of those of Japanese origin was deemed necessary because of the presence of an unascertained number of disloyal members of the group, most of whom we have no doubt were loyal to this country. It was because we could not reject the finding of the military authorities that it was impossible to bring about an immediate segregation of the disloyal from the loyal that we sustained the validity of the curfew order as applying to the whole group. In the instant case, temporary exclusion of the entire group was rested by the military on the same ground. The judgment that exclusion of the whole group was for the same reason a military imperative answers the contention that the exclusion was in the nature of group punishment based on antagonism to those of Japanese origin. That there were members of the group who retained loyalties to Japan has been confirmed by investigations made subsequent to the exclusion. Approximately five thousand American citizens of Japanese ancestry refused to swear unqualified allegiance to the United States and to renounce allegiance to the Japanese Emperor, and several thousand evacuees requested repatriation to Japan.

We uphold the exclusion order . . . In doing so, we are not unmindful of the hardships imposed by it upon a large group of American citizens. But hardships are part of war, and war is an aggregation of hardships. All citizens alike, both in and out of uniform, feel the impact of war in greater or lesser measure. Citizenship has its responsibilities as well as its privileges, and in time of war the burden is always heavier. Compulsory exclusion of large groups of citizens from their homes, except under circumstances of direst emergency and peril, is inconsistent with our basic governmental institutions. But when under conditions of modern warfare our shores are threatened by hostile forces, the power to protect must be commensurate with the threatened danger. . . .

It is said that we are dealing here with the case of imprisonment of a citizen in a concentration camp solely because of his ancestry, without evidence or inquiry concerning his loyalty and good disposition towards the United States. Our task would be

Japanese American civilians, with whatever possessions they could carry, arrive at a Los Angeles pickup point from which they would be transferred by bus to inland detention centers in 1942. The evacuation of individuals of Japanese descent from the Pacific Coast states was upheld by the Supreme Court in *Korematsu v. United States* (1944).

AP Images

simple, our duty clear, were this a case involving the imprisonment of a loyal citizen in a concentration camp because of racial prejudice. Regardless of the true nature of the assembly and relocation centers—and we deem it unjustifiable to call them concentration camps with all the ugly connotations that term implies—we are dealing specifically with nothing but an exclusion order. To cast this case into outlines of racial prejudice, without reference to the real military dangers which were presented, merely confuses the issue. Korematsu was not excluded from the Military Area because of hostility to him or his race. He *was* excluded because we are at war with the Japanese Empire, because the properly constituted military authorities feared an invasion of our West Coast and felt constrained to take proper security measures, because they decided that the military urgency of the situation demanded that all citizens of Japanese ancestry be segregated from the West Coast temporarily,

and finally, because Congress, reposing its confidence in this time of war in our military leaders—as inevitably it must—determined that they should have the power to do just this.

There was evidence of disloyalty on the part of some, the military authorities considered that the need for action was great, and time was short. We cannot—by availing ourselves of the calm perspective of hindsight—now say that at that time these actions were unjustified.

Affirmed.

MR. JUSTICE MURPHY, DISSENTING.

This exclusion of "all persons of Japanese ancestry, both alien and non-alien," from the Pacific Coast area on a plea of military necessity in the absence of martial law ought not to be approved. Such exclusion goes over "the very brink of constitutional power" and falls into the ugly abyss of racism.

In dealing with matters relating to the prosecution and progress of a war, we must accord great respect and consideration to the judgments of the military authorities who are on the scene and who have full knowledge of the military facts. . . .

At the same time, however, it is essential that there be definite limits to military discretion, especially where martial law has not been declared. Individuals must not be left impoverished of their constitutional rights on a plea of military necessity that has neither substance nor support. Thus, like other claims conflicting with the asserted constitutional rights of the individual, the military claim must subject itself to the judicial process of having its reasonableness determined and its conflicts with other interests reconciled . . .

The judicial test of whether the Government, on a plea of military necessity, can validly deprive an individual of any of his constitutional rights is whether the deprivation is reasonably related to a public danger that is so "immediate, imminent, and impending" as not to admit of delay and not to permit the intervention of ordinary constitutional processes to alleviate the danger. [The Exclusion Order] banishing from a prescribed area of the Pacific Coast "all persons of Japanese ancestry, both alien and non-alien," clearly does not meet that test. Being an obvious racial discrimination, the order deprives all those within its scope of the equal protection of the laws . . . It further deprives these individuals of their constitutional rights to live and work where they will, to establish a home where they choose and to move about freely. In excommunicating them without benefit of hearings, this order also deprives them of all their constitutional rights to procedural due process. Yet no reasonable relation to an "immediate, imminent, and impending" public danger is evident to support this racial restriction which is one of the most sweeping and complete deprivations of constitutional rights in the history of this nation in the absence of martial law.

It must be conceded that the military and naval situation in the spring of 1942 was such as to generate a very real fear of invasion of the Pacific Coast, accompanied by fears of sabotage and espionage in that area. The military command was therefore justified in adopting all reasonable means necessary to combat these dangers. In adjudging the military action taken in light of the then apparent dangers, we must not erect too high or too meticulous standards; it is necessary only that the action have some reasonable relation to the removal of the dangers of invasion, sabotage and espionage. But the exclusion, either temporarily or permanently, of all persons with Japanese blood in their veins has no such reasonable relation. And that relation is lacking because the exclusion order necessarily must rely for its reasonableness upon the assumption that *all* persons of Japanese ancestry may have a dangerous tendency to commit sabotage and espionage and to aid our Japanese enemy in other

ways. It is difficult to believe that reason, logic or experience could be marshalled in support of such an assumption.

That this forced exclusion was the result in good measure of this erroneous assumption of racial guilt rather than bona fide military necessity is evidenced by the Commanding General's Final Report on the evacuation from the Pacific Coast area. In it he refers to all individuals of Japanese descent as "subversive," as belonging to "an enemy race" whose "racial strains are undiluted," and as constituting "over 112,000 potential enemies . . . at large today" along the Pacific Coast. . . .

The main reasons relied upon by those responsible for the forced evacuation, therefore, do not prove a reasonable relation between the group characteristics of Japanese Americans and the dangers of invasion, sabotage and espionage. The reasons appear, instead, to be largely an accumulation of much of the misinformation, half-truths and insinuations that for years have been directed against Japanese Americans by people with racial and economic prejudices—the same people who have been among the foremost advocates of the evacuation. A military judgment based upon such racial and sociological considerations is not entitled to the great weight ordinarily given the judgments based upon strictly military considerations . . . .

The military necessity which is essential to the validity of the evacuation order thus resolves itself into a few intimations that certain individuals actively aided the enemy, from which it is inferred that the entire group of Japanese Americans could not be trusted to be or remain loyal to the United States. . . . To give constitutional sanction to that inference in this case, however well-intentioned may have been the military command on the Pacific Coast, is to adopt one of the cruelest of the rationales used by our enemies to destroy the dignity of the individual and to encourage and open the door to discriminatory actions against other minority groups in the passions of tomorrow. . . .

I dissent, therefore, from this legalization of racism. Racial discrimination in any form and in any degree has no justifiable part whatever in our democratic way of life. It is unattractive in any setting but it is utterly revolting among a free people who have embraced the principles set forth in the Constitution of the United States. All residents of this nation are kin in some way by blood or culture to a foreign land. Yet they are primarily and necessarily a part of the new and distinct civilization of the United States. They must accordingly be treated at all times as the heirs of the American experiment and as entitled to all the rights and freedoms guaranteed by the Constitution.

MR. JUSTICE JACKSON, DISSENTING.

Korematsu was born on our soil, of parents born in Japan. The Constitution makes him a citizen of the United States by nativity and a citizen of California by residence. No claim is made that he is not loyal to this country. There is no suggestion that apart from the matter involved here he is not law-abiding and well disposed. Korematsu, however, has been convicted of an act not commonly a crime. It consists merely of being present in the state whereof he is a citizen, near the place where he was born, and where all his life he has lived.

Even more unusual is the series of military orders which made this conduct a crime. They forbid such a one to remain, and they also forbid him to leave . . . .

A citizen's presence in the locality, however, was made a crime only if his parents were of Japanese birth. Had Korematsu been one of four—the others being, say, a German alien enemy, an Italian alien enemy, and a citizen of American-born ancestors, convicted of treason but out on parole—only Korematsu's presence would have violated the order. The difference between their innocence and his crime would result, not from anything he did, said, or thought, different than they, but only in that he was born of different racial stock.

Now, if any fundamental assumption underlies our system, it is that guilt is personal and not inheritable. Even if all of one's antecedents had been convicted of treason, the Constitution forbids its penalties to be visited upon him, for it provides that "no attainder of treason shall work corruption of blood, or forfeiture except during the life of the person attainted." But here is an attempt to make an otherwise innocent act a crime merely because this prisoner is the son of parents as to whom he had no choice, and belongs to a race from which there is no way to resign. If Congress in peace-time legislation should enact such a criminal law, I should suppose this Court would refuse to enforce it. . . .

It would be impracticable and dangerous idealism to expect or insist that each specific military command in an area of probable operations will conform to conventional tests of constitutionality. When an area is so beset that it must be put under military control at all, the paramount consideration is that its measures be successful, rather than legal. The armed services must protect a society, not merely its Constitution. The very essence of the military job is to marshal physical force, to remove every obstacle to its effectiveness, to give it every strategic advantage. Defense measures will not, and often should not, be held within the limits that bind civil authority in peace. No court can require such a commander in such circumstances to act as a reasonable man; he may be unreasonably cautious and exacting. Perhaps he should be. But a commander in temporarily focusing the life of a community on defense is carrying out a military program; he is not making law in the sense the courts know the term. He issues orders, and they may have a certain authority as military commands, although they may be very bad as constitutional law.

But if we cannot confine military expedients by the Constitution, neither would I distort the Constitution to approve all that the military may deem expedient. This is what the Court appears to be doing, whether consciously or not. I cannot say, from any evidence before me, that the orders of General DeWitt were not reasonably expedient military precautions, nor could I say that they were. But even if they were permissible military procedures, I deny that it follows that they are constitutional. If, as the Court holds, it does follow, then we may as well say that any military order will be constitutional and have done with it.

The limitation under which courts always will labor in examining the necessity for a military order are illustrated by this case. How does the Court know that these orders have a reasonable basis in necessity? No evidence whatever on that subject has been taken by this or any other court. There is sharp controversy as to the credibility of the DeWitt report. So the Court, having no real evidence before it, has no choice but to accept General DeWitt's own unsworn, self-serving statement, untested by any cross-examination, that what he did was reasonable. And thus it will always be when courts try to look into the reasonableness of a military order.

In the very nature of things, military decisions are not susceptible of intelligent judicial appraisal. They do not pretend to rest on evidence, but are made on information that often would not be admissible and on assumptions that could not be proved. Information in support of an order could not be disclosed to courts without danger that it would reach the enemy. Neither can courts act on communications made in confidence. Hence, courts can never have any real alternative to accepting the mere declaration of the authority that issued the order that it was reasonably necessary from a military viewpoint.

Much is said of the danger to liberty from the Army program for deporting and detaining these citizens of Japanese extraction. But a judicial construction of the due process clause that will sustain this order is a far more subtle blow to liberty than the promulgation of the order itself. A military order, however unconstitutional, is not apt to last longer than the military emergency. Even during that period a succeeding commander may revoke it all. But once a judicial opinion rationalizes such an order to show that it conforms to the Constitution, or rather rationalizes the Constitution to show that the Constitution sanctions such an order, the Court for all time has validated the principle of racial discrimination in criminal procedure and of transplanting American citizens. The principle then lies about like a loaded weapon ready for the hand of any authority that can bring forward a plausible claim of an urgent need. . . .

I should hold that a civil court cannot be made to enforce an order which violates constitutional limitations even if it is a reasonable exercise of military authority. The courts can exercise only the judicial power, can apply only law, and must abide by the Constitution, or they cease to be civil courts and become instruments of military policy. . . .

My duties as a justice as I see them do not require me to make a military judgment as to whether General DeWitt's evacuation and detention program was a reasonable military necessity. I do not suggest that the courts should have attempted to interfere with the Army in carrying out its task. But I do not think they may be asked to execute a military expedient that has no place in law under the Constitution. I would reverse the judgment and discharge the prisoner.

Legal scholars and civil libertarians have severely criticized the *Korematsu* decision, and in 1988 Congress approved $20,000 in reparations for each living Japanese American who was interned during the war *(see Box 5-4)*. Three decades later, in 2018 the Court finally ended the possibility of Korematsu lying "about like a loaded weapon," as Justice Jackson famously put it in his dissent. In *Trump v. Hawaii,* the majority finally overruled Korematsu with these words:

> [We] express what is already obvious: *Korematsu* was gravely wrong the day it was decided, has been overruled in the court of history, and— to be clear—"has no place in law under the Constitution." (Jackson, J., dissenting).

The Korean Conflict

During the war in Korea the justices were called on to decide the constitutional validity of yet another executive action taken in the name of national security. As you read Justice Black's opinion for the Court in *Youngstown Sheet & Tube Co. v. Sawyer* (1952), compare it to his opinion in *Korematsu*. Both involved actions the president took to strengthen war efforts. Does it make sense to you that the Court approved the detention of more than 110,000 individuals on the basis of national origin but ruled that the government could not take nominal possession of the steel mills? Note the analysis provided in Justice Jackson's concurring opinion, in which he lays out an approach for deciding questions of presidential power in relation to congressional action. Consider, too, the dissenting opinion of Chief Justice Fred Vinson, who concludes that the national emergency justified the president's actions.

Youngstown Sheet & Tube Co. v. Sawyer

343 U.S. 579 (1952)
http://caselaw.findlaw.com/us-supreme-court/343/579.html
Vote: 6 (Black, Burton, Clark, Douglas, Frankfurter, Jackson)
*   3 (Minton, Reed, Vinson)*

OPINION OF THE COURT: *Black*

CONCURRING OPINIONS: *Burton, Clark, Douglas, Frankfurter, Jackson*

DISSENTING OPINION: *Vinson*

In 1951 a labor dispute began in the steel industry. In December the United Steelworkers Union announced that it would call a strike at the end of that month, when its contract with the steel companies expired. For the next several months the Federal Mediation and Conciliation Service and the Federal Wage Stabilization Board tried to work out a settlement, but the efforts were unsuccessful. On April 4, 1952, the union said that its strike would begin on April 9.

President Harry S. Truman was not about to let a strike hit the steel industry. The nation was engaged in a war in Korea, and steel production was necessary to produce weapons and other military equipment. Only hours before the strike was to begin, Truman issued an executive order commanding Secretary of Commerce Charles Sawyer to seize the nation's steel mills and keep them in operation. Sawyer in turn ordered the mill owners to continue to run their facilities as operators for the United States.

Truman's seizure order cited no statutory authority for his action because there was none. Federal statutes allowed government seizure of industrial plants for certain specified reasons, but the settlement of a labor dispute was not one of them. In fact, the Taft-Hartley Act of 1947 rejected the idea that labor disputes could be resolved by such means. Instead, the act authorized the

The attorney representing the steel industry, John W. Davis Jr., left, arriving at the Supreme Court May 13, 1952, with acting attorney general Philip B. Perlman. Davis was the Democratic nominee for the presidency in 1924, capturing 29 percent of the popular vote in a loss to Calvin Coolidge. He later represented the school board defendants in the 1954 school desegregation cases.

BOX 5-4

Aftermath . . . Fred Korematsu

Following his arrest and conviction in 1942 for refusing to leave his northern California home in compliance with President Franklin D. Roosevelt's evacuation orders, Fred T. Korematsu was sentenced to five years' probation. He was also sent with other Japanese Americans to an isolated internment camp in Topaz, Utah. After the war, he returned to his home in San Leandro, California, married, and continued his work as a welder.

Almost forty years later, documents were discovered providing evidence that officials of the U.S. Navy and the Justice Department had intentionally deceived the Supreme Court by suppressing information showing that Japanese Americans posed no threat during World War II. Based on this new evidence, lawyers representing Korematsu filed a legal action to clear his name. In November 1983 a federal district court in San Francisco overturned Korematsu's conviction. Charges against Gordon Hirabayashi for violating a curfew imposed on Japanese Americans, upheld by the Supreme Court in 1942, were similarly reversed by a Seattle federal court in 1986. These legal actions helped fuel a movement that led Congress in 1988 to approve $20,000 in reparations for each living Japanese American who was interned during the war.

In 1998 President Bill Clinton awarded Korematsu, then seventy-eight years old, the Presidential Medal of Freedom, the nation's highest civilian award. "In the long history of our country's constant search for justice," Clinton said, "some names of ordinary citizens stand for

President Bill Clinton stands with Fred Korematsu after awarding him the Presidential Medal of Freedom, January 15, 1998.

millions of souls. Plessy, Brown, Parks. To that distinguished list, today we add the name of Fred Korematsu." Korematsu died in Marin County, California, on March 30, 2005, at the age of eighty-six.

Sources: *New York Times,* January 31, 1983, November 11, 1983, August 11, 1988, February 19, 1992; *San Francisco Chronicle,* January 16, 1998, April 10, 2005.

---

president to impose an eighty-day cooling-off period as a way to postpone any strike that seriously threatened the public interest. Truman, however, had little regard for the Taft-Hartley Act, which Congress had passed over his veto. The president ignored the cooling-off period alternative and took the direct action of seizing the mills. The authority vested to him as president and commander in chief was enough, in Truman's view, to authorize the action.

Congress might have improved the president's legal ground by immediately passing legislation authorizing such seizures retroactively, but it did not (nor did it take any action to stop the president's seizures). The mill owners complied with the seizure orders under protest and filed suit in federal court to have Truman's action declared unconstitutional. The district court ruled in favor of the steel industry, enjoining the secretary from seizing the plants, but the same day the court of appeals stayed the injunction.

> **MR. JUSTICE BLACK DELIVERED THE OPINION OF THE COURT.**

We are asked to decide whether the President was acting within his constitutional power when he issued an order directing the

Secretary of Commerce to take possession of and operate most of the Nation's steel mills. The mill owners argue that the President's order amounts to lawmaking, a legislative function which the Constitution has expressly confided to the Congress and not to the President. The Government's position is that the order was made on findings of the President that his action was necessary to avert a national catastrophe which would inevitably result from a stoppage of steel production, and that in meeting this grave emergency the President was acting within the aggregate of his constitutional powers as the Nation's Chief Executive and the Commander in Chief of the Armed Forces of the United States. . . .

The President's power, if any, to issue the order must stem either from an act of Congress or from the Constitution itself. There is no statute that expressly authorizes the President to take possession of property as he did here. Nor is there any act of Congress to which our attention has been directed from which such a power can fairly be implied. Indeed, we do not understand the Government to rely on statutory authorization for this seizure. There are two statutes which do authorize the President to take both personal and real property under certain conditions. However, the Government admits that these conditions were not met, and that the President's order was not rooted in either of the statutes. The Government refers to the seizure provisions of one of these statutes (the Defense Production Act) as "much too cumbersome, involved, and time-consuming for the crisis which was at hand."

Moreover, the use of the seizure technique to solve labor disputes in order to prevent work stoppages was not only unauthorized by any congressional enactment; prior to this controversy, Congress had refused to adopt that method of settling labor disputes. When the Taft-Hartley Act was under consideration in 1947, Congress rejected an amendment which would have authorized such governmental seizures in cases of emergency. Apparently it was thought that the technique of seizure, like that of compulsory arbitration, would interfere with the process of collective bargaining . . .

It is clear that, if the President had authority to issue the order he did, it must be found in some provision of the Constitution . . . Particular reliance is placed on provisions in Article II which say that "The executive Power shall be vested in a President . . ."; that "he shall take Care that the Laws be faithfully executed"; and that he "shall be Commander in Chief of the Army and Navy of the United States."

The order cannot properly be sustained as an exercise of the President's military power as Commander in Chief of the Armed Forces. The Government attempts to do so by citing a number of cases upholding broad powers in military commanders engaged in day-to-day fighting in a theater of war. Such cases need not concern us here. Even though "theater of war" be an expanding concept, we cannot with faithfulness to our constitutional system hold that the Commander in Chief of the Armed Forces has the ultimate power

as such to take possession of private property in order to keep labor disputes from stopping production. This is a job for the Nation's lawmakers, not for its military authorities.

Nor can the seizure order be sustained because of the several constitutional provisions that grant executive power to the President. In the framework of our Constitution, the President's power to see that the laws are faithfully executed refutes the idea that he is to be a lawmaker. The Constitution limits his functions in the lawmaking process to the recommending of laws he thinks wise and the vetoing of laws he thinks bad. And the Constitution is neither silent nor equivocal about who shall make laws which the President is to execute. The first section of the first article says that "All legislative Powers herein granted shall be vested in a Congress of the United States. . .

The President's order does not direct that a congressional policy be executed in a manner prescribed by Congress—it directs that a presidential policy be executed in a manner prescribed by the President . . .

The Founders of this Nation entrusted the lawmaking power to the Congress alone in both good and bad times. It would do no good to recall the historical events, the fears of power and the hopes for freedom that lay behind their choice. Such a review would but confirm our holding that this seizure order cannot stand.

The judgment of the District Court is

Affirmed.

MR. JUSTICE JACKSON, CONCURRING IN THE JUDGMENT AND OPINION OF THE COURT.

That comprehensive and undefined presidential powers hold both practical advantages and grave dangers for the country will impress anyone who has served as legal adviser to a President in time of transition and public anxiety. While an interval of detached reflection may temper teachings of that experience, they probably are a more realistic influence on my views than the conventional materials of judicial decision which seem unduly to accentuate doctrine and legal fiction. But, as we approach the question of presidential power, we half overcome mental hazards by recognizing them. The opinions of judges, no less than executives and publicists, often suffer the infirmity of confusing the issue of a power's validity with the cause it is invoked to promote, of confounding the permanent executive office with its temporary occupant. The tendency is strong to emphasize transient results upon policies—such as wages or stabilization—and lose sight of enduring consequences upon the balanced power structure of our Republic.

A judge, like an executive adviser, may be surprised at the poverty of really useful and unambiguous authority applicable to concrete problems of executive power as they actually present themselves. Just what our forefathers did envision, or would have envisioned had they foreseen modern conditions, must be divined from materials almost as enigmatic as the dreams Joseph was called upon to interpret for Pharaoh. A century and a half of partisan debate and scholarly speculation yields no net result but only supplies more or less apt quotations from respected sources on each side of any question. They largely cancel each other. And court decisions are indecisive because of the judicial practice of dealing with the largest questions in the most narrow way.

The actual art of governing under our Constitution does not, and cannot, conform to judicial definitions of the power of any of its branches based on isolated clauses, or even single Articles torn from context. While the Constitution diffuses power the better to secure liberty, it also contemplates that practice will integrate the dispersed powers into a workable government. It enjoins upon its branches separateness but interdependence, autonomy but reciprocity. Presidential powers are not fixed but fluctuate depending upon their disjunction or conjunction with those of Congress. We may well begin by a somewhat over-simplified grouping of practical situations in which a President may doubt, or others may challenge, his powers, and by distinguishing roughly the legal consequences of this factor of relativity.

1. When the President acts pursuant to an express or implied authorization of Congress, his authority is at its maximum, for it includes all that he possesses in his own right plus all that Congress can delegate. In these circumstances, and in these only, may he be said (for what it may be worth) to personify the federal sovereignty. If his act is held unconstitutional under these circumstances, it usually means that the Federal Government, as an undivided whole, lacks power. A seizure executed by the President pursuant to an Act of Congress would be supported by the strongest of presumptions and the widest latitude of judicial interpretation, and the burden of persuasion would rest heavily upon any who might attack it.

2. When the President acts in absence of either a congressional grant or denial of authority, he can only rely upon his own independent powers, but there is a zone of twilight in which he and Congress may have concurrent authority, or in which its distribution is uncertain. Therefore, congressional inertia, indifference or quiescence may sometimes, at least as a practical matter, enable, if not invite, measures on independent presidential responsibility. In this area, any actual test of power is likely to depend on the imperatives of events and contemporary imponderables rather than on abstract theories of law.

3. When the President takes measures incompatible with the expressed or implied will of Congress, his power is at its lowest ebb, for then he can rely only upon his own constitutional powers minus any constitutional powers of Congress over the matter. Courts can sustain exclusive presidential control in such a case only by disabling the Congress from acting upon the subject. Presidential claim to a power at once so conclusive and preclusive must be scrutinized with caution, for what is at stake is the equilibrium established by our constitutional system.

Into which of these classifications does this executive seizure of the steel industry fit? It is eliminated from the first by admission, for it is conceded that no congressional authorization exists for this seizure. . . .

Can it then be defended under flexible tests available to the second category? It seems clearly eliminated from that class because Congress has not left seizure of private property an open field but has covered it by . . . statutory policies inconsistent with this seizure. . . .

This leaves the current seizure to be justified only by the severe tests under the third grouping, where it can be supported only by any remainder of executive power after subtraction of such powers as Congress may have over the subject. In short, we can sustain the President only by holding that seizure of such strike-bound industries is within his domain and beyond control by Congress. Thus, this Court's first review of such seizures occurs under circumstances which leave presidential power most vulnerable to attack and in the least favorable of possible constitutional postures. . . .

The Solicitor General seeks the power of seizure in three clauses of the Executive Article, the first reading, "The executive Power shall be vested in a President of the United States of America." Lest I be thought to exaggerate, I quote the interpretation which his brief puts upon it: "In our view, this clause constitutes a grant of all the executive powers of which the Government is capable." If that be true, it is difficult to see why the forefathers bothered to add several specific items, including some trifling ones.

. . . I cannot accept the view that this clause is a grant in bulk of all conceivable executive power, but regard it as an allocation to the presidential office of the generic powers thereafter stated.

The clause on which the Government next relies is that "The President shall be Commander in Chief of the Army and Navy of the United States. . . ." These cryptic words have given rise to some of the most persistent controversies in our constitutional history. Of course, they imply something more than an empty title. But just what authority goes with the name has plagued presidential advisers who would not waive or narrow it by nonassertion, yet cannot say where it begins or ends. It undoubtedly puts the Nation's armed forces under presidential command. Hence, this loose appellation is sometimes advanced as support for any presidential action, internal or external, involving use of force, the idea being that it vests power to do anything, anywhere, that can be done with an army or navy . . .

I cannot foresee all that it might entail if the Court should indorse this argument. Nothing in our Constitution is plainer than that declaration of a war is entrusted only to Congress. Of course, a state of war may, in fact, exist without a formal declaration. But no doctrine that the Court could promulgate would seem to me more sinister and alarming than that a President whose conduct of foreign affairs is so largely uncontrolled, and often even is unknown, can vastly enlarge his mastery over the internal affairs of the country by his own commitment of the Nation's armed forces to some foreign venture. . . .

The third clause in which the Solicitor General finds seizure powers is that "he shall take Care that the Laws be faithfully executed. . . . That authority must be matched against words of the Fifth Amendment that "No person shall be . . . deprived of life, liberty or property, without due process of law. . . ." One gives a governmental authority that reaches so far as there is law, the other gives a private right that authority shall go no farther. These signify about all there is of the principle that ours is a government of laws, not of men, and that we submit ourselves to rulers only if under rules.

The Solicitor General lastly grounds support of the seizure upon nebulous, inherent powers never expressly granted, but said to have accrued to the office from the customs and claims of preceding administrations. The plea is for a resulting power to deal with a crisis or an emergency according to the necessities of the case, the unarticulated assumption being that necessity knows no law . . .

The appeal . . . that we declare the existence of inherent powers *ex necessitate* to meet an emergency asks us to do what many think would be wise, although it is something the forefathers omitted. They knew what emergencies were, knew the pressures they engender for authoritative action, knew, too, how they afford a ready pretext for usurpation. We may also suspect that they suspected that emergency powers would tend to kindle emergencies. Aside from suspension of the privilege of the writ of habeas corpus in time of rebellion or invasion, when the public safety may require it, they made no express provision for exercise of extraordinary authority because of a crisis. I do not think we rightfully may so amend their work, and, if we could, I am not convinced it would be wise to do so, although many modern nations have forthrightly recognized that war and economic crises may upset the normal balance between liberty and authority. . . .

But [contemporary foreign experience] suggests that emergency powers are consistent with free government only when their control is lodged elsewhere than in the Executive who exercises them. That is the safeguard that would be nullified by our adoption of the "inherent powers" formula. Nothing in my experience convinces me that such risks are warranted by any real necessity, although such powers would, of course, be an executive convenience.

In the practical working of our Government, we already have evolved a technique within the framework of the Constitution by which normal executive powers may be considerably expanded to meet an emergency. Congress may and has granted extraordinary authorities which lie dormant in normal times but may be called into play by the Executive in war or upon proclamation of a national emergency. . . .

In view of the ease, expedition and safety with which Congress can grant and has granted large emergency powers, certainly ample to embrace this crisis, I am quite unimpressed with the argument that we should affirm possession of them without statute. Such power either has no beginning or it has no end. If it exists, it need submit to no legal restraint. I am not alarmed that it would plunge us straightway into dictatorship, but it is at least a step in that wrong direction. . . .

I cannot be brought to believe that this country will suffer if the Court refuses further to aggrandize the presidential office, already so potent and so relatively immune from judicial review, at the expense of Congress.

But I have no illusion that any decision by this Court can keep power in the hands of Congress if it is not wise and timely in meeting its problems. A crisis that challenges the President equally, or perhaps primarily, challenges Congress. If not good law, there was worldly wisdom in the maxim attributed to Napoleon that "The tools belong to the man who can use them." We may say that power to legislate for emergencies belongs in the hands of Congress, but only Congress itself can prevent power from slipping through its fingers.

MR. CHIEF JUSTICE VINSON, WITH WHOM MR. JUSTICE REED AND MR. JUSTICE MINTON JOIN, DISSENTING.

The District Court ordered the mills returned to their private owners on the ground that the President's action was beyond his powers under the Constitution.

This Court affirms. . . . Because we cannot agree that affirmance is proper on any ground, and because of the transcending importance of the questions presented not only in this critical litigation, but also to the powers of the President and of future Presidents to act in time of crisis, we are compelled to register this dissent . . .

A review of executive action demonstrates that our Presidents have on many occasions exhibited the leadership contemplated by the Framers when they made the President Commander in Chief, and imposed upon him the trust to "take Care that the Laws be faithfully executed." With or without explicit statutory authorization, Presidents have at such times dealt with national emergencies by acting promptly and resolutely to enforce legislative programs, at least to save those programs until Congress could act. Congress and the courts have responded to such executive initiative with consistent approval.

Our first President displayed at once the leadership contemplated by the Framers. When the national revenue laws were openly flouted in some sections of Pennsylvania, President

Washington, without waiting for a call from the state government, summoned the militia and took decisive steps to secure the faithful execution of the laws . . . .

Some six months before Pearl Harbor, a dispute at a single aviation plant at Inglewood, California, interrupted a segment of the production of military aircraft. In spite of the comparative insignificance of this work stoppage to total defense production, as contrasted with the complete paralysis now threatened by a shutdown of the entire basic steel industry, and even though our armed forces were not then engaged in combat, President [Franklin] Roosevelt ordered the seizure of the plant pursuant to the powers vested in [him] by the Constitution and laws of the United States, as President of the United States of America and Commander in Chief of the Army and Navy of the United States.

The Attorney General ([Robert] Jackson) vigorously proclaimed that the President had the moral duty to keep this Nation's defense effort a "going concern." His ringing moral justification was coupled with a legal justification equally well stated:

The Presidential proclamation rests upon the aggregate of the Presidential powers derived from the Constitution itself and from statutes enacted by the Congress . . .

Focusing now on the situation confronting the President . . ., we cannot but conclude that the President was performing his duty under the Constitution to "take Care that the Laws be faithfully executed" . . .

The absence of a specific statute authorizing seizure of the steel mills as a mode of executing the laws . . . has not until today been thought to prevent the President from executing the laws. Unlike . . . the head of a department when administering a particular statute, the President is a constitutional officer charged with taking care that a "mass of legislation" be executed. Flexibility as to mode of execution to meet critical situations is a matter of practical necessity. This practical construction of the "Take Care" clause [was] adopted by this Court in *In re Neagle* . . . and other cases . . .

In this case, there is no statute prohibiting the action taken by the President in a matter not merely important, but threatening the very safety of the Nation. Executive inaction in such a situation, courting national disaster, is foreign to the concept of energy and initiative in the Executive as created by the Founding Fathers . . .

The Framers knew, as we should know in these times of peril, that there is real danger in Executive weakness . . .

[Yet, the Court says that] [t]he broad executive power granted by Article II to an officer on duty 365 days a year cannot . . . be invoked to avert disaster. Instead, the President must confine himself to sending a message to Congress recommending action. Under this messenger-boy concept of the Office, the President cannot even act to preserve legislative programs from destruction so that Congress will have something left to act upon. . . .

Presidents have been in the past, and any man worthy of the Office should be in the future, free to take at least interim action

necessary to execute legislative programs essential to survival of the Nation. A sturdy judiciary should not be swayed by the unpleasantness or unpopularity of necessary executive action, but must independently determine for itself whether the President was acting, as required by the Constitution, to "take Care that the Laws be faithfully executed."

Youngstown is interesting in at least two regards. First, the justices were sharply divided over the nature of executive power—a subject we covered earlier in the chapter. Two members of the Court (Douglas and Black) adopted the "mere designation" or enumerated approach, writing, "The President's power, if any, to issue the order must stem either from an act of Congress or from the Constitution itself." Three justices (Vinson, Stanley Reed, and Sherman Minton) took the opposite position. In their opinion, the take care clause of Article II provided the president with a sufficient constitutional basis for his actions: he was taking steps that were in the best interest of the country until Congress could act. Finally, Jackson's famous concurrence settled somewhere between the two extremes. Jackson's concurrence is especially interesting. Although he seems to read the vesting clause of Article II as a mere designation of office, as do Black and Douglas, Jackson concedes that other clauses in Article II can and should be interpreted flexibly to accommodate the modern presidency. But, in contrast to the dissenters, he argued that President Truman could not seize the mills because he had acted against the "implied" desires of Congress. As Jackson puts it, "When the President takes measures incompatible with the expressed or implied will of Congress, his power is at its lowest ebb, for then he can rely only upon his own constitutional powers minus any constitutional powers of Congress over the matter." In other words, when the president is at odds with Congress, he must show that he alone has conclusive and exclusive power, and Congress has none (since Congress withdrew whatever it has).

A second interesting point is this: although it is typically the majority opinion that establishes precedent for the nation, in *Youngstown* legal analysts regard Jackson's concurrence as the most important statement coming out of the case. Indeed, some scholars deem it the most important concurrence ever written. The explanation, it seems, is that Jackson provided a useful framework for dealing with presidential power vis-à-vis Congress.

Foreign Policy in the Middle East

Would the Court adopt the Jackson framework in other disputes involving foreign policy? ***Zivotofsky*** *v. Kerry* (2015) provides some answers.[20] *Zivotofsky* originates from President Truman's decision in 1948 not to recognize Israeli sovereignty over Jerusalem. All subsequent presidents have followed suit, and State Department policy on passports reflects the president's position. Because the United States does not recognize any country as having sovereignty over Jerusalem, the State Department instructs employees to record the place of birth for U.S. citizens born in Jerusalem as "Jerusalem"—not Israel. In 2002, though, Congress passed the Foreign Relations Authorization Act, which attempted to override State Department policy by allowing citizens born in Jerusalem to list their place of birth as "Israel."

Despite this law, President George W. Bush and his secretary of state said that "U.S. policy regarding Jerusalem had not changed"; the government would continue to list only Jerusalem, and not Israel, on passports. The Zivotofskys, U.S. citizens whose child, Menachem, had been born in Jerusalem objected. They argued that the 2002 congressional law gave Menachem the right to have "Israel" recorded as his place of birth in his passport. The secretary of state responded that the case presented a nonjusticiable political question or, in the alternative, that the law violated the Constitution by interfering with the president's constitutional power to "receive Ambassadors and other public Ministers," which embraced the power to recognize a foreign sovereign.

The district court dismissed the ***Zivotofsky v. Clinton*** (2012) case on the grounds that it raised a political question. After the court of appeals affirmed, the case went to the Supreme Court in 2012. By an 8–1 vote (with only Justice Breyer dissenting), the Court vacated and remanded the case, holding that "the Judiciary must decide if Zivotofsky's

interpretation of the statute is correct, and whether the statute is constitutional"—not whether Jerusalem is, in fact, part of Israel.

On remand the court of appeals agreed with the secretary of state (and the president), ruling that the law unconstitutionally infringed on the president's authority to grant formal recognition to a foreign sovereign. Zivotofsky again appealed to the U.S. Supreme Court.

In the Supreme Court, Zivotosky drew on Justice Jackson's concurring opinion in *Youngstown Sheet & Tube Co. v. Sawyer* to argue that this dispute fell in Justice Jackson's third category, where presidential power is at his "lowest ebb." Writing for the Court, Justice Anthony M. Kennedy agreed that this dispute fell into category 3; the executive branch had indeed taken "measures incompatible with the expressed . . . will of Congress." But, unlike in *Youngstown*, the Court ruled in favor of the president. Why? Because Jackson's third category does not mean that the president can never take action incompatible with Congress's will; it rather means that when the president does act in this way, he must rely on "his own constitutional powers minus any constitutional powers of Congress over the matter." In other words, the president's asserted power must be both "exclusive" and "conclusive." Based on an analysis of the Constitution's text and structure, along with precedent and historical practice, the majority concluded that the president has exclusive authority to recognize foreign states and their governments, as well as the territorial limits of their sovereignty.

What should we make of *Zivotofsky?* First, it provides direct evidence that Justice Jackson's third category will not always lead the Court to nullify presidential action (as it did in *Youngstown*). Here the president demonstrated that his power to recognize foreign governments belonged exclusively to him, and for that reason the Court invalidated the congressional law as an encroachment on his power. Second, and despite ruling in the president's favor, Justice Kennedy acknowledged the role that Congress plays in foreign affairs: "It remains true . . . that many decisions affecting foreign relations—including decisions that may determine the course of our relations with recognized countries—require congressional action."

The War on Terrorism

The cases and materials we have considered so far have special relevance for post–September 11, 2001,

---

[20]See also *Dames & Moore v. Regan* (1981). In *Dames*, the justices considered an appeal based on a serious foreign policy problem from the Carter administration—the Iran hostage crisis. *Dames & Moore* involved the power of the president to seize Iranian assets and use them as a bargaining chip to help resolve an international stalemate. To preserve the assets under his control, President Carter disallowed any lawsuits by U.S. citizens and corporations, requesting that the assets be used to pay off judgments against Iran. Was the president acting within his legitimate foreign policy powers or had he gone too far? Using both Black's majority views and Jackson's concurrence in *Youngstown*, then Justice Rehnquist—a former law clerk to Justice Jackson—ruled in favor of the president in part because Congress had implicitly approved the practice of claim settlement by executive agreement.

In 2004 the Supreme Court upheld the military detention of Yaser Hamdi, a U.S. citizen captured during hostilities in Afghanistan, but also ruled that Hamdi must be given an opportunity to rebut the government's designation of him as an "enemy combatant."

America. In the process of waging a "war on terrorism"—a battle that may endure far longer than any other conflict Americans have experienced—the George W. Bush administration sent military forces into two countries, Afghanistan and Iraq. The president also took steps to restrict the rights and liberties of Americans and foreigners alike.

Among the more controversial was the government's policy on captured enemy combatants. The Bush administration took the position that supporters of the enemy could be detained indefinitely without access to the civilian courts. Such policies ultimately brought to the Supreme Court disputes similar to those the justices faced in *Ex parte Milligan* during the Civil War and *Ex parte Quirin* during World War II. One of the most important was *Hamdi v. Rumsfeld*. As you read the excerpt below, note the justices' interest, not unlike Justice Jackson's in *Youngstown*, in whether Congress had authorized the detentions ordered by the president or whether the president had acted on his own.

Hamdi v. Rumsfeld

542 U.S. 507 (2004)
http://caselaw.findlaw.com/us-supreme-court/542/507.html
Oral arguments available at https://www.oyez.org/
  cases/2003/03-6696
On the question of the validity of Hamdi's detention:
Vote: 5 (Breyer, Kennedy, O'Connor, Rehnquist, Thomas)
  4 (Ginsburg, Scalia, Souter, Stevens)
On the question of Hamdi's access to courts and lawyers:
Vote: 8 (Breyer, Ginsburg, Kennedy, O'Connor, Rehnquist, Scalia,
  Souter, Stevens)
  1 (Thomas)

OPINION ANNOUNCING THE JUDGMENT OF THE COURT:
O'Connor

OPINION CONCURRING IN PART, DISSENTING IN PART, AND CONCURRING IN THE JUDGMENT: *Souter*

DISSENTING OPINIONS: *Scalia, Thomas*

One week after the September 11, 2001, al-Qaeda terrorist attacks on the United States, Congress passed the Authorization for Use of Military Force resolution (AUMF), which gave the president authority to "use all necessary and appropriate force against those nations, organizations, or persons he determines planned, authorized, committed, or aided the terrorist attacks" or "harbored such organizations or persons, in order to prevent any future acts of international terrorism against the United States." On the basis of this congressional grant of authority, President Bush ordered American armed forces to Afghanistan to attack al-Qaeda and the Taliban regime that supported it.

During this military effort, Afghan elements supporting the United States captured twenty-year-old Yaser Esam Hamdi and delivered him to U.S. forces. Hamdi was an American citizen by virtue of his birth in Louisiana, but his family had moved to Saudi Arabia when he was a child. After being interrogated in Afghanistan, Hamdi was transferred first to the U.S. naval base at Guantánamo Bay, Cuba, then to military prisons in Norfolk, Virginia, and Charleston, South Carolina. The government claimed that Hamdi was an "enemy combatant" and as such could be held indefinitely without formal charges, court proceedings, access to counsel, or the freedom to communicate with anyone beyond the prison walls.

On what grounds did the administration justify the detention? It made two kinds of arguments. First, the administration said it did not require congressional authorization for its actions. Under its interpretation of presidential wartime authority and Supreme Court decisions, it believed that Article II provided the executive with plenary authority to detain the enemy combatants. This is a position embraced by some of the cases and opinions we have considered, especially

Curtiss-Wright. But it is an argument that Justice Jackson's concurrence in *Youngstown Sheet & Tube* could be seen to reject.

There was another problem, too, with Bush's claim of authority to hold enemy combatants (at least those who were U.S. citizens) without formal charges: a federal law (U.S. Code Title 18, §4001(a)) that said, "No citizen shall be imprisoned or otherwise detained by the United States except pursuant to an Act of Congress." This law was enacted to overturn an act of the Cold War Act era, the Emergency Detention Act of 1950, which had authorized the attorney general, in time of emergency, to detain anyone reasonably thought likely to engage in espionage or sabotage. Congress replaced it with §4001(a) in 1971 out of fear that the 1950 law could "authorize a repetition of the World War II internment of citizens of Japanese ancestry."[21] Congress meant to preclude another episode like the one described in *Korematsu v. United States* (1944).

In the face of these potential difficulties, the administration had a back-up argument. Government lawyers claimed that §4001(a) was, in fact, satisfied because Congress had in fact authorized the use of detentions through the AUMF, its resolution authorizing the use of military force.

Believing otherwise, in June 2002 Hamdi's father, Esam Fouad Hamdi, filed a petition for habeas corpus on behalf of his son against Secretary of Defense Donald Rumsfeld. He claimed the continued detention without formal charges or access to lawyers or the courts violated the younger Hamdi's constitutional right to due process of law. Hamdi's father argued that his son was not engaged in military activity but had gone to Afghanistan as a relief worker. The United States countered that Hamdi had received military training in Afghanistan and had joined a Taliban unit prior to his capture in a theater of war. The government's allegations as to Hamdi's participation in Taliban activities were submitted in the form of a statement by Michael Mobbs, a Defense Department official. This document, referred to as the Mobbs Declaration, contained little in the way of direct factual evidence.

After a series of hearings at the district and circuit court levels, the U.S. Court of Appeals for the Fourth Circuit ruled in favor of the government's position, holding that Hamdi could be detained and was entitled only to the limited judicial determination of whether the government had acted properly under its war powers. Hamdi's lawyers appealed to the Supreme Court.

> **JUSTICE O'CONNOR ANNOUNCED THE JUDGMENT OF THE COURT AND DELIVERED AN OPINION, IN WHICH THE CHIEF JUSTICE, JUSTICE KENNEDY, AND JUSTICE BREYER JOIN.**

At this difficult time in our Nation's history, we are called upon to consider the legality of the Government's detention of a United States citizen on United States soil as an "enemy combatant" and to address the process that is constitutionally owed to one who seeks to challenge his classification as such. . . . We hold that although Congress authorized the detention of combatants in the narrow circumstances alleged here, due process demands that a citizen held in the United States as an enemy combatant be given a meaningful opportunity to contest the factual basis for that detention before a neutral decisionmaker. . . .

The threshold question before us is whether the Executive has the authority to detain citizens who qualify as "enemy combatants." There is some debate as to the proper scope of this term, and the Government has never provided . . . the full criteria that it uses in classifying individuals as such. It has made clear, however, that, for purposes of this case, the "enemy combatant" that it is seeking to detain is an individual who, it alleges, was "'part of or supporting forces hostile to the United States or coalition partners'" in Afghanistan and who "'engaged in an armed conflict against the United States'" there. We therefore answer only the narrow question before us: whether the detention of citizens falling within that definition is authorized.

The Government maintains that no explicit congressional authorization is required, because the Executive possesses plenary authority to detain pursuant to Article II of the Constitution. We do not reach the question whether Article II provides such authority, however, because we agree with the Government's alternative position, that Congress has in fact authorized Hamdi's detention, through the AUMF [the Authorization for Use of Military Force resolution] . . . and that the AUMF satisfied §4001(a)'s requirement that a detention be "pursuant to an Act of Congress."

The AUMF authorizes the President to use "all necessary and appropriate force" against "nations, organizations, or persons" associated with the September 11, 2001, terrorist attacks. There can be no doubt that individuals who fought against the United States in Afghanistan as part of the Taliban, an organization known to have supported the al Qaeda terrorist network responsible for those attacks, are individuals Congress sought to target in passing the AUMF. We conclude that detention of individuals falling into the limited category we are considering, for the duration of the particular conflict in which they were captured, is so fundamental and accepted an incident to war as to be an exercise of the "necessary and appropriate force" Congress has authorized the President to use.

The capture and detention of lawful combatants and the capture, detention, and trial of unlawful combatants, by "universal agreement and practice," are "important incident[s] of war." *Ex parte Quirin* [1942]. The purpose of detention is to prevent captured individuals from returning to the field of battle and taking up arms once again. . . .

There is no bar to this Nation's holding one of its own citizens as an enemy combatant. In *Quirin,* one of the detainees, Haupt, alleged that he was a naturalized United States citizen. We held that

---

[21]See Justice Souter's opinion in *Hamdi v. Rumsfeld.*

"[c]itizens who associate themselves with the military arm of the enemy government, and with its aid, guidance and direction enter this country bent on hostile acts, are enemy belligerents within the meaning of . . . the law of war." While Haupt was tried for violations of the law of war, nothing in *Quirin* suggests that his citizenship would have precluded his mere detention for the duration of the relevant hostilities. Nor can we see any reason for drawing such a line here. A citizen, no less than an alien, can be "part of or supporting forces hostile to the United States or coalition partners" and "engaged in an armed conflict against the United States"; such a citizen, if released, would pose the same threat of returning to the front during the ongoing conflict.

In light of these principles, it is of no moment that the AUMF does not use specific language of detention. Because detention to prevent a combatant's return to the battlefield is a fundamental incident of waging war, in permitting the use of "necessary and appropriate force," Congress has clearly and unmistakably authorized detention in the narrow circumstances considered here.

Hamdi objects, nevertheless, that Congress has not authorized the *indefinite* detention to which he is now subject. . . . As the Government concedes, "given its unconventional nature, the current conflict is unlikely to end with a formal cease-fire agreement." The prospect Hamdi raises is therefore not far-fetched. If the Government does not consider this unconventional war won for two generations, and if it maintains during that time that Hamdi might, if released, rejoin forces fighting against the United States, then the position it has taken throughout the litigation of this case suggests that Hamdi's detention could last for the rest of his life . . .

Hamdi contends that the AUMF does not authorize indefinite or perpetual detention. Certainly, we agree that indefinite detention for the purpose of interrogation is not authorized. Further, we understand Congress' grant of authority for the use of "necessary and appropriate force" to include the authority to detain for the duration of the relevant conflict, and our understanding is based on longstanding law-of-war principles [that detention may last no longer than active hostilities]. If the practical circumstances of a given conflict are entirely unlike those of the conflicts that informed the development of the law of war, that understanding may unravel. But that is not the situation we face as of this date. Active combat operations against Taliban fighters apparently are ongoing in Afghanistan. The United States may detain, for the duration of these hostilities, individuals legitimately determined to be Taliban combatants who "engaged in an armed conflict against the United States." If the record establishes that United States troops are still involved in active combat in Afghanistan, those detentions are part of the exercise of "necessary and appropriate force," and therefore are authorized by the AUMF.

Ex parte Milligan (1866) does not undermine our holding about the Government's authority to seize enemy combatants, as we define that term today. In that case, the Court made repeated reference to the fact that its inquiry into whether the military tribunal had jurisdiction to try and punish Milligan turned in large part on the fact that Milligan was not a prisoner of war, but a resident of Indiana arrested while at home there. That fact was central to its conclusion. Had Milligan been captured while he was assisting Confederate soldiers by carrying a rifle against Union troops on a Confederate battlefield, the holding of the Court might well have been different. The Court's repeated explanations that Milligan was not a prisoner of war suggest that had these different circumstances been present he could have been detained under military authority for the duration of the conflict, whether or not he was a citizen. . . .

Even in cases in which the detention of enemy combatants is legally authorized, there remains the question of what process is constitutionally due to a citizen who disputes his enemy-combatant status. . . .

Though they reach radically different conclusions on the process that ought to attend the present proceeding, the parties begin on common ground. All agree that, absent suspension, the writ of habeas corpus remains available to every individual detained within the United States. Only in the rarest of circumstances has Congress seen fit to suspend the writ. At all other times, it has remained a critical check on the Executive, ensuring that it does not detain individuals except in accordance with law. All agree suspension of the writ has not occurred here. . . .

. . . [A]s critical as the Government's interest may be in detaining those who actually pose an immediate threat to the national security of the United States during ongoing international conflict, history and common sense teach us that an unchecked system of detention carries the potential to become a means for oppression and abuse of others who do not present that sort of threat. See *Ex parte Milligan*. . . . We reaffirm today the fundamental nature of a citizen's right to be free from involuntary confinement by his own government without due process of law, and we weigh the opposing governmental interests against the curtailment of liberty that such confinement entails.

On the other side of the scale are the weighty and sensitive governmental interests in ensuring that those who have in fact fought with the enemy during a war do not return to battle against the United States. . . . [T]he law of war and the realities of combat may render such detentions both necessary and appropriate, and our due process analysis need not blink at those realities. Without doubt, our Constitution recognizes that core strategic matters of war making belong in the hands of those who are best positioned and most politically accountable for making them . . .

Striking the proper constitutional balance here is of great importance to the Nation during this period of ongoing combat. But it is equally vital that our calculus not give short shrift to the values that this country holds dear or to the privilege that is American citizenship. It is during our most challenging and uncertain moments that our Nation's commitment to due process is most severely tested; and it is in those times that we must preserve our commitment at home to the principles for which we fight abroad. . . .

We therefore hold that a citizen-detainee seeking to challenge his classification as an enemy combatant must receive notice of the factual basis for his classification, and a fair opportunity to rebut the Government's factual assertions before a neutral decisionmaker. These essential constitutional promises may not be eroded.

At the same time, the exigencies of the circumstances may demand that, aside from these core elements, enemy combatant proceedings may be tailored to alleviate their uncommon potential to burden the Executive at a time of ongoing military conflict. [T]he Constitution would not be offended, [for example], by a presumption in favor of the Government's evidence, so long as that presumption remained a rebuttable one and fair opportunity for rebuttal were provided. Thus, once the Government puts forth credible evidence that the habeas petitioner meets the enemy combatant criteria, the onus could shift to the petitioner to rebut that evidence with more persuasive evidence that he falls outside the criteria. A burden-shifting scheme of this sort would meet the goal of ensuring that the errant tourist, embedded journalist, or local aid worker has a chance to prove military error while giving due regard to the Executive once it has put forth meaningful support for its conclusion that the detainee is in fact an enemy combatant. . . .

We think it unlikely that this basic process will have the dire impact on the central functions of warmaking that the Government forecasts. The parties agree that initial captures on the battlefield need not receive the process we have discussed here; that process is due only when the determination is made to *continue* to hold those who have been seized. . . . While we accord the greatest respect and consideration to the judgments of military authorities in matters relating to the actual prosecution of a war, and recognize that the scope of that discretion necessarily is wide, it does not infringe on the core role of the military for the courts to exercise their own time-honored and constitutionally mandated roles of reviewing and resolving claims like those presented here. . . .

In so holding, we necessarily reject the Government's assertion that separation of powers principles mandate a heavily circumscribed role for the courts in such circumstances. Indeed, the position that the courts must forgo any examination of the individual case and focus exclusively on the legality of the broader detention scheme cannot be mandated by any reasonable view of separation of powers, as this approach serves only to *condense* power into a single branch of government. We have long since made clear that a state of war is not a blank check for the President when it comes to the rights of the Nation's citizens. . . . Likewise, we have made clear that, unless Congress acts to suspend it, the Great Writ of habeas corpus allows the Judicial Branch to play a necessary role in maintaining this delicate balance of governance, serving as an important judicial check on the Executive's discretion in the realm of detentions. . . .

. . . Plainly, the "process" Hamdi has received is not that to which he is entitled under the Due Process Clause.

There remains the possibility that the standards we have articulated could be met by an appropriately authorized and properly constituted military tribunal. . . .

Hamdi asks us to hold that the Fourth Circuit also erred by denying him immediate access to counsel upon his detention and by disposing of the case without permitting him to meet with an attorney. Since our grant of certiorari in this case, Hamdi has been appointed counsel, with whom he has met for consultation purposes on several occasions, and with whom he is now being granted unmonitored meetings. He unquestionably has the right to access to counsel in connection with the proceedings on remand. No further consideration of this issue is necessary at this stage of the case.

The judgment of the United States Court of Appeals for the Fourth Circuit is vacated, and the case is remanded for further proceedings.

It is so ordered.

JUSTICE SOUTER, WITH WHOM JUSTICE GINSBURG JOINS, CONCURRING IN PART, DISSENTING IN PART, AND CONCURRING IN THE JUDGMENT.

The threshold issue is how broadly or narrowly to read §4001(a), . . . the tone of which is severe: "No citizen shall be imprisoned or otherwise detained by the United States except pursuant to an Act of Congress." . . . The fact that Congress intended to guard against a repetition of the World War II internments when it . . . gave us §4001(a) provides a powerful reason to think that §4001(a) was meant to require clear congressional authorization before any citizen can be placed in a cell. . . .

Under this principle of reading §4001(a) robustly to require a clear statement of authorization to detain, [the government's arguments do not] suffice to justify Hamdi's detention. . . .

Since the [AUMF] was adopted one week after the attacks of September 11, 2001, it naturally speaks with some generality, but its focus is clear, and that is on the use of military power. It is fairly read to authorize the use of armies and weapons, whether against other armies or individual terrorists. But . . . it never so much as uses the word detention, and there is no reason to think Congress might have perceived any need to augment Executive power to deal with dangerous citizens within the United States, given the well-stocked statutory arsenal of defined criminal offenses covering the gamut of actions that a citizen sympathetic to terrorists might commit.

Because I find Hamdi's detention . . . unauthorized by the Force Resolution, I would not reach any questions of what process he may be due in litigating disputed issues in a proceeding under the habeas statute or prior to the habeas enquiry itself. For me, it suffices that the Government has failed to justify holding him in the absence of a further Act of Congress, criminal charges, [or] a showing that the detention conforms to the laws of war. . . .

Since this disposition does not command a majority of the Court, however, the need to give practical effect to the conclusions of eight members of the Court rejecting the Government's position calls for me to join with the plurality in ordering remand on terms closest to those I would impose. Although I think litigation of Hamdi's status as an enemy combatant is unnecessary, the terms of the plurality's remand will allow Hamdi to offer evidence that he is not an enemy combatant, and he should at the least have the benefit of that opportunity.

Subject to these qualifications, I join with the plurality in a judgment of the Court vacating the Fourth Circuit's judgment and remanding the case.

JUSTICE SCALIA, WITH WHOM JUSTICE STEVENS JOINS, DISSENTING.

This case brings into conflict the competing demands of national security and our citizens' constitutional right to personal liberty. Although I share the Court's evident unease as it seeks to reconcile the two, I do not agree with its resolution.

Where the Government accuses a citizen of waging war against it, our constitutional tradition has been to prosecute him in federal court for treason or some other crime. Where the exigencies of war prevent that, the Constitution's Suspension Clause, Art. I, §9, c1.2, allows Congress to relax the usual protections temporarily. Absent suspension, however, the Executive's assertion of military exigency has not been thought sufficient to permit detention without charge. No one contends that the congressional Authorization for Use of Military Force, on which the Government relies to justify its actions here, is an implementation of the Suspension Clause. Accordingly, I would reverse the decision below. . . .

JUSTICE O'CONNOR, writing for a plurality of this Court, asserts that captured enemy combatants (other than those suspected of war crimes) have traditionally been detained until the cessation of hostilities and then released. That is probably an accurate description of wartime practice with respect to enemy *aliens.* The tradition with respect to American citizens, however, has been quite different. Citizens aiding the enemy have been treated as traitors subject to the criminal process. . . .

. . . [T]he reasoning and conclusion of [*Ex parte*] *Milligan* logically cover the present case. The Government justifies imprisonment of Hamdi on principles of the law of war and admits that, absent the war, it would have no such authority. But if the law of war cannot be applied to citizens where courts are open, then Hamdi's imprisonment without criminal trial is no less unlawful than Milligan's trial by military tribunal. . . .

. . . Hamdi is entitled to a habeas decree requiring his release unless (1) criminal proceedings are promptly brought, or (2) Congress has suspended the writ of habeas corpus. A suspension of the writ could, of course, lay down conditions for continued detention, similar to those that today's opinion prescribes under the Due Process Clause. But there is a world of difference between the people's representatives' determining the need for that suspension (and prescribing the conditions for it), and this Court's doing so.

The plurality finds justification for Hamdi's imprisonment in the Authorization for Use of Military Force. . . .

This is not remotely a congressional suspension of the writ, and no one claims that it is . . . . The Suspension Clause of the Constitution, which carefully circumscribes the conditions under which the writ can be withheld, would be a sham if it could be evaded by congressional prescription of requirements *other than the common-law requirement of committal for criminal prosecution* that render the writ, though available, unavailing. If the Suspension Clause does not guarantee the citizen that he will either be tried or released, unless the conditions for suspending the writ exist and the grave action of suspending the writ has been taken; if it merely guarantees the citizen that he will not be detained unless Congress by ordinary legislation says he can be detained; it guarantees him very little indeed. . . .

There is a certain harmony of approach in the plurality's making up for Congress's failure to invoke the Suspension Clause and its making up for the Executive's failure to apply what it says are needed procedures—an approach that reflects what might be called a Mr. Fix-it Mentality. The plurality seems to view it as its mission to Make Everything Come Out Right, rather than merely to decree the consequences, as far as individual rights are concerned, of the other two branches' actions and omissions. Has the Legislature failed to suspend the writ in the current dire emergency? Well, we will remedy that failure by prescribing the reasonable conditions that a suspension should have included. And has the Executive failed to live up to those reasonable conditions? Well, we will ourselves make that failure good, so that this dangerous fellow (if he is dangerous) need not be set free. The problem with this approach is not only that it steps out of the courts' modest and limited role in a democratic society; but that by repeatedly doing what it thinks the political branches ought to do it encourages their lassitude and saps the vitality of government by the people.

Several limitations give my views in this matter a relatively narrow compass. They apply only to citizens, accused of being enemy combatants, who are detained within the territorial jurisdiction of a federal court. This is not likely to be a numerous group. . . . Where the citizen is captured outside and held outside the United States, the constitutional requirements may be different. Moreover, even within the United States, the accused citizen-enemy combatant may lawfully be detained once prosecution is in progress or in contemplation. . . .

I frankly do not know whether these tools are sufficient to meet the Government's security needs, including the need to obtain intelligence through interrogation. It is far beyond my competence, or the Court's competence, to determine that. But it is not beyond Congress's. If the situation demands it, the Executive can ask Congress to authorize suspension of the writ—which can be made subject to whatever conditions Congress deems appropriate, including even the procedural novelties invented by the plurality today. To be sure, suspension is limited by the Constitution to cases of rebellion or invasion. But whether the attacks of September 11, 2001, constitute an "invasion," and whether those attacks still justify suspension several years later, are questions for Congress rather than this Court. If civil rights are to be curtailed during wartime, it must be done openly and democratically, as the Constitution requires, rather than by silent erosion through an opinion of this Court. . . .

Many think it not only inevitable but entirely proper that liberty give way to security in times of national crisis—that, at the extremes of military exigency, *inter arma silent leges*. Whatever the general merits of the view that war silences law or modulates its voice, that view has no place in the interpretation and application of a Constitution designed precisely to confront war and, in a manner that accords with democratic principles, to accommodate it. Because the Court has proceeded to meet the current emergency in a manner the Constitution does not envision, I respectfully dissent.

JUSTICE THOMAS, DISSENTING.

The Executive Branch, acting pursuant to the powers vested in the President by the Constitution and with explicit congressional approval, has determined that Yaser Hamdi is an enemy combatant and should be detained. This detention falls squarely within the Federal Government's war powers, and we lack the expertise and capacity to second-guess that decision. As such, petitioners' habeas challenge should fail, and there is no reason to remand the case. The plurality reaches a contrary conclusion by failing adequately to consider basic principles of the constitutional structure as it relates to national security and foreign affairs. . . . I do not think that the Federal Government's war powers can be balanced away by this Court. Arguably, Congress could provide for additional procedural protections, but until it does, we have no right to insist upon them. But even if I were to agree with the general approach the plurality takes, I could not accept the particulars. The plurality utterly fails to account for the Government's compelling interests and for our own institutional inability to weigh competing concerns correctly. I respectfully dissent.

Although the justices were divided over Hamdi's detention, they were nearly unanimous in their belief that "a state of war is not a blank check for the President when it comes to the rights of the Nation's citizens." They ruled that even though the government could detain Hamdi as an enemy combatant, he was entitled to challenge his classification and to be afforded "a fair opportunity to rebut the Government's factual assertions before a neutral decisionmaker." But Hamdi never received that opportunity. Following the Court's decision, his lawyers and the government reached an agreement that allowed him to return to Saudi Arabia in exchange for renouncing his American citizenship.

Hamdi answered questions about the rights of U.S. citizens who are captured during military conflict, but it did not address similar issues with respect to noncitizens. The justices considered this aspect of the president's war powers in *Rasul v. Bush* (2004), decided the same day as *Hamdi*.

The *Rasul* case centered on the status of some six hundred men who had been captured during hostilities in Afghanistan and transported to the naval detention facilities at Guantánamo Bay. The United States occupies and completely controls the naval base pursuant to a lease and treaty, but Cuba retains ultimate sovereignty over the land. The prisoners were detained without formal charges and without access to courts or attorneys. The relatives of two Australians and twelve Kuwaitis held at Guantánamo filed habeas corpus petitions on the detainees' behalf, claiming they were illegally incarcerated. The lower federal courts dismissed these lawsuits, holding that the federal courts have no jurisdiction outside the United States. The relatives of the detainees requested Supreme Court review.

A six-justice majority reversed, ruling that U.S. law confers jurisdiction on the federal courts over such habeas corpus petitions. Federal authority extends to areas under the control of the United States, such as the Guantánamo naval base, as well as to the military custodians of the detainees. Under the Court's decision, incarcerated captives, whether American citizens or aliens, have the right to challenge their imprisonment in federal court.

The decision in *Rasul* was based on an interpretation of federal statutes, not on the Constitution. The ruling is important, however, because it allows access to the courts where the constitutional validity of the detainees' continued imprisonment may be challenged.

Hamdi and *Rasul* dealt with the government's power to detain suspected terrorists and limit challenges in the federal courts to their detention. They were not, however, the Court's last words on the executive power in the war against terrorism. Just as Lincoln and Roosevelt resorted to military tribunals or commissions, so, too, did President George W. Bush; and just as during those earlier wartime administrations—recall *Milligan* and *Quirin*—the president's actions were challenged. In **Hamdan v. Rumsfeld** (2006) the Court considered a military order issued by President Bush that subjected "enemy combatants" to military commissions. For purposes of the order, an enemy combatant is any noncitizen for whom the president determines there is reason to believe the individual (1) is or was a member of al-Qaeda or (2) has engaged in activities aimed at or harmful to the United States.

Justice Stevens, writing for the majority, outlawed the use of these commissions, reiterating the view that even during wars the "executive is bound to comply with the Rule of Law."[22] The Court did not, however, entirely shut the door. Part of the majority's concern about the commissions was that Congress had not authorized them. But under the Court's ruling, as Justice Breyer noted, "[n]othing prevents the President from returning to Congress to seek the authority he believes necessary." And, in fact, the administration took that step—with success. Within months of the Court's decision in *Hamdan*, Congress passed the Military Commissions Act (MCA), which authorized the use of military commissions for trying suspected terrorists and denied federal courts jurisdiction to hear the detainees' habeas corpus applications.

Based in part on their review of the history and origins of the writ of habeas corpus, the justices struck down parts of the MCA in **Boumediene v. Bush** (2008). In a closely divided vote, they held that the Guantánamo Bay detainees have a right to challenge their imprisonment in the federal courts. Writing for the majority, Justice Kennedy declared:

The laws and Constitution are designed to survive, and remain in force, in extraordinary times. Liberty and security can be reconciled; and in our system they are reconciled within the framework of the law. The Framers decided that habeas corpus, a right of first importance, must be a part of that framework, a part of that law.

Kennedy held that "if the privilege of habeas corpus is to be denied to the detainees now before us, Congress must act in accordance with the requirements of the Suspension Clause." In other words, Congress must suspend the writ.

The four dissenters objected strongly to Kennedy's analysis. Justice Scalia wrote, "The game of bait-and-switch that today's opinion plays upon the Nation's Commander in Chief will make the war harder on us. It will almost certainly cause more Americans to be killed." President Bush, not surprisingly, said that while his administration would "abide by the Court's decision," he did not agree with it.

What are the lessons of *Hamdi, Rasul, Hamdan,* and *Boumediene*—all of which the executive lost in part or in full? Are they in line with other cases you have read in this chapter? Is the central idea one that follows from Jackson's concurrence in *Youngstown,* that in the interest of the nation's security, the justices may be willing to allow the president to take actions during times of war that they would otherwise prohibit, but generally only if he has the backing of Congress? If so, do you agree that this is the appropriate way for the justices to proceed? On one hand, why would legislative approval be so important if the president believes he is acting in the country's best interest? On the other, should the Court allow the president, even with Congress's support, to curtail rights and liberties? Keep in mind that in *Boumediene* the Court took the position that it should not: Congress had approved of the detentions, but the Court still ruled against the executive.

President Bush, of course, was not the last president to claim broad constitutional authority for the executive in such circumstances. His successor, Barack Obama, continued to assert authority to detain terrorist suspects who "substantially supported terrorist organizations." And although Obama's Justice Department dropped the term *enemy combatant*, President Trump restored it, tweeting that "building a great Border Wall, with drugs (poison) and enemy combatants pouring into our Country, is all about National Defense."[23]

---

[22]In addition to the issue of the constitutionality of the military commissions, *Hamdan* raised a jurisdictional issue. Shortly after the Court agreed to hear *Hamdan*, however, on December 30, 2005, Congress enacted the Detainee Treatment Act (DTA), which said that "no court, justice, or judge shall have jurisdiction to hear or consider" habeas corpus petitions filed by Guantánamo detainees. Although the act was silent about pending cases, the Bush administration believed that it removed the Supreme Court's jurisdiction to resolve Hamdan's suit. Accordingly, the administration asked the justices to dismiss the writ of certiorari. In light of the government's request, some commentators thought that *Hamdan* presented an opportunity for the Court to clarify its ruling in *Ex parte McCardle* and, more generally, the appropriate reading of the exceptions clause. Justice Stevens, however, writing for himself and Justices Breyer, Ginsburg, Kennedy, and Souter, said that it was "unnecessary" to consider the various constitutional arguments about *McCardle* and the exceptions clause because the DTA did not expressly cover pending cases. Justice Scalia (and Justice Alito), in contrast, believed that Congress had taken away the Court's jurisdiction to hear the case.

[23]@realDonaldTrump, March 25, 2018.

In 2017 Trump also took the step of issuing a proclamation (a type of directive) titled "Enhancing Vetting Capabilities and Processes for Detecting Attempted Entry Into the United States by Terrorists or Other Public-Safety Threats." As its name suggests, the proclamation restricted people from eight countries from entering the United States (Chad, Iran, Iraq, Libya, North Korea, Syria, Venezuela, and Yemen). Those eight countries, according to the President, had inadequate systems managing and sharing information about their nationals.

Trump claimed that he had authority to issue the directive under the Immigration and Nationality Act (INA), which gives the president authority to restrict the entry of aliens whenever he finds that their entry "would be detrimental to the interests of the United States." In *Trump v. Hawaii* (2018) (the travel ban case), the state of Hawaii and the Muslim Association of Hawaii, among others, argued that the directive violated the INA. They also claimed that the directive violated the religious establishment clause of the First Amendment because most of the countries covered by the Proclamation have Muslim-majority populations. On their theory, the president singled out Muslims for disfavored treatment, and they used Trump's own public statements to back up their claim.

Writing for a 5–4 Court, Chief Justice John G. Roberts held for the president. He found, first, that the directive falls "squarely within the scope of Presidential authority under the INA." "By its plain language, the chief justice wrote, the INA "grants the President broad discretion to suspend the entry of aliens into the United States." Second, out of a belief that "judicial inquiry into the national-security realm raises concerns for the separation of powers by intruding on the President's constitutional responsibilities in the area of foreign affairs," Roberts applied a very deferential standard of review to evaluate the religious establishment claim. It could only succeed, he wrote, if the proclamation lacked "any purpose other than a 'bare . . . desire to harm a politically unpopular group.'" But, to the majority, it did have other purposes—legitimate purposes grounded in "national security concerns, quite apart from any religious hostility."

Justice Sotomayor, in dissent, vehemently disagreed, comparing the majority's holding to that of *Korematsu v. United States* (1944):

In *Korematsu*, the Court gave "a pass [to] an odious, gravely injurious racial classification" authorized by an executive order. As here, the Government invoked an ill-defined national-security threat to justify an exclusionary policy of sweeping proportion. As here, the exclusion order was rooted in dangerous stereotypes about a particular group's supposed inability to assimilate and desire to harm the United States. . . . And as here, there was strong evidence that impermissible hostility and animus motivated the Government's policy . . .

Roberts did not let Sotomayor's claim go unaddressed:

Whatever rhetorical advantage the dissent may see in [invoking *Korematsu*], *Korematsu* has nothing to do with this case. The forcible relocation of U.S. citizens to concentration camps, solely and explicitly on the basis of race, is objectively unlawful and outside the scope of Presidential authority. But it is wholly inapt to liken that morally repugnant order to a facially neutral policy denying certain foreign nationals the privilege of admission. The entry suspension is an act that is well within executive authority and could have been taken by any other President—the only question is evaluating the actions of this particular President in promulgating an otherwise valid Proclamation.

As we noted earlier, Roberts concluded by overruling *Korematsu*, a step that Sotomayor approved but, she wrote, one "does not make the majority's decision here acceptable or right. . . . It "merely replaces one 'gravely wrong' decision with another."

Trump v. Hawaii will not be the last word on the constitutionality of government actions in wartime and over foreign affairs, nor will it be the last time the Court debates these matters. Just as authority over external relations presents an invitation to struggle between the president and Congress, it also has generated differences of opinion, to say the least, among the justices over their appropriate role.

ANNOTATED READINGS

General treatments of Article II, executive authority, and theories of presidential power include Joseph Bessette and Jeffrey Tulis, eds., *The Constitutional Presidency* (Baltimore: Johns Hopkins University Press, 2009); Steven G. Calabresi and Christopher S. Yoo, *The Unitary Executive: Presidential Power from Washington to Bush* (New Haven, CT: Yale University Press, 2008); Phillip J. Cooper, *By Order of the President: The Use and Abuse of Executive Direct Action* (Lawrence: University Press of Kansas, 2002); Edward S. Corwin, *The President: Office and Powers*, 5th rev. ed. (New York: New York University Press, 1984); Matthew J. Dickinson, *Bitter Harvest: FDR, Presidential Power and the Growth of the Presidential Branch* (Cambridge: Cambridge University Press, 1999); Heidi Kitrosser, *Reclaiming Accountability: Transparency, Executive Power, and the U.S. Constitution* (Chicago: University of Chicago Press, 2015); Eric A. Posner and Adrian Vermeule, *The Executive Unbound: After the Madisonian Republic* (New York: Oxford University Press, 2011); Saikrishna Bangalore Prakash, *Imperial from the Beginning: The Constitution of the Original Executive* (New Haven, CT: Yale University Press, 2015).

Books covering more specific domestic powers are Raoul Berger, *Executive Privilege: A Constitutional Myth* (Cambridge, MA: Harvard University Press, 1974); Michael J. Gerhardt, *The Federal Impeachment Process: A Constitutional and Historical Analysis* (Chicago: University of Chicago Press, 2000); Howard Gillman, *The Votes That Counted: How the Court Decided the 2000 Presidential Election* (Chicago: University of Chicago Press, 2001); Katy J. Harriger, *Independent Justice: The Federal Special Prosecutor in American Politics* (Lawrence: University Press of Kansas, 1992); Scott M. Matheson, Bush v. Gore: *Exposing the Hidden Crisis in American Democracy* (Lawrence: University Press of Kansas, 2008); Merrill McLoughlin, ed., *The Impeachment and Trial of President Clinton* (New York: Random House, 1999); Richard A. Posner, *An Affair of State: The Investigation, Impeachment, and Trial of President Clinton* (Cambridge, MA: Harvard University Press, 1999); William H. Rehnquist, *Grand Inquests: The Historic Impeachments of Justice Samuel Chase and President Andrew Johnson* (New York: William Morrow, 1999); Mark J. Rozell and Clyde Wilcox, *The Clinton Scandal and the Future of American Government* (Washington, DC: Georgetown

University Press, 2000); Mitchel A. Sollenberger, *The President Shall Nominate: How Congress Trumps Executive Power* (Lawrence: University Press of Kansas, 2008); Donald Grier Stephenson Jr., *Campaigns and the Court: The U.S. Supreme Court in Presidential Elections* (New York: Columbia University Press, 1999).

For readings on foreign affairs or war, see David Gray Adler and Larry N. George, eds., *The Constitution and the Conduct of American Foreign Policy* (Lawrence: University Press of Kansas, 1996); Howard Ball, *Bush, the Detainees, and the Constitution: The Battle over Presidential Power in the War on Terrorism* (Lawrence: University Press of Kansas, 2007); Burrus M. Carnahan, *Lincoln on Trial: Southern Civilians and the Law of War* (Lexington: University Press of Kentucky, 2010); John Hart Ely, *War and Responsibility: Constitutional Lessons of Vietnam and Its Aftermath* (Princeton, NJ: Princeton University Press, 1993); Louis Fisher, *Presidential War Power*, 2nd ed. (Lawrence: University Press of Kansas, 2004); Louis Fisher, *Supreme Court Expansion of Presidential Power: Unconstitutional Leanings* (Lawrence: University Press of Kansas, 2017); Kimberly L. Fletcher, *The Collision of Political and Legal Time: Foreign Affairs and the Supreme Court's Transformation of Executive Authority* (Philadelphia: Temple University Press, 2018); Louis Henkin, *Foreign Affairs and the Constitution* (Mineola, NY: Foundation Press, 1972); Peter Irons, *Justice at War: The Story of the Japanese American Internment Cases* (New York: Oxford University Press, 1983); Elizabeth D. Leonard, *Lincoln's Avengers: Justice, Revenge, and Reunion after the Civil War* (New York: W. W. Norton, 2004); Maeva Marcus, *Truman and the Steel Seizure Case: The Limits of Presidential Power* (Durham, NC: Duke University Press, 1994); Scott M. Matheson, *Presidential Constitutionalism in Perilous Times* (Cambridge, MA: Harvard University Press, 2009); Christopher May, *In the Name of War: Judicial Review and the War Powers since 1918* (Cambridge, MA: Harvard University Press, 1989); Brian McGinty, *Lincoln and the Court* (Cambridge, MA: Harvard University Press, 2008); Eric A. Posner and Adrian Vermeule, *Terror in the Balance: Security, Liberty, and the Courts* (New York: Oxford University Press, 2007); William H. Rehnquist, *All the Laws but One: Civil Liberties in Wartime* (New York: Knopf, 1998);

W. Taylor Reveley III, *War Powers of the President and Congress* (Charlottesville: University Press of Virginia, 1981); Martin S. Sheffer, *The Judicial Development of Presidential War Powers* (Westport, CT: Praeger, 1999); Gordon Silverstein, *Imbalance of Powers: Constitutional Interpretation and the Making of American Foreign Policy* (New York: Oxford University Press, 1996); Geoffrey R. Stone, *War and Liberty: An American Dilemma* (New York: W. W. Norton, 2007).

For work on the writ of habeas corpus, see Eric M. Freedman, *Habeas Corpus: Rethinking the Great Writ of Liberty* (New York: New York University Press, 2003); Nancy J. King and Joseph L. Hoffmann, *Habeas for the Twenty-first Century: Uses, Abuses, and the Future of the Great Writ* (Chicago: University of Chicago Press, 2011); Justin J. Wert, *Habeas Corpus in America: The Politics of Individual Rights* (Lawrence: University Press of Kansas, 2011).

NATION-STATE RELATIONS

I F WE WERE TO CATALOG THE TYPES of national governments that exist in the world today, we would have a fairly diverse list. Some are unitary systems in which power is located in a central authority that may or may not mete out some power to its subdivisions. Others are virtually the opposite, with authority resting largely with local governments and only certain powers reserved to national authority. When the framers drafted the Constitution, they had to make some basic decisions about the allocation of government power between the states and the national government they were creating. Their choice, generally speaking, was federalism: a system in which government power is divided between a national government and several subnational units, with each given a sphere of authority.

That decision turned out to be a wise one, and we reap the advantages of it today. For example, because the government is multilayered, Americans have many points of access to influence the system. If your state enacts legislation you do not like, you might find grounds to challenge it in federal court or lobby your representative in Congress urging federal action to counter it. You could even "vote with your feet" and move to a state that has laws you prefer. Moreover, the system provides for further checks on the exercise of government power because federal, state, and even local systems are all involved in policy making. Finally, federalism encourages experimentation and provides for flexibility. Justice Louis Brandeis once wrote, "It is one of the happy incidents of the federal system that a single courageous State may, if its citizens choose, serve as a laboratory; and try novel social and economic experiments without risk to the rest of the country."[1] Because of their proximity to many problems, state and local governments may be better positioned to fashion effective public policy than is the federal government. If successful, such policy innovations may be copied by other states or even adopted nationwide. The states were first to implement tougher

laws to discourage drunk driving, policies to protect workers' rights, welfare reforms, and so forth. Other problems, such as those associated with foreign policy, are better left to the national government, which can act on behalf of the entire country.

But federalism is not perfect. It can add considerable inefficiency to government operations. The implementation of certain kinds of policies might require the coordination of the national government, fifty state governments, and numerous subdivisions, which inevitably slows down the process.

For our purposes, the most relevant concern about federalism is its complexity. It is quite difficult for citizens to keep abreast of such a decentralized system. People may not understand which level of government makes specific policies. In addition, government may seem so remote to some citizens that they may not even know the names of their representatives. At the other end of the spectrum, governments sometimes do not understand or abide by the boundaries of their own power. American history is full of state allegations that the federal government has gone too far in regulating "their" business; indeed, this was one issue over which the Civil War, the most extreme disagreement, was fought.

Yet, in most circumstances, it is neither war that has resolved these disputes nor the entities themselves that have shed light on their complexities. Rather, since the nation's founding, the U.S. Supreme Court has played a substantial role in delineating and defining the contours of American federalism. The chapters that follow discuss why and how the Court has done so. Chapter 6 focuses on the various theories of federal-state relations with which the Court has dealt. Chapters 7 and 8 consider the exercise of government power over the most contentious issues: the regulation of commerce and the power to tax and spend.

But first, we explore several issues emanating from our discussion so far: the kind of system the framers adopted, the amending of that system, and its complexity. These issues have often led to the involvement of "neutral" arbiters—judges and Supreme Court justices.

---

[1]Dissenting opinion in *New State Ice Co. v. Liebmann* (1932).

THE FRAMERS AND FEDERALISM

We have already mentioned that the framers selected federalism from among several alternative forms of government, although the word *federalism* does not appear in the Constitution. The founders had a general vision of the sort of government they wanted—or, more to the point, the sort they did not want. They rejected a unitary system as wholly incompatible with basic values and traditions already existing within the states. They also rejected a confederation in which power would reside with the states; after all, that is what they had under the Articles of Confederation, the charter they came to Philadelphia to revise.

How to divide power, then, became the delegates' central concern. In the end, they wrote into the document a rather elaborate "pattern of allocation." What does this system look like? In other words, who gets what? Table III-1 depicts the allocation of powers emanating from the Constitution. As we can see, the different levels of government have some exclusive and some concurrent powers, but they are also prohibited from operating in certain spheres. The powers of the federal government are those that are enumerated in the Constitution, broadly defined according to provisions such as the necessary and proper clause. Unless otherwise restricted by the Constitution, the states retain broad governing authority, which includes the "police powers"—the general authority to regulate for the health, safety, morals, and general welfare of their citizens.

Despite the framers' attempt to allocate power, ambiguity resulted. One source of this confusion was the question of constitutional relationships; that is, in the parlance of the eighteenth century, the framers looked at the Constitution as a contract, but a contract between whom? Some commentators argue that it specifies the relationship between the people and the national government and that the former empower the latter. Justice Joseph Story wrote:

> The constitution of the United States was ordained and established, not by the states in their sovereign capacities, but emphatically, as the preamble of the constitution declares, by "the people of the United States." . . . The constitution was not, therefore, necessarily carved out of existing state sovereignties, nor a surrender of powers already existing in state institutions.[2]

---
[2]*Martin v. Hunter's Lessee* (1816).

Others suggest that the contract is between the states and the nation. In a 1798 resolution of the Virginia Assembly, James Madison wrote:

> That this Assembly doth explicitly and peremptorily declare that it views the powers of the Federal Government as resulting from the compact, to which the States are parties, as limited by the plain sense and intention of the instrument constituting that compact; as no further valid than they are authorized by the grants enumerated in that compact; and that in case of deliberate, palpable, and dangerous exercise of other powers not granted by the said compact, the States, who are the parties thereto, have the right, and are in duty bound, to interpose for arresting the progress of the evil, and for maintaining within their respective limits, the authorities, rights, and liberties appertaining to them.[3]

This debate is not abstract. It has real consequences. In its most violent incarnation, the Civil War, Southern leaders took Madison's logic to its limit. They argued that the Constitution represented a contract between the states and the federal government, with the states creating the national government. When the federal government—controlled by the Northern states—abrogated its end of the agreement, the contract was no longer valid. The Civil War ended that particular dispute, but the principle continued to flare up in less extreme, but still important, forms. The history of some Southern states refusing to abide by federal civil rights laws is one example.

This problem continues to manifest itself largely because the Constitution supports both sides and therefore neither. Those who favor the national government-people approach point to the document's preamble: "*We the people* [our italics] of the United States . . . do ordain and establish this Constitution." To support the national government-state argument, proponents turn to the language of Article VII, that the ratification of *nine states* "shall be sufficient for the Establishment of this Constitution between the States so ratifying." When issues of the contractual nature of the Constitution arise, therefore, many look to the Supreme Court to resolve them. As we shall see in the next chapter, different Courts have approached this debate in varying ways, adopting

---
[3]Reprinted in Melvin I. Urofsky, ed., *Documents of American Constitutional and Legal History*, vol. 1 (New York: Knopf, 1989), 159.

Table III-1   The Constitutional Allocation of Government Power

Powers Specified within the Constitution or by Court Interpretation

Powers Exclusive to the Federal Government	Powers Exclusive to State Governments	Concurrent Powers to both Federal and State Governments
Coin money	Administer elections	Tax
Regulate interstate and foreign commerce	Regulate intrastate commerce	Borrow money
Tax imports	Establish republican forms of state and local governments	Establish courts
Make treaties	Protect public health, safety, and morals	Charter banks and corporations
Make all laws "necessary and proper"	All powers not delegated to the national government or denied to the states by the Constitution	Make and enforce laws
Make war		Take property (power of eminent domain)
Regulate postal system		

Powers Denied by the Constitution or by Court Interpretation

Expressly Prohibited to the Federal Government	Expressly Prohibited to State Governments	Expressly Prohibited to Both
Tax exports	Tax imports and exports	Pass bills of attainder
Change state boundaries	Coin money	Pass ex post facto laws
	Enter into treaties	Grant titles of nobility
	Impair obligation of contracts	Impose religious tests
		Pass laws in conflict with the Bill of Rights and subsequent amendments

Sources: Adapted from J. W. Peltason and Sue Davis, *Corwin and Peltason's Understanding the Constitution,* 15th ed. (Belmont, CA: Wadsworth, 2000), chaps. 1 and 2; and C. Herman Pritchett, *Constitutional Law of the Federal System* (Englewood Cliffs, NJ: Prentice-Hall, 1984), 58.

one view over the other at distinct points in American history.

THE TENTH AND ELEVENTH AMENDMENTS

Arguments over who the parties to the constitutional contract are may never be fully resolved, but another point of ambiguity was thought so onerous that it could not be left to interpretation. That area is the balance of power between the states and the federal government. The original charter, in the view of some, placed too much authority with the federal government. In particular, states' rights advocates pointed to two clauses in the Constitution as working against their interests.

The first is the necessary and proper clause: Congress has the power "[t]o make all Laws which shall be necessary and proper for carrying into Execution [its] Powers, and all other Powers vested by this Constitution in the Government of the United States, or in any Department or Officer thereof."

The other is the supremacy clause: "This Constitution, and the Laws of the United States which shall be made in Pursuance thereof; and all Treaties made, or which shall be made, under the Authority of the United States, shall be the supreme Law of the Land; and the Judges in every State shall be bound thereby, any Thing in the Constitution or Laws of any State to the Contrary notwithstanding."

These clauses seem to allocate a great deal of power to the national government. Yet, as Madison wrote in *Federalist* No. 45:

The powers delegated by the proposed Constitution to the Federal Government, are few and defined. Those which are to remain in the State Governments are numerous and indefinite. The former will be exercised principally on external objects, as war, peace, negotiation, and foreign commerce; with which last the power of taxation will for the most part be connected. The powers reserved to the several States will extend to all the objects, which, in the ordinary course of affairs, concern the lives, liberties, and properties of the people; and the internal order, improvement, and prosperity of the State.

Nevertheless, states remained concerned that the national government would attempt to cut into their power and sovereignty, and the language of the Constitution did little to allay their fears. At worst, it suggested that the federal institutions would always be supreme; at best, it was highly ambiguous. Even Madison recognized its lack of clarity when he wrote in *Federalist* No. 39:

> The proposed Constitution therefore . . . is in strictness neither a national nor a federal Constitution; but a composition of both. In its foundation it is federal, not national; in the sources from which the ordinary powers of the Government are drawn, it is partly federal, and partly national: in the operation of these powers, it is national, not federal. In the extent of them, again, it is federal; not national: And finally in the authoritative mode of introducing amendments, it is neither wholly federal, nor wholly national.

Madison clearly thought this ambiguity was an asset of the new system of government, an advantage that made it fit compatibly into the overall philosophies of separation of powers and checks and balances. But this argument proved insufficient; when the perceived unfair balance of power became an obstacle to the ratification of the Constitution, those favoring its adoption promised to remedy it.

This remedy took the form of the Tenth Amendment, which—depending on the interpretation—seems quite different from the rest of the Bill of Rights. The first nine amendments deal mainly with the rights of the people vis-à-vis the federal government, such as the First Amendment, "Congress shall make no law respecting an establishment of religion." But the Tenth Amendment states, "The powers not delegated to the United States by the Constitution, nor prohibited by it to the States, are reserved to the States respectively, or to the people." With these words in place, states' rights advocates were mollified, at least temporarily. To be sure, some understood the Tenth Amendment to do little more than to affirm that the Constitution created a federal government limited to its "delegated" powers. In the view of some states' rights advocates, however, the amendment established the rights of states, creating a protected area—an enclave—for state power.[4]

We will have many opportunities to explore this debate in the chapters to come. For now, it is worth noting that supporters of state authority quickly learned that the Tenth Amendment did not offer the states complete protection against federal encroachment. Just three years after the amendment was ratified, the Supreme Court in **Chisholm v. Georgia** (1793) upheld the authority of the federal courts to hear cases that citizens of a state brought against another state. The idea that a federal tribunal could decide the fortunes of a state was unacceptable to state power advocates. They demanded constitutional protection against such intrusions. The result was the Eleventh Amendment, ratified in 1795, which restricted the power of the federal courts to hear disputes brought against a state by the citizens of another state or by citizens of other nations. As history would quickly show, however, neither the Tenth nor the Eleventh Amendment settled the perennial question of the proper distribution of political power between the federal government and the states.

Why not? Given the elaborate system of American federalism depicted in Table III-1, why is the division of power the center of so much controversy? In part, the answer takes us back to the contractual nature of the Constitution. As we shall see in the following chapter, which explores general theoretical approaches to federalism, the Court has had some difficulty determining the parties to the contract, and its confusion has encouraged litigation. In more concrete terms, no matter how elaborate the design, the contract does not (and perhaps cannot) address the range of real disputes that arise between nation and state.

---

[4]For more on the Tenth Amendment as an enclave, see Martin H. Redish, *The Constitution as Political Structure* (New York: Oxford University Press, 1995). We should note that Redish rejects this interpretation of the amendment.

Indeed, the irony here is that the complexity of the system, coupled with the language of the Constitution, is what fosters the need for interpretation. We must ask, where do state powers begin and federal powers end and vice versa? States have the authority to regulate intrastate commerce, and the federal government regulates interstate commerce, but is it so easy to delineate those boundaries? Which entity controls the manufacturing of goods in one state that are shipped to another? And, more to the point, what happens when the state and federal governments have different ideas regarding how to regulate the manufacturing?

If that problem is not enough, compare the constitutional language of the Tenth Amendment with that of the necessary and proper and supremacy clauses. The supremacy clause prohibits states from passing laws that directly conflict with the Constitution, federal laws, and so forth. But so often the issues are not that clear. Is the federal authority supreme only in its sphere of operations—those activities where it has clear constitutional mandates—as some argue the Tenth Amendment

dictates? Or is it the case that every time the federal government enters into a particular realm, it automatically preempts the actions of states? Or, going further, does the answer depend on the intent of Congress—that is, whether it intended to preempt state action?

It should be clear that American federalism is something of a two-edged sword. On one hand, the balance of power the framers created pacified those who were opposed to ratifying the Constitution, and this balance continues to define the contours of the U.S. system of government. On the other hand, the complexity of federalism has given rise to tensions between the levels of government, often leading to disputes that require settlement by the courts. It may be that the system has been resilient because it constantly requires fresh interpretation. But we will leave that for you to decide as we now turn to how the Supreme Court has formulated theories and specific rulings in response to two distinct but interrelated issues: the general contours of state-federal relations and the important powers to regulate commerce and to tax and spend.

CHAPTER SIX

FEDERALISM

DURING THE 1960s Congress amended the Fair Labor Standards Act of 1938 (FLSA) to require state governments to pay virtually all their employees a specified minimum wage and to compensate them for overtime work. Were these amendments constitutional? Does Congress have the constitutional power to dictate to the states how they should treat their own government employees? Or does such congressional action interfere with state autonomy and authority? The answer depends on how we view the letter and spirit of the Constitution. We would reach very different conclusions depending on whether we subscribed to the *dual* or *cooperative* approach to nation-state relations *(see Table 6-1)*.

Proponents of dual federalism would want the Court to strike down the law. As advocates of states' rights, they would argue that the Constitution represents an agreement between the states and the federal government in which the states empower the central government and that, therefore, states are not subservient to the federal government. In other words, because each state is supreme within its own sphere, the federal government could no more impose minimum wage requirements on state governments than the states could impose them on the federal government. To support their theory, dual federalists invoke the Tenth Amendment, arguing that it creates an "enclave" of states' rights that Congress may not invade—especially if Congress encroaches on a traditional state function.[1]

Cooperative federalism takes the opposite view. Proponents argue that the people, not the states, created and animated the federal government. This view holds that the supremacy clause and the necessary and proper clause, not the Tenth Amendment, control the balance of power between the federal government and the states. That amendment, according to cooperative federalism, grants no additional powers to the states. It serves only to emphasize that the federal government is limited to the powers the Constitution assigns to it. As long as Congress bases the law regulating wages and hours on an enumerated (or implied) power, the law passes constitutional muster. The Tenth Amendment creates no bar, or so the argument goes.

The history of nation-state relations issues before the Supreme Court has been characterized by swings back and forth between variants of cooperative federalism and dual federalism. In fact, a sharply divided Supreme Court voted 5–4 to strike down the amendments to the Fair Labor Standards Act in 1976. The case was **National League of Cities v. Usery**, in which the majority held that the provisions violated the Tenth Amendment and were an unconstitutional interference with states. Just nine years later, however, in another 5–4 decision, the Court upheld the maximum hours and minimum wage provisions of the law in *Garcia v. San Antonio Metropolitan Transit Authority* (1985), which effectively overruled the 1976 decision.

But only fourteen years after *Garcia*, in **Alden v. Maine** (1999), the Court held that state employees could not bring a federal suit against their nonconsenting state for alleged violations of the overtime pay provisions of the labor act. The decision by no means overruled *Garcia*, but it certainly made it more difficult for employees to take advantage of the law.

---

[1]See Martin H. Redish, *The Constitution as Political Structure* (New York: Oxford University Press, 1995). The idea here is that even if Congress possessed the power, it would be unable to exercise it if it impinged on the "enclave."

Table 6-1 A Comparison of Dual and Cooperative Federalism

	Dual Federalism	Cooperative Federalism
General view	Operates under the assumption that the two levels of government are coequal sovereigns, each supreme within its own sphere.	Operates under the assumption that the national government is supreme even if its actions touch state functions. States and the federal government are "partners," but the latter largely sets policy for the nation.
View of the Constitution	It is a compact among the states and a contract between the states and the federal government.	Rejecting the view of it as a "compact," the people, not the states, empower the national government.
Constitutional support	Tenth Amendment reserves certain powers to the states and thus limits the national government to those powers specifically delegated to it. Necessary and proper clause is to be read narrowly.	Tenth Amendment does not provide additional powers to the states. Necessary and proper clause is to be read expansively and loosely. Supremacy clause means that the national government is supreme within its own sphere, even if its actions touch on state functions.

The Court's about-face from *National League of Cities* to *Garcia* to *Alden* is not an anomaly in this area of the law; rather, it is a symptom of the general confusion that has surrounded American federalism since the eighteenth century. As depicted in Table 6-2, throughout U.S. history the Supreme Court's allegiance has shifted from cooperative federalism to dual federalism (or one of their variants) and back again. As a consequence, the justices have moved between states' rights and national supremacy positions over time.

This chapter examines the components of that cycle. As you read the cases, consider not only which doctrine governed each decision but also why the philosophies have grown stronger or weaker. What forces—legal, political, and historical—have led the justices to choose one approach over the other?

FEDERAL POWER, STATE SOVEREIGNTY, AND THE TENTH AMENDMENT

From our introduction to this part of the book, you learned that the Tenth Amendment was included in the

Bill of Rights to allay concerns that the national government would run roughshod over the states. Vexing from the start, however, has been the question of how to interpret its words: "The powers not delegated to the United States by the Constitution, nor prohibited by it to the States, are reserved to the States respectively, or to the people." As the discussion above suggests, to dual federalists it is a states' rights amendment—one that creates an enclave of authority protected from unwarranted federal intrusions. To cooperative federalists, it does little more than confirm that the Constitution created a federal government limited to its "delegated" powers.

Many of the debates over how to interpret the Tenth Amendment have occurred in cases involving Congress's power to tax and spend and especially to regulate commerce, as our example of the FLSA litigation suggests. We examine these areas in the next two chapters. Here, our goal is broader: to highlight chronologically the doctrinal cycle of nation-state relations with reference to some of the most important cases involving the Tenth Amendment and other claims of state sovereignty. The questions these cases raise directly implicate the very nature of the Constitution. To dual federalists, it is a

Table 6-2 Doctrinal Cycles of Nation-State Relations

Court Era	General Approach Adopted
Marshall Court (1801–1835)	Cooperative federalism (as long as Congress can ground a law in its enumerated or implied powers, the Tenth Amendment does not serve as a bar)
Taney Court (1836–1864)	Dual federalism (state rights)
Civil War/Reconstruction Courts (1865–1895)	Cooperative federalism
Laissez-faire Courts (1896–1936)	Dual federalism (grounded in laissez-faire philosophy)
Post–New Deal Courts (1937–1975)	Cooperative federalism
Burger Court: *National League of Cities v. Usery* (1976)	Dual federalism (traditional state functions)
Burger Court: *Garcia v. SAMTA* (1985)	Cooperative federalism (the electoral process serves as a check on Congress)
Rehnquist Court (1986–2005)	A milder version of dual federalism, holding, for example, that states cannot be treated as administrative units of the federal government and that the federal government cannot "commandeer" state authority
Roberts Court (2005–)	A general continuation of the Rehnquist Court's approach

contract between the federal government and the states; to those espousing the cooperative view, it is a contract between the federal government and the people—not the states. This is a debate, as we shall see, that has had, and may continue to have, serious implications for American society.

The Marshall Court and the Rise of National Supremacy

An ardent Federalist, Chief Justice John Marshall was true to his party's tenets over the course of his long career on the Court. In case after case he was more than willing to elevate the powers of the federal government above those of the states. Perhaps his most significant statement on national supremacy came in *McCulloch v. Maryland* (1819). In chapter 4 we saw how he used this case to assert firmly that Congress has implied powers. Here, we shall see that *McCulloch* also served as his vehicle to expound the notion of national supremacy; note in particular his view of the Tenth Amendment. A brief review of the essential facts is offered to remind you of the issues in this case.

McCulloch v. Maryland

17 U.S. (Wheat.) 316 (1819)
http://caselaw.findlaw.com/us-supreme-court/17/316.html
Vote: 6 (Duvall, Johnson, Livingston, Marshall, Story, Washington)
    0

OPINION OF THE COURT: *Marshall*

NOT PARTICIPATING: *Todd*

Congress established the Second Bank of the United States in 1816. Because of inefficiency and corruption, the bank was very unpopular, and many blamed it for the nation's economic problems. To show its displeasure, the Maryland legislature passed a law saying that banks operating in the state that were not chartered by the state—in other words, the national bank—could issue banknotes only on special paper, which the state taxed. The Maryland law was clearly a state attack on an operation of the federal government. Was it constitutional for the state to use its authority to impede a federal program?

This question became a legal dispute when James McCulloch, the cashier of the Baltimore branch of the Bank of the United States, refused to pay the tax, and Maryland took legal action to enforce its law. The United States challenged the constitutionality of the Maryland tax, and in return Maryland disputed the constitutionality of the bank.[2]

MR. CHIEF JUSTICE MARSHALL DELIVERED THE OPINION OF THE COURT.

The constitution of our country, in its most interesting and vital parts, is to be considered; the conflicting powers of the government of the Union and of its members, as marked in that constitution, are to be discussed; and an opinion given, which may essentially influence the great operations of the government. . . .

In discussing this . . . the counsel for the state of Maryland have deemed it of some importance, in the construction of the constitution, to consider that instrument not as emanating from the people, but as the act of sovereign and independent states. The powers of the general government, it has been said, are delegated by the states, who alone are truly sovereign; and must be exercised in subordination to the states, who alone possess supreme dominion.

It would be difficult to sustain this proposition. The convention which framed the constitution was indeed elected by the state legislatures. But the instrument, when it came from their hands, was a mere proposal, without obligation, or pretensions to it. It was reported to the then existing Congress of the United States, with a request that it might "be submitted to a convention of delegates, chosen in each state by the people thereof, under the recommendation of its legislature, for their assent and ratification." This mode of proceeding was adopted; and by the convention, by Congress, and by the state legislatures, the instrument was submitted to the people. They acted upon it in the only manner in which they can act safely, effectively, and wisely, on such a subject, by assembling in convention. It is true, they assembled in their several states—and where else should they have assembled? No political dreamer was ever wild enough to think of breaking down the lines which separate the states, and of compounding the American people into one common mass. Of consequence, when they act, they act in their states. But the measures they adopt do not, on that account, cease to be the measures of the people themselves, or become the measures of the state governments. . . .

The government of the Union, then . . . is, emphatically, and truly, a government of the people. . . .

It is the government of all; its powers are delegated by all; it represents all, and acts for all. Though any one state may be willing to control its operations, no state is willing to allow others to control them. The nation, on those subjects on which it can act, must necessarily bind its component parts. But this question is not left to mere reason; the people have, in express terms, decided it by saying, "this constitution, and the laws of the United States, which shall be made in pursuance thereof," "shall be the supreme law of the land," and by requiring that the members of the state legislatures, and the officers of the executive and judicial departments of the states shall take the oath of fidelity to it. The government of the United States, then, though limited in its powers, is supreme; and its laws, when made in pursuance of the constitution, form the supreme law of the land, "anything in the constitution or laws of any State to the contrary notwithstanding."

Among the enumerated powers, we do not find that of establishing a bank or creating a corporation. But there is no phrase in the instrument which, like the articles of confederation, excludes incidental or implied powers; and which requires that everything granted shall be expressly and minutely described. Even the 10th amendment, which was framed for the purpose of quieting the excessive jealousies which had been excited, omits the word "expressly," and declares only that the powers "not delegated to the United States, nor prohibited to the states, are reserved to the states or to the people" thus leaving the question, whether the particular power which may become the subject of contest has been delegated to the one government, or prohibited to the other, to depend on a fair construction of the whole instrument. The men who drew and adopted this amendment had experienced the embarrassments resulting from the insertion of this word in the articles of confederation, and probably omitted it to avoid those embarrassments. A constitution, to contain an accurate detail of all the subdivisions of which its great powers will admit, and of all the means by which they may be carried into execution, would partake of a prolixity of a legal code, and could scarcely be embraced by the human mind. It would probably never be understood by the public. Its nature, therefore, requires, that only its great outlines should be marked, its important objects designated, and the minor ingredients which compose those objects be deduced from the nature of the objects themselves. That this idea was entertained by the framers of the American constitution, is not only to be inferred from the nature of the instrument, but from the language. . . .

After this declaration, it can scarcely be necessary to say that the existence of state banks can have no possible influence on the question. No trace is to be found in the constitution of an intention to create a dependence of the government of the Union on those of the states, for the execution of the great powers assigned to it. Its means are adequate to its ends; and on those means alone was it expected to rely for the accomplishment of its ends. To impose on it the necessity of resorting to means which it cannot control, which another government may furnish or withhold, would render its course precarious; the result of its measures uncertain, and create

---

[2]The first part of Marshall's opinion deals with the question of whether Congress had the power to create the bank *(see the excerpt in chapter 4).* The second part, excerpted here, deals with the constitutionality of the Maryland tax. Marshall clearly delineates this division in his opinion.

a dependence on other governments, which might disappoint its most important designs and is incompatible with the language of the constitution. But were it otherwise, the choice of means implies a right to choose a national bank in preference to state banks, and Congress alone can make the election.

After the most deliberate consideration, it is the unanimous and decided opinion of this court that the act to incorporate the bank of the United States is a law made in pursuance of the constitution, and is part of the supreme law of the land. . . .

It being the opinion of the court, that the act incorporating the bank is constitutional; and that the power of establishing a branch in the State of Maryland might be properly exercised by the bank itself, we proceed to inquire . . . whether the State of Maryland may, without violating the constitution, tax that branch? . . .

The argument on the part of the State of Maryland, is, not that the States may directly resist a law of Congress, but that they may exercise their acknowledged powers upon it, and that the constitution leaves them this right in the confidence that they will not abuse it.

That the power to tax involves the power to destroy; that the power to destroy may defeat and render useless the power to create; that there is a plain repugnance, in conferring on one government a power to control the constitutional measures of another, which other, with respect to those very measures, is declared to be supreme over that which exerts the control, are propositions not to be denied. But all inconsistencies are to be reconciled by the magic of the word CONFIDENCE. Taxation, it is said, does not necessarily and unavoidably destroy. To carry it to the excess of destruction would be an abuse, to presume which, would banish that confidence which is essential to all government.

But is this a case of confidence? Would the people of any one State trust those of another with a power to control the most insignificant operations of their State government? We know they would not. Why, then, should we suppose that the people of any one State should be willing to trust those of another with a power to control the operations of a government to which they have confided their most important and most valuable interests? In the legislature of the Union alone, are all represented. The legislature of the Union alone, therefore, can be trusted by the people with the power of controlling measures which concern all, in the confidence that it will not be abused. This, then, is not a case of confidence, and we must consider it as it really is.

If we apply the principle for which the State of Maryland contends, to the constitution generally, we shall find it capable of changing totally the character of that instrument. We shall find it capable of arresting all the measures of the government, and of prostrating it at the foot of the States. The American people have declared their constitution, and the laws made in pursuance thereof, to be supreme; but this principle would transfer the supremacy, in fact, to the States.

If the States may tax one instrument, employed by the government in the execution of its powers, they may tax any and every other instrument. They may tax the mail; they may tax the mint; they may tax patent rights; they may tax the papers of the custom-house; they may tax judicial process; they may tax all the means employed by the government, to an excess which would defeat all the ends of government. This was not intended by the American people. They did not design to make their government dependent on the States. . . .

It has also been insisted, that, as the power of taxation in the general and State governments is acknowledged to be concurrent, every argument which would sustain the right of the general government to tax banks chartered by the States, will equally sustain the right of the States to tax banks chartered by the general government.

But the two cases are not on the same reason. The people of all the States have created the general government, and have conferred upon it the general power of taxation. The people of all the States, and the States themselves, are represented in Congress, and, by their representatives, exercise this power. When they tax the chartered institutions of the States, they tax their constituents; and these taxes must be uniform. But, when a State taxes the operations of the government of the United States, it acts upon institutions created, not by their own constituents, but by people over whom they claim no control. It acts upon the measures of a government created by others as well as themselves, for the benefit of others in common with themselves. The difference is that which always exists, and always must exist, between the action of the whole on a part, and the action of a part on the whole— between the laws of a government declared to be supreme, and those of a government which, when in opposition to those laws, is not supreme.

But if the full application of this argument could be admitted, it might bring into question the right of Congress to tax the State banks, and could not prove the right of the States to tax the Bank of the United States.

The court has bestowed on this subject its most deliberate consideration. The result is a conviction that the states have no power, by taxation or otherwise, to retard, impede, burden, or in any manner control the operations of the constitutional laws enacted by Congress to carry into execution the powers vested in the general government. This is, we think, the unavoidable consequence of that supremacy which the constitution has declared.

We are unanimously of opinion that the law passed by the legislature of Maryland, imposing a tax on the Bank of the United States, is unconstitutional and void.

Constitutional scholars regard *McCulloch* as an unequivocal statement of national power over the states.

Its strength lies in Marshall's treatment of the three relevant constitutional provisions: the necessary and proper clause, the Tenth Amendment, and the supremacy clause.

First, as you may recall from chapter 4, according to *McCulloch*, the necessary and proper clause permits Congress to pass legislation implied by its enumerated functions, bounded chiefly in this way: "Let the end be legitimate, let it be within the scope of the constitution, and all means which are appropriate, which are plainly adapted to that end, which are not prohibited, but consist with the letter and spirit of the constitution, are constitutional."

Second, because the Tenth Amendment reserves to the states or to the people only power that has not been delegated to Congress (expressly or otherwise), it stands as no significant bar to Congress's exercise of its powers, including those that are implied. Given Marshall's treatment of the necessary and proper clause, implied powers seem quite expansive. This also seems to be an explicit rejection of the "enclave" approach to the Tenth Amendment.

Third, the supremacy clause places the national government at the top within its sphere of operation, a sphere that, again according to Marshall's interpretation of the necessary and proper clause, is expansive. If the supremacy clause means anything, it means that no state may "retard, impede, burden, or in any manner control the operations of the constitutional laws enacted by Congress." Note, too, Marshall's view of the constitutional arrangement. As one would expect, he fully endorses the position that the charter represents a contract between the federal government and the people—not the states.

McCulloch's holdings—supporting congressional creation of the bank and negating state taxation of it—were not particularly surprising. Most observers thought the Marshall Court would rule the way it did. It was the chief justice's language and the constitutional theories he offered that sparked a serious debate in a states' rights newspaper, the *Richmond Enquirer*. The argument started just weeks after *McCulloch* was decided, as a barrage of states' rights advocates wrote letters to the newspaper's editor condemning the ruling. Apparently concerned that if their views took hold, the Union would revert back to its form under Articles of Confederation, Marshall took an unusual step for a Supreme Court justice: he responded to his critics. Initially, he wrote two articles, carried by a Philadelphia newspaper, defending *McCulloch*. But when an old enemy, Spencer Roane, a Virginia Supreme Court judge, launched an unbridled attack, Marshall responded with nine essays published under the pseudonym "A Friend of the Constitution."[3]

The Taney Court and States' Rights

While Marshall was chief justice of the United States, it was his view of nation-state relations, not Roane's, that prevailed. But their dispute foreshadowed a series of events that took place from the 1830s through the 1860s, events that would change the country forever (*see Table 6-3*). The first occurred in November 1832. After Congress passed a tariff act that the South thought unfairly burdensome, South Carolina adopted an ordinance that nullified the federal law. Several days later, the state said it was prepared to enforce its nullification by military force and, if necessary, secession from the Union. It is not surprising that South Carolina took the lead in the battle for state sovereignty. The state was the home of John C. Calhoun, a former vice president of the United States and an outspoken proponent of slavery and states' rights. Indeed, Calhoun is best remembered as an advocate of the doctrine of concurrent majorities, a view that would provide states with a veto over federal policies. This doctrine was the underpinning for South Carolina's ordinance of nullification.

The president, Andrew Jackson, was no great nationalist; rather, he believed that states' rights were not incompatible with the powers of the federal government. But even he took issue with South Carolina's ordinance. Just a month after the state acted, as Table 6-3 illustrates, Jackson issued a proclamation warning the state that it could not secede from the Union. The president's action infuriated South Carolina, but it temporarily averted a major crisis, as no other state attempted to act on the nullification doctrine.

Another event that would have major implications was Chief Justice Marshall's death and Roger B. Taney's ascension to the chief justiceship in 1835. In some ways Marshall and Taney were alike. Both had begun their political careers in their respective states—Virginia and Maryland—and then held major positions within the executive branch of the national government. Both were committed partisan activists. The difference was that they were committed to opposing concepts of government structure, particularly of nation-state relations. In contrast to Marshall's Federalist sentiments, Taney

[3]For records of Marshall's essays, see Gerald Gunther, ed., *John Marshall's Defense of* McCulloch v. Maryland (Stanford, CA: Stanford University Press, 1969).

Table 6-3 Selected Events Leading to the Civil War

Date	Event	Result
November 1832	South Carolina adopts ordinance of nullification.	Suggests that states can nullify acts of the federal government and, if necessary, secede from the Union.
December 1832	Jackson issues proclamation warning South Carolina against secession.	Temporarily halts secession crisis, as no state follows South Carolina's lead.
December 1835	Jackson nominates Taney to be chief justice of the United States.	Delays Senate confirming Taney, a former slaveholder, until March 1836.
May 1854	Congress repeals the Missouri Compromise.	Allows territories to enter the Union with or without slavery.
March 1857	Supreme Court issues final judgment in *Scott v. Sandford*.	Increases tension between the North and South, as the former loudly denounces the decision.
November 1860	Lincoln is elected president.	Prompts the South's proclamation that secession is inevitable.
December 1860	South Carolina issues ordinance of secession.	Precipitates secession by six other Southern states within the following six weeks and four more by June 1861.

was a Jacksonian Democrat, a full believer in the ideas espoused by President Jackson, under whom he had served as attorney general, secretary of war, and secretary of the Treasury, and who had appointed him chief justice. The two chief justices' views on the Bank of the United States provide a clear example of their political ideas in action. In 1819 in *McCulloch* Marshall lent his full support to the bank; in 1832 Taney helped write President Jackson's veto message in which he "condemned the Second Bank of the United States" and refused to recharter it.[4]

Had Taney been Jackson's only appointment to the Court, the course of federalism might not have been altered. But that was not the case. The Court had changed from being composed of justices from the Federalist and Jeffersonian party eras to becoming dominated by Jacksonian Democrats. By 1841 Joseph Story was the only justice remaining from the Marshall Court that decided *McCulloch*. The others, like Taney, were schooled in Jacksonian democracy. It was, as R. Kent Newmyer has noted, no longer "the Marshall Court. But,

then again it was not the age of Marshall."[5] This observation holds on two levels: doctrinally and politically. The Taney Court ushered in substantial legal changes, especially in federal-state relations. Although there is no true Taney corollary to Marshall's opinion in *McCulloch*, examples of Taney's views abound. In many opinions he explicated the doctrine of dual federalism, that national and state governments are equivalent sovereigns within their own spheres of operation. Unlike Marshall, Taney read the Tenth Amendment in a broad sense, asserting that it did, in fact, reserve to the states certain powers and limited the power of the federal government over the states.

Early Taney Court decisions were not politically controversial. They may have represented a break from previous doctrine, but they matched the tenor of the times. Although Jackson had his feuds with the states (as his battle with South Carolina illustrates), his general philosophical approach to federalism and to governance aligned with popular opinion.

The issue of slavery was another matter. It had been the cause of acrimony at the Philadelphia

---

[4]R. Kent Newmyer, *The Supreme Court under Marshall and Taney* (New York: Crowell, 1968), 93.

[5]Ibid., 94.

convention in 1787, and animosity between the North and the South had continued. The country remained united only through compromises, such as the "three-fifths" plan in the U.S. Constitution, by which a slave counted as three-fifths of a person for taxation and representation purposes, and the Missouri Compromise of 1820, which provided a plan for slavery in newly admitted states and the territories. By the 1850s old battles were heating up; for example, after California was admitted to the Union, South Carolina once again issued a secession call.

Slavery, therefore, represented the most immediate concern of the day, splitting the nation into two ideological camps. On a different level, however, it was a symptom of a larger problem: the growing resistance of Southern states to federal supremacy. As the North's criticism of slavery became more vocal, calls for secession or, at the very least, for adoption of Calhoun's "concurrent majority" doctrine, became more widespread in the South.

It was at this critical moment that the Taney-led Supreme Court interceded in both issues—slavery and federal supremacy. When, in the infamous case of **Scott v. Sandford** (1857), the Court planted its feet firmly in the states' rights camp, it may have contributed to the collapse of the Union.

Dred Scott, a slave bought in Missouri, was the property of Dr. John Emerson, an army surgeon. In 1834 Emerson took Scott to the free state of Illinois and in 1836 to the Upper Louisiana Territory, which was to remain free of slavery under the Missouri Compromise of 1820. Eventually, Scott and Emerson returned to Missouri, but the doctor died shortly thereafter, leaving title to Scott to his brother-in-law, John Sanford, a citizen of New York.[6] Believing that he no longer had slave status because he had lived on free soil, Scott sued for his freedom in a Missouri state court in 1846. He received a favorable decision at the trial court level but lost in the Missouri Supreme Court. Several years later, Scott and his lawyer decided to try again. This time they brought the case to a federal district court, contending that they had a diversity suit—Scott was a citizen of Missouri and Sanford of New York. Sanford argued that the suit should be dismissed because members of the "African race" could not be citizens.

By the time the case arrived at the U.S. Supreme Court for final judgment in 1856, the facts and the

political situation had become more complex. In 1854, under mounting pressure, Congress had repealed the Missouri Compromise, replacing it with legislation declaring congressional neutrality on the issue of slavery. Given this new law and the growing tensions between the North and the South and the free and the slave states, some observers speculated that the Court would decline to decide the case, as it had become highly controversial and overtly political.

For at least a year, the Court chose that route. In fact, historians have suggested that after hearing the case, the justices wanted simply to affirm the state court's decision, thereby evading the issue of slavery and citizenship for blacks. But when Justice James Wayne insisted that the Court deal with these concerns, the majority of the others—including Chief Justice Taney, a former slaveholder—went along.[7] Waiting until after the presidential election of 1856, a very divided Court (nine separate opinions were written) announced its decision.

At the end of the day, the Court held that Scott was still a slave. In his majority opinion, Taney offered several reasons for this holding.[8] First, although Scott could become a citizen of a state, he could not be considered, in a legal sense, to be a citizen of the United States; the nation's history and the words of the Constitution and other documents foreclosed that possibility. As a result, Scott could not sue in federal courts. As Taney put it, members of the slave class, emancipated or not, were considered from the beginning to be inferior and subordinate beings who "had no rights or privileges but such as those who held the power and the government might choose to grant them." Second, Congress had no constitutional power to regulate slavery in the territories (in reaching this result, the Court struck down the Missouri Compromise, which already had been repealed by Congress), and the Constitution protects the right to property, a category into which slaves, according to Taney, fell. Third, the status of slaves depended on the law of the state to which they voluntarily returned, regardless of where they had been. Because the Missouri Supreme Court ruled that Scott was a slave, the U.S. Supreme Court would follow suit. Although Taney did not explicitly cite the Tenth Amendment, his use of its

---

[6]The party's name, Sanford, was misspelled "Sandford" in the official records.

[7]Melvin I. Urofsky and Paul Finkelman, *A March of Liberty*, 2nd ed. (New York: Oxford University Press, 2002), 392.

[8]For additional discussion, see ibid., 384–391; and Walter Ehrlich, "*Scott v. Sandford*," in *The Oxford Companion to the Supreme Court*, 2nd ed., ed. Kermit L. Hall (New York: Oxford University Press, 2005), 887–889.

language made clear that he viewed it as a brake on the federal government.

Scott was decided as the nation was on the verge of collapse *(see Table 6-3)*. Taney's holding, coupled with his vision of the nature of the federal-state relationship, rather than calming matters, probably added fuel to the fire. From the perspective of Northerners and abolitionists, the opinion was among the most evil and heinous the Court ever issued. Opponents of slavery used the ruling to rally support for their position; they took aim at Taney and the Court, claiming that the institution was so pro-South that it could not be taken seriously. Northern newspapers aroused anti-Court sentiment around the country with stories about the decision. As one wrote:

> The whole slavery agitation was reopened by the proceedings in the Supreme Court today, and that tribunal voluntarily introduced itself into the political arena. . . . Much feeling is excited by this decree, and the opinion is freely expressed that a new element of sectional strife has been wantonly imposed upon the country.[9]

Members of Congress lambasted the Court for the raw and unnecessary display of judicial power it had exercised in striking down the Missouri Compromise. One history of the period asserted, "Never has the Supreme Court been treated with such ineffable contempt, and never has that tribunal so often cringed before the clamor of the mob."[10] As for the chief justice, his reputation was forever tarnished. Even after his death, Congress resisted commissioning a bust of Taney to sit beside those of other chief justices in the Capitol's Supreme Court room. At the time, Senator Charles Sumner said, "I object to that; that now an emancipated country should make a bust to the author of the Dred Scott decision. . . . (T)he name of Taney is to be hooted down the page of history. Judgment is beginning now; and an emancipated country will fasten upon him the stigma which he deserves."[11]

To Southerners, *Scott* was a cause for celebration. Indeed, Taney's notions of slavery and dual federalism

appeared in a more energized form just a few years later when South Carolina issued its Declaration of the Causes of Secession. President Abraham Lincoln presented precisely the opposite view—the Marshall approach—in his 1861 inaugural address, but his words could not prevent the outbreak of war.

At its core the Civil War was not only about slavery but also about the supremacy of the national government over the states. It was the culmination of the debates between the Federalists and Anti-Federalists, between Marshall and Roane, and so forth. When the Union won the war, it seemed to have also won the debate over the nature of federal-state relations. Cooperative federalism prevailed. In the immediate aftermath of the battle, the Court acceded, though not willingly, to congressional power over the defeated region.

THE POST–CIVIL WAR ERA AND THE RETURN OF DUAL FEDERALISM

Once the Civil War concluded, Congress moved swiftly to embed into the Constitution the victories that Union armies had won on the battlefield. Three constitutional amendments were proposed and ratified. The Thirteenth and Fifteenth Amendments focused on issues of slavery and race. The Thirteenth (1865) put an official end to slavery and the Fifteenth (1870) barred the denial of voting rights on account of race. The Fourteenth Amendment (1968) shifted much governmental authority from the states to the federal government. It also directly overruled Taney's *Dred Scott* opinion by declaring, "All persons born or naturalized in the United States, and subject to the jurisdiction thereof, are citizens of the United States and of the State wherein they reside." As a consequence, United States citizenship became superior to state citizenship. Constitutionally, the dual federalism of the Jacksonian era had ended.

Did the conclusion of the Civil War and the rise of national supremacy mean that Taney's dual federalism had seen its last days? Indeed, it remained under wraps for several decades, but then as the Court entered the era of the Industrial Revolution, the justices once again began articulating the dual federalism philosophy.

Take, for example, the justices' decision in *Coyle v. Smith* (1911). This dispute involved a congressional directive telling a newly admitted state where it must locate its capital. Did Congress's power to admit new states extend to placing such conditions on statehood? Or was the congressional order an unconstitutional intrusion

---

[9]Quoted in Charles Warren, *The Supreme Court in United States History*, vol. 2 (Boston: Little, Brown, 1926), 304.

[10]Quoted in Bernard Schwartz, *A History of the Supreme Court* (New York: Oxford University Press, 1993), 154.

[11]*Congressional Globe* (23 February 1865) 38th Cong., 2nd sess., 1012. It was not until 1874 that a bust of Taney was approved "without debate." See Warren, *The Supreme Court in United States History*, 393–394.

into state sovereignty? As you read Justice Lurton's opinion, note the vivid language of dual federalism, including the position that the national government is a "union of states" and that the states must be "equal in power, dignity and authority, each competent to exert that residuum of sovereignty not delegated to the United States by the Constitution itself." Lurton goes so far as to declare that "without the States in union, there could be no such political body as the United States." Finally, notice the Court's narrow interpretation of Congress's implied powers.

Coyle v. Smith

221 U.S. 559 (1911)
http://caselaw.findlaw.com/us-supreme-court/221/559.html
Vote: 7 (Day, Harlan, Hughes, Lamar, Lurton, Van Devanter, White)
   2 (Holmes, McKenna)

OPINION OF THE COURT: *Lurton*

Article IV, Section 3, of the Constitution authorizes Congress to admit new states. On June 16, 1906, Congress exercised this power by passing the Enabling Act inviting the Oklahoma territory to join the Union. The invitation, however, came with certain conditions. One of those conditions required that the state capital be in Guthrie, where the territorial capital was located, and that the state refrain from relocating the capital or making any provisions for relocation before 1913. The terms of the Enabling Act were to be "irrevocable."

Why this restriction was imposed is a bit uncertain, but it seemingly had to do with a Republican-dominated Congress granting statehood to a heavily Democratic territory. The city of Guthrie, however, was Oklahoma's lone Republican stronghold.

The territory accepted the terms of the invitation, and in 1907 Oklahoma became the forty-sixth state. But just three years later the state's voters supported a measure to move the capital to Oklahoma City. Democratic governor Charles Haskell and the state legislature did not wait until 1913 to take action on the voters' wishes, but immediately enacted implementing legislation and began securing the necessary funds to effect the relocation.

W. H. Coyle, a large Guthrie landowner who would suffer economic losses if the capital were to be moved, filed suit against Oklahoma secretary of state Thomas Smith to block the relocation. Oklahoma's supreme court upheld the state's actions, and Coyle requested Supreme Court review.

MR. JUSTICE LURTON DELIVERED THE OPINION OF THE COURT.

The only question for review by us is whether the provision of the enabling act was a valid limitation upon the power of the State after its admission which overrides any subsequent state legislation repugnant thereto.

The power to locate its own seat of government and to determine when and how it shall be changed from one place to another, and to appropriate its own public funds for that purpose, are essentially and peculiarly state powers. That one of the original thirteen States could now be shorn of such powers by an act of Congress would not be for a moment entertained. The question then comes to this: can a State be placed upon a plane of inequality with its sister States in the Union if the Congress chooses to impose conditions which so operate at the time of its admission? . . .

The power of Congress in respect to the admission of new States is found in the third section of the fourth Article of the Constitution. That provision is that "new States may be admitted by the Congress into this Union." The only expressed restriction upon this power is that no new State shall be formed within the jurisdiction of any other State, nor by the junction of two or more States, or parts of States, without the consent of such States, as well as of the Congress.

But what is this power? It is not to admit political organizations which are less or greater, or different in dignity or power, from those political entities which constitute the Union. It is, as strongly put by counsel, a "power to admit States."

The definition of "a State" is found in the powers possessed by the original States which adopted the Constitution, a definition emphasized by the terms employed in all subsequent acts of Congress admitting new States into the Union. The first two States admitted into the Union were the States of Vermont and Kentucky, one as of March 4, 1791, and the other as of June 1, 1792. No terms or conditions were exacted from either. Each act declares that the State is admitted "as a new and *entire member* of the United States of America." Emphatic and significant as is the phrase admitted as "an entire member," even stronger was the declaration upon the admission in 1796 of Tennessee, as the third new State, it being declared to be "one of the United States of America," "on an equal footing with the original States in all respects whatsoever," phraseology which has ever since been substantially followed in admission acts, concluding with the Oklahoma act, which declares that Oklahoma shall be admitted "on an equal footing with the original States."

The power is to admit "new States into *this* Union."

"This Union" was and is a union of States, equal in power, dignity and authority, each competent to exert that residuum of sovereignty not delegated to the United States by the Constitution itself. To maintain otherwise would be to say that the Union, through the power of Congress to admit new States, might come to be a union of States unequal in power, as including States whose powers were restricted only by the Constitution, with others whose powers had been further restricted by an act of Congress accepted as a condition of admission. Thus, it would result, first, that the powers of Congress would not be defined by the Constitution alone, but in respect to new States, enlarged or restricted by the conditions imposed upon new States by its own legislation admitting them into the Union; and, second, that such new States might not exercise all of the powers which had not been delegated by the Constitution, but only such as had not been further bargained away as conditions of admission.

The argument that Congress derives from the duty of "guaranteeing to each State in this Union a republican form of government," power to impose restrictions upon a new State which deprives it of equality with other members of the Union, has no merit. . . . [I]t obviously does not confer power to admit a new State which shall be any less a State than those which compose the Union. . . .

. . . The constitutional provision concerning the admission of new States is not a mandate, but a power to be exercised with discretion. From this alone, it would follow that Congress may require, under penalty of denying admission, that the organic laws of a new State at the time of admission shall be such as to meet its approval. A constitution thus supervised by Congress would, after all, be a constitution of a State, and, as such, subject to alteration and amendment by the State after admission. Its force would be that of a state constitution, and not that of an act of Congress. . . .

So far as this court has found occasion to advert to the effect of enabling acts as affirmative legislation affecting the power of new States after admission, there is to be found no sanction for the contention that any State may be deprived of any of the power constitutionally possessed by other States, as States, by reason of the terms in which the acts admitting them to the Union have been framed. . . .

. . . [W]hen a new State is admitted into the Union, it is so admitted with all of the powers of sovereignty and jurisdiction which pertain to the original States, and that such powers may not be constitutionally diminished, impaired or shorn away by any conditions, compacts or stipulations embraced in the act under which the new State came into the Union which would not be valid and effectual if the subject of congressional legislation after admission. . . .

. . . The legislation in the Oklahoma enabling act relating to the location of the capital of the State, if construed as forbidding a removal by the State after its admission as a State, is referable to no power granted to Congress over the subject, and if it is to be upheld at all, it must be implied from the power to admit new States. If power to impose such a restriction upon the general and undelegated power of a State be conceded as implied from the power to admit a new State, where is the line to be drawn against restrictions imposed upon new States? The insistence finds no support in the decisions of this court. . . .

Has Oklahoma been admitted upon an equal footing with the original States? If she has, she, by virtue of her jurisdictional sovereignty as such a State, may determine for her own people the proper location of the local seat of government. She is not equal in power to them if she cannot.

In *Texas v. White* [1869] Chief Justice Chase said in strong and memorable language that, "the Constitution, in all of its provisions, looks to an indestructible Union, composed of indestructible States."

In *Lane County v. Oregon* [1869], he said:

> The people of the United States constitute one nation, under one government, and this government, within the scope of the powers with which it is invested, is supreme. On the other hand, the people of each State compose a State having its own government, and endowed with all the functions essential to separate and independent existence. The States disunited might continue to exist. Without the States in union, there could be no such political body as the United States.

To this we may add that the constitutional equality of the States is essential to the harmonious operation of the scheme upon which the Republic was organized. When that equality disappears, we may remain a free people, but the Union will not be the Union of the Constitution.

Judgment affirmed.

The approach to federalism Justice Horace Harmon Lurton outlined was characteristic of this period of industrial expansion, but many decisions carried significantly more societal importance than the ability of a state to select the location of its own capital. The justices were well steeped in the laissez-faire economic theories of the day. From the 1890s through the mid-1930s, as we discuss more thoroughly in the next two chapters, the Court used dual federalism as a way to restrict the federal government's authority to regulate business activity. Frequently the Court concluded that congressional actions pertaining, for example, to manufacturing and labor invaded powers the Tenth Amendment reserved to the states.

The dual federalism of this laissez-faire period, however, differed markedly from Taney's philosophy. Taney viewed dual federalism as a way to equalize state and federal power, but the Supreme Court during the early twentieth century was more concerned with allowing business to continue its expansion unimpeded by government controls. Dual federalism was an effective way to blunt federal regulation, yet at the same time, the justices were using other sections of the Constitution, especially the due process clauses, to limit state regulation of business.

The justices' wholehearted support of business was as well suited to their day as Taney's ideology was to his, or so some have argued. At the very least, the Court's willingness to embrace a free enterprise philosophy reflected the general mood of Americans, some of whom were benefiting financially from the growth of the economy. When the economic boom of the 1920s turned into the Great Depression of the 1930s, citizens and their newly elected leaders clamored for change.

THE (RE)EMERGENCE OF NATIONAL SUPREMACY: COOPERATIVE FEDERALISM

The economic collapse of 1929 invariably meant that the days of dual federalism were numbered. Fueled by the electorate's demand for change, the national elections of 1932 brought Franklin Roosevelt to the White House and Democratic majorities to the House and Senate. As we will see in the next chapter, Roosevelt immediately proposed major changes in the way the federal government regulated business and the economy. Initially the Supreme Court resisted by striking down key parts of Roosevelt's New Deal program. By 1937, however, the Court's majority began shifting its position. It viewed the federal government's commerce, taxation, and spending powers more broadly and abandoned its use of the Tenth Amendment as a significant obstacle to federal regulatory efforts. In the important commerce clause case of *United States v. Darby* (1941), Justice Stone, writing for the Court, referred to the Tenth Amendment as "but a truism." The pendulum once again had swung away from dual federalism and returned to favoring the cooperative federalism approach.

For the next half-century dual federalism was out and cooperative federalism was in. Under this doctrine, at least theoretically, the various levels of government shared policy-making responsibilities. In practice it meant that the national government took the lead in formulating many policy goals, which it expected state and local officials to implement. Consistent with this new approach, the Court generally deferred to Congress in establishing economic regulatory policy. By the 1960s the federal government reigned supreme.

But change was in the wind. The election of Richard Nixon to the presidency in 1968 was an indication of growing dissatisfaction with an increasingly expansive federal government. Although Nixon was not a strong supporter of dual federalism, he favored increased state

participation in federal programs. When it came to judicial appointments, Nixon desired justices who exercised judicial restraint generally and leaned toward a law-and-order posture in particular. Such individuals also tended to have greater sympathy for the role of state governments than did the justices of the immediate post–New Deal era who preceded them. Nixon had the good fortune of being able to appoint a new chief justice, Warren Burger, and three associate justices, enough to alter the ideological makeup of the Court.

With Nixon's appointees taking their seats on the Court, advocates of dual federalism were encouraged that change might now be possible. And, in fact, the supporters of state authority won a surprising victory in *National League of Cities v. Usery* (1976), a decision that centered on the 1938 federal Fair Labor Standards Act (FLSA). This law regulated wages, hours, and other conditions for employees working in any form of interstate commerce. The Supreme Court had upheld the statute's constitutionality in 1941. *National League* crystallized when Congress in 1974 expanded the scope of the FLSA to require the state governments to pay all their employees the minimum wage and to disallow them from working in excess of maximum hours requirements. This, of course, represented a major change in the scope of the law. It was one thing for Congress to use its commerce power authority to regulate wages and hours for workers in the private sector, but it was a much different matter for the federal government to dictate how state governments must treat their own state employees.

Various cities and states challenged the constitutionality of the new amendments. In particular, they argued that the amendments represented a "collision" between federal expansion and states' rights in violation of the Tenth Amendment.

In their scrutiny of the FLSA, the four Nixon appointees plus Justice Potter Stewart provided an undeniable signal that dual federalism—in the form of a revival of the Tenth Amendment enclave—was far from dead. Writing for the Court, Justice William Rehnquist struck down the new extension of the FLSA as impinging on state sovereignty. Rehnquist's opinion did not question the validity of federal regulation of private employers. He concluded, however, that when Congress is regulating the states as states—even if the law falls within one of Congress's enumerated or implied powers—the Tenth Amendment enclave comes into play. "There are attributes of sovereignty attaching to every state government," he wrote, "which may not be impaired by Congress, not because Congress may lack an affirmative grant of legislative authority to reach the matter, but because the Constitution prohibits it from exercising the authority in that manner." For Rehnquist and other members of the *National League* majority, Congress lacks the authority to dictate the terms by which states carry out their traditional and essential government functions.

As it turned out, however, the victory enjoyed by supporters of state interests was short-lived. Less than a decade later in *Garcia v. San Antonio Metropolitan Transit Authority* (1985), the Court overruled *National League of Cities*. Part of the problem with *National League*, as Justice Harry Blackmun explained, was that it was difficult for the Court to distinguish traditional and essential state functions from those that are nontraditional and less essential. But, in upholding the federal law, did Blackmun give too much deference to Congress?

Garcia v. San Antonio Metropolitan Transit Authority

469 U.S. 528 (1985)
http://caselaw.findlaw.com/us-supreme-court/469/528.html
Oral arguments available at https://www.oyez.org/
    cases/1983/82-1913
Vote: 5 (Blackmun, Brennan, Marshall, Stevens, White)
    4 (Burger, O'Connor, Powell, Rehnquist)

OPINION OF THE COURT: *Blackmun*

DISSENTING OPINIONS: *Powell, O'Connor, Rehnquist*

Garcia was virtually a carbon copy of *National League of Cities*. That latter case arose when Congress in 1974 expanded the scope of the FLSA and brought virtually all state public employees, who were excluded in the original legislation, under its reach. Various cities and states and two organizations representing their collective interests, the National League of Cities and the National Governors' Conference, challenged the constitutionality of the new amendments. In particular, they argued that the amendments represented a "collision" between federal expansion and states' rights in violation of the Tenth Amendment. The Court, in *National League of Cities,* agreed.

Garcia, too, centered on amendments to the FLSA, in this case amendments that obligated states to meet minimum wage and overtime requirements for almost all public employees. The facts, however, were a bit more complicated than those in *National League of Cities.*

To understand this case, more background information is needed. The San Antonio Transit System (SATS) began operation in 1959. At first the mass transit system was a moneymaking venture,

but by 1969 it was operating at a loss and turned to the federal government for assistance. The federal Urban Mass Transit Administration (UMTA) subsequently provided it with a $4 million grant. In 1978 the city replaced SATS with the San Antonio Metropolitan Transit Authority (SAMTA), which federal grants also subsidized. Between 1970 and 1980 the transit system received more than $51 million, or 40 percent of its costs, from the federal government. The *Garcia* case thus started in 1979 when, "in response to a specific inquiry about the applicability of the FLSA to employees of SAMTA," the U.S. Department of Labor issued an opinion holding that SAMTA must abide by the act's wage provisions. SAMTA filed a challenge to the department's holding, and Joe G. Garcia and other SAMTA employees, in turn, initiated a suit against their employer for overtime pay.

When this case and a companion, *Donovan v. San Antonio Metropolitan Transit Authority,* reached the U.S. Supreme Court, SAMTA relied heavily on *National League of Cities.* It argued that "transit is a traditional [city] function," and, as the operator of that function, it was not covered by FLSA amendments. The U.S. government and Garcia countered by arguing that *National League of Cities* was not necessarily applicable. In their view, application of the FLSA to public transit did not violate the Tenth Amendment because (1) operation of a transit system is not a traditional government function, and (2) operation of a transit system is not a core government function that must be exempted from federal commerce power legislation to preserve the states' independence.

> **JUSTICE BLACKMUN DELIVERED THE OPINION OF THE COURT.**

We revisit in these cases an issue raised in *National League of Cities v. Usery* (1976). In that litigation, this Court, by a sharply divided vote, ruled that the Commerce Clause does not empower Congress to enforce the minimum-wage and overtime provisions of the Fair Labor Standards Act (FLSA) against the States "in areas of traditional government functions." Although *National League of Cities* supplied some examples of "traditional governmental functions," it did not offer a general explanation of how a "traditional" function is to be distinguished from a "nontraditional" one. Since then, federal and state courts have struggled with the task, thus imposed, of identifying a traditional function for purposes of state immunity under the Commerce Clause.

In the present cases, a Federal District Court concluded that municipal ownership and operation of a mass-transit system is a traditional governmental function and thus, under *National League of Cities,* is exempt from the obligations imposed by the FLSA. Faced with the identical question, three Federal Courts of Appeals and one state appellate court have reached the opposite conclusion.

Our examination of this "function" standard applied in these and other cases over the last eight years now persuades us that the attempt to draw the boundaries of state regulatory immunity in terms of "traditional governmental function" is not only unworkable but is also inconsistent with established principles of federalism and, indeed, with those very federalism principles on which *National League of Cities* purported to rest. That case, accordingly, is overruled. . . .

The central theme of *National League of Cities* was that the States occupy a special position in our constitutional system and that the scope of Congress' authority under the Commerce Clause must reflect that position. Of course, the Commerce Clause by its specific language does not provide any special limitation on Congress' actions with respect to the States. It is equally true, however, that the text of the Constitution provides the beginning rather than the final answer to every inquiry into questions of federalism, for "[b]ehind the words of the constitutional provisions are postulates which limit and control." *National League of Cities* reflected the general conviction that the Constitution precludes "the National Government [from] devour[ing] the essentials of state sovereignty." In order to be faithful to the underlying federal premises of the Constitution, courts must look for the "postulates which limit and control."

What has proved problematic is not the perception that the Constitution's federal structure imposes limitations on the Commerce Clause, but rather the nature and content of those limitations. One approach to defining the limits on Congress' authority to regulate the States under the Commerce Clause is to identify certain underlying elements of political sovereignty that are deemed essential to the States' "separate and independent existence." This approach obviously underlay the Court's use of the "traditional governmental function" concept in *National League of Cities*. It also has led to the separate requirement that the challenged federal statute "address matters that are indisputably 'attribute[s] of state sovereignty.'" . . . The opinion did not explain what aspects of such decisions made them such an "undoubted attribute," and the Court since then has remarked on the uncertain scope of the concept. The point of the inquiry, however, has remained to single out particular features of a State's internal governance that are deemed to be intrinsic parts of state sovereignty.

We doubt that courts ultimately can identify principled constitutional limitations on the scope of Congress' Commerce Clause powers over the States merely by relying on *a priori* definitions of state sovereignty. In part, this is because of the elusiveness of objective criteria for "fundamental" elements of state sovereignty, a problem we have witnessed in the search for "traditional governmental functions." There is, however, a more fundamental reason: the sovereignty of the States is limited by the Constitution itself. A variety of sovereign powers, for example, are withdrawn from the States by Article I, §10. Section 8 of the same Article works an equally sharp contraction of state sovereignty by authorizing Congress to exercise a wide range of legislative powers and (in conjunction with the Supremacy Clause of Article VI) to displace contrary state legislation. . . .

The States unquestionably do "retai[n] a significant measure of sovereign authority." They do so, however, only to the extent that the Constitution has not divested them of their original powers and transferred those powers to the Federal Government. . . .

As a result, to say that the Constitution assumes the continued role of the States is to say little about the nature of that role. . . . With rare exceptions, like the guarantee, in Article IV, §3, of state territorial integrity, the Constitution does not carve out express elements of state sovereignty that Congress may not employ its delegated powers to displace. . . . The power of the Federal Government is a "power to be respected" as well, and the fact that the States remain sovereign as to all powers not vested in Congress or denied them by the Constitution offers no guidance about where the frontier between state and federal power lies. In short, we have no license to employ freestanding conceptions of state sovereignty when measuring congressional authority under the Commerce Clause.

When we look for the States' "residuary and inviolable sovereignty," *The Federalist* No. 39 (J. Madison), in the shape of the constitutional scheme, rather than in predetermined notions of sovereign power, a different measure of state sovereignty emerges. Apart from the limitation on federal authority inherent in the delegated nature of Congress' Article I powers, the principal means chosen by the Framers to ensure the role of the States in the federal system lies in the structure of the Federal Government itself. It is no novelty to observe that the composition of the Federal Government was designed in large part to protect the States from overreaching by Congress. The Framers thus gave the States a role in the selection both of the Executive and the Legislative Branches of the Federal Government. The States were vested with indirect influence over the House of Representatives and the Presidency by their control of electoral qualifications and their role in Presidential elections. U.S. Const., Art. I, §2, and Art. II, §1. They were given more direct influence in the Senate, where each State received equal representation and each Senator was to be selected by the legislature of his State. Art. I, §3. The significance attached to the States' equal representation in the Senate is underscored by the prohibition of any constitutional amendment divesting a State of equal representation without the State's consent. Art. V. . . .

The effectiveness of the federal political process in preserving the States' interests is apparent even today in the course of federal legislation. . . . [T]he States have been able to direct a substantial proportion of federal revenues into their own treasuries in the form of general and program-specific grants in aid. . . . As a result, federal grants now account for about one-fifth of state and local government expenditures. The States have obtained federal funding for such services as police and fire protection, education, public health and hospitals, parks and recreation, and sanitation. . . . The fact that some federal statutes such as the FLSA extend general obligations to the States cannot obscure the extent to which the political position of the States in the federal system has served to minimize the burdens that the States bear under the Commerce Clause.

We realize that changes in the structure of the Federal Government have taken place since 1789, not the least of which has been the substitution of popular election of Senators by the adoption of the Seventeenth Amendment in 1913, and that these changes may work to alter the influence of the States in the federal political process. Nonetheless, against this background, we are convinced that the fundamental limitation that the constitutional scheme imposes on the Commerce Clause to protect the "States as States" is one of process, rather than one of result. Any substantive restraint on the exercise of Commerce Clause powers must find its justification in the procedural nature of this basic limitation, and it must be tailored to compensate for possible failings in the national political process, rather than to dictate a "sacred province of state autonomy."

Insofar as the present cases are concerned, then, we need go no further than to state that we perceive nothing in the overtime and minimum-wage requirements of the FLSA, as applied to SAMTA, that is destructive of state sovereignty or violative of any constitutional provision. SAMTA faces nothing more than the same minimum-wage and overtime obligations that hundreds of thousands of other employers, public as well as private, have to meet. . . .

Of course, we continue to recognize that the States occupy a special and specific position in our constitutional system and that the scope of Congress' authority under the Commerce Clause must reflect that position. But the principal and basic limit on the federal commerce power is that inherent in all congressional action—the built-in restraints that our system provides through state participation in federal governmental action. The political process ensures that laws that unduly burden the States will not be promulgated. In the factual setting of these cases the internal safeguards of the political process have performed as intended. . . .

We do not lightly overrule recent precedent. We have not hesitated, however, when it has become apparent that a prior decision has departed from a proper understanding of congressional power under the Commerce Clause. Due respect for the reach of congressional power within the federal system mandates that we do so now.

National League of Cities v. Usery (1976) is overruled. The judgment of the District Court is reversed, and these cases are remanded to that court for further proceedings consistent with this opinion.

It is so ordered.

JUSTICE POWELL, WITH WHOM THE CHIEF JUSTICE, JUSTICE REHNQUIST, AND JUSTICE O'CONNOR JOIN, DISSENTING.

Whatever effect the Court's decision may have in weakening the application of *stare decisis,* it is likely to be less important than what the Court has done to the Constitution itself. A unique feature of the United States is the federal system of government guaranteed by the Constitution and implicit in the very name of our country. Despite some genuflecting in the Court's opinion to the concept of federalism, today's decision effectively reduces the Tenth Amendment to meaningless rhetoric when Congress acts pursuant to the Commerce Clause. . . .

The Court apparently thinks that the States' success at obtaining federal funds for various projects and exemptions from the obligations of some federal statutes is indicative of the "effectiveness of the federal political process in preserving the States' interests. . . ." But such political success is not relevant to the question whether the political processes are the proper means of enforcing constitutional limitations. The fact that Congress generally does not transgress constitutional limits on its power to reach state activities does not make judicial review any less necessary to rectify the cases in which it does do so. The States' role in our system of government is a matter of constitutional law, not of legislative grace.

More troubling than the logical infirmities in the Court's reasoning is the result of its holding, i.e., that federal political officials, invoking the Commerce Clause, are the sole judges of the limits of their own power. This result is inconsistent with the fundamental principles of our constitutional system. See, e.g., *The Federalist* No. 78 (Hamilton). At least since *Marbury v. Madison* (1803), it has been the settled province of the federal judiciary "to say what the law is" with respect to the constitutionality of Acts of Congress. In rejecting the role of the judiciary in protecting the States from federal overreaching, the Court's opinion offers no explanation for ignoring the teaching of the most famous case in our history.

JUSTICE O'CONNOR, WITH WHOM JUSTICE POWELL AND JUSTICE REHNQUIST JOIN, DISSENTING.

It is worth recalling the . . . passage in *McCulloch v. Maryland* (1819) that lies at the source of the recent expansion of the commerce power. "Let the end be legitimate, let it be within the scope of the constitution," Chief Justice Marshall said, "and all means which are appropriate, which are plainly adapted to that end, which are not prohibited, but consist with the letter *and spirit* of the constitution, are constitutional" [emphasis added]. The *spirit* of the Tenth Amendment, of course, is that the States will retain their integrity in a system in which the laws of the United States are nevertheless supreme.

It is not enough that the "end be legitimate"; the means to that end chosen by Congress must not contravene the spirit of the Constitution. Thus many of this Court's decisions acknowledge that the means by which national power is exercised must take into account concerns for state autonomy. . . . The operative language of these cases varies, but the underlying principle is consistent: state autonomy is a relevant factor in assessing the means by which Congress exercises its powers.

This principle requires the Court to enforce affirmative limits on federal regulation of the States to complement the judicially crafted expansion of the interstate commerce power. *National League of Cities v. Usery* represented an attempt to define such limits. The Court today rejects *National League of Cities* and washes its hands of all efforts to protect the States. In the process, the Court opines that unwarranted federal encroachments on state authority are and will remain "'horrible possibilities that never happen in the real world.'" There is ample reason to believe to the contrary.

The last two decades have seen an unprecedented growth of federal regulatory activity, as the majority itself acknowledges. . . . Today, as federal legislation and coercive grant programs have expanded to embrace innumerable activities that were once viewed as local, the burden of persuasion has surely shifted, and the extraordinary has become ordinary. For example, recently the Federal Government has, with this Court's blessing, undertaken to tell the States the age at which they can retire their law enforcement officers, and the regulatory standards, procedures, and even the agenda which their utilities commissions must consider and follow. The political process has not protected against these encroachments on state activities, even though they directly impinge on a State's ability to make and enforce its laws. With the abandonment of *National League of Cities,* all that stands between the remaining essentials of state sovereignty and Congress is the latter's underdeveloped capacity for self-restraint.

The problems of federalism in an integrated national economy are capable of more responsible resolution than holding that the States as States retain no status apart from that which Congress chooses to let them retain. The proper resolution, I suggest, lies in weighing state autonomy as a factor in the balance when interpreting the means by which Congress can exercise its authority on the States as States. It is insufficient, in assessing the validity of congressional regulation of a State pursuant to the commerce power, to ask only whether the same regulation would be valid if enforced against a private party. That reasoning, embodied in the majority opinion, is inconsistent with the spirit of our Constitution. It remains relevant that a State is being regulated, as *National League of Cities* and every recent case have recognized. . . .

It has been difficult for this Court to craft bright lines defining the scope of the state autonomy protected by *National League of Cities.* Such difficulty is to be expected whenever constitutional concerns as important as federalism and the effectiveness of the commerce power come into conflict. Regardless of the difficulty, it is and will remain the duty of this Court to reconcile these concerns in the final instance. That the Court shuns the task today by appealing to the "essence of federalism" can provide scant comfort to those who believe our federal system requires something more than a unitary, centralized government. I would not shirk the duty acknowledged by *National League of Cities* and its progeny, and I

[along with Justice Rehnquist believe] that this Court will in time again assume its constitutional responsibility.

I respectfully dissent.

After *Garcia*, many thought that the Supreme Court's endorsement of cooperative federalism had permanently settled the issue of a proper balance of federal-state power. *National League* was but an anomalous blip; *Garcia* was now the law of the land. But it was not to remain so. *Garcia* proved to be the last major articulation of cooperative federalism of the post–New Deal period.

Dating back to the late 1960s, the national mood had begun shifting to more conservative positions. In all but four of the twenty-four years between 1969 and 1993, Republicans occupied the presidency. Each of those presidents appointed members of the Supreme Court who were generally more conservative than the justices they replaced. The only exception to the string of Republican electoral victories was the single term of Democrat Jimmy Carter, who had the unusual misfortune of having no opportunities to fill a Supreme Court vacancy.

Especially important were the early 1990s when four supporters of cooperative federalism—Justices William J. Brennan, Thurgood Marshall, Byron White, and Harry Blackmun—retired. New members, appointed by Presidents Ronald Reagan and George H. W. Bush, significantly changed the makeup of the Court. These justices joined a Court now led by recently elevated Chief Justice William Rehnquist, who had a strong history of supporting the interests of the states. A rekindling of the federalism debate was inevitable.

RETURN OF (A MILDER FORM OF) DUAL FEDERALISM

The first indication that the balance of power had shifted occurred in **New York v. United States** (1992). At issue was the 1980 Low-Level Radioactive Waste Policy Act, a federal law designed to confront the difficult problem of the disposal of radioactive waste generated by private industry, government, hospitals, and research institutions. The act provided incentives for state cooperation with certain waste disposal options, but states that failed to participate were required to "take title" to the radioactive waste generated inside their borders and be responsible for it. A six-justice majority struck down the "take title" portion of the law. Justice Sandra Day O'Connor, writing for the Court, explained that although the federal government was free to use its spending power to offer incentives for state participation, it could not direct the states to provide for the disposal of radioactive waste generated within their borders. O'Connor's words were direct and hard-hitting:

> Some truths are so basic that, like the air around us, they are easily overlooked.... States are not mere political subdivisions of the United States. State governments are neither regional offices nor administrative agencies of the Federal Government. The positions occupied by state officials appear nowhere on the Federal Government's most detailed organization chart. The Constitution instead "leaves to the several States a residuary and inviolable sovereignty."... Whatever the outer limits of that sovereignty may be, one thing is clear: The Federal Government may not compel the States to enact or administer a federal regulatory program.

The Court's decision in *New York* signaled that those justices sympathetic to the interests of the states had now formed a majority. Five years later the same majority ruled when the Court handed down its decision in *Printz v. United States* (1997), which centered on the federal government's response to another difficult problem of society: violence and firearms.

Executive Office of the President of the United States/Public domain/Wikimedia Commons

James S. Brady, former press secretary for President Reagan, who was wounded during an assassination attempt on the president, watches as President Clinton signs the Brady Bill gun control legislation in 1993.

Printz v. United States

521 U.S. 898 (1997)
http://caselaw.findlaw.com/us-supreme-court/521/898.html
Oral arguments available at https://www.oyez.org/ cases/1996/95-1478
Vote: 5 (Kennedy, O'Connor, Rehnquist, Scalia, Thomas)
4 (Breyer, Ginsburg, Souter, Stevens)

OPINION OF THE COURT: Scalia

CONCURRING OPINIONS: O'Connor, Thomas

DISSENTING OPINIONS: Breyer, Souter, Stevens

The Gun Control Act of 1968 forbids firearms dealers to transfer firearms to convicted felons, unlawful users of controlled substances, fugitives from justice, persons judged to be mentally defective, persons dishonorably discharged from the military, persons who have renounced their citizenship, and persons who have committed certain acts of domestic violence. In 1993, Congress amended the Gun Control Act with the Brady Handgun Violence Prevention Act. This act required the attorney general to establish by November 30, 1998, a national database allowing for an instant background check on anyone attempting to buy a handgun. In the interim, the Brady Act allowed gun dealers to sell firearms to buyers who already possessed state handgun permits or who lived in states with existing instant background check systems.

In states where these alternatives were not available, the law required certain actions by the local chief law enforcement officer (CLEO). It mandated that CLEOs receive firearm purchase forms from gun dealers and make a reasonable effort within five business days to verify that any proposed sale was not to a person unqualified under the law. Essentially, federal law required local CLEOs to conduct a background check on potential gun purchasers. When CLEOs determined that any particular proposed sale would violate the law, they were required upon request to submit a written report to the proposed purchaser stating the reasons for that determination. If CLEOs found no reason for objecting to a sale, they were required to destroy all records pertaining to it. These mandated responsibilities were to terminate in 1998 once the federal instant background check program became operative.

Jay Printz, sheriff of Ravalli County, Montana, and Richard Mack, sheriff of Graham County, Arizona, filed separate suits challenging the constitutionality of the Brady Act's interim provisions. They argued that the federal government had no authority to command state or local officials to administer a federal program. In each case the district court declared the act unconstitutional to the extent that it forced state officers to carry out federal policies. Other provisions of the law were left untouched. The court of appeals disagreed, finding no provisions of the law to violate the Constitution. The Supreme Court accepted the cases for review. Although the decision immediately affected only a temporary provision that was scheduled to become inoperative in 1998, it involved a meaningful constitutional issue.

JUSTICE SCALIA DELIVERED THE OPINION OF THE COURT.

The question presented in these cases is whether certain interim provisions of the Brady Handgun Violence Prevention Act, commanding state and local law enforcement officers to conduct background checks on prospective handgun purchasers and to perform certain related tasks, violate the Constitution. . . .

. . . [T]he Brady Act purports to direct state law enforcement officers to participate, albeit only temporarily, in the administration of a federally enacted regulatory scheme. . . .

The petitioners here object to being pressed into federal service, and contend that congressional action compelling state officers to execute federal laws is unconstitutional. Because there is no constitutional text speaking to this precise question, the answer to the CLEOs' challenge must be sought in historical understanding and practice, in the structure of the Constitution, and in the jurisprudence of this Court. . . .

Petitioners contend that compelled enlistment of state executive officers for the administration of federal programs is, until very recent years at least, unprecedented. The Government contends, to the contrary, that "the earliest Congresses enacted statutes that required the participation of state officials in the implementation of federal laws." . . .

The Government's contention demands our careful consideration, since early congressional enactments "provid[e] 'contemporaneous and weighty evidence' of the Constitution's meaning." . . . Conversely if, as petitioners contend, earlier Congresses avoided use of this highly attractive power, we would have reason to believe that the power was thought not to exist. . . .

Not only do the enactments of the early Congresses, as far as we are aware, contain no evidence of an assumption that the Federal Government may command the States' executive power in the absence of a particularized constitutional authorization, they contain some indication of precisely the opposite assumption. On September 23, 1789—the day before its proposal of the Bill of Rights—the First Congress enacted a law aimed at obtaining state assistance of the most rudimentary and necessary sort for the enforcement of the new Government's laws: the holding of federal prisoners in state jails at federal expense. Significantly, the law issued not a command to the States' executive, but a recommendation to their legislatures. Congress "recommended to the legislatures of the several States to pass laws, making it expressly the duty of the keepers of their gaols, to receive and safe keep therein all prisoners committed under the authority of the United States." . . .

In addition to early legislation, the Government also appeals to other sources we have usually regarded as indicative of the original understanding of the Constitution. It points to portions of *The Federalist* which . . . [state] that Congress will probably "make use of the State officers and State regulations, for collecting" federal taxes, *The Federalist* No. 36 (A. Hamilton) . . . The Government also invokes the *Federalist's* more general observations that the Constitution would "enable the [national] government to employ the ordinary magistracy of each [State] in the execution of its laws," No. 27 (A. Hamilton), and that it was "extremely probable that in other instances, particularly in the organization of the judicial power, the officers of the States will be clothed in the correspondent authority of the Union," No. 45 (J. Madison). But none of these statements necessarily implies—what is the critical point here—that Congress could impose these responsibilities *without the consent of the States*. They appear to rest on the natural assumption that the States would consent to allowing their officials to assist the Federal Government, an assumption proved correct by the extensive mutual assistance the States and Federal Government voluntarily provided one another in the early days of the Republic, including voluntary *federal implementation of state law*. . . .

. . . We turn next to consideration of the structure of the Constitution, to see if we can discern among its "essential postulate[s]" a principle that controls the present cases. . . .

It is incontestable that the Constitution established a system of "dual sovereignty." Although the States surrendered many of their powers to the new Federal Government, they retained "a residuary and inviolable sovereignty," *The Federalist* No. 39 (J. Madison). . . . Residual state sovereignty was also implicit, of course, in the Constitution's conferral upon Congress of not all governmental powers, but only discrete, enumerated ones, which implication was rendered express by the Tenth Amendment's assertion that "[t]he powers not delegated to the United States by the Constitution, nor prohibited by it to the States, are reserved to the States respectively, or to the people."

The Framers' experience under the Articles of Confederation had persuaded them that using the States as the instruments of federal governance was both ineffectual and provocative of federal-state conflict. . . . [T]he Framers rejected the concept of a central government that would act upon and through the States, and instead designed a system in which the state and federal governments would exercise concurrent authority over the people—who were, in Hamilton's words, "the only proper objects of government," *The Federalist* No. 15. . . . The great innovation of this design was that our citizens would have two political capacities, one state and one federal, each protected from incursion by the other. . . . The Constitution thus contemplates that a State's government will represent and remain accountable to its own citizens. . . .

This separation of the two spheres is one of the Constitution's structural protections of liberty. "Just as the separation and independence of the coordinate branches of the Federal Government serve to prevent the accumulation of excessive power in any one branch, a healthy balance of power between the States and the Federal Government will reduce the risk of tyranny and abuse from either front." . . . To quote Madison . . . :

"In the compound republic of America, the power surrendered by the people is first divided between two distinct governments, and then the portion allotted to each subdivided among distinct and separate departments. Hence a double security arises to the rights of the people. The different governments will control each other, at the same time that each will be controlled by itself." *The Federalist* No. 51

We have thus far discussed the effect that federal control of state officers would have upon the first element of the "double security" alluded to by Madison: the division of power between State and Federal Governments. It would also have an effect upon the second element: the separation and equilibration of powers between the three branches of the Federal Government itself. The Constitution does not leave to speculation who is to administer the laws enacted by Congress; the President, it says, "shall take Care that the Laws be faithfully executed," personally and through officers whom he appoints. . . . The Brady Act effectively transfers this responsibility to thousands of CLEOs in the 50 States, who are left to implement the program without meaningful Presidential control (if indeed meaningful Presidential control is possible without the power to appoint and remove). The insistence of the Framers upon unity in the Federal Executive—to insure both vigor and accountability—is well known. See *The Federalist* No. 70 (A. Hamilton). That unity would be shattered, and the power of the President would be subject to reduction, if Congress could act as effectively without the President as with him, by simply requiring state officers to execute its laws.

The dissent of course resorts to the last, best hope of those who defend *ultra vires* congressional action, the Necessary and Proper Clause. It reasons that the power to regulate the sale of handguns under the Commerce Clause, coupled with the power to "make all Laws which shall be necessary and proper for carrying into Execution the foregoing Powers," conclusively establishes the Brady Act's constitutional validity, because the Tenth Amendment imposes no limitations on the exercise of *delegated* powers but merely prohibits the exercise of powers "*not* delegated to the United States." What destroys the dissent's Necessary and Proper Clause argument, however, is not the Tenth Amendment but the Necessary and Proper Clause itself. When a "La[w] . . . for carrying into Execution" the Commerce Clause violates the principle of state sovereignty reflected in the various constitutional provisions we mentioned earlier it is not a "La[w] . . . *proper* for carrying into Execution the Commerce Clause," and is thus, in the words of *The Federalist*, "merely [an] ac[t] of usurpation" which "deserve[s] to be treated as such." *The Federalist* No. 33 (A. Hamilton).

Finally, and most conclusively in the present litigation, we turn to the prior jurisprudence of this Court. . . .

. . . In *New York* [v. *United* States we held that] "The Federal Government . . . may not compel the States to enact or administer a federal regulatory program."

The Government contends that *New York* is distinguishable on the following ground: unlike the "take title" provisions invalidated there, the background check provision of the Brady Act does not require state legislative or executive officials to make policy, but instead issues a final directive to state CLEOs. . . .

The Government's distinction between "making" law and merely "enforcing" it, between "policymaking" and mere "implementation," is an interesting one. . . . [But] [e]xecutive action that has utterly no policymaking component is rare, particularly at an executive level as high as a jurisdiction's chief law enforcement officer. Is it really true that there is no policymaking involved in deciding, for example, what "reasonable efforts" shall be expended to conduct a background check? . . .

The Government also maintains that requiring state officers to perform discrete, ministerial tasks specified by Congress does not violate the principle of *New York* because it does not diminish the accountability of state or federal officials. This argument fails even on its own terms. By forcing state governments to absorb the financial burden of implementing a federal regulatory program, Members of Congress can take credit for "solving" problems without having to ask their constituents to pay for the solutions with higher federal taxes. And even when the States are not forced to absorb the costs of implementing a federal program, they are still put in the position of taking the blame for its burdensomeness and for its defects. . . .

We held in *New York* [v. *United States*] that Congress cannot compel the States to enact or enforce a federal regulatory program. Today we hold that Congress cannot circumvent that prohibition by conscripting the State's officers directly. The Federal Government may neither issue directives requiring the States to address particular problems, nor command the States' officers, or those of their political subdivisions, to administer or enforce a federal regulatory program. . . . [S]uch commands are fundamentally incompatible with our constitutional system of dual sovereignty. Accordingly, the judgment of the Court of Appeals for the Ninth Circuit is reversed.

It is so ordered.

JUSTICE STEVENS, WITH WHOM JUSTICE SOUTER, JUSTICE GINSBURG, AND JUSTICE BREYER JOIN, DISSENTING.

When Congress exercises the powers delegated to it by the Constitution, it may impose affirmative obligations on executive and judicial officers of state and local governments as well as ordinary citizens. This conclusion is firmly supported by the text of the Constitution, the early history of the Nation, decisions of this Court, and a correct understanding of the basic structure of the Federal Government.

These cases do not implicate the more difficult questions associated with congressional coercion of state legislatures addressed in *New York v. United States* (1992). Nor need we consider the wisdom of relying on local officials rather than federal agents to carry out aspects of a federal program, or even the question whether such officials may be required to perform a federal function on a permanent basis. The question is whether Congress, acting on behalf of the people of the entire Nation, may require local law enforcement officers to perform certain duties during the interim needed for the development of a federal gun control program. . . .

The text of the Constitution provides a sufficient basis for a correct disposition of this case.

Article I, §8, grants the Congress the power to regulate commerce among the States. . . . [T]here can be no question that that provision adequately supports the regulation of commerce in handguns effected by the Brady Act. Moreover, the additional grant of authority in that section of the Constitution "[t]o make all Laws which shall be necessary and proper for carrying into Execution the foregoing Powers" is surely adequate to support the temporary enlistment of local police officers in the process of identifying persons who should not be entrusted with the possession of handguns. In short, the affirmative delegation of power in Article I provides ample authority for the congressional enactment.

Unlike the First Amendment, which prohibits the enactment of a category of laws that would otherwise be authorized by Article I, the Tenth Amendment imposes no restriction on the exercise of delegated powers. . . .

The Amendment confirms the principle that the powers of the Federal Government are limited to those affirmatively granted by the Constitution, but it does not purport to limit the scope or the effectiveness of the exercise of powers that are delegated to Congress. Thus, the Amendment provides no support for a rule that immunizes local officials from obligations that might be imposed on ordinary citizens. . . .

There is not a clause, sentence, or paragraph in the entire text of the Constitution of the United States that supports the proposition that a local police officer can ignore a command contained in a statute enacted by Congress pursuant to an express delegation of power enumerated in Article I. . . .

. . . [T]he Court's reasoning [also] contradicts *New York v. United States.*

That decision squarely approved of cooperative federalism programs, designed at the national level but implemented principally by state governments. *New York* disapproved of a particular *method* of putting such programs into place, not the *existence* of federal programs implemented locally. . . .

The provision of the Brady Act that crosses the Court's newly defined constitutional threshold is more comparable to a statute requiring local police officers to report the identity of missing children to the Crime Control Center of the Department of Justice than to an offensive federal command to a sovereign state. If Congress believes that such a statute will benefit the people of the Nation, and serve the interests of cooperative federalism better than an enlarged federal bureaucracy, we should respect both its policy judgment and its appraisal of its constitutional power.

Accordingly, I respectfully dissent.

Because of the scheduled date for the national background check system to become operative, *Printz* had little impact on gun control. The decision, however, gave a clear indication of the Rehnquist Court's position on federalism. Five conservative justices, all appointees of Republican presidents Ronald Reagan and George H. W. Bush, expressed their commitment to maintaining the view that the states are not merely administrative units of the federal government. Justice Antonin Scalia, for the majority, invoked the term "dual sovereignty" to describe the constitutionally mandated division of power between the central government and the states. Justice John Paul Stevens, writing for the four liberal justices in dissent, explicitly endorsed "cooperative federalism."

What of the Rehnquist Court's successor, the Roberts Court? Although significant personnel changes have occurred since *New York* and *Printz*, the Court's federalism jurisprudence seems to be relatively stable. For example, the Court in *National Federation of Independent Business v. Sebelius* (2012) struck down a provision of the Patient Protection and Affordable Care Act of 2010 (the federal health care law widely known as "Obamacare") judged to impose coercive financial pressure on the states to adopt expanded Medicaid coverage. As Chief Justice John G. Roberts wrote, "Congress has no authority to order the States to regulate according to its instructions. Congress may offer the States grants and require the States to comply with accompanying conditions, but the States must have a genuine choice whether to accept the offer. The States are given no such choice in this case: They must either accept a basic change in the nature of Medicaid, or risk losing all Medicaid funding." Though Roberts did not cite the Tenth Amendment, his opinion echoed the claim of the challenging states: that the threatened loss of all federal Medicaid funding violated the Tenth Amendment by coercing them into complying with the Medicaid expansion.

Still, the Supreme Court's shift back toward dual federalism should not be interpreted as a return to the pre–Civil War days of Roger B. Taney or to the laissez-faire philosophies that were popular prior to the New Deal. Rather, in cases such as *New York*, *Printz*, and *Sebelius*, the majority sought to remind us that under the U.S. constitutional system, the states retain significant independent sovereignty. Congress may achieve its goals by cooperating with the states or by providing incentives to encourage states to participate in the administration of federally established policies, but the federal government may not commandeer the states and order them to carry out federal directives.

THE ELEVENTH AMENDMENT

The federalism cases we have discussed thus far have centered on disputes arising when legislative actions of the federal government are challenged for encroaching on the constitutional prerogatives of the states (or vice versa). Similar friction between the states and the federal government has concerned questions of judicial power. On these questions, however, the primary constitutional provision of interest tends to be the Eleventh Amendment.

As background on the amendment and its notion of sovereign immunity, when the states were deciding whether to ratify the new U.S. Constitution, some expressed concern that federal judicial power would extend to suits brought against states by citizens of other states or even foreign countries. In *Federalist* No. 81 Alexander Hamilton tried to put such fears to rest: "It is inherent in the nature of sovereignty not to be amenable to the suit of an individual without its consent." Hamilton was referring to the principle of sovereign immunity, which holds that a government cannot be sued unless it has given permission to be sued. This principle had its origins in English common law, which held that a king was immune from lawsuits from his subjects because he had established the law and the legal system and, therefore, could not be held accountable in courts he created.

Quite early on, however, it appeared that the United States would not adhere to this principle. In 1793 the Supreme Court accepted original jurisdiction in **Chisholm v. Georgia**, a suit brought against the state of Georgia by two citizens of South Carolina trying to collect a debt. This action was based on Article III's authorization for federal courts to adjudicate controversies "between a State and Citizens of another State." Congress and the states strongly opposed the Court's action and reacted quickly by adopting the Eleventh Amendment, which gives states immunity from being sued, without their consent, in federal courts by "Citizens of another State, or by Citizens or Subjects of any Foreign State."

Soon afterward, however, the Supreme Court gave the Eleventh Amendment a "stingy" reading. In his opinion in **Cohens v. Virginia** (1821), Chief Justice Marshall stated his belief that the Eleventh Amendment did not preclude citizens from bringing suit in federal court against their own state. That view held sway with the Court until the post–Civil War case of *Hans v. Louisiana* (1890). The Court, in *Hans*, was aware of Marshall's "observation" in *Cohens* but deemed it dicta, "unnecessary to the decision," and therefore not binding. It went on to conclude that the Eleventh Amendment does, in fact, prohibit suits brought in federal court by citizens against their own state unless the state grants consent. According to the Court, even though the text of the amendment does not mention suits by a state's own citizens, it would be "anomalous"—especially given the furor over *Chisholm*—that a state may be sued in the federal courts by its own citizens in cases arising under the Constitution or federal laws but could not be sued under similar circumstances by the citizens of other states, or of a foreign state.

Although *Hans* seemed to expand state sovereign immunity protections, Congress, with the blessing of the Supreme Court, attempted to contract it. This trend continued into the 1980s. In case after case, the Court allowed Congress to make exceptions to the sovereign immunity established in the Eleventh Amendment. In *Fitzpatrick v. Bitzer* (1976) the Court held that because the Fourteenth Amendment expressly authorizes Congress to enforce the amendment "by appropriate legislation," Congress could, when exercising that authority, abrogate the states' immunity from suit under the Eleventh Amendment. Similarly, in *Pennsylvania v. Union Gas Co.* (1989) a divided Court ruled that the commerce clause (Article I, Section 8) permitted Congress to make an exception to the Eleventh Amendment's grant of immunity, holding that the power to regulate commerce "among the several States" would be "incomplete without the authority to render States liable in damages." These decisions, allowing Congress to pass legislation encroaching on state interests, were consistent with the philosophy of cooperative federalism that was accepted by the justices at that time.

But in 1996 the Court overruled *Union Gas* in **Seminole Tribe of Florida v. Florida**, a case involving the Indian Gaming Regulatory Act. This act requires that states negotiate in good faith with Native American tribes over gambling activities. If a tribe thinks a state is not doing so, the act permits the tribe to bring suit in a federal court to compel the state to negotiate in good faith. Writing for the Court, Chief Justice Rehnquist stated, "Even when the Constitution vests in Congress complete law-making authority over a particular area, the Eleventh Amendment prevents congressional authorization of suits by private parties against unconsenting States." In other words, the Court asserted that the specific terms of Article I of the constitutional text do not permit Congress to abrogate the states' immunity from suits commenced or prosecuted in the federal courts. This decision, of course, was in line with the Rehnquist Court's turn toward dual federalism.

Would the Court push *Seminole Tribe* even further, holding that Congress cannot subject nonconsenting states to private suits for damages even in their own courts? This question was at the heart of *Alden v. Maine* (1999). At issue was the federal Fair Labor Standards Act. Sixty-five probation officers brought a legal action against their employer, the state of Maine, for allegedly violating the overtime provisions of the FLSA. The officers filed their suit in state court, as authorized under the federal statute. The trial court judge dismissed the suit on the ground of sovereign immunity, the traditional principle that a government may not be sued without its permission. On appeal to the Supreme Court, the question was whether Congress, by legislation, could subject nonconsenting states to lawsuits in their own courts.

By the same 5–4 division that occurred in *Printz*, the Court ruled that Congress was without authority to strip the state of its sovereign immunity by compelling the state courts to accept such lawsuits. Because the state of Maine had not consented to be sued, its courts were without jurisdiction to hear the case. As a consequence of *Alden* and *Seminole Tribe*, state employees have a hard time asserting their rights under certain federal labor laws unless their states agree to be sued. Although the minority in *Alden* vigorously attacked the injustice that might result, the majority remained convinced that the principles of federalism left little room for Congress to eliminate a nonconsenting state's traditional immunity from lawsuit.[12]

Based on these cases and those we covered in the preceding section, it is apparent that the swing of the pendulum back toward the dual federalism position is closely associated with the Court's personnel changes. It seems that individual justices rarely change their positions. A justice who favors cooperative federalism—Justice Ruth Bader Ginsburg, for example—consistently tends to support the interests of the national government over the states, and justices with ideologies sympathetic to dual federalism—Justice Clarence Thomas, for example—repeatedly side with the states. How the Supreme Court interprets the Constitution's core principle of federalism is highly dependent on the values of appointees to the bench. In subsequent chapters we will see how the federalism debate has been fought when national and state interests have clashed over issues such as commerce and taxation.

---

[12]Something of a break in this trend came from the Court in a 2003 statement on the Eleventh Amendment. In **Nevada Department of Human Resources v. Hibbs** the justices surprised observers when they held that states are not immune from suits brought in federal court by their employees under the federal Family and Medical Leave Act of 1993, which provides employees with up to twelve workweeks of unpaid leave annually in the event of the onset of a "serious health condition" in a spouse and for other reasons.

ANNOTATED READINGS

General books on federalism, including the founding period and *McCulloch v. Maryland*, are Robert Allen, *The Ordeal of the Constitution: The Antifederalists and the Ratification Struggle of 1787–1788* (Norman: University of Oklahoma Press, 1966); Christopher P. Banks and John C. Blakeman, *The U.S. Supreme Court and New Federalism* (Lanham, MD: Rowman & Littlefield, 2012); Raoul Berger, *Federalism: The Founders' Design* (Norman: University of Oklahoma Press, 1987); Erwin Chemerinsky, *Enhancing Government: Federalism for the 21st Century* (Palo Alto, CA: Stanford University Press, 2008); Richard E. Ellis, *Aggressive Nationalism:* McCulloch v. Maryland *and the Foundation of Federal Authority in the Young Republic* (New York: Oxford University Press, 2007); Malcolm M. Feeley and Edward Rubin, *Federalism: Political Identity and Tragic Compromise* (Ann Arbor: University of Michigan Press, 2008); Michael J. Glennon and Robert D. Sloane, *Foreign Affairs Federalism: The Myth of National Exclusivity* (New York: Oxford University Press, 2016); Gerald Gunther, ed., *John Marshall's Defense of* McCulloch v. Maryland (Stanford, CA: Stanford University Press, 1969); Alison L. LaCroix, *The Ideological Origins of American Federalism* (Cambridge, MA: Harvard University Press, 2011); Laura Langer, *Judicial Review in State Supreme Courts: A Comparative Study* (Albany, NY: State University Press of America, 2002); Alpheus Mason, *The States Rights Debate: Antifederalism and the Constitution* (Englewood Cliffs, NJ: Prentice Hall, 1964); Robert F. Nagel, *The Implosion of American Federalism* (New York: Oxford University Press, 2001); John D. Nugent, *Safeguarding Federalism: How States Protect Their Interests in National Policy Making* (Norman: University of Oklahoma Press, 2009); David Brian Robertson, *Federalism and the Making of America* (New York: Routledge, 2018); John R. Schmidhauser, *The Supreme Court as Final Arbiter in Federal-State Relations, 1789–1957* (Chapel Hill: University of North Carolina Press, 1958); Anne Silverwood Twitty, *Before Dred Scott* (New York: Cambridge University Press, 2016); and Eric N. Waltenburg and Bill Swinford, *Litigating Federalism: The States before the U.S. Supreme Court* (Westport, CT: Greenwood Press, 1999).

On the Tenth and Eleventh Amendments, see Mark R. Killenbeck, ed., *The Tenth Amendment and State Sovereignty* (Lanham, MD: Rowman & Littlefield, 2002); and John V. Orth, *The Judicial Power of the United States: The Eleventh Amendment in American History* (New York: Oxford University Press, 1987).

CHAPTER SEVEN

THE COMMERCE POWER

OF ALL THE POWERS granted to government, perhaps none has caused more controversies and resulted in more litigation than the power to regulate commerce. Concern over the exercise of this power was present at the Constitution's birth and continues today. At each stage of the nation's development from an unorganized collection of thirteen separate colonies isolated from the world's commercial centers to a country of vast economic power, legal disputes of great significance tested the powers of government to regulate the economy.

During certain periods, such as John Marshall's chief justiceship, the decisions of the Supreme Court enhanced the role of the federal government in promoting economic development. At other times, such as in the early years of the Great Depression, the Court's interpretations thwarted the government's attempts to overcome economic collapse. From the earliest days of the nation, battles over the commerce power have raised basic questions. What is commerce? What is commerce among the states (now called interstate commerce)? How do we distinguish interstate commerce from intrastate commerce? What does it mean to regulate? What powers of commercial regulation does the Constitution grant to the federal government, and what role remains to be played by the states?

Rather than address these questions separately, in this chapter we explore the development of the commerce power chronologically. We take this approach because, as we just suggested, the Court has answered such questions in various ways in different eras, sometimes enhancing the federal government's power and sometimes curtailing it. These phases tend to correspond to the cyclical debate between dual and cooperative federalism that we considered in chapter 6. Keep in mind, however, that at times justices who adopt the tools of the dualist approach—especially the Tenth Amendment and narrower approaches to defining interstate commerce—are more committed to an antiregulation regime than they are to states' rights.

FOUNDATIONS OF THE COMMERCE POWER

A primary reason for the Constitutional Convention was the inability of the government under the Articles of Confederation to control the country's commercial activity effectively. Economic conditions were dismal following the Revolutionary War. The national and state governments were deeply in debt. The tax base of the newly independent nation was minimal, and commerce was undeveloped, leaving property taxes and customs duties as the primary sources of government funds.

The states were almost exclusively in charge of economic regulation. To raise enough revenue to pay their debts, the states imposed substantial taxes on land, placing farmers in an economically precarious situation. The states also erected trade barriers and imposed duties on the importation of foreign goods. Although such policies were enacted in part to promote the states' domestic businesses, the result was a general strangulation of commercial activity. Several states printed their own money and passed statutes canceling debts. With each of the states working independently, the national economy continued to slide into stagnation; for all practical purposes, the central government was powerless to respond effectively.

When agrarian interests reached their economic breaking point—culminating in the 1787 march on the federal arsenal at Springfield, Massachusetts, by a makeshift army of farmers led by Daniel Shays and others—it was clear that something had to be done. Congress called for a convention to reconsider the status of the Articles of Confederation, a convention that ultimately resulted in the drafting of the U.S. Constitution.

Commerce and the Constitutional Convention

The delegates to the Constitutional Convention recognized the necessity of giving the power to regulate the economy to the central government. The condition of the nation required that individual states no longer be allowed to pursue independent policies, each having a different impact on the country's economic health. To that end, Article I of the Constitution removed certain powers from the states and gave the federal government powers it did not have under the Articles of Confederation. States were stripped of the ability to print money, to impair the obligation of contracts, and to levy import duties. The federal government obtained the authority necessary to impose uniform regulations for the national economy. Among the powers granted to the central government were the authority to tax and impose customs duties, to spend and borrow, to develop and protect a single monetary system, and to regulate bankruptcies. Most important was the authority to regulate interstate and foreign commerce. Article I, Section 8, states: "The Congress shall have the power . . . to regulate Commerce with foreign Nations, and among the several States, and with the Indian Tribes."

The need for Congress to speak for the nation with a single voice on these matters was clear to the framers. Even Alexander Hamilton and James Madison, who disagreed on many questions of federalism, were in accord on the need for the central government to control interstate and foreign commerce. Hamilton wrote in *Federalist* No. 22:

> In addition to the defects already enumerated in the existing federal system, there are others of not less importance which concur in rendering it altogether unfit for the administration of the affairs of the Union.

> The want of a power to regulate commerce is by all parties allowed to be of the number.

Madison took a similar position in *Federalist* No. 42, arguing that the country's experience under the Articles of Confederation, as well as the experiences of the European nations, demonstrated that a central government without broad powers over the nation's commerce was destined to fail.

Congress quickly seized upon the authority to regulate commerce with other nations. Almost immediately, it imposed import duties as a means of raising revenue. The constitutional grant in this area was clear: the power to regulate foreign commerce, as well as other matters of foreign policy, was given unambiguously to the national government, and the role of the states was eliminated. Only on rare occasions since ratification have the states challenged congressional supremacy over foreign commerce.

The power to regulate interstate commerce, however, was a different story. Congress was slow in responding to this grant of authority, despite its constitutional power to regulate commerce among the states. For the first several decades, federal officials continued to view business as an activity occurring within the borders of individual states. In fact, Congress did not pass comprehensive legislation governing commerce among the states until the Interstate Commerce Act of 1887.

Marshall Defines the Commerce Power

The commerce clause gives Congress the power to "regulate commerce . . . among the Several states." But what do these terms—*regulate*, *commerce*, and *among*—mean? The history of the commerce clause is replete with disputes over definitions. Is "commerce" limited to the buying and selling of goods, or is its meaning broad enough to include other activities, such as manufacturing and production? What about "among"? How should we distinguish *inter*state commerce, which, according to the Constitution, the federal government regulates, from *intra*state commerce, over which the states may retain regulatory power? Problems associated with such distinctions were difficult enough in the early years, but they became even more complex as the economy grew and the country changed from agrarian to industrialized. As many constitutional law cases illustrate, disputes over commercial regulatory authority often involve power struggles between the national government and the states.

Disputes over the meaning of the commerce clause came before the Supreme Court even during the early years of nationhood. The justices probed the constitutional definition of "commerce" and the proper division of federal and state power to regulate it. Of the commerce cases decided by the Supreme Court in those early decades, none was more important than *Gibbons v. Ogden*

(1824). This dispute involved some of the nation's most prominent and powerful businessmen and attorneys. A great deal was at stake, both economically and politically. In his opinion for the Court, Chief Justice John Marshall responded to the fundamental problems of defining commerce and allocating the power to control it. His answers to the questions presented in this case are still very much a part of the American constitutional fabric.

Gibbons v. Ogden

22 U.S. (9 Wheat.) 1 (1824)
http://caselaw.findlaw.com/us-supreme-court/22/1.html
Vote: 6 (Duvall, Johnson, Marshall, Story, Todd, Washington)
    0

OPINION OF THE COURT: *Marshall*

CONCURRING OPINION: *Johnson*

NOT PARTICIPATING: *Thompson*

This complicated litigation can be traced back to 1798, when the New York legislature granted the wealthy and prominent Robert R. Livingston a monopoly to operate steamboats on all waters within the state, including the two most important commercial waterways, New York Harbor and the Hudson River. New York officials did not see the monopoly grant as particularly important because no one had yet developed a steamship that could operate reliably and profitably. But Livingston joined forces with Robert Fulton, and together they produced a commercially viable steamship. This mode of transportation became extremely popular and very profitable for the partners. When they obtained a similar monopoly over the port of New Orleans in 1811, they had significant control over the nation's two most important harbors.

The rapid westward expansion taking place at that time fueled the need for modern transportation systems. The Livingston-Fulton monopoly, however, put a damper on the use of steam engines in the evolution of such a system. The New York monopoly was so strong and so vigorously enforced that other states enacted retaliatory laws, which refused to let steam-powered vessels from New York use their waters. Especially hostile relations developed between New York and New Jersey, and violence between the crews of rival companies became common. Livingston died in 1813, followed two years later by Fulton, but their monopoly lived on.

In 1817 Aaron Ogden, a former governor of New Jersey, and Thomas Gibbons, a successful Georgia lawyer, entered into a partnership to carry passengers between New York City and Elizabethtown, New Jersey. Ogden had purchased the right to operate in New York waters from the Livingston-Fulton monopoly, and Gibbons had a federal permit issued under the 1793 Coastal Licensing Act to operate steamships along the coast. With these grants of authority the two partners could carry passengers between

Aaron Ogden

Thomas Gibbons

New York and New Jersey. The New York monopoly, however, pressured Ogden to terminate his relationship with Gibbons, and the partnership dissolved.

Gibbons then joined forces with Cornelius Vanderbilt, and they became fierce competitors with Ogden and the New York monopoly interests. Gibbons and Vanderbilt entered New York waters in violation of the monopoly whenever they could, picking up as much New York business as possible. In response, Ogden successfully persuaded the New York courts to enjoin Gibbons from entering New York waters. Gibbons appealed this ruling to the U.S. Supreme Court.

To press their case, Gibbons and Vanderbilt acquired the services of two of the best lawyers of the day, William Wirt and Daniel Webster. Wirt, the attorney general of the United States, argued that the federal permit issued to Gibbons took precedence over any state-issued monopoly and therefore Gibbons had the right to enter New York waters. Webster took a more radical position, explicitly stating that the commerce clause of the Constitution gave Congress exclusive power over commerce and that the state-granted monopoly was a violation of that clause. Ogden's lawyer responded that navigation was not commerce under the meaning of the Constitution but instead was an intrastate enterprise left to the states to regulate. The oral arguments in the case lasted four and a half days, an unusually long time.

MR. CHIEF JUSTICE MARSHALL DELIVERED THE OPINION OF THE COURT.

The appellant contends that this decree is erroneous, because the laws which purport to give the exclusive privilege it sustains, are repugnant to the constitution and laws of the United States.

They are said to be repugnant:

To that clause in the constitution which authorizes Congress to regulate commerce. . . .

The words are, "Congress shall have power to regulate commerce with foreign nations, and among the several States, and with the Indian tribes."

The subject to be regulated is commerce; and our constitution being . . . one of enumeration, and not of definition, to ascertain the extent of the power, it becomes necessary to settle the meaning of the word. The counsel for the appellee would limit it to traffic, to buying and selling, or the interchange of commodities, and do not admit that it comprehends navigation. This would restrict a general term, applicable to many objects, to one of its significations. Commerce, undoubtedly, is traffic, but it is something more: it is intercourse. It describes the commercial intercourse between nations, and parts of nations, in all its branches, and is regulated by prescribing rules for carrying on that intercourse. The mind can scarcely conceive a system for regulating commerce between

nations, which shall exclude all laws concerning navigation, which shall be silent on the admission of the vessels of the one nation into the ports of the other, and be confined to prescribing rules for the conduct of individuals, in the actual employment of buying and selling, or of barter.

If commerce does not include navigation, the government of the Union has no direct power over that subject, and can make no law prescribing what shall constitute American vessels, or requiring that they shall be navigated by American seamen. Yet this power has been exercised from the commencement of the government, has been exercised with the consent of all, and has been understood by all to be a commercial regulation. All America understands, and has uniformly understood, the word "commerce," to comprehend navigation. It was so understood, and must have been so understood, when the constitution was framed. The power over commerce, including navigation, was one of the primary objects for which the people of America adopted their government, and must have been contemplated in forming it. The convention must have used the word in that sense, because all have understood it in that sense; and the attempt to restrict it comes too late. . . .

The word used in the constitution, then, comprehends, and has been always understood to comprehend, navigation within its meaning; and a power to regulate navigation, is as expressly granted, as if that term had been added to the word "commerce."

To what commerce does this power extend? The constitution informs us, to commerce "with foreign nations, and among the several States, and with the Indian tribes."

It has, we believe, been universally admitted, that these words comprehend every species of commercial intercourse between the United States and foreign nations. No sort of trade can be carried on between this country and any other, to which this power does not extend. It has been truly said, that commerce, as the word is used in the constitution, is a unit, every part of which is indicated by the term.

If this be the admitted meaning of the word, in its application to foreign nations, it must carry the same meaning throughout the sentence, and remain a unit, unless there be some plain intelligible cause which alters it.

The subject to which the power is next applied, is to commerce "among the several States." The word "among" means intermingled with. A thing which is among others, is intermingled with them. Commerce among the States, cannot stop at the external boundary line of each State, but may be introduced into the interior.

It is not intended to say that these words comprehend that commerce, which is completely internal, which is carried on between man and man in a State, or between different parts of the same State, and which does not extend to or affect other States. Such a power would be inconvenient, and is certainly unnecessary.

Comprehensive as the word "among" is, it may very properly be restricted to that commerce which concerns more States than one.

The phrase is not one which would probably have been selected to indicate the completely interior traffic of a State, because it is not an apt phrase for that purpose; and the enumeration of the particular classes of commerce, to which the power was to be extended, would not have been made, had the intention been to extend the power to every description. The enumeration presupposes something not enumerated; and that something, if we regard the language or the subject of the sentence, must be the exclusively internal commerce of a State. The genius and character of the whole government seem to be, that its action is to be applied to all the external concerns of the nation, and to those internal concerns which affect the States generally; but not to those which are completely within a particular State, which do not affect other States, and with which it is not necessary to interfere, for the purpose of executing some of the general powers of the government. The completely internal commerce of a State, then, may be considered as reserved for the State itself.

But, in regulating commerce with foreign nations, the power of Congress does not stop at the jurisdictional lines of the several States. It would be a very useless power, if it could not pass those lines. The commerce of the United States with foreign nations, is that of the whole United States. Every district has a right to participate in it. The deep streams which penetrate our country in every direction, pass through the interior of almost every State in the Union, and furnish the means of exercising this right. If Congress has the power to regulate it, that power must be exercised whenever the subject exists. If it exists within the States, if a foreign voyage may commence or terminate at a port within a State, then the power of Congress may be exercised within a State.

This principle is, if possible, still more clear, when applied to commerce "among the several States." They either join each other, in which case they are separated by a mathematical line, or they are remote from each other, in which case other States lie between them. What is commerce "among" them; and how is it to be conducted? Can a trading expedition between two adjoining States, commence and terminate outside of each? And if the trading intercourse be between two States remote from each other, must it not commence in one, terminate in the other, and probably pass through a third? Commerce among the States must, of necessity, be commerce with the States. . . .

We are now arrived at the inquiry—What is this power?

It is the power to regulate; that is, to prescribe the rule by which commerce is to be governed. This power, like all others vested in Congress, is complete in itself, may be exercised to its utmost extent, and acknowledges no limitations, other than are prescribed in the constitution. . . . If, as has always been understood, the sovereignty of Congress, though limited to specified objects, is plenary as to those objects, the power over commerce with foreign nations, and among the several States, is vested in Congress as absolutely as it would be in a single government, having in its constitution the same restrictions on the exercise of the power as are found in the constitution of the United States. The wisdom and the discretion of Congress, their identity with the people, and the influence which their constituents possess at elections, are, in this, as in many other instances, as that, for example, of declaring war, the sole restraints on which they have relied, to secure them from its abuse. They are the restraints on which the people must often rely solely, in all representative governments.

The power of Congress, then, comprehends navigation, within the limits of every State in the Union; so far as that navigation may be, in any manner, connected with "commerce with foreign nations, or among the several States, or with the Indian tribes." It may, of consequence, pass the jurisdictional line of New-York, and act upon the very waters to which the prohibition now under consideration applies.

But it has been urged with great earnestness, that, although the power of Congress to regulate commerce with foreign nations, and among the several States, be coextensive with the subject itself, and have no other limits than are prescribed in the constitution, yet the States may severally exercise the same power, within their respective jurisdictions. In support of this argument, it is said, that they possessed it as an inseparable attribute of sovereignty, before the formation of the constitution, and still retain it, except so far as they have surrendered it by that instrument; that this principle results from the nature of the government, and is secured by the tenth amendment; that an affirmative grant of power is not exclusive, unless in its own nature it be such that the continued exercise of it by the former possessor is inconsistent with the grant, and that this is not of that description.

The appellant, conceding these postulates, except the last, contends, that full power to regulate a particular subject, implies the whole power, and leaves no residuum; that a grant of the whole is incompatible with the existence of a right in another to any part of it. . . .

In discussing the question, whether this power is still in the States, in the case under consideration, we may dismiss from it the inquiry, whether it is surrendered by the mere grant to Congress, or is retained until Congress shall exercise the power. We may dismiss that inquiry, because it has been exercised, and the regulations which Congress deemed it proper to make, are now in full operation. The sole question is, can a State regulate commerce with foreign nations and among the States, while Congress is regulating it?

The counsel for the respondent answer this question in the affirmative, and rely very much on the restrictions in the 10th section, as supporting their opinion. . . .

It has been contended by the general counsel for the appellant, that, as the word "to regulate" implies in its nature, full power over the thing to be regulated, it excludes, necessarily, the action of all others that would perform the same operation on the same thing. That regulation is designed for the entire result, applying to those parts which remain as they were, as well as to those which are altered. It produces a uniform whole, which is as much disturbed and deranged by changing what the regulating power designs to leave untouched, as that on which it has operated.

There is great force in this argument, and the Court is not satisfied that it has been refuted.

Since, however, in exercising the power of regulating their own purely internal affairs, whether of trading or police, the States may sometimes enact laws, the validity of which depends on their interfering with, and being contrary to, an act of Congress passed in pursuance of the constitution, the Court will enter upon the inquiry, whether the laws of New York, as expounded by the highest tribunal of that State, have, in their application to this case, come into collision with an act of Congress, and deprived a citizen of a right to which that act entitles him. Should this collision exist, it will be immaterial whether those laws were passed in virtue of a concurrent power "to regulate commerce with foreign nations and among the several States," or, in virtue of a power to regulate their domestic trade and police. In one case and the other, the acts of New-York must yield to the law of Congress; and the decision sustaining the privilege they confer, against a right given by a law of the Union, must be erroneous. . . .

But the framers of our constitution foresaw this state of things, and provided for it, by declaring the supremacy not only of itself, but of the laws made in pursuance of it. The nullity of any act, inconsistent with the constitution, is produced by the declaration, that the constitution is the supreme law. The appropriate application of that part of the clause which confers the same supremacy on laws and treaties, is to such acts of the State Legislatures as do not transcend their powers, but, though enacted in the execution of acknowledged State powers, interfere with, or are contrary to the laws of Congress, made in pursuance of the constitution, or some treaty made under the authority of the United States. In every such case, the act of Congress, or the treaty, is supreme; and the law of the State, though enacted in the exercise of powers not controverted, must yield to it. . . .

But all inquiry into this subject seems to the Court to be put completely at rest, by the act already mentioned, entitled, "An act for the enrolling and licensing of steam boats."

This act authorizes a steam boat employed, or intended to be employed, only in a river or bay of the United States, owned wholly or in part by an alien, resident within the United States, to be enrolled and licensed as if the same belonged to a citizen of the United States.

This act demonstrates the opinion of Congress, that steam boats may be enrolled and licensed, in common with vessels using sails. They are, of course, entitled to the same privileges, and can no more be restrained from navigating waters, and entering ports which are free to such vessels, than if they were wafted on their voyage by the winds, instead of being propelled by the agency of fire. The one element may be as legitimately used as the other, for every commercial purpose authorized by the laws of the Union; and the act of a State inhibiting the use of either to any vessel having a license under the act of Congress, comes, we think, in direct collision with that act.

Like his opinions in *Marbury* and *McCulloch*, Marshall's opinion in *Gibbons* laid a constitutional foundation that remains in place today. The decision made several important points. First, commerce involves more than buying and selling. It includes the commercial intercourse between nations and states; therefore, transportation and navigation clearly fall within the definition of commerce. Second, commerce among the states begins in one state and ends in another; it does not stop when the act of crossing a state border is completed. Consequently, commerce that occurs within a state may be part of a larger interstate process. Third, once an act is considered part of interstate commerce, Congress, according to the Constitution, may regulate it. The power to regulate interstate commerce is complete and has no limitation other than what may be found in other constitutional provisions. But note that Marshall rejects Ogden's argument that the Tenth Amendment serves as such a limit. In line with his opinion in *McCulloch*, Marshall does not find that the amendment creates an "enclave" of state power. Instead, he emphasizes that Congress is limited to its delegated powers (*see chapter 6*)—in this case, the power to regulate interstate commerce, however broadly defined. This brings us to the fourth point: because the text of the commerce clause grants Congress the power to regulate commerce only among the states, the power to regulate commerce that occurs completely within the boundaries of a single state and does not extend to or affect other states belongs to the states.

Gibbons v. Ogden was a substantial victory for national power. It broadly construed the definitions of both commerce and interstate commerce. But Marshall did not go as far as Daniel Webster had urged. The opinion asserts only that Congress has complete power to regulate interstate commerce and that federal regulations are superior to any state laws. The decision does not answer the question of the legitimacy of states regulating interstate commerce in the absence of federal action. That controversy was left for future justices to decide.

ATTEMPTS TO DEFINE THE COMMERCE POWER IN THE WAKE OF THE INDUSTRIAL REVOLUTION

Marshall provided a clear, if expansive, framework for the exercise of congressional commerce power, but it was not invoked much immediately after *Gibbons* because federal commerce clause cases did not become major items on the Supreme Court's agenda until the latter half of the nineteenth century. By this time, small intrastate businesses were giving way to large interstate corporations. Industrial expansion blossomed, and the interstate railroad and pipeline systems were well under way. The infamous captains of industry were creating large monopolistic trusts that dominated huge segments of the national economy, squeezing out small businesses and discouraging new entrepreneurs. The industrial combines that controlled the railroads also, in effect, ruled agriculture and other interests that relied on the rails to transport goods to market. This commercial growth brought great prosperity to some, but it also caused horrendous social problems. Children worked in sweatshops, and unsafe working conditions and low wages plagued employees of all ages, eventually leading to the formation of labor unions.

In light of these developments, Congress sought to exert some control over both the economic and the social concerns following from the rise of big business. To deal with the former, it passed several laws—aimed at regulating business practices—based in its commerce power. In the case of social problems, it began to make use of the commerce clause as a federal police power—that is, the government's authority to regulate for the health, safety, morals, and general welfare of its citizens.

How did the Court respond to these laws? When it came to efforts to regulate the nation's interstate railroads, the justices had little difficulty ruling for Congress. To the Court it was clear that railroads were "instruments of interstate commerce" over which Congress could exert federal power.[1] When it came to efforts to regulating manufacturing and production, however, the Court took a harder line. In **United States v. E. C. Knight Co.** (1895), for example, the Court rejected the federal government's efforts to break up a sugar trust that controlled over 98 percent of the sugar refining business in the United States. The government claimed that the trust operated as a monopoly in violation of the Sherman Anti-Trust Act, which was designed to break up monopolies that restrained trade. Nonetheless, the Court ruled that the antitrust law could not be imposed on the sugar refining industry. Refining was manufacturing. It was production that occurred within the boundaries of a single state. It made no difference that the sugar

---

[1]See, e.g., **Houston, E. & W. Texas Railway Co. v. United States** (1914), better known as the Shreveport Rate Case.

trust controlled 98 percent of the nation's sugar supply or that the processed sugar was destined to be sold in interstate commerce. Manufacturing was not interstate commerce. In Chief Justice Melville Fuller's words for the Court, "Commerce succeeds to manufacture, and is not a part of it."

What about congressional efforts to use the commerce power as a police power? These were quite controversial. On the one hand, it was clear that state governments possessed general police powers prior to the adoption of the federal Constitution and so retained them when the national government was created. As a result, states may pass laws for the general welfare without any specific grant of power to do so as long as their legislation does not run afoul of specific constitutional limitations (such as the Bill of Rights).

The federal government, on the other hand, is a government of delegated powers. It does not possess any general police power. For an act of Congress to be valid, it must rest on a specific grant of authority—an enumerated, implied, or inherent power. Madison described the situation aptly in *Federalist* No. 45: the "powers delegated by the proposed Constitution to the federal government are few and defined. Those which are to remain in the State governments are numerous and indefinite."

Congress dealt with this potential obstacle by adding an "interstate" requirement to some of its laws; and, at least initially, that was enough to satisfy the Court. **Champion v. Ames** (1903) provides an example. At issue in this case was an 1895 law in which Congress regulated lotteries by prohibiting the shipment (or carrying) of lottery tickets in interstate or foreign commerce. Federal authorities charged Charles Champion with violating this act. Champion had arranged for a shipment of lottery tickets, supposedly printed in Paraguay, to be transported from Texas to California by Wells Fargo. He challenged his arrest on several grounds, but mostly on the ground that the law was not a regulation of commerce but rather a "suppression of an alleged evil."

Writing for the Court, Justice John Marshall Harlan rejected Champion's argument. Under existing precedent, including *Gibbons*, he held that as long as Congress was regulating "commerce . . . among the states," it could use its power to prohibit what Congress thought was an immoral trade. As he wrote, "We are of opinion that lottery tickets are subjects of traffic and therefore are subjects of commerce, and the regulation of the carriage of such tickets from State to State, at least by independent carriers, is a regulation of commerce among the several States." The four dissenters disagreed. They argued that

Congress was not regulating commerce at all; instead, it was trying to prohibit lotteries, a matter for the police powers of the state to address.

Champion set the precedent that Congress may indeed use the commerce clause in much the same manner as states use their police powers. In the years following *Champion*, the legislature passed a number of laws designed to accomplish social, not economic, goals through the exercise of the commerce power. For example, in 1910, as a method of curtailing interstate prostitution rings, Congress passed the Mann Act. In *Hoke v. United States* (1913) the Court unanimously ruled that the federal government has the authority under the commerce clause to prohibit taking women across state lines for purposes of prostitution or other immoral activities. In addition, Congress passed various laws that federalized criminal activity that extends beyond the boundaries of a single state. Kidnapping that crosses state lines, interstate transportation of stolen property, and even interstate flight to avoid prosecution are all federal crimes because of Congress's power to regulate commerce among the states.

And yet, just when it seemed that the Court would continue to allow Congress to develop federal police powers via the commerce clause, it dealt Congress a significant blow in the case of *Hammer v. Dagenhart* (1918).

Hammer v. Dagenhart

247 U.S. 251 (1918)
http://caselaw.findlaw.com/us-supreme-court/247/251.html
Vote: 5 (Day, McReynolds, Pitney, Van Devanter, White)
  4 (Brandeis, Clarke, Holmes, McKenna)

OPINION OF THE COURT: *Day*

DISSENTING OPINION: *Holmes*

In the 1880s America entered the industrial age, which was characterized by the unfettered growth of the private-sector economy. The Industrial Revolution changed the United States for the better in countless ways, but it also had a downside. Lacking any significant government controls, many businesses had less-than-benevolent relations with their workers. Some forced employees to work more than fourteen hours a day at absurdly low wages and under dreadful conditions. They also had no qualms about employing children under the age of sixteen.

Americans were divided over these practices. On one side were the entrepreneurs, stockholders, and others who gained from worker exploitation. By employing children, paying low wages, and

providing no benefits, they minimized expenses and maximized profits. On the other side were the progressives, reformist groups, and individuals who sought to persuade the states and the federal government to enact laws to protect workers. These two camps repeatedly clashed in their struggle to attain diametrically opposed policy ends.[2]

One of the first battles came in 1915, when Congress was considering the Federal Child Labor Act. The bill prohibited shipment in interstate commerce of factory products made by children under the age of fourteen or by children ages fourteen to sixteen who worked more than eight hours a day. Numerous progressive groups supported the legislation, but it faced substantial opposition from employer associations such as the Executive Committee of Southern Cotton Manufacturers. This group was made up of militant mill owners who organized in 1915 solely to defeat federal child labor legislation. Its first attempt failed, and Congress passed the child labor law in 1916. The committee's leader, David Clark, vowed that his group would challenge the constitutionality of the act in court. He then sought the right test case to challenge the law. Eventually, he decided on a suit involving the Fidelity Manufacturing Company and retained a corporate law firm that held a laissez-faire philosophy to advance his argument.

The case Clark brought was perfect for the committee's needs. Roland Dagenhart and his two minor sons were employed at Fidelity, a cotton mill in North Carolina. Under state law, both of Dagenhart's sons were permitted to work up to eleven hours a day. Under the new federal act, however, the older boy could work only eight hours, and the younger one could not work at all. Not only were the facts relating to the Dagenharts advantageous, but Clark also secured the cooperation of the company, which had equal disdain for the law, in planning the litigation. One month before the effective date of the law, the company posted the new federal regulations on its door and "explained" to affected employees that they would be unable to continue to work. A week later, having already secured the consent of the Dagenharts and the factory, the committee's attorneys filed an injunction against the company and William C. Hammer, a U.S. attorney, to prevent enforcement of the law.

Within a month, the district court heard arguments and ruled the act unconstitutional. The judge did not write an opinion, but when he handed down his decision, he fully agreed with the committee's arguments, suggesting that the federal government had usurped state power.

Once the district court stayed enforcement of the act, both the committee and the U.S. Justice Department began to plan

---

[2]We derive what follows from Lee Epstein, *Conservatives in Court* (Knoxville: University of Tennessee Press, 1985); and Stephen B. Wood, *Constitutional Politics in the Progressive Era* (Chicago: University of Chicago Press, 1968).

the strategies they would use before the U.S. Supreme Court. The committee argued that Congress had no authority to impose its policies on the states. Solicitor General John W. Davis led the government's defense. One of the great attorneys of the day, Davis made a strong case for the law, although he probably opposed it. Not only did he argue that the regulation of child labor fell squarely within Congress's purview, but he also supplied the Court with data indicating that the states themselves had sought to eliminate the exploitation of young children by employers. His brief pointed out that only three states placed no age limit on factory employees, and only ten allowed those between the ages of fourteen and sixteen to work.

MR. JUSTICE DAY DELIVERED THE OPINION OF THE COURT.

It is . . . contended that the authority of Congress may be exerted to control interstate commerce in the shipment of child-made goods because of the effect of the circulation of such goods in other states where the evil of this class of labor has been recognized by local legislation, and the right to thus employ child labor has been more rigorously restrained than in the state of production. In other words, that the unfair competition thus engendered may be controlled by closing the channels of interstate commerce to manufacturers in those states where the local laws do not meet what Congress deems to be the more just standard of other states.

There is no power vested in Congress to require the states to exercise their police power so as to prevent possible unfair competition. Many causes may co-operate to give one state, by

Young girls working in a clothing factory. Congressional attempts to curb child labor by taxing the items produced or prohibiting their interstate shipment initially were rebuffed by the Supreme Court.

reason of local laws or conditions, an economic advantage over others. The commerce clause was not intended to give to Congress a general authority to equalize such conditions. In some of the states laws have been passed fixing minimum wages for women; in others the local law regulates the hours of labor of women in various employments. Business done in such states may be at an economic disadvantage when compared with states which have no such regulations; surely, this fact does not give Congress the power to deny transportation in interstate commerce to those who carry on business where the hours of labor and the rate of compensation for women have not been fixed by a standard in the use in other states and approved by Congress.

The grant of power to Congress over the subject of interstate commerce was to enable it to regulate such commerce, and not to give it authority to control the states in their exercise of the police power over local trade and manufacture.

The grant of authority over a purely Federal matter was not intended to destroy the local power always existing and carefully reserved to the states in the 10th Amendment to the Constitution. . . .

That there should be limitations upon the right to employ children in mines and factories in the interest of their own and the public welfare, all will admit. That such employment is generally deemed to require regulation is shown by the fact that the brief of counsel states that every state in the Union has a law upon the subject, limiting the right to thus employ children. In North Carolina, the state wherein is located the factory in which the employment was had in the present case, no child under twelve years of age is permitted to work.

. . . The maintenance of the authority of the states over matters purely local is as essential to the preservation of our institutions as is the conservation of the supremacy of the Federal power in all matters intrusted to the nation by the Federal Constitution.

In interpreting the Constitution it must never be forgotten that the nation is made up of states, to which are intrusted the powers of local government. And to them and to the people the powers not expressly delegated to the national government are reserved. The power of the states to regulate their purely internal affairs by such laws as seem wise to the local authority is inherent, and has never been surrendered to the general government. To sustain this statute would not be, in our judgment, a recognition of the lawful exertion of congressional authority over interstate commerce, but would sanction an invasion by the Federal power of the control of a matter purely local in its character, and over which no authority has been delegated to Congress in conferring the power to regulate commerce among the states.

We have neither authority nor disposition to question the motives of Congress in enacting this legislation. The purposes intended must be attained consistently with constitutional limitations, and not by an invasion of the powers of the states. This

Courtesy of the Library of Congress, Prints & Photographs Division

court has no more important function than that which devolves upon it the obligation to preserve inviolate the constitutional limitations upon the exercise of authority, Federal and state, to the end that each may continue to discharge, harmoniously with the other, the duties intrusted to it by the Constitution.

In our view the necessary effect of this act is, by means of a prohibition against the movement in interstate commerce of ordinary commercial commodities, to regulate the hours of labor of children in factories and mines within the states,—a purely state authority. Thus the act in a twofold sense is repugnant to the Constitution. It not only transcends the authority delegated to Congress over commerce, but also exerts a power as to a purely local matter to which the Federal authority does not extend. The far-reaching result of upholding the act cannot be more plainly indicated than by pointing out that if Congress can thus regulate matters intrusted to local authority by prohibition of the movement of commodities in interstate commerce, all freedom of commerce will be at an end, and the power of the states over local matters may be eliminated, and thus our system of government be practically destroyed.

For these reasons we hold that this law exceeds the constitutional authority of Congress. It follows that the decree of the District Court must be affirmed.

MR. JUSTICE HOLMES, DISSENTING.

The act does not meddle with anything belonging to the states. They may regulate their internal affairs and their domestic commerce as they like. But when they seek to send their products across the state line they are no longer within their rights. If there were no Constitution and no Congress their power to cross the line would depend upon their neighbors. Under the Constitution such commerce belongs not to the states, but to Congress to regulate. It may carry out its views of public policy whatever indirect effect they may have upon the activities of the states. Instead of being encountered by a prohibitive tariff at her boundaries, the state encounters the public policy of the United States which it is for Congress to express. The public policy of the United States is shaped with a view to the benefit of the nation as a whole. . . . The national welfare as understood by Congress may require a different attitude within its sphere from that of some self-seeking state. It seems to me entirely constitutional for Congress to enforce its understanding by all the means at its command.

If William Day's opinion was a total victory for the Executive Committee, it meant little to the Dagenharts (*see Box 7-1*). More important is what it meant for congressional power under the commerce clause. First, it perpetuated the distinction drawn in *E. C. Knight*

between the manufacturing/production of goods, which the Court regarded as intrastate commerce and therefore to be regulated only by the states, and their shipment in interstate commerce, which Congress could regulate. In *Hammer* the Court saw the law as a regulation of the manufacturing stage rather than a regulation of interstate commerce. Seen in this way, some say the decision was not so much a rejection of the power of Congress to regulate social matters as it was a reminder that the justices would treat these types of laws as they did the antitrust law at issue in *E. C. Knight:* Congress must show it is not regulating manufacturing or production. On the other hand, Day seemed to reprimand Congress for using the commerce power to invade state police power. As he wrote, "The grant of power to Congress over the subject of interstate commerce was to enable it to regulate such commerce, and not to give it authority to control the states in their exercise of the police power over local trade and manufacture." This is related to another striking aspect of *Hammer:* the Court's use of the Tenth Amendment as, seemingly, an independent brake on the commerce power.

THE SUPREME COURT AND THE NEW DEAL

The related moves of narrowing the definition of commerce and invoking the Tenth Amendment in *E. C. Knight* and *Hammer* probably reflected less a commitment to states' rights than a willingness on the part of the Court to embrace a free enterprise philosophy. If so, this matched the general mood of the public, as at least some Americans were benefiting so much from the economic boom of the 1920s that they opposed regulation. Calvin Coolidge famously put it this way: "After all, the chief business of the American people is business."

This changed almost overnight when the New York Stock Exchange crashed on October 29, 1929. The crash set in motion a series of events that shook the American economy and drove the nation into a deep depression. For the next two years, the stock market continued to tumble, with the Standard & Poor's Industrial Average falling 75 percent. The gross national product declined 27 percent over three years, and the unemployment rate rose from a healthy 3.2 percent in 1929 to a catastrophic 24.9 percent in 1933.

The Republican Party, which had been victorious in the 1928 elections, controlled the White House and both houses of Congress. The party attempted to cope

BOX 7-1

Aftermath . . . *Hammer v. Dagenhart*

Five years after the Supreme Court's decision in *Hammer v. Dagenhart* striking down the child labor law, a journalist interviewed Reuben Dagenhart, whose father had sued to prevent Congress from interfering with his sons' jobs in a North Carolina cotton mill. Reuben was twenty when he was interviewed. Excerpts follow:

"What benefit . . . did you get out of the suit which you won in the United States Supreme Court?"

"I don't see that I got any benefit. I guess I'd be a lot better off if they hadn't won it.

"Look at me! A hundred and five pounds, a grown man, and no education. I may be mistaken, but I think the years I've put in the cotton mills have stunted my growth. They kept me from getting any schooling. I had to stop school after the third grade and now I need the education I didn't get."

"Just what did you and John get out of that suit then?" he was asked.

"Why, we got some automobile rides when them big lawyers from the North was down here. Oh yes, and they bought both of us a Coca-Cola! That's all we got out of it."

"What did you tell the judge when you were in court?"

"Oh, John and me was never in court. Just Paw was there. John and me was just little kids in short pants. I guess we wouldn't have looked like much in court. . . . We were working in the mill while the case was going on."

Reuben hasn't been to school in years, but his mind has not been idle.

"It would have been a good thing for all the kids in this state if that law they passed had been kept. Of course, they do better now than they used to. You don't see so many babies working in the factories, but you see a lot of them that ought to be going to school."

Source: Labor, November 17, 1923, 3, quoted in Leonard F. James, *The Supreme Court in American Life,* 2nd ed. (Glenview, IL: Scott, Foresman, 1971), 74.

---

with the Great Depression by following philosophies of government that had been successful during the previous years of prosperity, with dismal results. The economic forces against which the Republicans fought were enormous. A different political approach was necessary to battle the collapse, and the American people were demanding such a change.

The Depression and Political Change

In the 1932 presidential election, Democratic candidate Franklin D. Roosevelt was swept into office by a huge margin as the voters rejected the incumbent, Herbert Hoover. With new Democratic majorities in the House and Senate, the president began combating the Great Depression with his New Deal policies. The overwhelming Democratic margins in Congress gave Roosevelt all the political clout he needed to gain approval of his radical new approach to boosting the economy. His programs were so popular with the American people that in 1936 they reelected Roosevelt

by an even greater margin and provided him with even larger Democratic majorities in Congress, reducing the Republicans almost to minor party status *(see Figure 7-1).*

The U.S. Supreme Court, however, did not change. In 1929, just before the stock market crashed, the Court had six Republicans and three Democrats. The economic conservatives (William Howard Taft, Willis Van Devanter, James C. McReynolds, Pierce Butler, George Sutherland, and Edward Sanford) held control and clearly outnumbered the justices more sympathetic to political and economic change (Oliver Wendell Holmes, Louis Brandeis, and Harlan Fiske Stone). By 1932 the Court had three new justices. Hughes succeeded Taft as chief justice, Benjamin Cardozo took Holmes's seat, and Owen Roberts replaced Sanford. Although these changes reduced the Republican majority to five, the ideological balance of the Court underwent no appreciable change. Hoover had filled all three of these vacancies, which occurred before Roosevelt took office. Inaugurated in March 1933, Roosevelt had no opportunity to name a

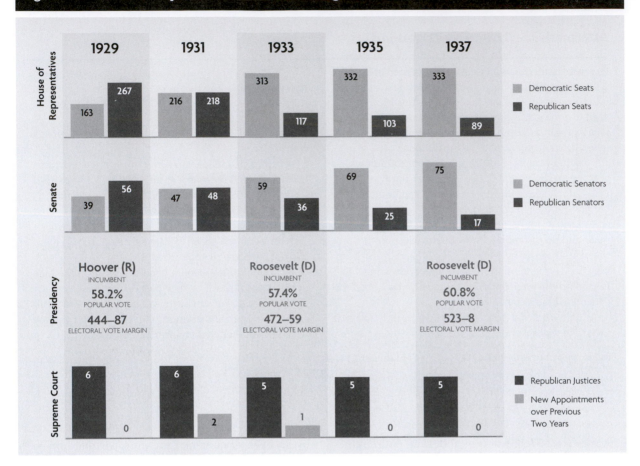

Figure 7-1   The Great Depression and Political Change

House of Representatives

	1929	1931	1933	1935	1937
Democratic Seats	163	216	313	332	333
Republican Seats	267	218	117	103	89

Senate

	1929	1931	1933	1935	1937
Democratic Senators	39	47	59	69	75
Republican Senators	56	48	36	25	17

Presidency

Hoover (R)	Roosevelt (D)	Roosevelt (D)
INCUMBENT	INCUMBENT	INCUMBENT
58.2%	57.4%	60.8%
POPULAR VOTE	POPULAR VOTE	POPULAR VOTE
444–87	472–59	523–8
ELECTORAL VOTE MARGIN	ELECTORAL VOTE MARGIN	ELECTORAL VOTE MARGIN

Supreme Court

	1929	1931	1933	1935	1937
Republican Justices	6	6	5	5	5
New Appointments over Previous Two Years	0	2	1	0	0

Supreme Court justice until Van Devanter retired in June 1937. Roosevelt's first appointment, Hugo Black, assumed his seat in August of that year. Not until 1940 did the Court have a majority appointed from the period after Roosevelt's first election.

In the executive branch, Roosevelt assembled a cadre of young, creative people to devise novel ways of approaching the ailing economy, and these New Deal Democrats quickly set out to develop, enact, and implement their programs. Congress passed the first legislation, the Emergency Banking Act of 1933, just five days after Roosevelt's inauguration, and a string of statutes designed to control all major sectors of the nation's economy followed, including the Social Security Act and the National Labor Relations Act. It also created the Federal Communications Commission and the Securities and Exchange Commission, among others. In adopting these programs, Congress relied on a number of constitutional powers, including the powers to tax, spend, and regulate interstate and foreign commerce.

The new political majority that dominated the legislative and executive branches espoused philosophies that called for the government to take a significantly more active role in economic regulation. The Supreme Court remained firmly in the control of representatives of the old order, whose views on the relationship between government and the economy were at odds with those of the political branches. A clash between the president and the Court was inevitable.

The Court Attacks the New Deal

As soon as the New Deal programs came into being, conservative business interests began to challenge their constitutional validity. In just two years the appeals started to reach the Court's doorstep. Beginning in 1935 and lasting for two long, tense years, the Court and the New Deal Democrats fought over the constitutionality of an expanded federal role in managing the economy.

During this period, the justices struck down many important New Deal statutes. Of ten major programs challenged, the Court approved only two—the Tennessee Valley Authority and the emergency monetary laws. Four hard-line conservative justices, Van Devanter, McReynolds, Sutherland, and Butler, formed the heart of the Court's opposition. Many thought their obstruction of New Deal initiatives would bring about the nation's ruin. As a consequence, they became known as the Four Horsemen of the Apocalypse, a reference to the end of the world as depicted in the Bible's book of Revelation. Two of the four, McReynolds and Butler, were Democrats (*see Box 7-2*).

Naturally, these four justices by themselves could not declare void any act of Congress. They needed the vote of at least one other justice. As indicated in Table 7-1, they had little trouble attracting others to their cause. Of the eight major 1935–1936 decisions striking down congressional policies, three were by 5–4 votes in which the four were able to attract Justice Roberts to their side. In one additional case, Roberts and Hughes voted with the conservatives. But in three of these significant decisions, the Court was unanimous, with even the more liberal Brandeis, Cardozo, and Stone voting to strike down the challenged legislation.

The first salvo in the war between the two branches occurred on January 7, 1935, when the Supreme Court, by an 8–1 vote in **Panama Refining Company v. Ryan**, struck down a section of the National Industrial Recovery Act (NIRA) as an improper delegation of congressional power to the executive branch. The section in question was a major New Deal weapon for regulating the oil industry. It gave the president the power to prohibit interstate shipment of oil and petroleum products that were produced or stored in a manner illegal under state law. The justices found fault with the act because it did not provide sufficiently clear standards to guide the executive branch; rather, it gave the president almost unlimited discretion in applying the prohibitions. *Panama Refining* was the first case in which the Court struck down legislation because it was an improper delegation of power.

Although the decision in *Panama Refining* was restricted to the delegation question and did not focus on Congress's interstate commerce authority, it promised bad days ahead for the administration. Not only was the decision a disappointment for the president, but also the vote was lopsided. Only Justice Cardozo voted to approve the law.

Then, on May 27, 1935—a date that became known as Black Monday—the justices dealt three significant blows to the administration's efforts to fight the Depression—all by unanimous votes. First, in **Humphrey's Executor v. United States** the Court declared that the president did not have the power to remove a member of the Federal Trade Commission. Second, the justices invalidated the Frazier-Lemke Act, which provided mortgage relief, especially to farmers.[3]

Finally, in **A. L. A. Schechter Poultry Corp. v. United States** the Court handed the president the most stinging defeat of all when it held that another section of the NIRA, Section 3, exceeded Congress' commerce power.[4] That section called for the creation of codes of fair competition for business. The codes would regulate trade practices, wages, hours, and other business activities within various industries. Trade associations and other industry groups had the responsibility for drafting the codes, which were submitted to the president for approval. In the absence of the private sector's recommendations, the president was authorized to draft codes himself. Once approved by the president, the codes had the force of law, and violators faced fines and even jail.

---

[3] *Louisville Bank v. Radford* (1935).

[4] The Court also found that the section was an unconstitutional delegation of power. According to Chief Justice Hughes, who wrote the opinion of the Court:

Section 3 of the Recovery Act is without precedent. It supplies no standards for any trade, industry or activity. It does not undertake to prescribe rules of conduct to be applied to particular states of fact determined by appropriate administrative procedure. Instead of prescribing rules of conduct, it authorizes the making of codes to prescribe them. For that legislative undertaking, §3 sets up [almost] no standards. . . In view of the scope of that broad declaration, and of the nature of the few restrictions that are imposed, the discretion of the President in approving or prescribing codes, and thus enacting laws for the government of trade and industry throughout the country, is virtually unfettered.

BOX 7-2

The Four Horsemen

Willis Van Devanter (1910–1937)

Republican from Wyoming. Born 1859. University of Cincinnati Law School. Wyoming state legislator and state supreme court judge. Federal appeals court judge. Appointed by William Howard Taft.

James Clark McReynolds (1914–1941)

Democrat from Tennessee. Born 1862. University of Virginia Law School. U.S. attorney general. Appointed by Woodrow Wilson.

George Sutherland (1922–1938)

Republican from Utah. Born 1862. University of Michigan Law School. State legislator, U.S. representative, U.S. senator. Appointed by Warren G. Harding.

Pierce Butler (1922–1939)

Democrat from Minnesota. Born 1866. No law school, studied privately. Corporate attorney. Appointed by Warren G. Harding.

A. L. A. Schechter Poultry Corp. involved a poultry slaughtering business in Brooklyn. Slaughterhouse operators such as Schechter Poultry purchased large numbers of live chickens from local poultry dealers who imported the fowl from out of state to be killed and dressed for sale.

Government officials found Schechter Poultry in violation of the Poultry Code, created under the NIRA, on numerous counts: The business ignored the code's wage and hour provisions, failed to comply with government record-keeping requirements, and did not conform to the slaughter regulations. Its worst offense, however, was selling unsanitary poultry that the government found unfit for human consumption. For this reason, *Schechter Poultry* became known as the "sick chicken case."

Writing for the Court, Chief Justice Hughes found that the code regulated intrastate, not interstate commerce. He also wrote that the code had only an indirect effect on commerce:

> In determining how far the federal government may go in controlling intrastate transactions upon the ground that they "affect" interstate commerce, there is a necessary and well-established distinction between direct and indirect effects. The precise line can be drawn only as individual cases arise, but the distinction is clear in principle. Direct effects are illustrated by the railroad cases. . . But where the effect of intrastate transactions upon interstate commerce is merely indirect, such transactions remain within the domain of state power. If the commerce clause were construed to reach all enterprises and transactions which could be said to have an indirect effect upon interstate commerce, the federal authority would embrace practically all the activities of the people and the authority of the State over its domestic concerns would exist only by sufferance of the federal government.

The decision in *Schechter* closely paralleled the *E. C. Knight* decision. In *E. C. Knight* the Court held that sugar refining was a manufacturing stage, not part of interstate commerce, and, therefore, the federal government could not regulate it. In *Schechter* the Court classified the slaughtering and local sale of chickens as intrastate commerce. In *Schechter* the interstate movement of the poultry had ceased. Once the distributor had sold to local processors

Table 7-1   The Supreme Court and the New Deal

Listed below are eight major decisions handed down by the Supreme Court in 1935 and 1936 declaring parts of the New Deal legislative program unconstitutional.

Case (Decision Date)	Acts Ruled Unconstitutional (Grounds)	Majority	Dissent
Panama Refining Co. v. Ryan (January 7, 1935)	Portions of the National Industrial Recovery Act (improper delegation of congressional powers)	Brandeis, Butler, Hughes, McReynolds, Roberts, Stone, Sutherland, Van Devanter	Cardozo
Railroad Retirement Board v. Alton Railroad Co. (May 6, 1935)	Railroad Retirement Act of 1934 (exceeded commerce clause powers; Fifth Amendment due process violations)	Butler, McReynolds, Roberts, Sutherland, Van Devanter	Brandeis, Cardozo, Hughes, Stone
A. L. A. Schechter Poultry Corp. v. United States (May 27, 1935)	Portions of the National Industrial Recovery Act (a regulation of intrastate commerce and improper delegation of congressional power)	Brandeis, Butler, Cardozo, Hughes, McReynolds, Roberts, Stone, Sutherland, Van Devanter	
Louisville Bank v. Radford (May 27, 1935)	Frazier-Lemke Act of 1934 extending bankruptcy relief (Fifth Amendment property rights)	Brandeis, Butler, Cardozo, Hughes, McReynolds, Roberts, Stone, Sutherland, Van Devanter	
Hopkins Savings Association v. Cleary (December 12, 1935)	Home Owners Loan Act of 1933 (Tenth Amendment)	Brandeis, Butler, Cardozo, Hughes, McReynolds, Roberts, Stone, Sutherland, Van Devanter	
United States v. Butler (January 6, 1936)	Agricultural Adjustment Act (taxing and spending power violations)	Butler, Hughes, McReynolds, Roberts, Sutherland, Van Devanter	Brandeis, Cardozo, Stone
Carter v. Carter Coal Co. (May 18, 1936)	Bituminous Coal Conservation Act (a regulation of intrastate commerce; improper delegation of congressional power)	Butler, McReynolds, Roberts, Sutherland, Van Devanter	Brandeis, Cardozo, Hughes, Stone
Ashton v. Cameron County District Court (May 25, 1936)	Municipal Bankruptcy Act (Tenth Amendment; Fifth Amendment property rights)	Butler, McReynolds, Roberts, Sutherland, Van Devanter	Brandeis, Cardozo, Hughes, Stone

like the Schechter company, the chickens had reached their state of final destination and became a part of intrastate commerce. Also consistent with *E. C. Knight* was the justices' conclusion that the poultry slaughter business had only an indirect effect on interstate commerce.

Through the remaining months of 1935 and into 1936, the Court continued to strike down federal legislation designed to cope with the Depression. In some cases the Court found the statutes defective for violating the federal taxing and spending power or for depriving individuals of their right to property without due process of law, topics covered in later chapters. But throughout this period, the Court was concerned with congressional actions that went beyond constitutional authority to regulate interstate commerce. Congress could not constitutionally legislate local business activity, such as manufacturing, processing, or refining, unless that activity had a direct effect on interstate commerce. The Court supported congressional regulation when the commerce was in movement from one state to another, but, as demonstrated in *Schechter*, the justices were unwilling to allow Congress to act on commerce after it had completed its interstate journey. *Schechter* examined when interstate commerce ends; in May 1936, with its decision in **Carter v. Carter Coal Company**, the Court taught the administration a lesson in when interstate commerce begins.

Congress passed the Bituminous Coal Conservation Act in August 1935, following the *Schechter* decision. This law replaced the NIRA coal codes, which had been reasonably effective in bringing some stability to the depressed coal industry. The new act called for establishing a commission empowered to develop regulations regarding fair competition, production, wages, hours, and labor relations. The commission included representatives from the coal producers, coal miners, and the public. To fund the program, Congress imposed a tax at the mines of 15 percent of the value of the coal produced. As was not the case with the NIRA codes, compliance with the new code regulations was voluntary. There was, however, an incentive for joining the program: companies that participated were given a rebate of 90 percent of the taxes levied by the act.

James W. Carter and other shareholders urged their company, Carter Coal, not to participate in the program. The board of directors did not want to join, but it believed that the company could not afford to pay the 15 percent tax and forgo the participation rebate. Carter and the stockholders sued to prevent the company from joining the program on the ground that the Coal Act was unconstitutional. Of Carter's several attacks on the law, the most deadly was the charge that coal mining was not interstate commerce.

By a 5–4 vote the justices struck down the law. The majority held that coal mining was not interstate commerce because the activity occurred within a single state. The stream of commerce doctrine was inapplicable because the movement of the coal to other states had not yet begun. Furthermore, the justices concluded that the production of coal did not have a direct effect on interstate commerce. For these reasons, the Court invalidated federal regulation of coal mining. But *Carter v. Carter Coal* was to be Roosevelt's last major defeat at the hands of the Four Horsemen and their allies.

The Court-Packing Plan

The Court entered its summer recess in 1936 having completed a year and a half of dealing with Roosevelt's legislative program and striking down several of the New Deal's most significant programs. The Four Horsemen constituted a solid bloc, and in important cases they could count on the support of at least one other member—usually Roberts. Roosevelt was understandably frustrated with what he viewed as the Court's obstructionism; he was also impatient that no vacancies had occurred that he might fill with appointees sympathetic to the New Deal.

The national elections took center stage in fall 1936, with little doubt that Roosevelt would be reelected and that the Democrats would continue to control Congress. The only question was how big the margin was going to be. Roosevelt won by a landslide, capturing 98 percent of the electoral votes. His Republican opponent, Alf Landon of Kansas, carried only Maine and Vermont. The congressional elections were another triumph for the Democrats. When the legislature reconvened in early 1937, they controlled approximately 80 percent of the seats in both houses. With such an impressive mandate from the people and such strong party support in Congress, Roosevelt was willing to proceed with his planned attack on the Court. If no vacancies on the Supreme Court occurred naturally, Roosevelt would try to create some.

On February 5, 1937, the president announced his plan to reorganize the federal court system. Among other proposals, the president asked Congress to authorize the creation of one new seat on the Court for every justice who had attained the age of seventy but remained in active service. These expanded positions would have an upper limit of six, bringing the potential size of the Court to a maximum of fifteen. At the time of his proposal, six sitting justices were older than seventy. If Roosevelt could appoint six New Deal advocates to the Court, they probably could attract the votes of at least two others and form a majority that would give constitutional approval to the president's programs. Although Roosevelt attempted to justify his proposal on the ground that the advanced age of several sitting justices called for the addition of younger, more vigorous colleagues, everyone saw the plan for what it was—an attempt to pack the Court.

The reaction was not favorable.[5] Public opinion polls taken during the course of the debate over the plan

---

[5] See Gregory A. Caldeira, "Public Opinion and the U.S. Supreme Court: FDR's Court-Packing Plan," *American Political Science Review* 81 (December 1987): 1139–1153.

On March 9, 1937, President Franklin D. Roosevelt delivered a Fireside Chat, proposing to expand the size of the U.S. Supreme Court. Frustrated that the justices had struck down significant portions of his New Deal programs, he argued that the Court needed younger justices with "a present-day sense of the Constitution."

revealed that at no time did a majority of Americans support Roosevelt's proposal. Members of the organized bar were overwhelmingly opposed. Even with large Democratic majorities in both houses of Congress, Roosevelt had difficulty selling his proposal to the legislature. Chief Justice Hughes wrote a public letter criticizing the proposal to Senator Burton Wheeler of Montana, a leader of Democrats opposing the president.[6] The press expressed sharp disapproval. In spite of the general support the people gave Roosevelt and the New Deal, they did not appreciate his tampering with the structure of government to get his way.

---

[6]The letter, dated March 21, 1937, is reprinted in Joan Biskupic and Elder Witt, eds., *Guide to the U.S. Supreme Court*, 3rd ed. (Washington, DC: Congressional Quarterly, 1997), 1039–1040.

The Switch in Time That Saved Nine

The battle in Congress over the president's plan was closely fought.[7] A continuation of the confrontation was averted in large measure by the actions of the Supreme Court itself. On March 29 the Court signaled that changes were in the making. The first indication was the 5–4 decision in *West Coast Hotel v. Parrish* (1937), which upheld the validity of a Washington State law regulating wages and working conditions for women and children. Although this case involved a state law rather than a

---

[7]See William E. Leuchtenburg, "The Origins of Franklin D. Roosevelt's 'Court-Packing' Plan," in *Supreme Court Review 1966*, ed. Philip B. Kurland (Chicago: University of Chicago Press, 1966), 347–400; and Leuchtenburg, *Franklin D. Roosevelt and the New Deal, 1932–1940* (New York: Harper & Row, 1963).

federal statute and focused on a Fourteenth Amendment issue rather than the commerce clause, it had great significance. The voting coalitions on the Court had changed. Justice Roberts, so long an ally of the Four Horsemen, deserted the conservatives and voted with the liberal bloc to approve the legislation. Just months earlier Roberts had voted with the conservatives in a 5–4 decision striking down a New York law that was nearly a carbon copy of the one he now approved.[8]

Two weeks later Roberts proved that his *West Coast Hotel* vote was not an aberration. On April 12 the Court issued its ruling in *National Labor Relations Board v. Jones & Laughlin Steel Corporation*. Once again Roberts joined Hughes, Brandeis, Cardozo, and Stone to form a majority, this time upholding a major piece of New Deal legislation. This decision is among the most significant economic rulings handed down during the twentieth century. In it the Court announced a break from the past and ushered in a new era in the constitutional relationship between the government and the economy.

National Labor Relations Board v. Jones & Laughlin Steel Corporation

301 U.S. 1 (1937)
http://caselaw.findlaw.com/us-supreme-court/301/1.html
Vote: 5 (Brandeis, Cardozo, Hughes, Roberts, Stone)
 4 (Butler, McReynolds, Sutherland, Van Devanter)

OPINION OF THE COURT: *Hughes*

DISSENTING OPINION: *McReynolds*

In 1935 Congress passed the National Labor Relations Act, more commonly known as the Wagner Act. The purpose of the legislation was to help workers achieve gains in wages and working conditions through the collective bargaining process. The act's primary aim was to protect the rights of employees to organize and join labor unions and to provide a means for the enforcement of those rights. The law authorized the creation of the National Labor Relations Board (NLRB), which was empowered to hear complaints of unfair labor practices and impose certain corrective measures. The act was based on the power of Congress to regulate interstate commerce and on the assertion that labor unrest and strikes caused interruptions in such commerce that Congress had the right to prevent.

Jones & Laughlin was one of the nation's largest steel producers. Its operations were fully integrated, extending into many

---

[8] *Morehead v. New York ex rel. Tipaldo* (1936).

states and involving every aspect of steel production, from mining through production and distribution. Complaints were filed against the company for engaging in unfair labor practices at its plant in Aliquippa, Pennsylvania. The charges included discriminating against workers who wanted to join a labor union. The NLRB ruled against the company and ordered it to reinstate ten workers who had been dismissed because of their union activities. The company refused, claiming that the National Labor Relations Act was unconstitutional. Steel production facilities, according to the company, were engaged in a manufacturing activity that the Supreme Court declared to be intrastate commerce and thus outside the regulatory authority of Congress. The lower courts, applying existing Supreme Court precedent, ruled in favor of the company, and the NLRB appealed.

MR. CHIEF JUSTICE HUGHES DELIVERED THE OPINION OF THE COURT.

The scope of the Act.—The Act is challenged in its entirety as an attempt to regulate all industry, thus invading the reserved powers of the States over their local concerns. It is asserted that the references in the Act to interstate and foreign commerce are colorable at best; that the Act is not a true regulation of such commerce or of matters which directly affect it but on the contrary has the fundamental object of placing under the compulsory supervision of the federal government all industrial labor relations within the nation. . . .

If this conception of terms, intent and consequent inseparability were sound, the Act would necessarily fall by reason of the limitation upon the federal power which inheres in the constitutional grant, as well as because of the explicit reservation of the Tenth Amendment. The authority of the federal government may not be pushed to such an extreme as to destroy the distinction, which the commerce clause itself establishes, between commerce "among the several States" and the internal concerns of a State. That distinction between what is national and what is local in the activities of commerce is vital to the maintenance of our federal system. . . .

We think it clear that the National Labor Relations Act may be construed so as to operate within the sphere of constitutional authority. The jurisdiction conferred upon the Board, and invoked in this instance, is found in §10 (a), which provides:

> "Sec. 10 (a). The Board is empowered, as hereinafter
> provided, to prevent any person from engaging
> in any unfair labor practice (listed in section 8)
> affecting commerce." The critical words of this
> provision, prescribing the limits of the Board's
> authority in dealing with the labor practices, are
> "affecting commerce." The Act specifically defines the
> "commerce" to which it refers (§2 (6)):

"The term 'commerce' means trade, traffic, commerce, transportation, or communication among the several States, or between the District of Columbia or any Territory of the United States and any State or other Territory, or between any foreign country and any State, Territory, or the District of Columbia, or within the District of Columbia or any Territory, or between points in the same State but through any other State or any Territory or the District of Columbia or any foreign country."

There can be no question that the commerce thus contemplated by the Act (aside from that within a Territory or the District of Columbia) is interstate and foreign commerce in the constitutional sense. The Act also defines the term "affecting commerce" (§2 (7)):

"The term 'affecting commerce' means in commerce, or burdening or obstructing commerce or the free flow of commerce or having led or tending to lead to a labor dispute burdening or obstructing commerce or the free flow of commerce."

This definition is one of exclusion as well as inclusion. The grant of authority to the Board does not purport to extend to the relationship between all industrial employees and employers. Its terms do not impose collective bargaining upon all industry regardless of effects upon interstate and foreign commerce. It purports to reach only what may be deemed to burden or obstruct that commerce and, thus qualified, it must be construed as contemplating the exercise of control within constitutional bounds. It is a familiar principle that acts which directly burden or obstruct interstate or foreign commerce, or its free flow, are within the reach of the congressional power. Acts having that effect are not rendered immune because they grow out of labor disputes. It is the effect upon commerce, not the source of the injury, which is the criterion. Whether or not particular action does affect commerce in such a close and intimate fashion as to be subject to federal control, and hence to lie within the authority conferred upon the Board, is left by the statute to be determined as individual cases arise. We are thus to inquire whether in the instant case the constitutional boundary has been passed. . . .

The application of the Act to employees engaged in production.—The principle involved.—Respondent says that whatever may be said of employees engaged in interstate commerce, the industrial relations and activities in the manufacturing department of respondent's enterprise are not subject to federal regulation. The argument rests upon the proposition that manufacturing in itself is not commerce.

The Government [argued that] various parts of respondent's enterprise are . . . interdependent and as thus involve[e] "a great movement of iron ore, coal and limestone along well-defined paths to the steel mills. . . . It is urged that these activities constitute a "stream" or "flow" of commerce, of which the Aliquippa

manufacturing plant is the focal point, and that industrial strife at that point would cripple the entire government. . . .

We do not find it necessary to determine whether these features of defendant's business [are the] "stream of commerce" cases. . . . The congressional authority to protect interstate commerce from burdens and obstructions is not limited to transactions which can be deemed to be an essential part of a "flow" of interstate or foreign commerce. Burdens and obstructions may be due to injurious action springing from other sources. The fundamental principle is that the power to regulate commerce is the power to enact "all appropriate legislation" for "its protection and advancement"; to adopt measures "to promote its growth and insure its safety"; "to foster, protect, control and restrain." That power is plenary and may be exerted to protect interstate commerce "no matter what the source of the dangers which threaten it."

Although activities may be intrastate in character when separately considered, if they have such a close and substantial relation to interstate commerce that their control is essential or appropriate to protect that commerce from burdens and obstructions, Congress cannot be denied the power to exercise that control. . . .

It is thus apparent that the fact that the employees here concerned were engaged in production is not determinative. The question remains as to the effect upon interstate commerce of the labor practice involved. . . .

Effects of the unfair labor practice in respondent's enterprise.— . . . In view of respondent's far-flung activities, it is idle to say that the effect would be indirect or remote. It is obvious that it would be immediate and might be catastrophic. We are asked to shut our eyes to the plainest facts of our national life and to deal with the question of direct and indirect effects in an intellectual vacuum. Because there may be but indirect and remote effects upon interstate commerce in connection with a host of local enterprises throughout the country, it does not follow that other industrial activities do not have such a close and intimate relation to interstate commerce as to make the presence of industrial strife a matter of the most urgent national concern. When industries organize themselves on a national scale, making their relation to interstate commerce the dominant factor in their activities, how can it be maintained that their industrial labor relations constitute a forbidden field into which Congress may not enter when it is necessary to protect interstate commerce from the paralyzing consequences of industrial war? We have often said that interstate commerce itself is a practical conception. It is equally true that interferences with that commerce must be appraised by a judgment that does not ignore actual experience.

Experience has abundantly demonstrated that the recognition of the right of employees to self-organization and to have representatives of their own choosing for the purpose of collective bargaining is often an essential condition of industrial peace. Refusal to confer and negotiate has been one of the most prolific causes of strife. This is such an outstanding fact in the history of labor disturbances that it is a proper subject of judicial notice and requires no citation of instances. . . .

These questions have frequently engaged the attention of Congress and have been the subject of many inquiries. The steel industry is one of the great basic industries of the United States, with ramifying activities affecting interstate commerce at every point. The Government aptly refers to the steel strike of 1919–1920 with its far-reaching consequences. The fact that there appears to have been no major disturbance in that industry in the more recent period did not dispose of the possibilities of future and like dangers to interstate commerce which Congress was entitled to foresee and to exercise its protective power to forestall. It is not necessary again to detail the facts as to respondent's enterprise. Instead of being beyond the pale, we think that it presents in a most striking way the close and intimate relation which a manufacturing industry may have to interstate commerce and we have no doubt that Congress had constitutional authority to safeguard the right of respondent's employees to self-organization and freedom in the choice of representatives for collective bargaining. . . .

Reversed.

MR. JUSTICE MCREYNOLDS DELIVERED THE FOLLOWING DISSENTING OPINION IN THE CASES PRECEDING.

MR. JUSTICE VAN DEVANTER, MR. JUSTICE SUTHERLAND, MR. JUSTICE BUTLER and I are unable to agree with the decisions just announced. . . .

The Constitution still recognizes the existence of states with indestructible powers; the Tenth Amendment was supposed to put them beyond controversy.

We are told that Congress may protect the "stream of commerce" and that one who buys raw material without the state, manufactures it therein, and ships the output to another state is in that stream. Therefore it is said he may be prevented from doing anything which may interfere with its flow.

This . . . goes beyond the constitutional limitations heretofore enforced. If a man raises cattle and regularly delivers them to a carrier for interstate shipment, may Congress prescribe the conditions under which he may employ or discharge helpers on the ranch? The products of a mine pass daily into interstate commerce; many things are brought to it from other states. Are the owners and miners within the power of Congress in respect of the miners' tenure and discharge? May a mill owner be prohibited from closing his factory or discontinuing his business because so to do would stop the flow of products to and from his plant in interstate commerce? May employees in a factory be restrained from quitting work in a body because this will close the factory and thereby stop the flow

of commerce? May arson of a factory be made a Federal offense whenever this would interfere with such flow? If the business cannot continue with the existing wage scale, may Congress command a reduction? If the ruling of the Court just announced is adhered to, these questions suggest some of the problems certain to arise. . . .

That Congress has power by appropriate means, not prohibited by the Constitution, to prevent direct and material interference with the conduct of interstate commerce is settled doctrine. But the interference struck at must be direct and material, not some mere possibility contingent on wholly uncertain events; and there must be no impairment of rights guaranteed. . . .

It seems clear to us that Congress has transcended the powers granted.

The decisions in *West Coast Hotel v. Parrish* and *NLRB v. Jones & Laughlin Steel* took the energy out of Roosevelt's drive to pack the Court. It no longer appeared necessary, as the Court was now looking with greater approval at state and federal legislation aimed at correcting the failing economy. In addition, on May 18, 1937, Justice Van Devanter, a consistent foe of Roosevelt's New Deal programs, announced that he would retire from the Court at the end of the term. At long last the president would have an opportunity to put a justice of his own choosing on the Court.

Much has been said and written about Justice Roberts's change in position. At the time, it was described as "the switch in time that saved nine," because his move from the conservative to the liberal wing of the Court was largely responsible for killing the Court-packing plan and preserving the Court as a nine-justice institution. Such a characterization is not flattering for a judge, who is not supposed to make decisions on the basis of external political pressures. Nevertheless, it would certainly be understandable for a justice to rethink his or her views if the future of the Court as an institution were at stake.

More contemporary analyses of Roberts's switch assert that the notion that he caved in to the pressures of the president's plan is simplistic. Although the decision in *West Coast Hotel* was announced after Roosevelt sent his proposal to Congress, it was argued and initially voted upon weeks before the president made his plans public. Roosevelt had kept the Court-packing proposal carefully under wraps before he announced it, and there is little likelihood that the justices had advance knowledge of it. Furthermore, Owen Roberts was not a doctrinaire conservative. Although he joined the Court's right wing in several important decisions, he did not have the

Justice Owen Roberts. He cast critical votes in 1937 Supreme Court cases that expanded the authority of the federal government to regulate the economy.

Harris & Ewing/Library of Congress/Public domain/Wikimedia Commons

he had has something to do with it."[11] Whatever the reasons for his switch, it broke the conservatives' domination of the Court.

THE ERA OF EXPANSIVE COMMERCE CLAUSE JURISPRUDENCE

Van Devanter's retirement was followed over the next four years by the retirements of Justices Sutherland and Brandeis and the deaths of Justices Cardozo and Butler. By 1940 Franklin Roosevelt had appointed a majority of the sitting justices. And in 1941 Justice McReynolds, the last of the Four Horsemen, retired.

With *NLRB v. Jones & Laughlin Steel* showing the way, the increasingly liberal Court upheld many New Deal programs. It also continued to expand the concept of interstate commerce. Gone were the old notions that production, manufacturing, mining, and processing were exclusively intrastate affairs with insufficient direct effects on interstate commerce to activate federal commerce powers. Precedents such as *E. C. Knight*, *Dagenhart*, *Panama Refining*, *Schechter Poultry*, and *Carter Coal* were substantially overruled, discredited, or severely limited.

Of all the cases during this period, two are considered among the Court's most important statements on congressional commerce power: *United States v. Darby* (1941) and *Wickard v. Filburn* (1942). Not only do they provide insight into the modern commerce clause doctrine, but they also serve to illustrate how far the Court had moved from its pre-1937 idea of interstate commerce. As you read *Darby*, keep in mind decisions such as *Hammer v. Dagenhart*, in which the Court struck down an act prohibiting the shipment in interstate commerce of products made by children. Regulating child labor, the Court reasoned, was not "expressly" delegated to the federal government and so, by virtue of the Tenth Amendment, belonged to the states. As you compare *Wickard* to earlier rulings, recall that in *E. C. Knight* a sugar trust that controlled 98 percent of the nation's sugar refining was considered to be operating in intrastate commerce. And in *Carter v. Carter Coal* the entire coal mining industry was said to be outside the power of Congress to regulate interstate commerce. How do these industries compare with Roscoe Filburn's farm?

laissez-faire zeal of the Four Horsemen. In fact, Roberts had voted on many occasions in support of state efforts to combat economic problems.[9] Some observers now conclude that Roberts's change of position was primarily a matter of his growing disenchantment with the hard-line conservative view and that he followed "his sound judicial intuition to a well-reasoned position in keeping with the public interest."[10] As for Roberts's own explanation, he maintained traditional judicial silence. When asked in a 1946 interview why he had altered his position, he deflected the question by responding, "Who knows what causes a judge to decide as he does? Maybe the breakfast

---

[9]See, for example, his opinion for the Court in *Nebbia v. New York* (1934).

[10]Merlo J. Pusey, "Justice Roberts' 1937 Turnaround," in *Yearbook of the Supreme Court Historical Society* (Washington, DC: Supreme Court Historical Society, 1983), 107.

---

[11]Quoted in ibid., 106.

United States v. Darby

312 U.S. 100 (1941)

http://caselaw.findlaw.com/us-supreme-court/312/100.html
Vote: 8 (Black, Douglas, Frankfurter, Hughes, Murphy, Reed,
    Roberts, Stone)
    0

OPINION OF THE COURT: *Stone*

In 1938 Congress, under its power to regulate interstate commerce, enacted a major piece of New Deal legislation, the Fair Labor Standards Act (FLSA). It provided that all employers "engaged in interstate commerce, or in the production of goods for that commerce" must pay all their employees a minimum wage of twenty-five cents per hour and not permit employees to work longer than forty-four hours per week without paying them one and one-half times their regular pay. In November 1939 the federal government sought and obtained an indictment against Fred W. Darby for violating the FLSA. The indictment alleged that Darby, the owner of a lumber company, was engaged in the production and manufacturing of goods shipped out of state, but that he had not abided by either of the FLSA's principal pay requirements.

Darby did not dispute the charges but invoked the logic of *Hammer v. Dagenhart* and other pre-1937 cases. The government responded with legal and pragmatic arguments consistent with the new commerce clause precedents set in *NLRB v. Jones Laughlin Steel* (1937) and subsequent rulings.

MR. JUSTICE STONE DELIVERED THE OPINION OF THE COURT.

The two principal questions raised by the record in this case are, first, whether Congress has constitutional power to prohibit the shipment in interstate commerce of lumber manufactured by employees whose wages are less than a prescribed minimum or whose weekly hours of labor at that wage are greater than a prescribed maximum [Section 15(1)], and, second, whether it has power to prohibit the employment of workmen in the production of goods "for interstate commerce" at other than prescribed wages and hours [Section 15(a)(2)]. . . .

The prohibition of shipment of the proscribed goods in interstate commerce.

Section 15(a)(1) prohibits, and the indictment charges, the shipment in interstate commerce, of goods produced for interstate commerce by employees whose wages and hours of employment do not conform to the requirements of the Act. [T]he only question arising under the commerce clause with respect to such shipments is whether Congress has the constitutional power to prohibit them.

While manufacture is not, of itself, interstate commerce, the shipment of manufactured goods interstate is such commerce, and the prohibition of such shipment by Congress is indubitably a regulation of the commerce. The power to regulate commerce is the power "to prescribe the rule by which commerce is governed." *Gibbons v. Ogden.* It extends not only to those regulations which aid, foster and protect the commerce, but embraces those which prohibit it. It is conceded that the power of Congress to prohibit transportation in interstate commerce includes noxious articles, *Lottery Case, Hoke v. United States* . . ., kidnapped persons and articles, such as intoxicating liquor or convict made goods, traffic in which is forbidden or restricted by the laws of the state of destination.

But it is said that the present prohibition falls within the scope of none of these categories; that, while the prohibition is nominally a regulation of the commerce, its motive or purpose is regulation of wages and hours of persons engaged in manufacture, the control of which has been reserved to the states. . . . [It is said that] under the guise of a regulation of interstate commerce, [Congress] undertakes to regulate wages and hours within the state contrary to the policy of the state which has elected to leave them unregulated.

The power of Congress over interstate commerce "is complete in itself, may be exercised to its utmost extent, and acknowledges no limitations other than are prescribed in the Constitution." *Gibbons v. Ogden.* That power can neither be enlarged nor diminished by the exercise or nonexercise of state power. Congress, following its own conception of public policy concerning the restrictions which may appropriately be imposed on interstate commerce, is free to exclude from the commerce articles whose use in the states for which they are destined it may conceive to be injurious to the public health, morals or welfare, even though the state has not sought to regulate their use.

Such regulation is not a forbidden invasion of state power merely because either its motive or its consequence is to restrict the use of articles of commerce within the states of destination, and is not prohibited unless by other Constitutional provisions. It is no objection to the assertion of the power to regulate interstate commerce that its exercise is attended by the same incidents which attend the exercise of the police power of the states.

The motive and purpose of the present regulation are plainly to make effective the Congressional conception of public policy that interstate commerce should not be made the instrument of competition in the distribution of goods produced under substandard labor conditions, which competition is injurious to the commerce and to the states from and to which the commerce flows. The motive and purpose of a regulation of interstate commerce are matters for the legislative judgment upon the exercise of which the Constitution places no restriction, and over which the courts are given no control. . . .

In the more than a century which has elapsed since the decision of *Gibbons v. Ogden,* these principles of constitutional interpretation have been so long and repeatedly recognized by this

Court as applicable to the Commerce Clause that there would be little occasion for repeating them now were it not for the decision of this Court twenty-two years ago in *Hammer v. Dagenhart.* In that case, it was held by a bare majority of the Court, over the powerful and now classic dissent of Mr. Justice Holmes setting forth the fundamental issues involved, that Congress was without power to exclude the products of child labor from interstate commerce. The reasoning and conclusion of the Court's opinion there cannot be reconciled with the conclusion which we have reached, that the power of Congress under the Commerce Clause is plenary to exclude any article from interstate commerce subject only to the specific prohibitions of the Constitution.

Hammer v. Dagenhart has not been followed. The distinction on which the decision was rested, that Congressional power to prohibit interstate commerce is limited to articles which in themselves have some harmful or deleterious property—a distinction which was novel when made and unsupported by any provision of the Constitution—has long since been abandoned. . . .

The conclusion is inescapable that *Hammer v. Dagenhart* was a departure from the principles which have prevailed in the interpretation of the Commerce Clause both before and since the decision, and that such vitality, as a precedent, as it then had, has long since been exhausted. It should be, and now is, overruled.

Validity of the wage and hour requirements.

Section 15(a)(2) [requires] employers to conform to the wage and hour provisions with respect to all employees engaged in the production of goods for interstate commerce. As appellee's employees are not alleged to be "engaged in interstate commerce," the validity of the prohibition turns on the question whether the employment, under other than the prescribed labor standards, of employees engaged in the production of goods for interstate commerce is so related to the commerce, and so affects it, as to be within the reach of the power of Congress to regulate it. . . .

The obvious purpose of the Act was not only to prevent the interstate transportation of the proscribed product, but to stop the initial step toward transportation, production with the purpose of so transporting it. Congress was not unaware that most manufacturing businesses shipping their product in interstate commerce make it in their shops without reference to its ultimate destination, and then, after manufacture, select some of it for shipment interstate and some intrastate, according to the daily demands of their business, and that it would be practically impossible, without disrupting manufacturing businesses, to restrict the prohibited kind of production to the particular pieces of lumber, cloth, furniture or the like which later move in interstate, rather than intrastate, commerce.

There remains the question whether such restriction on the production of goods for commerce is a permissible exercise of the commerce power. The power of Congress over interstate commerce is not confined to the regulation of commerce among the states.

It extends to those activities intrastate which so affect interstate commerce or the exercise of the power of Congress over it as to make regulation of them appropriate means to the attainment of a legitimate end, the exercise of the granted power of Congress to regulate interstate commerce. *See McCulloch v. Maryland.*

While this Court has many times found state regulation of interstate commerce, when uniformity of its regulation is of national concern, to be incompatible with the Commerce Clause even though Congress has not legislated on the subject, the Court has never implied such restraint on state control over matters intrastate not deemed to be regulations of interstate commerce or its instrumentalities even though they affect the commerce. In the absence of Congressional legislation on the subject, state laws which are not regulations of the commerce itself or its instrumentalities are not forbidden, even though they affect interstate commerce.

But it does not follow that Congress may not, by appropriate legislation, regulate intrastate activities where they have a substantial effect on interstate commerce. A recent example is the National Labor Relations Act for the regulation of employer and employee relations in industries in which strikes, induced by unfair labor practices named in the Act, tend to disturb or obstruct interstate commerce. *See National Labor Relations Board v. Jones & Laughlin Steel Corp.* But, long before the adoption of the National Labor Relations Act, this Court had many times held that the power of Congress to regulate interstate commerce extends to the regulation through legislative action of activities intrastate which have a substantial effect on the commerce or the exercise of the Congressional power over it. In such legislation, Congress has sometimes left it to the courts to determine whether the intrastate activities have the prohibited effect on the commerce, as in the Sherman Act. . . . In passing on the validity of legislation of the class last mentioned, the only function of courts is to determine whether the particular activity regulated or prohibited is within the reach of the federal power.

Congress having by the present Act adopted the policy of excluding from interstate commerce all goods produced for the commerce which do not conform to the specified labor standards, it may choose the means reasonably adapted to the attainment of the permitted end even though they involve control of intrastate activities. Such legislation has often been sustained with respect to powers other than the commerce power granted to the national government when the means chosen, although not themselves within the granted power, were nevertheless deemed appropriate aids to the accomplishment of some purpose within an admitted power of the national government. A familiar like exercise of power is the regulation of intrastate transactions which are so commingled with or related to interstate commerce that all must be regulated if the interstate commerce is to be effectively controlled. *Shreveport Case.*

We think also that §15(a)(2), now under consideration, is sustainable independently of §15(a)(1), which prohibits shipment or transportation of the proscribed goods. As we have said, the evils aimed at by the Act are the spread of substandard labor conditions through the use of the facilities of interstate commerce for competition by the goods so produced with those produced under the prescribed or better labor conditions, and the consequent dislocation of the commerce itself caused by the impairment or destruction of local businesses by competition made effective through interstate commerce. The Act is thus directed at the suppression of a method or kind of competition in interstate commerce which it has, in effect, condemned as "unfair," . . . made effective through interstate commerce.

The Sherman Act and the National Labor Relations Act are familiar examples of the exertion of the commerce power to prohibit or control activities wholly intrastate because of their effect on interstate commerce. . . .

The means adopted by §15(a)(2) for the protection of interstate commerce by the suppression of the production of the condemned goods for interstate commerce is so related to the commerce, and so affects it, as to be within the reach of the commerce power. Congress, to attain its objective in the suppression of nationwide competition in interstate commerce by goods produced under substandard labor conditions, has made no distinction as to the volume or amount of shipments in the commerce or of production for commerce by any particular shipper or producer. It recognized that, in present day industry, competition by a small part may affect the whole, and that the total effect of the competition of many small producers may be great. The legislation, aimed at a whole, embraces all its parts.

So far as *Carter v. Carter Coal Co.* is inconsistent with this conclusion, its doctrine is limited in principle by the decisions under the Sherman Act and the National Labor Relations Act, which we have cited and which we follow.

Our conclusion is unaffected by the Tenth Amendment, which provides:

The powers not delegated to the United States by the Constitution, nor prohibited by it to the States, are reserved to the States respectively, or to the people.

The amendment states but a truism that all is retained which has not been surrendered. There is nothing in the history of its adoption to suggest that it was more than declaratory of the relationship between the national and state governments as it had been established by the Constitution before the amendment, or that its purpose was other than to allay fears that the new national government might seek to exercise powers not granted, and that the states might not be able to exercise fully their reserved powers.

From the beginning and for many years, the amendment has been construed as not depriving the national government of authority to resort to all means for the exercise of a granted power which are appropriate and plainly adapted to the permitted end. *McCulloch v. Maryland.* . . .

Reversed.

Wickard v. Filburn

317 U.S. 111 (1942)

http://caselaw.findlaw.com/us-supreme-court/317/111.html

Vote: 9 (Black, Byrnes, Douglas, Frankfurter, Jackson, Murphy, Reed, Roberts, Stone)

 0

OPINION OF THE COURT: *Jackson*

The 1938 Agricultural Adjustment Act, as amended, allowed the secretary of agriculture to establish production limits for various grains. Under these limits, acreage allotments were assigned to individual farmers. The purpose of the law was to stop wild swings in grain prices by eliminating surpluses and shortfalls.

Roscoe Filburn owned a small farm in Montgomery County, Ohio. For many years he raised dairy cattle and chickens, selling the milk, poultry, and eggs the farm produced. He also raised winter wheat on a small portion of his farm. He sold some of the wheat and used the rest to feed his cattle and chickens, make flour for home consumption, and produce seeds for the next planting.

In July 1940, Secretary of Agriculture Claude R. Wickard set the wheat production limits for the 1941 crop. Filburn was allotted 11.1 acres to be planted in wheat with a yield of 20.1 bushels per acre. He planted not only his allotted acres but also some other land to produce the wheat for home consumption. In total Filburn planted 23 acres in wheat, from which he harvested 239 bushels more than the government allowed him. For this excess planting Filburn was fined $117.11. He refused to pay the fine, claiming that Congress had exceeded its powers under the commerce clause by regulating the planting by an individual of wheat on his own property for on-farm consumption. The lower court ruled in Filburn's favor, and Secretary Wickard appealed.

MR. JUSTICE JACKSON DELIVERED THE OPINION OF THE COURT.

It is urged that under the Commerce Clause of the Constitution, Article I, §8, clause 3, Congress does not possess the power it has in this instance sought to exercise. The question would merit little consideration since our decision in *United States v. Darby* sustaining the federal power to regulate production of goods for commerce, except for the fact that this Act extends federal regulation to production not intended in any part for commerce but wholly for consumption on the farm. The Act includes a definition of "market" and its derivatives, so that as related to wheat, in addition to its conventional meaning, it also means to dispose of "by feeding (in any form) to poultry or livestock which, or the products of which, are sold, bartered, or exchanged, or to be so disposed of." Hence,

Roscoe Filburn, the Ohio farmer who unsuccessfully argued that Congress lacked the constitutional power to regulate the production of wheat intended for on-farm consumption.

marketing quotas not only embrace all that may be sold without penalty but also what may be consumed on the premises. Wheat produced on excess acreage is designated as "available for marketing" as so defined, and the penalty is imposed thereon. Penalties do not depend upon whether any part of the wheat, either within or without the quota, is sold or intended to be sold. The sum of this is that the Federal Government fixes a quota including all that the farmer may harvest for sale or for his own farm needs, and declares that wheat produced on excess acreage may neither be disposed of nor used except upon payment of the penalty, or except it is stored as required by the Act or delivered to the Secretary of Agriculture.

Appellee says that this is a regulation of production and consumption of wheat. Such activities are, he urges, beyond the reach of Congressional power under the Commerce Clause, since they are local in character, and their effects upon interstate commerce are at most "indirect." In answer the Government argues that the statute regulates neither production nor consumption, but only marketing; and, in the alternative, that if the Act does go beyond the regulation of marketing it is sustainable as a "necessary and proper" implementation of the power of Congress over interstate commerce.

The Government's concern lest the Act be held to be a regulation of production or consumption, rather than of marketing, is attributable to a few dicta and decisions of this Court which might be understood to lay it down that activities such as "production," "manufacturing," and "mining" are strictly "local" and, except in special circumstances which are not present here, cannot be regulated under the commerce power because their effects upon interstate commerce are, as matter of law, only "indirect." Even today, when this power has been held to have great latitude, there is no decision of this Court that such activities may be regulated where no part of the product is intended for interstate commerce or intermingled with the subjects thereof. We believe that a review of the course of decision under the Commerce Clause will make plain, however, that questions of the power of Congress are not to be decided by reference to any formula which would give controlling force to nomenclature such as "production" and "indirect" and foreclose consideration of the actual effects of the activity in question upon interstate commerce.

At the beginning Chief Justice Marshall described the federal commerce power with a breadth never yet exceeded. *Gibbons v. Ogden*. He made emphatic the embracing and penetrating nature of this power by warning that effective restraints on its exercise must proceed from political rather than from judicial processes.

For nearly a century, however, decisions of this Court under the Commerce Clause dealt rarely with questions of what Congress might do in the exercise of its granted power under the Clause, and almost entirely with the permissibility of state activity which it was claimed discriminated against or burdened interstate commerce. During this period there was perhaps little occasion for the affirmative exercise of the commerce power, and the influence of the Clause on American life and law was a negative one, resulting almost wholly from its operation as a restraint upon the powers of the states. In discussion and decision the point of reference, instead of being what was "necessary and proper" to the exercise by Congress of its granted power, was often some concept of sovereignty thought to be implicit in the status of statehood. Certain activities such as "production," "manufacturing," and "mining" were occasionally said to be within the province of state governments and beyond the power of Congress under the Commerce Clause.

It was not until 1887, with the enactment of the Interstate Commerce Act, that the interstate commerce power began to exert positive influence in American law and life. This first important federal resort to the commerce power was followed in 1890 by the Sherman Anti-Trust Act and, thereafter, mainly after 1903, by many others. These statutes ushered in new phases of adjudication, which required the Court to approach the interpretation of the Commerce Clause in the light of an actual exercise by Congress of its power thereunder.

When it first dealt with this new legislation, the Court adhered to its earlier pronouncements, and allowed but little scope to the power of Congress. *United States v. Knight Co.* These earlier pronouncements also played an important part in several of the five cases in which this Court later held that Acts of Congress under the Commerce Clause were in excess of its power.

Even while important opinions in this line of restrictive authority were being written, however, other cases called forth broader interpretations of the Commerce Clause destined to supersede the earlier ones, and to bring about a return to the principles first enunciated by Chief Justice Marshall in *Gibbons v. Ogden.* . . .

Whether the subject of the regulation in question was "production," "consumption," or "marketing" is . . . not material for purposes of deciding the question of federal power before us. That an activity is of local character may help in a doubtful case to determine whether Congress intended to reach it. The same consideration might help in determining whether in the absence of Congressional action it would be permissible for the state to exert its power on the subject matter, even though in so doing it to some degree affected interstate commerce. But even if appellee's activity be local and though it may not be regarded as commerce, it may still, whatever its nature, be reached by Congress if it exerts a substantial economic effect on interstate commerce, and this irrespective of whether such effect is what might at some earlier time have been defined as "direct" or "indirect." . . .

The effect of consumption of home-grown wheat on interstate commerce is due to the fact that it constitutes the most variable factor in the disappearance of the wheat crop. Consumption on the farm where grown appears to vary in an amount greater than 20 per cent of average production. The total amount of wheat consumed as food varies but relatively little, and use as seed is relatively constant.

The maintenance by government regulation of a price for wheat undoubtedly can be accomplished as effectively by sustaining or increasing the demand as by limiting the supply. The effect of the statute before us is to restrict the amount which may be produced for market and the extent as well to which one may forestall resort to the market by producing to meet his own needs. That appellee's own contribution to the demand for wheat may be trivial by itself is not enough to remove him from the scope of federal regulation where, as here, his contribution, taken together with that of many other similarly situated, is far from trivial.

It is well established by decisions of this Court that the power to regulate commerce includes the power to regulate the prices at which commodities in that commerce are dealt in and practices affecting such prices. One of the primary purposes of the Act in question was to increase the market price of wheat, and to that end to limit the volume thereof that could affect the market. It can hardly be denied that a factor of such volume and variability as home-consumed wheat would have a substantial influence on price and market conditions. This may arise because being in marketable condition such wheat overhangs the market and, if induced by rising prices, tends to flow into the market and check price increases. But

if we assume that it is never marketed, it supplies a need of the man who grew it which would otherwise be reflected by purchases in the open market. Homegrown wheat in this sense competes with wheat in commerce. The stimulation of commerce is a use of the regulatory function quite as definitely as prohibitions or restrictions thereon. This record leaves us in no doubt that Congress may properly have considered that wheat consumed on the farm where grown, if wholly outside the scheme of regulation, would have a substantial effect in defeating and obstructing its purpose to stimulate trade therein at increased prices. . . .

Reversed.

With the *Darby* and *Wickard* decisions, the Court entered a new era of commerce clause interpretation. No longer would the justices grapple with issues such as direct versus indirect effects or stream of commerce concerns. Under the modern interpretations very little commercial activity could be defined as purely intrastate. The justices made clear, as Stone wrote in *Darby*, that "[t]he power of Congress over interstate commerce is not confined to the regulation of commerce among the states. It extends to those activities intrastate which so affect interstate commerce or the exercise of the power of Congress over it as to make regulation of them appropriate means to the attainment of a legitimate end, the exercise of the granted power of Congress to regulate interstate commerce."

Why would the Court allow Congress to regulate activities that were purely local in nature when the commerce clause speaks only of activities "among the states"? Stone's invocation of the language of *McCulloch* provides the answer. For Congress to regulate the interstate activities, it may be "necessary and proper" for it to regulate the local activities. This, according to Stone, was the case in *Darby*, and according to Jackson it held in *Wickard*, too. If every farmer acted as Filburn did, it would affect demand for wheat, which, in turn, would have a substantial effect in "defeating and obstructing" the congressional regulatory scheme of stabilizing prices. As Jackson put it, that Filburn's "own contribution to the demand for wheat may be trivial by itself is not enough to remove him from the scope of federal regulation where, as here, his contribution, taken together with that of many other similarly situated, is far from trivial." Under this approach very little commercial activity could be defined as purely intrastate. For, as *Darby*, *Wickard*, and the commerce clause cases to come in the 1960s and 1970s suggest, as long as the local activities are part of a class of activities that *Congress decides* in the aggregate have a substantial effect on interstate commerce, Congress may regulate. Finally, as our emphasis on "Congress decides" suggests, no longer would the Court decide whether the local activities, taken in the aggregate, substantially affect interstate commerce in fact, but only whether Congress reasonably thinks it does (or whether it has a "rational basis" for so concluding, as more modern Courts have termed it). This approach sat comfortably with the Court's new approach to economic legislation, whether passed by Congress or by the states (*see chapter 10*).

Note, too, *Darby*'s return to the Court's approach in *Gibbons*, that the power of Congress over interstate commerce "is complete in itself, may be exercised to its utmost extent, and acknowledges no limitations other than are prescribed in the Constitution." To the *Darby* Court, Congress was free to use commerce power as a federal police power, excluding from "commerce articles whose use in the states for which they are destined it may conceive to be injurious to the public health, morals or welfare." A law falling into this category, as Stone wrote, is "not a forbidden invasion of state power merely because either its motive or its consequence is to restrict the use of articles of commerce within the states of destination, and is not prohibited unless by other constitutional provisions." But, to Justice Stone, other "constitutional provisions" do not include the Tenth Amendment. In contrast to the Court's earlier approach in *Hammer*, Stone wrote in *Darby* that the Tenth Amendment is not an enclave to which the litigants can turn when Congress is making constitutional use of its commerce power; it is but a "truism."

Taken together, these cases gave Congress substantial authority to regulate under the commerce clause without fear of the Court invalidating its law. Congress took great advantage of this new deference by enacting a vast number of laws regarding activities that earlier Courts might have considered outside the definition of interstate commerce and thus federal purview.

Many of these were in the economic realm, but with the expansive definition of interstate commerce that occurred after 1936 came a commensurate expansion of the federal police powers. These changes gave Congress sufficient power to combat social problems that it otherwise would have been unable to fight effectively.

Modern civil rights laws provide a good example. The constitutional protections against discrimination are found primarily in the equal protection clause of the Fourteenth Amendment and the due process clause of the Fifth, which have erected powerful barriers against invidious discrimination. But their exclusive target is discrimination perpetuated by the government. The words of the Fourteenth Amendment are clear: "Nor shall any state . . . deny to any person within its jurisdiction the equal protection of the laws." Nothing in the Fifth or Fourteenth Amendment prohibits discrimination by private parties. These amendments were not intended to prohibit a private citizen from being discriminatory, but only to bar discriminatory government action. Although the Fourteenth Amendment includes a clause giving Congress the authority to enforce the provision with appropriate legislation, the Supreme Court has ruled that such enforcement legislation may not extend beyond the scope of the amendment itself. Consequently, the amendment does not empower Congress to regulate private discriminatory behavior.

When the civil rights activists of the 1950s and 1960s campaigned for the elimination of discriminatory conditions, high on their list was the eradication of discrimination by private parties who operated public accommodations. The movement targeted the owners of hotels, restaurants, movie theaters, recreation areas, and transportation systems. With the decision in *Brown v. Board of Education* (1954), governments could no longer maintain laws mandating segregation of such facilities, but private operators could still impose discrimination on their own. In the South, where segregation was the way of life, no one expected the states to pass civil rights statutes prohibiting private parties from discriminating. Therefore, civil rights advocates pressured Congress to act.

Congress responded by enacting the Civil Rights Act of 1964, the most comprehensive legislation of its type ever passed. The act, as amended, is still the nation's strongest statute aimed at eliminating discrimination. The primary authority for passing this groundbreaking legislation, however, was not a clause in the Bill of Rights or one of the Civil War amendments, but the commerce clause. Because the Court had treated commerce clause legislation favorably since 1937, members of Congress had confidence that the Civil Rights Act would withstand a legal challenge. Opponents of the legislation argued that Congress had misused its power to regulate commerce by invoking it to justify a civil rights law. Obviously, they said, the framers, many of whom owned slaves, did not intend the power to regulate commerce among the states to be used to enact civil rights legislation.

Was Congress on solid ground in doing so? The primary test of the law's constitutionality was *Heart of Atlanta Motel, Inc. v. United States* (1964). As you read this case, note Justice Tom C. Clark's description of how racial discrimination has a negative impact on interstate commerce. Also note the Court's expansive view of interstate commerce and its conclusion that the commerce clause can be used to combat moral wrongs.

Heart of Atlanta Motel, Inc. v. United States

379 U.S. 241 (1964)
http://caselaw.findlaw.com/us-supreme-court/379/241.html
Oral arguments are available at https://www.oyez.org/
cases/1964/515
Vote: 9 (Black, Brennan, Clark, Douglas, Goldberg, Harlan,
Stewart, Warren, White)
0

OPINION OF THE COURT: *Clark*

CONCURRING OPINIONS: *Black, Douglas, Goldberg*

Title II of the 1964 Civil Rights Act in its original form prohibited discrimination on the basis of race, color, religion, or national origin by certain public accommodations that operated in or affected interstate commerce. The accommodations specifically included were as follows:

1. Inns, hotels, motels, or other lodging facilities of five rooms or more. Because they served the traveling public, these facilities were considered part of interstate commerce by definition.

2. Restaurants and cafeterias, if they served interstate travelers or if a substantial portion of their food or other products had moved in interstate commerce.

3. Motion picture houses, if they presented films that had moved in interstate commerce.

4. Any facility physically located within any of the other covered accommodations, which included operations such as hotel shops and theater snack bars.

The Heart of Atlanta Motel was a 216-room facility in Atlanta, Georgia, owned by a group of investors led by Moreton Rolleston Jr. Located near the commercial center of the city, it had easy access to two interstate highways and two major state roads. The motel advertised for business in national publications and maintained more than fifty billboards and highway signs around the state. Both the government and the motel agreed that the facility met the act's definition of a public accommodation in interstate commerce.

The motel admitted that prior to the enactment of the civil rights law it practiced a policy of racial discrimination. Furthermore, it acknowledged that it intended to continue its policy of not serving blacks. To secure its right to do so, the motel filed suit to have the 1964 Civil Rights Act declared unconstitutional.

MR. JUSTICE CLARK DELIVERED THE OPINION OF THE COURT.

THE BASIS OF CONGRESSIONAL ACTION

While the Act as adopted carried no congressional findings the record of its passage through each house is replete with evidence of the burdens that discrimination by race or color places upon interstate commerce. This testimony included the fact that our people have become increasingly mobile with millions of people of all races traveling from State to State; that Negroes in particular have been the subject of discrimination in transient accommodations, having to travel great distances to secure the same; that often they have been unable to obtain accommodations and have had to call upon friends to put them up overnight; and that these conditions had become so acute as to require the listing of available lodging for Negroes in a special guidebook which was itself "dramatic testimony to the difficulties" Negroes encounter in travel. These exclusionary practices were found to be nationwide, the Under Secretary of Commerce testifying that there is "no question that this discrimination in the North still exists to a large degree" and in the West and Midwest as well. This testimony indicated a qualitative as well as a quantitative effect on interstate travel by Negroes. The former was the obvious impairment of the Negro traveler's pleasure and convenience that resulted when he continually was uncertain of finding lodging. As for the latter, there was evidence that this uncertainty stemming from racial discrimination had the effect of discouraging travel on the part of a substantial portion of the Negro community. This was the conclusion not only of the Under Secretary of Commerce but also of the Administrator of the Federal Aviation Agency who wrote the Chairman of the Senate Commerce Committee that it was his "belief that air commerce is adversely affected by the denial to a substantial segment of the traveling public of adequate and desegregated public accommodations." We shall not burden this opinion with further details since the voluminous testimony presents overwhelming evidence that discrimination by hotels and motels impedes interstate travel.

THE POWER OF CONGRESS OVER INTERSTATE TRAVEL

The power of Congress to deal with these obstructions depends on the meaning of the Commerce Clause. Its meaning was first enunciated 140 years ago by the great Chief Justice John Marshall in *Gibbons v. Ogden* (1824), in these words:

"The subject to be regulated is commerce;
and . . . to ascertain the extent of the power, it

becomes necessary to settle the meaning of the word. The counsel for the appellee would limit it to traffic, to buying and selling, or the interchange of commodities . . . but it is something more: it is intercourse . . . between nations, and parts of nations, in all its branches, and is regulated by prescribing rules for carrying on that intercourse.

"To what commerce does this power extend? The constitution informs us, to commerce 'with foreign nations and among the several States, and with the Indian tribes.'

"It has, we believe, been universally admitted, that these words comprehend every species of commercial intercourse. . . . No sort of trade can be carried on . . . to which this power does not extend.

"The subject to which the power is next applied, is to commerce 'among the several States,' The word 'among' means intermingled." . . .

In short, the determinative test of the exercise of power by the Congress under the Commerce Clause is simply whether the activity sought to be regulated is "commerce which concerns more States than one" and has a real and substantial relation to the national interest. Let us now turn to this facet of the problem.

That the "intercourse" of which the Chief Justice spoke included the movement of persons through more States than one was settled as early as 1849, in the *Passenger Cases,* where Mr. Justice McLean stated: "That the transportation of passengers is a part of commerce is not now an open question." Again in 1913 Mr. Justice McKenna, speaking for the Court, said: "Commerce among the States, we have said, consists of intercourse and traffic between their citizens, and includes the transportation of persons and property. . . . Nor does it make any difference whether the transportation is commercial in character." . . .

The same interest in protecting interstate commerce which led Congress to deal with segregation in interstate carriers and the white-slave traffic has prompted it to extend the exercise of its power to gambling; to criminal enterprises; to deceptive practices in the sale of products; to fraudulent security transactions; to misbranding of drugs; to wages and hours; to members of labor unions; to crop control; to discrimination against shippers; to the protection of small business from injurious price cutting; to resale price maintenance; to professional football; and to racial discrimination by owners and managers of terminal restaurants.

That Congress was legislating against moral wrongs in many of these areas rendered its enactments no less valid. In framing Title II of this Act Congress was also dealing with what it considered a moral problem. But that fact does not detract from the overwhelming evidence of the disruptive effect that racial discrimination has had

on commercial intercourse. It was this burden which empowered Congress to enact appropriate legislation, and, given this basis for the exercise of its power, Congress was not restricted by the fact that the particular obstruction to interstate commerce with which it was dealing was also deemed a moral and social wrong.

It is said that the operation of the motel here is of a purely local character. But . . . the power of Congress to promote interstate commerce also includes the power to regulate the local incidents thereof, including local activities in both the States of origin and destination, which might have a substantial and harmful effect upon that commerce. One need only examine the evidence which we have discussed above to see that Congress may—as it has—prohibit racial discrimination by motels serving travelers, however "local" their operations may appear. . . .

We, therefore, conclude that the action of the Congress in the adoption of the Act as applied here to a motel which concededly serves interstate travelers is within the power granted it by the Commerce Clause of the Constitution, as interpreted by this Court for 140 years. It may be argued that Congress could have pursued other methods to eliminate the obstructions it found in interstate commerce caused by racial discrimination. But this is a matter of policy that rests entirely with the Congress not with the courts. How obstructions in commerce may be removed—what means are to be employed—is within the sound and exclusive discretion of the Congress. It is subject only to one caveat—that the means chosen by it must be reasonably adapted to the end permitted by the Constitution. We cannot say that its choice here was not so adapted. The Constitution requires no more.

Affirmed.

Employing the same sweeping language as the Court used in *Wickard* and especially *Darby,* Justice Clark's opinion gave Congress broad powers to use the commerce clause as authority to regulate moral wrongs that occur in interstate commerce. The Heart of Atlanta Motel complied with the Court's decision *(see Box 7-3),* and a new era of civil rights in public accommodations began.

With its decisions in *Heart of Atlanta,* along with *Wickard and Darby,* the Court affirmed Congress' efforts to turn the commerce clause into one of the most powerful weapons in the federal government's regulatory arsenal. Nonetheless, several individual justices occasionally expressed doubts about the expansiveness of the modern definitions of interstate commerce.

Justice Potter Stewart's dissent in *Perez v. United States* (1971) provides an example.[12] This case involved the Consumer Credit Protection Act, which Congress

---

[12]See also Justice Black's dissent in **Daniel v. Paul** (1969).

BOX 7-3

Aftermath . . . Heart of Atlanta Motel

The Heart of Atlanta Motel, built in 1956, was owned by a group of Atlanta investors. One of the co-owners was Moreton Rolleston Jr., a former lieutenant commander in the U.S. Navy and a longtime Atlanta lawyer. Rolleston was a strong supporter of racial segregation. It was no coincidence, therefore, that the Heart of Atlanta Motel refused to serve black customers or that the motel did not cooperate with a consortium of fourteen downtown hotels whose owners agreed in 1963 to accommodate conventions that included blacks.

When it appeared certain that Congress would pass the 1964 Civil Rights Act, Rolleston, who also served as the motel's attorney, prepared a lawsuit to challenge the act's constitutionality. He filed the suit just two hours after Lyndon Johnson signed the bill into law.

In August 1964, after losing in the district court, the owners complied with the court's ruling and began operating the motel on an integrated basis. At the same time, they pressed an appeal to the U.S. Supreme Court. Rolleston, arguing before the justices, claimed that the Civil Rights Act was an unconstitutional intrusion by the federal government into an area reserved to the states and a violation of the rights of business owners. When the Supreme Court unanimously upheld the law on December 14, 1964, Rolleston lamented, "The decision opens the frightful door to unlimited power of a centralized government in Washington, in which the individual citizen and his personal liberty are of no importance."

Several years later Rolleston bought out his fellow investors and became the motel's sole owner. In 1973 the motel was sold and razed. A large, modern hotel now occupies the land where the Heart of Atlanta Motel once stood.

Rolleston continued to practice law in Atlanta well into his eighties. In 2000 he was briefly a Republican candidate for the U.S. Senate. Seven years later, the Georgia Supreme Court disbarred the eighty-nine-

Moreton Rolleston Jr.

year-old Rolleston for abusing the legal process by excessive litigation in a property dispute that was ongoing for more than two decades. The legal battle included Rolleston's attempts to stop film producer and actor Tyler Perry from building a 30,000-square-foot mansion on a seventeen-acre riverfront parcel of land that Rolleston claimed to own, a claim that the courts repeatedly rejected. In addition, Rolleston lost a $5.4 million malpractice ruling in 1995, and he suffered a $4.1 million judgment in 1998. In defiance of the disbarment action, Rolleston pledged to continue practicing law.

Rolleston died on August 19, 2013, at the age of ninety-five.

Sources: Richard C. Cortner, *Civil Rights and Public Accommodations: The Heart of Atlanta Motel and McClung Cases* (Lawrence: University Press of Kansas, 2001); *Atlanta Journal-Constitution,* May 14, 1991; May 16, 1991; December 25, 1991; March 23, 1995; February 8, 1996; March 5, 1998; August 8, 2000; October 10, 2007; October 24, 2007.

passed under its commerce clause power to criminalize extortionate means to collect payments on loans. Congress based its use of the commerce clause on its conclusion that "loan sharks"—lenders who use threats of violence to ensure the repayment of loans—are in a class largely controlled by organized crime, which exerts an adverse effect on interstate commerce. Alcides Perez was convicted under the act for attempting to extort money from the owner of a butcher shop. Perez challenged the law, claiming that Congress may not use its commerce power to regulate purely local loan-sharking.

The Supreme Court disagreed. Writing for a majority of eight, Justice William O. Douglas began by setting out his understanding of what the Court had said about the reach of the commerce clause:

> The Commerce Clause reaches, in the main, three categories of problems. First, the use of channels of interstate or foreign commerce which Congress deems are being misused. Second, protection of the instrumentalities of interstate commerce. Third, those activities affecting commerce. It is with this last category that we are here concerned.

By "channels . . . being misused" Douglas meant, for example, using airline routes to ship stolen goods or interstate highways to transport people who have been kidnapped. (*Champion v. Ames*, the lottery case, provides another example.) The "instrumentalities" of interstate commerce include things (or even persons) that move in the channels of interstate commerce. Neither of these ideas is especially controversial.[13] The Court had long held that "transportation and its instrumentalities" are appropriate subjects of the commerce power.

The chief concerns in *Perez*, as in so many cases, are raised by Douglas's last category. How do we know whether an activity that seems local, such as the activity at issue here, affects commerce? For Douglas, the answer lay in the Court's post–New Deal decisions in *NLRB*, *Wickard*, and *Darby:* Congress had concluded that loan-sharking, although a purely local activity, had, by virtue of being part of a "class of activities," a substantial effect on interstate commerce, and that was enough to sustain the law.

Justice Stewart cast the lone dissent in the case. He agreed that Congress can use its commerce clause power to protect the instrumentalities and channels of commerce

and to regulate intrastate activities that have a substantial effect on interstate commerce. But he was concerned that under this law "a man can be convicted without any proof of interstate movement, of the use of the facilities of interstate commerce, or of facts showing that his conduct affected interstate commerce." He continued, "The Framers of the Constitution never intended that the National Government might define as a crime and prosecute such wholly local activity through the enactment of federal criminal laws." This power, in Stewart's view, belonged to the states unless Congress could "rationally have concluded that loan sharking is an activity with interstate attributes that distinguish it in some substantial respect from other local crime." In short, it was not enough for Stewart to say simply that loan-sharking has some interstate characteristics because "all crime is a national problem" and Congress cannot regulate "all crime."

Still, in spite of these occasional complaints that the Court had erased the distinction between inter- and intrastate commerce, the justices remained wedded to a broad interpretation of the congressional commerce power. The post–New Deal approach reflects Justice Cardozo's dissent in *Carter v. Carter Coal Co.*, in which he said the commerce power is "as broad as the need that evokes it."

LIMITS ON THE COMMERCE POWER: THE REPUBLICAN COURT ERA

That the Court remained loyal to this modern interpretation of the commerce power for six decades led constitutional scholars to conclude that it was "settled law." But, as we discussed in chapter 6, by the early 1990s changes in the Court's membership resulted in a shift in how the justices evaluated the state-federal relationship. And these changes had a direct impact on the justices' interpretation of the commerce clause. The new Republican majority had a more limited view of the breadth of the commerce power and a more respectful attitude toward the constitutional status of the states.

Even though it was clear that change was in the wind, the Court's decision in *United States v. Lopez* (1995) came as somewhat of a surprise. For the first time since the battles over the New Deal, the justices invalidated a federal statute as falling outside the authority granted to Congress by the commerce clause.[14]

---

[13]As Justice Scalia wrote in *Gonzales v. Raich* (2005), "The first two categories are self-evident, since they are the ingredients of interstate commerce itself. See *Gibbons v. Ogden* (1824)."

[14]In *National League of Cities* and *New York* (*see chapter 6*), the Court invalidated federal laws not because they were beyond Congress's power to regulate interstate commerce but because they violated the Tenth Amendment.

United States v. Lopez

514 U.S. 549 (1995)
http://caselaw.findlaw.com/us-supreme-court/514/549.html
*Oral arguments available at https://www.oyez.org/
cases/1994/93-1260*
Vote: 5 (Kennedy, O'Connor, Rehnquist, Scalia, Thomas)
4 (Breyer, Ginsburg, Souter, Stevens)

OPINION OF THE COURT: *Rehnquist*

CONCURRING OPINIONS: *Kennedy, Thomas*

DISSENTING OPINIONS: *Breyer, Souter, Stevens*

On March 10, 1992, Alfonso Lopez Jr. came to Edison High School carrying a concealed .38 caliber handgun and five rounds of ammunition. Acting on an anonymous tip, officials at the San Antonio school confronted the twelfth-grade student, and he admitted having the weapon. Lopez claimed that he had been given the gun by a person who instructed him to deliver it to another individual. The gun was to be used in gang-related activities. Lopez was arrested for violating the federal Gun-Free School Zones Act.

Lopez, who had no record of previous criminal activity, was convicted in federal district court and sentenced to six months in prison, two years of supervised release, and a $50 fine. His attorneys appealed to the Fifth Circuit Court of Appeals, claiming that Congress had no constitutional authority to pass the Gun-Free School Zones Act. Attorneys for the United States countered by arguing that the law was an appropriate exercise of congressional power to regulate interstate commerce. The appeals court held in favor of Lopez, and the government asked the Supreme Court to review that ruling.

Congress passed the Gun-Free School Zones Act—section 922(q) of chapter 18 of the United States Code—in 1990. In passing the act, Congress did not issue any findings showing a relationship between gun possession on school property and commerce. The federal government argued that such findings should not be required, and that it would be sufficient if Congress could reasonably conclude that gun-related violence in schools affects interstate commerce directly or indirectly. Lopez countered by arguing that the simple possession of a weapon on school grounds is not a commercial activity that reasonably falls under commerce clause jurisdiction. Furthermore, the regulation of crime and education are traditional areas of state, not federal, jurisdiction.

**CHIEF JUSTICE REHNQUIST DELIVERED
THE OPINION OF THE COURT.**

In the Gun-Free School Zones Act of 1990, Congress made it a federal offense "for any individual knowingly to possess a firearm at a place that the individual knows, or has reasonable cause to believe, is a school zone." The Act neither regulates a commercial activity nor contains a requirement that the possession be connected in any way to interstate commerce. We hold that the Act exceeds the authority of Congress "[t]o regulate Commerce . . . among the several States." . . .

We start with first principles. The Constitution creates a Federal Government of enumerated powers. As James Madison wrote, "[t]he powers delegated by the proposed Constitution to the federal government are few and defined. Those which are to remain in the State governments are numerous and indefinite." This constitutionally mandated division of authority "was adopted by the Framers to ensure protection of our fundamental liberties." *Gregory v. Ashcroft* (1991). . . .

. . . The Court, through Chief Justice Marshall, first defined the nature of Congress' commerce power in *Gibbons v. Ogden* (1824):

> "Commerce, undoubtedly, is traffic, but it is something
> more: it is intercourse. It describes the commercial
> intercourse between nations, and parts of nations, in
> all its branches, and is regulated by prescribing rules
> for carrying on that intercourse."

The commerce power "is the power to regulate; that is, to prescribe the rule by which commerce is to be governed. This power, like all others vested in Congress, is complete in itself, may be exercised to its utmost extent, and acknowledges no limitations, other than are prescribed in the constitution." Id. . . .

. . . [I]n the watershed case of *NLRB v. Jones & Laughlin Steel Corp.* (1937), the Court upheld the National Labor Relations Act against a Commerce Clause challenge, and in the process, departed from the distinction between "direct" and "indirect" effects on interstate commerce. The Court held that intrastate activities that "have such a close and substantial relation to interstate commerce that their control is essential or appropriate to protect that commerce from burdens and obstructions" are within Congress' power to regulate.

In *United States v. Darby* (1941), the Court upheld the Fair Labor Standards Act, stating:

> "The power of Congress over interstate commerce is
> not confined to the regulation of commerce among
> the states. It extends to those activities intrastate
> which so affect interstate commerce or the exercise
> of the power of Congress over it as to make regulation
> of them appropriate means to the attainment of a
> legitimate end, the exercise of the granted power of
> Congress to regulate interstate commerce."

In *Wickard v. Filburn,* the Court upheld the application of amendments to the Agricultural Adjustment Act of 1938 to the production and consumption of homegrown wheat. The *Wickard* Court explicitly rejected earlier distinctions between direct and indirect effects on interstate commerce, stating:

> "[E]ven if appellee's activity be local and though it may not be regarded as commerce, it may still, whatever its nature, be reached by Congress if it exerts a substantial economic effect on interstate commerce, and this irrespective of whether such effect is what might at some earlier time have been defined as 'direct' or 'indirect.'"

The *Wickard* Court emphasized that although Filburn's own contribution to the demand for wheat may have been trivial by itself, that was not "enough to remove him from the scope of federal regulation where, as here, his contribution, taken together with that of many others similarly situated, is far from trivial."

Jones & Laughlin Steel, Darby, and *Wickard* ushered in an era of Commerce Clause jurisprudence that greatly expanded the previously defined authority of Congress under that Clause. In part, this was a recognition of the great changes that had occurred in the way business was carried on in this country. Enterprises that had once been local or at most regional in nature had become national in scope. But the doctrinal change also reflected a view that earlier Commerce Clause cases artificially had constrained the authority of Congress to regulate interstate commerce.

But even these modern-era precedents which have expanded congressional power under the Commerce Clause confirm that this power is subject to outer limits. In *Jones & Laughlin Steel,* the Court warned that the scope of the interstate commerce power "must be considered in the light of our dual system of government and may not be extended so as to embrace effects upon interstate commerce so indirect and remote that to embrace them, in view of our complex society, would effectually obliterate the distinction between what is national and what is local and create a completely centralized government." See also *Darby* (Congress may regulate intrastate activity that has a "substantial effect" on interstate commerce); *Wickard* (Congress may regulate activity that "exerts a substantial economic effect on interstate commerce"). Since that time, the Court has heeded that warning and undertaken to decide whether a rational basis existed for concluding that a regulated activity sufficiently affected interstate commerce. . . .

Consistent with this structure, we have identified three broad categories of activity that Congress may regulate under its commerce power. First, Congress may regulate the use of the channels of interstate commerce. Second, Congress is empowered to regulate and protect the instrumentalities of interstate commerce, or persons or things in interstate commerce, even though the threat may come only from intrastate activities. Finally, Congress' commerce authority includes the power to regulate those activities having a substantial relation to interstate commerce.

Within this final category, admittedly, our case law has not been clear whether an activity must "affect" or "substantially affect" interstate commerce in order to be within Congress' power to regulate it under the Commerce Clause. We conclude, consistent with the great weight of our case law, that the proper test requires an analysis of whether the regulated activity "substantially affects" interstate commerce.

We now turn to consider the power of Congress, in the light of this framework, to enact §922(q). The first two categories of authority may be quickly disposed of: §922(q) is not a regulation of the use of the channels of interstate commerce, nor is it an attempt to prohibit the interstate transportation of a commodity through the channels of commerce; nor can §922(q) be justified as a regulation by which Congress has sought to protect an instrumentality of interstate commerce or a thing in interstate commerce. Thus, if §922(q) is to be sustained, it must be under the third category as a regulation of an activity that substantially affects interstate commerce.

First, we have upheld a wide variety of congressional Acts regulating intrastate economic activity where we have concluded that the activity substantially affected interstate commerce. . . . Where economic activity substantially affects interstate commerce, legislation regulating that activity will be sustained. . . .

Section 922(q) is a criminal statute that by its terms has nothing to do with "commerce" or any sort of economic enterprise, however broadly one might define those terms. Section 922(q) is not an essential part of a larger regulation of economic activity, in which the regulatory scheme could be undercut unless the intrastate activity were regulated. It cannot, therefore, be sustained under our cases upholding regulations of activities that arise out of or are connected with a commercial transaction, which viewed in the aggregate, substantially affects interstate commerce.

Second, §922(q) contains no jurisdictional element which would ensure, through case-by-case inquiry, that the firearm possession in question affects interstate commerce. For example, in *United States v. Bass* (1971), the Court interpreted former 18 U.S.C. §1202(a), which made it a crime for a felon to "receiv[e], posses[s], or transpor[t] in commerce or affecting commerce . . . any firearm." The Court interpreted the possession component of §1202(a) to require an additional nexus to interstate commerce both because the statute was ambiguous and because "unless Congress conveys its purpose clearly, it will not be deemed to have significantly changed the federal-state balance." . . . Unlike the statute in *Bass,* §922(q) has no express jurisdictional element which might limit its reach to a discrete set of firearm possessions that additionally have an explicit connection with or effect on interstate commerce.

Although as part of our independent evaluation of constitutionality under the Commerce Clause we of course consider legislative findings, and indeed even congressional committee findings, regarding effect on interstate commerce, the Government concedes that "[n]either the statute nor its legislative history contain[s] express congressional findings regarding the effects upon interstate commerce of gun possession in a school zone." We agree with the Government that Congress normally is not required to make formal findings as to the substantial burdens that an activity has on interstate commerce. But to the extent that congressional findings would enable us to evaluate the legislative judgment that the activity in question substantially affected interstate commerce, even though no such substantial effect was visible to the naked eye, they are lacking here. . . .

The Government's essential contention, *in fine,* is that we may determine here that §922(q) is valid because possession of a firearm in a local school zone does indeed substantially affect interstate commerce. The Government argues that possession of a firearm in a school zone may result in violent crime and that violent crime can be expected to affect the functioning of the national economy in two ways. First, the costs of violent crime are substantial, and, through the mechanism of insurance, those costs are spread throughout the population. Second, violent crime reduces the willingness of individuals to travel to areas within the country that are perceived to be unsafe. The Government also argues that the presence of guns in schools poses a substantial threat to the educational process by threatening the learning environment. A handicapped educational process, in turn, will result in a less productive citizenry. That, in turn, would have an adverse effect on the Nation's economic well-being. As a result, the Government argues that Congress could rationally have concluded that §922(q) substantially affects interstate commerce.

We pause to consider the implications of the Government's arguments. The Government admits, under its "costs of crime" reasoning, that Congress could regulate not only all violent crime, but all activities that might lead to violent crime, regardless of how tenuously they relate to interstate commerce. Similarly, under the Government's "national productivity" reasoning, Congress could regulate any activity that it found was related to the economic productivity of individual citizens: family law (including marriage, divorce, and child custody), for example. Under the theories that the Government presents in support of §922(q), it is difficult to perceive any limitation on federal power, even in areas such as criminal law enforcement or education where States historically have been sovereign. Thus, if we were to accept the Government's arguments, we are hard pressed to posit any activity by an individual that Congress is without power to regulate. . . .

Admittedly, a determination whether an intrastate activity is commercial or noncommercial may in some cases result in legal uncertainty. But, so long as Congress' authority is limited to those powers enumerated in the Constitution, and so long as those enumerated powers are interpreted as having judicially enforceable outer limits, congressional legislation under the Commerce Clause always will engender "legal uncertainty." . . .

These are not precise formulations, and in the nature of things they cannot be. But we think they point the way to a correct decision of this case. The possession of a gun in a local school zone is in no sense an economic activity that might, through repetition elsewhere, substantially affect any sort of interstate commerce. Respondent was a local student at a local school; there is no indication that he had recently moved in interstate commerce, and there is no requirement that his possession of the firearm have any concrete tie to interstate commerce.

To uphold the Government's contentions here, we would have to pile inference upon inference in a manner that would bid fair to convert congressional authority under the Commerce Clause to a general police power of the sort retained by the States. Admittedly, some of our prior cases have taken long steps down that road, giving great deference to congressional action. The broad language in these opinions has suggested the possibility of additional expansion, but we decline here to proceed any further. To do so would require us to conclude that the Constitution's enumeration of powers does not presuppose something not enumerated, and that there never will be a distinction between what is truly national and what is truly local. This we are unwilling to do.

For the foregoing reasons the judgment of the Court of Appeals is

Affirmed.

JUSTICE BREYER, WITH WHOM JUSTICE STEVENS, JUSTICE SOUTER, AND JUSTICE GINSBURG JOIN, DISSENTING.

The issue in this case is whether the Commerce Clause authorizes Congress to enact a statute that makes it a crime to possess a gun in, or near, a school. In my view, the statute falls well within the scope of the commerce power as this Court has understood that power over the last half century.

In reaching this conclusion, I apply three basic principles of Commerce Clause interpretation. First, the power to "regulate Commerce . . . among the several States" encompasses the power to regulate local activities insofar as they significantly affect interstate commerce. . . . I use the word "significant" because the word "substantial" implies a somewhat narrower power than recent precedent suggests. But, to speak of "substantial effect" rather than "significant effect" would make no difference in this case.

Second, in determining whether a local activity will likely have a significant effect upon interstate commerce, a court must consider, not the effect of an individual act (a single instance of gun possession), but rather the cumulative effect of all similar instances (i.e., the effect of all guns possessed in or near schools). . . .

Third, the Constitution requires us to judge the connection between a regulated activity and interstate commerce, not directly, but at one remove. Courts must give Congress a degree of leeway in determining the existence of a significant factual connection between the regulated activity and interstate commerce—both because the Constitution delegates the commerce power directly to Congress and because the determination requires an empirical judgment of a kind that a legislature is more likely than a court to make with accuracy. The traditional words "rational basis" capture this leeway. Thus, the specific question before us, as the Court recognizes, is not whether the "regulated activity sufficiently affected interstate commerce," but, rather, whether Congress could have had "*a rational basis*" for so concluding. . . .

Applying these principles to the case at hand, we must ask whether Congress could have had a *rational basis* for finding a significant (or substantial) connection between gun-related school violence and interstate commerce. . . .

As long as one views the commerce connection, not as a "technical legal conception," but as "a practical one," the answer to this question must be yes. . . .

For one thing, reports, hearings, and other readily available literature make clear that the problem of guns in and around schools is widespread and extremely serious. . . . Congress obviously could have thought that guns and learning are mutually exclusive. Congress could therefore have found a substantial educational problem—teachers unable to teach, students unable to learn—and concluded that guns near schools contribute substantially to the size and scope of that problem.

Having found that guns in schools significantly undermine the quality of education in our Nation's classrooms, Congress could also have found, given the effect of education upon interstate and foreign commerce, that gun-related violence in and around schools is a commercial, as well as a human, problem. Education, although far more than a matter of economics, has long been inextricably intertwined with the Nation's economy. . . .

The economic links I have just sketched seem fairly obvious. Why then is it not equally obvious, in light of those links, that a widespread, serious, and substantial physical threat to teaching and learning also substantially threatens the commerce to which that teaching and learning is inextricably tied? . . .

Specifically, Congress could have found that gun-related violence near the classroom poses a serious economic threat (1) to consequently inadequately educated workers who must endure low paying jobs, and (2) to communities and businesses that might (in today's "information society") otherwise gain, from a well-educated work force, an important commercial advantage, of a kind that location near a railhead or harbor provided in the past. . . . The violence-related facts, the educational facts, and the economic facts, taken together, make this conclusion rational. And, because under our case law, the sufficiency of the constitutionally necessary Commerce Clause link between a crime of violence and interstate

commerce turns simply upon size or degree, those same facts make the statute constitutional.

The majority's holding—that [the law] falls outside the scope of the Commerce Clause—creates three serious legal problems. First, the majority's holding runs contrary to modern Supreme Court cases that have upheld congressional actions despite connections to interstate or foreign commerce that are less significant than the effect of school violence. . . .

The second legal problem the Court creates comes from its apparent belief that it can reconcile its holding with earlier cases by making a critical distinction between "commercial" and noncommercial "transaction[s]." That is to say, the Court believes the Constitution would distinguish between two local activities, each of which has an identical effect upon interstate commerce, if one, but not the other, is "commercial" in nature. . . .

The third legal problem created by the Court's holding is that it threatens legal uncertainty in an area of law that, until this case, seemed reasonably well settled. . . .

. . . For these reasons, I would reverse the judgment of the Court of Appeals. Respectfully, I dissent.

Just how far-reaching was *United States v. Lopez*? How did it fit into the Court's evolving commerce clause jurisprudence? Some interpreted it quite narrowly, simply as a warning to Congress that it must justify its legislation by showing the relationship between the activities regulated and interstate commerce. Had Congress explicitly demonstrated that it was responding to the negative impact school violence has on the economy, they asserted, it is likely that the Court would have found no fault with the law. These commentators saw the decision as little more than a detour and not a full-scale retreat from the body of commerce clause jurisprudence that flows almost seamlessly from *NLRB v. Jones & Laughlin Steel Corporation* onward (the Tenth Amendment cases of *National League of Cities* and *New York v. United States* being the chief exceptions).

Others viewed the decision as more sweeping, a signal that the Court would no longer allow Congress to regulate whatever it wished on the ground that all activities somehow affect interstate commerce. These critics concluded that *Lopez* was not an isolated ruling; rather, it should be considered in conjunction with **New York v. United States** (1992) and *Printz v. United States* (1997) (*excerpted in chapter 6*)—other decisions in which a majority of the Court ruled against federal action that was seen as encroaching on the states.

The justices themselves seemed divided on what the case represented. In their concurring opinions, Justice Anthony M. Kennedy called *Lopez* a "limited holding," but Justice Clarence Thomas declared that it was time "to modify our Commerce Clause jurisprudence." The Court's 5–4 vote contributed additional uncertainty. Whether *Lopez* was an aberration or a signal that the Court was following Thomas's advice became clearer five years later, when the Court issued its decision in **United States v. Morrison**.

In *Morrison* (2000) the Court, by the same 5–4 voting split that occurred in *Lopez*, struck down the Violence Against Women Act of 1994. The majority found that Congress was without authority under the commerce clause to pass a criminal law against gender-motivated crimes of violence. Such crimes are in no sense economic activity. Therefore, the states, not the federal government, should exercise criminal law jurisdiction over such acts.

Morrison was quickly followed by *Jones v. United States* (2000), which held that a federal criminal statute against arson, passed pursuant to the commerce power, could not be applied to a man who tossed a Molotov cocktail into his cousin's house. Because the target of the arson was a private residence not used in any commercial activity, the Court concluded that Congress under the commerce clause had no authority to regulate.

The decisions in *Lopez, Morrison,* and *Jones,* taken together with other Rehnquist Court federalism and taxation decisions, clearly demonstrate that the justices had modified their commerce clause jurisprudence *(see Box 7-4)*. Following the New Deal revolution, the federal government was given wide latitude to regulate in the name of interstate commerce. But in more recent decisions the Court has cautioned that the commerce clause does not give Congress a blank check.

The importance of this evolution in doctrine remains to be seen. Although the Court has enunciated a revised interpretation of the commerce power, its application of that standard in no way resembles the breadth of the Court's attack on federal authority in the period prior to 1937. In fact, some of its decisions have been quite consistent with its earlier post–New Deal jurisprudence. Take, for example, *Gonzales v. Raich* (2005), a controversial ruling on the validity of state laws that allow the medical use of marijuana. Despite a vigorous attack from the dissenters, the majority applied the precedent of *Wickard v. Filburn* and other New Deal cases.

AP Images/Noah Berger

Angel Raich, shown here at a 2004 press conference, sued to block the U.S. attorney general from enforcing the federal Controlled Substances Act against her. Raich, suffering from a brain tumor and other serious medical conditions, used marijuana under California's Compassionate Use Act to combat her pain and discomfort.

AP Images/Rich Pedroncelli

Diane Monson joined Angel Raich in asking the Supreme Court to uphold California's medicinal marijuana law. Monson, under a physician's direction, regularly used marijuana to alleviate chronic back pain.

BOX 7-4

Major Stages in the Evolution of Interstate Commerce Clause Doctrine

Marshall Interpretation	
Gibbons v. Ogden (1824) Marshall opinion for a 6–0 Court	Commerce begins in one state and ends in another. It does not stop when the act of crossing a state border is completed. Commerce occurring within a state may be part of a larger interstate process.

Shreveport Doctrine	

Manufacturing Excluded from Interstate Commerce	
United States v. E. C. Knight Co. (1895) Fuller opinion for an 8–1 Court *Schechter Poultry v. United States* (1935) Hughes opinion for a 9–0 Court *Carter v. Carter Coal Co.* (1936) Sutherland opinion for a 5–4 Court	Manufacturing, processing, and mining activities are local by nature and not a part of interstate commerce. Their effect on interstate commerce is indirect. That an article is intended for interstate commerce does not make its manufacture part of interstate commerce. "Commerce succeeds to manufacture, and is not a part of it."

Modern Interpretation of Interstate Commerce	
NLRB v. Jones & Laughlin Steel Corp. (1937) Hughes opinion for a 5–4 Court	Congress may enact all appropriate legislation to protect, advance, promote, and ensure interstate commerce. "Although activities may be intrastate in character when separately considered, if they have such a close and substantial relation to interstate commerce that their control is essential or appropriate to protect that commerce from burdens and obstructions, Congress cannot be denied the power to exercise that control."
United States v. Darby (1941) Stone opinion for an 8–0 Court	"The power of Congress over interstate commerce is not confined to the regulation of commerce among the states. It extends to those intrastate activities that so affect interstate commerce, or the exercise of the power of Congress over it, as to make regulation of them an appropriate means to the attainment of a legitimate end, the exercise of the granted power of Congress to regulate interstate commerce."
Wickard v. Filburn (1942) Jackson opinion for a 9–0 Court	Even if an activity is local and not regarded as commerce, "it may still, whatever its nature, be reached by Congress if it exerts a substantial economic effect on interstate commerce, and this is irrespective of whether such effect is what might at some earlier time have been defined as 'direct' or 'indirect.' . . . That [an individual's] own contribution [to interstate commerce] may be trivial by itself is not enough to remove him from the scope of federal regulation where [his] contribution, taken together with that of many others similarly situated, is far from trivial."

(Continued)

(Continued)

Modern Interpretation of Interstate Commerce	
Lopez (see below) and *Gonzales v. Raich* (2005) Stevens opinion for a 6–3 Court	"In assessing the scope of Congress' authority under the Commerce Clause, we stress that the task before us is a modest one. We need not determine whether [the] activities, taken in the aggregate, substantially affect interstate commerce in fact, but only whether a 'rational basis' exists for so concluding."
Modern Commerce Power Limitations	
United States v. Lopez (1995) Rehnquist opinion for a 5–4 Court *United States v. Morrison* (2000) Rehnquist opinion for a 5–4 Court	Federal legislation is constitutionally suspect if it does not regulate an economic activity that, in the aggregate, substantially affects interstate commerce.
National Federation of Independent Business v. Sebelius (2012) Roberts opinion for a 5–4 Court	"The power to regulate commerce presupposes the existence of commercial activity to be regulated." Congress cannot compel individuals "to become active in commerce by purchasing a product," even if their failure to do so affects interstate commerce.

Gonzales v. Raich

545 U.S. 1 (2005)
http://caselaw.findlaw.com/us-supreme-court/545/1.html
Oral arguments available at https://www.oyez.org/
    cases/2004/03-1454
Vote: 6 (Breyer, Ginsburg, Kennedy, Scalia, Souter, Stevens)
    3 (O'Connor, Rehnquist, Thomas)

OPINION OF THE COURT: *Stevens*

OPINION CONCURRING IN THE JUDGMENT: *Scalia*

DISSENTING OPINIONS: *O'Connor, Thomas*

In 1996 California voters passed Proposition 215, commonly known as the Compassionate Use Act (CUA). The law allowed seriously ill state residents to use marijuana for medical purposes. The act also created an exemption from criminal prosecution for patients, physicians, and caregivers who cultivate and possess marijuana for medical reasons.

Californian Angel Raich suffered from more than ten serious and possibly life-threatening medical conditions, including an inoperable brain tumor. On the advice of her doctor she used marijuana

to help ease her suffering. Too ill to produce her own supply, Raich depended on two caregivers to grow and provide marijuana without charge.

Diane Monson, another California resident following her physician's advice, had been using marijuana in compliance with the CUA for five years to combat chronic spinal pain. She grew about six cannabis plants to maintain a supply of the drug.

In 2002 county deputy sheriffs and federal drug agents came to Monson's home. After an investigation, the local officials found no evidence of illegal activity under California law. The federal agents, however, concluded that Monson's possession of marijuana violated the federal Controlled Substances Act (CSA). They seized and destroyed her marijuana plants.

Raich and Monson sued Attorney General Alberto Gonzales and the head of the U.S. Drug Enforcement Administration to bar enforcement of the CSA to the extent that it prevented them from obtaining and possessing marijuana for medical purposes. The federal government claimed that its constitutional power to regulate commerce was sufficiently broad to regulate the use of the substance. Raich and Monson argued that the federal commerce power does not extend to the medical use of marijuana, a purely local and noncommercial activity regulated by state law. They further claimed that their marijuana plants were grown and processed only with water, nutrients, supplies, and equipment originating in California. The court of appeals ruled in favor of Raich and Monson, and the federal government asked the Supreme Court to reverse.

JUSTICE STEVENS DELIVERED THE OPINION OF THE COURT.

California is one of at least nine States that authorize the use of marijuana for medicinal purposes. The question presented in this case is whether the power vested in Congress by Article I, §8, of the Constitution "[t]o make all Laws which shall be necessary and proper for carrying into Execution" its authority to "regulate Commerce with foreign Nations, and among the several States" includes the power to prohibit the local cultivation and use of marijuana in compliance with California law. . . .

Respondents in this case do not dispute that passage of the CSA, as part of the Comprehensive Drug Abuse Prevention and Control Act, was well within Congress' commerce power. Nor do they contend that any provision or section of the CSA amounts to an unconstitutional exercise of congressional authority. Rather, respondents' challenge is actually quite limited; they argue that the CSA's categorical prohibition of the manufacture and possession of marijuana as applied to the intrastate manufacture and possession of marijuana for medical purposes pursuant to California law exceeds Congress' authority under the Commerce Clause. . . .

In assessing the validity of congressional regulation, none of our Commerce Clause cases can be viewed in isolation. As charted in considerable detail in *United States v. Lopez* [1995], our understanding of the reach of the Commerce Clause, as well as Congress' assertion of authority thereunder, has evolved over time. . . .

. . . [We have now] identified three general categories of regulation in which Congress is authorized to engage under its commerce power. First, Congress can regulate the channels of interstate commerce. *Perez v. United States* (1971). Second, Congress has authority to regulate and protect the instrumentalities of interstate commerce, and persons or things in interstate commerce. *Ibid.* Third, Congress has the power to regulate activities that substantially affect interstate commerce. *Ibid.; NLRB v. Jones & Laughlin Steel Corp.* (1937). Only the third category is implicated in the case at hand.

Our case law firmly establishes Congress' power to regulate purely local activities that are part of an economic "class of activities" that have a substantial effect on interstate commerce. See, *e.g., Perez* [*v. United States* (1971)]; *Wickard v. Filburn* (1942). As we stated in *Wickard,* "even if appellee's activity be local and though it may not be regarded as commerce, it may still, whatever its nature, be reached by Congress if it exerts a substantial economic effect on interstate commerce." We have never required Congress to legislate

with scientific exactitude. When Congress decides that the "'total incidence'" of a practice poses a threat to a national market, it may regulate the entire class. . . .

Our decision in *Wickard* is of particular relevance. . . .

Wickard . . . establishes that Congress can regulate purely intrastate activity that is not itself "commercial," in that it is not produced for sale, if it concludes that failure to regulate that class of activity would undercut the regulation of the interstate market in that commodity.

The similarities between this case and *Wickard* are striking. Like the farmer in *Wickard,* respondents are cultivating, for home consumption, a fungible commodity for which there is an established, albeit illegal, interstate market. . . . In *Wickard,* we had no difficulty concluding that Congress had a rational basis for believing that, when viewed in the aggregate, leaving home-consumed wheat outside the regulatory scheme would have a substantial influence on price and market conditions. Here too, Congress had a rational basis for concluding that leaving home-consumed marijuana outside federal control would similarly affect price and market conditions.

More concretely, one concern prompting inclusion of wheat grown for home consumption in the 1938 Act was that rising market prices could draw such wheat into the interstate market, resulting in lower market prices. The parallel concern making it appropriate to include marijuana grown for home consumption in the CSA is the likelihood that the high demand in the interstate market will draw such marijuana into that market. While the diversion of homegrown wheat tended to frustrate the federal interest in stabilizing prices by regulating the volume of commercial transactions in the interstate market, the diversion of homegrown marijuana tends to frustrate the federal interest in eliminating commercial transactions in the interstate market in their entirety. In both cases, the regulation is squarely within Congress' commerce power because production of the commodity meant for home consumption, be it wheat or marijuana, has a substantial effect on supply and demand in the national market for that commodity. . . .

In assessing the scope of Congress' authority under the Commerce Clause, we stress that the task before us is a modest one. We need not determine whether respondents' activities, taken in the aggregate, substantially affect interstate commerce in fact, but only whether a "rational basis" exists for so concluding. Given the enforcement difficulties that attend distinguishing between marijuana cultivated locally and marijuana grown elsewhere and concerns about diversion into illicit channels, we have no difficulty concluding that Congress had a rational basis for believing that failure to regulate the intrastate manufacture and possession of marijuana would leave a gaping hole in the CSA. Thus, as in *Wickard,* when it enacted comprehensive legislation to regulate the interstate market in a fungible commodity, Congress was acting well within its authority to "make all Laws which shall be necessary and proper" to "regulate Commerce . . . among the several States." That the regulation ensnares some purely intrastate activity is of no moment. As we have done many times before, we refuse to excise individual components of that larger scheme.

To support their contrary submission, respondents rely heavily on two of our more recent Commerce Clause cases. In their myopic focus, they overlook the larger context of modern-era Commerce Clause jurisprudence preserved by those cases. Moreover, even in the narrow prism of respondents' creation, they read those cases far too broadly. Those two cases, of course, are [*United States v.*] *Lopez* [1995] and [*United States v.*] *Morrison* [2000]. . . .

Unlike those at issue in *Lopez* and *Morrison,* the activities regulated by the CSA are quintessentially economic. "Economics" refers to "the production, distribution, and consumption of commodities." *Webster's Third New International Dictionary* 720 (1966). The CSA is a statute that regulates the production, distribution, and consumption of commodities for which there is an established, and lucrative, interstate market. Prohibiting the intrastate possession or manufacture of an article of commerce is a rational (and commonly utilized) means of regulating commerce in that product. . . . Because the CSA is a statute that directly regulates economic, commercial activity, our opinion in *Morrison* casts no doubt on its constitutionality. . . .

The exemption for cultivation by patients and caregivers can only increase the supply of marijuana in the California market. The likelihood that all such production will promptly terminate when patients recover or will precisely match the patients' medical needs during their convalescence seems remote; whereas the danger that excesses will satisfy some of the admittedly enormous demand for recreational use seems obvious. Moreover, that the national and international narcotics trade has thrived in the face of vigorous criminal enforcement efforts suggests that no small number of unscrupulous people will make use of the California exemptions to serve their commercial ends whenever it is feasible to do so. Taking into account the fact that California is only one of at least nine States to have authorized the medical use of marijuana, . . . Congress could have rationally concluded that the aggregate impact on the national market of all the transactions exempted from federal supervision is unquestionably substantial.

. . . Thus the case for the exemption comes down to the claim that a locally cultivated product that is used domestically rather than sold on the open market is not subject to federal regulation. Given the findings in the CSA and the undisputed magnitude of the commercial market for marijuana, our decisions in *Wickard v. Filburn* and the later cases endorsing its reasoning foreclose that claim. . . .

. . . [T]he judgment of the Court of Appeals must be vacated. The case is remanded for further proceedings consistent with this opinion.

It is so ordered.

JUSTICE O'CONNOR, WITH WHOM THE CHIEF JUSTICE AND JUSTICE THOMAS JOIN . . . , DISSENTING.

We enforce the "outer limits" of Congress' Commerce Clause authority not for their own sake, but to protect historic spheres of state sovereignty from excessive federal encroachment and thereby to maintain the distribution of power fundamental to our federalist system of government. One of federalism's chief virtues, of course, is that it promotes innovation by allowing for the possibility that "a single courageous State may, if its citizens choose, serve as a laboratory; and try novel social and economic experiments without risk to the rest of the country." *New State Ice Co. v. Liebmann* (1932) (Brandeis, J., dissenting).

This case exemplifies the role of States as laboratories. The States' core police powers have always included authority to define criminal law and to protect the health, safety, and welfare of their citizens. Exercising those powers, California (by ballot initiative and then by legislative codification) has come to its own conclusion about the difficult and sensitive question of whether marijuana should be available to relieve severe pain and suffering. Today the Court sanctions an application of the federal Controlled Substances Act that extinguishes that experiment, without any proof that the personal cultivation, possession, and use of marijuana for medicinal purposes, if economic activity in the first place, has a substantial effect on interstate commerce and is therefore an appropriate subject of federal regulation. In so doing, the Court announces a rule that gives Congress a perverse incentive to legislate broadly pursuant to the Commerce Clause—nestling questionable assertions of its authority into comprehensive regulatory schemes—rather than with precision. That rule and the result it produces in this case are irreconcilable with our decisions in *Lopez* and *Morrison*. . . .

The Court's definition of economic activity is breathtaking. It defines as economic any activity involving the production, distribution, and consumption of commodities. And it appears to reason that when an interstate market for a commodity exists, regulating the intrastate manufacture or possession of that commodity is constitutional either because that intrastate activity is itself economic, or because regulating it is a rational part of regulating its market. . . . [T]he Court's definition of economic activity for purposes of Commerce Clause jurisprudence threatens to sweep all of productive human activity into federal regulatory reach.

The Court uses a dictionary definition of economics to skirt the real problem of drawing a meaningful line between "what is national and what is local." It will not do to say that Congress may regulate noncommercial activity simply because it may have an effect on the demand for commercial goods, or because the noncommercial endeavor can, in some sense, substitute for commercial activity. Most commercial goods or services have some sort of privately producible analogue. Home care substitutes for daycare. Charades games substitute for movie tickets. Backyard or windowsill gardening substitutes for going to the supermarket. To draw the line wherever private activity affects the demand for market goods is to draw no line at all, and to declare everything economic. . . .

The Government has not overcome empirical doubt that the number of Californians engaged in personal cultivation, possession, and use of medical marijuana, or the amount of marijuana they produce, is enough to threaten the federal regime. Nor has it shown that Compassionate Use Act marijuana users have been or are realistically likely to be responsible for the drug's seeping into the market in a significant way. . . .

Relying on Congress' abstract assertions, the Court has endorsed making it a federal crime to grow small amounts of marijuana in one's own home for one's own medicinal use. This overreaching stifles an express choice by some States, concerned for the lives and liberties of their people, to regulate medical marijuana differently. If I were a California citizen, I would not have voted for the medical marijuana ballot initiative; if I were a California legislator I would not have supported the Compassionate Use Act. But whatever the wisdom of California's experiment with medical marijuana, the federalism principles that have driven our Commerce Clause cases require that room for experiment be protected in this case. For these reasons I dissent.

JUSTICE THOMAS, DISSENTING.

Respondents Diane Monson and Angel Raich use marijuana that has never been bought or sold, that has never crossed state lines, and that has had no demonstrable effect on the national market for marijuana. If Congress can regulate this under the Commerce Clause, then it can regulate virtually anything—and the Federal Government is no longer one of limited and enumerated powers. . . .

Even the majority does not argue that respondents' conduct is itself "Commerce among the several States." Monson and Raich neither buy nor sell the marijuana that they consume. They cultivate their cannabis entirely in the State of California—it never crosses state lines, much less as part of a commercial transaction. Certainly no evidence from the founding suggests that "commerce" included the mere possession of a good or some purely personal activity that did not involve trade or exchange for value. In the early days of the Republic, it would have been unthinkable that Congress could prohibit the local cultivation, possession, and consumption of marijuana. . . .

Moreover, even a Court interested more in the modern than the original understanding of the Constitution ought to resolve cases based on the meaning of words that are actually in the document. Congress is authorized to regulate "Commerce," and respondents' conduct does not qualify under any definition of that term. The majority's opinion only illustrates the steady drift away from the text of the Commerce Clause. There is an inexorable expansion from "'commerce,'" to "commercial" and "economic" activity, and

finally to all "production, distribution, and consumption" of goods or services for which there is an "established . . . interstate market." Federal power expands, but never contracts, with each new locution. The majority is not interpreting the Commerce Clause, but rewriting it. . . .

. . . I respectfully dissent.

The decision in *Raich* still allows federal agents to prosecute medical marijuana cases. But in October 2009 the Obama administration announced that it would no longer prosecute such cases *if* the individuals involved are in compliance with state law. When the Trump administration took office in 2017, the Justice Department announced that it would begin enforcing the federal law against marijuana possession and distribution. The president, however, quickly reversed that policy as it pertained to activities that are legal under state law. The decision of an increasing number of states, beginning with Colorado and Washington, to remove bans on recreational use of marijuana certainly widens the policy gap between the legalizing states and federal statutes. Clearly, under *Gonzales v. Raich* the federal government can enforce federal laws prohibiting the distribution and possession of marijuana no matter what state law provides. For the present, federal authorities have chosen not to prosecute such violations. Whether that nonenforcement policy will continue for the long term remains to be seen.

Raich demonstrates that *Lopez, Morrison,* and *Jones* should not be seen as a wholesale repudiation of commerce clause jurisprudence as it has developed since 1937. Rather, the six-justice majority in *Raich*, which included conservatives Scalia and Kennedy, held fast to the precedent set in *Wickard v. Filburn:* the production of commercially viable items, when considered in the aggregate, has a sufficiently substantial relationship with interstate commerce to trigger the use of congressional regulatory authority. But when Congress under the commerce clause attempts to regulate noneconomic activity (such as gun possession, rape, or arson) without showing that the regulation is a necessary part of a broader regulation of interstate commerce, it may impermissibly infringe on powers reserved for the states.

The justices were faced with a legal dispute in 2012 that required them to go well beyond the distinction between economic and noneconomic activity. In *National Federation of Independent Business v. Sebelius,* the Court considered whether Congress has the power to regulate economic *inactivity* that affects interstate commerce. At issue was the constitutionality of the Patient Protection and Affordable Care Act of 2010. The attacked legislation imposed comprehensive reforms on the nation's medical care and health insurance sectors. The law was exceptionally controversial and became a political issue that affected the 2010–2016 congressional and presidential elections. A core question in the case was whether Congress constitutionally can require unwilling individuals to purchase health insurance.

In deciding the case the justices had to consider congressional powers under the commerce clause, the necessary and proper clause, and the taxing and spending clauses, as well as important federalism questions. In the following excerpt, we provide the Court's analysis of congressional authority to act under the commerce clause and the necessary and proper clause. As you will see, the majority concludes that these constitutional provisions do not empower Congress to regulate commercial inactivity. In so ruling, the Roberts Court interpreted the commerce power rather narrowly. But the commerce clause ruling did not settle the case. As we will see in the next chapter, the health insurance purchase requirement, while not constitutional under the commerce power, was found to be a valid regulation under Congress's authority to tax and spend.

National Federation of Independent Business v. Sebelius

567 U.S. _____ (2012)
http://caselaw.findlaw.com/us-supreme-court/11-393.html
Oral arguments available at https://www.oyez.org/
cases/2011/11-393
Vote on the commerce clause challenge to the Affordable Care
Act:
5 (Alito, Kennedy, Roberts, Scalia, Thomas)
4 (Breyer, Ginsburg, Kagan, Sotomayor)

OPINION ANNOUNCING THE JUDGMENT OF THE COURT AND THE OPINION OF THE COURT: *Roberts*

OPINION CONCURRING IN PART AND DISSENTING IN PART: *Ginsburg*

JOINT OPINION CONCURRING ON THE COMMERCE CLAUSE ISSUE BUT DISSENTING FROM THE FINAL CASE OUTCOME: *Alito, Kennedy, Scalia, Thomas*

DISSENTING OPINION: *Thomas*

In 2010, Congress passed the Patient Protection and Affordable Care Act (ACA). The purpose of the law was to increase the number of Americans covered by health insurance and to decrease the cost of health care. The law was passed along partisan lines, with Democrats supporting the bill and Republicans opposed. The American public also was closely divided over the policies the act implemented. The legislation was quite complex, with the statute running to more than nine hundred pages in length. It introduced major changes in the health insurance industry, expanded insurance coverage and benefits, eliminated coverage limitations for preexisting conditions, and significantly enlarged Medicaid.

At the heart of the ACA was a requirement known as the "individual mandate" (also known as the "minimum coverage" requirement). This provision directed that most Americans purchase "minimum essential" health insurance coverage for themselves and their dependents if they did not receive such coverage from their employers. Those who failed to comply with this provision were required to make a "shared responsibility" payment to the federal government. The act provided that this "penalty" be paid to the Internal Revenue Service and "shall be assessed and collected in the same manner" as tax penalties. The mandate was intended to ensure that health costs were evenly distributed throughout the population and to prohibit individuals from refusing to buy health insurance until they developed medical conditions requiring treatment.

Almost immediately after President Obama signed the bill into law, a series of lawsuits were filed challenging the constitutionality of the ACA. The lower federal courts reached differing opinions on the validity of law. In order to resolve this conflict, the Supreme Court granted a petition to review a decision of the Eleventh Circuit Court of Appeals striking down portions of the law but allowing the balance of the statute to remain in effect. The appealed decision involved a suit initiated by the National Federation of Independent Business, twenty-six state governments, and several individuals against Kathleen Sebelius, the secretary of health and human services.

Challengers of the law argued that Congress exceeded its commerce clause powers by compelling individuals to purchase insurance when they may not wish to do so. Commercial inactivity, they argued, is not commerce. Secretary Sebelius responded that health care is an integral part of the national economy. Therefore, the commerce clause and the necessary and proper clause give Congress ample authority to enact a comprehensive health care law that includes an individual mandate. She asserted that the ACA was also a legitimate action under Congress's constitutional power to tax and spend. In another line of attack, the challengers claimed that the expansion of the federal Medicaid program unconstitutionally infringed on the powers of the states.

In the excerpted material appearing here, we focus exclusively on the question of whether the individual mandate provision can legitimately rest on Congress's power to regulate interstate commerce and the necessary and proper clause. In the next chapter we will return to this decision and highlight arguments related to the authority of Congress to tax and spend.

In our federal system, the National Government possesses only limited powers; the States and the people retain the remainder. Nearly two centuries ago, Chief Justice Marshall observed that "the question respecting the extent of the powers actually granted" to the Federal Government "is perpetually arising, and will probably continue to arise, as long as our system shall exist." *McCulloch v. Maryland* (1819). In this case we must again determine whether the Constitution grants Congress powers it now asserts, but which many States and individuals believe it does not possess. Resolving this controversy requires us to examine both the limits of the Government's power, and our own limited role in policing those boundaries.

The Federal Government "is acknowledged by all to be one of enumerated powers." Ibid. That is, rather than granting general authority to perform all the conceivable functions of government, the Constitution lists, or enumerates, the Federal Government's powers. Congress may, for example, "coin Money," "establish Post Offices," and "raise and support Armies." Art. I, §8, cls. 5, 7, 12. The enumeration of powers is also a limitation of powers, because "[t]he enumeration presupposes something not enumerated." *Gibbons v. Ogden* (1824). The Constitution's express conferral of some powers makes clear that it does not grant others. And the Federal Government "can exercise only the powers granted to it." *McCulloch.*

. . . If no enumerated power authorizes Congress to pass a certain law, that law may not be enacted, even if it would not violate any of the express prohibitions in the Bill of Rights or elsewhere in the Constitution.

. . . The Federal Government has expanded dramatically over the past two centuries, but it still must show that a constitutional grant of power authorizes each of its actions. See, e.g., *United States v. Comstock* (2010).

The same does not apply to the States, because the Constitution is not the source of their power. . . . The States thus can and do perform many of the vital functions of modern government—punishing street crime, running public schools, and zoning property for development, to name but a few—even though the Constitution's text does not authorize any government to do so. Our cases refer to this general power of governing, possessed by the States but not by the Federal Government, as the "police power." See, e.g., *United States v. Morrison* (2000). . . .

This case concerns . . . powers that the Constitution does grant the Federal Government, but which must be read carefully to avoid creating a general federal authority akin to the police power. The Constitution authorizes Congress to "regulate Commerce with foreign Nations, and among the several States, and with the Indian Tribes." Our precedents read that to mean that Congress may regulate "the channels of interstate commerce," "persons or things in interstate commerce," and "those activities that substantially affect interstate commerce." *Morrison.* The power over activities that substantially affect interstate commerce can be expansive. That power has been held to authorize federal regulation of such seemingly local matters as a farmer's decision to grow wheat for himself and his livestock, and a loan shark's extortionate collections from a neighborhood butcher shop. See *Wickard v. Filburn* (1942); *Perez v. United States* (1971). . . .

The reach of the Federal Government's enumerated powers is broader still because the Constitution authorizes Congress to "make all Laws which shall be necessary and proper for carrying into Execution the foregoing Powers." We have long read this provision to give Congress great latitude in exercising its powers: "Let the end be legitimate, let it be within the scope of the constitution, and all means which are appropriate, which are plainly adapted to that end, which are not prohibited, but consist with the letter and spirit of the constitution, are constitutional." *McCulloch.* . . .

Our permissive reading of these powers is explained in part by a general reticence to invalidate the acts of the Nation's elected leaders. . . .

Our deference in matters of policy cannot, however, become abdication in matters of law. "The powers of the legislature are defined and limited; and that those limits may not be mistaken, or forgotten, the constitution is written." *Marbury v. Madison* (1803). Our respect for Congress's policy judgments thus can never extend so far as to disavow restraints on federal power that the Constitution carefully constructed. . . . And there can be no question that it is the responsibility of this Court to enforce the limits on federal power by striking down acts of Congress that transgress those limits. *Marbury v. Madison.*

The questions before us must be considered against the background of these basic principles. . . .

The Government's . . . argument is that the individual mandate is a valid exercise of Congress's power under the Commerce Clause and the Necessary and Proper Clause. According to the Government, the health care market is characterized by a significant cost-shifting problem. Everyone will eventually need health care at a time and to an extent they cannot predict, but if they do not have insurance, they often will not be able to pay for it. Because state and federal laws nonetheless require hospitals to provide a certain degree of care to individuals without regard to their ability to pay, hospitals end up receiving compensation for only a portion of the services they provide. To recoup the losses, hospitals pass on the cost to insurers through higher rates, and insurers, in turn, pass on the cost to policy holders in the form of higher premiums. Congress estimated that the cost of uncompensated care raises family health insurance premiums, on average, by over $1,000 per year. . . .

The Government contends that the individual mandate is within Congress's power because the failure to purchase insurance "has a substantial and deleterious effect on interstate commerce" by creating the cost-shifting problem. . . .

Given its expansive scope, it is no surprise that Congress has employed the commerce power in a wide variety of ways to address the pressing needs of the time. But Congress has never attempted to rely on that power to compel individuals not engaged in commerce to purchase an unwanted product. Legislative novelty is not necessarily fatal; there is a first time for everything. But sometimes "the most telling indication of [a] severe constitutional problem . . . is the lack of historical precedent" for Congress's action. *Free Enterprise Fund v. Public Company Accounting Oversight Bd.* (2010). At the very least, we should "pause to consider the implications of the Government's arguments" when confronted with such new conceptions of federal power. *Lopez.*

The Constitution grants Congress the power to "regulate Commerce." The power to regulate commerce presupposes the existence of commercial activity to be regulated. If the power to "regulate" something included the power to create it, many of the provisions in the Constitution would be superfluous. For example, the Constitution gives Congress the power to "coin Money," in addition to the power to "regulate the Value thereof." And it gives Congress the power to "raise and support Armies" and to "provide and maintain a Navy," in addition to the power to "make Rules for the Government and Regulation of the land and naval Forces." If the power to regulate the armed forces or the value of money included the power to bring the subject of the regulation into existence, the specific grant of such powers would have been unnecessary. The language of the Constitution reflects the natural understanding that the power to regulate assumes there is already something to be regulated.

Our precedent also reflects this understanding. As expansive as our cases construing the scope of the commerce power have been, they all have one thing in common: They uniformly describe the power as reaching "activity." . . .

The individual mandate, however, does not regulate existing commercial activity. It instead compels individuals to become active in commerce by purchasing a product, on the ground that their failure to do so affects interstate commerce. Construing the Commerce Clause to permit Congress to regulate individuals precisely because they are doing nothing would open a new and potentially vast domain to congressional authority. Every day individuals do not do an infinite number of things. In some cases they decide not to do something; in others they simply fail to do it. Allowing Congress to justify federal regulation by pointing to the effect of inaction on commerce would bring countless decisions an individual could potentially make within the scope of federal regulation, and—under the Government's theory—empower Congress to make those decisions for him.

Applying the Government's logic to the familiar case of *Wickard v. Filburn* shows how far that logic would carry us from the notion of a government of limited powers. In *Wickard,* the Court famously upheld a federal penalty imposed on a farmer for growing wheat for consumption on his own farm. That amount of wheat caused the farmer to exceed his quota under a program designed to support the price of wheat by limiting supply. The Court rejected the farmer's argument that growing wheat for home consumption was beyond the reach of the commerce power. It did so on the ground that the farmer's decision to grow wheat for his own use allowed him to avoid purchasing wheat in the market. That decision, when considered in the aggregate along with similar decisions of others, would have had a substantial effect on the interstate market for wheat.

Wickard has long been regarded as "perhaps the most far reaching example of Commerce Clause authority over intrastate activity," *Lopez,* but the Government's theory in this case would go much further. . . . The farmer in *Wickard* was at least actively engaged in the production of wheat, and the Government could regulate that activity because of its effect on commerce. The Government's theory here would effectively override that limitation, by establishing that individuals may be regulated under the Commerce Clause whenever enough of them are not doing something the Government would have them do.

Indeed, the Government's logic would justify a mandatory purchase to solve almost any problem. To consider a different example in the health care market, many Americans do not eat a balanced diet. That group makes up a larger percentage of the total population than those without health insurance. The failure of that group to have a healthy diet increases health care costs, to a greater extent than the failure of the uninsured to purchase insurance. Those increased costs are borne in part by other Americans who must pay more, just as the uninsured shift costs to the insured. Congress addressed the insurance problem by ordering everyone to buy insurance. Under the Government's theory, Congress could address the diet problem by ordering everyone to buy vegetables.

People, for reasons of their own, often fail to do things that would be good for them or good for society. Those failures—joined with the similar failures of others—can readily have a substantial effect on interstate commerce. Under the Government's logic, that authorizes Congress to use its commerce power to compel citizens to act as the Government would have them act.

That is not the country the Framers of our Constitution envisioned. . . . Congress already enjoys vast power to regulate much of what we do. Accepting the Government's theory would give Congress the same license to regulate what we do not do, fundamentally changing the relation between the citizen and the Federal Government.

To an economist, perhaps, there is no difference between activity and inactivity; both have measurable economic effects on commerce. But the distinction between doing something and doing nothing would not have been lost on the Framers, who were "practical statesmen," not metaphysical philosophers. . . . The Framers gave Congress the power to regulate commerce, not to compel it, and for over 200 years both our decisions and Congress's actions have reflected this understanding. There is no reason to depart from that understanding now.

The Government sees things differently. It argues that because sickness and injury are unpredictable but unavoidable, "the uninsured as a class are active in the market for health care, which they regularly seek and obtain." The individual mandate "merely regulates how individuals finance and pay for that active participation—requiring that they do so through insurance, rather than through attempted self-insurance with the back-stop of shifting costs to others." . . .

The individual mandate's regulation of the uninsured as a class is, in fact, particularly divorced from any link to existing commercial activity. The mandate primarily affects healthy, often young adults who are less likely to need significant health care and have other priorities for spending their money. It is precisely because these individuals, as an actuarial class, incur relatively low health care costs that the mandate helps counter the effect of forcing insurance companies to cover others who impose greater costs than their premiums are allowed to reflect. If the individual mandate is targeted at a class, it is a class whose commercial inactivity rather than activity is its defining feature.

The Government, however, claims that this does not matter. The Government regards it as sufficient to trigger Congress's authority that almost all those who are uninsured will, at some unknown point in the future, engage in a health care transaction. . . .

The proposition that Congress may dictate the conduct of an individual today because of prophesied future activity finds no support in our precedent. . . .

Everyone will likely participate in the markets for food, clothing, transportation, shelter, or energy; that does not authorize Congress to direct them to purchase particular products in those or other markets today. The Commerce Clause is not a general license to regulate an individual from cradle to grave, simply because he will predictably engage in particular transactions. . . .

The Government says that health insurance and health care financing are "inherently integrated." But that does not mean the compelled purchase of the first is properly regarded as a regulation of the second. No matter how "inherently integrated" health insurance and health care consumption may be, they are not the same thing: They involve different transactions, entered into at different times, with different providers. And for most of those targeted by the mandate, significant health care needs will be years, or even decades, away. The proximity and degree of connection between the mandate and the subsequent commercial activity is too lacking to justify an exception of the sort urged by the Government. The individual mandate forces individuals into commerce precisely because they elected to refrain from commercial activity. Such a law cannot be sustained under a clause authorizing Congress to "regulate Commerce."

The Government next contends that Congress has the power under the Necessary and Proper Clause to enact the individual mandate because the mandate is an "integral part of a comprehensive scheme of economic regulation." . . .

The power to "make all Laws which shall be necessary and proper for carrying into Execution" the powers enumerated in the Constitution vests Congress with authority to enact provisions "incidental to the [enumerated] power, and conducive to its beneficial exercise." *McCulloch.* Although the Clause gives Congress authority to "legislate on that vast mass of incidental powers which must be involved in the constitution," it does not license the exercise of any "great substantive and independent power[s]" beyond those specifically enumerated. Instead, the Clause is "merely a declaration, for the removal of all uncertainty, that the means of carrying into execution those [powers] otherwise granted are included in the grant." *Kinsella v. United States ex rel. Singleton* (1960).

As our jurisprudence under the Necessary and Proper Clause has developed, we have been very deferential to Congress's determination that a regulation is "necessary." We have thus upheld laws that are "'convenient, or useful' or 'conducive' to the authority's 'beneficial exercise.'" *Comstock.* But we have also carried out our responsibility to declare unconstitutional those laws that undermine the structure of government established by the Constitution. Such laws, which are not "consist[ent] with the letter and spirit of the constitution," *McCulloch,* are not "proper [means] for carrying into Execution" Congress's enumerated powers. Rather, they are, "in the words of The Federalist, 'merely acts of usurpation' which 'deserve to be treated as such.'" *Printz v. United States* (1997).

Applying these principles, the individual mandate cannot be sustained under the Necessary and Proper Clause as an essential component of the insurance reforms. Each of our prior cases upholding laws under that Clause involved exercises of authority derivative of, and in service to, a granted power. For example, we have upheld provisions permitting continued confinement of those already in federal custody when they could not be safely released. *Comstock.* The individual mandate, by contrast, vests Congress with the extraordinary ability to create the necessary predicate to the exercise of an enumerated power.

This is in no way an authority that is "narrow in scope," *Comstock,* or "incidental" to the exercise of the commerce power, *McCulloch.* Rather, such a conception of the Necessary and Proper Clause would work a substantial expansion of federal authority. No longer would Congress be limited to regulating under the Commerce Clause those who by some preexisting activity bring themselves within the sphere of federal regulation. Instead, Congress could reach beyond the natural limit of its authority and draw within its regulatory scope those who otherwise would be outside of it. Even if the individual mandate is "necessary" to the Act's insurance reforms, such an expansion of federal power is not a "proper" means for making those reforms effective. . . .

Just as the individual mandate cannot be sustained as a law regulating the substantial effects of the failure to purchase health insurance, neither can it be upheld as a "necessary and proper" component of the insurance reforms. The commerce power thus does not authorize the mandate.

JUSTICE GINSBURG, WITH WHOM JUSTICE SOTOMAYOR JOINS, AND WITH WHOM JUSTICE BREYER AND JUSTICE KAGAN JOIN, . . . CONCURRING IN PART, CONCURRING IN THE JUDGMENT IN PART, AND DISSENTING IN PART.

Unlike The Chief Justice, . . . I would hold . . . that the Commerce Clause authorizes Congress to enact the minimum coverage provision. . . .

Since 1937, our precedent has recognized Congress' large authority to set the Nation's course in the economic and social welfare realm. See *United States v. Darby* (1941); *NLRB v. Jones & Laughlin Steel Corp.* (1937). The Chief Justice's crabbed reading of the Commerce Clause harks back to the era in which the Court routinely thwarted Congress' efforts to regulate the national economy in the interest of those who labor to sustain it. It is a reading that should not have staying power.

In enacting the Patient Protection and Affordable Care Act (ACA), Congress comprehensively reformed the national market for health-care products and services. By any measure, that market is immense. Collectively, Americans spent $2.5 trillion on health care in 2009, accounting for 17.6% of our Nation's economy. Within the next decade, it is anticipated, spending on health care will nearly double.

The health-care market's size is not its only distinctive feature. Unlike the market for almost any other product or service, the market for medical care is one in which all individuals inevitably participate. Virtually every person residing in the United States, sooner or later, will visit a doctor or other health-care professional. . . .

When individuals make those visits, they face another reality of the current market for medical care: its high cost. In 2010, on average, an individual in the United States incurred over $7,000 in health-care expenses. Over a lifetime, costs mount to hundreds of thousands of dollars. . . .

Although every U.S. domiciliary will incur significant medical expenses during his or her lifetime, the time when care will be needed is often unpredictable. . . .

To manage the risks associated with medical care—its high cost, its unpredictability, and its inevitability—most people in the United States obtain health insurance. . . .

Not all U.S. residents, however, have health insurance. In 2009, approximately 50 million people were uninsured, either by choice or, more likely, because they could not afford private insurance and did not qualify for government aid. As a group, uninsured individuals annually consume more than $100 billion in health-care services, nearly 5% of the Nation's total. Over 60% of those without insurance visit a doctor's office or emergency room in a given year.

The large number of individuals without health insurance, Congress found, heavily burdens the national health-care market. . . . Unlike markets for most products, however, the inability to pay for care does not mean that an uninsured individual will receive no care. Federal and state law, as well as professional obligations and embedded social norms, require hospitals and physicians to provide care when it is most needed, regardless of the patient's ability to pay.

As a consequence, medical-care providers deliver significant amounts of care to the uninsured for which the providers receive no payment. In 2008, for example, hospitals, physicians, and other health-care professionals received no compensation for $43 billion worth of the $116 billion in care they administered to those without insurance.

Health-care providers do not absorb these bad debts. Instead, they raise their prices, passing along the cost of uncompensated care to those who do pay reliably: the government and private insurance companies. In response, private insurers increase their premiums, shifting the cost of the elevated bills from providers onto those who carry insurance. The net result: Those with health insurance subsidize the medical care of those without it. As economists would describe what happens, the uninsured "free ride" on those who pay for health insurance.

The size of this subsidy is considerable. Congress found that the cost-shifting just described "increases family [insurance] premiums by on average over $1,000 a year." Higher premiums, in turn, render health insurance less affordable, forcing more people to go without insurance and leading to further cost-shifting. . . .

States cannot resolve the problem of the uninsured on their own. . . .

Aware that a national solution was required, . . . Congress enacted the ACA, a solution that retains a robust role for private insurers and state governments. To make its chosen approach work, however, Congress had to use some new tools, including a requirement that most individuals obtain private health insurance coverage. . . . [B]y employing these tools, Congress was able to achieve a practical, altogether reasonable, solution. . . .

. . . Congress passed the minimum coverage provision as a key component of the ACA to address an economic and social problem that has plagued the Nation for decades: the large number of U.S. residents who are unable or unwilling to obtain health insurance. Whatever one thinks of the policy decision Congress made, it was Congress' prerogative to make it. Reviewed with appropriate deference, the minimum coverage provision, allied to the guaranteed-issue and community-rating prescriptions, should survive measurement under the Commerce and Necessary and Proper Clauses.

The Commerce Clause, it is widely acknowledged, "was the Framers' response to the central problem that gave rise to the Constitution itself." Under the Articles of Confederation, the Constitution's precursor, the regulation of commerce was left to the States. This scheme proved unworkable, because the individual States, understandably focused on their own economic interests, often failed to take actions critical to the success of the Nation as a whole.

. . . The Framers' solution was the Commerce Clause, which, as they perceived it, granted Congress the authority to enact economic legislation "in all Cases for the general Interests of the Union, and also in those Cases to which the States are separately incompetent." . . .

Consistent with the Framers' intent, we have repeatedly emphasized that Congress' authority under the Commerce Clause is dependent upon "practical" considerations, including "actual experience." We afford Congress the leeway "to undertake to solve national problems directly and realistically."

Until today, this Court's pragmatic approach to judging whether Congress validly exercised its commerce power was guided by two familiar principles. First, Congress has the power to regulate economic activities "that substantially affect interstate commerce." *Gonzales v. Raich* (2005). This capacious power extends even to local activities that, viewed in the aggregate, have a substantial impact on interstate commerce.

Second, we owe a large measure of respect to Congress when it frames and enacts economic and social legislation. When appraising such legislation, we ask only (1) whether Congress had a "rational basis" for concluding that the regulated activity substantially affects interstate commerce, and (2) whether there is a "reasonable connection between the regulatory means selected and the asserted ends." In answering these questions, we presume the statute under review is constitutional and may strike it down only on a "plain showing" that Congress acted irrationally.

Straightforward application of these principles would require the Court to hold that the minimum coverage provision is proper Commerce Clause legislation. Beyond dispute, Congress had a rational basis for concluding that the uninsured, as a class, substantially affect interstate commerce. Those without insurance consume billions of dollars of health-care products and services each year. Those goods are produced, sold, and delivered largely by national and regional companies who routinely transact business across state lines. The uninsured also cross state lines to receive care. Some have medical emergencies while away from home. Others, when sick, go to a neighboring State that provides better care for those who have not prepaid for care.

Not only do those without insurance consume a large amount of health care each year; critically, as earlier explained, their inability to pay for a significant portion of that consumption drives up market prices, foists costs on other consumers, and reduces market efficiency and stability. Given these far-reaching effects on interstate commerce, the decision to forgo insurance is hardly inconsequential or equivalent to "doing nothing"; it is, instead, an economic decision Congress has the authority to address under the Commerce Clause.

The minimum coverage provision, furthermore, bears a "reasonable connection" to Congress' goal of protecting the health-care market from the disruption caused by individuals who fail to obtain insurance. By requiring those who do not carry insurance to pay a toll, the minimum coverage provision gives individuals a strong incentive to insure. This incentive, Congress had good reason to believe, would reduce the number of uninsured and, correspondingly, mitigate the adverse impact the uninsured have on the national health-care market.

Congress also acted reasonably in requiring uninsured individuals, whether sick or healthy, either to obtain insurance or to pay the specified penalty. As earlier observed, because every person is at risk of needing care at any moment, all those who lack insurance, regardless of their current health status, adversely affect the price of health care and health insurance. . . .

Rather than evaluating the constitutionality of the minimum coverage provision in the manner established by our precedents, The Chief Justice relies on a newly minted constitutional doctrine. The commerce power does not, The Chief Justice announces, permit Congress to "compe[l] individuals to become active in commerce by purchasing a product."

The Chief Justice's novel constraint on Congress' commerce power gains no force from our precedent and for that reason alone warrants disapprobation. But even assuming, for the moment, that Congress lacks authority under the Commerce Clause to "compel individuals not engaged in commerce to purchase an unwanted product," such a limitation would be inapplicable here. Everyone will, at some point, consume health-care products and services. Thus, if The Chief Justice is correct that an insurance-purchase requirement can be applied only to those who "actively" consume health care, the minimum coverage provision fits the bill. . . .

Our decisions . . . acknowledge Congress' authority, under the Commerce Clause, to direct the conduct of an individual today (the farmer in *Wickard,* stopped from growing excess wheat; the plaintiff in *Raich,* ordered to cease cultivating marijuana) because of a prophesied future transaction (the eventual sale of that wheat or marijuana in the interstate market). Congress' actions are even more rational in this case, where the future activity (the consumption of medical care) is certain to occur, the sole uncertainty being the time the activity will take place. . . .

For the reasons explained above, the minimum coverage provision is valid Commerce Clause legislation. When viewed as a component of the entire ACA, the provision's constitutionality becomes even plainer.

The Necessary and Proper Clause "empowers Congress to enact laws in effectuation of its [commerce] powe[r] that are not within its authority to enact in isolation." Hence, "[a] complex regulatory program . . . can survive a Commerce Clause challenge without a showing that every single facet of the program is independently and directly related to a valid congressional goal." "It is enough that the challenged provisions are an integral part of the regulatory program and that the regulatory scheme when considered as a whole satisfies this test."

Recall that one of Congress' goals in enacting the Affordable Care Act was to eliminate the insurance industry's practice of charging higher prices or denying coverage to individuals with preexisting medical conditions. The commerce power allows Congress to ban this practice, a point no one disputes.

Congress knew, however, that simply barring insurance companies from relying on an applicant's medical history would not work in practice. Without the individual mandate, Congress learned, guaranteed-issue and community-rating requirements would trigger an adverse-selection death-spiral in the health-insurance market: Insurance premiums would skyrocket, the number of uninsured would increase, and insurance companies would exit the market. When complemented by an insurance mandate, on the other hand, guaranteed issue and community rating would work as intended, increasing access to insurance and reducing uncompensated care. The minimum coverage provision is thus an "essential par[t] of a larger regulation of economic activity"; without the provision, "the regulatory scheme [w]ould be undercut." *Raich.* Put differently, the minimum coverage provision, together with the guaranteed-issue and community-rating requirements, is "'reasonably adapted' to the attainment of a legitimate end under the commerce power": the elimination of pricing and sales practices that take an applicant's medical history into account.

Asserting that the Necessary and Proper Clause does not authorize the minimum coverage provision, The Chief Justice focuses on the word "proper." A mandate to purchase health insurance is not "proper" legislation, The Chief Justice urges, because the command "undermine[s] the structure of government established by the Constitution." If long on rhetoric, The Chief Justice's argument is short on substance. . . .

The Chief Justice [does not] pause to explain *why* the power to direct either the purchase of health insurance or, alternatively, the payment of a penalty collectible as a tax is more far-reaching than other implied powers this Court has found meet under the Necessary and Proper Clause. These powers include the power to enact criminal laws; the power to imprison, including civil imprisonment, see, *e.g., Comstock;* and the power to create a national bank, see *McCulloch.*

In failing to explain why the individual mandate threatens our constitutional order, The Chief Justice disserves future courts. How is a judge to decide, when ruling on the constitutionality of a federal statute, whether Congress employed an "independent power," or merely a "derivative" one. Whether the power used is "substantive," or just "incidental"? The instruction The Chief Justice, in effect, provides lower courts: You will know it when you see it. . . .

In the early 20th century, this Court regularly struck down economic regulation enacted by the peoples' representatives in both the States and the Federal Government. See, e.g., *Carter Coal Co., Dagenhart, Lochner v. New York* (1905). The Chief Justice's Commerce Clause opinion, and even more so the joint dissenters' reasoning, bear a disquieting resemblance to those long-overruled decisions.

JOINT OPINION OF JUSTICE SCALIA, JUSTICE KENNEDY, JUSTICE THOMAS, AND JUSTICE ALITO, DISSENTING.

Congress has set out to remedy the problem that the best health care is beyond the reach of many Americans who cannot afford it. It can assuredly do that, by exercising the powers accorded to it under the Constitution. The question in this case, however, is whether the complex structures and provisions of the Patient Protection and Affordable Care Act go beyond those powers. We conclude that they do.

. . . What is absolutely clear, affirmed by the text of the 1789 Constitution, by the Tenth Amendment ratified in 1791, and by innumerable cases of ours in the 220 years since, is that there are structural limits upon federal power—upon what it can prescribe with respect to private conduct, and upon what it can impose upon the sovereign States. . . .

That clear principle carries the day here. The striking case of *Wickard v. Filburn* (1942), which held that the economic activity of growing wheat, even for one's own consumption, affected commerce sufficiently that it could be regulated, always has been regarded as the *ne plus ultra* of expansive Commerce Clause jurisprudence. To go beyond that, and to say the failure to grow wheat (which is not an economic activity, or any activity at all) nonetheless affects commerce and therefore can be federally regulated, is to make mere breathing in and out the basis for federal prescription and to extend federal power to virtually all human activity. . . .

Article I, §8, of the Constitution gives Congress the power to "regulate Commerce . . . among the several States." The Individual Mandate in the Act commands that every "applicable individual shall for each month beginning after 2013 ensure that the individual, and any dependent of the individual who is an applicable individual, is covered under minimum essential coverage." If this provision "regulates" anything, it is the failure to maintain minimum essential coverage. One might argue that it regulates that failure by requiring it to be accompanied by payment of a penalty. But that failure—that abstention from commerce—is not "Commerce." To be sure, purchasing insurance is "Commerce"; but one does not regulate commerce that does not exist by compelling its existence. . . .

. . . Congress has impressed into service third parties, healthy individuals who could be but are not customers of the relevant industry, to offset the undesirable consequences of the regulation. Congress' desire to force these individuals to purchase insurance is motivated by the fact that they are further removed from the market than unhealthy individuals with pre-existing conditions, because they are less likely to need extensive care in the near future. If Congress can reach out and command even those furthest removed from an interstate market to participate in the market, then the Commerce Clause becomes a font of unlimited power, or in Hamilton's words, "the hideous monster whose devouring jaws . . . spare neither sex nor age, nor high nor low, nor sacred nor profane." *The Federalist* No. 3. . . .

Wickard v. Filburn has been regarded as the most expansive assertion of the commerce power in our history. A close second is *Perez v. United States* (1971), which upheld a statute criminalizing the eminently local activity of loan-sharking. Both of those cases, however, involved commercial activity. To go beyond that, and to say that the failure to grow wheat or the refusal to make loans affects commerce, so that growing and lending can be federally compelled, is to extend federal power to virtually everything. All of us consume food, and when we do so the Federal Government can prescribe what its quality must be and even how much we must pay. But the mere fact that we all consume food and are thus, sooner or later, participants in the "market" for food, does not empower the Government to say when and what we will buy. That is essentially what this Act seeks to do with respect to the purchase of health care. It exceeds federal power.

What should we make of the Court's decision striking down a provision of federal law requiring individuals purchase a commercial product? First, it is important to realize that while Roberts held that the mandate could not be sustained as an exercise of congressional commerce power, he did uphold it as a tax, as we will see in chapter 8.[15] Moreover, even the holding on the commerce power may not be so far-reaching, because Congress has rarely forced people into commerce.[16] Finally, even if Congress does pass another law of this kind, it is not altogether clear that the Court would stand by the distinction drawn by Justice Roberts: it could adopt Ginsburg's dissenting position. For, as we have seen, commerce clause doctrine has not moved in a straight line; rather, it has varied greatly depending on the philosophies of the sitting justices.

[15]As we note in chapter 8, while the majority upheld the mandate as a tax, in 2018 the Congress repealed it as part of the Tax Cuts and Jobs Act.

[16]Rarely is not never. For some early examples, see Einer Elhauge, "If Health Insurance Mandates Are Unconstitutional, Why Did the Founding Fathers Back Them?," *New Republic*, April 13, 2012.

ANNOTATED READINGS

For pre–New Deal studies, see Maurice G. Baxter, *The Steamboat Monopoly: Gibbons v. Ogden* (New York: Knopf, 1972); Felix Frankfurter, *The Commerce Clause under Marshall, Taney, and Waite* (Chapel Hill: University of North Carolina Press, 1937); Tony A. Freyer, *The Passenger Cases and the Commerce Clause* (Lawrence: University Press of Kansas, 2014); Calvin H. Johnson, *Righteous Anger at the Wicked States: The Meaning of the Founders' Constitution* (New York: Cambridge University Press, 2005); Herbert Alan Johnson, *Gibbons v. Ogden: John Marshall, Steamboats, and the Commerce Clause* (Lawrence: University Press of Kansas, 2010); Stephen B. Wood, *Constitutional Politics in the Progressive Era: Child Labor and the Law* (Chicago: University of Chicago Press, 1968).

On the New Deal period, see Leonard Baker, *Back to Back: The Duel between FDR and the Supreme Court* (New York: Macmillan, 1967); Richard Cortner, *The Wagner Act Cases* (Knoxville: University of Tennessee Press, 1964); Edward S. Corwin, *The Commerce Power versus States' Rights* (Princeton, NJ: Princeton University Press, 1936); Barry Cushman, *Rethinking the New Deal Court: The Structure of a Constitutional Revolution* (New York: Oxford University Press, 1998); Nelson Dawson, *Louis D. Brandeis, Felix Frankfurter, and the New Deal* (Hamden, CT: Archon Books, 1980); Robert Himmelberg, *The Origins of the National Recovery Administration* (New York: Fordham University Press, 1976); Peter H. Irons, *New Deal Lawyers* (Princeton,

NJ: Princeton University Press, 1982); William E. Leuchtenburg, *The Supreme Court Reborn: The Constitutional Revolution in the Age of Roosevelt* (New York: Oxford University Press, 1995); Drew Pearson and Robert S. Allen, *The Nine Old Men* (Garden City, NY: Doubleday, 1936); C. Herman Pritchett, *The Roosevelt Court: A Study in Judicial Politics and Values* (New York: Macmillan, 1948); Ronen Shamir, *Managing Legal Uncertainty: Elite Lawyers in the New Deal* (Durham, NC: Duke University Press, 1995).

Books that address the post–New Deal era include Fritz Allhoff and Mark A. Hall, eds., *The Affordable Care Act Decision* (New York: Routledge, 2014); Richard Cortner, *Civil Rights and Public Accommodations: The* Heart of Atlanta Motel *and* McClung *Cases* (Lawrence: University Press of Kansas, 2001); Thomas M. Keck, *The Most Activist Supreme Court in History* (Chicago: University of Chicago Press, 2004); and Robert D. Loevy, ed., *The Civil Rights Act of 1964: The Passage of the Law That Ended Racial Segregation* (Albany: State University of New York Press, 1997).

CHAPTER EIGHT

THE POWER TO TAX AND SPEND

PERHAPS NO GOVERNMENT POWER affects Americans more directly than the authority to tax and spend. Each year federal, state, and local governments collect trillions of dollars in taxes imposed on a wide variety of activities, transactions, and goods. The federal government reminds us of its power to tax when we receive our paychecks, to say nothing of every April 15, the deadline for filing tax returns. Many state governments lay taxes on our incomes as well, and a majority of them also impose a levy each time we make a retail purchase. If we own a house, we must annually pay a tax on its value. We pay state and/or federal excise taxes whenever we put gas in the car, buy an airline ticket, or purchase anything from a long list of other products and services. When we buy goods from abroad, the price includes a duty imposed on imports.

Given the importance the public places on these issues, it is not surprising that government fiscal policies are often at the center of political battles. Recent national elections, for example, largely focused on taxing and spending policies. How should we deal with the growing national debt? What constitutes a fair income tax rate? What should be done to reform government spending on entitlement programs such as Social Security, Medicare, and Medicaid? Do we spend too much (or too little) on national defense? Should government use the taxing and spending power to reform health care? Is it better to increase government spending to stimulate the economy, or is cutting taxes a more effective alternative to encourage growth?

Today the government's power to tax and spend is firmly established and has reasonably well-defined contours, but this was not always the case. Some of the country's greatest constitutional battles were fought over the fiscal powers. The results of these legal disputes have significantly shaped the range of powers American political institutions exercise. In this chapter, we examine the Supreme Court's interpretations of the twin fiscal powers of taxation and spending.

THE CONSTITUTIONAL POWER TO TAX AND SPEND

The government under the Articles of Confederation was ineffective in part because it had no authority to levy taxes. It could only request funds from the states and had no power to collect payment if the states refused to cooperate. The taxing authority resided solely with the states, which left the national government unable to execute public policies unless the states overwhelmingly supported them, a situation that did not often occur. It was clear that the central government would have to gain some revenue-gathering powers under the new constitution while the states retained concurrent authority to impose taxes.

Federal Fiscal Authority

Article I, Section 8, of the Constitution enumerates the powers of the federal government, and the first of those listed is the power to tax and spend:

> The Congress shall have the Power to lay and collect Taxes, Duties, Imposts and Excises, to pay the Debts and provide for the common Defence and general Welfare of the United States.

The wording of this grant of authority is quite broad. The revenue function breaks into three categories. The first is the general grant of taxation power. The second is the authority to collect duties and imposts, which generally refers to taxes levied on imports, the primary source of revenue at the time of the nation's founding. The third is the power to impose excises, which are taxes on the manufacture, sale, or use of goods, or on occupational or other activities.

The power to spend is similarly written in broad terms. The revenues gathered through the various taxing mechanisms may be used to pay government debts, to fund the nation's defense, and to provide for the general welfare. Although James Madison (and others) argued that the framers intended the spending power to be limited to funding those government activities explicitly authorized in the Constitution, the wording of Article I, Section 8, does not impose any such restriction. In fact, Alexander Hamilton believed that, in order to address issues that the framers could not foresee, Congress would need to have broad discretion in its spending authority.[1] That Congress may spend federal funds to provide for the general welfare means that the national government can employ the power of the purse to effect far-reaching policies, some of which are arguably the domain of the states.

This is not to say that the federal power to tax and spend is without limits. The framers were sufficiently wary of the dangers of a strong central government that they imposed some restrictions.

First, Article I, Section 8, stipulates that "all Duties, Imposts and Excises shall be uniform throughout the United States." The purpose of this provision is to prevent Congress from imposing different tax rates on various regions or requiring the citizens of one state to pay a tax rate higher than the citizens of other states. Geographical uniformity is the only stated constitutional requirement for excise taxes and taxes on imports. If this standard is met, the tax is likely to be valid.

Second, Article I, Section 9, holds that "[n]o Tax or Duty shall be laid on Articles exported from any State." Consistent with the prevailing philosophy of increased commerce and trade, the framers wanted to ensure that the products of the states would move freely without the burden of federal taxes being placed on them. Although this clause may appear absolute, the Supreme Court on occasion has been called upon to enforce it. In **United States v. United States Shoe Corp.** (1998) the justices struck down the harbor maintenance tax imposed by the federal Water Resources Development Act of 1986.

The law imposed a tax of 0.125 percent on the value of commercial cargo passing through the nation's ports. The proceeds were used for harbor maintenance and improvements. Rejecting the government's argument that the program imposed a legitimate user fee and not a tax, the Court unanimously found the law to be a direct violation of the constitutional prohibition against the taxation of exports.

Third, Article I, Section 9, also dictates that "[n]o capitation, or other direct, Tax shall be laid, unless in Proportion to the Census or Enumeration herein before directed to be taken." This same admonition is found in Article I, Section 2, where the framers wrote, "[D]irect Taxes shall be apportioned among the several States . . . according to their respective Numbers" as determined by the national census. The term *direct tax* is not defined in the Constitution, and it is a difficult concept to understand. When the framers referred to direct taxes they most likely meant a head tax—a tax imposed on each person—or a tax on land. As we shall see in the next section of this chapter, the requirement that direct taxes be apportioned on the basis of population has proved troublesome, and consequently Congress has not often resorted to such levies.

State Fiscal Authority

The framers generally allowed the states to retain their taxing authority as it existed prior to the ratification of the Constitution. Consequently, state and local governments today tax a wide array of activities and goods, including individual and corporate incomes, personal property, real estate, retail sales, investment holdings, and inheritances. But the Constitution imposed some new restraints on state taxing authority. These limitations specifically removed from the states any power to place a tax on certain forms of commerce. Article I, Section 10, prohibits the states from imposing any duty on imports or exports, as well as any tax on the cargo capacity of vessels using the nation's ports. The framers were interested in the promotion of commerce, and these provisions meant that states could not retard commerce by using foreign trade as a source of tax revenue. These provisions also reserved for the federal government the exclusive authority to tax goods coming into the United States from other countries.

In addition to these specific restrictions, state and federal taxation must be consistent with the other provisions of the Constitution. It would be a violation of the Constitution if a state or the federal government taxed

[1]Theodore Sky, *To Provide for the General Welfare: A History of the Federal Spending Power* (Newark: University of Delaware Press, 2008), p. 94.

the exercise of a constitutional right, such as the freedom of speech or the exercise of religion. By the same token, if the government imposed varying tax rates based on sex or race, such levies would be in violation of the constitutional rights of due process and equal protection of the laws.

State taxation policies must also be consistent with the dictates of the commerce clause. The framers were well aware that, under the Articles of Confederation, states imposed protectionist tariffs that penalized interstate trade and frustrated national economic growth. By granting the national government the power to regulate interstate commerce, the framers deprived the states of the ability to use their taxing powers to inhibit trade that crossed state lines. Although states have the authority to tax commercial activity within their borders, they may not discriminate by taxing local aspects of interstate commerce at higher rates than purely intrastate business.[2] Nor may they devise taxation systems that protect intrastate businesses from interstate competition.[3]

DIRECT TAXES AND THE POWER TO TAX INCOME

The Constitution stipulates two standards for assessing federal taxes. The first is geographical uniformity. Duties, imposts, and excise taxes all must be applied according to this standard. If Congress taxes a particular product entering the ports of the United States, the tax rate on the article must be the same regardless of the point of entry. Excise taxes—taxes paid by businesses that are typically incorporated into the price of a product—also must be applied uniformly throughout the nation. If an excise is placed on automobiles, the amount assessed must be the same in California as it is in Tennessee.

The second standard for imposing taxes is population distribution. The Constitution says that all direct taxes must be apportioned among the states on the basis of population, which simply means that, regardless of what is being taxed, each state must contribute a share of the revenue equal to its proportion of the U.S. population. The document does not provide a precise description of what the term *direct tax* means, but we know that historically the concept was considered at a minimum

to include a tax levied on every individual (often called a capitation tax or a head tax) and taxes on land. If every individual paid the same capitation tax, states with larger populations would contribute more, and smaller states would contribute less.

The delegates from the sparsely populated states supported this provision because they feared that the larger states, with greater representation in the House of Representatives, would craft tax measures in such a way that the burden would fall disproportionately upon the citizens of the smaller states. Southern states particularly supported the requirement that direct taxes be apportioned on the basis of population. These states had smaller populations than the Northern states and were larger in geographical size. Without apportioning on the basis of population, for example, the South would be much harder hit by a federal tax on land than would the North. The apportionment requirement also led the Southern states to demand that slaves be counted as less than full persons for taxation purposes. Counting a slave as three-fifths of a person, as the Constitution ultimately did, would reduce the tax liability of the Southern states in the event that Congress imposed a head tax or other direct tax.

Do direct taxes include more than just taxes on individual persons and taxes on land? The question is an important one. As Box 8-1 illustrates, whether a tax is levied uniformly (as the Constitution requires for excise taxes) or is apportioned on the basis of population (required for direct taxes) makes a great deal of difference as to who pays how much. In *Federalist* No. 21, Alexander Hamilton claimed that direct taxes were only those imposed on land and buildings, but Hamilton's opinion did not settle the issue. It required a Supreme Court decision to do that.

Defining Direct Taxation

In one of the Court's earliest cases, **Hylton v. United States** (1796), the justices defined the term *direct tax*. The dispute stemmed from a carriage tax Congress passed on June 5, 1794. The statute classified the tax as an excise and, therefore, applied the same rate on carriages nationwide. The Federalist majorities in Congress passed the statute over Anti-Federalist opposition, and the tax was completely partisan. The Federalists generally represented the states in the Northeast with large populations but relatively few carriages; the Anti-Federalist strongholds were the less densely populated and more agricultural states with larger numbers of carriages. Because the

---

[2] See *Complete Auto Transit v. Brady* (1977).

[3] See *Oregon Waste Systems v. Department of Environmental Quality of the State of Oregon* (1994); *West Lynn Creamery v. Healy* (1994).

BOX 8-1

Direct and Indirect Taxes: Apportionment versus Geographical Uniformity

This example demonstrates the difference between direct and indirect taxing methods. The facts and figures used are purely hypothetical.

Assume that Congress decides to raise $1 million through a tax on the nation's 100,000 thoroughbred horses. If this tax is considered an excise tax, it must conform to the constitutional requirement of geographical uniformity. In order to meet the $1 million goal, Congress would have to require that all thoroughbred horse owners pay a tax of $10 per horse. The rate would be the same in Maine as in Oregon. If, however, the tax on thoroughbred horses is classified as a direct tax, a different set of calculations would have to be made to meet the constitutionally required apportionment standard.

Three factors would need to be known: first, the amount of money Congress intends to raise; second, the proportion of the national population residing in each state; and third, the number of thoroughbred horses in each state. Apportionment means that the proportion of the revenue obtained from a state must equal the proportion of the country's population living there.

The following calculations show the differing impacts of apportionment in the application of the $1 million horse tax to three states. State A is a densely populated, urban state with few horses. State B is a moderately populated state with some ranching areas. State C is a sparsely populated, primarily agricultural state, with a relatively large number of thoroughbreds.

State	Percentage of National Population	Taxes Due from State	Number of Horses in State	Tax rate per Horse
State A	10	$100,000	100	$1,000
State B	5	$50,000	1,000	$50
State C	1	$10,000	10,000	$1

Obviously, the horse owners in State A would be greatly disadvantaged if the horse tax were classified as a direct tax and apportioned among the states on the basis of population. State C, on the other hand, would be greatly benefited. Because State C has only 1 percent of the nation's population, it would be responsible for raising only 1 percent of the desired tax revenues. Furthermore, that smaller tax obligation would be distributed over a disproportionately large number of horses.

Horse owners in State A clearly would prefer that the tax on thoroughbreds be defined as an excise tax, with its required geographical uniformity. State C's thoroughbred owners obviously would want the horse tax to be considered a direct tax and thus apportioned among the states on the basis of population.

---

carriage tax was deemed an excise, the Anti-Federalist areas would pay a much greater share of it than would the residents of the Northeast. The Anti-Federalists would have preferred to classify the measure as a direct tax and apportion it on the basis of population, the result of which would be to shift much of the tax burden to the more densely populated Northern states.

Daniel Hylton, a resident of Virginia, challenged the constitutionality of the assessment, claiming that it was a direct tax, not an excise, and should have been apportioned on the basis of population. The government took the position that, as a tax on an article, the carriage tax was an excise.

By almost every rule of judicial authority developed since that time, the Court should have refused to hear the dispute.[4] The evidence showed that the case did not

---

[4]See Melvin I. Urofsky and Paul Finkelman, *A March of Liberty: A Constitutional History of the United States*, 2nd ed. (New York: Oxford University Press, 2002), 160–162.

involve adverse parties. In fact, the suit appeared to be little more than a ploy by the government to obtain Court approval of its interpretation of the taxation provisions of the Constitution. Both sides to the dispute agreed that Hylton owned 125 carriages exclusively for his private use. In reality, he owned only one, but the tax due on a single carriage was insufficient to meet the threshold for federal court jurisdiction. If Hylton owned 125 carriages, the taxes and penalties due would reach $2,000, enough for federal court action. This jurisdictional point was important because Federalist judges dominated the federal courts, and they were likely to give the law a sympathetic hearing. Administration officials also agreed that if the tax were found valid, they would demand that Hylton pay only $16. Perhaps an even greater indication of collusion was that the government paid the fees of the attorneys for both sides.

Former secretary of the Treasury Alexander Hamilton presented the government's case. Hamilton was one of the most vigorous supporters of a strong national government and of broad federal taxation powers. He understood the problems associated with apportioning taxes on the basis of population and consequently wanted the Court to set down a very narrow definition of direct taxes.

Hamilton's side was victorious. The three judges who participated in the decision each voted in favor of the statute and in agreement with Congress's determination that the carriage tax was an excise tax.[5] As was the custom in the years before John Marshall became chief justice, each justice wrote a separate opinion explaining his vote.[6] The opinions of James Iredell and Samuel Chase stressed the inappropriateness of attempting to apportion a tax on carriages and the inevitable inequities that would result. William Paterson's opinion emphasized the intention of the framers. His opinion had particular credibility because Paterson, who had been a New Jersey delegate to the Constitutional Convention, was one of the framers.[7] All three agreed that only two kinds of taxes fell into the direct tax category: capitation taxes and taxes on land.

Apportioning taxes on the basis of population is very cumbersome and almost inevitably leads to unjust tax burdens. The *Hylton* decision, by limiting the kinds of taxes that fell into the direct taxation category, significantly strengthened federal taxation powers. It freed Congress from having to apply unpopular apportionment standards to most taxes. So difficult is the apportionment problem that Congress only rarely has attempted to use a direct tax, and such efforts generally have been unsatisfactory. In fact, Congress has imposed taxes requiring apportionment on only five occasions, the last time occurring in 1861.[8]

Hylton is also historically noteworthy because it was the first case in which the Supreme Court heard a challenge to the constitutionality of a federal statute; the decision predated *Marbury v. Madison* by seven years. It is clear from the arguments before the Court and the justices' opinions that the law was tested for its constitutionality. *Hylton* is not as well-known as *Marbury* because the act of Congress was found to be valid.

The Constitutionality of the Income Tax

From *Hylton* to the 1860s federal taxing authority remained generally unchanged. The national government financed its activities largely through import duties and excise taxes. The Civil War, however, placed a tremendous financial strain on the federal government. Between 1858 and the end of the war, the government ran unusually high budget deficits and needed to find new sources of revenue to fund the war effort. In response, Congress in 1862 and 1864 imposed the first taxes on individual incomes. **Springer v. United States** (1881) involved a challenge to the validity of the 1864 income tax act. William M. Springer, an attorney, claimed that the income tax was a direct tax and should have been apportioned on the basis of population. The

---

[5]The other three members of the Court were absent for various reasons. Oliver Ellsworth had just been sworn in as chief justice and, because he had missed some of the arguments, did not participate in the decision. Justice James Wilson heard arguments but did not vote in the case because he had participated in the lower court decision upholding the tax. Justice William Cushing was not present for the arguments and therefore did not vote on the merits.

[6]Having each justice write a separate opinion explaining his views was a practice borrowed from the British courts. When John Marshall became chief justice, he moved away from the use of these seriatim opinions to the current practice of a single opinion explaining the views of the majority. Marshall believed that the presentation of a single opinion increased the Court's status and effectiveness.

[7]Justice Wilson also was a delegate at the Constitutional Convention and, therefore, one of the framers. Although he did not participate in *Hylton* at the Supreme Court level, Wilson earlier had voted in the lower court to uphold the tax as an excise.

[8]Robert F. Cushman, *Cases in Constitutional Law*, 7th ed. (Englewood Cliffs, NJ: Prentice Hall, 1989), 178. The direct tax issue, however, is still occasionally raised. As we will see later in this chapter, it was one of the arguments made against the constitutional validity of the Patient Protection and Affordable Care Act of 2010.

justices unanimously rejected this position, once again holding that only capitation taxes and taxes on land were direct taxes. Although the challenged tax was a levy on the income of individuals, it could not be considered a capitation tax within the normal meaning of that term because it was not a tax levied equally on all individuals. *Springer*, then, set the precedent that the federal government had the power to tax incomes.

As the government reduced its war debts, Congress in 1872 was able to repeal the income tax law and rely upon tariffs as a principal revenue stream.[9] But the issue of taxing incomes did not go away. Tariffs, which made international trade more expensive, enabled many business interests to solidify their control of their respective markets without the fear of foreign competition. Sensing that tariffs were benefiting the wealthy few, the Democratic Party began advocating for a less regressive tax structure, one that would fall more heavily on corporations and affluent Americans.[10] In response to these demands, Congress enacted an income tax law in 1894. The statute, which was passed as part of the Wilson-Gorman Tariff Act, imposed a 2 percent tax on all corporate profits and on individual incomes. Income derived from salaries and wages, gifts, inheritances, dividends, rents, and interest, including interest from state and municipal bonds, was subject to this tax. People with annual incomes of less than $4,000 paid no tax. This exemption, set at a figure much higher than what the average worker earned, meant that most of the burden fell upon the wealthy. For this reason, the tax received overwhelming support from rank-and-file citizens and bitter opposition from businesses and high-income individuals. The wealthy classes, in fact, claimed that the income tax would destroy the very fabric of the nation, replacing the historical principle of respect for private property with communism and socialism.

The income tax law was promptly challenged in Court in an 1895 appeal, *Pollock v. Farmers' Loan & Trust Co.* One of the primary arguments of the law's opponents was that the income tax was a direct tax, and because Congress had not apportioned it, the law was unconstitutional. Given precedents such as *Hylton* and *Springer*, would you anticipate that this position would be successful?

[9]For an excellent review of the history of the income tax in the United States, see John F. Witte, *The Politics and Development of the Federal Income Tax* (Madison: University of Wisconsin Press, 1985).

[10]W. Elliot Brownlee, *Federal Taxation in America: A Short History*, 2nd ed. (New York: Cambridge University Press, 2009), pp. 41–45.

Pollock v. Farmers' Loan & Trust Co.

158 U.S. 601 (1895)
http://caselaw.findlaw.com/us-supreme-court/158/601.html
Vote: 5 (Brewer, Field, Fuller, Gray, Shiras)
    4 (Brown, Harlan, Jackson, White)

OPINION OF THE COURT: *Fuller*

DISSENTING OPINIONS: *Brown, Harlan, Jackson, White*

Charles Pollock, a shareholder in Farmers' Loan & Trust Company of New York, filed suit on behalf of himself and his fellow stockholders to block the company from paying the national income tax on the ground that the tax was unconstitutional. The lawsuit was obviously collusive: the company no more wanted to pay the tax than did its shareholders. Opponents of the law claimed (1) that taxing income from state and city bonds was an unconstitutional encroachment on the state's power to borrow money, (2) that a tax on income from real property was a direct tax and must be apportioned on the basis of population, and (3) that these two taxes were so integral to the entire tax act that the whole law should be declared unconstitutional.

The Court heard arguments in the *Pollock* case twice. In its first decision, the majority declared the tax on state and municipal bonds unconstitutional.[11] It further ruled that a tax on income from land was essentially the same as taxing land itself. Because a tax on land is a direct tax, so, too, is a tax on the income from land; therefore, such taxes must be apportioned on the basis of population. But the Court was unable to reach a decision on whether the entire law should be declared unconstitutional. On this question the justices divided 4–4 because Justice Howell Jackson, ill with tuberculosis, was absent.

Pollock filed a petition for a second hearing, and Jackson made it known that he would be present for it. The second decision reviewed much of what the Court concluded in the first, but this time the Court ruled on the question of the general constitutionality of the income tax act.

Farmers' Loan & Trust made no attempt to defend the law. It only urged the Court to decide the case expeditiously. In its place, U.S. Justice Department attorneys presented the case supporting the constitutionality of the income tax.

The *Pollock* decision was one of the most controversial and important of its day. It contained all the elements of high drama. The case pitted the interests of business and wealthy individuals against those supporting social and fiscal reform. Both sides believed that a victory for their opponents would have disastrous consequences for the nation. Newspapers editorialized with enthusiasm. Because

[11]*Pollock v. Farmers' Loan & Trust Co.*, 157 U.S. 429 (1895).

the first decision ended in a tie, the suspense surrounding the second hearing grew tremendously. The human interest factor was heightened when Justice Jackson was transported to Washington to cast what he thought would be the deciding vote in favor of the tax. (Jackson died three months later.) Oral arguments took place from May 6 to May 8. The justices did not act in a manner consistent with detached objectivity. As political science professor Loren Beth has described it, "[Justice John Marshall] Harlan wrote privately that Justice Stephen J. Field acted like a 'madman' throughout the case, but the dissenters' own opinions were similarly emotional."[12] In the end the opponents of the tax were victorious. Although Jackson, as expected, voted to uphold the law, Justice George Shiras, who had supported the tax in the first hearing, changed positions and became the crucial fifth vote to strike it down.

MR. CHIEF JUSTICE FULLER DELIVERED THE OPINION OF THE COURT.

Whenever this court is required to pass upon the validity of an act of Congress as tested by the fundamental law enacted by the people, the duty imposed demands in its discharge the utmost deliberation and care, and invokes the deepest sense of responsibility. And this is especially so when the question involves the exercise of a great governmental power, and brings into consideration, as vitally affected by the decision, that complex system of government, so sagaciously framed to secure and perpetuate "an indestructible Union, composed of indestructible States." . . .

As heretofore stated, the Constitution divided Federal taxation into two great classes, the class of direct taxes, and the class of duties, imposts and excises; and prescribed two rules which qualified the grant of power as to each class.

The power to lay direct taxes apportioned among the several States in proportion to their representation in the popular branch of Congress, a representation based on population as ascertained by the census, was plenary and absolute; but to lay direct taxes without apportionment was forbidden. The power to lay duties, imposts, and excises was subject to the qualification that the imposition must be uniform throughout the United States.

Our previous decision was confined to the consideration of the validity of the tax on the income from real estate, and on the income from municipal bonds. The question thus limited was whether such taxation was direct or not, in the meaning of the Constitution; and the court went no farther, as to the tax on the income from real estate, than to hold that it fell within the same class as the source whence the income was derived, that is, that a tax upon the realty

and a tax upon the receipts therefrom were alike direct; while as to the income from municipal bonds, that could not be taxed because of want of power to tax the source, and no reference was made to the nature of the tax as being direct or indirect.

We are now permitted to broaden the field of inquiry, and to determine to which of the two great classes a tax upon a person's entire income, whether derived from rents, or products, or otherwise, of real estate, or from bonds, stocks, or other forms of personal property, belongs; and we are unable to conclude that the enforced subtraction from the yield of all the owner's real or personal property, in the manner prescribed, is so different from a tax upon the property itself, that it is not a direct, but an indirect tax, in the meaning of the Constitution. . . .

The reasons for the clauses of the Constitution in respect of direct taxation are not far to seek. The States, respectively, possessed plenary powers of taxation. They could tax the property of their citizens in such manner and to such extent as they saw fit; they had unrestricted powers to impose duties or imposts on imports from abroad, and excises on manufactures, consumable commodities, or otherwise. They gave up the great sources of revenue derived from commerce; they retained the concurrent power o[f] levying excises, and duties if covering anything other than excises; but in respect of them the range of taxation was narrowed by the power granted over interstate commerce, and by the danger of being put at disadvantage in dealing with excises on manufactures. They retained the power of direct taxation, and to that they looked as their chief resource; but even in respect of that, they granted the concurrent power, and if the tax were placed by both governments on the same subject, the claim of the United States had preference. Therefore, they did not grant the power of direct taxation without regard to their own condition and resources as States; but they granted the power of apportioned direct taxation, a power just as efficacious to serve the needs of the general government, but securing to the States the opportunity to pay the amount apportioned, and to recoup from their own citizens in the most feasible way, and in harmony with their systems of local self-government. . . .

The founders anticipated that the expenditures of the States, their counties, cities, and towns, would chiefly be met by direct taxation on accumulated property, while they expected that those of the Federal government would be for the most part met by indirect taxes. And in order that the power of direct taxation by the general government should not be exercised, except on necessity; and, when the necessity arose, should be so exercised as to leave the States at liberty to discharge their respective obligations, and should not be so exercised, unfairly and discriminatingly, as to particular States or otherwise, by a mere majority vote, possibly of those whose constituents were intentionally not subjected to any part of the burden, the qualified grant was made. . . .

It is said that a tax on the whole income of property is not a direct tax in the meaning of the Constitution, but a duty, and, as a

[12]Loren P. Beth, "*Pollock v. Farmers' Loan & Trust Co.*," in *The Oxford Companion to the Supreme Court*, ed. Kermit L. Hall (New York: Oxford University Press, 1992), 655.

duty, leviable without apportionment, whether direct or indirect. We do not think so. Direct taxation was not restricted in one breath, and the restriction blown to the winds in another. . . .

We have unanimously held in this case that, so far as this law operates on the receipts from municipal bonds, it cannot be sustained, because it is a tax on the power of the States, and on their instrumentalities to borrow money, and consequently repugnant to the Constitution. But if, as contended, the interest when received has become merely money in the recipient's pocket, and taxable as such without reference to the source from which it came, the question is immaterial whether it could have been originally taxed at all or not. This was admitted by the Attorney General with characteristic candor; and it follows that, if the revenue derived from municipal bonds cannot be taxed because the source cannot be, the same rule applies to revenue from any other source not subject to the tax; and the lack of power to levy any but an apportioned tax on real and personal property equally exists as to the revenue therefrom.

This 1895 editorial cartoon, published after the Supreme Court's decision in *Pollock v. Farmers' Loan & Trust,* illustrates the defeat of the federal income tax law. In 1913, however, the situation was reversed when the states ratified the Sixteenth Amendment, which gave the federal government the power to tax income regardless of source.

Admitting that this act taxes the income of property irrespective of its source, still we cannot doubt that such a tax is necessarily a direct tax in the meaning of the Constitution. . . .

We are not here concerned with the question whether an income tax be or be not desirable, nor whether such a tax would enable the government to diminish taxes on consumption and duties on imports, and to enter upon what may be believed to be a reform of its fiscal and commercial system. Questions of that character belong to the controversies of political parties, and cannot be settled by judicial decision. In these cases our province is to determine whether this income tax on the revenue from property does or does not belong to the class of direct taxes. If it does, it is, being unapportioned, in violation of the Constitution, and we must so declare. . . .

Being of opinion that so much of the sections of this law as lays a tax on income from real and personal property is invalid, we are brought to the question of the effect of that conclusion upon these sections as a whole.

It is elementary that the same statute may be in part constitutional and in part unconstitutional, and if the parts are wholly independent of each other, that which is constitutional may stand while that which is unconstitutional will be rejected. And in the case before us there is no question as to the validity of this act, except sections twenty-seven to thirty-seven, inclusive, which relate to the subject which has been under discussion; and as to them we think . . . that if the different parts "are so mutually connected with and dependent on each other, as to warrant a belief that the legislature intended them as a whole, and that, if all could not be carried into effect, the legislature would not pass the residue independently, and some parts are unconstitutional, all the provisions which are thus dependent, conditional or connected, must fall with them." . . .

According to the census, the true valuation of real and personal property in the United States in 1890 was $65,037,091,197, of which real estate with improvements thereon made up $39,544,544,333. Of course, from the latter must be deducted, in applying these sections, all unproductive property and all property whose net yield does not exceed four thousand dollars; but, even with such deductions, it is evident that the income from realty formed a vital part of the scheme for taxation embodied therein. If that be stricken out, and also the income from all invested personal property, bonds, stocks, investments of all kinds, it is obvious that by far the largest part of the anticipated revenue would be eliminated, and this would leave the burden of the tax to be borne by professions, trades, employments, or vocations; and in that way what was intended as a tax on capital would remain in substance a tax on occupations and labor. We cannot believe that such was the intention of Congress. We do not mean to say that an act laying by apportionment a direct tax on all real estate and personal property, or the income thereof, might not also lay excise taxes on business, privileges, employments, and vocations. But this is not such an act; and the scheme must be considered as a whole. Being invalid as to the greater part, and falling, as the tax would, if any part were held valid, in a direction which could not have been contemplated except in connection with the taxation considered as an entirety, we are constrained to conclude that sections twenty-seven to thirty-seven, inclusive, of the act, which became a law without the signature of the President on August 28, 1894, are wholly inoperative and void.

Our conclusions may, therefore, be summed up as follows:

First. We adhere to the opinion already announced, that, taxes on real estate being indisputably direct taxes, taxes on the rents or income of real estate are equally direct taxes.

Second. We are of opinion that taxes on personal property, or on the income of personal property, are likewise direct taxes.

Third. The tax imposed by sections twenty-seven to thirty-seven, inclusive, of the act of 1894, so far as it falls on the income of real estate and of personal property, being a direct tax within the meaning of the Constitution, and, therefore, unconstitutional and void because not apportioned according to representation, all those sections, constituting one entire scheme of taxation, are necessarily invalid.

MR. JUSTICE HARLAN, DISSENTING.

Assuming it to be the settled construction of the constitution that the general government cannot tax lands, . . . except by apportioning the tax among the states according to their respective numbers, does it follow that a tax on incomes derived from rents is a direct tax on the real estate from which such rents arise?

In my judgment, a tax on income derived from real property ought not to be, and until now has never been, regarded by any court as a direct tax on such property, within the meaning of the constitution. As the great mass of lands in most of the states do not bring any rents, and as incomes from rents vary in the different states, such a tax cannot possibly be apportioned among the states, on the basis merely of numbers, with any approach to equality of right among taxpayers, any more than a tax on carriages or other personal property could be so apportioned. And in view of former adjudications, beginning with the *Hylton Case*, and ending with the *Springer Case*, a decision now that a tax on income from real property can be laid and collected only by apportioning the same among the states on the basis of numbers may not improperly be regarded as a judicial revolution that may sow the seeds of hate and distrust among the people of different sections of our common country. . . .

. . . While a tax on the land itself, whether at a fixed rate applicable to all lands, without regard to their value, or by the acre, or according to their market value, might be deemed a direct tax, within the meaning of the constitution, as interpreted in the *Hylton Case,* a duty on rents is a duty on something distinct and entirely separate from, although issuing out of, the land. . . .

But the court, by its judgment just rendered, goes far in advance, not only of its former decisions, but of any decision heretofore rendered by an American court. . . .

In my judgment,—to say nothing of the disregard of the former adjudications of this court, and of the settled practice of the government,—this decision may well excite the gravest apprehensions. It strikes at the very foundations of national authority, in that it denies to the general government a power which is or may become vital to the very existence and preservation of the Union in a national emergency, such as that of war with a great commercial nation, during which the collection of all duties upon imports will cease or be materially diminished. It tends to re-establish that condition of helplessness in which congress found itself during the period of the Articles of Confederation, when it was without authority, by laws operating directly upon individuals, to lay and collect, through its own agents, taxes sufficient to pay the debts and defray the expenses of government, but was dependent in all such matters upon the good will of the states, and their promptness in meeting requisitions made upon them by congress.

Why do I say that the decision just rendered impairs or menaces the national authority? The reason is so apparent that it need only be stated. In its practical operation this decision withdraws from national taxation not only all incomes derived from real estate, but tangible personal property, "invested personal property, bonds, stocks, investments of all kinds," and the income that may be derived from such property. This results from the fact that, by the decision of the court, all such personal property and all incomes from real estate and personal property are placed beyond national taxation otherwise than by apportionment among the states on the basis simply of population. No such apportionment can possibly be made without doing gross injustice to the many for the benefit of the favored few in particular states. Any attempt upon the part of congress to apportion among the states, upon the basis simply of their population, taxation of personal property or of incomes, would tend to arouse such indignation among the freemen of America that it would never be repeated. When, therefore, this court adjudges, as it does now adjudge, that congress cannot impose a duty or tax upon personal property, or upon income arising either from rents of real estate or from personal property, including invested personal property, bonds, stocks, and investments of all kinds, except by apportioning the sum to be so raised among the states according to population, it practically decides that, without an amendment of the constitution,—two-thirds of both houses of congress and three-fourths of the states concurring,—such property and incomes can never be made to contribute to the support of the national government. . . .

. . . I dissent from the opinion and judgment of the court.

The Sixteenth Amendment

The decision to invalidate the entire income tax act was quite unpopular. Because that statute had placed a greater obligation on the wealthy, the ruling convinced the middle and working classes that the Supreme Court was little more than the defender of the rich. Various political groups immediately began working to reverse the impact of the Court's decision through either a constitutional amendment or revised federal legislation. Labor and farming interests supported a new income tax, as did progressive Republicans and Democratic populists. Opposition came primarily from conservative Republicans in the Northeast.

In 1909 Congress began serious work on an income tax measure. There were sufficient votes in the legislature to reform the tax structure, moving the federal government away from excessive reliance on regressive tariffs and excise taxes. The major question was whether to pass another income tax bill or to propose a constitutional amendment. Finding themselves in a minority, conservative Republicans threw their support to an amendment. They hoped the state legislatures would not ratify it, but even if the states approved, the process would take several years to complete.

Congress proposed a constitutional amendment to authorize a federal income tax in July 1909 by overwhelming votes of 77–0 in the Senate and 318–14 in the House. The amendment received the required number of approvals from the state legislatures in February 1913 and became the Sixteenth Amendment to the U.S. Constitution:

> The Congress shall have power to lay and collect taxes on incomes, from whatever source derived, without apportionment among the several States, and without regard to any census or enumeration.

The amendment, which effectively ended the debate over direct taxation of income, is one of only four designed to overturn a Supreme Court precedent. It gave Congress sufficient taxing authority to fund the federal government without having to resort to the cumbersome process of apportioning tax obligations by state population. The Constitution now made all sources of income readily subject to Congress's taxing power.

Congress wasted no time. In 1913 the legislature imposed a 1 percent tax rate on individual incomes in excess of $3,000 and on incomes of married couples over $4,000. Not surprisingly, the statute's constitutionality was challenged in the Supreme Court, but the justices upheld the law three years later in *Brushaber v. Union Pacific Railroad* (1916) by a 7–2 vote. As shown in Table 8-1, the income tax is now the primary source of federal revenue.

Table 8-1 Federal Tax Revenues: The Impact of the Sixteenth Amendment

Source	1800	1850	1900	1950	2000	2020 (EST.)
Customs duties	83.7	91.0	41.1	1.0	1.0	1.3
Excises	7.5	—	50.1	18.4	3.4	3.0
Gifts and inheritances	—	—	—	1.7	1.4	0.5
Individual incomes	—	—	—	38.5	49.6	50.0
Corporate incomes	—	—	—	25.5	10.2	7.0
Insurance trust (Social Security, etc.)	—	—	—	10.7	32.2	35.6
Other income	8.8	9.0	8.8	4.2	2.2	2.6

Sources: Historical Statistics of the United States: Colonial Times to 1970 (Washington, DC: U.S. Bureau of the Census, 1975); Budget of the United States (Washington, DC: Office of Management and Budget, various years).

Note: The data represent the percentage of total federal revenues for each of seven sources of taxation. The data prior to ratification of the Sixteenth Amendment in 1913 demonstrate the federal government's reliance on customs duties and excise taxes. Data from the period after 1913 illustrate the shift to income taxes as the primary sources for federal tax dollars.

INTERGOVERNMENTAL TAX IMMUNITY

The operation of a federal system carries within it inherent risks of conflict between the national government and the states. When both levels of government are authorized to tax, one government could use the power as a weapon against the other. No specific provision of the Constitution prohibits the federal government from taxing state governments or vice versa, but for the federal system to operate effectively, the entities need to avoid such conflicts.

Establishing the Tax Immunity Doctrine

The issue of intergovernmental tax immunity was first raised in *McCulloch v. Maryland* (1819), which tested the constitutional validity of the national bank. We have already discussed its significance for the development of congressional power and the concept of federalism, but *McCulloch* also is relevant to understanding whether one level of government may tax another.

McCulloch involved a challenge to a Maryland tax imposed on the Bank of the United States, a creation of the federal government. Supporters of federal power argued that the Union could not be maintained if the states were permitted to place debilitating taxes on any operations of the federal government they disapproved. States' rights advocates claimed that the power of the states to tax within their own borders was absolute and that there was no constitutional bar to such taxes. The Court ruled in favor of the federal government; declaring the state tax unconstitutional, the justices held that a single state could not use its taxing authority to control national policy. With his hard-hitting opinion for a unanimous Court, Chief Justice Marshall put an immediate stop to a conflict that would have severely weakened the Union if allowed to continue.

In doing so, Marshall created the doctrine of intergovernmental tax immunity. He wrote, "[T]he power to tax involves the power to destroy; . . . the power to destroy may defeat and render useless the power to create; . . . there is plain repugnance, in conferring on one government a power to control the constitutional measures of another." The ability of the states to tax the legitimate operations of the federal government is simply incompatible with the framers' intent of creating viable government units at both the national and state levels.

Marshall's decision in *McCulloch* was consistent with his general philosophy of favoring a strong national government. But was the doctrine of intergovernmental tax immunity a two-way street? Marshall's opinion fell short of proclaiming that the national government was prohibited from taxing the legitimate operations of the states. He was more concerned in this case with reinforcing principles of federal supremacy. Yet a strong case can be made that it would also violate the principles of the Constitution for the federal government to be permitted to destroy the states through its taxing power.

The first case that tested whether the states enjoyed immunity from federal taxation was ***Collector v. Day*** (1871), which stemmed from an application of the Civil War federal income tax law. Judge J. M. Day of the probate court in Massachusetts objected to paying a federal tax on his income on grounds of intergovernmental tax immunity. Three decades earlier the Supreme Court had ruled that the state governments could not tax the income of federal officeholders,[13] and Day was now asking the Court to adopt the converse of that ruling. The Supreme Court held, in an 8–1 vote, that Day's judicial income was immune from federal taxation. The Court reasoned that the Constitution protects the legitimate functions of the state. The federal government cannot use its taxation powers to curtail or destroy the operations or instruments of the state, and the probate court system is a legitimate and necessary agency of state government. As far as the Court was concerned, the federal government was not simply taxing the income of an employee of Massachusetts; it was taxing the state itself. To allow the federal government to tax the income of state judges would be to open the door for Congress to tax all state government functions.

For several decades the justices vigorously maintained the doctrine that the Constitution did not allow one government to tax the essential functions of another. In the *Pollock* income tax decisions, as we have already seen, the Court struck down a federal tax on interest income from state and municipal bonds as an unconstitutional burden on the state's authority to borrow. The Court struck down state taxes on income from federal land leases and federally granted patents and copyrights, and on the sales of petroleum products to the federal government.[14] It also invalidated a federal tax on

---

[13]*Dobbins v. Commissioners of Erie County* (1842).

[14]*Gillespie v. Oklahoma* (1922) and *Long v. Rockwood* (1928) concerned patents and copyrights; *Panhandle Oil Co. v. Mississippi* (1928) dealt with petroleum sales.

revenues derived from the sales of goods to state agencies.[15] The only significant standard the Court imposed in this line of cases was that immunity covered only essential government functions. Consequently, the justices upheld a federal tax on the profits of South Carolina's state-run liquor stores.[16] As a merchant of alcoholic beverages, the state was acting as a private business, not exercising a government function, and therefore was not immune from federal taxation.

Erosion of the Tax Immunity Doctrine

During the New Deal period, support for the tax immunity doctrine began to wane. A series of Supreme Court decisions modified or reversed the earlier rulings that had established an almost impenetrable barrier against the taxation by one government of the instruments or operations of another.

In *Helvering v. Gerhardt* (1938) the Court overruled *Dobbins v. Commissioners of Erie County* (1842) and permitted states to tax the income of federal officials. The justices then overruled *Collector v. Day* in **Graves v. New York ex rel. O'Keefe** (1939), holding that there was no constitutional bar to the federal government's taxation of the income of state employees. "The theory," said the Court, "that a tax on income is legally or economically a tax on its source, is no longer tenable." Also falling were bans on taxing profits from doing business with state or federal government agencies. The Supreme Court went so far as to allow a state to impose taxes on a federal contractor even when those taxes were passed on to the federal government through a cost-plus contract (that is, a contract that separately specifies the amounts of expenses and profits to be paid).[17]

Although these rulings seriously weakened the doctrine of intergovernmental tax immunity, the principle still has some vitality. It would be unconstitutional for a state to place a tax on cases filed in the federal courts operating within its boundaries, or for the federal government to impose an excise tax on the traffic citations issued by a state highway patrol. But aside from these obvious examples, where is the line between permissible and impermissible taxation? The Supreme Court helped answer that question in **South Carolina v. Baker** (1988), which involved a challenge to a federal law taxing the income from long-term state and city bonds.

Bonds are a mechanism that governments can use to borrow money. State and local governments issue bonds, and the purchasers of those bonds, in effect, lend their money to the government, with a promise that the money will be repaid, after some period of time, with interest. In 1982 Congress passed a tax act that removed the federal tax exemption for interest earned on publicly offered long-term bonds issued by state and local governments unless the bonds and their owners were registered. The registration requirement was intended to identify owners of such bonds so that capital gains and estate taxes could be better monitored. The taxing of interest from unregistered state and municipal bonds ran directly contrary to the *Pollock* decision. South Carolina objected to the law as a direct violation of the intergovernmental tax immunity doctrine. The federal tax, it argued, placed a direct burden on the ability of state and local governments to raise revenue.

By a 7–1 vote, with only Justice Sandra Day O'Connor in dissent, the Supreme Court upheld the law and explicitly overruled *Pollock*. For the Court, Justice William J. Brennan Jr. explained that precedents since *Pollock* had repudiated the position that a tax on those doing business with the state was the equivalent of a tax on the state. The justices could see no reason for treating persons who receive interest on state bonds any differently from persons receiving income from other kinds of contracts with the state.

The decision in *South Carolina v. Baker* continued a long-standing trend of the Court toward eroding the doctrine of intergovernmental tax immunity. A statement of the contemporary status of the doctrine, in Justice Brennan's words, is that "the States can never tax the United States directly but can tax any private parties with whom it does business, even though the financial burden falls on the United States, as long as the tax does not discriminate against the United States or those with whom it deals." A similar, although not quite as rigid, prohibition applies to federal taxes on the states.

Even in those cases that, like *South Carolina v. Baker*, have limited intergovernmental tax immunity, the Court repeatedly has stressed the principle that taxes must be nondiscriminatory. If a state wishes to tax a company's profits from a business transaction with the federal government, for example, the tax obligation must be the same as that imposed on profits from business with nongovernmental parties. This bar against discriminatory taxation was reinforced in **Davis v. Michigan Department of Treasury** (1989), in which the Court struck down a state law that taxed income that residents

---

[15]*Indian Motorcycle Co. v. United States* (1931).

[16]*South Carolina v. United States* (1905).

[17]*Alabama v. King and Boozer* (1941).

received from federal retirement plans but exempted income from state retirement programs.

Fourteen other states had similar tax laws, and as a result of this decision they were required to revise those laws, choosing either to extend the tax exemptions to retired federal employees or eliminate the exemption granted to state and local retirees. The Court's decision in *Davis* reminds us that the tax immunity doctrine remains viable in spite of decisions that have imposed limitations on it.

TAXATION AS A REGULATORY POWER

Normally, we think of taxation as a method of funding the government. Yet Marshall's well-known statement that the "power to tax involves the power to destroy" was an early recognition that taxes can be used for purposes other than raising revenue. Excessive taxation can make the targeted activities so unprofitable that it is no longer feasible to engage in them. The converse also is true: favorable tax status, including tax exemptions, can encourage preferred activities. These observations prompt several important constitutional questions regarding the taxation powers of the federal government. Is it proper for the United States to impose taxes for reasons other than revenue raising? Is it constitutional for the government to use taxation as a method of regulation? Is it valid for Congress to enact tax laws as a means of controlling activities not otherwise within the jurisdiction of the federal government?

From the beginning, Congress has used its authority to tax for purposes other than raising revenue. Before the ratification of the Sixteenth Amendment, the federal government relied heavily on customs duties. As secretary of the Treasury, Alexander Hamilton supported tariffs on imports as a means of enabling fledging industries in the American economy to develop the capacity to compete with their more established foreign counterparts. Thus, certain industries received protection from imports and were able to grow with little foreign competition. The practice of combining revenue gathering with other policy objectives continues to this day.

Deciding that Congress may impose import duties with regulatory purposes does not necessarily answer a similar question with respect to domestic excise taxes. Customs duties, after all, have a limited range. They can be applied only to those goods that are brought into the country from abroad. Excise taxes, by contrast, can be applied to the broad spectrum of domestic goods, services, and activities. The only restriction on such taxes explicitly mentioned in the Constitution is that they be geographically uniform. But is there an implied requirement that excise taxes be generated only for revenue purposes, or may Congress regulate through the use of the excise? If Congress is allowed to regulate domestic activities through the power to tax, does that not give the federal government the equivalent of a police power that the framers reserved to the states?

Initially, the Court took the position that Congress had wide latitude in exercising the taxing power. In *Veazie Bank v. Fenno* (1869) the justices upheld a 10 percent tax on notes issued by state banks. The law was intended to protect the newly chartered national bank from state competition by making notes far too costly for state banks to issue. In **McCray v. United States** (1904) the Court held valid a federal tax on oleomargarine designed primarily to protect the dairy industry from competition from the less expensive butter substitute. The justices refused to examine the motives of the legislators in passing the act. In the words of Justice Edward White, "The decisions of this court from the beginning lend no support whatever to the assumption that the judiciary may restrain the exercise of lawful power on the assumption that a wrongful purpose or motive has caused the power to be exerted." The tax was clearly an excise tax, and as such was subject to only one constitutional limitation— geographical uniformity. That requirement having been met, the federal tax on margarine was constitutional.

Later, in **Bailey v. Drexel Furniture Co.** (1922), the Court seemingly changed course. At issue was a federal tax on the profits of any company hiring child labor. In striking down the tax, the justices took into consideration the motives behind the legislation. They concluded that the legislature violated principles of federalism by using the power to tax as a means of regulating activities that were outside Congress's proper authority. As Chief Justice William Howard Taft explained, "So here the so-called tax is a penalty to coerce the people of a State to act as Congress wishes them to act in respect of a matter completely the business of the state government under the Federal Constitution."

The decision in *Drexel* was a reversal of the position on excise taxes the Court had held since the early 1800s. It generally proved to be out of line with Supreme Court rulings both before and after. The Court repeatedly has faced the question of taxation and regulation and generally has ruled in favor of the federal power to tax and even acknowledged that all taxes to some degree have regulatory effects. In a number of cases, the Court has upheld Congress's use of its taxing power as a means of discouraging various activities. In *United States v. Doremus* (1919) and *Nigro v. United States* (1928) the Court upheld federal excise taxes on narcotics, and in *United States v. Sanchez* (1950) it upheld a tax on marijuana. Similarly, an excise tax on objectionable firearms was declared valid in *Sonzinsky v. United States* (1937), even though the Court admitted that the law had an unmistakable "legislative purpose to regulate rather than to tax." The justices found no constitutional defects with an excise levied on professional gamblers in *United States v. Kahriger* (1953). These taxes expand federal regulatory powers. If Congress has the power to impose a tax, then the federal government also has the power to enforce the tax laws, creating, to an extent, "police powers" within the federal government that originally resided with the states.

TAXING AND SPENDING FOR THE GENERAL WELFARE

The Constitution authorizes Congress to tax and spend for the general welfare. Whether the term *general welfare* was intended to expand the powers of Congress beyond those explicitly stated in the Constitution is subject to debate. James Madison argued that the Constitution's use of the term was only a reference to the other enumerated powers. Because the United States is a government of limited and specified powers, he asserted, the authority to tax and spend must be confined to those spheres of authority the Constitution explicitly granted. Alexander Hamilton took the opposite position. He interpreted the power to tax and spend for the general welfare to be a separate power altogether. For Hamilton, taxing and spending authority was given in addition to the other granted powers, not limited by them. The conflict between these two opposing interpretations was the subject of legal disputes throughout much of the nation's history, and the last battle between them was waged during the constitutional crisis over legislation passed during the New Deal.

Many of the programs Franklin Roosevelt recommended to reestablish the nation's economic strength involved regulatory activity far more extensive than ever before proposed. Several depended on the power of the federal government to tax and spend for the general welfare. Opponents of the New Deal claimed that these programs, while ostensibly based on the taxing and spending authority, in reality were regulations of matters the Constitution reserved for the states.

During the Great Depression, agriculture was one of the hardest hit sectors of the economy. At that time agriculture was responsible for a much larger proportion of the nation's economy than it is today, and conditions in the farming sector had dire effects on the general welfare of the entire country. The nation's farmers were overproducing, which caused prices for farm products to drop. In many cases the cost of production was higher than the income from crop sales, leaving farmers in desperate straits. Most of their farms were mortgaged, and all owed taxes on their lands. The farther the farmers fell behind economically, the more they attempted to produce to improve their situation. This strategy further increased production, making matters even worse.

In response, Roosevelt proposed and Congress passed the Agricultural Adjustment Act (AAA), a statute that combined the taxing and spending powers to combat the agricultural crisis. The central purpose of the plan was to reduce the amount of acreage being farmed. To accomplish this goal, the federal government would "rent" a percentage of the nation's farmland and leave this acreage unplanted. In effect, the government would pay the farmers not to farm. If the plan succeeded, production would drop, prices would rise, and the farmers would have a sufficient income. Making payments to the nation's farmers in order to "rent" their land was an expensive proposition, and to fund these expenditures the AAA imposed an excise tax on the processing of agricultural products.

The program was a success until William M. Butler challenged the constitutionality of the law. Butler was the bankruptcy receiver for Hoosac Mills Corporation, a cotton processor. When the government imposed the processing tax on Hoosac, Butler took legal action to avoid payment, claiming that the AAA exceeded the taxing and spending powers granted to the federal government.

In **United States v. Butler** (1936) the Court concluded that the federal government had broad powers to tax and spend for the general welfare. The justices decided, consistent with Hamilton's position, that Congress's fiscal authority was not limited to those subjects specifically enumerated in Article I. This philosophy did not, however, mean that congressional powers had no limits. The majority in *Butler* ruled that the law was unconstitutional because what it imposed was not truly a tax. Instead, the government was taking money from one group (the processors) to give to another (the farmers), and it was doing this to regulate farm production, a matter of intrastate commerce reserved for state regulation. The decision dealt a severe blow to the New Deal, but only temporarily.

Butler's impact was short-lived. Following the Court's dramatic change in position after Roosevelt's threat to add new members, the justices ruled that agriculture could be regulated under the commerce power.[18] As for the power to tax and spend for the general welfare, the position taken in *Butler* was reevaluated the very next year in *Steward Machine Co. v. Davis* (1937) and *Helvering v. Davis* (1937), challenges to the constitutionality of the newly formed Social Security system. The Social Security Act shared several characteristics with the Agricultural Adjustment Act that the Court had condemned in *Butler*. Both used the taxing and spending powers to combat the effects of the Depression, both took money from one group of people to give to another, and both regulated areas previously thought to be reserved to the states. The radical change in position occurred largely because Chief Justice Charles Evans Hughes and Justice Owen Roberts deserted the *Butler* majority and joined with the liberal wing of the Court to forge a new constitutional interpretation. Just as these two justices had abandoned the conservative Four Horsemen in *National Labor Relations Board v. Jones & Laughlin Steel* (1937) to uphold a more broad use of Congress's power to regulate interstate commerce, so, too, did they support a more generous interpretation of Congress's fiscal authority in *Steward Machine* and *Helvering*.

The Social Security cases firmly established that the taxing and spending powers are to be broadly construed. If Congress decides that the general welfare of the United States demands a program requiring the use of these fiscal powers, the Supreme Court likely will find that program constitutionally valid unless parts of the law violate specific provisions of the Constitution. Since these 1937 decisions, Congress has used the spending authority to expand greatly the role of the federal government.

Because the justices now tend to defer to Congress on such matters, serious challenges to federal spending programs have become unusual, but occasionally a battle erupts over federal and state authority with respect to spending programs. *South Dakota v. Dole* (1987) provides an important example. This dispute involved a conflict over federal spending power and the state's authority to regulate highway safety and alcoholic beverages. The use of federal funds to encourage the states to take particular policy positions was attacked in much the same

William M. Butler, receiver for Hoosac Mills, objected to paying the federal tax on processing cotton. His lawsuit successfully challenged the constitutionality of the Agricultural Adjustment Act of 1933.

manner that several of the Roosevelt New Deal programs were challenged. It is interesting to note that Chief Justice William Rehnquist, who was considered a strong defender of states' rights, wrote the majority opinion upholding the exercise of federal authority over the states. Not surprising was the stinging dissent registered by Justice O'Connor on behalf of state interests.

South Dakota v. Dole

483 U.S. 203 (1987)
http://caselaw.findlaw.com/us-supreme-court/483/203.html
Oral arguments available at https://www.oyez.org/
cases/1986/86-260
Vote: 7 (Blackmun, Marshall, Powell, Rehnquist, Scalia,
Stevens, White)
2 (Brennan, O'Connor)

OPINION OF THE COURT: *Rehnquist*

DISSENTING OPINIONS: *Brennan, O'Connor*

---

[18]See *Mulford v. Smith* (1939) and *Wickard v. Filburn* (1942).

In 1984 Congress passed a statute (23 U.S.C. sec. 158) directing the secretary of transportation to withhold a portion of federal highway funds from any state that did not establish a minimum age of twenty-one years for the legal consumption of alcoholic beverages. The purpose of the law was to decrease the number of serious automobile collisions among young people, a group that statistics showed had a high percentage of accidents. The legislators correctly believed that withholding federal dollars would be an effective way of encouraging the states to comply with the federal program.

South Dakota, which allowed the purchase of beer containing 3.2 percent alcohol by persons nineteen years or older, objected to the statute, arguing that Congress was infringing on the rights of the states. The Twenty-first Amendment, which repealed Prohibition in 1933, gave full authority to the states to regulate alcoholic beverages; therefore, South Dakota claimed, Congress had no authority to set a minimum drinking age. According to the state, the federal government was using its considerable spending power to coerce the states into enacting laws that were otherwise outside congressional authority.

The state sued Secretary of Transportation Elizabeth Dole, asking the courts to declare the law unconstitutional. Both the district court and the court of appeals ruled against the state and upheld the law.

CHIEF JUSTICE REHNQUIST DELIVERED THE OPINION OF THE COURT.

The Constitution empowers Congress to "lay and collect Taxes, Duties, Imposts, and Excises, to pay the Debts and provide for the common Defence and general Welfare of the United States." Art. I, §8, cl. 1. Incident to this power, Congress may attach conditions on the receipt of federal funds, and has repeatedly employed the power "to further broad policy objectives by conditioning receipt of federal moneys upon compliance by the recipient with federal statutory and administrative directives." The breadth of this power was made clear in *United States v. Butler* (1936), where the Court, resolving a longstanding debate over the scope of the Spending Clause, determined that "the power of Congress to authorize expenditure of public moneys for public purposes is not limited by the direct grants of legislative power found in the Constitution." Thus, objectives not thought to be within Article I's "enumerated legislative fields" may nevertheless be attained through the use of the spending power and the conditional grant of federal funds.

The spending power is of course not unlimited, but is instead subject to several general restrictions articulated in our cases. The first of these limitations is derived from the language of the Constitution itself: the exercise of the spending power must be in pursuit of "the general welfare." In considering whether a particular expenditure is intended to serve general public purposes, courts should defer substantially to the judgment of Congress. Second, we have required that if Congress desires to condition the States' receipt of federal funds, it "must do so unambiguously . . . , enabl[ing] the States to exercise their choice knowingly, cognizant of the consequences of their participation." Third, our cases have suggested (without significant elaboration) that conditions on federal grants might be illegitimate if they are unrelated "to the federal interest in particular national projects or programs." Finally, we have noted that other constitutional provisions may provide an independent bar to the conditional grant of federal funds.

South Dakota does not seriously claim that §158 is inconsistent with any of the first three restrictions mentioned above. We can readily conclude that the provision is designed to serve the general welfare, especially in light of the fact that "the concept of welfare or the opposite is shaped by Congress. . . ." Congress found that the differing drinking ages in the States created particular incentives for young persons to combine their desire to drink with their ability to drive, and that this interstate problem required a national solution. The means it chose to address this dangerous situation were reasonably calculated to advance the general welfare. The conditions upon which States receive the funds, moreover, could not be more clearly stated by Congress. And the State itself, rather than challenging the germaneness of the condition to federal purposes, admits that it "has never contended that the congressional action was . . . unrelated to a national concern in the absence of the Twenty-first Amendment." Indeed, the condition imposed by Congress is directly related to one of the main purposes for which highway funds are expended—safe interstate travel. This goal of the interstate highway system had been frustrated by varying drinking ages among the States. . . . By enacting §158, Congress conditioned the receipt of federal funds in a way reasonably calculated to address this particular impediment to a purpose for which the funds are expended.

The remaining question about the validity of §158—and the basic point of disagreement between the parties—is whether the Twenty-first Amendment constitutes an "independent constitutional bar" to the conditional grant of federal funds. Petitioner, relying on its view that the Twenty-first Amendment prohibits direct regulation of drinking ages by Congress, asserts that "Congress may not use the spending power to regulate that which it is prohibited from regulating directly under the Twenty-first Amendment." But our cases show that this "independent constitutional bar" limitation on the spending power is not of the kind petitioner suggests. *United States v. Butler,* for example, established that the constitutional limitations on Congress when exercising its spending power are less exacting than those on its authority to regulate directly. . . .

. . . [T]he "independent constitutional bar" limitation on the spending power is not, as petitioner suggests, a prohibition on the indirect achievement of objectives which Congress is not empowered to achieve directly. Instead, we think that the language in our earlier opinions stands for the unexceptionable proposition that the power may not be used to induce the States to engage in activities that would themselves be unconstitutional. Thus, for example, a grant of federal funds conditioned on invidiously discriminatory state action or the infliction of cruel and unusual punishment would be an illegitimate exercise of the Congress' broad spending power. But no such claim can be or is made here. Were South Dakota to succumb to the blandishments offered by Congress and raise its drinking age to 21, the State's action in so doing would not violate the constitutional rights of anyone.

Our decisions have recognized that in some circumstances the financial inducement offered by Congress might be so coercive as to pass the point at which "pressure turns into compulsion." Here, however, Congress has directed only that a State desiring to establish a minimum drinking age lower than 21 lose a relatively small percentage of certain federal highway funds. Petitioner contends that the coercive nature of this program is evident from the degree of success it has achieved. We cannot conclude, however, that a conditional grant of federal money of this sort is unconstitutional simply by reason of its success in achieving the congressional objective.

When we consider, for a moment, that all South Dakota would lose if she adheres to her chosen course as to a suitable minimum drinking age is 5% of the funds otherwise obtainable under specified highway grant programs, the argument as to coercion is shown to be more rhetoric than fact. . . .

Here Congress has offered relatively mild encouragement to the States to enact higher minimum drinking ages than they would otherwise choose. But the enactment of such laws remains the prerogative of the States not merely in theory but in fact. Even if Congress might lack the power to impose a national minimum drinking age directly, we conclude that encouragement to state action found in §158 is a valid use of the spending power. Accordingly, the judgment of the Court of Appeals is

Affirmed.

JUSTICE O'CONNOR, DISSENTING.

The Court today upholds the National Minimum Drinking Age Amendment, 23 U.S.C. §158, as a valid exercise of the spending power conferred by Article I, §8. But §158 is not a condition on spending reasonably related to the expenditure of federal funds and cannot be justified on that ground. Rather, it is an attempt to regulate the sale of liquor, an attempt that lies outside Congress' power to regulate commerce because it falls within the ambit of §2 of the Twenty-first Amendment. . . .

When Congress appropriates money to build a highway, it is entitled to insist that the highway be a safe one. But it is not entitled to insist as a condition of the use of highway funds that the State impose or change regulations in other areas of the State's social and economic life because of an attenuated or tangential relationship to highway use or safety. Indeed, if the rule were otherwise, the Congress could effectively regulate almost any area of a State's social, political, or economic life on the theory that use of the interstate transportation system is somehow enhanced. If, for example, the United States were to condition highway moneys upon moving the state capital, I suppose it might argue that interstate transportation is facilitated by locating local governments in places easily accessible to interstate highways—or, conversely, that highways might become overburdened if they had to carry traffic to and from the state capital. In my mind, such a relationship is hardly more attenuated than the one which the Court finds supports §158.

There is a clear place at which the Court can draw the line between permissible and impermissible conditions on federal grants. It is the line identified in the Brief for the National Conference of State Legislatures et al. as *Amici Curiae:*

"Congress has the power to *spend* for the general welfare, it has the power to *legislate* only for the delegated purposes." . . .

This approach harks back to *United States v. Butler* (1936), the last case in which this Court struck down an Act of Congress as beyond the authority granted by the Spending Clause. . . .

While *Butler*'s authority is questionable insofar as it assumes that Congress has no regulatory power over farm production, its discussion of the spending power and its description of both the power's breadth and its limitations remain sound. The Court's decision in *Butler* also properly recognizes the gravity of the task of appropriately limiting the spending power. If the spending power is to be limited only by Congress' notion of the general welfare, the reality, given the vast financial resources of the Federal Government, is that the Spending Clause gives "power to the Congress to tear down the barriers, to invade the states' jurisdiction, and to become a parliament of the whole people, subject to no restrictions save such as are self-imposed." This, of course, as *Butler* held, was not the Framers' plan and it is not the meaning of the Spending Clause. . . .

The immense size and power of the Government of the United States ought not obscure its fundamental character. It remains a Government of enumerated powers. Because 23 U.S.C. §158 cannot be justified as an exercise of any power delegated to the Congress, it is not authorized by the Constitution. The Court errs in holding it to be the law of the land, and I respectfully dissent.

JUSTICE BRENNAN, DISSENTING.

I agree with Justice O'CONNOR that regulation of the minimum age of purchasers of liquor falls squarely within the ambit of those powers reserved to the States by the Twenty-first Amendment. Since States possess this constitutional power, Congress cannot condition a federal grant in a manner that abridges this right. The Amendment, itself, strikes the proper balance between federal and state authority. I therefore dissent.

Rehnquist's opinion gave strong support to the federal spending power. The majority held that there are only five basic requirements that must be met for a federal spending statute to be valid: (1) the expenditure must be for the general welfare, (2) any conditions imposed on the expenditure must be unambiguous, (3) the conditions must be reasonably related to the purpose of the expenditure, (4) the legislation must not violate any independent constitutional provision, and (5) the financial inducement offered by Congress cannot be so coercive as to pass the point at which federally imposed pressure on the states to adopt a particular public policy turns into compulsion. These are minimal requirements indeed, especially because the Court acknowledged a policy of deferring to the legislature's determinations of what promotes the general welfare. O'Connor's dissent, which praised much of what the Court concluded in *Butler*, is not likely to find a great deal of support today.

As the Court entered the twenty-first century, it had established a firm pattern of giving wide latitude to Congress's use of the taxing and spending powers. In fact, the justices had not invalidated any federal spending legislation since 1936, when, in *United States v. Butler*, they struck down the Agricultural Adjustment Act. In cases such as *South Dakota v. Dole*, the Court gave considerable discretion to Congress to use the fiscal powers to provide incentives for states to cooperate with federal policies.

Yet the continuing judicial support for federal taxing and spending programs seemed to be running at odds with another line of decisions. In cases such as **New York v. United States** (1992), *United States v. Lopez* (1995), and *Printz v. United States* (1997) the justices applied principles of federalism to strike down congressional actions that encroached on the authority of the states. These cases served as a caution to the national government that it could not take control of the resources or decision making of states. What would happen if Congress provided financial incentives that the states viewed as being excessive, leaving the states no choice but to participate in particular federal programs?

Would the Court under these circumstances continue to support federal use of the taxing and spending powers? Or would the Court find such incentives to have a coercive effect that would be destructive to the traditional relationship between the federal government and the states? A major clash over just these questions occurred in 2012 when the justices reviewed the constitutionality of the Affordable Care Act.

We introduced the case of *National Federation of Independent Business v. Sebelius* in the previous chapter, focusing on the federal government's argument that Congress has ample authority under the commerce clause to require all Americans not already covered by medical insurance to buy a health care policy or pay a "shared responsibility" penalty for failure to do so. We saw that the Court concluded that the commerce power did not extend so far as to allow Congress to command unwilling individuals to purchase a commercial product. The Court's ruling, however, did not invalidate the Affordable Care Act. The government had an alternative position, an argument that Congress could enact the individual mandate through the use of the constitutional power to tax.

Another significant provision of the Affordable Care Act involved an enlargement of Medicaid, the government program to provide health care for the poor. This section of the ACA expanded both the number of persons eligible for Medicaid and the benefits provided. Because the federal and state governments jointly financed Medicaid, an expansion of the program would be costly to the states. The law stipulated that state participation in the expanded program was voluntary, but the penalty for refusing to participate was the loss of all federal Medicaid money. The federal government argued that the spending clause gave Congress ample authority to impose this requirement as a condition for receiving federal dollars. But a number of states objected, claiming that the nonparticipation penalty was not the kind of mild financial inducement upheld in *South Dakota v. Dole*. The threatened loss of all Medicaid funding, they argued, was instead precisely the kind of coercive policy that was forbidden by that decision.

In the excerpt that appears below we highlight the Court's response to the taxing power justification for the individual mandate and the spending power rationale for the Medicaid expansion. Throughout the opinions in this decision, you will see reference to many of the perennial taxing and spending power issues the Court has confronted since the beginning of the Republic.

National Federation of Independent Business v. Sebelius

567 U.S. 519 (2012)
http://caselaw.findlaw.com/us-supreme-court/11-393.html
Oral arguments available at https://www.oyez.org/
   cases/2011/11-393
Vote on the taxing power challenge to the Affordable Care Act:
   5 (Breyer, Ginsburg, Kagan, Roberts, Sotomayor)
   4 (Alito, Kennedy, Scalia, Thomas)
Vote on the expansion of Medicaid:
   7 (Alito, Breyer, Kagan, Kennedy, Roberts, Scalia, Thomas)
   2 (Ginsburg, Sotomayor)

OPINION ANNOUNCING THE JUDGMENT OF THE COURT AND THE OPINION OF THE COURT: *Roberts*

OPINION CONCURRING IN PART, CONCURRING IN JUDGMENT, AND DISSENTING IN PART: *Ginsburg*

JOINT OPINION DISSENTING: *Alito, Kennedy, Scalia, Thomas*

DISSENTING OPINION: *Thomas*

In 2010, Congress passed the Patient Protection and Affordable Care Act with the goal of increasing the number of Americans covered by medical insurance and decreasing the cost of health care. The constitutionality of the law was challenged in several suits, including this one filed by the National Federation of Independent Business, twenty-six state governments, and several individuals against Kathleen Sebelius, the secretary of health and human services.

Two provisions of the ACA provoked the most significant constitutional attacks. The first was the "individual mandate," which directs most Americans to purchase "minimum essential" health insurance coverage for themselves and their dependents if they do not receive such coverage from their employers. Section 5000A directs that those who do not comply with this provision are required to make a "shared responsibility" payment to the federal government. The act provides that this "penalty" will be paid to the Internal Revenue Service and "shall be assessed and collected in the same manner" as tax penalties.

The challengers argued that Congress exceeded its constitutional power in passing the law. The government countered that Congress acted properly under its power to regulate interstate commerce and its power to tax. In the previous chapter we presented an excerpt from this decision in which the Court concluded that the commerce clause did not give Congress the authority to compel inactive individuals to enter into commercial transactions. In the excerpt below, we focus on the Court's reaction to the government's

alternative claim that the power to tax allows Congress to impose the individual mandate.

The second provision in this controversy called for an expansion of Medicaid. This program, administered by the states but jointly funded by state and federal governments, provides health care for the poor. It is by far the largest source of federal dollars granted to the states. About two-thirds of all Medicaid funds come from the federal government. Medicaid expenditures constitute a state's largest budget item, accounting for about 20 percent of a typical state's expenditures.

The ACA called for an enlarged Medicaid program that would expand the health care services available to the poor. It would also increase the number of people eligible for program benefits by including all those whose incomes fall below 133 percent of the federal poverty line. Once the program was fully implemented, the federal government would cover 90 percent of the costs of the newly eligible persons. To the objecting states, the Medicare expansion provisions were not compatible with the principles articulated in *South Dakota v. Dole*. The threat to strip nonparticipating states of all Medicare funds, they argued, amounted to unconstitutionally excessive pressure on the states to bow to the federal government's policy wishes.

The Eleventh Circuit Court of Appeals upheld the Medicaid expansion but struck down the individual mandate. The Supreme Court granted review.

CHIEF JUSTICE ROBERTS ANNOUNCED THE JUDGMENT OF THE COURT AND DELIVERED . . . AN OPINION WITH RESPECT TO [THE AUTHORITY OF CONGRESS TO IMPOSE THE INDIVIDUAL MANDATE UNDER THE TAXING POWER AND THE CONSTITUTIONALITY OF THE MEDICAID EXPANSION].

Today we resolve constitutional challenges to two provisions of the Patient Protection and Affordable Care Act of 2010: the individual mandate, which requires individuals to purchase a health insurance policy providing a minimum level of coverage; and the Medicaid expansion, which gives funds to the States on the condition that they provide specified health care to all citizens whose income falls below a certain threshold. . . .

The exaction the Affordable Care Act imposes on those without health insurance looks like a tax in many respects. The "[s]hared responsibility payment," as the statute entitles it, is paid into the Treasury by "taxpayer[s]" when they file their tax returns. It does not apply to individuals who do not pay federal income taxes because their household income is less than the filing threshold in the Internal Revenue Code. For taxpayers who do owe the payment, its amount is determined by such familiar factors as taxable income, number of dependents, and joint filing status. The requirement to pay is found in the Internal Revenue Code and enforced by the IRS, which . . . must assess and collect it "in the same manner as taxes." This process yields the essential feature of any tax: it produces at least some revenue for the Government. Indeed, the payment is expected to raise about $4 billion per year by 2017.

It is of course true that the Act describes the payment as a "penalty," not a "tax." But [this] does not determine whether the payment may be viewed as an exercise of Congress's taxing power. . . .

We have . . . held that exactions not labeled taxes nonetheless were authorized by Congress's power to tax. In the *License Tax Cases* [1866], for example, we held that federal licenses to sell liquor and lottery tickets—for which the licensee had to pay a fee—could be sustained as exercises of the taxing power. And in *New York v. United States* [1992] we upheld as a tax a "surcharge" on out-of-state nuclear waste shipments, a portion of which was paid to the Federal Treasury. We thus ask whether the shared responsibility payment falls within Congress's taxing power, "[d]isregarding the designation of the exaction, and viewing its substance and application." *United States v. Constantine* (1935).

Our cases confirm this functional approach. For example, in [*Bailey v.*] *Drexel Furniture* [1922], we focused on three practical characteristics of the so-called tax on employing child laborers that convinced us the "tax" was actually a penalty. First, the tax imposed an exceedingly heavy burden—10 percent of a company's net income—on those who employed children, no matter how small their infraction. Second, it imposed that exaction only on those who knowingly employed underage laborers. Such scienter requirements are typical of punitive statutes, because Congress often wishes to punish only those who intentionally break the law. Third, this "tax" was enforced in part by the Department of Labor, an agency responsible for punishing violations of labor laws, not collecting revenue.

The same analysis here suggests that the shared responsibility payment may for constitutional purposes be considered a tax, not a penalty: First, for most Americans the amount due will be far less than the price of insurance, and, by statute, it can never be more. It may often be a reasonable financial decision to make the payment rather than purchase insurance, unlike the "prohibitory" financial punishment in *Drexel Furniture.* Second, the individual mandate contains no scienter requirement. Third, the payment is collected solely by the IRS through the normal means of taxation—except that the Service is not allowed to use those means most suggestive of a punitive sanction, such as criminal prosecution. The reasons the Court in *Drexel Furniture* held that what was called a "tax" there was a penalty support the conclusion that what is called a "penalty" here may be viewed as a tax.

None of this is to say that the payment is not intended to affect individual conduct. Although the payment will raise considerable revenue, it is plainly designed to expand health insurance coverage. But taxes that seek to influence conduct are nothing new. Some of our earliest federal taxes sought to deter the purchase of imported manufactured goods in order to foster the growth of domestic industry. Today, federal and state taxes can compose more than half the retail price of cigarettes, not just to raise more money, but to encourage people to quit smoking. And we have upheld such obviously regulatory measures as taxes on selling marijuana and sawed-off shotguns. Indeed, "[e]very tax is in some measure regulatory. To some extent it interposes an economic impediment to the activity taxed as compared with others not taxed." That §5000A seeks to shape decisions about whether to buy health insurance does not mean that it cannot be a valid exercise of the taxing power.

In distinguishing penalties from taxes, this Court has explained that "if the concept of penalty means anything, it means punishment for an unlawful act or omission." *United States v. Reorganized CF&I Fabricators of Utah, Inc.* (1996). While the individual mandate clearly aims to induce the purchase of health insurance, it need not be read to declare that failing to do so is unlawful. Neither the Act nor any other law attaches negative legal consequences to not buying health insurance, beyond requiring a payment to the IRS. The Government agrees with that reading, confirming that if someone chooses to pay rather than obtain health insurance, they have fully complied with the law.

Indeed, it is estimated that four million people each year will choose to pay the IRS rather than buy insurance. We would expect Congress to be troubled by that prospect if such conduct were unlawful. That Congress apparently regards such extensive failure to comply with the mandate as tolerable suggests that Congress did not think it was creating four million outlaws. It suggests instead that the shared responsibility payment merely imposes a tax citizens may lawfully choose to pay in lieu of buying health insurance. . . .

Even if the taxing power enables Congress to impose a tax on not obtaining health insurance, any tax must still comply with other requirements in the Constitution. Plaintiffs argue that the shared responsibility payment does not do so, citing Article I, §9, clause 4. That clause provides: "No Capitation, or other direct, Tax shall be laid, unless in Proportion to the Census or Enumeration herein before directed to be taken." This requirement means that any "direct Tax" must be apportioned so that each State pays in proportion to its population. According to the plaintiffs, if the individual mandate imposes a tax, it is a direct tax, and it is unconstitutional because Congress made no effort to apportion it among the States. . . .

A tax on going without health insurance does not fall within any recognized category of direct tax. It is not a capitation. Capitations are taxes paid by every person, "without regard to property, profession, or any other circumstance." *Hylton* [*v. United States* (1796)]. The whole point of the shared responsibility payment is that it is triggered by specific circumstances—earning a certain amount of income but not obtaining health insurance. The payment is also plainly not a tax on the ownership of land or personal property. The shared responsibility payment is thus not a direct tax that must be apportioned among the several States.

There may, however, be a more fundamental objection to a tax on those who lack health insurance. Even if only a tax, the payment under §5000A(b) remains a burden that the Federal Government imposes for an omission, not an act. If it is troubling to interpret the Commerce Clause as authorizing Congress to regulate those who abstain from commerce, perhaps it should be similarly troubling to permit Congress to impose a tax for not doing something.

. . . [I]t is abundantly clear the Constitution does not guarantee that individuals may avoid taxation through inactivity. A capitation, after all, is a tax that everyone must pay simply for existing, and capitations are expressly contemplated by the Constitution. The Court today holds that our Constitution protects us from federal regulation under the Commerce Clause so long as we abstain from the regulated activity. But from its creation, the Constitution has made no such promise with respect to taxes. . . .

The Affordable Care Act's requirement that certain individuals pay a financial penalty for not obtaining health insurance may reasonably be characterized as a tax. Because the Constitution permits such a tax, it is not our role to forbid it, or to pass upon its wisdom or fairness.

. . . The Federal Government does have the power to impose a tax on those without health insurance. Section 5000A is therefore constitutional, because it can reasonably be read as a tax.

* * *

The States also contend that the Medicaid expansion exceeds Congress's authority under the Spending Clause. They claim that Congress is coercing the States to adopt the changes it wants by threatening to withhold all of a State's Medicaid grants, unless the State accepts the new expanded funding and complies with the conditions that come with it. This, they argue, violates the basic principle that the "Federal Government may not compel the States to enact or administer a federal regulatory program." *New York.* . . .

The Spending Clause grants Congress the power "to pay the Debts and provide for the . . . general Welfare of the United States." We have long recognized that Congress may use this power to grant federal funds to the States, and may condition such a grant upon the States' "taking certain actions that Congress could not require them to take." Such measures "encourage a State to regulate in a particular way, [and] influenc[e] a State's policy choices." *New York.* The conditions imposed by Congress ensure that the funds are used by the States to "provide for the . . . general Welfare" in the manner Congress intended.

At the same time, our cases have recognized limits on Congress's power under the Spending Clause to secure state compliance with federal objectives. . . . [The] "Constitution has never been understood to confer upon Congress the ability to require the States to govern according to Congress' instructions." *New York.* Otherwise the two-government system established by the Framers would give way to a system that vests power in one central government, and individual liberty would suffer.

That insight has led this Court to strike down federal legislation that commandeers a State's legislative or administrative apparatus for federal purposes. See, e.g., *Printz* [*v. United States* (1997)], *New York.* It has also led us to scrutinize Spending Clause legislation to ensure that Congress is not using financial inducements to exert a "power akin to undue influence." *Steward Machine Co. v. Davis* (1937). Congress may use its spending power to create incentives for States to act in accordance with federal policies. But when "pressure turns into compulsion," the legislation runs contrary to our system of federalism. "[T]he Constitution simply does not give Congress the authority to require the States to regulate." *New York.* That is true whether Congress directly commands a State to regulate or indirectly coerces a State to adopt a federal regulatory system as its own.

Permitting the Federal Government to force the States to implement a federal program would threaten the political accountability key to our federal system. . . . Spending Clause programs do not pose this danger when a State has a legitimate choice whether to accept the federal conditions in exchange for federal funds. In such a situation, state officials can fairly be held politically accountable for choosing to accept or refuse the federal offer. But when the State has no choice, the Federal Government can achieve its objectives without accountability, just as in *New York* and *Printz.* Indeed, this danger is heightened when Congress acts under the Spending Clause, because Congress can use that power to implement federal policy it could not impose directly under its enumerated powers. . . .

The States . . . object that Congress has "crossed the line distinguishing encouragement from coercion," *New York,* in the way it has structured the funding: Instead of simply refusing to grant the new funds to States that will not accept the new conditions, Congress has also threatened to withhold those States' existing Medicaid funds. The States claim that this threat serves no purpose other than to force unwilling States to sign up for the dramatic expansion in health care coverage effected by the Act.

Given the nature of the threat and the programs at issue here, we must agree. . . .

In *South Dakota v. Dole,* we considered a challenge to a federal law that threatened to withhold five percent of a State's federal highway funds if the State did not raise its drinking age to 21. . . .

We accordingly asked whether "the financial inducement offered by Congress" was "so coercive as to pass the point at which 'pressure turns into compulsion.'" By "financial inducement" the Court meant the threat of losing five percent of highway funds; no new money was offered to the States to raise their drinking ages. We found that the inducement was not impermissibly coercive, because

Congress was offering only "relatively mild encouragement to the States." *Dole.* We observed that "all South Dakota would lose if she adheres to her chosen course as to a suitable minimum drinking age is 5%" of her highway funds. In fact, the federal funds at stake constituted less than half of one percent of South Dakota's budget at the time. . . .

In this case, the financial "inducement" Congress has chosen is much more than "relatively mild encouragement"—it is a gun to the head. Section 1396c of the Medicaid Act provides that if a State's Medicaid plan does not comply with the Act's requirements, the Secretary of Health and Human Services may declare that "further payments will not be made to the State." A State that opts out of the Affordable Care Act's expansion in health care coverage thus stands to lose not merely "a relatively small percentage" of its existing Medicaid funding, but all of it. Medicaid spending accounts for over 20 percent of the average State's total budget, with federal funds covering 50 to 83 percent of those costs. The Federal Government estimates that it will pay out approximately $3.3 trillion between 2010 and 2019 in order to cover the costs of pre-expansion Medicaid. In addition, the States have developed intricate statutory and administrative regimes over the course of many decades to implement their objectives under existing Medicaid. It is easy to see how the *Dole* Court could conclude that the threatened loss of less than half of one percent of South Dakota's budget left that State with a "prerogative" to reject Congress's desired policy, "not merely in theory but in fact." The threatened loss of over 10 percent of a State's overall budget, in contrast, is economic dragooning that leaves the States with no real option but to acquiesce in the Medicaid expansion. . . .

Nothing in our opinion precludes Congress from offering funds under the Affordable Care Act to expand the availability of health care, and requiring that States accepting such funds comply with the conditions on their use. What Congress is not free to do is to penalize States that choose not to participate in that new program by taking away their existing Medicaid funding. . . . In light of the Court's holding, the Secretary cannot . . . withdraw existing Medicaid funds for failure to comply with the requirements set out in the expansion. . . .

We have no way of knowing how many States will accept the terms of the expansion, but we do not believe Congress would have wanted the whole Act to fall, simply because some may choose not to participate. The other reforms Congress enacted, after all, will remain "fully operative as a law" and will still function in a way "consistent with Congress' basic objectives in enacting the statute." Confident that Congress would not have intended anything different, we conclude that the rest of the Act need not fall in light of our constitutional holding.

* * *

The Affordable Care Act is constitutional in part and unconstitutional in part. The individual mandate cannot be upheld as an exercise of Congress's power under the Commerce Clause. That Clause authorizes Congress to regulate interstate commerce, not to order individuals to engage in it. In this case, however, it is reasonable to construe what Congress has done as increasing taxes on those who have a certain amount of income, but choose to go without health insurance. Such legislation is within Congress's power to tax.

As for the Medicaid expansion, that portion of the Affordable Care Act violates the Constitution by threatening existing Medicaid funding. Congress has no authority to order the States to regulate according to its instructions. Congress may offer the States grants and require the States to comply with accompanying conditions, but the States must have a genuine choice whether to accept the offer. The States are given no such choice in this case: They must either accept a basic change in the nature of Medicaid, or risk losing all Medicaid funding. The remedy for that constitutional violation is to preclude the Federal Government from imposing such a sanction. That remedy does not require striking down other portions of the Affordable Care Act.

The Framers created a Federal Government of limited powers, and assigned to this Court the duty of enforcing those limits. The Court does so today. But the Court does not express any opinion on the wisdom of the Affordable Care Act. Under the Constitution, that judgment is reserved to the people.

The judgment of the Court of Appeals for the Eleventh Circuit is affirmed in part and reversed in part.

It is so ordered.

JUSTICE GINSBURG, . . . CONCURRING IN PART, CONCURRING IN THE JUDGMENT IN PART, AND DISSENTING IN PART.

I agree with The Chief Justice that the . . . minimum coverage provision is a proper exercise of Congress' taxing power. . . . I would also hold that the Spending Clause permits the Medicaid expansion exactly as Congress enacted it. . . .

The Spending Clause authorizes Congress "to pay the Debts and provide for the . . . general Welfare of the United States." To ensure that federal funds granted to the States are spent "to 'provide for the . . . general Welfare' in the manner Congress intended," Congress must of course have authority to impose limitations on the States' use of the federal dollars. This Court, time and again, has respected Congress' prescription of spending conditions, and has required States to abide by them. In particular, we have recognized Congress' prerogative to condition a State's receipt of Medicaid funding on compliance with the terms Congress set for participation in the program.

The ACA . . . relates solely to the federally funded Medicaid program; if States choose not to comply, Congress has not

On June 28, 2012, a woman in Chicago expresses her thanks to the majority of justices who, that day, had issued an opinion upholding the Patient Protection and Affordable Care Act.

Todd Bannor/Alamy Stock Photo

threatened to withhold funds earmarked for any other program. Nor does the ACA use Medicaid funding to induce States to take action Congress itself could not undertake. The Federal Government undoubtedly could operate its own health-care program for poor persons, just as it operates Medicare for seniors' health care.

That is what makes this such a simple case, and the Court's decision so unsettling. Congress, aiming to assist the needy, has appropriated federal money to subsidize state health-insurance programs that meet federal standards. The principal standard the ACA sets is that the state program cover adults earning no more than 133% of the federal poverty line. Enforcing that prescription ensures that federal funds will be spent on health care for the poor in furtherance of Congress' present perception of the general welfare. . . .

Congress has broad authority to construct or adjust spending programs to meet its contemporary understanding of "the general Welfare." *Helvering v. Davis* (1937). Courts owe a large measure of respect to Congress' characterization of the grant programs it establishes. See *Steward Machine*. . . .

At bottom, my colleagues' position is that the States' reliance on federal funds limits Congress' authority to alter its spending programs. This gets things backwards: Congress, not the States, is tasked with spending federal money in service of the general welfare. And each successive Congress is empowered to appropriate funds as it sees fit. When the 110th Congress reached a conclusion about Medicaid funds that differed from its predecessors' view, it abridged no State's right to "existing," or "pre-existing," funds. For, in fact, there are no such funds. There is only money States anticipate receiving from future Congresses.

Congress has delegated to the Secretary of Health and Human Services the authority to withhold, in whole or in part, federal Medicaid funds from States that fail to comply with the Medicaid Act as originally composed and as subsequently amended. The Chief Justice, however, holds that the Constitution precludes the Secretary from withholding "existing" Medicaid funds based on States' refusal to comply with the expanded Medicaid program. . . .I disagree that any such withholding would violate the Spending Clause. Accordingly, I would affirm the decision of the Court of Appeals for the Eleventh Circuit in this regard.

But in view of The Chief Justice's disposition, I agree with him that the Medicaid Act's severability clause determines the appropriate remedy. That clause provides that "[i]f any provision of [the Medicaid Act], or the application thereof to any person or circumstance, is held invalid, the remainder of the chapter, and the application of such provision to other persons or circumstances shall not be affected thereby." . . .

JOINT OPINION OF JUSTICE SCALIA, JUSTICE KENNEDY, JUSTICE THOMAS, AND JUSTICE ALITO, DISSENTING.

The Government contends . . . that "the minimum coverage provision is independently authorized by Congress's taxing power." The phrase "independently authorized" suggests the existence of a creature never hitherto seen in the United States Reports: A penalty for constitutional purposes that is *also* a tax for constitutional purposes. In all our cases the two are mutually exclusive. The provision challenged under the Constitution is either a penalty or else a tax. . . . The issue is not whether Congress had the power to frame the minimum-coverage provision as a tax, but whether it did so.

In answering that question we must, if "fairly possible," construe the provision to be a tax rather than a mandate-with-penalty, since that would render it constitutional rather than unconstitutional. But we cannot rewrite the statute to be what it is not. "[A]lthough this Court will often strain to construe legislation so as to save it against constitutional attack, it must not and will not carry this to the point of perverting the purpose of a statute . . . or judicially rewriting it." *Commodity Futures Trading Comm'n v. Schor* (1986). In this case, there is simply no way, "without doing violence to the fair meaning of the words used," to escape what Congress enacted: a mandate that individuals maintain minimum essential coverage, enforced by a penalty.

Our cases establish a clear line between a tax and a penalty: "[A] tax is an enforced contribution to provide for the support of government; a penalty . . . is an exaction imposed by statute as punishment for an unlawful act." *United States v. Reorganized CF&I Fabricators of Utah, Inc.* (1996). . . .

So the question is, quite simply, whether the exaction here is imposed for violation of the law. It unquestionably is. The minimum-coverage provision is . . . entitled "Requirement to maintain minimum essential coverage." It commands that every "applicable individual shall . . . ensure that the individual . . . is covered under minimum essential coverage." And the immediately following provision states that, "[i]f . . . an applicable individual . . . fails to meet the requirement of subsection (a) . . . there is hereby imposed . . . a penalty." And several of Congress' legislative "findings" with regard to §5000A confirm that it sets forth a legal requirement and constitutes the assertion of regulatory power, not mere taxing power. . . .

Quite separately, the fact that Congress (in its own words) "imposed . . . a penalty," for failure to buy insurance is alone sufficient to render that failure unlawful. . . .

. . . [T]o say that the Individual Mandate merely imposes a tax is not to interpret the statute but to rewrite it.

We now consider respondents' second challenge to the constitutionality of the ACA, namely, that the Act's dramatic expansion of the Medicaid program exceeds Congress' power to attach conditions to federal grants to the States.

The ACA does not legally compel the States to participate in the expanded Medicaid program, but the Act authorizes a severe sanction for any State that refuses to go along: termination of all the State's Medicaid funding. For the average State, the annual federal Medicaid subsidy is equal to more than one-fifth of the State's expenditures. A State forced out of the program would not only lose this huge sum but would almost certainly find it necessary to increase its own health-care expenditures substantially, requiring either a drastic reduction in funding for other programs or a large increase in state taxes. And these new taxes would come on top of the federal taxes already paid by the State's citizens to fund the Medicaid program in other States. . . .

When federal legislation gives the States a real choice whether to accept or decline a federal aid package, the federal-state relationship is in the nature of a contractual relationship. And just as a contract is voidable if coerced, "[t]he legitimacy of Congress' power to legislate under the spending power . . . rests on whether the State voluntarily and knowingly accepts the terms of the 'contract.'" If a federal spending program coerces participation the States have not "exercise[d] their choice"—let alone made an "informed choice."

Coercing States to accept conditions risks the destruction of the "unique role of the States in our system." "[T]he Constitution has never been understood to confer upon Congress the ability to require the States to govern according to Congress' instructions." Congress may not "simply commandeer the legislative processes of the States by directly compelling them to enact and enforce a federal regulatory program." Congress effectively engages in this impermissible compulsion when state participation in a federal spending program is coerced, so that the States' choice whether to enact or administer a federal regulatory program is rendered illusory.

Where all Congress has done is to "encourag[e] state regulation rather than compe[l] it, state governments remain responsive to the local electorate's preferences; state officials remain accountable to the people. [But] where the Federal Government compels States to regulate, the accountability of both state and federal officials is diminished." . . .

. . . [T]he legitimacy of attaching conditions to federal grants to the States depends on the voluntariness of the States' choice to accept or decline the offered package. Therefore, if States really have no choice other than to accept the package, the offer is coercive, and the conditions cannot be sustained under the spending power. And as our decision in *South Dakota v. Dole* makes clear, theoretical voluntariness is not enough. . . .

. . . When a heavy federal tax is levied to support a federal program that offers large grants to the States, States may, as a practical matter, be unable to refuse to participate in the federal program and to substitute a state alternative. Even if a State believes that the federal program is ineffective and inefficient, withdrawal would likely force the State to impose a huge tax increase on its residents, and this new state tax would come on top of the federal taxes already paid by residents to support subsidies to participating States. . . .

Whether federal spending legislation crosses the line from enticement to coercion is often difficult to determine, and courts should not conclude that legislation is unconstitutional on this ground unless the coercive nature of an offer is unmistakably clear. In this case, however, there can be no doubt. In structuring the ACA, Congress unambiguously signaled its belief that every State would have no real choice but to go along with the Medicaid Expansion. If the anticoercion rule does not apply in this case, then there is no such rule. . . .

In sum, it is perfectly clear from the goal and structure of the ACA that the offer of the Medicaid Expansion was one that Congress understood no State could refuse. The Medicaid Expansion therefore exceeds Congress' spending power and cannot be implemented. . . .

For the reasons here stated, we would find the Act invalid in its entirety. We respectfully dissent.

National Federation of Independent Business v. Sebelius was a landmark ruling on the power of Congress, one that can be understood as both a victory and a defeat for the legislative branch. On the one hand, it reinforced the ability of Congress to utilize its taxing power as a regulatory tool, justifying legislation that Congress might not otherwise have the authority to enact. On the other hand, aside from narrowing the range of federal regulatory power under the commerce clause, the justices—for the first time in seventy-five years—struck down a federal spending initiative, finding that the Medicaid expansion violated the principles of federalism by coercing the states to participate in a federal program.

The Supreme Court's decision on the Affordable Care Act made significant contributions to our understanding of the commerce clause, the power to tax and spend, and the constitutional relationship between the federal government and the states. Subsequent political events, however, significantly altered the law itself. The 2016 national elections gave Republicans control of both houses of Congress and ushered Donald Trump into the White House. These electoral victories provided members of the party an opening to fulfill their pledge to repeal and replace "Obamacare." Initially they were unsuccessful, but in 2018 the controversial individual mandate's tax penalty, a major component of the law's foundation, was not exactly repealed but was set at zero dollars, leaving the viability of the health care law in some doubt. In fact, in late 2019 the U.S. Court of Appeals for the Fifth Circuit held the individual mandate unconstitutional: "because it can no longer be read as a tax, and there is no other constitutional provision that justifies this exercise of congressional power."

As for the Medicaid expansion provisions, thirty-seven states (including the District of Columbia) elected to participate in the new coverage opportunities. However, fourteen states, mostly located in the South, took advantage of the Supreme Court's decision and decided not to expand coverage. These events rendered the country's health care policy somewhat unstable and guaranteed that the issue would remain high on the national political agenda.

ANNOTATED READINGS

A number of good works focus on the history and development of tax law and policy, including W. Elliot Brownlee, *Federal Taxation in America: A Short History*, 2nd ed. (New York: Cambridge University Press, 2009); Gerald Carson, "The Income Tax and How It Grew," *American Heritage*, December 1973, 4–7, 79–88; Jasper L. Cummings Jr., *The Supreme Court, Federal Taxation, and the Constitution* (Washington, DC: American Bar Association, 2013); Ajay K. Merota, *Making the Modern American Fiscal State: Law, Politics, and the Rise of Progressive Taxation, 1877-1929* (New York: Cambridge University Press, 2013); Ann Mumford, *Taxing Culture: Toward a Theory of Tax Collection Law* (Burlington, VT: Ashgate, 2002); Sheldon D. Pollack, *War, Revenue, and State Building: Financing the Development of the American State* (Ithaca, NY: Cornell University Press, 2009); Steven R. Weisman, *The Great Tax Wars: Lincoln to Wilson—The Fierce Battles over Money and Power* (New York: Simon & Schuster, 2001); John F. Witte, *The Politics and Development of the Federal Income Tax* (Madison: University of Wisconsin Press, 1985); Joseph F. Zimmerman, *The Silence of Congress: State Taxation of Interstate Commerce* (Albany: State University of New York Press, 2007).

Other studies focus on monetary and spending policy, such as Edward S. Corwin, "The Spending Power of Congress—Apropos the Maternity Act," *Harvard Law Review* 36 (1923): 548–582; Gerald T. Dunne, *Monetary Decisions of the Supreme Court* (New Brunswick, NJ: Rutgers University Press, 1960); Robert M. Howard, *Getting a Poor Return: Courts, Justice, and Taxes* (Albany: State University of New York Press, 2009); James Willard Hurst, *A Legal History of Money in the United States, 1774–1970* (Lincoln: University of Nebraska Press, 1973); Dennis S. Ippolito, *Deficit, Debt, and the New Politics of Tax Policy* (New York: Cambridge University Press, 2012); Theodore Sky, *To Provide for the General Welfare: A History of Federal Spending Power* (Newark: University of Delaware Press, 2003).

ECONOMIC LIBERTIES

IF ASKED WHAT THEY ADMIRE about the United States, many Americans would say the freedoms of speech, press, and religion. But when asked to make political decisions—to choose elected officials, for example—Americans may put other considerations ahead of these cherished freedoms. As the old adage goes, people tend to vote their pocketbooks. Americans might not admit that the state of the economy drives their behavior, but it is perhaps the single most important determinant in their voting decisions.

That Americans hold economic well-being as a priority is not surprising. In Part III we saw that economic issues—commerce, taxing, and spending—have been major sources of friction between the federal government and the states virtually from the beginning of U.S. history.

Economic questions, however, are not the exclusive domain of the Supreme Court's federalism cases—quite the contrary. The Supreme Court often has heard constitutional challenges in which individuals claim that government actions have violated their personal economic liberties. In such cases the justices must determine how much power federal and state governments have to seize private property, to alter freely made contracts, and to restrict private employment agreements about wages and hours. Seen in this way, there is a strong relationship between civil liberties, such as the freedom of speech, and economic liberties, such as the right to own private property. Indeed, both provoke the same fundamental question: To what extent can government enact legislation that infringes on personal rights? Both also involve the same perennial conflict between individual interests and the government's view of the common good.

Even so, most Americans, including elected officials and even Supreme Court justices, tend to separate economic liberties from other civil liberties. We consider the right to express our views as significantly different from the right to conduct business. The framers, however, viewed both as equally important. Indeed, like the English philosopher John Locke—who regarded "life, liberty, and property" as natural rights—the framers saw civil and economic rights as fundamental freedoms that government was obligated to respect. According to James Madison, one of the framers' most important objectives as they gathered in Philadelphia in 1787 was to provide "more effectively for the security of private rights and the steady dispensation of justice within the states. Interference with these were the evils which had, more perhaps than anything else, produced this convention."

But, as Madison's comment implies, the framers' conception of liberties and what interfered with their exercise was somewhat different from ours. They equated liberty with the protection of private property, and in their view the states, not the new national government, posed the greater threat. Given the economic chaos under the Articles of Confederation, we can easily understand the founders' concerns. They believed the states had "crippled" both the government and the economy, and they wanted to create a national government strong enough to protect economic liberty from aggressive state governments. We must also keep in mind that many who attended the convention were wealthy men who wanted to protect their own economic advantage. In short, the framers were concerned that the unpropertied masses might succeed in taking control of state legislatures and pass legislation that would jeopardize the economic advantages of the upper classes. Indeed, in an important (albeit controversial) work published in 1913, *An Economic Interpretation of the Constitution*, historian Charles A. Beard depicted the founders as self-serving, even greedy, men who viewed the Constitution as a vehicle for the protection of their property interests.

Other analysts have taken issue with Beard's interpretation. Some contend that we cannot necessarily equate modern definitions of property with those the framers used; that is, the property interests they sought to protect were probably more encompassing than those we envision today. Although we may consider property as something tangible, or of clear monetary value, the framers—at least some of them—used the term *property* as "shorthand for an expanse of personal freedoms that need only be tangentially related, if at all, to economic activity."[1]

To protect these paramount property rights, however conceptualized, the framers inserted several

---

[1] Walter F. Murphy, James E. Fleming, and William F. Harris II, *American Constitutional Interpretation*, 2nd ed. (Mineola, NY: Foundation Press, 1995), 1071.

provisions into the Constitution. An important provision, which we examine in chapter 9, is the contract clause. Under Article I, Section 10, "No State shall . . . pass any . . . Law impairing the Obligation of Contracts." To understand the meaning of the clause, we must consider its language within the context of the day. As one source suggests:

> For the generation of 1787–91, property was a natural right, though the constitutional text did not so label it. And, because the right to property included rights to use and increase property, that basic right included a cognate right to contract with other property holders. Thus did the right to contract borrow a measure of moral status from the broader right in which it originated: the obligation to keep one's contracts was a duty flowing from the natural right to property.[2]

If the contract clause was one of the ways the framers sought to protect property interests against the "evils" of government interference, it was effective, at least initially. For the Marshall Court the contract clause, in particular, was an effective vehicle for promoting federal supremacy and economic growth. That Court understood Article I, Section 10, to prohibit state action that infringed on property rights and thereby impeded economic development.

But this interpretation was short-lived. With the end of the Marshall Court and the ascendancy of the Taney Court in the mid-1830s, use of the contract clause as a vehicle to protect property interests waned. Why that occurred is considered fully in chapter 9; for now, it is important to note that the "death" of the contract clause did not mean that courts were no longer interested in protecting economic liberties. They simply turned to another section of the Constitution to do so, the Fourteenth Amendment.

The Fourteenth Amendment's due process clause says no state shall "deprive any person of life, liberty, or property, without due process of law." Under the doctrine of substantive due process, which we address in chapter 10, between the 1890s and the 1930s the Supreme Court used the Fourteenth Amendment to prohibit states' interference with "liberty" interests. It struck down legislation mandating maximum work hours on the ground that such legislation interfered with the rights of employers to enter into contracts with their employees. Like the Court's interpretation of the contract clause, this treatment of the Fourteenth

Amendment—at least in the economic realm—eventually fell into disrepute. In chapter 10 we examine the reasons for its decline (but see chapter 16 for discussion of its use in cases implicating the right to privacy).

More recently, the Court has taken a serious look at yet another provision of the Constitution designed to protect property interests—the takings clause of the Fifth Amendment. Whereas in the contract clause the framers sought to prevent governments from infringing on contractual agreements, in the takings clause they tried to protect owners of private property from bearing the burden of governmental programs: "nor shall private property be taken for public use without just compensation." The founders recognized that the government needed the power to confiscate property—to construct roads or erect government buildings, for example—but wanted to ensure that property owners had some form of protection from abusive government practices.

Although the heyday of the contract clause and economic substantive due process has long since passed, the takings clause is enjoying a renaissance. As described in chapter 11, some recent justices, particularly the late Antonin Scalia and Clarence Thomas, sought to revitalize the takings clause as a significant vehicle for protecting property rights.

When the Court faces questions involving personal property rights today, it continues to confront the fundamental issue that bedeviled its predecessors: the complex relationship between "vested rights" and "community interests." We know that in a mature democratic society the pursuit of the collective good may occasionally conflict with individual property interests. For example, if a state enacts a law setting a minimum wage, that statute affects the individual liberty of employers, who believe it would be in their best interest, economically speaking, to pay their employees as little as possible. As a result, employers may argue that minimum wage laws violate their constitutional guarantees. But is there another interest at stake? What are the results of paying workers the lowest wage the market will bear? Does the state have a responsibility to promote the "health, safety, and welfare" of its citizens by enacting legislation that raises that wage?

The clash between these two interests—individual liberty (vested rights) and the state (community well-being)—has been a primary reason for the Court's involvement in this area. Over the long sweep of the institution's history, as we shall see, the Court has swung back and forth, during some eras exalting property rights above those of the community, and during others taking precisely the opposite approach.

---

[2]Ibid., 1073.

CHAPTER NINE

THE CONTRACT CLAUSE

SUPPOSE A FRIEND OF YOURS accepted a position some years ago with a large corporation. One of the reasons she took this particular job was that the company took advantage of a state-authorized program to offer an attractive retirement savings plan as a fringe benefit. Under the terms of the savings plan contract, your friend regularly placed a portion of her income into the fund, and the company matched her contributions. Money deposited in the fund belonged to the individual savers, and the company had no authority to use the funds for any corporate purpose. Over the years, your friend's savings account grew steadily. Then, in a national recession, the company's fortunes reversed and it, along with many others, faced bankruptcy. The state rushed to the relief of the troubled businesses by passing a law that allowed them unilaterally to use the assets in employee savings plans to finance operations until the economy regained its strength. The company took advantage of this statute, but, after spending all of the savings plan funds, the company still went bankrupt.

This hypothetical scenario raises some basic questions. How can the state pass a law that releases a company from its contractual obligations? With the state granting permission, the company stripped the employees of their savings. Why would anyone participate in any investment or commercial activity without some assurance that the state will not intervene and change the provisions of valid contractual agreements or nullify them altogether?

One of the hallmarks of a society that values commercial activity is the right to enter into legally binding contracts. It would be hard to imagine a market-based economy that did not recognize and protect such agreements. In most instances, we would expect the government to enforce contracts and not authorize parties who wished to break them.

The individuals who drafted the Constitution felt much the same way. Disturbed by the actions of state governments in the economic upheaval that followed the Revolution, the delegates to the Constitutional Convention moved to block state interference with contractual obligations. They did this by drafting the contract clause, one of the most important provisions of the Constitution during the nation's formative years.

THE FRAMERS AND THE CONTRACT CLAUSE

It might be difficult to find a group of people more supportive of the right to enter into binding agreements than the delegates to the Constitutional Convention. For the most part, these individuals represented the propertied classes, and they assembled in Philadelphia at a time of economic turmoil. Many of them feared that, in times of economic upheaval, state governments would resort to measures that would affect contractual obligations. In fact, as the delegates met in Philadelphia, some states were already adopting such policies.

After the Revolutionary War the economy was very unstable, and the government under the Articles of Confederation was powerless to correct the situation. Hardest hit were small farmers, many of whom had taken out large loans they could not repay. When creditors started foreclosing on real estate and some debtors were even jailed for failing to pay, farmers and others faced with unmanageable obligations began to agitate for relief. Several states responded by passing laws to help them. Among these were bankruptcy laws that erased certain debt obligations or extended the time to pay—legal obstacles that blocked creditors from asserting their contractual rights against their debtors. To complicate matters, states often issued their own fiat money—paper money that is not tied to the value of a commodity, like gold—and these state currencies were not always a reliable means of exchange. Some states issued paper money, only to see it quickly decline in value.[1]

These policies hurt the creditors, many of whom were wealthy landowners. In response, they called for a strengthening of the national government to deal with economic problems and a ban on states nullifying contractual obligations. This issue was among the more important factors prompting Congress to support a convention for the purpose of recommending changes in the Articles of Confederation. Once assembled, the delegates went much further than originally authorized and created the Constitution of the United States. The document drafted in Philadelphia clearly reflected the economic interests of the delegates. Among the provisions they wrote was a protection of contracts against state government infringement. Article I, Section 10, declares: "No State shall . . . pass any . . . Law impairing the obligation of contracts."

The eighteenth century's understanding of the term *contract* was much the same as today's understanding. A contract is an agreement voluntarily entered into by two or more parties in which a promise is made and something of value is given or pledged. Contractual agreements are made in almost every commercial transaction, such as a mining company's promise to deliver a quantity of iron ore to a steel mill in return for a particular sum of money, or a lawyer's promise to represent a client at a specified rate of compensation.

For the framers, the right to enter into contracts was an important freedom closely tied to the right of private property. The ownership of private property implies the right to buy, sell, divide, occupy, lease, and use it, but one cannot effectively exercise these various property rights without the ability to enter into legally binding arrangements with others. In commercial transactions the parties rely on each other to carry out the contractual provisions. During the nation's formative years, those who failed to live up to contractual promises were dealt with harshly; for instance, individuals who could not meet their obligation were often sent to debtor prisons.

In the minds of the propertied classes of the eighteenth century, this was entirely appropriate, since the government, they believed, should not be allowed to intervene in such private arrangements.

Evidence from the convention indicates that the framers adopted the contract clause as a means of protecting agreements between private parties from state interference. At that time, however, contracts also were a means of carrying out public policy. Because governments then were much more limited than they are today, the states regularly entered into contracts with individuals or corporations to carry out government policy or to distribute government benefits. These state actions included land grants, commercial monopolies, and licenses to construct roads and bridges. An individual who entered into a contractual agreement with the state expected it to live up to its obligations and not abrogate the arrangement or unilaterally change the terms. In spite of what the framers might have intended, the contract clause is worded generally and therefore offers protection both to contracts among private parties and to agreements made between private parties and state governments.

Importantly, the framers drafted the contract clause to apply only to the states and not to the national government. There were two reasons they targeted the states in this way. First, the framers had recent experience with states passing laws that nullified contractual provisions, and so they saw the states as the more likely threat to the importance of contractual relationships. Second and more practically, given the nature of business activity at that time, the framers envisioned that most economic regulatory efforts would occur at the state level.

To be sure, there were delegates to the convention who regarded the contract clause as essential to the protection of property rights. In *Federalist* No. 7, Alexander Hamilton justified the prohibition against state impairment of contract obligations by claiming, "Laws in violation of private contracts . . . may be considered as another probable source of hostility." James Madison declared in *Federalist* No. 44, "[L]aws impairing the obligation of contracts are contrary to the first principles of the social compact and to every principle of sound legislation." At the same time, there were others who wanted to ensure that states had the ability to intervene in economic emergencies to protect borrowers from financial ruin. Luther Martin believed, "The times have been such as to render regulations of this kind necessary in most or all of the states, to prevent the wealthy creditor and the moneyed man from totally destroying the poor, though industrious debtor."

---

[1]See Edward J. Perkins, *American Public Finance and Financial Services, 1700-1815* (Columbus: Ohio State University Press, 1994), Chapter 7.

The contract clause became an important legal force in the early years of the nation's development. As political majorities changed from election to election, it was not unusual for state legislatures to enter into contracts with private parties, only to break or change those agreements in subsequent legislative sessions. In addition, state governments often adopted policies that ran contrary to contracts among private individuals. When such actions occurred, injured parties would challenge the state in court. As a result, the contract clause was one of the most litigated constitutional provisions in the first decades of U.S. history. In a number of cases, for instance, the Court evaluated various state laws that changed the legal remedies available to parties of contracts that existed before those laws went into effect.[2] One study concluded that roughly 40 percent of all Supreme Court cases prior to 1889 that attacked the validity of state legislation did so on the basis of contract clause arguments.[3]

JOHN MARSHALL AND THE CONTRACT CLAUSE

Under the Marshall Court, the significance of the contract clause increased dramatically. As a Federalist, Chief Justice John Marshall had strong views on private property, economic development, and the role of the federal government. He consistently supported aggressive policies that would result in vigorous economic expansion. Underlying this position was a philosophy that elevated private property to the level of a natural right that government had little authority to limit. Furthermore, Marshall firmly believed that the nation's interests would be best served if the federal government rather than the states became the primary agent for economic policy making. As we have seen in the areas of federalism and commerce, Marshall could be counted on to uphold actions taken by the federal government and to favor it over competing state interests. Marshall's ideology predisposed him to champion the contract clause, which he viewed as essential to the right to private property. Moreover, the limitations the clause placed on state regulatory powers appealed to his views on federalism. Given Marshall's domination of the Court for more than three decades, it is not surprising that the contract clause achieved an elevated status during those years.

Establishing the Importance of the Contract Clause

The first major Supreme Court decision to consider the contract clause was *Fletcher v. Peck* (1810), which concerned whether a state could nullify a public contract. The suit flowed from one of the most notorious incidents of corruption and bribery in the nation's early history—the Yazoo River land fraud. In this litigation the beneficiaries of the scheme sought to use the contract clause to protect their gains.

This dispute had its roots in the 1795 session of the Georgia legislature. Clearly motivated by wholesale bribery, the legislators sold about 35 million acres of public lands to several land companies. The territory that Georgia owned encompassed most of what is now Mississippi and Alabama. Some of the nation's most prominent public figures, including members of Congress, supported this transaction or invested in it. The citizens of Georgia were outraged by the sale and turned out most of their state legislators in the next election. In 1796 the newly elected legislature promptly rescinded the sales contract and moved to repossess the land. Unfortunately, by this time the land companies had sold numerous parcels to third-party investors and settlers, none of whom were parties to Georgia's original corrupt sale. A massive and complicated set of legal actions ensued to determine ownership of the disputed lands. Attempts to negotiate a settlement proved unsuccessful. Even the president, Thomas Jefferson, was drawn into the controversy as he tried to work out a compromise settlement that would satisfy the state of Georgia as well as the investors.

Fletcher v. Peck was a lawsuit filed to obtain a judicial determination of the ownership question. John Peck acquired a parcel of the land in question from James Gunn, one of the original buyers in the Georgia land sales. Peck in turn sold the land to Robert Fletcher. When the state repealed the sale and resumed control of the land, Fletcher sued Peck for return of the purchase price. The real issue, however, rested squarely on the meaning of the contract clause: May a state that has entered into a valid contract later rescind that contract?

John Quincy Adams, who would become the sixth president of the United States, Joseph Story, who subsequently became the youngest person ever appointed to the Supreme Court, and former South Carolina

---

[2]Robert L. Hale, "The Supreme Court and the Contract Clause," *Harvard Law* Review 57 (1944): 512–557.

[3]Benjamin F. Wright, *The Contract Clause of the Constitution* (Cambridge, MA: Harvard University Press, 1938).

congressman Robert Goodloe Harper represented Peck and the interests of the others who had purchased the land. They argued that the contract clause barred the state from rescinding the original sales agreements. Attorneys supporting Georgia's repudiation of the land sale maintained that the state was empowered to declare the sale void because the original transaction was based on fraud. Furthermore, they contended that the contract clause was intended to protect against the abrogation of private contracts, not those made by the states.

Chief Justice Marshall was caught in a bind. To give force to the contract clause would be to rule in favor of those who profited from state government corruption. To rule against the unpopular fraudulent transactions would be to hand down a precedent significantly curtailing the meaning of the provision.

Marshall's choice, supported by each of the other four justices participating in the decision, was to uphold the land sales. The Court did not question the general ability of a legislature to repeal what a previous legislature had done. But when the law is in the form of "a contract, when absolute rights have vested under that contract, a repeal of the law cannot devest those rights." In Marshall's view, Georgia was not simply enacting a law; it was using its legislative power to void a contract and in so doing impaired the obligation of contracts in violation of Article I, Section 10.

Marshall's opinion gave considerable force to the contract clause. Although he acknowledged that the original transactions were based on bribery and corruption, Marshall concluded that such matters are beyond the power of the courts to control. He concentrated instead on the validity of a state's rescinding a previously passed, binding agreement. According to the Court's holding in this case, the Constitution prohibits the states from impairing the obligation of any contract, even a contract that is contrary to the public good. In striking down the 1796 Georgia statute, the Supreme Court for the first time nullified a state law on constitutional grounds. *Fletcher v. Peck* established the contract clause as an important provision of the new Constitution and encouraged the use of the clause in challenges to states' economic regulations. As illustrated in Box 9-1, however, it took several additional years for the legal confusion over the Yazoo land titles to be settled.

In 1819 the Marshall Court heard *Sturges v. Crowninshield,* an appeal that presented issues hitting squarely on the concerns the delegates at the Constitutional Convention expressed. Richard Crowninshield, whose business enterprises had suffered hard times, received two loans from Josiah Sturges totaling approximately $1,500. The loans were secured by promissory notes. When Crowninshield became insolvent, he sought relief from his debts by invoking New York's recently passed bankruptcy law. Sturges objected, claiming that the New York law was a state impairment of the obligation of contracts in violation of the Constitution. The New York bankruptcy law was an example of just what the framers had intended to prohibit—states interfering with agreements between debtors and creditors.

The case presented two issues to the Supreme Court. The first was whether a state may enact a bankruptcy law at all. Article I, Section 8, Clause 4, of the Constitution expressly gave the federal government power to enact such legislation. Did this power preclude the states' acting? For a unanimous Court, Chief Justice Marshall wrote that in the absence of any federal action, the states were free to enact bankruptcy laws. The second issue was whether the New York law was invalid as an impairment of contracts. Here the Court found the law defective. The New York law discharged Crowninshield's contractual indebtedness entered into prior to the passage of the statute, which, according to the Court, was beyond the power of the state.[4]

Corporate Charters as Contracts

The same year the Court decided *Sturges,* the justices announced their decision in **Trustees of Dartmouth College v. Woodward** (1819), perhaps the most famous of the Marshall-era contract clause cases. The *Dartmouth College* case presented a question of particular significance to the business community: Is a corporation charter a contract protected against state impairment? The case had added intrigue because it involved a bitter partisan battle between the Republicans and the Federalists.

In 1769 King George III issued a corporate charter establishing Dartmouth College in New Hampshire. The charter designated a board of trustees as the ultimate governing body. The board was self-perpetuating, with the power to fill its own vacancies. The founder and first president of Dartmouth was Eleazar Wheelock, a Congregational minister whose school for the Christian

---

[4]Eight years later, however, the Court held in *Ogden v. Saunders* (1827) that state bankruptcy laws did not violate the contract clause if the contract was entered into after the enactment of the bankruptcy statute. That meant that, while states cannot interfere with contracts already established, they can enact rules under which subsequent contracts are made.

BOX 9-1

Aftermath . . . The Yazoo Lands Controversy

The Supreme Court's decision in *Fletcher v. Peck* (1810) provided a landmark ruling on the meaning of the contract clause, but it did not fully resolve the issues surrounding the Yazoo land claims. In the period between the Georgia legislature's original land sale in 1795 and the state's voiding of the sale in 1796, parcels were bought and sold in a climate of feverish land speculation. About 60 percent of the purchasers were New England residents eager to participate in western land investments. After Georgia repealed the original sale, titles to the Yazoo lands were in considerable doubt. The issue was complicated not only by the actions of the Georgia legislature but also by claims made by Indian tribes, old Spanish interests, squatters, and those who had been granted lands by Georgia governors over the years. Bogus titles and sales of nonexistent land further complicated matters.

When purchasers learned that Georgia had passed legislation canceling the original sale, they pressured Congress to provide compensation if their titles proved to be invalid. Northern representatives favored a compensation program to provide relief to constituents who had purchased property, but southerners, especially representatives from Georgia, opposed any compensation as rewarding those who sought to benefit from the original acts of bribery and fraud. *Fletcher v. Peck* was first filed in federal circuit court in Massachusetts in 1803 in an attempt to have the judiciary settle the matter. Action on the lawsuit and subsequent appeals were delayed, with the parties hoping that Congress would resolve the dispute by passing a compensation act. When legislation failed in 1804, 1805, and 1806, it appeared that the courts would have to answer the lingering questions. By the time the Supreme Court decided *Fletcher v. Peck*, fifteen years had elapsed since the original sales, and determining valid title to each parcel of land was next to impossible.

The decision in *Fletcher v. Peck* was unpopular in many circles. Some thought the Court should not uphold contracts based on wholesale corruption. Thomas Jefferson used the decision as an opportunity to renew his attacks on Marshall. He claimed the chief justice's opinion was filled with "twistifications," "cunning," and "sophistry." According to Jefferson, it illustrated once again "how dexterously [Marshall] can reconcile law to his personal biases."

The decision, however, put pressure on Congress to bring closure to the controversy. Northerners again demanded a compensation program, but southerners still resisted. In 1814 Congress appropriated $5 million from federal land sales to compensate those who held title to the Yazoo lands. Investors released their land claims in return for monetary compensation. It took four years for the claims to be settled. Northern representatives had obtained relief for their constituents, but resolving the confusion over the Yazoo lands also cleared the way for organizing the Mississippi Territory, which was admitted to the Union as a slaveholding state in 1817.

Sources: C. Peter Magrath, *Yazoo: Law and Politics in the New Republic* (Providence, RI: Brown University Press, 1966); see also Charles F. Hobson, *The Great Yazoo Lands Sale: The Case of* Fletcher v. Peck (Lawrence: University Press of Kansas, 2016).

---

education of Native Americans was expanded with financial support from the Earl of Dartmouth. Reverend Wheelock had authority to designate his own successor, and he chose his son, John Wheelock, who assumed the presidency upon Eleazar's death. John Wheelock was ill suited for the position, and for years friction existed between him and the board of trustees.

To shore up his position, Wheelock made political alliances with the Jeffersonian Republicans, who had gained control of the state legislature in 1816. The Republicans gladly took his side in the dispute with the Federalist-dominated board of trustees and passed a law radically changing the governing structure of the college. The law called for an expansion of the board from twelve to twenty-one, with members to be appointed by the governor, and it created a supervisory panel with veto power over the actions of the trustees. This reorganization of the college essentially rendered the old trustees powerless. In effect, the legislature converted Dartmouth College—renamed Dartmouth University under the new law—from a private to a public institution. The result was chaos. The students and faculty for the most part remained loyal to the old trustees, but the state essentially took over the buildings and records of the college. As might be expected, the college soon found itself on the edge of fiscal collapse.

To resolve the situation, the old trustees hired Daniel Webster to represent them. Webster, an 1801 Dartmouth graduate, agreed to take the case for a fee of $1,000, a considerable sum of money in those days. The trustees sued William Woodward, the secretary of the college, who had in his possession the college charter, records, and seal. Webster and the old trustees lost in the state courts and then appealed to the U.S. Supreme Court. When the case was argued in March 1818, Webster engaged in four hours of brilliant oratory before the justices. At times his argument was quite emotional, and he is said to have brought tears to the eyes of those present when he spoke his often-quoted line, "It is, sir, as I have said, a small college, and yet there are those that love it." The justices did not act in the heat of emotion, however; almost a year passed before they announced their decision. By the time the opinion was released, both John Wheelock and William Woodward had died.

With only one justice dissenting, the Court supported Webster's position. The grant by the English Crown setting up the college was a contract, Marshall declared, and the governing structure of the college was part of that contract. When the state of New Hampshire restructured the college with the 1816 legislation, it impaired the original contract. The statute was repugnant to the contract clause and therefore void.

As a result of this decision, the old trustees regained control of the college, and Webster's reputation as one of the nation's leading legal advocates was firmly established. Politically, the decision was also a victory for business interests. By holding that corporate charters were contracts under the meaning of Article I, Section 10, the Court gave businesses considerable protection against state regulation. The decision, however, was not totally one-sided. Marshall acknowledged the power of the state to include in its contracts and charters provisions reserving the right to make future changes.

The importance of the contract clause reached its zenith under the Marshall Court. These early decisions protecting contractual agreements helped spur the nation's economic development and expansion. But an inevitable battle was on the horizon, a battle between the constitutional sanctity of contracts and a state's authority to regulate for the public good.

THE DECLINE OF THE CONTRACT CLAUSE

The Marshall years ended when the chief justice died on July 6, 1835, at the age of seventy-nine. Marshall had been appointed in 1801 in one of the last acts of the once-dominant Federalist Party, and he had imposed his political philosophy on the Court's constitutional interpretations for more than three decades. His decisions in contract clause disputes, as well as in other areas of federalism and economic regulation, encouraged economic development and fostered entrepreneurial activity. Those decisions, however, often thwarted the regulatory efforts of the states.

Elevating the Public Good

The days of the Federalist philosophy sympathetic to the interests of business and the economic elite had passed. Andrew Jackson now occupied the White House. Jackson came from the American frontier and was committed to policies beneficial to ordinary citizens; he had little sympathy for the moneyed classes of the Northeast. Within a short period, Jackson had the opportunity to change the course of the Supreme Court. During his presidency he filled not only the center chair left vacant by Marshall's death but also those of five associate justices. The new appointees all held ideologies consistent with principles of Jacksonian democracy, especially the new chief justice, Roger Brooke Taney, a Maryland Democrat who had served in several posts in the Jackson administration.[5] Changes in constitutional interpretation were inevitable, although in the final analysis the Taney Court did not veer as far from Marshall Court precedents as many had predicted it would.

Given the differences between Federalist and Jacksonian values, however, the Taney Court was likely to reevaluate the contract clause. Its first opportunity to do so came in *Proprietors of Charles River Bridge v. Proprietors of Warren Bridge* (1837). As you read the Court's opinion, compare it with the positions the Court took during the Marshall era. Although Taney certainly did not repudiate Marshall's rulings, his opinion in *Charles River Bridge* struck a new balance between the inviolability of contracts and the power of the state to legislate for the public good. The Court also held that contracts should be strictly construed, a position at odds with Marshall's rather

---

[5] Taney was also the first Roman Catholic named to the Court, which, prior to his appointment, had consisted entirely of Protestants.

BOX 9-2

Daniel Webster (1782–1852)

Daniel Webster played an influential role in the development of American law and politics during a public career that spanned almost fifty years. Born in Salisbury, New Hampshire, January 18, 1782, and educated at Phillips Exeter Academy and Dartmouth College, he was admitted to the bar in 1805 and immediately began the practice of law in his home state.

In 1813 Webster was first elected to Congress as a Federalist representative from New Hampshire. This office was only the beginning of an illustrious series of important positions, including the following:

United States representative, New Hampshire, 1813–1817

Monroe delegate to Electoral College, 1820

United States representative, Massachusetts, 1823–1827

United States senator, Massachusetts, 1827–1841

Presidential candidate, 1836

Secretary of state (Harrison and Tyler administrations), 1841–1843

United States senator, Massachusetts, 1845–1850

Secretary of state (Fillmore administration), 1850–1852

Courtesy of the Library of Congress, Prints & Photographs Division

Webster was perhaps best known for his role as an advocate before the Supreme Court and for the brilliant oratorical skills he displayed both in Congress and in the courts. Webster appeared before the Supreme Court in 168 cases, winning about half of them. In twenty-four of his appearances he was an advocate in a major constitutional dispute. Among his most celebrated cases were the following:

McCulloch v. Maryland (1819)

Dartmouth College v. Woodward (1819)

Cohens v. Virginia (1821)

Gibbons v. Ogden (1824)

Osborn v. Bank of the United States (1824)

Ogden v. Saunders (1827)

Wheaton v. Peters (1834)

Charles River Bridge v. Warren Bridge (1837)

Swift v. Tyson (1842)

West River Bridge v. Dix (1848)

Luther v. Borden (1849)

Note: For a review of Webster's legal career, see Maurice G. Baxter, Daniel Webster and the Supreme Court (Amherst: University of Massachusetts Press, 1966).

expansive interpretations of contractual obligations. Justice Story, who had appeared as an attorney in *Fletcher v. Peck* and had supported Marshall's views of the contract clause since he joined the Court in 1811, dissented from this change in doctrine.

Proprietors of Charles River Bridge v. Proprietors of Warren Bridge

36 U.S. (11 Pet.) 420 (1837)
http://caselaw.findlaw.com/us-supreme-court/36/420.html
Vote: 5 (Baldwin, Barbour, McLean, Taney, Wayne)
　　2 (Story, Thompson)

OPINION OF THE COURT: *Taney*

CONCURRING OPINION: *McLean*

DISSENTING OPINIONS: *Story, Thompson*

In 1785 the Massachusetts legislature decided to build a bridge across the Charles River, between Boston and Charlestown. To pay for the bridge, the state created by charter the Charles River Bridge Company, whose investors would underwrite construction. The charter gave the company the right to construct the bridge and to collect tolls for its use. This agreement replaced a ferry franchise between the two cities that the colonial legislature had granted to Harvard College in 1650, and under this agreement, Harvard was compensated for its lost revenue. In 1792 the legislature extended the charter. Because of the population growth in the Boston area, the bridge received heavy use, and its investors prospered. In 1828, when traffic congestion on the bridge became a significant problem, the legislature decided that a second bridge was needed. Consequently, the state incorporated the Warren Bridge Company and authorized it to construct a bridge to be located about a hundred yards from the first. This company operated in exactly the same fashion as the Charles River Bridge Company, but with one important difference: the Warren Bridge investors would collect tolls to pay for the expense of construction plus an agreed-upon profit, but in no more than six years the state was to assume ownership of the Warren Bridge and then operate it on a toll-free basis.

Charles River Bridge Company opposed the construction of a second bridge. It claimed that its charter conferred the exclusive right to build and operate a bridge between Boston and Charlestown. The charter did not explicitly state that the company had exclusive rights, but why would Massachusetts compensate Harvard for its lost ferry revenue if it did not? A second bridge, eventually to be operated without tolls, would deprive the company of profits to which they alone were entitled. The second charter, the company claimed, was

a violation of the contract clause. To represent it, Charles River Bridge Company hired Daniel Webster, who had won the Dartmouth College case two decades earlier *(see Box 9-2)*. When the Massachusetts courts failed to grant relief, the Charles River Bridge Company took its case to the U.S. Supreme Court.

The case was first argued in March 1831, John Marshall still led the Court at that time, and Webster understandably felt confident of victory. But the justices could not agree on a decision, and the case was scheduled for reargument in 1833. Once again, no decision was reached. Before a third hearing could be scheduled, deaths and resignations had changed the ideological complexion of the Court. When Jackson announced Taney as his choice for chief justice, Webster is said to have proclaimed, "The Constitution is gone." From Webster's perspective perhaps that was true. The Taney justices scheduled arguments on the bridge case in 1837, and Webster no longer had a sympathetic audience for his strong contract clause position.

MR. CHIEF JUSTICE TANEY DELIVERED THE OPINION OF THE COURT.

The plaintiffs in error insist . . . [t]hat . . . the acts of the legislature of Massachusetts . . . by their true construction, necessarily implied that the legislature would not authorize another bridge, and especially a free one, by the side of this, and placed in the same line of travel, whereby the franchise granted to the "proprietors of the Charles River Bridge" should be rendered of no value; and the plaintiffs in error contend, that the grant of the ferry to the college, and of the charter to the proprietors of the bridge, are both contracts on the part of the state; and that the law authorizing the erection of the Warren Bridge in 1828, impairs the obligation of one or both of these contracts. . . .

. . . [W]e are not now left to determine, for the first time, the rules by which public grants are to be construed in this country. The subject has already been considered in this Court . . . and the principle recognized, that in grants by the public, nothing passes by implication. . . .

. . . [T]he object and end of all government is to promote the happiness and prosperity of the community by which it is established; and it can never be assumed, that the government intended to diminish its power of accomplishing the end for which it was created. And in a country like ours, free, active, and enterprising, continually advancing in numbers and wealth; new channels of communication are daily found necessary, both for travel and trade; and are essential to the comfort, convenience, and prosperity of the people. A state ought never to be presumed to surrender this power, because, like the taxing power, the whole community have an interest in preserving it undiminished.

The Charles River Bridge ran from Prince Street in Boston to Charlestown. The bridge, considered a very advanced design at the time of its construction, was built on seventy-five oak piers and was more than 1,500 feet long.

And when a corporation alleges, that a state has surrendered for seventy years, its power of improvement, and public accommodation, in a great and important line of travel, along which a vast number of its citizens must daily pass; the community have a right to insist, in the language of this Court above quoted, "that its abandonment ought not to be presumed, in a case, in which the deliberate purpose of the state to abandon it does not appear." The continued existence of a government would be of no great value, if by implications and presumptions, it was disarmed of the powers necessary to accomplish the ends of its creation; and the functions it was designed to perform, transferred to the hands of privileged corporations. The rule of construction announced by the Court, was not confined to the taxing power; nor is it so limited in the opinion delivered. On the contrary, it was distinctly placed on the ground that the interests of the community were concerned in preserving, undiminished, the power then in question; and whenever any power of the state is said to be surrendered or diminished, whether it be the taxing power or any other affecting the public interest, the same principle applies, and the rule of construction must be the same. No one will question that the interests of the great body of the people of the state, would, in this instance, be affected by the surrender of this great line of travel to a single corporation, with the right to exact toll, and exclude competition for seventy years. While the rights of private property are sacredly guarded, we must not forget that the community also have rights, and that the happiness and well being of every citizen depends on their faithful preservation.

Adopting the rule of construction above stated as the settled one, we proceed to apply it to the charter of 1785, to the proprietors of the Charles River Bridge. This act of incorporation is in the usual form, and the privileges such as are commonly given to corporations of that kind. It confers on them the ordinary faculties of a corporation, for the purpose of building the bridge; and establishes certain rates of toll, which the company are authorized to take. This is the whole grant. There is no exclusive privilege given to them over the waters of Charles river, above or below their bridge. No right to erect another bridge themselves, nor to prevent other persons from erecting one. No engagement from the state, that another shall not be erected; and no undertaking not to sanction competition, nor to make improvements that may diminish the amount of its income. Upon all these subjects the charter is silent; and nothing is said in it about a line of travel, so much insisted on in the argument, in which they are to have exclusive privileges. No words are used, from which an intention to grant any of these rights can be inferred. If the plaintiff is entitled to them, it must be implied, simply, from the nature of the grant; and cannot be inferred from the words by which the grant is made.

The relative position of the Warren Bridge has already been described. It does not interrupt the passage over the Charles River Bridge, nor make the way to it or from it less convenient. None of the faculties or franchises granted to that corporation, have been revoked by the legislature; and its right to take the tolls granted by the charter remains unaltered. In short, all the franchises and rights of property enumerated in the charter, and there mentioned to have been granted to it, remain unimpaired. But its income is destroyed by the Warren Bridge; which, being free, draws off the passengers and property which would have gone over it, and renders their franchise of no value. This is the gist of the complaint. For it is not pretended, that the erection of the Warren Bridge would have done them any injury, or in any degree affected their right of property; if it had not diminished the amount of their tolls. In order then to entitle themselves to relief, it is necessary to show, that the legislature contracted not to do the act of which they complain; and that they impaired, or in other words, violated that contract by the erection of the Warren Bridge.

The inquiry then is, does the charter contain such a contract on the part of the state? Is there any such stipulation to be found in that instrument? It must be admitted on all hands, that there is none—no words that even relate to another bridge or to the diminution of their tolls, or to the line of travel. If a contract on that subject can be gathered from the charter, it must be by implication; and cannot be found in the words used. Can such an agreement be implied? The rule of construction before stated is an answer to the question. In charters of this description, no rights are taken from the public, or given to the corporation, beyond those which the words of the charter, by their natural and proper construction, purport to convey. There are no words which import such a contract as the plaintiffs in error contend for, and none can be implied. . . .

Indeed, the practice and usage of almost every state in the Union, old enough to have commenced the work of internal improvement, is opposed to the doctrine contended for on the part of the plaintiffs in error. Turnpike roads have been made in succession, on the same line of travel; the later ones interfering materially with the profits of the first. These corporations have, in some instances, been utterly ruined by the introduction of newer and better modes of transportation, and travelling. In some cases, rail roads have rendered the turnpike roads on the same line of travel so entirely useless, that the franchise of the turnpike corporation is not worth preserving. Yet in none of these cases have the corporations supposed that their privileges were invaded, or any contract violated on the part of the state. Amid the multitude of cases which have occurred, and have been daily occurring for the last forty or fifty years, this is the first instance in which such an implied contract has been contended for, and this Court called upon to infer it from an ordinary act of incorporation, containing nothing more than the usual stipulations and provisions to be found in every such law. The absence of any such controversy, when there must have been so many occasions to give rise to it, proves that neither states, nor individuals, nor corporations, ever imagined that such a contract could be implied from such charters. It shows that the men who voted for these laws, never imagined that they were forming such a contract; and if we maintain that they have made it, we must create

it by a legal fiction, in opposition to the truth of the fact, and the obvious intention of the party. We cannot deal thus with the rights reserved to the states; and by legal intendments and mere technical reasoning, take away from them any portion of that power over their own internal police and improvement, which is so necessary to their well being and prosperity. . . .

The judgment of the supreme judicial court of the commonwealth of Massachusetts, dismissing the plaintiff's bill, must, therefore, be affirmed, with costs.

MR. JUSTICE STORY, DISSENTING.

I maintain, that, upon the principles of common reason and legal interpretation, the present grant carries with it a necessary implication that the legislature shall do no act to destroy or essentially to impair the franchise; that, (as one of the learned judges of the state court expressed it,) there is an implied agreement that the state will not grant another bridge between Boston and Charlestown, so near as to draw away the custom from the old one; and, (as another learned judge expressed it,) that there is an implied agreement of the state to grant the undisturbed use of the bridge and its tolls so far as respects any acts of its own, or of any persons acting under its authority. In other words, the state, impliedly, contracts not to resume its grant, or to do any act to the prejudice or destruction of its grant. I maintain, that there is no authority or principle established in relation to the construction of crown grants, or legislative grants; which does not concede and justify this doctrine. Where the thing is given, the incidents, without which it cannot be enjoyed, are also given. . . . I maintain that a different doctrine is utterly repugnant to all the principles of the common law, applicable to all franchises of a like nature; and that we must overturn some of the best securities of the rights of property, before it can be established. I maintain, that the common law is the birthright of every citizen of Massachusetts, and that he holds the title deeds of his property, corporeal, and incorporeal, under it. I maintain, that under the principles of the common law, there exists no more right in the legislature of Massachusetts, to erect the Warren Bridge, to the ruin of the franchise of the Charles River Bridge than exists to transfer the latter to the former, or to authorize the former to demolish the latter. If the legislature does not mean in its grant to give any exclusive rights, let it say so, expressly; directly; and in terms admitting of no misconstruction. The grantees will then take at their peril, and must abide the results of their overweening confidence, indiscretion, and zeal.

My judgment is formed upon the terms of the grant, its nature and objects, its design and duties; and, in its interpretation, I seek for no new principles, but I apply such as are as old as the very rudiments of the common law.

In spite of Justice Story's protest that the majority had rendered the contract clause meaningless, the Taney Court allowed the states more leeway in regulating for the public good. As Taney noted in *Charles River Bridge*, "While the rights of private property are sacredly guarded, we must not forget that the community also have rights, and that the happiness and well being of every citizen depends on their faithful preservation."

The Taney justices, however, did not totally abandon the Marshall Court's posture favoring business, nor did they repeal the contract clause by judicial fiat; instead, the Court took a more balanced position. The state could have explicitly granted the Charles River Bridge Company exclusive rights, but it did not, and Taney was unwilling to infer such rights. By contrast, when the contractual provisions were clear, the Taney Court often struck down state regulations on contract clause grounds.

Decline in the Post–Civil War Period

After the Taney years, the Court continued to move away from strongly enforcing the contract clause and according the states increased freedom to exercise their police powers. ***Northwestern Fertilizing Co. v. Hyde Park*** (1878) provides a good illustration. The Illinois state legislature passed a statute on March 8, 1867, creating Northwestern Fertilizing Company. The charter authorized the company to operate within a designated territory a facility that converted dead animals to fertilizer and other products. The charter also gave the company the right to transport dead animals and animal parts (offal) through the territory. Acting on this authority, the company operated its plant in a sparsely populated, swampy area.

The facility was, however, located within the boundaries of the village of Hyde Park, a Chicago-area township that was beginning to experience considerable population growth. In 1869 the legislature upgraded the village charter, giving it full powers of local government, including the authority to "define or abate nuisances which are, or may be, injurious to the public health." Recognizing its charter with Northwestern, the legislature stipulated that no village regulations could be applied to the company for at least two years. At the end of the two years, the village of Hyde Park passed an ordinance that said, "No person shall transfer, carry, haul, or convey any offal, dead animals, or other offensive or unwholesome matter or material, into or through the village of Hyde Park." Parties in violation of the law were subject to fines. In 1873, following the arrest and conviction of railroad workers hauling dead animals to its plant, Northwestern filed suit, claiming that its original charter was a contract that could not be abrogated by the state or its local governments. The company was unsuccessful in the state courts and appealed to the U.S. Supreme Court.

Justice Noah H. Swayne's opinion made clear at the outset that the company faced a difficult task in its attempt to convince the justices:

> The rule of construction in this class of cases is that it shall be most strongly against the corporation. Every reasonable doubt is to be resolved adversely. Nothing is to be taken as conceded but what is given in unmistakable terms, or by an implication equally clear. The affirmative must be shown. Silence is negation, and doubt is fatal to the claim. This doctrine is vital to the public welfare.

The Court then went on to rule against the contract clause arguments of the company. The justices had no doubt that the transportation of offal was a public nuisance or that the state had ample police power to combat such an offensive practice. According to Swayne:

> That power belonged to the States when the Federal Constitution was adopted. They did not surrender it, and they all have it now. . . . It rests upon the fundamental principle that every one shall so use his own as not to wrong and injure another. To regulate and abate nuisances is one of its ordinary functions.

The states, the Court was implying, could not contract away their inherent powers to regulate for their citizens' health, safety, and welfare.

Two years later, the justices addressed a similar appeal, this time dealing with questions of public morality. ***Stone v. Mississippi*** (1880) focused on the use of the state's police power to combat lotteries, a form of gambling that much of the population considered evil at that time.

In 1867 the post–Civil War provisional state legislature chartered the Mississippi Agricultural, Educational, and Manufacturing Aid Society. In spite of its name, the society's only purpose was to operate a lottery. The charter gave the society authority to run a lottery in Mississippi for twenty-five years, and, in return, the society paid an initial sum of cash to the state, an additional annual payment for each year of operation, plus a percentage of the lottery receipts. In 1868 a state convention drafted a new constitution, which the people ratified the next year. This constitution contained provisions explicitly outlawing lotteries and stated, "Nor shall any lottery heretofore authorized be permitted to be drawn or tickets therein to be sold." On July 16, 1870, the legislature passed a statute providing for enforcement of the antilottery provisions, and four years later, on March 17, 1874, the state attorney general filed charges against John B. Stone and others associated with the Mississippi Agricultural, Educational, and Manufacturing Aid Society for being in violation of state law. The state admitted that the company was operating within the provisions of its 1867 charter but contended that the new constitution and subsequent enforcement legislation effectively repealed that grant. Stone countered that the U.S. Constitution's contract clause explicitly prohibited the state from negating the provisions of the charter.

A unanimous Supreme Court ruled in favor of the state. In his opinion, Chief Justice Waite emphasized that the states possess police powers that allow them to regulate for the health, safety, morals, and general welfare of their citizens and that a legislature, by means of a contract, cannot bargain away those police powers. Lotteries are proper subjects for police power regulation. Thus, anyone contracting with a state to conduct a lottery does so with the implied understanding that the people, through their properly constituted state agencies, may later exercise the power to regulate or even prohibit such gambling.

Following *Stone v. Mississippi* it was clear that the Court would no longer be sympathetic to contract clause attacks on state regulatory statutes. With contract clause avenues closing, opponents of the state regulation of business and commercial activities turned to another provision of the Constitution, the due process clause of the Fourteenth Amendment. From the 1890s to the 1930s (a period of Court history discussed in chapter 10), the Court heard and often responded favorably to these arguments under the guise of what became known as substantive due process.

The Depression and the Abrogation of Contracts

The contract clause reached its lowest status during the Great Depression of the 1930s. With the stock market crash of 1929, the nation entered the worst economic crisis in its history; most Americans were placed in serious financial jeopardy. The 1932 election of Franklin Roosevelt ushered in the New Deal, and under that broad banner, the federal government began to implement innovative economic programs to combat the Depression. At the same time, various states were developing their own programs to protect their citizens against the economic ravages the country was experiencing.

What people feared most during the Depression was losing the family home. Homeowners did what they could to meet their mortgage obligations, but many were out of work and unable to make their payments. Financial institutions had little choice but to foreclose on these properties as stipulated in the mortgage contracts. To provide relief, several states passed statutes aimed at increasing homeowners' chances of saving their houses. Banks and other creditors opposed these assistance measures. They asserted that such intervention by the state was a direct violation of the constitutional ban against impairment of contracts.

The showdown between the contract clause and a state government's authority to cope with economic crisis occurred in *Home Building and Loan Association v. Blaisdell* (1934). As you read Chief Justice Charles Evans Hughes's opinion for the Court, think about the Constitutional Convention and the concerns that led the framers to adopt the contract clause. Would they agree with the Court that the Constitution should bend in the face of national crises, or would they side with Justice George Sutherland's dissent that the provisions of the Constitution should be interpreted the same way regardless of the conditions of the times?

Home Building and Loan Association v. Blaisdell

290 U.S. 398 (1934)
http://caselaw.findlaw.com/us-supreme-court/290/398.html
Vote: 5 (Brandeis, Cardozo, Hughes, Roberts, Stone)
    4 (Butler, McReynolds, Sutherland, Van Devanter)

OPINION OF THE COURT: *Hughes*

DISSENTING OPINION: *Sutherland*

During the Great Depression, the nation faced high unemployment, low prices for agricultural and manufactured products, a stagnation of business, and a scarcity of credit. In response to these conditions, the Minnesota legislature declared that a state of economic emergency existed demanding the use of extraordinary police powers for the protection of the people. One of the legislature's actions was passage of the Minnesota Mortgage Moratorium Act, which was designed to protect homeowners from losing their houses when they could not make their mortgage payments. The act allowed homeowners who were behind in their payments to petition a state court for an extension of time to meet their mortgage obligations. During the period of the extension, the homeowners would not make normal mortgage payments but instead would pay a reasonable rental amount to the mortgage holder. The maximum extension was two years. The act was to be in effect only as long as the economic emergency continued. Its provisions applied to all mortgages, including those signed prior to the passage of the statute. Stated simply, Minnesota was altering (at least temporarily) contractual relationships between borrowers and lenders.

John and Rosella Blaisdell owned a house in Minneapolis that was mortgaged to Home Building and Loan Association. They lived in one part of the house and rented out the other part. When the Blaisdells were unable to keep their payments current or to obtain additional credit, they requested an extension in accordance with the moratorium law. After initially denying the request and then having it reversed by the state supreme court, the trial court granted the Blaisdells a two-year moratorium on mortgage payments. During this period the Blaisdells were ordered to pay $40 per month, which would be applied to taxes, insurance, interest, and mortgage principal.

Throughout this process Home Building and Loan Association opposed the extension, claiming that the law was an impairment of contracts in violation of the contract clause of the federal Constitution. The Minnesota high court conceded that the law impaired the obligation of contracts but concluded that the statute was within the police powers of the state because of the severe economic emergency. Home Building and Loan appealed to the U.S. Supreme Court.

MR. CHIEF JUSTICE HUGHES DELIVERED THE OPINION OF THE COURT.

In determining whether the provision for this temporary and conditional relief exceeds the power of the State by reason of the clause in the Federal Constitution prohibiting impairment of the obligations of contracts, we must consider the relation of emergency to constitutional power, the historical setting of the contract clause, the development of the jurisprudence of this Court in the construction of that clause, and the principles of construction which we may consider to be established.

Emergency does not create power. Emergency does not increase granted power or remove or diminish the restrictions imposed upon power granted or reserved. The Constitution was adopted in a period of grave emergency. Its grants of power to the Federal Government and its limitations of the power of the States were determined in the light of emergency and they are not altered by emergency. What power was thus granted and what limitations were thus imposed are questions which have always been, and always will be, the subject of close examination under our constitutional system.

While emergency does not create power, emergency may furnish the occasion for the exercise of power. "Although an emergency may not call into life a power which has never lived, nevertheless emergency may afford a reason for the exertion of a living power already enjoyed." *Wilson v. New* (1917). The constitutional question presented in the light of an emergency is whether the power possessed embraces the particular exercise of it in response to particular conditions. Thus, the war power of the Federal Government is not created by the emergency of war, but it is a power given to meet that emergency.

It is a power to wage war successfully, and thus it permits the harnessing of the entire energies of the people in a supreme cooperative effort to preserve the nation. But even the war power does not remove constitutional limitations safeguarding essential liberties. When the provisions of the Constitution, in grant or restriction, are specific, so particularized as not to admit of construction, no question is presented. Thus, emergency would not permit a State to have more than two Senators in the Congress, or permit the election of President by a general popular vote without regard to the number of electors to which the States are respectively entitled, or permit the States to "coin money" or to "make anything but gold and silver coin a tender in payment of debts." But where constitutional grants and limitations of power are set forth in general clauses, which afford a broad outline, the process of construction is essential to fill in the details. That is true of the contract clause. The necessity of construction is not obviated by the fact that the contract clause is associated in the same section with other and more specific prohibitions. Even the grouping of subjects in the same clause may not require the same application to each of the subjects, regardless of differences in their nature.

In the construction of the contract clause, the debates in the Constitutional Convention are of little aid. But the reasons which led to the adoption of that clause, and of the other prohibitions of Section 10 of Article I, are not left in doubt and have frequently been described with eloquent emphasis. The widespread distress following the revolutionary period, and the plight of debtors, had called forth in the States an ignoble array of legislative schemes for the defeat of creditors and the invasion of contractual obligations.

Legislative interferences had been so numerous and extreme that the confidence essential to prosperous trade had been undermined and the utter destruction of credit was threatened. "The sober people of America" were convinced that some "thorough reform" was needed which would "inspire a general prudence and industry, and give a regular course to the business of society." *The Federalist,* No. 44. It was necessary to impose the restraining power of a central authority in order to secure the foundations even of "private faith." . . .

But full recognition of the occasion and general purpose of the clause does not suffice to fix its precise scope. Nor does an examination of the details of prior legislation in the States yield criteria which can be considered controlling. To ascertain the scope of the constitutional prohibition we examine the course of judicial decisions in its application. These put it beyond question that the prohibition is not an absolute one and is not to be read with literal exactness like a mathematical formula. . . .

The legislature cannot "bargain away the public health or the public morals." Thus, the constitutional provision against the impairment of contracts was held not to be violated by an amendment of the state constitution which put an end to a lottery theretofore authorized by the legislature. The lottery was a valid enterprise when established under express state authority, but the legislature in the public interest could put a stop to it. A similar rule has been applied to the control by the State of the sale of intoxicating liquors. The States retain adequate power to protect the public health against the maintenance of nuisances despite insistence upon existing contracts. Legislation to protect the public safety comes within the same category of reserved power. This principle has had recent and noteworthy application to the regulation of the use of public highways by common carriers and "contract carriers," where the assertion of interference with existing contract rights has been without avail. . . .

It is manifest from this review of our decisions that there has been a growing appreciation of public needs and of the necessity of finding ground for a rational compromise between individual rights and public welfare. The settlement and consequent contraction of the public domain, the pressure of a constantly increasing density of population, the interrelation of the activities of our people and the complexity of our economic interests, have inevitably led to an increased use of the organization of society in order to protect the very bases of individual opportunity. Where, in earlier days, it was thought that only the concerns of individuals or of classes were involved, and that those of the State itself were touched only remotely, it has later been found that the fundamental interests of the State are directly affected; and that the question is no longer merely that of one party to a contract as against another, but of the use of reasonable means to safeguard the economic structure upon which the good of all depends.

It is no answer to say that this public need was not apprehended a century ago, or to insist that what the provision of the Constitution meant to the vision of that day it must mean to the vision of our time.

If by the statement that what the Constitution meant at the time of its adoption it means today, it is intended to say that the great clauses of the Constitution must be confined to the interpretation which the framers, with the conditions and outlook of their time, would have placed upon them, the statement carries its own refutation. It was to guard against such a narrow conception that Chief Justice Marshall uttered the memorable warning—"We must never forget that it is a *constitution* we are expounding" (*McCulloch v. Maryland*)—"a constitution intended to endure for ages to come, and consequently, to be adapted to the various crises of human affairs." When we are dealing with the words of the Constitution, said this Court in *Missouri v. Holland,* "we must realize that they have called into life a being the development of which could not have been foreseen completely by the most gifted of its begetters. . . . The case before us must be considered in the light of our whole experience and not merely in that of what was said a hundred years ago."

Nor is it helpful to attempt to draw a fine distinction between the intended meaning of the words of the Constitution and their intended application. When we consider the contract clause and the decisions which have expounded it in harmony with the essential reserved power of the States to protect the security of their peoples, we find no warrant for the conclusion that the clause has been warped by these decisions from its proper significance or that the founders of our Government would have interpreted the clause differently had they had occasion to assume that responsibility in the conditions of the later day. The vast body of law which has been developed was unknown to the fathers, but it is believed to have preserved the essential content and the spirit of the Constitution. With a growing recognition of public needs and the relation of individual right to public security, the court has sought to prevent the perversion of the clause through its use as an instrument to throttle the capacity of the States to protect their fundamental interests. This development is a growth from the seeds which the fathers planted. . . . The principle of this development is . . . that the reservation of the reasonable exercise of the protective power of the State is read into all contracts and there is no greater reason for refusing to apply this principle to Minnesota mortgages than to New York leases.

Applying the criteria established by our decisions we conclude:

1. An emergency existed in Minnesota which furnished a proper occasion for the exercise of the reserved power of the State to protect the vital interests of the community. . . .

2. The legislation was addressed to a legitimate end, that is, the legislation was not for the mere advantage of particular individuals but for the protection of a basic interest of society.

3. In view of the nature of the contracts in question— mortgages of unquestionable validity—the relief

afforded and justified by the emergency, in order not to contravene the constitutional provision, could only be of a character appropriate to that emergency and could be granted only upon reasonable conditions.

4. The conditions upon which the period of redemption is extended do not appear to be unreasonable. . . .

5. The legislation is temporary in operation. It is limited to the exigency which called it forth. . . .

We are of the opinion that the Minnesota statute as here applied does not violate the contract clause of the Federal Constitution. Whether the legislation is wise or unwise as a matter of policy is a question with which we are not concerned. . . .

The judgment of the Supreme Court of Minnesota is affirmed.

MR. JUSTICE SUTHERLAND, DISSENTING.

Few questions of greater moment than that just decided have been submitted for judicial inquiry during this generation. He simply closes his eyes to the necessary implications of the decision who fails to see in it the potentiality of future gradual but ever-advancing encroachments upon the sanctity of private and public contracts. The effect of the Minnesota legislation, though serious enough in itself, is of trivial significance compared with the far more serious and dangerous inroads upon the limitations of the Constitution which are almost certain to ensue as a consequence naturally following any step beyond the boundaries fixed by that instrument. And those of us who are thus apprehensive of the effect of this decision would, in a matter so important, be neglectful of our duty should we fail to spread upon the permanent records of the court the reasons which move us to the opposite view.

A provision of the Constitution, it is hardly necessary to say, does not admit of two distinctly opposite interpretations. It does not mean one thing at one time and an entirely different thing at another time. If the contract impairment clause, when framed and adopted, meant that the terms of a contract for the payment of money could not be altered . . . by a state statute enacted for the relief of hardly pressed debtors to the end and with the effect of postponing payment or enforcement during and because of an economic or financial emergency, it is but to state the obvious to say that it means the same now. This view, at once so rational in its application to the written word, and so necessary to the stability of constitutional principles, though from time to time challenged, has never, unless recently, been put within the realm of doubt by the decisions of this court. . . .

The provisions of the Federal Constitution, undoubtedly, are pliable in the sense that in appropriate cases they have the capacity of bringing within their grasp every new condition which falls within their meaning. But, their *meaning* is changeless; it is only their *application* which is extensible. . . .

A statute which materially delays enforcement of the mortgagee's contractual right of ownership and possession does not modify the remedy merely; it destroys, for the period of delay, all remedy so far as the enforcement of that right is concerned. The phrase, "obligation of a contract," in the constitutional sense imports a legal duty to perform the specified obligation of *that* contract, not to substitute and perform, against the will of one of the parties, a different, albeit equally valuable, obligation. And a state, under the contract impairment clause, has no more power to accomplish such a substitution than has one of the parties to the contract against the will of the other. It cannot do so either by acting directly upon the contract, or by bringing about the result under the guise of a statute in form acting only upon the remedy. If it could, the efficacy of the constitutional restriction would, in large measure, be made to disappear. . . .

I quite agree with the opinion of the court that whether the legislation under review is wise or unwise is a matter with which we have nothing to do. Whether it is likely to work well or work ill presents a question entirely irrelevant to the issue. The only legitimate inquiry we can make is whether it is constitutional. If it is not, its virtues, if it have any, cannot save it; if it is, its faults cannot be invoked to accomplish its destruction. If the provisions of the Constitution be not upheld when they pinch as well as when they comfort, they may as well be abandoned. Being unable to reach any other conclusion than that the Minnesota statute infringes the constitutional restriction under review, I have no choice but to say so.

The Court upheld the Minnesota statute because the majority concluded that the economic emergency justified the state's use of extensive police powers. In reaching that conclusion, the justices only inquired whether the law was a reasonable means of achieving a legitimate end, a standard developed in *McCulloch v. Maryland* (1819). That test of constitutionality—the rational basis test— is the easiest for the state to satisfy; it need only show that its action (the mortgage relief law) is a plausible way of achieving an appropriate governmental objective (addressing the adverse effects of dire economic circumstances). Does the contract clause retain any vitality under such an interpretation? Or did the *Home Building and Loan Association* decision render it virtually meaningless? After all, legislatures would have little reason to pass such statutes in good economic times.

The conditions that prompted passage of the Minnesota Mortgage Moratorium Act were repeated when a severe economic recession and its aftermath gripped the United States from 2008 to 2012, and the subject of mortgages and foreclosures claimed the nation's attention. Although this downturn did not match the catastrophic proportions of the Great Depression, the nation at one point suffered unemployment rates in excess of 10 percent, the freezing of credit markets, and the collapse of hundreds of banks. Even after the worst had passed, economic recovery was exceedingly slow. Once again the loss of the family home became one of Americans' greatest fears as joblessness sapped many of the ability to meet their mortgage obligations. Foreclosures skyrocketed, and the people turned to the government for relief. The federal government responded by expanding the monetary supply, increasing government spending, bailing out failing financial institutions, and pressuring banks to restructure mortgage contracts to stem the tide of foreclosures. Because housing market relief came primarily from the federal government, contract clause objections did not become an issue. This situation reminds us that the Constitution bars the states from impairing the obligation of contracts, but it does not impose the same restraint on the federal government.

MODERN APPLICATIONS OF THE CONTRACT CLAUSE

For decades following the *Home Building and Loan Association* decision, parties challenging state laws rarely rested their arguments on the contract clause. It made little practical sense to do so when the justices were reluctant to use the provision to strike down state legislation designed to promote the economic welfare of the citizens. Litigants who attempted to invoke the clause usually were unsuccessful.

But to conclude that the contract clause had been erased from the Constitution effectively and forever would be incorrect. In the decades following the New Deal, the Court was dominated by justices who took generally liberal positions on economic matters. They were philosophically opposed to allowing business interests to use the clause as a weapon to strike down legislation benefiting the people at large. The Court's liberal majority began to unravel, however, when Chief Justice Earl Warren retired in 1969 and President Richard Nixon appointed Warren Burger to replace him. As succeeding appointments brought more conservative and business-oriented justices to the Court, the prospects for a revitalized contract clause grew. This fact was not lost on enterprising lawyers, who began to consider raising contract clause issues once again.

In the late 1970s, the Court handed down two decisions that some considered an indication that the justices might be reviving the relevance of the contract clause. First, in *United States Trust Co. v. New Jersey* (1977) the Court invalidated laws New York and New Jersey had passed repealing a 1962 contractual promise made to New York Port Authority bondholders that the authority's revenues pledged as security for existing bonds would never be used for railroad expenditures. Second, in *Allied Structural Steel Co. v. Spannaus* (1978) the justices declared unconstitutional a Minnesota law that changed retroactively the contractual provisions of employee retirement plans, making many employees immediately eligible for pensions. These decisions signaled the states that they could not alter contractual obligations with abandon.

In them, the Court also articulated a two-step approach to analyzing modern contract clause claims. First, the justices will determine the extent to which the state's action impairs contractual obligations. In Justice Potter Stewart's words in *Allied Structural Steel*, "the severity of the impairment measures the height of the hurdle the state legislation must clear." If the impairment is found to be a substantial one, the Court will then consider the nature and purpose of the legislation, asking whether the law is drawn in an "appropriate" and "reasonable" way to advance "a significant and legitimate public purpose." Additionally, the justices made it clear in *United States Trust* that they will be especially skeptical when a state alters to its advantage the terms of a contract to which it is a party. These principles neither return the contract clause to the preferred position it once enjoyed nor substantially strip it of its meaning.

In his opinion for the Court, Justice Potter Stewart explained that, unlike the law in *Blaisdell* that was designed to deal with a broad social problem, the state seemed simply to be enacting legislation to benefit employees—and at a substantial and unanticipated cost to employers.

In the years following *Allied Structural Steel* the Court has continued to take a moderate approach. The justices have generally expressed a sensitivity to the need of the states to use their police powers to combat social problems. In *Energy Reserves Group, Inc. v. Kansas Power and Light Co.* (1983) the Court upheld a state law dictating an energy pricing system that conflicted with existing contracts. And in *Keystone Bituminous Coal Association v. DeBenedictis* (1987) the justices gave constitutional approval to a state law requiring coal mine operators to leave 50 percent of the coal in the ground beneath certain structures to provide support. The regulation was at odds with existing contracts between the mining companies and landowners that allowed the companies to extract a higher proportion of the coal in the ground. In both cases the Court recognized the need of the states to use their police powers to remedy social or economic problems, like those presented in *Blaisdell*. The contract clause, according to the Court, prohibits only those state actions—such as the vast changes in employee retirements in *Spannaus*—that "substantially impair the contractual arrangement." And even such substantial impairment can be justified if there is a significant and legitimate public purpose behind the regulation.

When regulations pose only minor interference with contracts, they are more readily sustained. In *Sveen v. Melin* (2018), the justices turned back a contract clause challenge to a Minnesota law that automatically revoked a spouse as an insurance beneficiary when a couple is divorced. The Court reasoned that this was only a minimal intrusion into contractual relationships; most policyholders intend to remove former spouses from their policies when they get divorced, and even if they do not, the law made it a simple matter to reinstate the original beneficiaries.

Decisions such as these have signaled potential litigants that successfully challenging state laws on contract clause grounds remains a difficult task. As a consequence, parties wishing to defend private property rights against state regulation have turned to other constitutional provisions. Frequently, the due process clauses of the Fifth and Fourteenth Amendments and the Fifth Amendment's takings clause have served as vehicles for such challenges. These subjects are addressed in chapters 10 and 11.

ANNOTATED READINGS

A number of important works have examined the historical evolution of the contract clause and how it contributes to the general protection of property rights. Among these are Bruce Ackerman, *Private Property and the Constitution* (New Haven, CT: Yale University Press, 1977); James W. Ely Jr., *The Contract Clause: A Constitutional History* (Lawrence: University Press of Kansas, 2016); James W. Ely, *Property Rights in American History* (New York: Garland, 1997); Kermit L. Hall, ed., *Law, Economy, and the Power of Contract: Major Historical Interpretations* (New York: Garland, 1987); Morton J. Horowitz, *The Transformation of American Law, 1780–1860* (Cambridge, MA: Harvard University Press, 1977); Warren B. Hunting, *The Obligation of Contracts Clause of the United States Constitution* (Baltimore: Johns Hopkins University Press, 1919); Harry N. Scheiber, ed., *The State and Freedom of Contract* (Stanford, CA: Stanford University Press, 1999); Benjamin F. Wright, *The Contract Clause of the Constitution* (Cambridge, MA: Harvard University Press, 1938).

Other works have focused on specific landmark rulings by the U.S. Supreme Court or the contributions to the Court's contract clause jurisprudence by specific justices. Examples are Morgan D. Dowd, "Justice Story, the Supreme Court, and the Obligation of Contract," *Case Western Reserve Law Review* 19 (1968): 493–527; John A. Fliter and Derek S. Hoff, *Fighting Foreclosure: The Blaisdell Case, the Contract Clause, and the Great Depression* (Lawrence: University Press of Kansas, 2012); Horace H. Hagin, "*Fletcher vs. Peck*," *Georgetown Law Journal* 16 (November 1927): 1–40; Charles F. Hobson, *The Great Yazoo Lands Sale: The Case of* Fletcher v. Peck (Lawrence: University Press of Kansas, 2016); Nathan Isaacs, "John Marshall on Contracts: A Study in Early American Juristic Theory," *Virginia Law Review* 7 (March 1921): 413–428; Stanley I. Kutler, *Privilege and Creative Destruction: The Charles River Bridge Case* (Philadelphia, PA: J. B. Lippincott, 1971); C. Peter Magrath, *Yazoo: Law and Politics in the New Republic* (Providence, RI: Brown University Press, 1966); Francis N. Stites, *Private Interest and Public Gain: The Dartmouth College Case, 1819* (Amherst: University of Massachusetts Press, 1972).

CHAPTER TEN

ECONOMIC SUBSTANTIVE DUE PROCESS

The concept of due process of law has a long history in Anglo-American law. Its roots can be traced to the England's Magna Carta of 1215, and it became an explicit right under a 1354 British law guaranteeing that "No man . . . shall be put out of his lands or tenements nor taken, nor disinherited, nor put to death, without he be brought to answer by due process of law." The American colonists considered the concept a fundamental one, and the phrase can be found in legal documents of the early American states.

Not surprisingly the due process guarantee was included in the Bill of Rights ratified in 1791 as a protection against actions of the federal government. The language of the Fifth Amendment reads: "No person shall . . . be deprived of life, liberty or property without due process of law." In 1868 in the aftermath of the Civil War, similar language explicitly applying to the states was included in the Fourteenth Amendment.

But what does the due process guarantee mean? The terminology is vague, and its definition is not self-evident. As the following example illustrates, two different interpretations have been advanced.

Suppose that federal and state agents receive a tip that the owners of a factory are violating the federal law that prohibits the employment of children younger than sixteen. Without stopping to obtain a search warrant, the agents enter the factory and observe that underage employees are indeed working there. The agents arrest the factory owners. Based on evidence collected by the investigators, a court convicts the owners of violating child labor laws and imposes a heavy fine. But the owners challenge their conviction on two similarly named, but distinct, grounds—procedural due process and substantive due process.

Citing the first ground, the factory owners allege that the procedure the agents used to obtain evidence against them—entering the factory without a warrant—violated guarantees in the Constitution, including sections of the Fifth and Fourteenth Amendments that prohibit government from depriving persons of "life, liberty, or property, without due process of law." For many, the term *due process* is synonymous with procedural fairness. The American system of justice is based on the idea that even people guilty of violating the law deserve fair treatment. This particular characterization of due process, known as *procedural due process*, is the most traditional and widely accepted use of the term. The government must proceed in fair ways if it is to convict an individual of a crime or otherwise deprive that person of life, liberty, or property. Evidence must be gathered according to prescribed procedures, and trials must take place following established rules of procedural fairness. Unless this procedural due process standard is met, a conviction cannot be sustained.

What is the second ground on which the factory owners base their appeal? None other than due process of law. Under this approach, due process means more than just adhering to fair procedures. Instead, the due process clauses are seen as guaranteeing certain substantive rights. This theory, known as *substantive due process*, holds that the Constitution is violated when government unreasonably or arbitrarily denies rights that are inherent in the freedom of the individual. In our example, the factory owners might argue that the law prohibiting child labor violates due process guarantees by unreasonably infringing on their freedom to do business and arbitrarily abridging their right to enter into employment agreements with willing workers. In their view, the child labor law cannot stand because it is inherently not just and not fair, and the Constitution requires that the substance of the law must be just and must not unfairly deprive persons of their life, liberty, or property.

In this chapter we examine the development and decline of substantive due process. We shall see that in the modern era the Supreme Court for the most part has made it exceedingly difficult to challenge laws governing economic relationships on substantive due process grounds. But for approximately forty years, between the 1890s and the 1930s, the Court read due process in substantive terms and used the principle to strike down many laws that allegedly infringed on economic rights.

If economic substantive due process is now a discredited doctrine, why should we devote an entire chapter to it? There are several reasons. First, its rise in and fall from the Court's grace constitutes an intriguing part of legal history. The adoption of substantive due process came about gradually and resulted from the push and pull of the legal and political environment of the day.

Second, looking at economic substantive due process provides us with an opportunity to revisit the concept of judicial activism. During the latter half of the twentieth century, judicial activism was associated with liberalism, but the justices from the 1890s to the 1930s actively used the doctrine of substantive due process to impose their conservative ideology on American society. The Court overturned many laws that legislatures passed to regulate businesses for the general good. Substantive due process became associated with the Court's strong support of business interests.

Third, the topic of substantive due process offers us a way to reexamine the cycles of history we have already discussed. As depicted in Table 10-1, substantive due

Table 10-1 The Legal Tools of the Laissez-Faire Courts, 1890s to 1930s: Some Examples

	1890–1899	1900–1909	1910–1919	1920–1929	1930–1939
Used to Strike State Laws					
Substantive due process	*Allgeyer v. Louisiana* (1897)	*Lochner v. New York* (1905)			*Morehead v. New York ex rel. Tipaldo* (1936)
Used to Strike Federal Laws					
Delegation of powers					*Panama Refining Co. v. Ryan* (1935) *Schechter Poultry v. United States* (1935)
Commerce clause			*Hammer v. Dagenhart* (1918)		*Panama Refining Co. v. Ryan* (1935) *Schechter Poultry v. United States* (1935) *Carter v. Carter Coal* (1936)
Taxing and Spending				*Bailey v. Drexel Furniture* (1922)	*United States v. Butler* (1936)
Tenth Amendment			*Hammer v. Dagenhart* (1918)		

process was an additional weapon in the Court's laissez-faire arsenal. While it was using delegation of power doctrines (chapter 4), the Tenth Amendment (chapter 6), the commerce clause (chapter 7), and taxing and spending provisions (chapter 8) to strike down federal regulation of business, the Court was also invoking substantive due process to hold against similar legislation passed by the states. This use was particularly ironic because, at the time, the Court was espousing notions of dual federalism, striking down federal regulations on the grounds that they encroached on powers reserved to the states. In other words, the Court found ways to strike down all sorts of economic regulation, even though, in so doing, it often took contradictory stances. Therefore, substantive due process provides a way to tie together much of what we have already covered in this book.

Finally, although the doctrine of substantive due process largely has been discredited, it continues to have some relevance today. The Court has used it to justify the protection of certain civil liberties, such as the right to privacy, and to nullify excessive monetary judgments juries have awarded in civil cases. We shall consider these issues at the end of the chapter, but first we review substantive due process chronologically—how it developed, why the Court embraced it, and what led to its demise.

THE DEVELOPMENT OF SUBSTANTIVE DUE PROCESS

Prior to the adoption of the Fourteenth Amendment, judges generally interpreted due process guarantees contained in the Fifth Amendment and in state constitutions as procedural in intent and nature. As historian Kermit L. Hall has observed, "Before the Civil War [due process] had essentially one meaning," that people were "entitled" to fair and orderly proceedings, particularly criminal proceedings.[1] But in the post–Civil War era, expanded understandings of the due process guarantee began to emerge.

Initial Interpretation of the Fourteenth Amendment's Due Process Clause

The social ills that flowed from the nation's transition from an agrarian to an industrial economy after the Civil War prompted state legislatures to consider new

regulations on commerce, but business interests feared that increased regulation would inevitably lead to a reduction in corporate profits. With the decline of the contract clause as a defense against state interference with business, it is not surprising that corporate interests looked to other parts of the Constitution for protection. Business advocates began arguing that unreasonable state limitations on the freedom of individuals to conduct their commercial activities as they so desired constituted a deprivation of liberty and property without due process of law.

The first attempt to invoke due process as a shield against government actions that business viewed as unreasonable occurred in *Butchers' Benevolent Association v. Crescent City Livestock Landing and Slaughter House Company* (1873), usually referred to as the **Slaughterhouse Cases**. Although industrialization had many benefits, it also had some unpleasant side effects. In this case the Louisiana state legislature claimed that the Mississippi River had become polluted because New Orleans butchers dumped garbage into it. To remedy this problem (or, as some have suggested, to use it as an excuse to create a monopolistic enterprise), the legislature created Crescent City Livestock Landing and Slaughter House Company and gave it the exclusive right to receive and slaughter all city livestock for twenty-five years. No longer could independent butchers carry out these traditional occupational activities.

Because the butchers were forced to use the company facilities and to pay top dollar for the privilege, they formed their own organization, the Butchers' Benevolent Association, and hired an attorney, former U.S. Supreme Court justice John A. Campbell, to sue the corporation. In his arguments, Campbell sought to apply the Fourteenth Amendment to the butchers' cause. In general terms, he asserted that the amendment, although passed in the wake of the Civil War, was not meant solely to protect former slaves. Rather, he said, its language was broad enough to encompass all citizens. In addition to presenting arguments based on the amendment's privileges and immunities and equal protection clauses, Campbell claimed that the Louisiana law violated the due process clause because it arbitrarily deprived his clients of their fundamental right to pursue their business. This unreasonable legislation, he argued, deprived the butchers of the liberty to practice a traditional occupation and the property (income) that flowed from their labors.

Writing for the Court's majority, Justice Samuel Miller rejected these claims. He relied on history to confirm the true purpose of the Fourteenth Amendment—to protect African Americans—and to refute Campbell's

---

[1] Kermit L. Hall, *The Magic Mirror* (New York: Oxford University Press, 1989), 232.

basic position. Miller focused his opinion on showing why the privileges and immunities claim was inapplicable, but he also rejected the due process clause argument. As he asserted,

> [I]t is sufficient to say that under no construction of that provision that we have ever seen, or any that we deem admissible, can the restraint imposed by the state of Louisiana upon the exercise of their trade by the butchers of New Orleans be held to be a deprivation of property within the meaning of that provision.

Why did Miller take such a hard-line position? In large measure, it was because he did not want to see the Court become a "superlegislature," a censor imposing its own judgment on what laws were arbitrary or unreasonable. That was a job best left to elected state legislatures.

Two of the four dissenters, Justices Joseph Bradley and Stephen Field, wrote especially important opinions, taking issue with Miller's claims. Bradley, in particular, countered the majority's position that the due process clause was inapplicable to the dispute:

> In my view, a law which prohibits a large class of citizens from adopting a lawful employment, or from following a lawful employment previously adopted, does deprive them of liberty as well as property, without due process of law. Their right of choice is a portion of their liberty; their occupation is their property.

It was Miller's view, however, that for the moment carried the day—there was no substance in due process.

The Beginning of Substantive Due Process: The Court Opens a Window

Substantive due process advocates suffered a major defeat in the *Slaughterhouse Cases*, but that did not prevent attorneys, representing increasingly desperate business interests, from continuing to make substantive due process arguments. From their perspective, the environment held promise for the eventual adoption of such arguments. Within legal circles, for example, there was much discussion of several theories that lent themselves to Bradley's dissenting position in *Slaughterhouse*. One was expressed in a book by Thomas M. Cooley, a nineteenth-century legal scholar and jurist. His influential *Constitutional Limitations*, first published in 1868, singled

out the word *liberty* within the due process clause as an important constitutional right. The protection of this right, in Cooley's eyes, required a substantive reading of the Fourteenth Amendment, which, in turn, would serve as a mechanism for protecting property rights and for restricting government regulation. Cooley's theory was specific, but nineteenth-century philosopher Herbert Spencer offered a more general view. Called social Darwinism, it treated social evolution in the same terms that Charles Darwin used to explain biological evolution: "If left to themselves, the best of mankind, 'the fittest,' would survive and prosper."[2] This proposition had a natural compatibility with laissez-faire economic theories: if government does not interfere, the best will prosper. Interpreting the Fifth and Fourteenth Amendments in substantive due process terms would prohibit a great deal of government interference with business activity.

Social Darwinism may have influenced some scholars, the social elite, and business, but most Americans did not buy into its tenets. Instead, the general public supported government regulation of commercial activities. The state legislatures responded to the people by continuing to pass legislation designed to alleviate the adverse social conditions America's rapid industrialization produced. Business reacted to these regulatory reforms by challenging them in court.

In addition, the Court itself contributed to the mounting number of substantive due process attacks on state regulation of business. Take, for example, the Court's ruling in **Munn v. Illinois** (1877). In this case, the justices considered an 1871 Illinois law that regulated the grain storage industry, a business sector that increasingly had become engaged in corrupt practices. The regulations included the imposition of an upper limit on the fees that warehouses could charge for storage of grain. The state justified the law as compatible with its constitution, which specified that public warehouses were subject to regulation. But companies forced to comply with the law disliked it. Ira Munn, co-owner of one of the more successful grain warehouses, challenged the law as a violation of the Fourteenth Amendment's due process clause.

In his opinion for the Court, Chief Justice Morrison Waite upheld the law and, in so doing, seemed to reject substantive due process completely, asserting that most regulatory legislation should be presumed valid. The decision, in fact, elicited an acrimonious dissent

[2]Walter F. Murphy, James E. Fleming, and William F. Harris II, *American Constitutional Interpretation*, 2nd ed. (Mineola, NY: Foundation Press, 1995), 1075.

from Justice Field that largely reflected Bradley's in *Slaughterhouse:* the law was "nothing less than a bold assertion of absolute power by the state to control at its discretion the property and business of the citizen." So it is not surprising that Waite's majority opinion "has generally been regarded as a great victory for liberalism and a judicial refusal to recognize due process as a limit on the substance of legislative regulatory power."[3]

That description is not entirely accurate, however. Although Waite could have taken the same approach as Miller in *Slaughterhouse*—complete rejection of the due process claim—he did not. Instead, Waite qualified his opinion, asserting first that state regulations of private property should not deprive owners of their right to due process, but "under some circumstances they may." What differentiated "some circumstances" from others? In Waite's opinion, the answer lay in the nature of the business being regulated: "We find that when private property is 'affected with a public interest it ceases to be [of private right] only.'" Waite used this approach, often called the "business affected with a public interest doctrine," to find against Ira Munn's claim. The grain elevator business played a crucial role in the distribution of foodstuffs to the nation; as such, it was an industry that was affected with the public interest. Private businesses of this kind are subject to regulation, including state limits on the right of the business owners to determine the prices charged.

But holding that businesses affected with the public interest could be constitutionally regulated implied that businesses not meeting this description could raise a due process defense against unreasonable state regulation. With his opinion Waite unwittingly provided a loophole that lawyers representing business clients who were unhappy with state regulation attempted to open even further. By avoiding a hard-line stance of the sort Miller took in *Slaughterhouse*, Waite's "maybe yes, maybe no" approach in the end provided some elbow room for the concept of substantive due process.

In two cases coming a decade or so after *Munn*, the Court moved closer to the concession only implied by Waite. In the first, **Mugler v. Kansas** (1887), the Court considered a state law prohibiting the manufacture and sale of liquor. Although the majority upheld the regulation against a substantive due process challenge, the Court's opinion represented something of a break from *Munn*. First, it articulated the view that not "every

statute enacted ostensibly for the promotion of [the public interest] is to be accepted as a legitimate exertion of police powers of the state." This opinion was far more explicit than Waite's: there were clear limits to state regulatory power. Second, and more important, it took precisely the opposite position from that of the majority in *Slaughterhouse*. Recall that Justice Miller wanted to avoid having the Court become a "superlegislature," scrutinizing and perhaps censoring state action. But in *Mugler*, that is precisely what the Court said it would do:

> There are . . . limits beyond which legislation cannot rightfully go. . . . If, therefore, a statute purporting to have been enacted to protect the public health, the public morals, or the public safety, has no real or substantial relation to those objects, or is a palpable invasion of rights secured by the fundamental law, *it is the duty of the courts to so adjudge*, and thereby give effect to the Constitution [emphasis added].

In *Mugler* the Court did not fully adopt the doctrine of substantive due process; it even upheld the state regulation on liquor. Yet the Court established its intent to review legislation to determine whether it was a "reasonable" exercise of state power. In essence, the Court would balance the interests of the state against those of individual due process guarantees—a course of action *Slaughterhouse* rejected.

The legislation tested in *Mugler* was deemed reasonable, but in **Chicago, Milwaukee & St. Paul Railway v. Minnesota** (1890), decided three years later, the Court went the other way: the justices struck down a state regulation on the ground that it interfered with due process guarantees. At first glance, *Chicago, Milwaukee & St. Paul Railway* bears a distinct resemblance to *Munn v. Illinois.* Strong lobbying efforts by farm groups led Minnesota in 1887 to establish a railroad and warehouse commission to set "equal and reasonable" rates for railroad transportation of goods and for warehouse storage. When the commission, and later the state courts, ruled that Chicago, Milwaukee & St. Paul Railway Company was charging dairy farmers unreasonable rates to ship their milk, the railroad took its case to the U.S. Supreme Court, where it argued that the commission had interfered with "its property" without providing it with due process of law.

Writing for the majority, Justice Samuel Blatchford examined the law in terms of the reasonableness standard promulgated in *Mugler*: "The question of the reasonableness of a rate of charge for transportation by a

---

[3]C. Herman Pritchett, *The American Constitution* (New York: McGraw-Hill, 1959), 557.

railroad company . . . is eminently a question for judicial investigation, requiring due process of law for its determination." Blatchford found that the law deprived the company of its property in an unfair way: "If the company is deprived of the power of charging reasonable rates . . . and such deprivation takes place in the absence of an investigation by judicial machinery, it is deprived of the lawful use of its property, and thus, in substance and effect, of the property itself, without due process of law."

Chicago, Milwaukee & St. Paul Railway highlights how much the Court's treatment of substantive due process had evolved over the two decades since the *Slaughterhouse Cases*. This change in position prompts us to ask why the Court did such a turnabout. The most obvious answer is personnel changes. By the time the Court decided *Mugler*, only one member of the *Slaughterhouse* majority, Justice Miller, remained. By 1890 Miller also was gone, as was Chief Justice Waite, who, despite the loophole in the *Munn* opinion, generally favored state regulatory power. Their replacements were quite different. Some had been corporate attorneys schooled in the philosophies of Cooley and Spencer and were quite willing to borrow from the briefs of their former colleagues who argued against state regulation. Given the backgrounds of the new appointees, it also is not surprising to find that the views of the *Slaughterhouse* dissenters went on to rule the day.

But there may have been more to it. By asserting the standard it did, the Court was engaging in judicial activism, ruling against the strong public sentiment that prompted the state legislatures to pass regulatory policies.

It is fair to say, though, that the justices did not see it this way; rather, they viewed the political pressures of the day as coming from particularized, radical "socialistic" elements that did not reflect majority interests. If this was their perception, it had a solid foundation. Some legislation had resulted from the lobbying efforts of farm and labor movements and later, as we shall see, of the Progressives and New Dealers. In the minds of many conservatives of the day, including some of the justices, such pressures were illegitimate because they sought to subvert the free enterprise system. In short, while the populists, Progressives, and New Dealers, in the opinion of conservatives, tried to put the brakes on businesses and inculcate the government with socialistic legislation, the conservatives strongly believed that the best interests of the country lay with a free market, unregulated by the government.

A fundamental change was in the wind, and many point to the Court's decision in ***Allgeyer v. Louisiana*** (1897) as the turning point. This case involved a Louisiana

law that barred the state's citizens and corporations from doing business with out-of-state insurance companies unless those companies complied with a specified set of requirements. The Allgeyer Company wanted to purchase insurance protection to cover one hundred bales of cotton it was shipping to a foreign port. When the company secured such a policy from a New York insurer that was not approved to do business in Louisiana, state government attorneys alleged that Allgeyer had violated the law.

The state argued that the purpose of the law was to prevent fraud, but Allgeyer did not see it that way and challenged the constitutionality of the law on Fourteenth Amendment due process grounds. In the company's view, the term *liberty* included the right to use and enjoy all "endowments" without constraint, and the term *property* included the right to acquire property and engage in business. Here, Allgeyer's attorney alleged, the law acted as a significant and unconstitutional curtailment of the legitimate business activity of the company.

In some ways, the opinion that Justice Rufus Peckham wrote for the Court was not so different from the majority's opinion in *Chicago, Milwaukee & St. Paul Railway*. It struck down the state law in part on the ground that the law was not reasonable. But Peckham went much further: he merged substantive due process with freedom of contract by reading the term *liberty* to mean economic liberty, encompassing the right to "enter into all contracts." As he wrote:

> Has not a citizen of a state, under the [due process clause of the Fourteenth Amendment], a right to contract outside of the state for insurance on his property—a right of which state legislation cannot deprive him? . . . When we speak of the liberty to contract for insurance or to do an act to effectuate such a contract already existing, we refer to and have in mind the facts of this case, where the contract was made outside the state, and as such was a valid and proper contract. . . . To deprive the citizen of such a right as herein described without due process of law is illegal. Such a statute as this in question is not due process of law, because it prohibits an act which under the Federal Constitution the defendants had a right to perform. This does not interfere in any way with the acknowledged right of the state to enact such legislation in the legitimate exercise of its police or other powers as to it

may seem proper. In the exercise of such right, however, care must be taken not to infringe upon those other rights of the citizen which are protected by the Federal Constitution.

In other words, Peckham adopted the position that businesses had been pressing since the demise of the contract clause as a source of protection. Now their right to do business, to set their own rates, and to enter into contracts with other businesses and perhaps even with employees had the highest level of legal protection.

THE ROLLER-COASTER RIDE OF SUBSTANTIVE DUE PROCESS: 1898–1923

However explicit *Allgeyer* was, the true test of its importance would come in its application. Some read the decision to mean that the Court would not uphold legislation that infringed on economic "liberty," but **Holden v. Hardy**, decided the very next year, dispelled this notion. In this case, the Court examined a Utah law prohibiting mining companies from working their employees more than eight hours a day, except in emergency situations. Attorneys challenging the law claimed that the legislature had no authority to prevent competent people from voluntarily entering into employment contracts even if the work to be performed was considered dangerous. The state asserted that the challenged statute was a "health regulation" and within the state's power because it was aimed at "preserving to a citizen his ability to work and support himself."

In *Holden* the Court reiterated its *Mugler* position: "The question in each case is whether the legislature has adopted the statute in exercise of a reasonable discretion or whether its actions be a mere excuse for an unjust discrimination." The Supreme Court, now acting as the nation's "superlegislature," deemed the legislation "reasonable"; that is, it did not impinge on the liberty of contract because the state had a well-justified interest in protecting its citizens from the unique health and safety problems caused by working in mines.

Holden was a victory for the still-forming Progressive movement and emerging labor groups, which were vigorously lobbying state legislatures to pass laws protecting workers. As the Industrial Revolution wore on, they argued that the necessity for such laws was increasing because corporations were growing ever more profit

oriented and, as a result, more likely to exploit employees. Although social reformers succeeded in persuading many state legislatures to enact laws like Utah's, they still feared that the courts would strike down such legislation. *Holden* gave them hope that the threat of judicial review was not as serious as they had thought.

But what did *Holden* really mean? Was the Court turning away from the strong substantive due process position it had taken in *Allgeyer?* Or were the justices only acknowledging that they would look more favorably on such legislation if the protected employees were engaged in especially dangerous tasks or working under unhealthy conditions? The justices provided a response to these questions seven years later in *Lochner v. New York* (1905).

Lochner v. New York

198 U.S. 45 (1905)
http://caselaw.findlaw.com/us-supreme-court/198/45.html
Vote: 5 (Brewer, Brown, Fuller, McKenna, Peckham)
    4 (Day, Harlan, Holmes, White)

OPINION OF THE COURT: Peckham

DISSENTING OPINIONS: Harlan, Holmes

To promote safe and healthy working conditions, New York passed the Bakeshop Act, a law that prohibited employees of bakeries from working more than ten hours per day and sixty hours per week. The state justified the law on two grounds. First, New York had the authority under its police powers to regulate working conditions while taking into account local circumstances and community standards. Second, the state, through the police power, had the authority to regulate for the health of both consumers and workers.

Joseph Lochner owned Lochner's Home Bakery in Utica, New York. In 1899, he was convicted of violating the Bakeshop Act by requiring an employee to work more than sixty hours a week and was fined $25. Two years later he was charged with his second offense of overworking his employees. Once again found guilty, Lochner was sentenced to a fine of $50 or fifty days in jail if he failed to pay the fine. This time Lochner decided to fight the charges and appealed. After he lost in the state's highest court, he asked the Supreme Court to reverse his conviction on the ground that the Bakeshop Act violated the due process clause of the Fourteenth Amendment. In part, he alleged the following:

1. Employees and employer have the right to agree upon hours and wages, and the use of the police power by New York to interfere with such agreements is so "paternal" as to violate the due process clause of the Fourteenth Amendment.

After Joseph Lochner, the owner of a bakery located in Utica, New York, was convicted of failing to comply with a state maximum hours work law, he asked the U.S. Supreme Court to strike down the law as violative of his constitutional rights. In *Lochner v. New York* (1905) the justices agreed. The majority found that the law impermissibly interfered with the right of employers to enter into contracts with their employees.

2. Regardless of the state's asserted interests, the "most cherished rights of American citizenship"—freedom of contract and property rights—"should be most closely and jealously scrutinized by this court." Since the state's interests here are not sufficiently "clear and apparent," the Court should strike the law.

MR. JUSTICE PECKHAM ... DELIVERED THE OPINION OF THE COURT.

The mandate of the statute, that "no employee shall be required or permitted to work," is the substantial equivalent of an enactment that "no employee shall contract or agree to work," more than ten hours per day; and, as there is no provision for special emergencies, the statute is mandatory in all cases. It is not an act merely fixing the number of hours which shall constitute a legal day's work, but an absolute prohibition upon the employer permitting, under any circumstances, more than ten hours' work to be done in his establishment. The employee may desire to earn the extra money which would arise from his working more than the prescribed time, but this statute forbids the employer from permitting the employee to earn it.

The statute necessarily interferes with the right of contract between the employer and employees, concerning the number of hours in which the latter may labor in the bakery of the employer. The general right to make a contract in relation to his business is part of the liberty of the individual protected by the 14th Amendment of the Federal Constitution. *Allgeyer v. Louisiana.* Under that provision no state can deprive any person of life, liberty, or property without due process of law. The right to purchase or to sell labor is part of the liberty protected by this amendment, unless there are circumstances which exclude the right. There are, however, certain powers, existing in the sovereignty of each state in the Union, somewhat vaguely termed police powers, the exact description and limitation of which have not been attempted by the courts. Those powers, broadly stated, and without, at present, any attempt at a more specific limitation, relate to the safety, health, morals, and general welfare of the public. Both property and liberty are held on such reasonable conditions as may be imposed by the governing power of the state in the exercise of those powers, and with such conditions the 14th Amendment was not designed to interfere.

This court has recognized the existence and upheld the exercise of the police powers of the states in many cases which might fairly be considered as border ones, and it has, in the course of its determination of questions regarding the asserted invalidity of such statutes, on the ground of their violation of the rights secured by the Federal Constitution, been guided by rules of a very liberal nature, the application of which has resulted, in numerous instances, in upholding the validity of state statutes thus assailed. Among the later cases where the state law has been upheld by this court is that of *Holden v. Hardy.* A provision in the act of the legislature of Utah was there under consideration, the act limiting the employment of workmen in all underground mines or workings, to eight hours per day, "except in cases of emergency, where life or property is in imminent danger." It also limited the hours of labor in smelting and other institutions for the reduction or refining of ores or metals to eight hours per day, except in like cases of emergency. The act was held to be a valid exercise of the police powers of the state . . . [because the] law applies only to the classes subjected by their employment to the peculiar conditions and effects attending underground mining and work in smelters, and other works for the reduction and refining of ores.

There is nothing in *Holden v. Hardy* which covers the case now before us. . . .

It must, of course, be conceded that there is a limit to the valid exercise of the police power by the state. There is no dispute concerning this general proposition. Otherwise the 14th Amendment would have no efficacy and the legislatures of the states would have unbounded power, and it would be enough to say that any piece of legislation was enacted to conserve the morals, the health, or the safety of the people; such legislation would be valid, no matter how absolutely without foundation the claim might be. The claim of the police power would be a mere pretext,—become another and delusive name for the supreme sovereignty of the state to be exercised free from constitutional restraint. This is not contended for. In every case that comes before this court, therefore, where legislation of this character is concerned, and where the protection of the Federal Constitution is sought, the question necessarily arises: Is this a fair, reasonable, and appropriate exercise of the police power of the state, or is it an unreasonable, unnecessary, and arbitrary interference with the right of the individual to his personal liberty, or to enter into those contracts in relation to labor which may seem to him appropriate or necessary for the support of himself and his family? Of course the liberty of contract relating to labor includes both parties to it. The one has as much right to purchase as the other to sell labor.

This is not a question of substituting the judgment of the court for that of the legislature. If the act be within the power of the state it is valid, although the judgment of the court might be totally opposed to the enactment of such a law. But the question would still remain: Is it within the police power of the state? and that question must be answered by the court.

The question whether this act is valid as a labor law, pure and simple, may be dismissed in a few words. There is no reasonable ground for interfering with the liberty of person or the right of free contract, by determining the hours of labor, in the occupation of a baker. There is no contention that bakers as a class are not equal in intelligence and capacity to men in other trades or manual occupations, or that they are not able to assert their rights and care for themselves without the protecting arm of the state, interfering with their independence of judgment and of action. They are in no sense wards of the state. Viewed in the light of a purely labor law, with no reference whatever to the question of health, we think that a law like the one before us involves neither the safety, the morals, nor the welfare, of the public, and that the interest of the public is

not in the slightest degree affected by such an act. The law must be upheld, if at all, as a law pertaining to the health of the individual engaged in the occupation of a baker. It does not affect any other portion of the public than those who are engaged in that occupation. Clean and wholesome bread does not depend upon whether the baker works but ten hours per day or only sixty hours a week. The limitation of the hours of labor does not come within the police power on that ground.

It is a question of which of two powers or rights shall prevail,—the power of the state to legislate or the right of the individual to liberty of person and freedom of contract. The mere assertion that the subject relates, though but in a remote degree, to the public health, does not necessarily render the enactment valid. The act must have a more direct relation, as a means to an end, and the end itself must be appropriate and legitimate, before an act can be held to be valid which interferes with the general right of an individual to be free in his person and in his power to contract in relation to his own labor. . . .

We think the limit of the police power has been reached and passed in this case. There is, in our judgment, no reasonable foundation for holding this to be necessary or appropriate as a health law to safeguard the public health, or the health of the individuals who are following the trade of a baker. If this statute be valid, and if, therefore, a proper case is made out in which to deny the right of an individual . . . as employer or employee, to make contracts for the labor of the latter under the protection of the provisions of the Federal Constitution, there would seem to be no length to which legislation of this nature might not go. . . .

We think that there can be no fair doubt that the trade of a baker, in and of itself, is not an unhealthy one to that degree which would authorize the legislature to interfere with the right to labor, and with the right of free contract on the part of the individual, either as employer or employee. . . .

It is also urged, pursuing the same line of argument, that it is to the interest of the state that its population should be strong and robust, and therefore any legislation which may be said to tend to make people healthy must be valid as health laws, enacted under the police power. If this be a valid argument and a justification for this kind of legislation, it follows that the protection of the Federal Constitution from undue interference with liberty of person and freedom of contract is visionary, wherever the law is sought to be justified as a valid exercise of the police power. Scarcely any law but might find shelter under such assumptions, and conduct, properly so called, as well as contract, would come under the restrictive sway of the legislature. Not only the hours of employees, but the hours of employers, could be regulated, and doctors, lawyers, scientists, all professional men, as well as athletes and artisans, could be forbidden to fatigue their brains and bodies by prolonged hours of exercise, lest the fighting strength of the state be impaired. We mention these extreme cases because the contention is extreme.

We do not believe in the soundness of the views which uphold this law. On the contrary, we think that such a law as this, although passed in the assumed exercise of the police power, and as relating to the public health, or the health of the employees named, is not within that power, and is invalid. . . .

It was further urged on the argument that restricting the hours of labor in the case of bakers was valid because it tended to cleanliness on the part of the workers, as a man was more apt to be cleanly when not overworked, and if cleanly then his "output" was also more likely to be so. What has already been said applies with equal force to this contention. We do not admit the reasoning to be sufficient to justify the claimed right of such interference. The state in that case would assume the position of a supervisor, or *pater familias,* over every act of the individual, and its right of governmental interference with his hours of labor, his hours of exercise, the character thereof, and the extent to which it shall be carried would be recognized and upheld. In our judgment it is not possible in fact to discover the connection between the number of hours a baker may work in the bakery and the healthful quality of the bread made by the workman. The connection, if any exist, is too shadowy and thin to build any argument for the interference of the legislature. If the man works ten hours a day it is all right, but if ten and a half or eleven his health is in danger and his bread may be unhealthy, and, therefore, he shall not be permitted to do it. This, we think, is unreasonable and entirely arbitrary. When assertions such as we have adverted to become necessary in order to give, if possible, a plausible foundation for the contention that the law is a "health law," it gives rise to at least a suspicion that there was some other motive dominating the legislature than the purpose to subserve the public health or welfare. . . .

It is impossible for us to shut our eyes to the fact that many of the laws of this character, while passed under what is claimed to be the police power for the purpose of protecting the public health or welfare, are, in reality, passed from other motives. . . .

It is manifest to us that the limitation of the hours of labor provided for in this section of the statute under which the indictment was found, and the plaintiff in error convicted, has no such direct relation to, and no such substantial effect upon, the health of the employee, as to justify us in regarding the section as really a health law. It seems to us that the real object and purpose were simply to regulate the hours of labor between the master and his employees (all being men, *sui juris*), in a private business, not dangerous in any degree to morals, or in any real and substantial degree to the health of the employees. Under such circumstances the freedom of master and employee to contract with each other in relation to their employment, and in defining the same, cannot be prohibited or interfered with, without violating the Federal Constitution.

The judgment of the Court of Appeals of New York, as well as that of the Supreme Court and the County Court of Oneida County, must be reversed and the case remanded to the County Court for further proceedings not inconsistent with this opinion.

Reversed.

MR. JUSTICE HOLMES, DISSENTING.

This case is decided upon an economic theory which a large part of the country does not entertain. If it were a question whether I agreed with that theory I should desire to study it further and long before making up my mind. But I do not conceive that to be my duty, because I strongly believe that my agreement or disagreement has nothing to do with the right of a majority to embody their opinions in law. It is settled by various decisions of this court that state constitutions and state laws may regulate life in many ways which we as legislators might think as injudicious or if you like as tyrannical as this, and which equally with this interfere with the liberty to contract. . . . The Fourteenth Amendment does not enact Mr. Herbert Spencer's Social Statics. . . . United States and state statutes and decisions cutting down the liberty to contract by way of combination are familiar to this court. Two years ago we upheld the prohibition of sales of stock on margins or for future delivery in the constitution of California. *Otis v. Parker.* The decision sustaining an eight hour law for miners is still recent. *Holden v. Hardy.* Some of these laws embody convictions or prejudices which judges are likely to share. Some may not. But a constitution is not intended to embody a particular economic theory, whether of paternalism and the organic relation of the citizen to the State or of *laissez faire.* It is made for people of fundamentally differing views, and the accident of our finding certain opinions natural and familiar or novel and even shocking ought not to conclude our judgment upon the question whether statutes embodying them conflict with the Constitution of the United States.

General propositions do not decide concrete cases. The decision will depend on a judgment or intuition more subtle than any articulate major premise. But I think that the proposition just stated, if it is accepted, will carry us far toward the end. Every opinion tends to become a law. I think that the word liberty in the Fourteenth Amendment is perverted when it is held to prevent the natural outcome of a dominant opinion, unless it can be said that a rational and fair man necessarily would admit that the statute proposed would infringe fundamental principles as they have been understood by the traditions of our people and our law. It does not need research to show that no such sweeping condemnation can be passed upon the statute before us. A reasonable man might think it a proper measure on the score of health. Men whom I certainly could not pronounce unreasonable would uphold it as a first installment of a general regulation of the hours of work. Whether in the latter aspect it would be open to the charge of inequality I think it unnecessary to discuss.

Many scholars have called *Lochner* the Court's strongest expression of economic substantive due process. Although the Court said the question to be asked in this case is the same one it had been addressing since *Mugler*—whether the law is a fair, reasonable, and appropriate exercise of police power—its answer is quite different. By distinguishing *Holden* to the point of non-existence and by narrowing the scope of reasonable state regulations, the Court moved away from a strict "reasonableness" approach to one that reflected *Allgeyer*: an employer's right "to make a contract" with employees is nearly sacrosanct.

That the Court, although divided 5–4, accomplished this feat not by changing the legal question but by changing the answer creates something of a puzzle, particularly with regard to the immediate subject of the dispute—maximum work hours. Think about it this way: the Court upheld the Utah law at issue in *Holden* on the ground that the kind of employment (underground mining) and the character of the employees (miners) were such as to make the law reasonable and proper; it struck the *Lochner* law because bakers can "care for themselves" and the production of "clean and wholesome bread" is not affected. Was this distinction significant? Or was it merely a way to mask what the Court wanted to do: narrow the grounds on which states could reasonably regulate and, thereby, strike protective legislation as a violation of the right to contract? Justice Oliver Wendell Holmes's dissent certainly implies the latter. He goes so far as to accuse the Court of using the Fourteenth Amendment to "enact Mr. Herbert Spencer's Social Statics." Although many scholars agree with Holmes's assessment and argue that the justices in the *Lochner* majority were "motivated by their own policy preferences favoring laissez-faire economics and Social Darwinism," other analysts present a somewhat different picture.[4] They suggest that the Court was seeking to remain faithful to "a long-standing constitutional ideology that distinguished between valid economic regulation and invalid 'class,' or factional legislation."[5] In other words, *Lochner* represented a "principled effort" on the part of the justices to keep this area

of the law consistent and coherent, and not merely a statement of their ideological predilections.

Regardless of who is right, these issues moved to the fore in ***Muller v. Oregon*** (1908). This case began when the state of Oregon brought charges against Curt Muller for requiring his female laundry employees to work longer than the state maximum of ten hours per day. Once convicted, Muller decided to challenge the law. In the view of his attorneys, Oregon's regulation, which prohibited the employment of women, but not men, in laundries for more than ten hours a day, violated his right to enter into a contract with his employees.

Recognizing that, in light of *Lochner*, Muller's argument rested on strong legal grounds, the National Consumers League (NCL)—a group that had pressed states to pass maximum hours legislation—grew concerned. The organization was reluctant to see the Supreme Court nullify its hard work to attain passage of the Oregon law. To defend the law, the NCL contacted Louis Brandeis, a well-known attorney of the day and a future U.S. Supreme Court justice.

Because of the decision in *Lochner* and the lack of significant membership changes on the Court since that case had been decided, Brandeis believed that bold action was necessary. Instead of filling his brief with legal arguments, he would provide the Court with "*facts*, published by anyone with expert knowledge of industry in its relation to women's hours of labor," that indicated the evils of Muller's actions. In particular, the brief pointed out that forcing women to work long hours affected their health and their reproductive systems. In the end, with the help of the NCL, Brandeis produced an incredible document. Known in legal history as the Brandeis Brief, it contained 113 pages of sociological data and only 2 pages of legal argument.

To the surprise of some, the justices ruled in the NCL's favor. Why, given *Lochner*, did the Court affirm the Oregon law? One answer is that, in the Court's opinion, it did not depart from *Lochner*; it merely found that Oregon's regulations, unlike New York's, were a reasonable use of the state's power. But the Court applied the reasonableness approach in both *Lochner* and *Holden* and came to completely different conclusions. So, despite the Court's attempt to distinguish *Lochner*, how much can applying that standard possibly explain about *Muller*'s outcome? Another possibility is that Brandeis forced the Court to see the reasonableness of the Oregon regulation. By presenting a mass of statistical data, he kept the justices riveted on the law and diverted their attention from a substantive

---

[4]Quotation from C. Ian Anderson, "Courts and the Constitution," *Michigan Law Review* 92 (1994): 1438. For the different viewpoint, see, especially, Howard Gillman, *The Constitution Besieged: The Rise and Demise of Lochner Era Police Powers Jurisprudence* (Durham, NC: Duke University Press, 1993).

[5]Anderson, "Courts and the Constitution," 1439.

Curt Muller (with arms folded) made constitutional history when he asked the U.S. Supreme Court to strike down as violative of his rights an Oregon law regulating the number of hours female laundry workers could work at his cleaning establishment. In *Muller v. Oregon* (1908), however, the Court held that states may constitutionally enact maximum hours work laws for women.

due process approach. The strategy worked: the justices even commended the Brandeis Brief. Finally, *Muller* was different from *Lochner* in at least one important way: the law applied solely to women. This was a point stressed by Brandeis and by the Court. As the majority opinion put it,

> That woman's physical structure and the performance of maternal functions place her at a disadvantage in the struggle for subsistence is obvious. This is especially true when the burdens of motherhood are upon her. Even when they are not, by abundant testimony of the medical fraternity continuance for a long time on her feet at work, repeating this from day to day, tends to injurious effects upon the body, and, as healthy mothers are essential to vigorous offspring, the physical well-being of woman becomes an object of public interest and care in order to preserve the strength and vigor of the race.

Winning *Muller* gave a big boost to organizations like the NCL. Those who favored maximum hours work laws worried, however, that the decision depended on the fact that the law covered only women and that, when the Court had an opportunity to review a law covering all workers, it would apply *Lochner*. Their fears were greatly relieved when the justices in **Bunting v. Oregon** (1917) upheld an Oregon law that barred employees of mills, factories, or manufacturing facilities from working more than ten hours per day.

Once again the Court failed even to mention *Lochner*. And, given the Court's holding, many predicted the death of that decision; after all, it was wholly incompatible with *Bunting*. Perhaps the demise of substantive due process would follow. Indeed, throughout the period from *Mugler* (1887) up to about *Bunting*, it appeared that *Lochner* was more the exception than the rule. Between 1887 and 1910, the Court decided 558 cases involving due process claims challenging state regulations and upheld 83 percent of the laws. It seemed that *Lochner*, not *Muller*, was the unusual case.[6]

---

[6]Alfred H. Kelly, Winfred A. Harbison, and Herman Belz, *The American Constitution*, 7th ed. (New York: W. W. Norton, 1991), 405.

THE HEYDAY OF SUBSTANTIVE DUE PROCESS: 1923–1936

The *Bunting* funeral for *Lochner* proved to be premature. Within six years, not only did the Court virtually overrule *Bunting*, but also it seemed to be more committed to the *Lochner* version of due process than ever before. *Adkins v. Children's Hospital* (1923) provides an excellent illustration of the magnitude of this resurgence.

Adkins v. Children's Hospital

261 U.S. 525 (1923)
http://caselaw.findlaw.com/us-supreme-court/261/525.html
Vote: 5 (Butler, McKenna, McReynolds, Sutherland,
Van Devanter)
3 (Holmes, Sanford, Taft)

OPINION OF THE COURT: Sutherland

DISSENTING OPINIONS: Holmes, Taft

NOT PARTICIPATING: Brandeis

In 1918 Congress, with the support of progressive-oriented president Woodrow Wilson, enacted a law that established the Minimum Wage Board of the District of Columbia and gave it authority to set minimum wages for women and children in Washington, D.C.[7] The board, staffed by progressives, ordered that restaurants and hospitals pay women workers a minimum wage of 34.5 cents per hour, $16.50 per week, or $71.50 per month. According to the board, these rates would "supply the necessary cost of living to . . . women workers to maintain them in good health and morals."

Children's Hospital of the District of Columbia, which employed many women, refused to comply. In its opinion, the law violated the due process clause of the Fifth Amendment encompassing the liberty to enter into salary contracts with employees.[8]

Because of delay at the lower court level, the case did not reach the Supreme Court until 1923. An attorney for the Wage Board, assisted by NCL attorney (and future Supreme Court justice) Felix Frankfurter and other NCL staffers, sought to defend the 1918 law on grounds similar to Brandeis's in *Muller*. They offered the Court "impressive documentation on the cost of living and the desirability of good wages."

---

[7]We derive this account from Vose, *Constitutional Change*, 190–196.

[8]Because the District of Columbia is not a state, the due process clause of the Fourteenth Amendment did not apply.

MR. JUSTICE SUTHERLAND DELIVERED THE OPINION OF THE COURT.

The statute now under consideration is attacked upon the ground that it authorizes an unconstitutional interference with the freedom of contract included within the guaranties of the due process clause of the 5th Amendment. That the right to contract about one's affairs is a part of the liberty of the individual protected by this clause is settled by the decisions of this court, and is no longer open to question. . . .

There is, of course, no such thing as absolute freedom of contract. It is subject to a great variety of restraints. But freedom of contract is, nevertheless, the general rule and restraint the exception; and the exercise of legislative authority to abridge it can be justified only by the existence of exceptional circumstances. . . .

[The statute under consideration] is simply and exclusively a price-fixing law, confined to adult women . . . who are legally as capable of contracting for themselves as men. It forbids two parties having lawful capacity—under penalties as to the employer—to freely contract with one another in respect of the price for which one shall render service to the other in a purely private employment. . . .

The feature of this statute which, perhaps more than any other, puts upon it the stamp of invalidity is that it exacts from the employer an arbitrary payment for a purpose and upon a basis having no causal connection with his business, or the contract, or the work the employee engages to do. The declared basis . . . is not the value of the service rendered, but the extraneous circumstance that the employee needs to get a prescribed sum of money to insure her subsistence, health, and morals. . . . The moral requirement, implicit in every contract of employment, viz., that the amount to be paid and the service to be rendered shall bear to each other some relation of just equivalence, is completely ignored. The necessities of the employee are alone considered, and these arise outside of the employment, are the same when there is no employment, and as great in one occupation as in another. Certainly the employer, by paying a fair equivalent for the service rendered, though not sufficient to support the employee, has neither caused nor contributed to her poverty. . . . A statute requiring an employer to pay in money, to pay at prescribed and regular intervals, to pay the value of the services rendered, even to pay with fair relation to the extent of the benefit obtained from the service, would be understandable. But a statute which prescribes payment without regard to any of these things, and solely with relation to circumstances apart from the contract of employment, the business affected by it, and the work done under it, is so clearly the product of a naked, arbitrary exercise of power, that it cannot be allowed to stand under the Constitution of the United States. . . .

It has been said that legislation of the kind now under review is required in the interest of social justice, for whose ends freedom of contract may lawfully be subjected to restraint. The liberty of

In *Adkins v. Children's Hospital* (1923) the Supreme Court struck down a federal minimum wage law on substantive due process grounds. The corporation that managed the Children's Hospital of the District of Columbia filed the legal action to enjoin enforcement of the law.

the individual to do as he pleases, even in innocent matters, is not absolute. It must frequently yield to the common good, and the line beyond which the power of interference may not be pressed is neither definite nor unalterable, but may be made to move, within limits not well defined, with changing need and circumstance. Any attempt to fix a rigid boundary would be unwise as well as futile. But, nevertheless, there are limits to the power, and when these have been passed, it becomes the plain duty of the courts, in the proper exercise of their authority, to so declare. To sustain the individual freedom of action contemplated by the Constitution is not to strike down the common good, but to exalt it; for surely the good of society as a whole cannot be better served than by the preservation against arbitrary restraint of the liberties of its constituent members.

It follows from what has been said that the act in question passes the limit prescribed by the Constitution, and, accordingly, the decrees of the court below are affirmed.

MR. CHIEF JUSTICE TAFT, DISSENTING.

The right of the Legislature under the Fifth and Fourteenth Amendments to limit the hours of employment on the score of the health of the employee, it seems to me, has been firmly established. As to that, one would think, the line had been pricked out so that it has become a well formulated rule. In *Holden v. Hardy* it was applied to miners and rested on the unfavorable environment of employment in mining and smelting. In *Lochner v. New York* it was held that restricting those employed in bakeries to 10 hours a day was an arbitrary and invalid interference with the liberty of contract secured by the Fourteenth Amendment. Then followed a number of cases beginning with *Muller v. Oregon,* sustaining the validity of a limit on maximum hours of labor for women to which I shall hereafter allude, and following these cases came *Bunting v. Oregon.* In that case, this court sustained a law limiting the hours of labor of any person, whether man or woman, working in any mill, factory, or manufacturing establishment to 10 hours a day with a proviso as to further hours to which I shall hereafter advert. The law covered the whole field of industrial employment and certainly covered the case of persons employed in bakeries. Yet the opinion in the *Bunting* Case does not mention the *Lochner* Case. No one can suggest any constitutional distinction between employment in a bakery and one in any other kind of a manufacturing establishment which should make a limit of hours in the one invalid, and the same limit in the other permissible. It is impossible for me to reconcile the *Bunting* Case and the *Lochner* Case, and I have always supposed that the *Lochner* Case was thus overruled *sub silentio.* . . .

I am authorized to say that Mr. Justice SANFORD concurs in this opinion.

MR. JUSTICE HOLMES, DISSENTING.

The question in this case is the broad one, whether Congress can establish minimum rates of wages for women in the District of Columbia, with due provision for special circumstances, or whether we must say that Congress has no power to meddle with the matter at all. To me, notwithstanding the deference due to the prevailing judgment of the court, the power of Congress seems absolutely free from doubt. The end—to remove conditions leading to ill health, immorality, and the deterioration of the race—no one would deny to be within the scope of constitutional legislation. The means are means that have the approval of Congress, of many states, and of those governments from which we have learned our greatest lessons. When so many intelligent persons, who have studied the matter more than any of us can, have thought that the means are effective and are worth the price, it seems to me impossible to deny that the belief reasonably may be held by reasonable men. . . . [T]he only objection that can be urged is found within the vague contours of the 5th Amendment, prohibiting the depriving any person of liberty or property without due process of law. To that I turn.

The earlier decisions upon the same words in the 14th Amendment began within our memory, and went no farther than an unpretentious assertion of the liberty to follow the ordinary callings. Later that innocuous generality was expanded into the dogma, Liberty of Contract. Contract is not specially mentioned in the text that we have to construe. It is merely an example of doing what you want to do, embodied in the word "liberty." But pretty much all law consists in forbidding men to do some things that they want to do, and contract is no more exempt from law than other acts. . . .

I confess that I do not understand the principle on which the power to fix a minimum for the wages of women can be denied by those who admit the power to fix a maximum for their hours of work. I fully assent to the proposition that here, as elsewhere, the distinctions of the law are distinctions of degree; but I perceive no difference in the kind or degree of interference with liberty, the only matter with which we have any concern, between the one case

and the other. The bargain is equally affected whichever half you regulate. . . .

I am of opinion that the statute is valid.

Adkins represented the return of substantive due process; indeed, it made clear that *Muller* and *Bunting* were not major breaks from that doctrine. If anything, as Justice Holmes wrote in his *Adkins* dissent, it had come back stronger than ever, with the term "due process of law" evolving into the "dogma, Liberty of Contract."

Why the change? In large measure, it can be traced back to the political climate of the day. Following World War I, the U.S. economy boomed, and voters elected one president after another committed to a free market economy. These presidents, in turn, appointed justices, at least some of whom shared their economic point of view. Warren Harding made the first four of these new Supreme Court appointments. As scholar Clement E. Vose notes, "The most important single fact about the Harding appointments was that he named two ardent conservatives of the old school—Sutherland and Butler—to serve along with two justices similarly committed who were already sitting—Van Devanter and McReynolds."[9] By 1922 the Four Horsemen were all in place.

The entrenchment of substantive due process, as we mentioned at the beginning of this chapter, was but one manifestation of the impact of Supreme Court appointments by Republican presidents of that era. With their strong commitment to an utterly free market, these conservative justices also invoked creative theories of the limits of national power, especially dual federalism, to strike down federal regulatory efforts. In the hands of these business-oriented justices, the doctrines of dual federalism and substantive due process, along with a very restrictive view of the commerce clause, served as powerful weapons against state and federal regulatory legislation.

THE DEPRESSION, THE NEW DEAL, AND THE DECLINE OF ECONOMIC SUBSTANTIVE DUE PROCESS

The laissez-faire approach of the Court through the 1920s was in keeping with the times. The nation's economy continued to prosper, and voters elected politicians—President Herbert Hoover, for example—who

---

[9]Clement E. Vose, *Constitutional Change* (Lexington, MA: Lexington Books, 1972), 194.

were committed to a private-sector-based economy that advocates believed would thrive if left free from regulation. The Great Depression, triggered by the stock market crash of 1929, and the subsequent election of Franklin Roosevelt demonstrate just how quickly that perception changed. Roosevelt's election indicated the desire of the citizenry for greater regulation to get the nation back on its feet.

At first, it appeared as if the Court, although dominated by Republican-appointed justices, might go along with the Depression-fighting regulatory efforts of the new administration and of the states, which in part would require a repudiation of substantive due process. How could states exercise any control over employers if the Court continued to strike down the legislatures' efforts on "liberty of contract" grounds?

This was a central question in *Nebbia v. New York* (1934), and here the Court upheld a state law that created the Milk Control Board, a body empowered to fix retail milk prices. By a 5–4 vote, the justices rejected a substantive due process argument that the law unconstitutionally deprived the seller and the buyer of the freedom to negotiate the terms of a sale. Justice Owen Roberts, writing for the majority, seemed to invoke the spirit of Chief Justice Waite's opinion in *Munn v. Illinois:* milk was so important to the life and health of the community that its sale was "affected with the public interest" and therefore subject to regulation.

But the Court was not yet ready to relent altogether from the substantive due process doctrines of *Lochner* and *Adkins.* Just two years after *Nebbia*, the justices heard arguments in *Morehead v. New York ex rel. Tipaldo* (1936), which involved a challenge to a New York statute setting minimum wage standards for women. The Court struck down the law. Writing for a majority of five, Justice Butler was just as emphatic on the subject of substantive due process as the *Adkins* Court had been: "Freedom of contract is the general rule and restraint the exception." This decision strongly reinforced the doctrine of substantive due process, but the Court's rejection of that theory was just around the corner.

The Demise of Economic Substantive Due Process: *West Coast Hotel v. Parrish*

The Court's refusal to uphold federal New Deal legislation, as you recall from chapter 7, angered President Roosevelt. Its ruling in *Morehead* cut even deeper. As one commentator notes, "More than any other decision by the Court during the New Deal period, *Morehead* unleashed a

barrage of criticism from conservatives as well as from liberals" who sympathized with the plight of women and children workers.[10] Even the Republican Party's 1936 platform included a plank supporting adoption of minimum wage and maximum hours laws of the sort struck in *Morehead.*

Amid all this pressure, the Court did a major about-face on the constitutionality of New Deal programs. As part of that change came what would be the demise of the doctrine of substantive due process in *West Coast Hotel v. Parrish.*

West Coast Hotel v. Parrish

300 U.S. 379 (1937)
http://caselaw.findlaw.com/us-supreme-court/300/379.html
Vote: 5 (Brandeis, Cardozo, Hughes, Roberts, Stone)
　　4 (Butler, McReynolds, Sutherland, Van Devanter)

OPINION OF THE COURT: *Hughes*

DISSENTING OPINION: *Sutherland*

Elsie Parrish had worked intermittently as a chambermaid in a hotel in Washington State for a wage of 22 cents to 25 cents per hour.[11] When she was discharged in 1935, she asked the management for back pay of $216.19, the difference between what she had received and what she would have gotten if the hotel had abided by the Washington wage board's minimum wage rate of $14.30 per week.

The hotel offered her $17.00, but Parrish refused to settle. Because of the community property laws in the state, she and her husband jointly brought suit against the hotel. Parrish found an attorney willing to represent her, but the attorney could not generate much interest in her case among outside organizations. Even the National Consumers' League declined to participate, viewing the effort as a waste of time in light of *Adkins* and *Morehead.* The Washington Supreme Court, however, ruled in favor of Parrish, and the hotel sought U.S. Supreme Court review.

MR. CHIEF JUSTICE HUGHES DELIVERED THE OPINION OF THE COURT.

The appellant relies upon the decision of this Court in *Adkins v. Children's Hospital,* which held invalid the District of Columbia

---

[10]Peter H. Irons, *The New Deal Lawyers* (Princeton, NJ: Princeton University Press, 1982), 278.

[11]We derive this account from William E. Leuchtenburg, "The Case of the Wenatchee Chambermaid," in *Quarrels That Have Shaped the Constitution,* rev. ed., ed. John A. Garraty (New York: Harper & Row, 1987).

Minimum Wage Act which was attacked under the due process clause of the Fifth Amendment. . . .

. . . The Supreme Court of Washington has upheld the minimum wage statute of that State. It has decided that the statute is a reasonable exercise of the police power of the State. In reaching that conclusion the state court has invoked principles long established by this Court in the application of the Fourteenth Amendment. The state court has refused to regard the decision in the *Adkins* Case as determinative and has pointed to our decisions both before and since that case as justifying its position. We are of the opinion that this ruling of the state court demands on our part a reexamination of the *Adkins* Case. The importance of the question, in which many States having similar laws are concerned, the close division by which the decision in the *Adkins* Case was reached, and the economic conditions which have supervened, and in the light of which the reasonableness of the exercise of the protective power of the State must be considered, make it not only appropriate, but we think imperative, that in deciding the present case the subject should receive fresh consideration. . . .

The principle which must control our decision is not in doubt. The constitutional provision invoked is the due process clause of the Fourteenth Amendment governing the States, as the due process clause invoked in the *Adkins* Case governed Congress. In each case the violation alleged by those attacking minimum wage regulation for women is deprivation of freedom of contract. What is this freedom? The Constitution does not speak of freedom of contract. It speaks of liberty and prohibits the deprivation of liberty without due process of law. In prohibiting that deprivation the Constitution does not recognize an absolute and uncontrollable liberty. Liberty in each of its phases has its history and connotation. But the liberty safeguarded is liberty in a social organization which requires the protection of law against the evils which menace the health, safety, morals and welfare of the people. Liberty under the Constitution is thus necessarily subject to the restraints of due process, and regulation which is reasonable in relation to its subject and is adopted in the interests of the community is due process.

This essential limitation of liberty in general governs freedom of contract in particular. More than twenty-five years ago we set forth the applicable principle in these words after referring to the cases where the liberty guaranteed by the Fourteenth Amendment had been broadly described:

"But it was recognized in the cases cited, as in many others, that freedom of contract is a qualified and not an absolute right. There is no absolute freedom to do as one wills or to contract as one chooses. The guaranty of liberty does not withdraw from legislative supervision that wide department of activity which consists of the making of contracts, or deny to government the power to provide restrictive safeguards. Liberty implies the absence of arbitrary restraint, not immunity from reasonable regulations and prohibitions imposed in the interests of the community." *Chicago, Burlington & Quincy R. Co. v. McGuire* [1911].

This power under the Constitution to restrict freedom of contract has had many illustrations. That it may be exercised in the public interest with respect to contracts between employer and employee is undeniable. . . . In dealing with the relation of employer and employed, the legislature has necessarily a wide field of discretion in order that there may be suitable protection of health and safety, and that peace and good order may be promoted through regulations designed to insure wholesome conditions of work and freedom from oppression.

The point that has been strongly stressed that adult employees should be deemed competent to make their own contracts was decisively met nearly forty years ago in *Holden v. Hardy,* where we pointed out the inequality in the footing of the parties. . . .

It is manifest that this established principle is peculiarly applicable in relation to the employment of women in whose protection the State has a special interest. That phase of the subject received elaborate consideration in *Muller v. Oregon* (1908). . . . In later rulings this Court sustained the regulation of hours of work of women employees.

This array of precedents and the principles they applied were thought by the dissenting Justices in the *Adkins* Case to demand that the minimum wage statute be sustained. The validity of the distinction made by the Court between a minimum wage and a maximum of hours in limiting liberty of contract was especially challenged. That challenge persists and is without any satisfactory answer. . . .

One of the points which was pressed by the Court in supporting its ruling in the *Adkins* Case was that the standard set up by the District of Columbia Act did not take appropriate account of the value of the services rendered. In the *Morehead* Case, the minority thought that the New York statute had met that point in its definition of a "fair wage" and that it accordingly presented a distinguishable feature which the Court could recognize within the limits which the *Morehead* petition for certiorari was deemed to present. The Court, however, did not take that view and the New York Act was held to be essentially the same as that for the District of Columbia. The statute now before us is like the latter, but we are unable to conclude that in its minimum wage requirement the State has passed beyond the boundary of its broad protective power.

The minimum wage to be paid under the Washington statute is fixed after full consideration by representatives of employers, employees and the public. It may be assumed that the minimum wage is fixed in consideration of the services that are performed in the particular occupations under normal conditions. Provision is made for special licenses at less wages in the case of women who are incapable of full service. The statement of Mr. Justice Holmes in the *Adkins* Case is pertinent: "This statute does not compel anybody to pay anything. It simply forbids employment at rates below those fixed as the minimum requirement of health and right living. It is safe to assume that women will not be employed at even the lowest wages allowed unless they earn them, or unless the employer's business can sustain the burden. In short the law in its character and operation is like hundreds of so-called police laws that have been upheld." . . .

We think that the views thus expressed are sound and that the decision in the *Adkins* Case was a departure from the true application of the principles governing the regulation by the State of the relation of employer and employed. Those principles have been reenforced by our subsequent decisions. . . .

With full recognition of the earnestness and vigor which characterize the prevailing opinion in the *Adkins* Case, we find it impossible to reconcile that ruling with these well-considered declarations. What can be closer to the public interest than the health of women and their protection from unscrupulous and overreaching employers? And if the protection of women is a legitimate end of the exercise of state power, how can it be said that the requirement of the payment of a minimum wage fairly fixed in order to meet the very necessities of existence is not an admissible means to that end? The legislature of the State was clearly entitled to consider the situation of women in employment, the fact that they are in the class receiving the least pay, that their bargaining power is relatively weak, and that they are the ready victims of those who would take advantage of their necessitous circumstances. The legislature was entitled to adopt measures to reduce the evils of the "sweating system," the exploiting of workers at wages so low as to be insufficient to meet the bare cost of living, thus making their very helplessness the occasion of a most injurious competition. The legislature had the right to consider that its minimum wage requirements would be an important aid in carrying out its policy of protection. The adoption of similar requirements by many States evidences a deep-seated conviction both as to the presence of the evil and as to the means adapted to check it. Legislative response to the conviction cannot be regarded as arbitrary or capricious and that is all we have to decide. Even if the wisdom of the policy be regarded as debatable and its effects uncertain, still the legislature is entitled to its judgment.

There is an additional and compelling consideration which recent economic experience has brought into a strong light. The exploitation of a class of workers who are in an unequal position with respect to bargaining power and are thus relatively defenceless against the denial of a living wage is not only detrimental to their health and well-being but casts a direct burden for their support upon the community. What these workers lose in wages the taxpayers are called upon to pay. The bare cost of living must be met. We may take judicial notice of the unparalleled demands for relief which arose during the recent period of depression and still continue to an alarming extent despite the degree of economic recovery which has been achieved. It is unnecessary to cite official statistics to establish what is of common knowledge through the length and breadth of the land. While in the instant case no factual brief has been presented, there is no reason to doubt that the State of Washington has encountered the same social problem that is present elsewhere. The community is not bound to provide what is in effect a subsidy for unconscionable employers. The community may direct its law-making power to correct the abuse which springs from their selfish disregard of the public interest. The argument that the legislation in question constitutes an arbitrary discrimination, because it does not extend to men, is unavailing. This Court has frequently held that the legislative authority, acting within its proper field, is not bound to extend its regulation to all cases which it might possibly reach. The legislature "is free to recognize degrees of harm and it may confine its restrictions to those classes of cases where the need is deemed to be clearest." . . .

Our conclusion is that the case of *Adkins v. Children's Hospital* should be, and it is, overruled. The judgment of the Supreme Court of the State of Washington is affirmed.

MR. JUSTICE SUTHERLAND, DISSENTING.

MR. JUSTICE VAN DEVANTER, MR. JUSTICE McREYNOLDS, MR. JUSTICE BUTLER, and I think the judgment of the court below should be reversed. . . .

Coming, then, to a consideration of the Washington statute, it first is to be observed that it is in every substantial respect identical with the statute involved in the *Adkins* Case. Such vices as existed in the latter are present in the former. And if the *Adkins* Case was properly decided, as we who join in this opinion think it was, it necessarily follows that the Washington statute is invalid. . . .

That the clause of the Fourteenth Amendment which forbids a state to deprive any person of life, liberty, or property without due process of law includes freedom of contract is so well settled as to be no longer open to question. Nor reasonably can it be disputed that contracts of employment of labor are included in the rule. . . .

In the *Adkins* Case we referred to this language, and said that while there was no such thing as absolute freedom of contract, but that it was subject to a great variety of restraints, nevertheless, freedom of contract was the general rule and restraint the exception; and that the power to abridge that freedom could only be justified by the existence of exceptional circumstances. This statement of the rule has been many times affirmed; and we do not understand that it is questioned by the present decision.

The Washington statute, like the one for the District of Columbia, fixes minimum wages for adult women. Adult men and their employers are left free to bargain as they please; and it is a significant and an important fact that all state statutes to which our attention has been called are of like character. The common-law rules restricting the power of women to make contracts have, under our system, long since practically disappeared. Women today stand upon a legal and political equality with men. There is no longer any reason why they should be put in different classes in respect of their legal right to make contracts; nor should they be denied, in effect, the right to compete with men for work paying lower wages which men may be willing to accept. And it is an arbitrary exercise of the legislative power to do so.

SUBSTANTIVE DUE PROCESS: CONTEMPORARY RELEVANCE

West Coast Hotel was an explicit repudiation of economic substantive due process. In one fell swoop, the justices overruled *Adkins* and changed the way the Court would view state regulatory efforts.

The modern Court has adopted a "rational basis" test that presumes the constitutionality of economic legislation and assigns responsibility to the law's challengers to show that no rational relationship exists between the law and a legitimate government function.[12] Under this test it is extremely difficult for attorneys to demonstrate "no conceivable rational relationship" between a challenged law and legitimate government function. Indeed, since 1937 the Court has rejected virtually all due process challenges to state and federal economic regulatory efforts. In short, the contemporary Court generally refuses to determine what is and is not in the public interest.

Williamson v. Lee Optical Co. (1955) provides a good example of how the Court now treats Fourteenth Amendment economic claims. Here, the Court upheld a 1953 Oklahoma law that made it "unlawful for any person . . . to fit, adjust, adapt, or to apply . . . lenses, frames . . . or any other optical appliances to the face" unless that person was a licensed ophthalmologist, "a physician who specializes in the care of eyes," or an optometrist, "one who examines eyes for refractory error . . . and fills prescriptions." An optician, an "artisan qualified to grind lenses to fill prescriptions," could do so only with a written prescription issued by an ophthalmologist or optometrist. Although the justices thought that the "law may exact a needless, wasteful requirement in many cases," Justice William O. Douglas noted in his majority opinion that "it is for the legislature, not the courts, to balance the advantages and disadvantages of the new requirement." Moreover, he said, "[t]he day is gone when this Court uses the Due Process Clause of the Fourteenth Amendment to strike down state laws, regulatory of business and industrial conditions, because they may be unwise, improvident, or out of harmony with a particular school of thought." The Court even quoted from Waite's opinion in *Munn*: "For protection against abuses by legislatures the people must resort to the polls, not to the courts."

Although *Williamson* was decided in 1955, it continues to characterize the Court's thinking on economic substantive due process. In ***Pennell v. City of San Jose*** (1988) the Court rejected the claims of a landlord who sought to invalidate a city rent control scheme on substantive due process grounds. In applying a rational basis standard, Chief Justice William Rehnquist concluded, "We have long recognized that a legitimate and rational goal of price or rate regulation is the protection of consumer welfare."

This is not to say that substantive due process has disappeared altogether. In fact, it has reemerged in at least two different contexts. The first is the issue of excessive monetary damages awarded by juries. In ***BMW of North America v. Gore*** (1996) the justices reviewed the outcome of a dispute between an automobile company and the purchaser of one of its cars. Ira Gore bought a new BMW from a dealership in Alabama. He later discovered that his car had been repainted prior to his purchase. He sued the manufacturer, claiming that it had failed to disclose the repainting and therefore should make a reasonable adjustment to the sale price. The jury decided in his favor, finding that the automobile was worth $4,000 less at the time of Gore's purchase than if it had not been repainted. In addition to the $4,000 in compensatory damages, the jury awarded Gore another $4 million because it found that BMW's nondisclosure policy amounted to "gross, oppressive, or malicious" fraud. The state supreme court reduced these punitive damages to $2 million, and BMW appealed to the Supreme Court, arguing that the jury award was so excessive as to violate due process of law. Over the objections of four dissenters who criticized the Court's use of substantive due process as a guide, the majority held that grossly unreasonable jury awards are contrary to the Fourteenth Amendment. The Court has continued to apply this reasoning to subsequent jury award appeals.[13]

---

[12]This position is consistent with the Court's rulings in related areas. Particularly important is the decision in *United States v. Carolene Products* (1938), in which the justices announced that they would henceforth generally defer to the legislature and give only minimal scrutiny to the reasonableness of economic regulations. In that same decision, the Court pledged to give more searching scrutiny to laws affecting civil liberties.

[13]See, for example, *State Farm Mutual Automobile Insurance Co. v. Campbell* (2003).

The second context in which the doctrine of substantive due process retains some relevance is in the Court's interpretation of personal privacy rights. Because the right to privacy is not explicitly mentioned anywhere in the Constitution, the Court struggled with the issue of whether it can be legitimately protected under a more general constitutional provision. In *Griswold v. Connecticut* (1965) the Court used privacy grounds to strike down a state law prohibiting the disbursement of birth control, but the justices divided on just how the Constitution protects privacy (see chapter 16 for a full discussion of the case). Indeed, at least some of the justices in the majority relied on substantive due process grounds to reach that result. Justice John Harlan wrote in a concurring opinion:

> In my view, the proper constitutional inquiry in this case is whether this Connecticut statute infringes the Due Process Clause of the Fourteenth Amendment because the enactment violates basic values "implicit in the concept of ordered liberty." . . . The Due Process Clause of the Fourteenth Amendment stands, in my opinion, on its own bottom.

Furthermore, Justice Harry A. Blackmun's 1973 opinion in *Roe v. Wade* legalizing abortion during the first two trimesters of pregnancy also invoked the due process clause:

> [The] right of privacy, whether it be founded in the Fourteenth Amendment's concept of personal liberty and restrictions upon state action, as we feel it is, or [another clause] . . . is broad enough to encompass a woman's decision whether or not to terminate her pregnancy.

That the *Roe* right rests, in part, on the due process clause has been a source of contention among legal scholars. Some, such as John Hart Ely, have accused Blackmun of "*Lochner*-ing," of returning to a discredited theory of individual rights as the peg on which to hang abortion rights.

In spite of such criticisms, the Court has continued to use a substantive due process approach to protect privacy rights. In *Lawrence v. Texas* (2003), for example, the justices struck down a Texas sodomy statute explicitly on due process grounds. For the majority, Justice Anthony M. Kennedy concluded:

> The petitioners are entitled to respect for their private lives. The State cannot demean their existence or control their destiny by making their private sexual conduct a crime. Their right to liberty under the Due Process Clause gives them the full right to engage in their conduct without intervention of the government. "It is a promise of the Constitution that there is a realm of personal liberty which the government may not enter."

Similarly, in *Obergefell v. Hodges* (2015) the Court, once again speaking through an opinion by Justice Kennedy, held that bans against same-sex marriage were unconstitutional in part because they denied liberty protected by due process of law guarantees. (Again, see chapter 16 for more in-depth discussions of *Lawrence* and *Obergefell*.)

Undoubtedly, the economic substantive due process doctrine—so exalted at the beginning of the twentieth century and so rejected in the post–New Deal period—has had a significant effect on the course of the law. What could have simply faded out of existence with Miller's *Slaughterhouse* opinion became the source of one of the most interesting episodes in constitutional law.

ANNOTATED READINGS

A number of works provide good discussions and critiques of substantive due process and related phenomena. These include Randy E. Barnett, *Restoring the Lost Constitution: The Presumption of Liberty* (Princeton, NJ: Princeton University Press, 2003); Raoul Berger, *Government by Judiciary* (Cambridge, MA: Harvard University Press, 1977); Michael Conant, *The Constitution and Economic Regulation* (New Brunswick, NJ: Transaction, 2008); Markus Dirk Dubber, *The Police Power: Patriarchy and the Foundations of American Government* (New York: Columbia University Press, 2005); Edward Keynes, *Liberty, Property, and Privacy: Toward a Jurisprudence of Substantive Due*

Process (University Park: Pennsylvania State University Press, 1996); John V. Orth, *Due Process of Law* (Lawrence: University Press of Kansas, 2003); Frank R. Strong, *Substantive Due Process of Law: A Dichotomy of Sense and Nonsense* (Durham, NC: Carolina Academic Press, 1986); E. Thomas Sullivan and Toni M. Massaro, *The Arc of Due Process in American Constitutional Law* (New York: Oxford University Press, 2013).

Other books approach substantive due process from a more historical perspective: Richard C. Cortner, *The Iron Horse and the Constitution: The Railroads and the Transformation of the Fourteenth Amendment* (Westport, CT: Greenwood Press, 1993); Herbert Hovenkamp, *Enterprise and American Law, 1836–1937* (Cambridge, MA: Harvard University Press, 1991); Morton Keller, *Affairs of State* (Cambridge, MA: Harvard University Press, 1977); Michael J. Phillips, *The* Lochner *Court, Myth and Reality: Substantive Due Process from the 1890s to the 1930s* (Westport, CT: Praeger, 2001); Timothy Sandefur, *The Right to Earn a Living: Economic Freedom and the Law* (Washington, DC: Cato Institute, 2010);

William F. Swindler, *Court and Constitution in the Twentieth Century* (Indianapolis, IN: Bobbs-Merrill, 1970); Clement E. Vose, *Constitutional Change* (Lexington, MA: Lexington Books, 1972); Christopher Wolfe, *The Rise of Modern Judicial Review* (New York: Basic Books, 1986).

Still other volumes provide in-depth analyses of specific cases that have been fundamental in the development and decline of substantive due process. Good examples are Howard Gillman, *The Constitution Besieged: The Rise and Demise of* Lochner *Era Police Powers Jurisprudence* (Durham, NC: Duke University Press, 1993); N. E. H. Hull, Roe v. Wade: *The Abortion Controversy in American History* (Lawrence: University Press of Kansas, 2001); John W. Johnson, Griswold v. Connecticut: *Birth Control and the Constitutional Right of Privacy* (Lawrence: University Press of Kansas, 2005); Paul Kens, *Judicial Power and Reform Politics: The Anatomy of* Lochner v. New York (Lawrence: University Press of Kansas, 1990); David Richards, *The Sodomy Cases:* Bowers v. Hardwick *and* Lawrence v. Texas (Lawrence: University Press of Kansas, 2009).

CHAPTER ELEVEN

THE TAKINGS CLAUSE

ONE DAY A CERTIFIED LETTER arrives at your house informing you that the government has decided to construct a new highway and that your property lies directly in its path. The letter further states that in return for your property the government will pay you $200,000—an amount it considers "fair market value" for your home. Finally, the letter instructs you to vacate the house within six months.

Does the government have the right to seize your property in this fashion? What if this house has been in your family for five generations and you do not want to sell? What if this is your dream home, just completed after years of saving and sacrificing? And what if you consider the government's offer to be much less than the property is worth? Can you challenge the amount offered? What about your rights to private property? The general answer to these questions is that the government indeed has the right to seize private property for a public purpose, such as the construction of a new road or a government building. This authority is referred to as the power of *eminent domain*. When federal, state, or local governments embark on new construction projects for roads, schools, military bases, or government offices, they usually must acquire private property. Sometimes they need to obtain only a single parcel or two, but at other times government projects require massive seizure (or condemnation) of property. Although property owners may feel mistreated when the government seizes their land, such government power is generally regarded as justified. Property owners, however, have an important protection. The Constitution contains a provision, known as the takings clause, that checks the authority of the government against the individual's right to property.

PROTECTING PRIVATE PROPERTY FROM GOVERNMENT SEIZURE

When the members of the First Congress proposed a listing of those rights considered important enough to merit constitutional protection, they included in the Fifth Amendment a significant private property guarantee—the takings clause—which states, "nor shall private property be taken for public use, without just compensation."

That the framers would have protected private property in this way is not surprising. The men who fashioned the U.S. Constitution supported a national government that would be stronger than it had been under the Articles of Confederation, knowing that without the power of eminent domain, individuals could hold government projects for ransom by refusing to sell or demanding unreasonable compensation. At the same time, the framers were firm believers in private property rights. For instance, James Madison, the primary author of the Bill of Rights, rejected the notion that government should have the absolute power to confiscate private property.[1] By requiring that governmental takings provide fair payment to property owners, the takings clause serves both to acknowledge the inherent power of the federal government to seize private property (a power that is not explicit in the Constitution) and to limit the exercise of that power by ensuring that property owners will not be unduly disadvantaged. As Justice Hugo

[1]James W. Ely Jr., *The Guardian of Every Other Right: A Constitutional History of Property Rights* (New York: Oxford University Press, 1992), 55.

Black explained, the takings clause "was designed to bar Government from forcing some people to bear public burdens which, in all fairness and justice, should be borne by the public as a whole."[2]

Because several states already protected private property against state government seizures, the takings clause was intended to apply only to federal government confiscations. This interpretation was endorsed by the Supreme Court in the case of *Barron v. Baltimore* in 1833. This dispute arose when the city of Baltimore initiated a series of street improvements that also necessitated altering several small streams. As a result, large amounts of sand and dirt were swept downstream into Baltimore Harbor, causing serious problems for the owners of wharves operating there. John Barron and John Craig were particularly damaged. Their wharf had been very profitable because its deepwater location enabled it to service large ships. The silt and waste accumulation near their wharf, though, was so great that the water became too shallow for large vessels, and Barron and Craig lost considerable business. They argued that Baltimore's municipal improvements had effectively destroyed their wharf, and they demanded compensation from the city for their loss. When the city refused, they sued, asking for $20,000 in damages. The local court awarded them $4,500, but a state appellate court reversed that decision. Barron and Craig appealed to the U.S. Supreme Court.

They claimed that the city's construction caused their wharf's loss of profitability. This constituted a "taking" under the meaning of the Fifth Amendment, and they deserved "just compensation." The justices, however, were not concerned with questions of whether a taking had occurred or what constituted just compensation. Instead, the Court focused on a more fundamental issue: Did the Fifth Amendment apply to state actions at all?

The Court concluded that it did not. In the words of Chief Justice John Marshall:

> We are of opinion that the provision in the fifth amendment to the constitution, declaring that private property shall not be taken for public use without just compensation, is intended solely as a limitation on the exercise of power

by the government of the United States, and is not applicable to the legislation of the states.[3]

For the next half century this interpretation remained the law of the land. The takings clause applied only to the federal government. If states did not impose similar restraints on themselves, they were free to exercise the power of eminent domain without providing adequate compensation to landowners whose property had been seized.

In the late 1800s, prompted by the ratification of the Fourteenth Amendment, the Court began to reconsider this position. The due process clause of the Fourteenth Amendment, you will recall, states, "nor shall any state deprive any person of life, liberty, or property, without due process of law." Lawyers began arguing that when states confiscated private property without giving the owners adequate compensation, they were depriving the owners of property without due process of law, a violation of the Fourteenth Amendment.

The Supreme Court adopted this position in *Chicago, Burlington & Quincy Railroad v. Chicago* (1897). The justices held that the takings clause of the U.S. Constitution was binding not only upon the federal government but also upon state and local governments. It affirmed the government's power of eminent domain but required the payment of adequate compensation whenever that power was exercised.[4] With this ruling, the takings clause became the first provision of the Bill of Rights to be made binding on the states.

The authority of government to take private property in order to carry out legitimate projects is now well established. One common issue that flows from government takings cases is what constitutes "just compensation." In the normal course of events, the government attempts to buy the necessary land from the owners.

---

[2] *Armstrong v. United States* (1960).

[3] The implications of this decision went far beyond the takings clause issue. In ruling as it did, the Supreme Court held that the states did not have to abide by any of the provisions of the Bill of Rights, that those sections of the Constitution limited federal government actions only. The states were governed only by their own bills of rights. Over time, the Court incrementally changed its position (through a process known as selective incorporation), but it took more than 130 years for it to conclude that the states were bound by almost all the provisions of the Bill of Rights.

[4] See David A. Schultz, *Property, Power, and American Democracy* (New Brunswick, NJ: Transaction, 1992).

If negotiations fail, the government may declare the power of eminent domain and take the property, giving the owners what it thinks is a fair price. The Supreme Court has concluded that fair market value is usually the appropriate standard, but it is not uncommon for owners to argue that the government's offer is inadequate. In such situations the owners may go to court to challenge the amount. Questions of just compensation normally are settled through negotiation or trial court action and rarely involve significant issues beyond the specific land under dispute.[5] Although legal battles may be fought over whether the offered compensation is just, there is no doubt about the power of the government to seize the property.

As we will see, two other questions have proven to be more problematic for the justices: What is a taking? And what constitutes a public use? Both questions have required authoritative answers by the Supreme Court.

WHAT CONSTITUTES A TAKING?

In most cases it is relatively easy to determine that a taking has occurred. If the federal government decides to build a new post office and must acquire a piece of privately owned property upon which to build, a taking is necessary if a voluntary sale is not negotiated. Similarly, a taking occurs when, to complete a water control project, the government needs to dam certain streams, which will cause privately owned land to become permanently flooded. In such situations the government takes private land and uses it for a public purpose. There is no question that the former owner has been deprived of ownership rights over the property.

But a taking may also occur if the government engages in some activity that destroys the use of private property without physically seizing it. *United States v.*

Causby (1946) arose in 1942, in the midst of World War II, when the federal government built a military airfield within 2,300 feet of a North Carolina chicken farm. The planes flew just 67 feet above the farmhouse; these flights almost skimmed the treetops and often blew the leaves from the trees. The constant noise and commotion as the planes took off and landed caused considerable disruption on the farm. The chickens became less productive, and many died when they flew into the walls of their coops out of fear and panic. In short, the property was no longer suitable for raising chickens.

The Supreme Court held that the government had "taken" this property. The path of the airplanes was so low and so close to the farm and residence as to deprive the owners of the use and enjoyment of their land. There was a diminution of the property's value that was directly and immediately attributable to the government's actions. Under such circumstances a taking has occurred and the landowners deserve compensation, even though the property, technically speaking, still belonged to the farm owner.

How far can the definition of a taking be legitimately extended? After all, every time the government passes a law regulating the use of property, the rights of owners are diminished. Does regulation constitute a taking? Justice Oliver Wendell Holmes addressed this question in *Pennsylvania Coal Co. v. Mahon* (1922). For Holmes, the answer depended on the extent of the regulation: "The general rule at least is, that while property may be regulated to a certain extent, if regulation goes too far it will be recognized as a taking." Holmes feared that, given too much discretion, the government might regulate "until the last private property disappears."[6]

Generally, government regulation that only incidentally infringes on the owner's use of property is not considered a taking, nor is regulation that outlaws the noxious or dangerous use of property. Obvious examples are zoning laws and other regulatory ordinances that make certain uses unlawful.[7] Owners may be distressed that they can no longer use their property in particular ways, but the Supreme Court has held that such statutes do not constitute a Fifth Amendment taking that deserves compensation. For example, the justices ruled

[5]Although disputes over compensation levels normally are settled at the trial court level, occasionally such controversies involve significant issues and large amounts of money. In *United States v. Sioux Nation of Indians* (1980) the Supreme Court settled a long-standing dispute over the abrogation of the Fort Laramie Treaty of 1868. The treaty had established the right of the Sioux nation to the Black Hills, but an 1877 act of Congress essentially took back those lands. The Court ruled that the treaty abrogation was governed by the takings clause and that the Sioux were entitled to the value of the land in 1877 plus 5 percent annual interest since that year, amounting to a total claim of some $100 million.

[6]See Ely, *The Guardian of Every Other Right*, chap. 6.

[7]See *Agins v. City of Tiburon* (1980).

that takings did not occur when a state ordered property owners to cut down standing cedar trees because a disease the cedars carried threatened nearby apple orchards; when a local government passed an ordinance removing an individual's right to use his land as a brickyard, a use seen as inconsistent with the surrounding neighborhood; or when for safety reasons a city prohibited a person from mining sand and gravel on his land.[8] In these and numerous similar cases the government's actions significantly reduced the way the land could be used and decreased its commercial value, yet the Court held that takings had not occurred. Instead, the government policies were instituted in response to social, economic, or environmental problems that could be addressed through the use of the government's police powers.

The questions of how far such regulation may go and for what reasons were addressed in *Penn Central Transportation Company v. City of New York* (1978). These issues are important. If the government imposes regulations that seriously curtail a landowner's economic use of his or her property, has a taking occurred? Although Justice William J. Brennan's opinion acknowledges that this area of the law has proved to be one of "considerable difficulty," it presents a good review of the principles the Court has developed to determine when a taking has occurred.

Penn Central Transportation Company v. City of New York

438 U.S. 104 (1978)
http://caselaw.findlaw.com/us-supreme-court/438/104.html
Oral arguments available at https://www.oyez.org/
  cases/1977/77-444
Vote: 6 (Blackmun, Brennan, Marshall, Powell, Stewart, White)
  3 (Burger, Rehnquist, Stevens)

OPINION OF THE COURT: *Brennan*

DISSENTING OPINION: *Rehnquist*

New York City passed the Landmarks Preservation Law in 1965 as part of an effort to protect historic buildings and districts. Each of the fifty states and more than five hundred cities had similar statutes. The Landmarks Preservation Commission administered the law, and the commission's task was to identify buildings and areas that held special historic or aesthetic value. These sites were

[8] *Miller v. Schoene* (1928), *Hadacheck v. Los Angeles* (1915), and *Goldblatt v. Hempstead* (1962), respectively.

then discussed in hearings to determine whether landmark status should be conferred on them. If a building or area was designated as historic, the owner's ability to change the property was restricted. Owners of landmark buildings were required to keep the exteriors in good repair and could not alter the buildings without first securing approval from the commission. Owners of such buildings received no direct compensation, but they were accorded enhanced development rights for other properties.

This case involved applying the preservation law to Grand Central Terminal, owned by Penn Central Transportation Company. The original terminal, constructed in the late nineteenth century by the shipping magnate, Cornelius Vanderbilt, required much of the station to be open-air, in order to accommodate the smoke generated by coal-fired trains. As electricity replaced steam, the station was rebuilt and moved all of it platforms underground. The renovated station—the largest in the world—opened in 1913 and is widely regarded as an example of ingenious engineering in response to problems presented by modern urban rail stations. It is also cited as a magnificent example of the French-inspired Beaux-Arts style. The terminal was designated a historic landmark in 1967, although Penn Central initially opposed the action.

As planes and automobiles became more popular, railways began to lose much of their profitability. So in 1968, to increase revenues, Penn Central entered into an agreement with UGP Properties to build a multistory office building above the terminal. The reason was obvious; Manhattan is a densely populated island, and the ability to build skyward makes real estate there enormously valuable. UGP and Penn Central presented two separate plans to the Landmarks Preservation Commission for its approval. One of the plans proposed a change in the facade of the building and the construction of a fifty-three-story office tower above it. The other envisioned a fifty-five-story office building cantilevered above the existing facade and resting on the roof of the terminal. The commission rejected both proposals.

In response, Penn Central and UGP filed suit claiming that the application of the Landmarks Preservation Law to the terminal constituted a taking of their property without just compensation. The New York courts denied their claims, with the state's highest court rejecting the notion that the property had been "taken" under the meaning of the Fifth Amendment.

MR. JUSTICE BRENNAN DELIVERED THE OPINION OF THE COURT.

Before considering appellants' specific contentions, it will be useful to review the factors that have shaped the jurisprudence of the Fifth Amendment injunction "nor shall private property be taken for public use, without just compensation." The question of what constitutes a "taking" for purposes of the Fifth Amendment has proved to be a problem of considerable difficulty. . . . [T]his Court, quite simply, has been unable to develop any "set formula" for determining when "justice and fairness" require that economic injuries caused by public action be compensated by the government, rather than remain disproportionately concentrated on a few persons. Indeed, we have frequently observed that whether a particular restriction will be rendered invalid by the government's failure to pay for any losses proximately caused by it depends largely "upon the particular circumstances [in that] case."

In engaging in these essentially ad hoc, factual inquiries, the Court's decisions have identified several factors that have particular significance. The economic impact of the regulation on the claimant and, particularly, the extent to which the regulation has interfered with distinct investment-backed expectations are, of course, relevant considerations. So, too, is the character of the government action. A "taking" may more readily be found when the interference with property can be characterized as a physical invasion by the government than when interference arises from some public program adjusting the benefits and burdens of economic life to promote the common good.

"Government hardly could go on if to some extent values incident to property could not be diminished without paying for every such change in the general law," *Pennsylvania Coal Co. v. Mahon* (1922), and this Court has accordingly recognized, in a wide variety of contexts, that government may execute laws or programs that adversely affect recognized economic values. Exercises of the taxing power are one obvious example. A second are the decisions in which this Court has dismissed "taking" challenges on the ground that, while the challenged government action caused economic harm, it did not interfere with interests that were sufficiently bound up with the reasonable expectations of the claimant to constitute "property" for Fifth Amendment purposes.

More importantly for the present case, in instances in which a state tribunal reasonably concluded that "the health, safety, morals, or general welfare" would be promoted by prohibiting particular contemplated uses of land, this Court has upheld land-use regulations that destroyed or adversely affected recognized real property interests. Zoning laws are, of course, the classic example. . . .

Zoning laws generally do not affect existing uses of real property, but "taking" challenges have also been held to be without merit in a wide variety of situations when the challenged governmental actions prohibited a beneficial use to which individual parcels had previously been devoted and thus caused substantial individualized harm. . . .

Pennsylvania Coal Co. v. Mahon (1922) is the leading case for the proposition that a state statute that substantially furthers important public policies may so frustrate distinct investment-backed expectations as to amount to a "taking." There the claimant had sold the surface rights to particular parcels of property, but expressly reserved the right to remove the coal thereunder.

A Pennsylvania statute, enacted after the transactions, forbade any mining of coal that caused the subsidence of any house, unless the house was the property of the owner of the underlying coal and was more than 150 feet from the improved property of another. Because the statute made it commercially impracticable to mine the coal, and thus had nearly the same effect as the complete destruction of rights claimant had reserved from the owners of the surface land, the Court held that the statute was invalid as effecting a "taking" without just compensation. . . .

In contending that the New York City law has "taken" their property in violation of the Fifth and Fourteenth Amendments, appellants make a series of arguments, which, while tailored to the facts of this case, essentially urge that any substantial restriction imposed pursuant to a landmark law must be accompanied by just compensation if it is to be constitutional. Before considering these, we emphasize what is not in dispute. Because this Court has recognized in a number of settings, that States and cities may enact land-use restrictions or controls to enhance the quality of life by preserving the character and desirable aesthetic features of a city, appellants do not contest that New York City's objective of preserving structures and areas with special historic, architectural, or cultural significance is an entirely permissible governmental goal. They also do not dispute that the restrictions imposed on its parcel are appropriate means of securing the purposes of the New York City law. Finally, appellants do not challenge any of the specific factual premises of the decision below. They accept for present purposes both that the parcel of land occupied by Grand Central Terminal must, in its present state, be regarded as capable of earning a reasonable return, and that the transferable development rights afforded the appellants by virtue of the Terminal's designation as a landmark are valuable, even if not as valuable as the rights to construct above the Terminal. In appellants' view none of these factors derogate from their claim that New York City's law has effected a "taking."

They first observe that the airspace above the Terminal is a valuable property interest, citing *United States v. Causby*. They urge that the Landmarks Law has deprived them of any gainful use of their "air rights" above the Terminal and that, irrespective of the value of the remainder of their parcel, the city has "taken" their right to this superadjacent airspace, thus entitling them to "just compensation" measured by the fair market value of these air rights.

Apart from our own disagreement with appellants' characterization of the effect of the New York City law, the submission that appellants may establish a "taking" simply by showing that they have been denied the ability to exploit a property interest that they heretofore had believed was available for development is quite simply untenable. . . . "Taking" jurisprudence does not divide a single parcel into discrete segments and attempt to determine whether rights in a particular segment have been entirely abrogated. In deciding whether a particular governmental action has effected a taking, this Court focuses rather both on the character of the action and on the nature and extent of the interference with rights in the parcel as a whole—here, the city tax block designated as the "landmark site."

Secondly, appellants, focusing on the character and impact of the New York City law, argue that it effects a "taking" because its operation has significantly diminished the value of the Terminal site. Appellants concede that the decisions sustaining other land-use regulations, which, like the New York City law, are reasonably related to the promotion of the general welfare, uniformly reject the proposition that diminution in property value, standing alone, can establish a "taking." . . . . [B]ut appellants argue that New York City's regulation of individual landmarks is fundamentally different from zoning or from historic-district legislation because the controls imposed by New York City's law apply only to individuals who own selected properties.

Stated baldly, appellants' position appears to be that the only means of ensuring that selected owners are not singled out to endure financial hardship for no reason is to hold that any restriction imposed on individual landmarks pursuant to the New York City scheme is a "taking" requiring the payment of "just compensation." Agreement with this argument would, of course, invalidate not just New York City's law, but all comparable landmark legislation in the Nation. We find no merit in it. . . .

Equally without merit is the related argument that the decision to designate a structure as a landmark "is inevitably arbitrary or at least subjective, because it is basically a matter of taste," thus unavoidably singling out individual landowners for disparate and unfair treatment. The argument has a particularly hollow ring in this case. . . . [A] landmark owner has a right to judicial review of any Commission decision, and, quite simply, there is no basis whatsoever for a conclusion that courts will have any greater difficulty identifying arbitrary or discriminatory action in the context of landmark regulation than in the context of classic zoning or indeed in any other context. . . .

In any event, appellants' repeated suggestions that they are solely burdened and unbenefited is factually inaccurate. This contention overlooks the fact that the New York City law applies to vast numbers of structures in the city in addition to the Terminal—all the structures contained in the 31 historic districts and over 400 individual landmarks, many of which are close to the Terminal. Unless we are to reject the judgment of the New York City Council that the preservation of landmarks benefits all New York citizens and all structures, both economically and by improving the quality of life in the city as a whole—which we are unwilling to do—we cannot conclude that the owners of the Terminal have in no sense been benefited by the Landmarks Law. . . .

. . . [T]he New York City law does not interfere in any way with the present uses of the Terminal. Its designation as a landmark not only permits but contemplates that appellants may continue to use the property precisely as it has been used for the past 65 years:

as a railroad terminal containing office space and concessions. So the law does not interfere with what must be regarded as Penn Central's primary expectation concerning the use of the parcel. More importantly, on this record, we must regard the New York City law as permitting Penn Central not only to profit from the Terminal but also to obtain a "reasonable" return on its investment. . . .

On this record, we conclude that the application of New York City's Landmarks Law has not effected a "taking" of appellants' property. The restrictions imposed are substantially related to the promotion of the general welfare and not only permit reasonable beneficial use of the landmark site but also afford appellants opportunities further to enhance not only the Terminal site proper but also other properties.

Affirmed.

MR. JUSTICE REHNQUIST, WITH WHOM THE CHIEF JUSTICE AND MR. JUSTICE STEVENS JOIN, DISSENTING.

Of the over one million buildings and structures in the city of New York, appellees have singled out 400 for designation as official landmarks. The owner of a building might initially be pleased that his property has been chosen by a distinguished committee of architects, historians, and city planners for such a singular distinction. But he may well discover, as appellant Penn Central Transportation Co. did here, that the landmark designation imposes upon him a substantial cost, with little or no offsetting benefit except for the honor of the designation. The question in this case is whether the cost associated with the city of New York's desire to preserve a limited number of "landmarks" within its borders must be borne by all of its taxpayers or whether it can instead be imposed entirely on the owners of the individual properties. . . .

The Fifth Amendment provides in part: "nor shall private property be taken for public use, without just compensation." In a very literal sense, the actions of appellees violated this constitutional prohibition. Before the city of New York declared Grand Central Terminal to be a landmark, Penn Central could have used its "air rights" over the Terminal to build a multistory office building, at an apparent value of several million dollars per year. Today, the Terminal cannot be modified in any form, including the erection of additional stories, without the permission of the Landmark Preservation Commission, a permission which appellants, despite good-faith attempts, have so far been unable to obtain. . . .

As Mr. Justice Holmes pointed out in *Pennsylvania Coal Co. v. Mahon,* "the question at bottom" in an eminent domain case "is upon whom the loss of the changes desired should fall." The benefits that appellees believe will flow from preservation of the Grand Central Terminal will accrue to all the citizens of New York City. There is no reason to believe that appellants will enjoy a substantially greater share of these benefits. If the cost of preserving Grand Central

Terminal were spread evenly across the entire population of the city of New York, the burden per person would be in cents per year—a minor cost appellees would surely concede for the benefit accrued. Instead, however, appellees would impost the entire cost of several million dollars per year on Penn Central. But it is precisely this sort of discrimination that the Fifth Amendment prohibits. . . .

Over 50 years ago, Mr. Justice Holmes, speaking for the Court, warned that the courts were "in danger of forgetting that a strong public desire to improve the public condition is not enough to warrant achieving the desire by a shorter cut than the constitutional way of paying for the change." The Court's opinion in this case demonstrates that the danger thus foreseen has not abated. The city of New York is in a precarious financial state, and some may believe that the costs of landmark preservation will be more easily borne by corporations such as Penn Central than the overburdened individual taxpayers of New York. But these concerns do not allow us to ignore past precedents construing the Eminent Domain Clause to the end that the desire to improve the public condition is, indeed, achieved by a shorter cut than the constitutional way of paying for the change.

Justice Brennan's majority opinion in *Penn Central* represented the accepted view of regulatory takings at that time; the landmark preservation law was merely a land-use regulation enacted for the public good, and it did not diminish the existing value of Grand Central Terminal. Justice Rehnquist's dissent, however, signaled that the more conservative justices on the Court preferred to give greater weight to the interests of property owners. Eight years later the ideological balance on the Court shifted when Rehnquist was elevated to the chief justiceship and Antonin Scalia joined the Court as an associate justice. Both were strong advocates of private property rights and adhered to a much broader conception of what constitutes a taking.

The first signs of change appeared in 1987, when the Court handed down three takings clause decisions. The first, decided in March, was **Keystone Bituminous Coal Association v. DeBenedictis**. The majority upheld a state regulation of coal mining operations against takings clause and contract clause attacks, but Chief Justice Rehnquist's dissenting position attracted the support of three other justices, indicating that the conservative-minded members of the Court were poised to make a major assault on existing takings clause interpretations.

The second 1987 decision, *First English Evangelical Lutheran Church of Glendale v. County of Los Angeles,* was decided in June. Although this case involved a relatively minor point regarding the recovery of damages, the Court voted 6–3 to support the property owners who

claimed compensation. Rehnquist wrote the majority opinion in support of the property rights position. This decision was a clear invitation to private property interests that the Rehnquist Court was open to new takings clause appeals. Justice John Paul Stevens's dissenting opinion acknowledged this point: "One thing is certain. The Court's decision today will generate a great deal of litigation."

The final 1987 decision, **Nollan v. California Coastal Commission**, decided in late June, was the most important indication that the Rehnquist Court was about to resurrect property rights under the takings clause. James and Marilyn Nollan owned a beachfront lot in Ventura County, California, located between two public beaches. The Nollans' property included a small bungalow that they rented to summer vacationers. When the house fell into serious disrepair and could no longer be rented, the couple decided to replace it with a new structure. To do so, they needed a building permit from the California Coastal Commission.

The commission granted the Nollans permission to build their new house, but with one significant condition: a strip of land across the Nollan property was to be set aside for public use as a passageway between the two public beaches. The Nollans protested, but the commission remained firm. The Nollans then filed suit claiming that the public access condition constituted a taking under the Fifth Amendment. The Court, in an opinion by Justice Scalia for the 5–4 majority, ruled that the condition attached to the building permit was in fact a taking for which the Nollans must be compensated. In dissent, Justice Brennan condemned the decision as being out of step with the complex reality of natural resource protection in the twentieth century.

Brennan's hope that *Nollan* would be an aberration was not fulfilled. In the years following *Nollan,* the personnel on the Court continued to change. Justices Brennan and Thurgood Marshall retired. Both had been firm supporters of public interests over private property rights. Two supporters of private property joined the Court, Anthony M. Kennedy in 1988 and Clarence Thomas in 1991, and they strengthened Chief Justice Rehnquist's efforts to breathe new life into the Constitution's private property protections.

There is no invariable rule to assist courts in determining whether a challenged government regulation has gone too far and becomes a taking. Rather, in line with the *Penn Central* decision, courts engage in an ad hoc evaluation of the government's actions, weighing all relevant facts and circumstances, including the nature of the government's actions, the economic impact of the regulation on the claimant, and the extent to which the regulation has interfered with distinct investment-backed expectations.

However, there are two conditions under which courts find no need to engage in such a searching analysis. If either of these two conditions exists, there is no question that the government action constitutes a taking that requires compensation. The first condition is when the government's action completely deprives the owner of all economically beneficial use of the property. The second occurs when the government permanently occupies the property. Either situation categorically requires compensation. These are often referred to as *per se* takings.

The Court's decision in *Lucas v. South Carolina Coastal Council* (1992) involves a litigant who claimed that the state government's environmental regulations stripped his land of any economic value. Do you think the government's action was a reasonable regulation to protect the coastal environment, or do you agree with the Court's majority that a taking occurred requiring compensation?

Lucas v. South Carolina Coastal Council

505 U.S. 1003 (1992)
http://caselaw.findlaw.com/us-supreme-court/505/1003.html
Oral arguments available at https://www.oyez.org/
cases/1991/91-453
Vote: 6 (Kennedy, O'Connor, Rehnquist, Scalia, Thomas, White)
3 (Blackmun, Souter, Stevens)

OPINION OF THE COURT: *Scalia*

OPINION CONCURRING IN THE JUDGMENT: *Kennedy*

DISSENTING OPINIONS: *Blackmun, Stevens*

SEPARATE STATEMENT: *Souter*

In 1986 David Lucas paid $975,000 for two vacant oceanfront lots on the Isle of Palms, a barrier island near Charleston, South Carolina. He acquired the property with the intention of building single-family homes similar to those already built on adjacent lots. When Lucas bought the land there were no regulations prohibiting such use. Shortly thereafter, however, the state passed the Beachfront Management Act, an environmental law that gave the state coastal council increased authority to protect certain shoreline areas against erosion and other dangers. The council decided that the Lucas lots were in a "critical area" and prohibited any new construction on the lots. Since nothing could be built on them,

what were previously highly valued beach-front parcels were now, in economic terms, worthless.

There is no doubt that under its police powers, the state has the right to pass such legislation, but Lucas claimed that the new regulations amounted to a taking of his property for a public purpose. The Fifth Amendment, he argued, required the state to pay him for the loss of his property. A state trial judge agreed that the regulations had made the Lucas property essentially worthless and ordered the state to pay Lucas $1.23 million as just compensation for the loss. On appeal the South Carolina Supreme Court reversed the decision, holding that the environmental legislation was not a taking under the meaning of the Constitution. Lucas appealed to the U.S. Supreme Court.

JUSTICE SCALIA DELIVERED THE OPINION OF THE COURT.

Prior to Justice Holmes' exposition in *Pennsylvania Coal Co. v. Mahon* (1922), it was generally thought that the Takings Clause reached only a "direct appropriation" of property or the functional equivalent of a "practical ouster of [the owner's] possession." Justice Holmes recognized in *Mahon,* however, that, if the protection against physical appropriations of private property was to be meaningfully enforced, the government's power to redefine the range of interests included in the ownership of property was necessarily constrained by constitutional limits. If, instead, the uses of private property were subject to unbridled, uncompensated qualification under the police power, "the natural tendency of human nature [would be] to extend the qualification more and more until at last private property disappear[ed]." These considerations gave birth in that case to the oft-cited maxim that, "while property may be regulated to a certain extent, if regulation goes too far, it will be recognized as a taking."

Nevertheless, our decision in *Mahon* offered little insight into when, and under what circumstances, a given regulation would be seen as going "too far" for purposes of the Fifth Amendment. In 70-odd years of succeeding "regulatory takings" jurisprudence, we have generally eschewed any "'set formula'" for determining how far is too far, preferring to "engag[e] in . . . essentially *ad hoc,* factual inquiries," *Penn Central Transportation Co. v. New York City* (1978). We have, however, described at least two discrete categories of regulatory action as compensable without case-specific inquiry into the public interest advanced in support of the restraint. The first encompasses regulations that compel the property owner to suffer a physical "invasion" of his property. In general (at least with regard to permanent invasions), no matter how minute the intrusion, and no matter how weighty the public purpose behind it, we have required compensation. For example, in *Loretto v. Teleprompter Manhattan CATV Corp.* (1982), we determined that New York's law requiring landlords to allow television cable companies to emplace cable facilities in their apartment buildings constituted a taking, even though the facilities occupied, at most, only 1 1/2 cubic feet of the landlords' property.

The second situation in which we have found categorical treatment appropriate is where regulation denies all economically beneficial or productive use of land. As we have said on numerous occasions, the Fifth Amendment is violated when land use regulation "does not substantially advance legitimate state interests *or denies an owner economically viable use of his land.*"

We have never set forth the justification for this rule. Perhaps it is simply, as Justice Brennan suggested, that total deprivation of beneficial use is, from the landowner's point of view, the equivalent of a physical appropriation. Surely, at least, in the extraordinary circumstance when no productive or economically beneficial use of land is permitted, it is less realistic to indulge our usual assumption that the legislature is simply "adjusting the benefits and burdens of economic life" in a manner that secures an "average reciprocity of advantage" to everyone concerned. *Pennsylvania Coal Co. v. Mahon.* And the *functional* basis for permitting the government, by regulation, to affect property values without compensation—that Government hardly could go on if, to some extent, values incident to property could not be diminished without paying for every such change in the general law—does not apply to the relatively rare situations where the government has deprived a landowner of all economically beneficial uses.

On the other side of the balance, affirmatively supporting a compensation requirement, is the fact that regulations that leave the owner of land without economically beneficial or productive options for its use—typically, as here, by requiring land to be left substantially in its natural state carry with them a heightened risk that private property is being pressed into some form of public service under the guise of mitigating serious public harm. . . .

We think, in short, that there are good reasons for our frequently expressed belief that, when the owner of real property has been called upon to sacrifice *all* economically beneficial uses in the name of the common good, that is, to leave his property economically idle, he has suffered a taking.

The trial court found Lucas' two beachfront lots to have been rendered valueless by respondent's enforcement of the coastal-zone construction ban. Under Lucas' theory of the case, which rested upon our "no economically viable use" statements, that finding entitled him to compensation. Lucas believed it unnecessary to take issue with either the purposes behind the Beachfront Management Act or the means chosen by the South Carolina Legislature to effectuate those purposes. The South Carolina Supreme Court, however, thought otherwise. In its view, the Beachfront Management Act was no ordinary enactment, but involved an exercise of South Carolina's "police powers" to mitigate the harm to the public interest that petitioner's use of his land might occasion. . . .

It is correct that many of our prior opinions have suggested that "harmful or noxious uses" of property may be proscribed by government regulation without the requirement of compensation. For a number of reasons, however, we think the South Carolina Supreme Court was too quick to conclude that that principle decides the present case. . . .

Where the State seeks to sustain regulation that deprives land of all economically beneficial use, we think it may resist compensation only if the logically antecedent inquiry into the nature of the owner's estate shows that the proscribed use interests were not part of his title to begin with. This accords, we think, with our "takings" jurisprudence, which has traditionally been guided by the understandings of our citizens regarding the content of, and the State's power over, the "bundle of rights" that they acquire when they obtain title to property. It seems to us that the property owner necessarily expects the uses of his property to be restricted, from time to time, by various measures newly enacted by the State in legitimate exercise of its police powers; "[a]s long recognized, some values are enjoyed under an implied limitation, and must yield to the police power." *Pennsylvania Coal Co. v. Mahon.* . . . In the case of land, . . . we think the notion pressed by the Council that title is somehow held subject to the "implied limitation" that the State may subsequently eliminate all economically valuable use is inconsistent with the historical compact recorded in the Takings Clause that has become part of our constitutional culture.

Where "permanent physical occupation" of land is concerned, we have refused to allow the government to decree it anew (without compensation), no matter how weighty the asserted "public interests" involved, *Loretto v. Teleprompter Manhattan CATV Corp.*—though we assuredly *would* permit the government to assert a permanent easement that was a preexisting limitation upon the landowner's title. . . . We believe similar treatment must be accorded confiscatory regulations, *i.e.,* regulations that prohibit all economically beneficial use of land: any limitation so severe cannot be newly legislated or decreed (without compensation), but must inhere in the title itself, in the restrictions that background principles of the State's law of property and nuisance already place upon land ownership. A law or decree with such an effect must, in other words, do no more than duplicate the result that could have been achieved in the courts—by adjacent landowners (or other uniquely affected persons) under the State's law of private nuisance, or by the State under its complementary power to abate nuisances that affect the public generally, or otherwise.

On this analysis, the owner of a lakebed, for example, would not be entitled to compensation when he is denied the requisite permit to engage in a landfilling operation that would have the effect of flooding others' land. Nor the corporate owner of a nuclear generating plant, when it is directed to remove all improvements from its land upon discovery that the plant sits astride an earthquake fault. Such regulatory action may well have the effect of eliminating

Courtesy of William Fischel

One of two lots on the Isle of Palms that David Lucas purchased with the intention of building houses on them. Shortly after the sale was completed, the South Carolina Coastal Council determined that building on the lots would be detrimental to the environment and prohibited future development there. In 1992 the Supreme Court agreed with Lucas that the state's action violated the takings clause.

the land's only economically productive use, but it does not proscribe a productive use that was previously permissible under relevant property and nuisance principles. The use of these properties for what are now expressly prohibited purposes was *always* unlawful, and (subject to other constitutional limitations) it was open to the State at any point to make the implication of those background principles of nuisance and property law explicit. . . . When, however, a regulation that declares "off limits" all economically productive or beneficial uses of land goes beyond what the relevant background principles would dictate, compensation must be paid to sustain it.

The judgment is reversed, and the cause remanded for proceedings not inconsistent with this opinion.

So ordered.

JUSTICE BLACKMUN, DISSENTING.

Today the Court launches a missile to kill a mouse. . . .

The State of South Carolina prohibited petitioner Lucas from building a permanent structure on his property . . . . Relying on an unreviewed (and implausible) state trial court finding that this restriction left Lucas' property valueless, this Court granted review

to determine whether compensation must be paid in cases where the State prohibits all economic use of real estate. According to the Court, such an occasion never has arisen in any of our prior cases, and the Court imagines that it will arise "relatively rarely" or only in "extraordinary circumstances." Almost certainly, it did not happen in this case.

Nonetheless, the Court presses on to decide the issue, and as it does, it ignores its jurisdictional limits, remakes its traditional rules of review, and creates simultaneously a new categorical rule and an exception (neither of which is rooted in our prior case law, common law, or common sense). I protest not only the Court's decision, but each step taken to reach it. More fundamentally, I question the Court's wisdom in issuing sweeping new rules to decide such a narrow case. Surely . . . the Court could have reached the result it wanted without inflicting this damage upon our Takings Clause jurisprudence. . . .

The Court makes . . . , in my view, misguided and unsupported changes in our taking doctrine. While it limits these changes to the most narrow subset of government regulation—those that eliminate all economic value from land—these changes go far beyond what is necessary to secure petitioner Lucas' private benefit. One hopes they do not go beyond the narrow confines the Court assigns them to today.

I dissent.

Following *Lucas*, the Court continued to support takings clause claims against government regulations. In **Dolan v. City of Tigard** (1994) the Court considered a challenge to a municipality that had required the owner of a small store to devote a portion of her land to public green space and allow a pedestrian/bicycle path to cross her property in return for permission to expand her store and pave her parking lot. The justices, divided 5–4, ruled that the property owner's Fifth Amendment rights had been violated because the requirements for obtaining the permit were insufficiently related to the proposed store improvements.

In 2015, the Court in **Horne v. Department of Agriculture** reminded us that the takings clause applies not only to real property but to personal property as well. The case challenged a federal law allowing the Department of Agriculture to impose a reserve requirement obliging raisin growers to set aside a certain percentage of their crop for the government's use free of charge. The law dated back to the Great Depression and was intended to stabilize the raisin market by limiting their supply. In some sense, it was similar to the federal government's effort to control the price of wheat, an action upheld under the commerce clause in *Wickard v. Filburn* (1942). Unlike *Wickard*, however, where the government sought to control prices by restricting the amount of wheat a farmer could grow, the law at issue in *Horne* permitted raisin growers to harvest as much as they wished, and the government took ownership of any raisins grown in excess of farmers' allotments. The government made use of those reserved raisins by selling them in noncompetitive markets, donating them, or disposing of them by other means consistent with establishing an orderly market. The justices concluded that the government's seizure of privately owned raisins for its own purposes was a per se taking that required compensation.

But not all cases have been decided in favor of property owners. In **Tahoe-Sierra Preservation Council v. Tahoe Regional Planning Agency** (2002) the Court, in a 6–3 vote, ruled against private property interests. A regional planning agency had imposed a "temporary" moratorium on new construction in the Lake Tahoe basin while it conducted a study of appropriate land-use regulations. When the moratorium had been in effect

BOX 11-1

Aftermath . . . *Lucas v. South Carolina Coastal Council*

In 1986 David Lucas, a developer of residential properties, purchased two lots on the Isle of Palms in South Carolina for $975,000. He intended to build two houses on the land, keeping one for himself and selling the other. Because of environmental concerns, however, the state coastal council denied Lucas permission to build. In response, Lucas took legal action, demanding compensation for his economic loss. He won a $1.23 million judgment in the state trial court, but the state supreme court reversed that ruling. In 1992 the U.S. Supreme Court found that Lucas had been deprived of property for a public purpose and was entitled to compensation. The justices remanded the case back to the South Carolina courts for further proceedings.

Additional court action was not required, however. The state had lost on the essential issue presented in the case, and only the determination of adequate compensation remained to be decided. South Carolina was understandably eager to settle the dispute rather than prolong the legal battle. Lucas and the state came to a quick out-of-court settlement in which the state agreed to pay Lucas $1.5 million in return for the property.

To recoup the funds lost in the *Lucas* settlement and related litigation costs, the state decided to sell the properties. Ironically, to increase the lots' value prior to sale, the state announced that the new owners would be allowed to build houses on them. A new home of about 5,000 square feet now sits on one of the lots formerly owned by Lucas.

Sources: *Arizona Republic*, November 2, 1994; *Chicago Sun-Times*, July 28, 1995; *Christian Science Monitor*, September 27, 1993; *San Diego Union-Tribune*, July 21, 1993.

for thirty-two months, the landowners objected, claiming that a taking had occurred. The Supreme Court held otherwise, ruling that, because the moratorium was temporary—not like the permanent limitation in *Lucas*—the moratorium did not constitute a taking that required compensation.[9]

PUBLIC USE REQUIREMENT

Although the Fifth Amendment recognizes the government's power to take private property, it does not allow all such seizures. The takings clause stipulates quite explicitly that the government may take private property only for a "public use." Even if the government provides adequate compensation, it may not take property against the owner's will for the sole benefit of a private individual or organization. When the government plans to build a new courthouse, road, or park, the public use is clear, but it would be of doubtful constitutionality if a state seized a piece of private property under the power of eminent domain and gave it to a private fraternal organization to construct a new lodge.

Throughout most of the nation's history, the justices were relatively insistent about the public use requirement.[10] Beginning in the New Deal period, however, the Court initiated a policy giving greater deference to legislative authority by equating "public purpose" with "public use." In ***Berman v. Parker*** (1954) the Court upheld a federal urban renewal project in Washington, D.C., in which private property was seized, improved, and then transferred to another private party. The program's objective was to ameliorate conditions in a particularly blighted section of the city. Even though private property was taken and ultimately given to another private party, the Court accepted the conclusion of Congress that the program's urban renewal objectives constituted a public purpose, thereby satisfying the requirements of the takings clause.

The Court's deference to the legislature on public use questions was extended to the state level in ***Hawaii Housing Authority v. Midkiff*** (1984). Attacked here was Hawaii's plan to redistribute land, using the power of eminent domain to force large landowners to sell their properties to the people who leased them. The transfer of land was clearly from one private owner to another.

---

[9]See also *Stop the Beach Renourishment, Inc. v. Florida Department of Environmental Protection* (2010).

[10]See Schultz, *Property, Power, and American Democracy.*

The land distribution program was the state legislature's response to social and economic problems that had their origins in Hawaii's unusual past.

The Hawaiian Islands were settled by Polynesians who developed an economic system based on principles of feudalism. Ownership and control of the land rested with the islands' high chief, who distributed parcels to various lower-ranking chiefs. At the end of the chain were tenant farmers and their families, who lived on the land and worked it. Private ownership of real property was not permitted. Ultimate ownership of all lands rested with the royal family.

The monarchy was overthrown in 1893, and, after a brief period as a republic, the islands were annexed by the United States in 1898. When Hawaii became the fiftieth state in 1959, the land still remained in the hands of a few. In the mid-1960s the state and federal governments owned 49 percent of the land in the Hawaiian Islands, and just seventy-two private landowners held another 47 percent. On Oahu, the most commercially developed island, twenty-two landowners controlled more than 72 percent of the private real estate. The Hawaiian legislature determined that this concentration of landownership was detrimental to the state's economy and general welfare.

To encourage development, the legislature first decided to compel landowners to sell large portions of their holdings to those individuals who leased the land from them. The landowners opposed this plan because it would result in their having to pay exceedingly high capital gains taxes. The legislature revised its plans and passed the Land Reform Act of 1967. This legislation allowed the state to condemn tracts of residential real estate. The Hawaii Housing Authority (HHA) would then seize the condemned property, compensate the landowners for their loss, and sell the parcels to the private individuals who had been leasing the land. Compensation for land seized by the government enjoyed a more favorable tax status than did profits from outright sales, making the legislation more acceptable to the landowners.

Frank Midkiff and others owned a large tract of land that was condemned under the land reform program, but Midkiff and the HHA could not agree on a fair price. He and his co-owners filed suit in federal district court to have the Land Reform Act declared unconstitutional as a violation of the takings clause. Their primary argument was that taking land from one private owner to transfer to another private owner did not meet the Constitution's requirement that takings be for a public purpose.

A unanimous Supreme Court upheld the Hawaii program. Using much of the same logic as it did in

Berman, the Court concluded that the land reform plan served a public purpose. The crucial issue was not the transfer of property from one private party to another; rather, it was whether the program was rationally related to a public purpose. The justices conceded that the legislature was in the best position to determine public use and that the Court would normally defer to the legislature's judgment on that question. If Hawaii concluded that would-be buyers were unable to acquire land at fair market value, it was entitled to take legislative action to ameliorate the problem.

Decisions such as *Berman* and *Midkiff* represented significant changes in the way the Court dealt with takings clause appeals. No longer did the justices strictly examine the nature of the public purpose of the taking. Instead, the Court gave wide latitude to legislatures to determine what constitutes public use. To this extent, private property rights became political as well as legal questions, increasing the power of the legislature at the expense of traditional property considerations. These decisions also reduced the extent to which "public use" objections could be employed to thwart the legislative redistribution of wealth and property for the public good.[11]

The Court's announced policy of deferring to the elected branches on the question of public use encouraged governments to expand their exercise of eminent domain, especially at the local level. Cities and towns faced with declining economies and dwindling tax revenues saw economic redevelopment as a means of expanding job opportunities, revitalizing local business activity, and increasing tax revenues. Many attempted to lure new businesses, create industrial parks, and develop areas that combined commercial and residential facilities. Often these policies required local governments to acquire significant tracts of land, either by purchasing the necessary property or by seizing it under eminent domain if owners refused to sell.

Although a city instituting such policies saw its actions as benefiting the entire community, the targeted owners who did not want to give up their property did not see it that way. They argued that the city was using the power of eminent domain in an unconstitutional fashion. Their homes and land were being taken not because their property was blighted or being misused, but because the city ultimately wanted to turn the seized parcels over to private businesses that were willing to build new stores, hotels, factories, or higher-priced

residences. Advocates of private property rights believed that such development policies violated the Fifth Amendment because no true public purpose was advanced. In their view, these policies amounted to nothing more than local officials taking private property from individual owners and selling it to corporate business interests to raise city tax revenues. A major confrontation between municipalities and private property owners was inevitable. The Supreme Court tackled the issue in the case of *Kelo v. City of New London* (2005), a decision that resulted in widespread controversy.

Kelo v. City of New London

545 U.S. 469 (2005)
http://caselaw.findlaw.com/us-supreme-court/545/469.html
Oral arguments available at https://www.oyez.org/
    cases/2004/04-108
Vote: 5 (Breyer, Ginsburg, Kennedy, Souter, Stevens)
    4 (O'Connor, Rehnquist, Scalia, Thomas)

OPINION OF THE COURT: *Stevens*

CONCURRING OPINION: *Kennedy*

DISSENTING OPINIONS: *O'Connor, Thomas*

Situated on the Long Island Sound, the city of New London, Connecticut, was once a bustling seaport. From the colonial era until after the Civil War, it was central to the whaling industry. It then transformed into a successful manufacturing center. By the end of the twentieth century, however, the city had suffered decades of significant economic decline. In 1998 the city's unemployment rate was double that of the state as a whole, and the population had declined to 24,000, the same number of residents as in 1920. In response, state and local officials created the New London Development Corporation (NLDC) to devise strategies for economic advancement. Efforts to revitalize the city resulted in a tentative commitment by the Pfizer drug company to build a $300 million research facility in the city's Fort Trumbull area. Officials believed that this new development would not only bring jobs and tax revenues to the city but also encourage other economic revitalization efforts.

The NLDC developed a master plan for the area surrounding the proposed Pfizer operation. This plan, which the city adopted in 2000, called for a hotel, conference center, museum, restaurants, shops, office space, marina, river walk, and new residential housing. To begin the development, the city had to acquire approximately 115 privately owned parcels of land. The city successfully negotiated the purchase of most of this land, but some landowners refused to sell. The city responded by condemning their properties through the use of eminent domain.

---

[11]Ibid., 73–74.

Nine landowners who were unwilling to sell their homes filed suit, claiming the city's actions violated the Fifth Amendment's takings clause. Among them were Susette Kelo, who had owned her water-view house since 1997 and had spent considerable time and money renovating it, and Wilhelmina Dery, who had lived in her Fort Trumbull home since her birth in 1918. The properties involved were not blighted or in poor condition; the city condemned them only because they stood in the path of the redevelopment plan. The petitioners claimed that the plan failed to meet the Fifth Amendment's public use requirement. After the Connecticut Supreme Court ruled in favor of the city, Kelo and her fellow petitioners requested review by the U.S. Supreme Court.

JUSTICE STEVENS DELIVERED THE OPINION OF THE COURT.

Two polar propositions are perfectly clear. On the one hand, it has long been accepted that the sovereign may not take the property of A for the sole purpose of transferring it to another private party B, even though A is paid just compensation. On the other hand, it is equally clear that a State may transfer property from one private party to another if future "use by the public" is the purpose of the taking; the condemnation of land for a railroad with common-carrier duties is a familiar example. Neither of these propositions, however, determines the disposition of this case.

As for the first proposition, the City would no doubt be forbidden from taking petitioners' land for the purpose of conferring a private benefit on a particular private party. . . . Nor would the City be allowed to take property under the mere pretext of a public purpose, when its actual purpose was to bestow a private benefit. The takings before us, however, would be executed pursuant to a "carefully considered" development plan. The trial judge and all the members of the Supreme Court of Connecticut agreed that there was no evidence of an illegitimate purpose in this case. Therefore, as was true of the statute challenged in [*Hawaii Housing Authority v.*] *Midkiff,* the City's development plan was not adopted "to benefit a particular class of identifiable individuals."

On the other hand, this is not a case in which the City is planning to open the condemned land—at least not in its entirety—to use by the general public. Nor will the private lessees of the land in any sense be required to operate like common carriers, making their services available to all comers. But although such a projected use would be sufficient to satisfy the public use requirement, this "Court long ago rejected any literal requirement that condemned property be put into use for the general public." [*Midkiff.*] Indeed, while many state courts in the mid-19th century endorsed "use by the public" as the proper definition of public use, that narrow view steadily eroded over time. Not only was the "use by the public" test difficult to administer (*e.g.,* what proportion of the public need have

access to the property? at what price?), but it proved to be impractical given the diverse and always evolving needs of society. . . .

The disposition of this case therefore turns on the question whether the City's development plan serves a "public purpose." Without exception, our cases have defined that concept broadly, reflecting our longstanding policy of deference to legislative judgments in this field.

In *Berman v. Parker* (1954), this Court upheld a redevelopment plan targeting a blighted area of Washington, D.C., in which most of the housing for the area's 5,000 inhabitants was beyond repair. Under the plan, the area would be condemned and part of it utilized for the construction of streets, schools, and other public facilities. The remainder of the land would be leased or sold to private parties for the purpose of redevelopment, including the construction of low-cost housing. . . .

In *Hawaii Housing Authority v. Midkiff* (1984), the Court considered a Hawaii statute whereby fee title was taken from lessors and transferred to lessees (for just compensation) in order to reduce the concentration of land ownership. We unanimously upheld the statute and rejected the Ninth Circuit's view that it was "a naked attempt on the part of the state of Hawaii to take the property of A and transfer it to B solely for B's private use and benefit." Reaffirming *Berman*'s deferential approach to legislative judgments in this field, we concluded that the State's purpose of eliminating the "social and economic evils of a land oligopoly" qualified as a valid public use. Our opinion also rejected the contention that the mere fact that the State immediately transferred the properties to private individuals upon condemnation somehow diminished the public character of the taking. "[I]t is only the taking's purpose, and not its mechanics," we explained, that matters in determining public use. . . .

. . . For more than a century, our public use jurisprudence has wisely eschewed rigid formulas and intrusive scrutiny in favor of affording legislatures broad latitude in determining what public needs justify the use of the takings power.

Those who govern the City were not confronted with the need to remove blight in the Fort Trumbull area, but their determination that the area was sufficiently distressed to justify a program of economic rejuvenation is entitled to our deference. The City has carefully formulated an economic development plan that it believes will provide appreciable benefits to the community, including—but by no means limited to—new jobs and increased tax revenue. As with other exercises in urban planning and development, the City is endeavoring to coordinate a variety of commercial, residential, and recreational uses of land, with the hope that they will form a whole greater than the sum of its parts. To effectuate this plan, the City has invoked a state statute that specifically authorizes the use of eminent domain to promote economic development. Given the comprehensive character of the plan, the thorough deliberation that preceded its adoption, and the limited scope of our review, it is appropriate for us, as it was in *Berman,* to resolve the challenges of the individual owners, not on a

The home of Susette Kelo is shown here in February 2005, just four months before the Supreme Court ruled that the city of New London could seize it as part of an economic revitalization program.

piecemeal basis, but rather in light of the entire plan. Because that plan unquestionably serves a public purpose, the takings challenged here satisfy the public use requirement of the Fifth Amendment.

To avoid this result, petitioners urge us to adopt a new bright-line rule that economic development does not qualify as a public use. Putting aside the unpersuasive suggestion that the City's plan will provide only purely economic benefits, neither precedent nor logic supports petitioners' proposal. Promoting economic development is a traditional and long accepted function of government. There is, moreover, no principled way of distinguishing economic development from the other public purposes that we have recognized. . . . Clearly, there is no basis for exempting economic development from our traditionally broad understanding of public purpose.

Petitioners contend that using eminent domain for economic development impermissibly blurs the boundary between public and private takings. Again, our cases foreclose this objection. Quite simply, the government's pursuit of a public purpose will often benefit individual private parties. . . . "We cannot say that public ownership is the sole method of promoting the public purposes of community redevelopment projects." [*Berman*]

It is further argued that without a bright-line rule nothing would stop a city from transferring citizen A's property to citizen B for the sole reason that citizen B will put the property to a more productive use and thus pay more taxes. Such a one-to-one transfer of property, executed outside the confines of an integrated development plan, is not presented in this case. While such an unusual exercise of government power would certainly raise a suspicion that a private purpose was afoot, the hypothetical cases posited by petitioners can be confronted if and when they arise. They do not warrant the crafting of an artificial restriction on the concept of public use. . . .

Just as we decline to second-guess the City's considered judgments about the efficacy of its development plan, we also decline to second-guess the City's determinations as to what lands it needs to acquire in order to effectuate the project. "It is not for the courts to oversee the choice of the boundary line nor to sit in review on the size of a particular project area. Once the question of the public purpose has been decided, the amount and character of land to be taken for the project and the need for a particular tract to complete the integrated plan rests in the discretion of the legislative branch." [*Berman*]

The construction of the $300 million Pfizer Global Research and Development headquarters was the centerpiece of New London's revitalization program that culminated in the Supreme Court's takings clause ruling in *Kelo v. City of New London* (2005).

In affirming the City's authority to take petitioners' properties, we do not minimize the hardship that condemnations may entail, notwithstanding the payment of just compensation. We emphasize that nothing in our opinion precludes any State from placing further restrictions on its exercise of the takings power. Indeed, many States already impose "public use" requirements that are stricter than the federal baseline. Some of these requirements have been established as a matter of state constitutional law, while others are expressed in state eminent domain statutes that carefully limit the grounds upon which takings may be exercised. As the submissions of the parties and their *amici* make clear, the necessity and wisdom of using eminent domain to promote economic development are certainly matters of legitimate public debate. This Court's authority, however, extends only to determining whether the City's proposed condemnations are for a "public use" within the meaning of the Fifth Amendment to the Federal Constitution. Because over a century of our case law interpreting that provision dictates an affirmative answer to that question, we may not grant petitioners the relief that they seek.

The judgment of the Supreme Court of Connecticut is affirmed.

It is so ordered.

JUSTICE KENNEDY, CONCURRING.

I join the opinion for the Court and add these further observations.

This Court has declared that a taking should be upheld as consistent with the Public Use Clause as long as it is "rationally related to a conceivable public purpose." *Hawaii Housing Authority v. Midkiff* (1984); see also *Berman v. Parker* (1954). This deferential standard of review echoes the rational-basis test used to review economic regulation under the Due Process and Equal Protection Clauses. The determination that a rational-basis standard of review is appropriate does not, however, alter the fact that transfers intended to confer benefits on particular, favored private entities, and with only incidental or pretextual public benefits, are forbidden by the Public Use Clause.

A court applying rational-basis review under the Public Use Clause should strike down a taking that, by a clear showing, is intended to favor a particular private party, with only incidental or pretextual public benefits. . . .

This is not the occasion for conjecture as to what sort of cases might justify a more demanding standard, but it is appropriate to underscore aspects of the instant case that convince me no departure from *Berman* and *Midkiff* is appropriate here. This taking occurred in the context of a comprehensive development plan meant to address a serious city-wide depression, and the projected economic benefits of the project cannot be characterized as *de minimus.* The identity of most of the private beneficiaries were unknown at the time the city formulated its plans. The city complied with elaborate procedural requirements that facilitate review of the record and inquiry into the city's purposes. In sum, while there may be categories of cases in which the transfers are so suspicious, or the procedures employed so prone to abuse, or the purported benefits are so trivial or implausible, that courts should presume an impermissible private purpose, no such circumstances are present in this case.

JUSTICE O'CONNOR, WITH WHOM THE CHIEF JUSTICE, JUSTICE SCALIA, AND JUSTICE THOMAS JOIN, DISSENTING.

Over two centuries ago, just after the Bill of Rights was ratified, Justice Chase wrote:

> "An act of the Legislature (for I cannot call it a law) contrary to the great first principles of the social compact, cannot be considered a rightful exercise of legislative authority. . . . A few instances will suffice to explain what I mean. . . . [A] law that takes property from A. and gives it to B: It is against all reason and justice, for a people to entrust a Legislature with such powers; and, therefore, it cannot be presumed that they have done it." *Calder v. Bull* (1798).

Today the Court abandons this long-held, basic limitation on government power. Under the banner of economic development, all private property is now vulnerable to being taken and trans-ferred to another private owner, so long as it might be upgraded— *i.e.,* given to an owner who will use it in a way that the legislature deems more beneficial to the public—in the process. To reason, as the Court does, that the incidental public benefits resulting from the subsequent ordinary use of private property render economic development takings "for public use" is to wash out any distinction between private and public use of property—and thereby effec-tively to delete the words "for public use" from the Takings Clause of the Fifth Amendment. Accordingly I respectfully dissent. . . .

This case returns us for the first time in over 20 years to the hard question of when a purportedly "public purpose" taking meets the public use requirement. It presents an issue of first impression: Are economic development takings constitutional? I would hold that they are not. We are guided by two precedents about the taking of real property by eminent domain. In *Berman,* we upheld takings within a blighted neighborhood of Washington, D.C. The neighborhood had so deteriorated that, for example, 64.3%

of its dwellings were beyond repair. It had become burdened with "overcrowding of dwellings," "lack of adequate streets and alleys," and "lack of light and air." Congress had determined that the neighborhood had become "injurious to the public health, safety, morals, and welfare" and that it was necessary to "eliminat[e] all such injurious conditions by employing all means necessary and appropriate for the purpose," including eminent domain. Mr. Berman's department store was not itself blighted. Having approved of Congress' decision to eliminate the harm to the public emanating from the blighted neighborhood, however, we did not second-guess its decision to treat the neighborhood as a whole rather than lot-by-lot.

In *Midkiff,* we upheld a land condemnation scheme in Hawaii whereby title in real property was taken from lessors and transferred to lessees. At that time, the State and Federal Governments owned nearly 49% of the State's land, and another 47% was in the hands of only 72 private landowners. Concentration of land ownership was so dramatic that on the State's most urbanized island, Oahu, 22 landowners owned 72.5% of the fee simple titles. The Hawaii Legislature had concluded that the oligopoly in land ownership was "skewing the State's residential fee simple market, inflating land prices, and injuring the public tranquility and welfare," and therefore enacted a condemnation scheme for redistributing title. . . .

The Court's holdings in *Berman* and *Midkiff* were true to the principle underlying the Public Use Clause. In both those cases, the extraordinary, precondemnation use of the targeted property inflicted affirmative harm on society—in *Berman* through blight resulting from extreme poverty and in *Midkiff* through oligopoly resulting from extreme wealth. And in both cases, the relevant legislative body had found that eliminating the existing property use was necessary to remedy the harm. Thus a public purpose was realized when the harmful use was eliminated. Because each taking directly achieved a public benefit, it did not matter that the property was turned over to private use. Here, in contrast, New London does not claim that Susette Kelo's and Wilhelmina Dery's well-maintained homes are the source of any social harm. Indeed, it could not so claim without adopting the absurd argument that any single-family home that might be razed to make way for an apartment building, or any church that might be replaced with a retail store, or any small business that might be more lucrative if it were instead part of a national franchise, is inherently harmful to society and thus within the government's power to condemn.

In moving away from our decisions sanctioning the condemnation of harmful property use, the Court today significantly expands the meaning of public use. It holds that the sovereign may take private property currently put to ordinary private use, and give it over for new, ordinary private use, so long as the new use is predicted to generate some secondary benefit for the public—such as increased tax revenue, more jobs, maybe even aesthetic pleasure. But nearly any lawful use of real private property can be said to generate some incidental benefit to the public. Thus, if predicted (or even guaranteed) positive side-effects are enough to render transfer from one private party to another constitutional, then the words "for public use" do not realistically exclude any takings, and thus do not exert any constraint on the eminent domain power. . . .

Finally, . . . the Court suggests that property owners should turn to the States, who may or may not choose to impose appropriate limits on economic development takings. This is an abdication of our responsibility. States play many important functions in our system of dual sovereignty, but compensating for our refusal to enforce properly the Federal Constitution (and a provision meant to curtail state action, no less) is not among them. . . .

Any property may now be taken for the benefit of another private party, but the fallout from this decision will not be random. The beneficiaries are likely to be those citizens with disproportionate influence and power in the political process, including large corporations and development firms. As for the victims, the government now has license to transfer property from those with fewer resources to those with more. The Founders cannot have intended this perverse result.

JUSTICE THOMAS, DISSENTING.

Today's decision is simply the latest in a string of our cases construing the Public Use Clause to be a virtual nullity, without the slightest nod to its original meaning. In my view, the Public Use Clause, originally understood, is a meaningful limit on the government's eminent domain power. . . .

. . . I would revisit our Public Use Clause cases and consider returning to the original meaning of the Public Use Clause: that the government may take property only if it actually uses or gives the public a legal right to use the property.

The consequences of today's decision are not difficult to predict, and promise to be harmful. So-called "urban renewal" programs provide some compensation for the properties they take, but no compensation is possible for the subjective value of these lands to the individuals displaced and the indignity inflicted by uprooting them from their homes. Allowing the government to take property solely for public purposes is bad enough, but extending the concept of public purpose to encompass any economically beneficial goal guarantees that these losses will fall disproportionately on poor communities. Those communities are not only systematically less likely to put their lands to the highest and best social use, but are also the least politically powerful. If ever there were justification for intrusive judicial review of constitutional provisions that protect "discrete and insular minorities," *United States v. Carolene Products Co.* (1938), surely that principle would apply with great force to the powerless groups and individuals the Public Use Clause protects. The deferential standard this Court has adopted for the Public Use Clause is therefore deeply perverse. It encourages "those citizens

with disproportionate influence and power in the political process, including large corporations and development firms" to victimize the weak. (O'Connor, J., dissenting). . . .

The Court relies almost exclusively on this Court's prior cases to derive today's far-reaching, and dangerous, result. But the principles this Court should employ to dispose of this case are found in the Public Use Clause itself. . . . When faced with a clash of constitutional principle and a line of unreasoned cases wholly divorced from the text, history, and structure of our founding document, we should not hesitate to resolve the tension in favor of the Constitution's original meaning. For the reasons I have given, and for the reasons given in Justice O'Connor's dissent, the conflict of principle raised by this boundless use of the eminent domain power should be resolved in petitioners' favor. I would reverse the judgment of the Connecticut Supreme Court.

In its takings clause decisions the Court has consistently favored neither private property interests nor the government's power of eminent domain. With respect to defining a "taking," the justices have tended to favor property owners by expanding the range of government actions that come under the authority of the Fifth Amendment. The Court has, however, given broad latitude to the government to define what constitutes a "public use."

WHAT IS JUST COMPENSATION?

Just as the Supreme Court has had to confront the meaning of a "taking" and a "public use," so, too, has it been drawn into questions over what compensation is required by the takings clause. Governments and the individuals whose property they seize may have very different perspectives about fair compensation. Suppose a local government intends to take a private home in order to acquire the land on which to construct a public library building. By objective indicators, a modest house might be worth relatively little in the local housing market, but if it is an ancestral home in which several generations of the same family have lived, a strong sentimental attachment might incline the owners to value the property at a substantially higher price. Is it fair for local officials to pay the owners a price well below what they might otherwise demand? One might want to give some weight to the owners' expectations. At the same time, suppose the owners expect a price so high that the local government cannot afford to pay compensation? The property owners can, in effect, negate the government's power of

BOX 11-2

Aftermath . . . *Kelo v. City of New London*

The *Kelo* decision touched off a storm of protest by private property rights advocates, and public opinion ran decidedly against the decision. Taking the Court's admonishment that nothing in the decision prohibits the states from imposing their own limits, forty-four state legislatures reacted to the public opposition to *Kelo* by placing new restrictions on the power of eminent domain. Supporters of eminent domain, including the National League of Cities, countered by persuading legislators in several states to modify many of the more extreme anti-*Kelo* proposals.

Two months after the *Kelo* decision, its author, Justice John Paul Stevens, acknowledged that the ruling was "unwise" and that he would have opposed it had he been a legislator and not a federal judge bound by precedent.

Some protests were directed at the justices themselves. In Weare, New Hampshire, private property activists secured sufficient petition signatures to place a proposal on the ballot to have the town seize the two-hundred-year-old farmhouse home of Justice David Souter, who voted with the majority in *Kelo*. Under the proposal the property would be turned over to private investors who would build an inn to be named the "Lost Liberty Hotel," featuring the "Just Desserts" cafe. One of the proposal's supporters said, "It would be more like a bed and breakfast. . . . There would be nine suites, with a black robe in each of the closets." In March 2006 the Weare voters rejected the proposal 1,167–493, endorsing instead a resolution asking the state legislature to forbid the use of eminent domain approved in the *Kelo* decision.

In a related but also unsuccessful effort, members of the state Libertarian Party urged the city of Plainfield, New Hampshire, to seize a 167-acre vacation retreat owned by Justice Stephen Breyer. In its place they planned to create a "Constitution Park," including monuments to the U.S. and New Hampshire Constitutions.

In a reversal of sorts, the city of Hercules, California, in 2006 used *Kelo* in an attempt to stop development. Wal-Mart Stores, Inc., had purchased a 17-acre parcel near the town's waterfront for $15 million, intending to construct a 140,000-square-foot store on the property. The city council opposed the development and voted to seize the land to "ward off urban blight." Wal-Mart vowed to take legal action against this use of eminent domain. In 2009, however, the dispute ended when the city purchased the property from Wal-Mart for $13.5 million.

New London used its victory in *Kelo* to continue its program of redeveloping the Fort Trumbull neighborhood. Pfizer built a $300 million research complex that served as the centerpiece for the project. The condemned houses were torn down, but the city's dream that they would be replaced by new commercial, entertainment, lodging, and residential facilities did not materialize. In 2009, to the city's great disappointment, Pfizer announced that it would abandon the New London facility and move its projects and most of its 1,400 jobs to another Pfizer operation in nearby Groton, Connecticut. The New London research facility had been in operation only eight years.

As for Susette Kelo, the New London nurse continued the fight to save her home from government seizure. She was aided by the Institute for Justice, a Washington, D.C., organization committed to property rights and other libertarian causes. In the end Kelo was forced to leave her home, and she moved across the river to Groton. Her little pink house, however, avoided the city's wrecking ball. It was disassembled and moved to another location in New London, where it was rebuilt. With the support of private property advocates, it was named the Kelo House and a monument was placed outside the home to commemorate the legal battle against New London's use of eminent domain.

Kelo continues to oppose what she considers to be abuses of the power of eminent domain. "Do I feel like I won? No, I didn't win. But other people did win. They got their properties back. People tell me all the time about towns that have passed a law limiting eminent domain," she explains. "People have to be continually made aware of how wrong it was. It's still wrong today."

Sources: Associated Press, March 14, 2006; *Contra Costa Times,* April 16, 2009; *Financial Times,* January 26, 2006; *Los Angeles Times,* May 25, 2006; *Money,* September 2006, August 2012; *New York Times,* February 21, 2006, March 14, 2006, November 12, 2009; *Norwich Bulletin,* November 9, 2009; *San Francisco Chronicle,* May 25, 2006, May 30, 2006; *The Day,* November 11, 2009; *Valley News,* July 28, 2005.

eminent domain simply by claiming that the only just price is a price the city is unable to meet.

The Court's resolution to this kind of quandary has been to recognize the difference between the market value of a property and the personal value to its owners. The former can usually be calculated by various measures—property tax assessments by local governments, the recent sales prices of comparable homes—whereas the latter is highly particularistic. Justice Frankfurter explained this distinction in *Kimball Laundry Co. v. U.S.* (1949): "The value of property springs from subjective needs and attitudes; its value to the owner may therefore differ widely from its value to the taker. Most things, however, have a general demand which gives them a value transferable from one owner to another." Normally, the market value is the gauge for just compensation, that is, "what a willing buyer would pay in cash to a willing seller."

Even that standard can be a thorny issue, however. In *U.S. v. Miller* (1943), the federal government acquired a strip of land for a water reclamation project in California. After the government committed to the project, the land increased in value, and the property owners believed that the increase should have been reflected in their compensation. The justices disagreed, ruling that "compensation means the full and perfect equivalent in money of the property taken. The owner is to be put in as good position [financially] as he would have occupied if his property had not been taken." That meant that the owners were entitled only to what they had lost—the market value of the property at the time it was taken. A similar complication arose when the federal government requisitioned a tug boat to help supply oil for combat vessels during World War II. Because the government was acquiring private boats to aid in the war effort, their values necessarily increased, and the tug owner argued that his compensation should include that enhanced value. In *U.S. v. Cors* (1949), the justices held that the government was not required to pay increased compensation when it was the taking itself that magnified the tug's value. Stated differently, the government was only required to pay the fair market value for the tug, not the value created by the government's taking.

One of the interesting questions relating to just compensation concerns whether it should reflect only the market value of the property taken or also include the costs of acquiring a new comparable property. The state might be willing to pay for the value of a seized property—a home, a factory, an office building—but what if the cost of replacing that property turns out to be substantially more? Is it fair to ask property owners to

bear the financial burden of restoring themselves to their "pre-taking" condition?

United States v. 564.54 Acres of Land

441 U.S. 506 (1979)
https://caselaw.findlaw.com/us-supreme-court/441/506.html
Oral arguments available at https://www.oyez.org/
cases/1978/78-488
Vote: 8 (Blackmun, Brennan, Burger, Marshall, Rehnquist, Stevens, Stewart, White)
0

OPINION OF THE COURT: *Marshall*

CONCURRING OPINION: *White*

The Southeastern Pennsylvania Synod of the Lutheran Church in America owned three nonprofit summer camps on the Delaware River in Monroe County, Pennsylvania. The camps were nondenominational and offered children opportunities to engage in sports, nature activities, and arts and crafts. As a part of its development of a national recreation area, the federal government exercised its power of eminent domain and acquired these three camps. The government judged these properties to have a market value of $485,400, but the church claimed that it was entitled to substantially more, $5.8 million. The church reasoned that, since there were no comparable camping facilities available for purchase, it would have to construct entirely new facilities. When the original camps were built, a good many federal and state regulations regarding construction had not yet been established, and the church had been permitted to operate its facilities without being forced to conform to the more recent rules. Any new construction, however, would have to be undertaken in compliance with those rules and therefore would be considerably more expensive.

A federal trial court concluded that the church was not entitled to the compensation required to construct new facilities. But the appeals court ruled that, if it could be demonstrated that the camps provided an important benefit to the community that could not be served if the church were unable to purchase comparable facilities at the market price paid for its old camps, then the cost of constructing new camps could be a part of the church's compensation. It ordered a new trial, but the United States sought review from the Supreme Court.

JUSTICE MARSHALL DELIVERED THE OPINION OF THE COURT.

In giving content to the just compensation requirement of the Fifth Amendment, this Court has sought to put the owner of condemned property "in as good a position pecuniarily as if his property had not been taken." *Olson v. United States* (1934). However, this principle . . . has not been given its full and literal force. Because of serious practical difficulties in assessing the worth an individual places on particular property at a given time, we have recognized the need for a relatively objective working rule. The Court therefore has employed the concept of fair market value to determine the condemnee's loss. Under this standard, the owner is entitled to receive "what a willing buyer would pay in cash to a willing seller" at the time of the taking. *United States v. Miller* (1943).

. . . [T]he concept of fair market value has been chosen to strike a fair "balance between the public's need and the claimant's loss" upon condemnation of property for a public purpose. *United States v. Toronto, Hamilton & Buffalo Nav. Co.* (1949).

But . . . this Court has refused to designate market value as the sole measure of just compensation. For there are situations where this standard is inappropriate. As we held in *United States v. Commodities Trading Corp.* (1950):

"When market value has been too difficult to find, or when its application would result in manifest injustice to owner or public, courts have fashioned and applied other standards. . . . Whatever the circumstances under which such constitutional questions arise, the dominant consideration always remains the same: What compensation is 'just' both to an owner whose property is taken and to the public that must pay the bill?" . . . .

The instances in which market value is too difficult to ascertain generally involve property of a type so infrequently traded that we cannot predict whether the prices previously paid, assuming there have been prior sales, would be repeated in a sale of the condemned property. This might be the case, for example, with respect to public facilities such as roads or sewers. But respondent's property does not fall in this category. There was a market for camps, albeit not an extremely active one. The Government's expert witness presented evidence concerning recent sales of comparable facilities in the vicinity, and estimated that respondent's camps could have been sold within six months to a year after they were offered for sale. Indeed, respondent's own expert testified that he had prepared an appraisal of the camps' fair market value as of the date of the taking. . . . Thus, it seems clear that respondent's property had a readily discernible market value. . . .

Emphasizing that the primary value of the condemned property lies in the use to which it is put, respondent argues that compensating only for market value would be unjust in the present context. Because new facilities would bear financial burdens imposed by regulations to which the existing camps were not subject, an award of market value would preclude continuation of respondent's use. Respondent therefore concludes that such a recovery would be insufficient. . . .

However, it is not at all unusual that property uniquely adapted to the owner's use has a market value on condemnation which falls far short of enabling the owner to preserve that use. Such a situation may often arise, for example, where a family home has been built to the owner's tastes, but is old and deteriorated, or where property, like respondent's camps, is exempt from regulations applicable to new facilities. . . .

. . . . That respondent is a nonprofit organization may provide some basis for distinguishing it from business enterprises, since the uses to which commercial property is put can often be valued in terms of the [profits] produced. But there is no reason to treat respondent differently from the many private homeowners and other noncommercial property owners who neither derive earnings from their property nor hold it for investment purposes. Unless the Just Compensation Clause mandates a Government subsidy for nonprofit organizations, a proposition we find patently implausible, respondent's nonprofit status does not require us to reject application of the fair-market-value standard.

Nor is it relevant in this case whether respondent's camps were reasonably necessary to the public welfare. In condemnations of property owned by public entities, lower courts have applied the reasonable-necessity standard to determine if the entity has an obligation to continue providing the facilities taken. . . . If the condemnee has such a duty to replace the property, these courts have reasoned that only an award of the costs of developing requisite substitute facilities will compensate for the loss.

Whatever the merits of this reasoning with respect to public entities, it does not advance analysis here. For respondent is under no legal or factual obligation to replace the camps, regardless of their social worth. As a private entity, respondent is free to allocate its resources to serve its own institutional objectives, which may or may not correspond with community needs. Awarding replacement cost on the theory that respondent would continue to operate the camps for a public purpose would thus provide a windfall if substitute facilities were never acquired, or if acquired, were later sold or converted to another use.

Finally, that the camps may have benefited the community does not warrant compensating respondent differently from other private owners. The community benefit which the camps conferred might provide an indication of the public's loss upon condemnation of the property. But we cannot accept the Court of Appeals' conclusion that this loss is relevant to assessing the compensation due a private entity. . . . The guiding principle of just compensation . . . is that the owner of the condemned property "must be made whole but is not entitled to more." *Olson v. United States* (1934). . . . [M]any condemnees use their property in a manner that confers a benefit on the community, and there is no sound basis for considering this factor only in condemnations of property owned by nonprofit organizations. And to make the measure of compensation depend on a jury's subjective estimation of whether a particular use "benefits" the community would conflict with this Court's efforts to develop relatively objective valuation standards.

In sum, we find no circumstances here that require suspension of the normal rules for determining just compensation. Respondent, like other private owners, is not entitled to recover for nontransferable values arising from its unique need for the property. . . . Allowing respondent the fair market value of its property is thus consistent with the "basic equitable principles of fairness," *United States v. Fuller* (1973), underlying the Just Compensation Clause.

JUSTICE WHITE, CONCURRING.

The Court rejects the claim that the measure of compensation in this case is the cost of substitute facilities rather than the fair market value of the taken property, here camps owned by a private, nonprofit corporation. I am in full agreement. The substitute-facilities doctrine is unrelated to fair market value and does not depend on whether fair market value is readily ascertainable; rather, it unabashedly demands additional compensation over and above market value in order to allow the replacement of the condemned facility. In those cases where it has been applied, primarily where public facilities have been condemned, the basic premise is that the condemnee is under some obligation to continue the functions performed on the taken property. But I do not understand how a duty to replace the condemned facility justifies paying more than market value. Obviously, replacing the old with a new facility will cost more than the value of the old, but the new facility itself will be more valuable and last longer. This is true with respect to condemnation of any facility, whether or not there is an obligation to reproduce it, and I had not understood the Just Compensation Clause to guarantee subsidies to either private or public projects. Similarly, if more demanding building codes or other regulations will enhance the cost of replacement, it is reasonable to assume that compliance itself will be of some benefit to the owner and hence need not be financed by the condemnor. . . .

I thus agree with the Court that the Just Compensation Clause does not require payment of the cost of a substitute facility where the condemnee is a private organization, even if it could be said that such an owner is in some sense obligated to replace the property or that the public has a stake in the continuance of the function that is being conducted on the taken property. I also have substantial doubt

that the Clause should be any differently construed and applied where public property is condemned, whether or not the function conducted on the property must be continued at another location. That issue, however, is not before the Court and is expressly put aside for another day.

Justice White's concurring opinion suggests that the cost of replacing a taken property is not required by the Fifth Amendment, even if the government takes publicly owned facilities that provide a crucial public service. That view proved to be prescient. Only five years later, the Court decided *United States v. 50 Acres of Land* (1984). In that case, the federal government acquired land that the city of Duncanville, Texas, was using as a sanitary landfill. Because of its responsibility for waste management, the city argued that its compensation should include the cost of developing another environmentally conscious landfill. The Court ruled unanimously, however, that the federal government was obliged to pay the city no more than it would for a taking of private property—fair market value. On the question of just compensation, then, the justices have had little difficulty adhering to a legal standard.

Defining a taking and a public use, however, has proven more problematic. The Court's decisions on these issues have revealed deep internal divisions between those justices who place primary value on the rights of individual property owners and those who accord greater values on the interest of the larger community. Decisions such as *Kelo* have turned a once-obscure constitutional provision into a subject of intense political controversy (*see Box 11-2*). Local governments have stepped up their use of the power of eminent domain as a method of spurring economic development and raising tax revenues. With each such action, groups dedicated to private property rights have become more organized and politically involved. This political conflict ensures that takings clause disputes will continue to find their way to the Supreme Court's docket for some time to come.

ANNOTATED READINGS

A number of works have examined the history and constitutional foundations of private property rights in America. These include Bruce Ackerman, *Economic Foundations of Property Law* (Boston: Little, Brown, 1975); Bruce Ackerman, *Private Property and the Constitution* (New Haven, CT: Yale University Press, 1977); David Dana and Thomas W. Merrill, *Property: Takings* (New York: Foundation Press, 2002); James W. Ely Jr., *The Guardian of Every Other Right: A Constitutional History of Property Rights* (New York: Oxford University Press, 1992); Nicholas

Mercuro, *Taking Property and Just Compensation* (Boston: Kluwer, 1992); Jennifer Nedelsky, *Private Property and the Limits of American Constitutionalism: The Madisonian Framework and Its Legacy* (Chicago: University of Chicago Press, 1990); Ellen Frankel Paul, *Liberty, Property, and the Foundations of the American Constitution* (Albany: State University of New York Press, 1988); David A. Schultz, *Property, Power, and American Democracy* (New Brunswick, NJ: Transaction, 1992).

Other works have specifically focused on the power of eminent domain and the government's use of that authority. Examples are Alan T. Ackerman, *Current Condemnation Law: Takings, Compensation, and Benefits* (Chicago: American Bar Association, 1994); Richard A. Epstein, *Takings: Private Property and the Power of Eminent Domain* (Cambridge, MA: Harvard University Press, 1985); Steven Greenhut, *Abuse of Power: How the Government Misuses Eminent Domain* (Santa Ana, CA: Seven Locks Press, 2004); Robin Paul Malloy, ed., *Private Property, Community Development, and Eminent Domain* (Burlington, VT: Ashgate, 2008); Ellen Frankel Paul, *Property Rights and Eminent Domain* (New Brunswick, NJ: Transaction, 1987); John Ryskamp, *The Eminent Domain Revolt* (New York: Algora, 2007); William B. Stoebuck, *Nontrespassory Takings in Eminent Domain* (Charlottesville, VA: Michie, 1977).

The growing concern over the use of regulation as a form of property taking is explored in the following works: Darren Botello-Samson, *Regulatory Takings and the Environment: The Impact of Property Rights Litigation* (El Paso, TX: LFB Scholarly Publishing, 2010); Dennis J. Coyle, *Property Rights and the Constitution: Shaping Society through Land Use Regulation* (Albany: State University of New York Press, 1993); Steven J. Eagle, *Regulatory Takings* (Newark, NJ: LexisNexis, 2005); William A. Fischel, *Regulatory Takings: Law, Economics, and Politics* (Cambridge, MA: Harvard University Press, 1995); Thomas J. Miceli and Kathleen Segerson, *Compensation for Regulatory Takings* (Greenwich, CT: JAI Press, 1996); Alfred M. Olivetti, *This Land Is Your Land, This Land Is My Land: The Property Rights Movement and Regulatory Takings* (New York: LFB Scholarly Publishing, 2003).

Works examining individual cases that have been significant in developing the Court's takings clause jurisprudence are also available. See, for example, Jeff Benedict, *Little Pink House: A True Story of Defiance and Courage* (New York: Grand Central Publishing, 2009); Guy F. Burnett, *The Safeguard of Liberty and Property: The Supreme Court, Kelo v. New London, and the Takings Clause* (Lanham, MD: Lexington Books, 2014); Gerald Korngold and Andrew P. Morriss, eds., *Property Stories* (New York: Thomson Reuters/Foundation Press, 2009); Cara T. Main, *Bulldozed: "Kelo," Eminent Domain, and the American Lust for Land* (New York: Encounter Books, 2007); Dwight H. Merriam and Mary Massaron Ross, eds., *Eminent Domain Use and Abuse: Kelo in Context* (Chicago: American Bar Association, 2006); Thomas E. Roberts, ed., *Taking Sides on Takings Issues: The Impact of Tahoe-Sierra* (Chicago: American Bar Association, 2003); David A. Schultz, *Evicted: Property Rights and Eminent Domain in America* (Westport, CT: Praeger, 2009);); and Ilya Somin, *The Grasping Hand: Kelo v. City of New London and the Limits of Eminent Domain* (Chicago: University of Chicago Press, 2015).

CIVIL LIBERTIES

istockphoto.com/DanBrandenburg

THE NEXT FIVE CHAPTERS explore the Supreme Court's interpretation of the guarantees contained in the First and Second Amendments and those that have been seen as relating to the right of privacy. These constitutional provisions allow Americans to live their lives as they please; to worship in whatever manner they wish; to hold and express political and social views of their own conviction; to place demands upon the government; to join with others; to print, post, and read whatever satisfies them; and to keep government out of those areas of human affairs that are considered private and personal. In contemporary society, however, few freedoms are absolute. To maintain order and promote equality, the government must regulate in ways that may restrict some of these liberties. The history of the Supreme Court is a chronicle of how it has played its role as an interpreter of these fundamental rights and as an umpire between the often contradictory values of freedom, equality, and order.

As a student approaching the subject of civil liberties, perhaps for the first time, you might be wondering why we devote so much space in chapter 12 (on religion) and chapters 13 (on speech) and 14 (on the press) to the following few phrases:

> Congress shall make no law respecting an establishment of religion, or prohibiting the free exercise thereof; or abridging the freedom of speech, or of the press; or the right of the people peaceably to assemble, and to petition the Government for a redress of grievances.

After all, the guarantees contained in the First Amendment seem specific enough. Or are they? Suppose we read about a religion that required its members to smoke opium before religious services, or about students who were so fed up with university policies they blocked vehicles from entering campus, or about a website that released classified documents containing the identities of agents in enemy countries. Taking the opening words of the First Amendment, "Congress shall make no law," to heart, we might conclude that the amendment's language—the guarantees of freedom of religion, speech,

and press—protects these activities from government regulation. Is that conclusion correct? Is society obliged to accept such forms of expression? What our examples and the subsequent cases illustrate is that tension sometimes exists between the words of the First Amendment and the real-world situations in which they must be applied. Although the language of the amendment may seem straightforward, it can be difficult to administer across a wide array of actual circumstances.

In contrast, the constitutional problems the Second Amendment presents center on what exactly the amendment covers. The amendment reads: "A well regulated Militia, being necessary to the security of a free State, the right of the people to keep and bear Arms, shall not be infringed." Some argue that this language creates only a narrow right—that of the states to maintain "a well regulated militia"; others suggest that it creates a broader right that enables citizens to "keep and bear" guns. In chapter 15 we sort through these competing approaches, as well as the Court's current thinking on the subject.

The Supreme Court's formulation and interpretation of a right to privacy, as we shall see in chapter 16, present even more difficulties, primarily because the Constitution contains no explicit mention of such a guarantee. Even though most justices agree that a right to privacy exists, they have disagreed over various questions, including from what provision of the Constitution the right arises and how far it extends.

It is the tension between what the Constitution says (or does not say) and the kinds of questions litigants ask the Court to address that explains why we devote so much space to civil liberties. Because the meaning of those rights is less than crystal clear, the institution charged with interpreting and applying them—the Supreme Court of the United States—has approached its task in a somewhat erratic way. Throughout the Court's history, different justices have brought different modes of interpretation to the guarantees of freedom of religion, expression, and the press, and to the right to privacy, which in turn have significantly affected the ways citizens enjoy those rights.

The Supreme Court has interpreted basic civil liberties either broadly or narrowly depending, in part, on the tenor of the times and the philosophies of the Court's sitting justices. Since the 1950s we have seen two distinct Court periods. From 1953 to 1969 Chief Justice Earl Warren led the Court. During this period, the strains of the Cold War and the cultural clashes of the Vietnam era brought many cases to the Court's doorstep, and civil liberties flourished as the Supreme Court expanded the rights of individuals to engage in political association and expression with limited government restrictions. Similarly, the Court created greater protections for the press to publish a wide variety of materials. And as new social cleavages developed, the justices moved to impose a stricter separation of church and state and created a right to privacy that was not explicitly written into the Constitution. In more than two-thirds of the civil liberties cases brought to the Warren Court, the justices ruled in favor of the individuals or groups claiming that the government had unconstitutionally limited their freedoms.

The Warren Court era was followed by a period of more conservative Courts, under the leadership of Warren Burger (1969–1986), William Rehnquist (1986–2004), and John G. Roberts (appointed in 2005). This Republican Court era came about in part because the nation as a whole began to adopt more conservative political positions. In addition, the public reacted negatively to many of the Warren Court's rulings. The protection of various forms of political expression, the expansion of rights to publish and distribute sexually oriented literature and films, and the elimination of prayer in the public schools were among the Court's actions that met with disapproval among large segments of the population. As we will see in subsequent sections of this book, similar reactions occurred with respect to Warren Court opinions in the areas of discrimination and the rights of the criminally accused.

As a consequence of the nation's turn to the right, four Republicans (Richard Nixon, Gerald Ford, Ronald Reagan, and George H. W. Bush) ascended to the presidency and between 1969 and 1993 appointed more politically conservative individuals to the Court. It was not until Bill Clinton's presidency (1993–2001) and his two appointments to the Court that this conservative trend was interrupted—but only temporarily. In 2005 and 2006 President George W. Bush made two conservative appointments: Chief Justice John G. Roberts and Associate Justice Samuel Alito.

Changing times and new justices brought about a Court less sympathetic to those claiming that the government had deprived them of rights guaranteed by the Constitution. Although they did not necessarily roll back the liberal doctrines of the Warren era, the Burger-Rehnquist-Roberts Courts certainly demonstrated a reluctance to expand civil liberties and a greater deference to the actions the government took. There were, however, some noteworthy exceptions. After all, it was the Burger Court that handed down the decision in *Roe v. Wade* (1973) that expanded women's reproductive rights, the Rehnquist Court that held that desecrating the American flag as a means of political protest is expression protected by the First Amendment, and the Roberts Court that maintained the principle that even offensive and unpopular speech is constitutionally protected.

Today the Court's membership is ideologically divided, reflecting divisions in the nation more generally. The conservative hold on the Court was weakened by President Barack Obama's two more liberal appointees, Sonia Sotomayor (2009) and Elena Kagan (2010). But President Donald Trump's elevation of Neil Gorsuch (2017) and Brett Kavanaugh (2018) reinforced the influence of the Court's more conservative wing.

Whatever the ideological disagreements among the justices may be, civil liberties issues still occupy a prominent position on the Supreme Court's docket. About 10 percent of the decisions the justices handed down in recent years have involved appeals based on the First Amendment or the right to privacy. This is a much higher percentage than was seen in the pre–Warren Court eras. Even more important is the impact of the Court's civil liberties rulings. Disputes involving government aid to religious institutions, prayer in schools, the rights of protesters, hate speech, censorship of the press, libel, obscenity, and reproductive rights fall into this category. The Court's responses to these issues determine the extent to which the government can constitutionally impose regulations that impinge on personal freedom.

Each decade brings to the Court new questions regarding these fundamental freedoms, as well as novel approaches to more traditional issues. In Part V, we examine major controversies that the justices have been asked to settle. In some areas they have been successful in developing coherent and settled doctrine, whereas in others they have returned repeatedly to the same conflicts between personal freedoms and government authority without reaching conclusions that stand the test of time. This is not surprising. As you read the coming chapters you will discover that these issues are not easy to resolve; they present perplexing conflicts among values that go to the very core of what it means to be an American citizen.

CHAPTER TWELVE

RELIGION
Exercise and Establishment

"ON MY ARRIVAL in the United States," wrote Alexis de Tocqueville in the 1830s,

> the religious aspect of the country was the first thing that struck my attention; and the longer I stayed there, the more I perceived the great political consequences resulting from this new state of things. In France I had almost always seen the spirit of religion and the spirit of freedom marching in opposite directions. But in America I found they were intimately united and that they reigned in common over the same country.[1]

What Tocqueville observed almost two centuries ago remains true today: religion plays an important role in the lives of most Americans. In fact, nearly 80 percent of the population expresses a religious affiliation.[2]

Americans have always been concerned about the relationship between government and religion. The first settlers came to the New World to escape religious persecution in Europe and to worship freely in a new land. As the colonies developed during the seventeenth century, however, they, too, became intolerant toward "minority" religions: many passed anti-Catholic laws or imposed ecclesiastical views on their citizens. Prior to the adoption of the Constitution, only two states (Maryland and Rhode Island, later joined by Virginia) provided full religious freedoms—the remaining eleven had some restrictive laws, and six of those had established state religions. Puritanism was the official faith of the Massachusetts Bay Colony, as was Anglicanism in Virginia.

More tolerant attitudes toward religious liberty developed with time. After independence was declared, some states adopted constitutions that contained guarantees of religious freedom. North Carolina's 1776 constitution proclaimed that "[a]ll men have a natural and unalienable right to worship Almighty God according to the dictates of their own consciences." But other state constitutions continued to favor some religions over others. Although Delaware provided that "[t]here shall be no establishment of any religious sect in this State in preference to another," it forced all state officers to "profess faith in God the Father, and in Jesus Christ His Only Son."

It would be fair to say that when the framers gathered in Philadelphia, they—like modern-day Americans—held divergent views about the relationship between religion and the state. Even so, the subject of religion arose only occasionally during the course of the debates. After one particularly difficult session, Benjamin Franklin moved that the delegates pray "for the assistance of Heaven, and its blessings on our deliberations." With virtual unanimity, the delegates opposed Franklin, arguing that a prayer session might offend some members and that it would require them to pay a minister "to officiate in [the] service."[3] In the end, the founders mentioned religion only once in the Constitution. Article VI provides that all government officials must take an oath to "support this Constitution; but no religious Test shall ever be required as a Qualification to any Office or public Trust under the United States."

---

[1] Alexis de Tocqueville, *Democracy in America*, vol. 1 (New York: Vintage Books, 1954), 319.

[2] Data on religious affiliation from the Pew Research Center's Religion and Public Life Project based on 2014 surveys (http://pewforum.org).

[3] Quoted by Adam Clymer in "Congress Moves to Ease Curb on Religious Acts," *New York Times*, May 10, 1993, A9.

Some opponents of the proposed Constitution objected to the absence of a Bill of Rights and a lack of any guarantee of religious liberty, in particular. New York Anti-Federalists, for example, condemned the document for "not securing the rights of conscience in matters of religion, of granting the liberty of worshipping God agreeable to the mode thereby dictated."[4] Many states proposed amendments to the Constitution that centered on religious liberty.

In response to such criticism, the First Congress assumed the task of developing a proposed bill of rights. At the conclusion of congressional debate and the state ratification process, a prohibition against government endorsement of religion and a guarantee of religious tolerance were prominent features; the establishment and the free exercise clauses became the first two guarantees contained in the First Amendment of the Constitution: "Congress shall make no law respecting an establishment of religion, or prohibiting the free exercise thereof."

How has the Court interpreted the establishment and free exercise clauses? Are their meanings the same today as when the framers wrote them? In this chapter, we examine these and other questions associated with the First Amendment's religion clauses.

FREE EXERCISE OF RELIGION

The First Amendment ("Congress shall make no law . . . prohibiting the free exercise" of religion) appears to erect a solid barrier against government regulation of religious practice. But imagine a religious sect whose members engage in a practice that society might regard as dangerous—say, handling poisonous snakes in the belief that such activity demonstrates their faith in God. Should government prohibit such activity because it poses a risk to the public welfare? Or should snake handling fall under the umbrella of the free exercise of religion and therefore be deemed protected behavior?

A literal approach to the free exercise clause would suggest the latter; that is, religious denominations can pursue any exercise of their religion they desire. It seems clear, however, that the majority of Americans did not think the free exercise of religion meant any such thing at the time the clause was framed. Although we do not know specifically what the framers intended by the words "free exercise" (congressional debates over religious guarantees tended to focus on the establishment clause rather than the free exercise clause), writings and documents of the day point to a universally accepted limit.[5] As Thomas Jefferson set it out in 1802 in a letter to the Danbury Baptist Association: "[I believe] that religion is a matter which lies solely between man and his God; that he owes account to none other for his faith or his worship; that the legislative powers of the Government reach actions only, and not opinion."[6] In other words, the free exercise of religion is not limitless, as a literal reading of the amendment would suggest. Rather, at least under Jefferson's interpretation, governments can regulate "actions."

Initial Interpretations: The Belief/Action Distinction and the Valid Secular Policy Test

Like Jefferson, the Supreme Court has never taken a literal approach to the free exercise clause. Rather, in its first major decision in this area, it seized on Jefferson's words to proclaim that some religious activities lie beyond First Amendment protection. That case was **Reynolds v. United States** (1879), which involved the Mormon practice of polygamy. Mormons at that time believed that men "had the duty . . . to practice polygamy" and that failure to do so would result in "damnation in the life to come." But the nation considered polygamy to be a moral and social evil. As a consequence, in 1862 Congress passed and President Lincoln signed into law the Morrill Anti-Bigamy Act. This statute targeted the Mormons by not only prohibiting plural marriages in U.S. territories but also limiting property ownership by churches. Efforts to implement the law were delayed by the Civil War, but once enforcement began, the Mormon Church orchestrated a test case to challenge the law on First Amendment free exercise grounds. A devout Mormon official, George Reynolds, was selected to be the lead party. After Reynolds married his second wife in 1874, he was promptly arrested. In his defense, Reynolds, supported by the Church, argued that he was following the dictates of his faith, a right reserved to him under the free exercise clause. A jury, however, found him guilty.

---

[4]Address of the Albany Antifederal Committee, April 26, 1788, excerpted in Daniel A. Farber and Suzanna Sherry, *A History of the American Constitution*, 2nd ed. (St. Paul, MN: Thomson/West, 2005), 256.

[5]Michael W. McConnell, "Free Exercise as the Framers Understood It," in *The Bill of Rights: Original Meaning and Current Understanding*, ed. Eugene W. Hickok Jr. (Charlottesville: University Press of Virginia, 1991).

[6]Quoted in *Reynolds v. United States* (1879).

On appeal, the Supreme Court upheld the conviction. In a unanimous opinion, the justices rejected an absolutist interpretation of the clause and instead sought to draw a distinction between an abstract religious faith and the practices associated with that faith. Chief Justice Morrison Waite's opinion for the Court asserted, "Congress was deprived of all legislative power over mere opinion, but was left free to reach actions which were in violation of social duties or subversive of the good order." Based on this standard, the justices found plural marriage to be an "odious" practice that had been consistently rejected by Western societies, well before the founding of the Mormon Church in 1830. It could therefore be regulated. To be sure, Congress could not outlaw devotion to the principles of Mormonism, but it was certainly free to forbid any practices that it regarded as inconsistent with the public welfare.[7] The distinction between beliefs and actions became, as we shall see, the centerpiece of several future religion cases.

In *Cantwell v. Connecticut* (1940) the Court embellished the belief/action dichotomy. Here, the Court considered a Connecticut law that required those who wanted to solicit money from the public to obtain a "certificate of approval" from the secretary of the state's Public Welfare Council. The state charged this official with determining whether "the cause is a religious one" or one of a "*bona fide* object of charity." If the official found neither, he was authorized to withhold the necessary certificate.

In a predominantly Catholic area of New Haven, Connecticut, Newton Cantwell and his sons Jesse and Russell, members of the Jehovah's Witnesses faith, were soliciting contributions as well as playing recordings and distributing literature that were critical of the Catholic faith. Passersby took offense at the anti-Catholic messages in the materials and complained to local authorities. The Cantwells were arrested and later convicted of soliciting funds without first having received the required certificate of approval from the state.

Although the law was neutral—that is, it applied to all those engaging in solicitation for any religious or charitable cause—the Jehovah's Witnesses challenged it as a restriction on their free exercise rights. Members of this denomination consider themselves "ministers of the gospel to the 'gentiles'" and, as such, distribute pamphlets and solicit money. Accordingly, the Cantwells argued that the state regulation deprived them of "their right of freedom to worship Almighty God."

In a unanimous decision, the Court held for the Jehovah's Witnesses. First, the justices ruled that the states, through the Fourteenth Amendment, were obliged to comply with the free exercise clause; and second, the Court found that the Cantwells' religious freedom had been violated, requiring a reversal of their convictions. Yet Justice Owen Roberts's majority opinion was something less than a complete victory for the Witnesses. Roberts relied on the belief/action dichotomy, noting, "The first is absolute but, in the nature of things, the second cannot be." He then adopted a legal standard that was exceedingly easy for the government to meet: if the policy serves a legitimate governmental goal, not directed at any particular religion, the Court would uphold it, even if the legislation had the effect of conflicting with religious practices. Applying this principle (often referred to as the "valid secular policy" test) to *Cantwell*, Roberts asserted that the state was free to regulate the solicitation of funds, even if those funds were for a religious purpose, because the state has a valid interest in protecting its citizens from fraudulent appeals for contributions. The particular Connecticut law Cantwell challenged, however, was defective. It empowered a single administrative official to determine whether a cause was religious. This section of the law opened the potential for arbitrary and capricious action on the part of the official and also allowed the government to stifle religious expression prior to its exercise. Had the law not contained such a provision, the Court probably would have upheld it as a legitimate secular policy.

If the Court had upheld the law, the Jehovah's Witnesses would have found it more difficult to carry out the dictates of their religion. By the same token, all other would-be solicitors—charitable organizations and the like—would have been similarly affected. In other words, both the religious and the nonreligious would have been subject to the regulations. Looking at *Cantwell* this way reveals an important underpinning of the logic of the valid secular policy test: neutrality. If a secular policy is generally applicable and does not target any particular religion or religions generally, then, in the eyes of the justices, religions should not be exempt from its coverage simply because they are religions. Exempting them would give religions an elevated position in society. At the same time, the "valid secular policy" test offers an important qualification that was absent in *Reynolds*. There, the prohibition on polygamy was upheld, despite

---

[7]Ordinarily, matters of family law are handled by the states, not Congress. This case arose in Utah, which, at the time, was still a federal territory and therefore subject to the control of the national government.

its being motivated by hostility toward the Mormon faith. Under the rule adopted in *Cantwell*, such a law would presumably be invalid.

A notable feature of this test is that it only requires the government to act in furtherance of a "legitimate state interest." The state need not demonstrate that its goal is essential or even important; it merely needs to be an end that it is entitled to pursue. In *Cantwell*, for example, the prevention of fraud, the regulation of the time and manner of solicitation, and actions promoting "public safety, peace, comfort or convenience" are obvious functions of the state. Although the government lost in *Cantwell*, the Court soon demonstrated how readily the government could prevail under this precedent.

At issue in ***Minersville School District v. Gobitis*** (1940) were the recitation of the Pledge of Allegiance and the hand gesture or salute that accompanied it. For most individuals, particularly schoolchildren, the pledge and salute are noncontroversial routines that illustrate their loyalty to the basic tenets of American society. Such is not the case for Jehovah's Witnesses, who exalt religious laws over all others. They claim that the salute and the pledge violate a teaching from Exodus: "Thou shalt not make unto thee any graven image, or any likeness of anything that is in heaven above, or that is in earth beneath, or that is in the water under the earth; thou shalt not bow down thyself to them, nor serve them."

Bettmann/Contributor/Getty Images

Walter Gobitas sued the Minersville, Pennsylvania, school district after his children, William and Lillian, were expelled for refusing to salute the flag because of their Jehovah's Witnesses faith.

Accordingly, Jehovah's Witnesses do not want their children to recite the pledge or salute the flag. The problem, at the time of this case, was that a number of states made the pledge and salute to the flag mandatory for all children attending public schools. Flag salute laws became particularly pervasive after World War I as a show of patriotism. Before the war, only five states required flag salutes; by 1935 that figure had risen to eighteen, with many local school boards compelling the salute in the absence of state legislation.[8] As the nation entered World War II, public support for practices encouraging patriotism among America's youth became even stronger.

Many Jehovah's Witnesses asked their children not to salute the flag. Among these was Walter Gobitas,[9] whose two children—twelve-year-old Lillian and her younger brother, William—attended a Pennsylvania public school with a mandatory flag salute policy. When the children refused to salute the flag, they were expelled. Represented by attorneys from the Witnesses, Gobitas sued the school board, arguing that the expulsion violated his children's right to free exercise of religion. Writing for the Court, Justice Felix Frankfurter used the valid secular policy rationale to uphold the flag salute requirement. Frankfurter claimed that the state had a legitimate secular reason for requiring flag salutes: to foster patriotism. That the law affected the religious practice of the Jehovah's Witnesses did not, in Frankfurter's view, detract from its constitutionality.[10]

Prince v. Massachusetts (1940) provides a second example of the valid secular policy test, this time applied in the area of child welfare. *Prince* involved a Massachusetts law that prohibited minors (girls under age eighteen and boys under twelve) from selling "upon the streets or in other public places, any newspaper, magazines, periodicals, or other articles of merchandise." It also specified that any parent or guardian who allowed a minor to perform such activity would be engaging in criminal behavior. Sarah Prince, a Jehovah's Witness,

allowed her nine-year-old niece, Betty Simmons, for whom Prince was the legal guardian, to help her distribute religious pamphlets. Prince knew she was violating the law—she had been warned by school authorities—but she continued and was arrested.

At the trial court level, there was some doubt about whether the child actually had sold materials, but when the case reached the Supreme Court, it dealt exclusively with this question: Did the state law violate First Amendment principles? A divided Court held that it did not. Writing for a five-person majority, Justice Wiley Rutledge asserted:

> The State's authority over children's activities is broader than over like actions of adults. This is peculiarly true of public activities and in matters of employment. A democratic society rests . . . upon the healthy, well-rounded growth of young people into full maturity as citizens. . . . It may secure this against impeding restraints and dangers, within a broad range of selection. Among evils most appropriate for such action are the crippling effects of child employment . . . and the possible harms arising from other activities subject to all the diverse influences of the street. It is too late now to doubt that legislation appropriately designed to reach such evils is within the state's police power, whether against the parent's claim to control of the child or one that religious scruples dictate contrary action.

Clearly, legislatures can regulate religious practices of potential harm to children as well as those of questionable morality and safety; these are legitimate state interests. Such laws, in the eyes of the justices, represent a reasonable use of state police power, which is the ability of states to regulate in the best interests of their citizens. In other words, child labor laws constitute valid and neutral secular policy, and when such laws are in opposition to a free exercise claim, the free exercise claim falls.

The *Sherbert-Yoder* Compelling Interest Test

Cantwell, Gobitis, and *Prince* have several traits in common: they were brought by members of a minority religion (Jehovah's Witnesses); they were decided during the 1940s, a period when the Court was neither particularly conservative nor liberal in ideological outlook; and

---

[8]See Peter Irons, *The Courage of Their Convictions* (New York: Free Press, 1988), 16–24.

[9]The family name, Gobitas, was misspelled in the records.

[10]Three years later, in *West Virginia Board of Education v. Barnette* (1943), after the initial intensity of the war years had subsided and criticism of the decision from the legal community had made its mark, the justices overruled *Gobitis.* As we will see in chapter 13, however, *Barnette* was based primarily on freedom of speech grounds rather than on religious exercise. As such, the overruling of *Gobitis* had little direct effect on the valid secular policy test.

they involved free exercise arguments combined with other constitutional claims, such as freedom of expression. In addition, the Court's approaches to the cases were relatively consistent. The Court remained true to the belief/action dichotomy. Religious beliefs were not questioned, but when religious actions were at issue, the Court invoked the valid secular policy test to resolve the disputes. These approaches occasionally led the justices to strike down state policies (*Cantwell*), as well as to uphold them (*Gobitis, Prince*).

In the 1960s, however, major changes began to occur in the Supreme Court's religious exercise jurisprudence. The first sign of change came in ***Braunfeld v. Brown***, which was one of several cases the Court heard in 1961 involving "blue laws," or laws requiring businesses to close on Sundays. At issue in *Braunfeld* was Pennsylvania's blue law, which allowed only certain kinds of stores considered essential to remain open on Sundays. Abraham Braunfeld, an Orthodox Jew, owned a retail clothing and home furnishings store in Philadelphia. Because such stores were not among those permitted to remain open on Sundays, Braunfeld wanted the Court to issue a permanent injunction against the law. His religious principles dictated that he could not work on Saturday, the Jewish Sabbath, but he needed his store to be open six days a week to compete economically with non-Jewish store owners who were free to operate on Saturdays. He challenged the law as a violation of, among other things, his right to exercise his religion.

In an opinion for a plurality of the justices, Chief Justice Earl Warren upheld the constitutionality of the Sunday closing laws. He did so on the basis of the belief/action dichotomy and the valid secular policy test. His explanation of the latter, however, contained a new twist. It is constitutional for the government to pursue a valid secular policy even if it incidentally restricts religious exercise, Warren stated, but only if there is no alternative means available that is less burdensome to religious liberty. In other words, government could pursue a valid government interest, but the means it chose to achieve that goal had to pose the least possible interference with religious exercise. In this context, the government had an interest in promoting the public welfare by setting aside "a day of rest, repose, recreation and tranquility," and the law would be too difficult to administer if the state had to police store owners to certify genuine religious exceptions. In opposition to Warren's new interpretation of the valid secular policy test, Justices William J. Brennan and Potter Stewart wrote powerful dissents in which they criticized not only the outcome in *Braunfeld* but also the standard the Court used to decide the case. The valid secular policy test, they argued, provided inadequate protection of individual religious liberties.

The divided opinion over *Braunfeld* created something of a quandary for legal scholars: Was the Court signaling a change in the way it would resolve free exercise disputes? Or was *Braunfeld* an aberration? In *Sherbert v. Verner* (1963) the Court provided some answers.

Sherbert v. Verner

374 U.S. 398 (1963)
http://caselaw.findlaw.com/us-supreme-court/374/398.html
Oral arguments available at https://www.oyez.org/
cases/1962/526
Vote: 7 (Black, Brennan, Clark, Douglas, Goldberg, Stewart,
Warren)
2 (Harlan, White)

OPINION OF THE COURT: *Brennan*

CONCURRING OPINIONS: *Douglas, Stewart*

DISSENTING OPINION: *Harlan*

Adell Sherbert was a spool tender in a Spartanburg, South Carolina, textile mill—a job she had held for thirty-five years. She worked Monday through Friday from 7:00 A.M. to 3:00 P.M. She had the option of working Saturdays, but Sherbert was a member of the Seventh-day Adventist Church, which held that no work could be performed between sundown on Friday and sundown on Saturday. Since Saturday was her church's Sabbath, she chose not to work on that day.

In the summer of 1959, Sherbert's employer informed her that work on Saturdays would no longer be voluntary: to retain her job, she would need to report to the mill every Saturday. She continued to work Monday through Friday but, in accord with her religious beliefs, did not work on six successive Saturdays. At that point, her employer fired her.

Sherbert had tried to find a job at three other textile mills, but they too operated on Saturdays. So she filed for state unemployment benefits. Under South Carolina law, a claimant who is eligible for benefits must be "able to work . . . and available for work"; a claimant is ineligible for benefits if he or she has "failed, without good cause . . . to accept available suitable work when offered . . . by the employment office or the employer." The benefits examiner rejected her claim because she had failed, without good cause, to accept "suitable work when offered" by her employer. In other words, her religious preference was an insufficient justification for her refusal of a job.

Sherbert and her lawyers filed suit, asserting that the rejection of the unemployment benefits claim amounted to a violation of the free exercise clause. After unsuccessfully arguing this point in the state courts, her attorneys asked the U.S. Supreme Court to review the case. The appeal presented a fundamental question to the justices: May a state deny unemployment benefits to persons whose religious beliefs preclude their working on Saturdays?

MR. JUSTICE BRENNAN DELIVERED THE OPINION OF THE COURT.

The door of the Free Exercise Clause stands tightly closed against any governmental regulation of religious beliefs as such, *Cantwell v. Connecticut.* . . . On the other hand, the Court has rejected challenges under the Free Exercise Clause to governmental regulation of certain overt acts prompted by religious beliefs or principles, for "even when the action is in accord with one's religious convictions, [it] is not totally free from legislative restrictions." *Braunfeld v. Brown.* The conduct or actions so regulated have invariably posed some substantial threat to public safety, peace or order. See, *e.g., Reynolds v. United States; Prince v. Massachusetts.* . . .

We turn first to the question whether the disqualification for benefits imposes any burden on the free exercise of appellant's religion. We think it is clear that it does. . . . [It] forces her to choose between following the precepts of her religion and forfeiting benefits, on the one hand, and abandoning one of the precepts of her religion in order to accept work, on the other hand. Governmental imposition of such a choice puts the same kind of burden upon the free exercise of religion as would a fine imposed against appellant for her Saturday worship. . . .

We must next consider whether some compelling state interest enforced in the eligibility provisions of the South Carolina statute justifies the substantial infringement of appellant's First Amendment right. It is basic that no showing merely of a rational relationship to some colorable state interest would suffice; in this highly sensitive constitutional area, "[o]nly the gravest abuses, endangering paramount interests, give occasion for permissible limitation." . . . No such abuse or danger has been advanced in the present case. The appellees suggest no more than a possibility that the filing of fraudulent claims by unscrupulous claimants feigning religious objections to Saturday work might not only dilute the unemployment compensation fund but also hinder the scheduling by employers of necessary Saturday work. But that possibility is not apposite here because no such objection appears to have been made before the South Carolina Supreme Court . . . . [E]ven if the possibility of spurious claims did threaten to dilute the fund and disrupt the scheduling of work, it would plainly be incumbent upon the appellees to demonstrate that no alternative forms of regulation

would combat such abuses without infringing First Amendment rights. . . .

In these respects, then, the state interest asserted in the present case is wholly dissimilar to the interests which were found to justify the less direct burden upon religious practices in *Braunfeld v. Brown.* The Court recognized that the Sunday closing law which that decision sustained undoubtedly served "to make the practice of [the Orthodox Jewish merchants'] . . . religious beliefs more expensive." But the statute was nevertheless saved by a countervailing factor which finds no equivalent in the instant case—a strong state interest in providing one uniform day of rest for all workers. That secular objective could be achieved, the Court found, only by declaring Sunday to be that day of rest. Requiring exemptions for Sabbatarians, while theoretically possible, appeared to present an administrative problem of such magnitude, or to afford the exempted class so great a competitive advantage, that such a requirement would have rendered the entire statutory scheme unworkable. In the present case no such justifications underlie the determination of the state court that appellant's religion makes her ineligible to receive benefits. . . .

The judgment of the South Carolina Supreme Court is reversed and the case is remanded for further proceedings not inconsistent with this opinion.

It is so ordered.

MR. JUSTICE DOUGLAS, CONCURRING.

Some have thought that a majority of a community can, through state action, compel a minority to observe their particular religious scruples so long as the majority's rule can be said to perform some valid secular function. That was the essence of the Court's decision in the Sunday Blue Law Cases . . . a ruling from which I then dissented and still dissent.

That ruling of the Court travels part of the distance that South Carolina asks us to go now. She asks us to hold that when it comes to a day of rest a Sabbatarian must conform with the scruples of the majority in order to obtain unemployment benefits.

The result turns not on the degree of injury, which may indeed be nonexistent by ordinary standards. The harm is the interference with the individual's scruples or conscience—an important area of privacy which the First Amendment fences off from government.

MR. JUSTICE STEWART, CONCURRING IN THE RESULT.

My . . . difference with the Court's opinion is that I cannot agree that today's decision can stand consistently with *Braunfeld v. Brown.* The Court says that there was a "less direct burden upon religious practices" in that case than in this. With all respect, I think the Court is mistaken, simply as a matter of fact. The *Braunfeld* case involved a state criminal statute. The undisputed effect of that statute, as pointed out by MR. JUSTICE BRENNAN in his dissenting opinion in that case, was that "'Plaintiff, Abraham Braunfeld, will be unable to continue in his business if he may not stay open on Sunday and he will thereby lose his capital investment.' In other words, the issue in this case . . . is whether a State may put an individual to a choice between his business and his religion."

The impact upon the appellant's religious freedom in the present case is considerably less onerous. We deal here not with a criminal statute, but with the particularized administration of South Carolina's Unemployment Compensation Act. Even upon the unlikely assumption that the appellant could not find suitable non-Saturday employment, the appellant at the worst would be denied a maximum of 22 weeks of compensation payments. I agree with the Court that the possibility of that denial is enough to infringe upon the appellant's constitutional right to the free exercise of her religion. But it is clear to me that in order to reach this conclusion the Court must explicitly reject the reasoning of *Braunfeld v. Brown.* I think the *Braunfeld* case was wrongly decided and should be overruled, and accordingly I concur in the result reached by the Court in the case before us.

MR. JUSTICE HARLAN, WHOM MR. JUSTICE WHITE JOINS, DISSENTING.

Today's decision is disturbing both in its rejection of existing precedent and in its implications for the future. . . .

. . . What the Court is holding is that if the State chooses to condition unemployment compensation on the applicant's availability for work, it is constitutionally compelled to *carve out an exception*—and to provide benefits—for those whose unavailability is due to their religious convictions. Such a holding has particular significance in two respects.

First, despite the Court's protestations to the contrary, the decision necessarily overrules *Braunfeld v. Brown,* which held that it did not offend the "Free Exercise" Clause of the Constitution for a State to forbid a Sabbatarian to do business on Sunday. . . .

Second, the implications of the present decision are far more troublesome than its apparently narrow dimensions would indicate at first glance. The meaning of today's holding, as already noted, is that the State must furnish unemployment benefits to one who is unavailable for work if the unavailability stems from the exercise of religious convictions. The State, in other words, must *single out* for financial assistance those whose behavior is religiously motivated, even though it denies such assistance to others whose identical behavior (in this case, inability to work on Saturdays) is not religiously motivated. . . .

. . . Those situations in which the Constitution may require special treatment on account of religion are, in my view, few and far between, and this view is amply supported by the course of constitutional litigation in this area. . . . Such compulsion in the present case is particularly inappropriate in light of the indirect, remote, and insubstantial effect of the decision below on the exercise of appellant's religion and in light of the direct financial assistance to religion that today's decision requires.

For these reasons I respectfully dissent from the opinion and judgment of the Court.

Brennan's majority opinion represents a significant break from past free exercise claims. No longer would a mere secular legislative purpose suffice as a justification for restricting religious exercise, as it had in *Braunfeld.* *Sherbert* now added the requirement that the government demonstrate that its regulation was in pursuit an overriding governmental goal. The Court had now fully embraced both features of the legal standard known as strict scrutiny; the state would have to demonstrate that it was pursuing a compelling state interest test and that its method was the least restrictive alternative. As such, the *Sherbert* approach is much more favorable to religious exercise claims and much less sympathetic to government efforts to regulate religious practice.

The Warren Court ushered in the change in free exercise standards in *Sherbert,* but that Court heard very few free exercise cases after *Sherbert.* It was left to the justices of the Court led by Chief Justice Warren Burger to apply those standards.

The opportunity for the Burger Court to put its stamp on this area of the law arose early in the new chief's tenure. In 1972 the Court decided **Wisconsin v. Yoder**. At issue was a Wisconsin law mandating that children attend accredited public or private schools until the age of sixteen. This compulsory education law violated the norms of the Amish, who had been among the first religious groups to arrive in the United States. As a simple people who eschew technology, including automobiles and electricity, the Amish do not permit their children to attend school after the eighth grade, believing that such attendance would adversely expose the children to worldly influences contrary to their beliefs.

In challenging the Wisconsin law, attorneys representing the parents of Amish children raised two fundamental claims. First, they asserted that the Amish did not want their children to be uneducated or ignorant. In fact, Amish teenagers pursued rigorous home study after their public school education. Second, because education was continuing at home, the state could demonstrate no compelling reason to require the children to attend public school. In contrast, the attorney general of Wisconsin compared this case with *Prince v. Massachusetts,* in which the Court upheld child labor regulations. He claimed that the two laws were similar because both were enacted out of a legitimate concern for the welfare of children.

In his opinion for the Court, Chief Justice Burger held for the Amish.

He invoked *Sherbert*'s approach to find that the state's interest was not sufficiently compelling to outweigh the free exercise claim. In doing so, the Court eliminated any doubt that *Sherbert* represented a major change in free exercise jurisprudence. The *Sherbert-Yoder* test, as it became known, was now firmly established. A law prohibiting individuals from engaging in religious exercise can withstand constitutional challenge only if the government has a compelling interest in enforcing the law and uses the least restrictive means possible to achieve that end. It should not be surprising that when this test is used, the religious liberty claimant is almost always victorious.

The Burger Court continued to apply the *Sherbert-Yoder* compelling interest test in subsequent cases. Less than a decade after *Yoder*, the justices decided **Thomas v. Review Board of Indiana Employment Security Division** (1981), the facts of which bore a marked resemblance to *Sherbert*. Eddie Thomas was a Jehovah's Witness who worked in a steel mill. When the owners closed the mill down, they transferred Thomas to another plant. Because his new job required him to make tanks for use by the military, Thomas quit on religious grounds and filed for unemployment benefits, which the state denied. Writing for the Court, Chief Justice Burger acknowledged the parallels between *Sherbert* and this dispute: "Here, as in *Sherbert*, the employee was put to a choice between fidelity to his religious beliefs or cessation of work; the coercive impact on Thomas is indistinguishable from *Sherbert*." Accordingly, he said, "Unless we are prepared to overrule *Sherbert*, Thomas cannot be denied the benefits due him."

The *Smith* Test

Despite the Burger Court's apparent adoption of the compelling interest/least restrictive means standard, some of the justices wanted to rethink that standard or, at the very least, make it easier for the state to respond to free exercise challenges. As a result, in the 1980s the Court was deeply divided over whether to retain the *Sherbert-Yoder* test or return to a position that would allow more government regulation of religious activity.

The debate arose in 1982 with the Court's decision in **United States v. Lee**. This dispute began when Edwin Lee, a member of the Amish faith and owner of a farm and carpentry shop, refused to withhold Social Security taxes or pay the employer's share of those taxes. The Amish believe that they have a religious duty to care for their elderly and therefore object to a policy that places that obligation in the hands of the government. He argued that the payment of taxes and the receipt of Social Security benefits violated his religious tenets.

In a short opinion for the Court, Chief Justice Burger disagreed. To be sure, Burger conceded, "compulsory participation" in the Social Security system interferes with the free exercise rights of the Amish. But the government was able to justify that burden on religion by showing that compulsory participation is "essential to accomplish an overriding governmental interest" in the maintenance of the Social Security system in the United States. The taxing power is essential to the operation of government, and it be would impossible to administer the tax system if religious objections to particular taxes—of which there are certainly many—were a basis for opting out. As Burger put it, "To maintain an organized society that guarantees religious freedom to a great variety of faiths requires that some religious practices yield to the common good."

To many observers, *Lee* appeared inconsistent with the *Sherbert-Yoder* standard. After all, the Court had previously used that test to exempt Amish children from compulsory education laws. Why was an exemption from Social Security requirements not also required by the First Amendment's free exercise clause?

Four years later, in **Goldman v. Weinberger** (1986), the Court provided even more evidence that the justices were beginning to stray from the *Sherbert-Yoder* test. In this case, a U.S. Air Force captain was prohibited from wearing a yarmulke (skullcap) while in uniform. As an Orthodox Jew, the captain was required to keep his head covered at all times, but wearing the yarmulke violated the Air Force Dress Code, a 190-page regulation that describes in minute detail all of the various items of apparel that constitute the air force uniform.

His attorneys argued that the religious skullcap in no way interfered with his duties; he served as a clinical psychologist at an Air Force base. Lawyers for the military saw the issue differently. They argued that strict uniform regulations help maintain discipline, morale, and esprit de corps. Granting an exemption, they claimed, would lead others to request permission to wear turbans, dreadlocks, saffron robes, and the like.

Writing for the majority, Justice William Rehnquist agreed with the government and ruled against Goldman.

As he explained,

> Petitioner argues that [the dress code], as applied to him, prohibits religiously motivated conduct and should therefore be analyzed under the standard enunciated in *Sherbert v. Verner* (1963). . . . But "within the military community there is simply not the same [individual] autonomy as there is in the larger civilian community." . . . In the context of the present case, when evaluating whether military needs justify a particular restriction on religiously motivated conduct, courts must give great deference to the professional judgment of military authorities concerning the relative importance of a particular military interest.

The Court's decision in *Goldman* fueled academic and political debate. Taking up an invitation issued by Justice Brennan in a dissenting opinion ("The Court and the military have refused these servicemen their constitutional rights; we must hope that Congress will correct this wrong"), members of Congress introduced legislation allowing members of the armed forces "to wear an item of religious apparel while in uniform" so long as the item is "neat and conservative" and does not "interfere with the performance" of military duties. Congress passed the law in September 1987, exercising its power to regulate the military as a means of expanding the religious rights of those serving in the armed forces.

Congress may have ameliorated a difficulty for religiously devout members of the military, but debate in academic and legal circles over *Goldman* continued. Legal observers were less concerned with the outcome of the case and more troubled by the rationale the Court invoked to resolve the dispute. Was *Goldman* a substantial break from the *Sherbert* standard? Clearly, the four dissenters (Harry Blackmun, William J. Brennan, Thurgood Marshall, and Sandra Day O'Connor) saw it that way. According to Justice O'Connor, the majority was departing from the Court's free exercise principles; regardless of whether regulations were imposed in the military or civilian life, she argued, the government would need to show that religious exemptions harmed an important state interest. In contrast, some scholars (along with a few members of the Court) did not think *Goldman* represented a significant shift in Court opinion. They argued that *Goldman* was an exceptional case: it involved the interests of the armed forces, interests to which the justices traditionally defer. Accordingly, they predicted that

the Court would return to the compelling interest/least restrictive means standard in future cases.

Predictions of a return to the *Sherbert-Yoder* test proved to be inaccurate. In 1986 William Rehnquist, the author of the majority opinion in *Goldman*, became chief justice. Rehnquist's promotion was quickly followed by the appointments of conservative justices Antonin Scalia and Anthony M. Kennedy. The shift in the ideological balance of the Court set the stage for a serious rethinking of the Court's free exercise jurisprudence.

In 1990 the justices not only reconsidered their previous free exercise rulings but also completely rejected the *Sherbert-Yoder* standard. In *Employment Division, Department of Human Resources of Oregon v. Smith* (1990) the Court seemed to turn its back on nearly three decades of free exercise cases and adopt a new standard.

Employment Division, Department of Human Resources of Oregon v. Smith

494 U.S. 872 (1990)
http://caselaw.findlaw.com/us-supreme-court/494/872.html
Oral arguments available at https://www.oyez.org/
  cases/1989/88-1213
Vote: 6 (Kennedy, O'Connor, Rehnquist, Scalia, Stevens, White)
  3 (Blackmun, Brennan, Marshall)

OPINION OF THE COURT: *Scalia*

CONCURRING OPINION: *O'Connor*

DISSENTING OPINION: *Blackmun*

This case centers on the use of peyote, which is a controlled substance under Oregon law. Peyote is a hallucinogen produced by certain cactus plants found in the southwestern United States and northern Mexico, and it is illegal to possess the drug unless a physician prescribes it. Unlike other hallucinogenic drugs (such as LSD), peyote has never been widely used. One reason for this is that ingesting peyote involves eating the buds of certain cactus plants, which have an unpleasant taste and may cause nausea and vomiting.

There is, however, one group of citizens who ingest peyote on a regular basis—members of a bona fide religion, the Native American Church. To them peyote is a sacramental substance, an object of worship, and a source of divine protection. They use the substance during religious rituals.

Various governments have acknowledged the spiritual nature of the church's use of peyote. Twenty-three U.S. states—those with sizeable Native American populations—and the federal government exempt the religious use of peyote from laws criminalizing the

Alfred Smith, a member of the Klamath Tribe in Oregon, was a long-time activist for Native American rights. Along with coworker Galen Black, Smith unsuccessfully challenged the state's denial of unemployment benefits when the two were fired from a drug rehabilitation service for using peyote in a religious ceremony.

drug's general use. The federal government even issues licenses to grow peyote for sacramental purposes.

The dispute in *Smith* arose when two members of the Native American Church, Alfred Smith and Galen Black, were fired from their jobs as counselors at a private drug and alcohol abuse clinic after they had used peyote at a religious ceremony. Smith and Black applied for unemployment benefits, but the state of Oregon turned them down. They were found ineligible because they had been fired for "misconduct"; under state law, workers discharged for that reason cannot obtain benefits.

Smith and Black brought suit in state court, arguing successfully that under the precedents of *Sherbert* and *Thomas*, the state could not deny them unemployment benefits. The state appealed, and after an initial hearing in the U.S. Supreme Court, the justices

returned the case to the state supreme court, instructing it to determine whether the religious use of peyote was prohibited by Oregon law. This was an important consideration, the justices explained, because the individuals in *Sherbert* and *Thomas* had not violated the law; they had simply refused to work for religious reasons. Oregon's supreme court ruled that, while the use of peyote—for religious reasons or otherwise—was prohibited under state law, the denial of unemployment benefits still violated the free exercise clause. The state thought differently; it again sought review from the U.S. Supreme Court, arguing that it could deny the benefits—regardless of Smith and Black's free exercise claim—because the use of peyote was prohibited by a general criminal statute that was not aimed at inhibiting religion. Oregon also noted that it—like all other government entities—had a compelling interest in regulating drug use and that the state's law represented the least intrusive means of achieving that interest. When the case returned to the Court, both sides assumed that the justices would use the *Sherbet-Yoder* standard to resolve the dispute.

JUSTICE SCALIA DELIVERED THE OPINION OF THE COURT.

The free exercise of religion means, first and foremost, the right to believe and profess whatever religious doctrine one desires. Thus, the First Amendment obviously excludes all "governmental regulation of religious beliefs as such." . . .

But the "exercise of religion" often involves not only belief and profession but the performance of (or abstention from) physical acts: assembling with others for a worship service, participating in sacramental use of bread and wine, proselytizing, abstaining from certain foods or certain modes of transportation. It would be true, we think (though no case of ours has involved the point), that a state would be "prohibiting the free exercise [of religion]" if it sought to ban such acts or abstentions only when they are engaged in for religious reasons, or only because of the religious belief that they display. It would doubtless be unconstitutional, for example, to ban the casting of "statues that are to be used for worship purposes," or to prohibit bowing down before a golden calf.

Respondents in the present case, however, seek to carry the meaning of "prohibiting the free exercise [of religion]" one large step further. They contend that their religious motivation for using peyote places them beyond the reach of a criminal law that is not specifically directed at their religious practice, and that is concededly constitutional as applied to those who use the drug for other reasons. . . .

. . . We have never held that an individual's religious beliefs excuse him from compliance with an otherwise valid law prohibiting conduct that the State is free to regulate. On the contrary, the record of more than a century of our free exercise jurisprudence contradicts that proposition. . . . We first had occasion to assert that principle in *Reynolds v. United States* (1879), where we rejected the claim that criminal laws against polygamy could not be constitutionally applied to those whose religion commanded the practice. . . .

Subsequent decisions have consistently held that the right of free exercise does not relieve an individual of the obligation to comply with a "valid and neutral law of general applicability on the ground that the law proscribes (or prescribes) conduct that his religion prescribes (or proscribes)." *United States v. Lee* (1982). . . . In *Prince v. Massachusetts* (1944) we held that a mother could be prosecuted under the child labor laws for using her children to dispense literature in the streets, her religious motivation notwithstanding. We found no constitutional infirmity in "excluding [these children] from doing there what no other children may do." In *Braunfeld v. Brown* (1961) (plurality opinion) we upheld Sunday-closing laws against the claim that they burdened the religious practices of persons whose religions compelled them to refrain from work on other days. . . .

. . . Respondents urge us to hold, quite simply, that when otherwise prohibitable conduct is accompanied by religious convictions, not only the convictions but the conduct itself must be free from governmental regulation. We have never held that, and decline to do so now. There being no contention that Oregon's drug law represents an attempt to regulate religious beliefs, the communication of religious beliefs, or the raising of one's children in those beliefs, the rule to which we have adhered ever since *Reynolds* plainly controls. "Our cases do not at their farthest reach support the proposition that a stance of conscientious opposition relieves an objector from any colliding duty fixed by a democratic government." . . .

Respondents argue that even though exemption from generally applicable criminal laws need not automatically be extended to religiously motivated actors, at least the claim for a religious exemption must be evaluated under the balancing test set forth in *Sherbert v. Verner* (1963). Under the *Sherbert* test, governmental actions that substantially burden a religious practice must be justified by a compelling governmental interest. . . . Applying that test we have, on three occasions, invalidated state unemployment compensation rules that conditioned the availability of benefits upon an applicant's willingness to work under conditions forbidden by his religion. See *Sherbert v. Verner; Thomas v. Review Bd. of Indiana Employment Security Div.* (1981); *Hobbie v. Unemployment Appeals Comm'n of Florida* (1987). We have never invalidated any governmental action on the basis of the *Sherbert* test except the denial of unemployment compensation. Although we have sometimes purported to apply the *Sherbert* test in contexts other than that, we have always found the test satisfied. . . . In recent years we have abstained from applying the *Sherbert* test (outside the unemployment compensation field)

at all. . . . In *Goldman v. Weinberger* (1986) we rejected application of the *Sherbert* test to military dress regulations that forbade the wearing of yarmulkes. . . .

Even if we were inclined to breathe into *Sherbert* some life beyond the unemployment compensation field, we would not apply it to require exemptions from a generally applicable criminal law. The *Sherbert* test, it must be recalled, was developed in a context that lent itself to individualized governmental assessment of the reasons for the relevant conduct. . . .

. . . We conclude today that the sounder approach, and the approach in accord with the vast majority of our precedents, is to hold the test inapplicable to such challenges. The government's ability to enforce generally applicable prohibitions of socially harmful conduct, like its ability to carry out other aspects of public policy, "cannot depend on measuring the effects of a governmental action on a religious objector's spiritual development." . . . To make an individual's obligation to obey such a law contingent upon the law's coincidence with his religious beliefs, except where the State's interest is "compelling"— permitting him, by virtue of his beliefs, "to become a law unto himself," *Reynolds v. United States*—contradicts both constitutional tradition and common sense. . . .

. . . Precisely because "we are a cosmopolitan nation made up of people of almost every conceivable religious preference," *Braunfeld v. Brown,* and precisely because we value and protect that religious divergence, we cannot afford the luxury of deeming presumptively invalid, as applied to the religious objector, every regulation of conduct that does not protect an interest of the highest order. The rule respondents favor would open the prospect of constitutionally required religious exemptions from civic obligations of almost every conceivable kind—ranging from compulsory military service . . . to the payment of taxes . . . to health and safety regulation such as manslaughter and child neglect laws . . . compulsory vaccination laws . . . drug laws . . . and traffic laws . . . to social welfare legislation such as minimum wage laws . . . child labor laws . . . animal cruelty laws . . . environmental protection laws . . . and laws providing for equality of opportunity for the races. . . . The First Amendment's protection of religious liberty does not require this.

. . . It may fairly be said that leaving accommodation to the political process will place at a relative disadvantage those religious practices that are not widely engaged in; but that unavoidable consequence of democratic government must be preferred to a system in which each conscience is a law unto itself or in which judges weigh the social importance of all laws against the centrality of all religious beliefs.

Because respondents' ingestion of peyote was prohibited under Oregon law, and because that prohibition is constitutional, Oregon may, consistent with the Free Exercise Clause, deny respondents unemployment compensation when their dismissal results from use of the drug. The decision of the Oregon Supreme Court is accordingly reversed.

It is so ordered.

JUSTICE O'CONNOR . . . CONCURRING IN JUDGMENT. [JUSTICES BRENNAN, MARSHALL, AND BLACKMUN JOIN THIS OPINION IN SUPPORTING CONTINUED ADHERENCE TO THE SHERBERT-YODER TEST, BUT DISAGREE WITH THE OPINION'S CONCLUSION THAT THE STATE HAS SATISFIED THAT STANDARD.]

Although I agree with the result the Court reaches in this case, I cannot join its opinion. In my view, today's holding dramatically departs from well-settled First Amendment jurisprudence, appears unnecessary to resolve the question presented, and is incompatible with our Nation's fundamental commitment to individual religious liberty.

* * *

The Court today extracts from our long history of free exercise precedents the single categorical rule that "if prohibiting the exercise of religion . . . is . . . merely the incidental effect of a generally applicable and otherwise valid provision, the First Amendment has not been offended." Indeed, the Court holds that where the law is a generally applicable criminal prohibition, our usual free exercise jurisprudence does not even apply. To reach this sweeping result, however, the Court must not only give a strained reading of the First Amendment but must also disregard our consistent application of free exercise doctrine to cases involving generally applicable regulations that burden religious conduct.

The Free Exercise Clause of the First Amendment commands that "Congress shall make no law . . . prohibiting the free exercise [of religion].". . . Because the First Amendment does not distinguish between religious belief and religious conduct, conduct motivated by sincere religious belief, like the belief itself, must be at least presumptively protected by the Free Exercise Clause.

The Court today, however, interprets the Clause to permit the government to prohibit, without justification, conduct mandated by an individual's religious beliefs, so long as that prohibition is generally applicable. But a law that prohibits certain conduct—conduct that happens to be an act of worship for someone—manifestly does prohibit that person's free exercise of his religion. . . . Moreover, that person is barred from freely exercising his religion regardless of whether the law prohibits the conduct only when engaged in for religious reasons, only by members of that religion, or by all persons. . . . The Court responds that generally applicable laws are "one large step" removed from laws aimed at specific religious practices. The First Amendment, however, does not distinguish between laws that are generally applicable and laws that target particular religious practices. Indeed, few States would be so naive as to enact a law directly prohibiting or burdening a religious practice as such. Our free exercise cases have all concerned generally applicable laws that had the effect of significantly burdening a religious practice. If the First Amendment is to have any vitality, it ought not be construed to cover only the extreme and hypothetical situation in which a State directly targets a religious practice. . . .

To say that a person's right to free exercise has been burdened, of course, does not mean that he has an absolute right to engage in the conduct. Under our established First Amendment jurisprudence, we have recognized that the freedom to act, unlike the freedom to believe, cannot be absolute. See, *e.g., Cantwell; Reynolds v. United States* (1879). . . .

The Court attempts to support its narrow reading of the Clause by claiming that "[w]e have never held that an individual's religious beliefs excuse him from compliance with an otherwise valid law prohibiting conduct that the State is free to regulate." But as the Court later notes, as it must, in cases such as *Cantwell* and *Yoder* we have in fact interpreted the Free Exercise Clause to forbid application of a generally applicable prohibition to religiously motivated conduct. . . . Indeed, in *Yoder* we expressly rejected the interpretation the Court now adopts. . . .

In my view . . . the essence of a free exercise claim is relief from a burden imposed by government on religious practices or beliefs, whether the burden is imposed directly through laws that prohibit or compel specific religious practices, or indirectly through laws that, in effect, make abandonment of one's own religion or conformity to the religious beliefs of others the price of an equal place in the civil community. . . . A State that makes criminal an individual's religiously motivated conduct burdens that individual's free exercise of religion in the severest manner possible, for it "results in the choice to the individual of either abandoning his religious principle or facing criminal prosecution." . . . . Indeed, we have never distinguished between cases in which a State conditions receipt of a benefit on conduct prohibited by religious beliefs and cases in which a State affirmatively prohibits such conduct. The *Sherbert* compelling interest test applies in both kinds of cases. . . . Once it has been shown that a government regulation or criminal prohibition burdens the free exercise of religion, we have consistently asked the Government to demonstrate that unbending application of its regulation to the religious objector "is essential to accomplish an overriding governmental interest," or represents "the least restrictive means of achieving some compelling state interest." . . . To me, the sounder approach—the approach more consistent with our role as judges to decide each case on its individual merits—is to apply this test in each case to determine whether the burden on the specific plaintiffs before us is constitutionally significant and whether the particular criminal interest asserted by the State before us is compelling. . . . The Court today gives no convincing reason to depart from settled First Amendment jurisprudence. There is nothing talismanic about neutral laws of general applicability or general criminal prohibitions, for laws neutral toward religion can coerce a person to violate his religious conscience or intrude upon his religious duties just as effectively as laws aimed at religion. . . . The Court's parade of horribles not only fails as a reason for discarding the compelling interest test, it instead demonstrates just the opposite: that courts have been quite capable of applying our free exercise jurisprudence to strike sensible balances between religious liberty and competing state interests.

Finally, the Court today suggests that the disfavoring of minority religions is an "unavoidable consequence" under our system of government and that accommodation of such religions must be left to the political process. In my view, however, the First Amendment was enacted precisely to protect the rights of those whose religious practices are not shared by the majority and may be viewed with hostility. The history of our free exercise doctrine amply demonstrates the harsh impact majoritarian rule has had on unpopular or emerging religious groups such as the Jehovah's Witnesses and the Amish. . . .

* * *

The Court's holding today not only misreads settled First Amendment precedent; it appears to be unnecessary to this case. I would reach the same result applying our established free exercise jurisprudence.

There is no dispute that Oregon's criminal prohibition of peyote places a severe burden on the ability of respondents to freely exercise their religion. Peyote is a sacrament of the Native American Church and is regarded as vital to respondents' ability to practice their religion. . . .

There is also no dispute that Oregon has a significant interest in enforcing laws that control the possession and use of controlled substances by its citizens. . . .

Thus, the critical question in this case is whether exempting respondents from the State's general criminal prohibition "will unduly interfere with fulfillment of the governmental interest." . . . Although the question is close, I would conclude that uniform application of Oregon's criminal prohibition is "essential to accomplish" . . . its overriding interest in preventing the physical harm caused by the use of a . . . controlled substance. Oregon's criminal prohibition represents that State's judgment that the possession and use of controlled substances, even by only one person, is inherently harmful and dangerous. Because the health effects caused by the use of controlled substances exist regardless of the motivation of the user, the use of such substances, even for religious purposes, violates the very purpose of the laws that prohibit them. . . . Moreover, in view of the societal interest in preventing trafficking in controlled substances, uniform application of the criminal prohibition at issue

is essential to the effectiveness of Oregon's stated interest in preventing any possession of peyote. . . .

I would therefore adhere to our established free exercise jurisprudence and hold that the State in this case has a compelling interest in regulating peyote use by its citizens and that accommodating respondents' religiously motivated conduct "will unduly interfere with fulfillment of the governmental interest." . . .

Accordingly, I concur in the judgment of the Court.

JUSTICE BLACKMUN, WITH WHOM JUSTICE BRENNAN AND JUSTICE MARSHALL JOIN, DISSENTING.

This Court over the years painstakingly has developed a consistent and exacting standard to test the constitutionality of a state statute that burdens the free exercise of religion. Such a statute may stand only if the law in general, and the State's refusal to allow a religious exemption in particular, are justified by a compelling interest that cannot be served by less restrictive means.

Until today, I thought this was a settled and inviolate principle of this Court's First Amendment jurisprudence. The majority, however, perfunctorily dismisses it as a "constitutional anomaly." As carefully detailed in Justice O'Connor's concurring opinion, the majority is able to arrive at this view only by mischaracterizing this Court's precedents. . . . This distorted view of our precedents leads the majority to conclude that strict scrutiny of a state law burdening the free exercise of religion is a "luxury" that a well-ordered society cannot afford, and that the repression of minority religions is an "unavoidable consequence of democratic government." I do not believe the Founders thought their dearly bought freedom from religious persecution a "luxury," but an essential element of liberty—and they could not have thought religious intolerance "unavoidable," for they drafted the Religion Clauses precisely in order to avoid that intolerance. . . .

. . . The State cannot plausibly assert that unbending application of a criminal prohibition is essential to fulfill any compelling interest, if it does not, in fact, attempt to enforce that prohibition. In this case, the State actually has not evinced any concrete interest in enforcing its drug laws against religious users of peyote. Oregon has never sought to prosecute respondents, and does not claim that it has made significant enforcement efforts against other religious users of peyote. The State's asserted interest thus amounts only to the symbolic preservation of an unenforced prohibition. But a government interest in "symbolism, even symbolism for so worthy a cause as the abolition of unlawful drugs," cannot suffice to abrogate the constitutional rights of individuals. . . .

I dissent.

Smith represents a significant change in the standards governing free exercise disputes. For the first time since the *Sherbert* test was articulated, the Court explicitly rejected that test. To be sure, the justices had failed to apply it in cases such as *Goldman*, but here the Court was eradicating the *Sherbert-Yoder* lineage of cases and returning to the kind of analysis it used in *Reynolds v. United States*.

In place of the *Sherbert-Yoder* test, the Court now held that the free exercise clause does not relieve an individual from the obligation to comply with a valid and neutral law of general applicability, even if that law commands behavior inconsistent with the person's religious teachings. The articulation of this new standard meant, as one scholar put it, that the Court had "brought free exercise jurisprudence full circle by reaffirming the . . . doctrine of *Reynolds*" and rejecting the compelling interest approach of *Sherbert*.[11]

But had the Court really returned to the doctrine articulated in *Reynolds*? The opinion in *Smith* is certainly consistent with the belief/action distinction in that case; although the government could not target the principles of the Native American Church, it was free to prohibit actions that might be, for some, religious obligations. The ruling in *Smith*, however, only permits a "neutral law of general applicability," and the law in *Reynolds* was decidedly not neutral. Indeed, the Morrill Anti-Bigamy Act of 1862 was clearly motivated by hostility toward the Mormon Church. Antipolygamists in Congress, adhering to the prevailing Protestant morality, saw polygamy as a violation of biblical command. As Representative Thomas Nelson of Tennessee explained in a speech in 1860, "[W]e shall act only 'in subordination to the great Lawgiver, transcribing and publishing His precepts.' He has said, 'Thou shalt not commit adultery.' He has authorized marriage alone with one person at the same time, and when the relation is extended further against His law, it becomes adulterous."[12] Although justified as upholding an established cultural norm that protected women from subjugation, the Morrill Act was, in fact, designed to preserve a particular set of Christian principles.

Under *Smith*, the validity of such a law now seemed doubtful. Justice Scalia suggested as much in his opinion in *Smith* when he wrote, "It would be true, we think (though no case of ours has involved the point), that a state would be 'prohibiting the free exercise [of

religion]' if it sought to ban such acts . . . only when they are engaged in for religious reasons. . . ." Just three years after *Smith*, the Court confronted that situation. Having declared that religiously neutral laws only had to be plausibly connected to a legitimate state goal, the Court would have to decide what standard to employ when a state singled out religious acts for prohibition.

Church of the Lukumi Babalu Aye Inc. v. City of Hialeah

508 U.S. 520 (1993)
https://caselaw.findlaw.com/us-supreme-court/508/520.html
Oral arguments available at https://www.oyez.org/
  cases/1992/91-948
Vote: 9 (Blackmun, Kennedy, O'Connor, Rehnquist, Scalia, Souter, Stevens, Thomas, White)

OPINION OF THE COURT: *Kennedy*

CONCURRING OPINION: *Scalia*

CONCURRING OPINION: *Souter*

CONCURRING OPINION: *Blackmun*

Santeria is a religion that originated in Cuba. Its original practitioners were African slaves, who absorbed elements of Roman Catholicism into religious traditions that were native to their homeland, Yorubaland, which was comprised primarily of modern-day Nigeria. Adherents of Santeria, which means "the way of the saints," commune with deities known as orishas. To sustain a personal relationship with these orishas, practitioners of Santeria engage in animal sacrifice. In a variety of ceremonies—rituals related to birth, death, and marriage, for instance—they sacrifice small animals, such as chickens, goats, sheep, and turtles. After their sacrifice, most of the animals are cooked and eaten as part of a religious celebration.

Although there are relatively few Santerians, several thousand live in south Florida. In the Miami suburb of Hialeah, after a group of Santerians announced plans to open a church, the city council held an emergency meeting in which both residents and council members openly expressed their antagonism. One city official declared, "This community will not tolerate religious practices which are abhorrent to its citizens," and the president of the council asked, "What can we do to prevent the Church from opening?" In response, the city enacted regulations that ostensibly were designed to guard against animal cruelty and to limit the public health risks associated with the disposal of animal waste. These rules prohibited the killing of animals when the primary purpose was not consumption as food, and they also forbade the ritual slaughter of animals, regardless

---

[11]Frederick Mark Gedicks, "Religion," in *The Oxford Companion to the Supreme Court*, ed. Kermit L. Hall (New York: Oxford University Press, 1992), 725.

[12]Quoted in Sarah Barringer Gordon, *The Mormon Question: Polygamy and Constitutional Conflict in Nineteenth Century America* (Chapel Hill: University of North Carolina Press, 2002), 80.

of whether those animals were consumed. Since the Santerians ritually slaughtered animals—and since the primary purpose was to offer a sacrifice to the orishas, not food consumption—the city had effectively outlawed the practice of Santeria. By contrast, those who might kill animals for sport, for medical research, or solely for food (including Jews who slaughter animals according to religious tradition) were not affected by these new rules.

The Santerians challenged these regulations in federal court, arguing that they interfered with religious exercise, but the trial court upheld the rules; ensuring the humane treatment of animals and protecting the public against the health risks posed by keeping and slaughtering animals in potentially unsanitary conditions were compelling state interests that justified the city's actions. After that decision was upheld by an appeals court, the Santerians sought review from the U.S. Supreme Court. The city maintained that, since its regulations applied to anyone who might mistreat animals or slaughter them unnecessarily, its actions were consistent with *Smith*. The Santerians suggested that Hialeah actually had two set of rules—one that prohibited killing animals for religious purposes and one that permitted killing animals for secular purposes.

JUSTICE KENNEDY DELIVERED THE OPINION OF THE COURT.

In addressing the constitutional protection for free exercise of religion, our cases establish the general proposition that a law that is neutral and of general applicability need not be justified by a compelling governmental interest even if the law has the incidental effect of burdening a particular religious practice. *Employment Div., Dept. of Human Resources of Oregon v. Smith* (1990). Neutrality and general applicability are interrelated, and, as becomes apparent in this case, failure to satisfy one requirement is a likely indication that the other has not been satisfied. A law failing to satisfy these requirements must be justified by a compelling governmental interest, and must be narrowly tailored to advance that interest. These ordinances fail to satisfy the *Smith* requirements. We begin by discussing neutrality. . . .

The record in this case compels the conclusion that suppression of the central element of the Santeria worship service was the object of the ordinances. First, though use of the words "sacrifice" and "ritual" does not compel a finding of improper targeting of the Santeria religion, the choice of these words is support for our conclusion. There are further respects in which the text of the city council's enactments discloses the improper attempt to target Santeria. Resolution 87-66 . . . recited that "residents and citizens of the City of Hialeah have expressed their concern that certain religions may propose to engage in practices which are inconsistent with public morals, peace or safety," and "reiterate[d]" the city's commitment to prohibit "any and all [such] acts of any and

all religious groups." No one suggests, and, on this record, it cannot be maintained, that city officials had in mind a religion other than Santeria . . . .

It is a necessary conclusion that almost the only conduct subject to [regulation] is the religious exercise of Santeria church members. The [ordinance] . . . prohibits the sacrifice of animals, but defines sacrifice as "to unnecessarily kill . . . an animal in a public or private ritual or ceremony not for the primary purpose of food consumption." The definition excludes almost all killings of animals except for religious sacrifice, and the primary purpose requirement narrows the proscribed category even further, in particular by exempting Kosher slaughter. . . . The net result of the gerrymander is that few, if any, killings of animals are prohibited other than Santeria sacrifice, which is proscribed because it occurs during a ritual or ceremony and its primary purpose is to make an offering to the orishas, not food consumption. Indeed, careful drafting ensured that, although Santeria sacrifice is prohibited, killings that are no more necessary or humane in almost all other circumstances are unpunished. . . .

[The ordinance] incorporates the Florida animal cruelty statute. Its prohibition is broad on its face, punishing "[w]hoever . . . unnecessarily . . . kills any animal." The city claims that this ordinance is the epitome of a neutral prohibition. The problem, however, is the interpretation given to the ordinance by respondent and the Florida attorney general. Killings for religious reasons are deemed unnecessary, whereas most other killings fall outside the prohibition. The city . . . deems hunting, slaughter of animals for food, eradication of insects and pests, and euthanasia as necessary. . . . Thus, religious practice is being singled out for discriminatory treatment. . . .

The legitimate governmental interests in protecting the public health and preventing cruelty to animals could be addressed by restrictions stopping far short of a flat prohibition of all Santeria sacrificial practice. If improper disposal, not the sacrifice itself, is the harm to be prevented, the city could have imposed a general regulation on the disposal of organic garbage. It did not do so. Indeed, counsel for the city conceded at oral argument that, under the ordinances, Santeria sacrifices would be illegal even if they occurred in licensed, inspected, and zoned slaughterhouses. Thus, these broad ordinances prohibit Santeria sacrifice even when it does not threaten the city's interest in the public health. . . .

. . . With regard to the city's interest in ensuring the adequate care of animals, regulation of conditions and treatment, regardless of why an animal is kept, is the logical response to the city's concern, not a prohibition on possession for the purpose of sacrifice. The same is true for the city's interest in prohibiting cruel methods of killing. . . . [T]he subject of the regulation should be the method of slaughter itself, not a religious classification that is said to bear some general relation to it. . . .

In sum, the neutrality inquiry leads to one conclusion: the ordinances had as their object the suppression of religion. The pattern we have recited discloses animosity to Santeria adherents and their religious practices; the ordinances, by their own terms, target this religious exercise; the texts of the ordinances were gerrymandered with care to proscribe religious killings of animals but to exclude almost all secular killings; and the ordinances suppress much more religious conduct than is necessary in order to achieve the legitimate ends asserted in their defense. These ordinances are not neutral, and the court below committed clear error in failing to reach this conclusion.

We turn next to a second requirement of the Free Exercise Clause, the rule that laws burdening religious practice must be of general applicability. . . .

. . . Despite the city's proffered interest in preventing cruelty to animals, the ordinances are drafted with care to forbid few killings but those occasioned by religious sacrifice. Many types of animal deaths or kills for nonreligious reasons are either not prohibited or approved by express provision. For example, fishing—which occurs in Hialeah—is legal. Extermination of mice and rats within a home is also permitted. Florida law . . . sanctions euthanasia of "stray, neglected, abandoned, or unwanted animals" [and] the infliction of pain or suffering "in the interest of medical science." . . .

The city concedes that "neither the State of Florida nor the City has enacted a generally applicable ban on the killing of animals." It asserts, however, that animal sacrifice is "different" from the animal killings that are permitted by law. According to the city, it is "self-evident" that killing animals for food is "important"; the eradication of insects and pests is "obviously justified"; and the euthanasia of excess animals "makes sense." These [assertions] do not explain why religion alone must bear the burden of the ordinances, when many of these secular killings fall within the city's interest in preventing the cruel treatment of animals.

. . . [W]ith regard to the city's interest in public health, . . . [t]he health risks posed by the improper disposal of animal carcasses are the same whether Santeria sacrifice or some nonreligious killing preceded it. The city does not, however, prohibit hunters from bringing their kill to their houses, nor does it regulate disposal after their activity. Despite substantial testimony at trial that the same public health hazards result from improper disposal of garbage by restaurants, restaurants are outside the scope of the ordinances. Improper disposal is a general problem that causes substantial health risks, but which respondent addresses only when it results from religious exercise. . . .

We conclude, in sum, that each of Hialeah's ordinances pursues the city's governmental interests only against conduct motivated by religious belief. The ordinances "ha[ve] every appearance of a prohibition that society is prepared to impose upon [Santeria worshippers], but not upon itself." *The Florida Star v. B.J.F.* (SCALIA, J., concurring in part and concurring in judgment). This precise evil is what the requirement of general applicability is designed to prevent.

A law burdening religious practice that is not neutral or not of general application must undergo the most rigorous of scrutiny. To satisfy the commands of the First Amendment, a law restrictive of religious practice must advance "interests of the highest order," and must be narrowly tailored in pursuit of those interests. *Wisconsin v. Yoder* (1972). The compelling interest standard that we apply once a law fails to meet the *Smith* requirements is not "water[ed] . . . down" but "really means what it says." *Employment Div., Dept. of Human Resources of Oregon v. Smith* (1990). A law that targets religious conduct for distinctive treatment or advances legitimate governmental interests only against conduct with a religious motivation will survive strict scrutiny only in rare cases. It follows from what we have already said that these ordinances cannot withstand this scrutiny.

First, even were the governmental interests compelling, the ordinances are not drawn in narrow terms to accomplish those interests. . . . The proffered objectives are not pursued with respect to analogous nonreligious conduct, and those interests could be achieved by narrower ordinances that burdened religion to a far lesser degree. The absence of narrow tailoring suffices to establish the invalidity of the ordinances.

Respondent has not demonstrated, moreover, that, in the context of these ordinances, its governmental interests are compelling. Where government restricts only conduct protected by the First Amendment and fails to enact feasible measures to restrict other conduct producing substantial harm or alleged harm of the same sort, the interest given in justification of the restriction is not compelling. . . .

. . . Those in office must be resolute in resisting importunate demands and must ensure that the sole reasons for imposing the burdens of law and regulation are secular. Legislators may not devise mechanisms, overt or disguised, designed to persecute or oppress a religion or its practices. The laws here in question were enacted contrary to these constitutional principles, and they are void.

JUSTICE SCALIA, WITH WHOM THE CHIEF JUSTICE JOINS, CONCURRING IN PART AND CONCURRING IN THE JUDGMENT.

. . . As I have noted elsewhere, it is virtually impossible to determine the singular "motive" of a collective legislative body, see, e.g., *Edwards v. Aguillard* (1987) (SCALIA, J., dissenting), and this Court has a long tradition of refraining from such inquiries, see, e.g., *Fletcher v. Peck* (1810); *United States v. O'Brien* (1968).

Perhaps there are contexts in which determination of legislative motive must be undertaken. But I do not think that is true of analysis under the First Amendment (or the Fourteenth, to the extent it incorporates the First). The First Amendment does not refer to the purposes for which legislators enact laws, but to the effects of the laws enacted: "Congress shall make no law . . . prohibiting the free exercise [of religion]. . . ." This does not put us in the business of invalidating laws by reason of the evil motives of their authors. Had the Hialeah City Council set out resolutely to suppress the practices of Santeria, but ineptly adopted ordinances that failed to do so, I do not see how those laws could be said to "prohibi[t] the free exercise" of religion. Nor, in my view, does it matter that a legislature consists entirely of the pure-hearted, if the law it enacts in fact singles out a religious practice for special burdens. Had the ordinances here been passed with no motive on the part of any councilman except the ardent desire to prevent cruelty to animals (as might in fact have been the case), they would nonetheless be invalid.

JUSTICE SOUTER, CONCURRING IN PART AND CONCURRING IN THE JUDGMENT.

Since holding in 1940 that the Free Exercise Clause applies to the States, the Court repeatedly has stated that the Clause sets strict limits on the government's power to burden religious exercise, whether it is a law's object to do so or its unanticipated effect. *Smith* responded to these statements by suggesting that the Court did not really mean what it said. . . . I would have trouble concluding that the Court has not meant what it has said in more than a dozen cases over several decades, particularly when, in the same period, it repeatedly applied the compelling-interest test to require exemptions. . . . In sum, it seems to me difficult to escape the conclusion that, whatever *Smith*'s virtues, they do not include a comfortable fit with settled law.

. . . Save in a handful of passing remarks, the Court has not explored the history of the [Free Exercise] Clause since its early attempts in 1879 and 1890, attempts that recent scholarship makes clear were incomplete. The curious absence of history from our free exercise decisions creates a stark contrast with our cases under the Establishment Clause, where historical analysis has been so prominent.

This is not the place to explore the history that a century of free exercise opinions have overlooked, and it is enough to note that, when the opportunity to reexamine *Smith* presents itself, we may consider recent scholarship raising serious questions about the *Smith* rule's consonance with the original understanding and purpose of the Free Exercise Clause. There appears to be a strong argument from the Clause's development in the First Congress, from its origins in the post-Revolution state constitutions and pre-Revolution colonial charters, and from the philosophy of rights to which the Framers adhered, that the Clause was originally understood to preserve a right to engage in activities necessary to fulfill one's duty to one's God, unless those activities threatened the rights of others or the serious needs of the State. If, as this scholarship suggests, the Free Exercise Clause's original "purpose [was] to secure religious liberty in the individual by prohibiting any invasions thereof by civil authority," *School Dist. of Abington v. Schempp* (1963), then there would be powerful reason to interpret the Clause to accord with its natural reading, as applying to all laws prohibiting religious exercise in fact, not just those aimed at its prohibition . . . .

The extent to which the Free Exercise Clause requires government to refrain from impeding religious exercise defines nothing less than the respective relationships in our constitutional democracy of the individual to government and to God. "Neutral, generally applicable" laws, drafted as they are from the perspective of the nonadherent, have the unavoidable potential of putting the believer to a choice between God and government. Our cases now present competing answers to the question when government, while pursuing secular ends, may compel disobedience to what one believes religion commands. The case before us is rightly decided without resolving the existing tension, which remains for another day when it may be squarely faced.

JUSTICE BLACKMUN, WITH WHOM JUSTICE O'CONNOR JOINS, CONCURRING IN THE JUDGMENT.

When the State enacts legislation that intentionally or unintentionally places a burden upon religiously motivated practice, it must justify that burden by "showing that it is the least restrictive means of achieving some compelling state interest." *Thomas v. Review Bd. of Indiana Employment Security Div.* (1981). . . .

When a law discriminates against religion as such, as do the ordinances in this case, it automatically will fail strict scrutiny under *Sherbert v. Verner* (1963). This is true because a law that targets religious practice for disfavored treatment both burdens the free exercise of religion and, by definition, is not precisely tailored to a compelling governmental interest. . . .

It is only in the rare case that a state or local legislature will enact a law directly burdening religious practice as such. Because respondent here does single out religion in this way, the present case is an easy one to decide.

A harder case would be presented if petitioners were requesting an exemption from a generally applicable anticruelty law. The result in the case before the Court today, and the fact that every Member of the Court concurs in that result, does not necessarily reflect this Court's views of the strength of a State's interest in prohibiting cruelty to animals. This case does not present, and I therefore decline to reach, the question whether the Free Exercise Clause would require a religious exemption from a law that sincerely pursued the goal of protecting animals from cruel treatment.

In a legal sense, the result in this case is perhaps unsurprising. At least since *Sherbert*, the Court had intimated that prohibiting conduct because of its religious motivation required exacting scrutiny from the

Court; here, the justices simply made that rule explicit. Politically, however, this case was more highly charged. Even though the case involved a relatively small denomination with unorthodox practices, a fair number of more mainstream religious groups—the American Jewish Congress, the Baptist Joint Committee for Public Affairs, the Catholic League for Religious and Civil Rights, and the Church of Jesus Christ of Latter-day Saints, to name a few—aligned in support of the Santerians. The reason was that the *Smith* decision was still reverberating among religious organizations, and they hoped to use this case to articulate how, under the "neutral law of general application" standard, they remained vulnerable to restrictions of their own religious practices. Because *Smith* departed from the compelling interest/least restrictive means approach of *Sherbet* and *Yoder*, general laws that regulated such activities as education, employment, and medical care would now prevail over any sincere religious objections, and all manner of churches saw a potential loss of religious liberty.

Soon after the justices handed down their opinion in *Smith*, interest groups began to lobby Congress to overturn the decision. As Senator Edward M. Kennedy, D-Mass., put it, these groups feared that, under the new standard, "dry communities could ban the use of wine in communion services, government meat inspectors could require changes in the preparation of kosher food and school boards could force children to attend sex education classes [contrary to their religious beliefs]."[13] With support from politicians as varied in ideological approach as Senators Kennedy and Orrin Hatch, R-Utah, Congress began debating legislative options to counteract the Supreme Court's newly articulated position.

As a legislative reaction began to take shape, the Court was in the midst of deciding *Lukumi*. Given the uproar precipitated by *Smith*, some legal observers were hopeful that the justices would use the Santeria case to clarify—and perhaps even limit—the Court's new free exercise doctrine. Congress, however, was not going to wait; in March 1993, a few months before the Court would issue its *Lukumi* decision, the Religious Freedom Restoration Act (RFRA) was introduced in both houses of Congress, and by the fall it was enacted into law. The purpose of the statute was to counteract the Court's more pro-regulatory policies as manifested in *Smith*. The law's most important provision, which applied to both state and federal governments, reads as follows:

---

[13]Quoted in Adam Clymer, "Congress Moves to Ease Curb on Religious Acts," *New York Times*, May 10, 1993, A9.

Government shall not substantially burden a person's exercise of religion even if the burden results from a rule of general applicability [unless the government can show that the burden] (1) is in furtherance of a compelling governmental interest; and (2) is the least restrictive means of furthering that compelling governmental interest.

The language should sound familiar. The statute codified the compelling interest/least restrictive means test used in *Sherbert* and *Yoder*. It explicitly rejected the general applicability approach ushered in by *Smith*. Congress was, through legislation, extending more protection to religious exercise rights than the Court was offering through its interpretation of the First Amendment. And, it is important to note, the statute commanded that all state, local, and federal government officials, including judges, use this standard.

Although most religious groups praised RFRA, it troubled state and local officials, who exercise police powers in innumerable ways to promote the public welfare. Did the act mean that every routine law and regulation would be subject to its strict requirements? What would constitute a substantial burden on a person's religious exercise? What standards would be used to establish a compelling government interest and the least restrictive means?

It did not take long for the statute to be challenged. A dispute arose between St. Peter the Apostle Catholic Church and the city of Boerne, Texas. Based on its historic preservation policies, the city had denied the church permission to tear down its existing building and erect a new structure large enough to serve its expanding congregation. The Catholic archdiocese claimed that under RFRA the city was without power to block construction.

In **City of Boerne v. Flores** (1997), the Court dealt a blow to those who had hoped that RFRA would reinstate the *Sherbert* and *Yoder* standard. In enacting the law, Congress had relied upon the Fourteenth Amendment, which both prohibits states from "depriv[ing] any person of life, liberty, or property, without due process of law" and empowers Congress to enforce that prohibition. The free exercise of religion is a "liberty" that is insulated from infringement by the states, and as far as Congress was concerned this law merely protected that right. The justices, however, explained that Congress's power was limited to remedying violations of the Constitution, not determining the meaning of the Constitution. In enacting

Father Tony Cummins in front of St. Peter the Apostle Catholic Church in Boerne, Texas. In 1997 the church lost its battle to replace the structure, which the city had declared a historic landmark.

the law, Congress was not trying to redress widespread religious discrimination; indeed, the legislative history cited virtually no examples of state hostility to religious groups. Instead, Congress simply wanted to restore the free exercise clause to its pre-*Smith* understanding. The Court ruled that the meaning of the clause, like the rest of the Constitution, could only be determined by the judicial branch.

Although RFRA's provisions limiting the federal government were not at issue in *City of Boerne*—and therefore left untouched—the ruling that Congress had exceeded its Fourteenth amendment power signaled that states were still free to enact neutral laws. So, Congress decided to try again, this time relying upon its authority to regulate interstate commerce and to spend for the general welfare, and in 2000 the Religious Land Use and Institutionalized Persons Act (RLUIPA) was signed into law by President Bill Clinton as a supplement to the surviving portions of RFRA. The provisions of the law applied to any zoning activity or prison facility that received federal financial assistance or affected interstate or foreign commerce. Under the law, religious exercise rights could not be restricted without a compelling reason to do so using the least restrictive means possible. Since state and local governments are typically responsible for zoning decisions and prison administration, this

new law aimed to ensure that at least some of their decisions would be subject to strict scrutiny in cases involving religious freedom.

Shortly after RLUIPA was enacted, a group of inmates sued the Ohio Department of Rehabilitation and Correction for violating their rights under the statute. The prisoners, members of the Satanist, Wicca, and Asatru sects, along with adherents of the Church of Jesus Christ Christian, claimed that Ohio authorities discriminated against them. They were not allowed access to religious literature, opportunities for group worship, freedom to engage in religious dress, or the use of ceremonial items that were available to members of mainstream religions. In *Cutter v. Wilkinson* (2005), the Court unanimously ruled that Congress was within its authority to require accommodation of the religious liberty of persons institutionalized in prison systems receiving federal assistance.

By enacting the sister statutes of RFRA and RLUIPA, Congress provided broader statutory protections for religious liberty than the Supreme Court granted in its *Smith* test interpretation of the Constitution's free exercise clause. This, of course, created a more favorable option for those desiring to challenge federal government restrictions on religious practices. Litigants have used this opportunity with considerable success.

In *Gonzales v. O Centro Espirita Beneficente Uniao do Vegetal* (2006), for example, the Court upheld the application of RFRA to the federal government, ruling that U.S. Customs agents could not block importing controlled substances from the Amazon used to make hoasca tea, a drink traditionally used for sacramental purposes by a Christian Spiritist sect that originated in Brazil. Similarly, in *Holt v. Hobbs* (2015), an Arkansas inmate turned to RLUIPA for relief when corrections authorities refused his request to wear a short beard during his period of incarceration. The Supreme Court held unanimously that the devout Muslim's rights under the law had been violated.

The most controversial of the RFRA/RLUIPA decisions, however, was *Burwell v. Hobby Lobby* (2014). This dispute arose over a question of compliance with the 2010 Patient Protection and Affordable Care Act (often referred to as Obamacare). The law required companies to offer health insurance to their employees, including benefits for a range of contraceptive medications and devices.

David and Barbara Green founded Hobby Lobby, a family-owned chain of arts and crafts stores. The Greens are deeply committed Christians who believe that birth control methods that terminate the life of a fertilized embryo are against God's will, and they objected to some of the required contraceptive coverage. Because noncompliance potentially would trigger heavy government fines of up to $1.3 million per day, the Greens and their Hobby Lobby stores sought protection under the Religious Freedom Restoration Act.

The Supreme Court agreed with the Greens. The Affordable Care Act, a majority found, substantially infringed on religious liberty, forcing the owners to run the company contrary to their religious beliefs. Although the Court concluded that providing health care coverage was a compelling government interest, the justices ruled that the coverage mandate and its fines were not the least restrictive means to accomplish the government's goals; since the federal government already had an exemption for religious nonprofits that had objections to the law, it could simply extend that exemption to for-profit companies whose owners had similar concerns.

This decision shifted the political ground of religious protection. Prior to *Hobby Lobby*, the Religious Freedom Restoration Act was seen as a generally liberal piece of legislation that safeguarded the members of minority religions from unnecessary government regulation. Here, RFRA allowed members of a conservative Protestant faith to excuse themselves from obligations imposed by a major social reform program. Liberals feared that RFRA, to which they previously had given strong support, would now further arm conservative groups—groups that already enjoyed substantial memberships and financial support—to impede the implementation of progressive social policies.

It is important to bear in mind, however, that RFRA and RLUIPA are only statutory, not constitutional, protections of religious liberty; Congress is free to modify or even eliminate those laws. Under the Court's current doctrines, the free exercise clause only requires neutral laws that apply broadly (*Smith*), while laws that single out religion for disfavored treatment must meet the demands of strict scrutiny (*Lukumi*). This was illustrated in three of the Court's more recent free exercise decisions. In *Trinity Lutheran Church of Columbia, Inc. v. Comer* (2017), the Court held that Missouri's program offering nonprofit organizations playground surfaces made from recycled tires could not be denied to a preschool and daycare center because it was owned and operated by a church. Similarly, in *Espinoza v. Montana Department of Revenue* (2020), the justices invalidated a state policy that provided tuition assistance for parents to send their children to private secular schools but not private religious schools. And in

Masterpiece Cakeshop, Ltd. v. Colorado Civil Rights Commission (2018), which involved a claim of discrimination against a bakery owner who refused for religious reasons to make a cake for a same-sex wedding, the Court ruled that a state civil rights commission violated the free exercise clause when one of its members openly criticized the baker's religious beliefs. These cases highlight the problems created by policies that impose disabilities on religion. In *Christian Legal Society v. Martinez* (2010), by contrast, the Court noted that a state university that required campus organizations to be open to all students was not required to grant an exemption to a religious group that sought to exclude students who did not share its religious convictions. As long as the state adheres to neutrality, its actions will likely survive free exercise challenge.

There is a stark contrast between the Supreme Court's constitutional decisions, which tend to favor government regulations that incidentally tread on religion, and its statutory decisions, which more often support religious freedom. These disparate approaches leave the law governing religious exercise somewhat uncertain. Litigation initiated by members of both majority and minority faiths, combined with states adopting their own RFRA-style laws, will likely ensure that the justices will continue to be drawn into questions of religious liberty.

RELIGIOUS ESTABLISHMENT

In addition to its free exercise provision, the First Amendment contains a second religious guarantee, the establishment clause: "Congress shall make no law respecting an establishment of religion." But exactly what did the framers intend this clause to prohibit? In the letter he wrote to the Danbury Baptist Association in 1802, Thomas Jefferson proclaimed that the First Amendment built "a wall of separation between Church and State." But what sort of wall did Jefferson imagine? Did it mean, as some suggest, that government was only forbidden to establish a national religion? Or would it bar all cooperative interactions between church and state? Or something in between?

The answers to these questions are not clear, but three alternative interpretations have been advanced over the years:

1. The religious establishment clause erects a solid wall of separation between church and state, prohibiting most, if not all, forms of public aid for or support of religion.

2. The religious establishment clause may erect a wall of separation between church and state, but that wall forbids only the favoring by the state of one religion over another— not nondiscriminatory support or aid for all religions.

3. The religious establishment clause prohibits only the establishment of an official national religion.

Individuals who favor the most impenetrable partition between church and state subscribe to the first of these interpretations. These "separationists" believe that freedom is best served when government is completely barred from commingling with religious organizations. The second and third interpretations would allow more interaction between religious interests and the government. For example, these "accommodationist" positions would generally allow government aid to certain religion-sponsored activities as long as no particular religion is favored over any other religion. Similarly, religion itself could not be favored over irreligion.

Generally, the Court's decisions have fluctuated between the first and second of the alternative interpretations, but most constitutional experts have evaluated the justices' attempts to develop a consistent, coherent, and long-lasting interpretation of the establishment clause as disappointing. As one scholar has noted, "From a lawyer's point of view, the Establishment Clause is the most frustrating part of First Amendment law. The cases are an impossible tangle of divergent doctrines and seemingly conflicting results."[14]

The Court's quest to develop a sound establishment clause jurisprudence began in 1899 when it decided the case of **Bradfield v. Roberts**. At issue was a congressional appropriation of $30,000 to Providence Hospital in Washington, D.C., for the construction of facilities to be used to treat indigent patients who had contracted contagious diseases. The appropriation was challenged because the hospital was owned and operated by the Sisters of Charity, a religious order of Roman Catholic nuns. The justices, however, unanimously rejected the challenge. The Court found little relevance in the fact that Catholic nuns administered the hospital. Important to the Court was the purpose of the facility, and in this case the justices found the appropriated money to have a secular, nonreligious, purpose.

Bradfield is significant because it demonstrated from the very start that the Court was willing to allow some aid to religious institutions, especially if the aid was intended to advance a clear secular purpose. Although it emphasized the importance of considering the government's intent—something that would later figure prominently in the Court's establishment clause cases—the decision fell short of offering a comprehensive legal standard by which to adjudicate future claims.

The question of government aid to religious institutions, as *Bradfield* exemplifies, is just one of a number of issues that have come before the justices repeatedly. Others have included challenges to the use of public facilities by religious groups, prayer at government-sponsored events, the infusion of religious teachings into public school curricula, and government displays of religious symbols.

Establishment Clause Developments through the Warren Court Era

Almost fifty years elapsed between *Bradfield* and the next important religious establishment case, *Everson v. Board of Education* (1947). As you read the Court's decision in *Everson*, consider these questions: Did the Court establish any legal standards by which to determine whether state practices violate the establishment clause? What view of the relationship between church and state did the Court adopt?

Everson v. Board of Education

330 U.S. 1 (1947)
http://caselaw.findlaw.com/us-supreme-court/330/1.html
Vote: 5 (Black, Douglas, Murphy, Reed, Vinson)
    4 (Burton, Frankfurter, Jackson, Rutledge)

OPINION OF THE COURT: *Black*

DISSENTING OPINIONS: *Jackson, Rutledge*

In 1941 New Jersey passed a law authorizing local school boards that provided "any transportation for public school children to and from school" also to supply transportation to children living in the district who attended nonprofit private schools. At the time New Jersey enacted this legislation, at least fifteen other states had similar laws.

Ewing Township decided to use tax dollars to reimburse parents for transportation costs incurred in sending their children to

---

[14]Daniel A. Farber, *The First Amendment* (New York: Foundation Press, 1998), 263.

school. Because the township had no public high schools of its own, the reimbursement policy covered the transportation expenses of parents sending their children to three neighboring public high schools. It also covered expenses for students attending four private schools, all of which were affiliated with the Roman Catholic Church and provided regular religious instruction along with normal secular subjects. The average annual payment to parents sending their children to public or Catholic schools was $40 per student.

Arch Everson, a taxpayer living in the district, challenged the reimbursements to parents sending their children to religious schools. He claimed that this money supported religion in violation of the establishment clause of the First Amendment.

MR. JUSTICE BLACK DELIVERED THE OPINION OF THE COURT.

The meaning and scope of the First Amendment, preventing establishment of religion or prohibiting the free exercise thereof . . . have been several times elaborated by the decisions of this Court prior to the application of the First Amendment to the states by the Fourteenth. The broad meaning given the Amendment by these earlier cases has been accepted by this Court in its decisions concerning an individual's religious freedom rendered since the Fourteenth Amendment was interpreted to make the prohibitions of the First applicable to state action abridging religious freedom. There is every reason to give the same application and broad interpretation to the "establishment of religion" clause. . . .

The "establishment of religion" clause of the First Amendment means at least this: Neither a state nor the Federal Government can set up a church. Neither can pass laws which aid one religion, aid all religions, or prefer one religion over another. Neither can force nor influence a person to go to or to remain away from church against his will or force him to profess a belief or disbelief in any religion. No person can be punished for entertaining or professing religious beliefs or disbeliefs, for church attendance or nonattendance. No tax in any amount, large or small, can be levied to support any religious activities or institutions, whatever they may be called, or whatever form they may adopt to teach or practice religion. Neither a state nor the Federal Government can, openly or secretly, participate in the affairs of any religious organizations or groups and vice versa. In the words of Jefferson, the clause against establishment of religion by law was intended to erect "a wall of separation between Church and State."

We must consider the New Jersey statute in accordance with the foregoing limitations imposed by the First Amendment. But we must not strike that state statute down if it is within the state's constitutional power even though it approaches the verge of that power. New Jersey cannot consistently with the "establishment of religion" clause of the First Amendment contribute tax-raised funds to the support of an institution which teaches the tenets and faith of any church. On the other hand, other language of the amendment commands that New Jersey cannot hamper its citizens in the free exercise of their own religion. Consequently, it cannot exclude individual Catholics, Lutherans, Mohammedans, Baptists, Jews, Methodists, Non-believers, Presbyterians, or the members of any other faith, *because of their faith, or lack of it,* from receiving the benefits of public welfare legislation. While we do not mean to intimate that a state could not provide transportation only to children attending public schools, we must be careful, in protecting the citizens of New Jersey against state-established churches, to be sure that we do not inadvertently prohibit New Jersey from extending its general State law benefits to all its citizens without regard to their religious belief.

Measured by these standards, we cannot say that the First Amendment prohibits New Jersey from spending tax-raised funds to pay the bus fares of parochial school pupils as a part of a general program under which it pays the fares of pupils attending public and other schools. It is undoubtedly true that children are helped to get to church schools. There is even a possibility that some of the children might not be sent to the church schools if the parents were compelled to pay their children's bus fares out of their own pockets when transportation to a public school would have been paid for by the State. . . . Moreover, state-paid policemen, detailed to protect children going to and from church schools from the very real hazards of traffic, would serve much the same purpose and accomplish much the same result as state provisions intended to guarantee free transportation of a kind which the state deems to be best for the school children's welfare. And parents might refuse to risk their children to the serious danger of traffic accidents going to and from parochial schools, the approaches to which were not protected by policemen. Similarly, parents might be reluctant to permit their children to attend schools which the state had cut off from such general government services as ordinary police and fire protection, connections for sewage disposal, public highways and sidewalks. Of course, cutting off church schools from these services, so separate and so indisputably marked off from the religious function, would make it far more difficult for the schools to operate. But such is obviously not the purpose of the First Amendment. That Amendment requires the state to be a neutral in its relations with groups of religious believers and non-believers; it does not require the state to be their adversary. State power is no more to be used so as to handicap religions, than it is to favor them.

. . . The State contributes no money to the [religious] schools. It does not support them. Its legislation, as applied, does no more than provide a general program to help parents get their children, regardless of their religion, safely and expeditiously to and from accredited schools.

The First Amendment has erected a wall between church and state. That wall must be kept high and impregnable. We could not approve the slightest breach. New Jersey has not breached it here.

Affirmed.

MR. JUSTICE JACKSON, DISSENTING.

I find myself, contrary to first impressions, unable to join in this decision. I have a sympathy, though it is not ideological, with Catholic citizens who are compelled by law to pay taxes for public schools, and also feel constrained by conscience and discipline to support other schools for their own children. Such relief to them as this case involves is not in itself a serious burden to taxpayers and I had assumed it to be as little serious in principle. Study of this case convinces me otherwise. . . .

It seems to me that the basic fallacy in the Court's reasoning, which accounts for its failure to apply the principles it avows, is in ignoring the essentially religious test by which beneficiaries of this expenditure are selected. A policeman protects a Catholic, of course—but not because he is a Catholic; it is because he is a man and a member of our society. The fireman protects the Church school—but not because it is a Church school; it is because it is property, part of the assets of our society. Neither the fireman nor the policeman has to ask before he renders aid "Is this man or building identified with the Catholic Church?" But before these school authorities draw a check to reimburse for a student's fare they must ask just that question, and if the school is a Catholic one they may render aid because it is such, while if it is of any other faith or is run for profit, the help must be withheld. To consider the converse of the Court's reasoning will best disclose its fallacy. . . . Could we sustain an Act that said the police shall protect pupils on the way to or from public schools and Catholic schools but not while going to and coming from other schools, and firemen shall extinguish a blaze in public or Catholic school buildings but shall not put out a blaze in Protestant Church schools or private schools operated for profit? That is the true analogy to the case we have before us and I should think it pretty plain that such a scheme would not be valid.

The Court's holding is that this taxpayer has no grievance because the state has decided to make the reimbursement a public purpose and therefore we are bound to regard it as such. I agree that this Court has left, and always should leave to each state, great latitude in deciding for itself, in the light of its own conditions, what shall be public purposes in its scheme of things. It may socialize utilities and economic enterprises and make taxpayers' business out of what conventionally had been private business. It may make public business of individual welfare, health, education, entertainment or security. But it cannot make public business of religious worship or instruction, or of attendance at religious institutions of any character. . . .

MR. JUSTICE FRANKFURTER joins in this opinion.

MR. JUSTICE RUTLEDGE, WITH WHOM MR. JUSTICE FRANKFURTER, MR. JUSTICE JACKSON, AND MR. JUSTICE BURTON AGREE, DISSENTING.

"Congress shall make no law respecting an establishment of religion, or prohibiting the free exercise thereof. . . ." U.S. Const., Amend. I. . . .

"We, the General Assembly, do enact, That no man shall be compelled to frequent or support any religious worship, place, or ministry whatsoever, nor shall be enforced, restrained, molested, or burthened in his body or goods, nor shall otherwise suffer, on account of his religious opinions or belief. . . ." ["A Bill for Establishing Religious Freedom," General Assembly of Virginia, January 19, 1786.]

I cannot believe that the great author of those words, or the men who made them law, could have joined in this decision. Neither so high nor so impregnable today as yesterday is the wall raised between church and state by Virginia's great statute of religious freedom and the First Amendment, now made applicable to all the states by the Fourteenth. . . .

The Amendment's purpose was not to strike merely at the official establishment of a single sect, creed or religion, outlawing only a formal relation such as had prevailed in England and some of the colonies. Necessarily it was to uproot all such relationships. But the object was broader than separating church and state in this narrow sense. It was to create a complete and permanent separation of the spheres of religious activity and civil authority by comprehensively forbidding every form of public aid or support for religion. In proof the Amendment's wording and history unite with this Court's consistent utterances whenever attention has been fixed directly upon the question. . . .

Does New Jersey's action furnish support for religion by use of the taxing power? Certainly it does, if the test remains undiluted as Jefferson and Madison made it, that money taken by taxation from one is not to be used or given to support another's religious training or belief, or indeed one's own. Today as then the furnishing of "contributions of money for the propagation of opinions which he disbelieves" is the forbidden exaction; and the prohibition is absolute for whatever measure brings that consequence and whatever amount may be sought or given to that end. . . .

Two great drives are constantly in motion to abridge, in the name of education, the complete division of religion and civil authority which our forefathers made. One is to introduce religious education and observances into the public schools. The other, to obtain public funds for the aid and support of various private religious schools. In my opinion both avenues were closed by the Constitution. Neither should be opened by this Court. The matter is not one of quantity, to be measured by the amount of money expended. Now as in Madison's day it is one of principle, to keep separate the separate spheres as the First Amendment drew them; to prevent the first experiment upon our liberties; and to keep the question from becoming entangled in corrosive precedents. We should not be less strict to keep strong and untarnished the one side of the shield of religious freedom than we have been of the other.

The judgment should be reversed.

The *Everson* decision was rather curious in that it combined both separationist and accommodationist elements. In his opinion Justice Hugo Black built a strong case for a separation of church and state. He even cited Jefferson's notion of a high wall dividing religion and civic institutions and made a compelling case against using tax dollars to promote any religious activity. Even the dissenters largely agreed with this approach. Yet the majority ultimately decided that New Jersey's transportation support program had not breached the wall of separation.

This conclusion was based on a number of factors, most notably that the aid was secular in purpose (to provide safe transportation for students), that the aid was indirect (it was not paid directly to a religious institution), that the beneficiaries of the aid were children and their parents (not churches), and that the state was "neutral in its relations with groups of religious believers and non-believers" (all schoolchildren were eligible for aid). As we shall see, these themes recur in later Court opinions and foreshadow aspects of a legal standard the Court eventually formulated.

The outcome in *Everson* encouraged supporters of public aid to church-sponsored schools to campaign for additional assistance programs. They found a sympathetic audience in a number of state legislatures that devised various funding policies. When challenged in court, these assistance programs were generally approved as long as they met certain criteria.

Board of Education v. Allen (1968) serves as an example of the Warren Court's approach to these school aid disputes. The case concerned a New York State program that required local school authorities to purchase textbooks and then lend them free of charge to all children in grades 7 through 12 attending accredited schools, both public and private. The program was confined to textbooks used for secular subjects; religious books could not be distributed through the program. Based on the *Everson* precedent, the Supreme Court upheld the constitutionality of the New York textbook program against the challenge that aid going to students attending religious schools violated the establishment clause. The Court explained that, when the purpose of the aid is secular and the primary effect of the aid neither advances nor inhibits religion, a system of aid is likely to be constitutional. Employing that test, the majority determined that the program had the legitimate public purpose of promoting learning among the young and that the recipients of the aid were children and their parents, not the parochial schools attended. Justices Hugo Black (the author of the *Everson* decision), William O. Douglas, and Abe Fortas dissented. Although the law was limited to secular textbooks, Justice Douglas observed that it seemed to provide a mechanism by which the administrators of parochial schools could nevertheless obtain religious texts. These books, unlike transportation, had an ideological content; they were, he argued, the means "for propagating a particular religious creed or faith. How can we possibly approve such state aid to a religion?"

Although the justices of the Warren Court were open to certain school aid programs, the same cannot be said for the practice of prayer in the public schools. It was on this question that the Warren Court justices handed down some of their most controversial rulings, decisions that provoked strong opposition from the general public.

Throughout most of the nation's history, almost all public schools engaged in religious practices of some kind; they may have held devotional services, conducted Bible readings, or taught about religion. As the nation entered the 1960s these practices were particularly prevalent in the South, where three-quarters of public schools engaged in Bible reading, and along the East Coast, where two-thirds of the schools did so.[15] Separationist groups believed that such state-sponsored religious activities violated the establishment clause and set out to persuade the Supreme Court to eradicate them.

Their initial suit, ***Engel v. Vitale*** (1962), challenged a New York requirement that teachers each morning lead public school students in reciting a prayer written by the state's board of regents: "Almighty God, we acknowledge our dependence upon Thee, and we beg Thy blessings upon us, our parents, our teachers and our country." New York representatives argued that the prayer was nondenominational and that student participation was voluntary. The New York Civil Liberties Union, representing

---

[15]Frank J. Sorauf, *The Wall of Separation* (Princeton, NJ: Princeton University Press, 1976), 297.

parents from a Long Island school district, claimed that those considerations were irrelevant. What mattered was that the state had required reciting a prayer government officials had written, clearly a violation of the establishment clause.

The Court struck down the New York prayer requirement in a 6–1 vote.[16] Writing for the Court, Justice Black took a strong separationist stance:

> We think the constitutional prohibition against laws respecting the establishment of religion must at least mean that in this country it is no part of the business of government to compose official prayers for any group of the American people to recite as a part of a religious program carried out by the government.

Engel generated a tremendous public backlash. Less than 20 percent of the American public supported the Court's decision. Church leaders condemned it, and Congress considered proposing a constitutional amendment to overturn it. Most of the justices described themselves as "surprised and pained" by the negative reaction. Chief Justice Warren later wrote, "I vividly remember one bold newspaper headline, 'Court outlaws God.' Many religious leaders in this same spirit condemned the Court." Justice Tom Clark defended the Court's opinion in a public address: "Here was a state-written prayer circulated by the school district to state-employed teachers with instructions to have their pupils recite it. [The Constitution] provides that both state and Federal governments shall take no part respecting the establishment of religion. . . . 'No' means 'No.' That was all the Court decided."[17]

With all this uproar, it is no wonder that separationist groups were concerned when the Court agreed to hear arguments in *School District of Abington Township v. Schempp* and its companion case, *Murray v. Curlett*, appeals involving the more prevalent practice of Bible reading in public schools. Would the justices bow to public pressure and reverse their ruling in *Engel?*

---

[16]Justices Felix Frankfurter and Byron White did not participate in this case. Frankfurter had been incapacitated by a stroke, and the newly appointed White did not take his seat until after the case was argued.

[17]Both justices are quoted in Bernard Schwartz, *Super Chief* (New York: New York University Press, 1983), 441–442.

School District of Abington Township v. Schempp; Murray v. Curlett

374 U.S. 203 (1963)
http://caselaw.findlaw.com/us-supreme-court/374/203.html
*Oral arguments available at https://www.oyez.org/
cases/1962/142*
*Vote: 8 (Black, Brennan, Clark, Douglas, Goldberg, Harlan,
Warren, White)
1 (Stewart)*

OPINION OF THE COURT: *Clark*

CONCURRING OPINIONS: *Brennan, Douglas, Goldberg*

DISSENTING OPINION: *Stewart*

In 1956, Ellery Schempp, the eldest of Edward and Sidney Schempp's three children, objected to the Bible readings that were conducted each day at the school he attended, Abington High School. This practice was mandated by a Pennsylvania law that required that "at least ten verses from the Holy Bible shall be read, without comment, at the opening of each public school on each school day." Selected students read the Bible verses over the school's public-address system, and the reading was followed by a recitation of the Lord's Prayer, during which students stood and repeated the prayer in unison. Those students whose parents did not want them to participate could, under the law, leave the room.

Ellery decided to protest these devotional exercises. One morning during his junior year, he sat at his desk and read silently from the Koran as the Bible verses were broadcast over the school's intercom system. He remained seated and silent as his classmates stood to recite the Lord's Prayer. This protest led to his suspension from school.

Edward and Sidney supported their son's actions. They were not atheists; in fact, they were active members of a Unitarian church, where they regularly attended services. But they objected to the use of the King James Bible and what they saw as its presentation as a literal truth—Unitarians commonly believe that Jesus was only human, not divine—and they did not want Ellery or their younger children, Roger and Donna, to participate in this daily ritual. With the assistance of the American Civil Liberties Union, an organization of which they were members, the Schempps challenged the state law. As Ellery later explained, he believed the devotional exercises were "the establishment of the Christian religion or the Judeo-Christian religion."[18]

---

[18]Quoted in Stephen D. Solomon, *Ellery's Protest: How One Young Man Defied Tradition and Sparked the Battle over School Prayer* (Ann Arbor: University of Michigan Press, 2007), p. 24.

Sidney Schempp holds the Bible as her husband, Edward, and their younger children, Roger and Donna, look on at their home in Roslyn, Pennsylvania, on June 18, 1963, one day after the Supreme Court announced its decision in *School District of Abington Township v. Schempp*. The Court agreed with the Schempps that compulsory Bible reading in public schools violates the establishment clause.

The separationist groups representing the Schempps brought in religious leaders and other religious experts to support the claim that Bible reading inherently favored some religions over others and violated principles of religious establishment. Attorneys for the school board, on the other hand, sought to frame the case in moral rather than religious terms. They argued that it was a legitimate purpose of the public schools to foster among young people an understanding of the principles of right and wrong; the Bible could be understood as a resource from which to draw and illustrate those principles. By the time the case reached the Supreme Court, it was quite clear that they were asking the justices to overrule *Engel*.

Murray v. Curlett involved a similar challenge to a Maryland law that required daily readings from the Bible or the recitation of the Lord's Prayer in public schools. The suit was brought by prominent atheist Madalyn Murray on behalf of her son William J. Murray III *(see Box 12-1)*.

In the *Schempp* case, the federal district court in Pennsylvania struck down the public school Bible reading and prayer recitation requirement, but the Maryland Court of Appeals upheld the practice in the *Murray* case. The Supreme Court consolidated the two appeals into a single ruling.

MR. JUSTICE CLARK DELIVERED THE OPINION OF THE COURT.

[T]his Court has rejected unequivocally the contention that the Establishment Clause forbids only governmental preference of one religion over another. Almost 20 years ago in *Everson* the Court said that "[n]either a state nor the Federal Government can set up a church. Neither can pass laws which aid one religion, aid all religions, or prefer one religion over another." . . .

. . . In short, the Court held that the Amendment

"requires the state to be a neutral in its relations with groups of religious believers and non-believers; it does not require the state to be their adversary. State power is no more to be used so as to handicap religions than it is to favor them." . . .

The wholesome "neutrality" of which this Court's cases speak . . . stems from a recognition of the teachings of history that powerful sects or groups might bring about a fusion of governmental and religious functions or a concert or dependency of one upon the other to the end that official support of the State or Federal Government would be placed behind the tenets of one or of all orthodoxies. This the Establishment Clause prohibits. . . . As we have indicated, the Establishment Clause has been directly considered by this Court eight times in the past score of years and, with only one Justice dissenting on the point, it has consistently held that the clause withdrew all legislative power respecting religious belief or the expression thereof. The test may be stated as follows: what are the purpose and the primary effect of the enactment? If either is the advancement or inhibition of religion then the enactment exceeds the scope of legislative power as circumscribed by the Constitution. That is to say that to withstand the strictures of the Establishment Clause there must be a secular legislative purpose and a primary effect that neither advances nor inhibits religion. *Everson v. Board of Education.* . . .

Applying the Establishment Clause principles to the cases at bar we find that the States are requiring the selection and reading at the opening of the school day of verses from the Holy Bible and the recitation of the Lord's Prayer by the students in unison. These exercises are prescribed as part of the curricular activities of students who are required by law to attend school. They are held in the school buildings under the supervision and with the participation of teachers employed in those schools. . . . The trial court in [*Schempp*] has found that such an opening exercise is a religious ceremony and was intended by the State to be so. We agree with the trial court's finding as to the religious character of the exercises. Given that finding, the exercises and the law requiring them are in violation of the Establishment Clause. . . .

The conclusion follows that . . . the [law] require[s] religious exercises and such exercises are being conducted in direct violation of the rights of the appellees and petitioners. Nor are these required exercises mitigated by the fact that individual students may absent themselves upon parental request, for that fact furnishes no defense to a claim of unconstitutionality under the Establishment Clause. Further, it is no defense to urge that the religious practices here may be relatively minor encroachments on the First Amendment. The breach of neutrality that is today a trickling stream may all too soon become a raging torrent and, in the words of Madison, "it is proper to take alarm at the first experiment on our liberties."

It is insisted that unless these religious exercises are permitted[,] a "religion of secularism" is established in the schools. We agree of course that the State may not establish a "religion of secularism" in the sense of affirmatively opposing or showing hostility to religion, thus "preferring those who believe in no religion over those who do believe." . . . We do not agree, however, that this decision in any sense has that effect. In addition, it might well be said that one's education is not complete without a study of comparative religion or the history of religion and its relationship to the advancement of civilization. It certainly may be said that the Bible is worthy of study for its literary and historic qualities. Nothing we have said here indicates that such study of the Bible or of religion, when presented objectively as part of a secular program of education, may not be effected consistently with the First Amendment. But the exercises here do not fall into those categories. They are religious exercises, required by the States in violation of the command of the First Amendment that the Government maintain strict neutrality, neither aiding nor opposing religion. . . .

The place of religion in our society is an exalted one, achieved through a long tradition of reliance on the home, the church and the inviolable citadel of the individual heart and mind. We have come to recognize through bitter experience that it is not within the power of government to invade that citadel, whether its purpose or effect be to aid or oppose, to advance or retard. In the relationship between man and religion, the State is firmly committed to a position of neutrality. Though the application of that rule requires interpretation of a delicate sort, the rule itself is clearly and concisely stated in the words of the First Amendment. Applying that rule to the facts of these cases, we affirm the judgment in [*Schempp*]. In [*Murray*] the judgment is reversed and the cause remanded to the Maryland Court of Appeals for further proceedings consistent with this opinion.

It is so ordered.

MR. JUSTICE DOUGLAS, CONCURRING.

These regimes violate the Establishment Clause in two different ways. In each case, the State is conducting a religious exercise; and, as the Court holds, that cannot be done without violating the "neutrality" required of the State by the balance of power between individual, church and state that has been struck by the First Amendment. But the Establishment Clause is not limited to precluding the State itself from conducting religious exercises. It also forbids the State to employ its facilities or funds in a way that gives any church, or all churches, greater strength in our society than it would have by relying on its members alone. Thus, the present regimes must fall under that clause for the additional reason that public funds, though small in amount, are being used to promote a religious exercise. Through the mechanism of the State, all of the people are being required to finance a religious exercise that only some of the people want and that violates the sensibilities of others.

MR. JUSTICE BRENNAN, CONCURRING.

I join fully in the opinion and the judgment of the Court. I see no escape from the conclusion that the exercises called in question in these two cases violate the constitutional mandate. The reasons we gave only last Term in *Engel v. Vitale* for finding in the New York Regents' prayer an impermissible establishment of religion compel the same judgment of the practices at bar. The involvement of the secular with the religious is no less intimate here; and it is constitutionally irrelevant that the State has not composed the material for the inspirational exercises presently involved. It should be unnecessary to observe that our holding does not declare that the First Amendment manifests hostility to the practice or teaching of religion, but only applies prohibitions incorporated in the Bill of Rights in recognition of historic needs shared by Church and State alike. While it is my view that not every involvement of religion in public life is unconstitutional, I consider the exercises at bar a form of involvement which clearly violates the Establishment Clause.

MR. JUSTICE GOLDBERG, WITH WHOM MR. JUSTICE HARLAN JOINS, CONCURRING.

The practices here involved do not fall within any sensible or acceptable concept of compelled or permitted accommodation, and involve the state so significantly and directly in the realm of the sectarian as to give rise to those very divisive influences and inhibitions of freedom which both religion clauses of the First Amendment preclude. The state has ordained and has utilized its facilities to engage in unmistakably religious exercises—the devotional reading and recitation of the Holy Bible—in a manner having substantial and significant import and impact. That it has selected, rather than written, a particular devotional liturgy seems to me without constitutional import. The pervasive religiosity and direct governmental involvement inhering in the prescription of prayer and Bible reading in the public schools, during and as part of the curricular day, involving young impressionable children whose school attendance is statutorily compelled, and utilizing the prestige, power, and influence of school administration, staff, and authority, cannot realistically be termed simply accommodation, and must fall within the interdiction of the First Amendment.

MR. JUSTICE STEWART, DISSENTING.

. . . [I]t is important to stress that, strictly speaking, what is at issue here is a privilege rather than a right. In other words, the question presented is not whether exercises such as those at issue here are constitutionally compelled, but rather whether they are constitutionally invalid. And that issue, in my view, turns on the question of coercion.

It is clear that the dangers of coercion involved in the holding of religious exercises in a schoolroom differ qualitatively from those presented by the use of similar exercises or affirmations in ceremonies attended by adults. Even as to children, however, the duty laid upon government in connection with religious exercises in the public schools is that of refraining from so structuring the school environment as to put any kind of pressure on a child to participate in those exercises; it is not that of providing an atmosphere in which children are kept scrupulously insulated from any awareness that some of their fellows may want to open the school day with prayer, or of the fact that there exist in our pluralistic society differences of religious belief. . . .

Viewed in this light, it seems to me clear that the records in both of the cases before us are wholly inadequate to support an informed or responsible decision. Both cases involve provisions which explicitly permit any student who wishes, to be excused from participation in the exercises. There is no evidence . . . as to whether there would exist any coercion of any kind upon a student who did not want to participate. . . . What our Constitution indispensably protects is the freedom of each of us, be he Jew or Agnostic, Christian or Atheist, Buddhist or Freethinker, to believe or disbelieve, to worship or not worship, to pray or keep silent, according to his own conscience, uncoerced and unrestrained by government. It is conceivable that these school boards, or even all school boards, might eventually find it impossible to administer a system of religious exercises during school hours in such a way as to meet this constitutional standard—in such a way as completely to free from any kind of official coercion those who do not affirmatively want to participate. But I think we must not assume that school boards so lack the qualities of inventiveness and good will as to make impossible the achievement of that goal.

I would remand both cases for further hearings.

The *Schempp* decision, following on the heels of *Engel v. Vitale*, set firmly in American jurisprudence the principle that state-sponsored prayer in public schools violates the establishment clause. The public, however, did not welcome the rulings. Opinion polls taken in the aftermath of *Schempp* showed that only 24 percent of the public favored the Court's decision. Over time public approval has increased, but only moderately so; even after five decades, only 41 percent of Americans support the Court's ban on prayer and Bible reading in public schools.[19] Given the public antipathy toward *Engel* and *Schempp*, it is not surprising to find some school districts failing to comply with the Court's decisions. Responding to public opposition, members of Congress over the years have introduced about 150 constitutional amendment proposals to return prayer to the nation's classrooms. None has been successful.

The *Lemon* Test: Adoption and Discontent

As the Warren Court came to an end in 1969, religious establishment remained a major issue on the Court's agenda. State and local policies that provided aid and accommodation to faith-sponsored activities had increased in number, size, and, variety. Separationist groups were quick to challenge the constitutionality of these programs. Even as these conflicts continued to unfold, however, the Court had yet to agree on an appropriate test by which to judge establishment clause disputes.

As the new chief justice, conservative Warren Burger, took office, Court observers predicted that major changes were likely to occur in the justices' approach to establishment clause cases. The first significant establishment case to reach the Court under Burger's leadership was *Walz v. Tax Commission of the City of New York* (1970). *Walz* involved the property tax exemption enjoyed by religious institutions. Frederick Walz bought a small, useless lot on Staten Island, New York, for the sole purpose of challenging the state's laws that gave religious organizations exemptions from property taxes. Walz contended that the tax exemptions in effect forced property owners to make involuntary contributions to churches in violation of the establishment clause. After losing in the lower courts, Walz appealed to the U.S. Supreme Court.

Writing for a seven-person majority (only Justice Douglas dissented), Chief Justice Burger found in favor of the state. The outcome was not surprising; after all, had the Court ruled the other way, the tax status of every religious institution in the United States would have been dramatically altered. The startling aspect of *Walz* was that Burger, in his first writing on the establishment

---

[19]Lee Epstein, Jeffrey A. Segal, Harold J. Spaeth, and Thomas G. Walker, *The Supreme Court Compendium: Data, Decisions, and Developments*, 6th ed. (Thousand Oaks, CA: CQ Press, 2015), Table 8-26.

BOX 12-1

Aftermath . . . Madalyn Murray O'Hair

In 1963 the U.S. Supreme Court, in *School District of Abington Township v. Schempp* and its companion case, *Murray v. Curlett,* declared Bible reading and the recitation of the Lord's Prayer in public schools to be unconstitutional. *Murray v. Curlett* was a lawsuit brought by Madalyn Murray on behalf of her son William, then a fourteen-year-old student in Baltimore. Madalyn Murray O'Hair, as she became known after her marriage to Richard O'Hair, was no stranger to controversy or the courts. Dubbed by *Life* magazine in 1964 "the most hated woman in America," O'Hair initiated several lawsuits based on First Amendment claims, including legal actions to have the words "In God We Trust" removed from U.S. currency and to prohibit astronauts from praying in outer space. She described the Bible as "nauseating, historically inaccurate and replete with the ravings of madmen." O'Hair, an abrasive, profane woman, attempted to defect to the Soviet Union in 1960 and later became associated with Larry Flynt, the publisher of *Hustler* magazine. She is probably best known as the founder of American Atheists, Inc., a national organization devoted to advancing the interests of atheists, headquartered in Austin, Texas.

On August 28, 1995, O'Hair, seventy-six years old and in declining health, mysteriously vanished, along with her second son, Jon Murray, and granddaughter Robin. Nothing appeared to be missing from their house—clothes were in the closets and food on the table. Many thought that O'Hair and her family had fled from her organization's declining membership and troubled financial condition. Speculation was fueled by evidence that more than $500,000 of American Atheists funds, most in gold coins, were missing and allegations that O'Hair had hidden organization funds in bank accounts in New Zealand.

Law enforcement authorities, however, were convinced that O'Hair and the others were victims of foul play. The chief suspects were David Waters, Gary Karr, and Danny Fry. Waters, a former American Atheists employee, had pleaded guilty to stealing $54,000 from the organization and had a grudge against O'Hair. Karr and Fry were associates of Waters; all three had criminal records. Evidence mounted that the three suspects had kidnapped the O'Hair family members, held them hostage, and extorted $500,000 before murdering them. Fry was removed from the suspect list when a body discovered on the banks of the Trinity River was identified as

Madalyn Murray O'Hair with son Jon and granddaughter Robin.

his. The head and hands had been severed in an obvious attempt to block identification.

Police put continued pressure on Waters and Karr, both of whom had been imprisoned for crimes related to the O'Hair disappearance. Finally, in 2001 Waters agreed to cooperate with authorities as part of a plea bargain on the murder charges. He led police to a remote ranch west of San Antonio, where three dismembered and burned bodies were found in a shallow grave, along with a head and hands presumed to be Fry's. The bodies were identified through dental records and O'Hair's metal artificial hip. Police believed that the three victims had been killed in a north Austin storage unit and the remains discarded at the burial site.

In February 2003 Waters died in prison of cancer. Karr continues to serve a life sentence.

Another twist to the O'Hair story involves her son William Murray. After being treated for alcoholism, Murray publicly rejected atheism in May 1980 and became a Southern Baptist. For many years he has chaired the Religious Freedom Coalition, a conservative organization that supports, among other things, the reintroduction of prayer in the public schools. He once described his mother as "an evil person who led many to hell." As might be expected, Murray and his mother had been estranged for many years before her disappearance.

Sources: Arizona Republic, May 15, 2000; *Atlanta Journal-Constitution,* June 3, 2000; *Houston Chronicle,* December 29, 1996, March 3, 2000, March 16, 2001, February 5, 2003; *Washington Post,* March 28 and August 16–17, 1999; *Buffalo News,* April 25, 1999; *San Diego Union-Tribune,* October 22, 1999; *New York Times,* December 8, 1999, March 16, 2001; and William J. Murray, "The Madalyn Murray O'Hair Murder," statement issued by the Religious Freedom Coalition, April 5, 2011.

clause, sought to usher in a major change. The opinion started traditionally enough, with an examination of the primary purpose of the New York law—"The legislative purpose of property tax exemptions is neither the advancement nor the inhibition of religion"—but rather than stopping at this point, Burger extended his analysis by discussing an additional requirement:

> Determining that the legislative purpose of tax exemption is not aimed at establishing, sponsoring, or supporting religion does not end the inquiry, however. We must also be sure that the end result—the effect—is not an *excessive government entanglement with religion* [emphasis added].

According to Burger, the establishment clause forbade any kind of union between church and state in which the two were so intertwined that it was impossible to determine where one stopped and the other began. He ultimately found that property tax exemptions did not create such an entanglement with religion; to the contrary, even though tax exemptions to churches "necessarily operate to afford an indirect economic benefit," involvement with religion would be far greater if the exemptions did not exist. State officials might occasionally want to examine church records, or they might need to speak with clergy about expenditures, and so forth. As Burger concluded, the tax exemption "restricts the fiscal relationship between church and state, and tends to complement and reinforce the desired separation insulating each from the other."

In the end, then, *Walz* probably raised more questions about Burger and the fate of establishment clause litigation than it answered. Was Burger's insertion of the new criterion of "excessive entanglement" an attempt to move the Court to a more accommodationist position? Would excessive entanglement now become a part of the Court's analytic tool bag for examining establishment claims? Consider these questions as you read *Lemon v. Kurtzman* and its companion case, *Earley v. DiCenso*.

Lemon v. Kurtzman; Earley v. DiCenso

403 U.S. 602 (1971)
http://caselaw.findlaw.com/us-supreme-court/403/602.html
Oral arguments available at https://www.oyez.org/cases/1970/89
Vote in Lemon:
    8 (Black, Blackmun, Brennan, Burger, Douglas, Harlan, Stewart, White)
    0

OPINION OF THE COURT: *Burger*
CONCURRING OPINIONS: *Brennan, White*
NOT PARTICIPATING: *Marshall*

Vote in DiCenso:
    8 (Black, Blackmun, Brennan, Burger, Douglas, Harlan, Marshall, Stewart)
    1 (White)

OPINION OF THE COURT: *Burger*
CONCURRING OPINION: *Douglas*
DISSENTING OPINION: *White*

In *Lemon v. Kurtzman,* Alton Lemon brought suit against David Kurtzman, Pennsylvania state superintendent of schools. Lemon wanted the Court to declare unconstitutional a state law authorizing Kurtzman to use revenues from state taxes levied on cigarettes to reimburse nonpublic schools for expenses incurred for teachers' salaries, textbooks, and instructional materials. The state authorized such funding with certain restrictions: it would pay for secular expenses only—that is, secular books and teachers' salaries for the same courses taught in public schools. To receive payments, schools had to keep separate records identifying secular and nonsecular expenses.

The act took effect in July 1968. Up to the time the Supreme Court heard the case, Pennsylvania had spent about $5 million annually on the program. It reimbursed expenses at 1,181 nonpublic elementary and secondary schools attended by about a half million students, around 20 percent of the state's school population. About 96 percent of the students in nonpublic schools attended religious schools, primarily Roman Catholic ones.

The other case, *Earley v. DiCenso,* involved a challenge to the Rhode Island Salary Supplement Act. Aimed at improving the quality of private education, this law supplemented the salaries of teachers of secular subjects in private elementary schools by up to 15 percent of their current salaries; payments could be made only to those who agreed in writing not to teach religious subjects, and salaries could not exceed the maximum salaries paid to public school instructors. The plaintiffs claimed that this law violated the establishment clause, in part because 95 percent of the schools falling under the terms of the act were affiliated with the Roman Catholic Church. Moreover, all of the 250 teachers who had applied for salary supplements worked at Roman Catholic schools. And, as evidence submitted at trial indicated, about two-thirds of them were nuns of various religious orders.

MR. CHIEF JUSTICE BURGER DELIVERED THE OPINION OF THE COURT.

These two appeals raise questions as to Pennsylvania and Rhode Island statutes providing state aid to church-related elementary and secondary schools. Both statutes are challenged as violative of the Establishment and Free Exercise Clauses of the First Amendment and the Due Process Clause of the Fourteenth Amendment. . . .

The language of the Religion Clauses of the First Amendment is at best opaque, particularly when compared with other portions of the Amendment. Its authors did not simply prohibit the establishment of a state church or a state religion, an area history shows they regarded as very important and fraught with great dangers. Instead they commanded that there should be "no law *respecting* an establishment of religion." . . . A law "respecting" the proscribed result, that is, the establishment of religion, is not always easily identifiable as one violative of the Clause. A given law might not establish a state religion but nevertheless be one "respecting" that end in the sense of being a step that could lead to such establishment and hence offend the First Amendment.

In the absence of precisely stated constitutional prohibitions, we must draw lines with reference to the three main evils against which the Establishment Clause was intended to afford protection: "sponsorship, financial support, and active involvement of the sovereign in religious activity." *Walz v. Tax Commission* (1970).

Every analysis in this area must begin with consideration of the cumulative criteria developed by the Court over many years. Three such tests may be gleaned from our cases. First, the statute must have a secular legislative purpose; second, its principal or primary effect must be one that neither advances nor inhibits religion; finally, the statute must not foster "an excessive government entanglement with religion."

Inquiry into the legislative purposes of the Pennsylvania and Rhode Island statutes affords no basis for a conclusion that the legislative intent was to advance religion. On the contrary, the statutes themselves clearly state that they are intended to enhance the quality of the secular education in all schools covered by the compulsory attendance laws. There is no reason to believe the legislatures meant anything else. A State always has a legitimate concern for maintaining minimum standards in all schools it allows to operate. As in [*Board of Education v.*] *Allen* [1968], we find nothing here that undermines the stated legislative intent; it must therefore be accorded appropriate deference. . . .

The two legislatures, however, have also recognized that church-related elementary and secondary schools have a significant religious mission and . . . have therefore sought to create statutory restrictions designed to guarantee the separation between secular and religious educational functions and to ensure that State financial aid supports only the former. All these provisions are precautions taken in candid recognition that these programs approached, even if they did not intrude upon, the forbidden areas under the Religion Clauses. We need not decide whether these legislative precautions restrict the principal or primary effect of the programs to the point where they do not offend the Religion Clauses, for we conclude that the cumulative impact of the entire relationship arising under the statutes in each State involves excessive entanglement between government and religion. . . .

In order to determine whether the government entanglement with religion is excessive, we must examine the character and purposes of the institutions that are benefited, the nature of the aid that the State provides, and the resulting relationship between the government and the religious authority. . . . Here we find that both statutes foster an impermissible degree of entanglement.

Rhode Island program. The District Court made extensive findings on the grave potential for excessive entanglement that inheres in the religious character and purpose of the Roman Catholic elementary schools of Rhode Island, to date the sole beneficiaries of the Rhode Island Salary Supplement Act.

The church schools involved in the program are located close to parish churches. This understandably permits convenient access for religious exercises since instruction in faith and morals is part of the total educational process. The school buildings contain identifying religious symbols such as crosses on the exterior and crucifixes, and religious paintings and statues either in the classrooms or hallways. Although only approximately 30 minutes a day are devoted to direct religious instruction, there are religiously oriented extracurricular activities. Approximately two-thirds of the teachers in these schools are nuns of various religious orders. Their dedicated efforts provide an atmosphere in which religious instruction and religious vocations are natural and proper parts of life in such schools. . . .

The substantial religious character of these church-related schools gives rise to entangling church-state relationships of the kind the Religion Clauses sought to avoid. Although the District Court found that concern for religious values did not inevitably or necessarily intrude into the content of secular subjects, the considerable religious activities of these schools led the legislature to provide for careful governmental controls and surveillance by state authorities in order to ensure that state aid supports only secular education. . . .

Several teachers testified . . . that they did not inject religion into their secular classes. . . . But what has been recounted suggests the potential if not actual hazards of this form of state aid. The teacher is employed by a religious organization, subject to the direction and discipline of religious authorities, and works in a system dedicated to rearing children in a particular faith. These controls are not lessened by the fact that most of the lay teachers are of the Catholic faith. Inevitably some of a teacher's responsibilities hover on the border between secular and religious orientation. . . .

We do not assume, however, that parochial school teachers will be unsuccessful in their attempts to segregate their religious beliefs from their secular educational responsibilities. But the potential for impermissible fostering of religion is present. The Rhode Island Legislature has not, and could not, provide state aid on the basis of a mere assumption that secular teachers under religious discipline can avoid conflicts. The State must be certain, given the Religion

Clauses, that subsidized teachers do not inculcate religion—indeed the State here has undertaken to do so. To ensure that no trespass occurs, the State has therefore carefully conditioned its aid with pervasive restrictions. An eligible recipient must teach only those courses that are offered in the public schools and use only those texts and materials that are found in the public schools. In addition the teacher must not engage in teaching any course in religion.

A comprehensive, discriminating, and continuing state surveillance will inevitably be required to ensure that these restrictions are obeyed and the First Amendment otherwise respected. Unlike a book, a teacher cannot be inspected once so as to determine the extent and intent of his or her personal beliefs and subjective acceptance of the limitations imposed by the First Amendment. These prophylactic contacts will involve excessive and enduring entanglement between state and church. . . .

Pennsylvania program. The Pennsylvania statute also provides state aid to church-related schools for teachers' salaries. The complaint describes an educational system that is very similar to the one existing in Rhode Island. According to the allegations, the church-related elementary and secondary schools are controlled by religious organizations, have the purpose of propagating and promoting a particular religious faith, and conduct their operations to fulfill that purpose. . . .

As we noted earlier, the very restrictions and surveillance necessary to ensure that teachers play a strictly nonideological role give rise to entanglements between church and state. The Pennsylvania statute, like that of Rhode Island, fosters this kind of relationship. Reimbursement is not only limited to courses offered in the public schools and materials approved by state officials, but the statute excludes "any subject matter expressing religious teaching, or the morals or forms of worship of any sect." In addition, schools seeking reimbursements must maintain accounting procedures that require the State to establish the cost of the secular as distinguished from the religious instruction.

The Pennsylvania statute, moreover, has the further defect of providing state financial aid directly to the church-related schools. This factor distinguishes both *Everson* and *Allen,* for in both those cases the Court was careful to point out that state aid was provided to the student and his parents—not to the church-related school. . . .

The history of government grants of a continuing cash subsidy indicates that such programs have almost always been accompanied by varying measures of control and surveillance. The government cash grants before us now provide no basis for predicting that comprehensive measures of surveillance and controls will not follow. In particular the government's post-audit power to inspect and evaluate a church-related school's financial records and to determine which expenditures are religious and which are secular creates an intimate and continuing relationship between church and state. . . .

. . . The sole question is whether state aid to these schools can be squared with the dictates of the Religion Clauses. Under our system the choice has been made that government is to be entirely excluded from the area of religious instruction and churches excluded from the affairs of government. The Constitution decrees that religion must be a private matter for the individual, the family, and the institutions of private choice, and that while some involvement and entanglements are inevitable, lines must be drawn.

The judgment of the Rhode Island District Court . . . is affirmed. The judgment of the Pennsylvania District Court . . . is reversed, and the case is remanded for further proceedings consistent with this opinion.

MR. JUSTICE DOUGLAS, WHOM MR. JUSTICE BLACK JOINS, CONCURRING.

We said in unequivocal words in *Everson v. Board of Education* [1947], "No tax in any amount, large or small, can be levied to support any religious activities or institutions, whatever they may be called, or whatever form they may adopt to teach or practice religion." We reiterated the same idea in *Zorach v. Clauson* [1952] and in *McGowan v. Maryland* [1961] and in *Torcaso v. Watkins* [1961]. We repeated the same idea in *McCollum v. Board of Education* [1948] and added that a State's tax-supported public schools could not be used "for the dissemination of religious doctrines" nor could a State provide the church "pupils for their religious classes through use of the State's compulsory public school machinery."

Yet in spite of this long and consistent history there are those who have the courage to announce that a State may nonetheless finance the *secular* part of a sectarian school's educational program. That, however, makes a grave constitutional decision turn merely on cost accounting and bookkeeping entries. A history class, a literature class, or a science class in a parochial school is not a separate institute; it is part of the organic whole which the State subsidizes. The funds are used in these cases to pay or help pay the salaries of teachers in parochial schools; and the presence of teachers is critical to the essential purpose of the parochial school, *viz.,* to advance the religious endeavors of the particular church. It matters not that the teacher receiving taxpayers' money only teaches religion a fraction of the time. Nor does it matter that he or she teaches no religion. The school is an organism living on one budget. What the taxpayers give for salaries of those who teach only the humanities or science without any trace of proselytizing enables the school to use all of its own funds for religious training. . . .

In my view, the taxpayers' forced contribution to the parochial schools in the present cases violates the First Amendment.

Lemon and *DiCenso* cleared up some of the confusion over legal standards governing establishment clause cases. It now seemed that the justices planned to adhere to a three-pronged test, usually called the *Lemon* test: first, the statute must have a secular legislative purpose; second, the statute's primary effect must be one that neither advances nor inhibits religion; and third, the statute must not foster an excessive government entanglement with religion. None of these prongs was new; all had their genesis in earlier Supreme Court cases. Taken together, however, they formed a comprehensive standard that potentially could be applied to all establishment clause disputes; it required an evaluation of both the intent and the consequences of laws relating to government support of religion, and failure to satisfy any single prong of the test would be fatal.

How has this test fared over time? The results have been mixed. The *Lemon* test has remained the justices' official standard for evaluating establishment clause claims, but they have interpreted and applied it in many different ways, and its critics have been many, both on and off the Court. *Lemon* has survived primarily because of the inability of a Court majority to unite behind any single alternative test.

In the post–*Lemon* era the Court continued to confront difficult establishment clause questions. At the same time the ideological composition of the Court began to shift. Between the *Lemon* decision in 1971 and the mid-1980s, the justices, although sharply divided, tended to take a more separationist approach. In the area of aid to religious schools, for example, they struck down government funding of programs such as the administration of state-required examinations, counseling and therapy services, instructional materials, teachers' salaries, and remedial instruction.[20]

In 1986, however, the Court began to change positions, a shift that coincided with the promotion of William Rehnquist to the position of chief justice and the appointment of Antonin Scalia as associate justice. Although the Court was still internally divided, the balance of power now favored accommodationist positions. One way to achieve these accommodationist policies, the Court found, was to ask whether a program offered a widely available benefit on a neutral basis—something accessible to public and private interests alike. Such programs did not have the impermissible effect of advancing religion.[21] Another approach that favored accommodationist outcomes involved examining the actual

recipients of government benefits; support that went directly to school children or their parents, as opposed to the religious institutions they might choose to attend, did not pose establishment problems.[22] Even if the justices did not always rely explicitly on *Lemon*, they were still often concerned with one of its elements—the consequences of state policy—and determined that generally available state resources and direct aid to children did not result in unconstitutional benefits to religion.

As the Court's rulings signaled greater sympathy for programs that aided religious schools, states supporting such policies became increasingly aggressive in developing more expansive programs. This set the stage for a legal battle over the most controversial form of such aid, school vouchers, which the justices confronted in 2002 in *Zelman v. Simmons-Harris.*

Zelman v. Simmons-Harris

536 U.S. 639 (2002)
http://caselaw.findlaw.com/us-supreme-court/536/639.html
Oral arguments available at https://www.oyez.org/
    cases/2001/00-1751
Vote: 5 (Kennedy, O'Connor, Rehnquist, Scalia, Thomas)
    4 (Breyer, Ginsburg, Souter, Stevens)

OPINION OF THE COURT: *Rehnquist*

CONCURRING OPINIONS: *O'Connor, Thomas*

DISSENTING OPINIONS: *Breyer, Ginsburg, Souter, Stevens*

In the 1990s the Cleveland School District faced a crisis. The district served some seventy-five thousand children, most of them from low-income, minority families. Evaluation studies found it to be one of the worst-performing school districts in the nation. The district failed to meet any of the eighteen state standards for minimal acceptable performance. Only 10 percent of ninth graders could pass basic proficiency examinations. More than two-thirds of high school students either failed or dropped out before graduation. In 1995 the state of Ohio assumed control over the district.

In order to improve performance, the state enacted its Pilot Project Scholarship Program. This program allowed parents to choose among the following alternatives for their children:

1. Continue in Cleveland public schools as before.

2. Receive a scholarship (up to $2,250 per year) to attend an accredited, private, nonreligious school.

---

[20]See *Levitt v. CPEARL* (1973), *CPEARL v. Nyquist* (1973), *Meek v. Pittenger* (1975), *New York v. Cathedral Academy* (1977), *Grand Rapids School District v. Ball* (1985), and *Aguilar v. Felton (1985).*

[21]*Agostini v. Felton* (1997) and *Mitchell v. Helms* (2000).

[22]*Mueller v. Allen* (1983) and *Zobrest v. Catalina Foothills School District* (1993).

3. Receive a scholarship (up to $2,250 per year) to attend an accredited, private, religious school.

4. Remain in the Cleveland public schools and receive up to $500 in tutorial assistance.

5. Attend a public school outside the district. Other public school districts accepting Cleveland students would receive $2,250 from the Cleveland district in addition to normal state funding for each student enrolled.

Scholarship levels were adjusted according to family income levels. Tuition assistance checks went directly to the parents, who then endorsed the checks to the participating private schools that accepted their children. Parents were required to pay a small portion of the private school tuition expense. Private schools participating in the program could not charge more than $2,500 for tuition, and they retained their own admissions standards, although they were prohibited from discriminating on the basis of race, religion, or ethnic background. In separate actions the state created two additional educational alternatives: magnet public schools that specialized in certain subject areas and community schools governed by local boards independent of the regular public school district.

Although no public schools from adjacent districts opted to participate in the program, fifty-six private schools, 80 percent of them religious, did. Religious schools were the choice of the parents of 97 percent of the students who used tuition vouchers to attend private schools. Participants seemed motivated more by the quality of these schools than their religious orientation; a majority of students who used the scholarship program to enroll in religious schools were not of the same faith as the churches whose schools they attended.

Doris Simmons-Harris and other local citizens filed suit against Susan Tave Zelman, Ohio's superintendent of public instruction, charging that the voucher program violated the First Amendment's establishment clause. Both the federal district court and the court of appeals struck down the program. The state asked for Supreme Court review.

CHIEF JUSTICE REHNQUIST DELIVERED THE OPINION OF THE COURT.

The State of Ohio has established a pilot program designed to provide educational choices to families with children who reside in the Cleveland City School District. The question presented is whether this program offends the Establishment Clause of the United States Constitution. We hold that it does not. . . .

The Establishment Clause of the First Amendment, applied to the States through the Fourteenth Amendment, prevents a State from enacting laws that have the "purpose" or "effect" of advancing or inhibiting religion. *Agostini v. Felton* (1997). There is no dispute that the program challenged here was enacted for the valid secular purpose of providing educational assistance to poor children in a demonstrably failing public school system. Thus, the question presented is whether the Ohio program nonetheless has the forbidden "effect" of advancing or inhibiting religion.

To answer that question, our decisions have drawn a consistent distinction between government programs that provide aid directly to religious schools, *Mitchell v. Helms* (2000) (plurality opinion); *Agostini; Rosenberger v. Rector and Visitors of Univ. of Va.* (1995), and programs of true private choice, in which government aid reaches religious schools only as a result of the genuine and independent choices of private individuals, *Mueller v. Allen* (1983); *Witters v. Washington Dept. of Servs. for Blind* (1986); *Zobrest v. Catalina Foothills School Dist.* (1993). While our jurisprudence with respect to the constitutionality of direct aid programs has "changed significantly" over the past two decades, *Agostini*, our jurisprudence with respect to true private choice programs has remained consistent and unbroken. Three times we have confronted Establishment Clause challenges to neutral government programs that provide aid directly to a broad class of individuals, who, in turn, direct the aid to religious schools or institutions of their own choosing. Three times we have rejected such challenges.

In *Mueller*, we rejected an Establishment Clause challenge to a Minnesota program authorizing tax deductions for various educational expenses, including private school tuition costs, even though the great majority of the program's beneficiaries (96%) were parents of children in religious schools. We began by focusing on the class of beneficiaries, finding that because the class included "*all* parents," including parents with "children [who] attend nonsectarian private schools or sectarian private schools" (emphasis in original), the program was "not readily subject to challenge under the Establishment Clause." Then, viewing the program as a whole, we emphasized the principle of private choice, noting that public funds were made available to religious schools "only as a result of numerous, private choices of individual parents of school-age children." This, we said, ensured that "'no imprimatur of state approval' can be deemed to have been conferred on any particular religion, or on religion generally.". . . That the program was one of true private choice, with no evidence that the State deliberately skewed incentives toward religious schools, was sufficient for the program to survive scrutiny under the Establishment Clause.

In *Witters*, we used identical reasoning to reject an Establishment Clause challenge to a vocational scholarship program that provided tuition aid to a student studying at a religious institution to become a pastor. . . . We further remarked that, as in *Mueller*, "[the] program is made available generally without regard to the sectarian-nonsectarian, or public-nonpublic nature of the institution benefited." In light of these factors, we held that the program was not inconsistent with the Establishment Clause. . . .

AP Photo/Ron Schwane

Roberta Kitchen, right, and Rosa-Linda Demore-Brown, executive director of Cleveland Parents for School Choice, celebrate the Supreme Court's ruling in favor of school voucher programs that endorsed a six-year-old pilot program in inner-city Cleveland and provided parents with tax-supported education stipends.

Finally, in *Zobrest,* we applied *Mueller* and *Witters* to reject an Establishment Clause challenge to a federal program that permitted sign-language interpreters to assist deaf children enrolled in religious schools. . . . Looking once again to the challenged program as a whole, we observed that the program "distributes benefits neutrally to any child qualifying as 'disabled.'" Its "primary beneficiaries," we said, were "disabled children, not sectarian schools."

We further observed that "[b]y according parents freedom to select a school of their choice, the statute ensures that a government-paid interpreter will be present in a sectarian school only as a result of the private decision of individual parents." Our focus again was on neutrality and the principle of private choice, not on the number of program beneficiaries attending religious schools. Because the program ensured that parents were the ones to select a religious school as the best learning environment for their handicapped child, the circuit between government and religion was broken, and the Establishment Clause was not implicated.

Mueller, Witters, and *Zobrest* thus make clear that where a government aid program is neutral with respect to religion, and provides assistance directly to a broad class of citizens who, in turn, direct government aid to religious schools wholly as a result of their own genuine and independent private choice, the program is not readily subject to challenge under the Establishment Clause. A program that shares these features permits government aid to reach religious institutions only by way of the deliberate choices of numerous individual recipients. The incidental advancement of a religious mission, or the perceived endorsement of a religious message, is reasonably attributable to the individual recipient, not to the government, whose role ends with the disbursement of benefits. . . .

We believe that the program challenged here is a program of true private choice, consistent with *Mueller, Witters,* and *Zobrest,* and thus constitutional. As was true in those cases, the Ohio program is neutral in all respects toward religion. It is part of a general and multifaceted undertaking by the State of Ohio to provide educational opportunities to the children of a failed school district. It confers educational assistance directly to a broad class of individuals defined without reference to religion, *i.e.,* any parent of a school-age child who resides in the Cleveland City School District. The program permits the participation of *all* schools within the district, religious or nonreligious. Adjacent public schools also may participate and have a financial incentive to do so. Program benefits are available to participating families on neutral terms, with no reference to religion. The only preference stated anywhere in the program is a preference for low-income families, who receive greater assistance and are given priority for admission at participating schools.

There are no "financial incentive[s]" that "ske[w]" the program toward religious schools. . . . The program here in fact creates financial *dis*incentives for religious schools, with private schools receiving only half the government assistance given to community schools and one-third the assistance given to magnet schools. Adjacent public schools, should any choose to accept program students, are also eligible to receive two to three times the state funding of a private religious school. Families too have a financial disincentive to choose a private religious school. . . . Parents that choose to participate in the scholarship program and then to enroll their children in a private school (religious or nonreligious) must copay a portion of the school's tuition. Families that choose a community school, magnet school, or traditional public school pay nothing. Although such features of the program are not necessary to its constitutionality, they clearly dispel the claim that the program "creates . . . financial incentive[s] for parents to choose a sectarian school." *Zobrest.*

Respondents suggest that even without a financial incentive for parents to choose a religious school, the program creates a "public perception that the State is endorsing religious practices and beliefs." But we have repeatedly recognized that no reasonable observer would think a neutral program of private choice, where state aid reaches religious schools solely as a result of the numerous independent decisions of private individuals, carries with it the *imprimatur* of government endorsement. . . .

There also is no evidence that the program fails to provide genuine opportunities for Cleveland parents to select secular educational options for their school-age children. Cleveland schoolchildren enjoy a range of educational choices: They may remain in public school as before, remain in public school with publicly funded tutoring aid, obtain a scholarship and choose a religious school, obtain a scholarship and choose a nonreligious private school, enroll in a community school, or enroll in a magnet school. That 46 of the 56 private schools now participating in the program are religious schools does not condemn it as a violation of the Establishment Clause. The Establishment Clause question is whether Ohio is coercing parents into sending their children to religious schools, and that question must be answered by evaluating *all* options Ohio provides Cleveland schoolchildren, only one of which is to obtain a program scholarship and then choose a religious school. . . .

Respondents . . . claim that even if we do not focus on the number of participating schools that are religious schools, we should attach constitutional significance to the fact that 96% of scholarship recipients have enrolled in religious schools. They claim that this alone proves parents lack genuine choice, even if no parent has ever said so. We need not consider this argument in detail, since it was flatly rejected in *Mueller,* where we found it irrelevant that 96% of parents taking deductions for tuition expenses paid tuition at religious schools. . . . The constitutionality of a neutral educational aid program simply does not turn on whether and why, in a particular area, at a particular time, most private schools are run by religious organizations, or most recipients choose to use the aid at a religious school. . . .

This point is aptly illustrated here. The 96% figure upon which the respondents . . . rely discounts entirely (1) the more than 1,900 Cleveland children enrolled in alternative community schools, (2) the more than 13,000 children enrolled in alternative magnet schools, and (3) the more than 1,400 children enrolled in traditional public schools with tutorial assistance. Including some or all of these children in the denominator of children enrolled in nontraditional schools during the 1999–2000 school year drops the percentage enrolled in religious schools from 96% to under 20%. . . .

In sum, the Ohio program is entirely neutral with respect to religion. It provides benefits directly to a wide spectrum of individuals, defined only by financial need and residence in a particular school district. It permits such individuals to exercise genuine choice among options public and private, secular and religious. The program is therefore a program of true private choice. In keeping with an unbroken line of decisions rejecting challenges to similar programs, we hold that the program does not offend the Establishment Clause.

The judgment of the Court of Appeals is reversed.

It is so ordered.

JUSTICE THOMAS, CONCURRING.

Ten States have enacted some form of publicly funded private school choice as one means of raising the quality of education provided to underprivileged urban children. These programs address the root of the problem with failing urban public schools that disproportionately affect minority students. Society's other solution to these educational failures is often to provide racial preferences in higher education. Such preferences, however, run afoul of the Fourteenth Amendment's prohibition against distinctions based on race. By contrast, school choice programs that involve religious schools appear unconstitutional only to those who would twist the Fourteenth Amendment against itself by expansively incorporating the Establishment Clause. Converting the Fourteenth Amendment from a guarantee of opportunity to an obstacle against education reform distorts our constitutional values and disserves those in the greatest need.

JUSTICE O'CONNOR, CONCURRING.

In my view the . . . significant finding in these cases is that Cleveland parents who use vouchers to send their children to religious private schools do so as a result of true private choice. The Court rejects, correctly, the notion that the high percentage of voucher recipients who enroll in religious private schools necessarily demonstrates that parents do not actually have the option to send their children to nonreligious schools. . . .

Based on the reasoning in the Court's opinion, which is consistent with the realities of the Cleveland educational system, I am persuaded that the Cleveland voucher program affords parents of eligible children genuine nonreligious options and is consistent with the Establishment Clause.

JUSTICE BREYER, WITH WHOM JUSTICE STEVENS AND JUSTICE SOUTER JOIN, DISSENTING.

I write separately . . . to emphasize the risk that publicly financed voucher programs pose in terms of religiously based social conflict. I do so because I believe that the Establishment Clause concern for protecting the Nation's social fabric from religious conflict poses an overriding obstacle to the implementation of this well-intentioned school voucher program. . . .

. . . [T]he Court's 20th century Establishment Clause cases— both those limiting the practice of religion in public schools and those limiting the public funding of private religious education—focused directly upon social conflict, potentially created when government becomes involved in religious education. . . .

School voucher programs differ . . . in both kind and degree from aid programs upheld in the past. They differ in kind because they direct financing to a core function of the church: the teaching of religious truths to young children. For that reason the constitutional demand for "separation" is of particular constitutional concern. . . .

Vouchers also differ in degree. The aid programs recently upheld by the Court involved limited amounts of aid to religion. But the majority's analysis here appears to permit a considerable shift of taxpayer dollars from public secular schools to private religious schools. . . .

I do not believe that the "parental choice" aspect of the voucher program sufficiently offsets the concerns I have mentioned. Parental choice cannot help the taxpayer who does not want to finance the religious education of children. It will not always help the parent who may see little real choice between inadequate nonsectarian public education and adequate education at a school whose religious teachings are contrary to his own. It will not satisfy religious minorities unable to participate because they are too few in number to support the creation of their own private schools. It will not satisfy groups whose religious beliefs preclude them from participating in a government-sponsored program, and who may well feel ignored as government funds primarily support the education of children in the doctrines of the dominant religions. And it does little to ameliorate the entanglement problems or the related problems of social division. . . . Consequently, the fact that

the parent may choose which school can cash the government's voucher check does not alleviate the Establishment Clause concerns associated with voucher programs.

. . . In a society composed of many different religious creeds, I fear that this present departure from the Court's earlier understanding risks creating a form of religiously based conflict potentially harmful to the Nation's social fabric. Because I believe the Establishment Clause was written in part to avoid this kind of conflict, . . . I respectfully dissent.

JUSTICE SOUTER, WITH WHOM JUSTICE STEVENS, JUSTICE GINSBURG, AND JUSTICE BREYER JOIN, DISSENTING.

The occasion for the legislation . . . upheld is the condition of public education in the city of Cleveland. The record indicates that the schools are failing to serve their objective, and the vouchers in issue here are said to be needed to provide adequate alternatives to them. If there were an excuse for giving short shrift to the Establishment Clause, it would probably apply here. But there is no excuse. Constitutional limitations are placed on government to preserve constitutional values in hard cases, like these. "[C]onstitutional lines have to be drawn, and on one side of every one of them is an otherwise sympathetic case that provokes impatience with the Constitution and with the line. But constitutional lines are the price of constitutional government." *Agostini v. Felton* (1997) (SOUTER, J., dissenting). I therefore respectfully dissent.

The applicability of the Establishment Clause to public funding of benefits to religious schools was settled in *Everson v. Board of Ed. of Ewing* (1947), which inaugurated the modern era of establishment doctrine. The Court stated the principle in words from which there was no dissent:

> "No tax in any amount, large or small, can be levied to support any religious activities or institutions, whatever they may be called, or whatever form they may adopt to teach or practice religion."

The Court has never in so many words repudiated this statement, let alone, in so many words, overruled *Everson*.

Today, however, the majority holds that the Establishment Clause is not offended by Ohio's Pilot Project Scholarship Program, under which students may be eligible to receive as much as $2,250 in the form of tuition vouchers transferable to religious schools. In the city of Cleveland the overwhelming proportion of large appropriations for voucher money must be spent on religious schools if it is to be spent at all, and will be spent in amounts that cover almost all of tuition. The money will thus pay for eligible students' instruction not only in secular subjects but in religion as well, in schools that can fairly be characterized as founded to teach religious doctrine and to imbue teaching in all subjects with a religious dimension. Public tax money will pay at a systemic level for teaching the covenant with Israel and Mosaic law in Jewish schools, the primacy of the Apostle Peter and the Papacy in Catholic schools, the truth of reformed Christianity in Protestant schools, and the revelation to the Prophet in Muslim schools, to speak only of major religious groupings in the Republic.

How can a Court consistently leave *Everson* on the books and approve the Ohio vouchers? The answer is that it cannot. It is only by ignoring *Everson* that the majority can claim to rest on traditional law in its invocation of neutral aid provisions and private choice to sanction the Ohio law. It is, moreover, only by ignoring the meaning of neutrality and private choice themselves that the majority can even pretend to rest today's decision on those criteria. . . .

. . . *Everson*'s statement is still the touchstone of sound law, even though the reality is that in the matter of educational aid the Establishment Clause has largely been read away. True, the majority has not approved vouchers for religious schools alone, or aid earmarked for religious instruction. But no scheme so clumsy will ever get before us, and in the cases that we may see, like these, the Establishment Clause is largely silenced. I do not have the option to leave it silent, and I hope that a future Court will reconsider today's dramatic departure from basic Establishment Clause principle.

Zelman illustrates the Court's recent pattern of taking accommodationist positions on aid to religious schools. By focusing on the consequences of the Cleveland program—whether it had "the forbidden 'effect' of advancing or inhibiting religion"—the justices concluded that the voucher policy resulted only in public money being placed into the hands of parents. Whether that money ended up paying for tuition in religious schools was a result of the decisions of parents, not the state, and thus there was no violation of the establishment clause.

Just as accommodationist decisions of the Rehnquist era were often forged by considering the effects of government policy, they were also facilitated by evaluating whether the state was pursuing a valid secular purpose. The secular purpose requirement was, of course, another element of the *Lemon* test, and employing that standard, the Court often permitted a public acknowledgment of religion, which differed from public support of religion.

One illustration of this approach can be seen in a series of cases that involve challenges to religious symbols on public property. Among such symbols, the most pervasive are probably the public displays related to the Christmas season. During that time of year, local governments routinely decorate their main streets and municipal buildings. Are these displays meant to encourage citizens to celebrate Christmas as a religious holiday, or are they motivated by nonreligious purposes?

The Court confronted this issue in **Lynch v. Donnelly** (1984), a challenge to a crèche displayed by the city of Pawtucket, Rhode Island. The crèche—a nativity scene that is a physical representation of the biblical account of the birth of Jesus—was complete with the Christ child, Mary, Joseph, angels, animals, and the like. It was part of a larger exhibit that also included other, more secular seasonal symbols, such as Santa Claus, reindeer, carolers, and a Christmas tree.

Chief Justice Burger, speaking for a five-person majority, found that the display was not an impermissible breach of the establishment clause. The purpose of the crèche contained in the larger Christmas display, he concluded, was to depict the historical origins of the holiday, not to advocate a particular religious message. The city's goal was to take part in the celebration of a national holiday, not encourage devotion to Christianity. Seen in this way, Burger implied that Christmas was so much a part of our heritage that it came close to representing a national nonsectarian celebration (as it doubtless is for many) rather than a religious holiday.

In a noteworthy concurring opinion, Justice O'Connor offered a specific method for evaluating whether the government is pursuing a valid secular purpose, the endorsement test. "The proper inquiry under the purpose prong of *Lemon* . . . is whether the government intends to convey a message of endorsement or disapproval of religion." When that intent is scrutinized, "[e]very government practice must be judged in its unique circumstances. . . ." This means that a judge would not necessarily accept the state's declared secular intent; what the endorsement test requires is a kind of objective assessment of the actual purpose—"what viewers may fairly understand to be the purpose"—whether stated or not. As she elaborated in another case the following year, "The relevant issue is whether an objective observer, acquainted with [all the facts], would perceive it as a state endorsement of prayer in public schools."[23]

The endorsement test proved useful five years after *Lynch*, when the Rehnquist Court decided **County of Allegheny v. ACLU** (1989). At issue were two public holiday displays in Pittsburgh, Pennsylvania. The

---

[23]*Wallace v. Jaffree* (1985).

first was a crèche that belonged to a Roman Catholic group, the Holy Name Society. Beginning with the Christmas season of 1981, the city allowed the Holy Name Society to place the crèche on the grand staircase of the county courthouse, which is, by all accounts, the "main," "most beautiful," and "most public" part of the courthouse. It contained the typical elements of the manger scene and included an angel bearing a banner with the Latin phrase "Gloria in Excelsis Deo!" ("Glory to God in the Highest!") The second challenged display was located outside the Pittsburgh City-County Building, where the mayor and other city officials have their offices. It consisted of a forty-five-foot Christmas tree, complete with lights and ornaments, and an eighteen-foot Chanukah menorah, owned by a Jewish group but stored and erected by the city. Also included was a sign from the mayor indicating that "Pittsburgh salutes liberty."

Did these displays violate the establishment clause? Although the justices were divided over the proper standard to apply, the plurality relied explicitly on the endorsement test.

Evaluating, as the test requires, the case's "unique circumstances," the Court concluded that given its physical setting, the display of the crèche violated the establishment clause. It stood alone, in a place of particular prominence, communicating an unmistakable religious message; the county supported and promoted the nativity scene as representing the birth of the Son of God. But the Court found that the Christmas tree and menorah did not run afoul of the Constitution. Because the display included side-by-side symbols, one secular (the Christmas tree) and one religious (the menorah), there was little to indicate government endorsement of a particular religious message. Moreover, the mayor's "salute to liberty" served to affirm the secular purpose. In light of those facts, the justices thought it unlikely that a reasonable observer would regard the display as endorsing religious beliefs.

Controversies over religious displays are, however, not confined to holiday symbols; they have also flared over public exhibition of the Ten Commandments. In *Van Orden v. Perry*, the Court reviewed the constitutional propriety of such a monument erected on the grounds of the Texas state capitol. As you read the opinion in this case, pay attention not only to how the majority treats the issue of a religious display but also to the question of the appropriate standard to use in establishment clause cases.

Van Orden v. Perry

545 U.S. 677 (2005)
http://caselaw.findlaw.com/us-supreme-court/545/677.html
*Oral arguments available at https://www.oyez.org/
cases/2004/03-1500*
Vote: 5 (Breyer, Kennedy, Rehnquist, Scalia, Thomas)
 4 (Ginsburg, O'Connor, Souter, Stevens)

OPINION ANNOUNCING THE JUDGMENT OF THE COURT:
Rehnquist

CONCURRING OPINIONS: *Kennedy, Scalia, Thomas*

OPINION CONCURRING IN THE JUDGMENT: *Breyer*

DISSENTING OPINIONS: *Ginsburg, O'Connor,
Souter, Stevens*

The twenty-two-acre park surrounding the Texas capitol in Austin contains seventeen monuments and twenty-one historical markers commemorating the "people, ideals, and events that compose Texan identity." One of these is a six-foot-high monument displaying the text of the Ten Commandments. The Fraternal Order of Eagles gave the monument to the people of Texas in 1961 and paid for its construction and dedication.

Thomas Van Orden, a lawyer by training and a resident of Austin, frequently saw the monument on his walks through the capitol grounds. After doing so for about six years, he filed suit against Governor Rick Perry and other state officials asking a federal court to order the removal of the monument because its presence on the capitol grounds violated the establishment clause. The trial court judge rejected Van Orden's request, finding that the monument had a secular purpose and that no reasonable observer would conclude that the state was endorsing religion by allowing this passive monument to be placed on state property. The court of appeals affirmed, and the Supreme Court granted review.

> **CHIEF JUSTICE REHNQUIST ANNOUNCED THE JUDGMENT OF THE COURT AND DELIVERED AN OPINION, IN WHICH JUSTICE SCALIA, JUSTICE KENNEDY, AND JUSTICE THOMAS JOIN.**

The question here is whether the Establishment Clause of the First Amendment allows the display of a monument inscribed with the Ten Commandments on the Texas State Capitol grounds. We hold that it does. . . .

Our cases, Janus-like, point in two directions in applying the Establishment Clause. One face looks toward the strong role played by religion and religious traditions throughout our Nation's history. . . .

The other face looks toward the principle that governmental intervention in religious matters can itself endanger religious freedom.

This case, like all Establishment Clause challenges, presents us with the difficulty of respecting both faces. Our institutions presuppose a Supreme Being, yet these institutions must not press religious observances upon their citizens. One face looks to the past in acknowledgment of our Nation's heritage, while the other looks to the present in demanding a separation between church and state. Reconciling these two faces requires that we neither abdicate our responsibility to maintain a division between church and state nor evince a hostility to religion by disabling the government from in some ways recognizing our religious heritage. . . .

These two faces are evident in representative cases both upholding and invalidating laws under the Establishment Clause. Over the last 25 years, we have sometimes pointed to *Lemon v. Kurtzman* (1971) as providing the governing test in Establishment Clause challenges. Yet, just two years after *Lemon* was decided, we noted that the factors identified in *Lemon* serve as "no more than helpful signposts." *Hunt v. McNair* (1973). Many of our recent cases simply have not applied the *Lemon* test. See, *e.g.*, *Zelman v. Simmons-Harris* (2002); *Good News Club v. Milford Central School* (2001). Others have applied it only after concluding that the challenged practice was invalid under a different Establishment Clause test.

Whatever may be the fate of the *Lemon* test in the larger scheme of Establishment Clause jurisprudence, we think it not useful in dealing with the sort of passive monument that Texas has erected on its Capitol grounds. Instead, our analysis is driven both by the nature of the monument and by our Nation's history.

As we explained in *Lynch v. Donnelly* (1984): "There is an unbroken history of official acknowledgment by all three branches of government of the role of religion in American life from at least 1789." . . .

Recognition of the role of God in our Nation's heritage has also been reflected in our decisions. We have acknowledged, for example, that "religion has been closely identified with our history and government," *School Dist. of Abington Township v. Schempp* [1963], and that "[t]he history of man is inseparable from the history of religion," *Engel v. Vitale* (1962). This recognition has led us to hold that the Establishment Clause permits a state legislature to open its daily sessions with a prayer by a chaplain paid by the State. *Marsh v. Chambers* [1983]. . . . With similar reasoning, we have upheld laws, which originated from one of the Ten Commandments, that prohibited the sale of merchandise on Sunday. *McGowan v. Maryland* (1961).

In this case we are faced with a display of the Ten Commandments on government property outside the Texas State Capitol. Such acknowledgments of the role played by the Ten Commandments in our Nation's heritage are common throughout America. We need only look within our own Courtroom. Since 1935, Moses has stood, holding two tablets that reveal portions of the Ten Commandments written in Hebrew, among other lawgivers in the south frieze. Representations of the Ten Commandments adorn the metal gates lining the north and south sides of the Courtroom as well as the doors leading into the Courtroom. Moses also sits on the exterior east facade of the building holding the Ten Commandments tablets.

Similar acknowledgments can be seen throughout a visitor's tour of our Nation's Capitol. . . .

Of course, the Ten Commandments are religious—they were so viewed at their inception and so remain. The monument, therefore, has religious significance. According to Judeo-Christian belief, the Ten Commandments were given to Moses by God on Mt. Sinai. But Moses was a lawgiver as well as a religious leader. And the Ten Commandments have an undeniable historical meaning. . . . Simply having religious content or promoting a message consistent with a religious doctrine does not run afoul of the Establishment Clause.

There are, of course, limits to the display of religious messages or symbols. For example, we held unconstitutional a Kentucky statute requiring the posting of the Ten Commandments in every public schoolroom. *Stone v. Graham* (1980). . . . [I]t stands as an example of the fact that we have "been particularly vigilant in monitoring compliance with the Establishment Clause in elementary and secondary schools," *Edwards v. Aguillard* (1987). Indeed, *Edwards v. Aguillard* recognized that *Stone*—along with *Schempp* and *Engel*—was a consequence of the "particular concerns that arise in the context of public elementary and secondary schools." Neither *Stone* itself nor subsequent opinions have indicated that *Stone's* holding would extend to a legislative chamber or to capitol grounds.

The placement of the Ten Commandments monument on the Texas State Capitol grounds is a far more passive use of those texts than was the case in *Stone,* where the text confronted elementary school students every day. Indeed, Van Orden, the petitioner here, apparently walked by the monument for a number of years before bringing this lawsuit. The monument is therefore also quite different from the prayers involved in *Schempp* and *Lee v. Weisman* [1992]. Texas has treated her Capitol grounds monuments as representing the several strands in the State's political and legal history. The inclusion of the Ten Commandments monument in this group has a dual significance, partaking of both religion and government. We cannot say that Texas' display of this monument violates the Establishment Clause of the First Amendment.

The judgment of the Court of Appeals is affirmed.

It is so ordered.

This six-foot-tall stone slab bearing the Ten Commandments was the focal point of the Supreme Court's decision in *Van Orden v. Perry* (2005). The justices ruled that the placement of this monument on the state capitol grounds in Austin, Texas, did not violate the First Amendment's establishment clause.

JUSTICE SCALIA, CONCURRING.

I join the opinion of the Chief Justice because I think it accurately reflects our current Establishment Clause jurisprudence—or at least the Establishment Clause jurisprudence we currently apply some of the time. I would prefer to reach the same result by adopting an Establishment Clause jurisprudence that is in accord with our Nation's past and present practices, and that can be consistently applied—the central relevant feature of which is that there is nothing unconstitutional in a State's favoring religion generally, honoring God through public prayer and acknowledgment, or, in a nonproselytizing manner, venerating the Ten Commandments.

JUSTICE THOMAS, CONCURRING.

The Court holds that the Ten Commandments monument found on the Texas State Capitol grounds does not violate the Establishment Clause. Rather than trying to suggest meaninglessness where there is meaning, the Chief Justice rightly recognizes that the monument has "religious significance." He properly recognizes the role of religion in this Nation's history and the permissibility of government

displays acknowledging that history. For those reasons, I join the Chief Justice's opinion in full.

This case would be easy if the Court were willing to abandon the inconsistent guideposts it has adopted for addressing Establishment Clause challenges, and return to the original meaning of the Clause. I have previously suggested that the Clause's text and history "resis[t] incorporation" against the States. See *Elk Grove Unified School Dist. v. Newdow* (2004) (opinion concurring in judgment). If the Establishment Clause does not restrain the States, then it has no application here, where only state action is at issue.

Even if the Clause is incorporated, or if the Free Exercise Clause limits the power of States to establish religions, our task would be far simpler if we returned to the original meaning of the word "establishment" than it is under the various approaches this Court now uses. The Framers understood an establishment "necessarily [to] involve actual legal coercion." "In other words, establishment at the founding involved, for example, mandatory observance or mandatory payment of taxes supporting ministers." And "government practices that have nothing to do with creating or maintaining . . . coercive state establishments" simply do not "implicate the possible liberty interest of being free from coercive state establishments."

JUSTICE BREYER, CONCURRING IN THE JUDGMENT.

The case before us is a borderline case. It concerns a large granite monument bearing the text of the Ten Commandments located on the grounds of the Texas State Capitol. On the one hand, the Commandments' text undeniably has a religious message, invoking, indeed emphasizing, the Deity. On the other hand, focusing on the text of the Commandments alone cannot conclusively resolve this case. Rather, to determine the message that the text here conveys, we must examine how the text is used. And that inquiry requires us to consider the context of the display. . . .

Here the tablets have been used as part of a display that communicates not simply a religious message, but a secular message as well. The circumstances surrounding the display's placement on the capitol grounds and its physical setting suggest that the State itself intended the latter, nonreligious aspects of the tablets' message to predominate. And the monument's 40-year history on the Texas state grounds indicates that that has been its effect. . . .

The physical setting of the monument, moreover, suggests little or nothing of the sacred. The monument sits in a large park containing 17 monuments and 21 historical markers, all designed to illustrate the "ideals" of those who settled in Texas and of those who have lived there since that time. The setting does not readily lend itself to meditation or any other religious activity. But it does provide a context of history and moral ideals. It (together with the display's inscription about its origin) communicates to visitors that the State sought to reflect moral principles, illustrating a relation between ethics and law that the State's citizens, historically speaking, have endorsed. That is to say, the context suggests that the State intended the display's moral message—an illustrative message reflecting the historical "ideals" of Texans—to predominate. . . .

For these reasons, I believe that the Texas display—serving a mixed but primarily nonreligious purpose, not primarily "advanc[ing]" or "inhibit[ing] religion," and not creating an "excessive government entanglement with religion,"—might satisfy this Court's more formal Establishment Clause tests. But, as I have said, in reaching the conclusion that the Texas display falls on the permissible side of the constitutional line, I rely less upon a literal application of any particular test than upon consideration of the basic purposes of the First Amendment's Religion Clauses themselves. This display has stood apparently uncontested for nearly two generations. That experience helps us understand that as a practical matter of degree this display is unlikely to prove divisive. And this matter of degree is, I believe, critical in a borderline case such as this one.

At the same time, to reach a contrary conclusion here, based primarily upon . . . the religious nature of the tablets' text would, I fear, lead the law to exhibit a hostility toward religion that has no place in our Establishment Clause traditions. Such a holding might well encourage disputes concerning the removal of longstanding depictions of the Ten Commandments from public buildings across the Nation. And it could thereby create the very kind of religiously based divisiveness that the Establishment Clause seeks to avoid. . . .

I concur in the judgment of the Court.

JUSTICE STEVENS, WITH WHOM JUSTICE GINSBURG JOINS, DISSENTING.

The monolith displayed on Texas Capitol grounds cannot be discounted as a passive acknowledgment of religion, nor can the State's refusal to remove it upon objection be explained as a simple desire to preserve a historic relic. This Nation's resolute commitment to neutrality with respect to religion is flatly inconsistent with the plurality's wholehearted validation of an official state endorsement of the message that there is one, and only one, God. . . .

The judgment of the Court in this case stands for the proposition that the Constitution permits governmental displays of sacred religious texts. This makes a mockery of the constitutional ideal that government must remain neutral between religion and irreligion. If a State may endorse a particular deity's command to "have no other gods before me," it is difficult to conceive of any textual display that would run afoul of the Establishment Clause. . . .

I respectfully dissent.

JUSTICE SOUTER, WITH WHOM JUSTICE STEVENS AND JUSTICE GINSBURG JOIN, DISSENTING.[24]

. . . [A] pedestrian happening upon the monument at issue here needs no training in religious doctrine to realize that the statement of the Commandments, quoting God himself, proclaims that the will of the divine being is the source of obligation to obey the rules, including the facially secular ones. In this case, moreover, the text is presented to give particular prominence to the Commandments' first sectarian reference, "I am the Lord thy God." That proclamation is centered on the stone and written in slightly larger letters than the subsequent recitation. . . . What follows, of course, are the rules against other gods, graven images, vain swearing, and Sabbath breaking. And the full text of the fifth Commandment puts forward filial respect as a condition of long life in the land "which the Lord thy God giveth thee." These "[w]ords . . . make [the] . . . religious meaning unmistakably clear." *County of Allegheny v. American Civil Liberties Union, Greater Pittsburgh Chapter* (1989).

To drive the religious point home, and identify the message as religious to any viewer who failed to read the text, the engraved quotation is framed by religious symbols: two tablets with what

---

[24]In a separate statement, Justice O'Connor also expressed agreement with Souter's opinion.

appears to be ancient script on them, two Stars of David, and the superimposed Greek letters Chi and Rho as the familiar monogram of Christ. Nothing on the monument, in fact, detracts from its religious nature, and the plurality does not suggest otherwise. It would therefore be difficult to miss the point that the government of Texas is telling everyone who sees the monument to live up to a moral code because God requires it, with both code and conception of God being rightly understood as the inheritances specifically of Jews and Christians. . . .

Texas . . . says that the Capitol grounds are like a museum for a collection of exhibits, the kind of setting that several Members of the Court have said can render the exhibition of religious artifacts permissible, even though in other circumstances their display would be seen as meant to convey a religious message forbidden to the State. . . .

But 17 monuments with no common appearance, history, or esthetic role scattered over 22 acres is not a museum, and anyone strolling around the lawn would surely take each memorial on its own terms without any dawning sense that some purpose held the miscellany together more coherently than fortuity and the edge of the grass. One monument expresses admiration for pioneer women. One pays respect to the fighters of World War II. And one quotes the God of Abraham whose command is the sanction for moral law. The themes are individual grit, patriotic courage, and God as the source of Jewish and Christian morality; there is no common denominator. . . .

. . . The monument in this case sits on the grounds of the Texas State Capitol. There is something significant in the common term "statehouse" to refer to a state capitol building: it is the civic home of every one of the State's citizens. If neutrality in religion means something, any citizen should be able to visit that civic home without having to confront religious expressions clearly meant to convey an official religious position that may be at odds with his own religion, or with rejection of religion. . . .

I would reverse the judgment of the Court of Appeals.

The same day that the Court handed down the decision in *Van Orden*, it issued a ruling in a related case, *McCreary County v. American Civil Liberties Union of Kentucky* (2005). This case also involved the public display of the Ten Commandments, but unlike the monument included in the larger set of historical markers around the Texas capitol in *Van Orden*, the Commandments were hung by themselves in a county courthouse, placed there in a ceremony overseen by a county official and his pastor. After objections were raised by the ACLU, the county modified its display, supplementing it with secular items such as the Magna Carta, the Declaration of Independence, and the Bill of Rights and declaring it to be an exhibit honoring the foundations of American law. In a 5–4 decision, the justices ruled that, unlike the monument in *Van Orden*, this display was a violation of the establishment clause. What was the difference between the two cases? In *McCreary County*, the Court based its decision on the original purpose of the display, which the justices saw as clearly religious; the Commandments were installed with the assistance of a minister and shown in insolation with a citation to their biblical source in the Book of Exodus. True, the county had expanded the display to include important historical documents, but the Court regarded that change only as a reaction to the complaints made against the original display; the genuine initial purpose still remained. Invoking the language of the endorsement test, Justice Souter wrote, "No reasonable observer could swallow the claim that the [county] had cast off the objective so unmistakable in the earlier [display]."

In *Van Orden*, by contrast, the monument inscribed with the Ten Commandments was only one part of a more comprehensive exhibit representing significant societal influences, which over time had been woven into the fabric of Texas' culture. To be sure, the Commandments are a religious text, but many of the nation's early leaders were clearly animated by those religious principles, and Texas was entitled to recognize the role of those ideals in its own heritage. Although the justices did not rely explicitly on the endorsement test in this case, they did seem to acknowledge that, in appropriate circumstances, religious messages could serve secular ends. As Chief Justice Rehnquist explained, "The inclusion of the Ten Commandments monument in this [display] has a dual significance, partaking of both religion and government."

In his concurring opinion in *Van Orden*, Justice Stephen Breyer referred to the Texas monument as "a borderline case," one in which it was difficult to see precisely the constitutional division between separation and accommodation. Drawing that line became even more problematic in yet another controversy over the display of a religious symbol on public property. *American Legion v. American Humanist Association* (2019) asked whether the government's purpose could change over time. Could a religiously expressive monument, with the passage of time, shed its original character and serve a valid secular purpose? The Court—now under the leadership of Chief Justice John G. Roberts, who replaced Rehnquist shortly after his death in the summer of 2005—provided an answer.

American Legion v. American Humanist Association; Maryland-National Capital Park and Planning Commission v. American Humanist Association

588 U.S. _____ (2019)

https://caselaw.findlaw.com/us-supreme-court/17-1717.html

Oral arguments available at https://www.oyez.org/ cases/2018/17-1717

Vote: 7 (Alito, Breyer, Gorsuch, Kagan, Kavanaugh, Roberts, Thomas)

2 (Ginsburg, Sotomayor)

OPINION OF THE COURT: *Alito*

CONCURRING OPINIONS: *Breyer, Kagan, Kavanaugh*

OPINIONS CONCURRING IN THE JUDGMENT: *Thomas, Gorsuch*

DISSENTING OPINION: *Ginsburg*

The human toll of World War I was staggering. Among all combined military forces, nine million lost their lives, while more than twenty-one million were wounded. Germany and France suffered the heaviest losses, but the thousands of American military personnel who were interred overseas were grim reminders of the heavy costs of the war to the United States. At the end of the war, residents of Prince George's County, Maryland, decided to honor the sacrifice of their local soldiers by raising money for a memorial. With the help of the American Legion, they constructed a thirty-two-foot tall Latin cross with the words "Valor," "Endurance," "Courage," and "Devotion" inscribed around its base. A bronze plaque, listing the names of local servicemen who died, announced that the cross was "Dedicated to the heroes of Prince George's County, Maryland who lost their lives in the Great War for the liberty of the world." Since its completion in 1925, the Peace Cross, as it has come to be known, has been the location for various civic celebrations.

The cross was constructed on the banks of the Anacostia River, at an intersection near the city's eighteenth-century port landing. As this suburban area of Washington, D.C., developed, new and expanded roads left the cross at the center of a traffic island and difficult to access by pedestrians. To ensure traffic safety and to facilitate local development, the county planning authority took ownership of the cross in 1961. Since then, the county commission has spent thousands of dollars for its preservation and maintenance. In 2014, the American Humanist Association filed a lawsuit in federal court, claiming that the expenditure of such funds, as well as their personal objection to the presence of a religious symbol on public land, constituted a violation of the establishment clause. The court ruled that the commission had legitimate secular purposes—honoring lives lost in the World War I and maintaining traffic safety—but that decision was reversed by an appeals court, which was concerned with the "inherent religious meaning of the cross." Both the American Legion, which had retained the right to use the cross, and the commission sought review from the Supreme Court.

> **JUSTICE ALITO ANNOUNCED THE JUDGMENT OF THE COURT AND DELIVERED AN OPINION IN WHICH THE CHIEF JUSTICE, JUSTICE BREYER, JUSTICE KAGAN, AND JUSTICE KAVANAUGH JOIN. [JUSTICE KAGAN DID NOT SUPPORT THE OPINION'S CRITICISM OF *LEMON*.]**

Although the cross has long been a preeminent Christian symbol, its use in the Bladensburg memorial has a special significance. After the First World War, the picture of row after row of plain white crosses marking the overseas graves of soldiers who had lost their lives in that horrible conflict was emblazoned on the minds of Americans at home, and the adoption of the cross as the Bladensburg memorial must be viewed in that historical context. For nearly a century, the Bladensburg Cross has expressed the community's grief at the loss of the young men who perished, its thanks for their sacrifice, and its dedication to the ideals for which they fought. It has become a prominent community landmark . . . .

The Establishment Clause of the First Amendment provides that "Congress shall make no law respecting an establishment of religion." While the concept of a formally established church is straightforward, pinning down the meaning of a "law respecting an establishment of religion" has proved to be a vexing problem . . . . *Lemon* ambitiously attempted to distill from the Court's existing case law a test that would bring order and predictability to Establishment Clause decisionmaking. That test . . . called on courts to examine the purposes and effects of a challenged government action, as well as any entanglement with religion that it might entail. The Court later elaborated that the "effect[s]" of a challenged action should be assessed by asking whether a "reasonable observer" would conclude that the action constituted an "endorsement" of religion. *County of Allegheny* (1989) (O'Connor, J., concurring in part and concurring in judgment).

If the *Lemon* Court thought that its test would provide a framework for all future Establishment Clause decisions, its expectation has not been met. In many cases, this Court has either expressly declined to apply the test or has simply ignored it.

This pattern is a testament to the *Lemon* test's shortcomings. As Establishment Clause cases involving a great array of laws and practices came to the Court, it became more and more apparent that the *Lemon* test could not resolve them. . . . The test has been

AP Photo/Kevin Wolf

Roy Speckhardt, executive director of the American Humanist Association, which challenged the Peace Cross honoring soldiers lost in World War I as a violation of the establishment clause. The Court ruled that, after nearly one hundred years, it had become part of Bladensburg, Maryland's cultural heritage.

harshly criticized by Members of this Court, lamented by lower court judges, and questioned by a diverse roster of scholars.

. . . [T]he *Lemon* test presents particularly daunting problems in cases, including the one now before us, that involve the use, for ceremonial, celebratory, or commemorative purposes, of words or symbols with religious associations. . . .

. . . [A]s time goes by, the purposes associated with an established monument, symbol, or practice often multiply. Take the example of Ten Commandments monuments, the subject we addressed in *Van Orden* and *McCreary*. For believing Jews and Christians, the Ten Commandments are the word of God handed down to Moses on Mount Sinai, but the image of the Ten Commandments has also been used to convey other meanings. They have historical significance as one of the foundations of our legal system, and for largely that reason, they are depicted in the marble frieze in our courtroom and in other prominent public buildings in our Nation's capital. In *Van Orden* and *McCreary*, no Member of the court thought that these depictions are unconstitutional.

. . . Even if the original purpose of a monument was infused with religion, the passage of time may obscure that sentiment. As our society becomes more and more religiously diverse, a community may preserve such monuments, symbols, and practices for the sake of their historical significance or their place in a common cultural heritage.

. . . [C]onsider the many cities and towns across the United States that bear religious names. Religion undoubtedly motivated those who named Bethlehem, Pennsylvania; Las Cruces, New Mexico; Providence, Rhode Island; Corpus Christi, Texas; Nephi, Utah, and the countless other places in our country with names that are rooted in religion. Yet few would argue that this history requires that these names be erased from the map. . . . Familiarity itself can become a reason for preservation.

. . . [W]hen time's passage imbues a religiously expressive monument, symbol, or practice with this kind of familiarity and historical significance, removing it may no longer appear neutral, especially to the local community for which it has taken on particular meaning. A government that roams the land, tearing down monuments with religious symbolism and scrubbing away any reference to the divine will strike many as aggressively hostile to religion. . . .

These . . . considerations show that retaining established, religiously expressive monuments, symbols, and practices is quite different from erecting or adopting new ones. The passage of time gives rise to a strong presumption of constitutionality.

The role of the cross in World War I memorials is illustrative of each of [these] considerations. Immediately following the war, "[c]ommunities across America built memorials to commemorate those who had served the nation in the struggle to make the world safe for democracy." Although not all of these communities included a cross in their memorials, the cross had become a symbol closely linked to the war. "[T]he First World War witnessed a dramatic change in . . . the symbols used to commemorate th[e] service" of the fallen soldiers. In the wake of the war, the United States adopted the cross as part of its military honors, establishing the Distinguished Service Cross and the Navy Cross in 1918 and 1919, respectively. . . . And this relationship between the cross and the war undoubtedly influenced the design of the many war memorials that sprang up across the Nation.

This is not to say that the cross's association with the war was the sole or dominant motivation for the inclusion of the symbol in every World War I memorial that features it. But today, it is all but impossible to tell whether that was so. . . . And no matter what the original purposes for the erection of a monument, a community may wish to preserve it for very different reasons, such as the historic preservation and traffic-safety concerns the Commission has pressed here. . . .

Finally, as World War I monuments have endured through the years and become a familiar part of the physical and cultural landscape, requiring their removal would not be viewed by many as a neutral act. And an alteration like the one entertained by the Fourth Circuit—amputating the arms of the Cross—would be seen by many as profoundly disrespectful. . . . A monument may express many purposes and convey many different messages, both secular and religious. Thus, a campaign to obliterate items with religious associations may evidence hostility to religion even if those religious associations are no longer in the forefront. . . .

While the *Lemon* Court ambitiously attempted to find a grand unified theory of the Establishment Clause, in later cases, we have taken a more modest approach that focuses on the particular issue at hand and looks to history for guidance. . . .

As we have explained, the Bladensburg Cross carries special significance in commemorating World War I. Due in large part to the image of the simple wooden crosses that originally marked the graves of American soldiers killed in the war, the cross became a symbol of their sacrifice, and the design of the Bladensburg Cross must be understood in light of that background. That the cross originated as a Christian symbol and retains that meaning in many

contexts does not change the fact that the symbol took on an added secular meaning when used in World War I memorials.

Not only did the Bladensburg Cross begin with this meaning, but with the passage of time, it has acquired historical importance. It reminds the people of Bladensburg and surrounding areas of the deeds of their predecessors and of the sacrifices they made in a war fought in the name of democracy. As long as it is retained in its original place and form, it speaks as well of the community that erected the monument nearly a century ago and has maintained it ever since. The memorial represents what the relatives, friends, and neighbors of the fallen soldiers felt at the time and how they chose to express their sentiments. And the monument has acquired additional layers of historical meaning in subsequent years. The Cross now stands among memorials to veterans of later wars. It has become part of the community. . . .

The cross is undoubtedly a Christian symbol, but that fact should not blind us to everything else that the Bladensburg Cross has come to represent. For some, that monument is a symbolic resting place for ancestors who never returned home. For others, it is a place for the community to gather and honor all veterans and their sacrifices for our Nation. For others still, it is a historical landmark. For many of these people, destroying or defacing the Cross that has stood undisturbed for nearly a century would not be neutral and would not further the ideals of respect and tolerance embodied in the First Amendment. For all these reasons, the Cross does not offend the Constitution.

We reverse the judgment of the Court of Appeals for the Fourth Circuit and remand the cases for further proceedings.

It is so ordered.

JUSTICE BREYER, WITH WHOM JUSTICE KAGAN JOINS, CONCURRING.

I have long maintained that there is no single formula for resolving Establishment Clause challenges. The Court must instead consider each case in light of the basic purposes that the Religion Clauses were meant to serve: assuring religious liberty and tolerance for all, avoiding religiously based social conflict, and maintaining that separation of church and state that allows each to flourish in its "separate spher[e]."

I agree with the Court that allowing the State of Maryland to display and maintain the Peace Cross poses no threat to those ends. The Court's opinion eloquently explains why that is so. . . .

The case would be different, in my view, if there were evidence that the organizers had "deliberately disrespected" members of minority faiths or if the Cross had been erected only recently, rather than in the aftermath of World War I. But those are not the circumstances presented to us here, and I see no reason to order *this* cross torn down simply because *other* crosses would raise constitutional concerns.

. . . The Court appropriately . . . upholds the constitutionality of the Peace Cross only after considering its particular historical context and its long-held place in the community. A newer memorial, erected under different circumstances, would not necessarily be permissible under this approach.

JUSTICE KAVANAUGH, CONCURRING.

The Bladensburg Cross commemorates soldiers who gave their lives for America in World War I. I agree with the Court that the Bladensburg Cross is constitutional. At the same time, I have deep respect for the plaintiffs' sincere objections to seeing the cross on public land. I have great respect for the Jewish war veterans who in an amicus brief say that the cross on public land sends a message of exclusion. I recognize their sense of distress and alienation. Moreover, I fully understand the deeply religious nature of the cross. It would demean both believers and nonbelievers to say that the cross is not religious, or not all that religious. A case like this is difficult because it represents a clash of genuine and important interests. Applying our precedents, we uphold the constitutionality of the cross. In doing so, it is appropriate to also restate this bedrock constitutional principle: All citizens are equally American, no matter what religion they are, or if they have no religion at all.

The conclusion that the cross does not violate the Establishment Clause does not necessarily mean that those who object to it have no other recourse. The Court's ruling *allows* the State to maintain the cross on public land. The Court's ruling does not *require* the State to maintain the cross on public land. The Maryland Legislature could enact new laws requiring removal of the cross or transfer of the land. The Maryland Governor or other state or local executive officers may have authority to do so under current Maryland law. And if not, the legislature could enact new laws to authorize such executive action. The Maryland Constitution, as interpreted by the Maryland Court of Appeals, may speak to this question. And if not, the people of Maryland can amend the State Constitution.

Those alternative avenues of relief illustrate a fundamental feature of our constitutional structure: This Court is not the *only* guardian of individual rights in America. This Court fiercely protects the individual rights secured by the U. S. Constitution. But . . . [o]ther federal, state, and local government entities generally possess authority to safeguard individual rights above and beyond the rights secured by the U. S. Constitution.

JUSTICE KAGAN, CONCURRING IN PART.

. . . Although I agree that rigid application of the *Lemon* test does not solve every Establishment Clause problem, I think that test's focus on purposes and effects is crucial in evaluating government action in this sphere—as this very suit shows. . . . Although I too "look [ ] to history for guidance," I prefer at least for now to do so case-by-case, rather than to sign on to any broader statements about history's role in Establishment Clause analysis. But I find much to admire in this section of the opinion—particularly, its emphasis on whether longstanding monuments, symbols, and practices reflect "respect and tolerance for differing views, an honest endeavor to achieve inclusivity and nondiscrimination, and a recognition of the important role that religion plays in the lives of many Americans." Here, as elsewhere, the opinion shows sensitivity to and respect for this Nation's pluralism, and the values of neutrality and inclusion that the First Amendment demands.

JUSTICE THOMAS, CONCURRING IN THE JUDGMENT.

. . . The *sine qua non* of an establishment of religion is "actual legal coercion." *Van Orden* (opinion of Thomas, J.). At the founding, "[t]he coercion that was a hallmark of historical establishments of religion was coercion of religious orthodoxy and of financial support by force of law and threat of penalty." *Lee v. Weisman* (1992) (Scalia, J., dissenting). "In a typical case, attendance at the established church was mandatory, and taxes were levied to generate church revenue. Dissenting ministers were barred from preaching, and political participation was limited to members of the established church." *Town of Greece* (opinion of Thomas, J.). In an action claiming an unconstitutional establishment of religion, the plaintiff must demonstrate that he was actually coerced by government conduct that shares the characteristics of an establishment as understood at the founding.

Here, . . . [t]he local commission has not attempted to control religious doctrine or personnel, compel religious observance, single out a particular religious denomination for exclusive state subsidization, or punish dissenting worship. Instead, the commission has done something that the founding generation, as well as the generation that ratified the Fourteenth Amendment, would have found commonplace: displaying a religious symbol on government property. Lacking any characteristics of "the coercive state establishments that existed at the founding," the Bladensburg Cross is constitutional. . . .

As to the long-discredited test set forth in *Lemon* (1971), and reiterated in *County of Allegheny* (1989), the plurality rightly rejects its relevance to claims, like this one, involving "religious references or imagery in public monuments, symbols, mottos, displays, and ceremonies." I agree with that aspect of its opinion. I would take the logical next step and overrule the *Lemon* test in all contexts. . . . It is our job to say what the law is, and because the *Lemon* test is not good law, we ought to say so.

JUSTICE GORSUCH, WITH WHOM JUSTICE THOMAS JOINS, CONCURRING IN THE JUDGMENT.

The American Humanist Association wants a federal court to order the destruction of a 94 year-old war memorial because its members are offended. . . . In my judgment, however, it follows from the

Court's analysis that suits like this one should be dismissed for lack of standing. . . .

This "offended observer" theory of standing has no basis in law. Federal courts may decide only those cases and controversies that the Constitution and Congress have authorized them to hear. And to establish standing to sue consistent with the Constitution, a plaintiff must show: (1) injury-in-fact, (2) causation, and (3) redressability. . . .

Unsurprisingly, this Court has already rejected the notion that offense alone qualifies as a "concrete and particularized" injury sufficient to confer standing. We could hardly have been clearer: "The presence of a disagreement, however sharp and acrimonious it may be, is insufficient by itself to meet Art. III's requirements." *Diamond v. Charles* (1986). Imagine if a bystander disturbed by a police stop tried to sue under the Fourth Amendment. . . . Or envision a religious group upset about the application of the death penalty trying to sue to stop it. Does anyone doubt those cases would be rapidly dispatched for lack of standing?

It's not hard to see why this Court has refused suits like these. If individuals and groups could invoke the authority of a federal court to forbid what they dislike for no more reason than they dislike it, we would risk exceeding the judiciary's limited constitutional mandate and infringing on powers committed to other branches of government. Courts would start to look more like legislatures, responding to social pressures rather than remedying concrete harms, in the process supplanting the right of the people and their elected representatives to govern themselves. . . .

In a large and diverse country, offense can be easily found. Really, most every governmental action probably offends *somebody*. No doubt, too, that offense can be sincere, sometimes well taken, even wise. But recourse for disagreement and offense does not lie in federal litigation. Instead, in a society that holds among its most cherished ambitions mutual respect, tolerance, self-rule, and democratic responsibility, an "offended viewer" may . . . pursue a political solution. Today's decision represents a welcome step toward restoring this Court's recognition of these truths, and I respectfully concur in the judgment.

JUSTICE GINSBURG, WITH WHOM JUSTICE SOTOMAYOR JOINS, DISSENTING.

The Latin cross is the foremost symbol of the Christian faith, embodying the "central theological claim of Christianity: that the son of God died on the cross, that he rose from the dead, and that his death and resurrection offer the possibility of eternal life." Precisely because the cross symbolizes these sectarian beliefs, it is a common marker for the graves of Christian soldiers. For the same reason, using the cross as a war memorial does not transform it into a secular symbol, as the Courts of Appeals have uniformly recognized. Just as a Star of David is not suitable to honor Christians who died serving their country, so a cross is not suitable to honor those of other faiths who died defending their nation. Soldiers of all faiths "are united by their love of country, but they are not united by the cross."

By maintaining the Peace Cross on a public highway, the Commission elevates Christianity over other faiths, and religion over nonreligion. Memorializing the service of American soldiers is an "admirable and unquestionably secular" objective. *Van Orden* (Stevens, J., dissenting). But the Commission does not serve that objective by displaying a symbol that bears "a starkly sectarian message." *Salazar v. Buono* (2010) (Stevens, J., dissenting). . . .

In cases challenging the government's display of a religious symbol, the Court has tested fidelity to the principle of neutrality by asking whether the display has the "effect of 'endorsing' religion." *County of Allegheny*. The display fails this requirement if it objectively "convey[s] a message that religion or a particular religious belief is favored or preferred." To make that determination, a court must consider "the pertinent facts and circumstances surrounding the symbol and its placement." *Salazar*.

As I see it, when a cross is displayed on public property, the government may be presumed to endorse its religious content. The venue is surely associated with the State; the symbol and its meaning are just as surely associated exclusively with Christianity. . . . To non-Christians, nearly 30% of the population of the United States, the State's choice to display the cross on public buildings or spaces conveys a message of exclusion: It tells them they "are outsiders, not full members of the political community," *County of Allegheny*, (O'Connor, J., concurring in part and concurring in judgment). . . .

The Commission urges in defense of its monument that the Latin cross "is not merely a reaffirmation of Christian beliefs"; rather, "when used in the context of a war memorial," the cross becomes "a universal symbol of the sacrifices of those who fought and died."

The Commission's "[a]ttempts to secularize what is unquestionably a sacred [symbol] defy credibility and disserve people of faith." *Van Orden*, (Stevens, J., dissenting). The asserted commemorative meaning of the cross rests on—and is inseparable from—its Christian meaning: "the crucifixion of Jesus Christ and the redeeming benefits of his passion and death," specifically, "the salvation of man." . . .

Every Court of Appeals to confront the question has held that "[m]aking a . . . Latin cross a war memorial does not make the cross secular," it "makes the war memorial sectarian."

The Peace Cross is no exception. That was evident from the start. At the dedication ceremony, the keynote speaker analogized the sacrifice of the honored soldiers to that of Jesus Christ, calling the Peace Cross "symbolic of Calvary," where Jesus was crucified. Local reporters variously described the monument as "[a] mammoth cross, a likeness of the Cross of Calvary, as described in the Bible"; "a monster [C]alvary cross"; and "a huge sacrifice cross." The character of the monument has not changed with the passage of time.

The opinions in *American Legion* can be divided between those justices who believed that the meaning of religious monuments could evolve over time and those who did not. According to the majority view, Bladensburg's cross may have once had a religious motivation, but it had gradually evolved into a largely secular historic landmark. It is certainly true that elements of America's cultural heritage have lost their original religious orientation. For instance, in 1863 Abraham Lincoln officially declared the last Thursday in November to be a day of "Thanksgiving and Praise to our beneficent Father who dwelleth in the Heavens," but most contemporary Americans do not regard Thanksgiving—today an occasion for presidents to "pardon" turkeys—as a genuine religious holiday. At the same time, Justice Ginsburg's dissent notes that the cross is inescapably a Christian symbol that "makes no sense apart from the crucifixion, the resurrection, and Christianity's promise of eternal life." If the nativity scene, unaccompanied by secular seasonal items, conveys a Christian message about the birth of Jesus, why doesn't a cross, which likewise conveys a message about his death and resurrection, suggest the same religious endorsement?

Just as the justices disagreed about the outcome of this case, they were even more splintered over which rule to apply. Justice Alito's opinion offered a scathing evaluation of the *Lemon* test, noting that it has been unreliable, criticized, and disregarded, and Justice Thomas's concurrence urges his colleagues explicitly to overrule it. And yet the principal concern of the majority opinion—whether the purpose of a religious monument can transform to serve secular purposes—is drawn from *Lemon*, a decision which Justice Kagan made clear she still regards as a constructive precedent. The Court is evidently no nearer resolving the question of the appropriate legal standard for evaluating disputes over the establishment clause.

American Legion was the second leading establishment clause decision of the Roberts Court. Just five years earlier, in *Town of Greece v. Galloway* (2014), the justices followed a Rehnquist-era precedent permitting prayer before a state legislative session, extending that ruling to allow prayer before city council meetings, even when virtually all of those prayers were Christian in orientation.[25]

---

[25]In *Hosanna-Tabor Evangelical Lutheran Church and School v. EEOC* (2011), the Roberts Court also declared that employment discrimination law could not be applied to the decision of a church to dismiss a minister. Although that decision was primarily about the free exercise of religion, the Court also acknowledged that the establishment clause forbids the government from involving itself in such ecclesiastical decisions.

With the *American Legion* decision, it seems clear that, under Chief Justice John G. Roberts, the Supreme Court will continue the support for religious accommodation that began under his predecessor.

It would be wrong to generalize from these decisions, however, and conclude that the Court has been uniform in its willingness to see a legitimate role for religion in public life. Just as the Court has been more accommodationist in many establishment clause cases, it has been unwavering in its separationist approach in at least one area, religious activity in the public schools.

Some public schools have long sought to disseminate particular religious tenets by slanting the curriculum to favor religious views about secular subjects. The best-known and most enduring example is the way teachers address the origins of human life. Did humankind evolve, as scientists suggest (evolutionary theory), or did it come about as a result of some divine intervention, as various religions argue (scientific creationism or intelligent design)?

Two Supreme Court decisions illustrate the justices' consistent separationist position on this issue. In **Epperson v. Arkansas** (1968), the Court struck down a state law that made it a crime for any state university or public school instructor "to teach the theory or doctrine that mankind ascended or descended from a lower order of animals." The history of the law's adoption made it clear that its purpose was to further religious beliefs about the beginning of life by banning a particular theory seen as conflicting with the biblical account.

Despite the Court's clear statement in *Epperson*, some states devised other ways to teach creationism. In **Edwards v. Aguillard** (1987) the Court reviewed Louisiana's Balanced Treatment for Creation-Science and Evolution-Science in Public School Instruction Act. The law did not ban the teaching of evolution, but it prohibited schools from teaching evolutionary principles unless they also taught theories of scientific creationism. The state claimed that teaching both creationism and evolutionary theory would ensure that students were exposed to different ideas about the origins of humankind. Examining the legislative debates, however, the Court found that endorsing a particular set of religious beliefs was the clear intent of the law's sponsors. By a 7–2 vote, the Supreme Court struck down the law for its lack of a secular purpose.

The Court has taken similar separationist positions with respect to public school prayer. As we discussed in earlier sections of this chapter, the Supreme Court in *Engel v. Vitale* (1962), *School District of Abington Township v. Schempp* (1963), and *Murray v. Curlett* (1963) ruled that government-required prayer in public schools violated the establishment clause. Because these decisions have run sharply against mass opinion, some local school systems have attempted to circumvent the Court and revive school prayer in alternative forms. In every case, the Court has remained steadfast in its position that such exercises run counter to the commands of the establishment clause. Three decisions illustrate the continued adherence to the principles established in *Engel*, *Schempp*, and *Murray*.

First, in **Wallace v. Jaffree** (1985) the justices found unconstitutional an Alabama law that mandated a daily period of silence in all public schools "for meditation or voluntary prayer." The Court concluded that the law had no secular purpose, but instead had the explicit objective of encouraging prayer.

Second, in **Lee v. Weisman** (1992) the justices struck down the practice of state-sponsored prayer at public school graduations. A Rhode Island school district had attempted to make this practice constitutionally acceptable by rotating the opportunity to offer such prayers among the various denominations in the community and imposing strict guidelines to ensure that the prayers were inclusive and nonsectarian. Still, the justices found that the practice was a coercive, state-sponsored religious exercise.

Third, the decision in **Santa Fe Independent School District v. Doe** (2000) put an end to prayers at the beginning of high school football games. A Texas school district defended its practice of student-led invocations by arguing that the decision to have prayers was determined by student vote, not school officials. The Court concluded, however, that the school's underlying purpose was to encourage prayer at a school-sponsored event. Further, because the players, cheerleaders, and band members were required to attend the games—the school had argued attendance was voluntary—an element of coercion was present.

The Court's school prayer decisions show remarkable consistency in an area of the law where consistency is not common. Although the justices have squabbled over the most appropriate test to use, the outcomes of these cases have never been in doubt—prayer in public schools is unconstitutional.

The Supreme Court and the Establishment Clause

What can we conclude about the Court's handling of establishment clause litigation in general? It is difficult to characterize a Court that, on the one hand, takes a strong accommodationist position by permitting religious symbols on public land and, on the other hand, assumes an equally strong separationist position in striking down prayer at high school football games and graduation ceremonies. This doctrinal variation has been due in part to ideological divisions on the Court—conservatives tend to take a more permissive view on the role of religion in public affairs, and liberals, a more restrictive view—but it also reflects the justices' inability to arrive at a consensus regarding an acceptable, comprehensive standard to apply to a broad array of establishment clause questions. Nearly five decades ago the Court adopted the three-pronged *Lemon* test, and it survives as the last standard endorsed by a majority of the justices. Yet this test has failed to bring about consistency in the law. The Court has used *Lemon* to arrive at radically different case outcomes, and when the test has proven inconvenient, the justices sometimes have ignored it altogether. Yet each time the Court seems on the verge of eliminating the *Lemon* test, it reappears. As Justice Scalia noted in 1993, "Like some ghoul in a late-night horror movie that repeatedly sits up in its grave and shuffles abroad, after being repeatedly killed and buried, *Lemon* stalks our Establishment Clause jurisprudence. . . ."

Lemon remains because a majority of the justices have failed to coalesce around any standard to replace it. This has not occurred for lack of trying. Several justices have offered alternative approaches, without success. But even justices of the same ideological stripe often champion very different establishment clause tests. The positions taken usually reflect the individual justices' views of the purpose of the establishment clause, their understandings of the evils that the clause was designed to prevent, the traditions and history of the American people, and the religious divisions in contemporary America.

Chief Justice Rehnquist, for example, often argued for a nonpreferentialism standard, believing that the establishment clause was designed primarily to stop the government from officially favoring one religion over another. Justices O'Connor and Blackmun contended that a constitutional violation is triggered when the government sends a signal that it endorses a particular religious belief or undertaking. Justices Scalia and Thomas have focused on eliminating any government actions that might have the effect of coercing individuals to participate in religious activity. And Justice Breyer's establishment clause opinions frequently remind us of the societal cleavages and even wars that other nations have experienced as a result of government becoming too involved with religion.

Establishment clause cases are rife with contradictions and inconsistencies, and the justices have fully acknowledged the problems they have had in this area. As Chief Justice Burger admitted, "[W]e can only dimly perceive the lines of demarcation in this extraordinarily sensitive area of constitutional law." Scalia characterized the Court's record as "embarrassing," Kennedy labeled the decisions as "tangled," and Thomas described the Court's establishment clause jurisprudence as "in hopeless disarray."

Will the Court seek to resolve the law's inconsistencies in the religious establishment area? What standard or test will it invoke to do so? Will *Lemon* survive or be modified, overruled, or simply ignored? Will the Court adopt any of the competing standards, or will it embrace a new alternative? Now that you have read about many of the significant cases of the past, you probably realize that there are no easy answers. Perhaps for that reason, disputes over establishment clause questions continue to emerge and find their way to the Court's doorstep.

ANNOTATED READINGS

Much scholarship has been devoted to general reviews of the religion clauses and the various means the Supreme Court has used to interpret them. Representative works include the following: Robert S. Alley, *The Supreme Court on Church and State* (New York: Oxford University Press, 1988); Jesse H. Choper, *Securing Religious Liberty: Principles for Judicial Interpretation of the Religion Clauses* (Chicago: University of Chicago Press, 1995); Catharine Cookson, *Regulating Religion: The Courts and the Free Exercise Clause* (New York: Oxford University Press, 2001); Louis Fisher, *Religious Liberty in America: Political Safeguards* (Lawrence: University Press of Kansas, 2002); Kent Greenawalt, *When Free Exercise and Nonestablishment Conflict* (Cambridge, MA: Harvard University Press, 2017); Philip Hamburger, *Separation of Church and State* (Cambridge, MA: Harvard University Press, 2002); William Lee Miller, *The First Liberty: America's Foundation in Religious Freedom* (Washington, DC: Georgetown University Press, 2003); Stephen V. Monsma, *When Sacred and Secular Mix* (Lanham, MD: Rowman & Littlefield, 1996); John T. Noonan Jr., *The Lustre of Our Country: The American Experience of Religious Freedom* (Berkeley: University of California Press, 1998); Frank S. Ravitch, *Masters of Illusion: The Supreme Court and the Religion Clauses* (New York: New York University Press, 2007); Martin S. Sheffer, *God versus Caesar: Belief, Worship, and Proselytizing under the First Amendment* (Albany: State University of New York Press, 1999); Steven D. Smith, *Foreordained Failure: The Quest for a Constitutional Principle of Religious Freedom* (New York: Oxford University Press, 1995); and Garry Wills, *Under God* (New York: Simon & Schuster, 1990).

Other works have examined the influence of the nation's founders on religious liberties and the use of original intent in interpreting the First Amendment. These include Thomas J. Currey, *The First Amendment Freedoms: Church and State in America to the Passage of the First Amendment* (New York: Oxford University Press, 1986); Donald L. Drakeman, *Church, State, and Original Intent* (New York: Cambridge University Press, 2009); Daniel L. Dreisbach, *Thomas Jefferson and the Wall of Separation between Church and State* (New York: New York University Press, 2002); Mark Douglas McGarvie, *One Nation under Law: America's Early National Struggles to Separate Church and State* (DeKalb: Northern Illinois University Press, 2004); Vincent Phillip Muñoz, *God and the Founders: Madison, Washington, and Jefferson* (New York: Cambridge University Press, 2009).

Also available are a number of excellent studies that delve deeply into specific landmark cases. Examples of these are Paula Abrams, *Cross Purposes:* Pierce v. Society of Sisters *and the Struggle over Compulsory Education* (Ann Arbor: University of Michigan Press, 2009); Bruce J. Dierenfield, *The Battle over School Prayer: How* Engel v. Vitale *Changed America* (Lawrence: University Press of Kansas, 2007); Garrett Epps, *Peyote vs. the State: Religious Freedom on Trial* (Norman: University of Oklahoma Press, 2009); Peter Irons, *God on Trial: Dispatches from America's Religious Battlefields* (New York: Viking/Penguin, 2007); Carolyn N. Long, *Religious Freedom and Indian Rights: The Case of* Oregon v. Smith (Lawrence: University Press of Kansas, 2000); David B. Manwaring, *Render unto Caesar: The Flag Salute Controversy* (Chicago: University of Chicago Press, 1962); David M. O'Brien, *Animal Sacrifice and Religious Freedom:* Church of the Lukumi Babalu Aye v. City of Hialeah (Lawrence: University Press of Kansas, 2004); Shawn Francis Peters, *The* Yoder *Case: Religious Freedom, Education, and Parental Rights* (Lawrence: University Press of Kansas, 2003); Stephen D. Solomon, *Ellery's Protest: How One Young Man Defied Tradition and Sparked the Battle over School Prayer* (Ann Arbor: University of Michigan Press, 2007); and Wayne R. Swanson, *The Christ Child Goes to Court* (Philadelphia: Temple University Press, 1992).

CHAPTER THIRTEEN

FREEDOM OF SPEECH, ASSEMBLY, AND ASSOCIATION

While the Bill of Rights was making its way through Congress and the state legislatures, the First Amendment's freedom of expression provisions were hardly debated. The framers had a fundamental commitment to speech and press, especially as they related to public discussion of political and social issues. After all, vigorous public oratory had fueled the Revolution and helped shape the contours of the new government.

The constitutional language that the framers settled on was very bold: "Congress shall make no law . . . abridging the freedom of speech, or of the press; or the right of the people peaceably to assemble, and to petition the Government for a redress of grievances." These words would seem to provide an impregnable shield against government actions that would restrict any of the four components of freedom of expression: speech, press, assembly, and petition. In fact, some members of the Court have taken this language quite literally. Justice Hugo Black argued, "I read 'no law . . . abridging' to mean *no law abridging*. The First Amendment, which is the supreme law of the land, has thus fixed its own value on freedom of speech and press by putting these freedoms wholly 'beyond the reach' of federal power."[1] Similarly, Justice William O. Douglas believed that "[t]he First Amendment, its prohibition in terms absolute, was designed to preclude courts as well as legislatures from weighing the values of speech against silence. The First Amendment puts free speech in the preferred position."[2] By contrast, other members of the Supreme Court have recognized that, as vital as speech may be, it sometimes clashes with other worthy goals of society. Judges, therefore, should consider the costs of permitting expression and, when necessary, strike a balance. Justice Felix Frankfurter advocated this approach. "The demands of free speech in a democratic society," he explained, "are better served by candid and informed weighing of the competing interests."[3] Because the justices have interpreted the First Amendment in different ways, they have, not surprisingly, struggled to define the constitutional boundaries of speech.

As we will see, the Supreme Court's cases generally fall into one of two broad categories.[4] First, there are those cases in which the government is concerned about the problems that arise from the content of the ideas that are expressed—those potential harms that emerge from *what* people say. The Court has kept a vigilant eye on efforts to stifle or punish particular ideas, typically requiring the government to demonstrate that it is pursuing a vital state interest in a manner that treads as lightly as possible on expression. Second, conflict over free speech can also occur because of the context in which ideas are expressed. In these cases, the Court focuses not on the content of ideas but rather on *when*, *where*, and *how* they are expressed. In these instances, the Court displays a more lenient attitude toward speech regulations, as long as the government is trying to achieve an important goal, unrelated to the ideas that are expressed. It has hammered out these ideas over a long chronology of conflicts that have been enmeshed in historical circumstance and cultural change.

---

[1] *Smith v. California* (1959).

[2] *Roth v. United States* (1957).

[3] *Dennis v. United States* (1951).

[4] This discussion is drawn from Laurence H. Tribe, *American Constitutional Law*, 2nd ed. (Mineola, NY: Foundation Press, 1988), 789–794.

REGULATIONS OF THE CONTENT OF SPEECH: PUNISHING HARMFUL IDEAS

In 1859, the English philosopher John Stuart Mill wrote an extended essay titled "On Liberty." It was a vigorous defense of individual freedom, arguing that people ought to enjoy the widest possible liberty to decide how to live their lives, and one of Mill's central concerns was freedom of speech. In his view, full and open discussion of ideas was essential for advancing human understanding. When government censored expression, it was deciding for others what constituted "truth" and, in effect, declaring itself to be infallible. Because people are inherently fallible, the majority had no right to suppress unpopular views. "If all mankind minus one, were of one opinion, and only one person were of the contrary opinion, mankind would be no more justified in silencing that one person, than he, if he had the power, would be justified in silencing mankind." He acknowledged, however, that there was one condition to this freedom, "[t]hat the only purpose for which power can be rightfully exercised over any member of a civilized community, against his will, is to prevent harm to others."

Mill's essay recognizes the basic tension that the Supreme Court faces when deciding cases involving freedom of speech. On the one hand, democratic government assumes that the majority will make informed policies by considering competing ideas. Society benefits by a public discussion of alternatives, and so it is important to protect free expression. On the other hand, speech has consequences, and some of them are undesirable. It can lead to violence and disrupt public order. It can also result in airing views that many consider deeply offensive. How should the justices balance those interests? Must they protect speech, regardless of the consequences? If there are genuine harms from speech, how serious must the harms be before speech loses the protections of the First Amendment? We consider some of the categories of expression in which the members of the Court have attempted to resolve these questions.

Incitement and the Clear and Present Danger Test

In times of crisis, governments tend to respond by restricting personal liberties. When a nation faces war, economic collapse, natural catastrophe, or internal rebellion, its survival may be at stake. Because political dissent and opposition to the government can exacerbate instability, political leaders predictably place a priority on national unity and take firm action against criticism that might undermine that unity. Often these reactions take the form of policies that restrict the rights of the people to speak, publish, and organize.

The United States is no exception to this rule. In the early years of the American republic, the government was weak and vulnerable, and the economy was in disarray. England and Spain still controlled much of North America, and so Europe continued to pose a threat. The ruling Federalist Party was the target of much political criticism. In response, Congress passed one of the most restrictive laws in American history, the Sedition Act of 1798. This statute made it a crime to write, print, utter, or publish malicious material that would defame the federal government, the president, or members of Congress; that would bring them into disrepute; or that could excite the hatred of the people against them. Violations of the act were punishable by imprisonment for up to two years. Prominent citizens were prosecuted; Vermont congressman Matthew Lyon, a combative and crude critic of the Federalist Party, was indicted for writing articles denouncing the Adams administration. Minor characters were also targeted, including Luther Baldwin, a patron at a tavern in Newark, New Jersey, who drunkenly expressed his hope that a cannon salute for President Adams "fired thro' his arse."[5] Many were critical of the Sedition Act. James Madison and Thomas Jefferson, in particular, expressed their belief that the law violated the Constitution. The act expired in 1801, however, and the Supreme Court never had the opportunity to evaluate its validity.

In fact, the Supreme Court faced no significant disputes over freedom of expression during the nation's first century. Certainly there were unifying periods of national emergency, most notably the Civil War, and during these periods of stress the government took oppressive actions. President Abraham Lincoln pursued a number of policies to suppress "treacherous" behavior, believing "that the nation must be able to protect itself in war against utterances which actually cause insubordination."[6] But the Supreme Court had no opportunity to rule on the constitutionality of the president's actions, at least on First Amendment grounds.

---

[5]James Morton Smith, *Freedom's Fetters: The Alien and Sedition Law and American Civil Liberties* (Ithaca: Cornell University Press, 1956); Charles Slack, *Liberty's First Crisis: Adams, Jefferson, and the Misfits Who Saved Free Speech* (New York: Atlantic Monthly Press, 2015), 111–113, 295.

[6]Zechariah Chafee Jr., *Free Speech in the United States* (Cambridge, MA: Harvard University Press, 1941), 266.

Congressman Matthew Lyon, Democratic-Republican of Vermont, fighting with Congressman Roger Griswold, Federalist of Connecticut, on the floor of Congress Hall in Philadelphia. Lyon (pictured with fireplace tongs) was an outspoken critic of the Federalists and was the first person indicted under the Sedition Act.

Significant changes occurred with the outbreak of war in Europe in 1914 and the Russian Revolution in 1917. The United States turned its attention away from domestic programs and toward defense of the American system of government. The growing threats of communism and socialism touched off a wave of nationalism, and that fervor led to attacks against suspected subversives.

The patriotic passions unleashed by World War I were strong and pervasive. No American was immune, not even Supreme Court justices. Consider Chief Justice Edward D. White's response to an attorney who argued that the military draft, which Congress enacted in 1917, lacked public support: "I don't think your statement has anything to do with legal arguments and should not have been said in this Court. It is a very unpatriotic statement to make."[7] Members of Congress, too, were caught up

in the nationalist emotions gripping the country. They, like the founders, felt it necessary to enact legislation to ensure that Americans presented a unified front to the world. The Espionage Act of 1917 prohibited any attempt to "interfere with the operation or success of the military or naval forces of the United States . . . to cause insubordination . . . in the military or naval forces . . . or willfully obstruct the recruiting or enlistment service of the United States." A year later, Congress passed the Sedition Act, which prohibited the uttering, writing, or publishing of anything disloyal to the government, flag, or military forces of the United States.

Although the majority of Americans probably supported these laws, some groups and individuals thought they constituted intolerable infringements on civil liberties guarantees contained in the First Amendment. These dissenters, however, did not speak with one voice. Some, most notably the American Union Against Militarism (a predecessor of the American Civil Liberties Union),

---

[7]Quoted in John R. Schmidhauser, *Constitutional Law in American Politics* (Monterey, CA: Brooks/Cole, 1984), 325.

were blatantly pacifist; others, primarily leaders of the Progressive movement, were pure civil libertarians, opposed to any government intrusion into free expression; and finally there were the radicals—individuals who hoped to see the United States undergo a socialist or communist revolution. Regardless of their motivation, these various interests brought legal challenges to the repressive laws and pushed the Supreme Court into freedom of expression cases for the first time. The Court decided the first of the World War I cases, *Schenck v. United States*, in 1919, followed by three others the same year.

The case involved Charles Schenck, general secretary of the Socialist Party of Philadelphia, who had been convicted of violating the Espionage Act. Drawing from a newspaper listing of men eligible for military service, he mailed leaflets to potential draftees, encouraging them to evade conscription. The language of the leaflets suggested that compulsory military service violated the Thirteenth Amendment's prohibition of slavery and involuntary servitude. His message to young men was clear: "assert your rights" and "do not submit to intimidation." Because his actions were designed to obstruct military enlistment—which was plainly prohibited by federal law—he was convicted. His appeal to the Supreme Court asserted that his leaflets were protected expression under the First Amendment.

In upholding Schenck's conviction, the Court acknowledged that, in some circumstances, his speech might well enjoy constitutional protection, but it stressed that in times of war the government need not tolerate expression that hindered efforts to preserve the nation. Speaking for a unanimous Court, Justice Oliver Wendell Holmes provided a mechanism, known as the clear and present danger test, for framing such cases and a standard by which to adjudicate future claims:

> The question in every case is whether the words used are used in such circumstances and are of such a nature as to create a clear and present danger that they will bring about the substantive evils that Congress has a right to prevent. It is a question of proximity and degree.

Thus, although government may punish harms that result from speech—"the substantive evils"—it may do so only when there is a strong likelihood—"a clear and present danger"—that those harms will occur. But what makes for a "clear and present danger"? In developing the test, Holmes seems to have applied his understanding of

Courtesy of the Library of Congress, Prints & Photographs Division

Oliver Wendell Holmes Jr., who originated the clear and present danger test. Holmes is universally regarded as one of the Court's greatest justices due to his thirty years of distinctive service.

criminal attempts.[8] The law generally recognizes various offenses in which there is an unsuccessful effort to commit a crime; attempted murder and attempted robbery are examples. Punishing these acts requires that a person intend to commit the crime and come close to achieving it. Elsewhere, Justice Holmes had explained that government had the right to deal with such "substantive evils," provided the "intent and the consequent dangerous probability [of success] exist."[9]

Schenck was accused of attempting to obstruct military recruiting and enlistment. True, there was no showing that his leaflets actually convinced any of its recipients. What mattered was that he had intended to

---

[8]Edward J. Bloustein, "Criminal Attempts and the 'Clear and Present Danger' Theory of the First Amendment," *Cornell Law Review* 74 (September 1989): 1118–1150.

[9]*Swift & Co. v. United States* (1905). Holmes had presented a similar view as a state court judge in *Commonwealth v. Peaslee* (1901).

provoke draft resistance during time of war and that, under those circumstances, a jury could plausibly conclude that there was "the consequent dangerous probability" of success. Under Holmes's test, there was no constitutional barrier to punishing Schenck's speech.

Allowing speech to be punished, even if it does not have its intended harmful effect, might seem to give government a good deal of leeway in suppressing expression, but it is important to keep in mind the circumstances surrounding the Court's decision. The United States had just successfully completed a war effort in which more than four million troops were in uniform and more than a million had been sent to fight in Europe. The number of Americans killed or seriously wounded exceeded three hundred thousand, and public support for the war effort had been tremendous. Against that backdrop, it is not surprising that the Court would afford the government greater discretion and concede a potential danger to military readiness.

Although the clear and present danger test was seemingly designated as the approved standard for interpreting the First Amendment,[10] the manner in which the justices deployed it began to stray from Holmes's original formulation.

In *Abrams v. United States* (1919), Jacob Abrams, along with several other Russian immigrants, challenged their convictions under the 1918 Sedition Act. They had published and distributed leaflets, written in English and Yiddish, criticizing President Woodrow Wilson for sending U.S. troops into Russia. The leaflets were written in language characteristic of the anticapitalist rhetoric of the Russian Revolution, calling Wilson a "Kaiser" and urging workers to go on strike.

Writing for the Supreme Court, Justice John Clarke upheld the convictions. As in *Schenck*, the Court addressed the attempt to provoke unlawful behavior. Abrams and his associates were accused of "intend[ing] to incite, provoke and encourage resistance to the United States" in its war with Germany. As Clarke saw the speech of these self-described anarchists, "the plain purpose of their propaganda was to excite, at the supreme crisis of the war, disaffection, sedition, riots, and . . . revolution, in this country." Unlike *Schenck*, however, the Court did not concern itself with whether there was a "dangerous probability" that their speech would cause political mayhem. In fact, Justice Clarke's opinion made no mention of the

clear and present danger test. It only noted the defendants' argument—that the law was an unconstitutional violation of free speech—and cited *Schenck* to refute that claim.

The majority's failure to gauge the likely effect of Abrams's speech drew the ire of Justice Holmes. Joined by Justice Louis D. Brandeis, he wrote a vigorous dissent to counter Clarke's approach, which he believed extended the government far too much power to censor criticism. He argued that proper application of the clear and present danger test permitted government to punish only speech that creates "a present danger of immediate evil." In *Schenck*, the justices were clearly mindful of the "clear and present danger" of disrupting military enlistment; they concluded that, in the context of an ongoing war that depended upon efficient recruitment of the armed forces, advocacy against conscription—directed specifically to draftees—was sufficient to create the danger. Holmes had long believed that to punish criminal attempts, "there must be dangerous proximity to success,"[11] and here he saw no threat from Abrams's speech:

[N]obody can suppose that the surreptitious publishing of a silly leaflet by an unknown man, without more, would present any immediate danger that its opinions would hinder the success of the government arms or have any appreciable tendency to do so. . . . [I doubt] enough can be squeezed from these poor and puny anonymities to turn the color of legal litmus paper.

Abrams's call to rebellion did not present even a remote likelihood of success, said Holmes. Had the Court properly employed his test, he argued, it would not have permitted the infringement of free expression.

Holmes had failed to convince his colleagues in *Abrams*. Instead, Clarke's majority opinion used a standard known as the bad tendency test, an approach derived from English common law. It asks, "Might the natural and probable effect of the words have a *tendency* to bring about something evil?" rather than "Do the words *actually bring about* an immediate substantive evil?" So instead of considering the likelihood of speech producing harm, the Court asked whether the speaker would have known that it could be harmful. Why the majority shifted constitutional standards is a matter of speculation.

Regardless of their motivation, by the early 1920s it was obvious that a majority of justices rejected the clear and present danger standard in favor of constitutional

---

[10]Immediately after *Schenck*, the Court used the clear and present danger rationale to decide two other challenges to the Espionage Act, *Frohwerk v. United States* (1919) and *Debs v. United States* (1919).

[11]*Hyde v. United States* (1912).

interpretations that were less protective of expression. Two cases, *Gitlow v. New York* (1925) and *Whitney v. California* (1927), exemplify this shift, but with a slightly different twist. *Gitlow* and *Whitney* involved violations of state laws. Just as the federal government wanted to foster patriotism during wartime, the states also felt the need to promulgate their own versions of nationalism. The result was the passage of state criminal syndicalism laws, which made it a crime to advocate, teach, aid, or abet any activity designed to bring about the overthrow of the government by force or violence. The actual effect of such laws was to outlaw any association with views "abhorrent" to the interests of the United States, such as communism and socialism. Would the Court be willing to tolerate such state intrusions into free speech?

In *Gitlow* the Court heard the appeal of a socialist leader, Benjamin Gitlow, who had been convicted under a New York State criminal anarchy law for distributing a pamphlet that called for mass action to overthrow the capitalist system in the United States. The majority upheld the conviction, ruling that the state had the authority to punish expression that might lead to the violent overthrow of the government. In dissent, Holmes continued to press his clear and present danger standard, emphasizing that Gitlow's actions posed no immediate threat of harm.

Although the outcome represented an immediate defeat for Gitlow, the doctrine the Court adopted represented a more long-term victory for free speech. The majority in *Gitlow* held that for "present purposes we may and do assume that freedom of speech and of the press—which are protected by the First Amendment from abridgment by Congress—are among the fundamental personal rights and 'liberties' protected by the due process clause of the Fourteenth Amendment from impairment by the States." This sweeping incorporation vastly expanded constitutional guarantees for freedom of expression by ensuring that, in addition to Congress, states also had to respect the guarantees contained in the First Amendment.

In *Whitney v. California* the Court again used the bad tendency test to uphold the conviction of a political radical. Charlotte Whitney, a well-known California heiress and niece of former Supreme Court justice Stephen J. Field, was active in a number of socialist organizations and a founding member of the California Communist Labor Party. In 1919 she was arrested and later sentenced to fourteen years in San Quentin State Prison for being a member of an organization that was dedicated to overthrowing the U.S. government, a violation of the state syndicalism law.

Benjamin Gitlow, former vice presidential candidate for the Workers (Communist) Party, whose publication of the Left Wing Manifesto led to his arrest and conviction under New York's criminal anarchy act. The Supreme Court ruled that states were bound by the First Amendment's freedom of speech but upheld the conviction. Gitlow later became an active critic of communism. He is shown here testifying before the House Committee on Un-American Activities in 1939.

On appeal to the Supreme Court, her attorneys from the newly formed American Civil Liberties Union (ACLU) argued that the state law violated the freedom of speech provision of the First Amendment, but the justices upheld Whitney's conviction. The decision in *Whitney* went a step beyond previous decisions permitting punishment of those with unpopular political views. There was no evidence that Whitney had ever taken concrete actions to bring down the government; now, it seemed, not even an intent to bring about "substantive evils" was required. Her conviction was based exclusively on her membership in a subversive organization. Never before had the Court approved criminal charges based on mere membership alone. Whitney, however, ultimately avoided serving her prison sentence (*see Box 13-1*).

Throughout these cases Holmes and Brandeis continued to distance themselves from the majority by arguing in favor of the clear and present danger test in their dissenting and concurring opinions. But the majority refused to back away from the position that the restriction of expression that might produce evils was constitutionally permissible.

Regardless of the philosophical debates triggered by the series of cases from *Schenck* to *Whitney*, one fact remains clear: the justices seemed swept away by the wave of nationalism and patriotism in the aftermath of

World War I. They generally acceded to the wishes of Congress and the states—wishes that centered on the complementary goals of promoting national unity and suppressing radicalism.

As the pressures of World War I and its aftermath faded, the national debate over seditious speech was argued in calmer voices. As part of this general trend, the Supreme Court began to reevaluate its previous decisions. Especially important was a seemingly insignificant bit of writing—a footnote contained in Justice Harlan Fiske Stone's opinion in **United States v. Carolene Products Co.** (1938). This case concerned a federal ban on the shipment of a certain kind of milk—an economic,

not a First Amendment, issue. Stone wrote in the opinion's fourth footnote:

> There may be narrower scope for operation of the presumption of constitutionality when legislation appears on its face to be within a specific prohibition of the Constitution, such as those of the first ten Amendments, which are deemed equally specific when held to be embraced by the Fourteenth Amendment. . . .

He went on to suggest that, in cases involving the Bill of Rights, the Supreme Court should begin to look more closely at legislation in order to ensure the protection of individual liberties and minority rights.

What appeared to be an obscure footnote in a relatively minor case took on tremendous importance for civil liberties claims, especially those based on the First Amendment's expressive rights. As Alpheus Mason and Donald Grier Stephenson explain, the footnote contains powerful ideas regarding the status of constitutional rights.[12] It asserts that when a government regulation appears on its face to be in conflict with the Bill of Rights, the usual presumption that laws are constitutional should be reduced or waived altogether. It likewise declares that the judiciary has a special responsibility to defend the rights that are essential to the effective functioning of the political process as well as the rights of minorities and unpopular groups. The standard expressed in Footnote Four has become known as the preferred freedoms doctrine *(see Box 13-2)*. This doctrine has special significance for First Amendment claims, for it means that the judiciary will apply special scrutiny when faced with laws that restrict freedom of expression, especially as those laws may relate to the articulation of unpopular political views. Put another way, "Laws restricting fundamental rights . . . would be regarded as suspect and potentially dangerous to the functioning of democracy."[13]

In the years immediately following *Carolene Products* the Court applied the preferred freedoms doctrine to overturn many laws restricting speech, and it acknowledged that the test was built on the foundation laid by Holmes. As Justice Wiley Rutledge explained in **Thomas v. Collins** (1945), the Court now recognized "the preferred place given in our scheme to the great, the indispensable democratic freedoms secured by the First Amendment," and that speech restrictions would only be upheld in the face of a true "clear and present danger." But like previous tests, the preferred freedoms doctrine was short-lived, and by early 1950s the Court began to turn back toward more conservative interpretations of the First Amendment.

In large measure this shift was consistent with a change in the tenor of the times. In the aftermath of World War II, the nation was faced with the rise of the Soviet Union and the communist form of government it represented. Americans became deeply concerned about the threat of communism with its dictatorial government, atheistic philosophy, and imperialistic ambitions. The United States entered a cold war with the Soviet Union, and the public mood turned against any expression deemed subversive. Some politicians, led by Senator Joseph R. McCarthy, R-Wis., fed the fear by alleging that Communist Party sympathizers had infiltrated the upper echelons of the U.S. government. This fear manifested itself in many ways, including congressional enactment of several pieces of legislation designed to suppress communist and other forms of subversive activity in the United States.

When the justices received First Amendment challenges to the enforcement of some of these newly restrictive laws, they turned away from the preferred freedoms doctrine and began articulating new standards less supportive of free expression. The members of the Supreme Court, it turned out, were not immune to the effects of this altered political environment. In addition, changes in Court personnel led to a more sympathetic

Granger

Eugene Dennis and his wife, Peggy, arriving at a federal court in New York City in 1951. He was the general secretary of the Communist Party of the United States and convicted of violating the Smith Act, a federal law that prohibited advocating violent overthrow of the U.S. government. The Supreme Court upheld the convictions of Dennis and several other Communist leaders in *Dennis v. United States.*

---

[12]Alpheus Thomas Mason and Donald Grier Stephenson Jr., *American Constitutional Law*, 11th ed. (Englewood Cliffs, NJ: Prentice Hall, 1996), 307–308.

[13]Stanley I. Kutler, ed., *The Supreme Court and the Constitution* (New York: W. W. Norton, 1984), 429.

BOX 13-2

The Preferred Freedoms Doctrine

Justice Harlan Fiske Stone's famous Footnote Four in *United States v. Carolene Products* (1938) gave birth to the preferred freedoms doctrine. This doctrine holds that some constitutional rights, particularly those protected by the First Amendment, are so fundamental to a free society that they deserve an especially high degree of judicial protection.

Stone's position built on theories advanced by earlier justices. Justice Oliver Wendell Holmes Jr., for example, contended in several cases that, whereas government regulation of the economy required only a rational relation to achieving a legitimate government objective, regulation of speech could take place only if a "clear and present danger" could be shown. Justice Benjamin Cardozo argued in *Palko v. Connecticut* (1937) that certain rights are so fundamental as to be indispensable for our system of liberty. Stone expanded these arguments to enlarge the role of the judiciary as a protector of freedom and to carve out a special responsibility for the protection of minority rights.

The preferred freedoms doctrine became more prominent in the years immediately after *Carolene Products*. Several justices who sought expanded protection for First Amendment rights based their argument on the doctrine. In *Murdock v. Pennsylvania* (1943), Justice William O. Douglas declared, "Freedom of press, freedom of speech, freedom of religion are in a preferred position." Justice Hugo Black frequently stated that the rights contained in the First Amendment are the very heart of our government.

In contemporary times, the preferred freedoms doctrine is rarely applied in its original form, but its spirit lives on in subsequently adopted rules of judicial interpretation. The Court today often distinguishes between fundamental rights and other liberties, designating certain rights as deserving "strict scrutiny." Government may restrict such rights only if there is a compelling reason to do so. These doctrines flow directly from Stone's assertion in 1938 that the rights most central to our system of liberty deserve special status and protection.

Source: C. Herman Pritchett, "Preferred Freedoms Doctrine," in *The Oxford Companion to the Supreme Court of the United States*, ed. Kermit L. Hall (New York: Oxford University Press, 1992), 663–664.

position on governmental efforts to stem the tide of communism.

One of those new tests was promoted by Justice Felix Frankfurter. Calling the preferred freedoms doctrine a "mischievous phrase," Frankfurter articulated an alternative standard by which to review First Amendment claims. He argued that the liberty interest in free speech had to be weighed against the government's reason for regulating it. But, in Frankfurter's judgment, these competing claims were not of equal merit; the latter should be taken more seriously because legislators had already determined that the law in question met an important government interest. So, Frankfurter's approach almost always favored the government.

One method that the justices used to balance these competing interests was to consider the severity of the potential harm from expression in conjunction with its likelihood of occurring. In *Dennis v. United States* (1951), the Court explained that it would evaluate "whether the gravity of the 'evil,' discounted by its improbability, justifies such invasion of free speech as is necessary to avoid the danger." To punish expression under this formula, less serious harms would have to be more likely to occur, but more serious harms could be less likely to occur. Since the government typically sought to limit the rights of political subversives that might advocate violent overthrow of the state—an admittedly grave objective—their speech could be curtailed, even if violence or other illegal acts were unlikely to take place. The justices employing this calculation claimed that they were utilizing the clear and present danger test, but it was a far cry from what Holmes and Brandeis had advocated.

The Court's broad grant of discretion to the government for the regulation of expression prompted a hostile reaction from Justices Hugo Black and William O. Douglas. Both filed vigorous dissenting opinions in several cases. As noted at the beginning of this chapter, these two civil libertarians consistently opposed almost any regulation of speech and press rights, based on their literal reading of the First Amendment. When the

Court upheld federal and state regulation of the expressive rights of communists and other revolutionaries, Douglas and Black were consistently in the minority. In his dissenting opinion in **Dennis v. United States** (1951), Justice Black wrote:

> Public opinion being what it now is, few will protest the conviction of these Communist petitioners. There is hope, however, that in calmer times, when present pressures, passions and fears subside, this or some later Court will restore the First Amendment liberties to the high preferred place where they belong in a free society.

Black's words were prophetic. As the 1950s drew to a close, the high emotions of the anticommunist postwar period dissipated. Senator McCarthy, whose campaign against domestic communism had fueled much of the repressive legislation, was discredited and censured by the Senate. The nation remained concerned about the communist threat and the possibility of nuclear war, but the hysteria died down.

Once the red scare was over, the Supreme Court, now under the leadership of Chief Justice Earl Warren, began taking positions defending freedom of expression and association against the restrictive legislation passed during the McCarthy era. In short order, the justices eliminated laws requiring communists to register their membership with the government, struck down loyalty oaths aimed at subversives, and eliminated prohibitions on communists working in defense plants or holding passports.[14]

By the end of the 1960s, then, the Court had devalued many of its Cold War rulings. It struck down much of the federal and state anticommunist legislation still on the books, viewing those laws as violations of the freedom to speak, publish, or associate. In *Brandenburg v. Ohio* (1969), one of the Warren Court's last major decisions, the justices articulated the Court's current—and its most protective—standard for judging speech that advocates illegal behavior. Ironically, the *Brandenburg* decision had nothing to do with the Communist Party or other groups dedicated to violent overthrow of the U.S. government. Instead, the dispute involved a group with a much different purpose, the Ku Klux Klan. As you read this case, consider the legal test the Court adopts and how it shields expression from punishment. How does the standard differ from its predecessors?

---

[14]See, respectively, *Albertson v. Subversive Activities Control Board* (1965), *Elfbrandt v. Russell* (1966), *United States v. Robel* (1967), and *Aptheker v. Secretary of State* (1964).

Brandenburg v. Ohio

395 U.S. 444 (1969)
https://caselaw.findlaw.com/us-supreme-court/395/444.html
*Oral arguments available at https://www.oyez.org/
    cases/1968/492*
Vote: 8 (Black, Brennan, Douglas, Harland, Marshall, Stewart, Warren, White)
    0

PER CURIAM OPINION

CONCURRING OPINIONS: *Black, Douglas*

Clarence Brandenburg, the leader of an Ohio affiliate of the Ku Klux Klan, sought to obtain publicity for the group's goals by inviting a television reporter and camera crew to attend a rally held on a farm, just outside of Cincinnati. Local and national television stations later aired some of the footage from the rally, which showed at least a dozen hooded Klansmen gathered around a burning cross. Some were carrying firearms. Brandenburg delivered a speech to the group in which he said, "We're not a revengent organization, but if our President, our Congress, our Supreme Court, continues to suppress the white, Caucasian race, it's possible that there might have to be some revengeance taken." He also said, "Personally I believe the nigger should be returned to Africa, the Jew returned to Israel." Based on these films, Ohio authorities arrested Brandenburg for violating Ohio's criminal syndicalism law, which was passed in 1919 to prevent the spread of unpatriotic views. The Ohio act prohibited the advocacy of unlawful means of political reform. After his conviction was upheld by the state supreme court, Brandenburg appealed to the U.S. Supreme Court, arguing that the First Amendment protected his expression.

PER CURIAM.

The appellant, a leader of a Ku Klux Klan group, was convicted under the Ohio Criminal Syndicalism statute for "advocat[ing] . . . the duty, necessity, or propriety of crime, sabotage, violence, or unlawful methods of terrorism as a means of accomplishing industrial or political reform" and for "voluntarily assembl[ing] with any society, group, or assemblage of persons formed to teach or advocate the doctrines of criminal syndicalism." . . .

The Ohio Criminal Syndicalism Statute was enacted in 1919. From 1917 to 1920, identical or quite similar laws were adopted by 20 States and two territories. In 1927, this Court sustained the constitutionality of California's Criminal Syndicalism Act, the text of which is quite similar to that of the laws of Ohio. *Whitney v. California* (1927). The Court upheld the statute on the ground that, without more, "advocating" violent means to effect political and economic change involves such danger to the security of the State that the State may outlaw it. But *Whitney* has been thoroughly discredited by later decisions. These later decisions have fashioned the principle that the constitutional guarantees of free speech and free press do not permit a State to forbid or proscribe advocacy of the use of force or of law violation except where such advocacy is directed to inciting or producing imminent lawless action and is likely to incite or produce such action. As we said in *Noto v. United States* (1961), "the mere abstract teaching . . . of the moral propriety or even moral necessity for a resort to force and violence is not the same as preparing a group for violent action and steeling it to such action." A statute which fails to draw this distinction impermissibly intrudes upon the freedoms guaranteed by the First and Fourteenth Amendments. It sweeps within its condemnation speech which our Constitution has immunized from governmental control.

Measured by this test, Ohio's Criminal Syndicalism Act cannot be sustained. The Act punishes persons who "advocate or teach the duty, necessity, or propriety" of violence "as a means of accomplishing industrial or political reform"; or who publish or circulate or display any book or paper containing such advocacy; or who "justify" the commission of violent acts "with intent to exemplify, spread or advocate the propriety of the doctrines of criminal syndicalism"; or who "voluntarily assemble" with a group formed "to teach or advocate the doctrines of criminal syndicalism." Neither the indictment nor the trial judge's instructions to the jury in any way refined the statute's bald definition of the crime in terms of mere advocacy not distinguished from incitement to imminent lawless action.

Accordingly, we are here confronted with a statute which, by its own words and as applied, purports to punish mere advocacy and to forbid, on pain of criminal punishment, assembly with others merely to advocate the described type of action. Such a statute falls within the condemnation of the First and Fourteenth Amendments. The contrary teaching of *Whitney v. California* cannot be supported, and that decision is therefore overruled.

Reversed.

The Court overturns Brandenburg's conviction because the law allows punishment merely for advocating unlawful conduct. Not surprisingly, the justices use this case to overrule *Whitney*. The test the Court adopts in *Brandenburg* has two important elements, both of which must be satisfied in order to justify punishing speech that incites others to criminal behavior. First, the government must show that there is an intent to produce lawlessness, and second, it must show that there is "imminent lawless action." Thus, *Brandenburg* is a variation on Holmes's clear and present danger test.

Anonymous/AP/Shutterstock

Clarence Brandenburg, who led a Ku Klux Klan rally in rural Ohio. He was prosecuted for advocating criminal behavior, but the Supreme Court ruled in his favor, since no lawbreaking resulted from his speech.

In earlier cases, though, the Court was sometimes less concerned with the likelihood of harm, which made it easier for the government to prevail over unpopular ideas. Now, the Court was the saying that not even a probable harm—a "danger" of "substantive evil"—was enough; the harm would actually have to occur (or be at the point of occurring).

Compared to many of the Court's earlier cases involving incitement, this approach offers much greater protection under the First Amendment. By this standard, any attempt to incite listeners to break the law is protected speech—as long as listeners do not respond by actually breaking it.

Disruptive Speech

Preserving public order and protecting citizens from injury caused by violence are among the essential duties of government. The Preamble to the Constitution includes to "insure domestic Tranquility" among the six basic purposes for which the new government was formed. Yet free expression can threaten order. When faced with an unpopular opinion, listeners can be moved to agitation and anger, and the reaction can be hostile, even violent. Such a breakdown of public order may lead to bodily injury, destruction of property, interruption of the free movement of the public, or hindrance of the government's ability to carry out its duties. In such cases a conflict arises between the nation's commitment to freedom of expression and the government's duty to maintain order. What should the government do when speech provokes a disruption? Is it the duty of the state to protect the speaker? At what point is the government constitutionally justified in repressing expression in order to stop or prevent violence?

The justices have usually adhered to the position that, in the face of a controversial opinion, an audience does not have the right to silence a speaker. A number of cases illustrate the Court's rejection of what is usually termed "the heckler's veto." In *Terminiello v. Chicago* (1949), a suspended Catholic priest addressed a substantial crowd inside a Chicago auditorium. In a speech sponsored by the Christian Veterans of America, Father Arthur Terminiello launched into a tirade directed against Communism and Jews. Outside the auditorium, an even larger crowd had gathered in opposition to the speech. The crowd grew unruly, throwing bricks and bottles at the building and breaking several of the auditorium's windows. Some protestors attempted to overpower the substantial police presence and break down the door to the building. Terminiello was charged with "breach of the peace," defined by a city ordinance as action that "stirs the public to anger, invites dispute, brings about a condition of unrest, or creates a disturbance." In a 5–4 decision, the Court struck down the ordinance as a violation of the First Amendment. Justice Douglas's opinion explained that "a function of free speech under our system of government is to invite dispute. It may indeed best serve its high purpose when it induces a condition of unrest, creates dissatisfaction with conditions as they are, or even stirs people to anger." Similarly, the Court upheld speech rights in *Cox v. Louisiana* (1965), when civil rights marchers in Baton Rouge were accused of disturbing the peace under a law that permitted punishing those who "agitate . . . arouse . . . interrupt . . . [or] disquiet." That speech is upsetting to some, said the Court, is not a sufficient reason to punish the speaker.

At the same time, the justices have been sensitive to the practical realities of situations such as these. In *Feiner v. New York* (1951), the Court upheld a speaker's conviction for breach of the peace. A college student named Irving Feiner stood on a box and made an impromptu speech on a street corner in Syracuse. He criticized a number of public officials and encouraged blacks to demand equal rights. A crowd assembled, one large enough to block pedestrian traffic and spill onto the street, and some in the crowd began to threaten Feiner as well as one another. Two police officers on the scene determined that, to ensure public safety, Feiner should suspend his speech. When he refused, he was arrested. In this case, the Court upheld the conviction for breach of the peace. What distinguished this case was that, under the circumstances—the danger to pedestrian and vehicular traffic and the threats of violence—the officers were left with little alternative but to protect the peace. This was not a case of the state using a vaguely worded statute to punish a speaker merely because the message irritated listeners.

Although a genuine desire to preserve public order might justify limiting speech, the possibility of government using that authority to limit particular ideas almost always provokes the Court's skepticism. One useful illustration of that skepticism is *Forsyth County, Georgia v. Nationalist Movement* (1992). In this case, consider whether the government is genuinely concerned with limiting disruptive speech. Even if it is, do you think that the mechanism it chose can be used arbitrarily?

Forsyth County, Georgia v. Nationalist Movement

505 U.S. 123 (1992)
https://caselaw.findlaw.com/us-supreme-court/505/123.html
Oral arguments available at https://www.oyez.org/
cases/1991/91-538
Vote: 5 *(Blackmun, Kennedy, O'Connor, Souter, Stevens)*
    4 *(Rehnquist, Scalia, Thomas, White)*

OPINION OF THE COURT: *Blackmun*

DISSENTING OPINION: *Rehnquist*

In Cumming, Georgia, a white nationalist organization wanted to hold a demonstration opposing the federal holiday honoring the birthday of civil rights leader, Martin Luther King Jr. This group, the Nationalist Movement, proposed to "conduct a rally and speeches for one and a half to two hours" on the county courthouse steps. Like any group that aimed to use public property, the Nationalist Movement was required to obtain a permit, the cost of which helped defray the county's administrative and law enforcement expenses. There was no fixed fee for the permit; the county could vary the fee, according to its estimate of the likely cost of maintaining order, provided it did not exceed $1,000. Some organizations, like the Girls Scouts, were charged as little as $5, if they were charged at all. The Nationalist Movement was assessed a fee of $100. Rather than pay the fee, the group mounted a legal challenge to the county ordinance, arguing that it gave officials too much discretion; because the fee could be utilized to limit ideas based on their content, it violated the guarantee of free speech. The county maintained that it was a sensible and neutral way to have users of public property bear some of the costs for that use.

**JUSTICE BLACKMUN DELIVERED
THE OPINION OF THE COURT.**

In this case, . . . we must decide whether the free speech guarantees of the First and Fourteenth Amendments are violated by an assembly and parade ordinance that permits a government administrator to vary the fee for assembling or parading to reflect the estimated cost of maintaining public order. . . .

Respondent contends that the county ordinance is facially invalid because it does not prescribe adequate standards for the administrator to apply when he sets a permit fee. A government regulation that allows arbitrary application . . . "has the potential for becoming a means of suppressing a particular point of view." To curtail that risk, "a law subjecting the exercise of First Amendment freedoms to the prior restraint of a license" must contain "narrow, objective, and definite standards to guide the licensing authority."

The reasoning is simple: If the permit scheme "involves appraisal of facts, the exercise of judgment, and the formation of an opinion," by the licensing authority, "the danger of censorship and of abridgment of our precious First Amendment freedoms is too great" to be permitted. . . .

Based on the county's implementation and construction of the ordinance, it simply cannot be said that there are any "narrowly drawn, reasonable and definite standards," guiding the hand of the Forsyth County administrator. The decision how much to charge for police protection or administrative time—or even whether to charge at all—is left to the whim of the administrator. There are no articulated standards either in the ordinance or in the county's established practice. The administrator is not required to rely on any objective factors. He need not provide any explanation for his decision, and that decision is unreviewable. Nothing in the law or its application prevents the official from encouraging some views and discouraging others through the arbitrary application of fees. The First Amendment prohibits the vesting of such unbridled discretion in a government official.

The Forsyth County ordinance contains more than the possibility of censorship through uncontrolled discretion. As construed by the county, the ordinance often requires that the fee be based on the content of the speech.

The county envisions that the administrator, in appropriate instances, will assess a fee to cover "the cost of necessary and reasonable protection of persons participating in or observing said . . . activit[y]." In order to assess accurately the cost of security for parade participants, the administrator "must necessarily examine the content of the message that is conveyed," *FCC v. League of Women Voters of California* (1984), estimate the response of others to that content, and judge the number of police necessary to meet that response. The fee assessed will depend on the administrator's measure of the amount of hostility likely to be created by the speech based on its content. Those wishing to express views unpopular with bottle throwers, for example, may have to pay more for their permit.

Although petitioner agrees that the cost of policing relates to content, it contends that the ordinance is content neutral because it is aimed only at a secondary effect—the cost of maintaining public order. It is clear, however, that, in this case, it cannot be said that the fee's justification "ha[s] nothing to do with content." *Boos v. Barry* (1988) (opinion of O'Connor, J.).

The costs to which petitioner refers are those associated with the public's reaction to the speech. Listeners' reaction to speech is not a content neutral basis for regulation. Speech cannot be financially burdened, any more than it can be punished or banned, simply because it might offend a hostile mob.

This Court has held time and again: "Regulations which permit the Government to discriminate on the basis of *the content* of the message cannot be tolerated under the First Amendment." *Regan v. Time, Inc.* (1984). The county offers only one justification for this ordinance: raising revenue for police services. While this undoubtedly is an important government responsibility, it does not justify a content based permit fee.

Petitioner insists that its ordinance cannot be unconstitutionally content based because it contains much of the same language as did the state statute upheld in *Cox v. New Hampshire* (1941). Although the Supreme Court of New Hampshire had interpreted the statute at issue in *Cox* to authorize the municipality to charge a permit fee for the "maintenance of public order," no fee was actually assessed. Nothing in this Court's opinion suggests that the statute, as interpreted by the New Hampshire Supreme Court, called for charging a premium in the case of a controversial political message delivered before a hostile audience. In light of the Court's subsequent First Amendment jurisprudence, we do not read *Cox* to permit such a premium.

Petitioner, as well as the Court of Appeals and the District Court, all rely on the maximum allowable fee as the touchstone of constitutionality. Petitioner contends that the $1,000 cap on the fee ensures that the ordinance will not result in content based discrimination. The ordinance was found unconstitutional by the Court of Appeals because the $1,000 cap was not sufficiently low to be "nominal." Neither the $1,000 cap on the fee charged, nor even some lower nominal cap, could save the ordinance because in this context, the level of the fee is irrelevant. A tax based on the content of speech does not become more constitutional because it is a small tax. . . .

. . . [T]he provision of the Forsyth County ordinance relating to fees is invalid because it unconstitutionally ties the amount of the fee to the content of the speech and lacks adequate procedural safeguards; no limit on such a fee can remedy these constitutional violations.

The judgment of the Court of Appeals is affirmed.

It is so ordered.

CHIEF JUSTICE REHNQUIST, WITH WHOM JUSTICE WHITE, JUSTICE SCALIA, AND JUSTICE THOMAS JOIN DISSENTING.

We granted certiorari in this case to consider the following question:

Whether the provisions of the First Amendment to the United States Constitution limit the amount of a license fee assessed pursuant to the provisions of a county parade ordinance to a nominal sum or whether the amount of the license fee may take into account the actual expense incident to the administration of the ordinance and the maintenance of public order in the matter licensed, up to the sum of $1,000.00 per day of the activity. . . .

Instead of deciding the particular question on which we granted certiorari, the Court concludes that the county ordinance is facially unconstitutional because it places too much discretion in the hands of the county administrator and forces parade participants to pay for the cost of controlling those who might oppose their speech. . . .

. . . The Court worries . . . about the possibility that the administrator has the discretion to set fees based upon his approval of the message sought to be conveyed. . . . The Court apparently envisions a situation where the administrator would impose a $1,000 parade fee on a group whose message he opposed, but would waive the fee entirely for a similarly situated group with whom he agreed. . . . It is true that the Constitution does not permit a system in which the county administrator may vary fees at his pleasure, but there has been no lower court finding that that is what this fledgling ordinance creates. . . .

. . . There is nothing in the record to support this assumption, however, and I would remand for a hearing on this question.

For the foregoing reasons, I dissent.

The majority in *Forsyth County* did not challenge the government's right to deal with the potential disruption from speech. In fact, one could argue that the whole reason for charging a fee for the permit is to ensure that speakers, demonstrators, and parades will be protected by police—who will safeguard them from possible hostile reaction. The constitutional flaw, says Justice Blackmun, is that the mechanism affords too much discretion in its implementation. By varying the fee, the state could impose greater financial burdens on speech whose content it judges to be troublesome; without clear standards, the government could make some ideas more expensive to express than others. The dissenters, led by Chief Justice Rehnquist, did not deny that possibility, but because there was no indication that the county had actually abused its discretion, they were unwilling to invalidate the law. The Court's lesson here is that, if government officials want to promote public order in the face of controversial speech, their policies should confine themselves to an objective assessment of the potential disruption. In the absence of such rules, the state's power can be used as a tool to burden speech based simply on its content.

Of course, speech can provoke a hostile reaction in other ways. One type of expression that has sometimes concerned the Court is speech takes the form of personal insults, speech that is so inflammatory that it provokes a violent response from the listener. Such speech— formally known as "fighting words"—has long been considered subject to regulation. Indeed, in *Chaplinsky v. New*

Hampshire (1942), the Court ruled that such expression is not really speech at all. It does not involve a genuine discussion of ideas; it is instead a kind of verbal assault on another person that inflicts an injury. It is akin to lobbing verbal "projectiles."[15] Using speech to convey ideas is protected, but using it, in effect, to throw rocks is not.

Surprisingly, however, the Court has been reluctant to uphold convictions based on the use of fighting words.[16] The principal reason is that, when policy makers have written laws directed at such expression, they have usually crafted legislation that has been too vague or drawn so broadly that it ends up encompassing legitimate speech at the same time. The vagueness standard is employed when laws lack sufficient precision to give fair notice as to what is being regulated; if reasonable people have to guess what a statute means and come to varying conclusions about what it prohibits, the statute is unconstitutionally vague. Likewise, the Court's doctrine of overbreadth requires that regulations of speech be carefully tailored to meet the government's objectives; when they go beyond what is necessary to deal with the legislature's legitimate concern, they are invalidated. Thus, for example, in one year the justices struck down four different regulations of fighting words on the basis of vagueness or overbreadth. One law prohibited the use of "opprobrious words or abusive language," and the Court explained that such terms are "easily susceptible to improper application."[17]

Even if the state does draft clear-cut prohibitions of fighting words, it still has to ensure that its goal is to punish insulting speech that sparks a violent reaction, not to punish unpopular ideas. In ***R.A.V. v. City of St. Paul*** (1992), for example, the Court had little difficulty invalidating an ordinance enacted by the city of St. Paul, Minnesota, that restricted only those fighting words that were directed at a person's race, color, creed, religion, or gender. Writing for the Court, Justice Scalia pointed out that the law discriminated on the basis of the viewpoint expressed; it prohibited personal insults on one side of an issue while permitting them on the other. For instance, saying that "all religious fundamentalists are worthless morons" might be fighting words, but a reply that "all

Darwinists are worthless morons" would be protected. One statement insults a person's religion, and the other insults a person's scientific convictions. Both are derogatory expressions that might produce a violent reaction, and a law that genuinely sought to address that problem would punish them all.

These cases reflect a fairly consistent theme. The Court has always recognized the state's legitimate interest in dealing with the adverse effects speech; a loss of public order—violence, property damage, interference with traffic, and the like—can obviously be subject to governmental control. In promoting order, however, the justices have scrutinized such regulations quite closely to make certain that policy makers are not singling out unpopular ideas for special burdens.

This poses practical difficulties for government officials who are charged with promoting public safety while simultaneously securing free speech rights. The city of Charlottesville, Virginia, for example, experienced this tension in the summer of 2017, after the city council voted to remove a statute of Confederate general Robert E. Lee. That decision sparked a series of protests and counter-protests that culminated in a "Unite the Right" rally in August that drew the support of white supremacists, neo-Nazis, and members of the Ku Klux Klan. Despite efforts by police to minimize potential conflict, a violent clash with counter-protestors ensued, and numerous people were injured—and one young woman was killed—when a man plowed his car into a crowd. The city later commissioned an independent review of these events. That review acknowledged "the complicated terrain of political protest and public safety." Aware of the Court's doctrines related to disruptive speech, it encouraged the city "to develop proactive plans that both protect the core value of free speech and prevent disorder." But what plans might be acceptable? As you have seen, when government officials try to act in anticipation of possible unrest, they run the risk of assessing the content of speech and making unconstitutional policy choices based on that content. At the same time, when police try to give speakers wide latitude in expressing unpopular ideas, they increase the likelihood that lawful assemblies will ignite disruptions that threaten the public welfare.

Offensive Speech

Society establishes a variety of norms for appropriate behavior. Although standards and tastes might change over time, most people know the kinds of words or ideas

---

[15]Tribe, ibid., 837.

[16]We derive the discussion in this paragraph from Erwin Chemerinsky, *Constitutional Law: Principles and Policies*, 4th ed. (New York: Wolters Kluwer Law and Business, 2011), 1036.

[17]*Gooding v. Wilson* (1972). See also *Brown v. Oklahoma* (1972), *Lewis v. City of New Orleans* (1972), and *Rosenfeld v. New Jersey* (1972).

Westboro Baptist Church members protest outside the Baltimore federal courthouse in 2007 while the jury deliberates over a lawsuit filed against the church by Albert Snyder. Left to right: Margie M. Phelps; her husband, Pastor Fred Phelps; and their daughter, Margie J. Phelps.

that are acceptable for public use as well as those that are rude or impolite. Government policy will sometimes incorporate those norms, giving them actual legal force, and when that happens, issues of freedom of expression can arise. Justice Frankfurter once observed that the First Amendment protects "freedom to speak foolishly and without moderation,"[18] but does that protection include speech that is offensive?

The justices' first major case on this question came before the Burger Court. In *Cohen v. California* (1971), the Court ruled that government could not criminalize the use of profanity solely because it ran against the standards of society. Paul Cohen appeared in the Los Angeles County Courthouse wearing a jacket bearing the words "Fuck the Draft," a message that reflected his views on the Vietnam War. California had outlawed "offensive conduct" that might disturb the peace, but the justices explained that words are often chosen for their

emotional force and that allowing words to be punished because they offend would provide a ready means to squelch particular ideas.

This is not to say that offensive expression is beyond control; there needs to be a strong reason to justify it. So, for instance, the Court has allowed limits on broadcasts of vulgar language on the public airwaves. It has likewise permitted punishment of sexually provocative speech in the public schools. In both instances, the justices noted that the potential harm to children provided a justification for the regulation.[19]

More recently, in the case of *Snyder v. Phelps* (2011), the justices considered the right of demonstrators to express offensive messages while engaged in public picketing. In this case, members of the Westboro Baptist Church in Topeka, Kansas, traveled to Maryland to conduct a protest at the Catholic funeral service of a U.S. Marine

---

[18]*Baumgartner v. United States* (1944).

[19]See *Federal Communications Commission v. Pacifica Foundation* (1978) and *Bethel School District No. 403 v. Fraser* (1986), respectively.

who had been killed while serving in Iraq. The church, which otherwise subscribes to fundamentalist Protestant Christianity, teaches that God hates homosexuality and punishes the United States and its military for being tolerant of gays. In addition, the church often expresses its opposition to the Catholic Church. On public land near the funeral service, the protesters held homemade signs proclaiming "God Hates the USA," "Pope in Hell," "Fag Troops," "God Hates You," "You're Going to Hell," "Priests Rape Boys," "Thank God for IEDs," "Fags Doom Nations," and "Thank You God for Dead Soldiers." The father of the deceased Marine sued the protestors, claiming that they had engaged in the intentional infliction of emotional distress, an unlawful act under Maryland law. The Court held, however, that the First Amendment shielded the church members from liability. Chief Justice John G. Roberts explained that, because "Westboro's speech was at a public place on a matter of public concern, that speech is entitled to 'special protection' under the First Amendment. Such speech cannot be restricted simply because it is upsetting or arouses contempt."

To say that government cannot restrict offensive ideas does not necessarily mean that the government is obligated to facilitate or encourage their expression. Texas denied the Sons of Confederate Veterans' application for the creation of a specialty license plate containing the Confederate battle flag because it judged the flag to be offensive to many members of the public. In upholding the state's decision in *Walker v. Texas Division, Sons of Confederate Veteran, Inc.* (2015), the justices ruled that specialty license plates are government speech, not private speech. License plates supporting the Dallas Cowboys football team, Mothers Against Drunk Driving, the Girl Scouts, the University of Houston, Read to Succeed, Save the Texas Ocelots, and the like are actually statements made by a democratically elected government. If the state can decide which messages it wishes to endorse on its license plates, it can therefore decide against including what it judges to be offensive.

Suppose, however, that there is private offensive speech that requires government support in order to be expressed. That issue is raised in *Matal v. Tam* (2017), a case that involves the denial of a trademark to a rock band whose name was deemed racially insensitive by the government. As you read Justice Alito's opinion, consider how it distinguishes between government speech and private speech. Also, pay particular attention to Justice Anthony M. Kennedy's concurring opinion and his analysis of how offensiveness can become a basis for discriminating against particular ideas.

Matal v. Tam

582 U.S. _____ (2017)
https://caselaw.findlaw.com/us-supreme-court/15-1293.html
*Oral arguments available at https://www.oyez.org/
cases/2016/15-1293*
Vote: 8 *(Alito, Breyer, Ginsburg, Kagan, Kennedy, Roberts, Sotomayor, Thomas)*
0

OPINION OF THE COURT: *Alito*

CONCURRING OPINIONS: *Kennedy, Thomas*

According to the U.S. Patent and Trademark Office, "A trademark is generally a word, phrase, symbol, or design, or a combination thereof, that identifies and distinguishes the source of the goods of one party from those of others." When the federal government grants a trademark, it facilitates commerce; those who own the mark are assured that it cannot be used by others to mislead consumers, and consumers know that the mark reliably identifies a particular good or service. The golden arches of McDonald's, the multicolored letters of Google, and the green twin-tailed mermaid of Starbucks Coffee are all trademarked. Rock bands also have trademark protections; the lips-and-tongue design that embodies Mick Jagger is always recognized as an emblem of the Rolling Stones, and the "drop T" logo on Ringo Starr's bass drum is universally associated with the Beatles. In Portland, Oregon, Simon Tam wanted to trademark the name of his band. He and his fellow bandmates, all of Asian descent, formed a group called the Slants. Although the term *slant* is generally regarded as an insulting reference to Asians, Mr. Tam chose the name in an attempt to convert the word into a source of racial pride. He encountered a problem, however, in the form of the Lanham Act, the federal law that governs the granting of trademarks. That law contained a "disparagement clause" that permitted the government to deny trademarks that maligned or ridiculed individuals. Trademark officials denied Tam's application, because it was judged to be offensive to Asians. He challenged the denial of his trademark, arguing that the disparagement clause violates freedom of speech. As he saw it, the law discriminated on the basis of viewpoint; it permitted trademarks that were positive or neutral, but it denied trademarks that were negative. The United States maintained that a trademark is actually government speech, and therefore the government had the right to refuse to express an offensive message. And even if not government speech, the law did not single out Tam's message; it applied to all disparaging speech, regardless of the persons to whom the speech was directed.

JUSTICE ALITO DELIVERED THE OPINION OF THE COURT.

This case concerns a dance-rock band's application for federal trademark registration of the band's name, "The Slants." "Slants" is a derogatory term for persons of Asian descent, and members of the band are Asian-Americans. But the band members believe that by taking that slur as the name of their group, they will help to "reclaim" the term and drain its denigrating force.

The Patent and Trademark Office (PTO) denied the application based on a provision of federal law prohibiting the registration of trademarks that may "disparage . . . or bring . . . into contemp[t] or disrepute" any "persons, living or dead." We now hold that this provision violates the Free Speech Clause of the First Amendment. It offends a bedrock First Amendment principle: Speech may not be banned on the ground that it expresses ideas that offend. . . .

Under the Lanham Act, trademarks that are "used in commerce" may be placed on the "principal register," that is, they may be federally registered. . . . There are now more than two million marks that have active federal certificates of registration. . . .

The Lanham Act contains provisions that bar certain trademarks from the principal register. For example, a trademark cannot be registered if it is "merely descriptive or deceptively misdescriptive" of goods, or if it is so similar to an already registered trademark or trade name that it is "likely . . . to cause confusion, or to cause mistake, or to deceive."

At issue in this case is one such provision, which we will call "the disparagement clause." This provision prohibits the registration of a trademark "which may disparage . . . persons, living or dead, institutions, beliefs, or national symbols, or bring them into contempt, or disrepute." . . .

Tam sought federal registration of "THE SLANTS," on the principal register, but an examining attorney at the PTO rejected the request. . . . The examining attorney relied in part on the fact that "numerous dictionaries define 'slants' or 'slant-eyes' as a derogatory or offensive term." The examining attorney also relied on a finding that "the band's name has been found offensive numerous times"—citing a performance that was canceled because of the band's moniker and the fact that "several bloggers and commenters to articles on the band have indicated that they find the term and the applied-for mark offensive." . . .

Because the disparagement clause applies to marks that disparage the members of a racial or ethnic group, we must decide whether the clause violates the Free Speech Clause of the First Amendment. And at the outset, we must consider . . . arguments that would either eliminate any First Amendment protection or result in highly permissive rational-basis review. Specifically, the Government contends . . . that trademarks are government speech. . . .

The First Amendment prohibits Congress and other government entities and actors from "abridging the freedom of speech"; the First Amendment does not say that Congress and other government entities must abridge their own ability to speak freely. And our cases recognize that "[t]he Free Speech Clause . . . does not regulate government speech."

As we have said, . . . "[T]he First Amendment forbids the government to regulate speech in ways that favor some viewpoints or ideas at the expense of others," *Lamb's Chapel v. Center Moriches Union Free School Dist.* (1993), but imposing a requirement of viewpoint-neutrality on government speech would be paralyzing. When a government entity embarks on a course of action, it necessarily takes a particular viewpoint and rejects others. The Free Speech Clause does not require government to maintain viewpoint neutrality when its officers and employees speak about that venture.

Here is a simple example. During the Second World War, the Federal Government produced and distributed millions of posters to promote the war effort. There were posters urging enlistment, the purchase of war bonds, and the conservation of scarce resources. These posters expressed a viewpoint, but the First Amendment did not demand that the Government balance the message of these posters by producing and distributing posters encouraging Americans to refrain from engaging in these activities.

But while the government-speech doctrine is important—indeed, essential—it is a doctrine that is susceptible to dangerous misuse. If private speech could be passed off as government speech by simply affixing a government seal of approval, government could silence or muffle the expression of disfavored viewpoints. For this reason, we must exercise great caution before extending our government-speech precedents.

At issue here is the content of trademarks that are registered by the PTO, an arm of the Federal Government. The Federal Government does not dream up these marks, and it does not edit marks submitted for registration. Except as required by the statute involved here, an examiner may not reject a mark based on the viewpoint that it appears to express. Thus, unless [the disparagement clause] is thought to apply, an examiner does not inquire whether any viewpoint conveyed by a mark is consistent with Government policy or whether any such viewpoint is consistent with that expressed by other marks already on the principal register. Instead, if the mark meets the Lanham Act's viewpoint-neutral requirements, registration is mandatory. . . .

In light of all this, it is far-fetched to suggest that the content of a registered mark is government speech. If the federal registration of a trademark makes the mark government speech, the Federal Government is babbling prodigiously and incoherently. It is saying many unseemly things. It is unashamedly endorsing a vast array of commercial products and services. And it is providing Delphic advice to the consuming public.

For example, if trademarks represent government speech, what does the Government have in mind when it advises Americans to "make.believe" (Sony), "Think different" (Apple), "Just do it" (Nike), or "Have it your way" (Burger King)? Was the Government warning about a coming disaster when it registered the mark "EndTime Ministries"? . . .

. . . Trademarks have not traditionally been used to convey a Government message. With the exception of the enforcement of [the disparagement clause], the viewpoint expressed by a mark has not played a role in the decision whether to place it on the principal register. And there is no evidence that the public associates the contents of trademarks with the Federal Government.

This brings us to the case on which the Government relies most heavily, *Walker* [*v. Texas Division, Sons of Confederate Veteran, Inc.*], which likely marks the outer bounds of the government-speech doctrine. Holding that the messages on Texas specialty license plates are government speech, the *Walker* Court cited three factors . . . . First, license plates have long been used by the States to convey state messages. Second, license plates "are often closely identified in the public mind" with the State, since they are manufactured and owned by the State, generally designed by the State, and serve as a form of "government ID." Third, Texas "maintain[ed] direct control over the messages conveyed on its specialty plates." As explained above, none of these factors are present in this case.

In sum, the federal registration of trademarks is vastly different from . . . the specialty license plates in *Walker*. Holding that the registration of a trademark converts the mark into government speech would constitute a huge and dangerous extension of the government-speech doctrine. . . .

Perhaps the most worrisome implication of the Government's argument concerns the system of copyright registration. If federal registration makes a trademark government speech and thus eliminates all First Amendment protection, would the registration of the copyright for a book produce a similar transformation? . . .

Trademarks are private, not government, speech.

* * *

For these reasons, we hold that the disparagement clause violates the Free Speech Clause of the First Amendment. The judgment of the Federal Circuit is affirmed.

It is so ordered.

The Asian American band the Slants at the Old Town Chinatown gate, Portland, Oregon (L-R: Simon Tam, Ken Shima, Joe X. Jiang, Tyler Chen). The federal government denied an application to trademark the band's name because it was offensive. The Supreme Court voted unanimously to invalidate the federal law used to deny the trademark as a violation of freedom of speech.

Anthony Pidgeon/Redferns/Getty Images

JUSTICE KENNEDY, WITH WHOM JUSTICE GINSBURG, JUSTICE SOTOMAYOR, AND JUSTICE KAGAN JOIN, CONCURRRING IN PART AND CONURRING IN THE JUDGMENT.

Those few categories of speech that the government can regulate or punish—for instance, fraud, defamation, or incitement—are well established within our constitutional tradition. Aside from these and a few other narrow exceptions, it is a fundamental principle of the First Amendment that the government may not punish or suppress speech based on disapproval of the ideas or perspectives the speech conveys.

The First Amendment guards against laws "targeted at specific subject matter," a form of speech suppression known as content based discrimination. This category includes a subtype of laws that go further, aimed at the suppression of "particular views . . . on a subject." A law found to discriminate based on viewpoint is an "egregious form of content discrimination," which is "presumptively unconstitutional."

At its most basic, the test for viewpoint discrimination is whether—within the relevant subject category—the government has singled out a subset of messages for disfavor based on the views expressed. In the instant case, the disparagement clause the Government now seeks to implement and enforce identifies the relevant subject as "persons, living or dead, institutions, beliefs, or national symbols." Within that category, an applicant may register a positive or benign mark but not a derogatory one. The law thus reflects the Government's disapproval of a subset of messages it finds offensive. This is the essence of viewpoint discrimination.

The Government disputes this conclusion. It argues, to begin with, that the law is viewpoint neutral because it applies in equal measure to any trademark that demeans or offends. This misses the point. A subject that is first defined by content and then regulated or censored by mandating only one sort of comment is not viewpoint neutral. To prohibit all sides from criticizing their opponents makes a law more viewpoint based, not less so. The logic of the Government's rule is that a law would be viewpoint neutral even if it provided that public officials could be praised but not condemned. The First Amendment's viewpoint neutrality principle protects more than the right to identify with a particular side. It protects the right to create and present arguments for particular positions in particular ways, as the speaker chooses. By mandating positivity, the law here might silence dissent and distort the marketplace of ideas.

The Government next suggests that the statute is viewpoint neutral because the disparagement clause applies to trademarks regardless of the applicant's personal views or reasons for using the mark. Instead, registration is denied based on the expected reaction of the applicant's audience. In this way, the argument goes, it cannot be said that Government is acting with hostility toward a particular point of view. For example, the Government does not dispute that respondent seeks to use his mark in a positive way. Indeed, respondent endeavors to use The Slants to supplant a racial epithet, using new insights, musical talents, and wry humor to make it a badge of pride. Respondent's application was denied not because the Government thought his object was to demean or offend but because the Government thought his trademark would have that effect on at least some Asian-Americans.

The Government may not insulate a law from charges of viewpoint discrimination by tying censorship to the reaction of the speaker's audience. The Court has suggested that viewpoint discrimination occurs when the government intends to suppress a speaker's beliefs, but viewpoint discrimination need not take that form in every instance. The danger of viewpoint discrimination is that the government is attempting to remove certain ideas or perspectives from a broader debate. That danger is all the greater if the ideas or perspectives are ones a particular audience might think offensive, at least at first hearing. An initial reaction may prompt further reflection, leading to a more reasoned, more tolerant position.

Indeed, a speech burden based on audience reactions is simply government hostility and intervention in a different guise. The speech is targeted, after all, based on the government's disapproval of the speaker's choice of message. And it is the government itself that is attempting in this case to decide whether the relevant audience would find the speech offensive. For reasons like these, the Court's cases have long prohibited the government from justifying a First Amendment burden by pointing to the offensiveness of the speech to be suppressed.

The Government's argument in defense of the statute assumes that respondent's mark is a negative comment. In addressing that argument on its own terms, this opinion is not intended to imply that the Government's interpretation is accurate. From respondent's submissions, it is evident he would disagree that his mark means what the Government says it does. The trademark will have the effect, respondent urges, of reclaiming an offensive term for the

positive purpose of celebrating all that Asian-Americans can and do contribute to our diverse Nation. While thoughtful persons can agree or disagree with this approach, the dissonance between the trademark's potential to teach and the Government's insistence on its own, opposite, and negative interpretation confirms the constitutional vice of the statute. . . .

* * *

A law that can be directed against speech found offensive to some portion of the public can be turned against minority and dissenting views to the detriment of all. The First Amendment does not entrust that power to the government's benevolence. Instead, our reliance must be on the substantial safeguards of free and open discussion in a democratic society.

For these reasons, I join the Court's opinion in part and concur in the judgment.

Two important points emerge from the decision in *Matal*. First, as Justice Alito's opinion makes clear, trademarks are not government speech. Even though the Patent and Trademark Office is involved in the process of granting trademarks, it never considers the ideas that the applicants might wish to convey—unless of course those ideas are disparaging—and therefore what is largely a detached, bureaucratic process of considering trademark applications could not be considered government speech. Second, Justice Kennedy's opinion emphasizes that, since trademarks are private speech, the government has no right to judge what message it likes or does not like; it cannot disapprove of a message because it finds that message offensive.

In case there was any doubt about the Roberts Court view of the Lanham Act's effort to sanitize trademarks, just two years later, the Court handed down its ruling in *Iancu v. Brunetti* (2019). The founder of a clothing brand called FUCT—the letters were to be read sequentially, not read as a single word—was denied a trademark because of another provision of the law, one that forbade trademarks that were deemed "immoral" or "scandalous." Again unanimously, the Supreme Court invalidated this part of the law on the same rationale as *Matal*: it discriminated on the basis of viewpoint.[20]

These decisions serve to cement the Court's doctrine related to offensive expression. The justices are certainly aware that speech can cross the boundary lines of civil discourse. Yet that fact alone is not enough to deny it the

---

[20]The vote in *Matal* was 8–0, because Justice Gorsuch did not participate, having been appointed to the Court only a few weeks before the decision was issued. He joined his colleagues in the subsequent decision in *Iancu*.

protections of the First Amendment. Discriminating on the basis of content—that is, punishing words because they are offensive, as in *Cohen* and *Snyder*—is presumptively invalid. When a government regulation is found to discriminate on the basis of content, it is subject to "strict scrutiny," the highest and most exacting standard of judicial oversight; a government action subjected to strict scrutiny can only survive constitutional challenge if it imposes the least restriction of expression necessary to attain a compelling state objective.

As problematic as general content-based regulations may be, the Court regards it as especially egregious when content discrimination is based on the specific viewpoint expressed—that is, placing burdens on offensive words because of the opinions they convey, as in *Matal* and *Iancu*. In the Court's judgment, it is troublesome enough to single out offensive speech for special burdens. It is intolerable, from a constitutional perspective, when a law "distinguishes between two opposed sets of ideas: those aligned with conventional moral standards and those hostile to them."[21]

Compelled Speech

The most common freedom of speech case involves a claim that the government has unconstitutionally prohibited, limited, or punished expression. We have discussed a number of these restrictions, including the imposition of criminal penalties for incitement, punishment for speech that provokes hostile reactions, and burdens on hateful or offensive expression. But the government may also attempt to regulate expression in the opposite manner—by *requiring* individuals to express ideas with which they disagree. This is no less a regulation of the content of expression; the difference is that, when the government compels speech, it is prescribing content, not proscribing it. Does the First Amendment's guarantee of freedom of speech carry with it the freedom not to speak?

In some instances, societal norms will strongly encourage the expression of an idea; people sense that they are expected to join in a show of patriotism by singing the national anthem, for example. In other cases, that expectation carries the force of law. As we have noted, during World War II state and local officials often required public school children to salute the American flag and to recite the Pledge of Allegiance. Although the Court originally upheld those policies against religious objections,[22] changes in public mood (combined with changes in the Court's lineup) led the justices to reevaluate that position. In *West Virginia Board of Education v. Barnette* (1943), the Court revisited the question, this time considering whether these mandatory acts of national unity violated the freedom of speech. West Virginia required its public schools to teach courses that would increase students' knowledge of the American system of government and foster the spirit of Americanism. In support of this policy, the state board of education required that the American flag be saluted and the Pledge of Allegiance be recited each day in public school classrooms. Students who refused to participate could be expelled—and some indeed were.[23]

The Court invalidated this policy, ruling that the First Amendment prohibits government from compelling individuals to express the state's preferred views; a nation that requires its citizens to be patriotic, the Court suggested, might not have much faith in that nation's ability to inspire voluntary support for its principles. In one widely quoted passage, Justice Robert Jackson's majority opinion noted, "If there is any fixed star in our constitutional constellation, it is that no official, high or petty, can prescribe what shall be orthodox in politics, nationalism, religion, or other matters of opinion or force citizens to confess by word or act their faith therein." Freedom of speech includes the right not to speak.[24]

In *Wooley v. Maynard* (1977), the justices considered whether that right included covering a state's motto on its license plates. New Hampshire's licenses are embossed with the state slogan, "Live Free or Die," a message which one individual regarded as inconsistent with his personal beliefs. After he was fined for obscuring that motto with tape, he alleged that New Hampshire was forcing him to carry a message he saw as objectionable. Consistent with *Barnette*, the Court ruled that "the State may [not] constitutionally require an individual to participate in the dissemination of an ideological message."

At the same time, the Court has occasionally turned away claims of compelled speech made against both state and federal governments. In *Board of Regents of the University of Wisconsin System v. Southworth* (2000), the justices saw no First Amendment impediment to a state university charging student fees that are made

---

[21]Justice Kagan for the Court in *Iancu v. Brunetti* (2019).

[22]See **Minersville School District v. Gobitis** (1940), chapter 12.

[23]For more details on this case, see David Manwaring, *Render unto Caesar: The Flag Salute Controversy* (Chicago: University of Chicago Press, 1962).

[24]Relatedly, freedom of the press likewise protects newspapers from being forced by law to carry editorial content to which they object (*Miami Herald Publishing Co. v. Tornillo*, 1974).

available to campus organizations whose messages some students find objectionable. Likewise, in **Rumsfeld v. Forum for Academic and Institutional Rights** (2006), the Court upheld a federal statute requiring universities receiving federal funds to treat recruiters for the U.S. armed forces on an equal basis with other recruiting employers—despite faculty members' objection to the military's public stance, which (at the time) excluded homosexuals. In both cases, the justices ruled unanimously that laws mandating openness and equal treatment do not require (or even imply) that faculty and students support specific ideas.

One of the most significant questions of compelled speech was decided in *Janus v. American Federation of State, County, and Municipal Employees* (2018). Here, the justices were asked to upend a long-standing precedent that permitted state governments to require their employees to contribute to the labor unions that represented those employees. To some, requiring state workers to support a union helps guarantee that all public sector employees are given an effective voice in labor-management relations. To others, forcing people to support an organization with whom they disagree is compelled speech and violates the First Amendment.

Janus v. American Federation of State, County, and Municipal Employees

585 U.S. ___ (2018)
https://caselaw.findlaw.com/us-supreme-court/16-1466.html
Oral arguments available https://www.oyez.org/
cases/2017/16-1466
Vote: 5 (Alito, Gorsuch, Kennedy, Roberts, Thomas)
4 (Breyer, Ginsburg, Kagan, Sotomayor)

OPINION OF THE COURT: *Alito*

DISSENTING OPINIONS: *Kagan, Sotomayor*

Mark Janus worked for the state of Illinois in its Department of Healthcare and Family Services, and every month roughly $45 was deducted from his paycheck. That money was paid to the American Federation of State, County, and Municipal Employees (AFSCME), the union that represented the interests of about 35,000 public employees in the state. Janus was not a member of the union; under state law, he could not be required to join. Because AFSCME represented the interests of both members and nonmembers, however, state law permitted the union to charge nonmembers what is called an "agency fee"—money that would be used to pay the cost of bargaining for better wages, hours, benefits, and

working conditions. Otherwise, these employees would be "free riders," enjoying the benefits of the union without paying for it.

As far as Mr. Janus was concerned, the state was requiring him to support the advocacy of an organization that was contributing to the state's financial instability: "I don't see [the] union working totally for the good of Illinois government. For years it supported candidates who put Illinois into its current budget and pension crisis. Government unions have pushed for government spending that made the state's fiscal situation worse." Being compelled to pay the agency fee meant that he was subsidizing speech with which he disagreed. "Unfortunately," he explained, "I have no choice. To keep my job at the state, I have to pay monthly fees to . . . a public employee union that claims to 'represent' me."[25]

Standing in Janus's way was *Abood v. Detroit Board of Education* (1977), a Supreme Court precedent that held exactly the opposite. Under that Burger Court decision, requiring public sector workers to contribute to unions—even if they were not members—did not violate the freedom of expression, as long as those contributions went to support a union's bargaining efforts, not its political activities. In order to rule that the forced agency fees were compelled speech, Janus would have to convince the Court to overturn *Abood*, a decision that, after forty years, had become woven into how governments structured their relationships with many of their employees.

JUSTICE ALITO DELIVERED THE OPINION OF THE COURT.

The First Amendment, made applicable to the States by the Fourteenth Amendment, forbids abridgment of the freedom of speech. We have held time and again that freedom of speech "includes both the right to speak freely and the right to refrain from speaking at all." *Wooley v. Maynard*, (1977). The right to eschew association for expressive purposes is likewise protected. As Justice Jackson memorably put it: "If there is any fixed star in our constitutional constellation, it is that no official, high or petty, can prescribe what shall be orthodox in politics, nationalism, religion, or other matters of opinion or *force citizens to confess by word or act their faith therein.*" *West Virginia Bd. of Ed. v. Barnette*, (1943) (emphasis added).

Compelling individuals to mouth support for views they find objectionable violates that cardinal constitutional command, and in most contexts, any such effort would be universally condemned. Suppose, for example, that the State of Illinois required all residents to sign a document expressing support for a particular set of

---

[25]Mark Janus, "Why I don't want to pay union dues," *Chicago Tribune*, January 5, 2016, http://www.chicagotribune.com/news/opinion/commentary/ct-union-dues-supreme-court-afscme-perspec-0106-20160105-story.html

positions on controversial public issues—say, the platform of one of the major political parties. No one, we trust, would seriously argue that the First Amendment permits this.

Perhaps because such compulsion so plainly violates the Constitution, most of our free speech cases have involved restrictions on what can be said, rather than laws compelling speech. But measures compelling speech are at least as threatening.

Free speech serves many ends. It is essential to our democratic form of government. Whenever the Federal Government or a State prevents individuals from saying what they think on important matters or compels them to voice ideas with which they disagree, it undermines these ends.

When speech is compelled, however, additional damage is done. In that situation, individuals are coerced into betraying their convictions. Forcing free and independent individuals to endorse ideas they find objectionable is always demeaning, and for this reason, one of our landmark free speech cases said that a law commanding "involuntary affirmation" of objected-to beliefs would require "even more immediate and urgent grounds" than a law demanding silence. *Barnette*.

Compelling a person to subsidize the speech of other private speakers raises similar First Amendment concerns. As Jefferson famously put it, "to compel a man to furnish contributions of money for the propagation of opinions which he disbelieves and abhor[s] is sinful and tyrannical." We have therefore recognized that a "significant impingement on First Amendment rights" occurs when public employees are required to provide financial support for a union that "takes many positions during collective bargaining that have powerful political and civic consequences." *Knox* [*v. SEIU, Local 1000* (2012)]. . . .

In *Abood*, the main defense of the agency-fee arrangement was that it served the State's interest in "labor peace," By "labor peace," the *Abood* Court meant avoidance of the conflict and disruption that it envisioned would occur if the employees in a unit were represented by more than one union. In such a situation, the Court predicted, "inter-union rivalries" would foster "dissension within the work force," and the employer could face "conflicting demands from different unions." Confusion would ensue if the employer entered into and attempted to "enforce two or more agreements specifying different terms and conditions of employment." And a settlement with one union would be "subject to attack from [a] rival labor organizatio[n]."

We assume that "labor peace," in this sense of the term, is a compelling state interest, but *Abood* cited no evidence that the pandemonium it imagined would result if agency fees were not allowed, and it is now clear that *Abood*'s fears were unfounded. . . .

. . . [M]illions of public employees in the 28 States that have laws generally prohibiting agency fees are represented by unions that serve as the exclusive representatives of all the employees. Whatever may have been the case 41 years ago when *Abood*

was handed down, it is now undeniable that "labor peace" can readily be achieved "through means significantly less restrictive of associational freedoms" than the assessment of agency fees.

In addition to the promotion of "labor peace," *Abood* cited "the risk of 'free riders'" as justification for agency fees. Respondents and some of their amici endorse this reasoning, contending that agency fees are needed to prevent nonmembers from enjoying the benefits of union representation without shouldering the costs.

Petitioner strenuously objects to this free-rider label. He argues that he is not a free rider on a bus headed for a destination that he wishes to reach but is more like a person shanghaied for an unwanted voyage.

Whichever description fits the majority of public employees who would not subsidize a union if given the option, avoiding free riders is not a compelling interest. As we have noted, "free-rider arguments . . . are generally insufficient to overcome First Amendment objections." *Knox*. To hold otherwise across the board would have startling consequences. Many private groups speak out with the objective of obtaining government action that will have the effect of benefiting nonmembers. May all those who are thought to benefit from such efforts be compelled to subsidize this speech?

Suppose that a particular group lobbies or speaks out on behalf of what it thinks are the needs of senior citizens or veterans or physicians, to take just a few examples. Could the government require that all seniors, veterans, or doctors pay for that service even if they object? It has never been thought that this is permissible. . . . In simple terms, the First Amendment does not permit the government to compel a person to pay for another party's speech just because the government thinks that the speech furthers the interests of the person who does not want to pay. . . .

In sum, we do not see any reason to treat the free-rider interest any differently in the agency-fee context than in any other First Amendment context. We therefore hold that agency fees cannot be upheld on free-rider grounds.

Implicitly acknowledging the weakness of *Abood*'s own reasoning, proponents of agency fees have come forward with alternative justifications for the decision. . . .

The most surprising of these new arguments is . . . *Abood* was correctly decided because the First Amendment was not originally understood to provide any protection for the free speech rights of public employees. . . .

. . . The Union offers no persuasive founding-era evidence that public employees were understood to lack free speech protections. While it observes that restrictions on federal employees' activities have existed since the First Congress, most of its historical examples involved limitations on public officials' outside business dealings, not on their speech. . . .

Developments since *Abood* . . . have also "eroded" the decision's "underpinnings" and left it an outlier among our First Amendment cases. . . .

John J. Kim/Chicago Tribune/Tribune News Service via Getty Images

Mark Janus, the Illinois public employee whose challenge to being forced to support a public-sector union of which he was not a member resulted in overturning the Court's long-standing precedent, *Abood v. Detroit Board of Education* (1977). The Court ruled that the money taken from his paycheck resulted in compelled speech and therefore violated the First Amendment.

. . . [T]he Court decided *Abood* against a very different legal and economic backdrop. Public-sector unionism was a relatively new phenomenon in 1977. The first State to permit collective bargaining by government employees was Wisconsin in 1959, and public-sector union membership remained relatively low until a "spurt" in the late 1960's and early 1970's, shortly before *Abood* was decided. Since then, public-sector union membership has come to surpass private-sector union membership, even though there are nearly four times as many total private-sector employees as public-sector employees.

This ascendance of public-sector unions has been marked by a parallel increase in public spending. In 1970, total state and local government expenditures amounted to $646 per capita in nominal terms, or about $4,000 per capita in 2014 dollars. By 2014, that figure had ballooned to approximately $10,238 per capita. Not all that increase can be attributed to public-sector unions, of course, but the mounting costs of public-employee wages, benefits, and pensions undoubtedly played a substantial role. We are told, for example, that Illinois' pension funds are underfunded by $129 billion as a result of generous public-employee retirement packages. Unsustainable collective-bargaining agreements have also been blamed for multiple municipal bankruptcies. These developments, and the political debate over public spending and debt they have spurred, have given collective-bargaining issues a political valence that *Abood* did not fully appreciate.

Abood is also an "anomaly" in our First Amendment jurisprudence. . . . Our later cases involving compelled speech and association have also employed exacting scrutiny, if not a more demanding standard. . . .

Abood particularly sticks out when viewed against our cases holding that public employees generally may not be required to support a political party. The Court reached that conclusion despite a "long tradition" of political patronage in government. It is an odd feature of our First Amendment cases that political patronage has been deemed largely unconstitutional, while forced subsidization of union speech (which has no such pedigree) has been largely permitted. As Justice Powell observed: "I am at a loss to understand why the State's decision to adopt the agency shop in the public sector should be worthy of *greater* deference, when challenged on First Amendment grounds, than its decision to adhere to the *tradition* of political patronage." *Abood* (opinion concurring in judgment) (emphasis added). . . . By overruling *Abood*, we end the oddity of privileging compelled union support over compelled party support and bring a measure of greater coherence to our First Amendment law. . . .

* * *

We recognize that the loss of payments from nonmembers may cause unions to experience unpleasant transition costs in the short term, and may require unions to make adjustments in order to attract and retain members. But we must weigh these disadvantages against the considerable windfall that unions have received under *Abood* for the past 41 years. It is hard to estimate how many billions of dollars have been taken from nonmembers and transferred to public-sector unions in violation of the First Amendment. Those unconstitutional exactions cannot be allowed to continue indefinitely. . . .

* * *

Abood was wrongly decided and is now overruled. The judgment of the United States Court of Appeals for the Seventh Circuit is reversed, and the case is remanded for further proceedings consistent with this opinion.

It is so ordered.

JUSTICE KAGAN, WITH WHOM JUSTICE GINSBURG, JUSTICE BREYER, AND JUSTICE SOTOMAYOR JOIN, DISSENTING.

In many cases over many decades, this Court has addressed how the First Amendment applies when the government, acting not as sovereign but as employer, limits its workers' speech. Those decisions have granted substantial latitude to the government, in recognition of its significant interests in managing its workforce so as to best serve the public. *Abood* fit neatly with that caselaw, in both reasoning and result. Indeed, its reversal today creates a significant anomaly—an exception, applying to union fees alone, from the usual rules governing public employees' speech. . . .

. . . As we have explained: "Government employers, like private employers, need a significant degree of control over their employees' words" in order to "efficient[ly] provi[de] public services." *Garcetti* [*v. Ceballos,* (2006)]. Again, significant control does not mean absolute authority. In particular, the Court has guarded against government efforts to "leverage the employment relationship" to shut down its employees' speech as private citizens. But when the government imposes speech restrictions relating to workplace operations, of the kind a private employer also would, the Court reliably upholds them. . . .

. . . [T]he majority's distinction between compelling and restricting speech . . . lacks force. The majority posits that compelling speech always works a greater injury, and so always requires a greater justification. But the only case the majority cites for that reading of our precedent is possibly (thankfully) the most exceptional in our First Amendment annals: It involved the state forcing children to swear an oath contrary to their religious beliefs. *West Virginia Bd. of Ed. v. Barnette*, (1943). . . . [But here] the government is not compelling actual speech, but instead compelling a subsidy that others will use for expression. See Brief for Eugene Volokh et al. as Amici Curiae (offering many examples to show that the First Amendment "simply do[es] not guarantee that one's hard-earned dollars will never be spent on speech one disapproves of").

But the worse part of today's opinion is where the majority subverts all known principles of stare decisis. The majority makes plain, in the first 33 pages of its decision, that it believes *Abood* was wrong. . . .

. . . *Abood* is not just any precedent: It is embedded in the law . . . in a way not many decisions are. Over four decades, this Court has cited *Abood* favorably many times. . . . And indeed, the Court has relied on [it] when deciding cases involving compelled speech subsidies outside the labor sphere—cases today's decision does not question. . . .

. . . Stare decisis, this Court has held, "has added force when the legislature, in the public sphere, and citizens, in the private realm, have acted in reliance on a previous decision." That is because overruling a decision would then "require an extensive legislative response" or "dislodge settled rights and expectations." Both will happen here: The Court today wreaks havoc on entrenched legislative and contractual arrangements.

Over 20 States have by now enacted statutes authorizing fair-share provisions. . . . Every one of them will now need to come up with new ways—elaborated in new statutes—to structure relations between government employers and their workers. The majority responds, in a footnote no less, that this is of no proper concern to the Court. But in fact, we have weighed heavily against "abandon[ing] our settled jurisprudence" that "[s]tate legislatures have relied upon" it and would have to "reexamine [and amend] their statutes" if it were overruled.

. . . The majority undoes bargains reached all over the country. It prevents the parties from fulfilling other commitments they have made based on those agreements. It forces the parties—immediately—to renegotiate once-settled terms and create new tradeoffs. It does so knowing that many of the parties will have to revise (or redo) multiple contracts simultaneously. . . . It does so knowing that those renegotiations will occur in an environment of legal uncertainty, as state governments scramble to enact new labor legislation. It does so with no real clue of what will happen next—of how its action will alter public-sector labor relations. It does so even though the government services affected—policing, firefighting, teaching, transportation, sanitation (and more)—affect the quality of life of tens of millions of Americans. . . .

There is no sugarcoating today's opinion. The majority overthrows a decision entrenched in this nation's law—and in its economic life—for over 40 years. As a result, it prevents the American people, acting through their state and local officials, from making important choices about workplace governance. And it does so by weaponizing the First Amendment, in a way that unleashes judges, now and in the future, to intervene in economic and regulatory policy. . . .

. . . The majority has overruled *Abood* for no exceptional or special reason, but because it never liked the decision. It has overruled *Abood* because it wanted to.

Because, that is, it wanted to pick the winning side in what should be—and until now, has been—an energetic policy debate. . . . Yesterday, 22 States were on one side, 28 on the other (ignoring a couple of in-betweeners). Today, that healthy—that democratic—debate ends. The majority has adjudged who should prevail. Indeed, the majority is bursting with pride over what it has accomplished: Now those 22 States, it crows, "can follow the model of the federal government and 28 other States."

And maybe most alarming, the majority has chosen the winners by turning the First Amendment into a sword, and using it against workaday economic and regulatory policy. Today is not the first time the Court has wielded the First Amendment in such an aggressive way. And it threatens not to be the last. . . . [A]lmost all economic and regulatory policy affects or touches speech. So the majority's road runs long. And at every stop are black-robed rulers overriding citizens' choices. The First Amendment was meant for better things. It was meant not to undermine but to protect democratic governance—including over the role of public-sector unions.

The majority and minority opinions in *Janus* took vastly different approaches to the issue of mandatory contributions to unions representing public employees. To Justice Alito, those contributions resulted in compelled speech; by taking money from a nonmember and transferring it to a union whose goals he did not support, the government was forcing him to express ideas to which he did not subscribe. To Justice Kagan, these fees were a proven, sensible way of structuring the economic relationship between labor and management; the government was merely one of many employers that work with employees to manage how labor's interests will be represented at the bargaining table. As long as the money was restricted to advocating for improved wages, better working conditions, and the like—and not used to advocate political positions—there was no free speech violation. To Justice Alito, that was a distinction without a difference; when the union lobbies for higher salaries for government workers, is that a labor negotiating position or political advocacy?

Both opinions spoke to the costs of the outcome, but they focused on different ones. According to Justice Kagan's dissent—which is scathing in its criticism of the Court's disregard for stare decisis—overturning *Abood* will have a disruptive effect on millions of public employees and undo countless contractual arrangement nationwide. Justice Alito's view was that the costs of adhering to *Abood* have been equally severe, since the result has been billions of dollars being taken from the government's workers and utilized for compelled speech to which they did not agree.

Interestingly, Justice Kagan's reference to "weaponizing the First Amendment" perhaps reflects an ideological shift in the kinds of interests seeking judicial relief from compelled speech. In prior cases, such as *Barnette* and *Wooley*, those who objected to compelled speech could be characterized as politically liberal; both involved members of a minority religion (Jehovah's Witnesses) that has been subject to past discrimination. In *Janus*, by contrast, the challenge to compelled speech was decidedly more conservative in orientation; Janus was taking on organized labor, a historically liberal interest group. To the extent that the justices consider the politics of the litigants themselves, this shift might help to explain why the Court's five most conservative members saw a case of compelled speech in a state requirement that pro-life "crisis pregnancy centers" inform women about publicly funded contraception and abortion services; in *National Institute of Family and Life Advocates v. Becerra* (2018), those justices regarded the notice requirement as a content-based restriction. Writing for the majority, Justice Thomas explained, "Governments must not be allowed to force persons to express a message contrary to their deepest convictions." The Court's liberal members, by contrast, viewed the law as the same kind of disclosure requirement for health professionals that the Court has previously upheld.

Expressive Association

Individuals are not alone in expressing ideas. Groups form because their members share similar goals and ideas, and they, too, engage in expressive activities. There is nothing new about the tendency of Americans to join together to pursue a common objective. When he traveled the United States in the early nineteenth century, the French aristocrat Alexis de Tocqueville was impressed by the extent to which citizens united for all kinds of political purposes. As he wrote, "In no country in the world has the principle of association been more successfully used, or more unsparingly applied to a multitude of different objects, than in America."[26] He believed that the liberty of association was a protection against tyranny by majorities that might wish to limit opinions of one kind or another.

For its part, the Supreme Court has long regarded the right to join with like-minded individuals to advance mutual goals as essential to the exercise of political and social expression. As Justice Harlan explained in *NAACP v. Alabama* (1958), "Effective advocacy of both public and private points of view, particularly controversial ones, is undeniably enhanced by group association." The right of association is not explicit in the First Amendment, but "[i]t is beyond debate that freedom to engage in association for the advancement of beliefs and ideas is an inseparable aspect of the 'liberty' assured by the Due Process Clause of the Fourteenth Amendment." Thus, the justices have concluded that it is a right implicit in the First Amendment's freedoms of speech, press, assembly, and petition.[27]

Protecting the right of individuals to form groups for political or social purposes often means extending constitutional guarantees to organizations that hold unpopular or even dangerous views. In several cases during the 1960s the justices struck down government attempts to regulate membership in the Communist Party. Similarly, the Court has been vigilant in

---

[26]Alexis de Tocqueville, *Democracy in America*, vol. 1 (New York: D. Appleton, 1899), 197.

[27]In addition, the Court has invoked the relevance of association rights to the protection of intimate human relationships (marriage, family, and childbearing).

protecting the association rights of minority groups. In the early years of the civil rights movement, the justices invalidated efforts by southern states to interfere with the National Association for the Advancement of Colored People and its organizational activities.

Since then, conflicts have arisen between groups asserting First Amendment association rights and states enforcing legislation to reduce discrimination. Most frequently at issue are the policies of private organizations that restrict membership or services based on characteristics such as race, sex, sexual orientation, or religion. Country clubs, businessmen's clubs, fraternal organizations, and civic groups often have such membership restrictions. Do the members of private organizations have the constitutional right to impose whatever membership qualifications they desire? Or may the state, concerned that the exclusion of people could deprive them of opportunities for business and professional networking and advancement, enforce antidiscrimination statutes that would make such membership restrictions unlawful?

The justices addressed this question in **Roberts v. United States Jaycees** (1984). The Jaycees, established in 1920 as the Junior Chamber of Commerce, is a private civic organization that helps young men participate in the affairs of their communities. The Minnesota Department of Human Rights claimed that the organization's exclusion of women violated a state law prohibiting sex-based discrimination in public accommodations. The Jaycees argued that applying the Minnesota antidiscrimination law to its membership policies was a violation of the First Amendment freedom of association.

In a 7–0 decision, the Supreme Court ruled against the Jaycees. While acknowledging that freedom of association is a necessary component of the First Amendment, the Court said that the Jaycees "lack the distinctive characteristics that might afford constitutional protection to the decision of its members to exclude women." According to the Court, the group does not have specific views that would be jeopardized by admitting women; it is a large, national organization with no firm ideological orientations. Since Minnesota's law was not aimed at limiting expression, the state's interest in eliminating gender discrimination to expand civic opportunities for women justified its use.

The logic of that ruling—that state regulations that are unrelated to expression do not harm the association rights of large groups with nonideological purposes and nonselective membership policies—was applied in

AP Photo/Stuart Ramson

The Boy Scouts revoked the adult membership of James Dale because of his admitted homosexuality. In *Boy Scouts of America v. Dale*, the Court determined that the organization had the right to exclude him.

two similar disputes, each time with similar results.[28] Given the consistent (and unanimous) opinions in these cases, the Court created the impression that the law was relatively settled: freedom of association must give way to state interests in combating discrimination. That impression was weakened in 1995, however, when the justices decided **Hurley v. Irish-American Gay, Lesbian and Bisexual Group of Boston**. This dispute arose when a private association organizing a Saint Patrick's Day parade in Boston rejected the application of a gay rights group to march in the celebration. The gay rights group sued, claiming that its exclusion from the parade violated the Massachusetts antidiscrimination statute. The Supreme Court unanimously ruled in favor of the parade organizers. The justices held that the

---

[28]*Board of Directors of Rotary International v. Rotary Club of Duarte* (1987) and *New York State Club Association v. City of New York* (1988).

First Amendment is violated by a state law requiring private sponsors of a parade to include a group imparting a message that the organizers do not wish to convey. The Court applied the principles set in *Roberts* but came to quite a different result. Here the forced inclusion of the gay rights group was found to place a significant burden on the expressive rights of the parade organizers; because the parade sponsors intended to communicate a specific message—quite unlike the Jaycees, whose goals were more amorphous—they were entitled to control the content of that message.

This decision set the stage for the next major freedom of association dispute, *Boy Scouts of America v. Dale* (2000), a challenge to the dismissal of a Scout leader on sexual orientation grounds. Would the Court find the facts in this case similar to the exclusion of women in *Roberts*, or would the justices conclude that the Boy Scouts' membership policies were protected by the First Amendment's freedom of association?

Boy Scouts of America v. Dale

530 U.S. 640 (2000)
http://caselaw.findlaw.com/us-supreme-court/530/640.html
Oral arguments available at https://www.oyez.org/
    cases/1999/99-699
Vote: 5 (Kennedy, O'Connor, Rehnquist, Scalia, Thomas)
    4 (Breyer, Ginsburg, Souter, Stevens)

OPINION OF THE COURT: *Rehnquist*

DISSENTING OPINIONS: *Souter, Stevens*

James Dale began his involvement in the Boy Scouts organization in 1978, when, at the age of eight, he joined Cub Scout Pack 142 in Monmouth, New Jersey. He became a Boy Scout in 1981 and remained an active Scout until he turned eighteen. Dale was an exemplary member of the organization, being admitted to the prestigious Order of the Arrow and achieving the rank of Eagle Scout, Scouting's highest honor. In 1989 he became an adult member of the organization and was an assistant scoutmaster.

Around the same time, Dale left home to attend Rutgers University. While at college, Dale first acknowledged to himself and to others that he was gay. He joined and later became copresident of Rutgers University Gay/Lesbian Alliance. After attending a seminar devoted to gay/lesbian health issues in 1990, he was interviewed and photographed for a newspaper story in which he discussed the need for gay teenagers to have appropriate role models.

Shortly after the publication of the newspaper article, Dale received a letter from the Monmouth Council of the Boy Scouts

of America revoking his adult membership. When he requested a reason for this action, the council informed him that the Boy Scouts "specifically forbid membership to homosexuals." In 1992 Dale filed a complaint against the Boy Scouts claiming that the revocation of his membership violated a New Jersey law prohibiting discrimination based on sexual orientation in public accommodations. The Boy Scouts countered that as a private, nonprofit organization it had the right, under the freedom of association guarantees of the First Amendment, to deny membership to individuals whose views are not consistent with the group's values. The New Jersey Supreme Court ruled in favor of Dale, and the Boy Scouts asked for review by the U.S. Supreme Court.

CHIEF JUSTICE REHNQUIST DELIVERED THE OPINION OF THE COURT.

In *Roberts v. United States Jaycees* (1984), we observed that "implicit in the right to engage in activities protected by the First Amendment" is "a corresponding right to associate with others in pursuit of a wide variety of political, social, economic, educational, religious, and cultural ends." This right is crucial in preventing the majority from imposing its views on groups that would rather express other, perhaps unpopular, ideas. Government actions that may unconstitutionally burden this freedom may take many forms, one of which is "intrusion into the internal structure or affairs of an association" like a "regulation that forces the group to accept members it does not desire." Forcing a group to accept certain members may impair the ability of the group to express those views, and only those views, that it intends to express. Thus, "[f]reedom of association . . . plainly presupposes a freedom not to associate."

The forced inclusion of an unwanted person in a group infringes the group's freedom of expressive association if the presence of that person affects in a significant way the group's ability to advocate public or private viewpoints. *New York State Club Assn., Inc. v. City of New York* (1988). But the freedom of expressive association, like many freedoms, is not absolute. We have held that the freedom could be overridden "by regulations adopted to serve compelling state interests, unrelated to the suppression of ideas, that cannot be achieved through means significantly less restrictive of associational freedoms." *Roberts*.

To determine whether a group is protected by the First Amendment's expressive associational right, we must determine whether the group engages in "expressive association." The First Amendment's protection of expressive association is not reserved for advocacy groups. But to come within its ambit, a group must engage in some form of expression, whether it be public or private. . . .

. . . [T]he general mission of the Boy Scouts is clear: "[T]o instill values in young people." The Boy Scouts seeks to instill these values by having its adult leaders spend time with the youth members, instructing and engaging them in activities like camping, archery, and fishing. During the time spent with the youth members, the scoutmasters and assistant scoutmasters inculcate them with the Boy Scouts' values—both expressly and by example. It seems indisputable that an association that seeks to transmit such a system of values engages in expressive activity.

Given that the Boy Scouts engages in expressive activity, we must determine whether the forced inclusion of Dale as an assistant scoutmaster would significantly affect the Boy Scouts' ability to advocate public or private viewpoints. This inquiry necessarily requires us first to explore, to a limited extent, the nature of the Boy Scouts' view of homosexuality.

The values the Boy Scouts seeks to instill are "based on" those listed in the Scout Oath and Law. The Boy Scouts explains that the Scout Oath and Law provide "a positive moral code for living; they are a list of 'do's' rather than 'don'ts.'" The Boy Scouts asserts that homosexual conduct is inconsistent with the values embodied in the Scout Oath and Law, particularly with the values represented by the terms "morally straight" and "clean."

Obviously, the Scout Oath and Law do not expressly mention sexuality or sexual orientation. And the terms "morally straight" and "clean" are by no means self-defining. Different people would attribute to those terms very different meanings. . . .

The New Jersey Supreme Court analyzed the Boy Scouts' beliefs and . . . concluded that the exclusion of members like Dale "appears antithetical to the organization's goals and philosophy." But our cases reject this sort of inquiry; it is not the role of the courts to reject a group's expressed values because they disagree with those values or find them internally inconsistent.

The Boy Scouts asserts that it "teach[es] that homosexual conduct is not morally straight," and that it does "not want to promote homosexual conduct as a legitimate form of behavior." We accept the Boy Scouts' assertion. We need not inquire further to determine the nature of the Boy Scouts' expression with respect to homosexuality. But because the record before us contains written evidence of the Boy Scouts' viewpoint, we look to it as instructive, if only on the question of the sincerity of the professed beliefs.

A 1978 position statement to the Boy Scouts' Executive Committee . . . expresses the Boy Scouts' "official position" with regard to "homosexuality and Scouting":

" . . . The Boy Scouts of America is a private, membership organization and leadership therein is a privilege and not a right. We do not believe that homosexuality and leadership in Scouting are appropriate. We will continue to select only those who in our judgment meet our standards and qualifications for leadership."

Thus, at least as of 1978—the year James Dale entered Scouting—the official position of the Boy Scouts was that avowed homosexuals were not to be Scout leaders.

A position statement promulgated by the Boy Scouts in 1991 (after Dale's membership was revoked but before this litigation was filed) also supports its current view:

"We believe that homosexual conduct is inconsistent with the requirement in the Scout Oath that a Scout be morally straight and in the Scout Law that a Scout be clean in word and deed, and that homosexuals do not provide a desirable role model for Scouts."

This position statement was redrafted numerous times but its core message remained consistent. . . .

. . . We cannot doubt that the Boy Scouts sincerely holds this view.

We must then determine whether Dale's presence as an assistant scoutmaster would significantly burden the Boy Scouts' desire to not "promote homosexual conduct as a legitimate form of behavior." As we give deference to an association's assertions regarding the nature of its expression, we must also give deference to an association's view of what would impair its expression. That is not to say that an expressive association can erect a shield against antidiscrimination laws simply by asserting that mere acceptance of a member from a particular group would impair its message. But here Dale, by his own admission, is one of a group of gay Scouts who have "become leaders in their community and are open and honest about their sexual orientation." Dale was the copresident of a gay and lesbian organization at college and remains a gay rights activist. Dale's presence in the Boy Scouts would, at the very least, force the organization to send a message, both to the youth members and the world, that the Boy Scouts accepts homosexual conduct as a legitimate form of behavior. . . .

The New Jersey Supreme Court determined that the Boy Scouts' ability to disseminate its message was not significantly affected by the forced inclusion of Dale as an assistant scoutmaster. . . .

We disagree with the New Jersey Supreme Court's conclusion. . . .

First, associations do not have to associate for the "purpose" of disseminating a certain message in order to be entitled to the protections of the First Amendment. An association must merely engage in expressive activity that could be impaired in order to be entitled to protection. . . .

Second, even if the Boy Scouts discourages Scout leaders from disseminating views on sexual issues—a fact that the Boy Scouts disputes with contrary evidence—the First Amendment protects the Boy Scouts' method of expression. If the Boy Scouts wishes Scout leaders to avoid questions of sexuality and teach only by example, this fact does not negate the sincerity of its belief discussed above.

Third, the First Amendment simply does not require that every member of a group agree on every issue in order for the group's policy to be "expressive association." The Boy Scouts takes an official position with respect to homosexual conduct, and that is sufficient for First Amendment purposes. . . . The fact that the organization does not trumpet its views from the housetops, or that it tolerates dissent within its ranks, does not mean that its views receive no First Amendment protection.

Having determined that the Boy Scouts is an expressive association and that the forced inclusion of Dale would significantly affect its expression, we inquire whether the application of New Jersey's public accommodations law to require that the Boy Scouts accept Dale as an assistant scoutmaster runs afoul of the Scouts' freedom of expressive association. We conclude that it does. . . .

. . . The state interests embodied in New Jersey's public accommodations law do not justify such a severe intrusion on the Boy Scouts' rights to freedom of expressive association. That being the case, we hold that the First Amendment prohibits the State from imposing such a requirement through the application of its public accommodations law. . . .

We are not, as we must not be, guided by our views of whether the Boy Scouts' teachings with respect to homosexual conduct are right or wrong; public or judicial disapproval of a tenet of an organization's expression does not justify the State's effort to compel the organization to accept members where such acceptance would derogate from the organization's expressive message. . . .

The judgment of the New Jersey Supreme Court is reversed, and the cause remanded for further proceedings not inconsistent with this opinion.

It is so ordered.

JUSTICE STEVENS, WITH WHOM JUSTICE SOUTER, JUSTICE GINSBURG, AND JUSTICE BREYER JOIN, DISSENTING.

The majority holds that New Jersey's law violates BSA's [Boy Scouts of America's] right to associate and its right to free speech. But that law does not "impos[e] any serious burdens" on BSA's "collective effort on behalf of [its] shared goals," *Roberts v. United States Jaycees* (1984), nor does it force BSA to communicate any message that it does not wish to endorse. New Jersey's law, therefore, abridges no constitutional right of the Boy Scouts. . . .

In this case, Boy Scouts of America contends that it teaches the young boys who are Scouts that homosexuality is immoral. Consequently, it argues, it would violate its right to associate to force it to admit homosexuals as members, as doing so would be at odds with its own shared goals and values. This contention, quite plainly, requires us to look at what, exactly, are the values that BSA actually teaches.

. . . BSA describes itself as having a "representative membership," which it defines as "boy membership [that] reflects proportionately the characteristics of the boy population of its service area." In particular, the group emphasizes that "[n]either the charter nor the bylaws of the Boy Scouts of America permits the exclusion of any boy. . . . To meet these responsibilities we have made a commitment that our membership shall be representative of all the population in every community, district, and council." . . .

To bolster its claim that its shared goals include teaching that homosexuality is wrong, BSA directs our attention to two terms appearing in the Scout Oath and Law. The first is the phrase "morally straight," which appears in the Oath ("On my honor I will do my best . . . To keep myself . . . morally straight"); the second term is the word "clean," which appears in a list of 12 characteristics together comprising the Scout Law. . . .

It is plain as the light of day that neither one of these principles—"morally straight" and "clean"—says the slightest thing about homosexuality. Indeed, neither term in the Boy Scouts' Law and Oath expresses any position whatsoever on sexual matters.

BSA's published guidance on that topic underscores this point. Scouts, for example, are directed to receive their sex education at home or in school, but not from the organization. . . . In light of the BSA's self-proclaimed ecumenism, furthermore, it is even more difficult to discern any shared goals or common moral stance on homosexuality. . . .

BSA's claim finds no support in our cases. We have recognized "a right to associate for the purpose of engaging in those activities protected by the First Amendment—speech, assembly, petition for the redress of grievances, and the exercise of religion." *Roberts.* And we have acknowledged that "when the State interferes with individuals' selection of those with whom they wish to join in a common endeavor, freedom of association . . . may be implicated." But "[t]he right to associate for expressive purposes is not . . . absolute"; rather, "the nature and degree of constitutional protection afforded freedom of association may vary depending on the extent to which . . . the constitutionally protected liberty is at stake in a given case." Indeed, the right to associate does not mean "that in every setting in which individuals exercise some discrimination in choosing associates, their selective process of inclusion and exclusion is protected by the Constitution." *New York State Club Assn., Inc. v. City of New York* (1988). . . .

. . . [T]he majority insists that we must "give deference to an association's assertions regarding the nature of its expression" and "we must also give deference to an association's view of what would impair its expression." . . .

This is an astounding view of the law. I am unaware of any previous instance in which our analysis of the scope of a constitutional right was determined by looking at what a litigant asserts in his or her brief and inquiring no further. . . . But the majority insists that our inquiry must be "limited" because "it is not the role of the courts to reject a group's expressed values because they disagree with those values or find them internally inconsistent."

But nothing in our cases calls for this Court to do any such thing. An organization can adopt the message of its choice, and it is not this Court's place to disagree with it. But we must inquire whether the group is, in fact, expressing a message (whatever it may be) and whether that message (if one is expressed) is significantly affected by a State's antidiscrimination law. More critically, that inquiry requires our *independent* analysis, rather than deference to a group's litigating posture. . . .

There is, of course, a valid concern that a court's independent review may run the risk of paying too little heed to an organization's sincerely held views. But unless one is prepared to turn the right to associate into a free pass out of antidiscrimination laws, an independent inquiry is a necessity. . . .

In this case, no such concern is warranted. It is entirely clear that BSA in fact expresses no clear, unequivocal message burdened by New Jersey's law. . . .

. . . Over the years, BSA has generously welcomed over 87 million young Americans into its ranks. In 1992 over one million adults were active BSA members. The notion that an organization of that size and enormous prestige implicitly endorses the views that each of those adults may express in a non-Scouting context is simply mind boggling. . . .

Unfavorable opinions about homosexuals "have ancient roots." *Bowers v. Hardwick* (1986). . . .

That such prejudices are still prevalent and that they have caused serious and tangible harm to countless members of the class New Jersey seeks to protect are established matters of fact that neither the Boy Scouts nor the Court disputes. That harm can only be aggravated by the creation of a constitutional shield for a policy that is itself the product of a habitual way of thinking about strangers. As Justice Brandeis so wisely advised, "we must be ever on our guard, lest we erect our prejudices into legal principles."

If we would guide by the light of reason, we must let our minds be bold. I respectfully dissent.

Although a divided Court ruled in favor of the Boy Scouts, the decision did not change the standards set in *Roberts v. United States Jaycees*. They remained firmly in place. Rather, the sharp divisions among the justices in *Dale* rested on answers to questions about the actual beliefs of the Boy Scouts and the extent to which New Jersey's antidiscrimination law inhibited the right of expressive association. Although the Court's ruling settled the immediate dispute over James Dale's removal as a Scout leader, it certainly did not end the controversy over the Boy Scouts' policy *(see Box 13-3)*.

BOX 13-3

Aftermath . . . *Boy Scouts of America v. Dale*

Following the Supreme Court's decision, the Boy Scouts of America (BSA) became surrounded by controversy, with supporters praising the organization's decision to hold fast to its values and critics applying intense social pressure in favor of lifting the ban on gay members. Inside the organization, certain segments of the Scouting community began agitating for a change in the group's position. In addition, the Boy Scouts suffered a modest loss of membership and financial support. Subsequently, the BSA initiated a comprehensive study to reevaluate its policy.

In May 2013, delegates at the BSA National Council meeting voted to drop the ban on gay youth members effective January 1, 2014, but to keep in place its prohibition against openly gay men serving as Scout leaders. The policy change was supported by 60 percent of the delegates. The organization, however, emphasized its position that "any sexual conduct, whether heterosexual or homosexual, by youth of Scouting age is contrary to the virtues of Scouting."

In addition, the BSA selected former U.S. defense secretary and Eagle Scout Robert Gates to assume the presidency of the organization in 2014. Gates was instrumental in removing the military's "Don't Ask, Don't Tell" policy with respect to sexual orientation.

The Scouting organization consists of over 2 million youths and 1 million volunteers. Its nearly 100,000 local units are sponsored by businesses, community groups, and religious organizations. Two of the largest Scouting sponsors, the Church of Jesus Christ of Latter-day Saints and the Roman Catholic Church, generally agreed with the policy change and indicated their

(Continued)

(Continued)

intention to remain involved in Scouting. The Southern Baptist Convention expressed disappointment with the new policy but left to local churches the decision whether to remain in Scouting or to sever ties with the organization.

In response to the BSA's new policy, conservative groups formed an alternative organization, Trail Life USA, a Christian adventure, character-building, and leadership program. Trail Life USA actively welcomed former Boy Scout troops whose sponsors opposed the change in BSA membership policies.

From the liberal side of the political spectrum came general support for BSA's revised membership policy, but many remained at odds with the continued ban on gay Scout leaders. One critic was James Dale, whose challenge to the former membership policy was rejected by the Supreme Court. Dale said, "It sends a negative, destructive message to young gay kids that this is a youthful indiscretion, that they don't really know who they are as a young person if they think they are gay, and once they're an adult they're not good enough anymore."

In 2015, at President Gates's urging, the Scouts ended the ban on gay leaders but allowed troops sponsored by religious organizations to select local leaders who share their faith-based principles, even if this results in restricting these positions to heterosexual men. The Scouts further altered membership policies in January 2017, when the organization began accepting new scouts based on the sex listed on their applications, thus opening the door to transgender youths. And later that same year, it announced it would open its membership to girls—much to the consternation of the Girl Scouts. To reflect its more inclusive orientation, the Boys Scouts of America officially changed its name to Scouts BSA in 2019.

In the years leading up these changes, the organization had been dogged by allegations of sexual abuse. Facing a wave of lawsuits from alleged victims, the Boy Scouts filed for bankruptcy early in 2020.

Sources: Boy Scouts of American Annual Report, 2018; Mike Baker, "Boy Scouts Seek Bankruptcy to Survive a Deluge of Sex-Abuse Claims," *New York Times*, February 18, 2020; Niraj Chokshi, "Boy Scouts, Reversing Century-Old Stance, Will Allow Transgender Boys," *New York Times,* January 30, 2017; Cheryl K. Chumley, "Bible-Based Boys' Group Opens after Boy Scouts' Nod to Gays," *Washington Times,* January 3, 2014; David Crary and Nomaan Merchant, "Boy Scouts Open Ranks to Gay Youth on January 1," *USA Today*, December 29, 2013; J. D. Gallop, "Trail Life USA Formed after Boy Scouts Gay Ban Lift," *Florida Today*, January 5, 2014; Molly Hennessy-Fiske, "Gay Youths Now 'Safe' in Boy Scouts," *Los Angeles Times,* December 31, 2013; Marice Richter, "Boy Scouts Begin Allowing Gay Youth Scouts," *Reuters,* December 31, 2013; Rachel Siegel, "Boy Scouts Getting a New Name as They Welcome Girls," *Washington Post*, May 3, 2018; Tina Susman and Molly Hennessy-Fiske, "Ex-Scout James Dale: Boy Scouts Should Accept Gay Leaders," *Los Angeles Times,* May 24, 2013.

More broadly, what the Court's decisions on the expressive rights of groups reflect is a desire to protect the right of groups to communicate their views. As long as the justices are satisfied that a group has a clear, defined message that it seeks to advocate, it will not permit a countervailing government interest to override that message. Just like individuals, associations have the right to determine what they do and not stand for; they should remain free from state interference. At the same time, if a group's purposes, whatever they may be, do not include giving collective voice to shared principles or goals, there is no First Amendment barrier to the government regulating that group to promote legitimate state interests.

REGULATIONS OF THE CONTEXT OF SPEECH: TIME, PLACE, AND MANNER RESTRICTIONS

When the government tries to regulate speech, it is because it wants to address the potential harms that may result from expression. As we have seen, policy makers are often concerned with the harms that arise as a consequence of the specific ideas that are contained in speech. Because such regulations are content-based, the Supreme Court has usually subjected them to its most exacting scrutiny. Without such critical analysis, government might abuse its authority and limit the public's access to legitimate, competing viewpoints.

In many instances, however, the government's focus is harms that are unrelated to the opinions people express. Depending on the circumstances, speech can result in excessive noise, misuse of public property, interference with government services, obstruction of traffic, or the spread of litter. There is little doubt that government can utilize its power to deal with these problems. When the state regulates speech in order to deal with such undesirable consequences, the Court has taken a more lenient approach and afforded the government greater discretion—provided, of course, that the object of the regulation is the actual troublesome effects themselves, not the content of the speaker's message.

These types of limits on speech are called "time, place, and manner restrictions." They involve government regulating when, where, and how speech takes place. To resolve questions that arise under this heading, the justices have developed standards that make it a good deal easier for the government to achieve its goals—even if it incidentally treads upon expression. To be sure, these cases raise important issues of freedom of speech, but the flexibility of the justices in such cases is a recognition that they are less worried about the government acting as a censor to squelch unpopular ideas.

What specific criteria does the Court utilize to resolve such cases? Over a number of decisions, the justices have consistently emphasized a number of factors. First and foremost, a valid time, place, or manner restriction cannot be based on the subject matter or content of speech; if it is not content-neutral, then the justices will presume that it is unconstitutional and evaluate it with the same care that they do any other content-based policy. Second, the regulation must serve an important governmental interest. Whereas content-specific laws can only be justified by an overriding state objective, time, place, and manner laws can be sustained if the state's goal is sufficiently worthwhile to override a free speech claim. Obviously, people may differ over what qualifies as an "important governmental interest"—indeed, the justices themselves have not been particularly clear on this issue—but what is relevant is that the state is not obligated to demonstrate that its interest is so compelling that it is a vital function of government. Third, the regulations must be narrowly tailored. Unlike the requirement of strict scrutiny—that the law be the least restrictive alternative for achieving a goal—this criterion only requires that the law be well-fitted to the state's purpose, or as the Court has explained, the state must show that "the means chosen are not substantially broader than necessary to achieve that interest."[29] This, too, might seem a bit nebulous, but it generally means that the regulation must be reasonably suited to achieving its goal. Or, as Chief Justice Roberts put it, "The First Amendment requires that [the law] be narrowly tailored, not that it be 'perfectly tailored.'"[30] Finally, the Court frequently demands that a time, place, or manner restriction leave open ample alternatives for communication. If the government seeks to impose limits on speech, it cannot foreclose other ways of exercising speech; there must still be other ways for a speaker to convey the same message.

It is important to bear in mind that these considerations are typically employed whenever government tries to impose a regulation in what is called a traditional public forum, that is, places where individuals have historically been entitled to speak.[31] Sidewalks, streets, and parks are the most obvious examples. When time, place, and manner restrictions are applied to these settings, the justices will want to make sure that these various criteria are satisfied. That is not the case, however, when speech take place outside of a public forum. Individuals want to register their voices in all kinds of public places; they stage sit-ins in government buildings, or they protest at nuclear power plants, or they advocate for candidates or causes at the polls on Election Day. When regulations are applied in those settings, the justices only require that the laws be a rational way of pursuing a legitimate state goal—a standard that is very easy for the government to satisfy.

Regulating the Time and Place of Speech

Americans have always tried to muster support for their ideas by presenting them to a public audience. After all, in a democratic government, decisions are made based on popular support, and so it makes sense that individuals try to disseminate their ideas as widely as possible; speakers meet listeners, often face-to-face, seeking to inform and persuade, and persuasion in sufficient numbers translates into public policy. There are certain places where such advocacy usually occurs, and the Supreme Court—recognizing the connection between public discussion and policy making—has sought to protect the speech in those locations from unwarranted interference.

One of the Court's early acknowledgments of the need to preserve the right to speak in such places is *Hague v. Committee for Industrial Organization* (1939). In this case, a labor organization was prevented from having public meetings and distributing literature on the streets of Jersey City, New Jersey. The justices invalidated the city's actions, but the case is usually remembered for the concurring opinion of Justice Owen Roberts, which argues that individuals are entitled to express their views in traditional public forums:

> Wherever the title of streets and parks may rest, they have immemorially been held in

---

[29]*Ward v. Rock Against Racism* (1989).

[30]*Williams-Yulee v. Florida Bar* (2015).

[31]The government is permitted to *designate* a place as a public forum, even if it has not historically been such. For example, public school buildings opened for community use after school hours could be a designated public forum.

trust for the use of the public and, time out of mind, have been used for purposes of assembly, communicating thoughts between citizens, and discussing public questions. Such use of the streets and public places has, from ancient times, been a part of the privileges, immunities, rights, and liberties of citizens.

Roberts rejected the suggestion that the government was similar to a private property owner who could control how property is used and expel those who are unwelcome. These locations, he suggested, are the places where there is a historical expectation of speech; in such places, individuals have a basic right to assemble and to express their views.

The justices have reinforced this view in subsequent cases. In *United States v. Grace* (1983), for instance, the justices invalidated a restriction on speech outside the U.S. Supreme Court. Regulating the use the federal government's buildings in Washington, D.C., Congress prohibited public demonstrations on or around the grounds of the Court, including the sidewalks that surround the building. A protestor—carrying a sign with the text of the First Amendment, ironically—was told by police that she could not display her sign on the Court's sidewalk. In striking down the sidewalk restriction, the Court unanimously held that, because sidewalks are historic public forums, the government's ability to limit speech around the Court was very limited.

Not surprisingly, the justices can be especially emphatic in rejecting content-based restrictions in public forums, even if there may good reason for the limitations. Congress, exercising its explicit authority to define and punish offenses against the law of nations, sought to protect the representatives of foreign governments by making it unlawful to display a sign critical of another nation within 500 feet of its embassy in Washington. In *Boos v. Barry* (1988) the Court conceded that preserving the security of diplomats may be an important interest recognized by international law. As a content-based restriction on speech in a public forum, however, it could not survive strict scrutiny.

In recent years, the justices have confronted a number of restrictions in public forums that stem from debate over abortion. Abortion excites passionate voices on both sides of the issue, and the debate sometimes plays out in ways that produce unwelcome results. This is especially true when demonstrations occur near places where abortions are performed. Policy makers have tried to find ways to ensure that women have ready access to abortion

facilities while at the same time guaranteeing that people can express their views. The results have been mixed. The Court has sustained policies restricting noise levels of demonstrations during times when abortion surgeries are being performed.[32] The justices have also upheld a fixed fifteen-foot buffer zone around the entrances to abortion clinics. But they have invalidated fifteen-foot "floating" buffer zones around individuals entering and leaving a clinic; because they were not sufficiently tailored to the state's interests in ensuring access to abortion services and promoting public safety, they burdened more speech than necessary by preventing normal conversations in a public forum.[33]

The latest of these public forum decisions is *McCullen v. Coakley* (2014), a case in which the justices examined the efforts of Massachusetts to deal with the conflicts that inevitably develop outside abortion facilities. As you read this case, consider whether the law was a content-neutral regulation of where and when speech could take place or a content-based regulation directed at a particular subject.

McCullen v. Coakley

573 U.S. 464 (2014)
https://caselaw.findlaw.com/us-supreme-court/12-1168-nr2. html
Oral arguments available at *https://www.oyez.org/ cases/2013/12-1168*
Vote: 9 (Alito, Breyer, Ginsburg, Kagan, Kennedy, Roberts, Scalia, Sotomayor, Thomas)
0

OPINION OF THE COURT: *Roberts*

CONCURRING OPINIONS: *Alito, Scalia*

In 2007, Massachusetts amended its law relating to access to abortion facilities. Because it believed that its existing law did not adequately protect patients and staff entering and leaving abortion clinics, the revised law established thirty-five-foot buffer zones around their entrances and driveways. Eleanor McCullen was what is known as a sidewalk abortion counselor, someone who attempts to dissuade women from seeking abortions by a calm, concerned approach, as opposed to aggressive, antagonistic confrontation. She offered sidewalk counseling at the Planned Parenthood clinic in Boston. The buffer zone, marked by

---

[32]*Madsen v. Women's Health Center, Inc.* (1994).

[33]*Schenck v. Pro-Choice Network of Western New York* (1997)

a painted, yellow arc extending from the clinic's front entrance, was so wide that it made it difficult for Ms. McCullen to initiate conversations with women entering the clinic. Along with a number of other sidewalk counselors, she asked a federal court to strike down the law, arguing that the buffer zone violated the First Amendment's guarantee of free speech. Both the trial and appellate courts concluded that the law was a legitimate time, place, and manner restriction. She sought review from the Supreme Court.

CHIEF JUSTICE ROBERTS DELIVERED THE OPINION OF THE COURT.

By its very terms, the Massachusetts Act regulates access to "public way[s]" and "sidewalk[s]." Such areas occupy a "special position in terms of First Amendment protection" because of their historic role as sites for discussion and debate. These places—which we have labeled "traditional public fora"—"have immemorially been held in trust for the use of the public and, time out of mind, have been used for purposes of assembly, communicating thoughts between citizens, and discussing public questions." . . .

Consistent with the traditionally open character of public streets and sidewalks, we have held that the government's ability to restrict speech in such locations is "very limited." . . .

We have, however, afforded the government somewhat wider leeway to regulate features of speech unrelated to its content. "[E]ven in a public forum the government may impose reasonable restrictions on the time, place, or manner of protected speech, provided the restrictions 'are justified without reference to the content of the regulated speech, that they are narrowly tailored to serve a significant governmental interest, and that they leave open ample alternative channels for communication of the information.'" *Ward* [*v. Rock Against Racism* (1989)]. . . .

The Act applies only at a "reproductive health care facility," defined as "a place, other than within or upon the grounds of a hospital, where abortions are offered or performed." Given this definition, petitioners argue, "virtually all speech affected by the Act is speech concerning abortion," thus rendering the Act content based.

We disagree. To begin, the Act does not draw content-based distinctions on its face. . . . The Act would be content based if it required "enforcement authorities" to "examine the content of the message that is conveyed to determine whether" a violation has occurred. [*FCC v.*] *League of Women Voters of Cal.* (1984). But it does not. Whether petitioners violate the Act "depends" not "on what they say," but simply on where they say it. Indeed, petitioners can violate the Act merely by standing in a buffer zone, without displaying a sign or uttering a word. . . .

Petitioners do not really dispute that the Commonwealth's interests in ensuring safety and preventing obstruction are, as a general matter, content neutral. But petitioners note that these interests "apply outside every building in the State that hosts any activity that might occasion protest or comment," not just abortion clinics. By choosing to pursue these interests only at abortion clinics, petitioners argue, the Massachusetts Legislature evinced a purpose to "single[ ] out for regulation speech about one particular topic: abortion."

We cannot infer such a purpose from the Act's limited scope. The broad reach of a statute can help confirm that it was not enacted to burden a narrower category of disfavored speech. At the same time, however, "States adopt laws to address the problems that confront them. The First Amendment does not require States to regulate for problems that do not exist." *Burson v. Freeman* (1992). The Massachusetts Legislature amended the Act in 2007 in response to a problem that was, in its experience, limited to abortion clinics. There was a record of crowding, obstruction, and even violence outside such clinics. There were apparently no similar recurring problems associated with other kinds of healthcare facilities, let alone with "every building in the State that hosts any activity that might occasion protest or comment." In light of the limited nature of the problem, it was reasonable for the Massachusetts Legislature to enact a limited solution. When selecting among various options for combating a particular problem, legislatures should be encouraged to choose the one that restricts less speech, not more.

Even though the Act is content neutral, it still must be "narrowly tailored to serve a significant governmental interest." *Ward*. The tailoring requirement does not simply guard against an impermissible desire to censor. The government may attempt to suppress speech not only because it disagrees with the message being expressed, but also for mere convenience. Where certain speech is associated with particular problems, silencing the speech is sometimes the path of least resistance. But by demanding a close fit between ends and means, the tailoring requirement prevents the government from too readily "sacrific[ing] speech for efficiency."

For a content-neutral time, place, or manner regulation to be narrowly tailored, it must not "burden substantially more speech than is necessary to further the government's legitimate interests." Such a regulation, unlike a content-based restriction of speech, "need not be the least restrictive or least intrusive means of" serving the government's interests. But the government still "may not regulate expression in such a manner that a substantial portion of the burden on speech does not serve to advance its goals."

. . . We have . . . previously recognized the legitimacy of the government's interests in "ensuring public safety and order, promoting the free flow of traffic on streets and sidewalks, protecting property rights, and protecting a woman's freedom to seek pregnancy-related services." *Schenck v. Pro-Choice Network of Western N. Y.* (1997). The buffer zones clearly serve these interests.

At the same time, the buffer zones impose serious burdens on petitioners' speech. At each of the three Planned Parenthood clinics

Eleanor McCullen, sidewalk abortion counselor, stands at the edge of the thirty-five-foot buffer zone around Planned Parenthood in Boston on December 17, 2013. The Supreme Court invalidated Massachusetts' use of the buffer zone, because it was a substantial interference with McCullen's right to speak to women entering the clinic.

where petitioners attempt to counsel patients, the zones carve out a significant portion of the adjacent public sidewalks, pushing petitioners well back from the clinics' entrances and driveways. The zones thereby compromise petitioners' ability to initiate the close, personal conversations that they view as essential to "sidewalk counseling." . . .

. . . But while the First Amendment does not guarantee a speaker the right to any particular form of expression, some forms—such as normal conversation and leafletting on a public sidewalk—have historically been more closely associated with the transmission of ideas than others. . . .

The buffer zones burden substantially more speech than necessary to achieve the Commonwealth's asserted interests. . . .

The Commonwealth points to a substantial public safety risk created when protestors obstruct driveways leading to the clinics. That is, however, an example of its failure to look to less intrusive means of addressing its concerns. Any such obstruction can readily be addressed through existing local ordinances.

All of the foregoing measures are, of course, in addition to available generic criminal statutes forbidding assault, breach of the peace, trespass, vandalism, and the like. . . .

The Commonwealth also asserts an interest in preventing congestion in front of abortion clinics. According to respondents, even when individuals do not deliberately obstruct access to clinics, they can inadvertently do so simply by gathering in large numbers. But the Commonwealth could address that problem through more targeted means. Some localities, for example, have ordinances that require crowds blocking a clinic entrance to disperse when ordered to do so by the police, and that forbid the individuals to reassemble within a certain distance of the clinic for a certain period. . . .

And to the extent the Commonwealth argues that even these types of laws are ineffective, it has another problem. The portions of the record that respondents cite to support the anticongestion interest pertain mainly to one place at one time: the Boston Planned Parenthood clinic on Saturday mornings. Respondents point us to no evidence that individuals regularly gather at other clinics, or at other times in Boston, in sufficiently large groups to obstruct access. For a problem shown to arise only once a week in one city at one clinic, creating 35-foot buffer zones at every clinic across the Commonwealth is hardly a narrowly tailored solution.

The point is not that Massachusetts must enact all or even any of the proposed measures discussed above. The point is instead that the Commonwealth has available to it a variety of approaches that appear capable of serving its interests, without excluding individuals from areas historically open for speech and debate.

Respondents have but one reply: "We have tried other approaches, but they do not work." . . .

. . . As Captain [William B.] Evans [of the Boston Police Department] predicted in his legislative testimony, fixed buffer zones would "make our job so much easier."

Of course they would. But that is not enough to satisfy the First Amendment. To meet the requirement of narrow tailoring, the government must demonstrate that alternative measures that burden substantially less speech would fail to achieve the government's interests, not simply that the chosen route is easier. A painted line on the sidewalk is easy to enforce, but the prime objective of the First Amendment is not efficiency. . . .

Given the vital First Amendment interests at stake, it is not enough for Massachusetts simply to say that other approaches have not worked.

* * *

Petitioners wish to converse with their fellow citizens about an important subject on the public streets and sidewalks—sites that have hosted discussions about the issues of the day throughout history. Respondents assert undeniably significant interests in maintaining public safety on those same streets and sidewalks, as well as in preserving access to adjacent healthcare facilities. But here the Commonwealth has pursued those interests by the extreme step of closing a substantial portion of a traditional public forum to all speakers. It has done so without seriously addressing the problem through alternatives that leave the forum open for its time-honored purposes. The Commonwealth may not do that consistent with the First Amendment.

The judgment of the Court of Appeals for the First Circuit is reversed, and the case is remanded for further proceedings consistent with this opinion.

It is so ordered.

Today's opinion carries forward this Court's practice of giving abortion-rights advocates a pass when it comes to suppressing the free-speech rights of their opponents. There is an entirely separate, abridged edition of the First Amendment applicable to speech against abortion. . . .

Public streets and sidewalks are traditional forums for speech on matters of public concern. Therefore, as the Court acknowledges, they hold a "special position in terms of First Amendment protection." Moreover, "the public spaces outside of [abortion-providing] facilities . . . ha[ve] become, by necessity and by virtue of this Court's decisions, a forum of last resort for those who oppose abortion." *Hill* [*v. Colorado* (2000)] (Scalia, J., dissenting). It blinks reality to say, as the majority does, that a blanket prohibition on the use of streets and sidewalks where speech on only one politically controversial topic is likely to occur—and where that speech can most effectively be communicated—is not content based. Would the Court exempt from strict scrutiny a law banning access to the streets and sidewalks surrounding the site of the Republican National Convention? Or those used annually to commemorate the 1965 Selma-to-Montgomery civil rights marches? Or those outside the Internal Revenue Service? Surely not.

The majority says, correctly enough, that a facially neutral speech restriction escapes strict scrutiny, even when it "may disproportionately affect speech on certain topics," so long as it is "justified without reference to the content of the regulated speech." . . .

. . . The majority points only to the statute's stated purpose of increasing "'public safety'" at abortion clinics, and to the additional aims articulated by respondents before this Court—namely, protecting "patient access to healthcare . . . and the unobstructed use of public sidewalks and roadways." Really? Does a statute become "justified without reference to the content of the regulated speech" simply because the statute itself and those defending it in court say that it is? Every objective indication shows that the provision's primary purpose is to restrict speech that opposes abortion.

I begin, as suggested above, with the fact that the Act burdens only the public spaces outside abortion clinics. One might have expected the majority to defend the statute's peculiar targeting by arguing that those locations regularly face the safety and access problems that it says the Act was designed to solve. But the majority does not make that argument because it would be untrue. As the Court belatedly discovers in . . . its opinion, although the statute applies to all abortion clinics in Massachusetts, only one is known to have been beset by the problems that the statute supposedly addresses. . . .

. . . Showing that a law that suppresses speech on a specific subject is so far-reaching that it applies even when the asserted non-speech-related problems are not present is persuasive evidence that the law is content based. In its zeal to treat abortion-related speech as a special category, the majority distorts not only the First Amendment but also the ordinary logic of probative inferences.

The structure of the Act also indicates that it rests on content-based concerns. The goals of "public safety, patient access to healthcare, and the unobstructed use of public sidewalks and roadways," are already achieved by an earlier-enacted subsection of the statute, which provides criminal penalties for "[a]ny person who knowingly obstructs, detains, hinders, impedes or blocks another person's entry to or exit from a reproductive health care facility." As the majority recognizes, that provision is easy to enforce. Thus, the speech-free zones carved out . . . add nothing to safety and access; what they achieve, and what they were obviously designed to achieve, is the suppression of speech opposing abortion. . . .

In sum, the Act should be reviewed under the strict-scrutiny standard applicable to content-based legislation. That standard requires that a regulation represent "the least restrictive means" of furthering "a compelling Government interest." Respondents do not even attempt to argue that [the law] survives this test. "Suffice it to say that if protecting people from unwelcome communications"—the actual purpose of the provision—"is a compelling state interest, the First Amendment is a dead letter." *Hill* (Scalia, J., dissenting). . . .

* * *

The obvious purpose of the challenged portion of the Massachusetts Reproductive Health Care Facilities Act is to "protect" prospective clients of abortion clinics from having to hear abortion-opposing speech on public streets and sidewalks. The provision is thus unconstitutional root and branch and cannot be saved, as the majority suggests, by limiting its application to the single facility that has experienced the safety and access problems to which it is quite obviously not addressed. I concur only in the judgment that the statute is unconstitutional under the First Amendment.

Although the justices do vote unanimously to invalidate the Massachusetts law, they split over the rationale. Chief Justice Roberts, writing for the majority, sees the buffer zone as content-neutral: the law regulates not what people say but where they say it. True, the law applied only to speech outside of abortion clinics, but that was because Massachusetts had found those clinics to be the unique source of crowding, obstruction, and violence. As a time, place, and manner restriction, the law ran afoul of the First Amendment by failing the "narrow tailoring" requirement. The legislature was not required to select the means that would pose the least possible restriction on speech, but it was required to identify solutions that did not intrude excessively on expression. Under the circumstances, the thirty-five-foot buffer zone made it too difficult for people like Ms. McCullen to exercise their speech rights. By contrast, Justice Scalia concluded that the law was content-based, aimed specifically at the discussion of abortion. Why else, he asked, would the law affect only speech at abortion clinics? Since he judged the law to be content-based, he would have subjected it to strict scrutiny—an approach that would make it even harder for states to enact similar restrictions.

These disagreements about how to judge time, place, and manner restrictions take place in cases involving public forums. When similar restrictions are imposed on other types of public property, the justices have only required a plausible justification for the limitations. So, for example, candidates for public office can be prevented from campaigning on military bases when the base commander believes it will interfere with discipline or morale.[34] Students who wish to protest the arrest of their fellow demonstrators have no right to stage that protest on the grounds of a jail; the state has a safety interest in maintaining the jail and can restrict access if it chooses.[35] Airports are not traditional public forums, and thus the government may ban solicitations for money there as a way of promoting efficient air travel.[36] In cases such as these, "[t]he restriction need only be *reasonable*; it need not be the most reasonable or the only reasonable limitation." Outside the public forum context, then, such speech regulations are very easy to sustain.

Symbolic Speech

In the days of the Revolution, political protest customarily took the form of eloquent addresses, sharply worded editorials, and fiery pamphlets. Verbal expression and published communication were the methods of political debate, and the framers unambiguously sought to protect them from government encroachment by drafting and ratifying the First Amendment. But what if today someone wishes to communicate a message by means other than word of mouth or printed copy? If a point is made by action rather than by verbal expression, does the First Amendment still grant immunity from government regulation? These questions address the manner of expression—whether expressive conduct qualifies as speech under the First Amendment.

---

[34]*Greer v. Spock* (1976).

[35]*Adderley v. Florida* (1966).

[36]*International Society for Krishna Consciousness v. Lee* (1992).

Although symbolic speech cases did not become a consistent concern of the Court until the modern era, the justices entered that legal terrain much earlier. In ***Stromberg v. California*** (1931), the Supreme Court acknowledged that at least some forms of symbolic speech merit constitutional protection, when it reversed the conviction of a camp counselor who had raised a red flag in support of communism, an act which violated California law. Recognizing a constitutional protection of symbolic expression did not mean, however, that the First Amendment shielded from government regulation *any* act committed to express an idea or opinion. So, for example, placing a sound amplifier on the back of a truck—which is then used to broadcast a speech and loud music while driving through the streets of a community—is not beyond the reach of restriction, as the Court held in *Kovacs v. Cooper* (1948).

In the late 1960s, the turbulence of the civil rights movement and the Vietnam War protests expanded the ways in which political messages were communicated. Traditional forms of speech and press gave way to demonstrations, sit-ins, flag desecration, and other varieties of conduct designed to present the protesters' political messages in a graphic manner. The first case to address such expression was ***United States v. O'Brien*** (1968). In March of 1966, David O'Brien and three other antiwar activists burned their draft cards on the steps of a South Boston courthouse. These actions violated the Selective Service Act, which made it illegal to destroy or mutilate a draft card. O'Brien maintained that his actions were protected, symbolic expression, but the federal government argued that it was only conduct: calling it "'symbolic speech' does not transform it into activity entitled to the same kind of constitutional protection given to words and other modes of expression."

Writing for the Court, Chief Justice Warren dismissed the notion that conduct used to express an idea automatically merits First Amendment protection. He did say that when speech and symbolic acts were combined, those acts—the manner of expression—could be regulated when the government was pursuing a significant goal by a means tailored to that end. With only Justice Douglas dissenting, the Court had little difficulty concluding that the government had a substantial interest in exercising its authority over the nation's military and that the draft registration system was a reasonable means of achieving that goal. Moreover, the Selective Service Act was only concerned with military interests; the law was not designed to curtail expression. Consequently, the

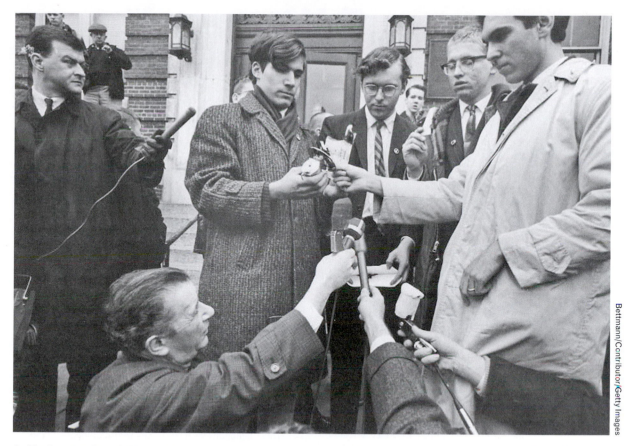

On March 31, 1966, David O'Brien and three other antiwar protesters demonstrated their opposition to U.S. military action in Vietnam by burning their draft cards. Their convictions for violating the Selective Service Act were affirmed in *United States v. O'Brien*.

government had the constitutional power to prosecute individuals who violated the Selective Service laws, even if the acts in question communicated a message of political protest.

This is not to suggest that these justices were hostile to claims of symbolic speech. To the contrary, the following year the Court decided ***Tinker v. Des Moines*** (1969), a decision upholding the right of public school children to wear black armbands to express their opposition to the Vietnam War. The Court explained that wearing an armband "was closely akin to pure speech." In the absence of any indication that such expressive activity was disruptive, the state was not justified in limiting it.

One subject that proved especially vexing for the justices during this era was the symbolic act of flag desecration. It is not hard to discern why; as a national symbol, the American flag evokes intense emotional feelings, especially among those who, like members of the Supreme Court, have long histories of public service, often in the military. Thus, in the two flag desecration cases decided in the context of civil rights and antiwar activism, even the justices who were most committed to freedom of speech indicated their discomfort in extending First Amendment protection to those who destroy the flag as a method of political expression.[37]

The most significant flag desecration case is *Texas v. Johnson* (1989). Unlike the two prior cases, this one was decided at a time of relative social and political calm, with few pressures on government to stifle radical expression. But sitting on the Court were some justices with quite conservative ideologies and several who had

---

[37]*Street v. New York* (1969) and *Spence v. Washington* (1974).

served in the armed forces. We would not expect them to be eager to extend constitutional protection to the desecration of the flag.

Texas v. Johnson

491 U.S. 397 (1989)
http://caselaw.findlaw.com/us-supreme-court/491/397.html
Oral arguments available https://www.oyez.org/
  cases/1988/88-155
Vote: 5 (Blackmun, Brennan, Kennedy, Marshall, Scalia)
  4 (O'Connor, Rehnquist, Stevens, White)

OPINION OF THE COURT: *Brennan*

CONCURRING OPINION: *Kennedy*

DISSENTING OPINIONS: *Rehnquist, Stevens*

The Republican Party held its 1984 national convention in Dallas, Texas, and overwhelmingly supported President Ronald Reagan's reelection bid. While the party was meeting, a group of demonstrators marched through the city to protest the Reagan administration's policies. One of the demonstrators gave an American flag to Gregory Lee Johnson, who also was marching. When the march ended, Johnson "unfurled the flag, doused it with kerosene and set it on fire." As it burned, others chanted, "America, the red, white, and blue, we spit on you." Authorities arrested Johnson, charging him with violating the Texas flag desecration law. He was convicted and sentenced to a one-year prison term and a $2,000 fine.

JUSTICE BRENNAN DELIVERED THE OPINION OF THE COURT.

The First Amendment literally forbids the abridgement only of "speech," but we have long recognized that its protection does not end at the spoken or written word. While we have rejected "the view that an apparently limitless variety of conduct can be labeled 'speech' whenever the person engaging in the conduct intends thereby to express an idea," we have acknowledged that conduct may be "sufficiently imbued with elements of communication to fall within the scope of the First and Fourteenth Amendments."

In deciding whether particular conduct possesses sufficient communicative elements to bring the First Amendment into play, we have asked whether "[a]n intent to convey a particularized message was present, and [whether] the likelihood was great that the message would be understood by those who viewed it." Hence, we have recognized the expressive nature of students' wearing of black armbands to protest American military involvement in Vietnam. . . .

Especially pertinent to this case are our decisions recognizing the communicative nature of conduct relating to flags. Attaching a peace sign to the flag, saluting the flag, and displaying a red flag, we have held, all may find shelter under the First Amendment. That we have had little difficulty identifying an expressive element in conduct relating to flags should not be surprising. The very purpose of a national flag is to serve as a symbol of our country; it is, one might say, "the one visible manifestation of two hundred years of nationhood." . . .

We have not automatically concluded, however, that any action taken with respect to our flag is expressive. Instead, in characterizing such action for First Amendment purposes, we have considered the context in which it occurred. . . .

. . . Johnson burned an American flag as part—indeed, as the culmination—of a political demonstration that coincided with the convening of the Republican Party and its renomination of Ronald Reagan for President. In these circumstances, Johnson's burning of the flag was conduct "sufficiently imbued with elements of communication" to implicate the First Amendment.

The Government generally has a freer hand in restricting expressive conduct than it has in restricting the written or spoken word. . . . "A law *directed* at the communicative nature of conduct must, like a law directed at speech itself, be justified by the substantial showing of need that the First Amendment requires." It is, in short, not simply the verbal or nonverbal nature of the expression, but the governmental interest at stake, that helps to determine whether a restriction on that expression is valid.

Thus, although we have recognized that where "'speech' and 'nonspeech' elements are combined in the same course of conduct, a sufficiently important governmental interest in regulating the nonspeech element can justify incidental limitations on First Amendment freedoms," . . . we have highlighted the requirement that the governmental interest in question be unconnected to expression. . . .

. . . [T]herefore, we must decide whether Texas has asserted an interest in support of Johnson's conviction that is unrelated to the suppression of expression. . . . The State offers two separate interests to justify this conviction: preventing breaches of the peace, and preserving the flag as a symbol of nationhood and national unity. We hold that the first interest is not implicated on this record and that the second is related to the suppression of expression.

Texas claims that its interest in preventing breaches of the peace justifies Johnson's conviction for flag desecration. However, no disturbance of the peace actually occurred or threatened to occur because of Johnson's burning of the flag. . . .

The State's position, therefore, amounts to a claim that an audience that takes serious offense at a particular expression is necessarily likely to disturb the peace and that the expression may be prohibited on this basis. Our precedents do not countenance such a presumption. On the contrary, they recognize that a principal "function of free speech under our system of government is to invite

Gregory Johnson on June 28, 1989, holding an American flag given to him by a well-wisher. One week earlier the U.S. Supreme Court had reversed his conviction for violating the Texas flag desecration statute.

AP Photo/David Cantor

dispute. It may indeed best serve its high purpose when it induces a condition of unrest, creates dissatisfaction with conditions as they are, or even stirs people to anger." . . .

Nor does Johnson's expressive conduct fall within that small class of "fighting words" that are "likely to provoke the average person to retaliation, and thereby cause a breach of the peace." No reasonable onlooker would have regarded Johnson's generalized expression of dissatisfaction with the policies of the Federal Government as a direct personal insult or an invitation to exchange fisticuffs.

We thus conclude that the State's interest in maintaining order is not implicated on these facts. The State need not worry that our holding will disable it from preserving the peace. We do not suggest that the First Amendment forbids a State to prevent "imminent lawless action." . . .

The State also asserts an interest in preserving the flag as a symbol of nationhood and national unity. In *Spence* [v. Washington, 1974], we acknowledged that the Government's interest in preserving the flag's special symbolic value "is directly related to expression in the context of activity" such as affixing a peace symbol to a flag. We are equally persuaded that this interest is related to expression in the case of Johnson's burning of the flag. The State, apparently, is concerned that such conduct will lead people to believe either that the flag does not stand for nationhood and national unity, but instead reflects other, less positive concepts, or that the concepts reflected in the flag do not in fact exist, that is, we do not enjoy unity as a Nation. These concerns blossom only when a person's treatment of the flag communicates some message, and thus are related "to the suppression of free expression." . . .

It remains to consider whether the State's interest in preserving the flag as a symbol of nationhood and national unity justifies Johnson's conviction. . . .

. . . Johnson's political expression was restricted because of the content of the message he conveyed. We must therefore subject the State's asserted interest in preserving the special symbolic character of the flag to "the most exacting scrutiny."

Texas argues that its interest in preserving the flag as a symbol of nationhood and national unity survives this close analysis. Quoting extensively from the writings of this Court chronicling the flag's historic and symbolic role in our society, the State emphasizes the "special place" reserved for the flag in our Nation. . . . [T]he State's claim is that it has an interest in preserving the flag as a symbol of *nationhood* and *national unity,* a symbol with a determinate range of meanings. According to Texas, if one physically treats the flag in a way that would tend to cast doubt on either the idea that nationhood and national unity are the flag's referents or that national unity actually exists, the message conveyed thereby is a harmful one and therefore may be prohibited.

If there is a bedrock principle underlying the First Amendment, it is that the Government may not prohibit the expression of an idea simply because society finds the idea itself offensive or disagreeable.

We have not recognized an exception to this principle even where our flag has been involved. In *Street v. New York* we held that a State may not criminally punish a person for uttering words critical of the flag. . . .

In short, nothing in our precedents suggests that a State may foster its own view of the flag by prohibiting expressive conduct relating to it. To bring its argument outside our precedents, Texas attempts to convince us that even if its interest in preserving the flag's symbolic role does not allow it to prohibit words or some expressive conduct critical of the flag, it does permit it to forbid the outright destruction of the flag. The State's argument cannot depend here on the distinction between written or spoken words and nonverbal conduct. That distinction, we have shown, is of no moment where the nonverbal conduct is expressive, as it is here, and where the regulation of that conduct is related to expression, as it is here. . . .

Texas' focus on the precise nature of Johnson's expression, moreover, misses the point of our prior decisions: their enduring lesson, that the Government may not prohibit expression simply because it disagrees with its message, is not dependent on the particular mode in which one chooses to express an idea. If we were to hold that a State may forbid flag-burning wherever it is likely to endanger the flag's symbolic role, but allow it wherever burning a flag promotes that role—as where, for example, a person ceremoniously burns a dirty flag—we would be saying that . . . the flag itself may be used as a symbol—as a substitute for the written or spoken word or a "short cut from mind to mind"—only in one direction. We would be permitting a State to "prescribe what shall be orthodox" by saying that one may burn the flag to convey one's attitude toward it and its referents only if one does not endanger the flag's representation of nationhood and national unity. . . .

There is, moreover, no indication—either in the text of the Constitution or in our cases interpreting it—that a separate juridical category exists for the American flag alone. Indeed, we would not be surprised to learn that the persons who framed our Constitution and wrote the Amendment that we now construe were not known for their reverence for the Union Jack. The First Amendment does not guarantee that other concepts virtually sacred to our Nation as a whole—such as the principle that discrimination on the basis of race is odious and destructive—will go unquestioned in the marketplace of ideas. We decline, therefore, to create for the flag an exception to the joust of principles protected by the First Amendment. . . .

We are tempted to say, in fact, that the flag's deservedly cherished place in our community will be strengthened, not weakened, by our holding today. Our decision is a reaffirmation of the principles of freedom and inclusiveness that the flag best reflects, and of the conviction that our toleration of criticism such as Johnson's is a sign and source of our strength. Indeed, one of the proudest images of our flag, the one immortalized in our own national anthem, is of the bombardment it survived at Fort McHenry. It is the Nation's resilience, not its rigidity, that Texas sees reflected in the flag—and it is that resilience that we reassert today.

The way to preserve the flag's special role is not to punish those who feel differently about these matters. It is to persuade them that they are wrong. . . . And, precisely because it is our flag that is involved, one's response to the flag-burner may exploit the uniquely persuasive power of the flag itself. We can imagine no more appropriate response to burning a flag than waving one's own, no better way to counter a flag-burner's message than by saluting the flag that burns, no surer means of preserving the dignity even of the flag that burned than by—as one witness here did—according its remains a respectful burial. We do not consecrate the flag by punishing its desecration, for in doing so we dilute the freedom that this cherished emblem represents.

Johnson was convicted for engaging in expressive conduct. The State's interest in preventing breaches of the peace does not support his conviction because Johnson's conduct did not threaten to disturb the peace. Nor does the State's interest in preserving the flag as a symbol of nationhood and national unity justify his criminal conviction for engaging in political expression. The judgment of the Texas Court of Criminal Appeals is therefore

Affirmed.

CHIEF JUSTICE REHNQUIST, WITH WHOM JUSTICE WHITE AND JUSTICE O'CONNOR JOIN, DISSENTING.

In holding this Texas statute unconstitutional, the Court ignores Justice Holmes' familiar aphorism that "a page of history is worth a volume of logic." *New York Trust Co. v. Eisner* (1921). For more than 200 years, the American flag has occupied a unique position as the symbol of our Nation, a uniqueness that justifies a governmental prohibition against flag burning in the way respondent Johnson did here. . . .

The American flag . . . has come to be the visible symbol embodying our Nation. It does not represent the views of any particular political party, and it does not represent any particular political philosophy. The flag is not simply another "idea" or "point of view" competing for recognition in the marketplace of ideas. Millions and millions of Americans regard it with an almost mystical reverence regardless of what sort of social, political, or philosophical beliefs they may have. I cannot agree that the First Amendment invalidates the Act of Congress, and the laws of 48 of the 50 States, which make criminal the public burning of the flag. . . .

. . . [T]he public burning of the American flag by Johnson was no essential part of any exposition of ideas, and at the same time it had a tendency to incite a breach of the peace. Johnson was free to make any verbal denunciation of the flag that he wished; indeed, he was free to burn the flag in private. He could publicly burn other symbols of the Government or effigies of political leaders. He did lead a march through the streets of Dallas, and conducted a rally in front of the Dallas City Hall. He engaged in a "die-in" to protest nuclear weapons. He shouted out various slogans during the march, including: "Reagan, Mondale which will it be? Either one means World War III"; "Ronald Reagan, killer of the hour, Perfect example of U.S. power"; and "red, white and blue, we spit on you, you stand for plunder, you will go under." For none of these acts was he arrested or prosecuted; it was only when he proceeded to burn publicly an American flag stolen from its rightful owner that he violated the Texas statute. . . .

. . . The Texas statute deprived Johnson of only one rather inarticulate symbolic form of protest—a form of protest that was profoundly offensive to many—and left him with a full panoply of other symbols and every conceivable form of verbal expression to express his deep disapproval of national policy. Thus, in no way can it be said that Texas is punishing him because his hearers—or any other group of people—were profoundly opposed to the message that he sought to convey. Such opposition is no proper basis for restricting speech or expression under the First Amendment. It was Johnson's use of this particular symbol, and not the idea that he sought to convey by it or by his many other expressions, for which he was punished. . . .

. . . Uncritical extension of constitutional protection to the burning of the flag risks the frustration of the very purpose for which organized governments are instituted. The Court decides that the American flag is just another symbol, about which not only must opinions pro and con be tolerated, but for which the most minimal public respect may not be enjoined. The government may conscript men into the Armed Forces where they must fight and perhaps die for the flag, but the government may not prohibit the public burning of the banner under which they fight. I would uphold the Texas statute as applied in this case.

To the majority in *Johnson*, the Texas flag desecration law was a content-based restriction on the manner of speech, which could not survive "the most exacting scrutiny." To the dissenters, there was no regulation of content, since Johnson was perfectly free to express any ideas he wished about the United States; he was simply limited in his conduct. To many Americans, the decision was an insult. President George H. W. Bush immediately condemned it, and public opinion polls indicated that Americans generally favored a constitutional amendment overturning the decision. But, after some politicking by civil liberties groups, senators, and representatives, Congress instead passed the Flag

Protection Act of 1989, which penalized by a one-year jail sentence and a $1,000 fine anyone who "knowingly mutilates, defaces, physically defiles, burns, maintains on the floor or ground, or tramples upon any flag of the United States."

Because the federal act differed from the Texas law at issue in *Johnson*—it banned flag desecration regardless of the motivation of the burner, whereas the Texas law did so only if a jury found the activity to be offensive—some thought it would meet approval in the Supreme Court. Others saw this difference as relatively insignificant, and, as it turned out, they were correct. In *United States v. Eichman* (1990) the Court, using the same reasoning expressed in *Johnson* and by the same vote, struck down this law as a violation of the First Amendment.

The Court's time, place, and manner cases have only grown in variety. The justices have evaluated prohibitions on overnight sleeping on the National Mall as a form of protest, limits on the wearing of political apparel at the polls on Election Day, permit requirements for the use of public parks, prohibitions on demonstrations in front of private homes, and volume restrictions on rock concerts, to name but a few examples. Given the expanding number of ways in which individuals communicate their ideas, such free speech questions will not disappear anytime soon.

Having discussed some of the principal issues surrounding the freedom of speech, we turn next to the final component of the freedom of expression—the right to a free press.

ANNOTATED READINGS

A number of works provide good general explorations of the Constitution's freedom of expression guarantees. Among them are Zechariah Chafee Jr., *Free Speech in the United States* (Cambridge, MA: Harvard University Press, 1941); Daniel A. Farber, *The First Amendment* (New York: Foundation Press, 1998); Stephen M. Feldman, *Free Expression and Democracy in America: A History* (Chicago: University of Chicago Press, 2008); Stanley Fish, *There's No Such Thing as Free Speech, and It's a Good Thing, Too* (New York: Oxford University Press, 1994); Karla K. Gower, *Liberty and Authority in Free Expression Law: The United States and Canada* (New York: LFB Scholarly Publishing,

2002); Mark A. Graber, *Transforming Free Speech* (Berkeley: University of California Press, 1991); Ken I. Kersch, *Freedom of Speech: Rights and Liberties under the Law* (Santa Barbara, CA: ABC-CLIO, 2003); Howard Schweber, *Speech, Conduct, and the First Amendment* (New York: Peter Lang, 2003); Steven H. Shiffrin, *What's Wrong with the First Amendment?* (Cambridge: Cambridge University Press, 2016); and Cass A. Sunstein, *Democracy and the Problem of Free Speech* (New York: Free Press, 1993).

The potential conflicts between freedom of expression and national security are explored in works such as Bruce Ackerman, *Before the Next Attack: Preserving Civil Liberties in an Age of Terrorism* (New Haven, CT: Yale University Press, 2006); Lee Epstein, Daniel E. Ho, Gary King, and Jeffrey A. Segal, "The Supreme Court during Crisis: How War Affects Only Nonwar Cases," *New York University Law Review* 80 (April 2005): 1–116; Ernest Freeberg, *Democracy's Prisoner: Eugene V. Debs, the Great War, and the Right to Dissent* (Cambridge, MA: Harvard University Press, 2009); Eric A. Posner and Adrian Vermeule, *Terror in the Balance: Security, Liberty, and the Courts* (New York: Oxford University Press, 2007); Richard A. Posner, *Not a Suicide Pact: The Constitution in a Time of National Emergency* (New York: Oxford University Press, 2006); Geoffrey R. Stone, *Perilous Times: Free Speech in Wartime from the Sedition Act of 1798 to the War on Terrorism* (New York: W. W. Norton, 2004); Geoffrey R. Stone, *War and Liberty: An American Dilemma, 1790 to the Present* (New York: W. W. Norton, 2007); and Patrick S. Washburn, *A Question of Sedition* (New York: Oxford University Press, 1986).

Offensive and hateful speech gives rise to the inevitable tension between the Constitution's commitment to liberty of expression and its commitment to the equality of all persons. Works that address these issues include Jeannine Bell, *Policing Hatred: Law Enforcement, Civil Rights, and Hate Crime* (New York: New York University Press, 2002); Erwin Chemerinsky and Howard Gillman, *Free Speech on Campus* (New Haven, CT: Yale University Press, 2018); Edward J. Cleary, *Beyond the Burning Cross: The First Amendment and the Landmark* R.A.V. *Case* (New York: Random House, 1994); Jon B. Gould, *Speak No Evil: The Triumph of Hate Speech Regulation* (Chicago: University of Chicago Press, 2005); Frederick M. Lawrence, *Punishing Hate: Bias Crimes under American Law* (Cambridge, MA: Harvard University Press, 2002); Catharine A. MacKinnon, *Only Words* (Cambridge, MA: Harvard University Press, 1993); Laura Beth Nielsen, *License to Harass: Law, Hierarchy, and Offensive Public Speech* (Princeton, NJ: Princeton University Press, 2004); Nadine Strossen, *Hate: Why We Should Resist It with Free Speech, Not Censorship* (New York: Oxford University Press, 2020); Philippa Strum, *When the Nazis Came to Skokie: Freedom for Speech We Hate* (Lawrence: University Press of Kansas, 1999); Keith Whittington, *Speak Freely: Why Universities Must Defend Free Speech* (Princeton, NJ: Princeton University Press, 2018); and Nicholas Wolfson, *Hate Speech, Sex Speech, Free Speech* (Westport, CT: Praeger, 1997).

The First Amendment's implications for the right of individuals not to speak is the subject of Haig Bosmajian, *The Freedom Not to Speak* (New York: New York University Press, 1999).

On the controversial issue of flag burning as a constitutionally protected means of expression, see Robert Justin Goldstein, *Burning the Flag: The Great 1989–1990 American Flag Desecration Controversy* (Kent, OH: Kent State University Press, 1996).

Examples of in-depth examinations of key cases dealing with the rights of students to express themselves freely in the public schools include James C. Foster, *BONG HiTS 4 JESUS: A Perfect Constitutional Storm in Alaska's Capital* (Fairbanks: University of Alaska Press, 2010); and John W. Johnson, *The Struggle for Student Rights: Tinker v. Des Moines and the 1960s* (Lawrence: University Press of Kansas, 1997).

CHAPTER FOURTEEN

FREEDOM OF THE PRESS

FREEDOM OF THE PRESS is perhaps the most visible manifestation of Americans exercising their expressive rights. Each day the print, broadcast, and electronic media blanket the nation with news, commentaries, and entertainment from varied perspectives. Newsstands, bookstores, and online booksellers flourish by offering publications devoted to every imaginable interest. Interactive media, such as talk radio, op-ed pages, letters to the editor, social media, and blogs, allow citizens to become participants in the press rather than just consumers. The result is a robust exchange of information and opinion.

Much of what appears in the media is critical of government, its leaders, and their policies. Unlike the situation in some other countries, in the United States those who criticize officials can do so without government censorship or fear of retaliation. They enjoy protection provided by the First Amendment's stipulation that "Congress shall make no law . . . abridging the freedom . . . of the press."

This constitutional provision may seem quaint in the modern age of the Internet. After all, it is implausible to think that the government could physically prevent journalists from posting material online (though the same may not hold for publishing material in newspapers, as the case excerpts in this chapter reveal). But it is hardly implausible to believe that government officials might try to pass laws, or take other action, that would punish journalists after the material appears. And this, among other reasons, is why the guarantee of a free press remains crucial today. It continues to reflect the framers' strong commitment to the importance of robust reporting. The framers saw the right to publish freely as important not only for its own sake but also because an independent press acts as a significant protection against the government's denying other political and personal liberties. The founders believed that the rights of speech and religion would be meaningless without a free press, the watchdog that sounds a warning when other rights are threatened. Thomas Jefferson was so certain of this precept that in 1816 he proclaimed, "When the press is free, and every man is able to read, all is safe."

As British colonists, the framers were well schooled in the values of a free press, and history had also taught them that this right could not be taken for granted. England had controlled the press from the fifteenth through the seventeenth centuries, and the government's repressive measures became well entrenched. Following the introduction of printing into England in the 1400s, Britain developed a licensing system under which nothing could be printed without prior approval from the government.[1] When these licensing laws expired in 1695, the right to publish materials free from censorship became recognized under common law, which led English jurist William Blackstone to write, "The liberty of the press consists in laying no previous restraint upon publications and not in freedom from censure for criminal matter when published."[2]

Although not fully embraced by the U.S. Supreme Court, Blackstone's words convey a significant message about freedom of the press, a message that the framers of the Constitution understood. They recognized that for a society to remain free, it must allow for the emergence of divergent views and opinions, which can be formed

---

[1] See Thomas I. Emerson, *The System of Freedom of Expression* (New York: Vintage Books, 1970), 504.

[2] Blackstone's *Commentaries on the Laws of England*, vol. 4 (London, 1765–1769), 151–152.

only through the open exchange of ideas. By censoring the press, government takes away a major mechanism (indeed, *the* major one during the eighteenth and nineteenth centuries) through which ideas can be openly shared; when the media are suppressed, the people know only what the government wants them to know. Under such circumstances, the press becomes an extension of government, not an independent observer, a check, or even a reliable source of information.

Why is this state of affairs so dangerous? Consider one of the most heinous regimes in the history of the world—Nazi Germany. How the Nazis came to power and carried out their deeds is still being debated, but certainly their ability to control the press and to use it as a propaganda tool is part of the explanation. The danger of government control of the press also can be seen closer to home. The Watergate scandal involved political manipulation and illegal behavior at the highest levels of government and led to President Richard Nixon's resignation in 1974. Although the Senate committee that investigated Watergate exposed many of the misdeeds of the President and his lieutenants, it was the press that first discovered the wrongdoing and brought it to light. If government could place prior restraints on the press—to censor material before it is published—the Watergate wrongdoing might not have been exposed.

In the first part of this chapter, we examine the right of the press to be free from government control prior to publication—in other words, to be free of prior restraint. Under what conditions, if any, may the government enjoin the press from freely printing and distributing its material? In the second part of the chapter, we explore special privileges the media claim. Reporters argue that they should enjoy a unique set of guarantees so that they can perform their jobs. How has the Court reacted to such claims? We then analyze those forms of expression that the Supreme Court historically has considered outside the free press protections of the First Amendment: obscenity and libel. To what extent can the government penalize those who distribute sexually explicit material or material that contains damaging falsehoods? We conclude with a look at the rapidly expanding opportunities for free expression the Internet provides and the constitutional issues surrounding online media.

PRIOR RESTRAINT

No concept is more important to an understanding of freedom of the press than prior restraint, which occurs when the government reviews material to determine whether its publication will be permitted. As a form of government censorship, prior restraint is antithetical to a free press. As Justice Lewis Powell explained, "The special vice of a prior restraint is that communication will be suppressed . . . before an adequate determination that it is unprotected by the First Amendment."[3] In other words, the government may punish press activity that violates legitimate civil or criminal laws, but such government sanctions may take place only *after* publication, not before.

The principle that prior restraint runs contrary to the Constitution was established in the formative case *Near v. Minnesota* (1931). The justices took a strong stance against censorship, but does their decision imply that the government may never block the publication of material it considers inappropriate or harmful? Are there exceptions to the constitutional prohibition against prior restraint? Consider these questions as you read Chief Justice Charles Evans Hughes's opinion in *Near*.

Near v. Minnesota

283 U.S. 697 (1931)
http://caselaw.findlaw.com/us-supreme-court/283/697.html
Vote: 5 (Brandeis, Holmes, Hughes, Roberts, Stone)
    4 (Butler, McReynolds, Sutherland, Van Devanter)

OPINION OF THE COURT: *Hughes*

DISSENTING OPINION: *Butler*

A 1925 Minnesota law provided for "the abatement, as a public nuisance, of a 'malicious, scandalous, and defamatory newspaper, magazine, or other periodical.'" In the fall of 1927, Floyd B. Nelson, a county attorney, asked a state judge to issue a restraining order banning publication of the *Saturday Press*. In the attorney's view, the newspaper, partly owned by Jay Near, was the epitome of a malicious, scandalous, and defamatory publication.[4] The *Saturday Press* committed itself to exposing corruption, bribery, gambling, and prostitution in Minneapolis, which Near often connected to Jews. The paper attacked specific city officials for being in league with gangsters and chided the established press for refusing to uncover the corruption. Near's racist, anti-Semitic attitudes colored these attacks. In one issue, Near wrote:

---

[3]*Pittsburgh Press Co. v. Pittsburgh Commission on Human Relations* (1973).

[4]For an in-depth account of this case, see Fred W. Friendly, *Minnesota Rag* (New York: Random House, 1981). The quotes in this and the next paragraph come from this account.

Floyd B. Olson, the attorney for Hennepin County, Minnesota. He used a nuisance law to seek a restraining order against the *Saturday Press* after it criticized him, the mayor, and the chief of police for not taking action against organized crime. The Supreme Court invalidated the statute, marking the first time the Court employed the First Amendment to strike a state law that imposed a prior restraint on a newspaper. Olson was later elected governor.

I simply state a fact when I say that ninety per cent of the crimes committed against society in this city are committed by Jew gangsters. . . . It is Jew, Jew, Jew, as long as one cares to comb over the records. I am launching no attack against the Jewish people AS A RACE. I am merely calling attention to a FACT. And if people of that race and faith wish to rid themselves of the odium and stigma THE RODENTS OF THEIR OWN RACE HAVE BROUGHT UPON THEM, they need only to step to the front and help the decent citizens of Minneapolis rid the city of these criminal Jews.

In a piece attacking establishment journalism, Near proclaimed: "Journalism today isn't prostituted so much as it is disgustingly flabby. I'd rather be a louse in the cotton shirt of a nigger than be a journalistic prostitute." Based on the paper's past record, a judge issued a temporary restraining order prohibiting the sale of printed and future editions. Believing that this action violated his rights,

Near contacted the American Civil Liberties Union, which agreed to take his case. He grew uncomfortable with the organization, however, and instead obtained assistance from the publisher of the *Chicago Tribune.* Together, they challenged the Minnesota law as a violation of the First Amendment freedom of press guarantee, arguing that the law was tantamount to censorship.

MR. CHIEF JUSTICE HUGHES DELIVERED THE OPINION OF THE COURT.

[The Minnesota] statute, for the suppression as a public nuisance of a newspaper or periodical, is unusual, if not unique, and raises questions of grave importance transcending the local interests involved in the particular action. . . . The object of the statute is not punishment, in the ordinary sense, but suppression of the offending newspaper or periodical. The reason for the enactment, as the state court has said, is that prosecutions to enforce penal statutes for libel do not result in "efficient repression or suppression of the evils of scandal." Describing the business of publication as a public nuisance does not obscure the substance of the proceeding which the statute authorizes. It is the continued publication of scandalous and defamatory matter that constitutes the business and the declared nuisance. In the case of public officers, it is the reiteration of charges of official misconduct, and the fact that the newspaper or periodical is principally devoted to that purpose, that exposes it to suppression. . . .

If we cut through mere details of procedure, the operation and effect of the statute in substance is that public authorities may bring the owner or publisher of a newspaper or periodical before a judge upon a charge of conducting a business of publishing scandalous and defamatory matter—in particular that the matter consists of charges against public officers of official dereliction—and, unless the owner or publisher is able and disposed to bring competent evidence to satisfy the judge that the charges are true and are published with good motives and for justifiable ends, his newspaper or periodical is suppressed and further publication is made punishable as a contempt. This is of the essence of censorship.

The question is whether a statute authorizing such proceedings in restraint of publication is consistent with the conception of the liberty of the press as historically conceived and guaranteed. In determining the extent of the constitutional protection, it has been generally, if not universally, considered that it is the chief purpose of the guaranty to prevent previous restraints upon publication. The struggle in England, directed against the legislative power of the licenser, resulted in renunciation of the censorship of the press. The liberty deemed to be established was thus described by Blackstone: "The liberty of the press is indeed essential to the nature of a free state; but this consists in laying no previous restraints upon publications, and not in freedom from censure for criminal matter when published." . . .

The fact that for approximately one hundred and fifty years there has been almost an entire absence of attempts to impose previous restraints upon publications relating to the malfeasance of public officers is significant of the deep-seated conviction that such restraints would violate constitutional right. Public officers, whose character and conduct remains open to debate and free discussion in the press, find their remedies for false accusations in actions under libel laws providing for redress and punishment, and not in proceedings to restrain the publication of newspapers and periodicals. . . .

. . . The fact that the liberty of the press may be abused by miscreant purveyors of scandal does not make any the less necessary the immunity of the press from previous restraint in dealing with official misconduct. Subsequent punishment for such abuses as may exist is the appropriate remedy, consistent with constitutional privilege. . . .

The statute in question cannot be justified by reason of the fact that the publisher is permitted to show, before injunction issues, that the matter published is true and is published with good motives and for justifiable ends. If such a statute, authorizing suppression and injunction on such a basis, is constitutionally valid, it would be equally permissible for the Legislature to provide that at any time the publisher of any newspaper could be brought before a court . . . and required to produce proof of the truth of his publication, or of what he intended to publish and of his motives, or stand enjoined. If this can be done, the Legislature may provide machinery for determining in the complete exercise of its discretion what are justifiable ends and restrain publication accordingly. And it would be but a step to a complete system of censorship. . . .

Equally unavailing is the insistence that the statute is designed to prevent the circulation of scandal which tends to disturb the public peace and to provoke assaults and the commission of crime. Charges of reprehensible conduct, and in particular of official malfeasance, unquestionably create a public scandal, but the theory of the constitutional guaranty is that even a more serious public evil would be caused by authority to prevent publication. . . . As was said in *New Yorker Staats-Zeitung v. Nolan,* "If the township may prevent the circulation of a newspaper for no reason other than that some of its inhabitants may violently disagree with it, and resent its circulation by resorting to physical violence, there is no limit to what may be prohibited." The danger of violent reactions becomes greater with effective organization of defiant groups resenting exposure, and, if this consideration warranted legislative interference with the initial freedom of publication, the constitutional protection would be reduced to a mere form of words.

For these reasons we hold the statute, so far as it authorized the proceedings in this action . . . , to be an infringement of the liberty of the press. . . .

Judgment reversed.

Chief Justice Hughes's opinion appears to take a definitive position against prior censorship. He wrote, "The statute not only seeks to suppress the offending newspaper . . . but to put the publisher under an effective censorship." But he acknowledged that there may be exceptional circumstances that may justify government censorship; for example, said Hughes, the government may legitimately prohibit the publication of certain material in times of war that it might not constitutionally regulate in times of peace. To see the Court's logic, suppose that during the war in Iraq, a major newspaper received classified information about a planned U.S.-led military effort in the northern part of that country and announced that it would publish the information so the American people would be fully informed about the war effort. The military would understandably be concerned that publication would give the enemy advance knowledge of the operation. Could the government take action to prohibit publication, or would it be confined to pursuing criminal charges against the paper for illegal dissemination of classified documents after publication? According to *Near,* the courts would likely rule in favor of the government.

Forty years after *Near,* the justices had the chance to consider whether national security would justify a prior restraint. **New York Times v. United States** (1971) concerned the government's attempt to stop the *New York Times* and the *Washington Post* from publishing classified documents pertaining to the Vietnam War.

The case began in June 1971, when the *Times* and the *Post* began publishing articles based on two government documents: a 1965 Defense Department depiction of the Gulf of Tonkin incident and the 1968 "History of U.S. Decision-Making Process on Viet Nam Policy," a Pentagon study that ran to seven thousand pages in forty-seven volumes. This secret study had been photocopied and presented to the press by a Defense Department employee, Daniel Ellsberg. Known as the Pentagon Papers, the documents constituted a history of U.S. involvement in the war in Indochina, a subject of acute interest among Americans in the early 1970s.

After the newspapers published several installments, the U.S. government asked a federal district court to order the papers to refrain from publishing any more installments. The government argued that the articles would cause "irreparable injury" to the country's national security. To support this assertion, the government said that the entire 1968 study was top secret, a classification "applied only to that information or material the defense aspect of which is paramount, and the unauthorized

Katharine Graham, publisher of the *Washington Post*, and Ben Bradlee, the newspaper's executive editor, leave U.S. District Court in Washington, D.C., in 1971, following the initial hearing on their legal challenge to the government's attempt to block publication of the Pentagon Papers. The Supreme Court ultimately ruled that the government's efforts to prohibit publication amounted to an unconstitutional prior restraint on the press.

disclosure of which could result in *exceptionally grave* damage to the Nation." The newspapers disagreed, arguing that the material was largely of historical, not current, interest, and that nothing in the documents related to a time period after 1968. As such, the government's attempt to enjoin publication amounted to nothing less than prior restraint.

Because the issues in this case were so important and the public controversy so intense, the judicial system responded to the dispute in a very unusual manner. The government's request to the district court was dated June 15, 1971, and the lower courts handled the case in an expedited fashion so that only nine days later the issue was before the Supreme Court. Although the justices were about to go into their summer recess, the Court extended its session and heard arguments on June 26. Four days later, the Court issued a short per curiam opinion announcing that the majority rejected the

government's demands. From start to finish, it took the federal judiciary only two weeks to decide this major constitutional dispute.

Six justices supported the claim of the newspapers, but they hardly agreed on the reasons for doing so. Justices Hugo Black and William O. Douglas took the most extreme position. Consistent with their view that First Amendment protections are absolute, they argued that the censorship the government requested was inappropriate. Justice Black emphatically stated, "I believe that every moment's continuance of the injunctions against these newspapers amounts to a flagrant, indefensible, and continuing violation of the First Amendment."

Justices William J. Brennan and Thurgood Marshall also strongly condemned the injunctions but without completely foreclosing the possibility that under extreme circumstances such censorship might be allowable. The government simply had failed to show that it was necessary in this case. Brennan wrote, "[T]he First Amendment stands as an absolute bar to the imposition of judicial restraints in circumstances of the kind presented by these cases. . . . Unless and until the Government has clearly made out its case, the First Amendment commands that no injunction may issue."

Justices Byron White and Potter Stewart took the most moderate position of those in the majority. They agreed that the injunctions should not be issued in the Pentagon Papers cases, but only because the government had not proven that publication would "result in direct, immediate, and irreparable damage to our Nation or its people." Both expressed concerns about letting the executive branch intervene against the press in this way. They explained that they would have been more open to the action the executive requested if Congress had passed legislation authorizing prior restraint in circumstances such as those presented by this case.

The three dissenting justices, Harry Blackmun, Warren Burger, and John Harlan, stressed two major points. First, they condemned the speed with which the case was decided. The Court, in their view, had been unable to give careful consideration to the difficult issues raised because the justices were rushed to arrive at a judgment. Second, they took the position that in matters of foreign policy, the Constitution rested primary authority in the executive branch. Therefore, when the executive branch, for foreign policy reasons, claims that it is necessary to impose certain limits on the press, deference should be given to that position. The dissenters would have preferred to have the case sent back to the lower courts for more lengthy study and with instructions that the courts give considerable latitude to the executive branch when it is "operating within the field of its constitutional prerogative."

The *New York Times* case has generated a great deal of debate among legal scholars. Some suggest that it was the Court's, or at least individual justices', strongest statement to date on freedom of the press, virtually eradicating Hughes's national security exception to prior restraint. Others disagree. C. Herman Pritchett notes, "While the result in *New York Times* was clear enough, the Court's opinions do not add up to a sound defense of freedom of the press."[5] At the very least, the justices were divided in their views. In fact, every justice wrote a separate opinion in the case.

A few years later in *United States v. Progressive, Inc.* (1979), the federal government tried to prevent the publication of a magazine article that detailed the workings of nuclear weapons. The United States argued that the article would harm national security and that, under the Non-Proliferation Treaty, the United States had an obligation to prevent non-nuclear nations from obtaining atomic weapons. These were exactly the sorts of considerations that some of the justices in the Pentagon Papers case thought might justify a prior restraint. The government was initially successful in blocking the magazine, but a similar article soon appeared in another publication; the case was abandoned before reaching the Court.

Since the *New York Times* case, the Court has had no other important cases dealing with prior restraint and national security concerns. Nevertheless, during contemporary military efforts, the government has not hesitated to impose constraints on the media. Depending on one's perspective, the 1991 Gulf War was either a high point or a low point in government-media relations: the government simply circumvented the need to censor the press by limiting its access to certain information.[6] During the war in Iraq that began in December 2003, six hundred embedded journalists enjoyed substantial, but not absolute, freedom. The Department of Defense requested that journalists refrain from publishing information that could harm America's national security and did not rule out the possibility of demanding to review reports before they were published or aired.

No one has yet mounted a serious legal challenge to these types of restrictions. But, given responses from journalists—including complaints that it is impossible for them to know whether coverage of particular military operations would, in fact, jeopardize national security—it seems likely that challenges will arise.

NEWS GATHERING AND SPECIAL RIGHTS

Challenging restraints on First Amendment rights is not the only battle the media have fought. For many years the news media have asked courts for "special rights" not normally accorded average citizens. These are prerogatives that journalists consider necessary if they are to provide "full and robust" coverage of local, national, and world events. The most important of these special

[5]C. Herman Pritchett, *Constitutional Civil Liberties* (Englewood Cliffs, NJ: Prentice Hall, 1984), 65.

[6]See, for example, Kevin A. Smith, "The Media at the Tip of the Spear," *Michigan Law Review* 102 (2004): 1329–1372.

rights is known as the reporter's privilege, a protection that prohibits the government from compelling reporters to supply information about their sources.

As far back as 1848 reporters asserted the need for unusual legal privileges. That year the Senate held a secret meeting to debate a proposed treaty to end the Mexican-American War. John Nugent, a reporter for the *New York Herald*, managed to obtain a copy of the proposed draft and mailed it to his editor. Outraged senators demanded to know the source of the leak and subpoenaed Nugent to testify. Nugent appeared, but he claimed First Amendment protection and refused to provide information about his source. In response the Senate had Nugent arrested and confined him to a congressional committee room. After about a month of unsuccessful efforts to convince Nugent to provide the requested information, a frustrated Senate released him.[7]

From time to time others faced the same fate as Nugent, but during the 1960s and 1970s claims of reporters' privilege increased. Some credit this growth to the federal subpoenas served on major networks, newspapers, and magazines to obtain information about the Chicago Seven, a group of individuals charged with starting a riot outside the arena where the Democratic National Convention was taking place in 1968. Others suggest that it was the Nixon administration's disdain for the press that led to the increase, and still others argue that the rise in investigative reporting ushered in by the Watergate scandal led reporters to assert their right to protect sources absolutely and unconditionally.

Whatever the cause, the debate over reporters' privilege was elevated in 1972 when the Supreme Court agreed to hear several cases involving such claims. The cases presented somewhat different issues, but the points of view were clear on both sides. The government asserted that reporters were just citizens and therefore not entitled to an exemption from the law: if ordinary citizens were forced to testify upon subpoena, then so should those working for the media. In response, the media pointed to other privileged relationships. Attorneys, for example, cannot be forced to reveal information about their clients, and patients are ensured of confidentiality by their doctors. Reporters also argued that, if they were forced to answer questions about their sources, those sources

would be reluctant to assist with news gathering. This would have a chilling effect on their ability to do their jobs and violate their free press guarantee.

Branzburg v. Hayes

408 U.S. 665 (1972)
http://caselaw.findlaw.com/us-supreme-court/408/665.html
Oral arguments available at https://www.oyez.org/
cases/1971/70-85
Vote: 5 (Blackmun, Burger, Powell, Rehnquist, White)
4 (Brennan, Douglas, Marshall, Stewart)

OPINION OF THE COURT: *White*

CONCURRING OPINION: *Powell*

DISSENTING OPINIONS: *Douglas, Stewart*

Paul M. Branzburg, a reporter for the Louisville, Kentucky, *Courier-Journal*, had written articles about his firsthand observations of the area's illegal drug trade. In one article, Branzburg wrote, "Larry, a young Louisville hippie, . . . and his partner, Jack, are engaged in a weird business that is a combination of capitalism, chemistry, and criminality." Branzburg described how they made hashish from marijuana and reaped a profit of about $5,000 for three weeks' work. The article contained the following passage:

> "I don't know why I am letting you do this story . . . To make the narcs mad I guess. That's the main reason." However, Larry and his partner *asked for and received a promise that their names would be changed* [emphasis added].

A second piece contained interviews Branzburg had conducted with numerous drug users in Frankfort, Kentucky. After these stories were published, a grand jury subpoenaed him. Branzburg appeared before the grand jury, but he refused to answer the following questions:

1. Who was the person or persons you observed in possession of marijuana, about which you wrote an article?

2. Who was the person or persons you observed compounding marijuana, producing same to a compound known as hashish?

State trial court judge J. Miles Pound then ordered Branzburg to answer the grand jury's questions. Branzburg again refused. Citing the First Amendment's press protection, he initiated legal

---

[7]Mark Neubauer, "The Newsmen's Privilege after *Branzburg*," *UCLA Law Review* 24 (1976): 160–192; Donald A. Ritchie, *Press Gallery: Congress and the Washington Correspondents* (Cambridge, MA: Harvard University Press, 1991); "Senate Arrests a Reporter— March 26, 1848," Senate Stories, 1801–1850, www.senate.gov.

action to stop the trial court from taking any action against him. The Kentucky Court of Appeals rejected his reporter's privilege claim, and he sought Supreme Court review. During the course of these proceedings, John P. Hayes replaced Judge Pound in office and also as respondent on the appeal.

MR. JUSTICE WHITE DELIVERED THE OPINION OF THE COURT.

The issue in these cases is whether requiring newsmen to appear and testify before state or federal grand juries abridges the freedom of speech and press guaranteed by the First Amendment. We hold that it does not. . . .

. . . Citizens generally are not constitutionally immune from grand jury subpoenas; and neither the First Amendment nor any other constitutional provision protects the average citizen from disclosing to a grand jury information that he has received in confidence. The claim is, however, that reporters are exempt from these obligations because if forced to respond to subpoenas and identify their sources or disclose other confidences, their informants will refuse or be reluctant to furnish newsworthy information in the future. This asserted burden on news gathering is said to make compelled testimony from newsmen constitutionally suspect and to require a privileged position for them.

It is clear that the First Amendment does not invalidate every incidental burdening of the press that may result from the enforcement of civil or criminal statutes of general applicability. Under prior cases, otherwise valid laws serving substantial public interests may be enforced against the press as against others, despite the possible burden that may be imposed. The Court has emphasized that "[t]he publisher of a newspaper has no special immunity from the application of general laws." . . .

A number of States have provided newsmen a statutory privilege of varying breadth, but the majority have not done so, and none has been provided by federal statute. Until now the only testimonial privilege for unofficial witnesses that is rooted in the Federal Constitution is the Fifth Amendment privilege against compelled self-incrimination. We are asked to create another by interpreting the First Amendment to grant newsmen a testimonial privilege that other citizens do not enjoy. This we decline to do. Fair and effective law enforcement aimed at providing security for the person and property of the individual is a fundamental function of government, and the grand jury plays an important, constitutionally mandated role in this process. On the records now before us, we perceive no basis for holding that the public interest in law enforcement and in ensuring effective grand jury proceedings is insufficient to override the consequential, but uncertain, burden on news gathering that is said to result from insisting that reporters, like other citizens, respond to relevant questions put to them in the course of a valid grand jury investigation or criminal trial. . . .

This conclusion itself involves no restraint on what newspapers may publish or on the type or quality of information reporters may seek to acquire, nor does it threaten the vast bulk of confidential relationships between reporters and their sources. Grand juries address themselves to the issues of whether crimes have been committed and who committed them. Only where news sources themselves are implicated in crime or possess information relevant to the grand jury's task need they or the reporter be concerned about grand jury subpoenas. Nothing before us indicates that a large number or percentage of *all* confidential news sources falls into either category. . . . The preference for anonymity of those confidential informants involved in actual criminal conduct is presumably a product of their desire to escape criminal prosecution, and this preference, while understandable, is hardly deserving of constitutional protection. It would be frivolous to assert—and no one does in these cases—that the First Amendment, in the interest of securing news or otherwise, confers a license on either the reporter or his news sources to violate valid criminal laws. . . .

The argument that the flow of news will be diminished by compelling reporters to aid the grand jury in a criminal investigation is not irrational, nor are the records before us silent on the matter. But we remain unclear how often and to what extent informers are actually deterred from furnishing information when newsmen are forced to testify before a grand jury. . . . Estimates of the inhibiting effect of such subpoenas on the willingness of informants to make disclosures to newsmen are widely divergent and to a great extent speculative. . . .

At the federal level, Congress has freedom to determine whether a statutory newsman's privilege is necessary and desirable and to fashion standards and rules as narrow or broad as deemed necessary to deal with the evil discerned and, equally important, to refashion those rules as experience from time to time may dictate. There is also merit in leaving state legislatures free, within First Amendment limits, to fashion their own standards in light of the conditions and problems with respect to the relations between law enforcement officials and press in their own areas. It goes without saying, of course, that we are powerless to bar state courts from responding in their own way and construing their own constitutions so as to recognize a newsman's privilege, either qualified or absolute. . . .

The decision . . . in *Branzburg v. Hayes* . . . must be affirmed. Here, petitioner refused to answer questions that directly related to criminal conduct that he had observed and written about. The Kentucky Court of Appeals noted that marijuana is defined as a narcotic drug by statute and that unlicensed possession or compounding of it is a felony punishable by both fine and imprisonment. It held that petitioner "saw the commission of the statutory felonies of unlawful possession of marijuana and the unlawful conversion of it into hashish." . . . [I]f what the petitioner wrote was true, he had direct information to provide the grand jury concerning the commission of serious crimes.

[Affirmed.]

MR. JUSTICE DOUGLAS, DISSENTING.

Today's decision will impede the wide-open and robust dissemination of ideas and counterthought which a free press both fosters and protects and which is essential to the success of intelligent self-government. Forcing a reporter before a grand jury will have two retarding effects upon the ear and the pen of the press. Fear of exposure will cause dissidents to communicate less openly to trusted reporters. And, fear of accountability will cause editors and critics to write with more restrained pens. . . .

A reporter is no better than his source of information. Unless he has a privilege to withhold the identity of his source, he will be the victim of governmental intrigue or aggression. If he can be summoned to testify in secret before a grand jury, his sources will dry up and the attempted exposure, the effort to enlighten the public, will be ended. If what the Court sanctions today becomes settled law, then the reporter's main function in American society will be to pass on to the public the press releases which the various departments of government issue. . . .

MR. JUSTICE STEWART, WITH WHOM MR. JUSTICE BRENNAN AND MR. JUSTICE MARSHALL JOIN, DISSENTING.

The Court's crabbed view of the First Amendment reflects a disturbing insensitivity to the critical role of an independent press in our society. The question whether a reporter has a constitutional right to a confidential relationship with his source is of first impression here, but the principles that should guide our decision are as basic as any to be found in the Constitution. . . . [T]he Court . . . holds that a newsman has no First Amendment right to protect his sources when called before a grand jury. The Court thus invites state and federal authorities to undermine the historic independence of the press by attempting to annex the journalistic profession as an investigative arm of government. Not only will this decision impair performance of the press' constitutionally protected functions, but it will, I am convinced, in the long run harm rather than help the administration of justice. . . .

Accordingly, when a reporter is asked to appear before a grand jury and reveal confidences, I would hold that the government must (1) show that there is probable cause to believe that the newsman has information that is clearly relevant to a specific probable violation of law; (2) demonstrate that the information sought cannot be obtained by alternative means less destructive of First Amendment rights; and (3) demonstrate a compelling and overriding interest in the information.

In *Branzburg* the majority emphatically denied the existence of reporters' privilege. The dissenters were distraught: Justice Potter Stewart, who in his youth had worked as a reporter for a Cincinnati newspaper and edited the *Yale Daily News* while in college, faulted his colleagues for "undermin[ing] the historic independence of the press." The reaction of the media was even more vehement, with an outpouring of condemnation of *Branzburg* and calls for federal and state statutes that would shield reporters from revealing their sources. The states responded to these calls, with forty passing laws that recognize a privilege for reporters to refuse to divulge information about certain news-gathering activities.[8] But because these shield laws often limit protections to specific circumstances, they may not necessarily be effective. Kentucky already had a shield law on the books at the time of Branzburg's grand jury proceedings, but it covered only sources of information and not personal observation. Journalists still face the threat of imprisonment if they refuse to answer questions pertaining to their stories—as Branzburg himself learned only a few months after the Supreme Court handed down the decision in his case *(see Box 14-1)*. In addition, Congress has yet to enact a federal shield law, despite immense pressure from a range of organized interests.

The ability to shield sources is not the only privilege reporters claim, but their assertions of privilege in other areas also have not fared particularly well. In **Zurcher v. Stanford Daily** (1978), the offices of Stanford University's student newspaper were subjected to a search when police sought news photographs that might help identify participants in an altercation on campus. The justices held that the media had no exemption from lawfully authorized searches. Several months after *Zurcher*, the Court decided **Houchins v. KQED, Inc.** (1978), which asked whether reporters have a right of access to inmates in a county jail, access that ordinarily would be denied to other individuals. Again, the Court decided that the press have no rights and privileges beyond those enjoyed by average citizens. As Chief Justice Burger explained in his plurality opinion, "There is an undoubted right to gather news 'from any source by means within the law,' but that affords no basis for the claim that the First Amendment compels others—private persons or governments—to supply information." Stated differently, the First Amendment prohibits government from *hindering* the press, but it does not require the government to *help* the press.

---

[8] For more details, see "Number of States with Shield Law Climbs to 40," Reporters Committee for Freedom of the Press, http://www.rcfp.org/browse-media-law-resources/news-media-law/news-media-law-summer-2011/number-states-shield-law-climbs.

BOX 14-1

Aftermath . . . Paul Branzburg

After the Supreme Court ruled that reporter Paul M. Branzburg of the Louisville *Courier-Journal* had no right to refuse to identify his confidential sources, Kentucky prosecutors again sought information from him concerning the drug users and dealers he had observed while researching his stories. Branzburg, who by this time had moved to Michigan to do investigative reporting for the *Detroit Free Press*, again declined to answer questions about his sources. On September 1, 1972, he was found in contempt of the Jefferson County court and was sentenced to six months in prison. When Branzburg refused to return to Kentucky voluntarily, state officials requested that Michigan authorities extradite him. Michigan's governor, William G. Milliken, denied the request, and Branzburg never served the six-month sentence.

THE BOUNDARIES OF FREE PRESS: LIBEL, OBSCENITY, AND EMERGING AREAS OF GOVERNMENT CONCERN

One of the Supreme Court's consistent teachings is that the First Amendment is not absolute, despite its seeming absolute language ("Congress shall make no law . . ."). As the Court has developed its doctrines of freedom of expression, it has periodically reminded us of the limits of the First Amendment; some varieties of expression, the justices have explained, fall outside of its protection and may be punished, usually on the basis of the harm they represent. One may not communicate military secrets to the enemy or make terrorist threats. One may not provide fraudulent information in commercial transactions or engage in discussions that amount to criminal conspiracies. One may not lie under oath or exchange insider information in securities transactions. In each of these cases, the expression falls outside the boundaries of First Amendment protection.

This section explores the limits of First Amendment protection by examining two types of expression that have presented the justices with perplexing constitutional questions: libel and obscenity. Agreement is almost universal that the framers did not intend the First Amendment to protect slanderous falsehoods or indecencies that offended public morals. Accepting this broad proposition, however, does not settle more particular questions. How do we define libel and obscenity? What distinguishes such expression from otherwise protected speech and press? What standards of evidence should be imposed? How can government regulate obscenity and libel without creating a chilling effect on protected expression? We end the chapter with a section on more recent attempts by the government to create new categories of unprotected press—media representations of cruelty and violence.

Libel

On any given day in the United States, we can buy a newspaper, navigate to a website, or turn on the television and find information on the activities of public officials, well-known figures, and even private citizens who have made the news for various reasons. Sometimes the reports imply criticism—for example, a newspaper article about a public official accused of wrongdoing. In other cases, the reports are blatantly false. To see this phenomenon we need go no farther than to a supermarket checkout line and read the tabloid headlines about the alleged doings of celebrities.

As we know from our readings on freedom of the press, government generally cannot prohibit the media from disseminating such information—true or false. But once stories are published or televised, do those who might be harmed by the stories have any recourse? Under U.S. law they do: they can bring libel actions against the offenders. If individuals believe that falsehoods in published or televised stories have defamed their character or caused a loss of their freedoms or financial assets, they can ask the courts to hold the media responsible for their actions. The injured individuals have this recourse because libelous statements fall outside the scope of First Amendment protections.

Defining the standards for libel has long been problematic. In 1798, the Federalist Congress enacted the Sedition Act, which outlawed seditious libel, defined as criticism of the government and of government officials (see chapter 13). Under this act, the government could bring criminal charges against those who made "false, scandalous, and malicious" statements that brought the United States or its representatives into "contempt or disrepute." Because President Thomas Jefferson later pardoned all those who had been convicted under the act, the Supreme Court never had an opportunity to rule on its constitutionality. For most of the nation's history, it was unclear whether seditious libel was protected or unprotected speech.[9] Indeed, the justices did not firmly established a position on libel until 1964.

Prior to that time, the states were free to determine their own standards for the most common form of libel—civil actions brought by individuals against other individuals, such as those running a newspaper. Some variation existed among state laws, but most allowed defamed individuals to seek two kinds of monetary damages: compensatory, for actual financial loss (e.g., an individual loses his or her job because of the story), and punitive, to punish the offender. To collect such damages, all the plaintiff generally had to demonstrate was that the story was false and damaging.

These criteria might sound like simple standards for plaintiffs to meet, but the simplicity further compounded the Court's problems. Many newspapers, television stations, and other media argued that the traditional standard had a chilling effect on their First Amendment guarantee of a free press. They feared printing anything critical of government or public officials, in particular, because if a story contained even the smallest factual error, they could face a costly lawsuit. Thus, the media felt constrained in their reporting of news. In *New York Times v. Sullivan*, the Court radically departed from its former position of permitting states to set their own standards and crafted a test of its own. What standard did the Court articulate? How did it alter existing libel law?

---

[9]See Zechariah Chafee Jr., *Free Speech in the United States* (Cambridge, MA: Harvard University Press, 1941); and Leonard W. Levy, *Legacy of Suppression* (Cambridge, MA: Harvard University Press, 1960). See also Levy's revised and enlarged edition, *Emergence of a Free Press* (New York: Oxford University Press, 1985).

New York Times *v. Sullivan*

376 U.S. 254 (1964)
http://caselaw.findlaw.com/us-supreme-court/376/254.html
Oral arguments available at https://www.oyez.org/cases/1963/39
Vote: 9 (Black, Brennan, Clark, Douglas, Goldberg, Harlan, Stewart, Warren, White)
0

OPINION OF THE COURT: *Brennan*

CONCURRING OPINIONS: *Black, Goldberg*

The March 29, 1960, edition of the *New York Times* ran a full-page advertisement (reprinted here) to publicize the struggle for civil rights and to raise money for the cause. L. B. Sullivan, the police commissioner of the city of Montgomery, Alabama, took offense at one portion of the ad. It did not mention Sullivan by name, but it offered highly critical references to police actions during a civil rights demonstration in Montgomery and suggested that in halting the demonstration, the police, who were under Sullivan's command, had engaged in wrongdoing.

Sullivan brought a libel action against the paper and various signatories to the ad, alleging that the ad contained falsehoods—which, in fact, it did. For example, it claimed that demonstrating students sang, "My Country, 'Tis of Thee," when they actually sang the "Star-Spangled Banner." In his charge to the jury, the judge said that the ad was "libelous per se," meaning that because it contained falsehoods, it was unprotected speech. In addition, he said, if the jury found that the statements were made "of and concerning" Sullivan, it could hold the *Times* liable. Taking these instructions to heart, the jury awarded Sullivan $500,000 in damages.

The Supreme Court of Alabama affirmed this judgment. It specified that words are libelous per se when they "tend to injure a person libeled by them in his reputation, profession, trade or business, or charge him with an indictable offense, or tend to bring the individual into public contempt." This definition was fairly typical. The *New York Times* sought Supreme Court review, challenging the lower court's definition because it "presumes malice and falsity. . . . Such a rule of liability works an abridgment of the free press." The paper's attorneys added, "It is implicit in this Court's decisions that speech which is critical of governmental action may not be repressed upon the ground that it diminishes the reputation of those officers whose conduct it deplores."

MR. JUSTICE BRENNAN DELIVERED THE OPINION OF THE COURT.

We are required in this case to determine for the first time the extent to which the constitutional protections for speech and press limit a

Heed Their Rising Voices

" The growing movement of peaceful mass demonstrations by Negroes is something new in the South, something understandable. . . . Let Congress heed their rising voices, for they will be heard."

—New York Times editorial Saturday, March 19, 1960

AS the whole world knows by now, thousands of Southern Negro students are engaged in widespread non-violent demonstrations in positive affirmation of the right to live in human dignity as guaranteed by the U. S. Constitution and the Bill of Rights. In their efforts to uphold these guarantees, they are being met by an unprecedented wave of terror by those who would deny and negate that document which the whole world looks upon as setting the pattern for modern freedom...

In Orangeburg, South Carolina, when 400 students peacefully sought to buy doughnuts and coffee at lunch counters in the business district, they were forcibly ejected, tear-gassed, soaked to the skin in freezing weather with fire hoses, arrested en masse and herded into an open barbed-wire stockade to stand for hours in the bitter cold.

In Montgomery, Alabama, after students sang "My Country, 'Tis of Thee" on the State Capitol steps, their leaders were expelled from school, and truckloads of police armed with shotguns and tear-gas ringed the Alabama State College Campus. When the entire student body protested to state authorities by refusing to re-register, their dining hall was padlocked in an attempt to starve them into submission.

In Tallahassee, Atlanta, Nashville, Savannah, Greensboro, Memphis, Richmond, Charlotte, and a host of other cities in the South, young American teenagers, in face of the entire weight of official state apparatus and police power, have boldly stepped forth as protagonists of democracy. Their courage and amazing restraint have inspired millions and given a new dignity to the cause of freedom.

Small wonder that the Southern violators of the Constitution fear this new, non-violent brand of freedom fighter... even as they fear the upswelling right-to-vote movement. Small wonder that they are determined to destroy the one man who, more than any other, symbolizes the new spirit now sweeping the South—the Rev. Dr. Martin Luther King, Jr., world-famous leader of the Montgomery Bus Protest. For it is his doctrine of non-violence which has inspired and guided the students in their widening wave of sit-ins; and it is this same Dr. King who founded and is president of the Southern Christian Leadership Conference—the organization which is spearheading the surging right-to-vote movement. Under Dr. King's direction the Leadership Conference conducts Student Workshops and Seminars in the philosophy and techniques of non-violent resistance.

Again and again the Southern violators have answered Dr. King's peaceful protests with intimidation and violence. They have bombed his home almost killing his wife and child. They have assaulted his person. They have arrested him seven times—for "speeding," "loitering" and similar "offenses." And now they have charged him with "perjury"—a *felony* under which they could imprison him for *ten years*. Obviously, their real purpose is to remove him physically as the leader to whom the students and millions of others—look for guidance and support, and thereby to intimidate *all* leaders who may rise in the South. Their strategy is to behead this affirmative movement, and thus to demoralize Negro Americans and weaken their will to struggle. The defense of Martin Luther King, spiritual leader of the student sit-in movement, clearly, therefore, is an integral part of the total struggle for freedom in the South.

Decent-minded Americans cannot help but applaud the creative daring of the students and the quiet heroism of Dr. King. But this is one of those moments in the stormy history of Freedom when men and women of good will must do more than applaud the rising-to-glory of others. The America whose good name hangs in the balance before a watchful world, the America whose heritage of Liberty these Southern Upholders of the Constitution are defending, is *our* America as well as theirs...

We must heed their rising voices—yes—but we must add our own.

We must extend ourselves above and beyond moral support and render the material help so urgently needed by those who are taking the risks, facing jail, and *even death* in a glorious re-affirmation of our Constitution and its Bill of Rights.

We urge you to join hands with our fellow Americans in the South by supporting, with your dollars, this combined appeal for all three needs—the defense of Martin Luther King—the support of the embattled students—and the struggle for the right-to-vote.

Your Help Is Urgently Needed . . . NOW!!

Stella Adler	Dr. Alan Knight Chalmers	Anthony Franciosa	John Killens	L. Joseph Overton	Maureen Stapleton
Raymond Pace Alexander	Richard Coe	Lorraine Hansbury	Eartha Kitt	Clarence Pickett	Frank Silvera
Harry Van Arsdale	Nat King Cole	Rev. Donald Harrington	Rabbi Edward Klein	Shad Polier	Hope Stevens
Harry Belafonte	Cheryl Crawford	Nat Hentoff	Hope Lange	Sidney Poitier	George Tabor
Julie Belafonte	Dorothy Dandridge	James Hicks	John Lewis	A. Philip Randolph	Rev. Gardner C.
Dr. Algernon Black	Ossie Davis	Mary Hinkson	Viveca Lindfors	John Raitt	Taylor
Marc Blitzstein	Sammy Davis, Jr.	Van Heflin	Carl Murphy	Elmer Rice	Norman Thomas
William Branch	Ruby Dee	Langston Hughes	Don Murray	Jackie Robinson	Kenneth Tynan
Marlon Brando	Dr. Philip Elliott	Morris Iushewitz	John Murray	Mrs. Eleanor Roosevelt	Charles White
Mrs. Ralph Bunche	Dr. Harry Emerson	Mahalia Jackson	A. J. Muste	Bayard Rustin	Shelley Winters
Diahann Carroll	Fosdick	Mordecai Johnson	Frederick O'Neal	Robert Ryan	Max Youngstein

We in the south who are struggling daily for dignity and freedom warmly endorse this appeal

Rev. Ralph D. Abernathy *(Montgomery, Ala.)*	Rev. Matthew D. McCollom *(Orangeburg, S.C.)*	Rev. Walter L. Hamilton *(Norfolk, Va.)*	Rev. A. L. Davis *(New Orleans, La.)*
Rev. Fred L. Shuttlesworth *(Birmingham, Ala.)*	Rev. William Holmes Borders *(Atlanta, Ga.)*	I. S. Levy *(Columbia, S.C.)*	Mrs. Katie E. Whickham *(New Orleans, La.)*
Rev. Kelley Miller Smith *(Nashville, Tenn.)*	Rev. Douglas Moore *(Durham, N.C.)*	Rev. Martin Luther King, Sr. *(Atlanta, Ga.)*	Rev. W. H. Hall *(Hattiesburg, Miss.)*
Rev. W. A. Dennis *(Chattanooga, Tenn.)*	Rev. Wyatt Tee Walker *(Petersburg, Va.)*	Rev. Henry C. Bunton *(Memphis, Tenn.)*	Rev. J. E. Lowery *(Mobile, Ala.)*
Rev. C. K. Steele *(Tallahassee, Fla.)*		Rev. S.S. Seay, Sr. *(Montgomery, Ala.)*	Rev. T. J. Jemison *(Baton Rouge, La.)*
		Rev. Samuel W. Williams *(Atlanta, Ga.)*	

COMMITTEE TO DEFEND MARTIN LUTHER KING AND THE STRUGGLE FOR FREEDOM IN THE SOUTH

312 West 125th Street, New York 27, N.Y. UNiversity 6-1700

Chairmen: A. Philip Randolph, Dr. Gardner C. Taylor; *Chairmen of Cultural Division:* Harry Belafonte, Sidney Poitier; *Treasurer:* Nat King Cole; *Executive Director:* Bayard Rustin; *Chairman of Church Division:* Father George B. Ford, Rev. Harry Emerson Fosdick, Rev. Thomas Kilgore, Jr., Rabbi Edward E. Klein; *Chairman of Labor Division:* Morris Iushewitz

Please mail this coupon TODAY!

Committee To Defend Martin Luther King
and
The Struggle For Freedom in The South
312 West 125th Street, New York 27, N.Y.
UNiversity 6-1700

I am enclosing my contribution of $_____ for the work of the Committee.

Name _____
Address _____
City _____ Zone _____ State _____

☐ I want to help ☐ Please send further information

Please make checks payable to:
Committee to Defend Martin Luther King

State's power to award damages in a libel action brought by a public official against critics of his official conduct. . . .

We may dispose at the outset of [t]he . . . contention . . . that the constitutional guarantees of freedom of speech and of the press are inapplicable here, at least so far as the *Times* is concerned, because the allegedly libelous statements were published as part of a paid, "commercial" advertisement. . . .

The publication here was not a "commercial" advertisement in the sense in which the word was used in [*Valentine v.*] *Chrestensen* [1942]. It communicated information, expressed opinion, recited grievances, protested claimed abuses, and sought financial support on behalf of a movement whose existence and objectives are matters of the highest public interest and concern. That the *Times* was paid for publishing the advertisement is as immaterial in this connection as is the fact that newspapers and books are sold. Any other conclusion would discourage newspapers from carrying "editorial advertisements" of this type, and so might shut off an important outlet for the promulgation of information and ideas by persons who do not themselves have access to publishing facilities—who wish to exercise their freedom of speech even though they are not members of the press. . . . To avoid placing such a handicap upon the freedoms of expression, we hold that if the allegedly libelous statements would otherwise be constitutionally protected from the present judgment, they do not forfeit that protection because they were published in the form of a paid advertisement.

Under Alabama law as applied in this case, a publication is "libelous per se" if the words "tend to injure a person . . . in his reputation" or to "bring [him] into public contempt"; the trial court stated that the standard was met if the words are such as to "injure him in his public office, or impute misconduct to him in his office, or want of official integrity, or want of fidelity to a public trust. . . ." The jury must find that the words were published "of and concerning" the plaintiff, but where the plaintiff is a public official his place in the governmental hierarchy is sufficient evidence to support a finding that his reputation has been affected by statements that reflect upon the agency of which he is in charge. Once "libel per se" has been established, the defendant has no defense as to stated facts unless he can persuade the jury that they were true in all their particulars.

The question before us is whether this rule of liability, as applied to an action brought by a public official against critics of his official conduct, abridges the freedom of speech and of the press that is guaranteed by the First and Fourteenth Amendments.

Respondent relies heavily, as did the Alabama courts, on statements of this Court to the effect that the Constitution does not protect libelous publications. Those statements do not foreclose our inquiry here. None of the cases sustained the use of libel laws to impose sanctions upon expression critical of the official conduct of public officials. . . . In deciding the question now, we are compelled by neither precedent nor policy to give any more weight to the epithet "libel" than we have to other "mere labels" of state law.

Like insurrection, contempt, advocacy of unlawful acts, breach of the peace, obscenity, solicitation of legal business, and the various other formulae for the repression of expression that have been challenged in this Court, libel can claim no talismanic immunity from constitutional limitations. It must be measured by standards that satisfy the First Amendment. . . .

. . . [W]e consider this case against the background of a profound national commitment to the principle that debate on public issues should be uninhibited, robust, and wide open, and that it may well include vehement, caustic, and sometimes unpleasantly sharp attacks on government and public officials. The present advertisement, as an expression of grievance and protest on one of the major public issues of our time, would seem clearly to qualify for the constitutional protection. The question is whether it forfeits that protection by the falsity of some of its factual statements and by its alleged defamation of respondent.

Authoritative interpretations of the First Amendment guarantees have consistently refused to recognize an exception for any test of truth—whether administered by judges, juries, or administrative officials—and especially one that puts the burden of proving truth on the speaker. The constitutional protection does not turn upon "the truth, popularity, or social utility of the ideas and beliefs which are offered." . . . That erroneous statement is inevitable in free debate, and that it must be protected if the freedoms of expression are to have the "breathing space" that they "need . . . to survive," was . . . recognized by the Court of Appeals for the District of Columbia Circuit in *Sweeney v. Patterson* [1942]. . . .

Injury to official reputation error affords no more warrant for repressing speech that would otherwise be free than does factual error. Where judicial officers are involved, this Court has held that concern for the dignity and reputation of the courts does not justify the punishment as criminal contempt of criticism of the judge or his decision. This is true even though the utterance contains "half-truths" and "misinformation." . . . If judges are to be treated as "men of fortitude, able to thrive in a hardy climate," surely the same must be true of other government officials, such as elected city commissioners. Criticism of their official conduct does not lose its constitutional protection merely because it is effective criticism and hence diminishes their official reputations.

If neither factual error nor defamatory content suffices to remove the constitutional shield from criticism of official conduct, the combination of the two elements is no less inadequate. This is the lesson to be drawn from the great controversy over the Sedition Act of 1798, which first crystallized a national awareness of the central meaning of the First Amendment. That statute made it a crime, punishable by a $5,000 fine and five years in prison, "if any person shall write, print, utter or publish . . . any false, scandalous and malicious writing or writings against the government of the United States, or either House of the Congress . . . or the President . . . , with intent to defame . . . or to bring them, or either of them, into contempt or disrepute; or to excite against them, or either or any of them, the hatred of the good people of the United States." . . .

Although the Sedition Act was never tested in this Court, the attack upon its validity has carried the day in the court of history. Fines levied in its prosecution were repaid by Act of Congress on the ground that it was unconstitutional. Calhoun, reporting to the Senate on February 4, 1836, assumed that its invalidity was a matter "which no one now doubts." Jefferson, as President, pardoned those who had been convicted and sentenced under the Act and remitted their fines, stating: "I discharged every person under punishment or prosecution under the sedition law, because I considered, and now consider, that law to be a nullity. . . ." The invalidity of the Act has also been assumed by Justices of this Court. These views reflect a broad consensus that the Act, because of the restraint it imposed upon criticism of government and public officials, was inconsistent with the First Amendment. . . .

The state rule of law is not saved by its allowance of the defense of truth. A defense for erroneous statements honestly made is . . . essential here. . . . A rule compelling the critic of official conduct to guarantee the truth of all his factual assertions—and to do so on pain of libel judgments virtually unlimited in amount—leads to a comparable "self-censorship." . . . Under such a rule, would-be critics of official conduct may be deterred from voicing their criticism, even though it is believed to be true and even though it is in fact true, because of doubt whether it can be proved in court or fear of the expense of having to do so. They tend to make only statements which "steer far wider of the unlawful zone." The rule thus dampens the vigor and limits the variety of public debate. It is inconsistent with the First and Fourteenth Amendments.

The constitutional guarantees require, we think, a federal rule that prohibits a public official from recovering damages for a defamatory falsehood relating to his official conduct unless he proves that the statement was made with "actual malice"—that is, with knowledge that it was false or with reckless disregard of whether it was false or not. An oft-cited statement of a like rule, which has been adopted by a number of state courts, [is] "where an article is published and circulated . . . for the sole purpose of giving what the defendant believes to be truthful information . . . , and the whole thing is done in good faith and without malice, the article is privileged, although the principal matters contained in the article may be untrue in fact and derogatory to the character of the plaintiff; and in such a case the burden is on the plaintiff to show actual malice in the publication of the article." . . .

We conclude that such a privilege is required by the First and Fourteenth Amendments.

We hold today that the Constitution delimits a State's power to award damages for libel in actions brought by public officials against critics of their official conduct. Since this is such an action, the rule requiring proof of actual malice is applicable . . .

Since respondent may seek a new trial, we deem that considerations of effective judicial administration require us to review the evidence in the present record to determine whether it could constitutionally support a judgment for respondent. This Court's duty is not limited to the elaboration of constitutional principles; we must also in proper cases review the evidence to make certain that those principles have been constitutionally applied. . . . Applying these standards, we consider that the proof presented to show actual malice lacks the convincing clarity which the constitutional standard demands, and hence that it would not constitutionally sustain the judgment for respondent under the proper rule of law. . . .

As to the *Times,* we . . . conclude that the facts do not support a finding of actual malice. The statement by the *Times'* Secretary that . . . he thought the advertisement was "substantially correct," affords no constitutional warrant for the Alabama Supreme Court's conclusion that it was a "cavalier ignoring of the falsity of the advertisement from which, the jury could not have but been impressed with the bad faith of the *Times,* and its maliciousness inferable therefrom." The statement does not indicate malice at the time of the publication; even if the advertisement was not "substantially correct"—although respondent's own proofs tend to show that it was—that opinion was at least a reasonable one, and there was no evidence to impeach the witness' good faith in holding it. . . .

The judgment of the Supreme Court of Alabama is reversed and the case is remanded to that court for further proceedings not inconsistent with this opinion.

Reversed and remanded.

MR. JUSTICE BLACK, WITH WHOM MR. JUSTICE DOUGLAS JOINS, CONCURRING.

I concur in reversing this half-million-dollar judgment against the New York Times Company and the four individual defendants. In reversing the Court holds that "the Constitution delimits a State's power to award damages for libel in actions brought by public officials against critics of their official conduct." I base my vote to reverse on the belief that the First and Fourteenth Amendments not merely "delimit" a State's power to award damages to "public officials against critics of their official conduct" but completely prohibit a State from exercising such a power. The Court goes on to hold that a State can subject such critics to damages if "actual malice" can be proved against them. "Malice," even as defined by the Court, is an elusive, abstract concept, hard to prove and hard to disprove. The requirement that malice be proved provides at best an evanescent protection for the right critically to discuss public affairs and certainly does not measure up to the sturdy safeguard embodied in the First Amendment. Unlike the Court, therefore, I vote to reverse exclusively on the ground that the Times and the individual defendants had an absolute, unconditional constitutional right to publish in the Times advertisement their criticisms of the Montgomery agencies and officials.

Many consider Brennan's opinion a tour de force on the subject of libel. By holding the Sedition Act of 1798 unconstitutional, however belatedly, Brennan said that the First Amendment protects seditious libel, that the government may not criminally punish individuals who speak out against public officials and their policies. But more important was the part of the opinion that dealt with civil actions. Brennan radically altered the standards that *public officials* acting in a *public capacity* had to meet before they could prove libel and receive damages. Calling previous rules of falsehood and defamation "constitutionally deficient," Brennan asserted that if plaintiffs were public officials, they had to demonstrate that the statement

was false, damaging, *and* "made with 'actual malice'—that is, with knowledge that it was false or with reckless disregard of whether it was false or not." In his view, such an exacting test—now called the *Sullivan* standard—was necessary because of a "profound national commitment to the principle that debate on public issues should be uninhibited, robust, and wide open." Brennan's opinion significantly altered libel law, making it quite difficult for public officials to bring actions against the media.

But the decision raised further questions—for example, who is considered a public official? In footnote 23 Brennan wrote, "We have no occasion here to determine how far down into lower ranks of government employees the 'public official' designation would extend." When an appropriate case presented itself, the Court would have to draw some distinctions. How it did so would have significant ramifications because, under the *Sullivan* test, only public officials had to prove actual malice; other plaintiffs were required only to show that published

Bettmann/Contributor/Getty Images

L. B. Sullivan, second from right, poses with his attorneys after winning his libel suit against the *New York Times*. The Supreme Court overturned the decision in 1964. Justice Brennan's opinion stated that in proving libel, public officials are held to a higher standard than private citizens.

statements about them were false and damaging. Equally difficult were other questions the decision raised: Did this new standard apply only to public officials engaged in their official duties? How could a public official prove actual malice? What did that term encompass?

In 1967 the Court decided two cases, **Curtis Publishing Company v. Butts** and **Associated Press v. Walker**, in hopes of clarifying its *Sullivan* ruling and to whom it applied. At issue in *Curtis* was a *Saturday Evening Post* article titled "The Story of a College Football Fix." The writer asserted that Wally Butts, the athletic director at the University of Georgia, had given Paul Bryant, the football coach at the University of Alabama, "the plays, defensive patterns, and all the significant secrets Georgia's football team possessed." According to the article, Butts was attempting to fix a 1962 game between the two schools. The story implied that Butts may have been wagering against his own school and assisting Alabama to ensure that his bet would pay off. The author claimed he had obtained this information from an Atlanta insurance salesman who accidentally overheard the conversation between Butts and Bryant. Butts initiated a libel suit against the publishing company, arguing that the article was false and damaging. And, although the Court had yet to hand down the *Sullivan* decision, Butts's suit also alleged that actual malice had occurred because the *Saturday Evening Post* "had departed greatly from the standards of good investigation and reporting." Evidence introduced at the trial showed that the *Saturday Evening Post* had done little to verify the insurance salesman's story. A jury awarded Butts $3,060,000 in damages, but the judge reduced the award to $460,000. The magazine later asked for a new trial on *Sullivan* grounds—that Butts was a public figure and should have to prove actual malice. The judge refused, asserting that Butts was not a public official—Butts was not technically a state employee—and, even if he were, there was sufficient evidence to conclude that the magazine had acted with "reckless disregard for the truth."

The companion case, *Associated Press v. Walker*, concerned a 1962 Associated Press story about riots at the University of Mississippi triggered by the government-ordered admission to the university of James Meredith, a black student. According to the story, retired army general Edwin Walker "took command of the violent crowd and . . . led a charge against federal marshals" who were in Mississippi to oversee the desegregation process. It also alleged that Walker gave the segregationists instructions on how to combat the effects of tear gas. Walker sued the Associated Press for $2 million in compensatory and punitive damages, arguing that the article was false and damaging. The jury awarded $500,000 in compensatory damages and $300,000 in punitive damages, but the judge set aside the latter on the grounds that Walker, while not a public official, was a public figure; his views on integration were well-known and, as such, he had to prove actual malice under the *Sullivan* standard.

Writing for the Court, Justice Harlan extended the press-protective *Sullivan* standard to public figures. Previously, the "actual malice" rule had been limited to government officials, thereby facilitating media scrutiny of individuals who must hold the public trust. Now, the Court ruled that well-known individuals must also overcome a high hurdle in order to wage successful libel suits. The specific requirements in *Sullivan*—demonstrate knowing falsity or reckless disregard for the truth—were not used by the Court here; public figures would have to show "highly unreasonable conduct constituting an extreme departure from the standards of investigation and reporting." But the underlying principle was the same: public officials and public persons would need to show negligence on the part of the press by their failure to follow the bare essentials of responsible journalism.

Applying these new rules, the Court ruled in favor of Butts's claim and against Walker's. Butts met this burden, because the *Saturday Evening Post* knew their source for the story was unreliable and made no effort to confirm his claims. Walker failed to prove such press improprieties; the press allegations against him were submitted by an established reporter who witnessed Walker's action firsthand.

Private individuals, meanwhile, remained covered by traditional libel rules. A person who does not qualify as a public official or public figure must prove only that the published statements were false. Drawing a line between public and private persons is not easy, and the Court itself has had a difficult time doing so. The justices, however, have helped to distinguish between the two categories. In **Gertz v. Welch, Inc.** (1974) the justices held that an attorney in private practice was not a public figure even though he represented a plaintiff in a controversial wrongful death suit. In **Time, Inc. v. Firestone** (1976) the Court ruled that a prominent socialite involved in a scandalous divorce suit retained her status as a private person and had not become a public figure under the *Sullivan* test approach to libel. And in *Hutchinson v. Proxmire* (1979), the Court determined that the notoriety surrounding a libel case does not convert a private individual alleging defamation into a public figure. In essence, the Court has taken a middle position.

It has given the media a significant shield against libel actions when they are carrying out their historic mission of reporting news about persons of legitimate, ongoing public interest, yet it has not imposed any additional burden on private individuals who are damaged by published falsehoods and turn to the judicial system for redress.

Obscenity

However difficult it was for the Court to settle on a framework for libel, obscenity presented even more vexing problems. According to Justice Harlan, "The subject of obscenity has produced a variety of views among the members of the Court unmatched in any other course of constitutional interpretation."[10] Justice Brennan, the member of the Court most associated with the subject, was even more candid. Discussing service on the Court, Brennan noted, "It takes a while before you can become even calm about approaching a job like this. Which is not to say you do not make mistakes. In my case, there has been the obscenity area."[11]

What is it about obscenity that has produced such extraordinary statements from these justices? After all, the Court uniformly has held that obscenity is not entitled to First Amendment protection. The problem is determining what makes a work obscene. In a general sense, it involves the use of sexually explicit material. (It does not include the use of profanity, i.e., "obscene" language.) Many books, magazines, and films portray sexual activity quite explicitly. So, how do we differentiate between protected material that is sexually oriented and unprotected obscene expression? The answer is important because it has broad implications for what we see, read, and hear. Although public standards may have changed over time, there continue to be challenges to books, movies, and music on obscenity grounds. Given the importance of the task, one might think the Court has set definitive policy in this area, but nothing could be further from reality. The Court has grappled with the issue for decades, particularly with fashioning a definition of obscenity. Before the 1950s the Court generally avoided the issue by adopting the British definition of obscenity. In *Regina v. Hicklin* (1868), which involved a pamphlet questioning the morals of Catholic priests, a British court promulgated the following test: "Whether the tendency of the matter charged as obscenity is to deprave and corrupt those whose minds are open to such immoral influences and into whose hands a publication of this sort might fall."

Under this standard, commonly referred to as the *Hicklin* test, the British court found the pamphlet obscene. That it did so is not surprising. First, the *Hicklin* test used a stringent level of acceptability—whether the material would be appropriate if a child were exposed to it. Second, the *Hicklin* test did not require that the publication be considered as a whole. Instead, a work could be declared obscene based on one of its parts. Third, the *Hicklin* test did not direct the courts to consider the social value of the work; rather, it provided only that the offensive sections have an immoral influence. As a result, the *Hicklin* standard left a wide range of expression unprotected. Initially, the U.S. Supreme Court not only adopted the *Hicklin* standard but strengthened it, as well. In *Ex parte Jackson* (1878) the Court upheld the Comstock Act, which made it a crime to send obscene materials, including information on abortion and birth control, through the U.S. mail. The justices applied the *Hicklin* test and extended its coverage to include materials discussing reproduction.

While the Supreme Court clung to *Hicklin*, some lower courts were attempting to liberalize it or even reject it. In 1926, the satirist H. L. Mencken was arrested in Boston for distributing copies of his magazine, the *American Mercury*, which contained an article about a prostitute. Dismissing the charge of obscenity against Mencken, the trial judge, James Parmenter, concluded that the article was a "rather frank discussion but at the same time an intellectual description of prostitution."[12] Another well-known example is *United States v. One Book Entitled "Ulysses" by James Joyce* (1934), in which Judge Augustus Hand argued that the proper standard should consider the work as whole, not simply isolated and potentially offensive passages. By that test *Ulysses*—unusual for its time but today often regarded as the greatest work of fiction of the twentieth century—could not be judged as obscene. The diverse rulings from the lower courts, coupled with the Supreme Court's silence on the issue, began to have an effect. By the 1950s the pornography business was flourishing in the United States, with little restriction on who could buy or view such material. This situation led to a backlash, with irate citizens clamoring for tighter controls. Others, particularly attorneys with the

[10]*Interstate Circuit v. Dallas* (1968).

[11]Quoted in Nat Hentoff, "Profiles: The Constitutionalists," *New Yorker*, March 12, 1990, 54.

[12]Neil Miller, *Banned in Boston: The Watch and Ward Society's Crusade against Books, Burlesque, and the Social Evil Paper* (Boston: Beacon Press, 2010), 91.

American Civil Liberties Union, pressured courts to move in precisely the opposite direction—to rule that the First Amendment covers all materials, including those previously adjudged obscene. By the late 1950s, these different interests were sending the same message to the justices: the time had come to deal with the issue.

In **Butler v. Michigan** (1957) the Court responded by declaring unconstitutional a state statute that defined obscenity along *Hicklin* test lines. The law made it a crime to distribute material "found to have a potentially deleterious influence on youth." The justices struck down the statute, finding fault with the child standard. It is incompatible with the First Amendment, the justices said, to reduce the reading material available to adults to that which is fit for children. To do so, according to Justice Felix Frankfurter's opinion, is "to burn the house to roast the pig."

H. L. Mencken, the journalist and satirist, who was arrested on a charge of obscenity for the sale of his magazine, the *American Mercury*. The Boston trial judge concluded that the magazine's discussion of prostitution was intellectual, not sexually offensive.

The *Butler* decision mortally wounded the *Hicklin* test, but the justices failed to provide an alternative until later that year, when the Court took its first stab at creating a contemporary American obscenity standard. The case was **Roth v. United States** (1957). This appeal stemmed from charges that Samuel Roth had sent "obscene, indecent, and filthy matter" through the mail. The trial judge told the jury that the federal law's use of the word "obscene" was meant to "signify that form of immorality which has relation to sexual impurity and has a tendency to excite lustful thoughts." The jury found Roth guilty on four of the counts, and the judge sentenced him to the maximum punishment: five years in prison and a $5,000 fine. Roth challenged his conviction, arguing that the standard imposed was inconsistent with First Amendment freedoms.

Although they were badly divided, a majority of the justices in *Roth* supported a new standard articulated by Justice Brennan in his opinion of the Court. Now known as the *Roth* test, Brennan's obscenity standard posed the following: "Whether to the average person, applying contemporary community standards, the dominant theme of the material taken as a whole appeals to prurient interest."

At first glance, Brennan's opinion seems to forge a compromise between competing views. On one hand, he appeased "decency" advocates by rejecting the view that nothing is obscene; on the other, he set a new standard of obscenity that was far less restrictive than *Hicklin*. The new *Roth* test was a significant departure from the *Hicklin* standard. First, *Roth* imposed an "average person" test, replacing *Hicklin*'s child standard with that of an adult. Second, the "contemporary community standards" criterion recognized the evolving nature of society's views on sexual morality. Third, the "dominant theme of the material taken as a whole" approach drew from the logic of the *Ulysses* decision, rejecting *Hicklin*'s notion that a work can be declared obscene based on the content of a single part. And finally, the "prurient interests" element ensured that only material with lurid sexual content would potentially fall under the obscenity rubric.

A majority supported Brennan's opinion, but the Court remained divided over the proper way to handle the obscenity issue. In the ensuing years, the Court confronted several appeals that provided opportunities for the justices to improve upon *Roth* or to agree on some alternative test. Attempts to replace *Roth*, however, were unsuccessful. The justices simply could not agree on an acceptable substitute. Although *Roth* survived, the justices did amplify and build upon its meaning. Perhaps the most significant of the post-*Roth* decisions were ***Jacobellis v. Ohio*** (1964) and ***Memoirs v. Massachusetts*** (1966). In *Jacobellis* the Court considered the appeal of Nico Jacobellis, the manager of a movie theater, who had been charged by Ohio authorities with showing an obscene film called *Les Amants* (*The Lovers*). The movie depicts a love affair between an archaeologist and a woman who leaves her husband and child for him. *Les Amants* contains one "explicit love scene."

Brennan's opinion in *Jacobellis* refined his *Roth* test by stating that contemporary community standards were those of the nation, not of a local community. In doing so, he not only held the film to be protected speech but also substantially liberalized the *Roth* test. It is bound to be the case that individual communities seeking to ban obscenity have stricter standards than those of the country at large. Under Brennan's refinement, Tulsa, Oklahoma, would be bound by the same obscenity standards as New York City. In addition, Brennan added a new provision to the *Roth* test: not only must material meet all of the provisions of the test to be legally obscene, but it also must be found to be "utterly without redeeming social importance."

In *Memoirs v. Massachusetts* the Court further explained what was required under its new social importance standard. This case reviewed the attempts of Massachusetts to declare obscene John Cleland's *Memoirs of a Woman of Pleasure*. This book, popularly known as *Fanny Hill*, dated from 1749. A concededly erotic novel, *Memoirs* traces the escapades of a London prostitute. The Massachusetts Supreme Court held that a book need not be "unqualifiedly worthless before it could be deemed obscene"; that is, just because *Memoirs* contained some nonerotic passages did not mean that it had redeeming value. Although divided, the U.S. Supreme Court disagreed. In his judgment for the Court, Brennan expanded the parameters of *Roth*. If a work had a "modicum of social value" it could not be adjudged obscene. This extended further protection to the press by requiring challenged works to be obscene in their totality. That meant that an otherwise sexually explicit book that temporarily digressed into a discussion of the virtues of the Pythagorean theorem would be free from the government's sanction.

By 1966, then, the justices, though hardly united, had substantially altered *Roth*, as shown in Box 14-2, which compares the test in 1957 to that articulated in 1966. Would anything be defined as obscene under the *Roth-Jacobellis-Memoirs* test? We might think that hardcore pornography would fall outside the test, but could

not a clever moviemaker, author, or publisher easily circumvent it?

The impact of these decisions was predictable. Expanded First Amendment protection prompted an explosion in sexually oriented materials. Adult movies, magazines, and books were more widely distributed than ever before. The fallout from these developments was also predictable. There was adverse reaction, primarily among more conservative citizens who were not pleased with the growing numbers of adult bookstores, theaters, and nightclubs and were disturbed that sexually explicit materials had become so widely available.

In the presidential election of 1968, the Republican candidate, Richard Nixon, delivered a campaign message that was quite critical of the Supreme Court. His expressed discontent with the justices covered a wide array of decisions, but the Court's obscenity decisions were a primary target for his campaign rhetoric. He promised the voters that if he became president he would appoint justices to the Court who were more conservative in their orientation. When he took office, he kept his promise. He had the opportunity to appoint four new justices to the Court, including a new chief justice, Warren Burger. Nixon's appointments turned the Court in a more conservative direction, and observers knew that eventually the justices would reconsider the line of liberal obscenity rulings that had begun with *Roth*. The anticipated change became apparent on June 21, 1973, when the justices announced their decision in *Miller v. California*.

Miller v. California

413 U.S. 15 (1973)
http://caselaw.findlaw.com/us-supreme-court/413/15.html
Oral arguments available at https://www.oyez.org/
cases/1971/70-73
Vote: 5 (Blackmun, Burger, Powell, Rehnquist, White)
4 (Brennan, Douglas, Marshall, Stewart)

OPINION OF THE COURT: *Burger*

DISSENTING OPINIONS: *Douglas, Brennan*

Marvin Miller, a vendor of so-called adult material, conducted a mass-mail campaign to drum up sales for his books. The pamphlets he sent out were fairly explicit, containing pictures of men and women engaging in various sexual activities, often with their genitals prominently displayed.

Had Miller sent the brochures to interested individuals only, he might not have been caught. But because he did a mass

BOX 14-2

Roth, *Jacobellis*, and *Memoirs* Compared

Roth:	"Whether to the average person, applying contemporary community standards, the dominant theme of the material taken as a whole appeals to prurient interest."		interest" and is "utterly without redeeming social importance."
Roth and *Jacobellis*:	"Whether to the average person applying" standards of "the society at large," the "dominant theme of the material taken as a whole appeals to prurient	*Roth, Jacobellis*, and *Memoirs*:	"Whether to the average person applying standards of the society at large," the "dominant theme of the material taken as a whole appeals to prurient interest" and "is utterly without redeeming social importance," possessing not "a modicum of social value."

mailing, some pamphlets predictably ended up in the hands of people who did not want them. Miller was arrested when the manager of a restaurant and his mother opened one of the envelopes and complained to the police.

**MR. CHIEF JUSTICE BURGER
DELIVERED THE OPINION OF THE COURT.**

This is one of a group of "obscenity-pornography" cases being reviewed by the Court in a re-examination of standards enunciated in earlier cases involving what Mr. Justice Harlan called "the intractable obscenity problem." . . .

This case involves the application of a State's criminal obscenity statute to a situation in which sexually explicit materials have been thrust by aggressive sales action upon unwilling recipients who had in no way indicated any desire to receive such materials. This Court has recognized that the States have a legitimate interest in prohibiting dissemination or exhibition of obscene material when the mode of dissemination carries with it a significant danger of offending the sensibilities of unwilling recipients or of exposure to juveniles. It is in this context that we are called on to define the standards which must be used to identify obscene material that a State may regulate without infringing on the First Amendment as applicable to the States through the Fourteenth Amendment. . . .

. . . [O]bscene material is unprotected by the First Amendment. We acknowledge, however, the inherent dangers of undertaking to regulate any form of expression. State statutes designed to regulate obscene materials must be carefully limited. As a result, we now confine the permissible scope of such regulation to works which

depict or describe sexual conduct. That conduct must be specifically defined by the applicable state law, as written or authoritatively construed. . . . The basic guidelines for the trier of fact must be: (a) whether "the average person, applying contemporary community standards" would find that the work, taken as a whole, appeals to the prurient interest; (b) whether the work depicts or describes, in a patently offensive way, sexual conduct specifically defined by the applicable state law; and (c) whether the work, taken as a whole, lacks serious literary, artistic, political, or scientific value. We do not adopt as a constitutional standard the "*utterly* without redeeming social value" test of *Memoirs v. Massachusetts;* that concept has never commanded the adherence of more than three Justices at one time. . . .

We emphasize that it is not our function to propose regulatory schemes for the States. That must await their concrete legislative efforts. It is possible, however, to give a few plain examples of what a state statute could define for regulation under part (b) of the standard announced in this opinion.

a. Patently offensive representations or descriptions of ultimate sexual acts, normal or perverted, actual or simulated.

b. Patently offensive representation or descriptions of masturbation, excretory functions, and lewd exhibition of the genitals.

Under the holdings announced today, no one will be subject to prosecution for the sale or exposure of obscene materials unless these materials depict or describe patently offensive "hard core" sexual conduct specifically defined by the regulating state law, as written or construed. We are satisfied that these specific prerequisites will provide fair notice to a dealer in such materials that his public and commercial activities may bring prosecution. If the inability to define regulated materials with ultimate, god-like precision altogether removes the power of the States or the Congress to regulate, then "hard core" pornography may be exposed without limit to the juvenile, the passerby, and the consenting adult alike. . . .

It is certainly true that the absence, since *Roth,* of a single majority view of this Court as to proper standards for testing obscenity has placed a strain on both state and federal courts. But today, for the first time since *Roth* was decided in 1957, a majority of this Court has agreed on concrete guidelines to isolate "hard core" pornography from expression protected by the First Amendment. Now we . . . attempt to provide positive guidance to federal and state courts alike.

This may not be an easy road, free from difficulty. But no amount of "fatigue" should lead us to adopt a convenient "institutional" rationale—an absolutist, "anything goes" view of the First Amendment—because it will lighten our burdens. "Such an abnegation of judicial supervision in this field would be inconsistent with our duty to uphold the constitutional guarantees." Nor should we remedy "tension between state and federal courts" by arbitrarily depriving the States of a power reserved to them under the Constitution, a power which they have enjoyed and exercised continuously from before the adoption of the First Amendment to this day. "Our duty admits of no 'substitute for facing up to the tough individual problems of constitutional judgment involved in every obscenity case.'" [*Jacobellis v. Ohio*]

Under a National Constitution, fundamental First Amendment limitations on the powers of the States do not vary from community to community, but this does not mean that there are, or should or can be, fixed, uniform national standards of precisely what appeals to the "prurient interest" or is "patently offensive." These are essentially questions of fact, and our Nation is simply too big and too diverse for this Court to reasonably expect that such standards could be articulated for all 50 States in a single formulation, even assuming the prerequisite consensus exists. When triers of fact are asked to decide whether "the average person, applying contemporary community standards" would consider certain materials "prurient," it would be unrealistic to require that the answer be based on some abstract formulation. . . . To require a State to structure obscenity proceedings around evidence of a *national* "community standard" would be an exercise in futility.

. . . [T]his case was tried on the theory that the California obscenity statute sought to incorporate the tripartite test of *Memoirs.* This, a "national" standard of First Amendment protection enumerated by a plurality of this Court, was correctly regarded at the time of trial as limiting state prosecution under the controlling case law. The jury, however, was explicitly instructed that, in determining whether the "dominant theme of the material as a whole . . . appeals

to the prurient interest" and in determining whether the material "goes substantially beyond customary limits of candor and affronts contemporary community standards of decency," it was to apply "contemporary community standards of the State of California."

We conclude that neither the State's alleged failure to offer evidence of "national standards," nor the trial court's charge that the jury consider state community standards, were constitutional errors. . . . It is neither realistic nor constitutionally sound to read the First Amendment as requiring that the people of Maine or Mississippi accept public depiction of conduct found tolerable in Las Vegas, or New York City. People in different States vary in their tastes and attitudes, and this diversity is not to be strangled by the absolutism of imposed uniformity. . . . We hold that the requirement that the jury evaluate the materials with reference to "contemporary standards of the State of California" serves this protective purpose and is constitutionally adequate.

The dissenting Justices sound the alarm of repression. But, in our view, to equate the free and robust exchange of ideas and political debate with commercial exploitation of obscene material demeans the grand conception of the First Amendment and its high purposes in the historic struggle for freedom. It is a "misuse of the great guarantees of free speech and free press. . . ." . . . [T]he public portrayal of hardcore sexual conduct for its own sake, and for the ensuing commercial gain, is a different matter. . . .

In sum, we (a) reaffirm the *Roth* holding that obscene material is not protected by the First Amendment; (b) hold that such material can be regulated by the States, subject to the specific safeguards enunciated above, without a showing that the material is "*utterly* without redeeming social value"; and (c) hold that obscenity is to be determined by applying "contemporary community standards," not "national standards." . . .

Vacated and remanded.

MR. JUSTICE DOUGLAS, DISSENTING.

Today we leave open the way for California to send a man to prison for distributing brochures that advertise books and a movie under freshly written standards defining obscenity which until today's decision were never the part of any law. . . .

Today the Court retreats from the earlier formulations of the constitutional test and undertakes to make new definitions. This effort, like the earlier ones, is earnest and well intentioned. The difficulty is that we do not deal with constitutional terms, since "obscenity" is not mentioned in the Constitution or Bill of Rights. And the First Amendment makes no such exception from "the press" which it undertakes to protect nor, as I have said on other occasions, is an exception necessarily implied for there was no recognized exception to the free press at the time the Bill of Rights was adopted which treated "obscene" publications differently from other types of papers, magazines, and books. So there are no constitutional guidelines for deciding what is and what is not "obscene." The Court is at large because we deal with tastes and standards of literature. What shocks me may be sustenance for my neighbor. What causes one person to boil up in rage over one pamphlet or movie may reflect only his neurosis, not shared by others. We deal here with a regime of censorship which, if adopted, should be done by constitutional amendment after full debate by the people. . . .

. . . Perhaps the people will decide that the path towards a mature, integrated society requires that all ideas competing for acceptance must have no censor. Perhaps they will decide otherwise. Whatever the choice, the courts will have some guidelines. Now we have none except our own predilections.

MR. JUSTICE BRENNAN, WITH WHOM MR. JUSTICE STEWART AND MR. JUSTICE MARSHALL JOIN, DISSENTING.

In the case before us, appellant was convicted of distributing obscene matter in violation of California Penal Code §311.2, on the basis of evidence that he had caused to be mailed unsolicited brochures advertising various books and a movie. I need not now decide whether a statute might be drawn to impose, within the requirements of the First Amendment, criminal penalties for the precise conduct at issue here. For it is clear that . . . the statute under which the prosecution was brought is unconstitutionally overbroad, and therefore invalid on its face.

The same day, the Court also handed down a decision in ***Paris Adult Theatre I v. Slaton,*** which involved a 1970 complaint filed by Atlanta, Georgia, against the Paris Adult Theatre, asserting that the theater was showing obscene films. The trial court judge viewed two of the offending films, which depicted simulated oral sex and group sexual intercourse. The judge ruled in favor of the theater, mainly because the owners did not admit to the theater anyone under the age of twenty-one.

After the Georgia Supreme Court reversed, the owners appealed to the U.S. Supreme Court. The justices, however, affirmed the ruling, refusing to extend the theater First Amendment protection, even though only consenting adults could see the films.

Miller (and *Paris Adult Theatre I*) substantially changed the constitutional definition of obscenity. In Table 14-1 we compare the *Roth* test (and its expansions) with the new *Miller* standard. Although the Court retained three important elements of the *Roth* test—the adult standard, the work taken as a whole, and the restriction of obscenity to sexually oriented materials—two major changes stand out. First, the *Miller* test specifically gives the states the authority to define what is obscene. The Court, therefore, emphasized local values rather than the national standard suggested in *Jacobellis.* Second, the Court did away with the notion that a work merited protection as long as it did not meet the "utterly without redeeming social value" criterion. Instead, the justices held that to receive First Amendment protection, sexually oriented materials must have serious literary, artistic, political, or scientific value. As a consequence, the new *Miller* test permitted much greater regulation of sexually explicit materials than did the *Roth* standard.

While a majority on the Burger Court ushered in a significant change in obscenity law, liberals from the Warren Court era also expressed a change in approach. Joined by Justices Thurgood Marshall and Potter Stewart, Justice Brennan wrote a dissenting opinion in *Paris Adult Theatre I* in which he urged the Court to abandon the issue of obscenity. After almost two decades of leading the Court in attempts to define obscenity, the author of *Roth* finally decided that it could not be done. Experience had taught him, he explained, that efforts to regulate "obscene" material inevitably led to unacceptable

Table 14-1 The Obscenity Standards of the Warren and Burger Courts Compared

	Warren Court	Burger Court
Relevant audience	Average person	Average person
Scope of consideration	Work taken as a whole	Work taken as a whole
Standard	Sexual material found patently offensive by the contemporary national standards of society at large	Sexual material found patently offensive by contemporary community standards as specifically defined by applicable state law
Value of the work	Utterly without redeeming social importance	Lacks serious literary, artistic, political, or scientific value

restrictions on protected expression. Consequently, state and federal authorities should be banned from regulating sexually oriented expression altogether—except to protect juveniles and unconsenting adults.

It would be difficult to imagine two more different positions than those the majority and the dissenters took in these obscenity cases, but they are alike in this respect: both sides wanted to extricate the Court from the business of resolving questions of obscenity. Brennan and the other dissenters advocated an almost total end to government regulation of obscenity, while the *Miller* majority wanted to put an end to federal obscenity cases by shifting authority to the states.

Since 1973 the *Miller* test has remained the authoritative definition of obscenity. The justices generally have refused to accept cases that have asked them to reconsider the definition of obscenity. In a very real sense, the *Miller* majority successfully removed the Court from the obscenity area and allowed the state and local governments greater leeway in dealing with it.

Despite its reluctance to revisit the obscenity standard, the Court still remains attuned to the potential harms of sexually explicit materials, especially when children are either exposed to it or used in producing it. In fact, the justices have permitted regulation of materials that depict sexual activity by children, even if those materials do not meet the *Miller* test's definition of obscenity. In *New York v. Ferber* (1982), for example, the Court unanimously affirmed government's authority to prohibit child pornography; liberals and conservatives alike recognize the state's overriding interest in protecting children from abuse and sexual exploitation.

These concerns about child welfare have only been amplified by the development of the Internet, which readily facilitates both the transmission and viewing of child pornography. Not surprisingly, many groups have pressured Congress and the states to regulate expression on the Internet, and lawmakers have responded with legislation designed to curtail the electronic dissemination of sexually explicit images of children or that appear to be of children. (They also responded with legislation designed to curtail electronic dissemination of sexually oriented material that is inappropriate for children to view. We consider these laws at the end of the chapter.) Opponents contended that, however well-intentioned, these laws restricted legitimate and protected expression. Indeed, the passage of state or federal laws limiting expression on the Internet have been met with immediate legal challenges. Newly formed organizations devoted to keeping the Internet free from regulation have joined with traditional civil liberties groups, such as the ACLU, to attack these restrictions as violations of the First Amendment.

Ashcroft v. Free Speech Coalition (2002) was the first major suit in this area. In this case, the justices considered a challenge to the constitutionality of the Child Pornography Prevention Act of 1996 (CPPA). Although *Ferber* gave strong support for legislative prohibitions against producing and distributing materials depicting children engaged in sexual activity, the CPPA had much greater breadth than the state statute upheld in that decision. The federal law not only prohibited using minors to create such materials but also barred the use of adult actors who looked like children as well as computer-generated images of youngsters. Under this law, critically acclaimed movies such as *American Beauty* and *Traffic*—both of which feature adult actresses portraying high school girls in sexual situations—would run afoul of the law, even if they were not obscene under *Miller*.

These provisions, according to the Court, went too far. The use of children engaging in real or simulated sexual activity is a crime of sexual abuse that can be punished, but similar activity involving adult actors or computer images is not a crime. Put another way, unless children are actually harmed in the production of such materials, otherwise legitimate films are protected by the First Amendment.

Congress "went back to the drawing board," as Justice Antonin Scalia put it, and enacted the PROTECT Act of 2003 to respond to *Ashcroft v. Free Speech Coalition*. (PROTECT is an acronym for Prosecutorial Remedies and Other Tools to End the Exploitation of Children Today.) This legislation was an attempt to remedy the defects in the 1996 law, in part by limiting it to anyone who knowingly "advertises, promotes, presents, distributes, or solicits . . . any material or purported material that reflects the belief, or that is intended to cause another to believe, that the material or purported material" contains illegal child pornography. When a challenge to the new law reached the Court in 2008 in *United States v. Williams*, Justices David Souter and Ruth Bader Ginsburg argued that the new law was just as problematic as the old one: it continued to criminalize virtual or "fake child pornography," which *Free Speech Coalition* had held came under First Amendment protection. The majority, however, disagreed. Writing for the Court, Justice Scalia noted that, rather than attempt to regulate the material itself, the new law targeted the speech of those who trafficked in child pornography. Under *Ferber*, the production, sale, and distribution—even the possession—of child pornography can be criminalized. So, speech that proposes a transaction involving child pornography (real or virtual) is not protected expression; such solicitations are "offers to engage in illegal transactions."

Cruelty and Violence

Obscenity and libel have long been considered outside the guarantees provided by the First Amendment, but of late there have been attempts to expand the list of unprotected genres of expression. In two cases, **United States v. Stevens** (2010) and *Brown v. Entertainment Merchants Association* (2011), the justices of the Roberts Court considered arguments by the federal and state governments to prohibit certain kinds of seemingly distasteful expression in the name of protecting vulnerable interests—in *Stevens* the sale of videos depicting cruelty to animals and in *Brown* the sale of violent video games to children. That is, the government asked the Court to treat these relatively new forms of expression as it does obscenity and place them beyond full First Amendment protection. In both cases, the justices declined to do so.

Stevens involved a 1999 federal law that criminalized the commercial creation, sale, or possession of certain depictions of animal cruelty. The statute addressed only portrayals of harmful acts, not the underlying conduct. It applied to any visual or auditory depiction "in which a living animal is intentionally maimed, mutilated, tortured, wounded, or killed," if that conduct violates federal or state law where "the creation, sale, or possession takes place." Another clause, following from the Court's obscenity cases, exempted depictions with "serious religious, political, scientific, educational, journalistic, historical, or artistic value."

In debating the law, Congress focused primarily on "crush videos," which feature the torture and killing of helpless animals.[13] Moreover, because he was concerned about its constitutionality under the First Amendment, President Bill Clinton, when he signed the law, told the Justice Department to focus on "wanton cruelty to animals designed to appeal to a prurient interest in sex." According to the president of the Humane Society of the United States, this had the effect of "almost immediately dr[ying] up the crush video industry."

Still, there were prosecutions, mostly against those compiling or selling videos depicting dogfights. Robert

Stevens was among those indicted, and upon conviction was sentenced to thirty-seven months in prison. Stevens argued that the law violated his rights under the First Amendment. The government responded by arguing that depictions of animal cruelty should be categorized as unprotected expression.

In an 8–1 decision (with Justice Alito dissenting), the Court rejected the government's claims. Writing for the majority, Chief Justice John G. Roberts declined to expand the list of unprotected expression to include depictions of animal cruelty and instead ruled that the law unconstitutionally singled out a particular subject matter for regulation. He was especially concerned about the breadth of the law, inasmuch as it permitted prosecution anywhere in the United States, as long as the acts depicted were against the law in the state where the video was created or sold. He provided the following example:

> In the District of Columbia . . . all hunting is unlawful. Other jurisdictions permit or encourage hunting, and there is an enormous national market for hunting-related depictions in which a living animal is intentionally killed. Hunting periodicals have circulations in the hundreds of thousands or millions. . . . Nonetheless, because the statute allows each jurisdiction to export its laws to the rest of the country, [the law] extends to *any* magazine or video depicting lawful hunting, so long as that depiction is sold within the Nation's Capital.

As Roberts explained, possession of a sporting magazine that contained photographs of an animal being killed could, in theory, serve as a basis for a prosecution in Washington, D.C., since hunting is illegal there. He found the law "alarming," since it could be used to punish a variety of materials in wide circulation.

In some ways, *Brown v. Entertainment Merchants Association*, excerpted below, is a broader decision. Not only did the Court reject the state of California's request to remove the sale of violent video games to minors from First Amendment protection, but the majority informed the state that all laws prohibiting the sale of such games would be subject to strict scrutiny (meaning that they could be very unlikely to survive; see chapter 13). Why? And why did Justice Alito's concurring opinion, not to mention the dissenters' commentary, take issue with this approach?

---

[13]We derive the information in this paragraph from Adam Liptak, "Justices Reject Ban on Videos of Animal Cruelty," *New York Times*, April 20, 2010, A1.

Brown v. Entertainment Merchants Association

564 U.S. 786 (2011)
http://caselaw.findlaw.com/us-supreme-court/08-1448.html
Oral arguments available at https://www.oyez.org/
cases/2010/08-1448
Vote: 7 (Alito, Ginsburg, Kagan, Kennedy, Roberts, Scalia,
Sotomayor)
2 (Breyer, Thomas)

OPINION OF THE COURT: *Scalia*

CONCURRING OPINION: *Alito*

DISSENTING OPINIONS: *Breyer, Thomas*

In 2005 the California assembly passed Bill 1179, which prohibited the direct sale or rental of violent video games to minors and required such games to be appropriately labeled. The act was designed to aid parents in restricting their children's access to increasingly gruesome video games. The legislative goals were to prevent violent, aggressive, and antisocial behavior, and to prevent psychological or neurological harm to minors who play violent video games. The legislature relied on social scientific studies that reported a link between playing violent video games and an increase in aggressive thoughts and behavior, antisocial behavior, and a desensitization to violence. Violators of the law were subject to a $1,000 fine for each count.

Borrowing directly from the Supreme Court's obscenity precedents, the statute defined violent video games as those games in which

> the range of options available to a player includes
> killing, maiming, dismembering, or sexually assaulting
> an image of a human being, if those acts are depicted
> in a manner that a reasonable person, considering
> the game as a whole, would find appeals to a deviant
> or morbid interest of minors, that is patently offensive
> to prevailing standards in the community as to what
> is suitable for minors, and that causes the game, as
> a whole to lack serious literary, artistic, political, or
> scientific value for minors.

Also coming under the provisions of this law were games that enable a player virtually to inflict serious injury upon images of human beings or characters with substantially human characteristics in a manner that is especially heinous, cruel, or depraved in that it involves torture or serious physical abuse to the victim.

The Entertainment Merchants Association, a not-for-profit international trade association dedicated to advancing the interests of the home entertainment industry, filed suit against the state in the name of the governor, claiming that Bill 1179 violated the freedom of speech clause of the First Amendment. The federal district court struck down the law, and the U.S. Court of Appeals for the Ninth Circuit affirmed.

**JUSTICE SCALIA DELIVERED
THE OPINION OF THE COURT.**

California correctly acknowledges that video games qualify for First Amendment protection. The Free Speech Clause exists principally to protect discourse on public matters, but we have long recognized that it is difficult to distinguish politics from entertainment, and dangerous to try. . . . Like the protected books, plays, and movies that preceded them, video games communicate ideas—and even social messages—through many familiar literary devices (such as characters, dialogue, plot, and music) and through features distinctive to the medium (such as the player's interaction with the virtual world). That suffices to confer First Amendment protection. Under our Constitution, "esthetic and moral judgments about art and literature . . . are for the individual to make, not for the Government to decree, even with the mandate or approval of a majority." *United States v. Playboy Entertainment Group, Inc.* (2000). And whatever the challenges of applying the Constitution to ever-advancing technology, "the basic principles of freedom of speech and the press, like the First Amendment's command, do not vary" when a new and different medium for communication appears.

The most basic of those principles is this: "[A]s a general matter, . . . government has no power to restrict expression because of its message, its ideas, its subject matter, or its content." *Ashcroft v. American Civil Liberties Union* (2002). There are of course exceptions. "'From 1791 to the present,' . . . the First Amendment has 'permitted restrictions upon the content of speech in a few limited areas,' and has never 'include[d] a freedom to disregard these traditional limitations.'" *United States v. Stevens* (2010). These limited areas—such as obscenity, *Roth v. United States* (1957), incitement, *Brandenburg v. Ohio* (1969), and fighting words, *Chaplinsky v. New Hampshire* (1942)—represent "well-defined and narrowly limited classes of speech, the prevention and punishment of which have never been thought to raise any Constitutional problem."

. . . California . . . wishes to create a wholly new category of content-based regulation that is permissible only for speech directed at children.

That is unprecedented and mistaken. "[M]inors are entitled to a significant measure of First Amendment protection, and only in relatively narrow and well-defined circumstances may government bar public dissemination of protected materials to them." No doubt a State possesses legitimate power to protect children from harm, *Ginsberg [v. New York,* 1968], but that does not include a free-floating power to restrict the ideas to which children may be exposed. "Speech that is neither obscene as to youths nor subject to some other legitimate proscription cannot be suppressed solely to protect the young from ideas or images that a legislative body thinks unsuitable for them."

California's argument would fare better if there were a longstanding tradition in this country of specially restricting children's access to depictions of violence, but there is none. Certainly the *books* we give children to read—or read to them when they are younger—contain no shortage of gore. Grimm's Fairy Tales, for example, are grim indeed. As her just deserts for trying to poison Snow White, the wicked queen is made to dance in red hot slippers "till she fell dead on the floor, a sad example of envy and jealousy." Cinderella's evil stepsisters have their eyes pecked out by doves. And Hansel and Gretel (children!) kill their captor by baking her in an oven.

High-school reading lists are full of similar fare. Homer's Odysseus blinds Polyphemus the Cyclops by grinding out his eye with a heated stake. In the *Inferno,* Dante and Virgil watch corrupt politicians struggle to stay submerged beneath a lake of boiling pitch, lest they be skewered by devils above the surface. And Golding's *Lord of the Flies* recounts how a schoolboy called Piggy is savagely murdered *by other children* while marooned on an island. . . .

California claims that video games present special problems because they are "interactive," in that the player participates in the violent action on screen and determines its outcome. The latter feature is nothing new: Since at least the publication of *The Adventures of You: Sugarcane Island* in 1969, young readers of choose-your-own-adventure stories have been able to make decisions that determine the plot by following instructions about which page to turn to. As for the argument that video games enable participation in the violent action, that seems to us more a matter of degree than of kind. . . .

Because the Act imposes a restriction on the content of protected speech, it is invalid unless California can demonstrate that it passes strict scrutiny—that is, unless it is justified by a compelling government interest and is narrowly drawn to serve that interest. The State must specifically identify an "actual problem" in need of solving, and the curtailment of free speech must be actually necessary to the solution. That is a demanding standard. "It is rare that a regulation restricting speech because of its content will ever be permissible."

California cannot meet that standard. At the outset, it acknowledges that it cannot show a direct causal link between violent video games and harm to minors. Rather, relying upon our decision in *Turner Broadcasting System, Inc. v. FCC* (1994), the State claims that it need not produce such proof because the legislature can make a predictive judgment that such a link exists, based on competing psychological studies. But reliance on *Turner Broadcasting* is misplaced. That decision applied *intermediate scrutiny* to a content-neutral regulation. California's burden is much

higher, and because it bears the risk of uncertainty, ambiguous proof will not suffice.

The State's evidence is not compelling. California relies primarily on the research of Dr. Craig Anderson and a few other research psychologists whose studies purport to show a connection between exposure to violent video games and harmful effects on children. These studies have been rejected by every court to consider them, and with good reason: They do not prove that violent video games *cause* minors to *act* aggressively (which would at least be a beginning). Instead, "[n]early all of the research is based on correlation, not evidence of causation, and most of the studies suffer from significant, admitted flaws in methodology." They show at best some correlation between exposure to violent entertainment and minuscule real-world effects, such as children's feeling more aggressive or making louder noises in the few minutes after playing a violent game than after playing a nonviolent game.

Even taking for granted Dr. Anderson's conclusions that violent video games produce some effect on children's feelings of aggression, those effects are both small and indistinguishable from effects produced by other media. . . .

Of course, California has (wisely) declined to restrict Saturday morning cartoons, the sale of games rated for young children, or the distribution of pictures of guns. The consequence is that its regulation is wildly underinclusive when judged against its asserted justification, which in our view is alone enough to defeat it. Underinclusiveness raises serious doubts about whether the government is in fact pursuing the interest it invokes, rather than disfavoring a particular speaker or viewpoint. Here, California has singled out the purveyors of video games for disfavored treatment—at least when compared to booksellers, cartoonists, and movie producers—and has given no persuasive reason why.

The Act is also seriously underinclusive in another respect—and a respect that renders irrelevant the contentions of the concurrence and the dissents that video games are qualitatively different from other portrayals of violence. The California Legislature is perfectly willing to leave this dangerous, mind-altering material in the hands of children so long as one parent (or even an aunt or uncle) says it's OK. And there are not even any requirements as to how this parental or avuncular relationship is to be verified; apparently the child's or putative parent's, aunt's, or uncle's say-so suffices. That is not how one addresses a serious social problem. . . .

. . . California cannot show that the Act's restrictions meet a substantial need of parents who wish to restrict their children's access to violent video games but cannot do so. The video-game industry has in place a voluntary rating system designed to inform consumers about the content of games. . . . This system does much to ensure that minors cannot purchase seriously violent games on their own, and that parents who care about the matter can readily evaluate the games their children bring home. Filling the remaining modest gap in concerned-parents' control can hardly be a compelling state interest.

And finally, the Act's purported aid to parental authority is vastly overinclusive. Not all of the children who are forbidden to purchase violent video games on their own have parents who care whether they purchase violent video games. While some of the legislation's effect may indeed be in support of what some parents of the restricted children actually want, its entire effect is only in support of what the State thinks parents *ought* to want. This is not the narrow tailoring to "assisting parents" that restriction of First Amendment rights requires.

California's effort to regulate violent video games is the latest episode in a long series of failed attempts to censor violent entertainment for minors. While we have pointed out above that some of the evidence brought forward to support the harmfulness of video games is unpersuasive, we do not mean to demean or disparage the concerns that underlie the attempt to regulate them— concerns that may and doubtless do prompt a good deal of parental oversight. We have no business passing judgment on the view of the California Legislature that violent video games (or, for that matter, any other forms of speech) corrupt the young or harm their moral development. Our task is only to say whether or not such works constitute a "well-defined and narrowly limited clas[s] of speech, the prevention and punishment of which have never been thought to raise any Constitutional problem," *Chaplinsky* (the answer plainly is no); and if not, whether the regulation of such works is justified by that high degree of necessity we have described as a compelling state interest (it is not). Even where the protection of children is the object, the constitutional limits on governmental action apply. . . .

We affirm the judgment below.

It is so ordered.

JUSTICE ALITO, WITH WHOM THE CHIEF JUSTICE JOINS, CONCURRING IN THE JUDGMENT.

. . . Although the California statute is well intentioned, its terms are not framed with the precision that the Constitution demands, and I therefore agree with the Court that this particular law cannot be sustained.

I disagree, however, with the approach taken in the Court's opinion. In considering the application of unchanging constitutional principles to new and rapidly evolving technology, this Court should proceed with caution. We should make every effort to understand the new technology. We should take into account the possibility that developing technology may have important societal implications that will become apparent only with time. We should not jump to the conclusion that new technology is fundamentally the same as some older thing with which we are familiar. And we should not hastily dismiss the judgment of legislators, who may be in a better position than we are to assess the implications of new technology. The opinion of the Court exhibits none of this caution. . . .

. . . Vague laws force potential speakers to "'steer far wider of the unlawful zone' . . . than if the boundaries of the forbidden areas were clearly marked."

Here, the California law does not define "violent video games" with the "narrow specificity" that the Constitution demands. In an effort to avoid First Amendment problems, the California Legislature modeled its violent video game statute on the New York law that this Court upheld in *Ginsberg v. New York* (1968)—a law that prohibited the sale of certain sexually related materials to minors. But the California Legislature departed from the *Ginsberg* model in an important respect, and the legislature overlooked important differences between the materials falling within the scope of the two statutes. . . .

There is a critical difference . . . between obscenity laws and laws regulating violence in entertainment. By the time of this Court's landmark obscenity cases in the 1960's, obscenity had long been prohibited, see *Roth*, and this experience had helped to shape certain generally accepted norms concerning expression related to sex.

There is no similar history regarding expression related to violence. As the Court notes, classic literature contains descriptions of great violence, and even children's stories sometimes depict very violent scenes.

Finally, the difficulty of ascertaining the community standards incorporated into the California law is compounded by the legislature's decision to lump all minors together. The California law draws no distinction between young children and adolescents who are nearing the age of majority. . . .

For these reasons, I conclude that the California violent video game law fails to provide the fair notice that the Constitution requires. And I would go no further.

JUSTICE THOMAS, DISSENTING.

The Court's decision today does not comport with the original public understanding of the First Amendment. The majority strikes down, as facially unconstitutional, a state law that prohibits the direct sale or rental of certain video games to minors because the law "abridg[es] the freedom of speech." But I do not think the First Amendment stretches that far. The practices and beliefs of the founding generation establish that "the freedom of speech," as originally understood, does not include a right to speak to minors (or a right of minors to access speech) without going through the minors' parents or guardians. I would hold that the law at issue is not facially unconstitutional under the First Amendment, and reverse and remand for further proceedings.

JUSTICE BREYER, DISSENTING.

California's law imposes no more than a modest restriction on expression. The statute prevents no one from playing a video game, it prevents no adult from buying a video game, and it prevents no child or adolescent from obtaining a game provided a parent is willing to help. All it prevents is a child or adolescent from buying, without a parent's assistance, a gruesomely violent video game of a kind that the industry *itself* tells us it wants to keep out of the hands of those under the age of 17.

The interest that California advances in support of the statute is compelling. As this Court has previously described that interest, it consists of both (1) the "basic" parental claim "to authority in their own household to direct the rearing of their children," which makes it proper to enact "laws designed to aid discharge of [parental] responsibility," and (2) the State's "independent interest in the well-being of its youth." *Ginsberg*. And where these interests work in tandem, it is not fatally "underinclusive" for a State to advance its interests in protecting children against the special harms present in an interactive video game medium through a default rule that still allows parents to provide their children with what their parents wish.

Both interests are present here. As to the need to help parents guide their children, the Court noted in 1968 that "'parental control or guidance cannot always be provided.'" Today, 5.3 million grade-school-age children of working parents are routinely home alone. Thus, it has, if anything, become more important to supplement parents' authority to guide their children's development. . . .

. . . In particular, extremely violent games can harm children by rewarding them for being violently aggressive in play, and thereby often teaching them to be violently aggressive in life. And video games can cause more harm in this respect than can typically passive media, such as books or films or television programs.

There are many scientific studies that support California's views. Social scientists, for example, have found *causal* evidence that playing these games results in harm. . . .

And "meta-analyses," *i.e.*, studies of all the studies, have concluded that exposure to violent video games "was positively associated with aggressive behavior, aggressive cognition, and aggressive affect," and that "playing violent video games is a *causal* risk factor for long-term harmful outcomes." Anderson et al., Violent Video Game Effects on Aggression, Empathy, and Prosocial Behavior in Eastern and Western Countries: A Meta-Analytic Review, 136 *Psychological Bulletin* (2010).

Some of these studies take care to explain in a common-sense way why video games are potentially more harmful than, say, films or books or television. In essence, they say that the closer a child's behavior comes, not to watching, but to *acting* out horrific violence, the greater the potential psychological harm. . . .

Unlike the majority, I would find sufficient grounds in these studies and expert opinions for this Court to defer to an elected legislature's conclusion that the video games in question are particularly likely to harm children. This Court has always thought it owed an elected legislature some degree of deference in respect to legislative facts of this kind, particularly when they involve technical matters that are beyond our competence, and even in First Amendment cases. The majority, in reaching its own, opposite conclusion about the validity of the relevant studies, grants the legislature no deference at all. . . .

The upshot is that California's statute, as applied to its heartland of applications (*i.e.*, buyers under 17; extremely violent, realistic video games), imposes a restriction on speech that is modest at most. That restriction is justified by a compelling interest (supplementing parents' efforts to prevent their children from purchasing potentially harmful violent, interactive material). And there is no equally effective, less restrictive alternative. California's statute is consequently constitutional on its face. . . .

I add that the majority's different conclusion creates a serious anomaly in First Amendment law. *Ginsberg* makes clear that a State can prohibit the sale to minors of depictions of nudity; today the Court makes clear that a State cannot prohibit the sale to minors of the most violent interactive video games. But what sense does it make to forbid selling to a 13-year-old boy a magazine with an image of a nude woman, while protecting a sale to that 13-year-old of an interactive video game in which he actively, but virtually, binds and gags the woman, then tortures and kills her? . . .

. . . Sometimes, children need to learn by making choices for themselves. Other times, choices are made for children—by their parents, by their teachers, and by the people acting democratically through their governments. In my view, the First Amendment does not disable government from helping parents make such a choice here—a choice not to have their children buy extremely violent, interactive video games, which they more than reasonably fear pose only the risk of harm to those children.

Although the vote in *Brown* was not especially divided, the range of opinions the justices expressed was nearly as diverse as in the pre-*Miller* obscenity cases. To Justice Scalia, video games are more akin to fairy tales, which "contain no shortage of gore," than they are to sexually explicit material. They deserve full First Amendment protection, meaning that the law can survive only if the state presents a compelling government interest and is narrowly drawn to serve that interest (*see chapter 13*). To Justice Scalia the social science evidence was not sufficiently compelling.

In his concurring opinion, Justice Alito took issue with the majority's broad ruling. He would have struck down the law as unconstitutionally vague, leaving open the possibility that the state could rewrite it (as the Court suggested in *Stevens*). Alito, too, thought the Court should not have necessarily treated video games as "the same as some older thing with which we are familiar." As he put it, "We should take into account the possibility that developing technology may have important societal implications that will become apparent only with time." Even the dissenters expressed divergent reasons for their disagreement with the majority. In accord with his version of originalism, Justice Clarence Thomas rejected the idea that the First Amendment included "a right to speak to minors (or a right of minors to access speech) without going through the minors' parents or guardians." Justice Stephen Breyer, in contrast, argued that the Court should have deferred to the state's findings about the potential harm associated with violent video games.

No doubt *Stevens* and *Brown* represent the first of what will be many cases generated by new technology, and perhaps the justices will reconsider whether changes in that technology necessitate declaring another category of expression to be unprotected. For the present, however, the Court seems content to stick to its position of defining only a limited number of categories as beyond the reach of the First Amendment—notably, obscenity and libel.

REGULATING THE INTERNET

As we have already hinted, the development of the Internet and other forms of electronic expression created entirely new methods of communication, combining elements of both speech and press. What began in 1969 as a military project has grown into an international network of interconnected computers. Internet communication is instantaneous and interactive. Unlike radio, electronic media can carry text, graphics, and sound. Unlike a television station, the Internet does not reside in a single location but is a network of communicators not confined by state or national boundaries. Unlike the broadcast media, which are restricted by the number of frequencies available, the Internet can accommodate communication by perhaps an infinite number of people. And unlike many other forms of expression, participating in electronic speech does not require a large expenditure of money. These factors make electronic communication potentially the most effective and participatory method of expression yet devised. The Internet carries the promise of creating a truly robust, free marketplace of ideas.

But electronic expression also carries certain dangers. We already have mentioned Congress's efforts to regulate the dissemination of child pornography. These efforts represent only one side of the equation, however—the other is Congress's attempts to prevent children from gaining *access* to sexually explicit material.

This issue is not new. Amid pressure from governments and various interest groups, the film, music, television, and gaming industries have adopted various rating and labeling systems. Perhaps because no one industry represents the worldwide Internet, Congress has stepped in, passing two types of laws. One, represented by the Communications Decency Act of 1996 (CDA) and the Child Online Protection Act of 1998 (COPA, sometimes called CDA II), generally attempts to regulate the transmission of certain kinds of material or messages to people under the age of eighteen. The other type involves the use of filtering devices to block minors from viewing certain material.

Reno v. American Civil Liberties Union (1997) presented a challenge to the first CDA, the Communications Decency Act of 1996. It is noteworthy not only because it provides some indication of the Court's thinking on regulating Internet access but also because it presented the justices' first opportunity to consider the legal status of the Internet. Would the justices characterize the Web as a medium akin to newspapers, or would they liken it to other more modern-day media, such as television and radio? This is an important question because the Court has ruled that the print media enjoy higher First Amendment protection than do the broadcast media.

Reno v. American Civil Liberties Union

521 U.S. 844 (1997)
http://caselaw.findlaw.com/us-supreme-court/521/844.html
Oral arguments available at https://www.oyez.org/
    cases/1996/96-511
Vote: 7 (Breyer, Ginsburg, Kennedy, Scalia, Souter,
    Stevens, Thomas)
    2 (O'Connor, Rehnquist)

OPINION OF THE COURT: *Stevens*

OPINION CONCURRING IN THE JUDGMENT IN PART AND DISSENTING IN PART: *O'Connor*

Passed in 1996 by large majorities in both houses of Congress and signed into law by President Bill Clinton, the Communications Decency Act—part of a larger legislative package regulating the telecommunications industry—sought to control children's access to sexually explicit material transmitted electronically, especially via the Internet. As soon as the law was passed, a coalition of about fifty organizations and businesses, led by the ACLU, filed suit, asserting that it violated the First Amendment.

Specifically, the lawsuit challenged two provisions of the act, known as the indecent transmission provision and the patently offensive display provision. The indecent transmission section prohibited online communication to minors that is indecent or obscene, "regardless of whether the user of such service . . . initiated the communication." The patently offensive display provision prohibited the transmission of messages that depict or describe, "in terms patently offensive as measured by community standards, sexual or excretory activities or organs" in a manner that "is available to a person under the age of eighteen." Violators of these provisions could be fined or imprisoned for two years, or both. The law recognized as a legitimate defense "good faith, reasonable, effective, and appropriate actions" to restrict minors' access to the prohibited communications.

Those attacking the law charged that terms such as *indecent* and *patently offensive* were unconstitutionally vague. They also argued that the law was not narrowly tailored to accomplish the goal of protecting minors; rather, it also unconstitutionally restricted adult access to sexually explicit communications.

A three-judge district court, although divided over the rationale, held that the law was unconstitutionally vague. Attorney General Janet Reno, representing the United States, appealed to the Supreme Court.

JUSTICE STEVENS DELIVERED THE OPINION OF THE COURT.

In *Southeastern Promotions, Ltd. v. Conrad* (1975), we observed that "each medium of expression . . . may present its own problems." Thus, some of our cases have recognized special justifications for regulation of the broadcast media that are not applicable to other speakers. In these cases, the Court relied on the history of extensive government regulation of the broadcast medium; the scarcity of available frequencies at its inception; and its "invasive" nature.

Those factors are not present in cyberspace. Neither before nor after the enactment of the CDA [Communications Decency Act] have the vast democratic fora of the Internet been subject to the type of government supervision and regulation that has attended the broadcast industry. Moreover, the Internet is not as "invasive" as radio or television. The District Court specifically found that "communications over the Internet do not 'invade' an individual's home or appear on one's computer screen unbidden. Users seldom encounter content 'by accident.'" . . .

. . . [U]nlike the conditions that prevailed when Congress first authorized regulation of the broadcast spectrum, the Internet can hardly be considered a "scarce" expressive commodity. It provides relatively unlimited, low-cost capacity for communication of all kinds. The Government estimates that "as many as 40 million people use the Internet today [1997], and that figure is expected to grow to 200 million by 1999." This dynamic, multifaceted category of communication includes not only traditional print and news services, but also audio, video, and still images, as well as interactive, real-time dialogue. Through the use of chat rooms, any person

with [Internet access] can become a town crier with a voice that resonates farther than it could from any soapbox. Through the use of Web pages, mail exploders, and newsgroups, the same individual can become a pamphleteer. As the District Court found, "the content on the Internet is as diverse as human thought." We agree with its conclusion that our cases provide no basis for qualifying the level of First Amendment scrutiny that should be applied to this medium.

. . . [T]he many ambiguities [of the CDA] concerning the scope of its coverage render it problematic for purposes of the First Amendment. For instance, each of the two parts of the CDA uses a different linguistic form. The first uses the word "indecent," while the second speaks of material that "in context, depicts or describes, in terms patently offensive as measured by contemporary community standards, sexual or excretory activities or organs." Given the absence of a definition of either term, this difference in language will provoke uncertainty among speakers about how the two standards relate to each other and just what they mean. Could a speaker confidently assume that a serious discussion about birth control practices, homosexuality . . . or the consequences of prison rape would not violate the CDA? This uncertainty undermines the likelihood that the CDA has been carefully tailored to the congressional goal of protecting minors from potentially harmful materials.

The vagueness of the CDA is a matter of special concern for two reasons. First, the CDA is a content-based regulation of speech. The vagueness of such a regulation raises special First Amendment concerns because of its obvious chilling effect on free speech. Second, the CDA is a criminal statute. In addition to the opprobrium and stigma of a criminal conviction, the CDA threatens violators with penalties including up to two years in prison for each act of violation. The severity of criminal sanctions may well cause speakers to remain silent rather than communicate even arguably unlawful words, ideas, and images. . . .

. . . [T]he CDA . . . presents a greater threat of censoring speech that, in fact, falls outside the statute's scope. Given the vague contours of the coverage of the statute, it unquestionably silences some speakers whose messages would be entitled to constitutional protection. That danger provides further reason for insisting that the statute not be overly broad. The CDA's burden on protected speech cannot be justified if it could be avoided by a more carefully drafted statute.

We are persuaded that the CDA lacks the precision that the First Amendment requires when a statute regulates the content of speech. In order to deny minors access to potentially harmful speech, the CDA effectively suppresses a large amount of speech that adults have a constitutional right to receive and to address to one another. That burden on adult speech is unacceptable if less restrictive alternatives would be at least as effective in achieving the legitimate purpose that the statute was enacted to serve.

In evaluating the free speech rights of adults, we have made it perfectly clear that "sexual expression which is indecent but not obscene is protected by the First Amendment." Indeed, [we have] admonished that "the fact that society may find speech offensive is not a sufficient reason for suppressing it."

It is true that we have repeatedly recognized the governmental interest in protecting children from harmful materials. See *Ginsberg* [*v. New York,* 1968]. But that interest does not justify an unnecessarily broad suppression of speech addressed to adults. As we have explained, the Government may not "reduce the adult population . . . to . . . only what is fit for children." . . .

In arguing that the CDA does not so diminish adult communication, the Government relies on the incorrect factual premise that prohibiting a transmission whenever it is known that one of its recipients is a minor would not interfere with adult-to-adult communication. The findings of the District Court make clear that this premise is untenable.

Given the size of the potential audience for most messages, in the absence of a viable age verification process, the sender must be charged with knowing that one or more minors will likely view it. Knowledge that, for instance, one or more members of a 100-person chat group will be a minor—and therefore that it would be a crime to send the group an indecent message—would surely burden communication among adults.

The District Court found that at the time of trial existing technology did not include any effective method for a sender to prevent minors from obtaining access to its communications on the Internet without also denying access to adults. The Court found no effective way to determine the age of a user who is accessing material through e-mail, mail exploders, newsgroups, or chat rooms. As a practical matter, the Court also found that it would be prohibitively expensive for noncommercial—as well as some commercial—speakers who have Web sites to verify that their users are adults. These limitations must inevitably curtail a significant amount of adult communication on the Internet. By contrast, the District Court found that "despite its limitations, currently available *user-based* software suggests that a reasonably effective method by which *parents* can prevent their children from accessing sexually explicit and other material which *parents* may believe is inappropriate for their children will soon be widely available" (emphases added).

The breadth of the CDA's coverage is wholly unprecedented. Unlike the regulations upheld in *Ginsberg* and [*FCC v.*] *Pacifica* [1978], the scope of the CDA is not limited to commercial speech or commercial entities. Its open ended prohibitions embrace all nonprofit entities and individuals posting indecent messages or displaying them on their own computers in the presence of minors. The general, undefined terms "indecent" and "patently offensive" cover large amounts of nonpornographic material with serious educational or other value. Moreover, the "community standards" criterion as applied to the Internet means that any communication available to a nationwide audience will be judged by the standards of the community most likely to be offended by the message. The regulated subject matter . . . may also extend to discussions about prison rape or safe sexual practices, artistic images that include nude subjects, and arguably the card catalogue of the Carnegie Library. . . .

In this Court, though not in the District Court, the Government asserts that—in addition to its interest in protecting children—its "equally significant" interest in fostering the growth of the Internet provides an independent basis for upholding the constitutionality of the CDA. The Government apparently assumes that the unregulated availability of "indecent" and "patently offensive" material on the Internet is driving countless citizens away from the medium because of the risk of exposing themselves or their children to harmful material.

We find this argument singularly unpersuasive. The dramatic expansion of this new marketplace of ideas contradicts the factual basis of this contention. The record demonstrates that the growth of the Internet has been and continues to be phenomenal. As a matter of constitutional tradition, in the absence of evidence to the contrary, we presume that governmental regulation of the content of speech is more likely to interfere with the free exchange of ideas than to encourage it. The interest in encouraging freedom of expression in a democratic society outweighs any theoretical but unproven benefit of censorship.

For the foregoing reasons, the judgment of the district court is affirmed.

It is so ordered.

Despite the Court's strong defense of First Amendment interests in *Reno,* reaction to its decision, at least among the CDA's congressional supporters, was harsh. As Senator Christopher Bond, R-Mo., put it, the ruling was "an unfortunate blow to those of us who want to protect our children from sexual predators using the Internet. . . . I believe Congress will try again, and that we'll get it right next time."[14]

Congress did try again. In 1998 it passed the Child Online Protection Act, which prohibited distribution on the Internet of "any communication for commercial purposes that is available to any minor and that includes any material that is harmful to minors."[15] Violators could face criminal prosecution, with fines of up to $50,000 a day.

[14]Quoted in the *St. Louis Post Dispatch,* June 27, 1997, A16.

[15]COPA defined material "harmful to minors" as "any communication, picture, image, graphic image file, article, recording, writing, or other matter of any kind that is obscene or that (A) the average person, applying contemporary community standards, would find, taking the material as a whole and with respect to minors, is designed to appeal to, or is designed to pander to, the prurient interest; (B) depicts, describes, or represents, in a manner patently offensive with respect to minors, an actual or simulated sexual act or sexual contact, an actual or simulated normal or perverted sexual act, or a lewd exhibition of the genitals or post-pubescent female breast; and (C) taken as a whole, lacks serious literary, artistic, political, or scientific value for minors."

A group of organizations that maintained websites containing sexually explicit materials challenged the law. Their concern was that COPA defined "harm to minors" in the context of "contemporary community standards," a feature of the Court's obscenity definition in *Miller*. Because the *Miller* ruling stipulated that "community standards" were determined by individual communities, not a hypothetical "national community," they feared that "any material that might be deemed harmful by the most puritan of communities in any state" might expose them to prosecution. In ***Ashcroft v. American Civil Liberties Union [I]*** (2002), the Court disagreed. Writing for the majority (or plurality, depending on the section of the opinion), Justice Clarence Thomas declared that the use of COPA's "community standards" to identify material harmful to children did not render the statute facially invalid. As he explained, "If a publisher chooses to send its material into a particular community, this Court's jurisprudence teaches that it is the publisher's responsibility to abide by that community's standards. The publisher's burden does not change simply because it decides to distribute its material to every community in the Nation." Thomas also noted that the law was less of a threat to protected expression, because COPA applied to a narrower class of material than did the CDA.

But that decision did not settle the matter. By its own reckoning, *Ashcroft* was "quite limited," stating only that the community standards criterion itself does not necessarily run afoul of the First Amendment. Indeed, the Court did not express an opinion on other questions—such as whether the law is unconstitutionally vague or would fail to pass a strict scrutiny analysis—and it sent the case back to the court of appeals, instructing it to evaluate the law more extensively.

The court of appeals held that COPA violated the First Amendment, ruling that it was not the "least restrictive" alternative available to accomplish Congress's goal of shielding children from harmful materials. In a second examination of the law, the Supreme Court agreed. Writing for a five-person majority in ***Ashcroft v. American Civil Liberties Union [II]*** (2004), Justice Anthony M. Kennedy agreed: "When plaintiffs challenge a content-based speech restriction, the burden is on the Government to prove that the proposed alternatives will not be as effective as the challenged statute." To Kennedy, the answer was straightforward: the government had not made its case that COPA was the least restrictive alternative. In particular, he pointed to the availability of blocking and filtering software that parents could use to limit minors' access to sexual material. These software programs "impose selective restrictions on speech at the receiving end, not universal restrictions at the source. . . . Above all, promoting the use of filters does not condemn as criminal any category of speech, and so the potential chilling effect is eliminated, or at least much diminished." He further argued that filters "also may well be more effective than COPA [because] they can prevent minors from seeing all pornography, not just pornography posted to the Web from America."

Kennedy's emphasis on filtering software was hardly coincidental. Just the year before *Ashcroft II*, the Court had issued a decision in *United States v. American Library Association* (2003). At issue in this case was the constitutionality of yet another congressional attempt to prevent children from visiting certain Internet sites: the Children's Internet Protection Act of 2000, which withholds federal financial aid to libraries that do not use "filtering" software to block "visual depictions" that are harmful to minors. Six of the justices voted to uphold the law, but Chief Justice William Rehnquist failed to obtain a majority for his view that restricting the ability of adult library users to access certain Internet sites was no more in violation of the First Amendment than placing limits on their ability to borrow books that librarians did not use their discretion to purchase. Two of the six, Justices Kennedy and Stephen Breyer, were a bit more circumspect. They agreed that the law was constitutional on its face, but they expressed some concerns about how it may work in practice. Both justices seemed aware that the blocking technology was imperfect and could result in preventing or delaying access to certain content by adult library patrons.

Given rapidly evolving technology, changes in the ways people use the Internet, and an ever-expanding range of online content, it is hard to estimate the First Amendment questions that will emerge. To date, as our discussion suggests, federal regulation of Internet content has focused on matters related to sexually explicit materials and the welfare of children. Potentially, however, legislation may touch upon many other aspects of Internet-based expression, including commercial regulation. Doubtless almost every attempt at Internet regulation will be challenged in court by groups that want this contemporary method of communication to remain as free and open as possible. Such challenges will require the nation's judges to apply constitutional principles to a medium of expression not even within the framers' imagination when they penned the First Amendment.

ANNOTATED READINGS

There is no shortage of interesting studies of the freedom of the press (broadly defined). Books containing histories of the free press clause, seminal cases, or both include Fred W. Friendly, *Minnesota Rag* (New York: Random House, 1981); Peter Charles Hoffer, *The Free Press Crisis of 1800: Thomas Cooper's Trial for Seditious Libel* (Lawrence: University Press of Kansas, 2011); Leonard W. Levy, *Emergence of a Free Press* (New York: Oxford University Press, 1985); Leonard W. Levy, ed., *Freedom of the Press from Zenger to Jefferson* (Durham, NC: Carolina Academic Press, 1996); Robert W. T. Martin, *The Founding of American Press Liberty, 1640–1880* (New York: New York University Press, 2001); Lucas A. Powe Jr., *The Fourth Estate and the Constitution* (Berkeley: University of California Press, 1991); John Prados and Margaret Pratt Porter, eds., *Inside the Pentagon Papers* (Lawrence: University Press of Kansas, 2004); David Rudenstine, *The Day the Presses Stopped: A History of the Pentagon Papers Case* (Berkeley: University of California Press, 1996); Mark R. Scherer, *Rights in the Balance: Free Press, Fair Trial, and* Nebraska Press Association v. Stuart (Lubbock: Texas Tech Press, 2008); Martin Shapiro, *The Pentagon Papers and the Courts* (San Francisco: Chandler, 1972); Jason M. Shepard, *Privileging the Press: Confidential Sources, Journalism Ethics, and the First Amendment* (El Paso, TX: LFB Scholarly Publishing, 2011); and Jeffery Alan Smith, *War and Press Freedom: The Problem of Prerogative Power* (New York: Oxford University Press, 1999).

For studies of libel law, see Renata Adler, *Reckless Disregard:* Westmoreland v. CBS et al., Sharon v. Time (New York: Vintage Books, 1986); Elmer Gertz, Gertz v. Robert Welch, Inc.: *The Story of a Landmark Libel Case* (Carbondale: Southern Illinois University Press, 1992); Donald M. Gillmor, *Power, Publicity, and the Abuse of Libel Law* (New York: Oxford University Press, 1992); Kermit L. Hall and Melvin I. Urofsky, New York Times v. Sullivan: *Civil Rights, Libel Law, and the Free Press* (Lawrence: University Press of Kansas, 2011); Peter E. Kane, *Errors, Lies, and Libel* (Carbondale: Southern Illinois University Press, 1992); Anthony Lewis, *Make No Law: The* Sullivan *Case and the First Amendment* (New York: Random House, 1991); Rodney A. Smolla, Jerry Falwell v. Larry Flynt: *The First Amendment on Trial* (Champaign: University of Illinois Press, 1990); David E Sumner, *Fumbled Call: The Bear Bryant-Wally Butts Football Scandal That Split the Supreme Court and Changed American Libel Law* (Jefferson, NC: McFarland &

Company, 2018); Russell L. Weaver, Andrew T. Kenyon, David F. Partlett, and Clive P. Walker, *The Right to Speak Ill: Defamation, Reputation, and Free Speech* (Durham, NC: Carolina Academic Press, 2006).

Books on obscenity and pornography include Brenda Cossman, Shannon Bell, Becki Ross, and Lise Gotell, *Bad Attitudes on Trial: Pornography, Feminism, and the* Butler *Decision* (Toronto, ON: University of Toronto Press, 1997); Steven J. Heyman, *Free Speech and Human Dignity* (New Haven, CT: Yale University Press, 2008); Richard F. Hixson, *Pornography and the Justices: The Supreme Court and the Intractable Obscenity Problem* (Carbondale: Southern Illinois University Press, 1996); Joseph F. Kobylka, *The Politics of Obscenity: Group Litigation in a Time of Legal Change* (New York: Greenwood Press, 1991); Catharine MacKinnon, *Only Words* (Cambridge, MA: Harvard University Press, 1993); Charles Rembar, *The End of Obscenity* (New York: Bantam Books, 1968); Kevin W. Saunders, *Degradation: What the History of Obscenity Tells Us about Hate Speech* (New York: New York University Press, 2011); Nadine Strossen, *Defending Pornography: Free Speech, Sex, and the Fight for Women's Rights* (New York: New York University Press, 2000); L. W. Sumner, *The Hateful and the Obscene: Studies in the Limits of Free Expression* (Toronto, ON: University of Toronto Press, 2004); James Weinstein, *Hate Speech, Pornography, and the Radical Attack on Free Speech Doctrine* (Boulder, CO: Westview Press, 1999); Amy Werbel, *Lust on Trial: Censorship and the Rise of American Obscenity in the Age of Anthony Comstock* (New York: Columbia University Press, 2018); Laura Wittern-Keller and Raymond Haberski Jr., *The Miracle Case: Film Censorship and the Supreme Court* (Lawrence: University Press of Kansas, 2008); Franklin E. Zimring and Gordon J. Hawkins, *Pornography in a Free Society* (New York: Cambridge University Press, 1991).

On evolving concepts of freedom of the press and new media, see Lee C. Bollinger, *Images of a Free Press* (Chicago: University of Chicago Press, 1991); Scott Gant, *We're All Journalists Now: The Transformation of the Press and the Reshaping of the Law in the Internet Age* (New York: Simon & Schuster, 2007); Stephen Gillers, *Journalism Under Fire: Protecting the Future of Investigative Reporting* (New York: Columbia University Press, 2018); Mike Godwin, *Cyber Rights:*

Defending Free Speech in the Digital Age (Cambridge, MA: MIT Press, 2003); Richard Reeves, *What the People Know: Freedom and the Press* (Cambridge, MA: Harvard University Press, 1999); and Joshua Rozenberg, *Privacy and the Press* (New York: Oxford University Press, 2004). For comparative analyses of the role of a free press, see Joseph Chappell, *Building the Fourth Estate: Democratization and the Rise of a Free Press* (Berkeley: University of California Press, 2002); Judith Lichtenberg, *Democracy and the Mass Media* (New York: Cambridge University Press, 1990); Jared Schroeder, *The Press Clause and Digital Technology's Fourth Wave: Media Law and the Symbiotic Web* (New York: Routledge, 2018); and B. R. Sharma, *Freedom of Press under the Indian Constitution* (Columbia, MO: South Asia Books, 1993).

Scholars and other commentators have published numerous books relating to the Internet and the First Amendment. Those focusing, in part or in full, on pornography include Yaman Akdeniz, *Internet Child Pornography and the Law: National and International Responses* (Burlington, VT: Ashgate, 2008); Mike Godwin, *Cyber Rights: Defending Free Speech in the Digital Age* (Cambridge, MA: MIT Press, 2003); Philip Jenkins, *Beyond Tolerance: Child Pornography Online* (New York: New York University Press, 2001). Other treatments include Scott Gant, *We're All Journalists Now: The Transformation of the Press and the Reshaping of the Law in the Internet Age* (New York: Simon & Schuster, 2007); Jack Goldsmith and Tim Wu, *Who Controls the Internet?* (New York: Oxford University Press, 2006); Jeremy Harris Lipschultz, *Free Expression in the Age of the Internet* (Boulder, CO: Westview Press, 2000); Daniel J. Solove, *The Future of Reputation: Gossip, Rumor, and Privacy on the Internet* (New Haven, CT: Yale University Press, 2007).

CHAPTER FIFTEEN

THE RIGHT TO KEEP AND BEAR ARMS

PROMINENTLY DISPLAYED in the literature the National Rifle Association (NRA) and similar groups distribute are statements invoking the Second Amendment. Advocates of gun ownership rights assert that this amendment protects the fundamental right of individuals to keep and bear arms. Supporters of gun control legislation, however, claim that the amendment guarantees no such thing. The conflict between these two points of view has continued without interruption since the earliest government attempts to limit gun ownership rights. In large measure the controversy rests on the ambiguity of the amendment's wording.

The Second Amendment states in full: "A well regulated Militia, being necessary to the security of a free State, the right of the people to keep and bear arms shall not be infringed." The form of this amendment makes it something of an oddity compared to other provisions of the Bill of Rights, because it comes with its own preamble. The structure gives rise to the question of the extent to which the preamble conditions the right itself.

As a result, two distinctly different interpretations of the amendment have been advanced. The first, often expressed by those who favor government restrictions on private gun ownership, emphasizes the first half of the amendment. According to this view, the amendment guarantees only a *collective* right of the states to arm their militias. No individual right to own firearms exists unless it is in conjunction with a state militia. This position, therefore, interprets the amendment's prefatory clause as significantly controlling the meaning of the right to keep and bear arms.

If, as gun control supporters argue, the amendment was intended as a barrier against the federal government disarming state militias, then the amendment has little relevance today. In the nation's early years, the states, with no standing armies in place, responded to emergencies by calling private persons to serve in their militias. When called into service, these individuals were often expected to bring their own weapons with them. But states no longer call on citizen militias. Whatever roles the state militias played in the nation's first century are now carried out by other institutions, such as the states' National Guard units.

The second interpretation, advocated by pro–gun ownership interests, emphasizes the second half of the amendment. It concludes that the Constitution guarantees an *individual* right to keep and bear arms. The preamble's reference to well-regulated state militias does not in any way limit the amendment's operative clause that explicitly guarantees "the right of the people" to own and carry weapons. The freedom to keep and bear arms, among other purposes, supports the inalienable right of individuals to engage in self-defensive behavior when necessary. As such, the Second Amendment is no less relevant today than it was when it was ratified in 1791.

The wording of the Second Amendment provides significant obstacles to understanding its meaning. Further complicating matters is the fact that historical records allow different interpretations of what Congress intended by proposing the amendment and what state legislators thought it meant when they ratified it. Until 2008 the Supreme Court had not offered much assistance, rarely accepting cases that call for an interpretation of gun ownership rights.

All the while, of course, the freedom to own and carry guns has been a significant political and social issue. Gun control supporters cite the social costs associated with the irresponsible use of firearms. These include mass shootings, gun-related crimes of violence, domestic abuse, and suicides as well as accidental injuries and deaths, often involving children. On the other side, advocates of gun ownership rights argue that the frequency of violent crime only underscores the need for responsible citizens to arm themselves for their personal protection.

In the United States gun ownership is widespread. According to recent surveys, about 30 percent of Americans own at least one gun, and an additional 13 percent do not own a firearm but share a household with someone who does.[1] Two-thirds of gun owners possess more than one weapon. Furthermore, of those not owning a gun, about half foresee the possibility of owning one in the future. The most cited reason for owning a firearm is personal protection.

Not surprisingly, the issue of gun ownership has always been associated with strong political views.[2] Today, about 60 percent of Americans support more stringent laws on guns; then again, only 28 percent support laws that would ban handgun possession. The nation is also sharply divided along partisan lines with 87 percent of Democrats but only 31 percent of Republican supporting stricter gun control laws.

INITIAL INTERPRETATIONS

Congress did little to regulate firearms prior to the twentieth century. Support for federal weapons restrictions began to grow in the 1920s, largely because of the increase in organized crime that occurred during Prohibition and into the Great Depression. Particularly significant in raising public awareness of the misuse of guns was a violent confrontation between warring criminal organizations in Chicago in the infamous 1929 St. Valentine's Day Massacre. Congress responded by first imposing a ban on the use of the postal service to transport certain weapons and then by passing the National Firearms Act of 1934 (NFA), the first significant piece of federal gun control legislation.

---

[1]The data in this paragraph come from Lydia Saad, "What Percentage of Americans Own Guns," Gallup (2019). https://news.gallup .com/poll/264932/percentage-americans-own-guns.aspx; and Kim Parker, Juliana Menasce Horowitz, Ruth Igielnik, J. Baxter Oliphant and Anna Brown, "America's Complex Relationship with Guns," Pew Research Center (2017). http://www.pewsocialtrends .org/2017/06/22/americas-complex-relationship-with-guns/

[2]The data in this paragraph come from RJ Reinhart, "Six in 10 Americans Support Stricter Gun Laws," Gallup (2018). https:// news.gallup.com/poll/243797/six-americans-support-stricter-gun-laws.aspx

The NFA was not a direct regulation of weapons. Rather, because federal authority over the possession of firearms was constitutionally suspect, Congress used its authority to levy taxes to justify the legislation. The law imposed an excise tax on certain particularly lethal weapons and required their registration. It further prohibited the interstate transportation of any unregistered firearm covered by the act.

With respect to its compatibility with the Constitution, the NFA was controversial. Many thought its provisions violated the Second Amendment. The constitutionality of the 1934 law was tested in **United States v. Miller** (1939). To decide this case, the justices were required to determine if the right to keep and bear arms was a personal liberty or only a collective right tied to the need for state militias.

The case began when Jack Miller and Frank Layton, two relatively insignificant career criminals, were indicted for transporting from Oklahoma to Arkansas a "shotgun having a barrel of less than eighteen inches in length"—that is, a sawed-off shotgun. A tax had not been paid on the weapon, and it was unregistered, both violations of the NFA.

The facts surrounding *Miller* allow the inference that it was a federally orchestrated test case.[3] The government was interested in expanding its gun control efforts, but it needed an authoritative decision by the Supreme Court to alleviate any Second Amendment concerns. Miller, the primary defendant, had a history of cooperating with the government as an informant in criminal cases. Federal district judge Heartsill Ragon, a former member of Congress who heard the case, was a strong proponent of gun regulation. Judge Ragon refused to accept guilty pleas from Miller and Layton, thereby ensuring that the case would be tried. Although Miller and Layton put up little defense, Ragon used the case to strike down the NFA for violating the Second Amendment. He did so by way of a memorandum opinion that provided no reasoning or argument to justify his decision. His opinion nicely set the stage for the federal government to ask the Supreme Court to reverse.

When the appeal reached the justices, only the federal government's position was presented. Among other arguments, the government, claimed that the Second Amendment was not applicable because that provision was designed only to cover weapons of the kind a state militia

---

[3]For an interesting analysis of this case, see Brian L. Frye, "The Peculiar Story of *United States v. Miller*," *NYU Journal of Law and Liberty* 3 (2008): 48–82.

use. The sawed-off, double-barreled shotgun in question had no relevance to any militia activity. No one represented the other side, so the position that the NFA violated the Second Amendment was not defended either by a coherent opinion from the lower court or by briefs and oral arguments on behalf of the defendants at the Supreme Court.

One could hardly imagine more favorable conditions for the federal government's position to prevail. And, in fact, the justices unanimously supported the federal government's position, holding that the NFA did not violate the Constitution. Through an opinion by Justice James C. McReynolds, the justices endorsed the government's claim that the law was a valid use of the power to tax. The Court further concluded that the Second Amendment was designed to cover only military-style weapons associated with the state militias. In rather direct language, McReynolds wrote:

> In the absence of any evidence tending to show that possession or use of a "shotgun having a barrel of less than eighteen inches in length" at this time has some reasonable relationship to the preservation or efficiency of a well regulated militia, we cannot say that the Second Amendment guarantees the right to keep and bear such an instrument. Certainly it is not within judicial notice that this weapon is any part of the ordinary military equipment or that its use could contribute to the common defense. . . .

> With obvious purpose to assure the continuation and render possible the effectiveness of [state militias] the declaration and guarantee of the Second Amendment were made. It must be interpreted and applied with that end in view.

On its face, the ruling seems unambiguous. The ruling offered strong support for the collective right theory of the Second Amendment—that is, the position that the right to keep and bear arms was guaranteed only as a means of supporting the state militias. Gun rights advocates, however, see the *Miller* decision much differently. They argue that the nation's early reliance on citizen soldiers to staff the state militias was predicated on private gun ownership.

THE SECOND AMENDMENT REVISITED

The *Miller* decision certainly did not end the controversy over the Second Amendment, though for decades the Supreme Court avoided cases that presented difficult Second Amendment issues. Not so of lawyers and historians who began, in the 1980s and 1990s, to reexamine the meaning of the Second Amendment. Earlier generations of scholars generally sided with the position that the Second Amendment guarantees only the collective right to keep and bear arms. Analyzing additional historical records, however, led several contemporary scholars to conclude that the NRA and its allies may have a stronger legal argument than previously thought.[4] As Justice Clarence Thomas put it in a footnote to his concurring opinion in *Printz v. United States* (1997), "Marshalling an impressive array of historical evidence, a growing body of scholarly commentary indicates that the 'right to keep and bear arms' is, as the amendment's text suggests, a personal right."

In *District of Columbia v. Heller* (2008), the Court finally addressed the varying approaches to the Second Amendment. As you read the opinions in this case, pay close attention to the justices' reasoning, especially their attempts to use historical analyses to establish what was understood to be the meaning of the amendment at the time it was proposed and ratified.

District of Columbia v. Heller

554 U.S. 570 (2008)
http://caselaw.findlaw.com/us-supreme-court/554/570.html
Oral arguments available at https://www.oyez.org/ cases/2007/07-290
Vote: 5 (Alito, Kennedy, Roberts, Scalia, Thomas)
  4 (Breyer, Ginsburg, Souter, Stevens)

OPINION OF THE COURT: *Scalia*

DISSENTING OPINIONS: *Breyer, Stevens*

In 1976 the District of Columbia, concerned with the high levels of gun-related crime, passed the nation's most restrictive gun control ordinance. The law essentially banned the private possession of handguns. Individuals could own shotguns and rifles, but only if the weapons were registered, kept unloaded, and disassembled or restricted by trigger locks. The law allowed the chief of police,

---

[4]See, for example, Joyce Lee Malcolm, *To Keep and Bear Arms: The Origins of an Anglo-American Right* (Cambridge, MA: Harvard University Press, 1996); William Van Alstyne, "The Second Amendment and the Personal Right to Arms," *Duke Law Journal* 43 (1994): 1236–1255; Don B. Kates, "Handgun Prohibition and the Original Meaning of the Second Amendment," *Michigan Law Review* 82 (1983): 204–273.

under certain circumstances, to issue a one-year certificate permitting an individual to carry a handgun.

Dick Heller, a D.C. police officer, had been granted a license to carry a handgun while on duty providing security at the Federal Judicial Center. Heller applied for permission to own a handgun for self-defense, but he was refused. Claiming that the D.C. statute violated his Second Amendment right to bear arms, Heller brought a suit against the District. The district court dismissed his case, but the U.S. Court of Appeals for the District of Columbia reversed, holding that the Second Amendment protected Heller's right to possess a firearm for self-defense.

Heller's case did not occur spontaneously; rather, it was orchestrated by Florida attorney Robert Levy, who wanted to test the constitutionality of the District's gun control law. Levy had become a wealthy man in his first career as a money manager. At age forty-nine he entered George Mason Law School, from which he graduated first in his class. After clerking for two federal judges, he devoted his professional life to libertarian causes. Levy, who had never owned a gun, saw the District's law as a violation of personal freedom and private property rights. He recruited six possible plaintiffs to challenge the law, but only Heller met the strict standing requirements to pursue legal action. To eliminate any possible influence over the case by the NRA or any other gun rights group, Levy funded the litigation out of his own pocket.

JUSTICE SCALIA DELIVERED THE OPINION OF THE COURT.

The Second Amendment is naturally divided into two parts: its prefatory clause and its operative clause. The former does not limit the latter grammatically, but rather announces a purpose. The Amendment could be rephrased, "Because a well regulated Militia is necessary to the security of a free State, the right of the people to keep and bear Arms shall not be infringed." . . . [O]ther legal documents of the founding era . . . commonly included a prefatory statement of purpose.

Logic demands that there be a link between the stated purpose and the command. . . . That requirement of logical connection may cause a prefatory clause to resolve an ambiguity in the operative clause. . . . But apart from that clarifying function, a prefatory clause does not limit or expand the scope of the operative clause. . . .

1. OPERATIVE CLAUSE

a. "Right of the People." The first salient feature of the operative clause is that it codifies a "right of the people." The unamended Constitution and the Bill of Rights use the phrase "right of the people" two other times, in the First Amendment's Assembly-and-Petition Clause and in the Fourth Amendment's Search-and-Seizure Clause. . . . All . . . of these instances unambiguously refer to individual rights, not "collective" rights, or rights that may be exercised only through participation in some corporate body. . . .

This contrasts markedly with the phrase "the militia" in the prefatory clause. As we will describe below, the "militia" in colonial America consisted of a subset of "the people"—those who were male, able bodied, and within a certain age range. Reading the Second Amendment as protecting only the right to "keep and bear Arms" in an organized militia therefore fits poorly with the operative clause's description of the holder of that right as "the people."

We start therefore with a strong presumption that the Second Amendment right is exercised individually and belongs to all Americans.

b. "Keep and bear Arms." We move now from the holder of the right—"the people"—to the substance of the right: "to keep and bear Arms."

Before addressing the verbs "keep" and "bear," we interpret their object: "Arms." The 18th-century meaning is no different from the meaning today. . . .

The term was applied, then as now, to weapons that were not specifically designed for military use and were not employed in a military capacity. . . .

. . . We turn to the phrases "keep arms" and "bear arms." [Dictionaries] defined "keep" as, most relevantly, "[t]o retain; not to lose," and "[t]o have in custody." Webster defined it as "[t]o hold; to retain in one's power or possession." No party has apprised us of an idiomatic meaning of "keep Arms." Thus, the most natural reading of "keep Arms" in the Second Amendment is to "have weapons." . . .

At the time of the founding, as now, to "bear" meant to "carry." When used with "arms," however, the term has a meaning that refers to carrying for a particular purpose—confrontation. In *Muscarello v. United States* (1998), in the course of analyzing the meaning of "carries a firearm" in a federal criminal statute, Justice Ginsburg wrote that "[s]urely a most familiar meaning is, as the Constitution's Second Amendment . . . indicate[s]: 'wear, bear, or carry . . . upon the person or in the clothing or in a pocket, for the purpose . . . of being armed and ready for offensive or defensive action in a case of conflict with another person.'" . . . Although the phrase implies that the carrying of the weapon is for the purpose of "offensive or defensive action," it in no way connotes participation in a structured military organization.

Dick Heller leaves police headquarters in Washington, D.C., on August 18, 2008, with his newly issued gun registration. Two months earlier, in *Heller v. District of Columbia*, the Supreme Court declared the District's handgun ban unconstitutional.

. . . In numerous instances, "bear arms" was unambiguously used to refer to the carrying of weapons outside of an organized militia. The most prominent examples are those most relevant to the Second Amendment: Nine state constitutional provisions written in the 18th century or the first two decades of the 19th, which enshrined a right of citizens to "bear arms in defense of themselves and the state" or "bear arms in defense of himself and the state." It is clear from those formulations that "bear arms" did not refer only to carrying a weapon in an organized military unit. . . . These provisions demonstrate—again, in the most analogous linguistic context—that "bear arms" was not limited to the carrying of arms in a militia. . . .

    c. Meaning of the Operative Clause. Putting all of these textual elements together, we find that they guarantee the individual right to possess and carry weapons in case of confrontation. This meaning is strongly confirmed by the historical background of the Second Amendment. We look to this because it has always been widely

understood that the Second Amendment, like the First and Fourth Amendments, codified a *pre-existing right*. . . .

There seems to us no doubt, on the basis of both text and history, that the Second Amendment conferred an individual right to keep and bear arms. . . .

2. PREFATORY CLAUSE

The prefatory clause reads: "A well regulated Militia, being necessary to the security of a free State. . . ."

    a. "Well-Regulated Militia." In *United States v. Miller* (1939), we explained that "the Militia comprised all males physically capable of acting in concert for the common defense." That definition comports with founding-era sources.

Petitioners take a seemingly narrower view of the militia, stating that "[m]ilitias are the state- and congressionally-regulated military forces described in the Militia Clauses. Although we agree with petitioners' interpretive assumption that "militia" means the same thing in Article I and the Second Amendment, we believe that petitioners identify the wrong thing, namely, the organized militia. Unlike armies and navies, which Congress is given the power to create, the militia is assumed by Article I already to be *in existence.* . . .

> b. "Security of a Free State." The phrase "security of a free state" meant "security of a free polity," not security of each of the several States. . . .

There are many reasons why the militia was thought to be "necessary to the security of a free state." First, of course, it is useful in repelling invasions and suppressing insurrections. Second, it renders large standing armies unnecessary—an argument that Alexander Hamilton made in favor of federal control over the militia. Third, when the able-bodied men of a nation are trained in arms and organized, they are better able to resist tyranny.

3. RELATIONSHIP BETWEEN PREFATORY CLAUSE AND OPERATIVE CLAUSE

We reach the question, then: Does the preface fit with an operative clause that creates an individual right to keep and bear arms? It fits perfectly, once one knows the history that the founding generation knew and that we have described above. That history showed that the way tyrants had eliminated a militia consisting of all the able-bodied men was not by banning the militia but simply by taking away the people's arms, enabling a select militia or standing army to suppress political opponents. . . .

The debate with respect to the right to keep and bear arms, as with other guarantees in the Bill of Rights, was not over whether it was desirable (all agreed that it was) but over whether it needed to be codified in the Constitution. During the 1788 ratification debates, the fear that the federal government would disarm the people in order to impose rule through a standing army or select militia was pervasive in Antifederalist rhetoric. . . . Federalists responded that because Congress was given no power to abridge the ancient right of individuals to keep and bear arms, such a force could never oppress the people. It was understood across the political spectrum that the right helped to secure the ideal of a citizen militia, which might be necessary to oppose an oppressive military force if the constitutional order broke down. . . .

. . . If, as the [petitioners] believe, the Second Amendment right is no more than the right to keep and use weapons as a member of an organized militia—if, that is, the *organized* militia is the sole institutional beneficiary of the Second Amendment's guarantee—it does not assure the existence of a "citizens' militia" as a safeguard against tyranny. For Congress retains plenary authority to organize the militia, which must include the authority to say who will belong to the organized force. . . . Thus, if petitioners are correct, the Second Amendment protects citizens' right to use a gun in an organization from which Congress has plenary authority to exclude them. . . .

Our interpretation is confirmed by analogous arms-bearing rights in state constitutions that preceded and immediately followed adoption of the Second Amendment. Four States adopted analogues to the Federal Second Amendment in the period between independence and the ratification of the Bill of Rights. . . .

We therefore believe that the most likely reading of [some] pre–Second Amendment state constitutional provisions is that they secured an individual right to bear arms for defensive purposes. Other States did not include rights to bear arms in their pre-1789 constitutions. . . .

The historical narrative that petitioners must endorse would thus treat the Federal Second Amendment as an odd outlier, protecting a right unknown in state constitutions or at English common law, based on little more than an over-reading of the prefatory clause.

We conclude that nothing in our precedents forecloses our adoption of the original understanding of the Second Amendment. It should be unsurprising that such a significant matter has been for so long judicially unresolved. For most of our history, the Bill of Rights was not thought applicable to the States, and the Federal Government did not significantly regulate the possession of firearms by law-abiding citizens. Other provisions of the Bill of Rights have similarly remained unilluminated for lengthy periods. . . .

Like most rights, the right secured by the Second Amendment is not unlimited. From Blackstone through the 19th-century cases, commentators and courts routinely explained that the right was not a right to keep and carry any weapon whatsoever in any manner whatsoever and for whatever purpose. . . . Although we do not undertake an exhaustive historical analysis today of the full scope of the Second Amendment, nothing in our opinion should be taken to cast doubt on longstanding prohibitions on the possession of firearms by felons and the mentally ill, or laws forbidding the carrying of firearms in sensitive places such as schools and government buildings, or laws imposing conditions and qualifications on the commercial sale of arms.

We also recognize another important limitation on the right to keep and carry arms. *Miller* said, as we have explained, that the sorts of weapons protected were those "in common use at the time." We think that limitation is fairly supported by the historical tradition of prohibiting the carrying of "dangerous and unusual weapons." . . .

. . . [T]he inherent right of self-defense has been central to the Second Amendment right. The handgun ban amounts to a prohibition of an entire class of "arms" that is overwhelmingly chosen by American society for that lawful purpose. The prohibition extends, moreover, to the home, where the need for defense of self, family, and property is most acute. Under any of the standards of scrutiny that we have applied to enumerated constitutional rights, banning from the home "the most preferred firearm in the nation to 'keep' and use for protection of one's home and family," would fail constitutional muster.

Few laws in the history of our Nation have come close to the severe restriction of the District's handgun ban. And some of those few have been struck down. . . .

. . . [T]he American people have considered the handgun to be the quintessential self-defense weapon. There are many reasons that a citizen may prefer a handgun for home defense: It is easier to store in a location that is readily accessible in an emergency; it cannot easily be redirected or wrestled away by an attacker; it is easier to use for those without the upper-body strength to lift and aim a long gun; it can be pointed at a burglar with one hand while the other hand dials the police. Whatever the reason, handguns are the most popular weapon chosen by Americans for self-defense in the home, and a complete prohibition of their use is invalid.

We must also address the District's requirement (as applied to respondent's handgun) that firearms in the home be rendered and kept inoperable at all times. This makes it impossible for citizens to use them for the core lawful purpose of self-defense and is hence unconstitutional. . . .

In sum, we hold that the District's ban on handgun possession in the home violates the Second Amendment, as does its prohibition against rendering any lawful firearm in the home operable for the purpose of immediate self-defense. Assuming that Heller is not disqualified from the exercise of Second Amendment rights, the District must permit him to register his handgun and must issue him a license to carry it in the home.

We are aware of the problem of handgun violence in this country, and we take seriously the concerns raised by the many *amici* who believe that prohibition of handgun ownership is a solution. The Constitution leaves the District of Columbia a variety of tools for combating that problem, including some measures regulating handguns. But the enshrinement of constitutional rights necessarily takes certain policy choices off the table. These include the absolute prohibition of handguns held and used for self-defense in the home. Undoubtedly some think that the Second Amendment is outmoded in a society where our standing army is the pride of our Nation, where well-trained police forces provide personal security, and where gun violence is a serious problem. That is perhaps debatable, but what is not debatable is that it is not the role of this Court to pronounce the Second Amendment extinct.

We affirm the judgment of the Court of Appeals.

It is so ordered.

JUSTICE STEVENS, WITH WHOM JUSTICE SOUTER, JUSTICE GINSBURG, AND JUSTICE BREYER JOIN, DISSENTING.

The Second Amendment was adopted to protect the right of the people of each of the several States to maintain a well-regulated militia. It was a response to concerns raised during the ratification of the Constitution that the power of Congress to disarm the state militias and create a national standing army posed an intolerable threat to the sovereignty of the several States. Neither the text of the Amendment nor the arguments advanced by its proponents evidenced the slightest interest in limiting any legislature's authority to regulate private civilian uses of firearms. Specifically, there is no indication that the Framers of the Amendment intended to enshrine the common-law right of self-defense in the Constitution.

. . . The view of the Amendment we took in *Miller*—that it protects the right to keep and bear arms for certain military purposes, but that it does not curtail the Legislature's power to regulate the nonmilitary use and ownership of weapons—is both the most natural reading of the Amendment's text and the interpretation most faithful to the history of its adoption.

Since our decision in *Miller,* hundreds of judges have relied on the view of the Amendment we endorsed there. . . . No new evidence has surfaced . . . supporting the view that the Amendment was intended to curtail the power of Congress to regulate civilian use or misuse of weapons. Indeed, a review of the drafting history of the Amendment demonstrates that its Framers *rejected* proposals that would have broadened its coverage to include such uses.

The opinion the Court announces today fails to identify any new evidence supporting the view that the Amendment was intended to limit the power of Congress to regulate civilian uses of weapons. . . .

Even if the textual and historical arguments on both sides of the issue were evenly balanced, respect for the well-settled views of all of our predecessors on this Court, and for the rule of law itself would prevent most jurists from endorsing such a dramatic upheaval in the law. . . .

Until today, it has been understood that legislatures may regulate the civilian use and misuse of firearms so long as they do not interfere with the preservation of a well-regulated militia. The Court's announcement of a new constitutional right to own and use firearms for private purposes upsets that settled understanding, but leaves for future cases the formidable task of defining the scope of permissible regulations. Today judicial craftsmen have confidently asserted that a policy choice that denies a "law-abiding, responsible citize[n]" the right to keep and use weapons in the home for self-defense is "off the table." Given the presumption that most citizens are law abiding, and the reality that the need to defend oneself may suddenly arise in a host of locations outside the home, I fear that the District's policy choice may well be just the first of an unknown number of dominoes to be knocked off the table. . . .

The Court properly disclaims any interest in evaluating the wisdom of the specific policy choice challenged in this case, but it fails to pay heed to a far more important policy choice—the choice made by the Framers themselves. The Court would have us believe that over 200 years ago, the Framers made a choice to limit the tools available to elected officials wishing to regulate civilian uses of weapons, and to authorize this Court to use the common-law process of case-by-case judicial lawmaking to define the contours of acceptable gun control policy. Absent compelling evidence that is nowhere to be found in the Court's opinion, I could not possibly conclude that the Framers made such a choice.

For these reasons, I respectfully dissent.

JUSTICE BREYER, WITH WHOM JUSTICE STEVENS, JUSTICE SOUTER, AND JUSTICE GINSBURG JOIN, DISSENTING.

. . . [T]he protection the [Second] Amendment provides is not absolute. The Amendment permits government to regulate the interests that it serves. Thus, irrespective of what those interests are—whether they do or do not include an independent interest in self-defense—the majority's view cannot be correct unless it can show that the District's regulation is unreasonable or inappropriate in Second Amendment terms. This the majority cannot do. . . .

. . . The law is tailored to the urban crime problem in that it is local in scope and thus affects only a geographic area both limited in size and entirely urban; the law concerns handguns, which are specially linked to urban gun deaths and injuries, and which are the overwhelmingly favorite weapon of armed criminals; and at the same time, the law imposes a burden upon gun owners that seems proportionally no greater than restrictions in existence at the time the Second Amendment was adopted. In these circumstances, the District's law falls within the zone that the Second Amendment leaves open to regulation by legislatures.

The majority in *Heller* rejected the collective right interpretation of the Second Amendment and held that the Constitution guarantees an individual the right to keep and bear arms. Justice Antonin Scalia's majority opinion, however, strongly states that the personal right to possess weapons is not absolute. It is a right that is subject to reasonable regulation. In the majority's view, the outright banning of handguns by the District of Columbia exceeded the degree of regulation the Second Amendment permits.

HELLER AND THE STATES

The Court's position in *Heller*, that the Second Amendment protects an individual's right to keep and bear arms, was a sharp break from the past. We should be mindful, however, that the case dealt only with the very restrictive gun control ordinance in Washington, D.C. Because the District of Columbia is ultimately controlled by the federal government and because the Second Amendment had yet to be incorporated, the Court's interpretation of the amendment in *Heller* had no direct effect on the authority of the states to regulate

firearms as they see fit. This, of course, raised the question of whether the justices ultimately would see fit to find that the right to keep and bear arms is a "fundamental" right and therefore applicable to the states through the due process clause of the Fourteenth Amendment.

The Court wasted little time before answering that question. Just two years after *Heller*, in **McDonald v. City of Chicago, Illinois** (2010), the justices heard a challenge to laws enacted by the city of Chicago and the village of Oak Park, a Chicago suburb, that effectively banned handgun possession by almost all private citizens. Writing for a 5–4 majority, Justice Samuel Alito left no doubt about the Second Amendment's application to the states: "We have previously held that most of the provisions of the Bill of Rights apply with full force to both the Federal Government and the States. Applying the standard that is well established in our case law, we hold that the Second Amendment right is fully applicable to the States."

The decisions in *Heller* and *McDonald* were major victories for those who support the personal right to keep and bear arms, but the Court's interpretation of the Second Amendment was not as wide-sweeping as gun advocates would have preferred. Importantly, in *Heller* the Court narrowly rested its decision on the right to self-defense. Because individuals are fundamentally entitled to protect themselves and their families, the federal government cannot prohibit the possession of handguns in the home. Outside of that context, however, reasonable regulation of firearms is constitutionally permissible. As Justice Alito reminded us in his *McDonald* opinion:

> It is important to keep in mind that *Heller*, while striking down a law that prohibited the possession of handguns in the home, recognized that the right to keep and bear arms is not "a right to keep and carry any weapon whatsoever in any manner whatsoever and for whatever purpose." We made it clear in *Heller* that our holding did not cast doubt on such longstanding regulatory measures as "prohibitions on the possession of firearms by felons and the mentally ill," "laws forbidding the carrying of firearms in sensitive places such as schools and government buildings, or laws imposing conditions and qualifications on the commercial sale of arms." We repeat those assurances here. Despite municipal respondents' doomsday proclamations, incorporation does not imperil every law regulating firearms.

But how far may governments go in regulating guns outside *Heller's* protected zone? Subsequent to the *Heller* and *McDonald* decisions, some states and cities have passed new ordinances curtailing gun ownership. Among these are restrictions on military-style assault weapons, gun show purchases, and magazine capacity. Other recent laws require gun owners to take safety courses, report lost or stolen guns, and undergo more extensive background checks. As these regulations have been enacted, they have often been challenged by gun rights advocates.

Thus far the Supreme Court has allowed the lower federal courts to develop answers to these questions. However, societal problems associated with guns, especially recent mass shootings in churches, entertainment venues, and schools, have heightened the call for more comprehensive regulation of firearms. As governments respond to demands for new laws, it is it is inevitable that the justices will find it necessary to return once again the Second Amendment issue.

ANNOTATED READINGS

The debate over the original meaning of the Second Amendment has generated a significant body of literature based on the studies and analyses of legal scholars, political scientists, and historians. Examples of some of the contributions to the discussion of this controversial issue are Randy E. Barnett and Don B. Kates, "Under Fire: The New Consensus on the Second Amendment," *Emory Law Journal* 45 (1996): 1140–1259; Saul Cornell, *Whose Right to Bear Arms Did the Second Amendment Protect?* (New York: St. Martin's Press, 2000); Stephen P. Halbrook, "The Right of the People or the Power of the State: Bearing Arms, Arming Militias, and the Second Amendment," *Valparaiso University Law Review* 26 (1991): 131–207; Nicholas J. Johnson, *Firearms Law and the Second Amendment* (New York: Wolters Kluwer, 2012); Don B. Kates, "Handgun Prohibition and the Original Meaning of the Second Amendment," *Michigan Law Review* 82 (1983): 204–273; Sanford Levinson, "The Embarrassing Second Amendment," *Yale Law Journal* 99 (1989): 637–659; Glenn Harlan Reynolds, "A Critical Guide to the Second Amendment," *Tennessee Law Review* 62 (1995): 461–512; Robert E. Shalhope, "The Ideological Origins of the Second Amendment," *Journal of American History* 6 (1982): 599–614; William Van Alstyne, "The Second Amendment and the Personal Right to Arms," *Duke Law Journal* 43 (1994): 1236–1255; Eugene Volokh, "The Amazing Vanishing Second Amendment," *New York University Law Review* 73 (1998): 831–840; and Eugene Volokh, "The Commonplace Second Amendment," *New York University Law Review* 73 (1998): 793–821.

Some scholars have arrived at conclusions about the Second Amendment based on historical analyses that have traced the development of the right and the conditions surrounding it. See, for example, Joseph Blocher and Darrell A. H. Miller, *The Positive Second Amendment: Rights, Regulation, and the Future of* Heller (New York: Cambridge University Press, 2018); Saul Cornell and Robert E. Shalhope, *Whose Right to Bear Arms Did the Second Amendment Protect?* (Boston, MA: Bedford/St. Martin's Press, 2000); Brian Doherty, *Gun Control on Trial: Inside the Supreme Court Battle over the Second Amendment* (Washington, DC: Cato Institute, 2008); Joyce Lee Malcolm, *To Keep and Bear Arms: The Origins of an Anglo-American Right* (Cambridge, MA: Harvard University Press, 1996); and H. Richard Uviller and William G. Merkel, *Militia and the Right to Arms: Or How the Second Amendment Fell Silent* (Durham, NC: Duke University Press, 2002); David C. Williams, *The Mythic Meanings of the Second Amendment* (New Haven, CT: Yale University Press, 2003).

Others have examined the right to keep and bear arms from a public policy perspective. See James B. Jacobs, *Can Gun Control Work?* (New York: Oxford University Press, 2002); and John R. Lott, *More Guns, Less Crime: Understanding Crime and Gun-Control Laws* (Chicago: University of Chicago Press, 2010).

For an interesting look at the National Rifle Association and other such groups, see Osha Gray Davidson, *Under Fire: The NRA and the Battle for Gun Control* (Iowa City: University of Iowa Press, 1998).

CHAPTER SIXTEEN

THE RIGHT TO PRIVACY

AMERICANS PLACE A HIGH VALUE on personal privacy. We believe that people have the right to be let alone; unnecessary government intrusion into people's private lives is generally unwelcome. But are the privacy interests of Americans protected by the Constitution?

Many are surprised to learn that privacy was not among the many liberties that the framers explicitly included in the Bill of Rights. In fact, the word *privacy* appears nowhere in the Constitution. Instead, the right to privacy became included among our protected liberties through judicial interpretation. In this chapter we discuss the right to privacy—its origins, constitutional status, and scope.

THE RIGHT TO PRIVACY: FOUNDATIONS

In today's legal and political context, the right to privacy has become almost synonymous with reproductive freedom. The reason may be that the case in which the Court first articulated a constitutional right to privacy, *Griswold v. Connecticut* (1965), involved birth control, and *Roe v. Wade* (1973), a decision coming on the heels of *Griswold*, legalized abortion.

Prior to these cases, the Court had contemplated privacy in somewhat different contexts. Following the common-law dictates that "a man's home is his castle" and all "have the right to be let alone," Louis Brandeis, a future Supreme Court justice, coauthored an 1890 *Harvard Law Review* article asserting that privacy rights should be applied to civil law cases of libel.[1] The article had enormous long-term influence, in no small part because it created a new legal "wrong"—the invasion of privacy.

After Brandeis joined the Court, he continued his quest to see a right to privacy etched into law. Among his best-known attempts was a dissent in ***Olmstead v. United States*** (1928), which involved the ability of federal agents to wiretap telephones without warrants. The Court ruled that neither the Fifth Amendment's protection against self-incrimination nor the Fourth Amendment's search and seizure provision protected individuals against wiretaps. Brandeis dissented, writing that the Fourth and Fifth Amendments prohibited such activity. He noted that the framers of the Constitution conferred on Americans "the right to be let alone—the most comprehensive of rights and the right most valued by civilized men."

Justices of earlier eras, however, had paid attention to a concept that would later become associated with privacy—the concept of liberty. The word *liberty* appears in the due process clauses of the Fifth and Fourteenth Amendments. The Fifth Amendment states that Congress shall not deprive any person of "life, liberty, or property, without due process of law," and the Fourteenth Amendment uses the same wording to apply to the states. In the early 1900s, the Supreme Court began making use of a doctrine known as substantive due process. Under substantive due process, the Court stresses the word *liberty* in the due process clauses to prevent governments from enacting certain kinds of laws. In the early 1900s, those laws were mostly economic; today, they are mostly in the personal privacy context.

Either way, the basic framework is the same: litigants argue that the word *liberty* in the due process clause *implies* the existence of a right that is not enumerated in the Constitution. Examples we will look at soon include the "right to contract" and the "right to privacy." The Court then must determine if the right exists and, if so,

---

[1] Louis Brandeis and Samuel Warren, "The Right of Privacy," *Harvard Law Review* 4 (1890): 193. William L. Prosser notes that Brandeis and Warren wrote this piece in response to the yellow journalism of the day. See William L. Prosser, "Privacy," *California Law Review* 48 (1960): 383–423.

whether it is a "fundamental" right—those the Court believes to be important in the concept of ordered liberty. If the right is not fundamental, the Court will simply ask whether a law is rationally related to a legitimate government interest. Under this rational basis standard, the Court will give high deference to the government and usually uphold its law. If the right is fundamental and the government has "directly and substantially" interfered with it, the Court will invalidate the law unless the government can meet a high standard. In earlier times, that standard was whether there was a "direct relation" between the law and a governmental interest. Today, it is called strict scrutiny. Under it, the Court asks whether the law is necessary to achieve a compelling government interest. These are very high hurdles for the government, as we shall see.

Lochner v. New York (1905) *(excerpted in chapter 10)* provides a famous early example how the Court used substantive due process in the economic sphere. In this case, recall, the Court struck down an 1897 New York law that limited the hours per day and per week that bakery employees could work. The Court said the law was an unreasonable interference with an employer's right of contract, which was protected in the liberty guarantee of the Fourteenth Amendment.

Lochner concerned an economic regulation—the primary target of substantive due process in the early 1900s. But there were some notable exceptions. In **Meyer v. Nebraska** (1923), the justices considered a state law, enacted after World War I, that forbade schools from teaching German and other foreign languages to students below the eighth grade. They invoked a substantive due process approach to strike down the law, reasoning that the word *liberty* in the Fourteenth Amendment protects more than the right to contract. It also covers

> the right of the individual . . . to engage in any of the common occupations of life, to acquire useful knowledge, to marry, establish a home and bring up children, to worship God according to the dictates of his own conscience, and generally to enjoy those privileges long recognized at common law as essential to the orderly pursuit of happiness by free men.

According to the Court, government cannot interfere with these liberties "under the guise of protecting the public interest, by legislative action which is arbitrary or without reasonable relation to some purpose within the competency of the State to that effect."

Meyer and *Lochner* are examples of substantive due process in action. Under this approach, the Court struck down legislation interfering with liberty unless governments could demonstrate a strong connection between the law and the reason for passing it, and the Court's judgment could not be "arbitrary," "capricious," or "unreasonable." To some analysts, this doctrine was the epitome of judicial activism because it allowed the Court to function as "superlegislature," the ultimate decider of what governments can and cannot do.

Through the 1930s the Court used the doctrine of substantive due process to nullify many laws, particularly those—as in *Lochner*—that sought to regulate businesses. The members of the Court were laissez-faire–oriented justices who believed that the government should not interfere with the business of business. During the New Deal, however, substantive due process fell into disrepute because the public demanded government involvement to straighten out the economy. And the Court ultimately revised its approach: the justices no longer treated the right to contract as sacrosanct (or fundamental, in today's parlance). As a result, they would allow states to adopt whatever economic policies they desired if the policies were reasonably related to legitimate government interests. This is the rational basis approach to the Fourteenth Amendment that we mentioned earlier. It differs significantly from the "direction relation" approach of yesteryear or the "compelling interest" approach of today because under it courts generally defer to governments and presume the validity of their policies.

Application of the rational basis test led the Court to uphold legislation such as minimum wage and maximum hours laws, which it had previously struck down on substantive due process—liberty—grounds, even if the laws did not necessarily seem reasonable to the justices. In one case, in fact, the justices characterized a particular state's economic policy as "needless" and "wasteful." They upheld the law anyway, proclaiming, "The day is gone when this Court uses the Due Process Clause of the Fourteenth Amendment to strike down state laws, regulatory of business and industrial conditions, because they may be unwise, improvident, or out of harmony with a particular school of thought."[2] The majority added that if the people did not like the legislation their governments passed, they should "resort to the polls, not to the courts."

---

[2]The case was *Williamson v. Lee Optical Company* (1955). The law at issue prohibited persons other than ophthalmologists and optometrists from fitting, adjusting, adapting, or applying eyeglass lenses and frames.

With this declaration, the Court seemed to strike the death knell for substantive due process. It would no longer substitute its "social and economic beliefs for the judgment of legislative bodies, who are elected to pass laws."[3]

But did the end of the *Lochner* era mean the end of finding fundamental liberty interests outside of economics? No. Justice John Marshall Harlan (II) transported ideas from that era to the privacy realm. Harlan was not an activist justice, and he was certainly no liberal, but he took great offense at the Court's handling of a 1961 case, **Poe v. Ullman**. At issue in *Poe* was the constitutionality of an 1879 Connecticut law prohibiting the use of birth control, even by married couples. A physician challenged the act on behalf of two women who wanted to use contraceptives for health reasons.

The majority of the Court voted to dismiss the case on procedural grounds. Several other justices disagreed with this holding, but Harlan's dissent was memorable. He argued that the Fourteenth Amendment's due process clause could be used to strike the law:

> I consider that this Connecticut
> legislation . . . violates the Fourteenth
> Amendment. . . . [It] involves what, by common
> understanding throughout the English-speaking
> world, must be granted to be the fundamental
> aspect of "liberty," the privacy of the home in
> its most basic sense, and it is this which requires
> that the statute be subjected to "strict scrutiny."

In making this claim, Harlan sought to demonstrate that the concepts of liberty and privacy were constitutionally bound together, that the word *liberty*, as used in the due process clauses, "embraced" a right to privacy. And, because that right was fundamental, laws that touched on liberty/privacy interests, such as the one at issue in *Poe*, must be subjected to "strict scrutiny." This means that the Court should presume that laws infringing on liberty/privacy were unconstitutional unless the state could show that the policies were the least restrictive means (that is, practically necessary) to accomplish a *compelling* interest.

Harlan's opinion was extraordinary in two ways. First, some scholars have pointed out that it resurrected the long-dead (and discredited) doctrine of substantive due process (used in *Lochner*), which the Court had buried in the 1930s. Now Harlan wanted to reinject some substance into the word *liberty*, but with a twist. In his view, rather than implying fundamental economic rights—such as the right to contract—due process

implies fundamental personal liberties. One of those—privacy—provides the second novel aspect of Harlan's opinion. As we have indicated, he was not writing on a blank slate; Brandeis had written about a right to privacy in the contexts of libel and search and seizure. In fact, Harlan cited—with approval—Brandeis's dissent in *Olmstead*. Still, Harlan's application of the doctrine to marital sexual relations was bold. As he wrote, "It is difficult to imagine what is more private or more intimate than a husband and wife's marital relations."

Harlan's assertion (and that by William O. Douglas, another dissenter in *Poe*[4]) of a constitutional and fundamental right to privacy proved too much, too soon for the Court; the majority of the justices were not yet willing to adopt it. But just four years later, in *Griswold v. Connecticut*, a dramatic change took place when the justices suddenly altered their views. More important is what they said about the right to privacy: the majority agreed that it existed, even if they disagreed over where it resides in the Constitution.

Bettmann/Contributor/Getty Images

Dr. C. Lee Buxton, center, medical director for the Planned Parenthood League of Connecticut, and Estelle Griswold, right, executive director of the organization, appear at police headquarters after their arrest. The two were held for violating the state's anticontraception law.

---

[3]*Ferguson v. Skrupa* (1963).

[4]In *Poe*, Douglas wrote, "Though I believe that 'due process' as used in the Fourteenth Amendment includes all of the first eight Amendments, I do not think it is restricted . . . to them. The right 'to marry, establish a home and bring up children' was said in *Meyer v. State of Nebraska* to come within the 'liberty' of the person protected by the Due Process Clause of the Fourteenth Amendment. . . . '[L]iberty' within the purview of the Fifth Amendment includes the right of 'privacy.' . . . This notion of privacy is not drawn from the blue. It emanates from the totality of the constitutional scheme under which we live."

Griswold v. Connecticut

381 U.S. 479 (1965)

http://caselaw.findlaw.com/us-supreme-court/381/479.html

*Oral arguments available at https://www.oyez.org/
    cases/1964/496*

Vote: 7 (Brennan, Clark, Douglas, Goldberg, Harlan,
    Warren, White)
    2 (Black, Stewart)

OPINION OF THE COURT: *Douglas*

CONCURRING OPINIONS: *Goldberg, Harlan, White*

DISSENTING OPINIONS: *Black, Stewart*

In *Poe v. Ullman,* physician C. Lee Buxton tested Connecticut's 1879 law banning contraceptives on behalf of two of his patients. The majority of the Court voted to dismiss the case on procedural grounds, with the opinion for the Court pointing out that no prosecutions under the law had been recorded even though contraceptives were apparently "commonly and notoriously sold in Connecticut drug stores."

Griswold v. Connecticut was virtually a carbon copy of *Poe,* with but a few differences designed to meet some of the shortcomings of the earlier case.[5] Estelle Griswold, the executive director of the Planned Parenthood League of Connecticut, and Buxton opened a birth control clinic in 1961 with the intent of being arrested for violating the same Connecticut law at issue in *Poe.* Three days later, Griswold was arrested for dispensing contraceptives to a married couple.

In the U.S. Supreme Court, Griswold's attorney, Yale Law School professor Thomas Emerson, challenged the Connecticut law on some of the same grounds set forth in the *Poe* dissent. Emerson took a substantive due process approach to the Fourteenth Amendment, arguing that the law infringed on an individual liberty—the right to privacy. He also argued that the right to privacy argument could be found in five amendments: the First, Third, Fourth, Ninth, and Fourteenth.

**MR. JUSTICE DOUGLAS DELIVERED
THE OPINION OF THE COURT.**

. . . [W]e are met with a wide range of questions that implicate the Due Process Clause of the Fourteenth Amendment. . . . We do not sit as a super-legislature to determine the wisdom, need, and

---

[5]For interesting accounts of *Griswold*, see Fred W. Friendly and Martha J. H. Elliot, *The Constitution: That Delicate Balance* (New York: Random House, 1984); and Bernard Schwartz, *The Unpublished Opinions of the Warren Court* (New York: Oxford University Press, 1985).

propriety of laws that touch economic problems, business affairs, or social conditions. This law, however, operates directly on an intimate relation of husband and wife and their physician's role in one aspect of that relation.

The association of people is not mentioned in the Constitution nor in the Bill of Rights. The right to educate a child in a school of the parents' choice—whether public or private or parochial—is also not mentioned. Nor is the right to study any particular subject or any foreign language. Yet the First Amendment has been construed to include certain of those rights.

By *Pierce v. Society of Sisters* [1925], the right to educate one's children as one chooses is made applicable to the States by the force of the First and Fourteenth Amendments. By *Meyer v. Nebraska* [1923], the same dignity is given the right to study the German language in a private school. In other words, the State may not, consistently with the spirit of the First Amendment, contract the spectrum of available knowledge. . . . Without those peripheral rights the specific rights would be less secure. . . .

. . . [Previous] cases suggest that specific guarantees in the Bill of Rights have penumbras, formed by emanations from those guarantees that help give them life and substance. Various guarantees create zones of privacy. The right of association contained in the penumbra of the First Amendment is one. . . . The Third Amendment in its prohibition against the quartering of soldiers "in any house" in time of peace without the consent of the owner is another facet of that privacy. The Fourth Amendment explicitly affirms the "right of the people to be secure in their persons, houses, papers, and effects, against unreasonable searches and seizures." The Fifth Amendment in its Self-Incrimination Clause enables the citizen to create a zone of privacy which government may not force him to surrender to his detriment. The Ninth Amendment provides: "The enumeration in the Constitution, of certain rights, shall not be construed to deny or disparage others retained by the people."

The Fourth and Fifth Amendments were described in *Boyd v. United States* as protection against all governmental invasions "of the sanctity of a man's home and the privacies of life." We recently referred to the Fourth Amendment as creating a "right to privacy, no less important than any other right carefully and particularly reserved to the people."

We have had many controversies over these penumbral rights of "privacy and repose." These cases bear witness that the right of privacy which presses for recognition here is a legitimate one.

The present case, then, concerns a relationship lying within the zone of privacy created by several fundamental constitutional guarantees. And it concerns a law which, in forbidding the *use* of contraceptives rather than regulating their manufacture or sale, seeks to achieve its goals by means having a maximum destructive impact upon that relationship. Such a law cannot stand in light of the familiar principle, so often applied by this Court, that a "governmental purpose to control or prevent activities constitutionally subject to state regulation may not be achieved by means which sweep unnecessarily broadly and thereby invade the area of protected freedoms." Would we allow the police to search the sacred precincts of marital bedrooms for telltale signs of the use of contraceptives? The very idea is repulsive to the notions of privacy surrounding the marriage relationship.

We deal with a right of privacy older than the Bill of Rights—older than our political parties, older than our school system. Marriage is a coming together for better or for worse, hopefully enduring, and intimate to the degree of being sacred. It is an association that promotes a way of life, not causes; harmony in living, not political faiths; bilateral loyalty, not commercial or social projects. Yet it is an association for as noble a purpose as any involved in our prior decisions.

Reversed.

MR. JUSTICE GOLDBERG, WITH WHOM THE CHIEF JUSTICE AND MR. JUSTICE BRENNAN JOIN, CONCURRING.

I agree with the Court that Connecticut's birth-control law unconstitutionally intrudes upon the right of marital privacy, and I join in its opinion and judgment. [I] agree that the concept of liberty protects those personal rights that are fundamental, and is not confined to the specific terms of the Bill of Rights. My conclusion that the concept of liberty is not so restricted and that it embraces the right of marital privacy though that right is not mentioned explicitly in the Constitution is supported both by numerous decisions of this Court, referred to in the Court's opinion, and by the language and history of the Ninth Amendment.

While this Court has had little occasion to interpret the Ninth Amendment, "it cannot be presumed that any clause in the constitution is intended to be without effect." The Ninth Amendment to the Constitution may be regarded by some as a recent discovery and may be forgotten by others, but since 1791 it has been a basic part of the Constitution which we are sworn to uphold. To hold that a right so basic and fundamental and so deep-rooted in our society as the right of privacy in marriage may be infringed because that right is not guaranteed in so many words by the first eight amendments to the Constitution is to ignore the Ninth Amendment and to give it no effect whatsoever. Moreover, a judicial construction that this fundamental right is not protected by the Constitution because it is not mentioned in explicit terms by one of the first eight amendments or elsewhere in the Constitution would violate the Ninth Amendment, which specifically states that "the enumeration in the Constitution, of certain rights shall not be *construed* to deny or disparage others retained by the people" (emphasis added). . . .

Nor am I turning somersaults with history in arguing that the Ninth Amendment is relevant in a case dealing with a State's infringement of a fundamental right. While the Ninth Amendment—and indeed the entire Bill of Rights—originally concerned restrictions upon federal power, the subsequently enacted Fourteenth Amendment prohibits the States as well from abridging fundamental personal liberties. And, the Ninth Amendment, in indicating that not all such liberties are specifically mentioned in the first eight amendments, is surely relevant in showing the existence of other fundamental personal rights, now protected from state, as well as federal, infringement. In sum, the Ninth Amendment simply lends strong support to the view that the "liberty" protected by the Fifth and Fourteenth Amendments from infringement by the Federal Government or the States is not restricted to rights specifically mentioned in the first eight amendments.

In determining which rights are fundamental, judges are not left at large to decide cases in light of their personal and private notions. Rather, they must look to the "traditions and [collective] conscience of our people" to determine whether a principle is "so rooted [there] as to be ranked as fundamental." The inquiry is whether a right involved is of such a character that it cannot be denied without violating those "fundamental principles of liberty and justice which lie at the base of all our civil and political institutions." "Liberty" also "gains content from the emanations of specific [constitutional] guarantees," and "from experience with the requirements of a free society." *Poe v. Ullman* (dissenting opinion of MR. JUSTICE DOUGLAS).

I agree fully with the Court that, applying these tests, the right of privacy is a fundamental personal right, emanating "from the totality of the constitutional scheme under which we live."

MR. JUSTICE HARLAN, CONCURRING IN THE JUDGMENT.

I fully agree with the judgment of reversal, but find myself unable to join the Court's opinion. . . .

In my view, the proper constitutional inquiry in this case is whether this Connecticut statute infringes the Due Process Clause of the Fourteenth Amendment because the enactment violates basic values "implicit in the concept of ordered liberty." For reasons stated at length in my dissenting opinion in *Poe v. Ullman,* I believe that it does. While the relevant inquiry may be aided by resort to one or more of the provisions of the Bill of Rights, it is not dependent on them or any of their radiations. The Due Process Clause of the Fourteenth Amendment stands, in my opinion, on its own bottom.

MR. JUSTICE BLACK, WITH WHOM MR. JUSTICE STEWART JOINS, DISSENTING.

The Court talks about a constitutional "right of privacy" as though there is some constitutional provision or provisions forbidding any law ever to be passed which might abridge the "privacy" of individuals. But there is not. There are, of course, guarantees in certain specific constitutional provisions which are designed in part to protect privacy at certain times and places with respect to certain activities. Such, for example, is the Fourth Amendment's guarantee against "unreasonable searches and seizures." But I think it belittles that Amendment to talk about it as though it protects nothing but "privacy." To treat it that way is to give it a niggardly interpretation, not the kind of liberal reading I think any Bill of Rights provision should be given. . . .

For these reasons I get nowhere in this case by talk about a constitutional "right of privacy" as an emanation from one or more constitutional provisions. I like my privacy as well as the next one, but I am nevertheless compelled to admit that government has a right to invade it unless prohibited by some specific constitutional provision. . . .I cannot agree with the Court's judgment and the reasons it gives for holding this Connecticut law unconstitutional. . . .

The due process argument . . . is based . . . on the premise that this Court is vested with power to invalidate all state laws that it considers to be arbitrary, capricious, unreasonable, or oppressive, or on this Court's belief that a particular state law under scrutiny has no "rational or justifying" purpose, or is offensive to a "sense of fairness and justice." If these formulas based on "natural justice," or others which mean the same thing, are to prevail, they require judges to determine what is or is not constitutional on the basis of their own appraisal of what laws are unwise or unnecessary. The power to make such decisions is of course that of a legislative body. While . . . our Court has constitutional power to strike down statutes, state or federal, that violate commands of the Federal Constitution, I do not believe that we are granted power by the Due Process Clause or any other constitutional provision or provisions to measure constitutionality by our belief that legislation is arbitrary, capricious or unreasonable, or accomplishes no justifiable purpose, or is offensive to our own notions of "civilized standards of conduct." Such an appraisal of the wisdom of legislation is an attribute of the power to make laws, not of the power to interpret them. The use by federal courts of such a formula or doctrine or whatnot to veto federal or state laws simply takes away from Congress and States the power to make laws based on their own judgment of fairness and wisdom and transfers that power to this Court for ultimate determination—a power which was specifically denied to federal courts by the convention that framed the Constitution. . . .

My Brother Goldberg has adopted the recent discovery that the Ninth Amendment as well as the Due Process Clause can be used by this Court as authority to strike down all state legislation which this Court thinks violates "fundamental principles of liberty and justice," or is contrary to the "traditions and [collective] conscience of our people." He also states, without proof satisfactory to me, that in making decisions on this basis judges will not consider "their personal and private notions." One may ask how they can avoid considering them. Our Court certainly has no machinery with which to take a Gallup Poll. And the scientific miracles of this age have not yet produced a gadget which the Court can use to determine what traditions are rooted in the "[collective] conscience of our people." . . . If any broad, unlimited power to hold laws

unconstitutional because they offend what this Court conceives to be the "[collective] conscience of our people" is vested in this Court by the Ninth Amendment, the Fourteenth Amendment, or any other provision of the Constitution, it was not given by the Framers, but rather has been bestowed on the Court by the Court. This fact is perhaps responsible for the peculiar phenomenon that for a period of a century and a half no serious suggestion was ever made that the Ninth Amendment, enacted to protect state powers against federal invasion, could be used as a weapon of federal power to prevent state legislatures from passing laws they consider appropriate to govern local affairs. Use of any such broad, unbounded judicial authority would make of this Court's members a day-to-day constitutional convention. . . .

I realize that many good and able men have eloquently spoken and written, sometimes in rhapsodical strains, about the duty of this Court to keep the Constitution in tune with the times. The idea is that the Constitution must be changed from time to time and that this Court is charged with a duty to make those changes. For myself, I must with all deference reject that philosophy. The Constitution makers knew the need for change and provided for it. Amendments suggested by the people's elected representatives can be submitted to the people or their selected agents for ratification. That method of change was good for our Fathers, and being somewhat old-fashioned I must add it is good enough for me. And so, I cannot rely on the Due Process Clause or the Ninth Amendment or any mysterious and uncertain natural law concept as a reason for striking down this state law. The Due Process Clause with an "arbitrary and capricious" . . . formula was liberally used by this Court to strike down economic legislation in the early decades of this century, threatening, many people thought, the tranquility and stability of the Nation. See, e.g., *Lochner v. New York.* That formula, based on subjective considerations of "natural justice," is no less dangerous when used to enforce this Court's views about personal rights than those about economic rights. I had thought that we had laid that formula, as a means for striking down state legislation, to rest once and for all.

MR. JUSTICE STEWART, WITH WHOM MR. JUSTICE BLACK JOINS, DISSENTING.

Since 1879 Connecticut has had on its books a law which forbids the use of contraceptives by anyone. I think this is an uncommonly silly law. As a practical matter, the law is obviously unenforceable, except in the oblique context of the present case. As a philosophical matter, I believe the use of contraceptives in the relationship of marriage should be left to personal and private choice, based upon each individual's moral, ethical, and religious beliefs. As a matter of social policy, I think professional counsel about methods of birth control should be available to all, so that each individual's choice can be meaningfully made. But we are not asked in this case to say whether we think this law is unwise, or even asinine. We are asked to hold that it violates the United States Constitution. And that I cannot do. . . .

What provision of the Constitution . . . does make this state law invalid? The Court says it is the right of privacy "created by several fundamental constitutional guarantees." With all deference, I can find no such general right of privacy in the Bill of Rights, in any other part of the Constitution, or in any case ever before decided by this Court. . . .

It is the essence of judicial duty to subordinate our own personal views, our own ideas of what legislation is wise and what is not. If, as I should surely hope, the law before us does not reflect the standards of the people of Connecticut, the people of Connecticut can freely exercise their true Ninth and Tenth Amendment rights to persuade their elected representatives to repeal it. That is the constitutional way to take this law off the books.

Griswold was a landmark decision because it found a right to privacy in the Constitution and deemed that right fundamental *(for how the decision affected the appellants, Griswold and Buxton, see Box 16-1)*. Under *Griswold*, governments may place limits on the right to privacy only if those limits survive "strict" constitutional scrutiny, which means that the government must demonstrate that its restrictions are necessary and narrowly tailored to serve a compelling government interest.

The justices, however, disagreed about where that right exists within the Constitution *(see Table 16-1)*. Douglas's opinion for the Court asserted that specific guarantees in the Bill of Rights have penumbras, formed by emanations from First, Third, Fourth, Fifth, and Ninth Amendment guarantees, "that help give them life and substance." In other words, Douglas claimed that even though the Constitution fails to mention privacy, clauses within the document create zones that give rise to the right. In making this argument, Douglas avoided reliance on the Fourteenth Amendment's due process clause. He apparently believed that grounding privacy in that clause would hearken back to the days of *Lochner* and substantive due process, a doctrine he explicitly rejected.

Arthur J. Goldberg, writing for Earl Warren and William J. Brennan Jr., did not dispute Douglas's penumbra theory but chose to emphasize the relevance of the Ninth Amendment. In Goldberg's view, that amendment could be read to contain a right to privacy. His logic was simple: the wording of the amendment, coupled with its history, suggested that it was "proffered to quiet expressed fears that a bill of specifically

Table 16-1	Where Is the Right to Privacy Located in the Constitution? The Splits in *Griswold*
Location of the Privacy Right	**Justices**
First, Third, Fourth, Fifth, and Ninth Amendments	Douglas, Clark
Ninth Amendment	Goldberg, Brennan, Warren
Fourteenth Amendment (due process clause)	Harlan, White
No general right to privacy in the Constitution	Black, Stewart

enumerated rights could not be sufficiently broad to cover all essential rights," including the right to privacy. Harlan reiterated his stance in *Poe* that the liberty interest in the due process clause of the Fourteenth Amendment embraces a right to privacy. In holding to his *Poe* opinion, however, Harlan went one step beyond the Goldberg concurrers. He rejected Douglas's penumbra theory and asserted, "While the relevant inquiry may be aided by resort to one or more of the provisions of the Bill of Rights, it is not dependent on them or any of their radiations." Byron White also filed a concurring opinion lending support to Harlan's due process view of privacy.

The *Griswold* opinions make clear that the justices did not speak with one voice. Seven agreed, more or less, that a right to privacy existed, but they located that right in three distinct constitutional spheres. The other two—Hugo L. Black and Potter Stewart—argued that the Constitution does not contain a general right to privacy, but they did more than that. They also took their colleagues to task for, in their view, reverting to the days of *Lochner* and substantive due process. Black and Stewart maintained that the people, not the courts, should pressure legislatures to change "unwise" laws.

Whether a right to privacy existed and where the right was located, however, were not the only questions raised by *Griswold*. Another issue concerned what this newly found right covered. Clearly, it protected "notions of privacy surrounding the marriage relationship," but beyond that observers could only speculate.

BOX 16-1

Aftermath . . . Estelle Griswold and C. Lee Buxton

After the Supreme Court ruled in their favor, it took Estelle Griswold and Lee Buxton a little more than three months to reopen the New Haven Planned Parenthood birth control clinic. On September 20, 1965, the clinic conducted its first birth control counseling session since its short-lived, ten-day stint in November 1961. This time, however, its activities were legal. Prior to the Supreme Court's ruling, Planned Parenthood legally could offer only transportation services from New Haven to birth control counselors in the neighboring states of Rhode Island and New York, where such counseling was permitted. Because its counseling services were in demand and little opposition was raised, Planned Parenthood soon opened additional clinics in other Connecticut communities. Physicians and staff working in these clinics no longer had to face arrest for dispensing contraceptive devices or information.

Lee Buxton, who served as medical director for the New Haven Clinic as well as chair of the Department of Obstetrics and Gynecology at the Yale University School of Medicine, had fallen into poor health by the time the Supreme Court issued its ruling. Plagued by depression and alcoholism, Buxton took a leave of absence from Yale in 1965. He was hospitalized several times over the next three years and died in July 1969.

Estelle Griswold turned sixty-five years old the day after the Court issued its opinion. She remained in her position as executive director of the Planned Parenthood League of Connecticut, but her tenure there was not a happy one. She had experienced long-standing disagreements with other birth control activists related

Granger

Estelle Griswold, left, and Cornelia D. Jahncke, president of the Planned Parenthood League of Connecticut, read a newspaper account of the 1965 Supreme Court decision establishing the constitutional right to privacy and striking down a Connecticut law banning the distribution of contraceptives.

both to policy issues and to her assertive leadership style. In the summer of 1965, shortly after the Court's ruling, she announced her intention to step down. By the end of that year, she had severed her relationship with the organization. Shortly after she retired, Griswold's husband, Richard, died after a long battle with emphysema. Griswold moved to Fort Myers, Florida, where she devoted her time to campaigning for the legalization of abortion and promoting the rights of senior citizens. She died in 1981 at the age of eighty-one.

Sources: Lori Ann Brass, "An Arrest in New Haven, Contraception and the Right to Privacy," *Yale Medicine* 41, no. 3 (Spring 2007); John W. Johnson, *Griswold v. Connecticut: Birth Control and the Constitutional Right to Privacy* (Lawrence: University Press of Kansas, 2005); Ernest Kohom, "The Department of Obstetrics and Gynecology at Yale: The First One Hundred Fifty Years, from Nathan Smith to Lee Buxton," *Yale Journal of Biology and Medicine* 66 (1993): 85–105; Susan Ware, ed., *Notable American Women: A Biographical Dictionary: Completing the Twentieth Century* (Cambridge, MA: Belknap Press, 2004).

In the remainder of this chapter, we examine the other areas where the Court has applied *Griswold*. We look first at *Griswold*'s role in the issue of abortion and then into its extensions into other private activities. Keep the *Griswold* precedent in mind. To which

interpretation of the right to privacy has the Court subscribed in the cases that follow? Has the Court's approach changed with its increasing conservatism, or do the majority of justices continue to adopt *Griswold*'s basic tenets?

Figure 16-1 Legislative Action on Abortion through the Early 1970s

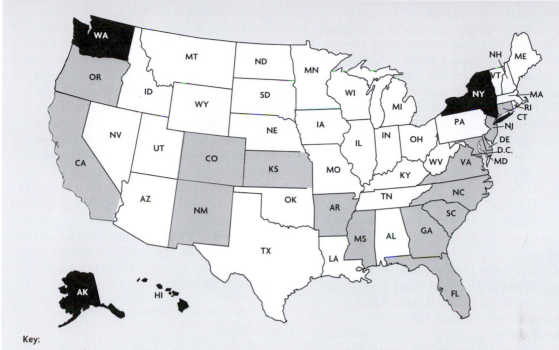

Key:

States in white: Retained existing law, which generally permitted abortions to save the life of the mother only.

States in gray: Altered existing abortion law, between 1966 and 1970, to permit abortion under certain circumstances, such as pregnancies resulting from rape or incest.

States in black: Repealed existing abortion law to allow for some form of "abortion on demand."

REPRODUCTIVE FREEDOM AND THE RIGHT TO PRIVACY: ABORTION

Although many right to privacy issues are hotly debated, few have caused emotional reactions of greater intensity or duration than has the debate over abortion initiated by the Court's decision in *Roe v. Wade* in 1973. Since this decision, abortion has taken center stage in public discourse. It has affected the outcomes of many political races; occupied preeminent places on legislative, executive, and judicial agendas; and become a heated topic for discussion in the nomination proceedings for Supreme Court and lower federal court judges.

What is particularly intriguing about the issue is that the Court generated the furor. Prior to the decision in *Roe*, abortion was not as salient a political issue

as it is today. As Figure 16-1 shows, many states had on their books laws enacted in the late 1800s that permitted abortion only to save the life of the mother. Other states had reformed their legislation in the 1960s to include legal abortion for pregnancies resulting from rape or incest or those in which there was a high likelihood of a deformed baby. The majority of states defined performing or obtaining an abortion, under all other circumstances, as criminal offenses. These conditions did not mean that states were under no pressure to change their laws. During the 1960s a growing pro-choice movement, consisting of groups such as the American Civil Liberties Union and the National Association for the Repeal of Abortion Laws (NARAL, later renamed the National Abortion Rights Action League and today known as NARAL Pro-Choice America), sought to persuade states to legalize the procedure fully—that is, allow abortion on demand.

When only a handful of states even considered taking such action, attorneys and leaders of the pro-choice movement supplemented their legislative lobbying with litigation, initiating dozens of suits in federal and state courts. These cases challenged restrictive abortion laws on several grounds, including the First Amendment's freedoms of association and speech for doctors (and patients) and the Fourteenth Amendment's equal protection clause (discrimination against women). But the most commonly invoked legal ground was *Griswold*'s right to privacy. Because it was unclear to attorneys which clause of the Constitution generated the right to privacy, in many cases pro-choice lawyers covered their bases by arguing on all three specific grounds. Their larger point was clear: the right to privacy was broad enough to encompass the right to obtain an abortion. Moreover, because the right to privacy was "fundamental," logic would hold that the right to obtain an abortion was also fundamental, meaning that states could proscribe the procedure only with a compelling interest. Such an interest, pro-choice attorneys asserted, did not exist.

The result of this legal activity was an avalanche of litigation. Pro-choice groups had flooded the U.S. courts with lawsuits—some on behalf of doctors, some for women—challenging both major kinds of abortion laws: those that permitted abortion only to save the life of the mother and those that allowed abortion in cases of rape or incest or to save the life of the mother. They were hoping that the Supreme Court would hear at least one.

Their wish was granted when the Court agreed to hear arguments in December of 1971 in two cases, *Roe v. Wade*, a challenge to a Texas law representing the most restrictive kinds of abortion laws, and *Doe v. Bolton*, a challenge to a Georgia law representing the newer, less restrictive laws. Because the Court had problems resolving these cases, they were reargued at the beginning of the next term.

In the meantime, the justices handed down a decision that had some bearing on the debate. In 1972 the Court struck down a Massachusetts law that prohibited the sale of contraceptives to unmarried people. Writing for a six-person majority (with only Chief Justice Warren Burger dissenting) in *Eisenstadt v. Baird*, Justice Brennan asserted that the law violated the "rights of single people" under the Fourteenth Amendment's equal protection clause. But, in dicta, he went much further:

If under *Griswold* the distribution of contraceptives to married persons cannot be prohibited, a ban on distribution to unmarried persons would be equally impermissible. It is true that in *Griswold* the right of privacy in question inhered in the marital relationship. Yet the marital couple is not an independent entity with a mind and heart of its own, but an association of two individuals each with separate intellectual and emotional makeup. If the right of privacy means anything, it is the right of the individual, married or single, to be free from unwarranted governmental intrusion into matters so fundamentally affecting a person as the decision whether to bear or beget a child.

Whether Brennan wrote this with *Roe* and *Doe* in mind we do not know, but clearly *Eisenstadt* heartened pro-choice forces. Their optimism was not misplaced, for, on January 22, 1973, when the Court handed down its decisions in *Roe* and *Doe*, they had won. As you read *Roe*, pay particular attention to the Court's logic. On what grounds did it strike down the Texas law?

Roe v. Wade

410 U.S. 113 (1973)
http://caselaw.findlaw.com/us-supreme-court/410/113.html
*Oral arguments available at https://www.oyez.org/
    cases/1971/70-18*
Vote: 7 (Blackmun, Brennan, Burger, Douglas, Marshall,
    Powell, Stewart)
    2 (Rehnquist, White)

OPINION OF THE COURT: *Blackmun*

CONCURRING OPINIONS: *Burger, Douglas, Stewart*

DISSENTING OPINIONS: *Rehnquist, White*

In August 1969 Norma McCorvey, a twenty-one-year-old carnival worker living in Texas, claimed to have been raped and to be pregnant as a result of that rape.[6] Her doctor refused to perform an abortion, citing an 1857 Texas law, revised in 1879, that made

---

[6]We draw this discussion from the papers of William J. Brennan Jr., Manuscript Division, Library of Congress; Lee Epstein and Joseph F. Kobylka, *The Supreme Court and Legal Change* (Chapel Hill: University of North Carolina Press, 1992); Lee Epstein and Jack Knight, *The Choices Justices Make* (Washington, DC: CQ Press, 1998); and Marion Faux, *Roe v. Wade* (New York: Macmillan, 1988). For other accounts, see Richard C. Cortner, *The Supreme Court and Civil Liberties Policy* (Palo Alto, CA: Mayfield, 1975); and Eva Rubin, *Abortion, Politics, and the Courts* (Westport, CT: Greenwood Press, 1987).

it a crime to "procure an abortion" unless it was necessary to save the life of a mother. He provided her with the name of a lawyer who handled adoptions. The lawyer, in turn, sent her to two other attorneys, Linda Coffee and Sarah Weddington, who he knew were interested in challenging the Texas law.

Coffee and Weddington went after the Texas law with a vengeance, challenging it on all possible grounds: privacy, women's rights, due process, and so forth. Their efforts paid off, and a three-judge district court panel ruled in their favor, mostly on Ninth Amendment privacy grounds. But because the district court ruling did not overturn the state law, McCorvey, using the pseudonym Jane Roe, and her attorneys appealed to the U.S. Supreme Court.

Once the Court agreed to hear the case, pro-choice and pro-life forces mobilized. On the pro-choice side, the ACLU and other groups helped Weddington and Coffee, who had never appeared before the Court, prepare their briefs and arguments. These groups also lined up numerous amici, ranging from the American College of Obstetricians and Gynecologists to the Planned Parenthood Federation to the American Association of University Women. In general, the pro-choice side wanted to convince the Court that abortion was a fundamental right under the *Griswold* doctrine. Unless Texas could provide a compelling and narrowly drawn interest, the law should fall. It also presented a mass of data indicating that physical and mental health risks are associated with restrictive abortion laws.

The state countered with arguments concerning the rights of fetuses. In its brief, it devoted twenty-four pages, along with nine photographs of fetuses at various stages of development, to depict the "humanness" of the unborn and to support its argument that a state has a compelling interest in protecting human life. The state's position was supported by several pro-life organizations, including the National Right to Life Committee and the League for Infants, Fetuses, and the Elderly, as well as by groups of doctors and nurses.

On December 13, 1971, the Supreme Court heard oral arguments, and three days later it met to decide the abortion cases. Only seven justices were present because President Richard Nixon's newest appointees, Lewis F. Powell Jr. and William H. Rehnquist, had not participated in oral arguments. Of the seven participating justices, a four-person majority (Brennan, Douglas, Thurgood Marshall, and Stewart) thought the abortion laws should be stricken, although for somewhat different reasons. Moreover, they were unsure about the "time problem"—whether a woman should be able to obtain an abortion anytime during her pregnancy or over a more limited period, such as the first six months. White came down most definitively in favor of the pro-life position. Burger and Harry A. Blackmun, who had joined the Court in 1969 and 1970, respectively, were less decisive; the chief justice leaned toward upholding laws prohibiting abortion, and Blackmun leaned toward the pro-choice camp. Although there was disagreement over the reasons the laws were unconstitutional and over the time frame for abortions, the result was clear: the pro-choice side would win by a 5–2

or 4–3 vote, depending on how Blackmun voted. Burger assigned the opinion to Blackmun, whom he had known since grade school.

This (mis)assignment triggered a series of events. The first was an irate letter from Douglas to Burger, in which Douglas had two bones to pick: first, as the senior member of the majority, he should have assigned the opinion, and, second, Blackmun should not have received the assignment in any event because Douglas's vote tallies put him in the minority. Burger responded that he would not change the assignment. He said:

> At the close of discussion of this case, I remarked to the Conference that there were, literally, not enough columns to mark up an accurate reflection of the voting. . . .I therefore marked down no votes and said this was a case that would have to stand or fall on the writing, when it was done. . . .This is still my view of how to handle . . . this sensitive case.

Still uncertain of how Blackmun would dispose of the case and of what rationale he would use, some of the justices began preparing opinions. Indeed, it took Douglas only a few weeks to circulate a memorandum to Brennan, who responded with some suggestions for revision and the admonition that Douglas hold on to the opinion until Blackmun circulated his.

It was a long wait. In mid-May 1972, Blackmun sent around his first draft in *Roe*—a draft that came to the "right" result in Brennan's and Douglas's minds but did so for the wrong (that is, narrowest possible) reason: that the restrictive Texas abortion law was void because it was vague, not because it interfered with any fundamental right. The four pro-choicers were disappointed and urged Blackmun to recast his draft. In so doing, they raised the opinion assignment issue again. Douglas wrote to Blackmun:

> In *Roe v. Wade,* my notes confirm what Bill Brennan wrote yesterday in his memo to you—that abortion statutes were invalid save as they required that an abortion be performed by a licensed physician within a limited time after conception.
>
> That was the clear view of a majority of the seven who heard argument. My notes also indicate that the Chief had the opposed view, which made it puzzling as to why he made the assignment at all except that he indicated he might affirm on vagueness. My notes indicate that Byron [White] was not firmly settled and that you might join the majority of four. So I think we should meet what Bill Brennan calls the "core constitutional issue."

At the same time, Douglas and the others were ready to sign Blackmun's draft, believing that it represented the best they could do.

They were happier with Blackmun's effort in *Doe v. Bolton,* the Georgia abortion case, because it adopted much of Douglas's and Brennan's beliefs about the importance of privacy and women's rights. Where they thought Blackmun went astray was in exploring the state's interest in protecting life. In this version, he stressed the point that somewhere around quickening (the point in pregnancy when fetal movement is first felt), a woman's right to privacy is no longer "unlimited. It must be balanced against the state. We cannot automatically strike down . . . features of the Georgia statute simply because they restrict any right on the part of the woman to have an abortion at will." Despite the qualms Brennan and Douglas had over such a balancing approach, they planned to sign the opinion; it led Blackmun to the "right" result. Douglas went so far as to "congratulate" Blackmun on his "fine job" and expressed the hope that "we can agree to get the cases down this Term, so that we can spend our energies next Term on other matters."[7]

Just when it appeared that a five-person majority would coalesce around Blackmun's opinion, on May 31 Burger initiated efforts to have the case reargued. Ostensibly, his reason was that "[t]hese cases . . . are not as simple for me as they appear for the others." He also "complained that part of his problem . . . resulted from the poor quality of oral argument." Brennan, Douglas, Stewart, and Marshall disagreed. In their view, Burger pushed for reargument because he was displeased with Blackmun's opinion in *Doe* and thought his side would stand a better chance of victory next term when Powell and Rehnquist would participate in oral arguments. Douglas later suggested that Burger believed the *Doe* opinion would prove embarrassing to President Nixon's reelection campaign and sought to minimize the damage. The same day Burger issued his memo, Blackmun also suggested that the cases be reargued. In a memo to conference, he wrote, "Although it would prove costly to me personally, in the light of energy and hours expended, I have now concluded, somewhat reluctantly, that reargument in both cases at an early date in the next term, would perhaps be advisable." Despite Brennan's and Douglas's attempts to thwart this action, after White and the two new appointees voted with Burger, on the last day of the 1971 term the Court ordered rearguments in both *Roe* and *Doe.*[8]

---

[7]This memo was, in part, a response to Burger's (and Blackmun's) suggestion that the cases be reargued.

[8]Both Brennan and Douglas wrote letters to Blackmun attempting to convince him that the cases should not be reargued. When Blackmun did not agree, Douglas warned Burger, "If the vote of Conference is to reargue, then I will file a statement telling what is happening to us and the tragedy it entails." He also accused Burger, in a memo to conference, of trying "to bend the Court to his will" and imperiling "the integrity of the institution." Douglas never carried through on his threat to take the matter public, but the *Washington Post* carried a story about it.

MR. JUSTICE BLACKMUN DELIVERED THE OPINION OF THE COURT.

We forthwith acknowledge our awareness of the sensitive and emotional nature of the abortion controversy, of the vigorous opposing views, even among physicians, and of the deep and seemingly absolute convictions that the subject inspires. One's philosophy, one's experiences, one's exposure to the raw edges of human existence, one's religious training, one's attitudes toward life and family and their values, and the moral standards one establishes and seeks to observe, are all likely to influence and to color one's thinking and conclusions about abortion.

In addition, population growth, pollution, poverty, and racial overtones tend to complicate and not to simplify the problem.

Our task, of course, is to resolve the issue by constitutional measurement, free of emotion and of predilection. We seek earnestly to do this, and, because we do, we have inquired into, and in this opinion place some emphasis upon, medical and medical-legal history and what that history reveals about man's attitudes toward the abortion procedure over the centuries. . . .

The principal thrust of appellant's attack on the Texas statutes is that they improperly invade a right, said to be possessed by the pregnant woman, to choose to terminate her pregnancy. Appellant would discover this right in the concept of personal "liberty" embodied in the Fourteenth Amendment's Due Process Clause in personal, marital, familial, and sexual privacy said to be protected by the Bill of Rights or its penumbras, see *Griswold v. Connecticut* (1965), or among those rights reserved to the people by the Ninth Amendment, *Griswold v. Connecticut.* . . .

It perhaps is not generally appreciated that the restrictive criminal abortion laws in effect in a majority of States today are of relatively recent vintage. Those laws, generally proscribing abortion or its attempt at any time during pregnancy except when necessary to preserve the pregnant woman's life, are not of ancient or even of common-law origin. Instead, they derive from statutory changes effected, for the most part, in the latter half of the 19th century. . . .

Three reasons have been advanced to explain historically the enactment of criminal abortion laws in the 19th century and to justify their continued existence.

It has been argued occasionally that these laws were the product of a Victorian social concern to discourage illicit sexual conduct. Texas, however, does not advance this justification in the present case, and it appears that no court or commentator has taken the argument seriously. . . .

A second reason is concerned with abortion as a medical procedure. When most criminal abortion laws were first enacted, the procedure was a hazardous one for the woman. This was particularly true prior to the development of antisepsis. . . .Thus, it has been argued that a State's real concern in enacting a criminal abortion law was to protect the pregnant woman, that is, to restrain her from submitting to a procedure that placed her life in serious jeopardy.

Modern medical techniques have altered this situation. . . . Consequently, any interest of the State in protecting the woman from an inherently hazardous procedure, except when it would be equally dangerous for her to forgo it, has largely disappeared. Of course, important state interests in the areas of health and medical standards do remain. The State has a legitimate interest in seeing to it that abortion, like any other medical procedure, is performed under circumstances that insure maximum safety for the patient. . . . Moreover, the risk to the woman increases as her pregnancy continues. Thus, the State retains a definite interest in protecting the woman's own health and safety when an abortion is proposed at a late stage of pregnancy.

The third reason is the State's interest—some phrase it in terms of duty—in protecting prenatal life. Some of the argument for this justification rests on the theory that a new human life is present from the moment of conception. The State's interest and general obligation to protect life then extends, it is argued, to prenatal life. Only when the life of the pregnant mother herself is at stake, balanced against the life she carries within her, should the interest of the embryo or fetus not prevail. Logically, of course, a legitimate state interest in this area need not stand or fall on acceptance of the belief that life begins at conception or at some other point prior to live birth. In assessing the State's interest, recognition may be given to the less rigid claim that as long as at least *potential* life is involved, the State may assert interests beyond the protection of the pregnant woman alone. . . .

It is with these interests, and the weight to be attached to them, that this case is concerned.

The Constitution does not explicitly mention any right of privacy. In a line of decisions, however, the Court has recognized that a right of personal privacy, or a guarantee of certain areas or zones of privacy, does exist under the Constitution. . . . These decisions make it clear that only personal rights that can be deemed "fundamental" or "implicit in the concept of ordered liberty" are included in this guarantee of personal privacy. They also make it clear that the right has some extension to activities relating to marriage, procreation, family relationships, and child rearing and education.

This right of privacy, whether it be founded in the Fourteenth Amendment's concept of personal liberty and restrictions upon state action, as we feel it is, or in the Ninth Amendment's reservation of rights to the people, is broad enough to encompass a woman's decision whether or not to terminate her pregnancy. The detriment that the State would impose upon the pregnant woman by denying this choice altogether is apparent. Specific and direct harm medically diagnosable even in early pregnancy may be involved. Maternity, or additional offspring, may force upon the woman a distressful life and future. Psychological harm may be imminent. Mental and physical health may be taxed by child care. There is also the

distress, for all concerned, associated with the unwanted child, and there is the problem of bringing a child into a family already unable, psychologically and otherwise, to care for it. In other cases, as in this one, the additional difficulties and continuing stigma of unwed motherhood may be involved. All these are factors the woman and her responsible physician necessarily will consider in consultation.

On the basis of elements such as these, appellant and some *amici* argue that the woman's right is absolute and that she is entitled to terminate her pregnancy at whatever time, in whatever way, and for whatever reason she alone chooses. With this we do not agree. Appellant's arguments that Texas either has no valid interest at all in regulating the abortion decision, or no interest strong enough to support any limitation upon the woman's sole determination, are unpersuasive. The Court's decisions recognizing a right of privacy also acknowledge that some state regulation in areas protected by that right is appropriate. [A] State may properly assert important interests in safeguarding health, in maintaining medical standards, and in protecting potential life. At some point in pregnancy, these respective interests become sufficiently compelling to sustain regulation of the factors that govern the abortion decision. The privacy right involved, therefore, cannot be said to be absolute. . . .

We . . . conclude that the right of personal privacy includes the abortion decision, but that this right is not unqualified and must be considered against important state interests in regulation. . . .

Texas urges that . . . life begins at conception and is present throughout pregnancy, and that, therefore, the State has a compelling interest in protecting that life from and after conception. We need not resolve the difficult question of when life begins. When those trained in the respective disciplines of medicine, philosophy, and theology are unable to arrive at any consensus, the judiciary, at this point in the development of man's knowledge, is not in a position to speculate as to the answer. . . .

[B]y adopting one theory of life, Texas may [not] override the rights of the pregnant woman that are at stake. [The] State does have an important and legitimate interest in preserving and protecting the health of the pregnant woman, whether she be a resident of the State or a non-resident who seeks medical consultation and treatment there, and that it has still another important and legitimate interest in protecting the potentiality of human life. These interests are separate and distinct. Each grows in substantiality as the woman approaches term and, at a point during pregnancy, each becomes "compelling."

With respect to the State's important and legitimate interest in the health of the mother, the "compelling" point, in the light of present medical knowledge, is at approximately the end of the first trimester. This is so because of the now-established medical fact . . . that until the end of the first trimester mortality in abortion may be less than mortality in normal childbirth. It follows that, from and after this point, a State may regulate the abortion procedure to the extent that the regulation reasonably relates to the preservation and protection of maternal health. Examples of permissible state regulation in this area are requirements as to the qualifications of the person who is to perform the abortion; as to the licensure of that person; as to the facility in which the procedure is to be performed, that is, whether it must be a hospital or may be a clinic or some other place of less-than-hospital status; as to the licensing of the facility; and the like.

This means, on the other hand, that, for the period of pregnancy prior to this "compelling" point, the attending physician, in consultation with his patient, is free to determine, without regulation by the State, that, in his medical judgment, the patient's pregnancy should be terminated. If that decision is reached, the judgment may be effectuated by an abortion free of interference by the State.

With respect to the State's important and legitimate interest in potential life, the "compelling" point is at viability. This is so because the fetus then presumably has the capability of meaningful life outside the mother's womb. State regulation protective of fetal life after viability thus has both logical and biological justifications. If the State is interested in protecting fetal life after viability, it may go so far as to proscribe abortion during that period, except when it is necessary to preserve the life or health of the mother.

Measured against these standards, . . . the Texas [law] . . . , in restricting legal abortions to those "procured or attempted by medical advice for the purpose of saving the life of the mother," sweeps too broadly. The statute makes no distinction between abortions performed early in pregnancy and those performed later, and it limits to a single reason, "saving" the mother's life, the legal justification for the procedure. The statute, therefore, cannot survive the constitutional attack made upon it here. . . .

To summarize . . . :

1. A state criminal abortion statute of the current Texas type, that excepts from criminality only a *life-saving* procedure on behalf of the mother, without regard to pregnancy stage and without recognition of the other interests involved, is violative of the Due Process Clause of the Fourteenth Amendment.

   a. For the stage prior to approximately the end of the first trimester, the abortion decision and its effectuation must be left to the medical judgment of the pregnant woman's attending physician.

   b. For the stage subsequent to approximately the end of the first trimester, the State, in promoting its interest in the health of the mother, may, if it chooses, regulate the abortion procedure in ways that are reasonably related to maternal health.

   c. For the stage subsequent to viability, the State in promoting its interest in the potentiality of human life may, if it chooses, regulate, and even proscribe,

abortion except where it is necessary, in appropriate medical judgment, for the preservation of the life or health of the mother. . . .

This holding, we feel, is consistent with the relative weights of the respective interests involved, with the lessons and examples of medical and legal history, with the lenity of the common law, and with the demands of the profound problems of the present day. The decision leaves the State free to place increasing restrictions on abortion as the period of pregnancy lengthens, so long as those restrictions are tailored to the recognized state interests. The decision vindicates the right of the physician to administer medical treatment according to his professional judgment up to the points where important state interests provide compelling justifications for intervention. Up to those points, the abortion decision in all its aspects is inherently, and primarily, a medical decision, and basic responsibility for it must rest with the physician. If an individual practitioner abuses the privilege of exercising proper medical judgment, the usual remedies, judicial and intra-professional, are available.[9]

Affirmed in part and reversed in part.

MR. JUSTICE REHNQUIST, DISSENTING.

. . . I have difficulty in concluding, as the Court does, that the right of "privacy" is involved in this case. Texas, by the statute here challenged, bars the performance of a medical abortion by a licensed physician on a plaintiff such as Roe. A transaction resulting in an operation such as this is not "private" in the ordinary usage of that word. Nor is the "privacy" that the Court finds here even a distant relative of the freedom from searches and seizures protected by the Fourth Amendment to the Constitution, which the Court has referred to as embodying a right to privacy.

If the Court means by the term "privacy" no more than that the claim of a person to be free from unwanted state regulation of consensual transactions may be a form of "liberty" protected by the

---

[9]*Authors' note:* In *Doe*, decided the same day as *Roe*, the Court reviewed a challenge to the newer abortion laws some states enacted in the 1960s. While Texas permitted abortion only to save a mother's life, Georgia allowed it under the following circumstances: (1) when a "duly licensed Georgia physician" determined in "his best clinical judgment" that carrying the baby to term would injure the mother's life or health; (2) when a high likelihood existed that the fetus would be born with a serious deformity; and (3) when the pregnancy was the result of rape. The law contained other requirements, the most stringent of which was that two other doctors agree with the judgment of the one performing the abortion. Reiterating his opinion in *Roe*, Blackmun struck down the Georgia law as a violation of Fourteenth Amendment guarantees. Once again, six other members of the Court agreed with his conclusion.

Fourteenth Amendment, there is no doubt that similar claims have been upheld in our earlier decisions on the basis of that liberty. I agree . . . that the "liberty," against deprivation of which without due process the Fourteenth Amendment protects, embraces more than the rights found in the Bill of Rights. But that liberty is not guaranteed absolutely against deprivation, only against deprivation without due process of law. The test traditionally applied in the area of social and economic legislation is whether or not a law such as that challenged has a rational relation to a valid state objective. . . .The Due Process Clause of the Fourteenth Amendment undoubtedly does place a limit, albeit a broad one, on legislative power to enact laws such as this. If the Texas statute were to prohibit an abortion even where the mother's life is in jeopardy, I have little doubt that such a statute would lack a rational relation to a valid state objective. . . .But the Court's sweeping invalidation of any restrictions on abortion during the first trimester is impossible to justify under that standard, and the conscious weighing of competing factors that the Court's opinion apparently substitutes for the established test is far more appropriate to a legislative judgment than to a judicial one.

MR. JUSTICE WHITE, WITH WHOM MR. JUSTICE REHNQUIST JOINS, DISSENTING.

With all due respect, I dissent. I find nothing in the language or history of the Constitution to support the Court's judgment. The Court simply fashions and announces a new constitutional right for pregnant women and, with scarcely any reason or authority for its action, invests that right with sufficient substance to override most existing state abortion statutes. The upshot is that the people and the legislatures of the 50 States are constitutionally disentitled to weigh the relative importance of the continued existence and development of the fetus, on the one hand, against a spectrum of possible impacts on the mother, on the other hand. As an exercise of raw judicial power, the Court perhaps has authority to do what it does today; but in my view its judgment is an improvident and extravagant exercise of the power of judicial review that the Constitution extends to this Court. . . .

In a sensitive area such as this, involving as it does issues over which reasonable men may easily and heatedly differ, I cannot accept the Court's exercise of its clear power of choice by interposing a constitutional barrier to state efforts to protect human life and by investing mothers and doctors with the constitutionally protected right to exterminate it. This issue, for the most part, should be left with the people and to the political processes the people have devised to govern their affairs.

Justice Blackmun's decisions in *Roe* and *Doe* were a tour de force on the subject of abortion. They provided a comprehensive history of government regulation of abortion and reviewed in some detail arguments for and against the procedure.[10] Most important was his conclusion: the right to privacy "is broad enough to encompass a woman's decision whether or not to terminate a pregnancy." Behind this assertion are several ideas. First, the Court, while not rejecting a Ninth Amendment theory of privacy, preferred to locate the right in the Fourteenth Amendment's due process clause, an approach suggested by Justices Harlan and White in their concurring opinions in *Griswold* (see Table 16-1). To put it another way, under the Court's approach the fundamental right to privacy follows from the "liberty" guaranteed in the due process clause, and that personal liberty includes the fundamental right to terminate a pregnancy.

Second, because the Court held that women have a fundamental right to abortion, it would use a strict scrutiny/a compelling interest test to assess the constitutionality of restrictions on that right. Under that approach, the state can burden a fundamental right—here the right to abortion—only if it has a compelling interest and its regulation is narrowly tailored to accommodate that interest. For the reasons Blackmun gave in his opinion, the state's interest in protecting the woman's health becomes compelling in the second trimester, and so it may regulate in ways that "are reasonably related to the mother's health." Its interest in protecting the "potentiality of human life" becomes compelling in the third trimester, and so it may regulate or even proscribe abortions at this point. This became known as the trimester approach to abortion (*see Table 16-2*).

In their dissents, Justices White and Rehnquist lambasted the trimester scheme, as well as almost every other aspect of the opinion. They thought it relied on "raw judicial power" to reach an "extravagant" and "improvident" decision. Rehnquist found that the Court's use of a compelling interest test to assess statutes under the Fourteenth Amendment's due process clause represented a return to the discredited doctrine of substantive due process as expressed in *Lochner v. New York*, a complaint that echoed Black's dissent in *Griswold*. Rehnquist would have preferred that the Court adopt a rational basis approach to the abortion right, as it had to regulations challenged on due process grounds after the fall of substantive due process. Under this approach, the Court would have to decide only whether the government had acted reasonably to achieve a legitimate government objective. Using a rational basis approach, as you can imagine, the Court generally defers to the

---

[10]Our excerpt omits the long history. For the full version see FindLaw at http://caselaw.findlaw.com/us-supreme-court/410/113.html.

Table 16-2	The *Roe v. Wade* Trimester Framework	
Stage of Pregnancy	**Degree of Permissible State Regulation of the Decision to Terminate Pregnancy**
Prior to the end of the first trimester (approximately months 1–3)	Almost none: "[T]he abortion decision and its effectuation must be left to [the woman and] the medical judgment of the pregnant woman's attending physician."
The end of the first trimester through "viability" (approximately months 4–6)	Some: "[T]he state, in promoting its interest in the health of the mother, may, if it chooses, regulate the abortion procedure in ways that are reasonably related to maternal health." But it cannot prohibit abortions.
Subsequent to viability (approximately months 7–9)	High: "[T]he state, in promoting its interest in the potentiality of human life, may, if it chooses, regulate, and even proscribe, abortion except where necessary, in appropriate medical judgment, for the preservation of the life or health of the mother."

government and presumes the validity of the government's action. Had the Court adopted this approach to the abortion right, it would have upheld the Texas and Georgia restrictions. White, joined by Rehnquist, thought the Court had gone well beyond the scope of its powers and of the text and history of the Constitution to generate a policy statement that smacked of judicial activism. To White, it was up to the people and their elected officials, not the Court, to determine the fate of abortion.

As Blackmun's opinion was nearly two years in the making, the other justices knew that it would be a comprehensive statement. Outsiders, however, were shocked; few expected such an opinion from a Nixon appointee. But Blackmun's opinion was not the only surprise. Burger's decision to go along with the majority also startled many observers. Moreover, White and Stewart cast rather puzzling votes given their opinions in *Griswold*. Stewart had dissented in *Griswold*, asserting that the Constitution does not guarantee a general right to privacy. If he believed that, how could he agree to the creation of the right to obtain legal abortions, a right that rested on privacy? White, on the other hand, had been in the majority in *Griswold*. But for him, apparently, the right to privacy was not broad enough to cover abortion.

What explains the justices' positions in *Roe* and *Doe* are matters of speculation, for, as Blackmun once noted, it is always hard to predict how a new justice will come down on the abortion issue. What is not a matter of speculation is that the responses to *Roe*—both positive and negative—were (and still are) among the strongest in the Court's history.

Reaction came from all quarters of American life. Some legal scholars applauded the *Roe* opinion, asserting that it indicated the Court's sensitivity to changing times. Others ripped it to shreds. They called

the trimester scheme unworkable and said that, as medical technology advanced, viability would come earlier in pregnancy. Others attacked the decision's use of the Fourteenth Amendment, agreeing with Rehnquist that it was a retreat to pre–New Deal days. Still others claimed it usurped the intention of *Griswold*. Legal scholar John Hart Ely wrote that a right to privacy against "governmental snooping" is legitimate, but a general freedom of "autonomy"—"to live one's life without governmental interference"—goes beyond the scope of *Griswold*.[11] Even Norma McCorvey (the Jane Roe in *Roe v. Wade*) surprisingly became an active critic of the decision (*see Box 16-2*).

Roe also divided the political community. Some legislators were relieved that the Court, and not they, had handled this political hot potato. Others were outraged on moral grounds (believing that abortion is murder) and still others on constitutional grounds (thinking that abortion rights should be a matter of public policy for legislators, not judges, to determine).

The public was split over its support for the Court's ruling, with about 50 percent of Americans supporting it and the rest either opposing it or offering no opinion. But divisions over abortion rights did not come about as a result of *Roe*. Political scientists Charles Franklin and Liane Kosaki show that all *Roe* did was intensify basic divisions over abortion: those who were pro-choice before the decision became even more so, and the same held true for those on the pro-life side.[12] Those divisions

[11]John Hart Ely, "The Wages of Crying Wolf: A Comment on *Roe v. Wade*," *Yale Law Journal* 82 (1973): 920.

[12]Charles H. Franklin and Liane C. Kosaki, "The Republican Schoolmaster: The Supreme Court, Public Opinion, and Abortion," *American Political Science Review* 83 (1989): 751–772. The Gallup Poll data cited in the paragraph are available at https://news.gallup.com/poll/1576/abortion.aspx.

BOX 16-2

Aftermath . . . Norma McCorvey

The life of Norma McCorvey, the pregnant carnival worker who, as Jane Roe, challenged Texas's abortion laws in the Supreme Court, took several interesting turns after *Roe v. Wade* was handed down.

At first, McCorvey's personal life was relatively untouched by the decision. She did not have an abortion, but gave her baby up for adoption. She remained anonymous, continuing to lead a life that included poverty, homelessness, drug and alcohol addiction, petty crimes, and attempted suicide. Then, in the 1980s McCorvey went public and announced that she was the real "Jane Roe." She also confessed that she had lied at the time of her case when she claimed that her pregnancy was the result of rape.

McCorvey worked for several years in Dallas abortion clinics, using her wages to help support her drug habit. She also dabbled in New Age religions and the occult and entered a romantic relationship with a store clerk who had caught her shoplifting.

In 1995 Operation Rescue, a Christian-based anti-abortion activist group, moved its headquarters to Dallas, taking office space next door to the abortion clinic where McCorvey worked. The Reverend Philip "Flip" Benham, an Operation Rescue leader, and other members of the group befriended McCorvey. Subsequently, she underwent a religious conversion, became an evangelical Christian, and joined Benham's nondenominational Hillcrest Church. Her 1995 baptism in a backyard swimming pool was nationally televised.

McCorvey left the abortion clinic and began working for Operation Rescue, proclaiming, "I don't have to go to the death camps anymore, to earn six bucks an hour." McCorvey also founded an organization, Roe No More Ministry, that provides information to anti-abortion groups. She experienced a second religious conversion in 1998 when she became a Roman Catholic. In 2000 McCorvey signed her name to a lawsuit asking the federal courts to declare that women seeking abortions have the right to be told that they are carrying a human being and to be shown a sonogram of the fetus. The lawsuit was unsuccessful.

McCorvey participated in numerous pro-life rallies and was arrested protesting a speech President

AP Photo/Ron Heflin

Norma McCorvey stands with nine-year-old Meredith Champion at an Operation Rescue rally in downtown Dallas in January 1997. McCorvey, the real Jane Roe of *Roe v. Wade* (1973), became pro-life and worked with the anti-abortion group.

Obama gave at Notre Dame University and also at Sonia Sotomayor's Senate confirmation hearings. She published two books, *I am Roe* and *Won by Love.*

Looking back at her participation in *Roe v. Wade,* McCorvey said that she felt exploited by the pro-choice movement. She claimed she met her lawyers in the case only twice, the first time over pizza and beer, and that she did not even know what the word *abortion* meant. "All I simply did was sign," she said. "I never appeared in any court. I never testified in front of any jury or judge."

McCorvey passed away on February 18, 2017, in Katy, Texas, at age 69.

Sources: St. Louis Post Dispatch, June 12, 1998; *Chicago Sun-Times,* July 27, 1998; *Boston Globe,* October 19, 1998; *Omaha World-Herald,* October 29 and 30, 1998; *Los Angeles Times,* December 8, 1999; *Houston Chronicle,* January 13, 2000; *Independent* (London), March 16, 2000; and *New York Times,* February 18, 2017.

persist today. For example, a 2019 Gallup Poll found that 53 percent of Americans believe that abortion should be legal under certain circumstances, such as if the pregnancy threatens a woman's life or health; 25 percent say it should be legal under any circumstances; and 21 percent think it should be illegal under all circumstances (2 percent had no opinion).

Although *Roe* may not have changed public opinion on abortion, it had the important effect of mobilizing the movement to oppose it. Before 1973 groups opposed to legalized abortion had lobbied successfully against efforts to liberalize state laws. When *Roe* nullified these legislative victories, these groups vowed to see the decision overturned; in short, *Roe* and *Doe* fanned the fire rather than extinguished it.

The Aftermath of *Roe*: Attempts to Limit the Decision

Pro-life groups remain dedicated to the eradication of *Roe v. Wade*, a goal that they can best accomplish in one of two ways: by persuading Congress to propose an amendment to the Constitution or by persuading the Court to overrule its decision. In the immediate aftermath of *Roe*, neither of these options was viable. Despite the public's mixed view of abortion, during the 1970s only about one-third of Americans supported a constitutional amendment to proscribe it. This lack of support may explain why Congress, ever cognizant of the polls, did not pass any of the "human life" amendments it considered in the 1970s. And, given the 7–2 vote in *Roe*, many changes in the Court's membership would have to occur for the Court to reconsider its stance on abortion.

Faced with this situation, pro-life groups determined that their best course of action was to seek limitations on the ways in which women could obtain and pay for abortions. They lobbied legislatures to enact restrictions on the right to an abortion. Two types of restrictions predominated—those that required consent of a woman's husband or a minor's parents and those that limited government funding for abortion services. These efforts were quite successful. During the 1970s, eighteen states required some form of consent, and thirty (along with the federal government) restricted funding. To put it another way, by 1978 only about fifteen states had not enacted laws requiring consent or restricting funding.

As you might expect, pro-choice groups responded with legal challenges to these limits on the abortion right, but, for the most part, they failed. Consider the consent laws. The first major post-*Roe* battle, ***Planned Parenthood of Central Missouri v. Danforth*** (1976), involved this subject—one the Court had not considered in *Roe*. The state of Missouri had passed legislation that required the written consent of the pregnant woman and her spouse or, for an unmarried minor, her parents, before an abortion could be performed.

The Court found no constitutional violation in requiring a woman to give her own consent to the procedure, but it struck down spousal and parental consent provisions as violative of the Constitution and inconsistent with *Roe*. Blackmun's majority opinion, however, gave the pro-life movement a little hope. It struck down Missouri's parental consent requirement, but it also stated, "We emphasize that our holding that parental consent is invalid does not suggest that every minor, regardless of age or maturity, may give effective consent for the termination of her pregnancy." With these words, Blackmun opened the door to the possibility of some form of required parental consent.

Pro-life forces took advantage of Blackmun's statement, persuading states to enact various parental and other consent requirements, many of which came before the Court. And, although the Court has continued to strike down laws forcing a woman to obtain the consent of or to notify her spouse/partner prior to obtaining an abortion, it has generally allowed states to require parental consent or notification, especially if the law allowed a minor to bypass the parent and instead to seek the consent of a judge.[13]

On funding for abortions, however, the Court's decisions are straightforward. In a trio of 1977 decisions, the Court upheld state or local restrictions on the funding of abortions.[14] Three years later, an even bigger battle erupted over the Hyde amendment, which limited federal Medicaid funding of abortions

---

[13]Moreover, in *Ayotte v. Planned Parenthood of Northern New England* (2006), the Court held that when states require parental notification, they must include exceptions if the minor's life or health is in danger.

[14]*Beal v. Doe* (upholding a Pennsylvania law limiting Medicaid funding "to those abortions that are certified by physicians as medically necessary"); *Maher v. Roe* (upholding a Connecticut Welfare Department regulation limiting state Medicaid "benefits for first trimester abortions [to those] . . . that are 'medically necessary'"); and *Poelker v. Doe* (upholding a St. Louis policy directive that barred city-owned hospitals from performing abortions). In all three cases, the Court rejected constitutional claims that the restrictions at issue interfered with the fundamental right to obtain an abortion as articulated in *Roe* and that they discriminated on the basis of socioeconomic status and against those choosing abortion over childbirth.

to those "where the life of the mother would be endangered if the fetus were carried to term." Pro-choice groups quickly challenged the regulation on two grounds: it violated due process because it impinged on a fundamental right, and it denied equal protection because it discriminated against women, especially poor women. In **Harris v. McCrae** (1980), however, a 5–4 Court rejected all three arguments and upheld the regulation. Writing for the majority, Justice Stewart asserted that the Court "cannot overturn duly enacted statutes simply because they may be unwise, improvident or out of harmony with a particular school of thought." More important, however, was the opinion's legal rationale:

> [R]egardless of whether the freedom of a woman to choose to terminate her pregnancy for health reasons lies at the core or the periphery of the due process liberty recognized in [*Roe v.*] *Wade*, it simply does not follow that a woman's freedom of choice carries with it a constitutional entitlement to the financial resources to avail herself of the full range of protected choices. . . . [A]lthough government may not place obstacles in the path of a woman's exercise of her freedom of choice, it need not remove those not of its own creation. Indigency falls in the latter category.

Attempts to Overturn *Roe*

In the early 1980s, pro-life forces had several reasons to feel optimistic. First, they had achieved considerable success in the funding decisions. Second, the 1980 elections placed Ronald Reagan, the first presidential contender ever to support, unequivocally, the goals of the pro-life movement, in the White House. It was almost assured that Reagan's judicial appointees would also oppose abortion. And third, personnel changes on the Supreme Court that were damaging to the pro-choice position had already taken place. John Paul Stevens replaced William O. Douglas. Although Stevens appeared to lean toward the pro-choice position, it seemed questionable whether he would embrace that view more enthusiastically than the man he replaced. Douglas, recall, had written the opinion in *Griswold* and supported the pro-choice position in every subsequent case. Sandra Day O'Connor, Reagan's first appointment, replaced Potter Stewart, who had voted with the *Roe* majority. O'Connor's position on abortion

was far from clear. Some pro-life groups alleged that O'Connor supported the pro-choice side, basing their argument on votes she had cast in the Arizona state legislature. But during her confirmation proceedings, she refused to answer questions on abortion, saying only that it was "a practice in which I would not have engaged." But, she added, she was "over the hill" and "not going to be pregnant any more . . . so perhaps it's easy for me to speak."

Given the changing context, pro-life forces began mounting a more direct attack on *Roe*, still hoping to overturn it. The first major battle occurred in **Akron v. Akron Center for Reproductive Health** (1983). At issue was a 1978 ordinance passed by the city council of Akron, Ohio, that contained five restrictions on the abortion right: (1) all post–first-trimester abortions must be performed in a hospital; (2) minors under the age of fifteen must obtain written consent of a parent or a court prior to an abortion; (3) a woman must give informed consent (for example, a physician must tell her that the "unborn child is a human life form from the moment of conception") prior to an abortion; (4) twenty-four hours must elapse between the time the pregnant woman signs the consent form and the abortion; and (5) doctors who perform abortions "shall insure that the remains of the unborn child are disposed of in a humane and sanitary manner."

Invoking the *Roe* precedent, the Court, in an opinion written by Powell and supported by five others (Brennan, Blackmun, Burger, Marshall, and Stevens), struck down the Akron law. The first four provisions were seen as unnecessary and unconstitutional impediments placed in the way of a woman's right to choose, and the fifth was struck down as unconstitutionally vague.

What is noteworthy, however, is that *Roe* had lost a vote. The 7–2 *Roe* majority was now 6–3, with O'Connor writing a dissent in *Akron* that was signed by Rehnquist and White. O'Connor's opinion was a scathing critique of *Roe*. Citing medical advances, she wrote that at the time of *Roe*, "viability before 28 weeks was considered unusual," but newer studies indicated viability as early as twenty-five weeks. This proved, she said, that because it is inherently tied to ever-changing medical technology, "the *Roe* framework . . . is clearly on a collision course with itself," and because lines separating viability from nonviability are fading, compelling state interests exist throughout pregnancy. O'Connor urged that the trimester framework be abandoned and replaced with one that "protects the woman from *unduly burdensome* interference with her freedom to decide whether to terminate

BOX 16-3

Proposed Approaches to Restrictive Abortion Laws

Approach	Exemplary Opinions	Definition
Strict scrutiny	Blackmun in *Roe*; Powell in *Akron*	The right to abortion is fundamental. So laws restricting that right must be the least restrictive means available to achieve a compelling state interest. In the abortion context, a state's interest grows more compelling as the pregnancy moves from the first to second to third trimesters.
Undue burden	O'Connor in *Akron*	The right to abortion may or may not be fundamental. Regardless, laws placing an undue burden on the woman's decision to terminate her pregnancy may be subject to strict scrutiny; other kinds of laws need only be rationally related to a legitimate state interest (rational basis test).
Rational basis	Rehnquist in *Roe*	The right to abortion is no different from economic rights claimed under the Fourteenth Amendment due process clause. So the law must be a reasonable measure designed to achieve a legitimate state interest.

her pregnancy" (emphasis added).[15] But what would O'Connor count as "unduly burdensome" regulation? Powell claimed that "the dissent would uphold virtually any abortion regulation under a rational-basis test," meaning that it would find constitutional any regulation that was reasonably related to a government interest. Such a standard, Powell noted, would gut *Roe*. O'Connor did not go that far. Rather, she suggested that if the law in question "unduly burdened" the fundamental right to seek an abortion, the Court should apply strict scrutiny;

if the law does not "unduly burden" the abortion right, then the Court should apply a rational basis test.

Therefore, as shown in Box 16-3, by 1983 the justices had proposed three different approaches to restrictive abortion laws. Although the majority of the justices continued to support *Roe*'s strict scrutiny standard, O'Connor's dissent raised questions. Would she stick with her undue burden standard? If so, would she be able to persuade other justices to adopt it? And what exactly did she mean by an "undue burden?" Would she use it as a vehicle to overrule *Roe?*

The answer would come nearly a decade later, in the landmark case of *Planned Parenthood of Southeastern Pennsylvania v. Casey* (1992). By the time the Court agreed to hear arguments in this case, two *Roe* supporters (Brennan and Marshall) had been replaced by two Republicans (David Souter and Clarence Thomas). These membership changes seemed to confirm the greatest hope and fear of the pro-life and pro-choice movements: *Roe* would finally go. Or would it?

---

[15]O'Connor's analysis paralleled the one that Reagan's solicitor general, Rex E. Lee, offered in an amicus curiae brief filed on behalf of the United States in *Akron*. Lee's reading of *Roe*'s progeny led him to conclude that from Danforth on, the justices had never really "applied" *Roe*'s "sweeping" language regarding first-trimester abortions but had made exceptions. He argued that the Court "has repeatedly adopted an 'unduly burdensome' analysis." That is, the Court had permitted state regulations of abortion as long as they did not "unduly burden" that decision.

Planned Parenthood of Southeastern Pennsylvania v. Casey

505 U.S. 833 (1992)
http://caselaw.findlaw.com/us-supreme-court/505/833.html
Oral arguments available at https://www.oyez.org/
cases/1991/91-744
Vote: 5 (Blackmun, Kennedy, O'Connor, Souter, Stevens)
4 (Rehnquist, Scalia, Thomas, White)

OPINION ANNOUNCING THE JUDGMENT OF THE COURT AND DELIVERING THE OPINION OF THE COURT: *Kennedy, O'Connor, Souter*

OPINIONS CONCURRING IN PART: *Blackmun, Rehnquist, Scalia, Stevens, Thomas, White*

OPINIONS DISSENTING IN PART: *Blackmun, Rehnquist, Scalia, Stevens, Thomas, White*

OPINIONS CONCURRING IN PART AND DISSENTING IN PART: *Blackmun, Rehnquist, Scalia, Stevens*

At issue in this case was a Pennsylvania law that required (1) informed consent and a twenty-four-hour waiting period before an abortion could be performed; (2) parental (or judicial) consent for minors; (3) spousal notification; and (4) comprehensive record keeping and reporting of the following information for each abortion performed: the name of the physician, the woman's age, the number of prior pregnancies or abortions the woman had had, the weight and age of the aborted fetus, whether the woman was married, and, if relevant, the reason(s) the woman failed to notify her spouse.

Before these provisions went into effect, five women's clinics challenged their constitutionality. A federal district court generally agreed with the clinics, but the U.S. Court of Appeals for the Third Circuit reversed, using O'Connor's undue burden standard, which—based on its reading of cases following in the wake of *Akron*—was "the law of the land." In the appeals court's opinion, the provisions, with the exception of spousal consent, did not place an undue burden on the decision of whether to terminate a pregnancy. The court applied a rational basis test under which the three provisions easily passed constitutional muster. The spousal consent provision, in the court's view, placed an undue burden on the abortion decision by exposing women to spousal abuse and violence. It therefore applied the strict scrutiny test and concluded that the provision could not stand. Judge Samuel Alito, who now sits on the Supreme Court, disagreed with his appellate court colleagues on

this portion of the decision. In a dissenting opinion, he wrote that he would have upheld the spousal consent provision:

> The Pennsylvania legislature could have rationally believed that some married women are initially inclined to obtain an abortion without their husbands' knowledge because of perceived problems—such as economic constraints, future plans or the husbands' previously expressed opposition—that may be obviated by discussion prior to the abortion.

As a result of this mixed opinion, the state and the clinics appealed to the Supreme Court. In a move designed to intensify the debate over abortion before the 1992 elections, Planned Parenthood asked the justices to issue an unambiguous decision: either affirm or overturn *Roe.* The state, joined by the George H. W. Bush administration's solicitor general, Kenneth Starr, also asked the Court "to end the current uncertainty" surrounding the abortion issue and overrule *Roe.* The state and the federal government wanted the Court to adopt a rational basis approach to abortion and to use that standard to uphold all of Pennsylvania's laws. Given the membership changes on the Court, many observers predicted the Court would do precisely that.

> **JUSTICE O'CONNOR, JUSTICE KENNEDY, AND JUSTICE SOUTER ANNOUNCED THE JUDGMENT OF THE COURT AND DELIVERED THE OPINION OF THE COURT WITH RESPECT TO PARTS I, II, III, V-A, V-C, AND VI, AN OPINION WITH RESPECT TO PART V-E, IN WHICH JUSTICE STEVENS JOINS, AND AN OPINION WITH RESPECT TO PARTS IV, V-B, AND V-D.**

[It] is common wisdom that the rule of *stare decisis* is not an "inexorable command," and certainly it is not such in every constitutional case. Rather, when this Court reexamines a prior holding, its judgment is customarily informed by a series of prudential and pragmatic considerations designed to test the consistency of overruling a prior decision with the ideal of the rule of law, and to gauge the respective costs of reaffirming and overruling a prior case. Thus, for example, we may ask whether the rule has proven to be intolerable simply in defying practical workability; whether the rule is subject to a kind of reliance that would lend a special hardship to the consequences of overruling and add inequity to the cost of repudiation; whether related principles of law have so far developed as to have left the old rule no more than a remnant of abandoned doctrine; or whether facts have so changed, or come to be seen so differently, as to have robbed the old rule of significant application or justification.

So in this case we may inquire whether *Roe*'s central rule has been found unworkable; whether the rule's limitation on state power could be removed without serious inequity to those who have relied upon it or significant damage to the stability of the society governed by the rule in question; whether the law's growth in the intervening years has left *Roe*'s central rule a doctrinal anachronism discounted by society; and whether *Roe*'s premises of fact have so far changed in the ensuing two decades as to render its central holding somehow irrelevant or unjustifiable in dealing with the issue it addressed.

1

Although *Roe* has engendered opposition, it has in no sense proven "unworkable," representing as it does a simple limitation beyond which a state law is unenforceable. While *Roe* has, of course, required judicial assessment of state laws affecting the exercise of the choice guaranteed against government infringement, and although the need for such review will remain as a consequence of today's decision, the required determinations fall within judicial competence.

2

The inquiry into reliance counts the cost of a rule's repudiation as it would fall on those who have relied reasonably on the rule's continued application. Since the classic case for weighing reliance heavily in favor of following the earlier rule occurs in the commercial context, where advance planning of great precision is most obviously a necessity, it is no cause for surprise that some would find no reliance worthy of consideration in support of *Roe*. . . .

To eliminate the issue of reliance that easily, however, one would need to limit cognizable reliance to specific instances of sexual activity. But to do this would be simply to refuse to face the fact that for two decades of economic and social developments, people have organized intimate relationships and made choices that define their views of themselves and their places in society, in reliance on the availability of abortion in the event that contraception should fail. The ability of women to participate equally in the economic and social life of the Nation has been facilitated by their ability to control their reproductive lives. The Constitution serves human values, and while the effect of reliance on *Roe* cannot be exactly measured, neither can the certain cost of overruling *Roe* for people who have ordered their thinking and living around that case be dismissed.

3

No evolution of legal principle has left *Roe*'s doctrinal footings weaker than they were in 1973. No development of constitutional law since the case was decided has implicitly or explicitly left *Roe* behind as a mere survivor of obsolete constitutional thinking. . . .

4

[T]ime has overtaken some of *Roe*'s factual assumptions: advances in maternal health care allow for abortions safe to the mother later in pregnancy than was true in 1973, and advances in neonatal care have advanced viability to a point somewhat earlier. But these facts go only to the scheme of time limits on the realization of competing interests, and the divergences from the factual premises of 1973 have no bearing on the validity of *Roe*'s central holding, that viability marks the earliest point at which the State's interest in fetal life is constitutionally adequate to justify a legislative ban on nontherapeutic abortions.

5

The sum of the precedential inquiry to this point shows *Roe*'s underpinnings unweakened in any way affecting its central holding. . . .

IV

. . . From what we have said so far it follows that it is a constitutional liberty of the woman to have some freedom to terminate her pregnancy. We conclude that the basic decision in *Roe* was based on a constitutional analysis which we cannot now repudiate. The woman's liberty is not so unlimited, however, that from the outset the State cannot show its concern for the life of the unborn, and at a later point in fetal development the State's interest in life has sufficient force so that the right of the woman to terminate the pregnancy can be restricted. . . .

We conclude the line should be drawn at viability, so that before that time the woman has a right to choose to terminate her pregnancy. We adhere to this principle for two reasons. First, as we have said, is the doctrine of *stare decisis*. . . .

The second reason is that the concept of viability, as we noted in *Roe,* is the time at which there is a realistic possibility of maintaining and nourishing a life outside the womb, so that the independent existence of the second life can in reason and all fairness be the object of state protection that now overrides the rights of the woman.

On the other side of the equation is the interest of the State in the protection of potential life. The *Roe* Court recognized the State's "important and legitimate interest in protecting the potentiality of human life."

The trimester framework [of *Roe*] no doubt was erected to ensure that the woman's right to choose not become so subordinate to the State's interest in promoting fetal life that her choice exists in theory but not in fact. We do not agree, however, that the trimester approach is necessary to accomplish this objective. A framework of this rigidity was unnecessary and in its later interpretation sometimes contradicted the State's permissible exercise of its powers.

We reject the trimester framework, which we do not consider to be part of the essential holding of *Roe*. . . .

The trimester framework suffers from basic flaws: in its formulation it misconceives the nature of the pregnant woman's interest; and in practice it undervalues the State's interest in potential life, as recognized in *Roe*. . . .

. . . Only where state regulation imposes an undue burden on a woman's ability to make this decision does the power of the State reach into the heart of the liberty protected by the Due Process Clause. . . .

Not all burdens on the right to decide whether to terminate a pregnancy will be undue. In our view, the undue burden standard is the appropriate means of reconciling the State's interest with the woman's constitutionally protected liberty.

The concept of an undue burden has been utilized by the Court as well as individual members of the Court, including two of us, in ways that could be considered inconsistent. . . . Because we set forth a standard of general application to which we intend to adhere, it is important to clarify what is meant by an undue burden.

A finding of an undue burden is a shorthand for the conclusion that a state regulation has the purpose or effect of placing a substantial obstacle in the path of a woman seeking an abortion of a nonviable fetus. A statute with this purpose is invalid because the means chosen by the State to further the interest in potential life must be calculated to inform the woman's free choice, not hinder it. And a statute which, while furthering the interest in potential life or some other valid state interest, has the effect of placing a substantial obstacle in the path of a woman's choice cannot be considered a permissible means of serving its legitimate ends. To the extent that the opinions of the Court or of individual Justices use the undue burden standard in a manner that is inconsistent with this analysis, we set out what in our view should be the controlling standard. . . .Understood another way, we answer the question, left open in previous opinions discussing the undue burden formulation, whether a law designed to further the State's interest in fetal life which imposes an undue burden on the woman's decision before fetal viability could be constitutional. The answer is no.

Some guiding principles should emerge. What is at stake is the woman's right to make the ultimate decision, not a right to be insulated from all others in doing so. Regulations which do no more than create a structural mechanism by which the State, or the parent or guardian of a minor, may express profound respect for the life of the unborn are permitted, if they are not a substantial obstacle to the woman's exercise of the right to choose. Unless it has that effect on her right of choice, a state measure designed to persuade her to choose childbirth over abortion will be upheld if reasonably related to that goal. Regulations designed to foster the health of a woman seeking an abortion are valid if they do not constitute an undue burden. . . .

. . . We give this summary:

a. To protect the central right recognized by *Roe v. Wade* while at the same time accommodating the State's profound interest in potential life, we will employ the undue burden analysis as explained in this opinion. An undue burden exists, and therefore a provision of law is invalid, if its purpose or effect is to place a substantial obstacle in the path of a woman seeking an abortion before the fetus attains viability.

b. We reject the rigid trimester framework of *Roe v. Wade*. To promote the State's profound interest in potential life, throughout pregnancy the State may take measures to ensure that the woman's choice is informed, and measures designed to advance this interest will not be invalidated as long as their purpose is to persuade the woman to choose childbirth over abortion. These measures must not be an undue burden on the right.

c. As with any medical procedure, the State may enact regulations to further the health or safety of a woman seeking an abortion. Unnecessary health regulations that have the purpose or effect of presenting a substantial obstacle to a woman seeking an abortion impose an undue burden on the right.

d. Our adoption of the undue burden analysis does not disturb the central holding of *Roe v. Wade*, and we reaffirm that holding. Regardless of whether exceptions are made for particular circumstances, a State may not prohibit any woman from making the ultimate decision to terminate her pregnancy before viability.

e. We also reaffirm *Roe's* holding that "subsequent to viability, the State in promoting its interest in the potentiality of human life may, if it chooses, regulate, and even proscribe, abortion except where it is necessary, in appropriate medical judgment, for the preservation of the life or health of the mother." *Roe v. Wade*.

These principles control our assessment of the Pennsylvania statute . . .

V

[In this section of the opinion the Court ruled on the law. It upheld the following provisions on the ground that they do not place an undue burden on the abortion right:

1. Informed Consent/24-hour waiting period (Part V-B); "Even the broadest reading of *Roe* . . . has not suggested that there is a constitutional right to abortion on demand. . . . Rather, the right protected by *Roe* is a right to decide to terminate a pregnancy free of undue interference by the State. Because the informed consent requirement facilitates the wise exercise of that right it cannot be classified as an interference with the right *Roe* protects. The informed consent requirement is not an undue burden on that right."

2. Parental Consent (Part V-D): "We have been over most of this ground before. Our cases establish, and we reaffirm today, that a State may require a minor seeking an abortion to obtain the consent of a parent or guardian, provided that there is an adequate judicial bypass procedure. . . ."

3. Recordkeeping and Reporting (Part V-E): "[A]ll the provisions at issue here except that relating to spousal notice are constitutional. The collection of information with respect to actual patients is a vital element of medical research, and so it cannot be said that the requirements serve no purpose other than to make abortions more difficult. Nor do we find that the requirements impose a substantial obstacle to a woman's choice. At most they might increase the cost of some abortions by a slight amount."

The Court struck the following provisions on the ground that they place an undue burden on the abortion right:

1. Spousal notification (V-C): "The spousal notification requirement is thus likely to prevent a significant number of women from obtaining an abortion. It does not merely make abortions a little more difficult or expensive to obtain; for many women, it will impose a substantial obstacle. We must not blind ourselves to the fact that the significant number of women who fear for their safety and the safety of their children are likely to be deterred from procuring an abortion as surely as if the Commonwealth had outlawed abortion in all cases."

2. Recordkeeping and Reporting (Part V-E): "Subsection (12) of the reporting provision requires the reporting of, among other things, a married woman's 'reason for failure to provide notice' to her husband. This provision in effect requires women, as a condition of obtaining an abortion, to provide the Commonwealth with the precise information we have already recognized that many women have pressing reasons not to reveal. Like the

spousal notice requirement itself, this provision places an undue burden on a woman's choice, and must be invalidated for that reason."]

Affirmed in part, reversed in part, and remanded.

JUSTICE BLACKMUN, CONCURRING IN PART, CONCURRING IN THE JUDGMENT IN PART, AND DISSENTING IN PART.

I join parts I, II, III, V-A, V-C, and VI of the joint opinion of JUSTICES O'CONNOR, KENNEDY, and SOUTER. . . .

Make no mistake, the joint opinion of JUSTICES O'CONNOR, KENNEDY, and SOUTER is an act of personal courage and constitutional principle. In contrast to previous decisions in which JUSTICES O'CONNOR and KENNEDY postponed reconsideration of *Roe v. Wade* (1973), the authors of the joint opinion today join JUSTICE STEVENS and me in concluding that "the essential holding of *Roe* should be retained and once again reaffirmed." In brief, five Members of this Court today recognize that "the Constitution protects a woman's right to terminate her pregnancy in its early stages." . . .

[But] . . . *Roe*'s requirement of strict scrutiny as implemented through a trimester framework should not be disturbed. No other approach has gained a majority, and no other is more protective of the woman's fundamental right. Lastly, no other approach properly accommodates the woman's constitutional right with the State's legitimate interests. . . .

Application of the strict scrutiny standard results in the invalidation of all the challenged provisions. Indeed, as this Court has invalidated virtually identical provisions in prior cases, *stare decisis* requires that we again strike them down. . . .

In one sense, the Court's approach is worlds apart from that of THE CHIEF JUSTICE and JUSTICE SCALIA. And yet, in another sense, the distance between the two approaches is short—the distance is but a single vote.

I am 83 years old. I cannot remain on this Court forever, and when I do step down, the confirmation process for my successor well may focus on the issue before us today. That, I regret, may be exactly where the choice between the two worlds will be made.

JUSTICE SCALIA, WITH WHOM THE CHIEF JUSTICE, JUSTICE WHITE, AND JUSTICE THOMAS JOIN, CONCURRING IN THE JUDGMENT IN PART AND DISSENTING IN PART.

The States may, if they wish, permit abortion on demand, but the Constitution does not *require* them to do so. The permissibility of abortion, and the limitations upon it, are to be resolved like most important questions in our democracy: by citizens trying to persuade one another and then voting. . . . A State's choice between two positions on which reasonable people can disagree is constitutional even when (as is often the case) it intrudes upon a "liberty" in the absolute sense. Laws against bigamy, for example—which entire societies of reasonable people disagree with—intrude upon men and women's liberty to marry and live with one another. But bigamy happens not to be a liberty specially "protected" by the Constitution.

That is, quite simply, the issue in this case: not whether the power of a woman to abort her unborn child is a "liberty" in the absolute sense; or even whether it is a liberty of great importance to many women. Of course it is both. The issue is whether it is a liberty protected by the Constitution of the United States. I am sure it is not. I reach that conclusion not because of anything so exalted as my views concerning the "concept of existence, of meaning, of the universe, and of the mystery of human life." Rather, I reach it for the same reason I reach the conclusion that bigamy is not constitutionally protected—because of two simple facts: (1) the Constitution says absolutely nothing about it, and (2) the longstanding traditions of American society have permitted it to be legally proscribed. . . .

We should get out of this area, where we have no right to be, and where we do neither ourselves nor the country any good by remaining.

What are we to make of *Casey?* On one hand, predictions of *Roe's* demise were wrong. The Court did not overrule *Roe;* to the contrary, it reaffirmed the "central holding" of the 1973 decision that a woman should have "some" freedom to terminate a pregnancy. And yet the "joint opinion" gutted the core of *Roe.* The trimester framework and its compelling interest analysis were gone. Under *Casey,* states may now enact laws—regulating the entire pregnancy—that further their interest in potential life so long as those laws do not put an undue burden on the right to terminate a pregnancy. If they do place an undue burden—a substantial obstacle—the Court will presumably invalidate them. This is akin to the approach that O'Connor proposed in 1983 in her *Akron* dissent, though it is not exactly the same. In *Akron,* she suggested that the Court apply rational basis analysis to laws that do not unduly burden the abortion choice and strict scrutiny to those that do. Here, that language is missing. The task for the Court, as O'Connor, Anthony M. Kennedy, and Souter set it out, is simply to determine whether the law does or does not unduly burden the abortion decision.

The Roberts Court and the Legal Future of Abortion

How the Court would perform that task remained to be seen, but what seemed clear—at least to the states—was that *Casey* gave them more latitude to regulate abortions. Nearly half took advantage of it by passing so-called Targeted Regulation of Abortion Providers (TRAP) laws. These laws come in different forms, but these two, enacted by the Texas legislature in 2013, are exemplary:

1. The "admitting-privileges requirement." Requires that doctors performing or inducing an abortion obtain admitting privileges at a hospital located no farther than 30 miles from the abortion facility.

2. The "surgical-center requirement." Requires an abortion facility to meet the minimum standards for ambulatory surgical centers under Texas law. These requirements include detailed specifications relating to the size of the nursing staff, building dimensions, and other building requirements. For example, facilities must include a full surgical suite with an operating room that has "a clear floor area of at least 240 square feet" in which "[t]he minimum clear dimension between built-in cabinets, counters, and shelves shall be 14 feet."

In **Whole Woman's Health v. Hellerstedt** (2016) a group of abortion providers brought suit claiming that the Texas regulations violated the Fourteenth Amendment's due process, as interpreted by the Supreme Court in *Planned Parenthood v. Casey* (1992). The providers argued that the provisions failed to meet *Casey's* "undue burden" standard because they are "unnecessary health regulations that have the purpose or effect of presenting a substantial obstacle to a woman seeking an abortion" and so "impose an undue burden on the right."

A federal district court agreed and enjoined the state from enforcing both provisions. But the U.S. Court of Appeals for the Fifth Circuit reversed. It interpreted *Casey's* standard to allow states to regulate abortion if the regulation was "reasonably related to a legitimate state interest." After the circuit court found that both requirements were rationally related to a compelling state interest in protecting women's health, the abortion providers asked the Supreme Court to hear their case.

In a 5–3 decision (the 2016 death of Justice Scalia had left the Court with only eight justices) the Court reversed the circuit court. Writing for the majority, Justice Breyer made an important contribution to abortion law by fleshing out *Casey's* undue burden standard.

To assess whether restrictions on abortion placed a substantial obstacle in front of women seeking to obtain a pre-viability abortion, the Court would consider whether the health benefits of the restrictions justified the burden they impose on women—in other words, the Court would perform something of a cost-benefit analysis. Or, as Ginsburg put it in a concurring opinion, "Targeted Regulation of Abortion Providers laws that 'do little or nothing for health, but rather strew impediments to abortion' cannot survive judicial inspection."

In the majority's view, both restrictions imposed too many burdens on women without sufficient off-setting benefits. For example, here's what Breyer had to say about the "admitting-privileges requirement."

> In our view, the [district court] record contains sufficient evidence that the admitting-privileges requirement led to the closure of half of Texas' clinics, or thereabouts. Those closures meant fewer doctors, longer waiting times, and increased crowding. Record evidence also supports the finding that after the admitting-privileges provision went into effect, the "number of women of reproductive age living in a county . . . more than 150 miles from a provider increased from approximately 86,000 to 400,000. . . ." We recognize that increased driving distances do not always constitute an "undue burden." But here, those increases are but one additional burden, which, when taken together with others that the closings brought about, and when viewed in light of the virtual absence of any health benefit, lead us to conclude that the record adequately supports the District Court's "undue burden" conclusion. . . .

Breyer reached a similar conclusion about the ambulatory surgical requirement.

The three dissenters (Alito, Thomas, and John G. Roberts) took issue not only with the majority's decision to invalidate the laws but also with its approach to *Casey's* undue burden standard. For example, after reiterating that he remained "fundamentally opposed to the Court's abortion jurisprudence," Thomas wrote, [This] free-form balancing test is contrary to *Casey*. . . . *Casey* did not balance the benefits and burdens of Pennsylvania's spousal and parental notification provisions. . . . Pennsylvania's spousal notification requirement, the plurality said, imposed an undue burden because findings established that the requirement would "likely . . . prevent a significant number of women from obtaining an abortion"— not because these burdens outweighed its benefits. . . .

What does *Whole Women's Health* tell us about the future of abortion in the Supreme Court? Clearly, support for *Roe's* central holding—that a woman has a right to choose to terminate her pregnancy—has diminished since 1973, as Table 16-3 shows. What began as a seven-person majority may now be down to four *if* Donald Trump's appointees, Kavanaugh and Gorsuch vote to overrule it. Whatever the future holds, it is doubtful that we have heard the last of the abortion controversy, and, as has consistently been the case, there are no easy answers.

PRIVATE ACTIVITIES AND THE APPLICATION OF *GRISWOLD*

Little doubt exists that many Americans now equate the right to privacy, first established in *Griswold v. Connecticut*, with reproductive freedom, especially the right to abortion. But the right to privacy, as it follows from the "liberty" guaranteed in the due process clauses, has implications for many other activities, including those we cover below: private sexual activities, same-sex marriage, and the right to die.

Private Sexual Activity

Private sexual activity was at the core of the 1986 case of **Bowers v. Hardwick** (1986). This dispute began in 1982 when an Atlanta police officer arrived at Michael Hardwick's home to serve an arrest warrant. When he entered the home with the permission of one of Hardwick's housemates, the officer witnessed Hardwick engaging in sodomy with another man. Hardwick was arrested for violating a Georgia law that prohibited the practice of oral or anal sex. The law applied to both same-sex and opposite-sex couples. Although the prosecutor dropped the charge, Hardwick, with the help of the ACLU, challenged the validity of the sodomy law.

Splitting 5–4, the Court upheld the Georgia law. Writing for himself and Burger, O'Connor, Powell, and Rehnquist, White said, "[F]undamental liberties . . . are characterized as those . . . that are 'deeply rooted in this Nation's history and tradition'"—a type of liberty that, according to White, "consensual homosexual sodomy" was not. Led by Harry Blackmun, the dissenters objected

Table 16-3 Support for *Roe*'s Central Holding

Roe v. *Wade* (1973)	Planned Parenthood v. *Casey* (1992)	*Whole Women's Health* v. *Hellerstedt* (2016)	*Current Court* (2020)
Blackmun	**Blackmun**	**Breyer**	**Breyer**
Brennan	**Souter**	**Sotomayor**	**Sotomayor**
Burger	*Rehnquist*	*Roberts*	*Roberts*
Douglas	**Stevens**	**Kagan**	**Kagan**
Marshall	*Thomas*	*Thomas*	*Thomas*
Powell	**Kennedy**	**Kennedy**	Kavanaugh (?)
Rehnquist	*Scalia*	————	Gorsuch (?)
Stewart	**O'Connor**	*Alito*	*Alito*
White	*White*	**Ginsburg**	**Ginsburg**

Key: Justices whose names appear in boldface support *Roe*, or at least its central holding; justices whose names appear in italics either voiced concerns about *Roe* or would overturn it.

to the Court's characterization of the issue. It was not, Blackmun argued, a matter of the right to engage in sodomy, but instead a question of privacy rights. Quoting with approval Justice Brandeis's dissent in *Olmstead v. United States* (1928), Blackmun wrote, "this case is about 'the most comprehensive of rights and the right most valued by civilized men,' namely, 'the right to be let alone.'"

The Court's decision in *Bowers* was quite controversial, and it politically energized the gay community. Organizations dedicated to advancing gay rights launched major efforts to change state laws regulating private sexual behavior. In addition, overturning *Bowers* became a high priority. The importance of this goal became even more salient to the gay community when the retired Lewis Powell, who had cast the swing vote in *Bowers*, admitted that he probably had made a mistake in siding with the majority *(see Box 16-4)*. Blackmun, in dissent, explicitly expressed his hope that the Court "will reconsider its analysis."

That reconsideration may not have come as quickly as Blackmun would have liked, but it did come. In *Lawrence v. Texas* (2003), the justices overruled *Bowers*. As you read the excerpt below, consider why you think the Court took the rare step of overturning one of its own decisions. Also consider the meaning of *Lawrence* for the development of privacy law.

Lawrence v. Texas

539 U.S. 558 (2003)
http://caselaw.findlaw.com/us-supreme-court/539/558.html
*Oral arguments available at https://www.oyez.org/
cases/2002/02-102*
Vote: 6 (Breyer, Ginsburg, Kennedy, O'Connor, Souter, Stevens)
3 (Rehnquist, Scalia, Thomas)

OPINION OF THE COURT: *Kennedy*

OPINION CONCURRING IN THE JUDGMENT: *O'Connor*

DISSENTING OPINIONS: *Scalia, Thomas*

In many ways, *Lawrence* is quite similar to *Bowers*. Like *Bowers*, this case began with a police visit to a private residence. After receiving a phone call about a possible weapons disturbance, police officers in Houston, Texas, entered John Geddes Lawrence's apartment, where they observed Lawrence and another man, Tyron Garner, engaging in a sexual act. The two men were arrested and eventually convicted of violating a Texas law that made it a crime for two persons of the same sex to engage in sodomy. This law, unlike the one at issue in *Bowers*, applied only to participants of the same sex.

Lawrence and Garner may have been rather unlikely litigants *(see Box 16-4)*, but they nonetheless challenged the statute as a violation of the equal protection clause of the Fourteenth Amendment, a similar provision of the Texas constitution, and the due process clause of the Fourteenth Amendment. After Texas courts, relying on the Supreme Court's decision in *Bowers,* rejected these claims, the two appealed to the U.S. Supreme Court.

Once the Supreme Court granted certiorari in *Lawrence,* numerous amici curiae entered the dispute, asking the Court to strike down the law. In some of the briefs, scholars criticized the historical premises on which the majority opinion and Chief Justice Burger's concurrence in *Bowers* relied. Others pointed to the changing circumstances of the two cases. For example, at the time the Court decided *Bowers,* half of the states outlawed sodomy; by 2003 that number was reduced to thirteen, of which four enforced their laws only against homosexual conduct.

JUSTICE KENNEDY DELIVERED THE OPINION OF THE COURT.

Liberty protects the person from unwarranted government intrusions into a dwelling or other private places. In our tradition the State is not omnipresent in the home. And there are other spheres of our lives and existence, outside the home, where the State should not be a dominant presence. Freedom extends beyond spatial bounds. Liberty presumes an autonomy of self that includes freedom of thought, belief, expression, and certain intimate conduct. The instant case involves liberty of the person both in its spatial and more transcendent dimensions. . . .

The petitioners were adults at the time of the alleged offense. Their conduct was in private and consensual.

We conclude the case should be resolved by determining whether the petitioners were free as adults to engage in the private conduct in the exercise of their liberty under the Due Process Clause of the Fourteenth Amendment to the Constitution [rather than the Fourteenth Amendment guarantee of equal protection of laws]. For this inquiry we deem it necessary to reconsider the Court's holding in *Bowers.* . . .

The [Bowers] Court began its substantive discussion in *Bowers* as follows: "The issue presented is whether the Federal Constitution confers a fundamental right upon homosexuals to engage in sodomy and hence invalidates the laws of the many States that still make such conduct illegal and have done so for a very long time." That statement, we now conclude, discloses the Court's own failure to appreciate the extent of the liberty at stake. To say that the issue in *Bowers* was simply the right to engage in certain sexual conduct demeans the claim the individual put forward, just as it would demean a married couple were it to be said marriage is simply about the right to have sexual intercourse. The laws involved in *Bowers* and here are, to be sure, statutes that purport to do no more than prohibit a particular sexual act. Their penalties and purposes, though, have more far-reaching consequences, touching upon the most private human conduct, sexual behavior, and in the most private of places, the home. The statutes do seek to control a personal relationship that, whether or not entitled to formal recognition in the law, is within the liberty of persons to choose without being punished as criminals.

This, as a general rule, should counsel against attempts by the State, or a court, to define the meaning of the relationship or to set its boundaries absent injury to a person or abuse of an institution the law protects. It suffices for us to acknowledge that adults may choose to enter upon this relationship in the confines of their homes and their own private lives and still retain their dignity as free persons. When sexuality finds overt expression in intimate conduct with another person, the conduct can be but one element in a personal bond that is more enduring. The liberty protected by the Constitution allows homosexual persons the right to make this choice.

Having misapprehended the claim of liberty there presented to it, and thus stating the claim to be whether there is a fundamental right to engage in consensual sodomy, the *Bowers* Court said: "Proscriptions against that conduct have ancient roots." In academic writings, and in many of the scholarly *amicus* briefs filed to assist the Court in this case, there are fundamental criticisms of the historical premises relied upon by the majority and concurring opinions in *Bowers.* We need not enter this debate in the attempt to reach a definitive historical judgment, but . . . it should be noted that there is no longstanding history in this country of laws directed at homosexual conduct as a distinct matter . . . [E]arly American sodomy laws were not directed at homosexuals as such but instead sought to prohibit nonprocreative sexual activity more generally. This does not suggest approval of homosexual conduct. It does tend to show that this particular form of conduct was not thought of as a separate category from like conduct between heterosexual persons. . . .

. . . [F]ar from possessing "ancient roots," American laws targeting same-sex couples did not develop until the last third of the 20th century. . . . It was not until the 1970's that any State singled out same-sex relations for criminal prosecution, and only nine States have done so. . . .

[T]he historical grounds relied upon in *Bowers* [then] are more complex than the majority opinion and the concurring opinion by Chief Justice Burger indicate. Their historical premises are not without doubt and, at the very least, are overstated. . . .

In all events we think that our laws and traditions in the past half century are of most relevance here. These references show an emerging awareness that liberty gives substantial protection to adult persons in deciding how to conduct their private lives in matters pertaining to sex.

This emerging recognition should have been apparent when *Bowers* was decided. In 1955 the American Law Institute promulgated the Model Penal Code and made clear that it did not recommend or provide for "criminal penalties for consensual sexual relations conducted in private." In 1961 Illinois changed its laws to conform to the Model Penal Code. Other States soon followed. . . .

. . . [A]lmost five years before *Bowers* was decided the European Court of Human Rights considered a case with parallels to *Bowers* and to today's case. An adult male resident in Northern Ireland alleged he was a practicing homosexual who desired to engage in consensual homosexual conduct. The laws of Northern Ireland forbade him that right. He alleged that he had been questioned, his home had been searched, and he feared criminal prosecution. The court held that the laws proscribing the conduct were invalid under the European Convention on Human Rights. Authoritative in all countries that are members of the Council of Europe (21 nations then, 45 nations now), the decision is at odds with the premise in *Bowers* that the claim put forward was insubstantial in our Western civilization.

In our own constitutional system the deficiencies in *Bowers* became even more apparent in the years following its announcement. The 25 States with laws prohibiting the relevant conduct referenced in the *Bowers* decision are reduced now to 13, of which 4 enforce their laws only against homosexual conduct. In those States where sodomy is still proscribed, whether for same-sex or heterosexual conduct, there is a pattern of nonenforcement with respect to consenting adults acting in private. The State of Texas admitted in 1994 that as of that date it had not prosecuted anyone under those circumstances.

Two principal cases decided after *Bowers* cast its holding into even more doubt. In *Planned Parenthood of Southeastern Pa. v. Casey* (1992), the Court reaffirmed the substantive force of the liberty protected by the Due Process Clause. The *Casey* decision again confirmed that our laws and tradition afford constitutional protection to personal decisions relating to marriage, procreation, contraception, family relationships, child rearing, and education. . . .

Persons in a homosexual relationship may seek autonomy for these purposes, just as heterosexual persons do. The decision in *Bowers* would deny them this right.

The second post-*Bowers* case of principal relevance is *Romer v. Evans* (1996). There the Court struck down class-based legislation directed at homosexuals as a violation of the Equal Protection Clause.[16] *Romer* invalidated an amendment to Colorado's constitution which named as a solitary class persons who were homosexuals, lesbians, or bisexual either by "orientation, conduct, practices or relationships," and deprived them of protection under state antidiscrimination laws. . . .

As an alternative argument in this case, counsel for the petitioners and some *amici* contend that *Romer* provides the basis for declaring the Texas statute invalid under the Equal Protection Clause. That is a tenable argument, but we conclude the instant case requires us to address whether *Bowers* itself has continuing validity.

---

[16] *Authors' note*: For an excerpt and discussion of *Romer*, see chapter 19.

Were we to hold the statute invalid under the Equal Protection Clause some might question whether a prohibition would be valid if drawn differently, say, to prohibit the conduct both between same-sex and different-sex participants.

Equality of treatment and the due process right to demand respect for conduct protected by the substantive guarantee of liberty are linked in important respects, and a decision on the latter point advances both interests. If protected conduct is made criminal and the law which does so remains unexamined for its substantive validity, its stigma might remain even if it were not enforceable as drawn for equal protection reasons. When homosexual conduct is made criminal by the law of the State, that declaration in and of itself is an invitation to subject homosexual persons to discrimination both in the public and in the private spheres. The central holding of *Bowers* has been brought in question by this case, and it should be addressed. Its continuance as precedent demeans the lives of homosexual persons. . . .

The foundations of *Bowers* have sustained serious erosion from our recent decisions in *Casey* and *Romer*. When our precedent has been thus weakened, criticism from other sources is of greater significance. In the United States criticism of *Bowers* has been substantial and continuing, disapproving of its reasoning in all respects, not just as to its historical assumptions. . . .

Bowers was not correct when it was decided, and it is not correct today. It ought not to remain binding precedent. *Bowers v. Hardwick* should be and now is overruled.

The present case does not involve minors. It does not involve persons who might be injured or coerced or who are situated in relationships where consent might not easily be refused. It does not involve public conduct or prostitution. It does not involve whether the government must give formal recognition to any relationship that homosexual persons seek to enter. The case involves two adults who, with full and mutual consent from each other, engaged in sexual practices common to a homosexual lifestyle. The petitioners are entitled to respect for their private lives. The State cannot demean their existence or control their destiny by making their private sexual conduct a crime. Their right to liberty under the Due Process Clause gives them the full right to engage in their conduct without intervention of the government. "It is a promise of the Constitution that there is a realm of personal liberty which the government may not enter." The Texas statute furthers no legitimate state interest which can justify its intrusion into the personal and private life of the individual.

Had those who drew and ratified the Due Process Clauses of the Fifth Amendment or the Fourteenth Amendment known the components of liberty in its manifold possibilities, they might have been more specific. They did not presume to have this insight. They knew times can blind us to certain truths and later generations can see that laws once thought necessary and proper in fact serve only to oppress. As the Constitution endures, persons in every generation can invoke its principles in their own search for greater freedom.

The judgment of the Court of Appeals for the Texas Fourteenth District is reversed, and the case is remanded for further proceedings not inconsistent with this opinion.

It is so ordered.

JUSTICE O'CONNOR, CONCURRING IN THE JUDGMENT.

The Court today overrules *Bowers v. Hardwick* (1986). I joined *Bowers,* and do not join the Court in overruling it. Nevertheless, I agree with the Court that Texas' statute banning same-sex sodomy is unconstitutional. Rather than relying on the substantive component of the Fourteenth Amendment's Due Process Clause, as the Court does, I base my conclusion on the Fourteenth Amendment's Equal Protection Clause.

The Equal Protection Clause of the Fourteenth Amendment "is essentially a direction that all persons similarly situated should be treated alike." Under our rational basis standard of review, "legislation is presumed to be valid and will be sustained if the classification drawn by the statute is rationally related to a legitimate state interest." . . .

Texas attempts to justify its law, and the effects of the law, by arguing that the statute satisfies rational basis review because it furthers the legitimate governmental interest of the promotion of morality. In *Bowers,* we held that a state law criminalizing sodomy as applied to homosexual couples did not violate substantive due process. We rejected the argument that no rational basis existed to justify the law, pointing to the government's interest in promoting morality. The only question in front of the Court in *Bowers* was whether the substantive component of the Due Process Clause protected a right to engage in homosexual sodomy. *Bowers* did not hold that moral disapproval of a group is a rational basis under the Equal Protection Clause to criminalize homosexual sodomy when heterosexual sodomy is not punished.

This case raises a different issue than *Bowers:* whether, under the Equal Protection Clause, moral disapproval is a legitimate state interest to justify by itself a statute that bans homosexual sodomy, but not heterosexual sodomy. It is not. Moral disapproval of this group, like a bare desire to harm the group, is an interest that is insufficient to satisfy rational basis review under the Equal Protection Clause. Indeed, we have never held that moral disapproval, without any other asserted state interest, is a sufficient rationale under the Equal Protection Clause to justify a law that discriminates among groups of persons. . . .

A law branding one class of persons as criminal solely based on the State's moral disapproval of that class and the conduct associated with that class runs contrary to the values of the Constitution and the Equal Protection Clause, under any standard of review. I therefore concur in the Court's judgment that Texas' sodomy law banning "deviate sexual intercourse" between consenting adults of the same sex, but not between consenting adults of different sexes, is unconstitutional.

JUSTICE SCALIA, WITH WHOM THE CHIEF JUSTICE AND JUSTICE THOMAS JOIN, DISSENTING.

Countless judicial decisions and legislative enactments have relied on the ancient proposition that a governing majority's belief that certain sexual behavior is "immoral and unacceptable" constitutes a rational basis for regulation. . . .

[I]n light of *Bowers'* validation of laws based on moral choices [state laws against bigamy, same-sex marriage, adult incest, prostitution, masturbation, adultery, fornication, bestiality, and obscenity] are called into question by today's decision; the Court makes no effort to cabin the scope of its decision to exclude them from its holding. The impossibility of distinguishing homosexuality from other traditional "morals" offenses is precisely why *Bowers* rejected the rational-basis challenge. "The law," it said, "is constantly based on notions of morality, and if all laws representing essentially moral choices are to be invalidated under the Due Process Clause, the courts will be very busy indeed." . . . What a massive disruption of the current social order, therefore, the overruling of *Bowers* entails. . . .

Having decided that it need not adhere to *stare decisis*, the Court still must establish that *Bowers* was wrongly decided and that the Texas statute, as applied to petitioners, is unconstitutional. [The statute] undoubtedly imposes constraints on liberty. So do laws prohibiting prostitution, recreational use of heroin, and, for that matter, working more than 60 hours per week in a bakery. But there is no right to "liberty" under the Due Process Clause, though today's opinion repeatedly makes that claim. . . .

Our opinions applying the doctrine known as "substantive due process" hold that the Due Process Clause prohibits States from infringing *fundamental* liberty interests, unless the infringement is narrowly tailored to serve a compelling state interest. We have held repeatedly, in cases the Court today does not overrule, that *only* fundamental rights qualify for this so-called "heightened scrutiny" protection—that is, rights which are "'deeply rooted in this Nation's history and tradition.'" All other liberty interests may be abridged or abrogated pursuant to a validly enacted state law if that law is rationally related to a legitimate state interest.

Bowers held, first, that criminal prohibitions of homosexual sodomy are not subject to heightened scrutiny because they do not implicate a "fundamental right" under the Due Process Clause. Noting that "[p]roscriptions against that conduct have ancient roots," that "[s]odomy was a criminal offense at common law and was forbidden by the laws of the original 13 States when they ratified the Bill of Rights," and that many States had retained their bans on sodomy, *Bowers* concluded that a right to engage in homosexual sodomy was not "'deeply rooted in this Nation's history and tradition.'"

The Court today does not overrule this holding. Not once does it describe homosexual sodomy as a "fundamental right" or a "fundamental liberty interest," nor does it subject the Texas statute to strict scrutiny. Instead, having failed to establish that the right to homosexual sodomy is "'deeply rooted in this Nation's history and tradition,'" the Court concludes that the application of Texas's statute to petitioners' conduct fails the rational-basis test, and overrules *Bowers'* holding to the contrary. "The Texas statute furthers no legitimate state interest which can justify its intrusion into the personal and private life of the individual." . . .

. . . This proposition is so out of accord with our jurisprudence—indeed, with the jurisprudence of *any* society we know—that it requires little discussion.

The Texas statute undeniably seeks to further the belief of its citizens that certain forms of sexual behavior are "immoral and unacceptable"—the same interest furthered by criminal laws against fornication, bigamy, adultery, adult incest, bestiality, and obscenity. . . .

Today's opinion is the product of a Court, which is the product of a law-profession culture, that has largely signed on to the so-called homosexual agenda, by which I mean the agenda promoted by some homosexual activists directed at eliminating the moral opprobrium that has traditionally attached to homosexual conduct. . . .

Let me be clear that I have nothing against homosexuals, or any other group, promoting their agenda through normal democratic means. Social perceptions of sexual and other morality change over time, and every group has the right to persuade its fellow citizens that its view of such matters is the best. That homosexuals have achieved some success in that enterprise is attested to by the fact that Texas is one of the few remaining States that criminalize private, consensual homosexual acts. But persuading one's fellow citizens is one thing, and imposing one's views in absence of democratic majority will is something else. I would no more *require* a State to criminalize homosexual acts—or, for that matter, display *any* moral disapprobation of them—than I would *forbid* it to do so.

At the end of its opinion—after having laid waste the foundations of our rational-basis jurisprudence—the Court says that the present case "does not involve whether the government must give formal recognition to any relationship that homosexual persons seek to enter." Do not believe it. . . . If moral disapproval of homosexual conduct is "no legitimate state interest" for purposes of proscribing that conduct; and if, as the Court coos (casting aside all pretense of neutrality), "[w]hen sexuality finds overt expression in intimate conduct with another person, the conduct can be but one element in a personal bond that is more enduring," what justification could there possibly be for denying the benefits of marriage to homosexual couples exercising "[t]he liberty protected by the Constitution." . . .

In *Lawrence,* the majority not only overruled prior precedent but also made the even rarer move of admitting that the Court had made a mistake in *Bowers.* Kennedy claimed that the *Bowers* justices "overstated" the historical premises on which their analyses relied, that they had failed "to appreciate the extent of the liberty interest at stake," and that they had not accounted for contemporaneous developments regarding the liberty of adults to decide how to conduct their private lives.

But *Lawrence* is noteworthy for other reasons, too. Linda Greenhouse of the *New York Times* declared, "While the political, social, and legal ramifications may take years to play out, there is no doubt that *Lawrence v. Texas* is a constitutional watershed."[17] As we shall see, the implications associated with *Lawrence* did not take years to play out: Just 12 years later, the Court invalidated bans on same-sex marriage—citing *Lawrence* over a dozen times. Greenhouse was right, however, about the importance of *Lawrence.* First, in overruling *Bowers,* the Court did not necessarily treat the right to same-sex sodomy as a fundamental right. But it did suggest that there is a significant liberty interest at stake—an interest grounded in privacy, dignity, and freedom from stigma—that the state's reason for curtailing could not justify. This is a substantial departure from *Bowers,* as Justice Antonin Scalia notes. In *Bowers,* the Court accepted the state's moral justification for criminalizing private consensual sexual acts as sufficient to uphold the sodomy law; in *Lawrence* it did not. In so concluding, Kennedy resisted the typical due process (and equal protection) tests of rational basis or heightened scrutiny. It is just that the moral justification cannot overcome *Lawrence*'s strong personal liberty interests.

Second, the Court declined the opportunity to rest the decision on the equal protection clause (though note Justice O'Connor's concurring opinion). As a result, although *Lawrence* was a major victory for privacy advocates, it did not significantly expand the meaning or scope of protection of the equal protection clause—the constitutional provision most frequently used to combat claims of discrimination. On the other hand, *Lawrence* played a consequential role in ultimately invalidating bans on same-sex marriage. Let's consider how.

Same-Sex Marriage

In his dissent in *Lawrence,* Justice Scalia offered the following forecast: "The Court says that the present case

---

[17]Linda Greenhouse, "In Momentous Term, Supreme Court Justices Remake Both Law and Themselves," *New York Times,* July 1, 2003, A18.

'does not involve whether the government must give formal recognition to any relationship that homosexual persons seek to enter.' Do not believe it."

Scalia was not wrong to think that same-sex marriage was on the horizon. On the heels of *Lawrence*, the highest court in Massachusetts held in *Goodridge v. Department of Public Health* (2003) that state laws allowing only heterosexual couples to marry discriminated against gay persons in violation of the state constitution. Shortly thereafter, the court clarified that allowing gay couples to enter into civil unions but not legal marriages was not an acceptable substitute for full equality. As a consequence, in 2004 Massachusetts became the first state to allow gay couples to marry. Although the Massachusetts court's opinion rested on state grounds, it quoted from Justice Kennedy's opinion in *Lawrence*, agreeing with his sentiment that "[o]ur obligation is to define the liberty of all, not to mandate our own moral code."

In the decade following the *Goodridge* ruling, countries throughout the world moved to legalize same-sex marriage, as did thirty-seven states and the District of Columbia. Most of the states (twenty-six) did so because judges invalidated their existing bans; in only eleven (plus D.C.) did the public or its representatives vote to legalize same-sex marriage. But public opinion was changing. In 2010, only 44% of Americans believed that same-sex marriages should be recognized by the law as valid; by 2014, that percentage had increased to 55 percent.[18] (As of this writing, the percentage is 63%.)

The Court seemed to be moving closer to recognition as well. In 2013 it heard two cases related to same-sex marriage. One, ***Hollingsworth v. Perry*** (2013), was a due process and equal protection challenge to an amendment to the California constitution banning same-sex marriage. While the Court dismissed the case for lack of standing, the majority's opinion, by not overturning the lower court's decision that the ban was unconstitutional, had the effect of permitting same-sex marriage in California. In the other, ***United States v. Windsor*** (2013), the Court struck down a section of the federal Defense of Marriage Act, which defined marriage as a legally recognized relationship between one man and one woman for purposes of the more than one thousand federal laws that address marital or spousal status. Writing for the majority, Justice Kennedy held that the due process clause of the Fifth Amendment precludes the federal government from refusing to recognize a same-sex marriage valid

under state law. He rested his conclusion on the primacy of the state over issues of marriage and the incompatibility of due process guarantees with the federal government's discrimination against marriages entered into by gay couples.

Although the majority in *Windsor* did not say whether the due process or equal protection clauses constitutionally oblige the states to permit same-sex marriages, all but one federal court read *Windsor* to suggest that the states could not constitutionally make distinctions based on sexual orientation. As a result, they invalidated state bans on same-sex marriage. The one exception was the Court of Appeals for the Sixth Circuit. When it upheld Ohio's ban on same-sex marriage, it created a split among the circuits, paving the way for the Supreme Court's decision in *Obergefell v. Hodges*. (The Eighth Circuit upheld a state ban on same-sex marriage, but its 2006 decision predated *Windsor*.)

Obergefell v. Hodges

576 U.S. ___ (2015)
http://caselaw.findlaw.com/us-supreme-court/14-556.html
*Oral arguments available at https://www.oyez.org/
    cases/2014/14-556*
*Vote: 5 (Breyer, Ginsburg, Kagan, Kennedy, Sotomayor)
    4 (Scalia, Alito, Roberts, Thomas)*

OPINION OF THE COURT: *Kennedy*

DISSENTING OPINIONS: *Alito, Roberts, Scalia, Thomas*

In 2004 voters in Ohio passed a ballot initiative adding to the state constitution an amendment that read, "Only a union between one man and one woman may be a marriage valid in or recognized by this state and its political subdivisions." This meant that the state not only banned same-sex marriages but also would not recognize same-sex marriages performed in other states where they were legal.

The petitioner in this case, James Obergefell, was a resident of Ohio. When Obergefell's partner of two decades, John Arthur, was diagnosed with terminal amyotrophic lateral sclerosis (ALS), they decided to get married before Arthur died. The couple boarded a medically equipped plane and traveled to Maryland, a state that licensed same-sex marriages. They were wed on the tarmac on July 11, 2013. Arthur died a few months later.

After they were married but before Arthur's death, the couple filed suit in a federal district court against Ohio officials, alleging that the state's marriage bans violated the due process and equal protection clauses of the Fourteenth Amendment. Among other things, Arthur and Obergefell were concerned that the state would not

---

[18]Gallup Historical Trends, Gay and Lesbian Rights, http://www.gallup.com/poll/1651/gay-lesbian-rights.aspx.

BOX 16-4

Aftermath . . . John Lawrence and Tyron Garner

In *Lawrence v. Texas* (2003), the Supreme Court decriminalized intimate relations between same-sex, consenting adults. But research by Minnesota law professor Dale Carpenter reveals that what happened on the night of September 17, 1998, when John Lawrence and Tyron Garner were arrested, may well have been much different than the official record reveals.[a]

Carpenter describes Lawrence and Garner as rather unlikely, almost accidental, Supreme Court litigants. Both came from Baptist families and neither had a history of participating in gay rights causes. Lawrence was a Navy veteran who worked as a medical technologist in Houston area hospitals. Garner was often unemployed and sometimes homeless, but he later sold barbecue from a street stand. Both had lives sprinkled with violations of the law, usually related to alcohol abuse. Throughout the litigation that bore their names, they remained quiet and out of the public spotlight.

On the night of their arrest, Lawrence, Garner, and two other men spent part of the evening watching television and drinking in Lawrence's apartment. Among those present was Robert Eubanks, with whom Garner had a stormy and sometimes violent romantic relationship. Eubanks became overcome with jealousy when he perceived Garner to be flirting with Lawrence. Eubanks left the apartment supposedly to get some soda, but while he was gone he called police and falsely reported that an out-of-control, armed black man was in the apartment and threatening neighbors. Four police officers quickly arrived and entered the apartment without a warrant, but they found no dangerous suspect. The officers did, however, arrest Lawrence and Garner on sodomy charges.

According to Carpenter's account, Lawrence claimed that he and Garner did not have sexual relations that evening. They were friends but were not in a romantic relationship. In fact, he claimed that they were clothed and not even physically close to each other when police arrived. Lawrence was deeply upset by police barging into his apartment without a warrant and unjustly making arrests. He and Garner pleaded not guilty on the grounds that no crime had been committed.

The two defendants soon became represented by attorneys from Lambda Legal, a gay rights organization, who were interested in using the case to challenge the constitutionality of the Texas statute. To do so, however, Lawrence and Garner would have to drop their not guilty pleas and instead enter a plea of no contest. This allowed their attorneys to focus on the constitutionality of the statute under which they were arrested without making any factual claims that might allow a court to sidestep the constitutional issue by finding the defendants not guilty of committing the crime. The lawyers also instructed Lawrence and Garner to remain silent during the course of the litigation. Emphasis had to be sharply focused on the challenged law, not on the litigants or what did or did not happen in the apartment that night.

Whatever the truth of that evening, the following years were not kind to any of the main participants. Tyron Garner contracted meningitis and died of septic shock at the age of thirty-nine, just three years after the Supreme Court ruling. John Lawrence passed away at age sixty-eight from a heart ailment five years after Garner's death. During his illness, Lawrence was cared for by his longtime partner, Jose Garcia. Robert Eubanks, the man who called the police, was convicted of filing a false report and served a two-week jail sentence. Long before the Supreme Court even received the appeal, Eubanks was found beaten to death. Tyron Garner was a prime suspect in the murder, but the crime remains unsolved.

Sources: Dale Carpenter, *Flagrant Conduct: The Story of* Lawrence v. Texas (New York: W. W. Norton 2012); Adam Liptak, "John Lawrence, Plaintiff in Gay Rights Case, Dies at 68," *New York Times,* December 23, 2011; Dahlia Lithwick, "Extreme Makeover: The Story behind the Story of *Lawrence v. Texas,*" *The New Yorker,* March 12, 2012; Douglas Martin, "Tyron Garner, 39, Plaintiff in Pivotal Sodomy Case, Dies, *New York Times,* September 14, 2006.

[a]For a much different account of the events of that evening, see Janice Law, *Sex Appealed* (Austin, TX: Eaton Press, 2005).

recognize their marriage on Arthur's death certificate. If Obergefell had been a woman, Ohio would have listed him as the surviving spouse. But because Arthur had married another man, the couple thought Ohio would treat them as if they were legally unconnected—strangers under the law.

The district court ruled in their favor. It held that Ohio's marriage bans violated the fundamental liberty protected by the due process clause to remain married without a rational justification. It also ruled that the bans discriminate on the basis of sexual orientation—discrimination that the state failed to justify under either heightened equal protection scrutiny or rational basis review (*see* chapter 19 for more on these standards of review).

The U.S. Court of Appeals for the Sixth Circuit reversed. Applying a deferential rational basis test, the court held that the state had sufficiently justified its bans: the bans further the government's legitimate interest in regulating male-female relationships because of their procreative capacity and "risk of unintended offspring." The court also emphasized the state's interest in letting the people, not the courts, decide an issue as important as same-sex marriage.

In so ruling, the Sixth Circuit became the only federal circuit court since *Windsor* to uphold bans on the right to marry and on recognition of out-of-state marriages of same-sex couples; the Fourth, Seventh, Ninth, and Tenth Circuits all invalidated state bans.

Obergefell appealed to the U.S. Supreme Court, as did other same-sex couples who wanted the Court to hold that prohibitions on same-sex marriage violate the due process clause, the equal protection, or both.

JUSTICE KENNEDY DELIVERED THE OPINION OF THE COURT.

The Constitution promises liberty to all within its reach, a liberty that includes certain specific rights that allow persons, within a lawful realm, to define and express their identity. The petitioners in these cases seek to find that liberty by marrying someone of the same sex and having their marriages deemed lawful on the same terms and conditions as marriages between persons of the opposite sex. . . .

Before addressing the principles and precedents that govern these cases, it is appropriate to note the history of the subject now before the Court. . . .

[M]arriage was once viewed as an arrangement by the couple's parents based on political, religious, and financial concerns; but by the time of the Nation's founding it was understood to be a voluntary contract between a man and a woman. As the role and status of women changed, the institution further evolved. Under the centuries-old doctrine of coverture, a married man and woman were treated by the State as a single, male-dominated legal entity. As women gained legal, political, and property rights, and as society began to understand that women have their own equal dignity, the law of coverture was abandoned. . . .

These new insights have strengthened, not weakened, the institution of marriage. Indeed, changed understandings of marriage are characteristic of a Nation where new dimensions of freedom become apparent to new generations, often through perspectives that begin in pleas or protests and then are considered in the political sphere and the judicial process.

This dynamic can be seen in the Nation's experiences with the rights of gays and lesbians. Until the mid–20th century, same-sex intimacy long had been condemned as immoral by the state itself in most Western nations, a belief often embodied in the criminal law. For this reason, among others, many persons did not deem homosexuals to have dignity in their own distinct identity. . . .

In the late 20th century, following substantial cultural and political developments, same-sex couples began to lead more open and public lives and to establish families. This development was followed by a quite extensive discussion of the issue in both governmental and private sectors and by a shift in public attitudes toward greater tolerance. As a result, questions about the rights of gays and lesbians soon reached the courts, where the issue could be discussed in the formal discourse of the law. . . .

Under the Due Process Clause of the Fourteenth Amendment, no State shall "deprive any person of life, liberty, or property, without due process of law." The fundamental liberties protected by this Clause include most of the rights enumerated in the Bill of Rights. In addition these liberties extend to certain personal choices central to individual dignity and autonomy, including intimate choices that define personal identity and beliefs. . . .

The identification and protection of fundamental rights is an enduring part of the judicial duty to interpret the Constitution. That responsibility . . . requires courts to exercise reasoned judgment in identifying interests of the person so fundamental that the State must accord them its respect. That process is guided by many of the same considerations relevant to analysis of other constitutional provisions that set forth broad principles rather than specific requirements. History and tradition guide and discipline this inquiry but do not set its outer boundaries. See *Lawrence v. Texas*. That method respects our history and learns from it without allowing the past alone to rule the present.

The nature of injustice is that we may not always see it in our own times. The generations that wrote and ratified the Bill of Rights and the Fourteenth Amendment did not presume to know the extent of freedom in all of its dimensions, and so they entrusted to future generations a charter protecting the right of all persons to enjoy liberty as we learn its meaning. When new insight reveals discord between the Constitution's central protections and a received legal stricture, a claim to liberty must be addressed.

Applying these established tenets, the Court has long held the right to marry is protected by the Constitution. In *Loving v. Virginia*

(1967), which invalidated bans on interracial unions, a unanimous Court held marriage is "one of the vital personal rights essential to the orderly pursuit of happiness by free men." Over time and in other contexts, the Court has reiterated that the right to marry is fundamental under the Due Process Clause. . . .

In defining the right to marry these cases have identified essential attributes of that right based in history, tradition, and other constitutional liberties inherent in this intimate bond. See, e.g., *Lawrence; Loving; Griswold.* And in assessing whether the force and rationale of its cases apply to same-sex couples, the Court must respect the basic reasons why the right to marry has been long protected.

This analysis compels the conclusion that same-sex couples may exercise the right to marry. The four principles and traditions to be discussed demonstrate that the reasons marriage is fundamental under the Constitution apply with equal force to same-sex couples.

A first premise of the Court's relevant precedents is that the right to personal choice regarding marriage is inherent in the concept of individual autonomy. This abiding connection between marriage and liberty is why *Loving* invalidated interracial marriage bans under the Due Process Clause. Like choices concerning contraception, family relationships, procreation, and childrearing, all of which are protected by the Constitution, decisions concerning marriage are among the most intimate that an individual can make.

The nature of marriage is that, through its enduring bond, two persons together can find other freedoms, such as expression, intimacy, and spirituality. This is true for all persons, whatever their sexual orientation. See *Windsor.* . . .

A second principle in this Court's jurisprudence is that the right to marry is fundamental because it supports a two-person union unlike any other in its importance to the committed individuals. This point was central to *Griswold v. Connecticut,* which held the Constitution protects the right of married couples to use contraception. . . .

Marriage responds to the universal fear that a lonely person might call out only to find no one there. It offers the hope of companionship and understanding and assurance that while both still live there will be someone to care for the other.

As this Court held in *Lawrence,* same-sex couples have the same right as opposite-sex couples to enjoy intimate association. . . . *Lawrence* confirmed a dimension of freedom that allows individuals to engage in intimate association without criminal liability, [but] it does not follow that freedom stops there. Outlaw to outcast may be a step forward, but it does not achieve the full promise of liberty.

A third basis for protecting the right to marry is that it safeguards children and families and thus draws meaning from related rights of childrearing, procreation, and education. . . . Under the laws of the several States, some of marriage's protections for children and families are material. But marriage also confers more

profound benefits. By giving recognition and legal structure to their parents' relationship, marriage allows children "to understand the integrity and closeness of their own family and its concord with other families in their community and in their daily lives." Marriage also affords the permanency and stability important to children's best interests. . . .

Without the recognition, stability, and predictability marriage offers, [the] children [of same-sex couples] suffer the stigma of knowing their families are somehow lesser. They also suffer the significant material costs of being raised by unmarried parents, relegated through no fault of their own to a more difficult and uncertain family life. The marriage laws at issue here thus harm and humiliate the children of same-sex couples.

That is not to say the right to marry is less meaningful for those who do not or cannot have children. . . . The constitutional marriage right has many aspects, of which childbearing is only one.

Fourth and finally, this Court's cases and the Nation's traditions make clear that marriage is a keystone of our social order. [J]ust as a couple vows to support each other, so does society pledge to support the couple, offering symbolic recognition and material benefits to protect and nourish the union. Indeed, while the States are in general free to vary the benefits they confer on all married couples, they have throughout our history made marriage the basis for an expanding list of governmental rights, benefits, and responsibilities. These aspects of marital status include: taxation; inheritance and property rights; rules of intestate succession; spousal privilege in the law of evidence; hospital access; medical decisionmaking authority; adoption rights; the rights and benefits of survivors; birth and death certificates; professional ethics rules; campaign finance restrictions; workers' compensation benefits; health insurance; and child custody, support, and visitation rules. The States have contributed to the fundamental character of the marriage right by placing that institution at the center of so many facets of the legal and social order.

There is no difference between same- and opposite-sex couples with respect to this principle. Yet by virtue of their exclusion from that institution, same-sex couples are denied the constellation of benefits that the States have linked to marriage. This harm results in more than just material burdens. Same-sex couples are consigned to an instability many opposite-sex couples would deem intolerable in their own lives. . . . It demeans gays and lesbians for the State to lock them out of a central institution of the Nation's society. . . .

The limitation of marriage to opposite-sex couples may long have seemed natural and just, but its inconsistency with the central meaning of the fundamental right to marry is now manifest. With that knowledge must come the recognition that laws excluding same-sex couples from the marriage right impose stigma and injury of the kind prohibited by our basic charter. . . .

The right of same-sex couples to marry that is part of the liberty promised by the Fourteenth Amendment is derived, too, from that

Amendment's guarantee of the equal protection of the laws. The Due Process Clause and the Equal Protection Clause are connected in a profound way, though they set forth independent principles. Rights implicit in liberty and rights secured by equal protection may rest on different precepts and are not always co-extensive, yet in some instances each may be instructive as to the meaning and reach of the other. In any particular case one Clause may be thought to capture the essence of the right in a more accurate and comprehensive way, even as the two Clauses may converge in the identification and definition of the right. This interrelation of the two principles furthers our understanding of what freedom is and must become.

The Court's cases touching upon the right to marry reflect this dynamic. In *Loving* the Court invalidated a prohibition on interracial marriage under both the Equal Protection Clause and the Due Process Clause. The Court first declared the prohibition invalid because of its unequal treatment of interracial couples. . . . With this link to equal protection the Court proceeded to hold the prohibition offended central precepts of liberty: "To deny this fundamental freedom on so unsupportable a basis as the racial classifications embodied in these statutes, classifications so directly subversive of the principle of equality at the heart of the Fourteenth Amendment, is surely to deprive all the State's citizens of liberty without due process of law." The reasons why marriage is a fundamental right became more clear and compelling from a full awareness and understanding of the hurt that resulted from laws barring interracial unions. . . .

Indeed, in interpreting the Equal Protection Clause, the Court has recognized that new insights and societal understandings can reveal unjustified inequality within our most fundamental institutions that once passed unnoticed and unchallenged. . . .

In *Lawrence* the Court acknowledged the interlocking nature of these constitutional safeguards in the context of the legal treatment of gays and lesbians. Although *Lawrence* elaborated its holding under the Due Process Clause, it acknowledged, and sought to remedy, the continuing inequality that resulted from laws making intimacy in the lives of gays and lesbians a crime against the State. *Lawrence* therefore drew upon principles of liberty and equality to define and protect the rights of gays and lesbians, holding the State "cannot demean their existence or control their destiny by making their private sexual conduct a crime."

This dynamic also applies to same-sex marriage. It is now clear that the challenged laws burden the liberty of same-sex couples, and it must be further acknowledged that they abridge central precepts of equality. Here the marriage laws enforced by the respondents are in essence unequal: same-sex couples are denied all the benefits afforded to opposite-sex couples and are barred from exercising a fundamental right. Especially against a long history of disapproval of their relationships, this denial to same-sex couples of the right to marry works a grave and continuing harm. The imposition of this disability on gays and lesbians serves to disrespect and subordinate them. And

the Equal Protection Clause, like the Due Process Clause, prohibits this unjustified infringement of the fundamental right to marry.

These considerations lead to the conclusion that the right to marry is a fundamental right inherent in the liberty of the person, and under the Due Process and Equal Protection Clauses of the Fourteenth Amendment couples of the same-sex may not be deprived of that right and that liberty. The Court now holds that same-sex couples may exercise the fundamental right to marry. No longer may this liberty be denied to them. . . . [The] State laws challenged by Petitioners in these cases are now held invalid to the extent they exclude same-sex couples from civil marriage on the same terms and conditions as opposite-sex couples. . . .

No union is more profound than marriage, for it embodies the highest ideals of love, fidelity, devotion, sacrifice, and family. In forming a marital union, two people become something greater than once they were. As some of the petitioners in these cases demonstrate, marriage embodies a love that may endure even past death. It would misunderstand these men and women to say they disrespect the idea of marriage. Their plea is that they do respect it, respect it so deeply that they seek to find its fulfillment for themselves. Their hope is not to be condemned to live in loneliness, excluded from one of civilization's oldest institutions. They ask for equal dignity in the eyes of the law. The Constitution grants them that right.

The judgment of the Court of Appeals for the Sixth Circuit is reversed.

It is so ordered.

CHIEF JUSTICE ROBERTS, WITH WHOM JUSTICE SCALIA AND JUSTICE THOMAS JOIN, DISSENTING.

Petitioners make strong arguments rooted in social policy and considerations of fairness. They contend that same-sex couples should be allowed to affirm their love and commitment through marriage, just like opposite-sex couples. That position has undeniable appeal; over the past six years, voters and legislators in eleven States and the District of Columbia have revised their laws to allow marriage between two people of the same sex.

But this Court is not a legislature. Whether same-sex marriage is a good idea should be of no concern to us. Under the Constitution, judges have power to say what the law is, not what it should be. The people who ratified the Constitution authorized courts to exercise "neither force nor will but merely judgment." The Federalist No. 78 (A. Hamilton)

Although the policy arguments for extending marriage to same-sex couples may be compelling, the legal arguments for requiring such an extension are not. The fundamental right to marry does not include a right to make a State change its definition of marriage. And a State's decision to maintain the meaning of marriage that has persisted in every culture throughout human history can hardly be called irrational. In short, our Constitution does not enact any one theory of marriage. The people of a State are free to expand marriage to include same-sex couples, or to retain the historic definition.

Today, however, the Court takes the extraordinary step of ordering every State to license and recognize same-sex marriage. Many people will rejoice at this decision, and I begrudge none their celebration. But for those who believe in a government of laws, not of men, the majority's approach is deeply disheartening. Supporters of same-sex marriage have achieved considerable success persuading their fellow citizens—through the democratic process—to adopt their view. That ends today. Five lawyers have closed the debate and enacted their own vision of marriage as a matter of constitutional law. Stealing this issue from the people will for many cast a cloud over same-sex marriage, making a dramatic social change that much more difficult to accept.

The majority's decision is an act of will, not legal judgment. The right it announces has no basis in the Constitution or this Court's precedent. The majority expressly disclaims judicial "caution" and omits even a pretense of humility, openly relying on its desire to remake society according to its own "new insight" into the "nature of injustice." As a result, the Court invalidates the marriage laws of more than half the States and orders the transformation of a social institution that has formed the basis of human society for millennia, for the Kalahari Bushmen and the Han Chinese, the Carthaginians and the Aztecs. Just who do we think we are?

It can be tempting for judges to confuse our own preferences with the requirements of the law. But as this Court has been reminded throughout our history, the Constitution "is made for people of fundamentally differing views." *Lochner v. New York* (1905) (Holmes, J., dissenting). Accordingly, "courts are not concerned with the wisdom or policy of legislation." The majority today neglects that restrained conception of the judicial role. It seizes for itself a question the Constitution leaves to the people, at a time when the people are engaged in a vibrant debate on that question. And it answers that question based not on neutral principles of constitutional law, but on its own "understanding of what freedom is and must become." I have no choice but to dissent.

Understand well what this dissent is about: It is not about whether, in my judgment, the institution of marriage should be changed to include same-sex couples. It is instead about whether, in our democratic republic, that decision should rest with the people acting through their elected representatives, or with five lawyers who happen to hold commissions authorizing them to resolve legal disputes according to law. The Constitution leaves no doubt about the answer. . . .

Allowing unelected federal judges to select which unenumerated rights rank as "fundamental"—and to strike down state laws on the basis of that determination—raises obvious concerns about the judicial role. Our precedents have accordingly insisted that judges "exercise the utmost care" in identifying implied fundamental rights, "lest the liberty protected by the Due Process Clause be subtly transformed into the policy preferences of the Members of this Court." *Washington v. Glucksberg.* . . .

The need for restraint in administering the strong medicine of substantive due process is a lesson this Court has learned the hard way. The Court first applied substantive due process to strike down a statute in *Dred Scott v. Sandford,* (1857). There the Court invalidated the Missouri Compromise on the ground that legislation restricting the institution of slavery violated the implied rights of slaveholders. The Court relied on its own conception of liberty and property in doing so. . . .

Dred Scott's holding was overruled on the battlefields of the Civil War and by constitutional amendment after Appomattox, but its approach to the Due Process Clause reappeared. In a series of early 20th-century cases, most prominently *Lochner v. New York,* this Court invalidated state statutes that presented "meddlesome interferences with the rights of the individual," and "undue interference with liberty of person and freedom of contract." In *Lochner* itself, the Court struck down a New York law setting maximum hours for bakery employees, because there was "in our judgment, no reasonable foundation for holding this to be necessary or appropriate as a health law." . . .

In the decades after *Lochner,* the Court struck down nearly 200 laws as violations of individual liberty, often over strong dissents contending that "[t]he criterion of constitutionality is not whether we believe the law to be for the public good." *Adkins v. Children's Hospital of D.C.,* (1923) (opinion of Holmes, J.). By empowering judges to elevate their own policy judgments to the status of constitutionally protected "liberty," the *Lochner* line of cases left "no alternative to regarding the court as a . . . legislative chamber." . . .

The majority acknowledges none of this doctrinal background, and it is easy to see why: Its aggressive application of substantive due process breaks sharply with decades of precedent and returns the Court to the unprincipled approach of *Lochner.* . . .

Perhaps recognizing how little support it can derive from precedent, the majority goes out of its way to jettison the "careful" approach to implied fundamental rights taken by this Court in *Glucksberg.* The majority's position requires it to effectively overrule *Glucksberg,* the leading modern case setting the bounds of substantive due process. At least this part of the majority opinion has the virtue of candor. Nobody could rightly accuse the majority of taking a careful approach.

Ultimately, only one precedent offers any support for the majority's methodology: *Lochner v. New York.* . . .

In the face of all this, a much different view of the Court's role is possible. That view is more modest and restrained. It is more skeptical that the legal abilities of judges also reflect insight into moral and philosophical issues. It is more sensitive to the fact that judges are unelected and unaccountable, and that the legitimacy of their power depends on confining it to the exercise of legal judgment.

It is more attuned to the lessons of history, and what it has meant for the country and Court when Justices have exceeded their proper bounds. And it is less pretentious than to suppose that while people around the world have viewed an institution in a particular way for thousands of years, the present generation and the present Court are the ones chosen to burst the bonds of that history and tradition.

If you are among the many Americans—of whatever sexual orientation—who favor expanding same-sex marriage, by all means celebrate today's decision. Celebrate the achievement of a desired goal. Celebrate the opportunity for a new expression of commitment to a partner. Celebrate the availability of new benefits. But do not celebrate the Constitution. It had nothing to do with it.

JUSTICE SCALIA, WITH WHOM JUSTICE THOMAS JOINS, DISSENTING.

I join THE CHIEF JUSTICE's opinion in full. I write separately to call attention to this Court's threat to American democracy.

Until the courts put a stop to it, public debate over same-sex marriage displayed American democracy at its best. Individuals on both sides of the issue passionately, but respectfully, attempted to persuade their fellow citizens to accept their views. Americans considered the arguments and put the question to a vote. . . .

But the Court ends this debate, in an opinion lacking even a thin veneer of law. Buried beneath the mummeries and straining-to-be-memorable passages of the opinion is a candid and startling assertion: No matter what it was the People ratified, the Fourteenth Amendment protects those rights that the Judiciary, in its "reasoned judgment," thinks the Fourteenth Amendment ought to protect. . . .

This is a naked judicial claim to legislative—indeed, super-legislative—power; a claim fundamentally at odds with our system of government. Except as limited by a constitutional prohibition agreed to by the People, the States are free to adopt whatever laws they like, even those that offend the esteemed Justices' "reasoned judgment." A system of government that makes the People subordinate to a committee of nine unelected lawyers does not deserve to be called a democracy.

JUSTICE THOMAS, WITH WHOM JUSTICE SCALIA JOINS, DISSENTING.

The majority's decision today will require States to issue marriage licenses to same-sex couples and to recognize same-sex marriages entered in other States largely based on a constitutional provision guaranteeing "due process" before a person is deprived of his "life, liberty, or property." I have elsewhere explained the dangerous fiction of treating the Due Process Clause as a font of substantive rights. *McDonald v. Chicago,* (THOMAS, J., concurring in part and concurring in judgment). It distorts the constitutional text, which guarantees only whatever "process" is "due" before a person is deprived of life, liberty, and property. U.S. Const., Amdt. 14, § 1. Worse, it invites judges to

do exactly what the majority has done here—"'roa[m] at large in the constitutional field' guided only by their personal views" as to the "'fundamental rights'" protected by that document. . . .

Even assuming that the "liberty" in those Clauses encompasses something more than freedom from physical restraint, it would not include the types of rights claimed by the majority. In the American legal tradition, liberty has long been understood as individual freedom from governmental action, not as a right to a particular governmental entitlement. . . .

To the extent that the Framers would have recognized a natural right to marriage that fell within the broader definition of liberty, it would not have included a right to governmental recognition and benefits. Instead, it would have included a right to engage in the very same activities that petitioners have been left free to engage in—making vows, holding religious ceremonies celebrating those vows, raising children, and otherwise enjoying the society of one's spouse—without governmental interference. . . .

The majority's inversion of the original meaning of liberty will likely cause collateral damage to other aspects of our constitutional order that protect liberty. . . .

Numerous amici—even some not supporting the States—have cautioned the Court that its decision here will "have unavoidable and wide-ranging implications for religious liberty." In our society, marriage is not simply a governmental institution; it is a religious institution as well. Today's decision might change the former, but it cannot change the latter. It appears all but inevitable that the two will come into conflict, particularly as individuals and churches are confronted with demands to participate in and endorse civil marriages between same-sex couples.

The majority appears unmoved by that inevitability. It makes only a weak gesture toward religious liberty in a single paragraph. And even that gesture indicates a misunderstanding of religious liberty in our Nation's tradition. Religious liberty is about more than just the protection for "religious organizations and persons . . . as they seek to teach the principles that are so fulfilling and so central to their lives and faiths." Religious liberty is about freedom of action in matters of religion generally, and the scope of that liberty is directly correlated to the civil restraints placed upon religious practice. . . .

JUSTICE ALITO, WITH WHOM JUSTICE SCALIA AND JUSTICE THOMAS JOIN, DISSENTING.

Today's decision . . . will be used to vilify Americans who are unwilling to assent to the new orthodoxy. In the course of its opinion, the majority compares traditional marriage laws to laws that denied equal treatment for African-Americans and women. The implications of this analogy will be exploited by those who are determined to stamp out every vestige of dissent.

Perhaps recognizing how its reasoning may be used, the majority attempts, toward the end of its opinion, to reassure those who oppose same-sex marriage that their rights of conscience will be protected. We will soon see whether this proves to be true. I assume that those who cling to old beliefs will be able to whisper their thoughts in the recesses of their homes, but if they repeat those views in public, they will risk being labeled as bigots and treated as such by governments, employers, and schools. . . .

Because it provided a definitive answer to the question of whether states can ban same-sex marriage, *Obergefell* is a landmark decision. But it—not to mention the strenuous dissents of the Court's four conservative justices—raises even more questions. What will happen when claims of equality based on sexual orientation collide with claims of religious freedom, such as when florists refuse to provide flowers for a gay wedding on religious ground? This and related questions will likely implicate freedom of religion laws in the states *(see chapter 12)*, state civil rights and accommodation laws (some of which cover sexual orientation), and the equal protection clause of the Fourteenth Amendment *(see chapter 19)*.

Obergefell also raises more general questions especially about the proper role of federal judges and justices in a democratic society, as do many of the other cases in this chapter. Note that here the four liberals joined with Justice Kennedy to invalidate all existing bans on same-sex marriage. But, in *Citizens United v. Federal Elections* (2010) *(excerpted in chapter 20)*, when the (conservative) majority invalidated a law that restricted corporations and unions from spending money in elections to support or oppose candidates, the liberals complained, "In a democratic society, the longstanding consensus on the need to limit corporate campaign spending should outweigh the wooden application of judge-made rules." Are they taking a different position here? Why or why not? You could ask the same questions of the conservatives, who voted to invalidate the campaign spending law in *Citizens United* but in *Obergefell* chided the majority for substituting its judgment for the will of the people.

Whatever you conclude, you should know that however important *Obergefell* and its precursor, *Lawrence*, are, they are not the only recent Court decisions touching on personal liberty and the right to privacy. In the past few decades, the justices rendered important rulings in another difficult privacy issue: the right to die.

The Right to Die

Right-to-die cases present many different kinds of questions. Do competent patients have a fundamental privacy right, grounded in the liberty guarantee in the due process clause, to refuse medical treatment, food, or water? What about incompetent patients? Can the families or guardians of an incapacitated individual exercise that right on his or her behalf? Should a physician (or even a nonphysician) have the right to assist a consenting individual in the commission of suicide? These are questions that faced the Rehnquist Court beginning with *Cruzan v. Director, Missouri Department of Health* (1990).

Cruzan v. Director, Missouri Department of Health

497 U.S. 261 (1990)
http://caselaw.findlaw.com/us-supreme-court/497/261.html
Oral arguments available at https://www.oyez.org/ cases/1989/88-1503
Vote: 5 (Kennedy, O'Connor, Rehnquist, Scalia, White)
4 (Blackmun, Brennan, Marshall, Stevens)

OPINION OF THE COURT: *Rehnquist*

CONCURRING OPINIONS: *O'Connor, Scalia*

DISSENTING OPINIONS: *Brennan, Stevens*

In January 1983 Nancy Beth Cruzan was in a serious car accident. When paramedics found her, she was "lying face down in a ditch without detectable respiratory or cardiac function." Although they were able to restore her breathing and heartbeat, Cruzan remained unconscious and was taken to a hospital. Both short- and long-term medical efforts failed, and, as a result, Cruzan degenerated to a persistent vegetative state, "a condition in which a person exhibits motor reflexes but evinces no indications of significant cognitive function." She required feeding and hydration tubes to stay alive. When Cruzan's case was presented before the Court, some experts suggested that she might live another thirty years, but no one predicted any improvement in her condition.

Her parents, Lester and Joyce Cruzan, asked doctors to remove her feeding tubes, a step that would lead to Nancy's death. The hospital staff refused, and the Cruzans sought permission from a state court. The Cruzans argued that "a person in Nancy's condition had a fundamental right to refuse or direct the withdrawal of 'death prolonging procedures.'" They presented evidence that when Nancy was twenty-five, she had told a friend that "she would not wish to continue her life unless she could live it at least halfway normally."

The trial court ruled in their favor, but the state supreme court reversed. It found no support in common law for a right to die, and it refused to apply privacy doctrines to the Cruzan situation. It also held that because the state had a strong interest in preserving life, the Cruzans would have to provide "clear and convincing evidence" that their daughter would have wanted her feeding tubes withdrawn.

CHIEF JUSTICE REHNQUIST DELIVERED THE OPINION OF THE COURT.

We granted certiorari to consider the question of whether Cruzan has a right under the United States Constitution which would require the hospital to withdraw life-sustaining treatment from her under these circumstances. . . .

The Fourteenth Amendment provides that no state shall "deprive any person of life, liberty, or property, without due process of law." The principle that a competent person has a constitutionally protected liberty interest in refusing unwanted medical treatment may be inferred from our prior decisions. . . .

But determining that a person has a "liberty interest" under the Due Process Clause does not end the inquiry; "whether respondent's constitutional rights have been violated must be determined by balancing his liberty interests against the relevant state interests."

Petitioners insist that under the general holdings of our cases, the forced administration of life-sustaining medical treatment, and even of artificially-delivered food and water essential to life, would implicate a competent person's liberty interest. Although we think the logic of the cases . . . would embrace such a liberty interest, the dramatic consequences involved in refusal of such treatment would inform the inquiry as to whether the deprivation of that interest is constitutionally permissible. But for purposes of this case, we assume that the United States Constitution would grant a competent person a constitutionally protected right to refuse lifesaving hydration and nutrition.

Petitioners go on to assert that an incompetent person should possess the same right in this respect as is possessed by a competent person. . . .

The difficulty with petitioners' claim is that in a sense it begs the question: an incompetent person is not able to make an informed and voluntary choice to exercise a hypothetical right to refuse treatment or any other right. Such a "right" must be exercised for her, if at all, by some sort of surrogate. Here, Missouri has in effect recognized that under certain circumstances a surrogate may act for the patient in electing to have hydration and nutrition withdrawn in such a way as to cause death, but it has established a procedural safeguard to assure that the action of the surrogate conforms as best it may to the wishes expressed by the patient while competent. Missouri requires that evidence of the incompetent's wishes as to the withdrawal of treatment be proved by clear and convincing evidence. The question, then, is whether the United States Constitution forbids the establishment of this procedural requirement by the State. We hold that it does not.

Whether or not Missouri's clear and convincing evidence requirement comports with the United States Constitution depends in part on what interests the State may properly seek to protect in this situation. Missouri relies on its interest in the protection and preservation of human life, and there can be no gainsaying this interest. As a general matter, the States—indeed, all civilized nations—demonstrate their commitment to life by treating homicide as a serious crime. Moreover, the majority of States in this country have laws imposing criminal penalties on one who assists another to commit suicide. We do not think a State is required to remain neutral in the face of an informed and voluntary decision by a physically-able adult to starve to death.

But in the context presented here, a State has more particular interests at stake. The choice between life and death is a deeply personal decision of obvious and overwhelming finality. We believe Missouri may legitimately seek to safeguard the personal element of this choice through the imposition of heightened evidentiary requirements. It cannot be disputed that the Due Process Clause protects an interest in life as well as an interest in refusing life-sustaining medical treatment. Not all incompetent patients will have loved ones available to serve as surrogate decision-makers. And even where family members are present, "there will, of course, be some unfortunate situations in which family members will not act to protect a patient." A State is entitled to guard against potential abuses in such situations. Similarly, a State is entitled to consider that a judicial proceeding to make a determination regarding an incompetent's wishes may very well not be an adversarial one, with the added guarantee of accurate factfinding that the adversary process brings with it. Finally, we think a State may properly decline to make judgments about the "quality" of life that a particular individual may enjoy, and simply assert an unqualified interest in the preservation of human life to be weighed against the constitutionally protected interests of the individual.

In our view, Missouri has permissibly sought to advance these interests through the adoption of . . . "an intermediate standard of proof—'clear and convincing evidence'—when the individual interests at stake in a state proceeding are both 'particularly important' and 'more substantial than mere loss of money.'"

We think it self-evident that the interests at stake in the instant proceedings are more substantial, both on an individual and societal level, than those involved in a run-of-the-mine civil dispute. But not only does the standard of proof reflect the importance of a particular adjudication, it also serves as "a societal judgment about how the risk of error should be distributed between the litigants." The more stringent the burden of proof a party must bear, the more that party bears the risk of an erroneous decision. We believe that Missouri may permissibly place an increased risk of an erroneous decision on those seeking to terminate an incompetent individual's life-sustaining treatment. An erroneous decision not to terminate results in a maintenance of the status quo; the possibility of subsequent developments such as advancements in medical science, the discovery of new evidence regarding the patient's intent, changes in the law, or simply the unexpected death of the patient despite the administration of life-sustaining treatment, at least create the potential that a wrong decision will eventually be corrected or its impact mitigated. An erroneous decision to withdraw life-sustaining treatment, however, is not susceptible of correction. . . .

It is also worth noting that most, if not all, States simply forbid oral testimony entirely in determining the wishes of parties in transactions which, while important, simply do not have the consequences that a decision to terminate a person's life does. At common law and by statute in most States, the parole evidence rule prevents the variations of the terms of a written contract by oral testimony. The statute of frauds makes unenforceable oral contracts to leave property by will, and statutes regulating the making of wills universally require that those instruments be in writing. There is no doubt that statutes requiring wills to be in writing, and statutes of frauds which require that a contract to make a will be in writing, on occasion frustrate the effectuation of the intent of a particular decedent, just as Missouri's requirement of proof in this case may have frustrated the effectuation of the not-fully-expressed desires of Nancy Cruzan. But the Constitution does not require general rules to work faultlessly; no general rule can.

In sum, we conclude that a State may apply a clear and convincing evidence standard in proceedings where a guardian seeks to discontinue nutrition and hydration of a person diagnosed to be in a persistent vegetative state. . . .

The Supreme Court of Missouri held that in this case the testimony adduced at trial did not amount to clear and convincing proof of the patient's desire to have hydration and nutrition withdrawn. In so doing, it reversed a decision of the Missouri trial court which had found that the evidence "suggest[ed]" Nancy Cruzan would not have desired to continue such measures, but which had not adopted the standard of "clear and convincing evidence" enunciated by the Supreme Court. The testimony adduced at trial consisted primarily of Nancy Cruzan's statements made to a housemate about a year before her accident that she would not want to live should she face life as a "vegetable," and other observations to the same effect. The observations did not deal in terms with withdrawal of medical treatment or of hydration and nutrition. We cannot say that the Supreme Court of Missouri committed constitutional error in reaching the conclusion that it did.

Petitioners alternatively contend that Missouri must accept the "substituted judgment" of close family members even in the absence of substantial proof that their views reflect the views of the patient. . . . Here again petitioners would seek to turn a decision which allowed a State to rely on family decisionmaking into a constitutional requirement that the State recognize such decisionmaking. But constitutional law does not work that way.

No doubt is engendered by anything in this record but that Nancy Cruzan's mother and father are loving and caring parents. If the State were required by the United States Constitution to repose a right of "substituted judgment" with anyone, the Cruzans would surely qualify. But we do not think the Due Process Clause requires the State to repose judgment on these matters with anyone but the patient herself. Close family members may have a strong feeling—a feeling not at all ignoble or unworthy, but not entirely disinterested, either—that they do not wish to witness the continuation of the life of a loved one which they regard as hopeless, meaningless, and even degrading. But there is no automatic assurance that the view of close family members will necessarily be the same as the patient's would have been had she been confronted with the prospect of her situation while competent. All of the reasons previously discussed for allowing Missouri to require clear and convincing evidence of the patient's wishes lead us to conclude that the State may choose to defer only to those wishes, rather than confide the decision to close family members.

The judgment of the Supreme Court of Missouri is

Affirmed.

JUSTICE O'CONNOR, CONCURRING.

I agree that a protected liberty interest in refusing unwanted medical treatment may be inferred from our prior decisions . . . and that the refusal of artificially delivered food and water is encompassed within that liberty interest. . . .

I . . . write separately to emphasize that the Court does not today decide the issue whether a State must also give effect to the decisions of a surrogate decisionmaker. In my view, such a duty may well be constitutionally required to protect the patient's liberty interest in refusing medical treatment. Few individuals provide explicit oral or written instructions regarding their intent to refuse medical treatment should they become incompetent. States which decline to consider any evidence other than such instructions may frequently fail to honor a patient's intent. Such failures might be avoided if the State considered an equally probative source of evidence: the patient's appointment of a proxy to make health care decisions on her behalf. Delegating the authority to make medical decisions to a family member or friend is becoming a common method of planning for the future. Several States have recognized the practical wisdom of such a procedure by enacting durable power of attorney statutes that specifically authorize an individual to appoint a surrogate to make medical treatment decisions. . . .

Today's decision, holding only that the Constitution permits a State to require clear and convincing evidence of Nancy Cruzan's desire to have artificial hydration and nutrition withdrawn, does not preclude a future determination that the Constitution requires the States to implement the decisions of a patient's duly appointed surrogate. Nor does it prevent States from developing other approaches for protecting an incompetent individual's liberty interest in refusing medical treatment. . . . [N]o national consensus has yet emerged on the best solution for this difficult and sensitive problem. Today we decide only that one State's practice does not violate the Constitution; the more challenging task of crafting appropriate procedures for safeguarding incompetents' liberty interests is entrusted to the "laboratory" of the States.

JUSTICE SCALIA, CONCURRING.

While I agree with the Court's analysis today, and therefore join in its opinion, I would have preferred that we announce, clearly and promptly, that the federal courts have no business in this field; that American law has always accorded the State the power to prevent, by force if necessary, suicide—including suicide by refusing to take appropriate measures necessary to preserve one's life; that the point at which life becomes "worthless," and the point at which the means necessary to preserve it become "extraordinary" or "inappropriate," are neither set forth in the Constitution nor known to the nine Justices of this Court any better than they are known to nine people picked at random from the Kansas City telephone directory; and hence, that even when it is demonstrated by clear and convincing evidence that a patient no longer wishes certain measures to be taken to preserve her life, it is up to the citizens of Missouri to decide, through their elected representatives, whether that wish will be honored. . . .

. . . This Court need not, and has no authority to, inject itself into every field of human activity where irrationality and oppression may theoretically occur, and if it tries to do so it will destroy itself.

JUSTICE BRENNAN, WITH WHOM JUSTICE MARSHALL AND JUSTICE BLACKMUN JOIN, DISSENTING.

Today the Court, while tentatively accepting that there is some degree of constitutionally protected liberty interest in avoiding unwanted medical treatment, including life-sustaining medical treatment such as artificial nutrition and hydration, affirms the decision of the Missouri Supreme Court. The majority opinion, as I read it, would affirm that decision on the ground that a State may require "clear and convincing" evidence of Nancy Cruzan's prior decision to forgo life-sustaining treatment under circumstances such as hers in order to ensure that her actual wishes are honored. Because I believe that Nancy Cruzan has a fundamental right to be free of unwanted artificial nutrition and hydration, which right is not outweighed by any interests of the State, and because I find that the improperly biased procedural obstacles imposed by the Missouri Supreme Court impermissibly burden that right, I respectfully dissent. Nancy Cruzan is entitled to choose to die with dignity. . . .

The question before this Court is a relatively narrow one: whether the Due Process Clause allows Missouri to require a now-incompetent patient in an irreversible persistent vegetative state

to remain on life-support absent rigorously clear and convincing evidence that avoiding the treatment represents the patient's prior, express choice. . . .

A State's inability to discern an incompetent patient's choice still need not mean that a State is rendered powerless to protect that choice. But I would find that the Due Process Clause prohibits a State from doing more than that. A State may ensure that the person who makes the decision on the patient's behalf is the one whom the patient himself would have selected to make that choice for him. And a State may exclude from consideration anyone having improper motives. But a State generally must either repose the choice with the person whom the patient himself would most likely have chosen as proxy or leave the decision to the patient's family.

As many as 10,000 patients are being maintained in persistent vegetative states in the United States, and the number is expected to increase significantly in the near future. . . . The 80% of Americans who die in hospitals are "likely to meet their end . . . in a sedated or comatose state; betubed nasally, abdominally and intravenously; and far more like manipulated objects than like moral subjects." A fifth of all adults surviving to age 80 will suffer a progressive dementing disorder prior to death.

. . . The new medical technology can reclaim those who would have been irretrievably lost a few decades ago and restore them to active lives. For Nancy Cruzan, it failed, and for others with wasting incurable disease it may be doomed to failure. In these unfortunate situations, the bodies and preferences and memories of the victims do not escheat to the State; nor does our Constitution permit the State or any other government to commandeer them. No singularity of feeling exists upon which such a government might confidently rely as *parens patriae*. . . . Missouri and this Court have displaced Nancy's own assessment of the processes associated with dying. They have discarded evidence of her will, ignored her values, and deprived her of the right to a decision as closely approximating her own choice as humanly possible. They have done so disingenuously in her name, and openly in Missouri's own. That Missouri and this Court may truly be motivated only by concern for incompetent patients makes no matter. . . .

I respectfully dissent.

In August 1990, two months after the Court's decision, the Cruzans petitioned a Missouri court for a new hearing. At the hearing, three of Nancy's former coworkers testified that she had said she would not want to live "like a vegetable." Despite protests from pro-life groups, a state court judge ruled December 14 that the Cruzans could have Nancy's feeding tube removed. The tube was removed, and Nancy died on December 26.

For the Cruzans the battle was over, but, as Justice Brennan pointed out in his dissent, there were approximately ten thousand "Nancy Cruzans" in the United States at that time, a figure that could increase exponentially as medical technology advances. Does the Court's opinion provide guidance for them and their families? Yes and no. On one hand, the Court ruled that the Fourteenth Amendment's due process clause permits a competent individual to terminate medical treatment, though the Court did not say whether the right was fundamental or not. As to incompetent patients, assuming they have a right to decline food and water, the Court held that the state does not violate that due process liberty right by requiring clear and convincing evidence of the patient's wish to terminate her life. To the majority, the state's interest in protecting life and ensuring that any decisions accurately reflect the patient's wishes are strong enough to justify the requirement. In short, the majority suggested that states may fashion their own standards, including those that require "clear and convincing evidence" of the patient's interests. Living wills, as O'Connor's concurrence notes, may be the best form of such evidence. Finally, the Court held that family members do not have an independent liberty right under the due process clause to act as surrogates.

Note, though, that the case did not call for the Court to address another dimension of the right-to-die question—suicides or assisted suicides for the terminally ill. Do terminally ill persons have a fundamental right to take their own life or arrange for a physician-assisted suicide when suffering from an incurable illness? In the 1990s this question took on unusual importance as the media were full of accounts of people with progressively debilitating diseases seeking to end their lives and of the assisted suicides conducted by Dr. Jack Kevorkian and others. Some of the justices' opinions provided hints as to how they would rule on "mercy killings," assisted suicides, and so forth. In a 1996 speech, Justice Scalia did more than provide a hint: he asserted his belief that the Constitution plainly provides "no right to die."[19]

Seven years after *Cruzan*, the Court had the opportunity to consider whether the right to privacy or "liberty interest" is broad enough to encompass a fundamental right of assisted suicide. That opportunity came in two 1997 cases, ***Washington v. Glucksberg*** and ***Vacco v. Quill***, both involving state laws making it a crime to assist another to commit suicide. By 9–0 votes, the justices held that terminally ill patients do not have a fun-

damental right to the assistance of a physician to hasten death because there are no deeply rooted traditions supporting "suicide"; actually there are long-standing traditions against it. As a result, the Court subjected the laws to a rational basis analysis and found that the bans were reasonably related to states' legitimate interests in preserving human life, protecting the integrity and ethics of the medical profession, safeguarding the vulnerable from coercion, and ensuring the value of life, even of those who are ready to die.

What should we learn from these decisions? On one hand, the justices made it crystal clear that states may maintain their existing bans on assisted suicides. On the other, they did not foreclose the possibility of future constitutional claims. In a concurring opinion, Justice O'Connor, for example, left open the possibility that the Court might respond positively to the question of "whether a mentally competent person who is experiencing great suffering has a constitutionally cognizable interest in controlling the circumstances of his or her imminent death." The suggestion here is that there could be a right to alleviate uncontrollable pain.

O'Connor turned out to be prophetic. In ***Gonzales v. Oregon*** (2006), the Court took up Oregon's Death with Dignity Act, which permits state-licensed physicians to dispense or prescribe a lethal dose of drugs upon the request of a terminally ill patient. Although the law had been in effect since 1994 and had survived a ballot initiative designed to repeal it, in 2001 Attorney General John Ashcroft issued a rule asserting that the statute was unlawful. He claimed that the Controlled Substances Act (CSA) of 1970, enacted by Congress to regulate the legitimate and illegitimate trafficking of drugs, criminalizes the use of controlled substances to assist suicide. Physicians dispensing drugs for this purpose, he declared, were not engaging in the legitimate practice of medicine and could lose their privilege to write prescriptions.

The state, a physician, a pharmacist, and some terminally ill state residents challenged the rule. By the time the case reached the Supreme Court, Ashcroft was no longer attorney general, but his successor, Alberto Gonzales, stood by Ashcroft's interpretation of the CSA.

In a 6–3 decision, the Supreme Court expressed its firm disagreement with the *Gonzales/Ashcroft* rule. Writing for the majority, Justice Kennedy explained:

> In deciding whether the CSA can be read as prohibiting physician-assisted suicide, we look to the statute's text and design. The statute and our case law amply support the conclusion that

---

[19]Antonin Scalia, "A Theory of Constitutional Interpretation," remarks at the Catholic University Law School, Washington, D.C., October 18, 1996.

Congress regulates medical practice insofar as it bars doctors from using their prescription-writing powers as a means to engage in illicit drug dealing and trafficking as conventionally understood. Beyond this, however, the statute manifests no intent to regulate the practice of medicine generally. The silence is understandable given the structure and limitations of federalism, which allow the States "'great latitude under their police powers to legislate as to the protection of the lives, limbs, health, comfort, and quiet of all persons.'"

Chief Justice Roberts did not write an opinion, but he joined a dissent by Justice Scalia (as did Justice Thomas). Scalia wrote that it was "easy to sympathize" with the position he thought the majority opinion reflected—"a feeling that the subject of assisted suicide is none of the Federal Government's business." But, unlike the majority, he believed that "unless we were to repudiate a long and well-established principle of our jurisprudence," it was well within Congress's power to prevent assisted suicide.

Gonzales v. Oregon will not be the last word on this subject. Indeed, Chief Justice Rehnquist's words in *Glucksberg* remain as true today as when he wrote them: "Throughout the Nation, Americans are engaged in an earnest and profound debate about the morality, legality, and practicality of physician-assisted suicide." He further noted that the Court's decision "permits this debate to continue, as it should in a democratic society." We might say the same about *Gonzales.* Now seven other states and the District of Columbia allow physicians to prescribe lethal drugs to terminal patients to self-administer (California, Colorado, Hawaii, Maine, New Jersey, Vermont, and Washington), and bills are pending in several more.

ANNOTATED READINGS

On the foundations of the right to privacy and ensuing debates, see Thomas I. Emerson, "Nine Justices in Search of a Doctrine," *Michigan Law Review* 64 (1965): 219–234; James E. Fleming, *Securing Constitutional Democracy: The Case for Autonomy* (Chicago: University of Chicago Press, 2006); John W. Johnson, Griswold v. Connecticut: *Birth Control and the Constitutional Right of Privacy* (Lawrence: University Press of Kansas, 2005); Daniel J. Solove, *Understanding Privacy* (Cambridge, MA: Harvard University Press, 2008); Philippa Strum, *Privacy: The Debate in the United States since 1945* (Fort Worth, TX: Harcourt Brace College Publishers, 1998); Mary Ziegler, *Beyond Abortion:* Roe v. Wade *and the Battle for Privacy* (Cambridge, MA: Harvard University Press, 2018).

Roe v. Wade, abortion, and reproductive freedom have generated no shortage of volumes. See, e.g., Susan R. Burgess, *Contest for Constitutional Authority: The Abortion and War Powers Debate* (Lawrence: University Press of Kansas, 1992); John Hart Ely, "The Wages of Crying Wolf: A Comment on *Roe v. Wade*," *Yale Law Journal* 82 (1973): 920–949; Lee Epstein and Joseph F. Kobylka, *The Supreme Court and Legal Change: Abortion and the Death Penalty* (Chapel Hill: University of North Carolina Press, 1992); David. J. Garrow, *Liberty and Sexuality: The Right to Privacy and the Making of* Roe v. Wade (Berkeley: University of California Press, 1998); Mark A. Graber, *Rethinking Abortion: Equal Choice, the Constitution, and Reproductive Politics* (Princeton, NJ: Princeton University Press, 1996); Linda Greenhouse and Reva Siegel, *Before* Roe v. Wade: *Voices That Shaped the Abortion Debate before the Supreme Court Ruling* (New York: Kaplan, 2010); N. E. H. Hull and Peter Charles Hoffer, Roe v. Wade: *The Abortion Rights Controversy in American History* (Lawrence: University Press of Kansas, 2010); Eileen L. McDonagh, *Breaking the Abortion Deadlock: From Choice to Consent* (New York: Oxford University Press, 1996); Richard L. Pacelle Jr., *Between Law & Politics: The Solicitor General and the Structuring of Race, Gender, and Reproductive Rights Litigation* (College Station: Texas A&M University Press, 2003); Leslie J. Reagan, *When Abortion Was a Crime: Women, Medicine and Law in the United States, 1867–1973* (Berkeley: University of California Press, 1997); Laurence H. Tribe, *Abortion: The Clash of Absolutes* (New York: W. W. Norton, 1990); Barbara M. Yarnold, *Abortion Politics in the Federal Courts: Right versus Right* (Westport, CT: Praeger, 1995); and Mary Ziegler, *After* Roe: *The Lost History of the Abortion Debate* (Cambridge, MA: Harvard University Press, 2015).

For studies centering on private sexual activities, see William N. Eskridge Jr., *Dishonorable Passions: Sodomy*

Laws in America, 1861–2003 (New York: Viking, 2008); William N. Eskridge, Jr., *Gaylaw: Challenging the Apartheid of the Closet* (Cambridge, MA: Harvard University Press, 1999); and David A. J. Richards, *The Case for Gay Rights: From* Bowers *to* Lawrence *and Beyond* (Lawrence: University Press of Kansas, 2009). For books specifically on questions related to same-sex marriage, see Carlos A. Ball, ed., *After Marriage Equality: The Future of LGBT Rights* (New York University Press, 2016); Nathaniel Frank, *Awakening: How Gays and Lesbians Brought Marriage Equality to America* (Cambridge, MA: Harvard University Press, 2017); Adam Liptak, *To Have and Uphold: The Supreme Court and the Battle for Same-Sex Marriage* (New York: New York Times, 2013); Joseph Mello, *The Courts, the Ballot Box, and Gay Rights: How Our Governing Institutions Shape the Same-Sex Marriage Debate* (Lawrence: University Press of Kansas, 2016); Daniel R. Pinello, *America's War on Same-Sex Couples and Their Families: And How the Courts Rescued Them* (New York: Cambridge University Press, 2017). See also chapter 19.

On the issues related to the right to die, see Susan M. Behuniak and Arthur G. Svenson, *Physician-Assisted Suicide: The Anatomy of a Constitutional Law Issue* (Lanham, MD: Rowman and Littlefield, 2003); Elizabeth Price Foley, *The Law of Life and Death* (Cambridge, MA: Harvard University Press, 2011); Elizabeth Atwood Gailey, *Write to Death: News Framing of the Right-to-Die Conflict from Quinlan's Coma to Kevorkian's Conviction* (Westport, CT: Praeger, 2003); Henry R. Glick, *The Right to Die: Policy Innovation and Its Consequences* (New York: Columbia University Press, 1992); Jennifer M. Scherer and Rita J. Simon, *Euthanasia and the Right to Die: A Comparative View* (Lanham, MD: Rowman and Littlefield, 1999); Melvin I. Urofsky, *Lethal Judgments: Assisted Suicide and American Law* (Lawrence: University Press of Kansas, 2000); Raymond Whiting, *A Natural Right to Die: Twenty-Three Centuries of Debate* (Westport, CT: Greenwood Press, 2002); and Marjorie B. Zucker, *The Right to Die Debate: A Documentary History* (Westport, CT: Greenwood Press, 1999).

THE RIGHTS OF THE CRIMINALLY ACCUSED

EQUAL · JUSTICE · UNDER

AMERICANS REGARD the Bill of Rights as an enumeration of cherished freedoms. The right to speak freely and to worship (or not) without undue interference from government are the guarantees to which politicians and citizens refer most often when they describe the unique character of the United States. We may need to be reminded, therefore, that four of the first eight amendments guarantee rights for the *criminally accused*. The framers of the Constitution placed great emphasis on criminal rights because they had grown to despise the abusive practices of British criminal procedure. They believed that agents of government should not enter private homes or search personal property without proper justification and that the accused should not be tried without the benefit of public scrutiny.

Consequently, the Fourth Amendment protects against unreasonable searches and prescribes the procedures by which law enforcement officials can obtain search warrants. The Fifth Amendment prohibits self-incrimination and double jeopardy and provides for grand juries and due process of law. The Sixth Amendment governs trial proceedings. It calls for speedy and public jury trials during which defendants can call witnesses and face their accusers. It also provides for the assistance of counsel. The Eighth Amendment prohibits excessive bail and monetary fines and any punishments that are cruel and unusual. So, in a number of important respects, the framers furnished constitutional guarantees that would protect all—the guilty as well as the innocent—against the potentially abusive prosecutorial powers of the government.

Just because these rights might not be the first that come to mind when we think about the Bill of Rights does not mean that they are any less important or less relevant to society. Most Americans are likely to participate in the criminal justice system at least once during their lives. Some may be the victims of crime. Others may serve as jurors in a criminal trial or be called to testify as witnesses. Still others may even be accused of a crime. Whatever the manner of participation in the justice system, it invariably intersects with the constitutional guarantees that relate to criminal procedure. The Supreme Court—ever mindful of the need to safeguard those guarantees—has devoted a great deal of time to the interpretation of the constitutional protections relating to the investigation, prosecution, and punishment of crime.

The two chapters that follow explore the constitutional rights of the criminally accused and the Supreme Court's interpretation of them. To appreciate their importance, however, we first take a brief look at the stages of the criminal justice process. Following that discussion, we describe trends in Supreme Court decision making in this area.

OVERVIEW OF THE CRIMINAL JUSTICE SYSTEM

Figure VI-1 provides a general overview of the criminal justice system and the constitutional rights effective at each stage. You should keep two points in mind. First, because the states have a degree of latitude in developing their criminal justice systems, these procedures may vary from jurisdiction to jurisdiction. Second, less than 10 percent of all criminal cases actually proceed through every stage of the system. At some point during the process, most criminal defendants plead guilty, thereby waiving their right to a jury trial, and proceed directly to sentencing. Most of these guilty pleas are the result of plea-bargaining deals in which the accused agrees to admit guilt in exchange for reduced charges or a lenient sentence.

These qualifications noted, the criminal process begins with the response of law enforcement officials to a suspected violation of a state or federal law. Many scholars and lawyers consider this part of the process to be of the utmost importance. The way police conduct their investigation and gather evidence affects all subsequent decisions lawyers, judges, and juries make. The police are also significant actors because of the conflicting roles society asks them to play. We expect police officers to act lawfully, within the confines of the Constitution. We do not want them to break down our doors and search our houses without proper cause, nor do we want them to single out people for special or ill treatment based on their race, gender, or ethnicity. But society also expects effective law enforcement, with the police having some, though

Figure VI-1 The American Criminal Justice System

Stage	Governing Amendment[a]
Reported or suspected crime ↓	
Investigation by law enforcement officials ↓	Fourth Amendment search and seizure rights Fifth Amendment self-incrimination clause
Arrest ↓	Sixth Amendment right to counsel clause
Booking ↓	
Decision to prosecute ↓	
Pretrial hearings (initial appearance, bail hearing, preliminary hearing, arraignment) ↓	Fifth Amendment grand jury clause Sixth Amendment notification clause Eighth Amendment bail clause
Trial ↓	Fifth Amendment self-incrimination clause Sixth Amendment speedy and public trial, jury, confrontation, and compulsory process clauses
Sentencing ↓	Eighth Amendment cruel and unusual punishment clause Eighth Amendment excessive fines clause
Appeals, postconviction stages	Fifth Amendment double jeopardy clause

[a] The right to due process of law is in effect throughout the process.

limited, discretion to make arrests and apply the laws. Law enforcement officers must understand the rules well enough to act without violating them, because when they make mistakes, the consequences can be considerable.

Once police make an arrest and take an individual into custody, the prosecuting attorney joins the process. The prosecutor of state crimes, commonly known as the district attorney, is an elected official having jurisdiction over criminal matters in a given local jurisdiction, usually a county. Prosecutors of federal offenses, whom the president appoints and the Senate confirms, are called U.S.

attorneys. Their assignments correspond to the geographical jurisdictions of the federal district courts, and they serve at the president's pleasure. These state and federal prosecutors decide whether the government will bring charges against the accused. In making this decision, a prosecutor might consider a number of factors, such as whether police acted properly in gathering evidence and making the arrest or whether the evidence is sufficiently strong to secure a conviction. If the prosecutor decides not to press charges, the police must release the suspect, and the process ends. If prosecution is initiated, the government brings the individual before a judge, who ensures that the accused has legal representation and understands the charges. The judge also must verify that police had adequate justification for holding the accused. The judge may set bail—a monetary guarantee that the accused will appear for trial if he or she is released from custody—or deny bail.

The system next provides a step to ensure that the prosecutor is not abusing the power to charge persons with crimes. This check on prosecutorial discretion takes place in one of two ways. An individual accused of committing a federal offense (or of violating the laws of some states) will receive a grand jury hearing in accordance with the Fifth Amendment. Composed of laypersons, the grand jury, without the accused being present, examines the prosecutor's case to determine whether the government's evidence is strong enough to support formal charges. If the grand jury decides that the prosecutor has satisfied the legal requirements, it issues a formal document, known as an *indictment*, ordering the accused to stand trial on specified charges. If the grand jury concludes that the prosecutor's case is insufficient, the defendant is released.

Because the right to a grand jury hearing is not one of the incorporated provisions of the Bill of Rights, states are free to develop other methods of checking the prosecutor. Several states use preliminary hearings, which more closely resemble trials than does the grand jury process. At such a hearing, both prosecution and defense may present their cases to a judge, who evaluates the adequacy of the government's evidence. If the judge agrees that the prosecutor's case justifies a trial, the prosecutor issues an *information*. Roughly the equivalent of an indictment, the information is a formal document that orders the accused to stand trial on certain specified violations of the criminal code. If the prosecutor's case is found inadequate to justify a trial, the judge may order the release of the defendant.

Once formally charged, the defendant proceeds to the arraignment stage. At arraignment, a judge reads the indictment or information to ensure that the defendant understands the charges and the applicable constitutional rights. The judge also asks if the defendant is represented by counsel. In some instances the judge will revisit and perhaps modify the bail amount, depending on the specific charges brought by the state. Finally, the judge accepts the defendant's plea: guilty, nolo contendere (an acceptance of punishment without an admission of guilt), or not guilty. Should the defendant plead guilty or nolo contendere, a trial is not necessary, and the court proceeds to sentencing of the defendant.

A plea of not guilty normally leads to a full trial governed by constitutional provisions found in the Fifth and Sixth Amendments. The accused is entitled to a fair, public, and speedy trial by jury. A judge presides over the trial, and the two opposing lawyers question witnesses and summarize case facts. When both sides have presented their cases, the jury deliberates to reach a verdict. If the individual is found guilty, the judge issues a sentence, which, under Eighth Amendment protections, may not be cruel and unusual.

If the defendant is found not guilty, the process ends. The Fifth Amendment prohibition against double jeopardy bars the government from putting an acquitted defendant through a criminal trial a second time for the same offense, and the prosecution has no right to appeal an acquittal verdict that the trial court reaches. Should the verdict be guilty, however, the defendant has the right to appeal the conviction to a higher court. The appeals court does not conduct a new trial; it is only concerned with whether the trial court conformed to the relevant legal standards. It reviews the trial procedures to determine whether any significant errors in law or procedure occurred. If dissatisfied with the findings of the appeals court, either side—the government or the defense—may try for a review by an even higher court. These requests may be denied, because the system generally provides for only one appeal as a matter of right. Subsequent appeals are left to the discretion of the appellate courts.

TRENDS IN SUPREME COURT DECISION MAKING

In the next two chapters, we examine each stage in the criminal justice system vis-à-vis the constitutional rights of the criminally accused. While reading the narrative and opinions, keep in mind that the four amendments governing criminal proceedings do not work in isolation. Rather, they fit into a larger scheme that includes law, politics, local custom, and the practical necessities of coping with crime in a contemporary society.

The rights accorded the criminally accused by the four amendments set limits that, in tandem with the legal system, define the criminal justice process. The system depends heavily upon the Supreme Court's interpretation of the several clauses contained in those amendments. As we have seen in other legal areas, however, the way the justices interpret constitutional rights is not determined exclusively by traditional legal factors such as precedent, the plain language of the law, or the intent of the framers. Historical circumstances, ideological stances, and pressure from other institutions and private groups also affect the course of law, which explains why jurisprudence varies from one Supreme Court era to the next or even from term to term.

Perhaps no issue illustrates this intersection of law and politics better than criminal rights. In the 1960s, with Chief Justice Earl Warren at the helm, the Supreme Court revolutionized criminal law by expanding the protections accorded those charged with crimes. The extent to which the Warren Court altered existing law will become clear as you read the cases to come. For now, note the high percentage of decisions favoring the criminally accused during the 1960s, as depicted in Figure VI-2.

The liberal trend did not go unnoticed. President Richard Nixon was among the first to recognize that expanded rights for the criminally accused upset a majority of Americans. During his presidential campaign of 1968 and once he was elected, Nixon emphasized a law-and-order theme, proclaiming to the voters that the liberal Warren Court had overvalued defendants' rights. In a 1968 speech, Nixon said:

> [I]t's time for some honest talk about the problem of order in the United States. Let us always respect, as I do, our courts and those who serve on them, but let us also recognize that some of our courts in their decisions have gone too far in weakening the peace forces as against the criminal forces in this country.

All who heard these words knew that Nixon was referring only to the Warren Court. Apparently, many voters agreed with the future president. Public opinion polls taken that election year showed that nearly two-thirds of Americans believed that the courts were not dealing with criminals harshly enough, compared with about 50 percent just three years earlier.[1] In short, Nixon

---

[1] Harold W. Stanley and Richard G. Niemi, *Vital Statistics on American Politics, 2015–2016* (Washington, DC: CQ Press, 2016), 164.

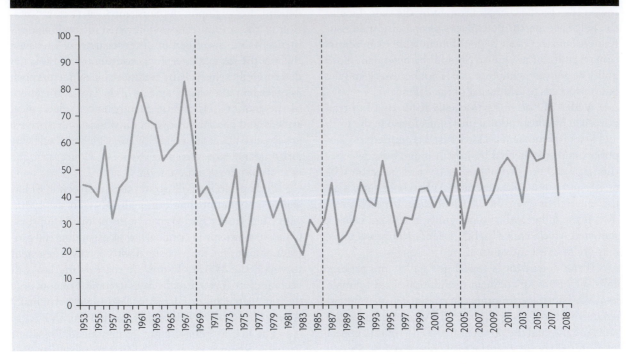

Source: Calculated by the authors from data available on the U.S. Supreme Court Judicial Database (http://supremecourtdatabase.org). Excludes per curiam opinions.

Note: Reference lines indicate the Warren, Burger, Rehnquist, and Roberts Courts.

had hit a nerve with U.S. citizens; he placed crime on the public agenda, where it remains.

Nixon also had the opportunity to keep his promise to restore law and order to American communities by changing the membership of the Supreme Court. One year before Nixon took office, Earl Warren had resigned to give President Lyndon Johnson the chance to appoint his successor. When Johnson's choice for that position, Justice Abe Fortas, failed to obtain Senate confirmation, the chief justiceship remained vacant for Nixon to fill. His choice was Warren Burger, a court of appeals judge who agreed with Nixon's stance on criminal law.

During the 1970s, those who sympathized with the liberal decisions of the Warren Court watched in dismay as Nixon appointed three more members of the Court, Justices Harry Blackmun, Lewis Powell, and William Rehnquist. The American Civil Liberties Union and various legal aid societies predicted that this new Court would not only stop the expansion of criminal rights

but also begin to retreat from Warren Court precedents. Figure VI-2 shows there may be some truth to this view. The Court proved less supportive of criminal rights under Burger's leadership than under Warren's. This trend continued when William Rehnquist replaced Burger as chief justice in 1986. Although there is some recent sign of increased liberalism in cases of criminal procedure, the Roberts Court overall still appears to be closer to its immediate predecessor, the Rehnquist Court, than to the earlier Warren Court. Since John G. Roberts became chief justice in the 2005 term, the Court has ruled for the defendant in only about 4.5 of every 10 cases (for the Rehnquist Court, slightly less than 4 of 10), compared with about 6 of every 10 during the Warren years. Some commentators have even suggested that the Roberts Court is continuing the Rehnquist Court's project of gradually limiting the application of landmark Warren Court decisions—disassembling defendants' rights precedents, such as *Miranda v. Arizona*, without explicitly overruling them.[2] If so, perhaps we should not be surprised. George W. Bush, a conservative Republican president, appointed Roberts and Samuel Alito, a former prosecutor. Both have turned out to give great deference to law enforcement officials. Roberts has supported the government in 66 percent of cases and Alito in 82 percent. So far, Barack Obama's appointees, Elena Kagan and Sonia Sotomayor, have tended to vote in favor of defendants in criminal cases. In fact, their levels of support for defendants' rights are close to those of some of the liberal justices of the Warren Court. Sotomayor (also a former prosecutor) has supported the accused 68 percent of the time, and Kagan, 65 percent.

Of course, you should keep in mind that the data depicted in Figure VI-2 present only an aggregated view of the Court's behavior. To understand whether, in fact, the Burger and Rehnquist Courts managed to alter existing precedent, we must examine the changes in particular areas of criminal law and procedure. As you read the next two chapters, note the date of each decision. Cases decided between 1953 and 1969 are Warren Court decisions, those between 1970 and 1986 are Burger Court opinions, those decided from that point through the 2004 term are Rehnquist Court cases, and all subsequent cases belong to the Roberts Court. Can you identify differences in interpretation? Have the Burger, Rehnquist, and now Roberts Courts weakened the pro-defendant precedents set by the Warren Court, as many civil libertarians predicted? If so, has this reaction imposed a reasonable balance between effective law enforcement and the rights of the accused, or has it gone too far in favoring the prosecution of criminal defendants?

---

[2]See, for example, Barry Friedman, "The Wages of Stealth Overruling (with Particular Attention to *Miranda v. Arizona*)," *Georgetown Law Journal* 99 (2010): 1–62.

CHAPTER SEVENTEEN

INVESTIGATIONS AND EVIDENCE

THE INVESTIGATION IS A CRITICAL stage in most criminal cases. It is during this early portion of the criminal process that police collect evidence of the crime. How strongly that evidence points to the accused and how lawfully it was obtained largely dictate what will occur at subsequent phases of the criminal process. If the police work is sound and the evidence of guilt is strong, a guilty plea or conviction is likely to result. But if the evidence is weak or gathered illegally, criminal charges may be dropped altogether.

The framers understood the importance of criminal investigations. They realized that effective law enforcement requires that the police be able to collect evidence of criminal behavior. At the same time, they were keenly aware of abusive investigatory tactics by law enforcement agents in England and other European countries. As a consequence, the framers included in the Bill of Rights certain protections for the criminally accused, protections that were meant to safeguard individual liberties without significantly weakening the ability of the police to investigate and solve crimes.

Most evidence of criminal behavior is either physical or testimonial. The collection of physical evidence is controlled by the Fourth Amendment, which prohibits unreasonable searches and seizures by the police. The gathering of testimonial evidence is limited by the Fifth Amendment, which protects suspects from having to give testimony against themselves. In this chapter we focus on these two crucial rights and on how the Supreme Court has interpreted and enforced them.

SEARCHES AND SEIZURES

To build a case against a criminal suspect a prosecutor often relies on physical evidence gathered by the police.

This evidence may assume many different forms: the money or goods taken during a theft, the weapons or tools used to carry out the crime, the clothing worn during the offense, illegal drugs, hair or blood samples, and the like. Physical evidence can be a powerful indicator of the guilt or innocence of a suspect. Given contemporary advances in technology, such as DNA testing, physical evidence today can yield much more information than was the case even in fairly recent years.

The founders recognized the importance of physical evidence to the criminal process, but they also understood that people's rights could be abused by overzealous law enforcement efforts to obtain such evidence. As a consequence, the Fourth Amendment, which deals exclusively with searches and seizures, became part of the Bill of Rights.

The Fourth Amendment has its genesis in the framers' resentment of an English institution, the writs of assistance. These writs were general search warrants that did not specify the places or things to be searched. The Crown in England authorized them beginning in the mid-1600s; by the early 1700s they were used in the colonies primarily to allow customs officials to conduct unrestricted searches. By authorizing these searches, Britain hoped to discourage smuggling by colonial merchants and to enforce existing restrictions on colonial trade.[1]

As general searches grew more common, some colonists began to express their disdain for what they felt were major intrusions on their personal privacy and political liberty. Shortly before the Declaration of Independence was issued, Samuel Adams said that opposition to these general searches was the "Commencement of the

---

[1]For more on the origins of the Fourth Amendment, see Melvin I. Urofsky and Paul Finkelman, *A March of Liberty*, 2nd ed. (New York: Oxford University Press, 2002), 43–44.

Controversy between Great Britain and America."[2] By the time James Madison proposed the Bill of Rights to Congress, it was clear that most Americans shared a contempt for general search warrants; even before he set about crafting his list of explicit limits on the power of the national government, almost all of the newly adopted state constitutions restricted government searches and seizures.

The Fourth Amendment contains two provisions, the first stating the basic right against unreasonable searches and seizures, and the second detailing the requirements for search warrants:

> [1] The right of the people to be secure in their persons, houses, papers, and effects, against unreasonable searches and seizures, shall not be violated, and [2] no Warrants shall issue, but upon probable cause, supported by Oath or affirmation, and particularly describing the place to be searched, and the persons or things to be seized.

The amendment clearly balances the government's need to gather evidence with the citizen's right not to suffer unnecessary government intrusions. The amendment does not stop police from searching and seizing; it simply outlaws such activities as are deemed "unreasonable." Moreover, it does not necessarily require that warrants be issued in order for searches to be considerable reasonable. But what distinguishes a reasonable from an unreasonable search? As in so many other areas, the task of applying important principles to concrete cases—that is, of giving meaning to the Constitution—has fallen to the Supreme Court. In fact, the justices have been called upon to clarify the meaning of the Fourth Amendment dozens of times, trying to balance the principles of its commands against the various and changing realities of law enforcement.

What Is a Search?

Most people are likely to imagine that searches follow a fairly standard set of procedures. The police have reason to believe that a search of a particular place will yield evidence relevant to a criminal investigation. They present their case to a judge, who evaluates whether there is a sufficient likelihood that a search will result in finding that evidence. If the search warrant is issued, police then conduct the search within the limits spelled out in that warrant.

But police can acquire evidence in a variety of ways. Someone else might uncover evidence and alert the police, or law enforcement might encounter evidence that is plainly visible to others. Or they might use a device—perhaps a special microphone that can isolate a conversation in a large crowd—to gather information that is in the open but otherwise hard to acquire. If methods such as these are not technically searches—if no "search" actually takes place—then the Fourth Amendment offers the accused no protection. Not surprisingly, the justices have sometimes been asked to determine what does and does not qualify as a search for the purposes of the Fourth Amendment.

In *Hester v. United States* (1924), the Court reviewed a conviction for possession of bootleg whiskey during Prohibition. When approached on the street by law enforcement officials, Hester attempted to flee with a gallon jug of moonshine, which he dropped when the officers gave chase. The officials retrieved the jug, and the illicit whiskey was used as a basis for his prosecution. Hester claimed that the evidence was the product of an illegal search, but the justices ruled that the whiskey was not obtained by any kind of search at all. In retrieving the jug, the officers did not rummage through Hester's belongings or invade his home. They only picked up what Hester had left behind for anyone to see. Justice Oliver Wendell Holmes, writing for the Court, ruled that the Fourth Amendment does not extend to open areas of property; it protects only "persons, houses, papers and effects."

The Court elaborated this position more fully a few years later in **Olmstead v. United States** (1928). Federal agents had reason to believe that Roy Olmstead and others were importing and selling alcohol in violation of the National Prohibition Act. To collect evidence against him, the agents, without first obtaining a search warrant, placed wiretaps on Olmstead's telephone lines. They did so without setting foot on Olmstead's property. One tap was applied in the basement of a large office building in which Olmstead rented space, and the other on a telephone line on the street outside Olmstead's home. Olmstead alleged a violation of the Fourth Amendment.

The Court decided in favor of the government, ruling that the Fourth Amendment did not protect Olmstead's conversations because it covered only searches of "material things—the person, the house, his papers or his effects." Therefore, "[t]he Amendment does not forbid what was done here. There was no searching.

[2]Quoted in Ira Glasser, *Visions of Liberty: The Bill of Rights for All Americans* (New York: Arcade, 1991), 166.

There was no seizure. The evidence was secured by the use of the sense of hearing and that only. There was no entry of the houses or offices of the defendants."

This logic was lost on four justices, who wrote dissenting opinions. Of these, Justice Louis Brandeis's is the best remembered. To him it was immaterial that agents had not needed to enter Olmstead's property to place the wiretaps. He declared, "The greatest dangers to liberty lurk in insidious encroachment by men of zeal, well-meaning but without understanding."

The Brandeis position, however, did not prevail. Instead, borrowing from the legal concept of trespass, the majority interpreted the Fourth Amendment to protect only against physical intrusions into constitutionally protected areas. As the Court had declared in *Hester*, as long as the police did not physically encroach on an individual's "person, houses, papers, or effects," evidence gathered without a search warrant could be used in court.

Over the next four decades the Court continued to use this trespass approach to the Fourth Amendment.[3] During this time, however, criticism was growing, especially within the legal community, that the *Olmstead* doctrine did not sufficiently protect individuals' rights. In response, the justices decided to reconsider their traditional approach to the question of what constitutes a search. They did so in **Katz v. United States** (1967).

Katz involved a federal investigation of Charles Katz, who was thought to be engaged in the organized transmission of wagering information by telephone from California to Miami and Boston. Based on observations of his behavior, law enforcement discovered that Katz made daily phone calls from two telephone booths on Sunset Boulevard in Los Angeles. Agents placed listening and recording devices on the exterior tops of the telephone booths to record Katz's conversations, which contained incriminating statements that were used against him in court. The government agents did not obtain a search warrant to conduct this investigation. They did not think they needed to do so; after all, the listening devices did not physically intrude on any constitutionally protected space.

Based on *Olmstead*, the agents were correct. But the Supreme Court had other ideas and handed down a decision that radically altered search and seizure law. The justices concluded that the *Olmstead* decision had misinterpreted the Fourth Amendment by placing too much emphasis on the "person, houses, papers, and effects" to be searched and not enough emphasis on the "right of

---

[3]See, for example, *Goldman v. United States* (1942).

the people." As a practical matter, did it make any difference that the listening devices were placed outside the telephone booths rather than inside? In either case, police could overhear private conversations.

Given this reality, the Court changed its interpretation of the Fourth Amendment by focusing on individual privacy rather than on the physical penetration of a person's constitutionally protected space. The Fourth Amendment, the Court concluded, "protects people, not places." Drawing upon Justice Brandeis's dissenting opinion in *Olmstead*, the Court ruled that whenever an individual has an expectation of privacy that society recognizes as reasonable, the Fourth Amendment applies. Thus, when Katz entered the phone booth and closed the door behind him, he had a reasonable expectation that his telephone conversations were private. The government invaded that privacy and therefore conducted a search.

Katz set a new standard for determining when a search occurs, but applying it in concrete cases has proven to be problematic, especially when the tools of law enforcement are used to enhance an investigation. In some cases, the justices have readily united behind a rationale. In *United States v. Knotts* (1983), for example, they unanimously ruled that it was not a search when the police used of an electronic transmitter to follow the transportation of chemicals used to manufacture illegal drugs. The police arranged for the transmitter to be hidden in a drum of chemicals and sold to a suspected drug dealer. The use of the transmitter, the Court determined, only made it easier to follow the movements of the suspect. It invaded no more privacy than if the police had surveilled the suspect by following him in a car, something that surely would not be labeled as a search.

In other cases, however, finding common ground has been difficult. The same justices who ruled unanimously on the use of the radio transmitter disagreed sharply on the issue of aerial photography to obtain evidence. In two cases, *California v. Ciraolo* (1986) and *Dow Chemical v. United States* (1986), the justices split on the question of whether flying over private property to observe illegal activity qualified as a search. The first case involved police flying over a suspect's home to photograph marijuana plants, and the second concerned the Environmental Protection Agency's reliance on pictures taken from a plane of a chemical company that had refused an inspection request. By identical 5–4 votes, the Court ruled that these actions did not violate a reasonable expectation of privacy; property owners know that their property can be observed from the air. Just like anyone else lawfully traveling in an airplane, police have the right to observe activity on the ground.

This reasoning drew a rebuke from Justice Powell, who suggested it was fanciful to think that the fleeting glances of fliers on commercial planes were comparable to the focused observation of the officials in these cases. In *Ciraolo*, he wrote:

> It is no accident that . . . many people build fences around their residential areas, but few build roofs over their backyards. Therefore, contrary to the Court's suggestion, people do not "knowingly expos[e]" their residential yards "to the public" merely by failing to build barriers that prevent aerial surveillance.

For its part, the Rehnquist Court seemed no closer to providing clarity, ruling in *Kyllo v. United States* (2001) that the use of thermal imaging technology to measure the heat emanating from a home qualified as a search. Federal agents suspected that a home was being used to cultivate marijuana and confirmed, through the thermal imager, that the abnormal amount of infrared radiation emanating from the home was consistent with the use of high-intensity lights to simulate sunlight. In a narrowly divided case, Justice Scalia admitted that the "question whether or not a Fourth Amendment 'search' has occurred is not so simple," but he went on to say that "any information regarding the home's interior that could not otherwise have been obtained without physical [invasion] constitutes a search." In dissent, Justice Stevens saw no invasive activity at all. Heat from a home is often visible to the naked eye—if snow is melted from the roof of one home but piled high on another, for example—and the device offered no intimate details. Drawing an analogy, he suggested that "it would be as if, in *Katz*, the listening device disclosed only the relative volume of sound leaving the booth, which presumably was discernible in the public domain."

More recently, the Roberts Court has been drawn into similar questions at the intersection of technology and the Fourth Amendment. In its efforts to define a search, it has actually developed a more protective approach to the Fourth Amendment than existed previously. *United States v. Jones* (2012) presented the question of whether placing a GPS tracking device on the automobile of a suspected drug dealer qualified as a search. Given the decision in *Knotts*, which held that a radio transmitter was not a search, one might have expected the Court to issue a similar ruling; why should it matter that police choose one method rather than the other to follow a suspect's movements? But in a 9–0 decision the justices ruled that use of the GPS device was, in fact, a search. Interestingly, Justice Scalia's opinion relied upon the *Olmstead* concept of trespass as a basis for the Court's ruling. A determining factor, he explained, was that the tracking device was placed on the suspect's car: "The Government physically occupied private property for the purpose of obtaining information. We have no doubt that such a physical intrusion would have been considered a 'search' within the meaning of the Fourth Amendment when it was adopted." In tying the decision to a protection against trespass, however, the Court was not turning its back on *Katz*. "[T]he *Katz* reasonable-expectation-of-privacy test has been added to, not substituted for, the common-law [trespass] test." According to the majority in *Jones*, the combination of these two standards expands Fourth Amendment protections beyond what would be covered if just one of the two tests were to be used exclusively.

No less than its predecessors, however, the Roberts Court can just as readily splinter in defining a search in light of increasingly sophisticated methods of acquiring information. *Carpenter v. United States* (2018) is a useful illustration. It raises questions about the ease with which law enforcement can acquire large amounts of digital data. Deciding whether a search took place is an especially thorny issue in this instance, since the digital records belonged to a cell phone carrier, not the person being investigated.

Carpenter v. United States

585 U.S. _____ (2018)
https://caselaw.findlaw.com/us-supreme-court/16-402.html
Oral arguments available at https://www.oyez.org/
   cases/2017/16-402
Vote: 5 (Breyer, Ginsburg, Kagan, Roberts, Sotomayor)
   4 (Alito, Gorsuch, Kennedy, Thomas)

OPINION OF THE COURT: *Roberts*

DISSENTING OPINIONS: *Alito, Gorsuch, Kennedy, Thomas*

Timothy Carpenter and several accomplices were suspected of robbing a number of electronics retailers in Michigan and Ohio. To aid in its investigation, the Federal Bureau of Investigation relied upon a law called the Stored Communications Act, which authorizes the federal government to acquire a suspect's cell phone records by demonstrating to a judge that those records are "relevant . . . to an ongoing investigation." Acting under this law, the FBI obtained Carpenter's "cell-site location information" (CSLI) from his cellular service provider. The CSLI consists of time-stamped data, marking the location of the cellular antennae that are used by a particular cell-phone user. Relying on these data, the government was able to establish that his location over a number of previous days was consistent with the times and places in which several of the robberies occurred. After his conviction, which was upheld by a court of appeals, he sought review from the Supreme Court, arguing that the government's use of the cell-cite data was a search. Searches typically require warrants, which are issued only when there is "probable cause," that is, good reason to believe that the search will produce evidence of criminal behavior. Here, the government only had to show that the cell-site data were "relevant to an investigation," a much easier standard for the government to satisfy.

CHIEF JUSTICE ROBERTS DELIVERED THE OPINION OF THE COURT.

The case before us involves the Government's acquisition of wireless carrier cell-site records revealing the location of Carpenter's cell phone whenever it made or received calls. This sort of digital data—personal location information maintained by a third party—does not fit neatly under existing precedents. Instead, requests for cell-site records lie at the intersection of two lines of cases, both of which inform our understanding of the privacy interests at stake.

The first set of cases addresses a person's expectation of privacy in his physical location and movements. In *United States v. Knotts* (1983), we considered the Government's use of a "beeper" to aid in tracking a vehicle through traffic. . . . Since the movements of the vehicle and its final destination had been "voluntarily conveyed to anyone who wanted to look," Knotts could not assert a privacy interest in the information obtained. . . .

Three decades later, the Court considered more sophisticated surveillance of the sort envisioned in *Knotts* and found that different principles . . . applied. In *United States v. Jones*, FBI agents installed a GPS tracking device on Jones's vehicle and remotely monitored the vehicle's movements for 28 days. The Court decided the case based on the Government's physical trespass of the vehicle. . . .

In a second set of decisions, the Court has drawn a line between what a person keeps to himself and what he shares with others. We have previously held that "a person has no legitimate expectation of privacy in information he voluntarily turns over to third parties." *Smith* [*v. Maryland*, (1979)]. That remains true "even if the information is revealed on the assumption that it will be used only for a limited purpose." *United States v. Miller* (1976). As a result, the Government is typically free to obtain such information from the recipient without triggering Fourth Amendment protections. . . .

The question we confront today is how to apply the Fourth Amendment to a new phenomenon: the ability to chronicle a person's past movements through the record of his cell phone signals. Such tracking partakes of many of the qualities of the GPS monitoring we considered in *Jones*. Much like GPS tracking of a vehicle, cell phone location information is detailed, encyclopedic, and effortlessly compiled.

At the same time, the fact that the individual continuously reveals his location to his wireless carrier implicates the third-party principle of *Smith* and *Miller*. But while the third-party doctrine applies to telephone numbers and bank records, it is not clear whether its logic extends to the qualitatively different category of cell-site records. After all, when *Smith* was decided in 1979, few could have imagined a society in which a phone goes wherever its owner goes, conveying to the wireless carrier not just dialed digits, but a detailed and comprehensive record of the person's movements.

We decline to extend *Smith* and *Miller* to cover these novel circumstances. . . . [W]e hold that an individual maintains a legitimate expectation of privacy in the record of his physical movements as captured through CSLI. . . .

Allowing government access to cell-site records contravenes that expectation. Although such records are generated for commercial purposes, that distinction does not negate Carpenter's anticipation of privacy in his physical location. Mapping a cell phone's location over the course of 127 days provides an all-encompassing record of the holder's whereabouts. . . . And like GPS monitoring, cell phone tracking is remarkably easy, cheap, and efficient compared to traditional investigative tools. With just the click of a button, the Government can access each carrier's deep repository of historical location information at practically no expense.

In fact, historical cell-site records present even greater privacy concerns than the GPS monitoring of a vehicle we considered in *Jones*. Unlike the bugged container in *Knotts* or the car in *Jones*, a cell phone—almost a "feature of human anatomy"—tracks nearly exactly the movements of its owner. . . . Accordingly, when the Government tracks the location of a cell phone it achieves near perfect surveillance, as if it had attached an ankle monitor to the phone's user.

Moreover, the retrospective quality of the data here gives police access to a category of information otherwise unknowable. In the past, attempts to reconstruct a person's movements were limited by a dearth of records and the frailties of recollection. With access to CSLI, the Government can now travel back in time to retrace a person's whereabouts, subject only to the retention policies of the wireless carriers, which currently maintain records for up to five years. Critically, because location information is continually logged for all of the 400 million devices in the United States—not just those belonging to persons who might happen to come under investigation—this newfound tracking capacity runs against everyone. Unlike with the GPS device in *Jones*, police need not even know in advance whether they want to follow a particular individual, or when.

Whoever the suspect turns out to be, he has effectively been tailed every moment of every day for five years, and the police may—in the Government's view—call upon the results of that surveillance without regard to the constraints of the Fourth Amendment. Only the few without cell phones could escape this tireless and absolute surveillance. . . .

At any rate, the rule the Court adopts "must take account of more sophisticated systems that are already in use or in development." *Kyllo*. While the records in this case reflect the state of technology at the start of the decade, the accuracy of CSLI is rapidly approaching GPS-level precision . . . .

The Government's primary contention to the contrary is that the third-party doctrine governs this case. In its view, cell-site records are fair game because they are "business records" created and maintained by the wireless carriers. . . .

The Government's position fails to contend with the seismic shifts in digital technology that made possible the tracking of not only Carpenter's location but also everyone else's, not for a short period but for years and years. . . . There is a world of difference between the limited types of personal information addressed in *Smith* and *Miller* and the exhaustive chronicle of location information casually collected by wireless carriers today. The Government thus is not asking for a straightforward application of the third-party doctrine, but instead a significant extension of it to a distinct category of information.

Neither does the second rationale underlying the third-party doctrine—voluntary exposure—hold up when it comes to CSLI. Cell phone location information is not truly "shared" as one normally understands the term. . . . [A] cell phone logs a cell-site record by dint of its operation, without any affirmative act on the part of the user beyond powering up. . . . Apart from disconnecting the phone from the network, there is no way to avoid leaving behind a trail of location data. As a result, in no meaningful sense does the user voluntarily "assume[ ] the risk" of turning over a comprehensive dossier of his physical movements. *Smith*. . . .

We decline to grant the state unrestricted access to a wireless carrier's database of physical location information. In light of the deeply revealing nature of CSLI, its depth, breadth, and comprehensive reach, and the inescapable and automatic nature of its collection, the fact that such information is gathered by a third party does not make it any less deserving of Fourth Amendment protection. The Government's acquisition of the cell-site records here was a search under that Amendment.

The judgment of the Court of Appeals is reversed, and the case is remanded for further proceedings consistent with this opinion.

It is so ordered.

JUSTICE KENNEDY, WITH WHOM JUSTICE THOMAS AND JUSTICE ALITO JOIN, DISSENTING.

This case involves new technology, but the Court's stark departure from relevant Fourth Amendment precedents and principles is, in

Cellular towers like these record information about the mobile phones that use them, including date, time, and general location. A cellular service provided the data it had recorded about one of its customers to the federal government, and those data were used to help convict him of various crimes. The Court ruled that acquiring the cell company's data was a search under the Fourth Amendment.

my submission, unnecessary and incorrect, requiring this respectful dissent. . . .

The Court has twice held that individuals have no Fourth Amendment interests in business records which are possessed, owned, and controlled by a third party. *United States v. Miller* (1976); *Smith v. Maryland* (1979). This is true even when the records contain personal and sensitive information. So when the Government uses a subpoena to obtain, for example, bank records, telephone records, and credit card statements from the businesses that create and keep these records, the Government does not engage in a search of the business's customers within the meaning of the Fourth Amendment. . . .

Cell-site records, however, are no different from the many other kinds of business records the Government has a lawful right to obtain by compulsory process. Customers like petitioner do not own, possess, control, or use the records, and for that reason have no reasonable expectation that they cannot be disclosed pursuant to lawful compulsory process. . . .

The Court today disagrees. It holds for the first time that by using compulsory process to obtain records of a business entity, the Government has not just engaged in an impermissible action, but has conducted a search of the business's customer. . . .

In concluding that the Government engaged in a search, the Court unhinges Fourth Amendment doctrine from the property-based concepts that have long grounded the analytic framework that pertains in these cases. In doing so it draws an unprincipled and unworkable line between cell-site records on the one hand and financial and telephonic records on the other. According to today's majority opinion, the Government can acquire a record of every credit card purchase and phone call a person makes over months or years without upsetting a legitimate expectation of privacy. But, in the Court's view, the Government crosses a constitutional line when it obtains a court's approval to issue a subpoena for more than six days of cell-site records in order to determine whether a person was within several hundred city blocks of a crime scene. That distinction is illogical and will frustrate principled application of the Fourth Amendment in many routine yet vital law enforcement operations. . . .

Here the only question necessary to decide is whether the Government searched anything of Carpenter's when it used compulsory process to obtain cell-site records from Carpenter's cell phone service providers. This Court's decisions in *Miller* and *Smith* dictate that the answer is no, as every Court of Appeals to have considered the question has recognized. . . .

Based on *Miller* and *Smith* and the principles underlying those cases, it is well established that subpoenas may be used to obtain a wide variety of records held by businesses, even when the records contain private information. Credit cards are a prime example. State and federal law enforcement, for instance, often subpoena credit card statements to develop probable cause to prosecute crimes ranging from drug trafficking and distribution to healthcare fraud to tax evasion. Subpoenas also may be used to obtain vehicle registration records, hotel records, employment records, and records of utility usage, to name just a few other examples. . . .

In fact, Carpenter's Fourth Amendment objection is even weaker than those of the defendants in *Miller* and *Smith*. Here the Government did not use a mere subpoena to obtain the cell-site records. It acquired the records only after it proved to a Magistrate Judge reasonable grounds to believe that the records were relevant and material to an ongoing criminal investigation. So even if . . . Carpenter [has] some attenuated interest in the records, the Government's conduct here would be reasonable under the standards governing subpoenas.

Under *Miller* and *Smith*, then, a search of the sort that requires a warrant simply did not occur when the Government used court-approved compulsory process, based on a finding of reasonable necessity, to compel a cell phone service provider, as owner, to disclose cell-site records.

JUSTICE ALITO, WITH WHOM JUSTICE THOMAS JOINS, DISSENTING.

I share the Court's concern about the effect of new technology on personal privacy, but I fear that today's decision will do far more harm than good. The Court's reasoning fractures two fundamental pillars of Fourth Amendment law, and in doing so, it guarantees a blizzard of litigation while threatening many legitimate and valuable investigative practices upon which law enforcement has rightfully come to rely.

First, the Court ignores the basic distinction between an actual search (dispatching law enforcement officers to enter private premises and root through private papers and effects) and an order merely requiring a party to look through its own records and produce specified documents. The former, which intrudes on personal privacy far more deeply, requires probable cause; the latter does not. Treating an order to produce like an actual search, as today's decision does, is revolutionary. It violates both the original understanding of the Fourth Amendment and more than a century of Supreme Court precedent. Unless it is somehow restricted to the particular situation in the present case, the Court's move will cause upheaval. Must every grand jury subpoena . . . be supported by probable cause? If so, investigations of terrorism, political corruption, white-collar crime, and many other offenses will be stymied. . . .

Second, the Court allows a defendant to object to the search of a third party's property. This also is revolutionary. The Fourth Amendment protects "[t]he right of the people to be secure in *their* persons, houses, papers, and effects" (emphasis added), not the persons, houses, papers, and effects of others. Until today, we have been careful to heed this fundamental feature of the Amendment's text. This was true when the Fourth Amendment was tied to property law, and it remained true after *Katz* broadened the Amendment's reach.

By departing dramatically from these fundamental principles, the Court destabilizes long-established Fourth Amendment doctrine. We will be making repairs—or picking up the pieces—for a long time to come.

Although the majority professes a desire not to "embarrass the future," we can guess where today's decision will lead.

One possibility is that the broad principles that the Court seems to embrace will be applied across the board. All subpoenas . . . and all other orders compelling the production of documents will require a demonstration of probable cause, and individuals will be able to claim a protected Fourth Amendment interest in any sensitive personal information about them that is collected and owned by third parties. Those would be revolutionary developments indeed.

The other possibility is that this Court will face the embarrassment of explaining in case after case that the principles on which today's decision rests are subject to all sorts of qualifications and limitations that have not yet been discovered. If we take this latter course, we will inevitably end up "mak[ing] a crazy quilt of the Fourth Amendment." *Smith*. . . .

The desire to make a statement about privacy in the digital age does not justify the consequences that today's decision is likely to produce.

Chief Justice John G. Roberts's opinion is Orwellian; it paints a picture of an unrestrained government exploiting vast hoards of readily available digital data to track anyone's movements—any time, any place, anywhere. He did not deny that the government had the right to subpoena information from third parties—to obtain, say, banking or business records—but here the sheer breadth of the electronic data available was too much for Roberts to stomach. Obtaining the cell-site data, even from a third party, was too invasive of the expectation of privacy—it was "detailed, encyclopedic, and effortlessly compiled"—and therefore qualified as a search.

The four dissenters each took a different tack in answering Roberts's opinion. Justice Anthony M. Kennedy saw no difference between cell-site data and any other information that the Court has allowed to be subpoenaed. In acquiring third-party information, the government conducted no search of Carpenter; the records obtained belonged to the cellular provider, not him. In his dissent, Justice Alito echoed Kennedy's concerns and predicted unhappy consequences. Lower courts will either disallow *all* requests for third-party data or create a hopeless mishmash of cases in which judges attempt to draw a line between the acceptable "request" and the unacceptable "search." Justices Thomas and Gorsuch both appealed for a return to a more traditional understanding of the Fourth Amendment. Thomas offered an extensive critique of *Katz*, urging his colleagues to focus on the amendment's textual limits, "persons, houses, papers, and effects," none of which, he believed, was involved here. Gorsuch shared Thomas's skepticism of the *Katz* doctrine, but he was a bit more circumspect, conceding that individuals still have a valid interest when their property is held by others and that such an interest might prevail in future cases.

The Court has come a long way in evaluating the question of what qualifies as a search. Nearly one hundred years ago, the justices considered whether the Coast Guard conducted a search by something as simple as shining a spotlight on a motorboat suspected of transporting illegal liquor. (It is not a search.[4]) Today, by contrast, the Court must confront a world of rapidly changing technology that encompasses a complex network of information acquisition, storage, and retrieval. Advances in computing, data science, and telecommunications—which the framers could scarcely have foreseen—will require the Court to continue to address their constitutional limits.

When Is a Search Reasonable?

The Fourth Amendment has two related, but independent guarantees. First, "[t]he right of the people to be secure in their persons, houses, papers, and effects, against unreasonable searches and seizures, shall not be violated." Second, it provides that "no Warrants shall issue, but upon probable cause, supported by Oath or affirmation, and particularly describing the place to be searched, and the persons or things to be seized." It does not say that the only reasonable searches are those authorized by a warrant. It does require that searches be reasonable—however they are conducted—and it also lays out the procedures that the government must follow for one particular category of search, those conducted under authority of a warrant.

The authors of the Fourth Amendment took great pains to describe search warrant procedures. So it is plausible to conclude that the framers preferred the use of warrants as a way to ensure that governments act without violating individual rights. What steps must the state take to adhere to this preferred method?

A police officer seeking approval to conduct a search must go before a judge or magistrate and swear under oath that he or she has reason to believe that a crime has been committed and evidence of the crime is located in a particular place. This information is often presented to the judge in the form of a sworn statement called an affidavit. The judge must then determine whether there is probable cause to believe the officer's petition. Normally the police bolster their requests with physical evidence or statements made during police interrogations that help establish the probability that the search will lead to the productive discovery of items related to the crime.[5] If the judge agrees that the probable cause standard has been met, he or she will issue a search warrant.

---

[4]*United States v. Lee* (1927).

[5]For a closer look at the Supreme Court's definition of probable cause, see *Illinois v. Gates* (1983).

Table 17-1 Exceptions to the Search Warrant Requirement

Exception	Conditions
Searches incident to a valid arrest	Police without a warrant may search a validly arrested person in order to disarm the suspect, prevent the destruction of evidence, and remove possible means of escape.
Searches under exigent circumstances	Police without a warrant may search and seize if delay would endanger lives, result in the loss of evidence that is about to be destroyed, or if the police are in "hot pursuit" of a suspect who might escape.
Consent searches	Police without a warrant may search upon receiving permission, voluntarily given.
Safety searches	Police without a warrant may search and seize if they believe there is a danger to themselves or the public.
Searches with a reduced expectation of privacy	Police without a warrant may search people at the U.S. border and, with probable cause, automobiles and their occupants.
Plain view seizures	Police without a warrant may seize evidence of a crime, contraband, or other seizable item that is openly visible and observed by a police officer who is lawfully present.

The Fourth Amendment is very definite about what the warrant must contain. It requires that the judge describe with specificity the place to be searched and the person or things to be seized. Armed with the judge's authorization, police may, in an orderly fashion, execute the warrant, searching only the area specified and seizing the designated items, if found.[6] When a judge issues a search warrant and the police act in a manner consistent with the terms of the warrant, the subsequent search will almost always be considered reasonable.

Not surprisingly, this is reflected in a number of the Supreme Court's decisions. Lawful warrants assure the Court that the government is playing by the rules. Thus, searches without a warrant, all else being equal, are viewed with great suspicion by the justices; usually the Court declares such searches invalid under the Fourth Amendment.[7]

At the same time, the Court has tried to allow its abstract legal doctrines to be informed by the practical realities of law enforcement. Indeed, the justices have acknowledged that police, acting conscientiously, may sometimes have justifiable reasons for conducting searches without a warrant. It has recognized what Justice Stewart referred to as "a few specifically established and well delineated exceptions." Table 17-1 describes the most significant of these exceptions.

Among these are searches conducted when a suspect is arrested; if a suspect has been apprehended on the street, it would be unrealistic to ask the arresting officer to delay a routine search of that suspect until after a warrant could be sought and issued. The same is true when the police believe there is an immediate danger to themselves or others; if officers believe that a person entering a bank has a shotgun concealed under a long coat, the police are justified—one might even say, obligated—to undertake a search. Relatedly, police often need to act quickly, leaving no time to obtain a search warrant. They are hardly abusing their discretion when they chase an armed suspect into a building without first obtaining judicial authorization.

In addition, there is little need to seek permission from judges if the people being searched themselves give permission. Consent, freely given, renders a search reasonable. Likewise, evidence that is in plain view obviates the need for a warrant. During a traffic stop, for instance, a police officer might see drug paraphernalia in the back seat of a car.

Finally, there are some contexts in which the justices have determined that a citizen's ordinary presumption of privacy is reduced. Automobiles have a diminished

[6]See *Wilson v. Arkansas* (1995) and *Richards v. Wisconsin* (1997) for rules pertaining to the proper execution of search warrants.

[7]See, for example, *Chimel v. California* (1969), *Johnson v. United States* (1947), *McDonald v. United States* (1948), and *Stoner v. California* (1964).

expectation of privacy. They are not private homes. They travel on the open road and are subject to extensive regulation and monitoring by the state. Police therefore can conduct certain warrantless searches of cars and the people in them when there is probable cause, that is, when law enforcement has sound reasons for believing that there is evidence of a crime or that a crime might be taking place. Privacy also contracts at the U.S. border. The government regards the protection of its borders as a vital interest, and the Court has sometimes supported that effort by permitting, at the point of entry into the United States, searches that could not lawfully be undertaken in the county's interior.

These exceptions should not be interpreted as license for law enforcement to conduct searches on just a slender pretext. The Court has been very precise in defining the conditions that trigger these exceptions, the reasons for allowing suspension of the warrant requirement, and the limitations placed on such searches.

If the purpose of the Fourth Amendment is to prevent the government from abusing its power of investigation, allowing the kinds of exceptions the justices have upheld seems sensible. For the most part, they occur in settings where a strong likelihood of harm merits police taking unilateral action. Moreover, some exceptions simply do not present the kinds of circumstances where police might misuse their authority.

Enforcing the Fourth Amendment: The Exclusionary Rule

So far, we have focused on the constitutional rules governing searches and seizures. We have shown that the Court has carved out numerous exceptions to the general principle that police should obtain warrants to conduct searches. Even so, the Court has placed limits on those exceptions. For example, assume that the police arrest a person at his or her home. If they wish to use the "incident to arrest" exception to conduct a warrantless search of the person and the suspect's immediate surroundings, then they must conduct that search at the time of the arrest. If police officers return later, after the suspect has been removed to the police station, and conduct a warrantless search of the suspect's home, the Court would not allow the "incident to arrest" exception to justify the search. The search would fail the requirement that such searches be contemporaneous with the arrest and be ruled unconstitutional.

But suppose that the police did go back to the house a day later, found evidence, and tried to justify the search under the incident to arrest exception. We know that

such a search would be illegal, but what is to prevent the police from doing it anyway? In England, if the police conduct an illegal search and seizure, the evidence they obtain may be used in court against the accused, although the person whose search and seizure rights have been violated can sue the police for damages. This system of police liability enables British citizens to enforce their search and seizure rights.

The United States employs a different remedy for police infractions. The provisions of the Fourth Amendment are enforced through the application of the *exclusionary rule*, a judicially created principle that removes any incentive the police might otherwise have for violating search and seizure rights. Under the exclusionary rule, evidence gathered illegally may not be admitted into court and so cannot be used by prosecutors to establish the suspect's guilt. The rationale behind the rule is straightforward: if the police know that evidence from an illegal search will be of no use, they have no incentive to violate the Fourth Amendment.

At one time, law enforcement officials faced no real consequences for conducting illegal searches and seizures. Unless individual state laws imposed some form of redress, the police were not held liable for their activities, nor was evidence obtained unconstitutionally excluded from trials. In 1914, however, the Supreme Court decided **Weeks v. United States**, a case that arose from a federal investigation into the activities of Fremont Weeks, who was suspected of illegally using the U.S. mail to transport lottery tickets. On two occasions, law enforcement officers searched Weeks's residence without a warrant and carried off boxes of his papers, letters, tax returns, business records, and various personal items, a clear violation of search and seizure rules. In addition, the materials seized were not narrowly selected for their relevance; they included voluminous business records and personal items through which authorities could conduct a fishing expedition in search of possible incriminating evidence.

Should the documents have been used as evidence against Weeks, even though the police and the marshal had gathered the materials in an illegal manner? Writing for the Court, Justice William R. Day announced:

> If letters and private documents can thus be seized
> and held and used as evidence against a citizen
> accused of an offense, the protection of the Fourth
> Amendment declaring his right to be secure
> against such searches and seizures is of no value,
> and, so far as those thus placed are concerned,
> might as well be stricken from the Constitution.

With this conclusion, the Court, through Justice Day, created the exclusionary rule: judges must exclude from trial any evidence gathered in violation of the Fourth Amendment. Although *Weeks* constituted a major decision, it was limited in scope, applying only to federal agents and federal judges in federal criminal cases. It was clear, however, that eventually the Court would be asked to apply the exclusionary rule to the states, because that is where most criminal prosecutions take place. But it was also the case that many states or their judges resisted adopting exclusionary rules. *People v. Defore* (1926) provides perhaps the most famous example. In that case, Benjamin Cardozo, then a judge on the New York Court of Appeals, rejected expanding the *Weeks* rule to apply to state criminal cases. In his opinion he wrote the now-famous lines disparaging the exclusionary rule: "The criminal is to go free because the constable has blundered. . . . A room is searched against the law, and the body of a murdered man is found. . . . The privacy of the home has been infringed, and the murderer goes free."

The issue of applying the exclusionary rule to the states first reached the Supreme Court in 1949 in **Wolf v. Colorado**. This case involved a Colorado physician who was suspected of performing illegal abortions. Because the police were unable to obtain sufficient solid evidence against him, a deputy sheriff surreptitiously took Wolf's appointment book and followed up on the names in it. Using this information, the police gathered enough evidence to convict him. Wolf's attorney argued that because the case against his client rested on illegally obtained evidence, the Court should dismiss it. To implement his arguments, the justices would have to rule that the Fourth Amendment applied to the states and then impose the exclusionary rule on them.

Writing for the Court, Justice Felix Frankfurter agreed that the states had to obey the Fourth Amendment. The right to be secure from unreasonable searches and seizures was deemed fundamental—"basic to a free society"—and the provisions of the amendment were applied to the states through the due process clause of the Fourteenth Amendment. The Court, however, refused to hold that the exclusionary rule was a necessary part of the Fourth Amendment. The rule was one method of enforcing search and seizure rights, but not the only one. In other words, although state law enforcement officials would have to abide by the guarantees contained in the Fourth Amendment, the states need not use a particular mechanism, such as the exclusionary rule, to ensure compliance. Frankfurter noted that the law in England, where there was no exclusionary rule—as well as in the states, the majority of which rejected the rule—proved that justice could be served without this specific check on police behavior. States were left free to adopt whatever procedures they wished to enforce search and seizure rights. The exclusionary rule was not mandatory.

Growing conflicts between the federal and various state search and seizure rules, coupled with changes in Court personnel, caused the Court to reconsider the applicability of the exclusionary rule to the states. As you read *Mapp v. Ohio* (1961), can you discern why it is one of the most significant rulings during the Warren Court era and why it was so controversial? Does Justice Tom Clark's majority opinion leave any room for exceptions?

Mapp v. Ohio

367 U.S. 643 (1961)
http://caselaw.findlaw.com/us-supreme-court/367/643.html
Oral arguments available at https://www.oyez.org/
    cases/1960/236
Vote: 6 (Black, Brennan, Clark, Douglas, Stewart, Warren)
    3 (Frankfurter, Harlan, Whittaker)

OPINION OF THE COURT: *Clark*

CONCURRING OPINIONS: *Black, Douglas, Stewart*

DISSENTING OPINION: *Harlan*

Dollree Mapp, a woman in her early twenties, was involved in myriad illegal activities, which she carried on in her Cleveland home. For several months the police had attempted to shut down her operations, but apparently Mapp was tipped off, because each time the police planned a raid, she managed to elude them.

On May 23, 1957, police officers, led by Sergeant Carl Delau, tried to enter Mapp's house, this time on the ground that she was harboring a fugitive from justice. (The fugitive was suspected of bombing the house of an alleged Cleveland numbers racketeer, Don King, who later became a prominent boxing promoter.)[8] When the police arrived, Mapp refused to let them in because they did not have a search warrant. Sgt. Delau returned to his car, radioed for a search warrant, and kept the house under surveillance. Three hours later, and with additional police officers, Delau again tried to enter. This time Mapp did not come to the door, so police forced it open.

At this point several events occurred almost simultaneously. Mapp's attorney, whom she had called when police first appeared, arrived and tried to see her. Police would not let him in. Hearing the police break in, Ms. Mapp came downstairs and began arguing

---

[8]See Fred W. Friendly and Martha J. H. Elliott, *The Constitution: That Delicate Balance* (New York: Random House, 1984), 128–133.

with them. Sgt. Delau held up a piece of paper, which he claimed was a search warrant. Mapp grabbed it and stuffed it down her blouse. A scuffle broke out, during which police handcuffed Mapp and searched the house. The police did not find any fugitive from justice, but they did seize some allegedly obscene pictures, which were illegal to possess under Ohio law. The existence of a valid search warrant was never established by the state. Ms. Mapp was found guilty of possession of obscene materials and sentenced to prison. Her attorney appealed to the U.S. Supreme Court, asking the justices to review Mapp's claim on First Amendment grounds, but the justices were more interested in exploring the search and seizure issue.[9]

MR. JUSTICE CLARK DELIVERED THE OPINION OF THE COURT.

Seventy-five years ago, in *Boyd v. United States* . . . [t]he Court noted that "constitutional provisions for the security of person and property should be liberally construed. . . . It is the duty of courts to be watchful for the constitutional rights of the citizen, and against any stealthy encroachments thereon."

In this jealous regard for maintaining the integrity of individual rights, the Court gave life to Madison's prediction that "independent tribunals of justice . . . will be naturally led to resist every encroachment upon rights expressly stipulated for in the Constitution by the declaration of rights." . . .

Less than 30 years after *Boyd,* this Court, in *Weeks v. United States* (1914), . . . stated that use of the seized evidence involved "a denial of the constitutional rights of the accused." Thus, in the year 1914, in the *Weeks* case, this Court "for the first time" held that "in a federal prosecution the Fourth Amendment barred the use of evidence secured through an illegal search and seizure." This Court has ever since required of federal law officers a strict adherence to that command which this Court has held to be a clear, specific, and constitutionally required—even if judicially implied—deterrent safeguard without insistence upon which the Fourth Amendment would have been reduced to "a form of words." It meant, quite simply, that "conviction by means of unlawful seizures and enforced confessions . . . should find no sanction in the judgments of the courts . . . ," that such evidence "shall not be used at all."

There are in the cases of this Court some passing references to the *Weeks* rule as being one of evidence. But the plain and unequivocal language of *Weeks*—and its later paraphrase in *Wolf*—to the effect that the *Weeks* rule is of constitutional origin, remains entirely undisturbed. . . .

In 1949, 35 years after *Weeks* was announced, this Court, in *Wolf v. People of State of Colorado,* again for the first time, discussed the effect of the Fourth Amendment upon the states through the operation of the Due Process Clause of the Fourteenth Amendment. It said: "[W]e have no hesitation in saying that were a State affirmatively to sanction such police incursion into privacy it would run counter to the guaranty of the Fourteenth Amendment."

Nevertheless, after declaring that the "security of one's privacy against arbitrary intrusion by the police" is "implicit in 'the concept of ordered liberty' and as such enforceable against the States through the Due Process Clause," and announcing that it "stoutly adhere[d]" to the *Weeks* decision, the Court decided that the *Weeks* exclusionary rule would not then be imposed upon the States as "an essential ingredient of the right." . . .

. . . While in 1949, prior to the *Wolf* case, almost two-thirds of the States were opposed to the use of the exclusionary rule, now, despite the *Wolf* case, more than half of those since passing upon it, by their own legislative or judicial decision, have wholly or partly adopted or adhered to the *Weeks* rule. Significantly, among those now following the rule is California, which, according to its highest court, was "compelled to reach that conclusion because other remedies have completely failed to secure compliance with the constitutional provisions. . . ." The experience of California that such other remedies have been worthless and futile is buttressed by the experience of other States. . . .

Likewise, time has set its face against what *Wolf* called the "weighty testimony" of *People v. Defore* (1926). There, Justice (then Judge) Cardozo, rejecting adoption of the *Weeks* exclusionary rule in New York, had said that "[t]he Federal rule as it stands is either too strict or too lax." However, the force of that reasoning has been largely vitiated by later decisions of this Court. . . .

It, therefore, plainly appears that the factual considerations supporting the failure of the *Wolf* Court to include the *Weeks* exclusionary rule . . . could not, in any analysis, now be deemed controlling.

Some five years after *Wolf,* in answer to a plea made here Term after Term that we overturn its doctrine on applicability of the *Weeks* exclusionary rule, this Court indicated that such should not be done until the States had "adequate opportunity to adopt or reject the [*Weeks*] rule." . . . Today we once again examine *Wolf*'s constitutional documentation of the right to privacy free from unreasonable state intrusion, and, after its dozen years on our books, are led by it to close the only courtroom door remaining open to evidence secured by official lawlessness in flagrant abuse of that basic right . . . . We hold that all evidence obtained by searches and

---

[9]Interestingly, the attorney for Mapp, while claiming that the police entered Mapp's home illegally, did not argue the exclusionary rule issue. Mapp's brief did not even cite *Wolf v. Colorado.* It was the ACLU, acting as an amicus in this case, that directly asked the justices in its brief and oral arguments to reconsider *Wolf. Mapp,* therefore, presents an excellent example of the effect amicus curiae briefs can have. It also illustrates how the justices can reach for an issue they want to decide even if it is not presented by the parties to the dispute.

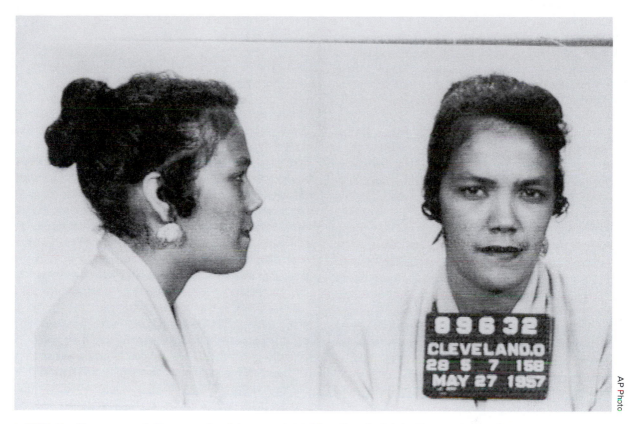

In 1957 Dollree Mapp was arrested for possession of obscene materials. The police seized vital evidence against her during an unconstitutional search. In *Mapp v. Ohio* (1961) the Supreme Court reversed her conviction, holding that evidence obtained through an illegal search could not be admitted in court.

seizures in violation of the Constitution is, by that same authority, inadmissible in a state court.

Since the Fourth Amendment's right of privacy has been declared enforceable against the States through the Due Process Clause of the Fourteenth, it is enforceable against them by the same sanction of exclusion as is used against the Federal Government. . . . To hold otherwise is to grant the right but in reality to withhold its privilege and enjoyment. Only last year the Court itself recognized that the purpose of the exclusionary rule "is to deter—to compel respect for the constitutional guaranty in the only effectively available way—by removing the incentive to disregard it." . . .

There are those who say, as did Justice (then Judge) Cardozo, that under our constitutional exclusionary doctrine "[t]he criminal is to go free because the constable has blundered." *People v. Defore*. In some cases this will undoubtedly be the result. But . . . "there is another consideration—the imperative of judicial integrity." The criminal goes free, if he must, but it is the law that sets him free. Nothing can destroy a government more quickly than its failure to observe its own laws, or worse, its disregard of the character of its own existence. Nor can it lightly be assumed that,

as a practical matter, adoption of the exclusionary rule fetters law enforcement. . . ."The federal courts themselves have operated under the exclusionary rule of *Weeks* for almost half a century; yet it has not been suggested either that the Federal Bureau of Investigation has thereby been rendered ineffective, or that the administration of criminal justice in the federal courts has thereby been disrupted." . . .

The ignoble shortcut to conviction left open to the State tends to destroy the entire system of constitutional restraints on which the liberties of the people rest. Having once recognized that the right to privacy embodied in the Fourth Amendment is enforceable against the States, and that the right to be secure against rude invasions of privacy by state officers is, therefore, constitutional in origin, we can no longer permit that right to remain an empty promise. Because it is enforceable in the same manner and to like effect as other basic rights secured by the Due Process Clause, we can no longer permit it to be revocable at the whim of any police officer who, in the name of law enforcement itself, chooses to suspend its enjoyment. Our decision, founded on reason and truth, gives to the individual no more than that which the Constitution guarantees him, to the police officer no less than that to which honest law enforcement is entitled, and, to the courts, that judicial integrity so necessary in the true administration of justice.

The judgment of the Supreme Court of Ohio is reversed and the cause remanded for further proceedings not inconsistent with this opinion.

Reversed and remanded.

MR. JUSTICE BLACK, CONCURRING.

I am still not persuaded that the Fourth Amendment, standing alone, would be enough to bar the introduction into evidence against an accused of papers and effects seized from him in violation of its commands. For the Fourth Amendment does not itself contain any provision expressly precluding the use of such evidence, and I am extremely doubtful that such a provision could properly be inferred from nothing more than the basic command against unreasonable searches and seizures. Reflection on the problem, however, in the light of cases coming before the Court since *Wolf,* has led me to conclude that when the Fourth Amendment's ban against unreasonable searches and seizures is considered together with the Fifth Amendment's ban against compelled self-incrimination, a constitutional basis emerges which not only justifies but actually requires the exclusionary rule.

The close interrelationship between the Fourth and Fifth Amendments, as they apply to this problem, has long been recognized and, indeed, was expressly made the ground for this Court's holding in *Boyd v. United States* [1866]. There the Court fully discussed this relationship and declared itself "unable to perceive that the seizure of a man's private books and papers to be used in evidence against him is substantially different from compelling him to be a witness against himself." It was upon this ground that Mr. Justice Rutledge largely relied in his dissenting opinion in the *Wolf* case. And, although I rejected the argument at that time, its force has, for me at least, become compelling with the more thorough understanding of the problem brought on by recent cases. In the final analysis, it seems to me that the *Boyd* doctrine, though perhaps not required by the express language of the Constitution strictly construed, is amply justified from an historical standpoint, soundly based in reason, and entirely consistent with what I regard to be the proper approach to interpretation of our Bill of Rights.

MR. JUSTICE HARLAN, WHOM MR. JUSTICE FRANKFURTER AND MR. JUSTICE WHITTAKER JOIN, DISSENTING.

I would not impose upon the States this federal exclusionary remedy. The reasons given by the majority for now suddenly turning its back on *Wolf* seem to me notably unconvincing. . . .

The preservation of a proper balance between state and federal responsibility in the administration of criminal justice demands patience on the part of those who might like to see things move faster among the States in this respect. Problems of criminal law enforcement vary widely from State to State. One State, in considering the totality of its legal picture, may conclude that the need for embracing the *Weeks* rule is pressing because other remedies are unavailable or inadequate to secure compliance with the substantive Constitutional principle involved. Another, though equally solicitous of Constitutional rights, may choose to pursue one purpose at a time, allowing all evidence relevant to guilt to be brought into a criminal trial, and dealing with Constitutional infractions by other means. . . . Further, a State after experimenting with the *Weeks* rule for a time may, because of unsatisfactory experience with it, decide to revert to a non-exclusionary rule. And so on. From the standpoint of Constitutional permissibility in pointing a State in one direction or another, I do not see at all why "time has set its face against" the considerations which led Mr. Justice Cardozo, then chief judge of the New York Court of Appeals, to reject for New York in *People v. Defore,* the *Weeks* exclusionary rule. For us the question remains, as it has always been, one of state power, not one of passing judgment on the wisdom of one state course or another. In my view this Court should continue to forbear from fettering the States with an adamant rule which may embarrass them in coping with their own peculiar problems in criminal law enforcement. . . .

I regret that I find so unwise in principle and so inexpedient in policy a decision motivated by the high purpose of increasing respect for Constitutional rights. But in the last analysis I think this Court can increase respect for the Constitution only if it rigidly respects the limitations which the Constitution places upon it, and respects as well the principles inherent in its own processes. In the present case I think we exceed both, and that our voice becomes only a voice of power, not of reason.

The application of the exclusionary rule to the states was a revolutionary decision of the Warren Court, not least because it accentuated the highly politicized nature of criminal law. Since 1961, when the Court informed states that they must adopt it, the rule has been both attacked and defended by scholars, lawyers, and judges. And of course it has obvious consequences for the accused *(see Box 17-1).* Supporters fear that if the exclusionary rule is eliminated, police will have no incentive to respect the law. Opponents of the rule agree with Cardozo and argue that letting a guilty person go free is too great a price for society to pay just because a police officer violated search and seizure guidelines.

The disagreement over the exclusionary rule expressed in academic circles and by the public also was evident among the justices. Six voted to overturn Mapp's conviction, but only five expressed full support for the exclusionary rule. Potter Stewart, who voted with the majority, explicitly did so on other grounds. When Chief Justice Earl Warren left the Court and was replaced by law-and-order-minded Warren Burger in 1969, legal scholars predicted that the Court might well overrule *Mapp*. With each additional Court appointment by Richard Nixon and then later by Ronald Reagan, speculation on the end of the exclusionary rule increased.

Predictions of the outright reversal of *Mapp* proved unfounded, but by the mid-1980s the situation had changed. The national mood had turned quite conservative, and pressure was mounting to alter liberal Warren Court rulings. In 1984 the Court imposed a major exception to the exclusionary rule.

United States v. Leon

468 U.S. 897 (1984)

http://caselaw.findlaw.com/us-supreme-court/468/897.html
Oral arguments available at https://www.oyez.org/
cases/1983/82-1771
Vote: 6 (Blackmun, Burger, O'Connor, Powell, Rehnquist, White)
3 (Brennan, Marshall, Stevens)

OPINION OF THE COURT: *White*

CONCURRING OPINION: *Blackmun*

DISSENTING OPINIONS: *Brennan, Stevens*

In 1981 police in Burbank, California, received a tip from a person of unproven reliability identifying two individuals, Patsy Stewart and Armando Sanchez, as drug dealers. According to the informant, the pair kept small quantities of drugs in their house on Price Drive in Burbank and a larger inventory at another residence in the same city. Police began a surveillance of the Price Drive residence, where they spotted a car belonging to Ricardo Del Castillo, who had a history of drug possession. Del Castillo's probation records led police to Alberto Leon, a known drug dealer. Based on observation, continued surveillance of various residences, and information from a second informant, Burbank narcotics investigator Cyril Rombach drew up an affidavit to obtain a search warrant, which a judge issued. With the warrant, police searched several residences and seized large quantities of drugs. Leon, Stewart, Sanchez, and Del Castillo were arrested.

At the trial stage, attorneys for the defendants argued that the search warrant was invalid. They claimed that because the original informant lacked established credibility, the judge did not have probable cause to issue the warrant. The government's lawyers admitted that the defendants had a valid point but argued that the courts should decline to throw out the entire case because of a defective warrant. They claimed that the officers had acted in "good faith"—that is, the police believed they had a legitimate warrant and acted accordingly.

JUSTICE WHITE DELIVERED THE OPINION OF THE COURT.

This case presents the question whether the Fourth Amendment exclusionary rule should be modified so as not to bar the use in the prosecution's case . . . of evidence obtained by officers acting in reasonable reliance on a search warrant issued by a detached and neutral magistrate but ultimately found to be unsupported by probable cause. To resolve this question, we must consider once again the tension between the sometimes competing goals of, on the one hand, deterring official misconduct and removing inducements to unreasonable invasions of privacy and, on the other, establishing procedures under which criminal defendants are "acquitted or convicted on the basis of all the evidence which exposes the truth." . . .

Whether the exclusionary sanction is appropriately imposed in a particular case, our decisions make clear, is "an issue separate from the question whether the Fourth Amendment rights of the party seeking to invoke the rule were violated by police conduct." Only the former question is currently before us, and it must be resolved by weighing the costs and benefits of preventing the use in the prosecution's case . . . of inherently trustworthy tangible evidence obtained in reliance on a search warrant issued by a detached and neutral magistrate that ultimately is found to be defective.

The substantial social costs exacted by the exclusionary rule for the vindication of Fourth Amendment rights have long been a source of concern. "Our cases have consistently recognized that unbending application of the exclusionary sanction to enforce ideals of governmental rectitude would impede unacceptably the truth-finding functions of judge and jury." An objectionable collateral consequence of this interference with the criminal justice system's truth-finding function is that some guilty defendants may go free or receive reduced sentences as a result of favorable plea bargains. Particularly when law enforcement officers have acted in objective good faith or their transgressions have been minor, the magnitude of the benefit conferred on such guilty defendants offends basic concepts of the criminal justice system. . . . Accordingly, "[a]s with any remedial device, the application of the rule has been restricted to those areas where its remedial objectives are thought most efficaciously served."

Close attention to those remedial objectives has characterized our recent decisions concerning the scope of the Fourth Amendment exclusionary rule. The Court has, to be sure, not seriously questioned,

"in the absence of a more efficacious sanction, the continued application of the rule to suppress evidence from the [prosecution's] case where a Fourth Amendment violation has been substantial and deliberate. . . ." Nevertheless, the balancing approach that has evolved in various contexts—including criminal trials—"forcefully suggest[s] that the exclusionary rule be more generally modified to permit the introduction of evidence obtained in the reasonable good-faith belief that a search or seizure was in accord with the Fourth Amendment." . . .

As yet, we have not recognized any form of good-faith exception to the Fourth Amendment exclusionary rule. But the balancing approach that has evolved during the years of experience with the rule provides strong support for the modification currently urged upon us. As we discuss below, our evaluation of the costs and benefits of suppressing reliable physical evidence seized by officers reasonably relying on a warrant issued by a detached and neutral magistrate leads to the conclusion that such evidence should be admissible in the prosecution's case. . . .

Because a search warrant "provides the detached scrutiny of a neutral magistrate, which is a more reliable safeguard against improper searches than the hurried judgment of a law enforcement officer 'engaged in often competitive enterprise of ferreting out crime,'" we have expressed a strong preference for warrants and declared that "in a doubtful or marginal case a search under a warrant may be sustainable where without one it would fall." Reasonable minds frequently may differ on the question whether a particular affidavit establishes probable cause, and we have thus concluded that the preference for warrants is most appropriately effectuated by according "great deference" to a magistrate's determination.

Deference to the magistrate, however, is not boundless. It is clear, first, that the deference accorded to a magistrate's finding of probable cause does not preclude inquiry into the knowing or reckless falsity of the affidavit on which that determination was based. Second, the courts must also insist that the magistrate purport to "perform his 'neutral and detached' function and not serve merely as a rubber stamp for the police." . . .

Third, reviewing courts will not defer to a warrant based on an affidavit that does not "provide the magistrate with a substantial basis for determining the existence of probable cause." . . . Even if the warrant application was supported by more than a "bare bones" affidavit, a reviewing court may properly conclude that, notwithstanding the deference that magistrates deserve, the warrant was invalid because the magistrate's probable-cause determination reflected an improper analysis of the totality of the circumstances or because the form of the warrant was improper in some respect.

Only in the first of these three situations, however, has the Court set forth a rationale for suppressing evidence obtained pursuant to a search warrant; in the other areas, it has simply excluded such evidence without considering whether Fourth Amendment interests will be advanced. To the extent that proponents of exclusion rely on its behavioral effects on judges and magistrates in these areas, their reliance is misplaced. First, the exclusionary rule is designed to deter police misconduct rather than to punish the errors of judges and magistrates. Second, there exists no evidence suggesting that judges and magistrates are inclined to ignore or subvert the Fourth Amendment or that lawlessness among these actors requires application of the extreme sanction of exclusion.

Third, and most important, we discern no basis, and are offered none, for believing that exclusion of evidence seized pursuant to a warrant will have a significant deterrent effect on the issuing judge or magistrate. . . . Judges and magistrates are not adjuncts to the law enforcement team; as neutral judicial officers, they have no stake in the outcome of particular criminal prosecutions. The threat of exclusion thus cannot be expected significantly to deter them. . . . If exclusion of evidence obtained pursuant to a subsequently invalidated warrant is to have any deterrent effect, therefore, it must alter the behavior of individual law enforcement officers or the policies of their departments. One could argue that applying the exclusionary rule in cases where the police failed to demonstrate probable cause in the warrant application deters future inadequate presentations or "magistrate shopping" and thus promotes the ends of the Fourth Amendment. Suppressing evidence obtained pursuant to a technically defective warrant supported by probable cause also might encourage officers to scrutinize more closely the form of the warrant and to point out suspected judicial errors. We find such arguments speculative and conclude that suppression of evidence obtained pursuant to a warrant should be ordered only on a case-by-case basis and only in those unusual cases in which exclusion will further the purposes of the exclusionary rule.

We have frequently questioned whether the exclusionary rule can have any deterrent effect when the offending officers acted in the objectively reasonable belief that their conduct did not violate the Fourth Amendment. . . . But even assuming that the rule effectively deters some police misconduct and provides incentives for the law enforcement profession as a whole to conduct itself in accord with the Fourth Amendment, it cannot be expected, and should not be applied, to deter objectively reasonable law enforcement activity. . . .

We conclude that the marginal or nonexistent benefits produced by suppressing evidence obtained in objectively reasonable reliance on a subsequently invalidated search warrant cannot justify the substantial costs of exclusion. We do not suggest, however, that exclusion is always inappropriate in cases where an officer has obtained a warrant and abided by its terms. . . . [I]t is clear that in some circumstances the officer will have no reasonable grounds for believing that the warrant was properly issued.

Suppression therefore remains an appropriate remedy if the magistrate or judge in issuing a warrant was misled by information in an affidavit that the affiant knew was false or would have known was false except for his reckless disregard of the truth. The exception we recognize today will also not apply in cases where the issuing magistrate wholly abandoned his judicial role. . . . [I]n such circumstances, no reasonably well trained officer should rely on the warrant. Nor would an officer manifest objective good faith in relying on a warrant based on an affidavit "so lacking in indicia of probable cause as to render official belief in its existence entirely unreasonable." Finally, depending on the circumstances of the particular case, a warrant may be so facially deficient—*i.e.,* in failing to particularize the place to be searched or the things to be seized—that the executing officers cannot reasonably presume it to be valid.

In so limiting the suppression remedy, we leave untouched the probable-cause standard and the various requirements for a valid warrant. . . . The good-faith exception for searches conducted pursuant to warrants is not intended to signal our unwillingness strictly to enforce the requirements of the Fourth Amendment, and we do not believe that it will have this effect. As we have already suggested, the good-faith exception, turning as it does on objective reasonableness, should not be difficult to apply in practice. . . .

When the principles we have enunciated today are applied to the facts of this case, it is apparent that the judgment of the Court of Appeals cannot stand. The Court of Appeals applied the prevailing legal standards to Officer Rombach's warrant application and concluded that the application could not support the magistrate's probable-cause determination. In so doing, the court clearly informed the magistrate that he had erred in issuing the challenged warrant. This aspect of the court's judgment is not under attack in this proceeding. . . .

In the absence of an allegation that the magistrate abandoned his detached and neutral role, suppression is appropriate only if the officers were dishonest or reckless in preparing their affidavit or could not have harbored an objectively reasonable belief in the existence of probable cause. . . .

Accordingly, the judgment of the Court of Appeals is

Reversed.

JUSTICE BRENNAN, WITH WHOM JUSTICE MARSHALL JOINS, DISSENTING.

Ten years ago in *United States v. Calandra* (1974), I expressed the fear that the Court's decision "may signal that a majority of my colleagues have positioned themselves to reopen the door [to evidence secured by official lawlessness] still further and abandon altogether the exclusionary rule in search-and-seizure cases." [Brennan, J., dissenting.] Since then, in case after case, I have witnessed the Court's gradual but determined strangulation of the rule. It now appears that the Court's victory over the Fourth Amendment is complete. That today's decision represents the *pièce de résistance* of the Court's past efforts cannot be doubted, for today the Court sanctions the use in the prosecution's case . . . of illegally obtained evidence against the individual whose rights have been violated—a result that had previously been thought to be foreclosed.

The Court seeks to justify this result on the ground that the "costs" of adhering to the exclusionary rule in cases like those before us exceed the "benefits." But the language of deterrence and of cost/benefit analysis, if used indiscriminately, can have a narcotic effect. It creates an illusion of technical precision and ineluctability. It suggests that not only constitutional principle but also empirical data support the majority's result. When the Court's analysis is examined carefully, however, it is clear that we have not been treated to an honest assessment of the merits of the exclusionary rule, but have instead been drawn into a curious world where the "costs" of excluding illegally obtained evidence loom to exaggerated heights and where the "benefits" of such exclusion are made to disappear with a mere wave of the hand.

The majority ignores the fundamental constitutional importance of what is at stake here. While the machinery of law enforcement and indeed the nature of crime itself have changed dramatically since the Fourth Amendment became part of the Nation's fundamental law in 1791, what the Framers understood then remains true today—that the task of combating crime and convicting the guilty will in every era seem of such critical and pressing concern that we may be lured by the temptations of expediency into forsaking our commitment to protecting individual liberty and privacy. It was for that very reason that the Framers of the Bill of Rights insisted that law enforcement efforts be permanently and unambiguously restricted in order to preserve personal freedoms. In the constitutional scheme they ordained, the sometimes unpopular task of ensuring that the government's enforcement efforts remain within the strict boundaries fixed by the Fourth Amendment was entrusted to the courts. . . . If those independent tribunals lose their resolve, however, as the Court has done today, and give way to the seductive call of expediency, the vital guarantees of the Fourth Amendment are reduced to nothing more than a "form of words." . . .

When the public, as it quite properly has done in the past as well as in the present, demands that those in government increase their efforts to combat crime, it is all too easy for those government officials to seek expedient solutions. . . . In the long run, however, we as a society pay a heavy price for such expediency, because as Justice Jackson observed, the rights guaranteed in the Fourth Amendment "are not mere second-class rights but belong in the catalog of indispensable freedoms." Once lost, such rights are difficult to recover. There is hope, however, that in time this or some later Court will restore these precious freedoms to their rightful place as a primary protection for our citizens against overreaching officialdom.

I dissent.

In *Leon* the Court authorized a good-faith exception to the exclusionary rule. If the police act in good faith, reasonably believing that they are following all of the appropriate rules and exhibiting no intent to violate the suspect's Fourth Amendment rights, then the evidence gathered will not be excluded should it later be determined that technical violations of the search and seizure rules occurred. Civil libertarians were dismayed by the *Leon* ruling. They agreed with Justice William J. Brennan's dissent that the Court had truly undermined the Fourth Amendment. Others, however, sided with Justice Byron White's majority opinion, believing that the decision did nothing more than bring a degree of reasonableness to the application of the rule.

The *Leon* decision placed a significant limitation on the exclusionary rule. As Table 17-2 illustrates, however, it was certainly not the only time the justices authorized an exception to the rules on the admissibility of evidence. Over the nearly six decades since *Mapp*, the Court has periodically eased the exclusionary rule, allowing for greater opportunities for evidence to be used. Conservative commentators have praised these changes as being reasonable accommodations in the interest of effective law enforcement. Critics of the Court, though, have argued that the cumulative effect of these exceptions has seriously undermined the rule's value as a deterrent to Fourth Amendment violations. Undoubtedly the debate over search and seizure rules will continue well into the future as each Supreme Court term sees new constitutional questions brought before the justices.

THE FIFTH AMENDMENT AND SELF-INCRIMINATION

As we now know, the Fourth Amendment governs the procedures by which police obtain evidence—generally physical evidence. But evidence used to make an arrest is not always physical or material. Very often arrests, and ultimately convictions, hinge on verbal evidence—testimony, confessions, and the like—the gathering of which is governed by the Fifth Amendment's self-incrimination clause: "No person . . . shall be compelled in any criminal case to be a witness against himself." Taken together, the Fourth (physical) and Fifth (verbal) Amendments dictate the procedures police use to gather most evidence against individuals.

The self-incrimination clause is violated by an involuntary admission of guilt. That is, there must be some form of testimonial evidence that incriminates the person who provides it. Likewise, the testimonial evidence must somehow be compelled by the government.

Table 17-2   Exceptions to the Exclusionary Rule

Mapp v. Ohio (1961) held that evidence obtained in violation of the **Fourth Amendment** is inadmissible in court. Over the years the justices have allowed certain exceptions to that rule. Listed below are some examples of those exceptions.

Decision	Exception
United States v. Calandra (1974)	The exclusionary rule does not apply to grand jury investigations.
United States v. Ceccolini (1978)	Evidence improperly obtained may be admitted if the connection between the evidence and the illegal means by which it was gathered is very remote.
United States v. Leon (1984)	Illegally seized evidence is admissible if law enforcement officers had a reasonable, good faith belief that they were acting consistent with appropriate legal authority, such as relying on a search warrant later proven to be defective.
Nix v. Williams (1984)	Evidence discovered as a result of an illegal search may still be admissible if it can be shown that the evidence inevitably would have been found had the violation not occurred.
Murray v. United States (1988)	Evidence obtained illegally may be admitted if the evidence was later independently obtained through legal means.
Arizona v. Evans (1995)	Evidence gathered in a search incident to a valid arrest may be admissible even if police based the arrest on information found in court records later determined to be inaccurate.
Hudson v. Michigan (2006)	Evidence from the search of a residence may be admissible where the police had authorization to search but entered the residence in violation of rules requiring them to knock and announce their presence.
Herring v. United States (2009)	Evidence gathered in a search incident to a valid arrest may be admissible even if the arrest was based on erroneous law enforcement records that the arresting officers relied upon as being accurate.

The protection against self-incrimination most commonly applies in two situations. First, no person may be forced to give testimony in any court case or other governmental hearing in which the truthful answering of questions will implicate the witness in a criminal act. For this reason a witness may decline to answer questions that would lead to self-incriminating answers. Furthermore, a defendant in a criminal case is exempt from testifying at all, and no inferences of guilt may be made on the basis of a defendant's decision not to speak in court.

The second common situation for which the Fifth Amendment is relevant involves police interrogation of suspects prior to trial. Certainly, police must be able to ask questions during the investigation of crimes, but constitutional disputes may arise if their interrogation tactics involve compulsion. The resulting legal challenges can require the Court to address difficult and controversial issues.

Even before the 1960s, the Supreme Court had established certain guidelines for police interrogations. For the most part, these dealt with instances of coercion, when confessions are forced from a suspect through physical torture or psychological duress.[10] These guidelines curtailed the most blatant forms of police misconduct, but they left considerable latitude for investigators to pry confessions out of poorly educated or naive suspects.

Several of the justices on the Warren Court believed that the balance was tipped decidedly in favor of the police. There were too many opportunities for police to obtain incriminating statements from unsuspecting potential defendants. As a consequence, the justices handed down two particularly important decisions in the mid-1960s designed to provide additional protections to

---

[10]See, for example, *Brown v. Mississippi* (1936); *Spano v. New York* (1959).

the criminally accused: *Escobedo v. Illinois* (1964) and *Miranda v. Arizona* (1966).

Danny Escobedo, a twenty-two-year-old of Mexican extraction and limited formal education, was accused of murder. The case began when Escobedo's brother-in-law was found fatally shot in a Chicago alley. The police quickly identified three potential suspects: Escobedo, his sister Grace, and his friend Benedict DiGerlando. The crime was motivated, police believed, by the deceased's long history of physically abusing Grace.

In the ten days following the murder all three suspects at various times were taken into custody for questioning. Eventually, DiGerlando told police that Escobedo had fired the fatal shots. As a consequence, police arrested Escobedo, told him what DiGerlando had said, and began a lengthy interrogation. Escobedo, feeling overwhelmed by the situation, asked to have his attorney present. Police told Escobedo that his attorney did not want to see him, even though the lawyer had arrived at the police station and asked to meet with his client. Although Escobedo was not subjected to any overt physical or psychological coercion, the questioning lasted more than fourteen hours, at the end of which Escobedo made incriminating statements. Against his attorney's objections, the incriminating statements, along with other evidence, were introduced at Escobedo's trial, and he was convicted of murder.

On appeal, Escobedo argued that his rights had been violated. The atmosphere at the police station surrounding the interrogation had been overwhelming. Without having his attorney present to provide advice, Escobedo broke down and incriminated himself. Under such conditions, he argued, the incriminating statements should be considered the product of coercion in violation of the Fifth Amendment.

By a 5–4 vote the Warren Court ruled that Escobedo's statements had been compelled. Coercion, the majority concluded, may take place even if overt physical or psychological pressure is not present. When arrested and brought to the police station for questioning, a suspect does not stand on equal footing with the law enforcement authorities. There is a clear power imbalance in favor of the police, and a poor and uneducated suspect is at a particular disadvantage and prone to make incriminating statements.

The justices decided that the right to counsel was the appropriate method of protecting the defendant's Fifth Amendment rights. Escobedo had repeatedly requested and was denied the opportunity to consult with his attorney; he was seeking guidance on how to protect his rights, guidance that was denied him by the

Danny Escobedo's 1960 arrest and conviction for the murder of his brother-in-law led to a Supreme Court decision that expanded constitutional protections for criminal defendants during police interrogations. This photograph of Escobedo was taken as he awaited processing on charges of burglarizing a hot dog stand not long after the Supreme Court issued its landmark ruling in *Escobedo v. Illinois* in 1964.

government. Instead, the police were urging him to incriminate himself. In those circumstances, he could not intelligently waive his Fifth Amendment privilege. A suspect, therefore, has the right to have an attorney present during any custodial interrogation.

Danny Escobedo had been denied his right to counsel, and the majority found this right to be a primary defense against violations of the protection against self-incrimination. The presence of an attorney serves to guard against both obvious and subtle methods to coerce a confession from a suspect. Escobedo was freed *(see Box 17-2)*.

The *Escobedo* majority held that, in order to safeguard against compelled admissions of guilt, the right to counsel begins at the accusatory stage of the process, defined as the point at which the investigation ceases to be general and focuses on a specific individual. The right is in effect for every critical stage of the process, which includes all interrogations. But once the Court had made this decision, it was

BOX 17-2

Aftermath . . . Danny Escobedo

Danny Escobedo's brush with the law for the murder of his brother-in-law, Manuel Valtierra, was neither his first nor his last encounter with the criminal justice system. In 1953 Escobedo, then sixteen, was incarcerated in a juvenile facility on theft charges. He was convicted of theft again in 1957 and of assault with a deadly weapon in 1958.

Escobedo had served four years of a twenty-year sentence for Valtierra's murder when the Supreme Court reversed his conviction. He then drifted from job to job in Chicago, at various times working as a plumber, a dockworker, a security guard, a carpenter, and a printer. He also had difficulty staying out of trouble with the law, a situation he blamed on police officers trying to advance their careers at his expense. Shortly after his release he was arrested for weapons violations, selling drugs to an undercover police officer, and robbing a hot dog stand. Each of these cases ended with dropped charges or acquittal. In 1967, however, Escobedo was convicted on narcotics charges, for which he spent seven years in federal prisons.

Escobedo was arrested again in 1984 when his thirteen-year-old stepdaughter claimed that he had molested her six different times. Escobedo denied the charges, alleging that they stemmed from a bitter custody battle over the girl. He was convicted of two counts of taking indecent liberties with a minor and sentenced

to twelve years in prison. He appealed his conviction, claiming that after his arrest, police handcuffed him to a wall for more than eight hours before allowing him to call his attorney.

While free on a $50,000 bond pending the appeal of his indecency conviction, Escobedo shot a man in a bar. He pleaded guilty to attempted murder and was sentenced to eleven years in prison.

In 1999, while on probation after his conviction for a federal weapons violation and also under investigation for the 1983 ice-pick stabbing of a Korean fur and leather dealer, Escobedo disappeared. He was placed on the U.S. Marshals Service's "fifteen most wanted fugitives" list. In 2001 a combined effort by the Marshals Service and Mexican police tracked Escobedo to a desolate rural area of Mexico, where the sixty-four-year-old fugitive was arrested. He was subsequently returned to the United States.

In 2003 Escobedo was convicted of the ice-pick murder and sentenced to forty years in prison. He had been arrested twenty-five times since his 1964 Supreme Court victory.

Escobedo's sister remarried after the famous decision of *Escobedo v. Illinois*. Her husband was later found shot to death by an unknown assailant.

Sources: New York Times, September 17, 1984, October 29, 1984, September 27, 1985, June 22, 2001; Washington Post, September 28, 1985; San Diego Union-Tribune, October 22, 1985; and Rocco J. Tresolini, These Liberties (Philadelphia: J. B. Lippincott, 1968).

---

faced, in *Miranda v. Arizona*, with a more difficult and far-reaching question: How should this new right be enforced?

Miranda v. Arizona

384 U.S. 436 (1966)
http://caselaw.findlaw.com/us-supreme-court/384/436.html
*Oral arguments available at https://www.oyez.org/
cases/1965/759*
Vote: 5 (Black, Brennan, Douglas, Fortas, Warren)
    4 (Clark, Harlan, Stewart, White)

OPINION OF THE COURT: Warren

OPINION DISSENTING IN PART: Clark

DISSENTING OPINIONS: Harlan, White, Stewart

Ernesto Miranda, a twenty-three-year-old indigent, nearly illiterate truck driver, allegedly kidnapped and raped a young woman outside Phoenix, Arizona. Ten days after the incident, police arrested him, took him to the station, and interrogated him. Within two hours of questioning, Miranda confessed. There was no evidence of any police misbehavior during the interrogation, and at no point during questioning did Miranda request an attorney. Miranda was convicted and received a sentence of twenty to thirty years. The conviction was based not only on the confession but also on other evidence, including the victim's positive identification of Miranda as her assailant.

Miranda's appeal reached the Supreme Court, where it was combined with three other cases presenting similar issues.[11] His

---

[11] Along with Miranda, the Court decided *Vignera v. New York*, *Westover v. United States*, and *California v. Stewart*.

attorneys claimed that, because the entire interrogation process is so inherently coercive, any individual will eventually succumb; the Court, they argued, should affirmatively protect the right against self-incrimination by adding to those protections already extended in *Escobedo*.

MR. CHIEF JUSTICE WARREN DELIVERED THE OPINION OF THE COURT.

The cases before us raise questions which go to the roots of our concepts of American criminal jurisprudence: the restraints society must observe consistent with the Federal Constitution in prosecuting individuals for crime. More specifically, we deal with the admissibility of statements obtained from an individual who is subjected to custodial police interrogation and the necessity for procedures which assure that the individual is accorded his privilege under the Fifth Amendment to the Constitution not to be compelled to incriminate himself.

We start here, as we did in *Escobedo,* with the premise that our holding is not an innovation in our jurisprudence, but is an application of principles long recognized and applied in other settings. We have undertaken a thorough reexamination of the *Escobedo* decision and the principles it announced, and we reaffirm it. That case was but an explication of basic rights that are enshrined in our Constitution—that "No person . . . shall be compelled in any criminal case to be a witness against himself," and that "the accused shall . . . have the Assistance of Counsel"—rights which were put in jeopardy in that case through official overbearing. . . .

It was necessary in *Escobedo,* as here, to insure that what was proclaimed in the Constitution had not become but a "form of words" in the hands of government officials. And it is in this spirit, consistent with our role as judges, that we adhere to the principles of *Escobedo* today. . . .

. . . [T]he modern practice of in-custody interrogation is psychologically rather than physically oriented. As we have stated before, "[T]his Court has recognized that coercion can be mental as well as physical, and that the blood of the accused is not the only hallmark of an unconstitutional inquisition." *Blackburn v. State of Alabama* (1960). Interrogation . . . takes place in privacy. Privacy results in secrecy and this in turn results in a gap in our knowledge as to what in fact goes on in the interrogation rooms. A valuable source of information about present police practices, however, may be found in various police manuals and texts which document procedures employed with success in the past, and which recommend various other effective tactics. . . .

The officers are told by the manuals that the "principal psychological factor contributing to a successful interrogation is privacy—being alone with the person under interrogation." . . .

To highlight the isolation and unfamiliar surroundings, the manuals instruct the police to display an air of confidence in the

Ernesto Miranda waits as the jury deliberates his case before finding him guilty of kidnapping and rape after he confessed to the crimes while in police custody. In a landmark ruling, *Miranda v. Arizona* (1966), the Supreme Court reversed the conviction because Miranda had not been told he had the right to remain silent and to have an attorney present during questioning.

suspect's guilt and from outward appearance to maintain only an interest in confirming certain details. The guilt of the subject is to be posited as a fact. The interrogator should direct his comments toward the reasons why the subject committed the act, rather than court failure by asking the subject whether he did it. Like other men, perhaps the subject has had a bad family life, had an unhappy childhood, had too much to drink, had an unrequited desire for women. The officers are instructed to minimize the moral seriousness of the offense, to cast blame on the victim or on society. These tactics are designed to put the subject in a psychological state where his story is but an elaboration of what the police purport to know already—that he is guilty. . . .

When the techniques described above prove unavailing, the texts recommend they be alternated with a show of some hostility. . . .

The interrogators sometimes are instructed to induce a confession out of trickery. . . .

Even without employing brutality, the "third degree" or the specific stratagems described above, the very fact of custodial interrogation exacts a heavy toll on individual liberty and trades on the weakness of individuals. . . .

. . . In each of the cases, the defendant was thrust into an unfamiliar atmosphere and run through menacing police interrogation procedures. The potentiality for compulsion is forcefully apparent, for example, in *Miranda,* where the indigent Mexican defendant was a seriously disturbed individual with pronounced sexual fantasies. . . . To be sure, the records do not evince overt physical coercion or patent psychological ploys. The fact remains that in none of these cases did the officers undertake to afford appropriate safeguards at the outset of the interrogation to insure that the statements were truly the product of free choice.

It is obvious that such an interrogation environment is created for no purpose other than to subjugate the individual to the will of his examiner. . . . Unless adequate protective devices are employed to dispel the compulsion inherent in custodial surroundings, no statement obtained from the defendant can truly be the product of his free choice.

From the foregoing, we can readily perceive an intimate connection between the privilege against self-incrimination and police custodial questioning. . . .

Today, then, there can be no doubt that the Fifth Amendment privilege is available outside of criminal court proceedings and serves to protect persons in all settings in which their freedom of action is curtailed in any significant way from being compelled to incriminate themselves. We have concluded that without proper safeguards the process of in-custody interrogation of persons suspected or accused of crime contains inherently compelling pressures which work to undermine the individual's will to resist and to compel him to speak where he would not otherwise do so freely. In order to combat these pressures and to permit a full opportunity to exercise the privilege against self-incrimination, the accused must be adequately and effectively apprised of his rights and the exercise of those rights must be fully honored. . . .

. . . [A] warning at the time of the interrogation is indispensable to overcome its pressures and to insure that the individual knows he is free to exercise the privilege at that point in time.

The warning of the right to remain silent must be accompanied by the explanation that anything said can and will be used against the individual in court. This warning is needed in order to make him aware not only of the privilege, but also of the consequences of forgoing it. It is only through an awareness of these consequences that there can be any assurance of real understanding and intelligent exercise of the privilege. . . .

The circumstances surrounding in-custody interrogation can operate very quickly to overbear the will of one merely made aware of his privilege by his interrogators. Therefore, the right to have counsel present at the interrogation is indispensable to the protection of the Fifth Amendment privilege under the system we delineate today. Our aim is to assure that the individual's right to choose between silence and speech remains unfettered throughout the interrogation process. . . . Even preliminary advice given to the accused by his own attorney can be swiftly overcome by the secret interrogation process. Thus, the need for counsel to protect the Fifth Amendment privilege comprehends not merely a right to consult with counsel prior to questioning, but also to have counsel present during any questioning if the defendant so desires.

. . . With a lawyer present the likelihood that the police will practice coercion is reduced, and if coercion is nevertheless exercised the lawyer can testify to it in court. The presence of a lawyer can also help to guarantee that the accused gives a fully accurate statement to the police and that the statement is rightly reported by the prosecution at trial.

An individual need not make a pre-interrogation request for a lawyer. . . . The accused who does not know his rights and therefore does not make a request may be the person who most needs counsel. . . .

Accordingly we hold that an individual held for interrogation must be clearly informed that he has the right to consult with a lawyer and to have the lawyer with him during interrogation under the system for protecting the privilege we delineate today. As with the warnings of the right to remain silent and that anything stated can be used in evidence against him, this warning is an absolute prerequisite to interrogation. . . . If an individual indicates that he wishes the assistance of counsel before any interrogation occurs, the authorities cannot rationally ignore or deny his request on the basis that the individual does not have or cannot afford a retained attorney. The financial ability of the individual has no relationship to the scope of the rights involved here. The privilege against self-incrimination secured by the Constitution applies to all individuals. The need for counsel in order to protect the privilege exists for the indigent as well as the affluent. In fact, were we to limit these constitutional rights to those who can retain an attorney, our decisions today would be of little significance. . . .

In order fully to apprise a person interrogated of the extent of his rights under this system then, it is necessary to warn him not only that he has the right to consult with an attorney, but also that if he is indigent a lawyer will be appointed to represent him. Without this additional warning, the admonition of the right to consult with counsel would often be understood as meaning only that he can consult with a lawyer if he has one or has the funds to obtain one. The warning of a right to counsel would be hollow if not couched in terms that would convey to the indigent—the person most often subjected to interrogation—the knowledge that he too has a right to have counsel present. . . . Once warnings have been given, the subsequent procedure is clear. If the individual indicates in any manner, at any time prior to or during questioning, that he wishes to remain silent, the interrogation must cease. At this point he has shown that he intends to exercise his Fifth Amendment privilege; any statement taken after the person invokes his privilege cannot be other than the product of compulsion, subtle or otherwise. . . . [T]he interrogation must cease until an attorney is present. At that time, the individual must have an opportunity to confer with the attorney and to have him present during any subsequent questioning. . . .

If the interrogation continues without the presence of an attorney and a statement is taken, a heavy burden rests on the government to demonstrate that the defendant knowingly and intelligently waived his privilege against self-incrimination and his right to retained or appointed counsel. . . .

To summarize, we hold that when an individual is taken into custody or otherwise deprived of his freedom by the authorities in any significant way and is subjected to questioning, the privilege against self-incrimination is jeopardized. Procedural safeguards must be employed to protect the privilege, and unless other fully effective means are adopted to notify the person of his right of silence and to assure that the exercise of the right will be scrupulously honored, the following measures are required. He must be warned prior to any questioning that he has the right to remain silent, that anything he says can be used against him in a court of law, that he has the right to the presence of an attorney, and that if he cannot afford an attorney one will be appointed for him prior to any questioning if he so desires. Opportunity to exercise these rights must be afforded to him throughout the interrogation. After such warnings have been given, and such opportunity afforded him, the individual may knowingly and intelligently waive these rights and agree to answer questions or make a statement. But unless and until such warnings and waiver are demonstrated by the prosecution at trial, no evidence obtained as a result of interrogation can be used against him. . . .

In announcing these principles, we are not unmindful of the burdens which law enforcement officials must bear, often under trying circumstances. We also fully recognize the obligation of all citizens to aid in enforcing the criminal laws. This Court, while protecting individual rights, has always given ample latitude to law enforcement agencies in the legitimate exercise of their duties. The limits we have placed on the interrogation process should not constitute an undue interference with a proper system of law enforcement. . . .

Judicial solutions to problems of constitutional dimension have evolved decade by decade. As courts have been presented with the need to enforce constitutional rights, they have found means of doing so. That was our responsibility when *Escobedo* was before us and it is our responsibility today. Where rights secured by the Constitution are involved, there can be no rule making or legislation which would abrogate them.

Reversed.

MR. JUSTICE WHITE, WITH WHOM MR. JUSTICE HARLAN AND MR. JUSTICE STEWART JOIN, DISSENTING.

The obvious underpinning of the Court's decision is a deep-seated distrust of all confessions. As the Court declares that the accused may not be interrogated without counsel present, absent a waiver of the right to counsel, and as the Court all but admonishes the lawyer to advise the accused to remain silent, the result adds up to a judicial judgment that evidence from the accused should not be used against him in any way, whether compelled or not. This is the not so subtle overtone of the opinion—that it is inherently wrong for the police to gather evidence from the accused himself. And this is precisely the nub of this dissent. I see nothing wrong or immoral, and certainly nothing unconstitutional, in the police's asking a suspect whom they have reasonable cause to arrest whether or not he killed his wife or in confronting him with the evidence on which the arrest was based, at least where he has been plainly advised that he may remain completely silent. Until today, "the admissions or confessions of the prisoner, when voluntarily and freely made, have always ranked high in the scale of incriminating evidence." . . .

This is not to say that the value of respect for the inviolability of the accused's individual personality should be accorded no weight or that all confessions should be indiscriminately admitted. This Court has long read the Constitution to proscribe compelled confessions, a salutary rule from which there should be no retreat. But I see no sound basis, factual or otherwise, and the Court gives none, for concluding that the present rule against the receipt of coerced confessions is inadequate for the task of sorting out inadmissible evidence and must be replaced by the per se rule which is now imposed. Even if the new concept can be said to have advantages of some sort over the present law, they are far outweighed by its likely undesirable impact on other very relevant and important interests.

The most basic function of any government is to provide for the security of the individual and of his property. These ends of society are served by the criminal laws which for the most part are aimed at the prevention of crime. Without the reasonably effective performance of the task of preventing private violence and retaliation, it is idle to talk about human dignity and civilized values. . . .

The rule announced today will measurably weaken the ability of the criminal law to perform [its] tasks. It is a deliberate calculus to prevent interrogations, to reduce the incidence of confessions and pleas of guilty and to increase the number of trials. . . . There is, in my view, every reason to believe that a good many criminal defendants who otherwise would have been convicted on what this Court has previously thought to be the most satisfactory kind of evidence will now, under this new version of the Fifth Amendment, either not be tried at all or will be acquitted if the State's evidence, minus the confession, is put to the test of litigation.

I have no desire whatsoever to share the responsibility for any such impact on the present criminal process.

BOX 17-3

Aftermath . . . Ernesto Miranda

In February 1967, following the Supreme Court's decision overturning his conviction on kidnapping and rape charges, Ernesto Miranda was retried, this time with his incriminating statements excluded. To mask his identity from the jurors, Miranda stood trial as "José Gomez." He was convicted and sentenced to twenty to thirty years in prison. Most damning was the testimony of his common-law wife, who claimed that Miranda had admitted to her that he had kidnapped and raped the victim. He was also convicted of an unrelated robbery of a woman at knifepoint and was sentenced to a concurrent term of twenty to twenty-five years.

In December 1972 Miranda was released on parole. Only two years later, he was arrested on drug and firearms charges after being stopped for a routine traffic violation. These charges were dropped because of Fourth Amendment violations and insufficient evidence. In 1975 he returned to prison for a short time on a parole violation.

Miranda's life ended in 1976. While drinking and playing cards in a Phoenix skid row bar, he became involved in a fight with two undocumented aliens. Miranda got the best of the fight and went to the restroom to wash his bloodied hands. When he returned, the two attacked him with a knife. Miranda was stabbed once in the chest and once in the abdomen. He collapsed and died. Miranda was thirty-four years old. Upon arresting his assailants, police read them their *Miranda* warnings.

Sources: New York Times, October 12, 1974; *Atlanta Journal*, December 13, 1972, February 1, 1976, February 2, 1976; and James A. Inciardi, *Criminal Justice*, 4th ed. (Fort Worth: Harcourt Brace Jovanovich, 1993).

Chief Justice Warren's majority opinion requires that police read the so-called *Miranda* warnings to suspects before any custodial interrogation takes place. The *Miranda* decision, in combination with subsequent rulings, means that whenever police take a suspect into custody for any crime, they are required to precede interrogation of the suspect with such warnings.[12] By "custody" the Court means any situation in which the suspect is under police control and may not freely leave—no matter where this may occur. Custody, therefore, is not confined to formal interrogation rooms at the police station.[13] Similarly, the justices have given a relatively broad interpretation of what is meant by "interrogation." Although most interrogations conform to the standard question-answer format, the justices have ruled that any police action designed to elicit statements from a suspect falls under the definition of interrogation and must be preceded by *Miranda* warnings.[14]

The Warren Court premised its decision in *Miranda* on the unavoidable inequities between the accused and the police during custodial interrogations. In 1966 the justices thought it too dangerous to ignore the likelihood that individuals would forgo their privilege against self-incrimination under intense and ultimately coercive police questioning. Thus, Miranda's confession could not be used against him, given that the police did not take the steps necessary to safeguard his rights (*see Box 17-3*).

Miranda triggered an enormous amount of litigation as individuals who had made incriminating statements to police claimed that their rights had been violated. In addition, the decision left many questions to be answered in future cases. By the time these follow-up cases reached the Supreme Court, Earl Warren had retired and a more conservative Court under Chief Justice Burger was in place.

Beginning in 1971 and extending well into the twenty-first century, the Court has frequently heard difficult appeals questioning the meaning of *Miranda*. The justices have responded by interpreting the precedent quite narrowly or by creating exceptions to it (*see Table 17-3*).

Although the Court has been prone to limit the application of *Miranda*, it has rejected attempts to overrule it altogether[15] and has vigorously enforced it when police have engaged in unfair tactics to evade the decision's central purpose. Take, for example, the case of *Missouri v. Seibert* (2004). The *Seibert* case had its origins in an earlier Supreme Court decision, *Oregon v. Elstad* (1985). *Elstad* involved a young burglary suspect who, while confronted by police in his home, blurted

---

[12]*Berkemer v. McCarty* (1984).

[13]*Orozco v. Texas* (1969).

[14]See *Brewer v. Williams* (1977); *Rhode Island v. Innis* (1980).

[15]*Dickerson v. United States* (2000).

Table 17-3 Exceptions to *Miranda*: Some Examples

Case	Facts	Ruling
Harris v. New York (1971)	An arrested drug suspect made incriminating statements without the benefit of *Miranda* warnings. At trial he gave an alibi at odds with his earlier statements. To impeach his credibility, the prosecutor introduced the suspect's initial statements.	Statements made without *Miranda* warnings may be used for the narrow purpose of counteracting perjury.
New York v. Quarles (1984)	A rape suspect was apprehended after a chase through a supermarket. Police discovered an empty holster and asked, "Where's the gun?" The suspect revealed where he dropped it. Police then read the suspect his *Miranda* warnings.	When there is a danger to public safety, police may ask questions to remove that danger prior to reading *Miranda* warnings. Answers to such questions may be used as evidence.
Illinois v. Perkins (1990)	An undercover police agent obtained incriminating statements from a prison inmate without first providing *Miranda* warnings.	*Miranda* warnings are not required when a suspect is unaware he or she is speaking to a law enforcement official and gives a voluntary statement.
New York v. Harris (1990)	Police unlawfully entered the home of a murder suspect without a warrant and without permission. They arrested the suspect and took him to the police station. He was read his *Miranda* warnings and subsequently signed a written confession.	The fact that police enter a home illegally to make an arrest does not taint a subsequent confession at the police station that takes place after *Miranda* warnings are given.
Davis v. United States (1994)	In the middle of an interrogation session a murder suspect, who had received proper *Miranda* warnings, commented, "Maybe I should talk to a lawyer." The questioning continued for about another hour, at which time the suspect said, "I think I want a lawyer before I say anything else." At that point the investigators terminated the interview.	*Miranda* does not require police to stop questioning when the suspect makes an ambiguous reference to an attorney.
United States v. Patane (2004)	An arrested suspect, who did not receive full *Miranda* warnings, was questioned at his home by police officers about a possible firearms violation. The suspect voluntarily admitted to having the pistol in question and gave the officers permission to retrieve it from his bedroom.	The failure to give full *Miranda* warnings does not require suppression of physical evidence obtained from information voluntarily supplied by the suspect in custody.
Montejo v. Louisiana (2009)	Although he remained silent and did not request a lawyer, an indigent charged with murder was automatically assigned counsel. After the appointment, but before the suspect ever consulted with his attorney, the suspect was read his *Miranda* warnings, cooperated in a police-initiated interrogation, and confessed.	Police are prevented from initiating custodial interrogations only after the suspect affirmatively asserts the right to counsel.
Howes v. Fields (2012)	Without first giving *Miranda* warnings, two armed sheriff's deputies interrogated an inmate in a prison conference room concerning a crime unrelated to his incarceration. The inmate confessed.	Because the inmate was informed that he could terminate the interrogation at any time and return to his cell, he was not "in custody" for *Miranda* purposes and therefore no warnings were required.
Salinas v. Texas (2013)	A homicide suspect being questioned by police refused to answer a question about whether ballistics tests would show that his shotgun was consistent with shell casings found at a murder scene.	Because he was not under arrest at the time he was questioned, he could not assert that his rights had been violated by police not providing *Miranda* warnings.

out incriminating comments before *Miranda* warnings could be given him. Police then transported Elstad to the police station, where he subsequently confessed after being provided *Miranda* warnings. The Supreme Court held that although Elstad's in-home comments were not admissible, his police station confession—because it had been preceded by proper warnings—could be used. An important factor in allowing the use of the later confession was that the in-home confession was not the product of police coercion; because there was no coercion for the first confession, his subsequent confession, accompanied by the *Miranda* warnings, could be seen as freely given.

Suppose, though, that the police decide to employ the coercive process of interrogation from the outset, with the aim of securing a confession. If the police successfully obtain incriminating statements—and then provide *Miranda* warnings—is a subsequent confession admissible? That is the question posed in *Seibert*.

about forty minutes, during which time she made incriminating statements. After giving her a twenty-minute coffee and cigarette break, Hanrahan turned on a tape recorder and gave Seibert her *Miranda* warnings. Seibert waived her rights, and Hanrahan resumed the questioning. He asked Seibert to repeat her incriminating statements, and she did. Prosecutors charged Seibert with first-degree murder.

Officer Hanrahan admitted that withholding the *Miranda* warnings was a conscious decision. He claimed he was following an interrogation technique he was taught: question first, then give the *Miranda* warnings, and finally question again with the goal of getting the suspect to repeat the incriminating statements.

Defense attorneys moved to suppress both the prewarning and postwarning statements, but the trial court, relying on *Oregon v. Elstad,* held that the postwarning statements could be admitted. The state supreme court reversed, ruling that the two interrogation sessions were nearly continuous and the statements made in the second session were clearly a product of the first. The state requested review by the U.S. Supreme Court.

Missouri v. Seibert

542 U.S. 600 (2004)
http://caselaw.findlaw.com/us-supreme-court/542/600.html
Oral arguments available at https://www.oyez.org/
  cases/2003/02-1371
Vote: 5 (Breyer, Ginsburg, Kennedy, Souter, Stevens)
  4 (O'Connor, Rehnquist, Scalia, Thomas)

OPINION OF THE COURT: *Souter*

CONCURRING OPINIONS: *Breyer, Kennedy*

DISSENTING OPINION: *O'Connor*

Patrice Seibert of Rolla, Missouri, had a twelve-year-old son, Jonathan, who suffered from cerebral palsy. When Jonathan died in his sleep, Seibert feared that she might be charged with child neglect because her son suffered a bad case of bedsores. To avoid such charges, Seibert, with her two teenage sons and two of their friends, devised a plan to conceal the facts. They decided to set Seibert's mobile home on fire to make it appear as if Jonathan had died in an accidental blaze. To guard against charges that Jonathan had been left unattended, they planned to leave Donald Rector, a mentally ill teenager living with the family, in the mobile home when the fire was set. Seibert's son Darian and a friend carried out the plan, and Rector died in the fire.

Five days later, Officer Kevin Clinton confronted Seibert at a local hospital where Darian was recovering from burns. He took her into custody, but on instructions from Officer Richard Hanrahan, Clinton did not provide Seibert with *Miranda* warnings. At the police station, Hanrahan interrogated Seibert for

In *Missouri v. Seibert*, the Supreme Court declared inadmissible the self-incriminating statements that led to Patrice Seibert's conviction on murder charges. The police interrogation techniques that produced those statements violated the *Miranda* ruling.

This case tests a police protocol for custodial interrogation that calls for giving no warnings of the rights to silence and counsel until interrogation has produced a confession. Although such a statement is generally inadmissible, since taken in violation of *Miranda v. Arizona* (1966), the interrogating officer follows it with *Miranda* warnings and then leads the suspect to cover the same ground a second time. The question here is the admissibility of the repeated statement. . . .

The technique of interrogating in successive, unwarned and warned phases raises a new challenge to *Miranda*. Although we have no statistics on the frequency of this practice, it is not confined to Rolla, Missouri. An officer of that police department testified that the strategy of withholding *Miranda* warnings until after interrogating and drawing out a confession was promoted not only by his own department, but by a national police training organization and other departments in which he had worked. . . .

When a confession so obtained is offered and challenged, attention must be paid to the conflicting objects of *Miranda* and question-first. *Miranda* addressed "interrogation practices . . . likely . . . to disable [an individual] from making a free and rational choice" about speaking, and held that a suspect must be "adequately and effectively" advised of the choice the Constitution guarantees. The object of question-first is to render *Miranda* warnings ineffective by waiting for a particularly opportune time to give them, after the suspect has already confessed.

. . . By any objective measure, applied to circumstances exemplified here, it is likely that if the interrogators employ the technique of withholding warnings until after interrogation succeeds in eliciting a confession, the warnings will be ineffective in preparing the suspect for successive interrogation, close in time and similar in content. After all, the reason that question-first is catching on is as obvious as its manifest purpose, which is to get a confession the suspect would not make if he understood his rights at the outset; the sensible underlying assumption is that with one confession in hand before the warnings, the interrogator can count on getting its duplicate, with trifling additional trouble. Upon hearing warnings only in the aftermath of interrogation and just after making a confession, a suspect would hardly think he had a genuine right to remain silent, let alone persist in so believing once the police began to lead him over the same ground again. . . . [T]elling a suspect that "anything you say can and will be used against you," without expressly excepting the statement just given, could lead to an entirely reasonable inference that what he has just said will be used, with subsequent silence being of no avail. Thus, when *Miranda* warnings are inserted in the midst of coordinated and continuing interrogation, they are likely to mislead and "depriv[e] a defendant of knowledge essential to his ability to understand the nature of his rights and the consequences of abandoning them." *Moran v. Burbine* (1986). . . .

Strategists dedicated to draining the substance out of *Miranda* cannot accomplish by training instructions what *Dickerson* [*v. United States* (2000)] held Congress could not do by statute. Because the question-first tactic effectively threatens to thwart *Miranda*'s purpose of reducing the risk that a coerced confession would be admitted, and because the facts here do not reasonably support a conclusion that the warnings given could have served their purpose, Seibert's postwarning statements are inadmissible. The judgment of the Supreme Court of Missouri is affirmed.

It is so ordered.

JUSTICE KENNEDY, CONCURRING IN THE JUDGMENT.

The police used a two-step questioning technique based on a deliberate violation of *Miranda*. The *Miranda* warning was withheld to obscure both the practical and legal significance of the admonition when finally given. As JUSTICE SOUTER points out, the two-step technique permits the accused to conclude that the right not to respond did not exist when the earlier incriminating statements were made. The strategy is based on the assumption that *Miranda* warnings will tend to mean less when recited midinterrogation, after inculpatory statements have already been obtained. This tactic relies on an intentional misrepresentation of the protection that *Miranda* offers and does not serve any legitimate objectives that might otherwise justify its use.

Further, the interrogating officer here relied on the defendant's prewarning statement to obtain the postwarning statement used against her at trial. The postwarning interview resembled a cross-examination. The officer confronted the defendant with her inadmissible prewarning statements and pushed her to acknowledge them. This shows the temptations for abuse inherent in the two-step technique. . . .

The technique used in this case distorts the meaning of *Miranda* and furthers no legitimate countervailing interest. The *Miranda* rule would be frustrated were we to allow police to undermine its meaning and effect. The technique simply creates too high a risk that postwarning statements will be obtained when a suspect was deprived of "knowledge essential to his ability to understand the nature of his rights and the consequences of abandoning them." *Moran v. Burbine* (1986). . . .

The admissibility of postwarning statements should continue to be governed by the principles of *Elstad* unless the deliberate two-step strategy was employed. If the deliberate two-step strategy has been used, postwarning statements that are related to the substance of prewarning statements must be excluded unless curative measures are taken before the postwarning statement is made. Curative measures should be designed to ensure that a reasonable person in the suspect's situation would understand the import and effect of the *Miranda* warning and of the *Miranda* waiver. For example, a substantial break in time and circumstances between the prewarning statement and the *Miranda* warning may suffice in most circumstances, as it allows the accused to distinguish the two contexts and appreciate that the interrogation has taken a new turn. Alternatively, an additional warning that explains the likely inadmissibility of the prewarning custodial statement may be sufficient. No curative steps were taken in this case, however, so the postwarning statements are inadmissible and the conviction cannot stand.

JUSTICE O'CONNOR, WITH WHOM THE CHIEF JUSTICE, JUSTICE SCALIA, AND JUSTICE THOMAS JOIN, DISSENTING.

I believe that we are bound by [*Oregon v.*] *Elstad* to reach a different result, and I would vacate the judgment of the Supreme Court of Missouri. . . .

I would analyze the two-step interrogation procedure under the voluntariness standards central to the Fifth Amendment and reiterated in *Elstad*. *Elstad* commands that if Seibert's first statement is shown to have been involuntary, the court must examine whether the taint dissipated through the passing of time or a change in circumstances: "When a prior statement is actually coerced, the time that passes between confessions, the change in place of interrogations, and the change in identity of the interrogators all bear on whether that coercion has carried over into the second

confession." In addition, Seibert's second statement should be suppressed if she showed that it was involuntary despite the *Miranda* warnings. . . .

Because I believe that the plurality gives insufficient deference to *Elstad* and that JUSTICE KENNEDY places improper weight on subjective intent, I respectfully dissent.

Now that you have seen how the Fifth Amendment's self-incrimination clause governs out-of-court "testimony," you should readily grasp why *Miranda* continues to be so controversial. Some individuals continue to argue that the decision binds the hands of police. Supporters make equally strong arguments in its favor. Marvin Zalman and Larry Siegel point out that *Miranda* has not, in fact, made it more difficult for police to obtain incriminating statements. Empirical investigations of the effect of *Miranda* in cities—both large and small—indicate that "equivalent proportions of confessions were obtained in the post-*Miranda* period as before and that police effectiveness did not appear to suffer."[16] Whatever its effects may be, the *Miranda* decision has clearly become an ingrained part of the criminal justice system.

[16]Marvin Zalman and Larry Siegel, *Criminal Procedure*, 2nd ed. (St. Paul, MN: West, 1997), 518. For a review of some of these studies, see Welsh S. White, "Defending Miranda: A Reply to Professor Caplan," *Vanderbilt Law Review* 39 (1986): 1–22.

ANNOTATED READINGS

A number of works provide in-depth discussion of the American criminal court system and the procedures pertaining to the collection and use of evidence. Among them are Craig M. Bradley, *The Failure of the Criminal Procedure Revolution* (Philadelphia: University of Pennsylvania Press, 1993); James A. Inciardi, *Criminal Justice*, 9th ed. (Fort Worth, TX: Harcourt Brace, 2009); David W. Neubauer and Henry F. Fradella, *America's Courts and the Criminal Justice System*, 10th ed. (Belmont, CA: Wadsworth, 2011); Frank Schmalleger, *Criminal Justice Today*, 12th ed. (Upper Saddle River, NJ: Pearson, 2012); and Jon R. Waltz, *Introduction to Criminal Evidence*, 4th ed. (Chicago: Nelson-Hall, 1997).

Excellent examples of literature covering the search and seizure provisions of the Fourth Amendment

are Akhil Reed Amar, *The Constitution and Criminal Procedure* (New Haven, CT: Yale University Press, 1997); Thomas K. Clancy, *The Fourth Amendment: Its History and Interpretation* (Durham, NC: Carolina Academic Press, 2014); Samuel Dash, *The Intruders: Unreasonable Searches and Seizures from King John to John Ashcroft* (New Brunswick, NJ: Rutgers University Press, 2004); Michael C. Gizzi and R. Craig Curtis, *The Fourth Amendment in Flux: The Roberts Court, Crime Control, and Digital Privacy* (Lawrence: University Press of Kansas, 2016); Carolyn N. Long, Mapp v. Ohio: *Guarding against Unreasonable Searches and Seizures* (Lawrence: University Press of Kansas, 2006); Tracey Maclin, *The Supreme Court and the Fourth Amendment's Exclusionary Rule* (New York: Oxford University Press, 2012); Thomas N. McInis, *Evolution of the Fourth*

Amendment (New York: Lexington Books, 2009); Darien A. McWhirter, *Search, Seizure, and Privacy: Exploring the Constitution* (Phoenix, AZ: Oryx Press, 1994); and Andrew E. Taslitz, *Reconstructing the Fourth Amendment: A History of Search and Seizure, 1789–1868* (New York: New York University Press, 2006).

The privilege against self-incrimination is explored in the following works: Liva Baker, Miranda: *Crime, Law, and Politics* (New York: Atheneum, 1983); R. H. Helmholz, Charles M. Gray, John H. Langbein, Eben Moglen, Henry E. Smith, and Albert W. Alschuler, *The Privilege against Self-Incrimination: Its Origins and Development* (Chicago: University of Chicago Press, 1997); Richard A. Leo and George C. Thomas III, eds., *The* Miranda *Debate: Law, Justice, and Policing* (Boston: Northeastern University Press, 1998); Richard J. Medalie, *From* Escobedo *to* Miranda (Washington, DC: Lerner Law Books, 1966); Steven M. Salky and Paul B. Hynes Jr., *The Privilege of Silence: Fifth Amendment Protections against Self-Incrimination* (Chicago: American Bar Association, 2014); and John B. Taylor, *The Right to Counsel and Privilege against Self-Incrimination: Rights and Liberties under the Law* (Santa Barbara, CA: ABC-CLIO, 2004).

CHAPTER EIGHTEEN

ATTORNEYS, TRIALS, AND PUNISHMENTS

THE FRAMERS CLEARLY understood the importance of fairness in evidence gathering; they also understood the need to ensure the integrity of the formal stages of the criminal process. Consequently, they included in the Bill of Rights specific guarantees to prohibit the government from abusing prosecuted defendants. These rights are among those we most value, such as the rights to be represented by counsel, to be tried by an impartial jury of peers, and to be protected against punishments that are cruel and unusual. Other guarantees, less well-known but no less important, also enjoy constitutional status—such as the right to a speedy and public trial and the right to confront an accuser in open court. Taken as a whole, these rights were designed to help achieve a universally valued goal—fundamentally fair criminal trials. In this chapter we discuss what the Constitution says about these important procedural guarantees and how they have evolved through Supreme Court interpretations over the years.

THE RIGHT TO COUNSEL

The Sixth Amendment states, "[I]n all criminal prosecutions, the accused shall enjoy the right . . . to have the Assistance of Counsel for his defence." At the time these words were written, the law was relatively uncomplicated, and lawyers in the new nation were scarce. Some individuals charged with crimes sought the advice of counsel, but most handled their own cases. Still, the framers understood the importance of legal representation well enough to include the right to counsel in the Bill of Rights.

Today, perhaps no other right guaranteed to the criminally accused is more important than the right to counsel. Until relatively recently, a lawyer representing a criminal client could do the job by appearing at trial and dealing with well-established principles of evidence and procedure. Today, however, appearing at trial is only a small part of what a criminal defense attorney must do. As we saw in the Fifth Amendment cases reviewed in chapter 17, the Supreme Court has repeatedly emphasized that the role of the defense attorney begins when police first interrogate a suspect. From arrest through appeal, there are critical and complicated stages during which a defendant's rights might be violated. It is counsel's responsibility to ensure that the interests of the defendant are not jeopardized. The defense attorney, therefore, is the primary guarantee that all of the other rights of criminal due process are observed.

The provisions of the Sixth Amendment are clear, and there has been little controversy over the right of an individual to have legal representation throughout the various stages of the criminal process. Historically, however, it was the responsibility of the accused person to secure a lawyer and to pay for the lawyer's services. Most controversy over legal representation in criminal matters has centered on the rights of those who cannot pay for legal assistance.

As the complexity of the U.S. system of justice increased, greater numbers of people retained lawyers to handle their cases. But as soon as this practice took hold, people began to complain about economic discrimination. Civil libertarians and reformers throughout the country argued that only those who could afford it were guaranteed the right to counsel; indigent defendants were denied their constitutional guarantee. Reformers claimed that the only way to eliminate this injustice would be through a Supreme Court decision that would force governments to appoint free counsel for poor defendants.

The plight of the nine "Scottsboro boys" arrested in rural Alabama in 1931 for raping two white females spawned numerous legal actions, including *Powell v. Alabama* (1932), which expanded the rights of indigents to legal representation. Samuel Leibowitz, a prominent attorney and later a judge, handled the defendants' cases after their original convictions. He is shown here conferring with seven of his clients. Deputy Sheriff Charles McComb stands to the left.

In ***Powell v. Alabama*** (1932) the Supreme Court considered this claim for the first time. The case began when nine young black men were charged with raping two white women while riding a freight train through Alabama. The defendants had little chance of avoiding conviction. They were uneducated, poor, and far away from home, with no friends or relatives to help them. Because of the nature of the charges, they faced a hostile environment. Much was at stake. In Alabama at that time, rape was punishable by death.

The young men did not have the funds to secure the services of an attorney, but under state law defendants in capital cases were entitled to a lawyer at government expense.[1] Instead of appointing a specific attorney to

prepare a defense, the trial court judge assigned all the lawyers in the town to represent the defendants. Not surprisingly, no one lawyer would accept the responsibility. When the trial was about to begin, the defendants were still without meaningful representation. At the last minute a Chattanooga lawyer, retained by the defendants' families to provide assistance, arrived in town and was permitted to represent them. His first request was for additional time to prepare. The request was denied, and the trial began. It should come as no surprise that the young men were convicted and sentenced to death.

With the assistance of civil rights groups and political organizations, the defendants acquired new representation and appealed to the Supreme Court. The Court reversed the conviction, holding that the young men did not receive effective counsel at trial. For the first time the justices held that the Constitution requires meaningful legal representation for indigent defendants. But

---

[1]Many states had laws mandating the appointment of counsel for capital crimes such as rape. In *Coker v. Georgia* (1977) the Supreme Court outlawed the use of the death penalty in rape cases.

the Court's decision was quite limited. Justice George Sutherland's opinion for the Court stressed that the right to a government-provided attorney was restricted to extreme situations. *Powell* certainly presented extreme circumstances—capital case, racially hostile environment, illiterate and indigent defendants with no family or friends in the area. It is easy to see why the Court concluded that under such conditions, a fair trial was not possible if the defendants were not provided with a competent lawyer who had an adequate opportunity to prepare a defense (for information on the fates of the "Scottsboro boys," see Box 18-1).

Six years after *Powell*, the Court went one step further. In *Johnson v. Zerbst* (1938) it ruled that indigent defendants involved in federal criminal prosecutions have the right to be represented by government-provided counsel. Federal criminal prosecutions account for only a small portion of all criminal cases. Therefore, although the *Johnson* decision was important, it did not affect most criminal defendants. Understandably, criminal defense attorneys wanted the Court to extend *Johnson* to state criminal courts, where the vast majority of prosecutions take place. The Court's first opportunity to do so occurred in **Betts v. Brady** (1942).

Indicted for robbery in Maryland, Smith Betts—a poor, uneducated, but literate white man—wanted an attorney at government expense. Like many states, Maryland provided indigents with counsel only in rape and murder cases. Betts conducted his own defense and was convicted. On appeal he asked the Supreme Court to apply *Johnson* to the states, thereby incorporating the Sixth Amendment guarantee. The Court refused, 6–3.

BOX 18-1

Aftermath . . . The Scottsboro Boys

The Supreme Court reversed their convictions in *Powell* in 1932, but the subsequent lives of the nine defendants known as the "Scottsboro boys" were filled with tragedy and additional criminal accusations. Even though one of the alleged rape victims later admitted that she had not been raped, the defendants were convicted following their second trial. This time the Supreme Court overturned the convictions in *Norris v. Alabama* (1935) because of racial discrimination in jury selection. Between 1936 and 1937, additional retrials took place, leading to the convictions of four of the original defendants, with sentences ranging from seventy-five years in prison to death.

In 1937 the rape charges were dropped against Olen Montgomery, Willie Roberson, and Eugene Williams. They subsequently fell into obscurity.

Charges against Roy Wright also were dismissed. In 1959 Wright stabbed his wife to death and then took his own life.

Rape charges against Ozie Powell were dropped. He was later convicted of shooting a law enforcement officer in the head. He received a long prison sentence but was paroled in 1946.

Charlie Weems, Andrew Wright, Haywood Patterson, and Clarence Norris were convicted of the rape charges on retrial. Weems and Patterson were sentenced to seventy-five years in prison, Wright to a term of ninety-nine years, and Norris to death.

Three of the convicted men were subsequently released from prison, and one escaped. Weems was paroled in 1943. Wright was paroled in 1944 but was returned to prison three times for parole violations. In 1951 Wright was accused of raping a thirteen-year-old girl, but he was acquitted and released. Patterson escaped from prison and fled to Michigan. In 1951 he was convicted of manslaughter and sentenced to prison. Shortly thereafter he died of lung cancer.

Norris had his death sentence commuted to life in prison in 1938. He was paroled in 1944 but was sent back to prison for leaving the state in violation of his parole agreement. Norris was paroled again in 1946 and almost immediately fled the state in violation of parole a second time. He lived undercover in New York City for many years. In 1976 the attorney general of Alabama acknowledged that subsequent studies of the case had concluded that Norris was not guilty of the original rape charge, and Governor George Wallace pardoned him. A bill to compensate Norris for wrongful conviction was defeated in the Alabama legislature. Norris died in 1989 at the age of seventy-six.

Source: James A. Inciardi, *Criminal Justice,* 4th ed. (Fort Worth, TX: Harcourt Brace Jovanovich, 1993), 372.

Writing for the majority, Justice Owen Roberts claimed that the framers never intended that the right to counsel be defined as a fundamental guarantee, just that it apply to extreme situations as in *Powell*. When Roberts compared Betts's claim to that of the Scottsboro defendants, he found that it came up short because Betts was not helpless or illiterate and was in no danger of the death penalty for his offense.

Justice Hugo L. Black dissented. He wrote:

Denial to the poor of the request for counsel in proceedings based on charges of serious crime has been long regarded as shocking to the "universal sense of justice" throughout this country. . . . Most . . . states have shown their agreement [and] assure that no man shall be deprived of counsel merely because of his poverty. Any other practice seems to me to defeat the promise of our democratic society to provide equal justice under law.

Twenty-one years later, a Court more sympathetic to the rights of the criminally accused reevaluated the wisdom of *Betts v. Brady*. As you read the landmark case of *Gideon v. Wainwright*, consider these questions: Why did the Court extend the right to government-provided attorneys to indigents accused of state crimes? Did something distinguish *Gideon* from *Betts*, or did other factors come into play?

Gideon v. Wainwright

372 U.S. 335 (1963)
http://caselaw.findlaw.com/us-supreme-court/372/335.html
Oral arguments available at https://www.oyez.org/
  cases/1962/155
Vote: 9 (Black, Brennan, Clark, Douglas, Goldberg, Harlan,
  Stewart, Warren, White)
  0

OPINION OF THE COURT: *Black*

CONCURRING OPINIONS: *Clark, Douglas, Harlan*

Florida officials charged Clarence Earl Gideon with breaking and entering a poolroom. The trial court refused to appoint counsel for him because Florida did not provide free lawyers to those charged with anything less than a capital offense. Gideon, like Betts, a poor, uneducated white man, tried to defend himself but failed. After studying the law in the prison library and attempting a number of

lower court actions, Gideon filed a petition for a writ of certiorari with the U.S. Supreme Court.[2] The petition was handwritten on prison notepaper, but the justices granted it a review.

Because Gideon was without counsel, the Court appointed Abe Fortas, a well-known attorney (and future Supreme Court justice), to represent him. Twenty-two states filed an amicus curiae brief, which was written by Minnesota's attorney general, Walter Mondale (and future senator and U.S. vice president), supporting Gideon's argument. Clarence Gideon went from being a poor convict facing a lonely court battle to a Supreme Court litigant represented by some of the country's best legal minds.

MR. JUSTICE BLACK DELIVERED THE OPINION OF THE COURT.

Since 1942, when *Betts v. Brady* was decided by a divided Court, the problem of a defendant's federal constitutional right to counsel in a state court has been a continuing source of controversy and litigation in both state and federal courts. To give this problem another review here, we granted certiorari. Since Gideon was proceeding in forma pauperis [without the funds to pursue the normal cost of criminal defense], we appointed counsel to represent him and requested both sides to discuss in their briefs and oral arguments the following: "Should this Court's holding in *Betts v. Brady* be reconsidered?"

Since the facts and circumstances of [this case and *Betts*] are so nearly indistinguishable, we think the *Betts v. Brady* holding if left standing would require us to reject Gideon's claim that the Constitution guarantees him the assistance of counsel. Upon full reconsideration we conclude that *Betts v. Brady* should be overruled.

The Sixth Amendment provides, "In all criminal prosecutions, the accused shall enjoy the right . . . to have the Assistance of Counsel for his defence." We have construed this to mean that in federal courts counsel must be provided for defendants unable to employ counsel unless the right is competently and intelligently waived. Betts argued that this right is extended to indigent defendants in state courts by the Fourteenth Amendment. . . . In order to decide whether the Sixth Amendment's guarantee of counsel is of this fundamental nature [and so applies to the states], the Court in *Betts* set out and considered "[r]elevant data on the subject . . . afforded by constitutional and statutory provisions subsisting in the colonies and the states prior to the inclusion of the Bill of Rights in the national Constitution, and in the constitutional, legislative, and judicial history of the states to the present date." On the basis of this historical data the Court concluded that

---

[2]See Anthony Lewis, *Gideon's Trumpet* (New York: Vintage Books, 1964).

"appointment of counsel is not a fundamental right, essential to a fair trial." . . .

We accept *Betts v. Brady's* assumption, based as it was on our prior cases, that a provision of the Bill of Rights which is "fundamental and essential to a fair trial" is made obligatory upon the States by the Fourteenth Amendment. We think the Court in *Betts* was wrong, however, in concluding that the Sixth Amendment's guarantee of counsel is not one of these fundamental rights. Ten years before *Betts v. Brady,* this Court, after full consideration of all the historical data examined in *Betts,* had unequivocally declared that "the right to the aid of counsel is of this fundamental character." *Powell v. Alabama* (1932). While the Court at the close of its *Powell* opinion did by its language, as this Court frequently does, limit its holding to the particular facts and circumstances of that case, its conclusions about the fundamental nature of the right to counsel are unmistakable. . . .

. . . In light of [this] and other prior decisions of the Court, . . . the Court in *Betts v. Brady* made an abrupt break with its own well considered precedents. In returning to these old precedents, sounder we believe than the new, we but restore constitutional principles established to achieve a fair system of justice. Not only these precedents but also reason and reflection require us to recognize that in our adversary system of criminal justice, any person haled [sic] into court, who is too poor to hire a lawyer, cannot be assured a fair trial unless counsel is provided for him. This seems to us to be an obvious truth. Governments, both state and federal, quite properly spend vast sums of money to establish machinery to try defendants accused of crime. Lawyers to prosecute are everywhere deemed essential to protect the public's interest in an orderly society. Similarly, there are few defendants charged with crime, few indeed, who fail to hire the best lawyers they can get to prepare and present their defenses. That government hires lawyers to prosecute and defendants who have the money hire lawyers to defend are the strongest indications of the widespread belief that lawyers in criminal courts are necessities, not luxuries. The right of one charged with crime to counsel may not be deemed fundamental and essential to fair trials in some countries, but it is in ours. From the very beginning, our state and national constitutions and laws have laid great emphasis on procedural and substantive safeguards designed to assure fair trials before impartial tribunals in which every defendant stands equal before the law. This noble ideal cannot be realized if the poor man charged with crime has to face his accusers without a lawyer to assist him. A defendant's need for a lawyer is nowhere better stated than [the Court's opinion in] *Powell v. Alabama.* . . .

The Court in *Betts v. Brady* departed from the sound wisdom upon which the Court's holding in *Powell v. Alabama* rested. Florida, supported by two other States, has asked that *Betts v. Brady* be left intact. Twenty-two States, as friends of the Court, argue that *Betts* was "an anachronism when handed down" and that it should now be overruled. We agree. The judgment is reversed and the cause is remanded to the Supreme Court of Florida for further action not inconsistent with this opinion.

Reversed.

Beyond its legal significance, *Gideon* is interesting for three reasons. First, the case provides another example of the Warren Court's revolution in criminal rights. The Court of 1963 took a carbon copy of *Betts* and came up with a radically different solution. *Gideon* completed a process of constitutional evolution in which the Court first applied a rule of law to the federal government, refused to extend that rule to the states, and then reversed its position and brought the states under the rule's applicability.

Second, *Gideon* is a classic example of the importance of dissents. Justice Hugo Black's minority position in *Betts* was finally written into law when the Court reversed itself in *Gideon.* How fitting it was that Black was still on the Court twenty-one years later and was given the opportunity to write the majority opinion in *Gideon.*

Finally, *Gideon v. Wainwright* has had a tremendous impact on the U.S. criminal justice system, in which 80 to 90 percent of the criminally accused are eligible for indigent defense. To comply with the Court's ruling, states had to alter their defender systems, creating mechanisms to provide lawyers for the accused. Many localities established public defender offices that mirrored their prosecuting attorneys' offices. In other words, the states hire lawyers to represent indigents. Other areas use court-appointed attorney systems in which judges assign members of the legal community to defend indigents.

Despite its importance, *Gideon* left several questions unanswered—most of which were addressed not by the justices of the Warren Court but by those of the Burger, Rehnquist, and Roberts Courts. First, what crimes does the ruling cover? Does it cover only serious offenses—felonies, such as the one Gideon was accused of committing—or does it apply to minor crimes as well? The Court dealt with this question in ***Argersinger v. Hamlin*** (1972) and ***Scott v. Illinois*** (1979). In these cases the Court developed the "loss of liberty" rule: an indigent charged with a crime that upon conviction will lead to incarceration for even one day is entitled to be represented by counsel at government expense. To put it another way, regardless of the range of penalties available to a judge, indigent criminal defendants may not be sentenced to incarceration unless they have been offered legal representation at government expense.

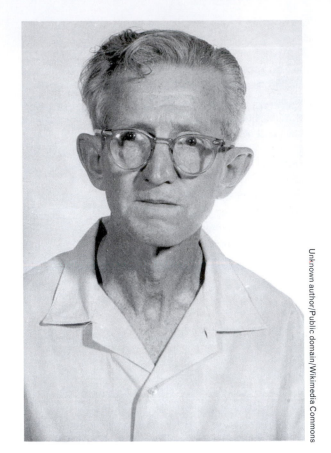

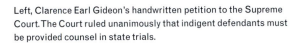

Left, Clarence Earl Gideon's handwritten petition to the Supreme Court. The Court ruled unanimously that indigent defendants must be provided counsel in state trials.

Right, Clarence Earl Gideon

Twenty-three years after *Scott v. Illinois*, in **Alabama v. Shelton** (2002), the justices of the Rehnquist Court reinforced this basic premise. LeReed Shelton, convicted of third-degree assault, was sentenced to a jail term of thirty days, which the trial court immediately suspended, placing Shelton on probation for two years. The question the Court addressed was whether the Sixth Amendment right to appointed counsel, as delineated in *Argersinger* and *Scott*, applies to a defendant in Shelton's situation. The majority answered in the affirmative, holding that "a suspended sentence that may 'end up in the actual deprivation of a person's liberty' may not be imposed unless the defendant was accorded 'the guiding hand of counsel' in the prosecution for the crime charged." To the four dissenters—Antonin Scalia, William Rehnquist, Anthony M. Kennedy, and Clarence Thomas—this logic turned *Argersinger* and *Scott* upside down: "Today's decision ignores this long and consistent jurisprudence,

extending the misdemeanor right to counsel to cases bearing the mere threat of imprisonment," Scalia wrote. "Respondent's 30-day suspended sentence, and the accompanying 2-year term of probation, are invalidated for lack of appointed counsel even though respondent has not suffered, and may never suffer, a deprivation of liberty."

A second unanswered question flowing from *Gideon* was this: To which stages of the process does the right to government-provided counsel apply? In his opinion in *Gideon*, Black said that an indigent accused of a criminal offense must be represented by counsel at trial. What Black did not address was whether that right extended through the appellate process. And if so, did such a right apply only to obligatory appeals (usually the first appeal after a trial) or also to discretionary appeals (subsequent appeals that the appellate court—usually a state supreme court—may or may not agree to hear)?

In *Douglas v. California* (1963) the Court answered part of this question, holding that the right indeed extended through the first obligatory appeal. Eleven years later, however, in *Ross v. Moffitt* (1974), the Burger Court—while not reversing the Warren Court—refused to extend the right to state-provided counsel for indigents to subsequent appeals.

FAIR TRIALS

From a quantitative perspective, trials are insignificant, as less than 10 percent of all criminal prosecutions go to trial. In the remaining 90 percent, defendants plead guilty, usually after arriving at plea-bargaining agreements with the prosecutors. In such an arrangement, the defendant waives the right to a jury trial and agrees to plead guilty in return for certain concessions made by the prosecutor. These concessions normally involve a reduction in the seriousness of the crimes charged, a reduction in the number of counts, or a recommendation for a lenient sentence. Although some commentators criticize this system,[3] the Supreme Court has sanctioned the practice of plea bargaining, and it remains the most common way criminal prosecutions are settled.

Qualitatively, however, trials are significant; the most serious crimes go to trial. In addition, trials serve a symbolic function and educate the public about crime and justice in the community. Further, they embody values that Americans treasure—openness and fundamental and objective fairness.

The framers clearly intended American trials to be the epitome of justice. They drafted the Sixth Amendment to correct the weaknesses they had observed in the English justice system, weaknesses that included closed proceedings, long delays, and few safeguards for defendants. Specifically, Sixth Amendment provisions governing trials state, "In all criminal prosecutions, the accused shall enjoy the right to a speedy and public trial, by an impartial jury of the State and district wherein the crime shall have been committed, . . . to be confronted with the witnesses against him; to have compulsory process for obtaining witnesses in his favor."[4]

In short, the Sixth Amendment provides strict guidelines for trial proceedings. In the next pages we consider how the Supreme Court has interpreted the rights specified in the amendment.

Speedy and Public Trials

Individuals accused of crimes have the right to their day in court, and if justice is to be meaningful, trials must be scheduled in a timely fashion. The framers considered it unfair for the government to lay criminal charges against suspects and then postpone their trials for months or even years. Consequently, the Sixth Amendment states that trials must be speedy.

But what constitutes "speedy"? In responding to this question the Supreme Court has refused to hold that a fixed number of days or months can be used to define what is a speedy trial. Instead, each case must be considered on its own merits. The Court has held that in determining whether the speedy trial provision has been violated, judges need to seek the answers to four basic questions: (1) How long was the delay? (2) What was the reason for the delay? (3) At what point did the defense begin objecting to the delay? and (4) Did the delay prejudice the defendant's case?[5] Balancing the answers to these questions will guide courts in determining whether the constitutional right to a speedy trial has been violated.[6]

---

[3]One of the many criticisms is that plea bargains favor prosecutors because they "overcharge" defendants in an effort to get them to accept plea deals. Justice Scalia noted as much in his dissent in *Lafler v. Cooper* (2012). Plea bargaining, he wrote, "presents grave risks of prosecutorial overcharging that effectively compels an innocent defendant to avoid massive risk by pleading guilty to a lesser offense; and for guilty defendants it often—perhaps usually—results in a sentence well below what the law prescribes for the actual crime." "But even so," Scalia went on to note, "we accept plea bargaining because many believe that without it our long and expensive process of criminal trial could not sustain the burden imposed on it, and our system of criminal justice would grind to a halt."

[4]These fair trial provisions of the Sixth Amendment are supported by two important rights found in the Fifth Amendment: the right against self-incrimination and the right to due process of law.

[5]*Barker v. Wingo* (1972). Nevertheless, questions over the application of *Barker* continue to emerge. In *Vermont v. Brillon* (2009) the Court considered whether delays caused solely by an indigent defendant's public defender could violate the defendant's speedy trial rights and be charged against the state pursuant to the test in *Barker*. The defendant, Michael Brillon, argued that the Court should answer in the affirmative because public defenders are paid by the state. Writing for a 7–2 Court, Justice Ginsburg held against Brillon. She noted that "assigned counsel generally are not state actors for purposes of a speedy-trial claim," and so in applying *Barker*, she attributed most of the delay to the defendant's counsel and not the state.

[6]Congress and many state legislatures have passed speedy trial laws that compel the prosecution to be ready to proceed with a trial within a specified number of days. The federal Speedy Trial Act of 1974 requires indictment within thirty days of arrest, arraignment within ten days after indictment, and trial within sixty days after arraignment. Failure to meet the requirements of the speedy trial law can lead to the dismissal of charges against the defendant.

Trials in the United States also must take place in public. The Sixth Amendment's right to a public trial was in direct reaction to the use of secret trials in England and other European countries. The underlying rationale for public trials is that abuse of authority is much less likely to occur when important proceedings can be witnessed by the public and the press. As a consequence, trials in the United States may not be closed affairs.

Jury Trials

As they had with many other aspects of law and procedure, the framers incorporated the British jury system into the U.S. Constitution. A jury trial means that the determination of whether a defendant is guilty is made by individuals drawn from the community, not by a government official. A jury that represents a cross section of the community is what we Americans consider a "jury of our peers."

To select a jury that is fair and representative, most jurisdictions follow a procedure that works this way:

1. Individuals living within a specified geographical area are called for jury duty. Most localities randomly select names from voter registration, property tax, or driver's license lists.

2. Those selected form the jury pool, or venire, the group from which attorneys choose the jury.

3. The judge may conduct initial interviews and excuse certain classes of people (those who have committed a felony, people who are illiterate, individuals with a mental illness) and certain occupational groups, as allowed under the laws of the particular jurisdiction.

4. The remaining individuals are available to be chosen to serve on a trial (petit) jury. In the final selection phase, the opposing attorneys interview the prospective jurors in the process called voir dire. During voir dire, attorneys can dismiss those individuals they believe would not vote in the best interests of their clients. The attorneys, therefore, select the jury.

During voir dire, attorneys have available two means of eliminating potential jurors. When a prospective juror appears to be unqualified to carry out the obligations of service, attorneys can *challenge for cause*. To do so, they must explain to the judge their reasons for requesting the disqualification of that prospective juror (for example, because of a conflict of interest, a bias against the defendant or the prosecution, or a stated refusal to follow the law). The judge can grant or deny the challenge for cause. Challenges for cause are unlimited. Attorneys also have a fixed number of *peremptory challenges*, which they may use to excuse jurors without stating reasons.

Traditionally, attorneys could use their peremptory challenges in whatever way and for whatever reasons they choose. Although that general rule remains in effect, the Supreme Court has intervened to limit lawyers' discretion in two important ways: lawyers may not use their peremptory challenges to dismiss prospective jurors on account of race or sex.[7] To exclude potential jurors systematically on the basis of race or sex violates the equal protection clause of the Fourteenth Amendment.

Generally, a jury consists of twelve individuals, and all jury decisions must be unanimous. Most jurisdictions follow this traditional format in major cases, but the Supreme Court has ruled that the Constitution does not require juries of twelve persons.[8] In response, many states began using six-person juries in minor cases. Some states even experimented with decision-making rules that allow for less than unanimity among jurors. But, in 2020, the Court held that the Constitution's Sixth Amendment requires unanimous jury verdicts in state cases involving serious crimes.[9]

Regardless of the specific configuration of the jury, however, it is fundamental to fair trials that juries deliberate and reach decisions in an atmosphere that allows detached and objective consideration of the evidence. Of particular concern are situations in which media coverage of criminal trials becomes so intense and extensive that the ends of justice are compromised. Given the constitutional guarantees of a public trial and freedom of the press, how can judges see to it that defendants receive fair, impartial jury trials? This question has major constitutional importance because it forces courts to deal with conflicting rights. The Sixth Amendment requires judges to regulate trials, ensuring, among other things, that the

---

[7]Race: **Batson v. Kentucky** (1986), *Powers v. Ohio* (1991), *Georgia v. McCullum* (1992), *Foster v. Chatman* (2016), **Flowers v. Mississippi** (2019); sex: *J. E. B. v. Alabama ex rel. T. B.* (1994).

[8]See *Williams v. Florida* (1970).

[9]**Ramos v. Louisiana** (2020), which overruled *Apodaca v. Oregon* (1972). The Court has long held that juries hearing federal criminal cases must reach unanimous verdicts.

jury is impartial. In a highly publicized case, the judge's task can become arduous. The judge must deal with the media, who are exercising their constitutional guarantee of a free press. How can judges keep trials fair without interfering with the rights of the press and the public?

Before the mid-1960s no balance existed between freedom of the press and the right to an impartial jury—the former far outweighed the latter. In cases involving well-known individuals or otherwise of interest to the public, the press descended on courtrooms and often behaved in a disruptive manner. Without well-defined rules, reporters, accompanied by crews carrying bulky, noisy equipment, simply showed up and interviewed and photographed witnesses and other participants at will. These activities often breached normal courtroom decorum and made objective, dispassionate analysis of evidence almost impossible for the jurors.

Not surprisingly, the Warren Court placed limitations on the media. In two important cases, *Estes v. Texas* (1965) and **Sheppard v. Maxwell** (1966), the Court reversed convictions based on media misbehavior and chastised lower court judges for allowing the press to jeopardize the integrity of the trials. As a result, judges around the country began to police their courtrooms more vigilantly to ensure that the press did not compromise the right of the defendant to receive a fair trial.

Although judges have an obligation to impose limitations on the activities of the press in covering trials, they cannot go too far. The press is still protected by the First Amendment in gathering and reporting the news. The justices have supported free press rights as long as they are compatible with the right to a fair trial.

TRIAL PROCEEDINGS

Once attorneys complete the voir dire and select the petit jury, the trial begins. Almost all trials follow the same format. First, the attorneys make opening statements. Each side (beginning with the prosecution because it has the burden of proof) presents an opening statement, typically setting forth the facts and a theory of the case or an explanation why the facts will support a verdict of either guilty or not guilty.

Next, each side presents its case, again beginning with the prosecution. At this point, attorneys call witnesses who testify for their side and then are cross-examined by the opposing attorney. This stage is the heart of the trial, and here, as in all other important parts of the criminal justice system, the Constitution affords

defendants a great many rights—not the least of which is the Sixth Amendment's guarantee that a defendant "shall enjoy the right. . . to be confronted with the witnesses against him." This provision, often called the confrontation clause, includes several guarantees. First, defendants have the right to be present during their trials; the United States generally does not permit trials in absentia.[10]

Second, the confrontation clause requires that prosecution witnesses appear in open court in the presence of the defendant to give their testimony under oath. As a consequence, the prosecution typically cannot obtain a conviction based on anonymous testimony or on information provided by witnesses who are unwilling to appear in court. This requirement appears to be both reasonable and necessary for most crimes, but it has received considerable criticism for crimes such as rape and child abuse. Rape victims, for example, may refuse to report their rapes to the police because they know that if they do so they may be required to give their testimony in open court. Similarly, many fear that children who have been abused will be traumatized by having to tell their stories in court with the persons who abused them visibly present.

Although the justices have generally adhered to the requirement that prosecution witnesses appear in court, they have been sympathetic to the situation facing children who may have been the victims of abuse. In **Maryland v. Craig** (1990), for example, the Court upheld a Maryland procedure that allowed abused children to testify via closed-circuit television. This procedure permitted the defendant to see the testimony of the alleged victim but protected the child witness from the trauma of face-to-face interaction with her accused abuser. For the majority, Justice Sandra Day O'Connor outlined the Court's reasoning:

> [W]e conclude that where necessary to
> protect a child witness from trauma that

---

[10]In *Illinois v. Allen* (1970), however, the Supreme Court considered the actions of a trial judge in response to a defendant's misbehavior in the courtroom. William Allen, on trial for armed robbery, verbally abused the judge and others in the courtroom, threw papers, continually talked loudly, and interrupted witnesses. After ample warning, the judge ordered Allen removed, and the trial continued in his absence. Allen was convicted, and he appealed on the grounds that he was not allowed to be present during his trial. A unanimous Court rejected his appeal. Justice Black's opinion explained that the right to confrontation can be waived by the defendant's own abusive behavior. Black indicated that in extreme cases a judge may order the defendant to be bound and gagged.

would be caused by testifying in the physical presence of the defendant, at least where such trauma would impair the child's ability to communicate, the Confrontation Clause does not prohibit use of a procedure that, despite the absence of face-to-face confrontation, ensures the reliability of the evidence by subjecting it to rigorous adversarial testing and thereby preserves the essence of effective confrontation. Because there is no dispute that the child witnesses in this case testified under oath, were subject to full cross-examination, and were able to be observed by the judge, jury, and defendant as they testified, we conclude that, to the extent that a proper finding of necessity has been made, the admission of such testimony would be consonant with the Confrontation Clause.

A third component of the right to confrontation is cross-examination. Not only does the prosecution have to produce witnesses who testify under oath in open court before the defendant, but those witnesses are also subject to questioning by the defense. This requirement is based on the theory that a jury will best be able to discern the truth if testimony—*even out-of-court testimony*, in some instances—is tested by vigorous examination from the opposing side. Justice Scalia, typically no friend of criminal defendants,[11] made this point emphatically in **Crawford v. Washington** (2004). The defendant, Michael Crawford, was accused of stabbing a man who allegedly tried to rape his wife, Sylvia. At his trial, the state played for the jury a recorded statement that Sylvia made during a police interrogation suggesting that the stabbing was not committed while her husband was defending her against a rape. Sylvia did not testify because of the state's marital privilege, which generally bars the spouse of a defendant from testifying without the defendant spouse's consent. Crawford objected to Sylvia's tape-recorded statement on the ground that his attorney never had an opportunity to cross-examine his wife and so admitting the evidence violated his Sixth Amendment right of confrontation.

The Court agreed with Michael Crawford. Writing for the majority, Justice Scalia drew two inferences from his extensive analysis of the historical underpinnings of the confrontation clause. "First, the principal evil at which the Confrontation Clause was directed was the use of *ex parte* examinations as evidence against the accused." To Scalia, this meant that the clause applies not only to any in-court testimony but also to any out-of-court statements introduced at trial. Thus, "Statements taken by police officers in the course of interrogations are . . . testimonial." Second, Scalia wrote that "the Framers would not have allowed admission of testimonial statements of a witness who did not appear at trial unless he was unavailable to testify, and the defendant had had a prior opportunity for cross-examination." Therefore, taken together, Crawford was denied the right to confrontation because the out-of-court statement amounted to testimony and Crawford's attorney never had a prior opportunity to cross-examine it.

The basic holding of *Crawford* seems simple enough. If witnesses providing testimonial evidence against the defendant cannot be cross-examined in open court, prosecutors can introduce their testimony only if the witnesses are unavailable and there was some prior opportunity for cross-examination. But what exactly is testimony? In *Crawford*, the majority wrote that the term "applies at a minimum to prior testimony at a preliminary hearing, before a grand jury, or at a former trial; and to police interrogations." Beyond that, it decided to "leave for another day any effort to spell out a comprehensive definition of 'testimonial.'"

That day came soon enough. In three cases coming on the heels of *Crawford*, the Court sought to clarify the meaning of testimony. In the first, **Davis v. Washington** (2006), the justices agreed that prosecutors could introduce victims' emergency phone calls to 911 even if the victims are not in court for cross-examination. In the same opinion, however, the Court refused to allow a victim's statement to police, given at the crime scene, to be used at trial unless the victim was willing to be cross-examined. The difference between the two, according to Justice Scalia's majority opinion, is that the phone call is not a "testimonial statement" covered by the confrontation clause, but the on-the-scene statement to police investigating a crime is.

At least to a majority of five, the second of the post-*Crawford* cases, **Melendez-Diaz v. Massachusetts** (2009), reaffirms this distinction. At Luis Melendez-Diaz's trial, the prosecution introduced sworn certificates of state laboratory analysts stating that material seized by police and connected to Melendez-Diaz was quite likely cocaine. Melendez-Diaz's attorney objected, claiming that under Supreme Court precedent, the analysts should testify in

---

[11]During his years on the Roberts Court, Scalia voted in favor of the defendant in only 33 percent of the 196 orally argued cases in which he participated. Only Thomas (24 percent), Roberts (32 percent), and Alito (19 percent) have lower percentages. By contrast, Ginsburg, Sotomayor, and Kagan have all supported defendants at a rate of 60 percent or higher.

person and face cross-examination. The Supreme Court agreed. Writing for a majority of five, Justice Scalia—who, as *Crawford* and *Davis* suggest, was taking the lead in developing the Court's confrontation clause jurisprudence—held that because the certificates fell within the "core class of testimonial statements," they were covered by the confrontation clause. The defendant should have had the chance to cross-examine the analysts.

The dissenters, led by Justice Kennedy, disagreed. To them *Davis* and *Crawford*

> stand for the proposition that formal statements made by a conventional witness—one who has personal knowledge of some aspect of the defendant's guilt—may not be admitted without the witness appearing at trial to meet the accused face to face. But *Davis* [does] not say . . . that anyone who makes a testimonial statement is a witness for purposes of the Confrontation Clause, even when that person has, in fact, witnessed nothing to give them personal knowledge of the defendant's guilt.

In 2011, a majority of the Court in **Michigan v. Bryant** moved closer to the dissenters in *Melendez-Diaz*. With Justice Sotomayor writing for the majority, the Court held that a statement made by a victim to police at a crime scene was nontestimonial even though the victim died before the start of the trial. The Court's reasoning in this instance was that the statement was nontestimonial in nature because it was made with the purpose of assisting the police in an ongoing emergency situation. Scalia (along with Ginsburg) now found himself in dissent. He accused the Court of distorting and confusing the confrontation clause doctrine that he had worked to build. To Scalia, because the victim's purpose was to ensure the arrest and prosecution of the defendant, the victim's statement clearly amounted to testimony for purposes of the confrontation clause. "No framing-era confrontation case," Scalia wrote, "that I know of, neither here nor in England, took such an enfeebled view of the right to confrontation."

Undoubtedly the debate over the nature of testimony will continue. It is important to know, however, that in addition to specific Sixth Amendment guarantees, defendants facing trial have rights under the Fifth Amendment's due process and self-incrimination clauses. As we have seen, the rather vague term *due process* has been used to ensure that police obtain evidence by fair means and as a way to apply constitutional guarantees to the states. The Court also has invoked it to guarantee that defendants receive fair treatment from prosecutors and courts.

SENTENCING AND THE EIGHTH AMENDMENT

If a criminal defendant pleads guilty or is convicted, the next stage of consequence is sentencing. The framers included many provisions in the Bill of Rights dealing with fair trials but only one section that focuses specifically on sentencing. The Eighth Amendment states: "Excessive bail shall not be required, nor excessive fines imposed, nor cruel and unusual punishment inflicted."

The most significant section of this amendment is its cruel and unusual punishment provision. Those who adopted the Bill of Rights clearly wanted to outlaw sentences that were not viewed as appropriate for a civilized society, those that were cruel and unusual. As a consequence, crucifixion, torture on the rack, drawing and quartering, tarring and feathering, dismemberment, and restraint in the stocks are not among the forms of punishment practiced in the United States. By our standards of decency today, these would violate the prohibition against cruel and unusual punishment.

Defining "Cruel and Unusual"

That the meaning of "cruel and unusual" is open to interpretation has not been missed by the Court. In **Solem v. Helm** (1983), it attempted to provide some guidance on what those words mean. In 1979 Jerry Helm was convicted of writing a $100 bad check. He had been convicted six previous times of such crimes as obtaining money under false pretenses and driving while intoxicated. None of his crimes was violent, none was a crime against a person, and all were related to a history of alcohol abuse. The judge, believing Helm to be beyond rehabilitation, invoked the South Dakota recidivism law and sentenced him to life in prison without possibility of parole. After two years of trying to get the governor to commute his sentence, Helm turned to the courts, claiming that his punishment was cruel and unusual.

By a 5–4 vote, the Supreme Court found that the life sentence violated the cruel and unusual punishment clause. Justice Lewis Powell's majority opinion held that the Eighth Amendment proscribes not only barbaric punishments but also sentences that are *disproportionate to the crime committed*. To determine whether a sentence is so disproportionate that it violates the Eighth Amendment, the justices said that they would consider three factors: "(i) the gravity of the offense and the harshness of the penalty; (ii) the sentences imposed on other criminals in the same jurisdiction; and (iii) the sentences imposed for commission of the same crime in other jurisdictions." As applied in this case, life in prison without parole was out of proportion to the bad check charges.

To some, the *Solem* approach was simply the Court's adaptation of the old adage, "Let the punishment fit the crime." However, all of the justices have not accepted the use of the *Solem* proportionality concept, and its application has not always been easy. In *Harmelin v. Michigan* (1991), for example, the justices rejected a convict's claim that a sentence of life in prison without possibility of parole for a first-time offense of cocaine possession violated the cruel and unusual punishment clause, but they could not agree on the reason this sentence was not grossly disproportionate.

In 2003 the issue returned to the Court in *Ewing v. California*. In this case the Court addressed the constitutionality of sentencing statutes popularly known as "three strikes and you're out" laws. Under such a scheme, a defendant convicted of a felony who has twice previously been convicted of a serious or violent felony can be sentenced to a long prison term, including life in prison. Such laws are designed to deter crime and to protect the public from habitual criminals by imprisoning them for long periods of time. In 1993 Washington became the first state to enact a three-strikes law when its voters approved such a proposal by a 3–1 margin. Over the next two years, twenty-four states and the federal government adopted similar measures.

The *Ewing* case was a constitutional challenge to California's three-strikes law. Gary Ewing had previous convictions for three burglaries and a robbery when he was arrested in 2000 for shoplifting three expensive golf clubs. Under California law, the prosecutor had the option of charging Ewing with a felony or a misdemeanor. The prosecutor decided that a felony grand theft charge was the appropriate alternative. Ewing was convicted of the felony charge and therefore became eligible for sentencing under the state's three-strikes statute. The judge sentenced him to a term of twenty-five years to life in prison. Ewing appealed, claiming that the sentence was disproportionate to the triggering offense of stealing three golf clubs.

The Supreme Court upheld the state law. In doing so, the justices gave wide deference to the state legislature's determination that recidivism is a matter of great state concern and that interests of public safety justify this harsh sentencing option. In considering whether the punishment as meted out to Ewing violated the proportionality standard, Justice O'Connor, announcing the judgment of the Court, explained that the long prison term was not imposed because Ewing stole three golf clubs. Rather, the penalty was based on the grand theft violation as part of a long history of criminal activity. Consequently, the sentence was not grossly disproportionate and did not violate the Eighth Amendment's prohibition on cruel and unusual punishment.

Not so in ***Graham v. Florida*** (2010), in which the Court considered whether the Constitution permits a juvenile offender to be sentenced to life in prison without parole for a nonhomicide crime. While on probation, Terrance Graham, a minor, was arrested for committing two robberies. Finding Graham in violation of his probation, the judge sentenced Graham to life. Because Florida had abolished its parole system, once sentenced to life imprisonment, Graham had no possibility of release. He challenged his sentence under the Eighth Amendment's cruel and unusual punishment clause.

The majority of the justices agreed with Graham. Writing for the Court, Justice Kennedy held that it was "grossly disproportionate" for a court to impose a sentence of life without parole on an offender less than eighteen years old unless the defendant had committed a homicide. As Kennedy put it, "The State has denied [Graham] any chance to later demonstrate that he is fit to rejoin society based solely on a nonhomicide crime that he committed while he was a child in the eyes of the law. This the Eighth Amendment does not permit."

The Death Penalty

The issue most frequently brought to the Court on Eighth Amendment grounds is the constitutionality of capital punishment. Death penalty cases have perplexed the Court for decades, presenting the justices with emotionally charged and legally complex questions.

The Court's opinions in death penalty cases tell us a great deal about what "cruel and unusual punishment" does and does not mean. Since 1947 the Court has held that the death penalty is inherently neither cruel nor unusual.[12] Never have a majority of the justices agreed that it is, but why not? The answer lies with the intent of the framers (at the time of ratification, death penalties were in use) and with the due process clauses of the Fifth and Fourteenth Amendments, which state that no person can be deprived of life without due process of law. Presumably, if due process is observed, life can be taken.

---

[12]See *Louisiana ex rel. Francis v. Resweber* (1947).

The majority of Americans also support use of the death penalty (56% at the time of this writing), but many interest groups have long been working to eliminate it. These groups believe that the death penalty constitutes cruel and unusual punishment, but, recognizing the Court's unwillingness to agree, they have tried to convince the justices that the way the death penalty is applied violates due process norms.

One of the first attempts to implement a due process strategy was undertaken by the NAACP Legal Defense and Educational Fund (LDF) in *Furman v. Georgia* (1972). This case involved William Furman, a black man accused of murdering a white man, the father of five children. Under Georgia law, it was completely up to the jury to determine whether a convicted murderer should be put to death. This system, the LDF argued, led to unacceptable disparities in sentencing; specifically, blacks convicted of murdering whites were far more likely to receive the death penalty than were whites convicted of the same crime.

A divided Supreme Court agreed with the LDF. In a short per curiam opinion deciding *Furman* and two companion cases, the justices said, "The Court holds that the imposition and carrying out of the death penalty in these cases constitutes cruel and unusual punishment." Following this terse statement, however, were nine separate opinions (five for the LDF and four against), running 243 pages (fifty thousand words)—the longest in Court history.[13]

The views presented in the opinions of the five-member majority varied considerably—three justices (William O. Douglas, Potter Stewart, and Byron R. White) thought capital punishment, as *currently* imposed, violated the Constitution, and two (William J. Brennan and Thurgood Marshall) said it was unconstitutional in all circumstances. Beyond this, the five justices agreed on only one major point of law: that states that allowed capital punishment applied it in an arbitrary manner, particularly with regard to race.

The dissenters, Harry A. Blackmun, Warren E. Burger, Lewis F. Powell, and William H. Rehnquist (the four Nixon appointees), were more uniform in their critiques. To a lesser or greater extent, all expressed the view that the Court was encroaching on legislative turf and that Americans had not "repudiated" the death penalty. Chief Justice Burger's opinion raised a unique issue: he noted that the plurality (Douglas, Stewart, and White) had not ruled that capital punishment under all

circumstances was unconstitutional and that it may be possible for states to rewrite their laws to meet their objections. Privately, however, Burger thought his suggestion futile, lamenting later, "There will never be another execution in this country."[14] This view was echoed in many quarters. A University of Washington law professor wrote, "My hunch is that *Furman* spells the complete end of capital punishment in this country."[15] LDF attorneys were ecstatic. One called it "the biggest step forward criminal justice has taken in 1,000 years."[16]

As it turned out, the abolitionists celebrated a bit too soon, because the Supreme Court was not finished with the death penalty. Just three years after *Furman*, the Court agreed to hear *Gregg v. Georgia* to consider the constitutionality of a new breed of death penalty laws written to overcome the defects of the old laws. Did these new laws reduce the chance for "wanton and freakish" punishment of the sort the Court found so distasteful in *Furman?* Consider this question as you read the facts and opinions in *Gregg v. Georgia.*

Gregg v. Georgia

428 U.S. 153 (1976)
http://caselaw.findlaw.com/us-supreme-court/428/153.html
*Oral arguments available at https://www.oyez.org/
cases/1975/74-6257*
Vote: 7 (Blackmun, Burger, Powell, Rehnquist, Stevens,
Stewart, White)
2 (Brennan, Marshall)

OPINION ANNOUNCING THE JUDGMENT OF THE COURT:
Stewart

CONCURRING OPINIONS: *Blackmun, Burger, Rehnquist, White*

DISSENTING OPINIONS: *Brennan, Marshall*

Taking cues from *Furman,* many states set out to revise their death penalty laws. Among the new plans was one proposed by Georgia (and other states). At the heart of this law was the "bifurcated trial," which consisted of two stages—the guilt phase and the penalty phase. Under such a system, the trial proceeds as usual, with a

---

[13]We adopt this discussion from Lee Epstein and Joseph F. Kobylka, *The Supreme Court and Legal Change: Abortion and the Death Penalty* (Chapel Hill: University of North Carolina Press, 1992), 78–80.

[14]Quoted in Bob Woodward and Scott Armstrong, *The Brethren* (New York: Simon & Schuster, 1979), 219.

[15]John M. Junker, "The Death Penalty Cases: A Preliminary Comment," *Washington Law Review* 48 (1972): 109.

[16]Quoted in Frederick Mann, "Anthony Amsterdam," *Juris Doctor* 3 (1973): 31–32.

jury finding the defendant guilty or not guilty. If the verdict is guilty, the prosecution can seek a death sentence at the penalty stage, in which the defense attorney presents the mitigating facts and the prosecution presents the aggravating facts. The defense is free to offer as mitigating factors any information that might reduce the seriousness or culpability of the crime. Mitigating facts often include such items as the individual's upbringing and personal history, family responsibilities, psychiatric evaluation, mental capacity, chances for rehabilitation, and age.[17] These factors are not specified in law. The prosecution, however, has to demonstrate that at least one codified aggravating factor was present.

The Georgia law specified ten aggravating factors, including (1) murders committed "while the offender was engaged in the commission of another capital offense"; (2) the murder of "a judicial officer . . . or . . . district attorney because of the exercise of his official duty"; and (3) murders that are "outrageously or wantonly vile, horrible, or inhumane." After hearing both sides, the jury determines whether the convicted individual receives the death penalty. By spelling out the conditions that must be present before a death penalty can be imposed, the law sought to reduce the jury's discretion and eliminate the arbitrary application of the death penalty that the Court found unacceptable in *Furman.* As a further safeguard, the Georgia Supreme Court was to review all jury determinations of death. This new law was applied to Troy Gregg and was quickly challenged by abolitionist interests.

Gregg and a friend were hitchhiking north in Florida. Two men picked them up, and the foursome was later joined by another passenger who rode with them as far as Atlanta, Georgia. The four then continued to a rest stop on the highway. The next day, the bodies of the two drivers were found in a nearby ditch. The individual let off in Atlanta identified Gregg and his friend as possible assailants. Gregg was tried under Georgia's new death penalty system. He was convicted of murder and sentenced to death, a penalty the state's highest court upheld.

> **JUDGMENT OF THE COURT, AND OPINIONS OF MR. JUSTICE STEWART, MR. JUSTICE POWELL, AND MR. JUSTICE STEVENS ANNOUNCED BY MR. JUSTICE STEWART.**

The issue in this case is whether the imposition of the sentence of death for the crime of murder under the law of Georgia violates the Eighth and Fourteenth Amendments. . . .

---

[17]In *Eddings v. Oklahoma* (1982), the Court agreed that age constituted a mitigating factor, which, at that point, meant that juries and judges may consider age before sentencing a minor to the death penalty. In fact, the Court has held that someone as young as sixteen at the time the crime was committed can be executed. See *Thompson v. Oklahoma* (1988) and *Stanford v. Kentucky* (1989). The Court overturned these decisions in 2005.

We address initially the basic contention that the punishment of death for the crime of murder is, under all circumstances, "cruel and unusual" in violation of the Eighth and Fourteenth Amendments of the Constitution. . . . [W]e . . . [also] consider the sentence of death imposed under the Georgia statutes at issue in this case.

The Court on a number of occasions has both assumed and asserted the constitutionality of capital punishment. In several cases that assumption provided a necessary foundation for the decision, as the Court was asked to decide whether a particular method of carrying out a capital sentence would be allowed to stand under the Eighth Amendment. But until *Furman v. Georgia* (1972), the Court never confronted squarely the fundamental claim that the punishment of death always, regardless of the enormity of the offense or the procedure followed in imposing the sentence, is cruel and unusual punishment in violation of the Constitution. Although this issue was presented and addressed in *Furman,* it was not resolved by the Court. Four Justices would have held that capital punishment is not unconstitutional *per se;* two Justices would have reached the opposite conclusion; and three Justices, while agreeing that the statutes then before the Court were invalid as applied, left open the question whether such punishment may ever be imposed. We now hold that the punishment of death does not invariably violate the Constitution.

. . . The phrase [cruel and unusual punishment] first appeared in the English Bill of Rights of 1689, which was drafted by Parliament at the accession of William and Mary. The English version appears to have been directed against punishments unauthorized by statute and beyond the jurisdiction of the sentencing court, as well as those disproportionate to the offense involved. The American draftsmen, who adopted the English phrasing in drafting the Eighth Amendment, were primarily concerned, however, with proscribing "tortures" and other "barbarous" methods of punishment.

In the earliest cases raising Eighth Amendment claims, the Court focused on particular methods of execution to determine whether they were too cruel to pass constitutional muster. The constitutionality of the sentence of death itself was not at issue, and the criterion used to evaluate the mode of execution was its similarity to "torture" and other "barbarous" methods.

But the Court has not confined the prohibition embodied in the Eighth Amendment to "barbarous" methods that were generally outlawed in the 18th century. Instead, the Amendment has been interpreted in a flexible and dynamic manner. The Court early recognized that "a principle to be vital must be capable of wider application than the mischief which gave it birth." Thus the Clause forbidding "cruel and unusual" punishments "is not fastened to the obsolete but may acquire meaning as public opinion becomes enlightened by a humane justice." . . .

It is clear from . . . [these] precedents that the Eighth Amendment has not been regarded as a static concept. As Mr. Chief Justice Warren said, in an oft-quoted phrase, "[t]he Amendment must draw its meaning from the evolving standards of decency that mark the progress of a maturing society." Thus, an assessment of contemporary values concerning the infliction of a challenged sanction is relevant to the application of the Eighth Amendment. As we develop below more fully, this assessment does not call for a subjective judgment. It requires, rather, that we look to objective indicia that reflect the public attitude toward a given sanction.

But our cases also make clear that public perceptions of standards of decency with respect to criminal sanctions are not conclusive. A penalty also must accord with "the dignity of man," which is the "basic concept underlying the Eighth Amendment." This means, at least, that the punishment not be "excessive." When a form of punishment in the abstract (in this case, whether capital punishment may ever be imposed as a sanction for murder) rather than in the particular (the propriety of death as a penalty to be applied to a specific defendant for a specific crime) is under consideration, the inquiry into "excessiveness" has two aspects. First, the punishment must not involve the unnecessary and wanton infliction of pain. Second, the punishment must not be grossly out of proportion to the severity of the crime.

Of course, the requirements of the Eighth Amendment must be applied with an awareness of the limited role to be played by the courts. This does not mean that judges have no role to play, for the Eighth Amendment is a restraint upon the exercise of legislative power. . . .

But, while we have an obligation to insure that constitutional bounds are not overreached, we may not act as judges as we might as legislators.

Therefore, in assessing a punishment selected by a democratically elected legislature against the constitutional measure, we presume its validity. We may not require the legislature to select the least severe penalty possible so long as the penalty selected is not cruelly inhumane or disproportionate to the crime involved. And a heavy burden rests on those who would attack the judgment of the representatives of the people. . . .

In the discussion to this point we have sought to identify the principles and considerations that guide a court in addressing an Eighth Amendment claim. We now consider specifically whether the sentence of death for the crime of murder is a *per se* violation of the Eighth and Fourteenth Amendments to the Constitution. We note first that history and precedent strongly support a negative answer to this question.

The imposition of the death penalty for the crime of murder has a long history of acceptance both in the United States and in England. . . .

It is apparent from the text of the Constitution itself that the existence of capital punishment was accepted by the Framers. At the time the Eighth Amendment was ratified, capital punishment was a common sanction in every State. . . . The Fifth Amendment, adopted at the same time as the Eighth, contemplated the continued existence of the capital sanction by imposing certain limits on the prosecution of capital cases:

> No person shall be held to answer for a capital, or otherwise infamous crime, unless on a presentment or indictment of a Grand Jury . . . ; nor shall any person be subject for the same offense to be twice put in jeopardy of life or limb; . . . nor be deprived of life, liberty, or property, without due process of law. . . .

And the Fourteenth Amendment, adopted over three-quarters of a century later, similarly contemplates the existence of the capital sanction in providing that no State shall deprive any person of "life, liberty, or property" without due process of law.

For nearly two centuries, this Court, repeatedly and often expressly, has recognized that capital punishment is not invalid *per se*. . . .

Four years ago, the petitioners in *Furman* and its companion cases predicated their argument primarily upon the asserted proposition that standards of decency had evolved to the point where capital punishment no longer could be tolerated. The petitioners in those cases said, in effect, that the evolutionary process had come to an end, and that standards of decency required that the Eighth Amendment be construed finally as prohibiting capital punishment for any crime regardless of its depravity and impact on society. . . .

The petitioners in the capital cases before the Court today renew the "standards of decency" argument, but developments during the four years since *Furman* have undercut substantially the assumptions upon which their argument rested. Despite the continuing debate, dating back to the 19th century, over the morality and utility of capital punishment, it is now evident that a large proportion of American society continues to regard it as an appropriate and necessary criminal sanction.

The most marked indication of society's endorsement of the death penalty for murder is the legislative response to *Furman*. The legislatures of at least 35 States have enacted new statutes that provide for the death penalty for at least some crimes that result in the death of another person. And the Congress of the United States, in 1974, enacted a statute providing the death penalty for aircraft piracy that results in death. These recently adopted statutes have attempted to address the concerns expressed by the Court in *Furman* primarily (i) by specifying the factors to be weighed and the procedures to be followed in deciding when to impose a capital sentence, or (ii) by making the death penalty mandatory for specified crimes. But all of the post-*Furman* statutes make clear that capital punishment itself has not been rejected by the elected representatives of the people. . . .

The jury also is a significant and reliable objective index of contemporary values because it is so directly involved. . . . [T]he actions of juries in many States since *Furman* are fully compatible with the legislative judgments, reflected in the new statutes, as to the continued utility and necessity of capital punishment in appropriate cases. At the close of 1974 at least 254 persons had been sentenced to death since *Furman,* and by the end of March 1976, more than 460 persons were subject to death sentences.

As we have seen, however, the Eighth Amendment demands more than that a challenged punishment be acceptable to contemporary society. The Court also must ask whether it comports with the basic concept of human dignity at the core of the Amendment. Although we cannot "invalidate a category of penalties because we deem less severe penalties adequate to serve the ends of penology," the sanction imposed cannot be so totally without penological justification that it results in the gratuitous infliction of suffering.

The death penalty is said to serve two principal social purposes: retribution and deterrence of capital crimes by prospective offenders.

In part, capital punishment is an expression of society's moral outrage at particularly offensive conduct. This function may be unappealing to many, but it is essential in an ordered society that asks its citizens to rely on legal processes rather than self-help to vindicate their wrongs. . . . "Retribution is no longer the dominant objective of the criminal law," but neither is it a forbidden objective nor one inconsistent with our respect for the dignity of men. . . .

Although some of the studies suggest that the death penalty may not function as a significantly greater deterrent than lesser penalties, there is no convincing empirical evidence either supporting or refuting this view. We may nevertheless assume safely that there are murderers, such as those who act in passion, for whom the threat of death has little or no deterrent effect. But for many others, the death penalty undoubtedly is a significant deterrent. There are carefully contemplated murders, such as murder for hire, where the possible penalty of death may well enter into the cold calculus that precedes the decision to act. And there are some categories of murder, such as murder by a life prisoner, where other sanctions may not be adequate. . . .

Finally, we must consider whether the punishment of death is disproportionate in relation to the crime for which it is imposed. There is no question that death as a punishment is unique in its severity and irrevocability. When a defendant's life is at stake, the Court has been particularly sensitive to insure that every safeguard is observed. But we are concerned here only with the imposition of capital punishment for the crime of murder, and when a life has been taken deliberately by the offender, we cannot say that the punishment is invariably disproportionate to the crime. It is an extreme sanction, suitable to the most extreme of crimes.

We hold that the death penalty is not a form of punishment that may never be imposed, regardless of the circumstances of the offense, regardless of the character of the offender, and regardless of the procedure followed in reaching the decision to impose it.

We now consider whether Georgia may impose the death penalty on the petitioner in this case.

While *Furman* did not hold that the infliction of the death penalty *per se* violates the Constitution's ban on cruel and unusual punishments, it did recognize that the penalty of death is different in kind from any other punishment imposed under our system of criminal justice. Because of the uniqueness of the death penalty, *Furman* held that it could not be imposed under sentencing procedures that created a substantial risk that it would be inflicted in an arbitrary and capricious manner. . . .

Furman mandates that where discretion is afforded a sentencing body on a matter so grave as the determination of whether a human life should be taken or spared, that discretion must be suitably directed and limited so as to minimize the risk of wholly arbitrary and capricious action. . . .

Jury sentencing has been considered desirable in capital cases in order "to maintain a link between contemporary community values and the penal system—a link without which the determination of punishment could hardly reflect 'the evolving standards of decency that mark the progress of a maturing society.'" But it creates special problems. Much of the information that is relevant to the sentencing decision may have no relevance to the question of guilt, or may even be extremely prejudicial to a fair determination of that question. This problem, however, is scarcely insurmountable. Those who have studied the question suggest that a bifurcated procedure—one in which the question of sentence is not considered until the determination of guilt has been made— is the best answer. . . . When a human life is at stake and when the jury must have information prejudicial to the question of guilt but relevant to the question of penalty in order to impose a rational sentence, a bifurcated system is more likely to ensure elimination of the constitutional deficiencies identified in *Furman*.

But the provision of relevant information under fair procedural rules is not alone sufficient to guarantee that the information will be properly used in the imposition of punishment, especially if sentencing is performed by a jury. Since the members of a jury will have had little, if any, previous experience in sentencing, they are unlikely to be skilled in dealing with the information they are given. To the extent that this problem is inherent in jury sentencing, it may not be totally correctable. It seems clear, however, that the problem will be alleviated if the jury is given guidance regarding the factors about the crime and the defendant that the State, representing organized society, deems particularly relevant to the sentencing decision.

While some have suggested that standards to guide a capital jury's sentencing deliberations are impossible to formulate, the fact is that such standards have been developed. . . . While such standards are by necessity somewhat general, they do provide guidance to the sentencing authority and thereby reduce the likelihood that it will impose a sentence that fairly can be called capricious or arbitrary. Where the sentencing authority is required to specify the factors it relied upon in reaching its decision, the further safeguard of meaningful appellate review is available to ensure that death sentences are not imposed capriciously or in a freakish manner.

In summary, the concerns expressed in *Furman* that the penalty of death not be imposed in an arbitrary or capricious manner can be met by a carefully drafted statute that ensures that the sentencing authority is given adequate information and guidance. As a general proposition these concerns are best met by a system that provides for a bifurcated proceeding at which the sentencing authority is apprised of the information relevant to the imposition of sentence and provided with standards to guide its use of the information. . . .

We now turn to consideration of the constitutionality of Georgia's capital-sentencing procedures. In the wake of *Furman,* Georgia amended its capital punishment statute but chose not to narrow the scope of its murder provisions. Thus, now as before *Furman,* in Georgia "[a] person commits murder when he unlawfully and with malice aforethought, either express or implied, causes the death of another human being." All persons convicted of murder "shall be punished by death or by imprisonment for life."

Georgia did act, however, to narrow the class of murderers subject to capital punishment by specifying 10 statutory aggravating circumstances, one of which must be found by the jury to exist beyond a reasonable doubt before a death sentence can ever be imposed. In addition, the jury is authorized to consider any other appropriate aggravating or mitigating circumstances. The jury is not required to find any mitigating circumstance in order to make a recommendation of mercy that is binding on the trial court, but it must find a *statutory* aggravating circumstance before recommending a sentence of death.

These procedures require the jury to consider the circumstances of the crime and the criminal before it recommends sentence. No longer can a Georgia jury do as *Furman*'s jury did: reach a finding of the defendant's guilt and then, without guidance or direction, decide whether he should live or die. Instead, the jury's attention is directed to the specific circumstances of the crime. . . . In addition, the jury's attention is focused on the characteristics of the person who committed the crime. . . . As a result, while some jury discretion still exists, "the discretion to be exercised is controlled by clear and objective standards so as to produce nondiscriminatory application."

As an important additional safeguard against arbitrariness and caprice, the Georgia statutory scheme provides for automatic appeal of all death sentences to the State's Supreme Court. That court is required by statute to review each sentence of death and determine whether it was imposed under the influence of passion or prejudice, whether the evidence supports the jury's finding of a statutory aggravating circumstance, and whether the sentence is disproportionate compared to those sentences imposed in similar cases.

In short, Georgia's new sentencing procedures require as a prerequisite to the imposition of the death penalty, specific jury findings as to the circumstances of the crime or the character of the defendant. Moreover, to guard further against a situation comparable to that presented in *Furman,* the Supreme Court of Georgia compares each death sentence with the sentences imposed on similarly situated defendants to ensure that the sentence of death in a particular case is not disproportionate. On their face these procedures seem to satisfy the concerns of *Furman.* No longer should there be "no meaningful basis for distinguishing the few cases in which [the death penalty] is imposed from the many cases in which it is not." . . .

The basic concern of *Furman* centered on those defendants who were being condemned to death capriciously and arbitrarily. Under the procedures before the Court in that case, sentencing authorities were not directed to give attention to the nature or circumstances of the crime committed or to the character or record of the defendant. Left unguided, juries imposed the death sentence in a way that could only be called freakish. The new Georgia sentencing procedures, by contrast, focus the jury's attention on the particularized nature of the crime and the particularized characteristics of the individual defendant. While the jury is permitted to consider any aggravating or mitigating circumstances, it must find and identify at least one statutory aggravating factor before it may impose a penalty of death. In this way the jury's discretion is channeled. No longer can a jury wantonly and freakishly impose the death sentence; it is always circumscribed by the legislative guidelines. In addition, the review function of the Supreme Court of Georgia affords additional assurance that the concerns that prompted our decision in *Furman* are not present to any significant degree in the Georgia procedure applied here.

For the reasons expressed in this opinion, we hold that the statutory system under which Gregg was sentenced to death does not violate the Constitution. Accordingly, the judgment of the Georgia Supreme Court is affirmed.

It is so ordered.

MR. JUSTICE WHITE, WITH WHOM THE CHIEF JUSTICE AND MR. JUSTICE REHNQUIST JOIN, CONCURRING IN THE JUDGMENT.

The Georgia Legislature has plainly made an effort to guide the jury in the exercise of its discretion, while at the same time permitting the jury to dispense mercy on the basis of factors too intangible to write into a statute, and I cannot accept the naked assertion that the effort is bound to fail. As the types of murders for which the death penalty may be imposed become more narrowly defined and are limited to those which are particularly serious or for which the death penalty is peculiarly appropriate as they are in Georgia by reason of the aggravating-circumstance requirement, it becomes reasonable to expect that juries—even given discretion *not* to impose the death penalty—will impose the death penalty in a substantial portion of the cases so defined. If they do, it can no longer be said that the penalty is being imposed wantonly and freakishly or so infrequently that it loses its usefulness as a sentencing device. There is, therefore, reason to expect that Georgia's current system would escape the infirmities which invalidated its previous system under *Furman.* However, the Georgia Legislature was not satisfied with a system which might, but also might not, turn out in practice to result in death sentences being imposed with reasonable consistency for certain serious murders. Instead, it gave the Georgia Supreme Court the power and the obligation to perform precisely the task which three Justices of this Court, whose opinions were necessary to the result, performed in *Furman:* namely, the task of deciding whether in fact the death penalty was being administered for any given class of crime in a discriminatory, standardless, or rare fashion.

. . . Indeed, if the Georgia Supreme Court properly performs the task assigned to it under the Georgia statutes, death sentences imposed for discriminatory reasons or wantonly or freakishly for any given category of crime will be set aside. Petitioner has wholly failed to establish, and has not even attempted to establish, that the Georgia Supreme Court failed properly to perform its task in this case or that it is incapable of performing its task adequately in all cases; and this Court should not assume that it did not do so.

MR. JUSTICE BRENNAN, DISSENTING.

My opinion in *Furman v. Georgia* concluded that . . . the punishment of death, for whatever crime and under all circumstances, is "cruel and unusual" in violation of the Eighth and Fourteenth Amendments of the Constitution. . . .

The fatal constitutional infirmity in the punishment of death is that it treats "members of the human race as nonhumans, as objects to be toyed with and discarded. [It is] thus inconsistent with the fundamental premise of the Clause that even the vilest criminal remains a human being possessed of common human dignity."

As such it is a penalty that "subjects the individual to a fate forbidden by the principle of civilized treatment guaranteed by the [clause]." I therefore would hold, on that ground alone, that death is today a cruel and unusual punishment prohibited by the Clause.

MR. JUSTICE MARSHALL, DISSENTING.

In *Furman v. Georgia* (1972) (concurring opinion), I set forth at some length my views on the basic issue presented to the Court in these cases. The death penalty, I concluded, is a cruel and unusual punishment prohibited by the Eighth and Fourteenth Amendments. That continues to be my view. . . .

. . . An excessive penalty is invalid under the Cruel and Unusual Punishments Clause "even though popular sentiment may favor it." The inquiry here, then, is simply whether the death penalty is necessary to accomplish the legitimate legislative purposes in punishment, or whether a less severe penalty—life imprisonment— would do as well.

The two purposes that sustain the death penalty as nonexcessive in the Court's view are general deterrence and retribution. In *Furman,* I canvassed the relevant data on the deterrent effect of capital punishment. . . . The available evidence, I concluded in *Furman,* was convincing that "capital punishment is not necessary as a deterrent to crime in our society." . . .

The other principal purpose said to be served by the death penalty is retribution. The notion that retribution can serve as a moral justification for the sanction of death finds credence in the opinion of my Brothers Stewart, Powell, and Stevens, and that of my Brother White. . . . It is this notion that I find to be the most disturbing aspect of today's unfortunate decisions.

The concept of retribution is a multifaceted one, and any discussion of its role in the criminal law must be undertaken with caution. On one level, it can be said that the notion of retribution or reprobation is the basis of our insistence that only those who have broken the law be punished, and in this sense the notion is quite obviously central to a just system of criminal sanctions. But our recognition that retribution plays a crucial role in determining who may be punished by no means requires approval of retribution as a general justification for punishment. It is the question whether retribution can provide a moral justification for punishment—in particular, capital punishment—that we must consider.

My Brothers Stewart, Powell, and Stevens, offer the following explanation of the retributive justification for capital punishment: "When people begin to believe that organized society is unwilling or unable to impose upon criminal offenders the punishment they 'deserve,' then there are sown the seeds of anarchy—of self-help, vigilante justice, and lynch law."

This statement is wholly inadequate to justify the death penalty. As my Brother Brennan stated in *Furman,* "There is no evidence whatever that utilization of imprisonment rather than death encourages private blood feuds and other disorders." It simply defies belief to suggest that the death penalty is necessary to prevent the American people from taking the law into their own hands. . . .

The death penalty, unnecessary to promote the goal of deterrence or to further any legitimate notion of retribution, is an excessive penalty forbidden by the Eighth and Fourteenth Amendments. I respectfully dissent from the Court's judgment upholding the sentences of death imposed upon the petitioners in these cases.

Despite the many opinions in *Gregg*, the majority of justices agreed that the Georgia law was constitutional; indeed, some members of the Court referred to it as a model death penalty scheme. Those who believed that *Furman* had signaled the end of capital punishment in the United States were clearly mistaken. *Furman* represented the rejection of a capital punishment system that allowed racial discrimination to influence sentencing, but, as *Gregg* demonstrates, *Furman* did not represent a judicial rejection of capital punishment per se. As for Troy Gregg, he was not executed under Georgia's revised capital punishment statute, but he did suffer a premature death *(see Box 18-2)*.

In the Aftermath of Gregg

In some ways, *Gregg* settled the death penalty issue: the Court asserted that capital punishment does not violate the Constitution, a position to which it still adheres. But opponents of the death penalty did not give up. In the immediate aftermath of *Gregg*, they continued to bring lawsuits, many of which were aimed at narrowing the application of capital punishment. In other words, this litigation challenged state procedures rather than the constitutionality of the death penalty.

Many of these challenges have not succeeded. In **McCleskey v. Kemp** (1987) the justices rejected a new attempt to strike down the death penalty because of continuing racial disparities. Furthermore, in *McCleskey v. Zant* (1991) the Court upheld limits on the right of convicts to use habeas corpus petitions to file additional legal actions to block the death penalty. In **Baze v. Rees** (2008) the justices rejected a challenge to the use of lethal injection as a method for executing those convicted of capital offenses. Writing for a deeply divided Court, Chief Justice John G. Roberts held, "Simply because an execution method may result in pain, either by accident or as an inescapable consequence of death, does not establish the sort of 'objectively intolerable risk of harm' that qualifies as cruel and unusual."

Capital punishment opponents have, however, also scored some victories in the courts, persuading the justices to be more attentive to the fairness of death penalty trials. In *Wiggins v. Smith* (2003) the Court overturned a death sentence because the accused did not receive effective counsel, and in *Ring v. Arizona* (2002) the justices rejected the authority of a single judge to impose capital punishment, holding that a death sentence can be issued only by a jury. One of the death penalty opponents'

more significant recent legal victories came in *Atkins v. Virginia* (2002), a case that presented the justices with an opportunity to revisit a 1989 decision that permitted the execution of convicted murderers suffering from intellectual disabilities.[18]

Atkins v. Virginia

536 U.S. 304 (2002)
http://caselaw.findlaw.com/us-supreme-court/536/304.html
Oral arguments available at https://www.oyez.org/
cases/2001/00-8452
Vote: 6 (Breyer, Ginsburg, Kennedy, O'Connor, Souter, Stevens)
3 (Rehnquist, Scalia, Thomas)

OPINION OF THE COURT: *Stevens*

DISSENTING OPINIONS: *Rehnquist, Scalia*

Close to midnight on August 16, 1996, Daryl Renard Atkins and William Jones, after a day spent drinking and smoking marijuana, walked to a convenience store intending to buy more alcohol. When they realized that they did not have enough money to make the purchase, they decided to rob a customer. Armed with a semiautomatic handgun, they abducted Eric Nesbitt, an airman from Langley Air Force Base. Atkins and Jones robbed Nesbitt of the money he was carrying and drove him to an automated teller machine, where they forced him to withdraw $200. That done, they drove Nesbitt to an isolated location and shot him eight times in the thorax, chest, abdomen, arms, and legs, resulting in his death.

Atkins and Jones were initially charged with capital murder, but prosecutors permitted Jones to plead guilty to first-degree murder in exchange for his testimony against Atkins. By pleading guilty, Jones was ineligible for the death penalty under Virginia law. At Atkins's trial, both men confirmed most of the details of the incident, with the important exception that each claimed that the other had shot Nesbitt. The jury believed Jones's account, convicting Atkins and sentencing him to death. The Virginia Supreme Court upheld the conviction but ordered a new penalty phase of the trial because the trial court had used an improper verdict form.

---

[18]In the *Atkins* opinion the Court uses the term *mental retardation*. Eight years after this decision, Congress passed and President Obama signed a statute known as Rosa's Law (124 Stat. 2643), which amended the United States Code by substituting the term *intellectual disability* wherever *mental retardation* appeared. The Supreme Court officially adopted this new terminology in *Hall v. Florida* (2014). Although the terminology has changed, both expressions refer to the same intellectual condition.

BOX 18-2

Aftermath . . . Troy Leon Gregg

On July 2, 1976, the Supreme Court upheld Troy Leon Gregg's death sentence for the robbery and murders of Fred Simmons and Bob Moore, who had provided a ride to the hitchhiking Gregg. Although Gregg would suffer a premature death, it would not be at the hands of the state executioner.

On July 28, 1980, shortly before he was scheduled for execution, Gregg and three other death row inmates (Timothy McCorquodale, Johnny L. Johnson, and David Jarrell) escaped from the Georgia State Prison in Reidsville. Dressed in pajamas modified to look like guard uniforms and wearing forged identification badges, the four condemned prisoners hacksawed through the bars of an exercise room window close to their fourth-floor cells. Under prison regulations this portion of the escape route was never to be left unattended by guards, but the four prisoners passed undetected. Once through the window, the inmates were able to gain access to fire escapes leading to the ground. After convincing an inquiring guard that they were doing a prison security check, the disguised escapees walked out of the prison unimpeded. Waiting for them outside was a car left by one of McCorquodale's relatives.

Shortly after the escape Gregg made a bragging telephone call to Charles Postell, a reporter for the *Albany Herald* who had written a number of articles based on interviews with death row inmates. At first Postell thought the call was a hoax, but he later became convinced when Gregg explained that the escapees would rather die than live one more day under the inhumane conditions on death row. Postell called the prison warden's office but initially was told, "Everyone is accounted for at this time. Gregg is in his cell. There has been no escape." Colonel William Lowe, deputy commissioner of the Department of Offender Rehabilitation, stated later that Postell's report of the escape "was the first time we knew about it."

Over the next two days, law enforcement tracked the fugitives to a house on North Carolina's Lake Wylie. Twenty local police and FBI agents surrounded the house. After spending six hours attempting to convince the escapees to give themselves up, the officers lobbed tear gas into the building, resulting in the peaceful arrest of McCorquodale, Johnson, and Jarrell. Also arrested was William Flamont, the renter of the house, who was charged with harboring the three.

Noticeably absent was Troy Gregg. Gregg had been beaten to death the previous day during a brawl in a North Carolina biker bar. His body was found by a

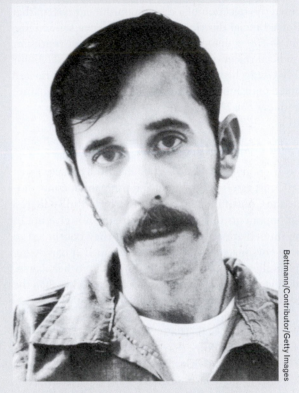

Convicted murderer Troy Leon Gregg

group of swimmers at the bottom of Mountain Island Lake, located about twelve miles from the house in which the others were hiding.

Nine individuals subsequently were indicted for helping the four convicts escape. Among them were a corrections officer, other inmates, and the escapees' relatives. Also indicted were *Albany Herald* reporter Charles Postell and his wife, Judi, who were accused of buying ten hacksaw blades and delivering them to Minnie Hunter, an aunt of one of the escapees, who mailed them to the prison, where they were intercepted by corrections officials. Another set of hacksaw blades mailed by a cousin of one of the inmates, however, did reach the prisoners. The charges against Postell and his wife were subsequently dropped when a key prosecution witness's credibility was tainted after he was linked to an attempt to extort $15,000 from Postell in return for favorable testimony.

Sources: Atlanta Daily World, August 17, 1980; *Christian Science Monitor,* August 29 and November 18, 1980; *New York Times,* July 29, July 31, August 28, and November 14, 1980; Kevin Clarke, "Suspended Sentence: How the U.S. Almost Put Capital Punishment to Death," *Salt of the Earth,* March/April 1997; *Washington Post,* July 29, August 28, and November 10, 1980.

Daryl Renard Atkins glances over his shoulder in a Virginia courtroom in February 1998 before being sentenced to death for carjacking and killing an airman. Four years later the Supreme Court would use the *Atkins* case to strike down Virginia's law permitting the execution of mentally retarded defendants.

At the second hearing, the jury heard testimony from a forensic psychologist, hired by the defense, that Atkins suffered a mild intellectual disability, with an IQ of 59 and an impaired capacity to interact successfully with his environment on a daily basis. A psychologist for the prosecution claimed, however, that although Atkins may have had an antisocial personality disorder, he was at least of average intelligence. The jury also heard about Atkins's sixteen prior felony convictions for robbery, attempted robbery, abduction, firearms violations, and maiming. After considering the evidence, the jurors sentenced Atkins to death.

Atkins's lawyers asked the Virginia Supreme Court to commute the sentence to life in prison on the ground that it is unconstitutional to execute an individual who is intellectually disabled. The Virginia court rejected this argument, relying on the U.S. Supreme Court's ruling in *Penry v. Lynaugh* (1989). The Supreme Court accepted the case in order to reconsider the *Penry* precedent.

JUSTICE STEVENS DELIVERED THE OPINION OF THE COURT.

Those mentally retarded persons who meet the law's requirements for criminal responsibility should be tried and punished when they commit crimes. Because of their disabilities in areas of reasoning, judgment, and control of their impulses, however, they do not act with the level of moral culpability that characterizes the most serious adult criminal conduct. Moreover, their impairments can jeopardize the reliability and fairness of capital proceedings against mentally retarded defendants. Presumably for these reasons, in the 13 years since we decided *Penry v. Lynaugh* (1989), the American public, legislators, scholars, and judges have deliberated over the question whether the death penalty should ever be imposed on a mentally retarded criminal. The consensus reflected in those deliberations informs our answer to the question presented by this case: whether such executions are "cruel and unusual punishments" prohibited by the Eighth Amendment to the Federal Constitution. . . .

The Eighth Amendment succinctly prohibits "excessive" sanctions. It provides: "Excessive bail shall not be required, nor excessive fines imposed, nor cruel and unusual punishments inflicted." In *Weems v. United States* (1910), we held that a punishment of 12 years jailed in irons at hard and painful labor for the crime of falsifying records was excessive. We explained "that it is a precept of justice that punishment for crime should be graduated and proportioned to the offense." We have repeatedly applied this proportionality precept in later cases interpreting the Eighth Amendment. . . .

A claim that punishment is excessive is judged not by the standards that prevailed in 1685 when Lord Jeffreys presided over the "Bloody Assizes" or when the Bill of Rights was adopted, but rather by those that currently prevail. As Chief Justice Warren explained in his opinion in *Trop v. Dulles* (1958): "The basic concept underlying the Eighth Amendment is nothing less than the dignity of man. . . . The Amendment must draw its meaning from the evolving standards of decency that mark the progress of a maturing society."

Proportionality review under those evolving standards should be informed by "objective factors to the maximum possible extent." We have pinpointed that the "clearest and most reliable objective evidence of contemporary values is the legislation enacted by the country's legislatures." *Penry.* Relying in part on such legislative evidence, we have held that death is an impermissibly excessive punishment for the rape of an adult woman, *Coker v. Georgia* (1977), or for a defendant who neither took life, attempted to take life, nor intended to take life, *Enmund v. Florida* (1982). . . .

We also acknowledged in *Coker* that the objective evidence, though of great importance, did not "wholly determine" the controversy, "for the Constitution contemplates that in the end our own judgment will be brought to bear on the question of the acceptability of the death penalty under the Eighth Amendment." . . . Thus, in cases involving a consensus, our own judgment is "brought to bear," by asking whether there is reason to disagree with the judgment reached by the citizenry and its legislators.

Guided by our approach in these cases, we shall first review the judgment of legislatures that have addressed the suitability of imposing the death penalty on the mentally retarded and then consider reasons for agreeing or disagreeing with their judgment.

The parties have not called our attention to any state legislative consideration of the suitability of imposing the death penalty on mentally retarded offenders prior to 1986. In that year, the public reaction to the execution of a mentally retarded murderer [Jerome Bowden] in Georgia apparently led to the enactment of the first state statute prohibiting such executions. In 1988, when Congress enacted legislation reinstating the federal death penalty, it expressly provided that a "sentence of death shall not be carried out upon a person who is mentally retarded." In 1989, Maryland enacted a similar prohibition. It was in that year that we decided *Penry,* and concluded that those two state enactments, "even when added to the 14 States that have rejected capital punishment completely, do not provide sufficient evidence at present of a national consensus."

Much has changed since then. Responding to the national attention received by the Bowden execution and our decision in *Penry,* state legislatures across the country began to address the issue. In 1990 Kentucky and Tennessee enacted statutes similar to those in Georgia and Maryland, as did New Mexico in 1991, and Arkansas, Colorado, Washington, Indiana, and Kansas in 1993 and 1994. In 1995, when New York reinstated its death penalty, it emulated the Federal Government by expressly exempting the mentally retarded. Nebraska followed suit in 1998. There appear to have been no similar enactments during the next two years, but in 2000 and 2001 six more States—South Dakota, Arizona, Connecticut, Florida, Missouri, and North Carolina—joined the procession. The Texas Legislature unanimously adopted a similar bill, and bills have passed at least one house in other States, including Virginia and Nevada.

It is not so much the number of these States that is significant, but the consistency of the direction of change. Given the well-known fact that anticrime legislation is far more popular than legislation providing protections for persons guilty of violent crime, the large number of States prohibiting the execution of mentally retarded persons (and the complete absence of States passing legislation reinstating the power to conduct such executions) provides powerful evidence that today our society views mentally retarded offenders as categorically less culpable than the average criminal. The evidence carries even greater force when it is noted that the legislatures that have addressed the issue have voted overwhelmingly in favor of the prohibition. Moreover, even in those States that allow the execution of mentally retarded offenders, the practice is uncommon. Some States, for example New Hampshire and New Jersey, continue to authorize executions, but none have been carried out in decades. Thus there is little need to pursue legislation barring the execution of the mentally retarded in those States. And it appears that even among those States that regularly execute offenders and that have no prohibition with regard to the mentally retarded, only five have executed offenders possessing a known IQ less than 70 since we

decided *Penry.* The practice, therefore, has become truly unusual, and it is fair to say that a national consensus has developed against it.*

To the extent there is serious disagreement about the execution of mentally retarded offenders, it is in determining which offenders are in fact retarded. In this case, for instance, the Commonwealth of Virginia disputes that Atkins suffers from mental retardation. Not all people who claim to be mentally retarded will be so impaired as to fall within the range of mentally retarded offenders about whom there is a national consensus. As was our approach in *Ford v. Wainwright* [1986], with regard to insanity, "we leave to the State[s] the task of developing appropriate ways to enforce the constitutional restriction upon its execution of sentences." . . .

. . . [O]ur death penalty jurisprudence provides two reasons consistent with the legislative consensus that the mentally retarded should be categorically excluded from execution. First, there is a serious question as to whether either justification that we have recognized as a basis for the death penalty applies to mentally retarded offenders. *Gregg v. Georgia* (1976) identified "retribution and deterrence of capital crimes by prospective offenders" as the social purposes served by the death penalty. Unless the imposition of the death penalty on a mentally retarded person "measurably contributes to one or both of these goals, it 'is nothing more than

---

*Additional evidence makes it clear that this legislative judgment reflects a much broader social and professional consensus. For example, several organizations with germane expertise have adopted official positions opposing the imposition of the death penalty upon a mentally retarded offender. See Brief for American Psychological Association et al. as *Amici Curiae*; Brief for AAMR et al. as *Amici Curiae*. In addition, representatives of widely diverse religious communities in the United States, reflecting Christian, Jewish, Muslim, and Buddhist traditions, have filed an amicus curiae brief explaining that even though their views about the death penalty differ, they all "share a conviction that the execution of persons with mental retardation cannot be morally justified." See Brief for United States Catholic Conference et al. as *Amici Curiae* in *McCarver v. North Carolina*. Moreover, within the world community, the imposition of the death penalty for crimes committed by mentally retarded offenders is overwhelmingly disapproved. Brief for The European Union as *Amicus Curiae* in *McCarver v. North Carolina*. Finally, polling data shows a widespread consensus among Americans, even those who support the death penalty, that executing the mentally retarded is wrong. R. Bonner & S. Rimer, "Executing the Mentally Retarded Even as Laws Begin to Shift," *N.Y. Times*, Aug. 7, 2000, p. A1; App. B to Brief for AAMR as *Amicus Curiae* in *McCarver v. North Carolina*, O.T. 2001, No. 00-8727 (appending approximately 20 state and national polls on the issue). Although these factors are by no means dispositive, their consistency with the legislative evidence lends further support to our conclusion that there is a consensus among those who have addressed the issue. See *Thompson v. Oklahoma* (1988) (considering the views of "respected professional organizations, by other nations that share our Anglo-American heritage, and by the leading members of the Western European community").

the purposeless and needless imposition of pain and suffering,' and hence an unconstitutional punishment." *Enmund.*

With respect to retribution—the interest in seeing that the offender gets his "just deserts"—the severity of the appropriate punishment necessarily depends on the culpability of the offender. Since *Gregg,* our jurisprudence has consistently confined the imposition of the death penalty to a narrow category of the most serious crimes. For example, in *Godfrey v. Georgia* (1980), we set aside a death sentence because the petitioner's crimes did not reflect "a consciousness materially more 'depraved' than that of any person guilty of murder." If the culpability of the average murderer is insufficient to justify the most extreme sanction available to the State, the lesser culpability of the mentally retarded offender surely does not merit that form of retribution. Thus, pursuant to our narrowing jurisprudence, which seeks to ensure that only the most deserving of execution are put to death, an exclusion for the mentally retarded is appropriate.

With respect to deterrence—the interest in preventing capital crimes by prospective offenders—"it seems likely that 'capital punishment can serve as a deterrent only when murder is the result of premeditation and deliberation,'" *Enmund.* Exempting the mentally retarded from that punishment will not affect the "cold calculus that precedes the decision" of other potential murderers. Indeed, that sort of calculus is at the opposite end of the spectrum from behavior of mentally retarded offenders. . . . Nor will exempting the mentally retarded from execution lessen the deterrent effect of the death penalty with respect to offenders who are not mentally retarded. Such individuals are unprotected by the exemption and will continue to face the threat of execution. Thus, executing the mentally retarded will not measurably further the goal of deterrence.

The reduced capacity of mentally retarded offenders provides a second justification for a categorical rule making such offenders ineligible for the death penalty. The risk "that the death penalty will be imposed in spite of factors which may call for a less severe penalty," *Lockett v. Ohio* (1978), is enhanced, not only by the possibility of false confessions, but also by the lesser ability of mentally retarded defendants to make a persuasive showing of mitigation in the face of prosecutorial evidence of one or more aggravating factors. Mentally retarded defendants may be less able to give meaningful assistance to their counsel and are typically poor witnesses, and their demeanor may create an unwarranted impression of lack of remorse for their crimes. . . . Mentally retarded defendants in the aggregate face a special risk of wrongful execution.

Our independent evaluation of the issue reveals no reason to disagree with the judgment of "the legislatures that have recently addressed the matter" and concluded that death is not a suitable punishment for a mentally retarded criminal. We are not persuaded that the execution of mentally retarded criminals will measurably advance the deterrent or the retributive purpose of the death penalty. Construing and applying the Eighth Amendment in the light of our "evolving standards of decency," we therefore conclude that such punishment is excessive and that the Constitution "places a substantive restriction on the State's power to take the life" of a mentally retarded offender.

The judgment of the Virginia Supreme Court is reversed and the case is remanded for further proceedings not inconsistent with this opinion.

It is so ordered.

JUSTICE SCALIA, WITH WHOM THE CHIEF JUSTICE AND JUSTICE THOMAS JOIN, DISSENTING.

Today's decision is the pinnacle of our Eighth Amendment death-is-different jurisprudence. Not only does it, like all of that jurisprudence, find no support in the text or history of the Eighth Amendment; it does not even have support in current social attitudes regarding the conditions that render an otherwise just death penalty inappropriate. Seldom has an opinion of this Court rested so obviously upon nothing but the personal views of its members. . . .

Under our Eighth Amendment jurisprudence, a punishment is "cruel and unusual" if it falls within one of two categories: "those modes or acts of punishment that had been considered cruel and unusual at the time that the Bill of Rights was adopted," and modes of punishment that are inconsistent with modern "standards of decency," as evinced by objective indicia, the most important of which is "legislation enacted by the country's legislatures," *Penry v. Lynaugh* (1989).

The Court makes no pretense that execution of the mildly mentally retarded would have been considered "cruel and unusual" in 1791. . . .

The Court is left to argue, therefore, that execution of the mildly retarded is inconsistent with the "evolving standards of decency that mark the progress of a maturing society." *Trop v. Dulles* (1958). Before today, our opinions consistently emphasized that Eighth Amendment judgments regarding the existence of social "standards" "should be informed by objective factors to the maximum possible extent" and "should not be, or appear to be, merely the subjective views of individual Justices." "First" among these objective factors are the "statutes passed by society's elected representatives," *Stanford v. Kentucky* (1989), because it "will rarely if ever be the case that the Members of this Court will have a better sense of the evolution in views of the American people than do their elected representatives," *Thompson* (SCALIA, J., dissenting).

The Court pays lip service to these precedents as it miraculously extracts a "national consensus" forbidding execution of the mentally retarded from the fact that 18 States—less than *half* (47%) of the 38 States that permit capital punishment (for whom the issue exists)—have very recently enacted legislation barring execution of the mentally retarded. . . .

. . . How is it possible that agreement among 47% of the death penalty jurisdictions amounts to "consensus"? Our prior cases have generally required a much higher degree of agreement before finding a punishment cruel and unusual on "evolving standards" grounds. In *Coker,* we proscribed the death penalty for rape of an adult woman after finding that only one jurisdiction, Georgia, authorized such a punishment. In *Enmund,* we invalidated the death penalty for mere participation in a robbery in which an accomplice took a life, a punishment not permitted in 28 of the death penalty States (78%). . . . What the Court calls evidence of "consensus" in the present case (a fudged 47%) more closely resembles evidence that we found *inadequate* to establish consensus in earlier cases. . . .

The Court attempts to bolster its embarrassingly feeble evidence of "consensus" with the following: "It is not so much the number of these States that is significant, but the *consistency* of the direction of change." But in what *other* direction *could we possibly* see change? Given that 14 years ago *all* the death penalty statutes included the mentally retarded, *any* change (except precipitate undoing of what had just been done) was *bound to be* in the one direction the Court finds significant enough to overcome the lack of real consensus. . . . In any event, reliance upon "trends," even those of much longer duration than a mere 14 years, is a perilous basis for constitutional adjudication. . . .

But the Prize for the Court's Most Feeble Effort to fabricate "national consensus" must go to its appeal (deservedly relegated to a footnote) to the views of assorted professional and religious organizations, members of the so-called "world community," and respondents to opinion polls. [T]he views of professional and religious organizations and the results of opinion polls are irrelevant. Equally irrelevant are the practices of the "world community," whose notions of justice are (thankfully) not always those of our people. "We must never forget that it is a Constitution for the United States of America that we are expounding. . . . [W]here there is not first a settled consensus among our own people, the views of other nations, however enlightened the Justices of this Court may think them to be, cannot be imposed upon Americans through the Constitution." *Thompson* (SCALIA, J., dissenting). . . .

. . . [T]he Court gives two reasons why the death penalty is an excessive punishment for all mentally retarded offenders. First, the "diminished capacities" of the mentally retarded raise a "serious question" whether their execution contributes to the "social purposes" of the death penalty, viz., retribution and deterrence. (The Court conveniently ignores a third "social purpose" of the death penalty—"incapacitation of dangerous criminals and the consequent prevention of crimes that they may otherwise commit in the future," *Gregg v. Georgia* (1976) But never mind; its discussion of even the other two does not bear analysis.) Retribution is not advanced, the argument goes, because the mentally retarded are *no more culpable* than the average murderer, whom we have already held lacks sufficient culpability to warrant the death penalty, see

Godfrey v. Georgia (1980). Who says so? Is there an established correlation between mental acuity and the ability to conform one's conduct to the law in such a rudimentary matter as murder? Are the mentally retarded really more disposed (and hence more likely) to commit willfully cruel and serious crime than others? In my experience, the opposite is true: being childlike generally suggests innocence rather than brutality. . . .

As for the other social purpose of the death penalty that the Court discusses, deterrence: That is not advanced, the Court tells us, because the mentally retarded are "less likely" than their non-retarded counterparts to "process the information of the possibility of execution as a penalty and . . . control their conduct based upon that information." . . . [T]he Court does not say that *all* mentally retarded individuals cannot "process the information of the possibility of execution as a penalty and . . . control their conduct based upon that information"; it merely asserts that they are "less likely" to be able to do so. But surely the deterrent effect of a penalty is adequately vindicated if it successfully deters many, but not all, of the target class. Virginia's death penalty, for example, does not fail of its deterrent effect simply because *some* criminals are unaware that Virginia *has* the death penalty. . . . I am not sure that a murderer is somehow less blameworthy if (though he knew his act was wrong) he did not fully appreciate that he could die for it; but if so, we should treat a mentally retarded murderer the way we treat an offender who may be "less likely" to respond to the death penalty because he was abused as a child. We do not hold him immune from capital punishment, but require his background to be considered by the sentencer as a mitigating factor. *Eddings v. Oklahoma* (1982).

The Court throws one last factor into its grab bag of reasons why execution of the retarded is "excessive" in all cases: Mentally retarded offenders "face a special risk of wrongful execution" because they are less able "to make a persuasive showing of mitigation," "to give meaningful assistance to their counsel," and to be effective witnesses. "Special risk" is pretty flabby language (even flabbier than "less likely")—and I suppose a similar "special risk" could be said to exist for just plain stupid people, inarticulate people, even ugly people. If this unsupported claim has any substance to it (which I doubt) it might support a due process claim in all criminal prosecutions of the mentally retarded; but it is hard to see how it has anything to do with an Eighth Amendment claim that execution of the mentally retarded is cruel and unusual.

Although the justices may agree that capital punishment is not inherently unconstitutional, they evince considerable conflict over specific applications of the death penalty relative to the constitutional ban against cruel and unusual punishments. As the opinions in *Atkins* demonstrate, the justices are often at loggerheads over the meaning of cruel and unusual punishment and how the nation's evolving standards of decency should be identified. To what should the justices look to determine changing societal standards? The actions of state legislatures? Jury verdicts? Public opinion polls? Is world opinion a relevant consideration? And how should we decide if the interests of retribution, deterrence, and incapacitation are advanced through the application of the death penalty? Undoubtedly the justices, and the nation as a whole, are a long way from arriving at final answers to these questions.

POSTTRIAL STAGES

Individuals who have been convicted of crimes can appeal their convictions in the hope that appellate judges will find errors in the trial courts' handling of their cases. Under the American concept of due process, someone convicted of a criminal offense is entitled to at least one appeal. A new trial might be granted if new evidence is discovered that brings into serious question the guilt of the defendant, although such instances are rare.

An additional guarantee governing the posttrial stage is the Fifth Amendment's ban against double jeopardy: "nor shall any person be subject for the same offence to be twice put in jeopardy of life or limb." The clause reflects the framers' belief that it is essentially unfair for any person to be tried twice for the same criminal charge. The government should have one attempt, and one attempt only, to convince a jury that the accused is guilty. A person who has been acquitted of an offense by a court of law cannot be tried a second time for that same offense. Also, the government may not prosecute a convicted person a second time in the hope of obtaining a more severe sentence. Once a trial on a given criminal charge is completed, the defendant is protected against any subsequent trial on that charge that might lead to more adverse consequences.

A great deal of the confusion surrounding the double jeopardy clause stems from the words "same offence." If a man sets fire to an apartment building, killing five residents, has he committed one homicide or five? If a man spends an evening robbing a series of liquor stores, has he committed a single offense or several? What does the double jeopardy clause mean when it prohibits trying a person more than once for the same offense? We find a partial answer in **Ashe v. Swenson** (1970). A group of individuals playing poker one night were robbed by three or four masked men. Several months later Bob Ashe was charged with the crime. The prosecutor first placed him on trial for robbing one of the card players. The jury found him not guilty because of insufficient evidence. Then the prosecutor charged him with robbing a second poker player. Ashe objected, claiming the second trial would violate the double jeopardy clause, and the Supreme Court agreed. The robbing of the poker party was a single act, and once acquitted of robbing the first poker player, Ashe could not be tried for robbing another member of the group that same evening. In Justice Stewart's words, the Fifth Amendment "surely protects a man who has been acquitted from having to 'run the gauntlet' a second time."

The double jeopardy clause does not, however, bar separate governments from prosecuting an individual for the same crime. In *Heath v. Alabama* (1985) the Court applied this dual sovereignty doctrine to Larry Gene Heath, who had arranged to have his wife, who was nine months pregnant, kidnapped and killed. The hired killers took Rebecca Heath from her home in Alabama and murdered her in Georgia. Heath was arrested in Georgia and pleaded guilty to murder charges as part of a plea-bargain arrangement to avoid the death penalty. Alabama authorities, independently investigating the crime, then indicted Heath for kidnapping and murder. Heath objected on double jeopardy grounds, but the Supreme Court held that the Fifth Amendment did not prohibit prosecution by Alabama. An act that offends the criminal laws of two jurisdictions may be punished by both.[19]

---

[19]See also **Gamble v. United States** (2019), in which the Court allowed prosecution in federal court and in state court for the same conduct (possession of a firearm as a convicted felon), thereby reaffirming the "separate sovereigns" approach to double jeopardy.

ANNOTATED READINGS

Of the topics we cover in this chapter, two have received substantial attention: the jury system and the death penalty. On juries, see Daniel Givelber and Amy Farrell, *Not Guilty:* *Are the Acquitted Innocent?* (New York: NYU Press, 2012); Reid Hastie, Steven D. Penrod, and Nancy Pennington, *Inside the Jury* (Cambridge, MA: Harvard University Press,

1983); Randolph N. Jonakait, *The American Jury System* (New Haven, CT: Yale University Press, 2003); Harry Kalven Jr. and Hans Zeisel, *The American Jury* (Boston: Little, Brown, 1966); and Neil Vidmar and Valerie P. Hans, *American Juries: The Verdict* (New York: Prometheus Books, 2007).

Books on the death penalty include David C. Baldus, George G. Woodworth, and Charles A. Pulaski Jr., *Equal Justice and the Death Penalty* (Boston: Northeastern University Press, 1990); Stuart Banner, *The Death Penalty: An American History* (Cambridge, MA: Harvard University Press, 2002); Frank R. Baumgartner, Suzanna L. DeBoef, and Amber E. Boydstun, *The Decline of the Death Penalty and the Discovery of Innocence* (New York: Cambridge University Press, 2008); Jennifer L. Culbert, *Dead Certainty: The Death Penalty and the Problem of Judgment* (Stanford, CA: Stanford University Press, 2007); Lee Epstein and Joseph F. Kobylka, *The Supreme Court and Legal Change: Abortion and the Death Penalty* (Chapel Hill: University of North Carolina Press, 1992); Stephen P. Garvey, ed., *Beyond Repair? America's Death Penalty* (Durham, NC: Duke University Press, 2002); Roger G. Hood, *Death Penalty: A Worldwide Perspective* (New York: Oxford University Press, 2002); Michael Meltsner, *Cruel and Unusual: The Supreme Court and Capital Punishment* (New York: Random House, 1973); David M. Oshinsky, *Capital Punishment on Trial: Furman v. Georgia and the Death Penalty in Modern America* (Lawrence: University Press of Kansas, 2010); Melynda J. Price, *Race, Religion, & Citizenship in the Politics of the Death Penalty* (Oxford, UK: Oxford University Press, 2015); Austin Sarat, *When the State Kills: Capital Punishment and the American Condition* (Princeton, NJ: Princeton University Press, 2001); Carol S. Streiker and Jordan M. Streiker, *Courting Death: The Supreme Court and Capital Punishment* (Cambridge, MA: Harvard University Press, 2016); and Thomas G. Walker, *Eligible for Execution: The Story of the Daryl Atkins Case* (Washington, DC: CQ Press, 2009).

Books on other topics relating to attorneys, trials, and punishments include George Fisher, *Plea Bargaining's Triumph* (Stanford, CA: Stanford University Press, 2004); Brandon L. Garrett, *Convicting the Innocent: Where Criminal Prosecutions Go Wrong* (Cambridge, MA: Harvard University Press, 2011); Milton Heumann, *Plea Bargaining* (Chicago: University of Chicago Press, 1978); Anthony Lewis, *Gideon's Trumpet* (New York: Vintage Books, 1964); Michael Lynch, Simon A. Cole, Ruth McNally, and Kathleen Jordan, *Truth Machine: The Contentious History of DNA Fingerprinting* (Chicago: University of Chicago Press, 2008); Keally McBride, *Punishment and Political Order* (Ann Arbor: University of Michigan Press, 2007); Jay A. Sigler, *Double Jeopardy: The Development of Legal and Social Policy* (Ithaca, NY: Cornell University Press, 1969); William J. Stuntz, *The Collapse of American Criminal Justice* (Cambridge, MA: Belknap Press, 2011); George C. Thomas, *Double Jeopardy: The History, the Law* (New York: Oxford University Press, 1998); George C. Thomas, *The Supreme Court on Trial: How the American Justice System Sacrifices Innocent Defendants* (Ann Arbor: University of Michigan Press, 2008); Mary Vogel, *Coercion to Compromise: Plea Bargaining, the Courts, and the Making of Political Authority* (New York: Oxford University Press, 2007); and Franklin E. Zimring, Gordon Hawkins, and Sam Kamin, *Punishment and Democracy: Three Strikes and You're Out in California* (New York: Oxford University Press, 2001).

CIVIL RIGHTS

EQUAL·JUSTICE·UNDER·LAW

IN MARKED CONTRAST to the colonial period, when most citizens came from British roots, Americans today are from many different backgrounds. Immigration has diversified the population, and this trend may continue. Americans are a people of wide-ranging religions, races, ethnic backgrounds, and levels of wealth. Given this diversity, the motto *E pluribus unum* ("One from many") sometimes appears to be more of a challenge than a statement of fact. In spite of the differences among Americans, however, the nation has pledged itself to fairness and equality. All Americans are to be free from unconstitutional discrimination, to have equal opportunity, and to be able to participate fully in the political process.

Even so, at times people feel they have been mistreated by their government, not because of what they have done but because of who they are. They claim that discrimination has occurred because of race, creed, national origin, gender, economic status, sexual orientation, or some other characteristic that government should not use as a basis for policy. When disputes over such charges arise, the court system provides a venue for their resolution. In the chapters in Part VII, we discuss the civil rights of Americans and how the Supreme Court has interpreted them. By *civil rights* we mean those legal provisions emanating from the concept of equality. Unlike civil liberties issues, which focus on personal freedoms protected by the Bill of Rights, civil rights issues involve the status of persons with shared characteristics who have been disadvantaged in some way. Civil rights laws attempt to guarantee full and equal citizenship for such persons and to protect them from arbitrary and capricious treatment. Chapter 19 examines discrimination, and chapter 20 explores the rights of political participation. Before we confront those subjects, however, a review of some basic concepts of history and law might be useful.

Today, we are used to hearing not only about charges of discrimination but also about Supreme Court rulings on the proper meaning of the Constitution governing such issues. These phenomena are comparatively recent. Colonial Americans discriminated in a number of ways that we now consider abhorrent—with the institution of slavery the most significant breach of fundamental equality. In spite of the Declaration of Independence, which proclaimed that all men are created equal, the enslavement of Africans brought to North America against their will was politically accepted, although not universally supported. The Constitution recognized this form of inequality, stipulating in Article I that a slave would be counted as three-fifths of a person for representation purposes; it also gave slavery a degree of protection by prohibiting any federal restrictions on the importation of slaves until 1808. Other forms of discrimination also were common. Voting qualifications, for example, were quite restrictive: only men could vote, and in some states only men who owned property could vote.

Guarantees of equality did not officially become part of the Constitution until after the Civil War. When the Radical Republicans took control of the legislative branch, three constitutional amendments, generally referred to as the Civil War amendments, were proposed and ratified. They incorporated into the Constitution what had been won on the battlefield and dramatically changed the concept of civil rights in the United States. The Thirteenth Amendment, ratified in 1865, unambiguously ended the institution of slavery. Although there have been some disputes over the involuntary servitude prohibition (in relation, for example, to the military draft), the slavery issue, over which the nation had been divided since the Constitutional Convention, finally was put to rest. The other two amendments, the Fourteenth and Fifteenth, have generated a great deal of litigation and many Supreme Court cases, and we discuss them in turn.

THE FOURTEENTH AMENDMENT

The Fourteenth Amendment, ratified in 1868, is unlike the other two Civil War amendments because of its length and complexity. The first section is the most significant: it states that U.S. citizenship is superior to state citizenship, constitutionally reinforcing the Civil War outcome of national superiority over states' rights. This idea was a dramatic change from the pre–Civil War concept that national citizenship was dependent on state citizenship. The first section also includes the due process clause and privileges or immunities clause we discussed in earlier chapters, as well as the equal protection clause. Because this last clause forms the basis of constitutional protections against discrimination, we describe it in some detail. The remaining parts of the Fourteenth Amendment require the former slaves to be fully counted for representational purposes, impose (with few exceptions) universal adult male suffrage, restrict the civil rights of certain participants in the rebellion, and guarantee the public debt resulting from the war.

The Supreme Court and Equal Protection of the Laws: An Overview

An analysis of the wording of the equal protection clause helps us to understand what it covers and what its limitations are. It says, "[N]or shall any State . . . deny to any person within its jurisdiction the equal protection of the laws."

The first significant element of the clause is the word *state*. The members of Congress who drafted the Fourteenth Amendment were concerned primarily with the danger of the states (especially those in the South) imposing discriminatory laws. With the Radical Republicans—who were deeply committed to the abolishment of slavery—in control of Congress and the White House, the legislators had little fear that the federal government would impose discriminatory policies. Consequently, the prohibitions of the clause apply only to the states and their political subdivisions, such as counties and cities. (This does not mean that the federal government is free to discriminate. As we will see momentarily, the Court has read the Fifth Amendment due process clause to contain an equal protection component.)

Second, the amendment protects *all* persons within a state's jurisdiction, not just former slaves. In an early dispute over the amendment, the Supreme Court acknowledged its broad applicability. ***Yick Wo v. Hopkins*** (1886) concerned the discriminatory enforcement of fire safety regulations in San Francisco. The Court held that the equal protection clause applies to persons other than African Americans, also protecting noncitizens who are targets of discrimination by the state.

Finally, the clause outlaws denying equal protection of the laws. It prohibits the government from drawing classifications—discriminating—in arbitrary and unreasonable ways.

The wording of the equal protection clause means that before an individual can legitimately assert a claim of unlawful discrimination, two important elements must be demonstrated. First, the aggrieved party must show that the law creates a classification that treats one group less fairly or equally than others. In other words, it discriminates.

Second, there must be state action—that is, the state or local government must have enacted or supported the classification. These two requirements have undergone substantial interpretation by the justices of the Supreme Court, and it is important to understand what each requirement includes.

Discrimination. Discrimination simply means to distinguish between people or things. It occurs in many forms, not all of which the Constitution prohibits. For example, in administering an admissions program, a state university must discriminate between—or classify—applicants. It admits some and rejects others. Decisions usually are based on applicants' high school grades, standardized test scores, and letters of recommendation. The university admits those who, based on valid predictors of performance, have the best chance to succeed. Those who are rejected usually accept the decision because the university's admissions criteria appear reasonable. But the reaction would be quite different if an applicant received a letter from a state college that said, "In spite of your demonstrated potential for college studies, we cannot admit you because of our policy not to accept students of your gender." In this case, the rejected applicant would rightly feel victimized by unreasonable discrimination.

What rule of law distinguishes acceptable discrimination from that which violates the Constitution? The Supreme Court answered this question by declaring that the equal protection clause goes no further than prohibiting "invidious discrimination"[1]—that is, discrimination that is arbitrary and capricious, unequal treatment that the state cannot adequately justify. Reasonable discrimination, on the other hand, is not unconstitutional. When the state treats two individuals differently, we need to ask why the state has created the classification. If two surgeons perform heart operations on patients and one surgeon is thrown in jail and the other is not, we might feel that the imprisoned person has not been treated fairly. Our opinion would change, however, if we learned that the jailed person had never been to medical school and was not licensed. Here the state would be classifying on

[1]See *Williamson v. Lee Optical* (1955).

the basis of legitimate, reasonable criteria. The equal protection clause demands that similarly situated persons be treated equally. The two surgeons, because of their vastly different qualifications, are not similarly situated, and consequently the Constitution does not require that they be treated the same.

Almost every government action involves some form of discrimination, classification, or line drawing. Most classifications or lines are perfectly legitimate, although all those affected might not agree. For example, when a state government passes an income tax law that imposes a higher rate on the wealthy than it does on the poor, the rich may feel they are the targets of unconstitutional discrimination. When individuals believe they have been denied equal protection at the hands of the state, the courts must decide if the government's discrimination runs afoul of the Fourteenth Amendment. When it comes to taxes, the courts have ruled that progressive rate structures are not invidious, but reasonable.

To assist the judiciary in deciding such disputes, the Supreme Court has developed three basic tests of the equal protection clause. As chapter 19 explains in more detail, the nature of the alleged discrimination and the government interests at stake guide which test the justices apply in any given case *(see also Table VII-1)*.

The traditional test used to decide discrimination cases is *rational basis* scrutiny. When using this approach to the Constitution, the justices ask, Is the challenged discrimination rational? Or is it arbitrary and capricious? If a state passes a law that says a person must be at least eighteen years old to enter a legally binding contract, it draws a classification based on age. Individuals under age eighteen are not granted the right to consummate legal agreements, whereas those over age eighteen are. If a dispute over the validity of this law were brought to court, the judge would have to decide whether the state had acted reasonably to achieve a legitimate government objective.[2] Using the rational basis test, the Court generally—though, as we shall see, not always—defers to the state and presumes the validity of the government's action. The burden of proof rests with the party challenging the law to establish that the statute is irrational. Unless the Court has determined otherwise, discrimination claims proceed according to the rules of the rational basis test.

The second test is called the *strict scrutiny* test. This test is used when the state discriminates against groups that make them more likely to be the targets of discrimination—perhaps because they faced discrimination in the past or because they are politically powerless, among other reasons.[3] Race falls into this "suspect class" category. For laws that classify on the basis of race, the Court does not apply the rational basis test but rather a strict scrutiny test. For a law to be valid under strict scrutiny, it must be found to advance a compelling state interest by the least restrictive means available. When the Court uses strict scrutiny, it presumes that the state action is unconstitutional, and the burden of proof is on the government to demonstrate that the law is constitutional—specifically, that it advances a compelling state interest and the law is necessary (the least restrictive means available) to advance that interest. The reason for moving racial discrimination from the rational basis test to the suspect class test is that the Supreme Court has concluded that racial criteria are inherently arbitrary, that compelling state interests are almost never served by treating people differently according to race. (Affirmative action programs are the key exceptions, as we will see in chapter 19.)

Given the rules associated with these two tests, it should be obvious that it is much easier to establish that a violation of the Constitution has occurred if the suspect class test is used. Therefore, many cases before the Supreme Court have been filed by attorneys representing groups seeking that classification—or at least something more than rational basis analysis. Although the Court has been stingy in recognizing other classifications as "suspect," it has acknowledged that some are "quasi-suspect," including gender.[4] This recognition has given rise to yet a third test of the equal protection clause, the *intermediate* or *heightened scrutiny* test. This test holds that to be valid, the unequal treatment must serve important government objectives and must be substantially related to the achievement of those objectives.[5] In recent years the Court has also suggested that under this test a state must provide an exceedingly persuasive justification for any discriminatory classifications. As such, this test falls somewhere between rational basis and strict scrutiny *(see Table VII-1)*.

This three-tiered approach can be confusing, and the Supreme Court has been neither clear nor consistent

---

[2]See *McGowan v. Maryland* (1961).

[3]See **United States v. Carolene Products** (1938) and *San Antonio Independent School District v. Rodriguez* (1973).

[4]See, for example, *Frontiero v. Richardson* (1973).

[5]*Craig v. Boren* (1976).

Table VII-1	Equal Protection Tests	
Test	**Example of Applicability**	**Validity Standard**
Rational basis scrutiny	Age discrimination	The law must be a *reasonable* measure designed to achieve a *legitimate* government purpose.
Intermediate or heightened scrutiny test	Sex discrimination	The law must be *substantially related* to the achievement of an *important* government objective.
Strict scrutiny	Race discrimination	The law must be the *least restrictive* means available to achieve a *compelling* state interest.

in applying the principles. Justice Thurgood Marshall in **Dunn v. Blumstein** (1972) acknowledged that the tests do not have the "precision of mathematical formulas." Justice Byron R. White hinted that in reality the Court may be using a spectrum of tests rather than three separate tests. Frustration over the status of the equal protection clause tests prompted Justice John Paul Stevens also to claim in his concurring opinion in *Cleburne v. Cleburne Living Center* (1985) that a continuum of standards was being used. Not persuaded of the wisdom of the Court's approach, Stevens argued that a single test should be adopted for all equal protection claims. In spite of these criticisms, the Court has stuck to the three-tiered approach, which reflects the belief that the more historically disadvantaged and politically powerless a class of people has been, the greater justification government must provide for any state action that discriminates against the members of that class.

State Action. As we noted, the equal protection clause specifically prohibits discrimination by any state. The Supreme Court has interpreted this concept to include a wide array of state actions—statutes, their enforcement

and administration, and the actions of state officials. We have already mentioned *Yick Wo v. Hopkins*, in which the Court struck down a fire safety regulation that was racially neutral as written but enforced in a discriminatory manner against Chinese laundry operators. State action includes the policies of political subdivisions such as towns, cities, counties, and special-purpose agencies. The states are prohibited from engaging in invidious discrimination either directly or indirectly. A city, for instance, may not run its municipal swimming pools in a racially segregated manner, nor may it donate the pools to a private organization that will restrict pool use to a particular racial group. In whatever form, however, some element of state action supporting invidious discrimination must be shown before a violation of the equal protection clause occurs.

This requirement means that discrimination by purely private individuals or organizations is not prohibited by the equal protection clause. A white apartment building owner who refuses to rent to an African American family does not violate the Constitution. Neither is a restaurant manager who will not serve Latinos, a private club that will not admit women, or an employer who will not hire applicants over forty years of age. In each of these cases there is ample evidence of irrational discrimination but no state action. The discrimination is conducted by private individuals or organizations. These forms of discrimination may well be in violation of any number of state or federal statutes (for some examples, *see Box VII-1*), but they do not offend the equal protection clause of the Fourteenth Amendment.

Moreover, because it is restricted to the states, the equal protection clause does not prohibit the federal government from engaging in discrimination. The Supreme Court, therefore, faced a difficult situation in 1954 in the school desegregation cases. The best-known of these is *Brown v. Board of Education of Topeka*, but *Brown* was only one of several cases involving the same basic question. In **Bolling v. Sharpe** the Court faced the thorny issue of racial segregation in the Washington, D.C., public schools. The District of Columbia is not a state, and in the 1950s Congress was the ultimate authority over Washington, as it is today. The equal protection clause was not applicable there. Given the political situation at the time, the Court had to find a way to declare *all* segregated schools unconstitutional.

The justices found a solution in the due process clause of the Fifth Amendment, which states, "No person shall . . . be deprived of life, liberty, or property, without due process of law." This guarantee of essential fairness applies to the federal government and was used by the justices in *Bolling* as a bar against racial discrimination. Chief Justice Earl Warren explained for a unanimous Court:

> The Fifth Amendment, which is applicable in the District of Columbia, does not contain an equal protection clause as does the Fourteenth Amendment which applies only to the states. But the concepts of equal protection and due process, both stemming from our American ideal of fairness, are not mutually exclusive. The "equal protection of the laws" is a more explicit safeguard of prohibited unfairness than "due process of law," and, therefore, we do not imply that the two are always interchangeable phrases. But, as this Court has recognized, discrimination may be so unjustifiable as to be violative of due process.

Although Warren cautioned that the due process clause and the equal protection clause could not be used interchangeably, the Court consistently has ruled that both provisions stand for the same general principles. In most areas of discrimination law (but not all), the justices have applied the same standards to both state and federal governments by using these two constitutional provisions. As a rule, any discriminatory action by a state found to be in violation of the equal protection clause would also be a violation of the Fifth Amendment if engaged in by the federal government. We should, however, understand which provision of the Constitution is offended when either a state government or the federal government practices invidious discrimination. If a state were to racially segregate a state park, for example, it would violate the equal protection clause of the Fourteenth Amendment. Were the federal government to do the same to campgrounds at Yellowstone, however, it would violate the due process clause of the Fifth Amendment. Worth noting, though, is that the Court sometimes refers to the "equal protection component" of the Fifth Amendment rather than the due process clause when it is adjudicating claims of discrimination by the federal government.[6]

Congressional Enforcement of the Fourteenth Amendment

The civil rights of Americans are defined and protected by more than just the Constitution. Over the years Congress has passed laws designed to enforce and extend constitutional guarantees (*see Box VII-1*). These laws expand prohibitions against discriminatory behavior, give the federal executive branch authority to enforce civil rights protections, and enlarge the opportunities for aggrieved parties to seek redress in the courts. The rules of evidence and procedure in some of these laws make it easier for litigants to prevail by proving a violation of a civil rights statute rather than a constitutional violation.

The authority for Congress to pass such laws can be found in several constitutional provisions. Each Civil War amendment contains a section granting Congress the power to enforce the amendment with appropriate legislation. Consequently, these amendments have had considerable impact not only because of their basic substantive content but also because they gave Congress new legislative power. Immediately following the Civil War, Congress used this authority to pass laws intended to give the new amendments teeth. For example, the Civil Rights Act of 1866, passed over the veto of President Andrew Johnson, guaranteed blacks the right to purchase, lease, and use real property. The Supreme Court upheld the law, ruling that the Thirteenth Amendment's enforcement section gave Congress the power not only to outlaw slavery but also to legislate against the "badges and incidents of slavery."[7] Much of the federal regulation on fair housing is based on this authority.

Congress learned by trial and error to ground legislation in the correct Civil War amendment. In 1883 the Supreme Court handed down its decisions in the ***Civil Rights Cases***, which involved challenges to the Civil Rights Act of 1875, a statute based on the Fourteenth Amendment that made discrimination in public accommodations unlawful. Because the law covered privately owned businesses, the owners of hotels, entertainment facilities, and transportation companies claimed that Congress had exceeded the authority granted to it by the amendment. The Court, with only one justice dissenting, struck down the statute, holding that any legislation based on the Fourteenth Amendment could regulate only discrimination promoted by state action. Discrimination by private individuals was not covered by the amendment, and, therefore, Congress could not prohibit it through an enforcement statute.

Congress eventually was able to pierce the private discrimination veil by finding a different constitutional grant of power upon which to base the Civil Rights Act of 1964. The most comprehensive civil rights statute ever,

---

[6]See, e.g., *Department of Agriculture v. Moreno* (1973) and **United States v. Windsor** (2013).

[7]Jones v. Alfred Mayer, Inc. (1968).

BOX VII-1

A Sample of Major Civil Rights Acts

Since the end of the Civil War, Congress has enacted scores of civil rights statutes. In what follows we describe a few of the more prominent acts.

Civil Rights Acts of 1866, 1870, 1871, and 1875

Congress passed these laws after the Civil War to provide African Americans with equal political and legal rights, but it later repealed many of them, and the Supreme Court struck down others. For example, in the *Civil Rights Cases* (1883) the Court invalidated the "public accommodation" provision of the 1875 act, which guaranteed "[t]hat citizens of every race and color," regardless of whether they had been slaves, "be entitled to the full and equal enjoyment of the accommodations, advantages, facilities, and privileges of inns, public conveyances on land or water, theaters, and other places of public amusement."

Today, a few major provisions remain from the acts of 1866 and 1871. One makes it a federal crime for any person acting under the authority of a state law to deprive another of any rights protected by the Constitution or by laws of the United States. Another authorizes suits for civil damages against state or local officials by persons whose rights are abridged. Others permit actions against persons who conspire to deprive people of their rights.

Civil Rights Acts of 1957 and 1960

These acts were the first major civil rights laws passed after the 1875 act, and they were largely (but not exclusively) designed to secure voting rights for African Americans. Many viewed them as weak and ultimately ineffective. The 1957 legislation did, however, create the Civil Rights Commission to investigate civil rights violations and make policy recommendations. The 1957 act also established the Civil Rights Division in the Department of Justice and empowered the U.S. attorney general to bring suit against any deprivation of voting rights.

Equal Pay Act of 1963

Passed as an amendment to the Fair Labor Standards Act, this law prohibits discrimination in wages based on sex. It mandates that men and women receive the same pay "for equal work on jobs, the performance of which requires equal skill, effort, and responsibility, and which are performed under similar working conditions." It excluded wages paid pursuant to seniority or merit systems, among other exceptions.

Civil Rights Acts of 1964 and 1968

Considered by some commentators to be one of the most important civil rights laws ever enacted by Congress, the Civil Rights Act of 1964 was designed to eradicate discrimination in many areas of American social, economic, and political life. One major provision of the 1964 act is Title I (on voting rights), which outlaws discrimination in voter registration and outlines procedures for expedited review of voting rights litigation. Title II (on public accommodations) guarantees that "all persons shall be entitled to the full and equal enjoyment of the goods, services, facilities, and privileges, advantages, and accommodations of any place of public accommodation, including hotels, restaurants, and theaters." Titles III and IV cover desegregation of public facilities and education and empower the attorney general to initiate desegregation suits. Title VI prohibits discrimination in projects funded by the federal government. Finally, Title VII guarantees equal opportunity in the employment context by making it illegal, for example, for employers with fifteen or more employees "to fail or refuse to hire or to discharge any individual, or otherwise to discriminate against any individual with respect to his compensation, terms, conditions, or privileges of employment, because of such individual's race, color, religion, sex, or national origin."

As comprehensive as it was, the Civil Rights Act of 1964 did not cover discrimination in housing. Four years later Congress enacted the Civil Rights Act of 1968, which prohibits discrimination in the sale, rental, advertising, and financing of housing based on race, religion, national origin, and (as later amended) sex, handicapped status, or presence of children in a household. Under the law, it is unlawful to refuse to sell a house to a buyer on any of these grounds (race, religion, and so on).

Voting Rights Act of 1965

Another major law, the Voting Rights Act of 1965 (and subsequent renewals) sought to eradicate racial discrimination in voting. For more on this law, see *South Carolina v. Katzenbach,* a 1966 case in which the Supreme Court upheld its constitutionality.

Age Discrimination in Employment Act of 1967

This act bans employment discrimination based on age. It covers individuals who are forty and older and applies to employers with twenty or more employees.

Title IX of the Education Amendments of 1972

This provision bars sex discrimination in federally funded education programs. It covers a range of programs, but it is probably best known for prohibiting sex discrimination in college sports.

Americans with Disabilities Act of 1990

Signed into law by President George H. W. Bush, this law (often called the ADA) sought to eliminate discrimination against individuals with disabilities in the spheres of employment and public services and accommodations. It defines disability as "a physical or mental impairment that substantially limits one or more of the major life activities."

Civil Rights Act of 1991

Congress enacted this law primarily to override several decisions the Supreme Court issued during its 1988 term, all of which made it more difficult for litigants to challenge discriminatory employment practices in the employment context. Legislators thought the Court's decisions had "weakened the scope and effectiveness of Federal civil rights protections" and set out to strengthen them.

Sources: William N. Eskridge Jr., Philip P. Frickey, Elizabeth Garrett and James Brudney, *Cases and Materials on Legislation and Regulation* (St. Paul, MN: West, 2014); Jody Feder, *Federal Civil Rights Statutes: A Primer, CRS Report for Congress,* September 9, 2005.

the law regulated discrimination in employment, education, and public accommodations. It placed restrictions on federal appropriations and programs to ensure that nondiscrimination principles were followed in any activity supported by the U.S. government. The act outlawed discrimination based not only on race but on other factors as well, such as sex, national origin, and religion. Much of what was regulated by the statute was private behavior, including prohibitions of discrimination by restaurants, hotels, and other privately run public accommodations. Rather than using the Fourteenth Amendment, Congress used the commerce clause of Article I. That clause gives the national legislature the power to regulate interstate commerce, and the provisions of the 1964 Civil Rights Act apply to all activities in interstate commerce. The Supreme Court upheld the constitutionality of the law and gave it increased effectiveness by broadly defining what is considered to fall within interstate commerce.[8]

Since then, Congress has expanded the scope of federal regulation over civil rights by passing amendments to the 1964 act and by enacting additional legislation (*see Box VII-1*). For example, the Civil Rights Act of 1968 attempted to remove discrimination in the sale, rental, or financing of housing, and the Americans with Disabilities Act of 1990 extended federal protections to the disabled in employment, public services, and access to public places. As a result of such legislative actions, a large portion of federal civil rights law is based on congressional statutes rather than on constitutional provisions.

Federal civil rights laws provide great opportunities for those who wish to challenge discriminatory behavior. Not only do these statutes regulate private-sector discrimination, but they also frequently impose thresholds of proof that are easier to satisfy than those the Supreme Court requires for constitutional challenges. For example, under the civil rights laws, a worker claiming employment discrimination based on race may not have to establish discriminatory intent (a requirement for a violation of the Constitution) but may instead submit statistical evidence that, regardless of intent, an employer's policies have a racially disparate impact. Because of the growth of civil rights laws, the federal courts today hear many more cases involving alleged violations of civil rights statutes than cases claiming a violation of the Constitution.

---

[8]In *Heart of Atlanta Motel v. United States* (1964), the Supreme Court upheld the public accommodations provisions of the law, thereby giving constitutional approval for Congress to expand civil rights protections by using the commerce power.

THE FIFTEENTH AMENDMENT

The Fifteenth Amendment removed race as a condition by which the right to vote could be denied. Unlike the Thirteenth Amendment, which was almost self-executing, the policy expressed so clearly in the Fifteenth Amendment in 1870 did not become a reality until almost a century later. Stubborn resistance by the southern states denied black citizens full participatory rights. It was not until the 1960s, when the nation renewed its commitment to civil rights, that equality in voting rights was substantially achieved.

The long delay in implementing the principles of the Fifteenth Amendment has several explanations. Although the nation's leaders seemed unshakably committed to equality rights after the Civil War, they soon turned their attention to other matters. Issues ranging from political corruption to the nation's industrialization moved to the top of the political agenda. At the same time, the white power structure of the prewar South began to reassert itself. Although forced to accept the Civil War amendments as a condition of rejoining the Union, the southern states survived Reconstruction and, once freed from the direct supervision of their victors, began to reinstitute discriminatory laws. Slavery was never again seriously considered, but, in its place, racial segregation became the official policy. For years the federal legislative and executive branches showed little interest in pursuing civil rights issues. And, even though the Supreme Court issued several important rulings, the nation did not turn its attention to freedom from discrimination and full participatory rights for all until the civil rights movement gained momentum in the 1960s.

The Fifteenth Amendment extended significant powers to the federal government to preserve fairness and equality in the political process. So, too, did the Nineteenth, Twenty-fourth, and Twenty-sixth Amendments, which, respectively, expanded the electorate by limiting state discrimination based on sex or on the ability to pay a tax and by lowering the voting age. From the enforcement provisions of these four voting rights amendments, Congress has passed a number of statutes ensuring the integrity of the election process. The most important of these is the Voting Rights Act of 1965, which had been strengthened by amendment over the years. This statute provided the machinery for federal enforcement and prosecution of voting rights violations. Its provisions have been the catalyst for significant growth in voter registration rates among segments of the population where political participation historically has been depressed.[9]

Because this book deals with constitutional law, our discussion of the various forms of discrimination focuses on the civil rights guarantees provided in the three Civil War amendments. As you read the cases and narrative to follow, however, keep in mind that in many areas Congress has passed statutes that extend those constitutional provisions to create various legal rights that go well beyond protections included in the Constitution itself.

---

[9]See chapter 20 for more detail on the Voting Rights Act of 1965, including an excerpt of Court's decision in *Shelby County v. Holder* (2013), which invalidated a section of the act.

CHAPTER NINETEEN

DISCRIMINATION

IN AN ADDRESS DELIVERED amid the planning for the bicentennial celebration of the Constitution, Justice Thurgood Marshall said that the document was "defective from the start." He claimed its first words—"We the People"—left out the majority of Americans because the phrase did not include women and blacks. He further alleged:

> These omissions were intentional. . . . The record of the Framers' debates on the slave question is especially clear: The Southern states acceded to the demands of the New England states for giving Congress broad power to regulate commerce in exchange for the right to continue the slave trade. The economic interests of the regions coalesced.

One does not have to agree with Marshall to believe that discrimination has been a difficult and persistent problem for the United States since its beginnings. Although the founders were considered the vanguard of enlightened politics, different treatment based on race, economic status, religious affiliation, and sex was the rule in the colonies, and issues of discrimination have persisted in the country's political agenda throughout the centuries. During the nineteenth century, slavery eroded national unity. Although officially abolished by the Civil War and the constitutional amendments that followed, racial inequity did not disappear. It continued through the Jim Crow era and the organized civil rights struggle, and it still exists today.

Recent years have seen the national spotlight turned on claims of unfair treatment based on sex, sexual orientation, and economic status, among other classifications. Attempts to force government to address these claims have engendered counterclaims by those who fear that a government overly sensitive to the needs of minorities will deprive the majority of its rights. With each new argument, the issues become more complex. This chapter explores the kinds of discrimination that have occurred (and continue to occur) in American society and how the Supreme Court has responded.

We begin with the Fourteenth Amendment's guarantee of equal protection and its historical relation to race discrimination. We then move forward to the framework the Court uses today to analyze claims under the equal protection clause. This discussion amounts to fleshing out the three levels of scrutiny that we introduced in the opener to this part of the book—rational basis, strict, and intermediate—and how the Court applies them to classifications based on race, gender, sexual orientation, and economic status.

RACE DISCRIMINATION AND THE FOUNDATIONS OF EQUAL PROTECTION

The institution of slavery is a blight on the record of a nation that otherwise has led the way in protecting individual rights. From 1619, when the first slaves were brought to Jamestown, to the ratification of the Civil War amendments 250 years later, people of African ancestry were considered an inferior race; they could be bought, sold, and used as personal property. Although some states extended various civil and political rights to emancipated slaves and their descendants, the national Constitution did not recognize African Americans as full citizens. In *Scott v. Sandford* (1857) Chief Justice Roger Brooke Taney, delivering the opinion of the Court, described the prevailing view of blacks when the Constitution was written:

> They had for more than a century before been regarded as beings of an inferior order, and altogether unfit to associate with the white race, either in social or political relations; and so far inferior, that they had no rights which the white man was bound to respect; and that the negro might justly and lawfully be reduced to slavery for his benefit. He was bought and sold, and treated as an ordinary article of merchandise and traffic, whenever a profit could be made by it. This opinion was at that time fixed and universal in the civilized portion of the white race.

Although the Court could have disavowed this view, the majority of justices did not. In *Scott* the majority interpreted the Constitution consistent with what they thought the framers intended: that a black slave could not become a full member of the political community and be entitled to the constitutional privileges of citizens. This interpretation not only undermined the legitimacy of the Court and damaged Taney's reputation forever but also set the stage for the Civil War. After Union victories on the battlefield reunited the country, the Thirteenth, Fourteenth, and Fifteenth Amendments were ratified. These amendments ended slavery, guaranteed equal protection of the laws, and conferred full national citizenship on African Americans (thereby overruling *Scott*).

Congress moved with dispatch to give force to the new amendments, but the Supreme Court did not act with the same level of zeal. Although the justices supported the claims of the newly emancipated blacks in some cases, they did not construe the new amendments broadly, nor did they enthusiastically support new legislation designed to enforce them. In the *Slaughterhouse Cases* (1873), for example, the Court interpreted the Fourteenth Amendment's privileges or immunities clause quite narrowly. A broader view might have provided opportunities for women and blacks to bring cases based on this clause to the Court. In *United States v. Harris* and the *Civil Rights Cases,* both decided in 1883, the justices nullified major provisions of the Ku Klux Klan Act of 1871 and the Civil Rights Act of 1875 for attempting to prevent discriminatory actions by private institutions. It was clear that the battle for legal equality of the races was far from over.

By the end of the nineteenth century, the Supreme Court still had not answered what was perhaps the most important question arising from the Fourteenth Amendment: What is equal protection? As the vitality of the Reconstruction Acts and federal efforts to enforce them gradually waned, the political forces of the old order began to reassert control in the South. From the 1880s to the 1950s, a period known as the Jim Crow era, what progress had been made toward achieving racial equality not only came to a halt but also began to be reversed. The South, where 90 percent of the black minority population lived, began to enact laws that reimposed an inferior legal status on African Americans and required a strict separation of the races. Northern liberals were of little help. With the battle against slavery won, they turned their attention to other issues.

Although the Constitution made it clear that slavery was dead and the right to vote could not be denied on the basis of race, the validity of many other racially based state actions remained unresolved. With more conservative political forces gaining power in Congress, it was left to the Court, still smarting from the *Scott* debacle, to give meaning to the phrase *equal protection of the laws*.

The most important case of this period was *Plessy v. Ferguson* (1896), which forced the justices to confront directly the meaning of equality under the Constitution. At odds were the equal protection clause of the Fourteenth Amendment and a host of segregation statutes by then in force in the southern and border states. While reading *Plessy*, note that the Court uses the reasonableness standard (rational basis test) to interpret the equal protection clause. Ironically, Justice Henry B. Brown, a Lincoln Republican and New Englander who supported the abolitionist movement, wrote the majority opinion upholding the separation standards of the South. Justice John Marshall Harlan, an aristocratic Kentuckian whose family had owned slaves, wrote the lone dissent. Harlan's opinion is considered a classic and one of the most prophetic dissents ever registered.

Plessy v. Ferguson

163 U.S. 537 (1896)
http://caselaw.findlaw.com/us-supreme-court/163/537.html
Vote: 7 (Brown, Field, Fuller, Gray, Peckham, Shiras, White)
    1 (Harlan)

OPINION OF THE COURT: *Brown*

DISSENTING OPINION: *Harlan*

NOT PARTICIPATING: *Brewer*

Following the lead of Florida, Mississippi, and Texas, Louisiana passed a statute in 1890 ordering the separation of the races on all railroads. In response, a group of New Orleans residents of black and mixed-race heritage formed the Citizens Committee to Test the Constitutionality of the Separate Car Law.[1] The railroads, which found compliance with the segregation law costly, supported the group's efforts. Attempts to have the judiciary invalidate the statute were partially successful when the Louisiana Supreme Court struck down the law as it applied to passengers crossing state lines because it placed an unconstitutional burden on interstate commerce. This decision, however, left unanswered the question of segregated travel wholly within the state's borders.

The committee hired Albion Tourgée, a former Union army officer, to lead the legal attack on the railroad segregation statute. Tourgée, who had served as a journalist, lawyer, and judge in North Carolina and New York, was one of the nation's most prominent civil rights advocates. Part of his strategy was to select an individual of mixed-race background to violate the segregation statute as it applied to intrastate travel. Homer Adolph Plessy, who had been active in civil rights efforts in New Orleans for some time, was selected. Plessy described himself as being "of seven-eighths Caucasian and one-eighth African blood."

On June 7, 1892, Plessy bought a first-class rail ticket from New Orleans to Covington, Louisiana. He took a seat in a car reserved for white passengers. Tourgée and the committee had enlisted the cooperation of the railroad to have Plessy arrested for violating the statute. He was taken off the train and held in a New Orleans jail to await trial.

Tourgée moved to block the trial on the ground that the segregation law was in violation of the U.S. Constitution's Thirteenth and Fourteenth Amendments. Judge John Ferguson denied the motion, and appeal was taken to the Louisiana Supreme Court. The state high court, under the leadership of Chief Justice Francis Tillou Nicholls, who, as governor two years earlier, had signed the segregation statute into law, denied Plessy's petition, and the case moved to the U.S. Supreme Court.

Attorney and equal rights activist Albion Tourgée, who argued Homer Plessy's case and lost in the Supreme Court. Justice Harlan's lone dissent said that the Constitution must be color-blind, a phrase suggested by Tourgée's brief.

MR. JUSTICE BROWN DELIVERED THE OPINION OF THE COURT.

This case turns upon the constitutionality of an act of the General Assembly of the State of Louisiana, passed in 1890, providing for separate railway carriages for the white and colored races. . . .

By the Fourteenth Amendment, all persons born or naturalized in the United States, and subject to the jurisdiction thereof, are made citizens of the United States and of the State wherein they reside; and the States are forbidden from making or enforcing any law which shall abridge the privileges or immunities of citizens of the United States, or shall deprive any person of life, liberty or property without due process of law, or deny to any person within their jurisdiction the equal protection of the laws. . . .

The object of the amendment was undoubtedly to enforce the absolute equality of the two races before the law, but in the nature of things it could not have been intended to abolish distinctions based upon color, or to enforce social, as distinguished from political equality, or a commingling of the two races upon terms unsatisfactory to either. Laws permitting, and even requiring, their separation in places where they are liable to be brought into contact do not necessarily imply the inferiority of either race to the other, and have been generally, if not universally, recognized as within the competency of the state legislatures in the exercise of their police power. The most common instance of this is connected with the establishment of separate schools for white and colored children, which has been held to be a valid exercise of the legislative power even by courts of States where the political rights of the colored race have been longest and most earnestly enforced.

One of the earliest of these cases is that of *Roberts v. City of Boston* [1849], in which the Supreme Judicial Court of Massachusetts held that the general school committee of Boston

---

[1]For a more complete description of the facts in this case, see Ellen Holmes Pearson, "Homer Plessy: Validation of Jim Crow," in *100 Americans Making Constitutional History*, ed. Melvin I. Urofsky (Washington, DC: CQ Press, 2004), 159–161.

had power to make provision for the instruction of colored children in separate schools established exclusively for them, and to prohibit their attendance upon the other schools. . . .

Laws forbidding the intermarriage of the two races may be said in a technical sense to interfere with the freedom of contract, and yet have been universally recognized as within the police power of the State.

The distinction between laws interfering with the political equality of the negro and those requiring the separation of the two races in schools, theatres and railway carriages has been frequently drawn by this court. Thus in *Strauder v. West Virginia* [1880] it was held that a law of West Virginia limiting to white male persons, 21 years of age and citizens of the State, the right to sit upon juries, was a discrimination which implied a legal inferiority in civil society, which lessened the security of the right of the colored race, and was a step toward reducing them to a condition of servility. Indeed, the right of a colored man that, in the selection of jurors to pass upon his life, liberty, and property, there shall be no exclusion of his race, and no discrimination against them because of color, has been asserted in a number of cases. . . .

So far, then, as a conflict with the Fourteenth Amendment is concerned, the case reduces itself to the question whether the statute of Louisiana is a reasonable regulation, and with respect to this there must necessarily be a large discretion on the part of the legislature. In determining the question of reasonableness it is at liberty to act with reference to the established usages, customs and traditions of the people, and with a view to the promotion of their comfort, and the preservation of the public peace and good order. Gauged by this standard, we cannot say that a law which authorizes or even requires the separation of the two races in public conveyances is unreasonable, or more obnoxious to the Fourteenth Amendment than the acts of Congress requiring separate schools for colored children in the District of Columbia, the constitutionality of which does not seem to have been questioned, or the corresponding acts of state legislatures.

We consider the underlying fallacy of the plaintiff's argument to consist in the assumption that the enforced separation of the two races stamps the colored race with a badge of inferiority. If this be so, it is not by reason of anything found in the act, but solely because the colored race chooses to put that construction upon it. The argument necessarily assumes that if, as has been more than once the case, and is not unlikely to be so again, the colored race should become the dominant power in the state legislature, and should enact a law in precisely similar terms, it would thereby relegate the white race to an inferior position. We imagine that the white race, at least, would not acquiesce in this assumption. The argument also assumes that social prejudices may be overcome by legislation, and that equal rights cannot be secured to the negro except by an enforced commingling of the two races. We cannot accept this proposition. If the two races are to meet upon terms of social equality, it must be the result of natural affinities, a mutual appreciation of each other's merits and a voluntary consent of individuals. . . . Legislation is powerless to eradicate racial instincts or to abolish distinctions based upon physical differences, and the attempt to do so can only result in accentuating the difficulties of the present situation. If the civil and political rights of both races be equal one cannot be inferior to the other civilly or politically. If one race be inferior to the other socially, the Constitution of the United States cannot put them upon the same plane. . . .

The judgment of the court below is, therefore,

Affirmed.

MR. JUSTICE HARLAN, DISSENTING.

In respect of civil rights, common to all citizens, the Constitution of the United States does not, I think, permit any public authority to know the race of those entitled to be protected in the enjoyment of such rights. Every true man has pride of race, and under appropriate circumstances when the rights of others, his equals before the law, are not to be affected, it is his privilege to express such pride and to take such action based upon it as to him seems proper. But I deny that any legislative body or judicial tribunal may have regard to the race of citizens when the civil rights of those citizens are involved. Indeed, such legislation, as that here in question, is inconsistent not only with that equality of rights which pertains to citizenship, National and State, but with the personal liberty enjoyed by every one within the United States.

The Thirteenth Amendment does not permit the withholding or the deprivation of any right necessarily inhering in freedom. It not only struck down the institution of slavery as previously existing in the United States, but it prevents the imposition of any burdens or disabilities that constitute badges of slavery or servitude. It decreed universal civil freedom in this country. This court has so adjudged. But that amendment having been found inadequate to the protection of the rights of those who had been in slavery, it was followed by the Fourteenth Amendment, which added greatly to the dignity and glory of American citizenship, and to the security of personal liberty. . . . These two amendments, if enforced according to their true intent and meaning, will protect all the civil rights that pertain to freedom and citizenship. Finally, and to the end that no citizen should be denied, on account of his race, the privilege of participating in the political control of his country, it was declared by the Fifteenth Amendment that "the right of citizens of the United States to vote shall not be denied or abridged by the United States or by any State on account of race, color or previous condition of servitude."

These notable additions to the fundamental law were welcomed by the friends of liberty throughout the world. They removed the race line from our governmental systems. They had, as this court has said, a common purpose, namely, to secure "to a race recently emancipated, a race that through many generations have been held in slavery, all the civil rights that the superior race enjoy." . . .

If a State can prescribe, as a rule of civil conduct, that whites and blacks shall not travel as passengers in the same railroad coach, why may it not so regulate the use of the streets of its cities and towns as to compel white citizens to keep on one side of a street and black citizens to keep on the other? Why may it not, upon like grounds, punish whites and blacks who ride together in street cars or in open vehicles on a public road or street? Why may it not require sheriffs to assign whites to one side of a courtroom and blacks to the other? And why may it not also prohibit the commingling of the two races in the galleries of legislative halls or in public assemblages convened for the consideration of the political questions of the day? Further, if this statute of Louisiana is consistent with the personal liberty of citizens, why may not the State require the separation in railroad coaches of native and naturalized citizens of the United States, or of Protestants and Roman Catholics? . . .

The white race deems itself to be the dominant race in this country. And so it is, in prestige, in achievements, in education, in wealth and in power. So, I doubt not, it will continue to be for all time, if it remains true to its great heritage and holds fast to the principles of constitutional liberty. But in view of the Constitution, in the eye of the law, there is in this country no superior, dominant, ruling class of citizens. There is no caste here. Our Constitution is color-blind, and neither knows nor tolerates classes among citizens. In respect of civil rights, all citizens are equal before the law. The humblest is the peer of the most powerful. The law regards man as man, and takes no account of his surroundings or of his color when his civil rights as guaranteed by the supreme law of the land are involved. It is, therefore, to be regretted that this high tribunal, the final expositor of the fundamental law of the land, has reached the conclusion that it is competent for a State to regulate the enjoyment by citizens of their civil rights solely upon the basis of race.

In my opinion, the judgment this day rendered will, in time, prove to be quite as pernicious as the decision made by this tribunal in the *Dred Scott* case. . . .

I am of opinion that the statute of Louisiana is inconsistent with the personal liberty of citizens, white and black, in that State, and hostile to both the spirit and letter of the Constitution of the United States. If laws of like character should be enacted in the several States of the Union, the effect would be in the highest degree mischievous. Slavery, as an institution tolerated by law, would, it is true, have disappeared from our country, but there would remain a power in the States, by sinister legislation, to interfere with the full enjoyment of the blessings of freedom; to regulate civil rights, common to all citizens, upon the basis of race; and to place in a condition of legal inferiority a large body of American citizens, now constituting a part of the political community called the People of the United States, for whom, and by whom through representatives, our government is administered. Such a system is inconsistent with the guarantee given by the Constitution to each State of a republican form of government, and may be stricken down by Congressional action, or by the courts in the discharge of their solemn duty to maintain the supreme law of the land, anything in the constitution or laws of any State to the contrary notwithstanding.

For the reason stated, I am constrained to withhold my assent from the opinion and judgment of the majority.

The *Plessy* decision's "separate but equal" doctrine ushered in full-scale segregation in the southern and border states. According to the Court, separation did not constitute inequality under the Fourteenth Amendment; if the facilities and opportunities were somewhat similar, the equal protection clause permitted the separation of the races. Encouraged by the ruling, the legislatures of the South passed a wide variety of statutes to keep blacks segregated from the white population. The segregation laws affected transportation, schools, hospitals, parks, public restrooms and water fountains, libraries, cemeteries, recreational facilities, hotels, restaurants, and almost every other public and commercial facility. These laws, coupled with segregated private lives, inevitably resulted in two separate societies.

During the first half of the twentieth century, the separate but equal doctrine dominated race relations law. The southern states continued to pass and enforce segregationist laws, largely insulated from legal attack. Over the years, however, it became clear that the "equality" part of the separate but equal doctrine was being ignored.

As the inequality of segregated public facilities grew worse, the disadvantages of the black population increased. The disparities extended to almost every area of life, but they were felt most keenly in education. Whites and blacks were given access to public schools, but the black schools, at all levels, received support and funding far inferior to that of the white institutions.

These conditions spurred the growth of civil rights groups dedicated to eradicating segregation. None was more prominent than the National Association for the Advancement of Colored People (NAACP) and its affiliate, the Legal Defense and Educational Fund (commonly referred to as the Legal Defense Fund, or LDF). Thurgood Marshall, who had been associated with the NAACP since he graduated first in his class at Howard University Law School, became the head of the LDF in 1940 and initiated a twenty-year campaign in the courts to win equal rights for black Americans. During those years, Marshall and his staff won substantial victories in the Supreme Court in civil rights cases concerning

Under the rule of law established in *Plessy v. Ferguson* (1896), states could require racial separation if facilities for blacks and whites were of equal quality. In public education, black schools were rarely equal to those reserved for whites.

housing, voting rights, public education, employment, and public accommodations. Marshall also served as a judge on the court of appeals and as U.S. solicitor general before being appointed in 1967 to the Supreme Court. He was the first African American justice.

When Marshall took over leadership of the LDF, the rule set in *Plessy* was already on shaky ground. In 1938 the Court had handed segregationist forces a significant defeat in **Missouri ex rel. Gaines v. Canada.** Lloyd Gaines, a Missouri resident who had graduated from the all-black Lincoln University, applied for admission to the University of Missouri's law school. He was denied admission because of his race. Missouri did not have a law school for its black citizens, so the state offered to finance the education of qualified black students who would attend law school in a neighboring state that did not have segregationist policies. The Supreme Court concluded, in a 7–2 vote, that the Missouri plan to provide educational opportunities out of state did not meet the obligations imposed by the equal protection clause.

The Supreme Court's message was reinforced in 1948 when, in two cases, *Sipuel v. Board of Regents* and

Fisher v. Hurst, the justices unanimously demanded that states provide equal facilities for blacks pursuing a legal education. Two years later the justices followed up with **Sweatt v. Painter**, in which the Court ruled that the University of Texas had violated the Constitution when its law school refused to admit a black applicant. The state had argued that its newly created law school for African Americans met the separate but equal requirement and allowed the state to continue to run the University of Texas law school on a whites-only basis. But the justices concluded that quality differences between the two schools were such that the black law school did not provide an education equal to that of the white law school. The same day the Court decided *Sweatt*, it also issued a ruling in **McLaurin v. Oklahoma State Regents for Higher Education** (1950), which took another step toward racial equality in higher education. Oklahoma, to comply with court orders, admitted some African American students to graduate programs at the University of Oklahoma, but the university kept the minority students segregated in special areas of classrooms, libraries, and dining halls. The Supreme Court unanimously found this segregated system in violation of the equal protection clause.[2]

By the early 1950s conditions were ripe for a final assault on the half-century-old separate but equal doctrine. Civil rights groups continued to marshal legal arguments and political support to eliminate segregation. Legal challenges to a wide array of discriminatory laws were filed throughout the country, and the Justice Department under President Harry S. Truman supported these efforts. The Supreme Court, through its unanimous rulings in favor of racial equality in higher education, appeared on the verge of seriously considering an end to *Plessy*. In addition, an important leadership change had occurred on the Court. Chief Justice Fred Vinson died on September 8, 1953, and was replaced by Earl Warren, a former governor of California, who was much more comfortable with activist judicial policies than was his predecessor.

All these factors combined to produce *Brown v. Board of Education of Topeka* (1954), which many consider to be the Supreme Court's most significant decision of the twentieth century. Unlike earlier civil rights cases that involved relatively small professional and graduate education programs, the *Brown* case challenged official racial segregation in the nation's primary and secondary public schools. The decision affected thousands of school districts concentrated primarily in the southern and border states. Moreover, it was apparent to all that the precedent to be set for public education would be extended to other areas as well.

As you read Warren's opinion for a unanimous Court, note how the concept of equality has changed. No longer does the Court examine only physical facilities and tangible items such as buildings, libraries, teacher qualifications, and funding levels; instead, it emphasizes the intangible negative impact of racial segregation on children. Warren's opinion includes a footnote listing social science references as authorities for his arguments. The opinion was criticized for citing sociological and psychological studies to support the Court's conclusions rather than confining the analysis exclusively to legal arguments. Are these criticisms valid? Should the Court take social science evidence into account in arriving at constitutional decisions? Note how similar Warren's opinion is to Justice Harlan's lone dissent in *Plessy*.

---

[2]For a discussion of the Supreme Court's decisions leading up to *Brown v. Board of Education of Topeka*, see Richard Kluger, *Simple Justice*, rev. ed. (New York: Knopf, 2004).

Brown v. Board of Education of Topeka

347 U.S. 483 (1954)
http://caselaw.findlaw.com/us-supreme-court/347/483.html
Vote: 9 (Black, Burton, Clark, Douglas, Frankfurter, Jackson, Minton, Reed, Warren)
    0

OPINION OF THE COURT: *Warren*

The Court consolidated five cases involving similar issues for consideration at the same time; *Brown v. Board of Education* was one of these cases. As part of the total desegregation litigation strategy orchestrated by Marshall and funded by the NAACP, these cases challenged the segregated public schools of Delaware, Kansas, South Carolina, Virginia, and the District of Columbia. The most prominent lawyers in the civil rights movement, Spottswood W. Robinson III, Louis Redding, Jack Greenberg, Constance Baker Motley, Robert L. Carter, and James M. Nabrit Jr., prepared them. As Marshall had expected, the suits were unsuccessful at the trial level, with the lower courts relying on *Plessy* as precedent. The leading lawyer for the states was John W. Davis, a prominent constitutional attorney who had been a Democratic candidate for president in 1924. (Davis had reportedly once been offered a nomination to the Court by President Warren G. Harding.)

Linda Carol Brown was an eight-year-old black girl whose father, Oliver Brown, was an assistant pastor of a Topeka church. The Browns lived in a predominantly white neighborhood only a short distance from an elementary school. Under Kansas law, cities with populations of more than fifteen thousand were permitted to administer racially segregated schools, and the Topeka Board of Education required its elementary schools to be racially divided. The Browns did not want their daughter to be sent to the school reserved for black students. It was far from home, and they considered the trip dangerous. In addition, their neighborhood school was a good one, and the Browns wanted their daughter to receive an integrated education. They filed suit challenging the segregated school system as violating their daughter's rights under the equal protection clause of the Fourteenth Amendment.

The *Brown* appeal was joined by those from the other four suits, and the cases were argued in December 1952. The following June, the Court asked the cases to be reargued in December 1953, with special emphasis to be placed on a series of questions dealing with the history and meaning of the Fourteenth Amendment. This delay also allowed the newly appointed Earl Warren to participate fully in the decision. Six months later, on May 17, 1954, the Court issued its ruling.

Pictured on the steps of the U.S. Supreme Court are the NAACP Legal Defense Fund lawyers who argued the school segregation cases that resulted in the May 17, 1954, *Brown v. Board of Education* precedent. Left to right: Howard Jenkins, James M. Nabrit Jr., Spottswood W. Robinson III, Frank Reeves, Jack Greenberg, Special Counsel Thurgood Marshall, Louis Redding, U. Simpson Tate, and George E. C. Hayes. Missing from the photograph is Robert L. Carter, who argued the Topeka, Kansas, case.

MR. CHIEF JUSTICE WARREN DELIVERED THE OPINION OF THE COURT.

In each of the cases, minors of the Negro race, through their legal representatives, seek the aid of the courts in obtaining admission to the public schools of their community on a nonsegregated basis. In each instance, they had been denied admission to schools attended by white children under laws requiring or permitting segregation according to race. This segregation was alleged to deprive the plaintiffs of the equal protection of the laws under the Fourteenth Amendment. . . .

The plaintiffs contend that segregated public schools are not "equal" and cannot be made "equal," and that hence they are deprived of the equal protection of the laws. Because of the obvious importance of the question presented, the Court took jurisdiction. Argument was heard in the 1952 Term, and reargument was heard this Term on certain questions propounded by the Court.

Reargument was largely devoted to the circumstances surrounding the adoption of the Fourteenth Amendment in 1868. It covered exhaustively consideration of the Amendment in Congress, ratification by the states, then existing practices in racial segregation, and the views of proponents and opponents of the Amendment. This discussion and our own investigation convince us that, although these sources cast some light, it is not enough to resolve the problem with which we are faced. At best, they are inconclusive. . . .

An additional reason for the inconclusive nature of the Amendment's history, with respect to segregated schools, is the status of public education at that time. In the South, the movement toward free common schools, supported by general taxation, had not yet taken hold. Education of white children was largely in the hands of private groups. Education of Negroes was almost nonexistent, and practically all of the race were illiterate. In fact, any education of Negroes was forbidden by law in some states. Today, in contrast, many Negroes have achieved outstanding success in

This photograph of Linda Brown, plaintiff in *Brown v. Board of Education*, was taken in 1952, when she was nine years old.

AP Photo

the arts and sciences as well as in the business and professional world. It is true that public school education at the time of the Amendment had advanced further in the North, but the effect of the Amendment on Northern States was generally ignored in the congressional debates. Even in the North, the conditions of public education did not approximate those existing today. The curriculum was usually rudimentary; ungraded schools were common in rural areas; the school term was but three months a year in many states; and compulsory school attendance was virtually unknown. As a consequence, it is not surprising that there should be so little in the history of the Fourteenth Amendment relating to its intended effect on public education.

In the first cases in this Court construing the Fourteenth Amendment, decided shortly after its adoption, the Court interpreted it as proscribing all state-imposed discriminations against the Negro race. The doctrine of "separate but equal" did not make its appearance in this Court until 1896 in the case of *Plessy v. Ferguson*, involving not education but transportation. American courts have since labored with the doctrine for over half a century. . . .

Here, unlike *Sweatt v. Painter,* there are findings below that the Negro and white schools involved have been equalized, or are being equalized, with respect to buildings, curricula, qualifications and salaries of teachers, and other "tangible" factors. Our decision, therefore, cannot turn on merely a comparison of these tangible factors in the Negro and white schools involved in each of the cases. We must look instead to the effect of segregation itself on public education.

In approaching this problem, we cannot turn the clock back to 1868 when the Amendment was adopted, or even to 1896 when *Plessy v. Ferguson* was written. We must consider public education in the light of its full development and its present place in American life throughout the Nation. Only in this way can it be determined if segregation in public schools deprives these plaintiffs of the equal protection of the laws.

Today, education is perhaps the most important function of state and local governments. Compulsory school attendance laws and the great expenditures for education both demonstrate our recognition of the importance of education to our democratic society. It is required in the performance of our most basic public responsibilities, even service in the armed forces. It is the very foundation of good citizenship. Today it is a principal instrument in awakening the child to cultural values, in preparing him for later professional training, and in helping him to adjust normally to his environment. In these days, it is doubtful that any child may reasonably be expected to succeed in life if he is denied the opportunity of an education. Such an opportunity, where the state has undertaken to provide it, is a right which must be made available to all on equal terms.

We come then to the question presented: Does segregation of children in public schools solely on the basis of race, even though the physical facilities and other "tangible" factors may be equal, deprive the children of the minority group of equal educational opportunities? We believe that it does.

In *Sweatt v. Painter,* in finding that a segregated law school of Negroes could not provide them equal educational opportunities, this Court relied in large part on "those qualities which are incapable of objective measurement but which make for greatness in a law school." In *McLaurin v. Oklahoma State Regents,* the Court, in requiring that a Negro admitted to a white graduate school be treated like all other students, again resorted to intangible considerations: " . . . his ability to study, to engage in discussions and exchange views with other students, and, in general, to learn his profession." Such considerations apply with added force to children in grade and high schools. To separate them from others of similar age and qualifications solely because of their race generates a feeling of inferiority as to their status in the community that may affect their hearts and minds in a way unlikely ever to be undone. The effect of this separation on their educational opportunities was well stated by a finding in the Kansas case by a court which nevertheless felt compelled to rule against the Negro plaintiffs:

> Segregation of white and colored children in public schools has a detrimental effect upon the colored children. The impact is greater when it has the sanction of the law; for the policy of separating the races is usually interpreted as denoting the inferiority of the negro group. A sense of inferiority affects the motivation of a child to learn. Segregation with the sanction of law, therefore, has a tendency to [retard] the educational and mental development of negro children and to deprive them of some of the benefits they would receive in a racial[ly] integrated school system.

Whatever may have been the extent of psychological knowledge at the time of *Plessy v. Ferguson,* this finding is amply supported by modern authority.* Any language in *Plessy v. Ferguson* contrary to this finding is rejected.

We conclude that in the field of public education the doctrine of "separate but equal" has no place. Separate educational facilities are inherently unequal. Therefore, we hold that the plaintiffs and others similarly situated for whom the actions have been brought are, by reason of the segregation complained of, deprived of the equal protection of the laws guaranteed by the Fourteenth Amendment. . . .

It is so ordered.

As is typical of many Supreme Court litigants, Linda Brown did not personally benefit from winning her case *(see Box 19-1).* Implementation of the *Brown* decision faced many barriers. Of obvious importance to the Court was public acceptance of the ruling. The Court has no formal enforcement powers, and the justices expected resistance, especially in the South. Chief Justice Warren went to great pains to obtain a unanimous vote and to unite the Court in a single opinion, written by him, demonstrating that the justices wanted to speak with all the

authority they could muster in the hopes of encouraging voluntary compliance.

The justices clearly realized that setting the constitutional standard was one thing, but gaining compliance with it was quite another. After issuing its ruling in *Brown*, the Court asked the parties to return the next year to argue the question of remedies. That is, once the segregationist policies were declared unconstitutional, how would the discriminatory system be dismantled? In **Brown v. Board of Education** (1955), commonly referred to as *Brown II*, the justices held that desegregation of the public schools must occur "with all deliberate speed." This rather ambiguous standard recognized that not all districts could be placed on the same timetable. The extent of segregation, the proportion of minority students, the size of the district, the district's resources, and other factors would have to be considered in the development of desegregation plans. Important to note is that the justices gave primary responsibility to the federal district courts to monitor the actions taken by local school boards to implement the *Brown* mandate.

The post-*Brown* era was marked by massive resistance to desegregation, especially in the South. School board members, most of whom were elected officials, did not pursue the implementation of *Brown* gladly. Federal district judges were often called upon to demand that school officials comply with the ruling.[3] Efforts to desegregate the schools were periodically marked by violence, and the mobilization of the National Guard and federal troops was sometimes necessary to enforce *Brown* in a reluctant region.

For the remaining years of the Warren Court, the justices held steadfast in their desegregation goals. In **Cooper v. Aaron** (1958) the Court responded firmly to popular resistance in Arkansas by declaring that violence or threats of violence would not be allowed to slow the progress toward full desegregation. In **Griffin v. Prince Edward County School Board** (1964) the Court stopped a Virginia plan to close down public schools rather than integrate them. In **Green v. School Board of New Kent County** (1968) the justices struck down a "freedom of choice" plan as failing to bring about a nondiscriminatory school system. By the mid-1960s the justices had begun to lose patience. Justice Hugo Black remarked in his opinion for the Court in *Griffin* that "there has been entirely too much deliberation and not enough speed" in enforcing *Brown*'s desegregation mandate.

---

*K. B. Clark, *Effect of Prejudice and Discrimination on Personality Development* (Midcentury White House Conference on Children and Youth, 1950); Witmer and Kotinsky, *Personality in the Making* (1952), c. VI; Deutscher and Chein, The Psychological Effects of Enforced Segregation: A Survey of Social Science Opinion, 26 *J. Psychol.* 259 (1948); Chein, What Are the Psychological Effects of Segregation Under Conditions of Equal Facilities? 3 *Int. J. Opinion and Attitude Res.* 229 (1949); Brameld, Educational Costs, in *Discrimination and National Welfare* (MacIver, ed., 1949), 44–48; Frazier, *The Negro in the United States* (1949), 674–681. And see generally Myrdal, *An American Dilemma* (1944).

[3]See J. W. Peltason, *Fifty-eight Lonely Men* (Urbana: University of Illinois Press, 1961); J. Harvie Wilkinson III, *The Supreme Court from* Brown *to* Bakke (New York: Oxford University Press, 1979).

BOX 19-1

One Child's Simple Justice

Linda Brown Buckner was eight years old in 1951 when her father, Oliver, included her in a lawsuit to desegregate public schools that led to the Supreme Court's landmark *Brown v. Board of Education* decision in 1954.

"I was just starting school when the local NAACP was recruiting people to join its case. Topeka had eighteen elementary schools for whites and four for African Americans. The closest school to my family was four blocks away, the Sumner School. But I went to Monroe Elementary School, which was two and a half miles across town. Often, I came home crying because it was so cold waiting for the bus.

"My father hadn't been involved with the NAACP, but he was upset with the distance I had to go. One of his childhood friends was Charles Scott, one of the attorneys for the case, and Dad agreed to try to enroll me at the Sumner School. Dad's name wasn't first alphabetically, and my sister Cheryl always suspected there was sexism involved in his name coming first in the court records: among the twelve other plaintiffs, he was the only man.

"The day the decision was handed down, my mother was home and heard it on the radio. The news was shared with the family, and there was a rally that evening at the Monroe School. But I never did go to the Sumner School. That fall I went to the junior-high school, which had been integrated in Topeka since 1879."

Source: U.S. News and World Report, L.P., 1993. Reprinted with permission.

In short, the justices of the Warren Court tried to make it clear that dilatory tactics would not be tolerated.[4] Yet they continued. The freedom given to district judges to approve desegregation plans led to a wide variety of schemes, some of which school officials criticized for going too far and some of which civil rights advocates disparaged for not going far enough. The specific methods of integration commonly were attacked for exceeding the powers of the district courts.

Clearing up the confusion was left to the Burger Court. In **Swann v. Charlotte-Mecklenburg County Board of Education** (1971) it approved a wide array of desegregation tools, including mandatory busing of students, teacher transfers, court supervision of spending and new construction, and the altering of attendance zones. *Swann* gave wide latitude to district judges to fashion desegregation programs appropriate to local conditions. But the Court made clear that such remedial actions could be imposed in a school district only if it could be proven that a violation of the Constitution had occurred there. This requirement made it difficult to impose effective desegregation plans in metropolitan areas with multiple school districts.[5]

The discrimination decisions of the Supreme Court in the post-*Brown* era have not focused exclusively on public education. Instead, the Court has regularly confronted questions of racial discrimination over a wide array of issues. The death of the separate but equal doctrine had widespread ramifications for American society because many states and local governments had laws that mandated segregated facilities. Other rules and restrictions, while not segregating the races, discriminated directly or indirectly against African Americans. Civil rights groups launched attacks on many of these discriminatory policies, as did the Justice Department.

As such challenges were brought before the Court, the justices faithfully applied the *Brown* precedent. If a case presented intentional discrimination by the government, the justices were not reluctant to declare that the Constitution had been violated. The Court presumed that racial classifications used to discriminate against African Americans violated the equal protection clause of the Fourteenth Amendment (state government discrimination) or the due process clause of the Fifth (federal government discrimination). Attempts to justify such actions faced a heavy burden of proof. Because race is a suspect classification, black litigants enjoyed the advantages of the strict scrutiny test. These factors made it difficult for federal, state, and local governments to withstand the attacks made against discriminatory

---

[4]See *Alexander v. Holmes Board of Education* (1969).

[5]See *Milliken v. Bradley* (1974).

policies and practices. One by one, the legal barriers between the races fell.

Since 1954 the Court has developed constitutional doctrine in many areas related to race. Some of these, such as the civil rights protesters' freedom of expression, we have already discussed; others, such as affirmative action and voting rights, will be covered in this chapter and the next. The justices have not always agreed, especially on how to eliminate the effects of past discrimination. But throughout the Court's post-*Brown* history, the justices have said consistently that the Constitution does not permit government classifications that penalize historically disadvantaged racial minorities or that impose distinctions that imply the racial inferiority of any group.

MODERN-DAY TREATMENT OF EQUAL PROTECTION CLAIMS

Brown v. Board of Education brought a legal conclusion to the separate-but-equal era, but it raised many questions about how the Court would treat other classifications— for example, those based on gender and sexual orientation.

Over time, the Court has established a three-tier framework for determining whether the government has engaged in unconstitutional discrimination. Figure 19-1 depicts this framework (see also Part VII Opener). Note that the triggering question in all equal protection cases is whether the government's law or action creates a classification that denies a right to some people while giving it to others—for example, a law that says only men can apply to become firefighters. In this example, the classification is based on gender.

Ultimately, the government must justify its classification, though as you can see from the boxes at the very bottom of the figure, its task will be harder or easier depending on the type of inequality. For almost all classifications—including those based on age and intelligence—the Court will presume that the law creating the classification is valid as long as it is rationally related to a legitimate state interest. If the classification involves race or national origin, the Court will apply the strict scrutiny test, and if it involves gender,[6] the

intermediate (or heightened) scrutiny test. Either way, the government will have a more difficult time justifying its line; it will have to show that its classification serves a compelling or important government interest.

Because there is only one equal protection clause, you might be wondering why the contemporary Court has developed three different tests to evaluate claims of discrimination. The genesis seems to lie in a footnote— Footnote Four in **United States v. Carolene Products Co.** (1938). After noting that the Court would give high deference to the government in economic cases in which classifications were challenged as violations of the due process clause or equal protection clause, the Court dropped a footnote, which read in part:

> [We need not] enquire whether similar considerations enter into the review of statutes directed at particular religious, or national or racial minorities: whether prejudice against discrete and insular minorities may be a special condition, which tends seriously to curtail the operation of those political processes ordinarily to be relied upon to protect minorities, and which may call for a correspondingly more searching judicial inquiry.

These few sentences contain some important ideas. First, certain groups are more likely than others to be the target of discrimination. Perhaps they have been historically subjected to prejudice or animus. Perhaps they bear discrete or immutable characteristics (for example, their skin color), which makes them easier to target for discriminatory treatment. Or perhaps they are insular, meaning that they do not or cannot disperse within society.[7] All in all, these groups may be politically powerless to generate change through normal democratic channels. This takes us to the second idea: because of these difficulties and obstacles, courts may not be able to trust legislatures (as they normally would) to draw classifications that reflect legitimate interests rather than bad motive in the form of prejudice.

Over time, the Court transformed these ideas into the strict scrutiny test. Only by forcing the government

---

[6]Illegitimacy also falls into this category. See, e.g., *Lalli v. Lalli* (1978), a challenge to a New York law that required illegitimate children to provide a proof of paternity before they could inherit from their fathers who died intestate. Legitimate children did not have to meet the same requirement. The Court applied an intermediate standard but nonetheless found that state's interest in providing "for the just and orderly disposition of property at death" justified the classification.

[7]These are factors that help the Court to decide on the level of scrutiny that it will apply. It has added others with time—for example, whether the characteristic prompting the discrimination is relevant to an individual's "ability to perform or contribute to society." This consideration led the Court to reject heightened scrutiny for "mentally retarded persons" (see *City of Cleburne v. Cleburne Living Center* [1985]) and for classifications based on age (see *Massachusetts Board of Retirement v. Murgia* [1976]).

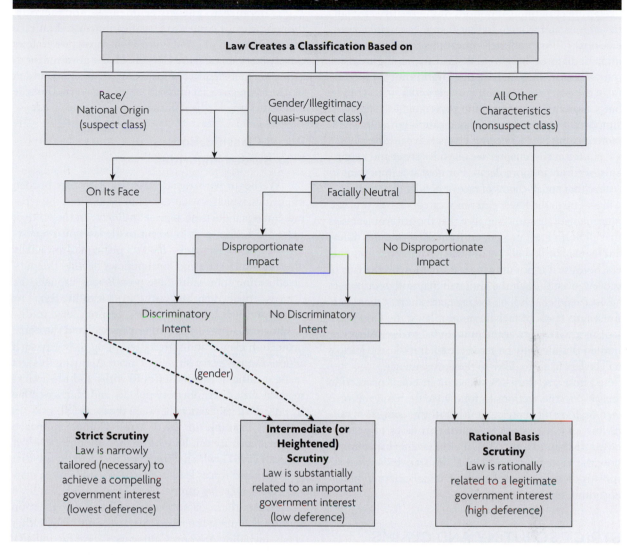

Figure 19-1 The Court's Framework for Analyzing Equal Protection Claims

Law Creates a Classification Based on

- Race/National Origin (suspect class)
- Gender/Illegitimacy (quasi-suspect class)
- All Other Characteristics (nonsuspect class)

On Its Face

Facially Neutral

Disproportionate Impact

No Disproportionate Impact

Discriminatory Intent

No Discriminatory Intent

(gender)

Strict Scrutiny
Law is narrowly tailored (necessary) to achieve a compelling government interest (lowest deference)

Intermediate (or Heightened) Scrutiny
Law is substantially related to an important government interest (low deference)

Rational Basis Scrutiny
Law is rationally related to a legitimate government interest (high deference)

Note: The authors thank Rebecca Brown, from whom they adapted this chart.

to show that its classification is narrowly tailored—necessary—to achieve a compelling interest can the Court be sure that the government's line does not reflect animus to a group that has, historically, faced discrimination.

Based on the material we just considered on the country's long history of race discrimination and on the characteristics identified in Footnote Four, you can see why the Court applies strict scrutiny to racial classifications. The justices have said that race and national origin are "factors . . . so seldom relevant to the achievement of any legitimate state interest" that they likely "reflect prejudice and antipathy—a view that those in the burdened class are not as worthy or deserving as others."[8]

Other groups have asked the Court to apply strict scrutiny to laws discriminating against them. Although the justices have resisted, they also have recognized that society has unfairly disadvantaged at least some other groups even if they do not meet all the factors identified in Footnote Four. Gender classifications fall into this category, not because women are "discrete and insular

---

[8]*Cleburne v. Cleburne Living Center* (1985).

minorities," but because "statutes distributing benefits and burdens between the sexes in different ways very likely reflect outmoded notions of the relative capabilities of men and women [rather than meaningful considerations]."[9] For gender classifications the Court applies intermediate or heightened scrutiny, as Figure 19-1 shows. Under this standard, the Court is not as mistrustful of the government's motive as it is under strict scrutiny, but it nonetheless requires the government to supply an "important" reason for the classification it has drawn or, more recently, an "exceedingly persuasive justification."[10]

Later in this chapter we consider strict and heightened scrutiny in more detail. For now, it is important to realize that not all claims of race or gender discrimination will end up in the lower deference categories of strict and intermediate scrutiny. Suppose that the government says that all firefighters must be six feet tall. This seems different than a law that allows only men to become firefighters, because it is not drawing a distinction on the face of the law, even though the law itself may still discriminate against women who, on average, are shorter than men. For these kinds of facially neutral laws, the Court will look to see if the government intended to discriminate or burden the allegedly targeted group. If it did, the justices will be less likely to defer to the government.

These are the basic steps in an equal protection analysis. In the sections to follow, we flesh out this process by looking at strict scrutiny in the context of race claims and intermediate scrutiny in cases of gender-based discrimination.[11] You'll also have a chance to see how the Court applies rational basis analysis when we turn to discrimination based on sexual orientation and economic status.

STRICT SCRUTINY AND CLAIMS OF RACE DISCRIMINATION

Under rational basis scrutiny the Court will usually defer to whatever classification the government has established. There are exceptions, notably *Romer v. Evans*, which involved sexual orientation. As we'll see later, the Court struck down the state amendment at issue in the case. But *Romer* is an exception, not the rule. It is not usual for the Court to invalidate classifications that it examines under the rational basis test.

Deference to the government is not the rule, though, when it comes to classifications based on race and national origin. As Figure 19-1 shows, when laws classify based on race, the Court holds the government to a much higher standard. This is true of laws that burden or disadvantage racial minorities, and today it is also true of laws designed to benefit them.

Racial Classifications That Burden Minorities

We begin with racial classifications that burden minorities, which is what the Court said about the separate but equal doctrine at issue in *Brown*. In the wake of these 1954 cases, parties began to file lawsuits requesting that the courts apply *Brown*'s principles to racially discriminatory state and local policies beyond the public education sphere. In these post-*Brown* disputes, the justices remained faithful to the strict scrutiny test. The Court presumed that racial classifications used to discriminate against African Americans violated the equal protection clause, and states attempting to justify such actions faced a heavy burden of proof. Applying this test made it difficult for the states to withstand the attacks made against discriminatory policies and practices. One by one, the legal barriers between the races fell.

One example of the Warren Court's approach to racial equality can be seen in the ruling in *Loving v. Virginia* (1967), which concerned that part of life that segregationist forces least wanted to see integrated: marriage. When *Loving* came to the Court, sixteen states, all of them southern or border states, had miscegenation statutes that made interracial marriages unlawful. Other states, including Arizona, California, Colorado, Indiana, and Oregon, had only recently repealed similar laws. The *Loving* case presents an interesting twist on the equality issue: Are blacks and whites treated equally if both are prohibited from marrying outside their respective races?

Loving v. Virginia

388 U.S. 1 (1967)
http://caselaw.findlaw.com/us-supreme-court/388/1.html
*Oral arguments available at https://www.oyez.org/
   cases/1966/395*
Vote: 9 (Black, Brennan, Clark, Douglas, Fortas, Harlan, Stewart,
   Warren, White)
   0

---

[9]Ibid.

[10]See *United States v. Virginia* (1996), excerpted later in the chapter.

[11]For examples of rational basis scrutiny, see *New York City Transit Authority v. Beazer* (1979) and *Cleburne v. Cleburne Living Center* (1985).

OPINION OF THE COURT: *Warren*

CONCURRING OPINION: *Stewart*

In June 1958, two Virginia residents, Mildred Jeter, a black woman, and Richard Loving, a white man, were married in Washington, D.C. They returned to Virginia to live, but later that year they were charged with evading the state's anti-miscegenation law by leaving the state to be married with the intent to return. The crime called for a sentence of up to five years in the state penitentiary. The Lovings pleaded guilty to the charge and were each sentenced to one year in jail. The judge suspended the sentences on condition that the Lovings leave Virginia and not return for twenty-five years. In handing down the sentence, the judge said:

> Almighty God created the races white, black, yellow, malay and red, and he placed them on separate continents. And but for the interference with his arrangement there would be no cause for such marriages. The fact that he separated the races shows that he did not intend for the races to mix.

The Lovings moved to Washington. In 1963, with the help of an American Civil Liberties Union attorney, they initiated a suit to have the sentence set aside on the ground that it violated their rights under the equal protection clause of the Fourteenth Amendment. The Virginia Supreme Court upheld the constitutionality of the law and affirmed the original convictions.

MR. CHIEF JUSTICE WARREN DELIVERED THE OPINION OF THE COURT.

This case presents a constitutional question never addressed by this Court: whether a statutory scheme adopted by the State of Virginia to prevent marriages between persons solely on the basis of racial classifications violates the Equal Protection and Due Process Clauses of the Fourteenth Amendment. For reasons which seem to us to reflect the central meaning of those constitutional commands, we conclude that these statutes cannot stand consistently with the Fourteenth Amendment. . . .

While the state court is no doubt correct in asserting that marriage is a social relation subject to the State's police power, the State does not contend in its argument before this Court that its powers to regulate marriage are unlimited notwithstanding the commands of the Fourteenth Amendment. Instead, the State argues that the meaning of the Equal Protection Clause, as illuminated by the statements of the Framers, is only that state penal laws containing an interracial element as part of the definition of the offense must apply equally to whites and Negroes in the sense that members of each race are punished to the same degree. Thus, the State contends that, because its miscegenation statutes punish equally both the white and the Negro participants in an interracial marriage, these statutes, despite their reliance on racial classifications, do not constitute an invidious discrimination based upon race. The second argument advanced by the State assumes the validity of its equal application theory. The argument is that, if the Equal Protection Clause does not outlaw miscegenation statutes because of their reliance on racial classifications, the question of constitutionality would thus become whether there was any rational basis for a State to treat interracial marriages differently from other marriages. On this question, the State argues, the scientific evidence is substantially in doubt and, consequently, this Court should defer to the wisdom of the state legislature in adopting its policy of discouraging interracial marriages.

Because we reject the notion that the mere "equal application" of a statute containing racial classifications is enough to remove the classifications from the Fourteenth Amendment's proscription of all invidious racial discriminations, we do not accept the State's contention that these statutes should be upheld if there is any possible basis for concluding that they serve a rational purpose. . . . In the case at bar, we deal with statutes containing racial classifications, and the fact of equal application does not immunize the statute from the very heavy burden of justification which the Fourteenth Amendment has traditionally required of state statutes drawn according to race. . . .

The State finds support for its "equal application" theory in the decision of the Court in *Pace v. Alabama* (1883). In that case, the Court upheld a conviction under an Alabama statute forbidding adultery or fornication between a white person and a Negro which imposed a greater penalty than that of a statute proscribing similar conduct by members of the same race. The Court reasoned that the statute could not be said to discriminate against Negroes because the punishment for each participant in the offense was the same. However, as recently as the 1964 Term, in rejecting the reasoning of that case, we stated *"Pace* represents a limited view of the Equal Protection Clause which has not withstood analysis in the subsequent decisions of this Court." As we there demonstrated, the Equal Protection Clause requires the consideration of whether the classifications drawn by any statute constitute an arbitrary and invidious discrimination. The clear and central purpose of the Fourteenth Amendment was to eliminate all official state sources of invidious racial discrimination in the States.

There can be no question but that Virginia's miscegenation statutes rest solely upon distinctions drawn according to race. The statutes proscribe generally accepted conduct if engaged in by members of different races. Over the years, this Court has consistently repudiated "[d]istinctions between citizens solely because of their ancestry" as being "odious to a free people whose institutions are founded upon the doctrine of equality." At the very least, the Equal Protection Clause demands that racial classifications, especially suspect in criminal statutes, be subjected to the "most rigid scrutiny," *Korematsu v. United States* (1944), and, if they are ever to be upheld, they must be shown to be necessary to the accomplishment of some permissible state objective, independent of the racial discrimination which it was the object of the Fourteenth Amendment to eliminate. . . .

There is patently no legitimate overriding purpose independent of invidious racial discrimination which justifies this classification. The fact that Virginia prohibits only interracial marriages involving white persons demonstrates that the racial classifications must stand on their own justification, as measures designed to maintain White Supremacy. We have consistently denied the constitutionality of measures which restrict the rights of citizens on account of race. There can be no doubt that restricting the freedom to marry solely because of racial classifications violates the central meaning of the Equal Protection Clause.

These statutes also deprive the Lovings of liberty without due process of law in violation of the Due Process Clause of the Fourteenth Amendment. The freedom to marry has long been recognized as one of the vital personal rights essential to the orderly pursuit of happiness by free men.

Marriage is one of the "basic civil rights of man," fundamental to our very existence and survival. To deny this fundamental freedom on so unsupportable a basis as the racial classifications embodied in these statutes, classifications so directly subversive of the principle of equality at the heart of the Fourteenth Amendment, is surely to deprive all the State's citizens of liberty without due process of law. The Fourteenth Amendment requires that the freedom of choice to marry not be restricted by invidious racial discriminations. Under our Constitution, the freedom to marry or not marry a person of another race resides with the individual and cannot be infringed by the State.

These convictions must be reversed.

It is so ordered.

Loving illustrates the Court's rejection of government policies that place minorities at a disadvantage or are based on racial stereotypes.[12] These almost never pass muster under strict scrutiny. No compelling state interest justified the prohibition on the Lovings' interracial marriage (*see Box 19-2*).

Today, cases akin to *Brown* and *Loving* are quite rare because laws that explicitly classify and burden minorities on the basis of race are virtually nonexistent, and, if they did exist, the Court would almost surely invalidate them. Rather, almost all contemporary constitutional race cases come in two varieties. One are laws or programs that draw lines on the basis of race but are designed to benefit, rather than burden, racial and ethnic minorities—the

---

[12]Another example is *Palmore v. Sidoti* (1984).

affirmative or diversity programs that we consider in the next section. The other are laws written in language that is racially neutral but that may, in their impact, disproportionately disadvantage a particular racial group. What about a law that is passed to accomplish a legitimate government purpose, with no racially discriminatory intent? Is such a law unconstitutional?

Washington v. Davis (1976) presented this question to the Court. At issue was a standard verbal ability, reading, and vocabulary examination that all applicants to the police force in Washington, D.C., were required to take. Unsuccessful black applicants challenged the exam, pointing out that the test had a disproportionately negative effect on black candidates; in fact, four times as many blacks as whites failed. A federal appeals court agreed. It held that the racially disproportionate impact of the examination, standing alone and without regard to proof of discriminatory intent, was sufficient to invalidate it on constitutional grounds. But, in a 7–2 decision, the Supreme Court reversed.

Writing for the Court, Justice Byron R. White emphasized that a successful constitutional challenge requires proof of discriminatory intent. Although disproportionate impact may be relevant to determining discriminatory intent, it is insufficient on its own to establish the presence of a discriminatory purpose. The Court's decision in *Washington v. Davis* was a blow to civil rights groups, making it more difficult than before for such groups to prevail in litigation. As Figure 19-1 shows, unless it can be proven that the government intended to discriminate, the Court evaluates laws that are racially neutral—even if their impact falls disproportionately on a racial group—under the rational basis test. (The same holds for claims of gender discrimination.)

Classifications that May Benefit Racial Minorities

Beginning in the late 1960s, many political bodies asserted that the Fifth and Fourteenth Amendments demanded more than the elimination of overt discrimination; they also required positive actions taken by government to ensure that equality is achieved and the effects of past discrimination are eliminated. This philosophy gave rise to the controversy over affirmative action.

Affirmative action programs generally take one of two approaches to reducing the effects of past discrimination. The first provides preferences for historically disadvantaged groups (racial and ethnic minorities) in hiring, promotion, and admission to education and

BOX 19-2

Richard Loving and Mildred Jeter

Richard Loving and Mildred Jeter first met in the early 1950s. She was eleven, and he was seventeen. Both were residents of rural Caroline County, Virginia. Loving was white. Jeter was of African American and Native American heritage. Contrary to the racial customs of that time, they began dating and in 1958 decided to marry. Because interracial marriages were not permitted in Virginia, the young couple drove to Washington, D.C., where such weddings were allowed. By then Richard was twenty-four years old and Mildred was still a teen.

Following the ceremony, the Lovings returned to Virginia to begin life as a wedded couple, believing that their marriage would be honored. They shared a home with Mildred's parents.

The Lovings' legal problems began one night in July of 1958 when they awoke at 2:00 A.M. with strange men hovering over their bed and flashlights aimed at their faces. It was the county sheriff along with his deputy and two others. They arrested the Lovings for violating the Virginia anti-miscegenation statute, and both were jailed. Mildred was five months pregnant.

What prompted the arrest is unknown. They had done nothing to aggravate local authorities or bring attention to themselves. Mildred later speculated, "Somebody had to tell, but I have no idea who it could have been. I guess we had one enemy."

In 1959, the Lovings appeared in court before Judge Leon M. Bazile. Their charged offense was a felony, punishable by up to five years in prison. Judge Bazile found them guilty and sentenced each to one year in prison. The judge, however, offered to suspend the sentence if the Lovings would leave the state and not return together for a period of twenty-five years.

Avoiding the prison term, Richard and Mildred moved to the District of Columbia. Richard worked in construction and as a mechanic, and Mildred focused on raising the couple's three children. However, they missed their home and relatives back in Virginia.

Finally, Mildred decided to take action. She wrote a letter to Attorney General Robert Kennedy asking for help. Kennedy recommended that she contact the American Civil Liberties Union. Mildred called the organization's Washington office and as a result the Lovings were introduced to Virginia civil rights attorney Bernard Cohen. Not long thereafter, Cohen joined forces with fellow ACLU attorney Philip Hirschkop, and the two law

Francis Miller/The LIFE Picture Collection/Getty Images

Richard and Mildred Loving at a press conference after the Supreme Court ruled in their favor, overturning Virginia's anti-miscegenation law.

yers initiated a legal assault against the state law. Cohen and Hirschkop donated their services, and the ACLU picked up other expenses.

The litigation ended on June 12, 1967, when the U.S. Supreme Court unanimously struck down the Virginia law. The decision came ten days after the Lovings celebrated their ninth wedding anniversary. Mildred reacted to the news: "I feel free now."

Tragically, Richard lost his life in June 1975. As the Lovings were returning home one evening, a drunk driver ran a stop sign and hit the Lovings' automobile. Richard died at the scene. Mildred suffered cuts to the face and the loss of her right eye.

Mildred Loving passed away of pneumonia on May 2, 2008. Although she was honored by several organizations, she always rejected the notion that she was a hero. Her goals were rather simple and straightforward. As she described, "Richard and I love one another, and we want the right to live in Virginia and raise our children there."

Sources: "Intermarriage Broken Up by Death," *Washington Post,* June 12, 1992; "Mildred Loving," biography.com; "Mildred Loving, Key Figure in Civil Rights Era, Dies," *PBS Newshour,* May 6, 2008; Peter Wallenstein, *Race, Sex, and the Freedom to Marry:* Loving v. Virginia (Lawrence: University Press of Kansas, 2014).

training programs. The second, often referred to as minority set-aside programs, requires that a certain proportion of government business be awarded to companies operated by minority owners. These programs, proponents argue, offer viable ways for women and minorities to become full participants in the nation's economy. Because of past discrimination, many minority businesses lack capital, management experience, and bonding eligibility. They cannot compete successfully with more solid, better-financed firms owned by whites. Consequently, minority set-aside programs propose, for a time, to reserve a percentage of government business and contracts for minority-owned enterprises. Opponents, however, see these policies as nothing more than unconstitutional race discrimination.

On what side would the Court come down? The answer, it seemed, would depend on which test the Court used. Under rational basis scrutiny, the programs would likely survive, while under strict scrutiny, they would perhaps fail. Thus, much of the earlier legal debate over affirmative action has focused on the appropriate level of scrutiny. Supporters of affirmative action tend to advocate against strict scrutiny. To them, strict scrutiny should be reserved for classifications that burden racial minorities because the entire point of strict scrutiny is to uncover racial animus. When the government, representing the majority, is seeking to advantage racial minorities, the Court need not worry about racial prejudice.[13]

Opponents of affirmative action contend that the Court should apply strict scrutiny. To them it is irrelevant whether the program benefits racial minorities; the only question is whether the program draws a classification on the basis of race. If it does, then it triggers strict scrutiny to ensure that "every person . . . be treated equally by each State regardless of the color of his skin," as Justice Potter Stewart once wrote.[14] To opponents, the application of strict scrutiny would signal the end of affirmative action because, as we've noted before, it is very difficult for government to convince the Court that it has a compelling reason that requires a classification based on race.

But very difficult is not impossible, at least not in the affirmative action context. Proponents have pointed to several possible compelling interests. One is that special programs and incentives for people from disadvantaged groups are warranted to eradicate and compensate for the effects of past discrimination. Another is that affirmative action plans do not benefit just one or two groups in society; they may benefit the entire community. Job-related programs may strengthen the country by taking advantage of the talents of all its citizens participating in a diverse political and economic system. And attempts by universities to increase the diversity of their student body may yield advantages for all students by preparing them to enter "an increasingly diverse workforce and society," among other benefits.[15]

The Court Enters the Fray

How would the Court navigate these competing positions? This question was very much on the minds of civil rights groups, scholars, and the public when the justices agreed to hear **Regents of the University of California v. Bakke** (1978), an equal protection clause challenge to the admissions policies of a public university's medical school, the University of California at Davis, which began operations in 1968. During its first two years, the school admitted only three minority students, all Asians. To improve minority participation, the school developed two admissions programs to fill the one hundred seats in its entry class—a regular admissions program and a special admissions program. The regular program worked in the customary way. The school evaluated applicants on the basis of undergraduate grades, standardized test scores, letters of recommendation, extracurricular activities, and an interview. The special program was for applicants who indicated that they were economically or educationally disadvantaged or were black, Chicano, Asian, or Native American. Such applicants could choose between going through the regular admissions process or being referred to a special admissions committee. Special admissions applicants were judged on the same characteristics as regular applicants, but they competed only against each other. The school reserved sixteen seats to be filled from the special admissions pool. Many white applicants, claiming poverty, indicated a desire to be considered by the special admissions committee, but none was admitted. Only members of the designated racial and ethnic minority groups qualified for special admittance.

---

[13]Justice Clarence Thomas, however, advances the position that such programs do not benefit but actually harm racial minorities. See, for example, his dissent in **Grutter v. Bollinger** (2003) and *Texas v. Fisher* (2016), excerpted later in the chapter.

[14]See Stewart's dissenting opinion in *Fullilove v. Klutznick* (1980). For support of this position, many point to Justice Harlan's assertion in his *Plessy v. Ferguson* dissent that the Constitution is "color-blind."

[15]See Justice Sandra Day O'Connor's opinion in *Grutter v. Bollinger* (2003).

Allan Bakke was a white man of Scandinavian descent. He graduated with honors in engineering from the University of Minnesota and was a veteran of the Vietnam War. He worked for the National Aeronautics and Space Administration and received his master's degree in engineering from Stanford. When he developed an interest in pursuing a medical career, Bakke took extra science courses and did volunteer work in a local hospital. At age thirty-three, he applied for admission to the 1973 entry class of the medical school at Davis. He was rejected. He applied in 1974 and was again rejected. Because applicants admitted under the special admissions program were, at least statistically, less qualified than he (see Table 19-1), Bakke sued for admission, claiming that the university's dual admissions program violated the equal protection clause of the Fourteenth Amendment.

The state trial court struck down the special program, declaring that race could not be constitutionally considered in deciding who would be admitted, but the court refused to order Bakke's admission. Both Bakke and the university appealed. The California Supreme Court found the special admissions program unconstitutional, holding that "no applicant may be rejected because of his race, in favor of another who is less qualified, as measured by standards applied without regard to race." The state supreme court's order to admit Bakke was stayed pending the university's appeal to the U.S. Supreme Court.

The stakes were high. For civil rights groups, the case represented a threat to the best way yet devised to eliminate the effects of past discrimination in education and promote minority students into professional positions. For opponents of affirmative action, it was an opportunity to overturn the growing burden of paying for the sins of the past and return to a system based on merit. Fifty-seven amicus briefs were filed by various organizations and interested parties.

At the end of the day, the justices were deeply divided. Four justices— Warren E. Burger, Potter Stewart, William H. Rehnquist, and John Paul Stevens— preferred not to address the constitutional issues in Bakke. Instead, they concluded that the university had violated Bakke's rights under Title VI of the Civil Rights Act of 1964, which states: "No person in the United States shall, on the ground of race, color, or national origin, be

Table 19-1 Admissions Data for the Entering Class of the Medical School of the University of California at Davis, 1973 and 1974

| | SGPA[a] | OGPA[b] | Mcat (Percentiles) | | | |
			Verbal	Quantitative	Science	General Information
Class Entering in 1973						
Bakke	3.44	3.46	96	94	97	72
Average of regular admittees	3.51	3.49	81	76	83	69
Average of special admittees	2.62	2.88	46	24	35	33
Class Entering in 1974						
Bakke	3.44	3.46	96	94	97	72
Average of regular admittees	3.36	3.29	69	67	82	72
Average of special admittees	2.42	2.62	34	30	37	18

Source: Regents of the University of California v. Bakke (1978).

[a]Science grade point average.

[b]Overall grade point average.

excluded from participation in, be denied the benefits of, or be subjected to discrimination under any program or activity receiving Federal financial assistance." By deciding for Bakke on statutory grounds, they argued, they avoided the controversy over the constitutionality of the affirmative action program. Four other justices, led by William J. Brennan, argued that intermediate scrutiny was the appropriate standard to use in "benign" discrimination cases and that the University of California's program was constitutional under that analysis.

This split left Justice Powell holding the balance of power. His opinion argued, first, that strict scrutiny was the appropriate standard. He further concluded that taking race and ethnicity into account in the admissions process is permissible because universities have a sufficiently compelling interest in achieving a diverse student body. But, to Powell, the use of quotas was an impermissible means of achieving that interest: applicants should be evaluated based on an individualized review of their credentials and may not be classified by racial characteristics alone. Under

his opinion, therefore, it violates the Constitution for the university to segregate minority applicants into a special admissions tract in which they compete only among themselves. Furthermore, absent a history of significant racial discrimination, it also offends the Fourteenth Amendment for the school to reserve a number of seats exclusively for minority candidates, seats for which majority applicants may not compete.

Because Powell's opinion failed to gather majority support, its precedential value seemed diminished, but over time the conclusions Powell reached became key guiding principles in the affirmative action controversy. Powell's opinion also was a victory for Allan Bakke, who won admission to the medical school at Davis after a long legal battle (see Box 19-3).

The *Bakke* decision struck down the use of racial quotas and found fault with programs reserved exclusively for minority individuals, but the decision permitted less extreme forms of affirmative action. This aspect of the decision encouraged government agencies as well

AP Photo/Walt Zeboski

Twice rejected for admission to the medical school of the University of California at Davis, Allan Bakke, center, filed suit challenging school policy that admitted minority students with grades and test scores lower than his. Bakke's suit led to the Supreme Court's first major statement on the constitutionality of affirmative action programs.

BOX 19-3

Aftermath . . . Allan Bakke

After securing his right to attend medical school, Allan Bakke asked the University of California to pay his legal expenses. When the university refused that request, Bakke sued. The California Superior Court ordered the university to compensate Bakke $183,089 to cover the fees of lead attorney Reynold Colvin and his associates. This was only a portion of the $437,295 Bakke had requested.

While the battle over legal fees was being fought, Bakke, at age thirty-eight and more than five years after his initial application for admission, entered the medical school at the University of California at Davis. When he arrived on campus in September 1978, more than one hundred demonstrators were protesting the Supreme Court's ruling, chanting, "Smash the *Bakke* decision now!" Bakke quietly entered the medical school building unrecognized by the protesters.

Bakke's medical school years were generally uneventful. His fellow students paid little attention to the manner in which he had gained acceptance to the school. The fact that Bakke was married and had three children distanced him somewhat from his classmates and many of their activities outside the classroom.

At age forty-two, four years after his admission, Allan Bakke graduated with his doctor of medicine degree. On March 18, 1982, the school held a ceremony during which the postgraduate assignments of the members of the graduating class were announced. One observer described Bakke as receiving the loudest applause of all when it was announced that he had been selected for a prestigious internship at the Mayo Clinic in his native state of Minnesota.

After completing his internship, Bakke continued at the Mayo Clinic for a four-year residency in anaesthesiology. He then went into private practice as an anaesthesiologist for the Olmsted Medical Group in Rochester, Minnesota. By nature a very quiet and private person, Bakke never discussed his famous lawsuit publicly.

Sources: Howard Ball, *The Bakke Case: Race, Education, and Affirmative Action* (Lawrence: University Press of Kansas, 2000); *New York Times,* December 6, 1981, March 19 and June 4, 1982, November 2, 1986; *San Francisco Chronicle,* November 3, 1986; *Washington Post,* January 15, 1980.

---

as private organizations and corporations to develop programs to benefit individuals from historically disadvantaged groups. Such programs gave rise to challenges that they violated the 1964 Civil Rights Act or the Constitution's equal protection guarantees. In the years immediately following *Bakke,* the Court was generally sympathetic to affirmative action programs—especially where a history of discrimination could be demonstrated. Under such circumstances the justices were more lenient with respect to the use of racial, ethnic, or gender classifications in both the public and private sectors.[16]

With the elevation of William Rehnquist to the chief justice position and the appointments of Antonin Scalia in 1986 and Anthony M. Kennedy in 1988, the ideological balance of the Court began to move in a more conservative direction that did not bode well for affirmative action programs. The first sign of this came in *City of Richmond v. J. A. Croson Co.* (1989). This dispute centered on a minority set-aside program. A variation on affirmative action, minority set-asides attempt to enhance the prospects of disadvantaged groups by granting them special considerations in the awarding of government contracts and benefits. The justification for such programs is the long history of discrimination against minority-owned businesses in general commercial activity and in providing goods and services for the government. Although the Court had approved federal minority set-aside programs in *Fullilove v. Klutznick* (1980), the justices applied strict scrutiny and struck down the program. In *Metro Broadcasting v. Federal Communications Commission* (1990), however, the Court approved the FCC's use of minority preferences. That was because Justice Brennan's opinion for the Court held the federal government to an intermediate scrutiny standard—a more lenient standard than strict scrutiny, which it applied to state programs in *Richmond.*

---

[17]Public sector, see, for example, *Johnson v. Transportation Agency of Santa Clara County, California* (1987); *private sector, see United Steelworkers of America v. Weber* (1979).

Would the Court continue to hold the federal government and the states to different standards? This question became all the more important because by the time the justices heard the 1995 minority set-aside case ***Adarand Constructors, Inc. v. Peña***, the Court's membership had changed. Justice Brennan's majority opinion in *Metro Broadcasting* was his last after an illustrious career of thirty-four years on the Court. During that time, he had been a steadfast defender of liberal principles in constitutional interpretation.

Brennan's 1990 retirement was followed the next year by Thurgood Marshall's. President George H. W. Bush appointed David Souter to Brennan's seat and Clarence Thomas to Marshall's. The Thomas-for-Marshall change turned out to be critical for affirmative action cases because Souter, like Brennan, seemed to support affirmative action, while Thomas, the second African American appointed to the Court, opposed it. With Thomas's vote, Sandra Day O'Connor was able to solidify a majority around her view that strict scrutiny applies regardless of whether the program is federal or state.

Applying Strict Scrutiny

Although *Adarand* did not strike down all affirmative action programs, the test of strict scrutiny seemed so difficult to meet that it cast considerable doubt on the constitutional viability of all affirmative action programs. Court observers began to speculate that the justices had turned away from the principles set in Justice Powell's opinion in *Bakke* and had become less open to minority preference programs of all kinds.

Answers soon came in 2003 when the justices took up two appeals challenging affirmative action policies at the University of Michigan. One suit, ***Gratz v. Bollinger***, attacked the university's undergraduate admissions policies, and the other, ***Grutter v. Bollinger***, challenged admissions to the university's law school. In both cases the admissions policies had been adopted voluntarily rather than in response to a court order to compensate for past constitutional violations.

Speculation on the outcome of the Court's deliberations generally conceded that the votes of seven of the nine justices were all but certain. Justices Stevens, Souter, Ruth Ginsburg, and Stephen Breyer had records of consistent support for the limited use of racial preferences. On the other side, Chief Justice Rehnquist, Scalia, and Thomas had consistently and vigorously opposed affirmative action. Most observers believed that O'Connor and Kennedy held the key to the outcome. For affirmative action to receive constitutional approval, at least one of these two moderate conservatives would have to vote with the Court's liberal bloc.

As it turned out, O'Connor was the pivotal justice. Although she agreed that strict scrutiny was the appropriate test for deciding racial preference cases and that a diverse student body is a sufficiently compelling state interest to justify taking race into account, application of this approach led her (and the Court) to uphold the program in *Grutter* and invalidate the program in *Gratz*. Contrary to the majority's findings in *Gratz*, she concluded that the law school's admissions process at issue in *Grutter* was based on a flexible, individualized consideration of applications in which race was only one of several diversity factors taken into account.

Toward the end of her opinion in *Grutter*, Justice O'Connor wrote, "We expect that 25 years from now, the use of racial preferences will no longer be necessary to further the interest approved today." Commentators have interpreted this sentence in different ways, but many seemed to think that it signaled the Court's departure from affirmative action cases for the next few decades.

This reading turned out to be incorrect. Just two years after Justice O'Connor retired and was replaced by the more conservative Samuel Alito, the Court seemed to begin backing off from its liberal *Grutter* decision. As we explain in *Fisher II* (2016) excerpted below, the Court in ***Fisher v. University of Texas*** (2013) seemed to advance an approach to strict scrutiny that would be even stricter than *Grutter*'s version. But, ultimately, when the case returned to the Court in 2016, the majority upheld the program. Why?

Fisher v. University of Texas

579 U.S. ___ (2016)
http://caselaw.findlaw.com/us-supreme-court/14-981.html
Oral arguments available at https://www.oyez.org/
    cases/2015/14-981
Vote: 4 (Breyer, Ginsburg, Kennedy, Sotomayor)
    3 (Alito, Roberts, Thomas)

OPINION OF THE COURT: *Kennedy*

DISSENTING OPINIONS: *Alito, Thomas*

NOT PARTICIPATING: *Kagan*

The University of Texas at Austin has used several different methods for evaluating applications for undergraduate admission. Before 1996, the university considered high school grades and standardized test scores and, to promote diversity, the race of the applicant. When, in 1996, the U.S. Court of Appeals for the Fifth Circuit held that the use of race violated the Fourteenth Amendment's equal protection clause, the university substituted a "Personal Achievement Index" (PAI) that considered factors such as leadership, work experience, awards, extracurricular activities, community service, and other special considerations. The state legislature further modified the process by enacting a law that gave automatic admission to all students in the top 10 percent of their class in accredited Texas high schools. Because high schools in Texas are often racially segregated, the 10-percent rule brought substantial racial diversity to the university, nearly equaling the effect of the explicit consideration of race used before 1996. In 2004, after the Supreme Court decided *Grutter v. Bollinger* and *Gratz v. Bollinger* (2003), the university again changed its admissions policies by explicitly adding race to the list of "plus" factors to be considered as part of an applicant's PAI score.

In 2008, 29,501 individuals applied for admission to the university. Of the 29,501, 12,843 were accepted and 6,717 enrolled. Among the rejected applicants was Abigail Noel Fisher, who is white. Fisher sued the university, arguing that the consideration of race in the admissions process violated the equal protection clause. The federal district court gave a victory to the university and the Fifth Circuit Court of Appeals affirmed, holding that *Grutter* required the court to give substantial deference to the university both with respect to identifying a compelling interest and determining a narrowly tailored plan to achieve that interest.

In 2013, the U.S. Supreme Court reviewed the Fifth Circuit's decision (*Fisher I*). As in *Grutter,* the Court applied strict scrutiny and, again as in *Grutter,* found that diversity was a sufficiently compelling interest. Writing for the majority, Justice Kennedy then turned to whether the plan the university chose to attain diversity is necessary to that goal. "On this point," he wrote, "the University receives no deference." Rather, the university must bear "the ultimate burden of demonstrating, before turning to racial classifications, that available, workable race-neutral alternatives do not suffice."

The Court did not invalidate the university's program. But it did send the case back to the lower court so that it could apply Kennedy's seemingly stricter version of strict scrutiny. After the Fifth Circuit once again upheld the plan, Fisher asked the Supreme Court to reverse the lower court's decision. Note that Justice Elena Kagan did not participate because she had worked on the case when she served as U.S. solicitor general.

JUSTICE KENNEDY DELIVERED THE OPINION OF THE COURT.

The Court is asked once again to consider whether the race-conscious admissions program at the University of Texas is lawful under the Equal Protection Clause. . . .

Fisher I [2013] set forth three controlling principles relevant to assessing the constitutionality of a public university's affirmative-action program. First, "because racial characteristics so seldom provide a relevant basis for disparate treatment, . . . [r]ace may not be considered [by a university] unless the admissions process can withstand strict scrutiny." Strict scrutiny requires the university to demonstrate with clarity that its "'purpose or interest is both constitutionally permissible and substantial, and that its use of the classification is necessary . . . to the accomplishment of its purpose.'"

Second, *Fisher I* confirmed that "the decision to pursue 'the educational benefits that flow from student body diversity' . . . is, in substantial measure, an academic judgment to which some, but not complete, judicial deference is proper." A university cannot impose a fixed quota or otherwise "define diversity as 'some specified percentage of a particular group merely because of its race or ethnic origin.'" Once, however, a university gives "a reasoned, principled explanation" for its decision, deference must be given "to the University's conclusion, based on its experience and expertise, that a diverse student body would serve its educational goals."

Third, *Fisher I* clarified that no deference is owed when determining whether the use of race is narrowly tailored to achieve the university's permissible goals. A university, *Fisher I* explained, bears the burden of proving a "nonracial approach" would not promote its interest in the educational benefits of diversity "about as well and at tolerable administrative expense." Though "[n]arrow tailoring does not require exhaustion of every conceivable race-neutral alternative" or "require a university to choose between maintaining a reputation for excellence [and] fulfilling a commitment to provide educational opportunities to members of all racial groups," it does impose "on the university the ultimate burden of demonstrating" that "race-neutral alternatives" that are both "available" and "workable" "do not suffice." *Fisher I*

Fisher I set forth these controlling principles, while taking no position on the constitutionality of the admissions program at issue in this case. The Court held only that the District Court and the Court of Appeals had "confined the strict scrutiny inquiry in too narrow a way by deferring to the University's good faith in its use of racial classifications." The Court remanded the case, with instructions to evaluate the record under the correct standard and to determine whether the University had made "a showing that its plan is narrowly tailored to achieve" the educational benefits that flow from diversity. On remand, the Court of Appeals determined that the program conformed with the strict scrutiny mandated by *Fisher I*.

The University's program is *sui generis*. Unlike other approaches to college admissions considered by this Court, it combines holistic review with a percentage plan. This approach gave rise to an unusual consequence in this case: The component of the University's admissions policy that had the largest impact on petitioner's chances of admission was not the school's consideration

Abigail Fisher, accompanied by her attorney Bert Rein, speaks to reporters on October 10, 2012, the day the affirmative action case of *Fisher v. University of Texas* was first orally argued.

of race under its holistic-review process but rather the Top Ten Percent Plan. Because petitioner did not graduate in the top 10 percent of her high school class, she was categorically ineligible for more than three-fourths of the slots in the incoming freshman class. It seems quite plausible, then, to think that petitioner would have had a better chance of being admitted to the University if the school used race-conscious holistic review to select its entire incoming class, as was the case in *Grutter*.

Despite the Top Ten Percent Plan's outsized effect on petitioner's chances of admission, she has not challenged it. For that reason, throughout this litigation, the Top Ten Percent Plan has been taken, somewhat artificially, as a given premise. . . .

In seeking to reverse the judgment of the Court of Appeals, petitioner makes four arguments. First, she argues that the University has not articulated its compelling interest with sufficient clarity. According to petitioner, the University must set forth more precisely the level of minority enrollment that would constitute a "critical mass." Without a clearer sense of what the University's ultimate goal is, petitioner argues, a reviewing court cannot assess whether the University's admissions program is narrowly tailored to that goal.

As this Court's cases have made clear, however, the compelling interest that justifies consideration of race in college admissions is not an interest in enrolling a certain number of minority students. Rather, a university may institute a race-conscious admissions program as a means of obtaining "the educational benefits that flow from student body diversity."

[E]nrolling a diverse student body "promotes cross-racial understanding, helps to break down racial stereotypes, and enables students to better understand persons of different races." Equally important, "student body diversity promotes learning outcomes, and better prepares students for an increasingly diverse workforce and society."

Increasing minority enrollment may be instrumental to these educational benefits, but it is not, as petitioner seems to suggest, a goal that can or should be reduced to pure numbers. Indeed, since the University is prohibited from seeking a particular number or quota of minority students, it cannot be faulted for failing to specify the particular level of minority enrollment at which it believes the educational benefits of diversity will be obtained.

On the other hand, asserting an interest in the educational benefits of diversity writ large is insufficient. A university's goals cannot be elusory or amorphous—they must be sufficiently measurable to permit judicial scrutiny of the policies adopted to reach them.

The record reveals that in first setting forth its current admissions policy, the University articulated concrete and precise goals. On the first page of its 2004 "Proposal to Consider Race and Ethnicity in Admissions," the University identifies the educational values it seeks to realize through its admissions process: the destruction of stereotypes, the "'promot[ion of] cross-racial understanding,'" the preparation of a student body "'for an increasingly diverse workforce and society,'" and the "'cultivat[ion of] a set of leaders with legitimacy in the eyes of the citizenry.'" All of these objectives, as a general matter, mirror the "compelling interest" this Court has approved in its prior cases.

The University has provided in addition a "reasoned, principled explanation" for its decision to pursue these goals. The University's 39-page proposal was written following a year-long study, which concluded that "[t]he use of race-neutral policies and programs ha[d] not been successful" in "provid[ing] an educational setting that fosters cross-racial understanding, provid[ing] enlightened discussion and learning, [or] prepar[ing] students to function in an increasingly diverse workforce and society." . . .

Second, petitioner argues that the University has no need to consider race because it had already "achieved critical mass" by 2003 using the Top Ten Percent Plan and race-neutral holistic review. Petitioner is correct that a university bears a heavy burden in showing that it had not obtained the educational benefits of diversity before it turned to a race-conscious plan. The record reveals, however, that, at the time of petitioner's application, the University could not be faulted on this score. Before changing its policy the University conducted "months of study and deliberation, including retreats, interviews, [and] review of data," and concluded that "[t]he use of race-neutral policies and programs ha[d] not been successful in achieving" sufficient racial diversity at the University. . . .

The record itself contains significant evidence, both statistical and anecdotal, in support of the University's position. . . . [T]he demographic data the University has submitted show consistent stagnation in terms of the percentage of minority students enrolling at the University from 1996 to 2002. In 1996, for example, 266 African-American freshmen enrolled, a total that constituted 4.1 percent of the incoming class. In 2003, the year *Grutter* was decided, 267 African-American students enrolled—again, 4.1 percent of the incoming class. . . .

In addition to this broad demographic data, the University put forward evidence that minority students admitted under the *Hopwood* regime experienced feelings of loneliness and isolation.

This anecdotal evidence is, in turn, bolstered by further, more nuanced quantitative data. In 2002, 52 percent of undergraduate classes with at least five students had no African-American students enrolled in them, and 27 percent had only one African-American student. In other words, only 21 percent of undergraduate classes with five or more students in them had more than one African-American student enrolled. Twelve percent of these classes had no Hispanic students, as compared to 10 percent in 1996. Though a college must continually reassess its need for race-conscious review, here that assessment appears to have been done with care, and a reasonable determination was made that the University had not yet attained its goals.

Third, petitioner argues that considering race was not necessary because such consideration has had only a "'minimal impact' in advancing the [University's] compelling interest." Again, the record does not support this assertion. In 2003, 11 percent of the Texas residents enrolled through holistic review were Hispanic and 3.5 percent were African-American. In 2007, by contrast, 16.9 percent of the Texas holistic-review freshmen were Hispanic and 6.8 percent were African-American. Those increases—of 54 percent and 94 percent, respectively—show that consideration of race has had a meaningful, if still limited, effect on the diversity of the University's freshman class.

In any event, it is not a failure of narrow tailoring for the impact of racial consideration to be minor. The fact that race consciousness played a role in only a small portion of admissions decisions should be a hallmark of narrow tailoring, not evidence of unconstitutionality.

Petitioner's final argument is that "there are numerous other available race-neutral means of achieving" the University's compelling interest. A review of the record reveals, however, that, at the time of petitioner's application, none of her proposed alternatives was a workable means for the University to attain the benefits of diversity it sought. For example, petitioner suggests that the University could intensify its outreach efforts to African-American and Hispanic applicants. But the University submitted extensive evidence of the many ways in which it already had intensified its outreach efforts to those students. The University has created three new scholarship programs, opened new regional admissions centers, increased its recruitment budget by half-a-million dollars, and organized over 1,000 recruitment events. Perhaps more significantly, in the wake of *Hopwood,* the University spent seven years attempting to achieve its compelling interest using race-neutral holistic review. None of these efforts succeeded, and petitioner fails to offer any meaningful way in which the University could have improved upon them at the time of her application. . . .

Petitioner's final suggestion is to uncap the Top Ten Percent Plan, and admit more—if not all—the University's students through a percentage plan. As an initial matter, petitioner overlooks the fact that the Top Ten Percent Plan, though facially neutral, cannot be understood apart from its basic purpose, which is to boost minority enrollment. . . .

Even if, as a matter of raw numbers, minority enrollment would increase under such a regime, petitioner would be hard-pressed to find convincing support for the proposition that college admissions would be improved if they were a function of class rank alone. That approach would sacrifice all other aspects of diversity in pursuit of enrolling a higher number of minority students. A system that selected every student through class rank alone would exclude the star athlete or musician whose grades suffered because of daily practices and training. It would exclude a talented young biologist who struggled to maintain above-average grades in humanities classes. And it would exclude a student whose freshman-year grades were poor because of a family crisis but who got herself back on track in her last three years of school, only to find herself just outside of the top decile of her class.

In short, none of petitioner's suggested alternatives—nor other proposals considered or discussed in the course of this litigation—have been shown to be "available" and "workable" means through which the University could have met its educational goals, as it understood and defined them in 2008. The University has thus met its burden of showing that the admissions policy it used at the time it rejected petitioner's application was narrowly tailored. . . .

A university is in large part defined by those intangible "qualities which are incapable of objective measurement but which make for greatness." Considerable deference is owed to a university in defining those intangible characteristics, like student body diversity, that are central to its identity and educational mission. But still, it remains an enduring challenge to our Nation's education system to reconcile the pursuit of diversity with the constitutional promise of equal treatment and dignity.

In striking this sensitive balance, public universities, like the States themselves, can serve as "laboratories for experimentation". . . . The University of Texas at Austin has a special opportunity to learn and to teach. The University now has at its disposal valuable data about the manner in which different approaches to admissions may foster diversity or instead dilute it. The University must continue to use this data to scrutinize the fairness of its admissions program; to assess whether changing demographics have undermined the need for a race-conscious policy; and to identify the effects, both positive and negative, of the affirmative-action measures it deems necessary.

The Court's affirmance of the University's admissions policy today does not necessarily mean the University may rely on that same policy without refinement. It is the University's ongoing obligation to engage in constant deliberation and continued reflection regarding its admissions policies.

The judgment of the Court of Appeals is affirmed.

It is so ordered.

JUSTICE THOMAS, DISSENTING.

I write separately to reaffirm that "a State's use of race in higher education admissions decisions is categorically prohibited by the Equal Protection Clause." "The Constitution abhors classifications based on race because every time the government places citizens on racial registers and makes race relevant to the provision of burdens or benefits, it demeans us all." That constitutional imperative does not change in the face of a "faddish theor[y]" that racial discrimination may produce "educational benefits." The Court was wrong to hold otherwise in *Grutter* v. *Bollinger.* I would overrule *Grutter* and reverse the Fifth Circuit's judgment.

JUSTICE ALITO, WITH WHOM THE CHIEF JUSTICE AND JUSTICE THOMAS JOIN, DISSENTING.

Something strange has happened since our prior decision in this case (*Fisher I*). In that decision, we held that strict scrutiny requires the University of Texas at Austin (UT or University) to show that its use of race and ethnicity in making admissions decisions serves compelling interests and that its plan is narrowly tailored to achieve those ends. . . . The University has still not identified with any degree of specificity the interests that its use of race and ethnicity is supposed to serve. Its primary argument is that merely invoking "the educational benefits of diversity" is sufficient and that it need not identify any metric that would allow a court to determine whether its plan is needed to serve, or is actually serving, those interests. This is nothing less than the plea for deference that we emphatically rejected in our prior decision. Today, however, the Court inexplicably grants that request.

To the extent that UT has ever moved beyond a plea for deference and identified the relevant interests in more specific terms, its efforts have been shifting, unpersuasive, and, at times, less than candid. . . .

At times, UT has claimed that its plan is needed to achieve a "critical mass" of African-American and Hispanic students, but it has never explained what this term means. According to UT, a critical mass is neither some absolute number of African-American or Hispanic students nor the percentage of African-Americans or Hispanics in the general population of the State. The term remains undefined, but UT tells us that it will let the courts know when the desired end has been achieved. This is a plea for deference—indeed, for blind deference—the very thing that the Court rejected in *Fisher I*.

UT has also claimed at times that the race-based component of its plan is needed because the Top Ten Percent Plan admits *the wrong kind* of African-American and Hispanic students, namely, students from poor families who attend schools in which the student body is predominantly African-American or Hispanic. As UT put it in its brief in *Fisher I*, the race-based component of its admissions plan is needed to admit "[t]he African-American or Hispanic child of successful professionals in Dallas."

After making this argument in its first trip to this Court, UT apparently had second thoughts, and in the latest round of briefing UT has attempted to disavow ever having made the argument. But it did, and the argument turns affirmative action on its head. Affirmative-action programs were created to help *disadvantaged* students.

Although UT now disowns the argument that the Top Ten Percent Plan results in the admission of the wrong kind of African-American and Hispanic students, the Fifth Circuit majority bought a version of that claim. As the panel majority put it, the Top Ten African-American and Hispanic admittees cannot match the holistic African-American and Hispanic admittees when it comes to "records of personal achievement," a "variety of perspectives" and "life experiences," and "unique skills." All in all, according to the panel majority, the Top Ten Percent students cannot "enrich the diversity of the student body" in the same way as the holistic admittees. . . .

The Fifth Circuit reached this conclusion with little direct evidence regarding the characteristics of the Top Ten Percent and holistic admittees. Instead, the assumption behind the Fifth Circuit's reasoning is that most of the African-American and Hispanic students admitted under the race-neutral component of UT's plan were able to rank in the top decile of their high school classes only because they did not have to compete against white and Asian-American students. This insulting stereotype is not supported by the record. African-American and Hispanic students admitted under the Top Ten Percent Plan receive higher college grades than the African-American and Hispanic students admitted under the race-conscious program.

It should not have been necessary for us to grant review a second time in this case, and I have no greater desire than the majority to see the case drag on. But that need not happen. When UT decided to adopt its race-conscious plan, it had every reason to know that its plan would have to satisfy strict scrutiny and that this meant that it would be *its burden* to show that the plan was narrowly tailored to serve compelling interests. UT has failed to make that showing. By all rights, judgment should be entered in favor of petitioner.

But if the majority is determined to give UT yet another chance, we should reverse and send this case back to the District Court. What the majority has now done—awarding a victory to UT in an opinion that fails to address the important issues in the case—is simply wrong. . . .

It is important to understand what is and what is not at stake in this case. *What is not at stake* is whether UT or any other university may adopt an admissions plan that results in a student body with a broad representation of students from all racial and ethnic groups. UT previously had a race-neutral plan that it claimed had "effectively compensated for the loss of affirmative action," and UT could have taken other steps that would have increased the diversity of its admitted students without taking race or ethnic background into account.

What is at stake is whether university administrators may justify systematic racial discrimination simply by asserting that such discrimination is necessary to achieve "the educational benefits of diversity," without explaining—much less proving—why the discrimination is needed or how the discriminatory plan is well crafted to serve its objectives. Even though UT has never provided any coherent explanation for its asserted need to discriminate on the basis of race, and even though UT's position relies on a series of unsupported and noxious racial assumptions, the majority concludes that UT has met its heavy burden. This conclusion is remarkable—and remarkably wrong.

Because UT has failed to satisfy strict scrutiny, I respectfully dissent.

For now, a slim majority of justices agree that universities can maintain affirmative action programs if they demonstrate that their program withstands strict scrutiny. That, of course, may change as the Court's membership has changed. Especially important may be the replacement of Justice Kennedy, the key vote in *Fisher*, with the Trump appointee, Brett Kavanaugh.

HEIGHTENED SCRUTINY AND CLAIMS OF GENDER DISCRIMINATION

Before *Brown v. Board of Education*, groups and individuals challenging practices as racially discriminatory had a major obstacle to overcome: *Plessy v. Ferguson*. Lawsuits based on claims of sex discrimination were also handicapped, and for even longer periods of time. Indeed, before the 1970s, the few sex discrimination cases that reached the Supreme Court often ended in decisions that reinforced traditional views of sex roles. In **Bradwell v. Illinois** (1873), for example, the Court heard a challenge to an action by the Illinois Supreme Court denying Myra Bradwell a license to practice law solely because of her sex. The Court, with only Chief Justice Salmon P. Chase dissenting, upheld the state action. Justice Joseph P. Bradley's concurring opinion, which Justices Noah H.

Swayne and Stephen J. Field joined, illustrates the attitude of the legal community toward women. Bradley said that he gave his "heartiest concurrence" to contemporary society's "multiplication of avenues for women's advancement." But, he added, "The natural and proper timidity and delicacy which belongs to the female sex evidently unfits it for many of the occupations of civil life." This condition, according to Bradley, was the product of divine ordinance. Two years later, in *Minor v. Happersett* (1875), the Court upheld Missouri's denial of voting rights to women, a precedent in effect until ratification of the Nineteenth Amendment in 1920.

Similar decisions came early in the twentieth century. The majority opinion in the 1908 case of **Muller v. Oregon**, in which the Court upheld a maximum work hours law that covered only women, echoed Justice Bradley's view of women.[17] Writing for the Court, Justice David J. Brewer noted:

> That woman's physical structure and the performance of maternal functions place her at a disadvantage in the struggle for subsistence is obvious. This is especially true when the burdens of motherhood are upon her. Even when they are not, by abundant testimony of the medical fraternity continuance for a long time on her feet at work, repeating this from day to day, tends to injurious effects upon her body, and, as healthy mothers are essential to vigorous offspring, the physical well-being of women becomes an object of public interest and care in order to preserve the strength and vigor of the race.

As late as 1948, the Court upheld the right of the state to ban women from certain occupations. In *Goesaert v. Cleary*, decided that year, the justices declared valid a Michigan law that barred a woman from becoming a bartender unless she was a member of the bar owner's immediate family. In explaining the ruling, Justice Felix Frankfurter wrote:

> The fact that women may now have achieved the virtues that men have long claimed as their prerogatives and now indulge in vices that men have long practiced, does not preclude the States from drawing a sharp line between the sexes,

Myra Bradwell studied law with her husband, a judge, and edited and published the *Chicago Legal News*, the most important legal publication in the Midwest. Although she passed the bar exam, the Illinois Supreme Court refused to admit her to the state bar because of her sex. She appealed to the U.S. Supreme Court but lost.

certainly in such matters as the regulation of the liquor traffic.

In a comparatively modern case, *Hoyt v. Florida* (1961), the justices upheld a Florida law that automatically exempted women from jury duty unless they asked to serve.

While the Court continued to articulate a traditional view of women, the growing strength of the women's movement in the 1960s prompted legislatures to act. Congress passed a number of federal statutes extending equal rights to women, among them the Equal Pay Act of 1963, which requires equal pay for equal work, and the 1964 Civil Rights Act, which forbids discrimination based on sex in the area of employment. Many states passed similar laws to eliminate discriminatory conditions in the marketplace and in state legal codes. In addition to these legislative actions, in 1972 Congress proposed an amendment to the Constitution. Known as the equal rights amendment (ERA), it declared, "Equality of rights under

---

[17]At the time of their implementation, statutes such as the one at issue in *Muller* were seen as a progressive step to protect women in the workforce. Today, this kind of law, based as it is on an assumption of the inferiority of women, is considered paternalistic.

the law shall not be denied or abridged by the United States or by any State on account of sex." Although the amendment ultimately failed to attain the support of the required number of states, the very fact that Congress proposed it (and later extended the deadline for ratification) indicated changing views toward women.

While continuing to press for the legislative change, women's rights organizations also turned to the courts for redress of their grievances. Like the advocates for African Americans, many in the women's movement believed that the due process and equal protection clauses held the potential for ensuring women's rights, and they began organizing to assert their claims in court.

One of the first such cases to reach the Supreme Court was *Reed v. Reed* (1971). In this case, the justices considered the validity of an Idaho inheritance statute that used sex classifications, which ACLU attorneys, including Ruth Bader Ginsburg, challenged as a violation of the equal protection clause of the Fourteenth Amendment.

It was clear from the outset that the same requirements that had developed in race relations cases would apply here: the statute's challenger would have to demonstrate both invidious discrimination and state action before a violation could be found. What was not so clear was the standard of scrutiny the justices would use. In the racial discrimination cases, the Court had declared strict scrutiny the appropriate standard. Racial minorities were considered a suspect class, and, therefore, classifications based on race were presumed to be unconstitutional. The state had a heavy burden of proof if it wished to show that a law based on race was the least restrictive means to achieve a compelling state interest. Much of the success civil rights groups enjoyed was due to this favorable legal status. Ginsburg and other advocates of equal rights for women hoped the Court would adopt the same standard for sex discrimination claims. Did the justices go along?

Reed v. Reed

404 U.S. 71 (1971)
http://caselaw.findlaw.com/us-supreme-court/404/71.html
Oral arguments available at www.oyez.org/cases/1971/70-4
Vote: 7 (Blackmun, Brennan, Burger, Douglas, Marshall, Stewart, White)
0

OPINION OF THE COURT: *Burger*

Richard Reed was Sally and Cecil Reed's adopted son. He died in 1967 at the age of sixteen in Ada County, Idaho, leaving no will. The Reeds, who had divorced several years before Richard's death, became involved in a legal dispute over who should administer his estate. The child's property was negligible, consisting of a few personal items and a small savings account. The total value was less than $1,000. The probate court judge appointed Cecil Reed administrator of the estate, in accordance with Idaho law. Section 15-312 of the Idaho code stipulated that when a person died intestate (without a will), an administrator would be appointed according to a list of priority relationships. First priority went to a surviving spouse, second priority to children, third to parents, and so forth. Section 15-314 of the statute stated that in the case of competing petitions from otherwise qualified individuals of the same priority relationship, "males must be preferred to females."

Sally Reed challenged the law as a violation of the equal protection clause of the Fourteenth Amendment. The state district court agreed with her argument, but the Idaho Supreme Court reversed. With the assistance of Ginsburg and other ACLU lawyers, Sally Reed and her attorney, Allen Derr, took the case to the U.S. Supreme Court. There they asked the justices to adopt a strict scrutiny approach to sex discrimination cases, but they also suggested that the law was unconstitutional even under a less rigorous standard.

Sally Reed, pictured with Boise attorney Allen Derr, who represented her in oral arguments before the Supreme Court, challenged an Idaho law that gave preference to males over females in designating administrators of estates. *Reed v. Reed* ushered in the modern era of sex discrimination litigation.

Having examined the record and considered the briefs and oral arguments of the parties, we have concluded that the arbitrary preference established in favor of males by §15-314 of the Idaho Code cannot stand in the face of the Fourteenth Amendment's command that no State deny the equal protection of the laws to any person within its jurisdiction.

Idaho does not, of course, deny letters of administration to women altogether. Indeed, under §15-312, a woman whose spouse dies intestate has a preference over a son, father, brother, or any other male relative of the decedent. Moreover, we can judicially notice that in this country, presumably due to the greater longevity of women, a large proportion of estates, both intestate and under wills of decedents, are administered by surviving widows.

Section 15-314 is restricted in its operation to those situations where competing applications for letters of administration have been filed by both male and female members of the same entitlement class established by §15-312. In such situations, §15-314 provides that different treatment be accorded to the applicants on the basis of their sex; it thus establishes a classification subject to scrutiny under the Equal Protection Clause.

In applying that clause, this Court has consistently recognized that the Fourteenth Amendment does not deny to States the power to treat different classes of persons in different ways. The Equal Protection Clause of that amendment does, however, deny to States the power to legislate that different treatment be accorded to persons placed by a statute into different classes on the basis of criteria wholly unrelated to the objective of that statute. A classification "must be reasonable, not arbitrary, and must rest upon some ground of difference having a fair and substantial relation to the object of the legislation, so that all persons similarly circumstanced shall be treated alike." The question presented by this case, then, is whether a difference in the sex of competing applicants for letters of administration bears a rational relationship to a state objective that is sought to be advanced by the operation of §§15-312 and 15-314.

In upholding the latter section, the Idaho Supreme Court concluded that its objective was to eliminate one area of controversy when two or more persons, equally entitled under §15-312, seek letters of administration and thereby present the probate court "with the issue of which one should be named." The court also concluded that where such persons are not of the same sex, the elimination of females from consideration "is neither an illogical nor arbitrary method devised by the legislature to resolve an issue that would otherwise require a hearing as to the relative merits . . . of the two or more petitioning relatives. . . ."

Clearly the objective of reducing the workload on probate courts by eliminating one class of contests is not without some legitimacy. The crucial question, however, is whether §15-314 advances that objective in a manner consistent with the command of the Equal Protection Clause. We hold that it does not. To give a mandatory preference to members of either sex over members of the other, merely to accomplish the elimination of hearings on the merits, is to make the very kind of arbitrary legislative choice forbidden by the Equal Protection Clause of the Fourteenth Amendment; and whatever may be said as to the positive values of avoiding intrafamily controversy, the choice in this context may not lawfully be mandated solely on the basis of sex.

We note finally that if §15-314 is viewed merely as a modifying appendage to §15-312 and aimed at the same objective, its constitutionality is not thereby saved. The objective of §15-312 clearly is to establish degrees of entitlement of various classes of persons in accordance with their varying degrees and kinds of relationship to the intestate. Regardless of their sex, persons within any one of the enumerated classes of that section are similarly situated with respect to that objective. By providing dissimilar treatment for men and women who are thus similarly situated, the challenged section violates the Equal Protection Clause. The judgment of the Idaho Supreme Court is reversed and the case remanded for further proceedings not inconsistent with this opinion.

Reversed and remanded.

The Court's unanimous decision in *Reed* applied two important principles to sex discrimination. First, the Court refused to accept Idaho's defense of its statute. The state had contended that it was inefficient to hold full court hearings on the relative merits of competing candidates to administer estates, especially small estates. Imposing arbitrary criteria saved court time and avoided intrafamily squabbles. The Supreme Court held that administrative convenience is no justification for violating the Constitution. Second, defenders of the Idaho law argued that the arbitrary favoring of males over females made sense because, in most cases, the male will have had more education and experience in financial matters than the competing female. In rejecting this argument, the justices said that laws containing overbroad, sex-based assumptions violate the equal protection clause.

The *Reed* case also signaled that the justices were receptive to sex discrimination claims and would not hesitate to strike down state laws that imposed arbitrary sex classifications. This turn of events was certainly good news for women's rights advocates, but the standard used in the case was not. Chief Justice Burger invoked the rational basis test (rather than strict scrutiny), holding that laws based on gender classifications must be reasonable and have a rational relationship to a state

Mark Walker, left, an Oklahoma State University student, joined with beer vendor Carolyn Whitener, middle, to challenge the state's drinking age law that treated males and females differently. When Walker turned twenty-one and was no longer adversely affected by the law, he persuaded freshman fraternity brother Curtis Craig, right, to join the lawsuit. Walker died in a car accident shortly before the Supreme Court decided *Craig v. Boren*.

objective. The Idaho law was sufficiently arbitrary to fail the rational basis test, but other laws and policies might well survive it.

Over the next several years, following *Reed*, many sex discrimination appeals reached the Court.[18] Although these cases dealt with differing subject matter, the most important question explicitly or implicitly presented to the justices had to do with the proper standard of scrutiny to use in sex discrimination cases. Women's rights organizations were committed to persuading the Court to elevate sex discrimination to suspect class test status. The justices were closely divided on the issue, however, and until 1976 no change occurred. In that year the Court decided *Craig v. Boren*, which was to change sex discrimination law fundamentally.

In *Craig* the justices adopted an entirely new standard of scrutiny for sex discrimination cases. This test, known as intermediate or heightened scrutiny, requires that laws that classify on the basis of sex be substantially related to an important government objective. It appealed especially to justices in the center of the Court who were not happy with either the more conservative rational basis test or the liberal suspect class test. Observe how William J. Brennan Jr., writing for the Court, justifies the new test as being consistent with *Reed* and how he treats the use

of social science evidence. Also, read carefully William Rehnquist's dissenting opinion rejecting the new test, especially as beneficially applied to men.

Craig v. Boren

429 U.S. 190 (1976)
http://caselaw.findlaw.com/us-supreme-court/429/190.html
*Oral arguments available at https://www.oyez.org/
    cases/1976/75-628*
*Vote: 7 (Blackmun, Brennan, Marshall, Powell, Stevens,
    Stewart, White)
    2 (Burger, Rehnquist)*

OPINION OF THE COURT: *Brennan*

CONCURRING OPINIONS: *Powell, Stevens*

OPINION CONCURRING IN THE JUDGMENT: *Stewart*

OPINION CONCURRING IN PART: *Blackmun*

DISSENTING OPINIONS: *Burger, Rehnquist*

In 1972 Oklahoma enacted a statute setting the age of legal majority for both males and females at eighteen. Before then, females reached legal age at eighteen and males at twenty-one.[19] The equalization statute, however, contained one exception. Males

---

[18]See, for example, *Frontiero v. Richardson* (1973), **Kahn v. Shevin** (1974), and *Stanton v. Stanton* (1975).

[19]For more on this case, see Lee Epstein and Jack Knight, *The Choices Justices Make* (Washington, DC: CQ Press, 1998).

could not purchase beer, even with the low 3.2 percent alcohol level, until they reached twenty-one; females could buy beer at eighteen. The state differentiated between the sexes in response to statistical evidence indicating a greater tendency for males ages eighteen to twenty-one to be involved in alcohol-related traffic accidents, including fatalities.

Viewing the Oklahoma law as a form of sex discrimination, Mark Walker, a twenty-year-old Oklahoma State University student who wanted to buy beer, and Carolyn Whitener, the owner of the Honk-N-Holler convenience store, who wanted to sell it, brought suit in federal trial court challenging the law on equal protection grounds. While the case slowly progressed, Walker turned twenty-one and was no longer subject to the state restrictions on purchasing alcohol. To protect against the case being declared moot, eighteen-year-old Curtis Craig replaced his friend Walker as the lead party.

Craig and Whitener argued that the Oklahoma law should be evaluated on the basis of strict scrutiny. The state disagreed. It urged the trial court to apply the rational basis test. Under that test, the law was clearly constitutional, the state claimed, because statistics demonstrated that compared to women, men in the eighteen-to-twenty age category "drive more, drink more, and commit more alcohol-related offenses."

While acknowledging that the U.S. Supreme Court decisions were murky, a three-judge district court ruled that the rational basis test was the appropriate standard to apply. In doing so the judges concluded that the statistical evidence supporting the differences in male and female drinking and driving behavior were sufficient to justify the state's sex-based alcohol policy. Craig and Whitener appealed to the U.S. Supreme Court.

The state continued to advocate for the continued use of the rational basis test, and Craig and Whitener for strict scrutiny. Craig and Whitener also opened the door to a compromise. Their brief cited a passage written by Justice Harry Blackmun in *Stanton v. Stanton* (1975), another dispute over sex differences and legal maturation. In deciding that case (and also avoiding the level of scrutiny issue) Blackmun wrote for the majority, "We therefore conclude that under any test—compelling state interest, or rational basis, or *something in between*—[the statute] does not survive an equal protection attack" (emphasis added). This suggested that the justices might be open to a compromise, some level of scrutiny between rational basis and strict scrutiny. An amicus curiae brief, written on behalf of the ACLU by Ruth Bader Ginsburg, also emphasized the possibility of an "in between" solution to the level of scrutiny standoff.

MR. JUSTICE BRENNAN DELIVERED THE OPINION OF THE COURT.

Analysis may appropriately begin with the reminder that *Reed* [*v. Reed,* (1971)] emphasized that statutory classifications that distinguish between males and females are "subject to scrutiny under the Equal Protection Clause." To withstand constitutional challenge, previous cases establish that classifications by gender must serve important governmental objectives and must be substantially related to achievement of those objectives. Thus, in *Reed,* the objectives of "reducing the workload on probate courts" and "avoiding intrafamily controversy" were deemed of insufficient importance to sustain use of an overt gender criterion in the appointment of administrators of intestate decedents' estates. Decisions following *Reed* similarly have rejected administrative ease and convenience as sufficiently important objectives to justify gender-based classifications. . . .

Reed v. Reed has also provided the underpinning for decisions that have invalidated statutes employing gender as an inaccurate proxy for other, more germane bases of classification. Hence, "archaic and overbroad" generalizations could not justify use of a gender line in determining eligibility for certain governmental entitlements. Similarly, increasingly outdated misconceptions concerning the role of females in the home rather than in the "marketplace and world of ideas" were rejected as loose-fitting characterizations incapable of supporting state statutory schemes that were premised upon their accuracy. In light of the weak congruence between gender and the characteristic or trait that gender purported to represent, it was necessary that the legislatures choose either to realign their substantive laws in a gender-neutral fashion, or to adopt procedures for identifying those instances where the sex-centered generalization actually comported with fact.

In this case, too, "*Reed,* we feel, is controlling. . . ." We turn then to the question whether, under *Reed,* the difference between males and females with respect to the purchase of 3.2% beer warrants the differential in age drawn by the Oklahoma statute. We conclude that it does not.

The District Court recognized that *Reed v. Reed* was controlling. In applying the teachings of that case, the court found the requisite important governmental objective in the traffic-safety goal proffered by the Oklahoma Attorney General. It then concluded that the statistics introduced by the appellees established that the gender-based distinction was substantially related to achievement of that goal.

. . . Clearly, the protection of public health and safety represents an important function of state and local governments. However, appellees' statistics in our view cannot support the conclusion that the gender-based distinction closely serves to achieve that objective and therefore the distinction cannot under *Reed* withstand equal protection challenge.

The appellees introduced a variety of statistical surveys. First, an analysis of arrest statistics for 1973 demonstrated that 18–20-year-old male arrests for "driving under the influence" and "drunkenness" substantially exceeded female arrests for that same age period. Similarly, youths aged 17–21 were found to be overrepresented among those killed or injured in traffic accidents, with males again numerically exceeding females in this regard. Third, a random roadside survey in Oklahoma City revealed that young males were more inclined to drive and drink beer than were their female counterparts. Fourth, Federal Bureau of Investigation nationwide statistics exhibited a notable increase in arrests for "driving under the influence." Finally, statistical evidence gathered in other jurisdictions, particularly Minnesota and Michigan, was offered to corroborate Oklahoma's experience by indicating the pervasiveness of youthful participation in motor vehicle accidents following the imbibing of alcohol. . . .

Even were this statistical evidence accepted as accurate, it nevertheless offers only a weak answer to the equal protection question presented here. The most focused and relevant of the statistical surveys, arrests of 18–20-year-olds for alcohol-related driving offenses, exemplifies the ultimate unpersuasiveness of this evidentiary record. Viewed in terms of the correlation between sex and the actual activity that Oklahoma seeks to regulate—driving while under the influence of alcohol—the statistics broadly establish that .18% of females and 2% of males in that age group were arrested for that offense. While such a disparity is not trivial in a statistical sense, it hardly can form the basis for employment of a gender line as a classifying device. Certainly if maleness is to serve as a proxy for drinking and driving, a correlation of 2% must be considered an unduly tenuous "fit." Indeed, prior cases have consistently rejected the use of sex as a decisionmaking factor even though the statutes in question certainly rested on far more predictive empirical relationships than this.

Moreover, the statistics exhibit a variety of other shortcomings that seriously impugn their value to equal protection analysis. Setting aside the obvious methodological problems, the surveys do not adequately justify the salient features of Oklahoma's gender-based traffic-safety law. None purports to measure the use and dangerousness of 3.2% beer as opposed to alcohol generally, a detail that is of particular importance since, in light of its low alcohol level, Oklahoma apparently considers the 3.2% beverage to be "nonintoxicating." Moreover, many of the studies, while graphically documenting the unfortunate increase in driving while under the influence of alcohol, make no effort to relate their findings to age-sex differentials as involved here. Indeed, the only survey that explicitly centered its attention upon young drivers and their use of beer—albeit apparently not of the diluted 3.2% variety—reached results that hardly can be viewed as impressive in justifying either a gender or age classification.

There is no reason to belabor this line of analysis. It is unrealistic to expect either members of the judiciary or state officials to be well versed in the rigors of experimental or statistical technique. But this merely illustrates that proving broad sociological propositions by statistics is a dubious business, and one that inevitably is in tension with the normative philosophy that underlies the Equal Protection Clause. Suffice to say that the showing offered by the appellees does not satisfy us that sex represents a legitimate, accurate proxy for the regulation of drinking and driving. In fact, when it is further recognized that Oklahoma's statute prohibits only the selling of 3.2% beer to young males and not their drinking the beverage once acquired (even after purchase by their 18–20-year-old female companions), the relationship between gender and traffic safety becomes far too tenuous to satisfy *Reed*'s requirement that the gender-based difference be substantially related to achievement of the statutory objective.

We hold, therefore, that under *Reed,* Oklahoma's 3.2% beer statute invidiously discriminates against males 18–20 years of age.

Reversed.

MR. JUSTICE REHNQUIST, DISSENTING.

The Court's disposition of this case is objectionable on two grounds. First is its conclusion that *men* challenging a gender-based statute which treats them less favorably than women may invoke a more stringent standard of judicial review than pertains to most other types of classifications. Second is the Court's enunciation of this standard, without citation to any source, as being that "classification by gender must serve *important* governmental objectives and must be *substantially* related to achievement of those objectives" (Emphasis added). The only redeeming feature of the Court's opinion, to my mind, is that it apparently signals a retreat by those who joined the plurality opinion in *Frontiero v. Richardson* (1973) from their view that sex is a "suspect" classification for purposes of equal protection analysis. I think the Oklahoma statute challenged here need pass only the "rational basis" equal protection analysis expounded in cases such as *McGowan v. Maryland* (1961) and *Williamson v. Lee Optical Co.* (1955), and I believe that it is constitutional under that analysis.

In *Frontiero v. Richardson,* the opinion for the plurality sets forth the reasons of four Justices for concluding that sex should be regarded as a suspect classification for purposes of equal protection analysis. These reasons center on our Nation's "long and unfortunate history of sex discrimination," which has been reflected in a whole range of restrictions on the legal rights of women, not the least of which have concerned the ownership of property and participation in the electoral process. Noting that the pervasive and persistent nature of the discrimination experienced by women is in part the result of their ready identifiability, the plurality rested its invocation of strict scrutiny largely upon the fact that "statutory distinctions between the sexes often have the effect of invidiously relegating the entire class of females to inferior legal status without regard to the actual capabilities of its individual members."

Subsequent to *Frontiero,* the Court has declined to hold that sex is a suspect class, and no such holding is imported by the Court's resolution of this case. However, the Court's application here of an elevated or "intermediate" level scrutiny, like that invoked in cases dealing with discrimination against females, raises the question of why the statute here should be treated any differently from countless legislative classifications unrelated to sex which have been upheld under a minimum rationality standard.

Most obviously unavailable to support any kind of special scrutiny in this case, is a history or pattern of past discrimination, such as was relied on by the plurality in *Frontiero* to support its invocation of strict scrutiny. There is no suggestion in the Court's opinion that males in this age group are in any way peculiarly disadvantaged, subject to systematic discriminatory treatment, or otherwise in need of special solicitude from the courts.

The Court does not discuss the nature of the right involved, and there is no reason to believe that it sees the purchase of 3.2% beer as implicating any important interest, let alone one that is "fundamental" in the constitutional sense of invoking strict scrutiny. Indeed, the Court's accurate observation that the statute affects the selling but not the drinking of 3.2% beer further emphasizes the limited effect that it has on even those persons in the age group involved. There is, in sum, nothing about the statutory classification involved here to suggest that it affects an interest, or works against a group, which can claim under the Equal Protection Clause that it is entitled to special judicial protection.

It is true that a number of our opinions contain broadly phrased dicta implying that the same test should be applied to all classifications based on sex, whether affecting females or males. However, before today, no decision of this Court has applied an elevated level of scrutiny to invalidate a statutory discrimination harmful to males, except where the statute impaired an important personal interest protected by the Constitution. There being no such interest here, and there being no plausible argument that this is a discrimination against females, the Court's reliance on our previous sex-discrimination cases is ill-founded. It treats gender classification as a talisman which—without regard to the rights involved or the persons affected—calls into effect a heavier burden of judicial review.

The Court's conclusion that a law which treats males less favorably than females "must serve important governmental objectives and must be substantially related to achievement of those objectives" apparently comes out of thin air. The Equal Protection Clause contains no such language, and none of our previous cases adopt that standard. I would think we have had enough difficulty with the two standards of review which our cases have recognized—the norm of "rational basis," and the "compelling state interest" required where a "suspect classification" is involved—so as to counsel weightily against the insertion of still another "standard" between those two. How is this Court to divine what objectives are important? How is it to determine whether a particular law is "substantially" related to the achievement of such objective, rather than related in some other way to its achievement? Both of the phrases used are so diaphanous and elastic as to invite subjective judicial preferences or prejudices relating to particular types of legislation, masquerading

as judgments whether such legislation is directed at "important" objectives or, whether the relationship to those objectives is "substantial" enough.

I would have thought that if this Court were to leave anything to decision by the popularly elected branches of the Government, where no constitutional claim other than that of equal protection is invoked, it would be the decision as to what governmental objectives to be achieved by law are "important," and which are not. As for the second part of the Court's new test, the Judicial Branch is probably in no worse position than the Legislative or Executive Branches to determine if there is *any* rational relationship between a classification and the purpose which it might be thought to serve. But the introduction of the adverb "substantially" requires courts to make subjective judgments as to operational effects, for which neither their expertise nor their access to data fits them. And even if we manage to avoid both confusion and the mirroring of our own preferences in the development of this new doctrine, the thousands of judges in other courts who must interpret the Equal Protection Clause may not be so fortunate.

The Court's ruling in *Craig v. Boren* had little impact on the parties to the case *(see Box 19-4)*, but the decision fundamentally changed sex discrimination law. The intermediate scrutiny test—requiring that laws that classify on the basis of sex be substantially related to an important government objective—was adopted by a narrow margin. Nevertheless, *Craig v. Boren* established the elevated level of scrutiny standard that has been used in sex discrimination cases ever since. The battle between strict scrutiny advocates and rational basis proponents ended with neither side able to claim a total victory.

In the years following *Craig* the Court confronted many claims of unconstitutional discrimination based on gender. In general, the Court continued to strike down laws and government actions that treated males and females differently simply because it was administratively convenient to do so. The Court also has taken a dim view of laws that include overbroad sex-based assumptions, particularly if a presumption of female inferiority appears to be the basis for the statute. For example, in **Orr v. Orr** (1979) the justices struck down an Alabama law that permitted courts to impose alimony obligations on husbands but not on wives. The law, according to Justice Brennan, speaking for the majority, contained an outdated stereotype that women are dependent on men. Similarly, in **Mississippi University for Women v. Hogan** (1982) the Court struck down the all-female admissions standard used by a state university because it was based on a presumption that female students were inferior and

BOX 19-4

Aftermath . . . *Craig v. Boren*

On January 12, 1976, the Supreme Court announced that it had accepted the case of *Craig v. Boren* for full consideration later that year. The news naturally excited Mark Walker, the former Oklahoma State University student who first initiated the legal action after becoming upset that a twenty-year-old male could be drafted and sent to war but could not buy a beer in Oklahoma. He eagerly awaited the oral arguments scheduled for October.

Tragically, however, Walker did not live to see the arguments or experience victory when the Supreme Court issued a ruling in his favor. On May 8, 1976, Mark Walker died in an auto accident. He was driving outside Stillwater when in the opposite lane one car was struck by another, causing the first vehicle to cross the median and crash head-on into the car driven by Walker.

Carolyn Whitener, the beer vendor who joined Walker's lawsuit challenging the constitutionality of the Oklahoma law, was owner of the Honk-N-Holler convenience store on Sixth and Knoblock Streets in Stillwater. At one time, together with her husband, she owned eleven such stores. Later the Whiteners sold the stores and went into the computer equipment business. Because of her role in the *Craig* case, Whitener was inducted into the Oklahoma Women's Hall of Fame in 2009 for her contributions to sexual equality.

Curtis Craig, Mark Walker's college friend who became the lead litigant when Walker turned twenty-one and was no longer affected by the challenged law, graduated with a BS degree from Oklahoma State University. He later received his law degree from the University of Tulsa. Craig subsequently had a long career as vice president and general counsel for the Tulsa-based Explorer Pipeline Company.

David Boren, who defended the state law against the constitutional challenge, was governor of Oklahoma from 1975 to 1979. In 1978 he won election to the U.S. Senate; he was reelected in 1984 and again in 1990, when he captured 83 percent of the vote. He stepped down from his Senate seat in 1994 to assume the presidency of the University of Oklahoma, a position he held until 2018.

Sources: R. Darcy and Jenny Sanbrano, "Oklahoma in the Development of Equal Rights: The ERA, 3.2% Beer, Juvenile Justice, and *Craig v. Boren*," *Oklahoma City University Law Review* 22 (1997): 1009–1049; Martindale.com, http://martindale.com; *Okie Women*, March 22, 2009; *Tulsa World*, March 25, 2009; University of Oklahoma, Office of the President, http://www.ou.edu/president/biography.html.

---

needed an academic environment without competition from males to succeed. The justices reemphasized this position in **United States v. Virginia** (1996), when they struck down the men-only admissions policy at Virginia Military Institute, a state-supported military college. The justices held that a state institution cannot constitutionally restrict participation to one sex on the ground that the educational experiences provided are inappropriate for the other.

In other cases, however, the Court has found some laws that discriminated between males and females to be valid because they recognized legitimate differences between the sexes. In **Michael M. v. Superior Court of Sonoma County** (1981) the justices, by a 5–4 vote, upheld a statutory rape law that applied to males only. The fact that only females can become pregnant was a significant sex difference that the majority took into account. In **Rostker v. Goldberg** (1981) the Court upheld the federal draft law that required men but not women to register for military service. Here the justices deferred to the judgment of the military and Congress that the nation required a system for quickly raising combat forces, and that men were better suited than women for combat.

DISCRIMINATION BASED ON SEXUAL ORIENTATION

Along with issues of race and gender, discrimination based on sexual orientation has been a subject of public controversy and legal disputes over the past several decades. Until the Supreme Court struck it down in **United States v. Windsor** (2013), a section of the 1996 Defense of Marriage Act denied federal recognition of same-sex marriages even for couples living in states that recognized such unions. That same federal statute permitted the states to refuse to recognize same-sex marriages legally performed in other states. Also in 1996, Congress refused to extend the remedies of the 1964 Civil Rights Act to sexual orientation, a move that would have prohibited job discrimination based on sexual orientation. These actions reflected public opinion at the time. In 1996 nearly two-thirds of Americans thought that sexual relations between two adults of the same sex was always or almost always wrong,[20] and only 27 percent believed that same-sex marriages should be recognized as valid.[21]

What about the Supreme Court? For years the justices avoided the issue in spite of efforts by gay rights groups to promote the expansion of legal protections for homosexuals. When the Court finally did decide a gay rights case, *Bowers v. Hardwick* (1986), it upheld laws against sodomy, as we mentioned in chapter 16.

In the years since *Bowers*, though, the Court has grown increasingly hostile to laws that classify or otherwise burden on the basis of sexual orientation. Table 19-2 highlights this point by identifying the major gay rights disputes, beginning with *Bowers* and ending with *Obergefell v. Hodges* (2015), in which the Court invalidated state bans on same-sex marriage. Recall from chapter 16, though, that in *Obergefell* (as well as in *Lawrence* and even *Windsor*), Justice Kennedy rested his majority opinion primarily on the due process clause, not on the equal protection clause.

As a result (and despite the importance of *Obergefell*), *Romer v. Evans* remains the Court's most significant interpretation of the equal protection clause as it applies to classifications based on sexual orientation. Note that the Court applied rational basis scrutiny to determine whether Colorado's constitutional amendment amounted to unconstitutional discrimination. When the Court applies this standard, it usually upholds the classification, but not here. Why?

Romer v. Evans

517 U.S. 620 (1996)

http://caselaw.findlaw.com/us-supreme-court/517/620.html

Oral arguments available at https://www.oyez.org/ cases/1995/94-103

Vote: 6 (Breyer, Ginsburg, Kennedy, O'Connor, Souter, Stevens)

3 (Rehnquist, Scalia, Thomas)

OPINION OF THE COURT: *Kennedy*

DISSENTING OPINION: *Scalia*

---

[20]Lee Epstein, et al. *The Supreme Court Compendium*, 6th ed. (Thousand Oaks, CA: CQ Press, 2015), Table 8-21.

[21]Gallup Historical Trends, Gay and Lesbian Rights, http://www.gallup.com/poll/1651/gay-lesbian-rights.aspx.

This case involved a challenge to an amendment to the Colorado state constitution, which had been adopted by statewide initiative. The initiative arose in response to local laws passed by communities such as Boulder, Aspen, and Denver, making sexual orientation an impermissible ground upon which to discriminate. In effect, the local laws gave sexual orientation the same status as race, sex, and other protected categories. To reverse this trend and remove the possibility of future legislation, a sufficient number of citizens signed a petition to place a proposed constitutional amendment on the ballot for the November 1992 elections. Known as Amendment 2, it passed with the support of 53.4 percent of those voting. The amendment stated:

> Neither the State of Colorado, through any of its branches or departments, nor any of its agencies, political subdivisions, municipalities or school districts, shall enact, adopt or enforce any statute, regulation, ordinance or policy whereby homosexual, lesbian or bisexual orientation, conduct, practices or relationships shall constitute or otherwise be the basis of or entitle any person or class of persons to have or claim any minority status, quota preferences, protected status or claim of discrimination. This Section of the Constitution shall be in all respects self-executing.

Almost immediately Richard G. Evans, a gay employee in the office of the mayor of Denver, other citizens, and several Colorado local governments sued Governor Roy Romer and the state of Colorado, claiming that the new amendment was in violation of the Fourteenth Amendment's equal protection clause. The amendment, they contended, prohibited gays from using the political process to secure legal protections against discrimination. The Colorado Supreme Court, 6–1, struck down the amendment, and the state appealed to the U.S. Supreme Court.

JUSTICE KENNEDY DELIVERED THE OPINION OF THE COURT.

One century ago, the first Justice Harlan admonished this Court that the Constitution "neither knows nor tolerates classes among citizens." *Plessy v. Ferguson* (1896) (dissenting opinion). Unheeded then, those words now are understood to state a commitment to the law's neutrality where the rights of persons are at stake. The Equal Protection Clause enforces this principle and today requires us to hold invalid a provision of Colorado's Constitution. . . .

Soon after Amendment 2 was adopted, this litigation to declare its invalidity and enjoin its enforcement was commenced in the District Court for the City and County of Denver. . . .

The trial court granted a preliminary injunction to stay enforcement of Amendment 2, and an appeal was taken to the

Table 19-2   The Court and Gay Rights Cases since 1986

Case	Outcome
Bowers v. Hardwick (1986). Georgia law that prohibited oral or anal sex challenged on the grounds that it violated the fundamental right to privacy embraced by the Fourteenth Amendment's due process clause.	5 (Burger, O'Connor, Powell, Rehnquist, **White**) to 4 (Blackmun, Brennan, Marshall, Stevens) to uphold the law. The majority held that consensual homosexual sodomy is not a fundamental right under the Fourteenth Amendment due process clause. Applying rational basis, the majority found that the state has a legitimate interest in morality.
Romer v. Evans (1996). Amendment to the Colorado state constitution that limited cities from enacting antidiscrimination ordinances based on sexual orientation challenged as violating the Fourteenth Amendment's equal protection clause.	6 (Breyer, Ginsburg, **Kennedy**, O'Connor, Souter, Stevens) to 3 (Rehnquist, Scalia, Thomas) to invalidate the amendment. The majority, applying rational basis scrutiny, found no legitimate justification for singling out sexual orientation for political disability and so inferred animus as a motivating factor.
Lawrence v. Texas (2003). Texas law that made it a crime for two persons of the same sex to engage in sodomy challenged as violation of the due process and equal protection clauses.	6 (Breyer, Ginsburg, **Kennedy**, O'Connor, Souter, Stevens) to 3 (Rehnquist, Scalia, Thomas) to invalidate the law. In overruling *Bowers,* the majority found that the state's moral justification for the law was insufficient to overcome the individual's protected liberty interest in privacy and dignity.
Perry v. Hollingsworth (2013). A due process and equal protection challenge to an amendment to the California constitution banning same-sex marriages.	5 (Breyer, Ginsburg, Kagan, **Roberts,** Scalia) to 4 (Alito, Kennedy, Sotomayor, Thomas) to vacate and remand. The Court dismissed the case on standing to sue grounds. Because the lower court had invalidated the amendment, the impact of the decision was to allow same-sex marriages to continue in California.
United States v. Windsor (2013). Federal Defense of Marriage Act (DOMA), which defined marriage as a legally recognized relationship between one man and one woman for purposes of the more than 1,000 federal laws that address marital or spousal status, challenged as a violation of the Fifth Amendment due process clause.	5 (Breyer, Ginsburg, Kagan, **Kennedy**, Sotomayor) to 4 (Alito, Roberts, Scalia, Thomas) to strike the law because the government had not supported it with any legitimate reason.
Obergefell v. Hodges (2015). Ohio's ban on same-sex marriage challenged as violating the equal protection and due process clauses of the Fourteenth Amendment.	5 (Breyer, Ginsburg, Kagan, **Kennedy**, Sotomayor) to 4 (Alito, Roberts, Scalia, Thomas) to invalidate the law, primarily as a denial of the dignity, personal choice, and autonomy interests protected by the due process clause.

Note: The majority opinion writer is in boldface.

Supreme Court of Colorado. Sustaining the interim injunction and remanding the case for further proceedings, the State Supreme Court held that Amendment 2 was subject to strict scrutiny under the Fourteenth Amendment because it infringed the fundamental right of gays and lesbians to participate in the political process. . . . On remand, the State advanced various arguments in an effort to show that Amendment 2 was narrowly tailored to serve compelling interests, but the trial court found none sufficient. It enjoined enforcement of Amendment 2, and the Supreme Court of Colorado, in a second opinion, affirmed the ruling. We granted certiorari and now affirm the judgment, but on a rationale different from that adopted by the State Supreme Court.

The State's principal argument in defense of Amendment 2 is that it puts gays and lesbians in the same position as all other persons. So, the State says, the measure does no more than deny homosexuals special rights. This reading of the amendment's language is implausible. We rely not upon our own interpretation of the amendment but upon the authoritative construction of Colorado's Supreme Court. The state court, deeming it unnecessary to determine the full extent of the amendment's reach, found it invalid even on a modest reading of its implications. The critical discussion of the amendment, set out . . . [by the Colorado Supreme Court], is as follows:

> The immediate objective of Amendment 2 is, at a minimum, to repeal existing statutes, regulations, ordinances, and policies of state and local entities that barred discrimination based on sexual orientation. . . .

> The "ultimate effect" of Amendment 2 is to prohibit any governmental entity from adopting similar, or more protective statutes, regulations, ordinances, or policies in the future unless the state constitution is first amended to permit such measures.

Sweeping and comprehensive is the change in legal status effected by this law. So much is evident from the ordinances that the Colorado Supreme Court declared would be void by operation of Amendment 2. Homosexuals, by state decree, are put in a solitary class with respect to transactions and relations in both the private and governmental spheres. The amendment withdraws from homosexuals, but no others, specific legal protection from the injuries caused by discrimination, and it forbids reinstatement of these laws and policies.

The change that Amendment 2 works in the legal status of gays and lesbians in the private sphere is far-reaching, both on its own terms and when considered in light of the structure and operation of modern anti-discrimination laws. That structure is well illustrated by contemporary statutes and ordinances prohibiting discrimination by providers of public accommodations. . . .

Amendment 2 bars homosexuals from securing protection against the injuries that these public-accommodations laws address. That in itself is a severe consequence, but there is more. Amendment 2, in addition, nullifies specific legal protections for this targeted class in all transactions in housing, sale of real estate, insurance, health and welfare services, private education, and employment.

Not confined to the private sphere, Amendment 2 also operates to repeal and forbid all laws or policies providing specific protection for gays or lesbians from discrimination by every level of Colorado government. . . . The repeal of these measures and the prohibition against their future reenactment demonstrates that Amendment 2 has the same force and effect in Colorado's governmental sector as it does elsewhere and that it applies to policies as well as ordinary legislation.

Amendment 2's reach may not be limited to specific laws passed for the benefit of gays and lesbians. It is a fair, if not necessary, inference from the broad language of the amendment that it deprives gays and lesbians even of the protection of general laws and policies that prohibit arbitrary discrimination in governmental and private settings. . . .

. . . [W]e cannot accept the view that Amendment 2's prohibition on specific legal protections does no more than deprive homosexuals of special rights. To the contrary, the amendment imposes a special disability upon those persons alone. Homosexuals are forbidden the safeguards that others enjoy or may seek without constraint. They can obtain specific protection against discrimination only by enlisting the citizenry of Colorado to amend the state constitution or perhaps, on the State's view, by trying to pass helpful laws of general applicability. This is so no matter how local or discrete the harm, no matter how public and widespread the injury. We find nothing special in the protections Amendment 2 withholds. These are protections taken for granted by most people either because they already have them or do not need them; these are protections against exclusion from an almost limitless number of transactions and endeavors that constitute ordinary civic life in a free society.

The Fourteenth Amendment's promise that no person shall be denied the equal protection of the laws must coexist with the practical necessity that most legislation classifies for one purpose or another, with resulting disadvantage to various groups or persons. We have attempted to reconcile the principle with the reality by stating that, if a law neither burdens a fundamental right nor targets a suspect class, we will uphold the legislative classification so long as it bears a rational relation to some legitimate end. See, *e.g., Heller v. Doe* (1993).

Amendment 2 fails, indeed defies, even this conventional inquiry. First, the amendment has the peculiar property of imposing a broad and undifferentiated disability on a single named group, an exceptional and, as we shall explain, invalid form of legislation. Second, its sheer breadth is so discontinuous with the reasons offered for it that the amendment seems inexplicable by anything but animus toward the class that it affects; it lacks a rational relationship to legitimate state interests.

Taking the first point, even in the ordinary equal protection case calling for the most deferential of standards, we insist on knowing the relation between the classification adopted and the object to be attained. The search for the link between classification and objective gives substance to the Equal Protection Clause; it provides guidance and discipline for the legislature, which is entitled to know what sorts of laws it can pass; and it marks the limits of our own authority. In the ordinary case, a law will be sustained if it can be said to advance a legitimate government interest, even if the law seems unwise or works to the disadvantage of a particular group, or if the rationale for it seems tenuous. . . . By requiring that the classification bear a rational relationship to an independent and legitimate legislative end, we ensure that classifications are not drawn for the purpose of disadvantaging the group burdened by the law.

Amendment 2 confounds this normal process of judicial review. It is at once too narrow and too broad. It identifies persons by a single trait and then denies them protection across the board. The resulting disqualification of a class of persons from the right to seek specific protection from the law is unprecedented in our jurisprudence. . . .

It is not within our constitutional tradition to enact laws of this sort. Central both to the idea of the rule of law and to our own Constitution's guarantee of equal protection is the principle that government and each of its parts remain open on impartial terms to all who seek its assistance. . . . Respect for this principle explains why laws singling out a certain class of citizens for disfavored legal status or general hardships are rare. A law declaring that in general it shall be more difficult for one group of citizens than for all others to seek aid from the government is itself a denial of equal protection of the laws in the most literal sense. . . .

. . . [L]aws of the kind now before us raise the inevitable inference that the disadvantage imposed is born of animosity toward the class of persons affected. . . . Even laws enacted for broad and ambitious purposes often can be explained by reference to legitimate public policies which justify the incidental disadvantages they impose on certain persons. Amendment 2, however, in making a general announcement that gays and lesbians shall not have any particular protections from the law, inflicts on them immediate, continuing, and real injuries that outrun and belie any legitimate justifications that may be claimed for it. We conclude that, in addition to the far-reaching deficiencies of Amendment 2 that we have noted, the principles it offends, in another sense, are conventional and venerable; a law must bear a rational relationship to a legitimate governmental purpose, and Amendment 2 does not.

The primary rationale the State offers for Amendment 2 is respect for other citizens' freedom of association, and in particular the liberties of landlords or employers who have personal or religious objections to homosexuality. Colorado also cites its interest in conserving resources to fight discrimination against other groups. The breadth of the Amendment is so far removed from these particular justifications that we find it impossible to credit them. We cannot say that Amendment 2 is directed to any identifiable legitimate purpose or discrete objective. It is a status-based enactment divorced from any factual context from which we could discern a relationship to legitimate state interests; it is a classification of persons undertaken for its own sake, something the Equal Protection Clause does not permit.

We must conclude that Amendment 2 classifies homosexuals not to further a proper legislative end but to make them unequal to everyone else. This Colorado cannot do. A State cannot so deem a class of persons a stranger to its laws. Amendment 2 violates the Equal Protection Clause, and the judgment of the Supreme Court of Colorado is affirmed.

It is so ordered.

JUSTICE SCALIA, WITH WHOM THE CHIEF JUSTICE AND JUSTICE THOMAS JOIN, DISSENTING.

The Court has mistaken a Kulturkampf [a cultural conflict between religious and civil authorities] for a fit of spite. The constitutional amendment before us here is not the manifestation of a "'bare . . . desire to harm'" homosexuals, but is rather a modest attempt by seemingly tolerant Coloradans to preserve traditional sexual mores against the efforts of a politically powerful minority to revise those mores through use of the laws. That objective, and the means chosen to achieve it, are not only unimpeachable under any constitutional doctrine hitherto pronounced (hence the opinion's heavy reliance upon principles of righteousness rather than judicial holdings); they have been specifically approved by the Congress of the United States and by this Court.

In holding that homosexuality cannot be singled out for disfavorable treatment, the Court contradicts a decision, unchallenged here, pronounced only 10 years ago, see *Bowers v. Hardwick,* and places the prestige of this institution behind the proposition that opposition to homosexuality is as reprehensible as racial or religious bias. Whether it is or not is *precisely* the cultural debate that gave rise to the Colorado constitutional amendment (and to the preferential laws against which the amendment was directed). Since the Constitution of the United States says nothing about this subject, it is left to be resolved by normal democratic means, including the democratic adoption of provisions in state constitutions. This Court has no business imposing upon all Americans the resolution favored by the elite class from which the Members of this institution are selected, pronouncing that "animosity" toward homosexuality is evil. I vigorously dissent. . . .

. . .The Court's opinion contains grim, disapproving hints that Coloradans have been guilty of "animus" or "animosity" toward homosexuality, as though that has been established as Unamerican. Of course it is our moral heritage that one should not hate any human being or class of human beings. But I had thought that one could consider certain conduct reprehensible—murder, for example, or polygamy, or cruelty to animals—and could exhibit even "animus" toward such conduct. Surely that is the only sort of "animus" at issue here: moral disapproval of homosexual conduct. . . .

But though Coloradans are, as I say, *entitled* to be hostile toward homosexual conduct, the fact is that the degree of hostility reflected by Amendment 2 is the smallest conceivable. The Court's portrayal of Coloradans as a society fallen victim to pointless, hate-filled "gay-bashing" is so false as to be comical. Colorado not only is one of the 25 States that have repealed their antisodomy laws, but was among the first to do so. But the society that eliminates criminal punishment for homosexual acts does not necessarily abandon the view that homosexuality is morally wrong and socially harmful; often, abolition simply reflects the view that enforcement of such criminal laws involves unseemly intrusion into the intimate lives of citizens. . . .

Today's opinion has no foundation in American constitutional law, and barely pretends to. The people of Colorado have adopted an entirely reasonable provision which does not even disfavor homosexuals in any substantive sense, but merely denies them preferential treatment. Amendment 2 is designed to prevent piecemeal deterioration of the sexual morality favored by a majority of Coloradans, and is not only an appropriate means to that legitimate end, but a means that Americans have employed before. Striking it down is an act, not of judicial judgment, but of political will. I dissent.

The majority's opinion is a strong statement against laws that single out homosexuals for discriminatory treatment. But the ruling is also important for other reasons. The justices explicitly distanced themselves from the "strict scrutiny" approach of the Colorado Supreme Court and did not even engage in a full discussion of the relative merits of the three equal protection tests as applied to gay rights. Instead, the Court concluded that Amendment 2 offends even the lowest level of scrutiny (rational basis), and because the state's justifications for singling out sexual orientation for political disability were weak, the majority could only infer that the amendment was driven by animus against gays and lesbians.

That same logic moved to the fore in **United States v. Windsor** (2013). Although that case, like *Obergefell*, rested on notions of human dignity

embraced in the due process clause (as well as the primacy of the state over issues of marriage), Justice Kennedy, writing for the majority, did note that the Defense of Marriage Act (DOMA) violated equal protection principles because it was "motivated by an improper animus or purpose." To find such a purpose, Kennedy did not have to look far. A congressional report on the law concluded that DOMA expresses "moral disapproval of homosexuality."

What might we conclude from *Romer*, *Windsor*, and the other gay rights cases listed in Table 19-2 (and discussed in chapter 16)? On the one hand, it is hard to deny that gays and lesbians have made significant progress in the Court since the 1990s. We only have to recall that as recently as 1986, the justices upheld bans on same-sex sodomy, while in 2015 they invalidated bans on same-sex marriage. On the other hand, because the Court has yet to decide whether classifications based on sexual orientation should be subject to strict or even intermediate scrutiny, questions remain about how the justices will treat these classifications moving forward—whether in employment, housing, jury selection, and many other spheres of American life where gays and lesbians do not have the benefit of federal civil rights laws, as do other groups.

DISCRIMINATION BASED ON ECONOMIC STATUS

As with matters of race, gender, and sexual orientation, society's views on economic status have changed. In the early days of our nation, wealth was considered a reflection of individual worth. The poor were thought to be less deserving. The free enterprise philosophy that emphasized personal economic responsibility discouraged public policies designed to help the less fortunate. The fact that people could be imprisoned for failure to pay debts—a contrast with today's more lenient treatment under the bankruptcy laws—reflects that period's hard-line approach to economic failure. Even a sitting Supreme Court justice, James Wilson, was imprisoned in 1796 because of a failure to satisfy his creditors. In *City of New York v. Miln* (1837) the Court supported the power of the state to take "precautionary measures against the moral pestilence of paupers."

As American society has evolved, the plight of the poor has become a major public policy concern.

Although opinions differ widely on the proper role of government in addressing poverty, housing, and health care, the U.S. political system has developed social programs that would have been inconceivable to leaders during the nation's formative years. Moreover, economic disadvantage, at least according to the Supreme Court, is no longer a justification for denying a person full political and social rights. We have already seen, for example, that the Court has extended certain rights, such as government-provided attorneys, to indigent criminal defendants. It has also ruled on government policies discriminating against the poor, including welfare programs that require individuals to live in a particular state for a specified amount of time before receiving benefits.

When the Court examines such policies, what standard of review does it use? The level of scrutiny varies depending on the nature of the right in question. If the classification burdens a "fundamental" right, the justices apply strict scrutiny; if not, they invoke the rational basis standard.

Shapiro v. Thompson (1969) nicely illustrates the point. This case involved the kind of law we just mentioned: some states required applicants to live in the state for one year in order to obtain welfare benefits. The states argued that the residency requirement was necessary for fiscal reasons. They claimed that those who require welfare assistance when they first move to a state are likely to become continuing burdens. If a state can deter such people from moving there by denying them welfare benefits during the first year, the state can continue to provide aid to longtime residents.

Writing for the Court, Justice Brennan disagreed. He concluded that the "states do not use and have no need to use the one-year requirement for the governmental purposes suggested. Thus, even under traditional equal protection tests a classification of welfare applicants according to whether they have lived in the State for one year would seem irrational and unconstitutional." But he went on to say that

[t]he traditional criteria do not apply in these cases. Since the classification here touches on the fundamental right of interstate movement, its constitutionality must be judged by the stricter standard of whether it promotes a compelling

state interest. Under this standard, the waiting-period requirement clearly violates the Equal Protection Clause.

In other words, a rational basis standard normally would be appropriate in cases involving classifications based on wealth, but when a fundamental right also is involved—here, the right to interstate travel—the standard is elevated. In *Saenz v. Roe* (1999) the Court reaffirmed *Shapiro v. Thompson* by striking down a California law that imposed similar economic disadvantages on new residents who moved into the state. The Court invoked the same logic in *Harper v. Virginia State Board of Elections* (1966), in which it struck down poll taxes as infringing on the fundamental right to vote.

When a fundamental right is not involved, however, the justices have tended to stick with the rational basis standard. An example is *San Antonio Independent School District v. Rodriguez* (1973), a case of enormous importance. First, it involved the right of children to receive a public education, the surest way for the disadvantaged to improve their prospects for economic and social advancement. Second, it questioned the constitutionality of the way Texas funded public schools. Education is the most expensive of all state programs, and any change in the method of distributing these funds can have a tremendous impact. Third, the Texas system challenged here was similar to schemes most states used to determine the allocation of education dollars. Whatever the Court decided, this case was going to be significant economically and socially.

At its heart was the contention that the Texas system for funding schools discriminated against the poor. It was undeniable that children who lived in wealthy school districts had access to a higher-quality education than children in poor districts. But did this difference violate the Constitution? In large measure, the answer depended on which equal protection standard was used. Under strict scrutiny the Texas funding system almost certainly would fail. But before strict scrutiny can be applied, as we now know, one of two requirements has to be met. Either the poor, like African Americans in the racial discrimination cases, would have to be declared a suspect class, or the right to an education would have to be declared a fundamental right. If the Court failed to support one of these positions, the rational basis test would control, and the

Demetrio Rodriguez and other Mexican American parents challenged the Texas public school financing system as discriminatory on the basis of economic status, but in 1973 the Supreme Court ruled against them.

state plan likely would stand. As you read Justice Powell's decision, think about his reasoning and conclusions on these two points.

San Antonio Independent School District v. Rodriguez

411 U.S. 1 (1973)
http://caselaw.findlaw.com/us-supreme-court/411/1.html
Oral arguments available at https://www.oyez.org/
    cases/1972/71-1332
Vote: 5 (Blackmun, Burger, Powell, Rehnquist, Stewart)
    4 (Brennan, Douglas, Marshall, White)

OPINION OF THE COURT: *Powell*

CONCURRING OPINION: *Stewart*

DISSENTING OPINIONS: *Brennan, Marshall, White*

Demetrio Rodriguez and other Mexican American parents whose children attended the public schools of the Edgewood Independent School District in San Antonio, Texas, were concerned about the quality of the local schools. The Edgewood district was about 90 percent Mexican American and quite poor. Efforts to improve the children's schools were unsuccessful due to insufficient funding. Because the state formula for distributing education funds resulted in low levels of financial support for economically depressed districts, the parents filed suit to declare the state funding system in violation of the equal protection clause. The funding program guaranteed each child in the state a minimum basic education by appropriating funds to local school districts through a complex formula designed to take into account economic variations across school districts. Local districts levied property taxes to meet their assigned contributions to the state program, but they also could use the property taxing power to obtain additional funds for the schools within their own districts.

The Edgewood district had an assessed property value per pupil of $5,960, the lowest in the San Antonio area. It taxed its residents at a rate of $1.05 per $100 in assessed valuation, the area's highest rate. This local tax yielded $26 per pupil above the contributions that had to be made to the state for the 1967–1968 school year. Funds from the state added $222 per pupil, and federal programs contributed $108. These sources combined for a total of $356 per pupil for the year. In the nearby Alamo Heights district, property values amounted to $49,000 per pupil, which was taxed at a rate of $0.85 per $100 of assessed valuation. These property taxes yielded $333 additional available revenues per pupil. Combined with $225 from state funds and $36 from federal sources, Alamo Heights enjoyed a total funding level of $594 per pupil.

The suit filed by Rodriguez and the other parents was based on these disparities. Although the residents of Edgewood taxed themselves at a much higher rate, the yield from local taxes in Alamo Heights was almost thirteen times greater. To achieve equal property tax dollars with Alamo Heights, Edgewood would have had to raise its tax rate to $13 per $100 in assessed valuation, but state law placed a $1.50 ceiling on such taxes. There was no way for the Edgewood parents to achieve funding equality.

A three-judge federal court agreed with the Rodriguez suit, finding that the Texas funding program invidiously discriminated against children on the basis of economic status. According to the federal court, the poor were a suspect class, and education was a fundamental right. The state appealed to the Supreme Court. Twenty-five states filed amicus curiae briefs supporting the Texas funding system. Groups such as the NAACP, the ACLU, and the American Education Association filed briefs backing Rodriguez.

MR. JUSTICE POWELL DELIVERED THE OPINION OF THE COURT.

Texas virtually concedes that its historically rooted dual system of financing education could not withstand the strict judicial scrutiny that this Court has found appropriate in reviewing legislative judgments that interfere with fundamental constitutional rights or that involve suspect classifications. If, as previous decisions have indicated, strict scrutiny means that the State's system is not entitled to the usual presumption of validity, that the State rather than the complainants must carry a "heavy burden of justification," that the State must demonstrate that its educational system has been structured with "precision," and is "tailored" narrowly to serve legitimate objectives and that it has selected the "less drastic means" for effectuating its objectives, the Texas financing system and its counterpart in virtually every other State will not pass muster. The State candidly admits that "[n]o one familiar with the Texas system would contend that it has yet achieved perfection." Apart from its concession that educational financing in Texas has "defects" and "imperfections," the State defends the system's rationality with vigor and disputes the District Court's finding that it lacks a "reasonable basis."

This, then, establishes the framework for our analysis. We must decide, first, whether the Texas system of financing public education operates to the disadvantage of some suspect class or impinges upon a fundamental right explicitly or implicitly protected by the Constitution, thereby requiring strict judicial scrutiny. If so, the judgment of the District Court should be affirmed. If not, the Texas scheme must still be examined to determine whether it rationally furthers some legitimate, articulated state purpose and therefore does not constitute an invidious discrimination in violation of the Equal Protection Clause of the Fourteenth Amendment. . . .

. . . [F]or the several reasons that follow, we find neither the suspect-classification nor the fundamental-interest analysis persuasive.

The wealth discrimination discovered by the District Court in this case, and by several other courts that have recently struck down school-financing laws in other States, is quite unlike any of the forms of wealth discrimination heretofore reviewed by this Court. Rather than focusing on the unique features of the alleged discrimination, the courts in these cases have virtually assumed their findings of a suspect classification through a simplistic process of analysis: since, under the traditional systems of financing public schools, some poorer people receive less expensive educations than other more affluent people, these systems discriminate on the basis of wealth. This approach largely ignores the hard threshold questions, including whether it makes a difference for purposes of consideration under the Constitution that the class of disadvantaged "poor" cannot be identified or defined in customary equal protection terms, and whether the relative—rather than absolute—nature of the asserted deprivation is of significant consequence. Before a State's laws and the justification for the classifications they create are subjected to strict judicial scrutiny, we think these threshold considerations must be analyzed more closely than they were in the court below. . . .

. . . First, in support of their charge that the system discriminates against the "poor," appellees have made no effort to demonstrate that it operates to the peculiar disadvantage of any class fairly definable as indigent, or as composed of persons whose incomes are beneath any designated poverty level. Indeed, there is reason to believe that the poorest families are not necessarily clustered in the poorest property districts. A recent and exhaustive study of school districts in Connecticut concluded that . . . the poor were clustered around commercial and industrial areas—those same areas that provide the most attractive sources of property tax income for school districts. Whether a similar pattern would be discovered in Texas is not known, but there is no basis on the record in this case for assuming that the poorest people—defined by reference to any level of absolute impecunity—are concentrated in the poorest districts.

Second, neither appellees nor the District Court addressed the fact that, unlike each of the foregoing cases, lack of personal resources has not occasioned an absolute deprivation of the desired benefit. The argument here is not that the children in districts having relatively low assessable property values are receiving no public education; rather, it is that they are receiving a poorer quality education than that available to children in districts having more assessable wealth. Apart from the unsettled and disputed question whether the quality of education may be determined by the amount of money expended for it, a sufficient answer to appellees' argument is that, at least where wealth is involved, the Equal Protection Clause does not require absolute equality or precisely equal advantages. . . .

For these two reasons—the absence of any evidence that the financing system discriminates against any definable category of "poor" people or that it results in the absolute deprivation of education—the disadvantaged class is not susceptible of identification in traditional terms. . . .

However described, it is clear that appellees' suit asks this Court to extend its most exacting scrutiny to review a system that allegedly discriminates against a large, diverse, and amorphous class, unified only by the common factor of residence in districts that happen to have less taxable wealth than other districts. The system of alleged discrimination and the class it defines have none of the traditional indicia of suspectness: the class is not saddled with such disabilities, or subjected to such a history of purposeful unequal treatment, or relegated to such a position of political powerlessness as to command extraordinary protection from the majoritarian political process.

We thus conclude that the Texas system does not operate to the peculiar disadvantage of any suspect class. But in recognition of the fact that this Court has never heretofore held that wealth discrimination alone provides an adequate basis for invoking strict scrutiny, appellees have not relied solely on this contention. They also assert that the State's system impermissibly interferes with the exercise of a "fundamental" right and that accordingly the prior decisions of this Court require the application of the strict standard of judicial review. It is this question—whether education is a fundamental right, in the sense that it is among the rights and liberties protected by the Constitution—which has so consumed the attention of courts and commentators in recent years. . . .

Nothing this Court holds today in any way detracts from our historic dedication to public education. We are in complete agreement with the conclusion of the three-judge panel below that "the grave significance of education both to the individual and to our society" cannot be doubted. But the importance of a service performed by the State does not determine whether it must be regarded as fundamental for purposes of examination under the Equal Protection Clause. . . .

. . . It is not the province of this Court to create substantive constitutional rights in the name of guaranteeing equal protection of the laws. Thus, the key to discovering whether education is "fundamental" is not to be found in comparisons of . . . relative societal significance. . . . Rather, the answer lies in assessing whether there is a right to education explicitly or implicitly guaranteed by the Constitution.

Education, of course, is not among the rights afforded explicit protection under our Federal Constitution. Nor do we find any basis for saying it is implicitly so protected. As we have said, the undisputed importance of education will not alone cause this Court to depart from the usual standard for reviewing a State's social and economic legislation. It is appellees' contention, however, that education is distinguishable from other services and benefits provided by the State because it bears a peculiarly close relationship to other rights and liberties accorded protection under the Constitution. Specifically, they insist that education is itself a fundamental personal right because it is essential to the effective exercise of First Amendment freedoms and to intelligent utilization of the right to vote. In asserting a nexus between speech and education, appellees urge that the right to speak is meaningless unless the speaker is capable of articulating his thoughts intelligently and persuasively. The "marketplace of ideas" is an empty forum for those lacking basic communicative tools. Likewise, they argue that

the corollary right to receive information becomes little more than a hollow privilege when the recipient has not been taught to read, assimilate, and utilize available knowledge. . . .

We need not dispute any of these propositions. The Court has long afforded zealous protection against unjustifiable governmental interference with the individual's rights to speak and to vote. Yet we have never presumed to possess either the ability or the authority to guarantee to the citizenry the most *effective* speech or the most *informed* electoral choice. That these may be desirable goals of a system of freedom of expression and of a representative form of government is not to be doubted. These are indeed goals to be pursued by a people whose thoughts and beliefs are freed from governmental interference. But they are not values to be implemented by judicial intrusion into otherwise legitimate state activities.

Even if it were conceded that some identifiable quantum of education is a constitutionally protected prerequisite to the meaningful exercise of either right, we have no indication that the present levels of educational expenditures in Texas provide an education that falls short. . . .

We have carefully considered each of the arguments supportive of the District Court's finding that education is a fundamental right or liberty and have found those arguments unpersuasive. . . .

In its reliance on state as well as local resources, the Texas system is comparable to the systems employed in virtually every other State. The power to tax local property for educational purposes has been recognized in Texas at least since 1883. When the growth of commercial and industrial centers and accompanying shifts in population began to create disparities in local resources, Texas undertook a program calling for a considerable investment of state funds. . . .

. . . While assuring a basic education for every child in the State, it permits and encourages a large measure of participation in and control of each district's schools at the local level. . . .

The persistence of attachment to government at the lowest level where education is concerned reflects the depth of commitment of its supporters. In part, local control means . . . the freedom to devote more money to the education of one's children. Equally important, however, is the opportunity it offers for participation in the decisionmaking process that determines how those local tax dollars will be spent. Each locality is free to tailor local programs to local needs. Pluralism also affords some opportunity for experimentation, innovation, and a healthy competition for educational excellence. An analogy to the Nation-State relationship in our federal system seems uniquely appropriate. Mr. Justice Brandeis identified as one of the peculiar strengths of our form of government each State's freedom to "serve as a laboratory; and try novel social and economic experiments." No area of social concern stands to profit more from a multiplicity of viewpoints and from a diversity of approaches than does public education.

Appellees do not question the propriety of Texas' dedication to local control of education. To the contrary, they attack the school-financing system precisely because, in their view, it does not provide the same level of local control and fiscal flexibility in all districts. Appellees suggest that local control could be preserved and promoted under other financing systems that resulted in more equality in educational expenditures. While it is no doubt true that reliance on local property taxation for school revenues provides less freedom of choice with respect to expenditures for some districts than for others, the existence of "some inequality" in the manner in which the State's rationale is achieved is not alone a sufficient basis for striking down the entire system. . . .

In sum, to the extent that the Texas system of school financing results in unequal expenditures between children who happen to reside in different districts, we cannot say that such disparities are the product of a system that is so irrational as to be invidiously discriminatory. Texas has acknowledged its shortcomings and has persistently endeavored—not without some success— to ameliorate the differences in levels of expenditures without sacrificing the benefits of local participation. The Texas plan is not the result of hurried, ill-conceived legislation. It certainly is not the product of purposeful discrimination against any group or class. On the contrary, it is rooted in decades of experience in Texas and elsewhere, and in major part is the product of responsible studies by qualified people. . . .

These practical considerations, of course, play no role in the adjudication of the constitutional issues presented here. But they serve to highlight the wisdom of the traditional limitations on this Court's function. The consideration and initiation of fundamental reforms with respect to state taxation and education are matters reserved for the legislative processes of the various States, and we do no violence to the values of federalism and separation of powers by staying our hand. We hardly need add that this Court's action today is not to be viewed as placing its judicial imprimatur on the status quo. The need is apparent for reform in tax systems which may well have relied too long and too heavily on the local property tax. And certainly innovative thinking as to public education, its methods, and its funding is necessary to assure both a higher level of quality and greater uniformity of opportunity. These matters merit the continued attention of the scholars who already have contributed much by their challenges. But the ultimate solutions must come from the lawmakers and from the democratic pressures of those who elect them.

Reversed.

MR. JUSTICE MARSHALL . . . , DISSENTING.

The Court today decides, in effect, that a State may constitutionally vary the quality of education which it offers its children in accordance with the amount of taxable wealth located in the school districts within which they reside. The majority's decision represents an abrupt departure from the mainstream of recent state and federal court decisions concerning the unconstitutionality of state educational financing schemes dependent upon taxable local wealth. More unfortunately, though, the majority's holding can only be seen as a retreat from our historic commitment to equality of educational opportunity and as unsupportable acquiescence in a system which deprives children in their earliest years of the chance to reach their full potential as citizens. The Court does this despite the absence of any substantial justification for a scheme which arbitrarily channels educational resources in accordance with the fortuity of the amount of taxable wealth within each district.

In my judgment, the right of every American to an equal start in life, so far as the provision of a state service as important as education is concerned, is far too vital to permit state discrimination on grounds as tenuous as those presented by this record. Nor can I accept the notion that it is sufficient to remit these appellees to the vagaries of the political process which, contrary to the majority's suggestion, has proved singularly unsuited to the task of providing a remedy for this discrimination. I, for one, am unsatisfied with the hope of an ultimate "political" solution sometime in the indefinite future while, in the meantime, countless children unjustifiably receive inferior educations that "may affect their hearts and minds in a way unlikely ever to be undone." I must therefore respectfully dissent. . . .

. . . I must . . . voice my disagreement with the Court's rigidified approach to equal protection analysis. The Court apparently seeks to establish today that equal protection cases fall into one of two neat categories which dictate the appropriate standard of review—strict scrutiny or mere rationality. But this Court's decisions in the field of equal protection defy such easy categorization. A principled reading of what this Court has done reveals that it has applied a spectrum of standards in reviewing discrimination allegedly violative of the Equal Protection Clause. This spectrum clearly comprehends variations in the degree of care with which the Court will scrutinize particular classifications, depending, I believe, on the constitutional and societal importance of the interest adversely affected and the recognized invidiousness of the basis upon which the particular classification is drawn. I find in fact that many of the Court's recent decisions embody the very sort of reasoned approach to equal protection analysis for which I previously argued—that is, an approach in which "concentration [is] placed upon the character of the classification in question, the relative importance to individuals in the class discriminated against of the governmental benefits that they do not receive, and the asserted state interests in support of the classification."

I therefore cannot accept the majority's labored efforts to demonstrate that fundamental interests, which call for strict scrutiny of the challenged classification, encompass only established rights which we are somehow bound to recognize from the text of the Constitution itself. To be sure, some interests which the Court has deemed to be fundamental for purposes of equal protection analysis are themselves constitutionally protected rights. . . . But it will not do to suggest that the "answer" to whether an interest is fundamental for purposes of equal protection analysis is always determined by whether that interest "is a right . . . explicitly or implicitly guaranteed by the Constitution."

I would like to know where the Constitution guarantees the right to procreate, *Skinner v. Oklahoma* (1942), or the right to vote in state elections, *e.g., Reynolds v. Sims* (1964), or the right to an appeal from a criminal conviction, *e.g., Griffin v. Illinois* (1956). These are instances in which, due to the importance of the interests at stake, the Court has displayed a strong concern with the existence of discriminatory state treatment. But the Court has never said or indicated that these are interests which independently enjoy full-blown constitutional protection. . . .

. . . [I]f the discrimination inherent in the Texas scheme is scrutinized with the care demanded by the interest and classification present in this case, the unconstitutionality of that scheme is unmistakable.

The decision in *Rodriguez* was a blow to civil rights advocates. It had a substantial impact on education by validating financing systems that perpetuated inequity.

Many states, however, reacted by adjusting their financing schemes to reduce funding disparities, and some state supreme courts even found unequal funding systems to violate state constitutional provisions.

In terms of constitutional development, the ruling introduced problems for future litigation. The Court expressly held that the poor were not a suspect class. Unlike other groups that were granted such status, such as African Americans and aliens, the poor were neither an easily identified group nor politically powerless; as a group they did not have a significant history of overt discrimination. The decision not to elevate the poor to suspect class status meant that a rational basis test would be used in economic discrimination cases in which a fundamental right was not at issue. This test provides the government with an advantage in demonstrating that challenged laws are valid.

In addition, the Court in *Rodriguez* held that education, unlike the right to interstate travel, was not a fundamental right under the Constitution. This holding also created potential problems for future cases. Advocates of the poor have concentrated their efforts on education because of its crucial role in human development. By not according it fundamental right status, the Court decreased the chances of successful legal action on behalf of the disadvantaged.

ANNOTATED READINGS

A rich and interesting literature focuses on unconstitutional discrimination and the history of civil rights in the United States. Some of these works trace the history of the struggle for equal rights, such as Paul Finkelman, *Supreme Injustice: Slavery in the Nation's Highest Court* (Cambridge, MA: Harvard University Press, 2018); Leslie F. Goldstein, *The U.S. Supreme Court and Racial Minorities: Two Centuries of Judicial Review on* Trial (Cheltenham, UK: Edward Elgar, 2017); Deborah Hellman, *When Is Discrimination Wrong?* (Cambridge, MA: Harvard University Press, 2008); Michael J. Klarman, *From Jim Crow to Civil Rights: The Supreme Court and the Struggle for Racial Equality* (New York: Oxford University Press, 2004); Richard Kluger, *Simple Justice*, rev. ed. (New York: Knopf, 2004); and Alexander Tsesis, *We Shall Overcome: A History of Civil Rights and the Law* (New Haven, CT: Yale University Press, 2008).

Other studies examine particular areas of civil rights law, including Terry H. Anderson, *The Pursuit of Fairness: A History of Affirmative Action* (New York: Oxford University Press, 2004); M. Kelly Carr, *The Rhetorical Invention of Diversity: Supreme Court Opinions, Public Arguments, and Affirmative* Action (East Lansing: Michigan State University Press, 2018); Susan Gluck Mezey,

Elusive Equality: Women's Rights, Public Policy, and the Law (Boulder, CO: Lynne Rienner, 2003); Susan Gluck Mezey, *Beyond Marriage: Continuing Battles for LGBT Rights* (Lanham, MD: Rowman & Littlefield, 2017); John S. Park, *Elusive Citizenship: Immigration, Asian Americans, and the Paradox of Civil Rights* (New York: New York University Press, 2004); Jason Pierceson, *Same-Sex Marriage in the United States: The Road to the Supreme Court* (Lanham, MD: Rowman & Littlefield, 2013); Daniel R. Pinello, *Gay Rights and American Law* (New York: Cambridge University Press, 2003); Girardeau A. Spann, *Race against the Court: The Supreme Court and Minorities in Contemporary America* (New York: New York University Press, 1993); Mark Strasser, *Same-Sex Unions across the United States* (Durham, NC: Carolina Academic Press, 2011); and John H. Vinzant, *The Supreme Court's Role in American Indian Policy* (El Paso, TX: LFB Scholarly Publishing, 2009).

Many other works provide in-depth studies of landmark Supreme Court decisions. Among them are

Howard Ball, *The* Bakke *Case: Race, Education, and Affirmative Action* (Lawrence: University Press of Kansas, 2000); Richard C. Cortner, *Civil Rights and Public Accommodations: The* Heart of Atlanta *and* McClung *Cases* (Lawrence: University Press of Kansas, 2001); Jeffrey D. Hockett, *A Storm over This Court: Law, Politics, and Supreme Court Decision-Making in* Brown v. Board of Education (Charlottesville: University of Virginia Press, 2013); William James and Hull Hoffer, Plessy v. Ferguson: *Race and Equality in Jim Crow America* (Lawrence: University Press of Kansas, 2012); Bernard Schwartz, *Swann's Way: The School Busing Case and the Supreme Court* (New York: Oxford University Press, 1986); Paul A. Sracic, San Antonio v. Rodriguez *and the Pursuit of Equal Education: The Debate over Discrimination and School Funding* (Lawrence: University Press of Kansas, 2006); and Philippa Strum, *Women in the Barracks: The VMI Case and Equal Rights* (Lawrence: University Press of Kansas, 2002).

CHAPTER TWENTY

VOTING AND REPRESENTATION

FOR ANY GOVERNMENT built on a foundation of popular sovereignty, voting and representation are of critical importance. Through these mechanisms the people express their political will and ultimately control the institutions of government. Representative democracy can function properly only when the citizenry has full rights to regular and meaningful elections and when the system is structured so that public officials act on behalf of their constituents. If any segment of society is denied the right to vote or is deprived of legitimate representation, the ideals of a republican form of government are not completely realized. Because elections and representation are the primary links between the people and their government, it is not surprising that the history of American constitutional law is replete with disputes over rights of political participation.

VOTING RIGHTS

When the framers met at the Constitutional Convention of 1787, the states already had election systems, with their own requirements for qualifying voters and procedures for selecting state and local officials. By European standards, the states were quite liberal in extending the right to vote.[1] But suffrage was not universal. Ballot access generally was granted only to free adult men, and in several states only to men who owned sufficient property. Women, slaves, Native Americans, minors, and the poor could not vote. Some states prohibited Jews and Catholics from voting as well.

With state systems in place, the framers saw no reason to create a separate set of qualifications for participating in federal elections. Because there was little uniformity from state to state and qualifications often changed, the addition of a new body of federal voting requirements could cause conflict. In addition, under the Constitution drafted at Philadelphia, only one agency of the new national government, the House of Representatives, was to be elected directly by the people—further reason the federal government need not develop its own voter rolls. In Article I, Section 2, the Constitution says with respect to House elections that "the Electors in each State shall have the Qualifications requisite for Electors of the most numerous Branch of the State Legislature." If citizens were qualified to cast ballots in their states' legislative elections, they were also qualified to vote in congressional elections. The authority of the states to set voting rights policy began to change after the Civil War, however, when this power started to shift steadily toward the federal government.

Ratification of four constitutional amendments substantially limited the states' authority to restrict the right to vote. The first was the Fifteenth Amendment in 1870. Part of the Reconstruction package initiated by the Radical Republicans after the Civil War, the Fifteenth Amendment prohibits the denial of the right to vote on the basis of race, color, or previous condition of servitude. It bars such discrimination by either the federal government or the states, but, at the time, the obvious target of the amendment was the South. Most members of the Reconstructionist Congress reasoned that, unless some action was taken to protect the political rights of the newly freed slaves, the white majority would reinstitute measures to deny black citizens full participation.

---

[1]Melvin I. Urofsky and Paul Finkelman, *A March of Liberty*, 2nd ed. (New York: Oxford University Press, 2002), 296.

Fifty years later the Constitution was again amended to expand the electorate. The Nineteenth Amendment, ratified in 1920, stipulates that the right to vote cannot be denied on account of sex. This amendment was the culmination of decades of effort by supporters of women's suffrage. Although some states already allowed women to vote, a change in the Constitution was necessary to extend that right uniformly across the nation.

The third voter qualification amendment went into effect in 1964. The Twenty-fourth Amendment denies the federal government and the states the power to impose a poll tax as a voter qualification for federal elections. The levying of a tax on the right to vote was a common practice in the South, and Congress identified this as one of many tactics used to keep African Americans from voting, thereby circumventing the clear intent of the Fifteenth Amendment.

In 1971 the last of the voting rights amendments, the Twenty-sixth, was ratified. It sets eighteen years as the minimum voting age for all state and federal elections. Before 1971 individual states determined the minimum voting age, which ranged from eighteen to twenty-one. Earlier, Congress had attempted to impose the eighteen-year minimum through legislation. The constitutionality of that act was challenged in **Oregon v. Mitchell** (1970). In a 5–4 vote, the justices held that Congress had the power under Article I to set a minimum age for voting in federal elections but lacked the constitutional authority to impose an age standard on state and local elections. Rather than face the possible confusion of conflicting sets of qualifications, Congress abrogated the *Mitchell* ruling by proposing the Twenty-sixth Amendment.

Each of these four constitutional changes altered the balance of authority over the establishment of voter qualifications. The states retained the basic right to set such qualifications, but with restrictions. States could no longer abridge voting rights by denying access to the ballot on the basis of race, sex, age, or ability to pay a tax; any actions by the states affecting voting rights were also constrained by the Fourteenth Amendment's guarantee of equal protection of the laws. In addition to limiting state power, the voting rights amendments increased congressional authority. Clauses in the Fourteenth, Fifteenth, Nineteenth, Twenty-fourth, and Twenty-sixth Amendments declared: "The Congress shall have the power to enforce this article by appropriate legislation." These enforcement clauses granted Congress authority over an area that originally had been left entirely to the states.

Congress has not been reluctant to use its enforcement authority. Shortly after ratification of the Fourteenth and Fifteenth Amendments, it demonstrated the federal government's interest in extending the franchise to African Americans by passing the Enforcement Act of 1870. This statute made it unlawful for state election officials to discriminate against black citizens in the application of state voting regulations. It also made acts of electoral corruption, including bribery, violence, and intimidation, federal crimes. The following year Congress passed the Enforcement Act of 1871, which allowed for federal supervision of congressional elections. The federal government also intervened to stem the growing incidence of private intimidation of black voters with the Ku Klux Klan Act of 1871, which gave the president broad powers to combat conspiracies against voting rights.

The Supreme Court's response to these post–Civil War enforcement statutes was mixed. In some of their decisions the justices questioned the breadth of the congressional actions that regulated state elections beyond the specific racial purposes of the Fifteenth Amendment. In *United States v. Reese* (1876) the justices declined to uphold the indictment of a Kentucky election official who refused to register a qualified black voter for a state election. The Court justified its conclusion on the ground that the Enforcement Act of 1870 was too broadly drawn. On the same day as *Reese*, and for the same reason, the Court in *United States v. Cruikshank* dismissed the federal indictments of ninety-six Louisiana whites who were charged with intimidating potential black voters by shooting them.

The Court also was reluctant to approve sanctions under the Ku Klux Klan Act when the prosecution centered on purely private behavior (*United States v. Harris*, 1883). In *Ex parte Yarbrough* (1884), however, the justices gave strong support to federal enforcement actions against even private behavior when the right to vote in national elections was abridged. Similarly, in *Ex parte Clark* (1880), *Ex parte Siebold* (1880), and *United States v. Gale* (1883) the Court approved criminal charges against state officials who compromised the integrity of federal elections.

Although these enforcement measures had an impact on the South, their influence was short-lived. By the 1890s the zeal behind the Reconstruction efforts had waned. White southerners had regained control of their home states and had begun passing measures to restrict black participation in state and federal elections; the Jim Crow era had begun. The Civil War amendments officially had reduced the power of the states to discriminate and given regulatory authority to the federal government, but full voting rights were not a reality until after the struggles of the civil rights movement of the mid-twentieth century.

State Restrictions on Voting

In 1869, during the congressional debate over the Fifteenth Amendment, Senator Waitman T. Willey, a Republican from West Virginia, proclaimed from the Senate floor:

> This amendment, when adopted, will settle the question for all time of negro suffrage in the insurgent States, where it has lately been extended under the pressure of congressional legislation, and will preclude the possibility of any future denial of this privilege by any change in the constitutions of those States.

In retrospect, it would be hard to imagine a more overly optimistic prediction of the effect of the Fifteenth Amendment. Although ratification meant that the states were constitutionally prohibited from engaging in racial discrimination in extending the right to vote, the southern states, once out from under the policies of Reconstruction, acted to keep African Americans from the voting booth.

Actions by the southern states to limit black participation in voting took many forms, including "white only" voting in Democratic Party primary elections, poll taxes, difficult registration requirements, literacy and understanding tests, and outright intimidation. These strategies were effective. African American participation at the ballot box in the South was negligible well into the middle of the twentieth century.

Beginning in the 1960s the federal government took measures to reduce racial discrimination in voting. All three branches were involved: Congress passed legislation to enforce voting rights and remove legal barriers to the ballot box, the executive branch brought suits against state governments and election officials who deprived blacks of their rights, and the judiciary heard legal disputes over claims of voter discrimination. In *Louisiana v. United States* (1965), for example, the Court struck down Louisiana's "understanding test," which permitted local voting registrars to determine whether individuals attempting to register had a sufficient understanding of state and federal constitutions to be qualified to vote. In making their decisions, these local voting officials discriminated notoriously on the basis of race. In striking down this practice, the Court gave a stern warning that it would no longer tolerate state schemes designed to deny individuals, particularly minorities, access to the ballot.

Racially discriminatory state practices were not the only barriers to voting that the Court struck down in the 1960s and 1970s. In *Harper v. Virginia State Board of Elections* (1966) the justices found that poll taxes imposed as a requirement to vote in *state elections* violated the Fourteenth Amendment. This decision, coupled with the Twenty-fourth Amendment's prohibition against poll taxes in *federal elections*, effectively eliminated the willingness or ability to pay a tax as a voting rights requirement. In *Kramer v. Union Free School District* (1969) the Court removed ownership or rental of real property as a requirement some states had imposed for voting on certain property tax issues. Similarly, in *Dunn v. Blumstein* (1972) the Court struck down state laws that established residency requirements of up to a year as a voting prerequisite. The justices held that a thirty-day requirement would be sufficient for the state to ensure that only bona fide residents voted.

The Voting Rights Act of 1965

Although Supreme Court decisions did much to define the right to vote and limit the state actions that restricted the franchise, court rulings alone were insufficient to prompt major changes—particularly with respect to voting participation among minorities. Too many alternative measures, many of them informal, were available to block or delay the effective exercise of the right to vote. Registration numbers in the southern states highlight the fact that court victories did not necessarily translate into social change. According to Justice Department statistics, between 1958 and 1964 black voter registration in Alabama rose from 14.2 percent to just 19.4 percent. From 1956 to 1965 Louisiana black registration remained virtually unchanged. And in Mississippi the ten years from 1954 to 1964 saw black registration rates rise to only 6.4 percent from 4.4 percent. In all of these states the registration rates for whites were fifty or more percentage points higher than the rates for African Americans. Figures such as these convinced Congress that its strategy of passing legislation to expand opportunities for taking civil rights claims to court had been ineffective and that a more aggressive policy was required. President Lyndon Johnson is reported to have instructed Attorney General Nicholas Katzenbach to "write the god-damnedest, toughest voting rights act that you can devise."[2] The result was the Voting Rights Act of 1965, the most comprehensive

---

[2]Quoted in Howard Ball, "The Voting Rights Act of 1965," in *The Oxford Companion to the Supreme Court of the United States*, ed. Kermit L. Hall (New York: Oxford University Press, 1992), 903.

statute Congress ever enacted to enforce the guarantees of the Fifteenth Amendment.

The act contained both general provisions that applied nationwide and special sections that targeted areas of the country having a history of voting rights discrimination. The general provisions prohibited all practices and procedures, including poll taxes and literacy tests, that had a discriminatory impact on voting rights. These provisions were to be enforced through litigation in the federal district courts. The act also allowed for the appointment of federal election examiners and observers where necessary to monitor elections and ensure compliance with the law.

The most stringent provisions of the statute applied to states or counties that qualified under the law's "coverage formula," found in Section 4 of the act. Covered jurisdictions were those that met the following two criteria: (1) that a discriminatory test or device was in operation in November 1964, and (2) that less than 40 percent of the voting-age population was registered to vote or voted in the 1964 presidential general election. In 1965 the states covered were Alabama, Alaska, Georgia, Louisiana, Mississippi, South Carolina, and Virginia, as well as portions of Arizona, Hawaii, Idaho, and North Carolina. As conditions have changed over time, various states and local governments have been added to and subtracted from the covered list. In 2012, Alabama, Alaska, Arizona, Georgia, Louisiana, Mississippi, South Carolina, Texas, and Virginia were covered under Section 4, as were portions of California, Florida, Michigan, New Hampshire, New York, North Carolina, and South Dakota.

States and local jurisdictions falling under the coverage formula were prohibited from implementing any changes in their election procedures without first gaining approval from the U.S. Justice Department or from a three-judge district court in Washington, D.C. Since states have historically taken the lead in developing election laws, this "preclearance" requirement essentially stripped the covered states of a bit of their sovereignty. Noncovered states were free to change their electoral systems at will, subject to possible legal challenge after the changes went into effect. The covered states, however, could not alter their electoral policies or procedures without first obtaining federal approval.

Immediately after the act was passed, South Carolina challenged its constitutionality, claiming that the law infringed on the right of states to determine voter eligibility, violated the fundamental principle of equality of statehood, and arbitrarily presumed racial discrimination to be the cause of low voting participation rates. The justices heard the case under the Supreme Court's original jurisdiction.

In *South Carolina v. Katzenbach* (1966) the Court with near unanimity upheld the validity of the law's general provisions as well as the sections applying to the covered states. The law, it ruled, was the product of Congress exercising its legitimate constitutional authority to enforce the mandates of the Fifteenth Amendment. The justices agreed with the argument the federal government offered, that the "blight of racial discrimination in voting" had infected the nation for so long that Congress appropriately responded under authority of the Fifteenth Amendment by passing a very comprehensive and forceful statute. The severity of the problem—"unremitting and ingenious defiance"—justified an unprecedented federal response. Only Justice Hugo Black, who expressed opposition to treating the covered states as if they were "conquered provinces," dissented from a portion of Chief Justice Earl Warren's majority opinion.

With the Court's approval of the Voting Rights Act, the federal government was free to launch a vigorous campaign to make the goals of the Fifteenth Amendment a reality. The executive branch actively enforced the law, and Congress periodically strengthened and extended its provisions. These efforts, coupled with large-scale voter registration drives conducted by civil rights organizations, resulted in voter registration and participation rates for African Americans in the southern states roughly equal to those of whites.

By the beginning of the twenty-first century, progress had been so significant that the states most affected by the law began arguing that portions of the statute were no longer necessary. The parts they found particularly objectionable were the coverage formula that determined which states were required to obtain prior federal approval of election law changes and the preclearance procedure itself. These states asserted that the discriminatory conditions of the 1960s that justified the Voting Rights Act no longer existed. Consequently, the most arduous sections of the law could no longer be justified. Civil rights advocates countered that the law remained necessary because discrimination still lingered, albeit in a more subtle form than in earlier eras. The controversy reached the Supreme Court in 2013 in the case of *Shelby County, Alabama v. Holder*.

Shelby County, Alabama v. Holder

570 U.S. _____ (2013)

http://caselaw.findlaw.com/us-supreme-court/12-96.html

Oral arguments available at https://www.oyez.org/
cases/2012/12-96

Vote: 5 (Alito, Kennedy, Roberts, Scalia, Thomas)
4 (Breyer, Ginsburg, Kagan, Sotomayor)

OPINION OF THE COURT: *Roberts*

CONCURRING OPINION: *Thomas*

DISSENTING OPINION: *Ginsburg*

Congress passed the Voting Rights Act of 1965 to protect the right to vote from the evils of racial discrimination. Three sections of the act are particularly relevant in this case. Section 2 bans any standard, practice, or procedure that results in a denial or abridgment of the right to vote on account of race. This section applies nationwide. It allows legal action to be taken against jurisdictions that engage in unlawful, discriminatory acts. Section 4 creates a coverage formula for determining which states and political subdivisions will be subject to additional scrutiny. The formula is based on the previous use of racially discriminatory practices and low voter registration or turnout. Finally, Section 5 specifies that no jurisdiction that qualifies under the coverage formula can implement any changes in voting procedures until such changes are approved by the U.S. Justice Department or a federal three-judge district court in the District of Columbia. This is known as the "preclearance" requirement. The coverage formula and the preclearance requirement originally were seen as temporary measures that would expire in five years. Congress, however, extended the life of these provisions several times, the most recent being a twenty-five-year extension enacted in 2006.

Shelby County, a covered jurisdiction in Alabama, sued the U.S. attorney general, asking the district court to strike down Sections 4 and 5 as unconstitutional, because the coverage formula was based on a 1965 environment of race relations that no

Supporters of the Voting Rights Act demonstrate in front of the U.S. Supreme Court on February 27, 2013, the day the justices heard oral arguments in *Shelby County, Alabama v. Holder*.

longer existed in 2006, when Congress extended the life of these provisions. The district court and the court of appeals rejected this argument, finding that Congress had ample evidence to justify the continuation of the challenged provisions and that Section 2 alone would be inadequate to protect the rights of minority voters.

CHIEF JUSTICE ROBERTS DELIVERED THE OPINION OF THE COURT.

The Voting Rights Act of 1965 employed extraordinary measures to address an extraordinary problem. Section 5 of the Act required States to obtain federal permission before enacting any law related to voting—a drastic departure from basic principles of federalism. And §4 of the Act applied that requirement only to some States—an equally dramatic departure from the principle that all States enjoy equal sovereignty. This was strong medicine, but Congress determined it was needed to address entrenched racial discrimination in voting, "an insidious and pervasive evil which had been perpetuated in certain parts of our country through unremitting and ingenious defiance of the Constitution." *South Carolina* v. *Katzenbach* (1966). As we explained in upholding the law, "exceptional conditions can justify legislative measures not otherwise appropriate." Reflecting the unprecedented nature of these measures, they were scheduled to expire after five years.

Nearly 50 years later, they are still in effect; indeed, they have been made more stringent, and are now scheduled to last until 2031. There is no denying, however, that the conditions that originally justified these measures no longer characterize voting in the covered jurisdictions. By 2009, "the racial gap in voter registration and turnout [was] lower in the States originally covered by §5 than it [was] nationwide." *Northwest Austin Municipal Util. Dist. No. One* v. *Holder* (2009). Since that time, Census Bureau data indicate that African-American voter turnout has come to exceed white voter turnout in five of the six States originally covered by §5, with a gap in the sixth State of less than one half of one percent.

At the same time, voting discrimination still exists; no one doubts that. The question is whether the Act's extraordinary measures, including its disparate treatment of the States, continue to satisfy constitutional requirements. . . .

* * *

In *Northwest Austin,* we stated that "the Act imposes current burdens and must be justified by current needs." And we concluded that "a departure from the fundamental principle of equal sovereignty requires a showing that a statute's disparate geographic coverage is sufficiently related to the problem that it targets." These basic principles guide our review of the question before us.

The Constitution and laws of the United States are "the supreme Law of the Land." State legislation may not contravene federal law. The Federal Government does not, however, have a general right to review and veto state enactments before they go into effect. A proposal to grant such authority to "negative" state laws was considered at the Constitutional Convention, but rejected in favor of allowing state laws to take effect, subject to later challenge under the Supremacy Clause.

Outside the strictures of the Supremacy Clause, States retain broad autonomy in structuring their governments and pursuing legislative objectives. Indeed, the Constitution provides that all powers not specifically granted to the Federal Government are reserved to the States or citizens. This "allocation of powers in our federal system preserves the integrity, dignity, and residual sovereignty of the States." But the federal balance "is not just an end in itself: Rather, federalism secures to citizens the liberties that derive from the diffusion of sovereign power."

More specifically, "'the Framers of the Constitution intended the States to keep for themselves, as provided in the Tenth Amendment, the power to regulate elections.'" *Gregory* v. *Ashcroft* (1991). . . .

Not only do States retain sovereignty under the Constitution, there is also a "fundamental principle of *equal* sovereignty" among the States. Over a hundred years ago, this Court explained that our Nation "was and is a union of States, equal in power, dignity and authority." *Coyle* v. *Smith* (1911). Indeed, "the constitutional equality of the States is essential to the harmonious operation of the scheme upon which the Republic was organized." . . .

The Voting Rights Act sharply departs from these basic principles. It suspends "*all* changes to state election law—however innocuous—until they have been precleared by federal authorities in Washington, D.C." States must beseech the Federal Government for permission to implement laws that they would otherwise have the right to enact and execute on their own, subject of course to any injunction in a §2 action. The Attorney General has 60 days to object to a preclearance request, longer if he requests more information. If a State seeks preclearance from a three-judge court, the process can take years.

And despite the tradition of equal sovereignty, the Act applies to only nine States (and several additional counties). While one State waits months or years and expends funds to implement a validly enacted law, its neighbor can typically put the same law into effect immediately, through the normal legislative process. Even if a noncovered jurisdiction is sued, there are important differences between those proceedings and preclearance proceedings; the preclearance proceeding "not only switches the burden of proof to the supplicant jurisdiction, but also applies substantive standards quite different from those governing the rest of the nation."

All this explains why, when we first upheld the Act in 1966, we described it as "stringent" and "potent." *Katzenbach.* We recognized that it "may have been an uncommon exercise of congressional power," but concluded that "legislative measures not otherwise appropriate" could be justified by "exceptional conditions." . . .

In 1966, we found these departures from the basic features of our system of government justified. The "blight of racial discrimination in voting" had "infected the electoral process in parts of our country for nearly a century." *Katzenbach.* Several States had enacted a variety of requirements and tests "specifically designed to prevent" African-Americans from voting. Case-by-case litigation had proved inadequate to prevent such racial discrimination in voting, in part because States "merely switched to discriminatory devices not covered by the federal decrees," "enacted difficult new tests," or simply "defied and evaded court orders." Shortly before enactment of the Voting Rights Act, only 19.4 percent of African-Americans of voting age were registered to vote in Alabama, only 31.8 percent in Louisiana, and only 6.4 percent in Mississippi. Those figures were roughly 50 percentage points or more below the figures for whites.

In short, we concluded that "[u]nder the compulsion of these unique circumstances, Congress responded in a permissibly decisive manner." We also noted then and have emphasized since that this extraordinary legislation was intended to be temporary, set to expire after five years.

At the time, the coverage formula—the means of linking the exercise of the unprecedented authority with the problem that warranted it—made sense. We found that "Congress chose to limit its attention to the geographic areas where immediate action seemed necessary." *Katzenbach.* The areas where Congress found "evidence of actual voting discrimination" shared two characteristics: "the use of tests and devices for voter registration, and a voting rate in the 1964 presidential election at least 12 points below the national average." We explained that "[t]ests and devices are relevant to voting discrimination because of their long history as a tool for perpetrating the evil; a low voting rate is pertinent for the obvious reason that widespread disenfranchisement must inevitably affect the number of actual voters." We therefore concluded that "the coverage formula [was] rational in both practice and theory." It accurately reflected those jurisdictions uniquely characterized by voting discrimination "on a pervasive scale," linking coverage to the devices used to effectuate discrimination and to the resulting disenfranchisement. The formula ensured that the "stringent remedies [were] aimed at areas where voting discrimination ha[d] been most flagrant."

* * *

Nearly 50 years later, things have changed dramatically. Shelby County contends that the preclearance requirement, even without regard to its disparate coverage, is now unconstitutional. Its arguments have a good deal of force. In the covered jurisdictions, "[v]oter turnout and registration rates now approach parity. Blatantly discriminatory evasions of federal decrees are rare. And minority candidates hold office at unprecedented levels." *Northwest Austin.* The tests and devices that blocked access to the ballot have been forbidden nationwide for over 40 years.

Those conclusions are not ours alone. Congress said the same when it reauthorized the Act in 2006, writing that "[s]ignificant progress has been made in eliminating first generation barriers experienced by minority voters, including increased numbers of registered minority voters, minority voter turnout, and minority representation in Congress, State legislatures, and local elected offices." . . . That Report also explained that there have been "significant increases in the number of African-Americans serving in elected offices"; more specifically, there has been approximately a 1,000 percent increase since 1965 in the number of African-American elected officials in the six States originally covered by the Voting Rights Act.

The following chart, compiled from the Senate and House Reports, compares voter registration numbers from 1965 to those from 2004 in the six originally covered States. These are the numbers that were before Congress when it reauthorized the Act in 2006:

	1965			2004		
	White	Black	Gap	White	Black	Gap
Alabama	69.2	19.3	49.9	73.8	72.9	0.9
Georgia	62.[6]	27.4	35.2	63.5	64.2	−0.7
Louisiana	80.5	31.6	48.9	75.1	71.1	4.0
Mississippi	69.9	6.7	63.2	72.3	76.1	−3.8
South Carolina	75.7	37.3	38.4	74.4	71.1	3.3
Virginia	61.1	38.3	22.8	68.2	57.4	10.8

There is no doubt that these improvements are in large part *because of* the Voting Rights Act. . . . Problems remain in these States and others, but there is no denying that, due to the Voting Rights Act, our Nation has made great strides.

Yet the Act has not eased the restrictions in §5 or narrowed the scope of the coverage formula in §4(b) along the way. Those extraordinary and unprecedented features were reauthorized—as if nothing had changed. In fact, the Act's unusual remedies have grown even stronger. When Congress reauthorized the Act in 2006, it did so for another 25 years on top of the previous 40—a far cry from the initial five-year period. . . .

* * *

Coverage today is based on decades-old data and eradicated practices. The formula captures States by reference to literacy tests and low voter registration and turnout in the 1960s and early 1970s. But such tests have been banned nationwide for over 40 years. And voter registration and turnout numbers in the covered

States have risen dramatically in the years since. Racial disparity in those numbers was compelling evidence justifying the preclearance remedy and the coverage formula. There is no longer such a disparity.

In 1965, the States could be divided into two groups: those with a recent history of voting tests and low voter registration and turnout, and those without those characteristics. Congress based its coverage formula on that distinction. Today the Nation is no longer divided along those lines, yet the Voting Rights Act continues to treat it as if it were. . . .

. . . By the time the Act was reauthorized in 2006, there had been 40 more years of it. In assessing the "current need" for a preclearance system that treats States differently from one another today, that history cannot be ignored. During that time, largely because of the Voting Rights Act, voting tests were abolished, disparities in voter registration and turnout due to race were erased, and African-Americans attained political office in record numbers. And yet the coverage formula that Congress reauthorized in 2006 ignores these developments, keeping the focus on decades-old data relevant to decades-old problems, rather than current data reflecting current needs.

The Fifteenth Amendment commands that the right to vote shall not be denied or abridged on account of race or color, and it gives Congress the power to enforce that command. The Amendment is not designed to punish for the past; its purpose is to ensure a better future. To serve that purpose, Congress—if it is to divide the States—must identify those jurisdictions to be singled out on a basis that makes sense in light of current conditions. It cannot rely simply on the past. We made that clear in *Northwest Austin,* and we make it clear again today. . . .

. . . If Congress had started from scratch in 2006, it plainly could not have enacted the present coverage formula. It would have been irrational for Congress to distinguish between States in such a fundamental way based on 40-year-old data, when today's statistics tell an entirely different story. And it would have been irrational to base coverage on the use of voting tests 40 years ago, when such tests have been illegal since that time. But that is exactly what Congress has done.

. . . Congress could have updated the coverage formula [when it reauthorized the Act], but did not do so. Its failure to act leaves us today with no choice but to declare §4(b) unconstitutional. The formula in that section can no longer be used as a basis for subjecting jurisdictions to preclearance.

Our decision in no way affects the permanent, nationwide ban on racial discrimination in voting found in §2. We issue no holding on §5 itself, only on the coverage formula. Congress may draft another formula based on current conditions. Such a formula is an initial prerequisite to a determination that exceptional conditions still exist justifying such an "extraordinary departure from the traditional course of relations between the States and the Federal Government." Our country has changed, and while any racial discrimination in voting is too much, Congress must ensure that the legislation it passes to remedy that problem speaks to current conditions.

The judgment of the Court of Appeals is reversed.

It is so ordered.

JUSTICE THOMAS, CONCURRING.

I join the Court's opinion in full but write separately to explain that I would find §5 of the Voting Rights Act unconstitutional as well. The Court's opinion sets forth the reasons. . . .

Today, our Nation has changed. "[T]he conditions that originally justified [§5] no longer characterize voting in the covered jurisdictions." As the Court explains: "'[V]oter turnout and registration rates now approach parity. Blatantly discriminatory evasions of federal decrees are rare. And minority candidates hold office at unprecedented levels.'"

In spite of these improvements, however, Congress *increased* the already significant burdens of §5. . . .

. . . However one aggregates the data compiled by Congress, it cannot justify the considerable burdens created by §5. . . . Section 5 is, thus, unconstitutional.

JUSTICE GINSBURG, WITH WHOM JUSTICE BREYER, JUSTICE SOTOMAYOR, AND JUSTICE KAGAN JOIN, DISSENTING.

In the Court's view, the very success of §5 of the Voting Rights Act demands its dormancy. Congress was of another mind. Recognizing that large progress has been made, Congress determined, based on a voluminous record, that the scourge of discrimination was not yet extirpated. The question this case presents is who decides whether, as currently operative, §5 remains justifiable, this Court, or a Congress charged with the obligation to enforce the post–Civil War Amendments "by appropriate legislation." With overwhelming support in both Houses, Congress concluded that, for two prime reasons, §5 should continue in force, unabated. First, continuance would facilitate completion of the impressive gains thus far made; and second, continuance would guard against backsliding. Those assessments were well within Congress' province to make and should elicit this Court's unstinting approbation.

"[V]oting discrimination still exists; no one doubts that." But the Court today terminates the remedy that proved to be best suited to block that discrimination. The Voting Rights Act of 1965 (VRA) has worked to combat voting discrimination where other remedies had been tried and failed. Particularly effective is the VRA's requirement of federal preclearance for all changes to voting laws in the regions of the country with the most aggravated records of rank discrimination against minority voting rights.

A century after the Fourteenth and Fifteenth Amendments guaranteed citizens the right to vote free of discrimination on the basis of race, the "blight of racial discrimination in voting" continued to "infec[t] the electoral process in parts of our country." Early attempts to cope with this vile infection resembled battling the Hydra. Whenever one form of voting discrimination was identified and prohibited, others sprang up in its place. This Court repeatedly encountered the remarkable "variety and persistence" of laws disenfranchising minority citizens. . . .

Congress learned from experience that laws targeting particular electoral practices or enabling case-by-case litigation were inadequate to the task. . . . Patently, a new approach was needed.

Answering that need, the Voting Rights Act became one of the most consequential, efficacious, and amply justified exercises of federal legislative power in our Nation's history. Requiring federal preclearance of changes in voting laws in the covered jurisdictions—those States and localities where opposition to the Constitution's commands were most virulent—the VRA provided a fit solution for minority voters as well as for States. . . .

Although the VRA wrought dramatic changes in the realization of minority voting rights, the Act, to date, surely has not eliminated all vestiges of discrimination against the exercise of the franchise by minority citizens. Jurisdictions covered by the preclearance requirement continued to submit, in large numbers, proposed changes to voting laws that the Attorney General declined to approve, auguring that barriers to minority voting would quickly resurface were the preclearance remedy eliminated. *City of Rome* v. *United States* (1980). . . . Efforts to reduce the impact of minority votes, in contrast to direct attempts to block access to the ballot, are aptly described as "second-generation barriers" to minority voting. . . .

. . . As the 1982 reauthorization approached its 2007 expiration date, Congress again considered whether the VRA's preclearance mechanism remained an appropriate response to the problem of voting discrimination in covered jurisdictions. . . .

After considering the full legislative record, Congress made the following findings: The VRA has directly caused significant progress in eliminating first-generation barriers to ballot access, leading to a marked increase in minority voter registration and turnout and the number of minority elected officials. But despite this progress, "second generation barriers constructed to prevent minority voters from fully participating in the electoral process" continued to exist, as well as racially polarized voting in the covered jurisdictions, which increased the political vulnerability of racial and language minorities in those jurisdictions. Extensive "[e]vidence of continued discrimination," Congress concluded, "clearly show[ed] the continued need for Federal oversight" in covered jurisdictions. The overall record demonstrated to the federal lawmakers that, "without the continuation of the Voting Rights Act of 1965 protections, racial and language minority citizens will be deprived of the opportunity to exercise their right to vote, or will have their votes diluted, undermining the significant gains made by minorities in the last 40 years."

Based on these findings, Congress reauthorized preclearance for another 25 years, while also undertaking to reconsider the extension after 15 years to ensure that the provision was still necessary and effective. . . .

True, conditions in the South have impressively improved since passage of the Voting Rights Act. Congress noted this improvement and found that the VRA was the driving force behind it. But Congress also found that voting discrimination had evolved into subtler second-generation barriers, and that eliminating preclearance would risk loss of the gains that had been made. Concerns of this order, the Court previously found, gave Congress adequate cause to reauthorize the VRA. *City of Rome*. . . .

. . . [T]he Court strikes §4(b)'s coverage provision because, in its view, the provision is not based on "current conditions." It discounts, however, that one such condition was the preclearance remedy in place in the covered jurisdictions, a remedy Congress designed both to catch discrimination before it causes harm, and to guard against return to old ways. . . . Throwing out preclearance when it has worked and is continuing to work to stop discriminatory changes is like throwing away your umbrella in a rainstorm because you are not getting wet. . . .

The sad irony of today's decision lies in its utter failure to grasp why the VRA has proven effective. The Court appears to believe that the VRA's success in eliminating the specific devices extant in 1965 means that preclearance is no longer needed. With that belief, and the argument derived from it, history repeats itself. The same assumption—that the problem could be solved when particular methods of voting discrimination are identified and eliminated—was indulged and proved wrong repeatedly prior to the VRA's enactment. Unlike prior statutes, which singled out particular tests or devices, the VRA is grounded in Congress' recognition of the "variety and persistence" of measures designed to impair minority voting rights. In truth, the evolution of voting discrimination into more subtle second-generation barriers is powerful evidence that a remedy as effective as preclearance remains vital to protect minority voting rights and prevent backsliding. . . .

. . . After exhaustive evidence-gathering and deliberative process, Congress reauthorized the VRA, including the coverage provision, with overwhelming bipartisan support. It was the judgment of Congress that "40 years has not been a sufficient amount of time to eliminate the vestiges of discrimination following nearly 100 years of disregard for the dictates of the 15th amendment and to ensure that the right of all citizens to vote is protected as guaranteed by the Constitution." That determination of the body empowered to enforce the Civil War Amendments "by appropriate legislation" merits this Court's utmost respect. In my judgment, the Court errs egregiously by overriding Congress' decision.

In some respects the Court's decision in *Shelby County* was limited. The decision did not strike down the nondiscrimination principles embedded in the Voting Rights Act. It did not reduce the opportunity for legal challenges to enacted state laws that might have a discriminatory impact on minority voting. It did not even declare that preclearance requirements are necessarily unconstitutional. The Court, however, did strike down the law's coverage formula, finding it to be based on conditions of a previous era with limited contemporary relevance. In Chief Justice John G. Roberts's opinion, the coverage formula failed the most basic test of constitutionality: it was irrational. Congress was relying on a set of procedures that were designed to address conditions that no longer existed. Thus, the Court left to Congress the task of revising the coverage formula based on contemporary data and thereby reactivating the preclearance procedure. To the dissenters, though, it was the coverage formula that ensured the law's past and present success. They believed that Congress's continued reliance on the formula deserved deference from the Court.

Although states previously targeted by the act were happy with the decision, civil rights advocates criticized it for eliminating the act's most effective provisions, those that applied to the jurisdictions with the most serious histories of discrimination. Without an effective preclearance requirement, they argued, discriminatory laws can be challenged only through expensive litigation and only after the laws go into effect. To the extent that there are sharp partisan divisions in Congress, there is little reason to expect that the law will be updated. In December 2019, for example, the Democrats in the House of Representatives were able to secure passage of a bill that sought to reinstate the preclearance procedures by revising the formula, but Republican opposition from the Senate and the president means that such legislation has no real prospect for success.[3]

CONTEMPORARY RESTRICTIONS ON THE RIGHT TO VOTE

Historically, racial discrimination has been a central voting rights concern, but in contemporary times other issues have commanded attention. One of the most controversial of these has been the issue of voter identification requirements. Following the bitter and closely contested 2000 presidential campaign, several states expressed concern about the potential risks of voter fraud. One of their responses was the enactment of legislation requiring voters to present government-issued photographic identification at the polls. Advocates of such laws argued that they would prohibit individuals from illegally casting ballots in the name of registered voters who might have died or moved to another state. Although such a requirement might seem reasonable on its face, critics claimed that it would impose an unwarranted hardship on the poor and the elderly, who are less likely to have such identification. Republicans tended to support this reform, while Democrats, who feared an adverse impact on groups of voters who traditionally support their party, opposed it. When the state of Indiana passed a voter identification law in 2005, the stage was set for a constitutional battle over the statute's validity.

Crawford v. Marion County Election Board

553 U.S. 181 (2008)
http://caselaw.findlaw.com/us-supreme-court/553/181.html
Oral arguments available at https://www.oyez.org/ cases/2007/07-21
Vote: 6 (Alito, Kennedy, Roberts, Scalia, Stevens, Thomas)
  3 (Breyer, Ginsburg, Souter)

OPINION ANNOUNCING THE JUDGMENT OF THE COURT: *Stevens*

OPINION CONCURRING IN THE JUDGMENT: *Scalia*

DISSENTING OPINIONS: *Breyer, Souter*

With the stated goals of discouraging and preventing voter fraud, the Republican-dominated Indiana legislature in 2005 enacted the Voter ID Law (SEA 483) requiring citizens to present government-issued photo identification at the polls in order to vote in any primary or general election. Exceptions were made for residents of state-licensed facilities such as nursing homes. A voter who had the required ID but failed to bring it to the polls could cast a provisional vote that would be counted if the voter brought proper identification to the circuit court clerk within ten days. Similar provisional ballot procedures were available for those who had religious objections to being photographed. The state Bureau of Motor Vehicles offered free photo identification cards to those who did not already possess a driver's license or other acceptable identification. A photo ID was not required to register to vote or to vote absentee.

[3]Sheryl Gay Stolberg and Emily Cochrane, "House Passes Voting Rights Bill despite Near Unanimous Republican Opposition," *New York Times*, December 6, 2019, https://www.nytimes .com/2019/12/06/us/politics/house-voting-rights.html

Shortly after the law's enactment, a coalition of individuals and groups representing the interests of minorities and the poor challenged the law. In addition, the Indiana and Marion County Democratic Party organizations filed suit to have the law declared unconstitutional. These parties claimed that the law violated the Fourteenth Amendment by substantially burdening the right to vote and arbitrarily disenfranchising voters who could not obtain the identification cards easily.

After consolidating these challenges into a single case, the district court ruled for the state and a divided court of appeals affirmed, concluding that the benefit of reducing the risk of fraud offset the burden on voters.

JUSTICE STEVENS ANNOUNCED THE JUDGMENT OF THE COURT AND DELIVERED AN OPINION IN WHICH THE CHIEF JUSTICE AND JUSTICE KENNEDY JOIN.

In *Harper v. Virginia Bd. of Elections* (1966), the Court held that Virginia could not condition the right to vote in a state election on the payment of a poll tax of $1.50. We rejected the dissenters' argument that the interest in promoting civic responsibility by weeding out those voters who did not care enough about public affairs to pay a small sum for the privilege of voting provided a rational basis for the tax. Applying a stricter standard, we concluded that a State "violates the Equal Protection Clause of the Fourteenth Amendment whenever it makes the affluence of the voter or payment of any fee an electoral standard." We used the term "invidiously discriminate" to describe conduct prohibited under that standard. . . . Although the State's justification for the tax was rational, it was invidious because it was irrelevant to the voter's qualifications.

Thus, under the standard applied in *Harper,* even rational restrictions on the right to vote are invidious if they are unrelated to voter qualifications. In *Anderson v. Celebrezze* (1983), however, we confirmed the general rule that "evenhanded restrictions that protect the integrity and reliability of the electoral process itself" are not invidious and satisfy the standard set forth in *Harper.* Rather than applying any "litmus test" that would neatly separate valid from invalid restrictions, we concluded that a court must identify and evaluate the interests put forward by the State as justifications for the burden imposed by its rule, and then make the "hard judgment" that our adversary system demands. . . .

. . . The State has a valid interest in participating in a nationwide effort to improve and modernize election procedures that have been criticized as antiquated and inefficient. The State also argues that it has a particular interest in preventing voter fraud in response to a problem that is in part the product of its own maladministration—namely, that Indiana's voter registration rolls include a large number of names of persons who are either

AP Photo/Joe Raymond

On May 6, 2008, polling inspector Julie McGuire, a Roman Catholic nun, was forced to turn away about a dozen of her fellow nuns from a nearby South Bend convent for not having proper identification. McGuire had frequently informed the sisters, most of them elderly, that under Indiana's new voter registration law, they would need to show an identification card from the state Bureau of Motor Vehicles before they could vote.

deceased or no longer live in Indiana. Finally, the State relies on its interest in safeguarding voter confidence. Each of these interests merits separate comment.

ELECTION MODERNIZATION

Two recently enacted federal statutes have made it necessary for States to reexamine their election procedures. Both contain provisions consistent with a State's choice to use government-issued photo identification as a relevant source of information concerning a citizen's eligibility to vote. . . .

Of course, neither [statute] required Indiana to enact SEA 483, but they do indicate that Congress believes that photo identification is one effective method of establishing a voter's qualification to vote and that the integrity of elections is enhanced through improved technology. That conclusion is also supported by a report issued shortly after the enactment of SEA 483 by the Commission on Federal Election Reform chaired by former President Jimmy Carter and former Secretary of State James A. Baker III. . . .

VOTER FRAUD

The only kind of voter fraud that SEA 483 addresses is in-person voter impersonation at polling places. The record contains no evidence of any such fraud actually occurring in Indiana at any time in its history. Moreover, petitioners argue that provisions of the Indiana Criminal Code punishing such conduct as a felony provide adequate protection against the risk that such conduct will occur in the future. It remains true, however, that flagrant examples of such fraud in other parts of the country have been documented throughout this Nation's history by respected historians and journalists, that occasional examples have surfaced in recent years, and that Indiana's own experience with fraudulent voting in the 2003 Democratic primary for East Chicago Mayor—though perpetrated using absentee ballots and not in-person fraud—demonstrate that not only is the risk of voter fraud real but that it could affect the outcome of a close election.

There is no question about the legitimacy or importance of the State's interest in counting only the votes of eligible voters. Moreover, the interest in orderly administration and accurate recordkeeping provides a sufficient justification for carefully identifying all voters participating in the election process. While the most effective method of preventing election fraud may well be debatable, the propriety of doing so is perfectly clear.

In its brief, the State argues that the inflation of its voter rolls provides further support for its enactment of SEA 483. . . . Indiana's lists of registered voters included the names of thousands of persons who had either moved, died, or were not eligible to vote because they had been convicted of felonies. . . . Even though Indiana's own negligence may have contributed to the serious inflation of its registration lists when SEA 483 was enacted, the fact of inflated voter rolls does provide a neutral and nondiscriminatory reason supporting the State's decision to require photo identification.

SAFEGUARDING VOTER CONFIDENCE

Finally, the State contends that it has an interest in protecting public confidence "in the integrity and legitimacy of representative government." While that interest is closely related to the State's interest in preventing voter fraud, public confidence in the integrity of the electoral process has independent significance, because it encourages citizen participation in the democratic process. . . .

States employ different methods of identifying eligible voters at the polls. Some merely check off the names of registered voters who identify themselves; others require voters to present registration cards or other documentation before they can vote; some require voters to sign their names so their signatures can be compared with those on file; and in recent years an increasing number of States have relied primarily on photo identification. A photo identification requirement imposes some burdens on voters that other methods of identification do not share. . . .

The burdens that are relevant to the issue before us are those imposed on persons who are eligible to vote but do not possess a current photo identification that complies with the requirements of SEA 483. The fact that most voters already possess a valid driver's license, or some other form of acceptable identification, would not save the statute under our reasoning in *Harper,* if the State required voters to pay a tax or a fee to obtain a new photo identification. But just as other States provide free voter registration cards, the photo identification cards issued by Indiana's BMV are also free. For most voters who need them, the inconvenience of making a trip to the BMV, gathering the required documents, and posing for a photograph surely does not qualify as a substantial burden on the right to vote, or even represent a significant increase over the usual burdens of voting.

Both evidence in the record and facts of which we may take judicial notice, however, indicate that a somewhat heavier burden may be placed on a limited number of persons. They include elderly persons born out-of-state, who may have difficulty obtaining a birth certificate; persons who because of economic or other personal limitations may find it difficult either to secure a copy of their birth certificate or to assemble the other required documentation to obtain a state-issued identification; homeless persons; and persons with a religious objection to being photographed. . . .

The severity of that burden is, of course, mitigated by the fact that, if eligible, voters without photo identification may cast provisional ballots that will ultimately be counted. To do so, however, they must travel to the circuit court clerk's office within 10 days to execute the required affidavit. It is unlikely that such a requirement would pose a constitutional problem unless it is wholly unjustified. . . .

Given the fact that petitioners have advanced a broad attack on the constitutionality of SEA 483, seeking relief that would invalidate the statute in all its applications, they bear a heavy burden of persuasion. . . .

Petitioners ask this Court, in effect, to perform a unique balancing analysis that looks specifically at a small number of voters who may experience a special burden under the statute and weighs their burdens against the State's broad interests in protecting election integrity. Petitioners urge us to ask whether the State's interests justify the burden imposed on voters who cannot afford or obtain a birth certificate and who must make a second trip to the circuit court clerk's office after voting. But on the basis of the evidence in the record it is not possible to quantify either the magnitude of the burden on this narrow class of voters or the portion of the burden imposed on them that is fully justified.

First, the evidence in the record does not provide us with the number of registered voters without photo identification. . . .

Further, the deposition evidence presented in the District Court does not provide any concrete evidence of the burden imposed on voters who currently lack photo identification. . . .

The record says virtually nothing about the difficulties faced by either indigent voters or voters with religious objections to being photographed. . . . The record does contain the affidavit of one homeless woman who has a copy of her birth certificate, but was denied a photo identification card because she did not have an address. But that single affidavit gives no indication of how common the problem is.

In sum, on the basis of the record that has been made in this litigation, we cannot conclude that the statute imposes "excessively burdensome requirements" on any class of voters. . . . When we consider only the statute's broad application to all Indiana voters we conclude that it "imposes only a limited burden on voters' rights." The "'precise interests'" advanced by the State are therefore sufficient to defeat petitioners' facial challenge to SEA 483. . . .

In their briefs, petitioners stress the fact that all of the Republicans in the General Assembly voted in favor of SEA 483 and the Democrats were unanimous in opposing it. . . . It is fair to infer that partisan considerations may have played a significant role in the decision to enact SEA 483. If such considerations had provided the only justification for a photo identification requirement, we may also assume that SEA 483 would suffer the same fate as the poll tax at issue in *Harper.*

But if a nondiscriminatory law is supported by valid neutral justifications, those justifications should not be disregarded simply because partisan interests may have provided one motivation for the votes of individual legislators. The state interests identified as justifications for SEA 483 are both neutral and sufficiently strong to require us to reject petitioners' facial attack on the statute. The application of the statute to the vast majority of Indiana voters is amply justified by the valid interest in protecting "the integrity and reliability of the electoral process."

The judgment of the Court of Appeals is affirmed.

It is so ordered.

JUSTICE SCALIA, WITH WHOM JUSTICE THOMAS AND JUSTICE ALITO JOIN, CONCURRING IN THE JUDGMENT.

The universally applicable requirements of Indiana's voter-identification law are eminently reasonable. The burden of acquiring, possessing, and showing a free photo identification is simply not severe, because it does not "even represent a significant increase over the usual burdens of voting." And the State's interests are sufficient to sustain that minimal burden. That should end the matter. That the State accommodates some voters by permitting (not requiring) the casting of absentee or provisional ballots is an indulgence—not a constitutional imperative that falls short of what is required.

JUSTICE SOUTER, WITH WHOM JUSTICE GINSBURG JOINS, DISSENTING.

Indiana's "Voter ID Law" threatens to impose nontrivial burdens on the voting right of tens of thousands of the State's citizens and a significant percentage of those individuals are likely to be deterred from voting. The statute is unconstitutional under the balancing standard of *Burdick v. Takushi* (1992): a State may not burden the right to vote merely by invoking abstract interests, be they legitimate, or even compelling, but must make a particular, factual showing that threats to its interests outweigh the particular impediments it has imposed. The State has made no such justification here, and as to some aspects of its law, it has hardly even tried. I therefore respectfully dissent from the Court's judgment sustaining the statute. . . .

Without a shred of evidence that in-person voter impersonation is a problem in the State, much less a crisis, Indiana has adopted one of the most restrictive photo identification requirements in the country. The State recognizes that tens of thousands of qualified voters lack the necessary federally issued or state-issued identification, but it insists on implementing the requirement immediately, without allowing a transition period for targeted efforts to distribute the required identification to individuals who need it. . . . It is impossible to say, on this record, that the State's interest in adopting its signally inhibiting photo identification requirement has been shown to outweigh the serious burdens it imposes on the right to vote. . . .

The Indiana Voter ID Law is thus unconstitutional: the state interests fail to justify the practical limitations placed on the right to vote, and the law imposes an unreasonable and irrelevant burden on voters who are poor and old.

JUSTICE BREYER, DISSENTING.

Indiana's statute requires registered voters to present photo identification at the polls. It imposes a burden upon some voters, but it does so in order to prevent fraud, to build confidence in the voting system, and thereby to maintain the integrity of the voting process. In determining whether this statute violates the Federal Constitution, I would balance the voting-related interests that the statute affects, asking "whether the statute burdens any one such interest in a manner out of proportion to the statute's salutary effects upon the others (perhaps, but not necessarily, because of the existence of a clearly superior, less restrictive alternative)." Applying this standard, I believe the statute is unconstitutional because it imposes a disproportionate burden upon those eligible voters who lack a driver's license or other statutorily valid form of photo ID.

After the Court's decision in *Crawford* upholding Indiana's voter identification requirements, other states passed such laws. Opponents continued to object, claiming that the requirements were little more than a partisan effort to depress electoral participation among certain classes of voters.

Most recently, states have found the Court equally receptive to laws that remove individuals from their voting rolls. States have an interest in maintaining accurate voter registration lists, and a common concern are those who remain on the voting list after moving, either from one part of a state to another or outside the state altogether. Ohio adopted a method of striking such names by identifying those who did not vote for two consecutive years. Those individuals were sent a notice, asking them to confirm their residence by returning the notice card. Those who failed to return the notice and then did not turn out to vote over the next four years were purged from the state's roll. Under a federal law known as the National Voter Registration Act, however, states are forbidden from using failure to vote as the sole basis for removing individuals from their registration lists. In *Husted v. A. Philip Randolph Institute* (2018), the justices ruled that Ohio's program was valid, since failure to vote was not the sole criterion it employed; it relied upon a failure to vote *and* a failure to return the notice card. Although this was not a constitutional issue—it was just a question of whether a state law was consistent with an act of Congress—the *Husted* decision serves to reinforce the Roberts Court's willingness to afford states greater discretion in setting the rules for voter eligibility.

ELECTION CAMPAIGN REGULATION

Following the 1972 presidential election and associated Watergate controversy, the integrity of federal elections became a national issue. In 1974 Congress moved to reform presidential elections, especially with respect to the role of campaign contributions and expenditures, by amending the Federal Election Campaign Act of 1971 (FECA). The law restricted how much individuals and groups could contribute to candidates, parties, and political action committees (PACs) for use in federal elections. It also imposed record-keeping requirements and provided for federal funding of presidential election campaigns. In **Buckley v. Valeo** (1976) the Supreme Court upheld these provisions but struck down others that limited independent campaign expenditures (i.e., direct campaign spending by individuals or groups not funneled through or coordinated with a candidate's campaign committee) and candidate expenditures of personal funds. The Court's decision rested on an assumption that restricting campaign expenditures was equivalent to limiting political speech. In addition, the justices balanced the need to secure the integrity of federal elections against the right to political expression. The Court concluded that reducing electoral corruption was a sufficient interest to limit campaign contributions but not to restrict campaign expenditures.

In the years following the implementation of the FECA, political strategists developed creative ways to circumvent the law. Campaign contributors were able to exploit a loophole that distinguished money given to a candidate's political campaign from contributions made to political party organizations for "party-building" activities or "get out the vote" drives. The amounts of money that could be given to campaign organizations in support of candidates ("hard money") were clearly regulated and limited by the FECA, but general funds given to political parties ("soft money") were not. Backed by unregulated soft money, political parties were able shrewdly to develop advertising campaigns that supported the election of candidates without explicit pleas to voters to cast their ballots for specific candidates. As a consequence, the use of soft money to fund campaign activities grew consistently and substantially for both political parties and undercut the goals of the FECA. By 2000, each party had more than doubled its reliance upon soft money, relative to hard money over the previous decade *(see Figure 20-1).*

In addition, interest groups and other entities launched "issue campaigns" that promoted certain public policies. These campaigns were unregulated because, at least on their face, they did not urge voters to cast their ballots for any particular candidate. In fact, as long as the advertisements avoided words such as "Vote for John Smith" or "Defeat Nancy Johnson," they were considered issue ads outside the reach of FECA regulation. Many such advertisements promoted or attacked policies or positions clearly associated with specific candidates and even praised or criticized the candidates themselves. They were often run during the heat of a political campaign. Again, these activities tended to undermine the policy goals of the FECA.

Increasing dissatisfaction with the inability of the FECA to control the growing problems related to soft-money contributions and issue advertising prompted Congress to pass the Bipartisan Campaign Reform Act of 2002 (BCRA). The new law contained several provisions that made it the most far-reaching reform of election campaigns since 1974.

Figure 20-1   Soft Money as a Percentage of Total Contributions

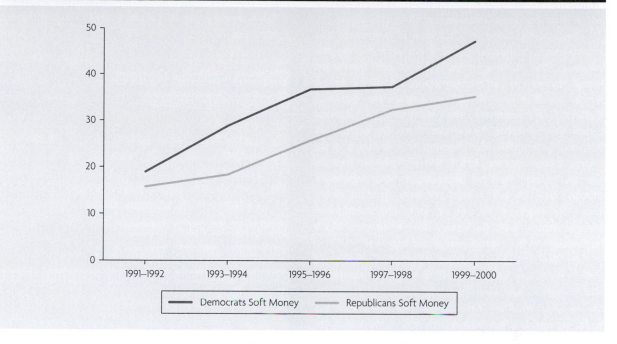

Sources: Federal Election Commission; "Debating McCain-Feingold," *CQ Weekly*, March 10, 2001, 524–526.

Note: These figures reflect soft-money contributions as a percentage of hard-money and soft-money combined. Although hard-money contributions given directly to candidates provided the bulk of money spent on political campaigns, soft-money donations to political party committees grew significantly in the years immediately preceding passage of the Bipartisan Campaign Reform Act of 2002.

First, the BCRA prohibited the national political parties from raising or spending soft money, barred officeholders and candidates for federal office from soliciting or receiving soft money, and prevented state and local party organizations from spending soft money to promote or attack candidates for federal office.

Second, the law prohibited labor unions and corporations, including incorporated interest groups, from using their general funds to engage in "electioneering communication," defined as advertising (primarily televised) clearly referring to a candidate for federal office that appears in the days leading up to an election.. This provision was intended to stop unions and corporations from funding candidate advertising thinly cloaked in the form of issue advocacy. The law also required comprehensive disclosure and record keeping related to such advertising. Exempt from these restrictions were media corporations as well as nonprofit organizations that took no contributions from for-profit corporations.

Third, the law sought to compensate political organizations for the loss of soft-money contributions. Thus, the law raised the ceiling on hard-money contributions—from $1,000 to $2,000 per election to a candidate, for example—and allowed the limits to be adjusted periodically for inflation. The law also limited a donor's aggregate contribution to candidates and groups, such as national party organizations and PACs.

Supporters of this new law had reason to be optimistic that it would survive a legal challenge. In *Buckley*, the Court had approved various campaign finance limits on the rationale that they reduced the likelihood of quid pro quos, where large donors use money to buy access to or favors from candidates once elected. The Court reinforced that reasoning in *Austin v. Michigan Chamber of Commerce* (1990). Because of "the corrosive and distorting effects of immense aggregations of wealth," the justices upheld a prohibition on corporate spending on behalf of candidates in elections. *Austin* involved a state law, not a federal regulation, but the Court's concern was much the same—"that huge corporate treasuries . . . will be used to influence unfairly the outcome of elections." Since the BCRA aimed to ensure public confidence in the electoral process—by reining in the excesses of large amounts of unregulated soft money and banning corporations for "electioneering"—this new law seemed consistent with the values embraced in those precedents.

Predictably, however, a number of individuals and organizations challenged the BCRA as soon as it became effective. The challengers included groups that rarely found themselves on the same side of public policy issues: the National Rifle Association, the National Right to Life Committee, the American Civil Liberties Union, the California Democratic Party, the Republican National Committee, the Chamber of Commerce of the United States, and the AFL/CIO. All believed that the new law violated the First Amendment. Most vigorously attacked were the soft-money and issue advocacy provisions. The attacks on the new law were consolidated into a single dispute, with the lawsuit filed by Senator Mitch McConnell, R-Ky., designated as the lead case.

In *McConnell v. Federal Election Commission* (2003) the Court upheld the BCRA against arguments that Congress had exceeded its authority and that the law violated the First Amendment, but the Court was badly fractured. A five-justice majority, representing the more liberal justices, reasoned that Congress had the authority to protect the integrity of the electoral process by imposing the restrictions included in the BCRA. The four dissenters, all from the Court's more conservative wing, expressed strong disagreement with the decision, calling it a sad day for the First Amendment. Crucial to the decision was Justice Sandra Day O'Connor, generally regarded as a swing vote. She decided in favor of the law's validity.

Five years later, in *Davis v. Federal Election Commission* (2008), the justices declared unconstitutional the so-called millionaire's amendment to the BCRA. This provision dealt with wealthy candidates who largely self-finance their campaigns. Under the law, supporters of the self-financing candidate's opponent were allowed to donate up to three times the regular contribution limits permitted under BCRA. Supporters of the self-financing candidate, by contrast, were required to abide by the normal contribution ceilings. The law was designed to reduce the advantage of wealthy candidates, but the justices found that it placed an impermissible burden on candidates' First Amendment rights to use their own money for campaign speech.

This gave way to speculation that the *McConnell* ruling no longer had the support of the Court's majority. In both decisions Justice Alito voted with the conservative bloc to strike down the campaign finance restrictions. It appeared that the Court now had a five-justice majority that opposed strong limitations on campaign finance on First Amendment grounds. That speculation was tested in the watershed case of *Citizens United v. Federal Election Commission*.

Citizens United v. Federal Election Commission

558 U.S. 310 (2010)
http://caselaw.findlaw.com/us-supreme-court/08-205.html
*Oral arguments available at https://www.oyez.org/
    cases/2008/08-205*
Vote: 5 (Alito, Kennedy, Roberts, Scalia, Thomas)
    4 (Breyer, Ginsburg, Sotomayor, Stevens)

OPINION OF THE COURT: *Kennedy*

CONCURRING OPINIONS: *Roberts, Scalia*

OPINIONS CONCURRING IN PART AND DISSENTING IN PART: *Stevens, Thomas*

In January 2008 Citizens United, a nonprofit corporation that receives some funding from for-profit organizations, released *Hillary: The Movie,* a documentary film critical of then-senator Hillary Clinton, a candidate for the Democratic presidential nomination. The film depicted Clinton as unfit for the presidency. Anticipating that it would make *Hillary* available on cable television through on-demand programming, Citizens United produced television advertisements promoting the documentary to run on broadcast and cable television. Concerned about possible civil and criminal penalties for violating campaign finance laws, Citizens United initiated legal action against the Federal Election Commission (FEC), arguing that (1) Section 203 of BCRA, which prohibits corporations and labor unions from using general treasury funds to finance independent electioneering communications, is unconstitutional as applied to *Hillary;* and (2) BCRA's disclaimer, disclosure, and reporting requirements (Sections 201 and 311) are unconstitutional as applied to *Hillary* and the advertisements. A three-judge district court ruled in favor of the FEC, and Citizens United appealed.

The full opinion in this case runs almost two hundred pages. The excerpt provided here focuses on the issue of the right of corporations to engage in political speech.

JUSTICE KENNEDY DELIVERED THE OPINION OF THE COURT.

In this case we are asked to reconsider *Austin* [v. *Michigan Chamber of Commerce* (1990)] and, in effect, *McConnell* [v. *Federal Election*

Commission (2003)]. It has been noted that "*Austin* was a significant departure from ancient First Amendment principles," *Federal Election Comm'n v. Wisconsin Right to Life, Inc.* (2007) [*WRTL*]. We agree with that conclusion and hold that *stare decisis* does not compel the continued acceptance of *Austin.* The Government may regulate corporate political speech through disclaimer and disclosure requirements, but it may not suppress that speech altogether. We turn to the case now before us. . . .

The law before us is an outright ban, backed by criminal sanctions. Section 441b [of the U.S. code] makes it a felony for all corporations—including nonprofit advocacy corporations—either to expressly advocate the election or defeat of candidates or to broadcast electioneering communications within 30 days of a primary election and 60 days of a general election. . . .

Section 441b's prohibition on corporate independent expenditures is thus a ban on speech. As a "restriction on the amount of money a person or group can spend on political communication during a campaign," that statute "necessarily reduces the quantity of expression by restricting the number of issues discussed, the depth of their exploration, and the size of the audience reached." *Buckley v. Valeo* (1976). Were the Court to uphold these restrictions, the Government could repress speech by silencing certain voices at any of the various points in the speech process. If §441b applied to individuals, no one would believe that it is merely a time, place, or manner restriction on speech. Its purpose and effect are to silence entities whose voices the Government deems to be suspect.

Speech is an essential mechanism of democracy, for it is the means to hold officials accountable to the people. The right of citizens to inquire, to hear, to speak, and to use information to reach consensus is a precondition to enlightened self-government and a necessary means to protect it. The First Amendment "'has its fullest and most urgent application' to speech uttered during a campaign for political office." *Eu v. San Francisco County Democratic Central Comm.* (1989).

Citizens United president David Bossie, right, stands outside the Supreme Court on January 21, 2010, after hearing the Court's ruling in *Citizens United v. FEC*.

For these reasons, political speech must prevail against laws that would suppress it, whether by design or inadvertence. Laws that burden political speech are "subject to strict scrutiny," which requires the Government to prove that the restriction "furthers a compelling interest and is narrowly tailored to achieve that interest." [*WRTL*] While it might be maintained that political speech simply cannot be banned or restricted as a categorical matter, the quoted language from *WRTL* provides a sufficient framework for protecting the relevant First Amendment interests in this case. We shall employ it here.

Premised on mistrust of governmental power, the First Amendment stands against attempts to disfavor certain subjects or viewpoints. Prohibited, too, are restrictions distinguishing among different speakers, allowing speech by some but not others. As instruments to censor, these categories are interrelated: Speech restrictions based on the identity of the speaker are all too often simply a means to control content.

Quite apart from the purpose or effect of regulating content, moreover, the Government may commit a constitutional wrong when by law it identifies certain preferred speakers. By taking the right to speak from some and giving it to others, the Government deprives the disadvantaged person or class of the right to use speech to strive to establish worth, standing, and respect for the speaker's voice. The Government may not by these means deprive the public of the right and privilege to determine for itself what speech and speakers are worthy of consideration. The First Amendment protects speech and speaker, and the ideas that flow from each.

The Court has upheld a narrow class of speech restrictions that operate to the disadvantage of certain persons, but these rulings were based on an interest in allowing governmental entities to perform their functions. The corporate independent expenditures at issue in this case, however, would not interfere with governmental functions, so these cases are inapposite. These precedents stand only for the proposition that there are certain governmental functions that cannot operate without some restrictions on particular kinds of speech. By contrast, it is inherent in the nature of the political process that voters must be free to obtain information from diverse sources in order to determine how to cast their votes. At least before *Austin,* the Court had not allowed the exclusion of a class of speakers from the general public dialogue.

We find no basis for the proposition that, in the context of political speech, the Government may impose restrictions on certain disfavored speakers. Both history and logic lead us to this conclusion.

The Court has recognized that First Amendment protection extends to corporations. [*First National Bank of Boston v.*] *Bellotti* [1978]; . . . *Doran v. Salem Inn, Inc.* (1975); *Southeastern Promotions, Ltd. v. Conrad* (1975); *Cox Broadcasting Corp. v. Cohn* (1975); *Miami Herald Publishing Co. v. Tornillo* (1974); *New York Times Co. v. United States* (1971); *Time, Inc. v. Hill* (1967); *New York Times Co. v. Sullivan* (1964); . . . *Turner Broadcasting System, Inc. v. FCC* (1997); . . . *Young v. American Mini Theatres, Inc.* (1976); *Gertz v. Robert Welch, Inc.* (1974). . . .

This protection has been extended by explicit holdings to the context of political speech. Under the rationale of these precedents, political speech does not lose First Amendment protection "simply because its source is a corporation." *Bellotti.* The Court has thus rejected the argument that political speech of corporations or other associations should be treated differently under the First Amendment simply because such associations are not "natural persons." . . .

"We thus find no support in the First . . . Amendment, or in the decisions of this Court, for the proposition that speech that otherwise would be within the protection of the First Amendment loses that protection simply because its source is a corporation that cannot prove, to the satisfaction of a court, a material effect on its business or property. . . . [That proposition] amounts to an impermissible legislative prohibition of speech based on the identity of the interests that spokesmen may represent in public debate over controversial issues and a requirement that the speaker have a sufficiently great interest in the subject to justify communication. [*Bellotti*]

"In the realm of protected speech, the legislature is constitutionally disqualified from dictating the subjects about which persons may speak and the speakers who may address a public issue." [*Bellotti*]

It is important to note that the reasoning and holding of *Bellotti* did not rest on the existence of a viewpoint-discriminatory statute. It rested on the principle that the Government lacks the power to ban corporations from speaking. . . .

Thus the law stood until *Austin. Austin* "uph[eld] a direct restriction on the independent expenditure of funds for political speech for the first time in [this Court's] history." There, the Michigan Chamber of Commerce sought to use general treasury funds to run a newspaper ad supporting a specific candidate. Michigan law, however, prohibited corporate independent expenditures that supported or opposed any candidate for state office. A violation of the law was punishable as a felony. The Court sustained the speech prohibition.

To bypass *Buckley* and *Bellotti,* the *Austin* Court identified a new governmental interest in limiting political speech: an antidistortion interest. *Austin* found a compelling governmental interest in preventing "the corrosive and distorting effects of immense aggregations of wealth that are accumulated with the help of the corporate form and that have little or no correlation to the public's support for the corporation's political ideas."

The Court is thus confronted with conflicting lines of precedent: a pre-*Austin* line that forbids restrictions on political speech based on the speaker's corporate identity and a post-*Austin* line that permits them. No case before *Austin* had held that Congress could prohibit independent expenditures for political speech based on the speaker's corporate identity. Before *Austin* Congress had enacted legislation for this purpose, and the Government urged the same proposition before this Court. [See *Federal Election Comm'n v. Massachusetts Citizens for Life, Inc.* (1986) and *California Medical Assn. v. Federal Election Comm'n* (1981).] In neither of these cases did the Court adopt the proposition.

In its defense of the corporate-speech restrictions in §441b, the Government notes the antidistortion rationale on which *Austin* and its progeny rest in part, yet it all but abandons reliance upon it. . . . [T]he Government does little to defend it. And with good reason, for the rationale cannot support §441b.

If the First Amendment has any force, it prohibits Congress from fining or jailing citizens, or associations of citizens, for simply engaging in political speech. If the antidistortion rationale were to be accepted, however, it would permit Government to ban political speech simply because the speaker is an association that has taken on the corporate form. The Government contends that *Austin* permits it to ban corporate expenditures for almost all forms of communication stemming from a corporation. If *Austin* were correct, the Government could prohibit a corporation from expressing political views in media beyond those presented here, such as by printing books. . . . This troubling assertion of brooding governmental power cannot be reconciled with the confidence and stability in civic discourse that the First Amendment must secure. . . .

Austin's antidistortion rationale would produce the dangerous, and unacceptable, consequence that Congress could ban political speech of media corporations. Media corporations are now exempt from §441b's ban on corporate expenditures. . . . [Yet] under the Government's reasoning, wealthy media corporations could have their voices diminished to put them on par with other media entities. There is no precedent for permitting this under the First Amendment. . . .

Austin interferes with the "open marketplace" of ideas protected by the First Amendment. It permits the Government to ban the political speech of millions of associations of citizens. Most of these are small corporations without large amounts of wealth. This fact belies the Government's argument that the statute is justified on the ground that it prevents the "distorting effects of immense aggregations of wealth." *Austin.* It is not even aimed at amassed wealth. . . .

The purpose and effect of this law is to prevent corporations, including small and nonprofit corporations, from presenting both facts and opinions to the public. . . .

Even if §441b's expenditure ban were constitutional, wealthy corporations could still lobby elected officials, although smaller corporations may not have the resources to do so. And wealthy individuals and unincorporated associations can spend unlimited amounts on independent expenditures. Yet certain disfavored associations of citizens—those that have taken on the corporate form—are penalized for engaging in the same political speech.

When Government seeks to use its full power, including the criminal law, to command where a person may get his or her information or what distrusted source he or she may not hear, it uses censorship to control thought. This is unlawful. The First Amendment confirms the freedom to think for ourselves. . . .

For the reasons above, it must be concluded that *Austin* was not well reasoned. The Government defends *Austin,* relying almost entirely on "the quid pro quo interest, the corruption interest or the shareholder interest," and not *Austin*'s expressed antidistortion rationale. When neither party defends the reasoning of a precedent, the principle of adhering to that precedent through *stare decisis* is diminished. . . .

Due consideration leads to this conclusion: *Austin* should be and now is overruled. We return to the principle established in *Buckley* and *Bellotti* that the Government may not suppress political speech on the basis of the speaker's corporate identity. No sufficient governmental interest justifies limits on the political speech of nonprofit or for-profit corporations.

Given our conclusion we are further required to overrule the part of *McConnell* that upheld . . . restrictions on corporate independent expenditures. The *McConnell* Court relied on the antidistortion interest recognized in *Austin* to uphold a greater restriction on speech than the restriction upheld in *Austin,* and we have found this interest unconvincing and insufficient. This part of *McConnell* is now overruled. . . .

[Affirmed in part; reversed in part.]

JUSTICE SCALIA, WITH WHOM JUSTICE ALITO JOINS, AND WITH WHOM JUSTICE THOMAS JOINS IN PART, CONCURRING.

The [First] Amendment is written in terms of "speech," not speakers. Its text offers no foothold for excluding any category of speaker, from single individuals to partnerships of individuals, to unincorporated associations of individuals, to incorporated associations of individuals—and the dissent offers no evidence about the original meaning of the text to support any such exclusion. We are therefore simply left with the question whether the speech at issue in this case is "speech" covered by the First Amendment. No one says otherwise. A documentary film critical of a potential Presidential candidate is core political speech, and its nature as such does not change simply because it was funded by a corporation. Nor does the character of that funding produce any reduction whatever in the "inherent worth of the speech" and "its capacity for informing the public[.]" *Bellotti.* Indeed, to exclude or impede corporate speech is to muzzle the principal agents of the modern free economy. We should celebrate rather than condemn the addition of this speech to the public debate.

JUSTICE STEVENS, WITH WHOM JUSTICE GINSBURG, JUSTICE BREYER, AND JUSTICE SOTOMAYOR JOIN, CONCURRING IN PART AND DISSENTING IN PART.

The real issue in this case concerns how, not if, the appellant may finance its electioneering. Citizens United is a wealthy nonprofit corporation that runs a political action committee (PAC) with millions of dollars in assets. Under the Bipartisan Campaign Reform Act of 2002 (BCRA), it could have used those assets to televise and promote *Hillary: The Movie* wherever and whenever it wanted to. It also could have spent unrestricted sums to broadcast *Hillary* at any time other than the 30 days before the last primary election. Neither Citizens United's nor any other corporation's speech has been "banned." All that the parties dispute is whether Citizens United had a right to use the funds in its general treasury to pay for broadcasts during the 30-day period. The notion that the First Amendment dictates an affirmative answer to that question is, in my judgment, profoundly misguided. Even more misguided is the notion that the Court must rewrite the law relating to campaign expenditures by *for-profit* corporations and unions to decide this case.

The basic premise underlying the Court's ruling is its iteration, and constant reiteration, of the proposition that the First Amendment bars regulatory distinctions based on a speaker's identity, including its "identity" as a corporation. While that glittering generality has rhetorical appeal, it is not a correct statement of the law. Nor does it tell us when a corporation may engage in electioneering that some of its shareholders oppose. It does not even resolve the specific question whether Citizens United may be required to finance some of its messages with the money in its PAC. The conceit that corporations must be treated identically to natural persons in the political sphere is not only inaccurate but also inadequate to justify the Court's disposition of this case.

In the context of election to public office, the distinction between corporate and human speakers is significant. Although they make enormous contributions to our society, corporations are not actually members of it. They cannot vote or run for office. Because they may be managed and controlled by nonresidents, their interests may conflict in fundamental respects with the interests of eligible voters. The financial resources, legal structure, and instrumental orientation of corporations raise legitimate concerns about their role in the electoral process. Our lawmakers have a compelling constitutional basis, if not also a democratic duty, to take measures designed to guard against the potentially deleterious effects of corporate spending in local and national races. . . .

I am not an absolutist when it comes to *stare decisis,* in the campaign finance area or in any other. No one is. But if this principle is to do any meaningful work in supporting the rule of law, it must at least demand a significant justification, beyond the preferences of five Justices, for overturning settled doctrine. "[A] decision to overrule should rest on some special reason over and above the belief that a prior case was wrongly decided." *Planned Parenthood of Southeastern Pa. v. Casey* (1992). No such justification exists in this case, and to the contrary there are powerful prudential reasons to keep faith with our precedents.

In the end, the Court's rejection of *Austin* and *McConnell* comes down to nothing more than its disagreement with their results. Virtually every one of its arguments was made and rejected in those cases, and the majority opinion is essentially an amalgamation of resuscitated dissents. The only relevant thing that has changed since *Austin* and *McConnell* is the composition of this Court. Today's ruling thus strikes at the vitals of *stare decisis,* "the means by which we ensure that the law will not merely change erratically, but will develop in a principled and intelligible fashion" that "permits society to presume that bedrock principles are founded in the law rather than in the proclivities of individuals." *Vasquez v. Hillery* (1986). . . .

Today's decision is backwards in many senses. It elevates the majority's agenda over the litigants' submissions, facial attacks over as-applied claims, broad constitutional theories over narrow statutory grounds, individual dissenting opinions over precedential holdings, assertion over tradition, absolutism over empiricism, rhetoric over reality. Our colleagues have arrived at the conclusion that *Austin* must be overruled and that §203 is facially unconstitutional only after mischaracterizing both the reach and rationale of those authorities, and after bypassing or ignoring rules of judicial restraint used to cabin the Court's lawmaking power. Their conclusion that the societal interest in avoiding corruption and the appearance of corruption does not provide an adequate justification for regulating corporate expenditures on candidate elections relies on an incorrect description of that interest, along with a failure to acknowledge the relevance of established facts and the considered judgments of state and federal legislatures over many decades.

In a democratic society, the longstanding consensus on the need to limit corporate campaign spending should outweigh the wooden application of judge-made rules. . . . At bottom, the Court's opinion is thus a rejection of the common sense of the American people, who have recognized a need to prevent corporations from undermining self-government since the founding, and who have fought against the distinctive corrupting potential of corporate electioneering since the days of Theodore Roosevelt. It is a strange time to repudiate that common sense. While American democracy is imperfect, few outside the majority of this Court would have thought its flaws included a dearth of corporate money in politics.

JUSTICE THOMAS, CONCURRING IN PART AND DISSENTING IN PART.

Political speech is entitled to robust protection under the First Amendment. Section 203 of the Bipartisan Campaign Reform Act of 2002 (BCRA) has never been reconcilable with that protection. By striking down §203, the Court takes an important first step toward restoring full constitutional protection to speech that is "indispensable to the effective and intelligent use of the processes of popular government." *McConnell.* I dissent from [a part] of the Court's opinion, however, because the Court's constitutional analysis does not go far enough. The disclosure, disclaimer, and reporting requirements in BCRA §§201 and 311 are also unconstitutional.

Supporters of campaign finance reform and especially those who favored reducing the influence of corporations in the electoral process vigorously opposed the *Citizens United* decision. President Barack Obama sharply criticized the ruling in his 2010 State of the Union address, with several of the justices in attendance. Clearly the fight over regulating elections and the meaning of the First Amendment was not fully settled by the Court's endorsement of constitutional protections for corporate political speech. In fact, new challenges to federal restrictions on campaign finance continued to reach the justices.

In **McCutcheon v. Federal Election Commission** (2014) the Court once again faced such a challenge. During the 2011–2012 election cycle, Shaun McCutcheon, the chief executive officer of an Alabama engineering company, contributed a total of $33,088 to sixteen different candidates. Each of the individual contributions was within the limits set by federal regulations. McCutcheon, however, wanted to make contributions to twelve additional candidates, each again within federal restrictions. However, doing so would have put McCutcheon over the $48,600 aggregate contribution limit imposed by the law. He faced similar aggregate limit restrictions in his desire to make contributions to various political organizations. McCutcheon sued the Federal Election Commission, claiming that the aggregate limits violated his First Amendment rights. In his words, "Somehow, I can give the individual limit, now $2,600, to 17 candidates without corrupting the system. But as soon as I give that same amount to an 18th candidate, our democracy is suddenly at risk." The Supreme Court struck down the aggregate limits imposed by the BCRA, finding that such restrictions violated McCutcheon's right to political expression. The majority reasoned that, while the limits on contributions to individual candidates may serve to reduce potential corruption, the aggregate limits do not.

In addition to invalidating some of the congressional attempts at campaign finance reform, the Roberts Court has also been skeptical of the efforts of states to regulate the role of money in elections, at least when it perceives those efforts to be overzealous. In **Randall v. Sorrell** (2006), for instance, the justices struck down a Vermont law that placed stringent ceilings on campaign contributions. Among its other provisions, the law limited individual donations to candidates for statewide office to $400 per two-year election cycle, with lower limits of $200 for some local offices. The law also put strict ceilings on the amount of money candidates could spend. The Court invalidated the law, saying that the Constitution is violated when contribution and spending limitations, like those imposed by the Vermont law, become so severe as to damage freedom of speech interests.

Alaska imposed similarly tight controls on campaign money, limiting individual contributions to $500 annually to any candidate or any group, other than a political party. Those restrictions were challenged in *Thompson v. Hebdon* (2019). The Court pointed out that Alaska's law exhibited some of the same "danger signs" that were characteristic of the Vermont law struck down in *Randall*; the contribution limits were substantially lower than other states and allowed no adjustment for inflation. Because the lower court had not relied upon *Randall* in reaching its judgment, the justices instructed that court to reconsider its decision, this time taking *Randall* into account. Although the Court did not explicitly say so, it strongly hinted that Alaska's law violated freedom of speech.

POLITICAL REPRESENTATION

Having the right to vote and the assurance of clean election campaigns does not guarantee that people share equally in political influence. The United States is not a direct democracy; consequently, few public policy decisions are made in the voting booth. In a republican form of government, most political decisions are made by officials who are elected by the people from defined geographical districts. The U.S. Congress, for example, reflects two types of geographic constituency, states in the Senate and congressional districts in the House. The duty of senators and representatives is to represent the interests of their respective constituencies in the policy-making process.

How well and how equitably this representational process works depends in part on how the boundary lines of political units are drawn. Because district lines determine political representation, the authority to draw those boundaries carries with it a great deal of political power. Skillful construction of political subdivisions can be used to great advantage, and politicians have never been reluctant to use this power to advance their own interests. Since 1812 the art of structuring legislative districts to ensure political success has been known as *gerrymandering*. The term refers to the political maneuverings of Governor Elbridge Gerry of Massachusetts, who persuaded the state legislature to draw district lines so that his partisan supporters would have a high probability of reelection. Gerrymandered districts frequently are characterized by the rather strange geographical configurations necessary to achieve the desired political ends.

Historically, the establishment or modification of district lines has been a political matter. Battles over drawing the boundaries of political subdivisions usually are fought within the halls of the state legislatures. Serious legal or even constitutional questions may arise when officials use inappropriate criteria for drawing boundaries, or when the process results in the discriminatory treatment of certain groups of voters. In such cases the courts may be called upon to intervene in what is otherwise a legislative duty.

The Reapportionment Controversy

In drafting Article I of the Constitution, the framers clearly intended that representation in the lower house of Congress would be based on population. Each state was allotted at least one representative, with additional

Courtesy of the Library of Congress, Prints & Photographs Division

In 1812 Elkanah Tinsdale lampooned the political maneuverings of Governor Elbridge Gerry of Massachusetts, who deftly engineered the construction of constituency boundaries to aid in the election of a member of his own party. Because the district resembled a mythological salamander in the cartoonist's illustration, the term *gerrymander* has come to mean the drawing of political district lines for political advantage.

seats based on the number of persons residing within state boundaries.

The delegates to the Constitutional Convention wisely anticipated that the nation would undergo considerable growth and experience significant population shifts. Consequently, they determined that the number of congressional seats allocated to each state would be reformulated every ten years following completion of the national census. States that grew in population would gain increased congressional representation, and those that lost population would lose representation. This process remains relatively unchanged today. The number of voting seats in the House of Representatives is fixed by federal law, currently at 435. Every ten years, when the Census Bureau completes its work, the allocation of those 435 seats among the states must be recalculated to reflect changes since the previous population count.

After the census has been taken, each state is told the number of representatives it will have for the next decade. The state legislature then geographically divides the state into separate congressional districts, each of which elects a member of Congress. This scheme of representation is known as the single-member constituency system. Equitable representation is guaranteed if the state legislature constructs the congressional districts so that all contain approximately the same number of residents.

The process of devising the legislative districts is called *apportionment*. When the legislature creates equally populated districts, the system is properly apportioned. When the districts are not in proper balance—that is, when some districts have larger populations and others have smaller populations—the districts are said to be malapportioned. A state can be malapportioned if the legislature does not draw the district lines properly or fails to adjust boundaries to keep pace with population shifts.

Representational districts are used not only for congressional seats but for other government units as well. State legislatures generally are based on the single-member constituency system, as are many county commissions and city councils. In each case, a legislative body must create districts from which representatives will be selected. The same apportionment concepts apply to these bodies as apply to the lower house of Congress.

Constitutional issues regarding apportionment rose to the surface after World War II. Spurred by industrialization, two major wars, and an economic depression, major population shifts took place during the first half of the twentieth century. Large numbers of Americans moved from rural areas and small towns to larger urban centers. Cities grew rapidly and agricultural areas declined, but state legislatures often failed to respond adequately to these migration patterns by reapportioning their congressional and state legislative districts. The more state legislatures were dominated by rural interests, the less incumbent legislators wished to consider redistricting; because proper apportionment would mean fewer legislative seats for the rural areas, some seats held by incumbents would have to be abolished. At the midpoint of the century, many states had not reapportioned since the 1900 census.

The first major apportionment case to come before the Supreme Court was **Colegrove v. Green** (1946), a challenge to the congressional districts in Illinois, where the most populous district had almost nine times as many residents as the least populous. This imbalance was challenged—by a political scientist at Northwestern University, Kenneth W. Colegrove—on the ground that it resulted in a system that violated the Constitution's guarantee of a republican form of government. The Supreme Court refused to rule on the case, holding that reapportionment was a political issue that should be resolved at the ballot box and not in court.

The Court's admonishment presented an insurmountable problem for urban residents living in disproportionately large districts. Many states were so badly malapportioned, and the dominant rural interests so opposed to change, that electing enough state legislators sympathetic to reapportionment was almost impossible. Meanwhile, the census figures for 1950 and 1960 indicated that the malapportionment problem was growing.

By 1958 only one of the four justices in the majority in *Colegrove*, Felix Frankfurter, remained on the bench. The Court, under the leadership of Earl Warren, radically changed its position on the issue. After a lower federal court had refused to hear a challenge to the badly malapportioned Tennessee state legislature, the justices in **Baker v. Carr** (1962) ruled that apportionment issues raise serious equal protection questions that are justiciable. In effect, the Court announced that it would welcome reapportionment challenges.

The first reapportionment dispute heard by the Supreme Court following *Baker* was **Wesberry v. Sanders** (1964), which questioned the way Georgia apportioned its congressional districts. This suit was filed by James P. Wesberry and other qualified voters of Georgia's Fifth Congressional District against Governor Carl Sanders and other state officials. The average population of the state's ten congressional districts was 394,312, but there was considerable variation around that average. The Fifth (metropolitan Atlanta) was the largest, with a population of 823,680. By comparison, the Ninth District had only 272,154 residents. This inequality meant that the Fifth District's legislator represented two to three times as many people as the other members of Congress from Georgia. Stated differently, the residents of the Fifth District had to "share" the time and attention of their representative with a lot more people, compared to the less populous Ninth. The districting scheme had been enacted by the state legislature in 1931, and no effort to bring the districts into balance had occurred since then.

The justices held that this condition of significant malapportionment violated Article I, Section 2, of the Constitution, which says, "The House of Representatives shall be composed of Members chosen every second Year by the People of the several States." To satisfy that constitutional provision, the Court ruled, the congressional districts within a state must be as equal in population as practicable. The decision required the state legislature to redraw its congressional districts to meet this standard.

Wesberry, however, did not fully resolve the reapportionment controversy. A more difficult and politically charged issue centered on malapportionment within the state legislatures. It was one thing for the federal courts to command the state legislators to alter the boundaries of congressional districts, but quite another to require them to reapportion their own legislative districts. Many legislators regarded such an action as an infringement on state sovereignty. In addition, the wholesale alteration of state legislative districts would mean that many state representatives would lose their districts or become politically vulnerable, and legislative power would shift from rural to urban interests. That the state legislatures were less than enthusiastic about such prospects is hardly surprising.

It did not take the Supreme Court long to address the issue. Only four months after *Wesberry*, the Court announced its decision in *Reynolds v. Sims*. Although *Reynolds* shares with *Wesberry* questions of representational equality, the legal bases for the two cases are very different. Article I, Section 2, of the Constitution, upon which the *Wesberry* outcome rested, deals only with the U.S. House of Representatives. Consequently, a challenge to state representational schemes had to be based on other grounds. In addition, all state legislatures except Nebraska's are bicameral, leaving open for dispute whether both houses of a state assembly must be based on population. Notice in Chief Justice Warren's majority opinion in *Reynolds* how the Court reaches a conclusion consistent with *Wesberry* while using entirely different constitutional analysis. Also, consider the Court's holding on the issue of bicameralism. Should a state be allowed to base representation in one house of the legislature on interests other than population alone? How compelling is Justice John Harlan's dissent?

Reynolds v. Sims

377 U.S. 533 (1964)

http://caselaw.findlaw.com/us-supreme-court/377/533.html
Oral arguments available at https://www.oyez.org/cases/1963/23
Vote: 8 (Black, Brennan, Clark, Douglas, Goldberg, Stewart,
*   Warren, White)*
*   1 (Harlan)*

OPINION OF THE COURT: *Warren*

CONCURRING OPINIONS: *Clark, Stewart*

DISSENTING OPINION: *Harlan*

Alabama's 1901 constitution authorized a state legislature of 106 House members and 35 senators. These legislators were to represent districts created generally on the basis of population. Although obliged under its state constitution to reapportion following each national census, the legislature had never altered the districts drawn following the 1900 census. Because of population shifts and a state constitutional requirement that each county, regardless of size, have at least one representative, Alabama had become severely malapportioned. For the state House of Representatives, the most populous legislative district had sixteen times as many people as the least populous. Conditions in the state Senate were even more inequitable. The largest senatorial district had a population forty-one times that of the smallest. As was the case in other states, rural areas enjoyed representation levels far in excess of what their populations warranted. For example, urban Jefferson County's single senator represented more than 600,000 residents, while rural Lowndes County's senator represented 15,417.

Voters in urban counties filed suit to have the Alabama system declared unconstitutional as a violation of the equal protection clause of the Fourteenth Amendment. Pressured by the threat of legal action in light of the Supreme Court's decision in *Baker v. Carr,* the state legislature offered two reapportionment plans to improve the situation. A three-judge district court declared the existing system unconstitutional and the proposed reforms inadequate. The trial court judges imposed a temporary reapportionment plan, and the state appealed to the U.S. Supreme Court. The *Reynolds* case was one of six state legislative reapportionment disputes the Court heard at the same time. The others came from Colorado, Delaware, Maryland, New York, and Virginia. The justices used the opinion in *Reynolds* as the primary vehicle for articulating the Court's position on the state redistricting issue.

> **MR. CHIEF JUSTICE WARREN DELIVERED THE OPINION OF THE COURT.**

Legislators represent people, not trees or acres. Legislators are elected by voters, not farms or cities or economic interests. As long as ours is a representative form of government, and our legislatures are those instruments of government elected directly by and directly representative of the people, the right to elect legislators in a free and unimpaired fashion is a bedrock of our political system. It could hardly be gainsaid that a constitutional claim had been asserted by an allegation that certain otherwise qualified voters had been entirely prohibited from voting for members of their state legislature. And, if a State should provide that the votes of citizens in one part of the State should be given two times, or five times, or 10 times the weight of votes of citizens in another part of the State, it could hardly be contended that the right to vote of those residing in the disfavored areas had not been effectively diluted. It would appear extraordinary to suggest that a State could be constitutionally permitted to enact a law providing that certain of the State's voters could vote two, five, or 10 times for their legislative representatives, while voters living elsewhere could vote only once. And it is inconceivable that a state law to the effect that, in counting votes for legislators, the votes of citizens in one part of the State would be multiplied by two, five, or 10 while the votes of persons in another area would be counted only at face value, could be constitutionally sustainable. Of course, the effect of state legislative districting schemes which give the same number of representatives to unequal numbers of constituents is identical. Overweighting and overvaluation of the votes of those living here has the certain effect of dilution and undervaluation of the votes of those living there. The resulting discrimination against those individual voters living in disfavored areas is easily demonstrable mathematically. Their right to vote is simply not the same right to vote as that of those living in a favored part of the State. Two, five, or 10 of them must vote before the effect of their voting is equivalent to that of their favored neighbor. Weighting the votes of citizens differently, by any method or means, merely because of where they happen to reside, hardly seems justifiable. One must be ever aware that the Constitution forbids "sophisticated as well as simple-minded modes of discrimination." . . .

Logically, in a society ostensibly grounded on representative government, it would seem reasonable that a majority of the people of a State could elect a majority of that State's legislators. To conclude differently, and to sanction minority control of state legislative bodies, would appear to deny majority rights in a way that far surpasses any possible denial of minority rights that might otherwise be thought to result. Since legislatures are responsible for enacting laws by which all citizens are to be governed, they should be bodies which are collectively responsive to the popular will. And the concept of equal protection has been traditionally viewed as requiring the uniform treatment of persons standing in the same relation to the governmental action questioned or challenged. With respect to the allocation of legislative representation, all voters, as citizens of a State, stand in the same relation regardless of where they live. . . . Since the achieving of fair and effective representation for all citizens is concededly the basic aim of legislative apportionment, we conclude that the Equal Protection Clause guarantees the opportunity for equal participation by all voters in the election of state legislators. Diluting the weight of votes because of place of residence impairs basic constitutional rights under the Fourteenth Amendment just as much as invidious discriminations based upon factors such as race or economic status. . . .

We are told that the matter of apportioning representation in a state legislature is a complex and many-faceted one. We are advised that States can rationally consider factors other than population in apportioning legislative representation. We are admonished not to restrict the power of the States to impose differing views as to political philosophy on their citizens. We are cautioned about the dangers of entering into political thickets and mathematical quagmires. Our answer is this: a denial of constitutionally protected rights demands judicial protection; our oath and our office require no less of us. . . . To the extent that a citizen's right to vote is debased, he is that much less a citizen. The fact that an individual lives here or there is not a legitimate reason for overweighting or diluting the efficacy of his vote. The complexions of societies and civilizations change, often with amazing rapidity. A nation once primarily rural in character becomes predominantly urban. Representation schemes once fair and equitable become archaic and outdated. But the basic principle of representative government remains, and must remain, unchanged—the weight of a citizen's vote cannot be made to depend on where he lives. Population is, of necessity, the starting point for consideration and the controlling criterion for judgment in legislative apportionment controversies. A citizen, a qualified voter, is no more nor no less so because he lives in the city or on the farm. This is the clear and strong command of our Constitution's Equal Protection Clause. This is an essential part of the concept of a government of laws and not men. This is at the heart of Lincoln's vision of "government of the people, by the people, [and] for the people." The Equal Protection Clause demands no less than substantially equal state legislative representation for all citizens, of all places as well as of all races.

We hold that, as a basic constitutional standard, the Equal Protection Clause requires that the seats in both houses of a bicameral state legislature must be apportioned on a population basis. Simply stated, an individual's right to vote for state legislators is unconstitutionally impaired when its weight is in a substantial fashion diluted when compared with votes of citizens living in other parts of the State. . . .

Legislative apportionment in Alabama is signally illustrative and symptomatic of the seriousness of this problem in a number of the States. At the time this litigation was commenced, there had been no reapportionment of seats in the Alabama Legislature for over 60 years. Legislative inaction, coupled with the unavailability of any political or judicial remedy, had resulted, with the passage of years, in the perpetuated scheme becoming little more than an irrational anachronism. Consistent failure by the Alabama Legislature to comply with state constitutional requirements as to the frequency of reapportionment and the bases of legislative representation resulted in a minority stranglehold on the State Legislature. Inequality of representation in one house added to the inequality in the other. . . . Since neither of the houses of the Alabama Legislature, under any of the three plans considered by the District Court, was apportioned on a population basis, we would be justified in proceeding no further. However, one of the proposed plans, that contained in the so-called 67-Senator Amendment, at least superficially resembles the scheme of legislative representation followed in the Federal Congress. Under this plan, each of Alabama's 67 counties is allotted one senator, and no counties are given more than one Senate seat. Arguably, this is analogous to the allocation of two Senate seats, in the Federal Congress, to each of the 50 States, regardless of population. Seats in the Alabama House, under the proposed constitutional amendment, are distributed by giving each of the 67 counties at least one, with the remaining 39 seats being allotted among the more populous counties on a population basis. This scheme, at least at first glance, appears to resemble that prescribed for the Federal House of Representatives, where the 435 seats are distributed among the States on a population basis, although each State, regardless of its population, is given at least one Congressman. Thus, although there are substantial differences in underlying rationale and results, the 67-Senator Amendment, as proposed by the Alabama Legislature, at least arguably presents for consideration a scheme analogous to that used for apportioning seats in Congress. . . .

We agree with the District Court, and find the federal analogy inapposite and irrelevant to state legislative districting schemes. Attempted reliance on the federal analogy appears often to be little more than an after-the-fact rationalization offered in defense of maladjusted state apportionment arrangements. The original constitutions of 36 of our States provided that representation in both houses of the state legislatures would be based completely, or predominantly, on population. And the Founding Fathers clearly had no intention of establishing a pattern or model for the apportionment of seats in state legislatures when the system of representation in the Federal Congress was adopted. . . .

The system of representation in the two Houses of the Federal Congress is one ingrained in our Constitution, as part of the law of the land. It is one conceived out of compromise and concession indispensable to the establishment of our federal republic. Arising from unique historical circumstances, it is based on the consideration that in establishing our type of federalism a group of formerly independent States bound themselves together under one national government. . . .

Political subdivisions of States—counties, cities, or whatever—never were and never have been considered as sovereign entities. Rather, they have been traditionally regarded as subordinate governmental instrumentalities created by the State to assist in the carrying out of state governmental functions. . . . The relationship of the States to the Federal Government could hardly be less analogous. . . .

By holding that as a federal constitutional requisite both houses of a state legislature must be apportioned on a population basis, we mean that the Equal Protection Clause requires that a State make an honest and good faith effort to construct districts, in both houses of its legislature, as nearly of equal population as is practicable. . . . A State may legitimately desire to maintain the integrity of various political subdivisions, insofar as possible, and provide for compact districts of contiguous territory in designing a legislative apportionment scheme. Valid considerations may underlie such aims. . . . Whatever the means of accomplishment, the overriding objective must be substantial equality of population among the various districts, so that the vote of any citizen is approximately equal in weight to that of any other citizen in the State.

History indicates, however, that many States have deviated, to a greater or lesser degree, from the equal-population principle in the apportionment of seats in at least one house of their legislatures. So long as the divergences from a strict population standard are based on legitimate considerations incident to the effectuation of a rational state policy, some deviations from the equal-population principle are constitutionally permissible with respect to the apportionment of seats in either or both of the two houses of a bicameral state legislature. But neither history alone, nor economic or other sorts of group interests, are permissible factors in attempting to justify disparities from population-based representation. Citizens, not history or economic interests, cast votes. Considerations of area alone provide an insufficient justification for deviations from the equal population principle. . . .

We find, therefore, that the action taken by the District Court in this case, in ordering into effect a reapportionment of both houses of the Alabama Legislature for purposes of the 1962 primary and general elections, by using the best parts of the two proposed plans which it had found, as a whole, to be invalid, was an appropriate and well-considered exercise of judicial power. Admittedly, the lower court's ordered plan was intended only as a temporary and provisional measure and the District Court correctly indicated that the plan was invalid as a permanent apportionment. In retaining jurisdiction while deferring a hearing on the issuance of a final injunction in order to give the provisionally reapportioned legislature an opportunity to act effectively, the court below proceeded in a proper fashion. . . .

Affirmed and remanded.

MR. JUSTICE HARLAN, DISSENTING.

In these cases the Court holds that seats in the legislatures of six States are apportioned in ways that violate the Federal Constitution. Under the Court's ruling it is bound to follow that the legislature in all but a few of the other 44 States will meet the same fate. These decisions, with *Wesberry v. Sanders,* involving congressional districting by the States, and *Gray v. Sanders,* relating to elections for statewide office, have the effect of placing basic aspects of state political systems under the pervasive overlordship of the federal judiciary. Once again, I must register my protest.

Today's holding is that the Equal Protection Clause of the Fourteenth Amendment requires every State to structure its legislature so that all the members of each house represent substantially the same number of people; other factors may be given play only to the extent that they do not significantly encroach on this basic "population" principle. Whatever may be thought of this holding as a piece of political ideology—and even on that score the political history and practices of this country from its earliest beginnings leave wide room for debate . . .—I think it demonstrable that the Fourteenth Amendment does not impose this political tenet on the States or authorize this Court to do so. . . .

Had the Court paused to probe more deeply into the matter, it would have found that the Equal Protection Clause was never intended to inhibit the States in choosing any democratic method they pleased for the apportionment of their legislatures. This is shown by the language of the Fourteenth Amendment taken as a whole, by the understanding of those who proposed and ratified it, and by the political practices of the States at the time the Amendment was adopted. It is confirmed by numerous state and congressional actions since the adoption of the Fourteenth Amendment, and by the common understanding of the Amendment as evidenced by subsequent constitutional amendments and decisions of this Court before *Baker v. Carr* made an abrupt break with the past in 1962. . . .

So far as the Federal Constitution is concerned, the complaints in these cases should all have been dismissed below for failure to state a cause of action because what has been alleged or proved shows no violation of any constitutional right.

Harlan's dissent in *Reynolds,* predicting that the legislatures of all the states would be affected by the Court's "one person, one vote" principle, proved to be accurate. At first, there was some disagreement with the Court's ruling. State advocates began a movement to amend the Constitution to provide states the authority to have at least one state legislative house based on factors other than population, but the proposal failed to garner sufficient support. As the states began the Court-imposed reapportion process, opposition started to wane. Today, reapportionment of congressional and state legislative districts occurs each decade following the national census. In addition, the reapportionment rulings have been extended to representation systems used at the local level, expanding the influence of decisions such as *Wesberry* and *Reynolds*.

Upon his retirement, Chief Justice Warren said that, in his opinion, the reapportionment decisions were the most significant rulings rendered during his sixteen-year tenure. That statement was remarkable, considering that under his leadership the Court handed down landmark decisions on race relations, criminal justice, obscenity, libel, and school prayer.

Political Representation and Minority Rights

So long as the "one person, one vote" principle is observed, the Supreme Court generally has allowed the states freedom in constructing representational districts. That latitude, however, is not without limit. The Court is aware that representational schemes satisfying standards of numerical equality may still offend basic constitutional principles. Plans that discriminate on the basis of race or ethnicity have been of particular concern. The justices have served notice that boundary lines cannot be drawn in ways that dilute the political power of minorities.

An early example of how lines can be drawn to reduce the influence of minorities is shown in *Gomillion v. Lightfoot* (1960). Prior to 1957 the city limits of Tuskegee, Alabama, were in the shape of a square that encompassed the entire urban area. With the growing civil rights activism of the time and the increasing tendency of black citizens to vote, the white establishment in Tuskegee feared a loss of political control. Consequently, members of the Alabama legislature sympathetic to the city's white leaders successfully sponsored a bill that changed the boundary lines. No longer a square, the altered city limits formed, in Justice Frankfurter's words, "an uncouth twenty-eight-sided figure."

The effect of the redistricting was extraordinary. The law removed from the city all but four or five of its four hundred African American voters, but no white voters. The black plaintiffs, now former residents of Tuskegee, claimed that their removal from the city denied them the right to vote on the basis of race and, therefore, violated their Fifteenth Amendment rights. The city did not deny that race was at issue but claimed that the state of Alabama had an unrestricted right to draw city boundaries as it saw fit and that the courts could not intervene to limit that authority. A unanimous Supreme Court ruled to the contrary, holding that when an otherwise lawful exercise of state power is used to circumvent a federally protected right, the courts may indeed intervene. A legislative act that removes citizens from the municipal voting rolls in a racially discriminatory fashion violates the Fifteenth Amendment.

Beginning in the 1970s the issue of race and representation took on a new twist when legislatures started to enact districting plans designed to *ensure* the election of minority officials. The legislatures created "majority-minority" districts, representational units in which a majority of the residents were members of a particular minority group. These districts virtually ensured the election of minority officeholders. In **United Jewish Organizations of Williamsburgh v. Carey** (1977), the Supreme Court upheld such legislative actions. For the Court, Justice Byron White declared:

> [T]he Constitution does not prevent a State subject to the Voting Rights Act from deliberately creating or preserving black majorities in particular districts. . . . [N]either the Fourteenth nor the Fifteenth Amendment mandates any per se rule against using racial factors in districting and apportionment. . . . The permissible use of racial criteria is not confined to eliminating the effects of past discriminatory districting or apportionment.

The decisions in *United Jewish Organizations* and subsequent cases encouraged state legislatures to engage in racially aware districting practices. Civil rights groups and other liberal organizations had been advocating this practice as the only meaningful way to guarantee African Americans, Hispanics, and other minorities a fair share of legislative seats.

In promoting this cause, advocates of increasing the political power of minorities received significant support from the Justice Department under Presidents Ronald Reagan and George H. W. Bush. Why would Republican administrations back efforts to increase the number of African American representatives, especially when these legislators probably would be Democrats? The answer is simple. When lines are drawn to create districts with high concentrations of African American voters, the other districts become more white and more Republican. In other words, by creating a few districts that are dominated by minorities, the state legislatures could also fashion other districts that are more likely to elect Republicans.

In many states the reapportionment battles that followed the 1990 census were not over one person, one vote issues; rather, they focused on drawing district boundary lines in a manner that would increase the number of minority officeholders. The successful creation of districts with heavy concentrations of racial and ethnic minorities had its intended effect. In the 1992 congressional elections, sixteen new African American representatives were elected, bringing the total membership of the Congressional Black Caucus to forty. Eight newly elected Hispanic representatives also took their seats after the 1992 elections.

To draw these new majority-minority districts, state legislatures often had to engage in very creative mapping methods. Critics contended that legislators went too far, frequently establishing districts that were highly irregular in shape and sprawled across large areas. It was one thing, they argued, to create districts that did not purposefully dilute minority voting strength, but a much different matter to base representational boundaries exclusively on race. As a consequence, lawsuits filed in Florida, Georgia, Louisiana, North Carolina, and Texas challenged the constitutionality of many new districts.

The first appeal to reach the Supreme Court was **Shaw v. Reno** (1993), a challenge to two majority-minority congressional districts in North Carolina, one of which had been created at the behest of the U.S. Department of Justice. Under the Voting Rights Act, the state was not permitted to make changes in its voting practices that would diminish the voting rights of minorities, and to ensure compliance, proposed changes had to receive approval from the federal government. After Attorney General Janet Reno informed the state that it needed to create a second majority-minority district, the legislature fashioned a district that snaked its way along Interstate 85, from Charlotte to Winston-Salem, Greensboro, and Durham. So narrow were the legislative boundary lines, one state legislator observed, "If you drove down the interstate with both car doors open, you'd kill most of the people in the district." The Court ruled that congressional districts created to maximize minority representation may be unconstitutional under some circumstances. States were still required to abide by federal anti-discrimination law, but they could not exceed the law's requirements by engaging in rank racial segregation. District lines that created bizarrely shaped configurations—classifying citizens simply on the basis of race— would be viewed with great skepticism from the Court. After establishing this new standard, the justices sent the case back to the lower courts for additional proceedings.

The decision in this case shocked the civil rights community. It was only a matter of time before the Court would receive an appeal requiring it to apply the *Shaw* principles. How much latitude would the Court give state legislatures in fashioning districts designed to enhance minority voting strength? To what extent would the *Shaw* standard allow race to be taken into account? The Court was not clear in *Shaw*, and its 5–4 vote left the districting waters muddy, but it did not take long for the Court to try again in a 1995 case challenging a majority-minority district in Georgia. As you read *Miller v. Johnson*, pay close attention to the different views expressed.

Miller v. Johnson

515 U.S. 900 (1995)
http://caselaw.findlaw.com/us-supreme-court/515/900.html
Oral arguments available at https://www.oyez.org/
cases/1994/94-631
Vote: 5 (Kennedy, O'Connor, Rehnquist, Scalia, Thomas)
4 (Breyer, Ginsburg, Souter, Stevens)

OPINION OF THE COURT: *Kennedy*

CONCURRING OPINION: *O'Connor*

DISSENTING OPINIONS: *Ginsburg, Stevens*

Following the 1990 census Georgia needed to redraw the lines of its eleven congressional districts. The first plan, passed by the state legislature in 1991, included two districts that had a majority of black voters. Because Georgia was subject to the provisions of the 1965 Voting Rights Act, the legislature submitted the plan to the Justice Department for approval (preclearance). The Justice Department rejected the plan, holding that it did not give sufficient attention to African American voting strength. The state revised its apportionment plan, but the new version again included only two majority-black districts, and this plan also failed to receive Justice Department approval. Finally, in 1992 the state passed, and the Justice Department approved, a new districting plan. This legislation created three majority-black districts: the Second (southwest Georgia), the Fifth (Atlanta), and the Eleventh, the district challenged in this case.

The Eleventh District ran diagonally across the state from the edge of Atlanta to the Atlantic Ocean. It included portions of urban Atlanta, Savannah, and Augusta, as well as sparsely populated, but overwhelmingly African American, rural areas in its central part. The Eleventh covered 6,784 square miles, splitting eight counties and five cities along the way. Numerous narrow land bridges were used to incorporate areas with significant African American populations into the district. The district was 60 percent black, and in the 1992 and 1994 elections, district voters sent Cynthia McKinney, an African American Democrat, to the House of Representatives.

In 1994 five white voters from the Eleventh District, including Davida Johnson, filed suit claiming that the legislature violated the equal protection clause of the Fourteenth Amendment by adopting a redistricting plan driven primarily by considerations of race. A three-judge federal court, applying principles articulated in *Shaw v. Reno,* struck down the district. The Constitution was violated, the judges ruled, because race was the overriding, predominant factor employed to determine the lines of the district. Governor Zell Miller, on behalf of the state, appealed to the Supreme Court.

JUSTICE KENNEDY DELIVERED THE OPINION OF THE COURT.

The Equal Protection Clause of the Fourteenth Amendment provides that no State shall "deny to any person within its jurisdiction the equal protection of the laws." Its central mandate is racial neutrality in governmental decisionmaking. See, e.g., *Loving v. Virginia* (1967); *McLaughlin v. Florida* (1964); see also *Brown v. Board of Education* (1954). Though application of this imperative raises

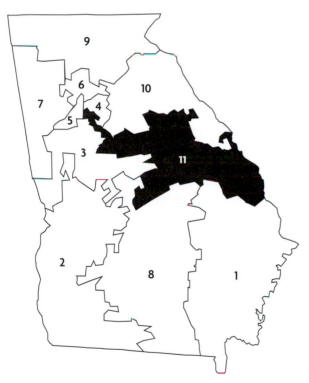

Georgia's Eleventh Congressional District was challenged in *Miller v. Johnson* (1995). Although the district is not generally irregular in shape, note the thin fingerlike extensions in its northwestern, northeastern, and western sections. These were designed to incorporate high concentrations of African American voters in Savannah, Augusta, and Atlanta.

difficult questions, the basic principle is straightforward: "Racial and ethnic distinctions of any sort are inherently suspect and thus call for the most exacting judicial examination. . . . This perception of racial and ethnic distinctions is rooted in our Nation's constitutional and demographic history." *Regents of Univ. of California v. Bakke* (1978) (opinion of Powell, J.). This rule obtains with equal force regardless of "the race of those burdened or benefited by a particular classification." *Richmond v. J. A. Croson Co.* (1989) (plurality opinion). Laws classifying citizens on the basis of race cannot be upheld unless they are narrowly tailored to achieving a compelling state interest.

In *Shaw v. Reno* [1993] we recognized that these equal protection principles govern a State's drawing of congressional districts, though, as our cautious approach there discloses, application of these principles to electoral districting is a most delicate task. Our analysis began from the premise that "[l]aws that explicitly distinguish between individuals on racial grounds fall within the core of [the Equal Protection Clause's] prohibition." This prohibition extends not just to explicit racial classifications, but also to laws neutral on their face but "'unexplainable on grounds other than race.'" Applying this basic Equal Protection analysis in the voting rights context, we held that "redistricting legislation that is so bizarre on its face that it is 'unexplainable on grounds other than race,' . . . demands the same close scrutiny that we give other state laws that classify citizens by race."

This case requires us to apply the principles articulated in *Shaw* to the most recent congressional redistricting plan enacted by the State of Georgia. . . .

. . . Just as the State may not, absent extraordinary justification, segregate citizens on the basis of race in its public parks, buses, golf courses, beaches, and schools, so did we recognize in *Shaw* that it may not separate its citizens into different voting districts on the basis of race. The idea is a simple one: "At the heart of the Constitution's guarantee of equal protection lies the simple command that the Government must treat citizens 'as individuals, not as simply components of a racial, religious, sexual or national class.'" *Metro Broadcasting, Inc. v. FCC* (1990) (O'CONNOR, J., dissenting). When the State assigns voters on the basis of race, it engages in the offensive and demeaning assumption that voters of a particular race, because of their race, "think alike, share the same political interests, and will prefer the same candidates at the polls." *Shaw;* see *Metro Broadcasting* (KENNEDY, J., dissenting). Race-based assignments "embody stereotypes that treat individuals as the product of their race, evaluating their thoughts and efforts— their very worth as citizens—according to a criterion barred to the Government by history and the Constitution." *Metro Broadcasting* (O'CONNOR, J., dissenting). They also cause society serious harm. As we concluded in *Shaw:*

> "Racial classifications with respect to voting carry particular dangers. Racial gerrymandering, even for

remedial purposes, may balkanize us into competing racial factions; it threatens to carry us further from the goal of a political system in which race no longer matters—a goal that the Fourteenth and Fifteenth Amendments embody, and to which the Nation continues to aspire. It is for these reasons that race-based districting by our state legislatures demands close judicial scrutiny."

Our observation in *Shaw* of the consequences of racial stereo-typing was not meant to suggest that a district must be bizarre on its face before there is a constitutional violation. . . . Shape is relevant not because bizarreness is a necessary element of the constitutional wrong . . . , but because it may be persuasive circumstantial evidence that race for its own sake, and not other districting principles, was the legislature's dominant and controlling rationale in drawing its district lines. The logical implication, as courts applying *Shaw* have recognized, is that parties may rely on evidence other than bizarreness to establish race-based districting.

Our reasoning in *Shaw* compels this conclusion. We recognized in *Shaw* that, outside the districting context, statutes are subject to strict scrutiny under the Equal Protection Clause not just when they contain express racial classifications, but also when, though race neutral on their face, they are motivated by a racial purpose or object. . . .

Shaw applied these same principles to redistricting. "In some exceptional cases, a reapportionment plan may be so highly irregular that, on its face, it rationally cannot be understood as anything other than an effort to 'segregat[e] . . . voters' on the basis of race." In other cases, where the district is not so bizarre on its face that it discloses a racial design, the proof will be more "difficul[t]." . . .

. . . Today's case requires us further to consider the requirements of the proof necessary to sustain this equal protection challenge.

. . . Electoral districting is a most difficult subject for legislatures, and so the States must have discretion to exercise the political judgment necessary to balance competing interests. Although race-based decisionmaking is inherently suspect, until a claimant makes a showing sufficient to support that allegation the good faith of a state legislature must be presumed. . . . The plaintiff's burden is to show, either through circumstantial evidence of a district's shape and demographics or more direct evidence going to legislative purpose, that race was the predominant factor motivating the legislature's decision to place a significant number of voters within or without a particular district. To make this showing, a plaintiff must prove that the legislature subordinated traditional race-neutral districting principles, including but not limited to compactness, contiguity, respect for political subdivisions or communities defined by actual shared interests, to racial considerations. Where these or other race-neutral considerations are the basis for redistricting legislation, and are not subordinated to race, a state can "defeat a claim that a district has been gerrymandered on racial lines." *Shaw.* These principles inform the plaintiff's burden of proof at trial. . . .

In our view, the District Court applied the correct analysis, and its finding that race was the predominant factor motivating the drawing of the Eleventh District was not clearly erroneous. The court found it was "exceedingly obvious" from the shape of the Eleventh District, together with the relevant racial demographics, that the drawing of narrow land bridges to incorporate within the District outlying appendages containing nearly 80% of the district's total black population was a deliberate attempt to bring black populations into the district. Although by comparison with other districts the geometric shape of the Eleventh District may not seem bizarre on its face, when its shape is considered in conjunction with its racial and population densities, the story of racial gerrymandering seen by the District Court becomes much clearer. . . . The District Court had before it considerable additional evidence showing that the General Assembly was motivated by a predominant, overriding desire to assign black populations to the Eleventh District and thereby permit the creation of a third majority-black district. . . .

The court found that "it became obvious," both from the Justice Department's objection letters and the three preclearance rounds in general, "that [the Justice Department] would accept nothing less than abject surrender to its maximization agenda." It further found that the General Assembly acquiesced and as a consequence was driven by its overriding desire to comply with the Department's maximization demands. . . .

In light of its well-supported finding, the District Court was justified in rejecting the various alternative explanations offered for the district. Although a legislature's compliance with "traditional districting principles such as compactness, contiguity, and respect for political subdivisions" may well suffice to refute a claim of racial gerrymandering, *Shaw,* appellants cannot make such a refutation where, as here, those factors were subordinated to racial objectives. Georgia's Attorney General objected to the Justice Department's demand for three majority-black districts on the ground that to do so the State would have to "violate all reasonable standards of compactness and contiguity." This statement from a state official is powerful evidence that the legislature subordinated traditional districting principles to race when it ultimately enacted a plan creating three majority-black districts, and justified the District Court's finding that "every [objective districting] factor that could realistically be subordinated to racial tinkering in fact suffered that fate."

Nor can the State's districting legislation be rescued by mere recitation of purported communities of interest. The evidence was compelling "that there are no tangible 'communities of interest' spanning the hundreds of miles of the Eleventh District." A comprehensive report demonstrated the fractured political, social, and economic interests within the Eleventh District's black population. It is apparent that it was not alleged shared interests but rather the object of maximizing the District's black population and obtaining Justice Department approval that in fact explained the General Assembly's actions. A State is free to recognize communities that have a particular racial makeup, provided its action is directed toward some common thread of relevant interests. . . . But where the State assumes from a group of voters' race that they "think alike, share the same political interests, and will prefer the same candidates at the polls," it engages in racial stereotyping at odds with equal protection mandates.

Race was, as the District Court found, the predominant, overriding factor explaining the General Assembly's decision to attach to the Eleventh District various appendages containing dense majority-black populations. As a result, Georgia's congressional redistricting plan cannot be upheld unless it satisfies strict scrutiny, our most rigorous and exacting standard of constitutional review.

To satisfy strict scrutiny, the State must demonstrate that its districting legislation is narrowly tailored to achieve a compelling interest. *Shaw*. There is a "significant state interest in eradicating the effects of past racial discrimination." *Shaw*. The State does not argue, however, that it created the Eleventh District to remedy past discrimination, and with good reason: there is little doubt that the State's true interest in designing the Eleventh District was creating a third majority-black district to satisfy the Justice Department's preclearance demands. . . . Whether or not in some cases compliance with the Voting Rights Act, standing alone, can provide a compelling interest independent of any interest in remedying past discrimination, it cannot do so here. As we suggested in *Shaw*, compliance with federal antidiscrimination laws cannot justify race-based districting where the challenged district was not reasonably necessary under a constitutional reading and application of those laws. The congressional plan challenged here was not required by the Voting Rights Act under a correct reading of the statute. . . .

We do not accept the contention that the State has a compelling interest in complying with whatever preclearance mandates the Justice Department issues. When a state governmental entity seeks to justify race-based remedies to cure the effects of past discrimination, we do not accept the government's mere assertion that the remedial action is required. Rather, we insist on a strong basis in evidence of the harm being remedied. "The history of racial classifications in this country suggests that blind judicial deference to legislative or executive pronouncements of necessity has no place in equal protection analysis." *Croson*. Our presumptive skepticism of all racial classifications, prohibits us as well from accepting on its face the Justice Department's conclusion that racial districting is necessary under the Voting Rights Act. Where a State relies on the Department's determination that race-based districting is necessary to comply with the Voting Rights Act, the judiciary retains an independent obligation in adjudicating consequent equal protection challenges to ensure that the State's actions are narrowly tailored to achieve a compelling interest. See *Shaw*. Were we to accept the Justice Department's objection itself as a compelling interest adequate to insulate racial districting from constitutional review, we would be surrendering to the Executive Branch our role in enforcing the constitutional limits on race-based official action. We may not do so. . . .

The Voting Rights Act, and its grant of authority to the federal courts to uncover official efforts to abridge minorities' right to vote, has been of vital importance in eradicating invidious discrimination from the electoral process and enhancing the legitimacy of our political institutions. Only if our political system and our society cleanse themselves of that discrimination will all members of the polity share an equal opportunity to gain public office regardless of race. As a Nation we share both the obligation and the aspiration of working toward this end. The end is neither assured nor well served, however, by carving electorates into racial blocs. "If our society is to continue to progress as a multiracial democracy, it must recognize that the automatic invocation of race stereotypes retards that progress and causes continued hurt and injury." *Edmondson v. Leesville Concrete Co.* (1991). It takes a shortsighted and unauthorized view of the Voting Rights Act to invoke that statute, which has played a decisive role in redressing some of our worst forms of discrimination, to demand the very racial stereotyping the Fourteenth Amendment forbids.

The judgment of the District Court is affirmed, and the case is remanded for further proceedings consistent with this decision.

It is so ordered.

JUSTICE GINSBURG, WITH WHOM JUSTICES STEVENS, BREYER . . . AND . . . SOUTER JOIN, DISSENTING.

Legislative districting is highly political business. This Court has generally respected the competence of state legislatures to attend to the task. When race is the issue, however, we have recognized the need for judicial intervention to prevent dilution of minority voting strength. Generations of rank discrimination against African-Americans, as citizens and voters, account for that surveillance. . . .

Today the Court expands the judicial role, announcing that federal courts are to undertake searching review of any district with contours "predominantly motivated" by race: "strict scrutiny" will be triggered not only when traditional districting practices are abandoned, but also when those practices are "subordinated to"—given less weight than—race. Applying this new "race-as-predominant-factor" standard, the Court invalidates Georgia's districting plan even though Georgia's Eleventh District, the focus of today's dispute, bears the imprint of familiar districting practices. Because I do not endorse the Court's new standard and would not upset Georgia's plan, I dissent. . . .

Before *Shaw v. Reno* this Court invoked the Equal Protection Clause to justify intervention in the quintessentially political task of legislative districting in two circumstances: to enforce the one-person-one-vote requirement, see *Reynolds v. Sims* (1964); and to prevent dilution of a minority group's voting strength.

In *Shaw,* the Court recognized a third basis for an equal protection challenge to a State's apportionment plan. The Court wrote cautiously, emphasizing that judicial intervention is exceptional: "[S]trict [judicial] scrutiny" is in order, the Court declared, if a district is "so extremely irregular on its face that it rationally can be viewed only as an effort to segregate the races for purposes of voting." . . .

The problem in *Shaw* was not the plan architects' consideration of race as relevant in redistricting. Rather, in the Court's estimation, it was the virtual exclusion of other factors from the calculus. Traditional districting practices were cast aside, the Court concluded, with race alone steering placement of district lines.

The record before us does not show that race similarly overwhelmed traditional districting practices in Georgia. Although the Georgia General Assembly prominently considered race in shaping the Eleventh District, race did not crowd out all other factors, as the Court found it did in North Carolina's delineation of the *Shaw* district.

In contrast to the snake-like North Carolina district inspected in *Shaw,* Georgia's Eleventh District is hardly "bizarre," "extremely irregular," or "irrational on its face." Instead, the Eleventh District's design reflects significant consideration of "traditional districting factors (such as keeping political subdivisions intact) and the usual political process of compromise and trades for a variety of nonracial reasons." . . .

Along with attention to size, shape, and political subdivisions, the Court recognizes as an appropriate districting principle, "respect for . . . communities defined by actual shared interests." The Court finds no community here, however, because a report in the record showed "fractured political, social, and economic interests within the Eleventh District's black population." But ethnicity itself can tie people together, as volumes of social science literature have documented—even people with divergent economic interests. For this reason, ethnicity is a significant force in political life. . . .

To accommodate the reality of ethnic bonds, legislatures have long drawn voting districts along ethnic lines. Our Nation's cities are full of districts identified by their ethnic character—Chinese, Irish, Italian, Jewish, Polish, Russian, for example. . . .

That ethnicity defines some of these groups is a political reality. Until now, no constitutional infirmity has been seen in districting Irish or Italian voters together, for example, so long as the delineation does not abandon familiar apportionment practices. If Chinese-Americans and Russian-Americans may seek and secure group recognition in the delineation of voting districts, then African-Americans should not be dissimilarly treated. Otherwise, in the name of equal protection, we would shut out "the very minority group whose history in the United States gave birth to the Equal Protection Clause." See *Shaw* (STEVENS, J., dissenting). . . .

Only after litigation—under either the Voting Rights Act, the Court's new *Miller* standard, or both—will States now be assured that plans conscious of race are safe. Federal judges in large numbers may be drawn into the fray. This enlargement of the judicial role is unwarranted. The reapportionment plan that resulted from Georgia's political process merited this Court's approbation, not its condemnation. Accordingly, I dissent.

With *Miller v. Johnson* the Court continued on its path of applying strict scrutiny standards to legislative redistricting designed to create majority-minority districts, majority-minority districts, such as those crafted in Georgia (*see Box 20-1*). Once again the decision was the result of a 5–4 voting split. The more conservative justices, Anthony M. Kennedy, Sandra Day O'Connor, William Rehnquist, Antonin Scalia, and Clarence Thomas, formed a solid bloc against districts with boundaries that are "unexplainable on grounds other than race" and where legislatures had "subordinated traditional race-neutral districting principles . . . to racial considerations." The same five-justice coalition had constituted the majority in *Shaw v. Reno* two years earlier. Liberal justices Stephen Breyer, Ruth Bader Ginsburg, David Souter, and John Paul Stevens expressed their solidarity with legislative and executive branch efforts to enhance the representation of historically disadvantaged minorities. As Figure 20-2 shows, these efforts have met with a degree of success.

More recently, the constitutional propriety of excessive partisan gerrymandering has been the center of legal battles. Of course, drawing district lines to enhance the prospects of the party in power has always been considered part of the real world of politics, but some have alleged that one political party using its power to limit the influence of another might violate the guarantee of equal protection. In *Davis v. Bandemer* (1986), the Court acknowledged that judges could at least address the issue, but almost twenty years later, the justices seemingly reversed course in *Vieth v. Jubelirer* (2004), suggesting that *Davis* should be overruled since courts had been unable to develop a workable standard for resolving such claims. In expressing that view, however, Justice Scalia was only able to muster the support of three of his fellow justices. By 2019, the Roberts Court was ready to make it official; in *Rucho v. Common Cause*, the justices, in effect, threw up their hands, declaring partisan gerrymandering to be a political question—an issue that could only be resolved by the political process.

THE 2000 PRESIDENTIAL ELECTION

As we have seen, the Court has never shied away from judging the constitutionality of laws or procedures that

BOX 20-1

Aftermath . . . *Miller v. Johnson*

The immediate impact of *Miller v. Johnson,* which struck down Georgia's redistricting plan, was to send the map back to the state legislature for revision. Despite numerous attempts, the lawmakers were unable to develop an acceptable plan, and the task of redesigning the congressional districts fell to the federal district court. After considering several plans, the court approved a scheme that included only one majority-black district. This judicially imposed redistricting plan was challenged by civil rights advocates. The Supreme Court upheld the plan in *Abrams v. Johnson* (1997), with the justices divided into the same 5–4 voting blocs that occurred in *Shaw v. Reno* and *Miller v. Johnson.*

Despite this legal setback, Georgia's three African American House members held their congressional positions in the next election. By 2013 Georgia's House delegation had increased to fourteen representatives. In 2017 four of those seats were held by African Americans.

Over the past three decades minority representation in the U.S. House of Representatives has grown considerably. Data for the entire House since 1985 show that the number of African American representatives has more than doubled, and the today there is a record number of Hispanic representatives, almost ten times the number from thirty-five years ago. These gains have been due to a number of factors, including increases in minority populations, higher levels of voting participation, and the creation of majority-minority districts. However, given their relative numbers in the general population (African Americans 13.4% and Latinos 18.3%), both groups remain underrepresented.

Figure 20-2   Number of Black and Hispanic Representatives in the U.S. House

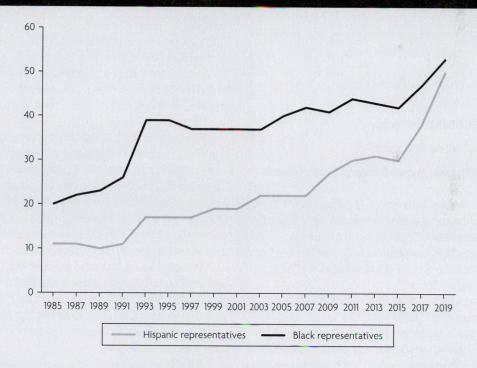

Sources: Norman J. Ornstein, Thomas E. Mann, and Michael J. Malbin, *Vital Statistics on Congress, 1999–2000* (Washington, DC: AEI Press, 2000); Michael Barone and Grant Ujifisa, with Richard E. Cohen and Charles E. Cook Jr., *The Almanac of American Politics 2000* (Washington, DC: National Journal, 1999); *Associated Press,* January 7, 2003; and "African, Hispanic (Latino), and Asian American Members of Congress," *Ethnic Majority,* http://www.ethnicmajority.com/congress.htm; Congressional Research Service.

affect citizens' rights to express their preferences at the polls. It has waded into disputes over legislative apportionment, campaign finance, racial discrimination in elections, and restrictions on voter qualifications. The various constitutional concerns that are implicated in these cases—disenfranchisement and denial of equal protection, enforcement of the Fifteenth Amendment, freedom of expression, and so forth—are significant in no small part because their resolution has broad implications for society. Whatever the specific constitutional questions, the cases decided by the Court on voting and representation have generally involved evaluating the electoral *process*, as opposed to electoral *outcomes*. As in most areas of the law, the justices are more concerned with providing legal guidance to large groups of nationwide interests and less concerned with the immediate consequences to a particular set of litigants. That, however, was not the case in 2000 when a dispute over vote count procedures in Florida led to the Supreme Court's decision in *Bush v. Gore*.

Bush v. Gore

531 U.S. 98 (2000)
http://caselaw.findlaw.com/us-supreme-court/531/98.html
Oral arguments available at https://www.oyez.org/
    cases/2000/00-949
Vote: 5 (Kennedy, O'Connor, Rehnquist, Scalia, Thomas)
    4 (Breyer, Ginsburg, Souter, Stevens)

OPINION OF THE COURT: *Per Curiam*

CONCURRING OPINION: *Rehnquist*

DISSENTING OPINIONS: *Breyer, Ginsburg, Souter, Stevens*

The presidential election of November 7, 2000, was one of the closest races in American history. On election night it became clear that the battle between Republican governor George W. Bush of Texas and Democratic vice president Al Gore for the 270 Electoral College votes necessary for victory would be decided by the outcome in the state of Florida.

Initial vote counts in Florida gave Governor Bush a lead of some 1,780 votes out of 6 million cast. This narrow margin triggered an automatic machine recount held on November 10. The results still gave Bush a victory, but the margin had slipped to a scant 250 votes, with absentee overseas ballots still to be counted. By this time charges and countercharges of voting irregularities had led to lawsuits and political protests. As the various issues sorted themselves out over the ensuing days, the outcome of the election appeared to hinge on one major issue: the large numbers of undercounted ballots in a select number of traditionally Democratic counties. Undercounted ballots (or undervotes) were those for which vote-counting machines did not register a presidential preference. In many cases such undercounting resulted from the voter's failure to perforate the computer-readable punch card ballot. In other cases, machine malfunction may have been the cause. Gore supporters demanded a hand recount of the undercounted ballots.

Three statutory deadlines imposed obstacles for the labor-intensive and time-consuming manual recounts. First, Florida law directed the secretary of state to certify the election results by November 18. Second, federal law provided that if all controversies and contests over a state's presidential electors were resolved by December 12, the state's slate would be considered conclusive and beyond challenge (the so-called safe harbor provision). And third, federal law set December 18 as the date Electoral College members would cast their ballots.

As the manual recounts proceeded, it became clear that the process would not be completed prior to the November 18 deadline for certification. Florida's Republican secretary of state, Katherine Harris, announced her intention to certify the vote on November 18 regardless of the ongoing recounts. Gore forces went to court to block Harris from doing so. A unanimous Florida Supreme Court, emphasizing that every cast vote should be counted, ruled that the recounts should continue and extended the certification date to November 26. Believing the Florida court had exceeded its authority, Bush's lawyers appealed this decision to the U.S. Supreme Court. On December 4 the justices set aside the Florida court's certification extension and asked the court to explain the reasoning behind its decision (*Bush v. Palm Beach Canvassing Board,* 2000). In the meantime, on November 26 Secretary Harris certified that Bush had won the state by 537 votes.

Four days after the U.S. Supreme Court's decision, the Florida high court, in response to an appeal by Vice President Gore, ordered a new statewide manual recount of all undervotes to begin immediately. The recounts were to be conducted by local officials guided only by the instruction to determine voter intent on each ballot. Governor Bush appealed this decision to the U.S. Supreme Court. On December 9 the justices scheduled the case for oral argument and ordered the recounts to stop, pending a final decision.

Two major issues dominated the case. First, did the Florida Supreme Court violate federal law by altering the election procedures in place prior to the election? Second, did it violate the equal protection clause of the Fourteenth Amendment when it ordered a recount to take place without setting a single uniform standard for determining voter intent?

A badly divided Supreme Court issued its ruling on December 12. The majority opinion focuses on the equal protection claim. The concurring and dissenting opinions include a wide range of views on the issues presented, and they debate what remedies should be imposed for any constitutional or statutory violations found.

Theresa LePore, Palm Beach County election supervisor, examines a ballot during the manual recount following the disputed 2000 presidential election in Florida.

PER CURIAM.

The closeness of this election, and the multitude of legal challenges which have followed in its wake, have brought into sharp focus a common, if heretofore unnoticed, phenomenon. Nationwide statistics reveal that an estimated 2% of ballots cast do not register a vote for President for whatever reason, including deliberately choosing no candidate at all or some voter error, such as voting for two candidates or insufficiently marking a ballot. In certifying election results, the votes eligible for inclusion in the certification are the votes meeting the properly established legal requirements.

This case has shown that punch card balloting machines can produce an unfortunate number of ballots which are not punched in a clean, complete way by the voter. After the current counting, it is likely legislative bodies nationwide will examine ways to improve the mechanisms and machinery for voting.

The individual citizen has no federal constitutional right to vote for electors for the President of the United States unless and until the state legislature chooses a statewide election as the means to implement its power to appoint members of the Electoral College. U.S. Const., Art. II, §1. This is the source for the statement in *McPherson v. Blacker* (1892) that the State legislature's power to select the manner for appointing electors is plenary; it may, if it so chooses, select the electors itself, which indeed was the manner used by State legislatures in several States for many years after the Framing of our Constitution. History has now favored the voter, and in each of the several States the citizens themselves vote for Presidential electors. When the state legislature vests the right to vote for President in its people, the right to vote as the legislature has prescribed is fundamental; and one source of its fundamental nature lies in the equal weight accorded to each vote and the equal dignity owed to each voter. The State, of course, after granting the franchise in the special context of Article II, can take back the power to appoint electors.

The right to vote is protected in more than the initial allocation of the franchise. Equal protection applies as well to the manner of its exercise. Having once granted the right to vote on equal terms, the State may not, by later arbitrary and disparate treatment, value one person's vote over that of another. . . .

There is no difference between the two sides of the present controversy on these basic propositions. Respondents say that the very purpose of vindicating the right to vote justifies the recount procedures now at issue. The question before us, however, is whether the recount procedures the Florida Supreme Court has adopted are consistent with its obligation to avoid arbitrary and disparate treatment of the members of its electorate.

Much of the controversy seems to revolve around ballot cards designed to be perforated by a stylus but which, either through error or deliberate omission, have not been perforated with sufficient precision for a machine to count them. In some cases a piece of the card—a chad—is hanging, say by two corners. In other cases there is no separation at all, just an indentation.

The Florida Supreme Court has ordered that the intent of the voter be discerned from such ballots. For purposes of resolving the equal protection challenge, it is not necessary to decide whether the Florida Supreme Court had the authority under the legislative scheme for resolving election disputes to define what a legal vote is and to mandate a manual recount implementing that definition. The recount mechanisms implemented in response to the decisions of the Florida Supreme Court do not satisfy the minimum requirement for non-arbitrary treatment of voters necessary to secure the fundamental right. Florida's basic command for the count of legally cast votes is to consider the "intent of the voter." This is unobjectionable as an abstract proposition and a starting principle. The problem inheres in the absence of specific standards to ensure its equal application. The formulation of uniform rules to determine intent based on these recurring circumstances is practicable and, we conclude, necessary.

The law does not refrain from searching for the intent of the actor in a multitude of circumstances; and in some cases the general command to ascertain intent is not susceptible to much further refinement. In this instance, however, the question is . . . how to interpret the marks or holes or scratches on an inanimate object, a piece of cardboard or paper which, it is said, might not have registered as a vote during the machine count. The factfinder confronts a thing, not a person. The search for intent can be confined by specific rules designed to ensure uniform treatment.

The want of those rules here has led to unequal evaluation of ballots in various respects. As seems to have been acknowledged at oral argument, the standards for accepting or rejecting contested ballots might vary not only from county to county but indeed within a single county from one recount team to another.

The record provides some examples. A monitor in Miami-Dade County testified at trial that he observed that three members of the county canvassing board applied different standards in defining a legal vote. And testimony at trial also revealed that at least one county changed its evaluative standards during the counting process. Palm Beach County, for example, began the process with a 1990 guideline which precluded counting completely attached chads, switched to a rule that considered a vote to be legal if any light could be seen through a chad, changed back to the 1990 rule, and then abandoned any pretense of a *per se* rule, only to have a court order that the county consider dimpled chads legal. This is not a process with sufficient guarantees of equal treatment. . . .

The State Supreme Court ratified this uneven treatment. It mandated that the recount totals from two counties, Miami-Dade and Palm Beach, be included in the certified total. The court also appeared to hold *sub silentio* that the recount totals from Broward County, which were not completed until after the original November 14 certification by the Secretary of State, were to be considered part of the new certified vote totals even though the county certification was not contested by Vice President Gore. Yet each of the counties used varying standards to determine what was a legal vote. Broward County used a more forgiving standard than Palm Beach County, and uncovered almost three times as many new votes, a result markedly disproportionate to the difference in population between the counties.

In addition, the recounts in these three counties were not limited to so-called undervotes but extended to all of the ballots. The distinction has real consequences. A manual recount of all ballots identifies not only those ballots which show no vote but also those which contain more than one, the so-called overvotes. Neither category will be counted by the machine. This is not a trivial concern. At oral argument, respondents estimated there are as many as 110,000 overvotes statewide. As a result, the citizen whose ballot was not read by a machine because he failed to vote for a candidate in a way readable by a machine may still have his vote counted in a manual recount; on the other hand, the citizen who marks two

candidates in a way discernable by the machine will not have the same opportunity to have his vote count, even if a manual examination of the ballot would reveal the requisite indicia of intent. Furthermore, the citizen who marks two candidates, only one of which is discernable by the machine, will have his vote counted even though it should have been read as an invalid ballot. The State Supreme Court's inclusion of vote counts based on these variant standards exemplifies concerns with the remedial processes that were under way.

That brings the analysis to yet a further equal protection problem. The votes certified by the court included a partial total from one county, Miami-Dade. The Florida Supreme Court's decision thus gives no assurance that the recounts included in a final certification must be complete. Indeed, it is respondent's submission that it would be consistent with the rules of the recount procedures to include whatever partial counts are done by the time of final certification, and we interpret the Florida Supreme Court's decision to permit this. This accommodation no doubt results from the truncated contest period established by the Florida Supreme Court in *Bush I,* at respondents' own urging. The press of time does not diminish the constitutional concern. A desire for speed is not a general excuse for ignoring equal protection guarantees.

In addition to these difficulties the actual process by which the votes were to be counted under the Florida Supreme Court's decision raises further concerns. That order did not specify who would recount the ballots. The county canvassing boards were forced to pull together ad hoc teams composed of judges from various Circuits who had no previous training in handling and interpreting ballots. Furthermore, while others were permitted to observe, they were prohibited from objecting during the recount.

The recount process, in its features here described, is inconsistent with the minimum procedures necessary to protect the fundamental right of each voter in the special instance of a statewide recount under the authority of a single state judicial officer. Our consideration is limited to the present circumstances, for the problem of equal protection in election processes generally presents many complexities.

The question before the Court is not whether local entities, in the exercise of their expertise, may develop different systems for implementing elections. Instead, we are presented with a situation where a state court with the power to assure uniformity has ordered a statewide recount with minimal procedural safeguards. When a court orders a statewide remedy, there must be at least some assurance that the rudimentary requirements of equal treatment and fundamental fairness are satisfied.

Given the Court's assessment that the recount process underway was probably being conducted in an unconstitutional manner, the Court stayed the order directing the recount so it could hear this case and render an expedited decision. The contest provision, as it was mandated by the State Supreme Court, is not well calculated to sustain the confidence that all citizens must have in the outcome of elections. The State has not shown that its procedures include the necessary safeguards. The problem, for instance, of the estimated 110,000 overvotes has not been addressed. . . .

Upon due consideration of the difficulties identified to this point, it is obvious that the recount cannot be conducted in compliance with the requirements of equal protection and due process without substantial additional work. It would require not only the adoption (after opportunity for argument) of adequate statewide standards for determining what is a legal vote, and practicable procedures to implement them, but also orderly judicial review of any disputed matters that might arise. In addition, the Secretary of State has advised that the recount of only a portion of the ballots requires that the vote tabulation equipment be used to screen out undervotes, a function for which the machines were not designed. If a recount of overvotes were also required, perhaps even a second screening would be necessary. Use of the equipment for this purpose, and any new software developed for it, would have to be evaluated for accuracy by the Secretary of State, as required by [Florida law].

The Supreme Court of Florida has said that the legislature intended the State's electors to "participat[e] fully in the federal electoral process," as provided in 3 U.S.C. §5. That statute, in turn, requires that any controversy or contest that is designed to lead to a conclusive selection of electors be completed by December 12. That date is upon us, and there is no recount procedure in place under the State Supreme Court's order that comports with minimal constitutional standards. Because it is evident that any recount seeking to meet the December 12 date will be unconstitutional for the reasons we have discussed, we reverse the judgment of the Supreme Court of Florida ordering a recount to proceed.

Seven Justices of the Court agree that there are constitutional problems with the recount ordered by the Florida Supreme Court that demand a remedy. The only disagreement is as to the remedy. Because the Florida Supreme Court has said that the Florida Legislature intended to obtain the safe-harbor benefits of 3 U.S.C. §5, JUSTICE BREYER's proposed remedy—remanding to the Florida Supreme Court for its ordering of a constitutionally proper contest until December 18—contemplates action in violation of the Florida election code, and hence could not be part of an "appropriate" order authorized by [Florida law].

None are more conscious of the vital limits on judicial authority than are the members of this Court, and none stand more in admiration of the Constitution's design to leave the selection of the President to the people, through their legislatures, and to the political sphere. When contending parties invoke the process of the courts, however, it becomes our unsought responsibility to resolve the federal and constitutional issues the judicial system has been forced to confront.

The judgment of the Supreme Court of Florida is reversed, and the case is remanded for further proceedings not inconsistent with this opinion.

CHIEF JUSTICE REHNQUIST, WITH WHOM JUSTICE SCALIA AND JUSTICE THOMAS JOIN, CONCURRING.

We join the *per curiam* opinion. . . .

We deal here not with an ordinary election, but with an election for the President of the United States. . . .

In most cases, comity and respect for federalism compel us to defer to the decisions of state courts on issues of state law. . . . But there are a few exceptional cases in which the Constitution imposes a duty or confers a power on a particular branch of a State's government. This is one of them. Article II, §1, cl. 2, provides that "[e]ach State shall appoint, in such Manner as the *Legislature* thereof may direct," electors for President and Vice President. (Emphasis added.) Thus, the text of the election law itself, and not just its interpretation by the courts of the States, takes on independent significance. . . .

In Florida, the legislature has chosen to hold statewide elections to appoint the State's 25 electors. Importantly, the legislature has delegated the authority to run the elections and to oversee election disputes to the Secretary of State (Secretary) and to state circuit courts. Isolated sections of the code may well admit of more than one interpretation, but the general coherence of the legislative scheme may not be altered by judicial interpretation so as to wholly change the statutorily provided apportionment of responsibility among these various bodies. In any election but a Presidential election, the Florida Supreme Court can give as little or as much deference to Florida's executives as it chooses, so far as Article II is concerned, and this Court will have no cause to question the court's actions. But, with respect to a Presidential election, the court must be both mindful of the legislature's role under Article II in choosing the manner of appointing electors and deferential to those bodies expressly empowered by the legislature to carry out its constitutional mandate. . . .

This inquiry does not imply a disrespect for state *courts* but rather a respect for the constitutionally prescribed role of state *legislatures*. To attach definitive weight to the pronouncement of a state court, when the very question at issue is whether the court has actually departed from the statutory meaning, would be to abdicate our responsibility to enforce the explicit requirements of Article II.

JUSTICE STEVENS, WITH WHOM JUSTICE GINSBURG AND JUSTICE BREYER JOIN, DISSENTING.

In the interest of finality . . . the majority effectively orders the disenfranchisement of an unknown number of voters whose ballots reveal their intent—and are therefore legal votes under state law—but were for some reason rejected by ballot-counting machines. It does so on the basis of the deadlines set forth in Title 3 of the United States Code. But . . . those provisions merely provide rules of decision for Congress to follow when selecting among conflicting slates of electors. They do not prohibit a State from counting what the majority concedes to be legal votes until a bona fide winner is determined. . . . Thus, nothing prevents the majority, even if it properly found an equal protection violation, from ordering relief appropriate to remedy that violation without depriving Florida voters of their right to have their votes counted. As the majority notes, "[a] desire for speed is not a general excuse for ignoring equal protection guarantees." . . .

What must underlie petitioners' entire federal assault on the Florida election procedures is an unstated lack of confidence in the impartiality and capacity of the state judges who would make the critical decisions if the vote count were to proceed. Otherwise, their position is wholly without merit. The endorsement of that position by the majority of this Court can only lend credence to the most cynical appraisal of the work of judges throughout the land. It is confidence in the men and women who administer the judicial system that is the true backbone of the rule of law. Time will one day heal the wound to that confidence that will be inflicted by today's decision. One thing, however, is certain. Although we may never know with complete certainty the identity of the winner of this year's Presidential election, the identity of the loser is perfectly clear. It is the Nation's confidence in the judge as an impartial guardian of the rule of law.

I respectfully dissent.

JUSTICE SOUTER, WITH WHOM JUSTICE BREYER JOINS AND WITH WHOM JUSTICE STEVENS AND JUSTICE GINSBURG JOIN WITH REGARD TO ALL BUT [THE PARAGRAPH DEALING WITH THE EQUAL PROTECTION ISSUE], DISSENTING.

The Court should not have reviewed either *Bush v. Palm Beach County Canvassing Bd.* or this case, and should not have stopped Florida's attempt to recount all undervote ballots by issuing a stay of the Florida Supreme Court's orders during the period of this review. If this Court had allowed the State to follow the course indicated by the opinions of its own Supreme Court, it is entirely possible that there would ultimately have been no issue requiring our review, and political tension could have worked itself out in the Congress. . . . The case being before us, however, its resolution by the majority is another erroneous decision. . . .

Petitioners have raised an equal protection claim, in the charge that unjustifiably disparate standards are applied in different electoral jurisdictions to otherwise identical facts. It is true that the Equal Protection Clause does not forbid the use of a variety of voting mechanisms within a jurisdiction, even though different mechanisms will have different levels of effectiveness in recording voters' intentions; local variety can be justified by concerns about cost, the potential value of innovation, and so on. But evidence in the record here suggests that a different order of disparity obtains under rules for determining a voter's intent that have been applied (and could continue to be applied) to identical types of ballots used in identical brands of machines and exhibiting identical physical characteristics (such as "hanging" or "dimpled" chads). I can

conceive of no legitimate state interest served by these differing treatments of the expressions of voters' fundamental rights. The differences appear wholly arbitrary.

In deciding what to do about this, we should take account of the fact that electoral votes are due to be cast in six days. I would therefore remand the case to the courts of Florida with instructions to establish uniform standards for evaluating the several types of ballots that have prompted differing treatments, to be applied within and among counties when passing on such identical ballots in any further recounting (or successive recounting) that the courts might order.

Unlike the majority, I see no warrant for this Court to assume that Florida could not possibly comply with this requirement before the date set for the meeting of electors, December 18. . . . To recount these [disputed votes] manually would be a tall order, but before this Court stayed the effort to do that the courts of Florida were ready to do their best to get that job done. There is no justification for denying the State the opportunity to try to count all disputed ballots now.

I respectfully dissent.

JUSTICE GINSBURG, WITH WHOM JUSTICE STEVENS, JUSTICE SOUTER, AND JUSTICE BREYER JOIN, . . . DISSENTING.

The extraordinary setting of this case has obscured the ordinary principle that dictates its proper resolution: Federal courts defer to state high courts' interpretations of their state's own law. This principle reflects the core of federalism, on which all agree. "The Framers split the atom of sovereignty. It was the genius of their idea that our citizens would have two political capacities, one state and one federal, each protected from incursion by the other." *Saenz v. Roe,* (1999). THE CHIEF JUSTICE's solicitude for the Florida Legislature comes at the expense of the more fundamental solicitude we owe to the legislature's sovereign. Were the other members of this Court as mindful as they generally are of our system of dual sovereignty, they would affirm the judgment of the Florida Supreme Court.

JUSTICE BREYER, WITH WHOM JUSTICE STVENS AND JUSTICE GINSBURG JOIN . . . AND WITH WHOM JUSTICE SOUTER JOINS, DISSENTING.

The Court was wrong to take this case. It was wrong to grant a stay. It should now vacate that stay and permit the Florida Supreme Court to decide whether the recount should resume.

The political implications of this case for the country are momentous. But the federal legal questions presented, with one exception, are insubstantial. . . .

. . . [T]here is no justification for the majority's remedy, which is simply to reverse the lower court and halt the recount entirely. An appropriate remedy would be, instead, to remand this case with instructions that, even at this late date, would permit the Florida Supreme Court to require recounting all undercounted votes in

Florida . . . and to do so in accordance with a single-uniform substandard. . . .

I respectfully dissent.

The Court's decision in *Bush v. Gore* became the final chapter in the presidential election controversy of 2000 (*see Box 20-2*). Although the extraordinary circumstances that gave birth to the case may limit the decision's applicability as a precedent, there is no doubt that it had important historical consequences. By stopping the Florida recount, the Court removed Vice President Gore's last hope of capturing the state's twenty-five electoral votes and guaranteed that Governor Bush would become the next president. Much of the nation was happy to see the election finally resolved, but the Court's action caused intense debate in political and academic circles. Not only was there a question of whether the Supreme Court should have heard the case in the first place, but also many believed that the justices' votes were excessively influenced by their own political preferences. The five-justice majority ruling in favor of Bush (Rehnquist, Kennedy, O'Connor, Scalia, and Thomas) was composed only of Republicans, and the Court's sole Democrats (Ginsburg and Breyer) favored Gore's position.

BOX 20-2

Aftermath . . . *Bush v. Gore*

Bush v. Gore (2000) effectively ended the 2000 presidential election controversy. On December 13, 2000, the day after the justices ruled, Vice President Al Gore announced that he was ending his campaign: "I accept the finality of this outcome. . . . And tonight, for the sake of our unity as a people and the strength of our democracy, I offer my concession."

Florida's 25 electoral votes gave George W. Bush a total of 271, just one more than he needed to become the forty-third president of the United States. He became only the fourth president in U.S. history to win the Electoral College while losing the popular vote to his chief opponent. Vice President Gore captured 48.39 percent of the popular vote to Governor Bush's 47.88 percent. Before Bush, only John Quincy Adams in 1824, Rutherford B. Hayes in 1876, and Benjamin Harrison in 1888 had been elected president without leading in the popular vote count. Subsequently, this phenomenon repeated itself in the 2016 presidential election when Donald Trump captured an Electoral College majority while losing the popular vote by almost 3 million ballots to Hillary Clinton.

Because of the voting controversies in Florida, many states revised their election laws and upgraded vote-counting equipment to avoid similar problems in future elections. The two Florida officials at the center of the controversy, Governor Jeb Bush and Secretary of State Katherine Harris, continued their political careers. Jeb Bush was reelected governor of Florida in 2002, and Harris won a congressional seat that same year. She ran unsuccessfully for the Senate in 2006. Theodore Olson, the lawyer who successfully argued George W. Bush's case before the Supreme Court, was appointed solicitor general of the United States by the new president.

George W. Bush was reelected to the presidency in 2004. Gore seriously considered undertaking a rematch against him, but in late 2002 he announced that he would not be a candidate. He instead focused his activities on environmental policy. *An Inconvenient Truth,* a film about global warming that Gore wrote and narrated, won the 2006 Academy Award for Best Documentary. In 2007 Gore received the Nobel Peace Prize for his efforts to combat global climate change.

Public opinion polls taken after the Court's ruling showed that a large majority of Americans accepted Bush as the legitimate president, and, contrary to many predictions, the polls failed to find any appreciable decline in public support for the Supreme Court as the result of its incursion into the 2000 presidential election.

A decade later, Al Gore's attorney David Boies and George W. Bush's lawyer Theodore Olson joined forces to represent the parties challenging a California state initiative that banned same-sex marriage. The Supreme Court ruled in their favor in *Hollingsworth v. Perry* (2013), although the decision was confined to a ruling on standing to sue. The consequence of the decision, however, was to allow same-sex marriages to resume in California. Two years later, in *Obergefell v. Hodges* (2015) the Supreme Court lifted the prohibition against same-sex marriages nationwide.

ANNOTATED READINGS

A great deal of scholarly attention has been devoted to the subject of voting rights, much of it dealing with various forms of discrimination. A representative sample of these works includes Charles V. Hamilton, *The Bench and Ballot: Southern Federal Judges and Black Voters* (New York: Oxford University Press, 1973); Richard L. Hasen, *The Supreme Court and Election Law: Judging Equality from* Baker v. Carr *to* Bush v. Gore (New York: New York University Press, 2003); Laurie Collier Hillstrom, *The Voting Rights Act of 1965* (Detroit, MI: Omnigraphics, 2009); David Michael Hudson, *Along Racial Lines: Consequences of the 1965 Voting Rights Act* (New York: Peter Lang, 1998); N. E. H. Hull, *Two Women Who Dared to Vote: The Trial of Susan B. Anthony* (Lawrence: University Press of Kansas, 2012); Alexander Keyssar, *The Right to Vote: The Contested History of Democracy in the United States* (New York: Basic Books, 2000); J. Morgan Kousser, *Colorblind Injustice: Minority Voting Rights and the Undoing of the Second Reconstruction* (Chapel Hill: University of North Carolina Press, 1999); Daniel McCool, Susan M. Olson, and Jennifer L. Robinson, *Native Vote: American Indians, the Voting Rights Act, and the Right to Vote* (New York: Cambridge University Press, 2007); Robert J. Norell, *Reaping the Whirlwind: The Civil Rights Movement in Tuskegee* (Chapel Hill: University of North Carolina Press, 1998); Anthony A. Peacock, *Deconstructing the Republic: Voting Rights, the Supreme Court, and the Founders' Republicanism Reconsidered* (Washington, DC: AEI Press, 2008); Donald Greer Stephenson Jr., *The Right to Vote: Rights and Liberties under the Law* (Santa Barbara, CA: ABC-CLIO, 2004); Richard M. Valelly, *Two Reconstructions: The Struggle for Black Enfranchisement* (Chicago: University of Chicago Press, 2004); and Charles L. Zelden, *The Battle for the Black Ballot:* Smith v. Allwright *and the Defeat of the Texas All-White Primary* (Lawrence: University Press of Kansas, 2004).

Other authors have focused on representation and apportionment issues. Their efforts have spanned a wide variety of topics, including historical development, limitations on judicial power, practical reapportionment problems, and the effects of malapportionment. Among these efforts are Dean Alfange Jr., "Gerrymandering and the Constitution: Into the Thorns of the Thicket at Last," *Supreme Court Review* (1986): 175–257; Dewey M. Clayton, *African Americans and the Politics of Congressional Redistricting* (New York: Garland, 2000); Richard C. Cortner, *The Apportionment Cases* (Knoxville: University of Tennessee Press, 1970); Bernard Grofman, *Political Gerrymandering and the Courts* (New York: Agathon Press, 1990); Anthony J. McGann, Charles Anthony Smith, Michael Latner, and Alex Keena, *Gerrymandering in America: The House of Representatives, the Supreme Court, and the Future of Popular Sovereignty* (New York: Cambridge University Press, 2016); Anthony Peacock, ed., *Affirmative Action and Representation:* Shaw v. Reno *and the Future of Voting Rights* (Durham, NC: Carolina Academic Press, 1997); Richard K. Scher, Jon L. Mills, and John J. Hotaling, *Voting Rights and Democracy: The Law and Politics of Districting* (Chicago: Nelson-Hall, 1997); Bernard Taper, Gomillion v. Lightfoot: *Apartheid in Alabama* (New York: McGraw-Hill, 1967); Dianne T. Thompson, *Congressional Redistricting in North Carolina: Reconsidering Traditional Criteria* (New York: LFB Scholarly Publishing, 2002); and Tinsley E. Yarbrough, *Race and Redistricting: The* Shaw-Cromartie *Cases* (Lawrence: University Press of Kansas, 2002).

The Supreme Court's role in the presidential election of 2000 has received a great deal of criticism and analysis. Some of the better examples include Alan M. Dershowitz, *Supreme Injustice: How the High Court Hijacked Election 2000* (New York: Oxford University Press, 2001); Howard Gillman, *The Votes That Counted: How the Court Decided the 2000 Presidential Election* (Chicago: University of Chicago Press, 2001); Abner Greene, *Understanding the 2000 Election: A Guide to the Legal Battles That Decided the Presidency* (New York: New York University Press, 2001); Richard A. Posner, *Breaking the Deadlock: The 2000 Election, the Constitution, and the Courts* (Princeton, NJ: Princeton University Press, 2001); and Charles Zeldin, Bush v. Gore: *Exposing the Hidden Crisis in American Democracy* (Lawrence: University Press of Kansas, 2010).

REFERENCE MATERIAL

Appendices

1. Constitution of the United States

2. The Justices

3. Glossary

4. Online Case Archive List

APPENDIX 1
Constitution of the United States

WE THE PEOPLE of the United States, in Order to form a more perfect Union, establish Justice, insure domestic Tranquility, provide for the common defence, promote the general Welfare, and secure the Blessings of Liberty to ourselves and our Posterity, do ordain and establish this Constitution for the United States of America.

ARTICLE I

Section 1. All legislative Powers herein granted shall be vested in a Congress of the United States, which shall consist of a Senate and House of Representatives.

Section 2. The House of Representatives shall be composed of Members chosen every second Year by the People of the several States, and the Electors in each State shall have the Qualifications requisite for Electors of the most numerous Branch of the State Legislature.

No Person shall be a Representative who shall not have attained to the age of twenty five Years, and been seven Years a Citizen of the United States, and who shall not, when elected, be an Inhabitant of that State in which he shall be chosen.

[Representatives and direct Taxes shall be apportioned among the several States which may be included within this Union, according to their respective Numbers, which shall be determined by adding to the whole Number of free Persons, including those bound to Service for a Term of Years, and excluding Indians not taxed, three fifths of all other Persons.][1] The actual Enumeration shall be made within three Years after the first Meeting of the Congress of the United States, and within every subsequent Term of ten Years, in such Manner as they shall by Law direct. The Number of Representatives shall not exceed one for every thirty Thousand, but each State shall have at Least one Representative; and until such enumeration shall be made, the State of New Hampshire shall be entitled to chuse three, Massachusetts eight, Rhode-Island and Providence Plantations one, Connecticut five, New-York six, New Jersey four, Pennsylvania eight, Delaware one, Maryland six, Virginia ten, North Carolina five, South Carolina five, and Georgia three.

When vacancies happen in the Representation from any State, the Executive Authority thereof shall issue Writs of Election to fill such Vacancies.

The House of Representatives shall chuse their Speaker and other Officers; and shall have the sole Power of Impeachment.

Section 3. The Senate of the United States shall be composed of two Senators from each State, [chosen by the Legislature thereof,][2] for six Years; and each Senator shall have one Vote.

Immediately after they shall be assembled in Consequence of the first Election, they shall be divided as equally as may be into three Classes. The Seats of the Senators of the first Class shall be vacated at the Expiration of the second Year, of the second Class at the Expiration of the fourth Year, and of the third Class at the Expiration of the sixth Year, so that one third may be chosen every second Year; [and if Vacancies happen by Resignation, or otherwise, during the Recess of the Legislature of any State, the Executive thereof may make temporary Appointments until the next Meeting of the Legislature, which shall then fill such Vacancies.][3]

No Person shall be a Senator who shall not have attained to the Age of thirty Years, and been nine Years a Citizen of the United States, and who shall not, when elected, be an Inhabitant of that State for which he shall be chosen.

---

[1]The part in brackets was changed by Section 2 of the Fourteenth Amendment.

[2]The part in brackets was changed by the first paragraph of the Seventeenth Amendment.

[3]The part in brackets was changed by the second paragraph of the Seventeenth Amendment.

The Vice President of the United States shall be President of the Senate, but shall have no Vote, unless they be equally divided.

The Senate shall chuse their other Officers, and also a President pro tempore, in the Absence of the Vice President, or when he shall exercise the Office of President of the United States.

The Senate shall have the sole Power to try all Impeachments. When sitting for that Purpose, they shall be on Oath or Affirmation. When the President of the United States is tried, the Chief Justice shall preside: And no Person shall be convicted without the Concurrence of two thirds of the Members present.

Judgment in Cases of Impeachment shall not extend further than to removal from Office, and disqualification to hold and enjoy any Office of honor, Trust or Profit under the United States: but the Party convicted shall nevertheless be liable and subject to Indictment, Trial, Judgment and Punishment, according to Law.

Section 4. The Times, Places and Manner of holding Elections for Senators and Representatives, shall be prescribed in each State by the Legislature thereof; but the Congress may at any time by Law make or alter such Regulations, except as to the Places of chusing Senators.

The Congress shall assemble at least once in every Year, and such Meeting shall [be on the first Monday in December],[4] unless they shall by Law appoint a different Day.

Section 5. Each House shall be the Judge of the Elections, Returns and Qualifications of its own Members, and a Majority of each shall constitute a Quorum to do Business; but a smaller Number may adjourn from day to day, and may be authorized to compel the Attendance of absent Members, in such Manner, and under such Penalties as each House may provide.

Each House may determine the Rules of its Proceedings, punish its Members for disorderly Behaviour, and, with the Concurrence of two thirds, expel a Member.

Each House shall keep a Journal of its Proceedings, and from time to time publish the same, excepting such Parts as may in their Judgment require Secrecy; and the Yeas and Nays of the Members of either House on any question shall, at the Desire of one fifth of those Present, be entered on the Journal.

Neither House, during the Session of Congress, shall, without the Consent of the other, adjourn for more than three days, nor to any other Place than that in which the two Houses shall be sitting.

Section 6. The Senators and Representatives shall receive a Compensation for their Services, to be ascertained by Law, and paid out of the Treasury of the United States. They shall in all Cases, except Treason, Felony and Breach of the Peace, be privileged from Arrest during their Attendance at the Session of their respective Houses, and in going to and returning from the same; and for any Speech or Debate in either House, they shall not be questioned in any other Place.

No Senator or Representative shall, during the Time for which he was elected, be appointed to any civil Office under the Authority of the United States, which shall have been created, or the Emoluments whereof shall have been encreased during such time; and no Person holding any Office under the United States, shall be a Member of either House during his Continuance in Office.

Section 7. All Bills for raising Revenue shall originate in the House of Representatives; but the Senate may propose or concur with Amendments as on other Bills.

Every Bill which shall have passed the House of Representatives and the Senate, shall, before it become a Law, be presented to the President of the United States; If he approve he shall sign it, but if not he shall return it, with his Objections to that House in which it shall have originated, who shall enter the Objections at large on their Journal, and proceed to reconsider it. If after such Reconsideration two thirds of that House shall agree to pass the Bill, it shall be sent, together with the Objections, to the other House, by which it shall likewise be reconsidered, and if approved by two thirds of that House, it shall become a Law. But in all such Cases the Votes of both Houses shall be determined by Yeas and Nays, and the Names of the Persons voting for and against the Bill shall be entered on the Journal of each House respectively. If any Bill shall not be returned by the President within ten Days (Sundays excepted) after it shall have been presented to him, the Same shall be a Law, in like Manner as if he had signed it, unless the Congress by their Adjournment prevent its Return, in which Case it shall not be a Law.

Every Order, Resolution, or Vote to which the Concurrence of the Senate and House of Representatives may be necessary (except on a question of Adjournment) shall be presented to the President of the United States; and before the Same shall take Effect, shall be approved by him, or being disapproved by him, shall be repassed by two thirds of the Senate and House of Representatives,

---

[4]The part in brackets was changed by Section 2 of the Twentieth Amendment.

according to the Rules and Limitations prescribed in the Case of a Bill.

Section 8. The Congress shall have Power To lay and collect Taxes, Duties, Imposts and Excises, to pay the Debts and provide for the common Defence and general Welfare of the United States; but all Duties, Imposts and Excises shall be uniform throughout the United States;

To borrow Money on the credit of the United States;

To regulate Commerce with foreign Nations, and among the several States, and with the Indian Tribes;

To establish an uniform Rule of Naturalization, and uniform Laws on the subject of Bankruptcies throughout the United States;

To coin Money, regulate the Value thereof, and of foreign Coin, and fix the Standard of Weights and Measures;

To provide for the Punishment of counterfeiting the Securities and current Coin of the United States;

To establish Post Offices and post Roads;

To promote the Progress of Science and useful Arts, by securing for limited Times to Authors and Inventors the exclusive Right to their respective Writings and Discoveries;

To constitute Tribunals inferior to the supreme Court;

To define and punish Piracies and Felonies committed on the high Seas, and Offences against the Law of Nations;

To declare War, grant Letters of Marque and Reprisal, and make Rules concerning Captures on Land and Water;

To raise and support Armies, but no Appropriation of Money to that Use shall be for a longer Term than two Years;

To provide and maintain a Navy;

To make Rules for the Government and Regulation of the land and naval Forces;

To provide for calling forth the Militia to execute the Laws of the Union, suppress Insurrections and repel Invasions;

To provide for organizing, arming, and disciplining, the Militia, and for governing such Part of them as may be employed in the Service of the United States, reserving to the States respectively, the Appointment of the Officers, and the Authority of training the Militia according to the discipline prescribed by Congress;

To exercise exclusive Legislation in all Cases whatsoever, over such District (not exceeding ten Miles square) as may, by Cession of particular States, and the Acceptance of Congress, become the Seat of the Government of the United States, and to exercise like Authority over all Places purchased by the Consent of the Legislature of the State in which the Same shall be, for the Erection of Forts, Magazines, Arsenals, dock-Yards, and other needful Buildings;—And

To make all Laws which shall be necessary and proper for carrying into Execution the foregoing Powers, and all other Powers vested by this Constitution in the Government of the United States, or in any Department or Officer thereof.

Section 9. The Migration or Importation of such Persons as any of the States now existing shall think proper to admit, shall not be prohibited by the Congress prior to the Year one thousand eight hundred and eight, but a Tax or duty may be imposed on such Importation, not exceeding ten dollars for each Person.

The Privilege of the Writ of Habeas Corpus shall not be suspended, unless when in Cases of Rebellion or Invasion the public Safety may require it.

No Bill of Attainder or ex post facto Law shall be passed.

No Capitation, or other direct, Tax shall be laid, unless in Proportion to the Census or Enumeration herein before directed to be taken.[5]

No Tax or Duty shall be laid on Articles exported from any State.

No Preference shall be given by any Regulation of Commerce or Revenue to the Ports of one State over those of another; nor shall Vessels bound to, or from, one State, be obliged to enter, clear, or pay Duties in another.

No Money shall be drawn from the Treasury, but in Consequence of Appropriations made by Law; and a regular Statement and Account of the Receipts and Expenditures of all public Money shall be published from time to time.

No Title of Nobility shall be granted by the United States: And no Person holding any Office of Profit or Trust under them, shall, without the Consent of the Congress, accept of any present, Emolument, Office, or Title, of any kind whatever, from any King, Prince, or foreign State.

Section 10. No State shall enter into any Treaty, Alliance, or Confederation; grant Letters of Marque and Reprisal; coin Money; emit Bills of Credit; make any Thing but gold and silver Coin a Tender in Payment of Debts; pass any Bill of Attainder, ex post facto Law, or

---

[5]The Sixteenth Amendment gave Congress the power to tax incomes.

Law impairing the Obligation of Contracts, or grant any Title of Nobility.

No State shall, without the Consent of the Congress, lay any Imposts or Duties on Imports or Exports, except what may be absolutely necessary for executing its inspection Laws: and the net Produce of all Duties and Imposts, laid by any State on Imports or Exports, shall be for the Use of the Treasury of the United States; and all such Laws shall be subject to the Revision and Controul of the Congress.

No State shall, without the Consent of Congress, lay any Duty of Tonnage, keep Troops, or Ships of War in time of Peace, enter into any Agreement or Compact with another State, or with a foreign Power, or engage in War, unless actually invaded, or in such imminent Danger as will not admit of delay.

ARTICLE II

Section 1. The executive Power shall be vested in a President of the United States of America. He shall hold his Office during the Term of four Years, and, together with the Vice President, chosen for the same Term, be elected, as follows

Each State shall appoint, in such Manner as the Legislature thereof may direct, a Number of Electors, equal to the whole Number of Senators and Representatives to which the State may be entitled in the Congress: but no Senator or Representative, or Person holding an Office of Trust or Profit under the United States, shall be appointed an Elector.

[The Electors shall meet in their respective States, and vote by Ballot for two Persons, of whom one at least shall not be an Inhabitant of the same State with themselves. And they shall make a List of all the Persons voted for, and of the Number of Votes for each; which List they shall sign and certify, and transmit sealed to the Seat of the Government of the United States, directed to the President of the Senate. The President of the Senate shall, in the Presence of the Senate and House of Representatives, open all the Certificates, and the Votes shall then be counted. The Person having the greatest Number of Votes shall be the President, if such Number be a Majority of the whole Number of Electors appointed; and if there be more than one who have such Majority, and have an equal Number of Votes, then the House of Representatives shall immediately chuse by Ballot one of them for President; and if no Person have a Majority, then from the five highest on the list the said

House shall in like Manner chuse the President. But in chusing the President, the Votes shall be taken by States, the Representation from each State having one Vote; A quorum for this Purpose shall consist of a Member or Members from two thirds of the States, and a Majority of all the States shall be necessary to a Choice. In every Case, after the Choice of the President, the Person having the greatest Number of Votes of the Electors shall be the Vice President. But if there should remain two or more who have equal Votes, the Senate shall chuse from them by Ballot the Vice President.][6]

The Congress may determine the Time of chusing the Electors, and the Day on which they shall give their Votes; which Day shall be the same throughout the United States.

No Person except a natural born Citizen, or a Citizen of the United States, at the time of the Adoption of this Constitution, shall be eligible to the Office of President; neither shall any Person be eligible to that Office who shall not have attained to the Age of thirty five Years, and been fourteen Years a Resident within the United States.

In Case of the Removal of the President from Office, or of his Death, Resignation, or Inability to discharge the Powers and Duties of the said Office,[7] the Same shall devolve on the Vice President, and the Congress may by Law provide for the Case of Removal, Death, Resignation or Inability, both of the President and Vice President, declaring what Officer shall then act as President, and such Officer shall act accordingly, until the Disability be removed, or a President shall be elected.

The President shall, at stated Times, receive for his Services, a Compensation, which shall neither be encreased nor diminished during the Period for which he shall have been elected, and he shall not receive within that Period any other Emolument from the United States, or any of them.

Before he enter on the Execution of his Office, he shall take the following Oath or Affirmation:—"I do solemnly swear (or affirm) that I will faithfully execute the Office of President of the United States, and will to the best of my Ability, preserve, protect and defend the Constitution of the United States."

Section 2. The President shall be Commander in Chief of the Army and Navy of the United States, and of the Militia of the several States, when called into the

---

[6]The part in brackets has been superseded by the Twelfth Amendment.

[7]This provision has been affected by the Twenty-fifth Amendment.

actual Service of the United States; he may require the Opinion, in writing, of the principal Officer in each of the executive Departments, upon any Subject relating to the Duties of their respective Offices, and he shall have Power to grant Reprieves and Pardons for Offences against the United States, except in Cases of Impeachment.

He shall have Power, by and with the Advice and Consent of the Senate, to make Treaties, provided two thirds of the Senators present concur; and he shall nominate, and by and with the Advice and Consent of the Senate, shall appoint Ambassadors, other public Ministers and Consuls, Judges of the supreme Court, and all other Officers of the United States, whose Appointments are not herein otherwise provided for, and which shall be established by Law: but the Congress may by Law vest the Appointment of such inferior Officers, as they think proper, in the President alone, in the Courts of Law, or in the Heads of Departments.

The President shall have Power to fill up all Vacancies that may happen during the Recess of the Senate, by granting Commissions which shall expire at the End of their next Session.

Section 3. He shall from time to time give to the Congress Information of the State of the Union, and recommend to their Consideration such Measures as he shall judge necessary and expedient; he may, on extraordinary Occasions, convene both Houses, or either of them, and in Case of Disagreement between them, with Respect to the Time of Adjournment, he may adjourn them to such Time as he shall think proper; he shall receive Ambassadors and other public Ministers; he shall take Care that the Laws be faithfully executed, and shall Commission all the Officers of the United States.

Section 4. The President, Vice President and all civil Officers of the United States, shall be removed from Office on Impeachment for, and Conviction of, Treason, Bribery, or other high Crimes and Misdemeanors.

ARTICLE III

Section 1. The judicial Power of the United States, shall be vested in one supreme Court, and in such inferior Courts as the Congress may from time to time ordain and establish. The Judges, both of the supreme and inferior Courts, shall hold their Offices during good Behaviour, and shall, at stated Times, receive for their Services, a Compensation, which shall not be diminished during their Continuance in Office.

Section 2. The judicial Power shall extend to all Cases, in Law and Equity, arising under this Constitution, the Laws of the United States, and Treaties made, or which shall be made, under their Authority;—to all Cases affecting Ambassadors, other public Ministers and Consuls;—to all Cases of admiralty and maritime Jurisdiction;—to Controversies to which the United States shall be a Party;—to Controversies between two or more States;—between a State and Citizens of another State;—between Citizens of different States;—between Citizens of the same State claiming Lands under Grants of different States, and between a State, or the Citizens thereof, and foreign States, Citizens or Subjects.[8]

In all Cases affecting Ambassadors, other public Ministers and Consuls, and those in which a State shall be Party, the supreme Court shall have original Jurisdiction. In all the other Cases before mentioned, the supreme Court shall have appellate Jurisdiction, both as to Law and Fact, with such Exceptions, and under such Regulations as the Congress shall make.

The Trial of all Crimes, except in Cases of Impeachment, shall be by Jury; and such Trial shall be held in the State where the said Crimes shall have been committed; but when not committed within any State, the Trial shall be at such Place or Places as the Congress may by Law have directed.

Section 3. Treason against the United States, shall consist only in levying War against them, or in adhering to their Enemies, giving them Aid and Comfort. No Person shall be convicted of Treason unless on the Testimony of two Witnesses to the same overt Act, or on Confession in open Court.

The Congress shall have Power to declare the Punishment of Treason, but no Attainder of Treason shall work Corruption of Blood, or Forfeiture except during the Life of the Person attainted.

ARTICLE IV

Section 1. Full Faith and Credit shall be given in each State to the public Acts, Records, and judicial Proceedings of every other State. And the Congress may by general Laws prescribe the Manner in which such Acts, Records and Proceedings shall be proved, and the Effect thereof.

Section 2. The Citizens of each State shall be entitled to all Privileges and Immunities of Citizens in the several States.

---

[8]These clauses were affected by the Eleventh Amendment.

A Person charged in any State with Treason, Felony, or other Crime, who shall flee from Justice, and be found in another State, shall on Demand of the executive Authority of the State from which he fled, be delivered up, to be removed to the State having Jurisdiction of the Crime.

[No Person held to Service or Labour in one State, under the Laws thereof, escaping into another, shall, in Consequence of any Law or Regulation therein, be discharged from such Service or Labour, but shall be delivered up on Claim of the Party to whom such Service or Labour may be due.][9]

Section 3. New States may be admitted by the Congress into this Union; but no new State shall be formed or erected within the Jurisdiction of any other State; nor any State be formed by the Junction of two or more States, or Parts of States, without the Consent of the Legislatures of the States concerned as well as of the Congress.

The Congress shall have Power to dispose of and make all needful Rules and Regulations respecting the Territory or other Property belonging to the United States; and nothing in this Constitution shall be so construed as to Prejudice any Claims of the United States, or of any particular State.

Section 4. The United States shall guarantee to every State in this Union a Republican Form of Government, and shall protect each of them against Invasion; and on Application of the Legislature, or of the Executive (when the Legislature cannot be convened) against domestic Violence.

ARTICLE V

The Congress, whenever two thirds of both Houses shall deem it necessary, shall propose Amendments to this Constitution, or, on the Application of the Legislatures of two thirds of the several States, shall call a Convention for proposing Amendments, which, in either Case, shall be valid to all Intents and Purposes, as Part of this Constitution, when ratified by the Legislatures of three fourths of the several States, or by Conventions in three fourths thereof, as the one or the other Mode of Ratification may be proposed by the Congress; Provided [that no Amendment which may be made prior to the Year One thousand eight hundred and eight shall in any Manner affect the first and fourth Clauses in the Ninth Section of the first Article; and][10] that no State, without its Consent, shall be deprived of its equal Suffrage in the Senate.

ARTICLE VI

All Debts contracted and Engagements entered into, before the Adoption of this Constitution, shall be as valid against the United States under this Constitution, as under the Confederation.

This Constitution, and the Laws of the United States which shall be made in Pursuance thereof; and all Treaties made, or which shall be made, under the Authority of the United States, shall be the supreme Law of the Land; and the Judges in every State shall be bound thereby, any Thing in the Constitution or Laws of any State to the Contrary notwithstanding.

The Senators and Representatives before mentioned, and the Members of the several State Legislatures, and all executive and judicial Officers, both of the United States and of the several States, shall be bound by Oath or Affirmation, to support this Constitution; but no religious Test shall ever be required as a Qualification to any Office or public Trust under the United States.

ARTICLE VII

The Ratification of the Conventions of nine States, shall be sufficient for the Establishment of this Constitution between the States so ratifying the Same. Done in Convention by the Unanimous Consent of the States present the Seventeenth Day of September in the Year of our Lord one thousand seven hundred and Eighty seven and of the Independence of the United States of America the Twelfth. IN WITNESS whereof We have hereunto subscribed our Names,

George Washington,
President and deputy from Virginia.

New Hampshire:	John Langdon, Nicholas Gilman.
Massachusetts:	Nathaniel Gorham, Rufus King.
Connecticut:	William Samuel Johnson, Roger Sherman.
New York:	Alexander Hamilton.

---

[9]This paragraph has been superseded by the Thirteenth Amendment.

[10]Obsolete.

New Jersey:	William Livingston, David Brearley, William Paterson, Jonathan Dayton.
Pennsylvania:	Benjamin Franklin, Thomas Mifflin, Robert Morris, George Clymer, Thomas FitzSimons, Jared Ingersoll, James Wilson, Gouverneur Morris.
Delaware:	George Read, Gunning Bedford Jr., John Dickinson, Richard Bassett, Jacob Broom.
Maryland:	James McHenry, Daniel of St. Thomas Jenifer, Daniel Carroll.
Virginia:	John Blair, James Madison Jr.
North Carolina:	William Blount, Richard Dobbs Spaight, Hugh Williamson.
South Carolina:	John Rutledge, Charles Cotesworth Pinckney, Charles Pinckney, Pierce Butler.
Georgia:	William Few, Abraham Baldwin.

[The language of the original Constitution, not including the Amendments, was adopted by a convention of the states on September 17, 1787, and was subsequently ratified by the states on the following dates: Delaware, December 7, 1787; Pennsylvania, December 12, 1787; New Jersey, December 18, 1787; Georgia, January 2, 1788; Connecticut, January 9, 1788; Massachusetts, February 6, 1788; Maryland, April 28, 1788; South Carolina, May 23, 1788; New Hampshire, June 21, 1788.

Ratification was completed on June 21, 1788.

The Constitution subsequently was ratified by Virginia, June 25, 1788; New York, July 26, 1788; North Carolina, November 21, 1789; Rhode Island, May 29, 1790; and Vermont, January 10, 1791.]

AMENDMENTS

Amendment I

(First ten amendments ratified December 15, 1791.)
Congress shall make no law respecting an establishment of religion, or prohibiting the free exercise thereof; or abridging the freedom of speech, or of the press; or the right of the people peaceably to assemble, and to petition the Government for a redress of grievances.

Amendment II

A well regulated Militia, being necessary to the security of a free State, the right of the people to keep and bear Arms, shall not be infringed.

Amendment III

No Soldier shall, in time of peace be quartered in any house, without the consent of the Owner, nor in time of war, but in a manner to be prescribed by law.

Amendment IV

The right of the people to be secure in their persons, houses, papers, and effects, against unreasonable searches and seizures, shall not be violated, and no Warrants shall issue, but upon probable cause, supported by Oath or affirmation, and particularly describing the place to be searched, and the persons or things to be seized.

Amendment V

No person shall be held to answer for a capital, or otherwise infamous crime, unless on a presentment or indictment of a Grand Jury, except in cases arising in the land or naval forces, or in the Militia, when in actual service in time of War or public danger; nor shall any person be subject for the same offence to be twice put in jeopardy of life or limb; nor shall be compelled in any criminal case to be a witness against himself, nor be deprived of life, liberty, or property, without due process of law; nor shall private property be taken for public use, without just compensation.

Amendment VI

In all criminal prosecutions, the accused shall enjoy the right to a speedy and public trial, by an impartial jury of the State and district wherein the crime shall have been committed, which district shall have been previously ascertained by law, and to be informed of the nature and cause of the accusation; to be confronted with the witnesses against him; to have compulsory process for obtaining witnesses in his favor, and to have the Assistance of Counsel for his defence.

Amendment VII

In Suits at common law, where the value in controversy shall exceed twenty dollars, the right of trial by jury shall be preserved, and no fact tried by a jury, shall be otherwise re-examined in any Court of the United States, than according to the rules of the common law.

Amendment VIII

Excessive bail shall not be required, nor excessive fines imposed, nor cruel and unusual punishments inflicted.

Amendment IX

The enumeration in the Constitution, of certain rights, shall not be construed to deny or disparage others retained by the people.

Amendment X

The powers not delegated to the United States by the Constitution, nor prohibited by it to the States, are reserved to the States respectively, or to the people.

Amendment XI

(Ratified February 7, 1795)
The Judicial power of the United States shall not be construed to extend to any suit in law or equity, commenced or prosecuted against one of the United States by Citizens of another State, or by Citizens or Subjects of any Foreign State.

Amendment XII

(Ratified June 15, 1804)
The Electors shall meet in their respective states and vote by ballot for President and Vice-President, one of whom, at least, shall not be an inhabitant of the same state with themselves; they shall name in their ballots the person voted for as President, and in distinct ballots the person voted for as Vice-President, and they shall make distinct lists of all persons voted for as President, and of all persons voted for as Vice-President, and of the number of votes for each, which lists they shall sign and certify, and transmit sealed to the seat of the government of the United States, directed to the President of the Senate;—The President of the Senate shall, in the presence of the Senate and House of Representatives, open all the certificates and the votes shall then be counted;—The person having the greatest number of votes for President, shall be the President, if such number be a majority of the whole number of Electors appointed; and if no person have such majority, then from the persons having the highest numbers not exceeding three on the list of those voted for

as President, the House of Representatives shall choose immediately, by ballot, the President. But in choosing the President, the votes shall be taken by states, the representation from each state having one vote; a quorum for this purpose shall consist of a member or members from two-thirds of the states, and a majority of all the states shall be necessary to a choice. [And if the House of Representatives shall not choose a President whenever the right of choice shall devolve upon them, before the fourth day of March next following, then the Vice-President shall act as President, as in the case of the death or other constitutional disability of the President.][11] The person having the greatest number of votes as Vice-President, shall be the Vice-President, if such number be a majority of the whole number of Electors appointed, and if no person have a majority, then from the two highest numbers on the list, the Senate shall choose the Vice President; a quorum for the purpose shall consist of two-thirds of the whole number of Senators, and a majority of the whole number shall be necessary to a choice. But no person constitutionally ineligible to the office of President shall be eligible to that of Vice President of the United States.

Amendment XIII

(Ratified December 6, 1865)
Section 1. Neither slavery nor involuntary servitude, except as a punishment for crime whereof the party shall have been duly convicted, shall exist within the United States, or any place subject to their jurisdiction.

Section 2. Congress shall have power to enforce this article by appropriate legislation.

Amendment XIV

(Ratified July 9, 1868)
Section 1. All persons born or naturalized in the United States, and subject to the jurisdiction thereof, are citizens of the United States and of the State wherein they reside. No State shall make or enforce any law which shall abridge the privileges or immunities of citizens of the United States; nor shall any State deprive any person of life, liberty, or property, without due process of law; nor deny to any person within its jurisdiction the equal protection of the laws.

Section 2. Representatives shall be apportioned among the several States according to their respective numbers, counting the whole number of persons in each

[11]The part in brackets has been superseded by Section 3 of the Twentieth Amendment.

State, excluding Indians not taxed. But when the right to vote at any election for the choice of electors for President and Vice President of the United States, Representatives in Congress, the Executive and Judicial officers of a State, or the members of the Legislature thereof, is denied to any of the male inhabitants of such State, being twenty-one years of age,[12] and citizens of the United States, or in any way abridged, except for participation in rebellion, or other crime, the basis of representation therein shall be reduced in the proportion which the number of such male citizens shall bear to the whole number of male citizens twenty-one years of age in such State.

Section 3. No person shall be a Senator or Representative in Congress, or elector of President and Vice President, or hold any office, civil or military, under the United States, or under any State, who, having previously taken an oath, as a member of Congress, or as an officer of the United States, or as a member of any State legislature, or as an executive or judicial officer of any State, to support the Constitution of the United States, shall have engaged in insurrection or rebellion against the same, or given aid or comfort to the enemies thereof. But Congress may by a vote of two-thirds of each House, remove such disability.

Section 4. The validity of the public debt of the United States, authorized by law, including debts incurred for payment of pensions and bounties for services in suppressing insurrection or rebellion, shall not be questioned. But neither the United States nor any State shall assume or pay any debt or obligation incurred in aid of insurrection or rebellion against the United States, or any claim for the loss or emancipation of any slave; but all such debts, obligations and claims shall be held illegal and void.

Section 5. The Congress shall have power to enforce, by appropriate legislation, the provisions of this article.

Amendment XV

(Ratified February 3, 1870)
Section 1. The right of citizens of the United States to vote shall not be denied or abridged by the United States or by any State on account of race, color, or previous condition of servitude.

Section 2. The Congress shall have power to enforce this article by appropriate legislation.

Amendment XVI

(Ratified February 3, 1913)

The Congress shall have power to lay and collect taxes on incomes, from whatever source derived, without apportionment among the several States, and without regard to any census or enumeration.

Amendment XVII

(Ratified April 8, 1913)
The Senate of the United States shall be composed of two Senators from each State, elected by the people thereof, for six years; and each Senator shall have one vote. The electors in each State shall have the qualifications requisite for electors of the most numerous branch of the State legislatures.

When vacancies happen in the representation of any State in the Senate, the executive authority of such State shall issue writs of election to fill such vacancies: *Provided*, That the legislature of any State may empower the executive thereof to make temporary appointments until the people fill the vacancies by election as the legislature may direct.

This amendment shall not be so construed as to affect the election or term of any Senator chosen before it becomes valid as part of the Constitution.

Amendment XVIII

(Ratified January 16, 1919)
Section 1. After one year from the ratification of this article the manufacture, sale, or transportation of intoxicating liquors within, the importation thereof into, or the exportation thereof from the United States and all territory subject to the jurisdiction thereof for beverage purposes is hereby prohibited.

Section 2. The Congress and the several States shall have concurrent power to enforce this article by appropriate legislation.

Section 3. This article shall be inoperative unless it shall have been ratified as an amendment to the Constitution by the legislatures of the several States, as provided in the Constitution, within seven years from the date of the submission hereof to the States by the Congress.[13]

Amendment XIX

(Ratified August 18, 1920)
The right of citizens of the United States to vote shall not be denied or abridged by the United States or by any State on account of sex.

---

[12]See the Nineteenth and Twenty-sixth Amendments.

[13]This amendment was repealed by Section 1 of the Twenty-first Amendment.

Congress shall have power to enforce this article by appropriate legislation.

Amendment XX

(Ratified January 23, 1933)

Section 1. The terms of the President and Vice President shall end at noon on the 20th day of January, and the terms of Senators and Representatives at noon on the 3d day of January, of the years in which such terms would have ended if this article had not been ratified; and the terms of their successors shall then begin.

Section 2. The Congress shall assemble at least once in every year, and such meeting shall begin at noon on the 3d day of January, unless they shall by law appoint a different day.

Section 3. If, at the time fixed for the beginning of the term of the President, the President elect shall have died, the Vice President elect shall become President. If a President shall not have been chosen before the time fixed for the beginning of his term, or if the President elect shall have failed to qualify, then the Vice President elect shall act as President until a President shall have qualified; and the Congress may by law provide for the case wherein neither a President elect nor a Vice President elect shall have qualified, declaring who shall then act as President, or the manner in which one who is to act shall be selected, and such person shall act accordingly until a President or Vice President shall have qualified.

Section 4. The Congress may by law provide for the case of the death of any of the persons from whom the House of Representatives may choose a President whenever the right of choice shall have devolved upon them, and for the case of the death of any of the persons from whom the Senate may choose a Vice President whenever the right of choice shall have devolved upon them.

Section 5. Sections 1 and 2 shall take effect on the 15th day of October following the ratification of this article.

Section 6. This article shall be inoperative unless it shall have been ratified as an amendment to the Constitution by the legislatures of three-fourths of the several States within seven years from the date of its submission.

Amendment XXI

(Ratified December 5, 1933)

Section 1. The eighteenth article of amendment to the Constitution of the United States is hereby repealed.

Section 2. The transportation or importation into any State, Territory, or possession of the United States for delivery or use therein of intoxicating liquors, in violation of the laws thereof, is hereby prohibited.

Section 3. This article shall be inoperative unless it shall have been ratified as an amendment to the Constitution by conventions in the several States, as provided in the Constitution, within seven years from the date of the submission hereof to the States by the Congress.

Amendment XXII

(Ratified February 27, 1951)

Section 1. No person shall be elected to the office of the President more than twice, and no person who has held the office of President, or acted as President, for more than two years of a term to which some other person was elected President shall be elected to the office of the President more than once. But this Article shall not apply to any person holding the office of President when this Article was proposed by the Congress, and shall not prevent any person who may be holding the office of President, or acting as President, during the term within which this Article becomes operative from holding the office of President or acting as President during the remainder of such term.

Section 2. This article shall be inoperative unless it shall have been ratified as an amendment to the Constitution by the legislatures of three-fourths of the several States within seven years from the date of its submission to the States by the Congress.

Amendment XXIII

(Ratified March 29, 1961)

Section 1. The District constituting the seat of Government of the United States shall appoint in such manner as the Congress may direct:

A number of electors of President and Vice President equal to the whole number of Senators and Representatives in Congress to which the District would be entitled if it were a State, but in no event more than the least populous State; they shall be in addition to those appointed by the States, but they shall be considered, for the purposes of the election of President and Vice President, to be electors appointed by a State; and they shall meet in the District and perform such duties as provided by the twelfth article of amendment.

Section 2. The Congress shall have power to enforce this article by appropriate legislation.

Amendment XXIV

(Ratified January 23, 1964)

Section 1. The right of citizens of the United States to vote in any primary or other election for President or Vice President, for electors for President or Vice President, or for Senator or Representative in Congress, shall not be denied or abridged by the United States or any State by reason of failure to pay any poll tax or other tax.

Section 2. The Congress shall have power to enforce this article by appropriate legislation.

Amendment XXV

(Ratified February 10, 1967)

Section 1. In case of the removal of the President from office or of his death or resignation, the Vice President shall become President.

Section 2. Whenever there is a vacancy in the office of the Vice President, the President shall nominate a Vice President who shall take office upon confirmation by a majority vote of both Houses of Congress.

Section 3. Whenever the President transmits to the President pro tempore of the Senate and the Speaker of the House of Representatives his written declaration that he is unable to discharge the powers and duties of his office, and until he transmits to them a written declaration to the contrary, such powers and duties shall be discharged by the Vice President as Acting President.

Section 4. Whenever the Vice President and a majority of either the principal officers of the executive departments or of such other body as Congress may by law provide, transmit to the President pro tempore of the Senate and the Speaker of the House of Representatives their written declaration that the President is unable to discharge the powers and duties of his office, the Vice President shall immediately assume the powers and duties of the office as Acting President.

Thereafter, when the President transmits to the President pro tempore of the Senate and the Speaker of the House of Representatives his written declaration that no inability exists, he shall resume the powers and duties of his office unless the Vice President and a majority of either the principal officers of the executive department or of such other body as Congress may by law provide, transmit within four days to the President pro tempore of the Senate and the Speaker of the House of Representatives their written declaration that the President is unable to discharge the powers and duties of his office. Thereupon Congress shall decide the issue, assembling within forty-eight hours for that purpose if not in session. If the Congress, within twenty-one days after receipt of the latter written declaration, or, if Congress is not in session, within twenty-one days after Congress is required to assemble, determines by two-thirds vote of both Houses that the President is unable to discharge the powers and duties of his office, the Vice President shall continue to discharge the same as Acting President; otherwise, the President shall resume the powers and duties of his office.

Amendment XXVI

(Ratified July 1, 1971)

Section 1. The right of citizens of the United States, who are eighteen years of age or older, to vote shall not be denied or abridged by the United States or by any State on account of age.

Section 2. The Congress shall have power to enforce this article by appropriate legislation.

Amendment XXVII

(Ratified May 7, 1992)

No law varying the compensation for the services of the Senators and Representatives shall take effect, until an election of Representatives shall have intervened.

Source: United States Government Manual, 1993–94 (Washington, DC: Government Printing Office, 1993), 5–20.

APPENDIX 2
The Justices

THE JUSTICES OF THE Supreme Court are listed below in alphabetical order, each with birth and death years, state from which he or she was appointed, political party affiliation at time of appointment, educational institutions attended, appointing president, confirmation date and vote, date of service termination, and significant preappointment offices and activities.

Alito, Samuel A., Jr. (1950–). New Jersey. Republican. Princeton, Yale. Nominated associate justice by George W. Bush; confirmed 2006 by 58–42 vote. U.S. attorney for New Jersey, federal appeals court judge.

Baldwin, Henry (1780–1844). Pennsylvania. Democrat. Yale. Nominated associate justice by Andrew Jackson; confirmed 1830 by 41–2 vote; died in office 1844. U.S. representative.

Barbour, Philip Pendleton (1783–1841). Virginia. Democrat. College of William and Mary. Nominated associate justice by Andrew Jackson; confirmed 1836 by 30–11 vote; died in office 1841. Virginia state legislator, U.S. representative, U.S. Speaker of the House, state court judge, federal district court judge.

Black, Hugo Lafayette (1886–1971). Alabama. Democrat. Birmingham Medical College, University of Alabama. Nominated associate justice by Franklin Roosevelt; confirmed 1937 by 63–16 vote; retired 1971. Alabama police court judge, county solicitor, U.S. senator.

Blackmun, Harry Andrew (1908–1999). Minnesota. Republican. Harvard. Nominated associate justice by Richard Nixon; confirmed 1970 by 94–0 vote; retired 1994. Federal appeals court judge.

Blair, John, Jr. (1732–1800). Virginia. Federalist. College of William and Mary, Middle Temple (England). Nominated associate justice by George Washington; confirmed 1789 by voice vote; resigned 1796. Virginia legislator, state court judge, delegate to Constitutional Convention.

Blatchford, Samuel (1820–1893). New York. Republican. Columbia. Nominated associate justice by Chester A. Arthur; confirmed 1882 by voice vote; died in office 1893. Federal district court judge, federal circuit court judge.

Bradley, Joseph P. (1813–1892). New Jersey. Republican. Rutgers. Nominated associate justice by Ulysses S. Grant; confirmed 1870 by 46–9 vote; died in office 1892. Private practice.

Brandeis, Louis Dembitz (1856–1941). Massachusetts. Republican. Harvard. Nominated associate justice by Woodrow Wilson; confirmed 1916 by 47–22 vote; retired 1939. Private practice.

Brennan, William Joseph, Jr. (1906–1997). New Jersey. Democrat. University of Pennsylvania, Harvard. Received recess appointment from Dwight Eisenhower to be associate justice 1956; confirmed 1957 by voice vote; retired 1990. New Jersey Supreme Court.

Brewer, David Josiah (1837–1910). Kansas. Republican. Wesleyan, Yale, Albany Law School. Nominated associate justice by Benjamin Harrison; confirmed 1889 by 53–11 vote; died in office 1910. Kansas state court judge, federal circuit court judge.

Breyer, Stephen G. (1938–). Massachusetts. Democrat. Stanford, Oxford, Harvard. Nominated associate justice by Bill Clinton; confirmed 1994 by 87–9 vote. Law professor; chief counsel, Senate Judiciary Committee; federal appeals court judge.

Brown, Henry B. (1836–1913). Michigan. Republican. Yale, Harvard. Nominated associate justice by Benjamin Harrison; confirmed 1890 by voice vote; retired 1906. Michigan state court judge, federal district court judge.

Burger, Warren Earl (1907–1995). Virginia. Republican. University of Minnesota, St. Paul College of Law.

Nominated chief justice by Richard Nixon; confirmed 1969 by 74–3 vote; retired 1986. Assistant U.S. attorney general, federal appeals court judge.

Burton, Harold Hitz (1888–1964). Ohio. Republican. Bowdoin College, Harvard. Nominated associate justice by Harry Truman; confirmed 1945 by voice vote; retired 1958. Ohio state legislator, mayor of Cleveland, U.S. senator.

Butler, Pierce (1866–1939). Minnesota. Democrat. Carleton College. Nominated associate justice by Warren G. Harding; confirmed 1922 by 61–8 vote; died in office 1939. Minnesota county attorney, private practice.

Byrnes, James Francis (1879–1972). South Carolina. Democrat. Privately educated. Nominated associate justice by Franklin Roosevelt; confirmed 1941 by voice vote; resigned 1942. South Carolina local solicitor, U.S. representative, U.S. senator.

Campbell, John Archibald (1811–1889). Alabama. Democrat. Franklin College (University of Georgia), U.S. Military Academy. Nominated associate justice by Franklin Pierce; confirmed 1853 by voice vote; resigned 1861. Alabama state legislator.

Cardozo, Benjamin Nathan (1870–1938). New York. Democrat. Columbia. Nominated associate justice by Herbert Hoover; confirmed 1932 by voice vote; died in office 1938. State court judge.

Catron, John (1786–1865). Tennessee. Democrat. Self-educated. Nominated associate justice by Andrew Jackson; confirmed 1837 by 28–15 vote; died in office 1865. Tennessee state court judge, state chief justice.

Chase, Salmon Portland (1808–1873). Ohio. Republican. Dartmouth. Nominated chief justice by Abraham Lincoln; confirmed 1864 by voice vote; died in office 1873. U.S. senator, Ohio governor, secretary of the Treasury.

Chase, Samuel (1741–1811). Maryland. Federalist. Privately educated. Nominated associate justice by George Washington; confirmed 1796 by voice vote; died in office 1811. Maryland state legislator, delegate to Continental Congress, state court judge.

Clark, Tom Campbell (1899–1977). Texas. Democrat. University of Texas. Nominated associate justice by Harry Truman; confirmed 1949 by 73–8 vote; retired 1967. Texas local district attorney, U.S. attorney general.

Clarke, John Hessin (1857–1945). Ohio. Democrat. Western Reserve University. Nominated associate justice by Woodrow Wilson; confirmed 1916 by voice vote; resigned 1922. Federal district judge.

Clifford, Nathan (1803–1881). Maine. Democrat. Privately educated. Nominated associate justice by James Buchanan; confirmed 1858 by 26–23 vote; died in office 1881. Maine state legislator, state attorney general, U.S. representative, U.S. attorney general, minister to Mexico.

Curtis, Benjamin Robbins (1809–1874). Massachusetts. Whig. Harvard. Nominated associate justice by Millard Fillmore; confirmed 1851 by voice vote; resigned 1857. Massachusetts state legislator.

Cushing, William (1732–1810). Massachusetts. Federalist. Harvard. Nominated associate justice by George Washington; confirmed 1789 by voice vote; died in office 1810. Massachusetts state court judge, Electoral College delegate.

Daniel, Peter Vivian (1784–1860). Virginia. Democrat. Princeton. Nominated associate justice by Martin Van Buren; confirmed 1841 by 22–5 vote; died in office 1860. Virginia state legislator, state Privy Council member, federal district court judge.

Davis, David (1815–1886). Illinois. Republican. Kenyon College, Yale. Nominated associate justice by Abraham Lincoln; confirmed 1862 by voice vote; resigned 1877. Illinois state legislator, state court judge.

Day, William Rufus (1849–1923). Ohio. Republican. University of Michigan. Nominated associate justice by Theodore Roosevelt; confirmed 1903 by voice vote; resigned 1922. Ohio state court judge, U.S. secretary of state, federal court of appeals judge.

Douglas, William Orville (1898–1980). Connecticut. Democrat. Whitman College, Columbia. Nominated associate justice by Franklin Roosevelt; confirmed 1939 by 62–4 vote; retired 1975. Law professor, Securities and Exchange Commission chairman.

Duvall, Gabriel (1752–1844). Maryland. Democratic-Republican. Privately educated. Nominated associate justice by James Madison; confirmed 1811 by voice vote; resigned 1835. Maryland state legislator, U.S. representative, state court judge, presidential elector, comptroller of the U.S. Treasury.

Ellsworth, Oliver (1745–1807). Connecticut. Federalist. Princeton. Nominated chief justice by George Washington; confirmed 1796 by 21–1 vote; resigned 1800. Connecticut state legislator, delegate to Continental Congress and Constitutional Convention, state court judge, U.S. senator.

Field, Stephen J. (1816–1899). California. Democrat. Williams College. Nominated associate justice by

Abraham Lincoln; confirmed 1863 by voice vote; retired 1897. California state legislator, California Supreme Court justice.

Fortas, Abe (1910–1982). Tennessee. Democrat. Southwestern College, Yale. Nominated associate justice by Lyndon Johnson; confirmed 1965 by voice vote; resigned 1969. Counsel for numerous federal agencies, private practice.

Frankfurter, Felix (1882–1965). Massachusetts. Independent. College of the City of New York, Harvard. Nominated associate justice by Franklin Roosevelt; confirmed 1939 by voice vote; retired 1962. Law professor, War Department law officer, assistant to secretary of war, assistant to secretary of labor, War Labor Policies Board chairman.

Fuller, Melville Weston (1833–1910). Illinois. Democrat. Bowdoin College, Harvard. Nominated chief justice by Grover Cleveland; confirmed 1888 by 41–20 vote; died in office 1910. Illinois state legislator.

Ginsburg, Ruth Bader (1933–). New York. Democrat. Columbia. Nominated associate justice by Bill Clinton; confirmed 1993 by 96–3 vote. Law professor, federal court of appeals judge.

Goldberg, Arthur J. (1908–1990). Illinois. Democrat. Northwestern. Nominated associate justice by John Kennedy; confirmed 1962 by voice vote; resigned 1965. U.S. secretary of labor.

Gorsuch, Neil (1967–). Colorado. Republican. Nominated associate justice by Donald J. Trump; confirmed 2017 by 54–45 vote. Federal court of appeals judge.

Gray, Horace (1828–1902). Massachusetts. Republican. Harvard. Nominated associate justice by Chester A. Arthur; confirmed 1881 by 51–5 vote; died in office 1902. Massachusetts Supreme Court justice.

Grier, Robert Cooper (1794–1870). Pennsylvania. Democrat. Dickinson College. Nominated associate justice by James Polk; confirmed 1846 by voice vote; retired 1870. Pennsylvania state court judge.

Harlan, John Marshall (1833–1911). Kentucky. Republican. Centre College, Transylvania University. Nominated associate justice by Rutherford B. Hayes; confirmed 1877 by voice vote; died in office 1911. Kentucky attorney general.

Harlan, John Marshall (1899–1971). New York. Republican. Princeton, Oxford, New York Law School. Nominated associate justice by Dwight Eisenhower; confirmed 1955 by 71–11 vote; retired 1971. Chief counsel for New York State Crime Commission, federal court of appeals judge.

Holmes, Oliver Wendell, Jr. (1841–1935). Massachusetts. Republican. Harvard. Nominated associate justice by Theodore Roosevelt; confirmed 1902 by voice vote; retired 1932. Law professor, Supreme Judicial Court of Massachusetts justice.

Hughes, Charles Evans (1862–1948). New York. Republican. Colgate, Brown, Columbia. Nominated associate justice by William Howard Taft; confirmed 1910 by voice vote; resigned 1916; nominated chief justice by Herbert Hoover; confirmed 1930 by 52–26 vote; retired 1941. New York governor, U.S. secretary of state, Court of International Justice judge.

Hunt, Ward (1810–1886). New York. Republican. Union College. Nominated associate justice by Ulysses S. Grant; confirmed 1872 by voice vote; retired 1882. New York state legislator, mayor of Utica, state court judge.

Iredell, James (1751–1799). North Carolina. Federalist. English schools. Nominated associate justice by George Washington; confirmed 1790 by voice vote; died in office 1799. Customs official, state court judge, state attorney general.

Jackson, Howell Edmunds (1832–1895). Tennessee. Democrat. West Tennessee College, University of Virginia, Cumberland University. Nominated associate justice by Benjamin Harrison; confirmed 1893 by voice vote; died in office 1895. Tennessee state legislator, U.S. senator, federal circuit court judge, federal court of appeals judge.

Jackson, Robert Houghwout (1892–1954). New York. Democrat. Albany Law School. Nominated associate justice by Franklin Roosevelt; confirmed 1941 by voice vote; died in office 1954. Counsel for Internal Revenue Bureau and Securities and Exchange Commission, U.S. solicitor general, U.S. attorney general.

Jay, John (1745–1829). New York. Federalist. King's College (Columbia University). Nominated chief justice by George Washington; confirmed 1789 by voice vote; resigned 1795. Delegate to Continental Congress, chief justice of New York, minister to Spain and Great Britain, U.S. secretary of foreign affairs.

Johnson, Thomas (1732–1819). Maryland. Federalist. Privately educated. Nominated associate justice by George Washington; confirmed 1791 by voice vote; resigned 1793. Delegate to Annapolis Convention and Continental Congress, Maryland governor, state legislator, state court judge.

Johnson, William (1771–1834). South Carolina. Democratic-Republican. Princeton. Nominated associate justice by Thomas Jefferson; confirmed 1804 by voice vote; died in office 1834. South Carolina state legislator, state court judge.

Kagan, Elena (1960–). Massachusetts. Democrat. Princeton, Oxford, Harvard. Nominated associate justice by Barack Obama; confirmed 2010 by 63–37 vote. Law professor and dean, solicitor general of the United States.

Kavanaugh, Brett Michael (1965–). Maryland. Republican. Yale. Nominated associate justice by Donald J. Trump; confirmed 2018 by 50–48 vote. Associate counsel, Office of the Independent Counsel; private practice; federal appeals court judge.

Kennedy, Anthony McLeod (1936–). California. Republican. Stanford, London School of Economics, Harvard. Nominated associate justice by Ronald Reagan; confirmed 1988 by 97–0 vote; retired 2018. Federal appeals court judge.

Lamar, Joseph Rucker (1857–1916). Georgia. Democrat. University of Georgia, Bethany College, Washington and Lee. Nominated associate justice by William Howard Taft; confirmed 1910 by voice vote; died in office 1916. Georgia state legislator, Georgia Supreme Court justice.

Lamar, Lucius Quintus Cincinnatus (1825–1893). Mississippi. Democrat. Emory College. Nominated associate justice by Grover Cleveland; confirmed 1888 by 32–28 vote; died in office 1893. Georgia state legislator, U.S. representative, U.S. senator, U.S. secretary of the interior.

Livingston, Henry Brockholst (1757–1823). New York. Democratic-Republican. Princeton. Nominated associate justice by Thomas Jefferson; confirmed 1806 by voice vote; died in office 1823. New York state legislator, state court judge.

Lurton, Horace Harmon (1844–1914). Tennessee. Democrat. University of Chicago, Cumberland. Nominated associate justice by William Howard Taft; confirmed 1909 by voice vote; died in office 1914. Tennessee Supreme Court justice, federal court of appeals judge.

Marshall, John (1755–1835). Virginia. Federalist. Privately educated, College of William and Mary. Nominated chief justice by John Adams; confirmed 1801 by voice vote; died in office 1835. Virginia state legislator, minister to France, U.S. representative, U.S. secretary of state.

Marshall, Thurgood (1908–1993). New York. Democrat. Lincoln University, Howard University. Nominated associate justice by Lyndon Johnson; confirmed 1967 by 69–11 vote; retired 1991. NAACP Legal Defense Fund chief counsel, federal court of appeals judge, U.S. solicitor general.

Matthews, Stanley (1824–1889). Ohio. Republican. Kenyon College. Nominated associate justice by Rutherford B. Hayes; no Senate action on nomination; renominated associate justice by James A. Garfield; confirmed 1881 by 24–23 vote; died in office 1889. Ohio state legislator, state court judge, U.S. attorney for southern Ohio, U.S. senator.

McKenna, Joseph (1843–1926). California. Republican. Benicia Collegiate Institute. Nominated associate justice by William McKinley; confirmed 1898 by voice vote; retired 1925. California state legislator, U.S. representative, federal court of appeals judge, U.S. attorney general.

McKinley, John (1780–1852). Alabama. Democrat. Self-educated. Nominated associate justice by Martin Van Buren; confirmed 1837 by voice vote; died in office 1852. Alabama state legislator, U.S. senator, U.S. representative.

McLean, John (1785–1861). Ohio. Democrat. Privately educated. Nominated associate justice by Andrew Jackson; confirmed 1829 by voice vote; died in office 1861. U.S. representative, Ohio Supreme Court justice, U.S. General Land Office commissioner, U.S. postmaster general.

McReynolds, James Clark (1862–1946). Tennessee. Democrat. Vanderbilt, University of Virginia. Nominated associate justice by Woodrow Wilson; confirmed 1914 by 44–6 vote; retired 1941. U.S. attorney general.

Miller, Samuel Freeman (1816–1890). Iowa. Republican. Transylvania University. Nominated associate justice by Abraham Lincoln; confirmed 1862 by voice vote; died in office 1890. Medical doctor, private law practice, justice of the peace.

Minton, Sherman (1890–1965). Indiana. Democrat. Indiana University, Yale. Nominated associate justice by Harry Truman; confirmed 1949 by 48–16 vote; retired 1956. U.S. senator, federal court of appeals judge.

Moody, William Henry (1853–1917). Massachusetts. Republican. Harvard. Nominated associate justice by Theodore Roosevelt; confirmed 1906 by voice vote; retired 1910. Massachusetts local district attorney, U.S. representative, secretary of the navy, U.S. attorney general.

Moore, Alfred (1755–1810). North Carolina. Federalist. Privately educated. Nominated associate justice by John Adams; confirmed 1799 by voice vote; resigned 1804. North Carolina legislator, state attorney general, state court judge.

Murphy, William Francis (Frank) (1880–1949). Michigan. Democrat. University of Michigan, London's Inn (England), Trinity College (Ireland). Nominated associate justice by Franklin Roosevelt; confirmed 1940 by voice vote; died in office 1949. Michigan state court judge, mayor of Detroit, governor of the Philippines, Michigan governor, U.S. attorney general.

Nelson, Samuel (1792–1873). New York. Democrat. Middlebury College. Nominated associate justice by John Tyler; confirmed 1845 by voice vote; retired 1872. Presidential elector, state court judge, New York Supreme Court chief justice.

O'Connor, Sandra Day (1930–). Arizona. Republican. Stanford. Nominated associate justice by Ronald Reagan; confirmed 1981 by 99–0 vote; retired 2006. Arizona state legislator, state court judge.

Paterson, William (1745–1806). New Jersey. Federalist. Princeton. Nominated associate justice by George Washington; confirmed 1793 by voice vote; died in office 1806. New Jersey attorney general, delegate to Constitutional Convention, U.S. senator, New Jersey governor.

Peckham, Rufus Wheeler (1838–1909). New York. Democrat. Albany Boys' Academy. Nominated associate justice by Grover Cleveland; confirmed 1895 by voice vote; died in office 1909. New York local district attorney, city attorney, state court judge.

Pitney, Mahlon (1858–1924). New Jersey. Republican. Princeton. Nominated associate justice by William Howard Taft; confirmed 1912 by 50–26 vote; retired 1922. U.S. representative, New Jersey state legislator, New Jersey Supreme Court justice, chancellor of New Jersey.

Powell, Lewis Franklin, Jr. (1907–1998). Virginia. Democrat. Washington and Lee, Harvard. Nominated associate justice by Richard Nixon; confirmed 1971 by 89–1 vote; retired 1987. Private practice, Virginia State Board of Education president, American Bar Association president, American College of Trial Lawyers president.

Reed, Stanley Forman (1884–1980). Kentucky. Democrat. Kentucky Wesleyan, Yale, University of Virginia, Columbia, University of Paris. Nominated associate justice by Franklin Roosevelt; confirmed 1938 by voice vote; retired 1957. Federal Farm Board general counsel, Reconstruction Finance Corporation general counsel, U.S. solicitor general.

Rehnquist, William Hubbs (1924–2005). Arizona. Republican. Stanford, Harvard. Nominated associate justice by Richard Nixon; confirmed 1971 by 68–26 vote; nominated chief justice by Ronald Reagan; confirmed 1986 by 65–33 vote; died in office 2005. Private practice, assistant U.S. attorney general.

Roberts, John G., Jr. (1955–). Maryland. Republican. Harvard. Nominated associate justice by George W. Bush 2005; nomination withdrawn; nominated chief justice by George W. Bush; confirmed 2005 by 78–22 vote. Deputy U.S. solicitor general, federal appeals court judge.

Roberts, Owen Josephus (1875–1955). Pennsylvania. Republican. University of Pennsylvania. Nominated associate justice by Herbert Hoover; confirmed 1930 by voice vote; resigned 1945. Private practice, Pennsylvania local prosecutor, special U.S. attorney.

Rutledge, John (1739–1800). South Carolina. Federalist. Middle Temple (England). Nominated associate justice by George Washington; confirmed 1789 by voice vote; resigned 1791. Nominated chief justice by George Washington August 1795 and served as recess appointment; confirmation denied and service terminated December 1795. South Carolina legislator, state attorney general, governor, chief justice of South Carolina, delegate to Continental Congress and Constitutional Convention.

Rutledge, Wiley Blount (1894–1949). Iowa. Democrat. Maryville College, University of Wisconsin, University of Colorado. Nominated associate justice by Franklin Roosevelt; confirmed 1943 by voice vote; died in office 1949. Law professor, federal court of appeals judge.

Sanford, Edward Terry (1865–1930). Tennessee. Republican. University of Tennessee, Harvard. Nominated associate justice by Warren G. Harding; confirmed 1923 by voice vote; died in office 1930. Assistant U.S. attorney general, federal district court judge.

Scalia, Antonin (1936–2016). Virginia. Republican. Georgetown, Harvard. Nominated associate justice by Ronald Reagan; confirmed 1986 by 98–0 vote; died in office 2016. Assistant U.S. attorney general, law professor, federal court of appeals judge.

Shiras, George, Jr. (1832–1924). Pennsylvania. Republican. Ohio University, Yale. Nominated associate justice by Benjamin Harrison; confirmed 1892 by voice vote; retired 1903. Private practice.

Sotomayor, Sonia (1954–). New York. Democrat. Princeton, Yale. Nominated associate justice by Barack Obama; confirmed 2009 by 68–31 vote. New York state assistant district attorney, federal district court judge, federal appeals court judge.

Souter, David Hackett (1939–). New Hampshire. Republican. Harvard, Oxford. Nominated associate justice by George H. W. Bush; confirmed 1990 by 90–9 vote; retired 2009. New Hampshire attorney general, state court judge, federal appeals court judge.

Stevens, John Paul (1920–2019). Illinois. Republican. University of Chicago, Northwestern. Nominated associate justice by Gerald Ford; confirmed 1975 by 98–0 vote; retired 2010. Federal court of appeals judge.

Stewart, Potter (1915–1985). Ohio. Republican. Yale, Cambridge. Received recess appointment from Dwight Eisenhower to be associate justice in 1958; confirmed 1959 by 70–17 vote; retired 1981. Cincinnati city council member, federal court of appeals judge.

Stone, Harlan Fiske (1872–1946). New York. Republican. Amherst College, Columbia. Nominated associate justice by Calvin Coolidge; confirmed 1925 by 71–6 vote; nominated chief justice by Franklin Roosevelt; confirmed 1941 by voice vote; died in office 1946. Law professor, U.S. attorney general.

Story, Joseph (1779–1845). Massachusetts. Democratic-Republican. Harvard. Nominated associate justice by James Madison; confirmed 1811 by voice vote; died in office 1845. Massachusetts state legislator, U.S. representative.

Strong, William (1808–1895). Pennsylvania. Republican. Yale. Nominated associate justice by Ulysses S. Grant; confirmed 1870 by voice vote; retired 1880. U.S. representative, Pennsylvania Supreme Court justice.

Sutherland, George (1862–1942). Utah. Republican. Brigham Young, University of Michigan. Nominated associate justice by Warren G. Harding; confirmed 1922 by voice vote; retired 1938. Utah state legislator, U.S. representative, U.S. senator.

Swayne, Noah Haynes (1804–1884). Ohio. Republican. Privately educated. Nominated associate justice by Abraham Lincoln; confirmed 1862 by 38–1 vote; retired 1881. Ohio state legislator, local prosecutor, U.S. attorney for Ohio, Columbus city council member.

Taft, William Howard (1857–1930). Connecticut. Republican. Yale, Cincinnati. Nominated chief justice by Warren G. Harding; confirmed 1921 by voice vote; retired 1930. Ohio local prosecutor, state court judge, U.S. solicitor general, federal court of appeals judge, governor of the Philippines, secretary of war, U.S. president.

Taney, Roger Brooke (1777–1864). Maryland. Democrat. Dickinson College. Nominated associate justice by Andrew Jackson; nomination not confirmed 1835; nominated chief justice by Andrew Jackson; confirmed 1836 by 29–15 vote; died in office 1864. Maryland state legislator, state attorney general, acting secretary of war, secretary of the Treasury (nomination later rejected by Senate).

Thomas, Clarence (1948–). Georgia. Republican. Holy Cross, Yale. Nominated associate justice by George H. W. Bush; confirmed 1991 by 52–48 vote. U.S. Department of Education assistant secretary for civil rights, Equal Employment Opportunity Commission chair, federal appeals court judge.

Thompson, Smith (1768–1843). New York. Democratic-Republican. Princeton. Nominated associate justice by James Monroe; confirmed 1823 by voice vote; died in office 1843. New York state legislator, state court judge, U.S. secretary of the navy.

Todd, Thomas (1765–1826). Kentucky. Democratic-Republican. Liberty Hall (Washington and Lee). Nominated associate justice by Thomas Jefferson; confirmed 1807 by voice vote; died in office 1826. Kentucky state court judge, state chief justice.

Trimble, Robert (1776–1828). Kentucky. Democratic-Republican. Kentucky Academy. Nominated associate justice by John Quincy Adams; confirmed 1826 by 27–5 vote; died in office 1828. Kentucky state legislator, state court judge, U.S. attorney, federal district court judge.

Van Devanter, Willis (1859–1941). Wyoming. Republican. Indiana Asbury University, University of Cincinnati. Nominated associate justice by William Howard Taft; confirmed 1910 by voice vote; retired 1937. Cheyenne city attorney, Wyoming Territory legislator, Wyoming Supreme Court justice, assistant U.S. attorney general, federal court of appeals judge.

Vinson, Frederick Moore (1890–1953). Kentucky. Democrat. Centre College. Nominated chief justice by Harry Truman; confirmed 1946 by voice vote; died in office 1953. U.S. representative, federal appeals court judge, director of Office of Economic Stabilization, secretary of the Treasury.

Waite, Morrison Remick (1816–1888). Ohio. Republican. Yale. Nominated chief justice by Ulysses S. Grant; confirmed 1874 by 63–0 vote; died in office 1888. Private practice, Ohio state legislator.

Warren, Earl (1891–1974). California. Republican. University of California. Recess appointment as chief justice by Dwight Eisenhower 1953; confirmed 1954 by voice vote; retired 1969. California local district attorney, state attorney general, governor.

Washington, Bushrod (1762–1829). Virginia. Federalist. College of William and Mary. Nominated associate justice by John Adams; confirmed 1798 by voice vote; died in office 1829. Virginia state legislator.

Wayne, James Moore (1790–1867). Georgia. Democrat. Princeton. Nominated associate justice by Andrew Jackson; confirmed 1835 by voice vote; died in office 1867. Georgia state legislator, mayor of Savannah, state court judge, U.S. representative.

White, Byron Raymond (1917–2000). Colorado. Democrat. University of Colorado, Oxford, Yale. Nominated associate justice by John Kennedy; confirmed 1962 by voice vote; retired 1993. Deputy U.S. attorney general.

White, Edward Douglass (1845–1921). Louisiana. Democrat. Mount St. Mary's College, Georgetown. Nominated associate justice by Grover Cleveland; confirmed 1894 by voice vote; nominated chief justice by William Howard Taft; confirmed 1910 by voice vote; died in office 1921. Louisiana state legislator, Louisiana Supreme Court justice, U.S. senator.

Whittaker, Charles Evans (1901–1973). Missouri. Republican. University of Kansas City. Nominated associate justice by Dwight Eisenhower; confirmed 1957 by voice vote; retired 1962. Federal district court judge, federal appeals court judge.

Wilson, James (1742–1798). Pennsylvania. Federalist. University of St. Andrews (Scotland). Nominated associate justice by George Washington; confirmed 1789 by voice vote; died in office 1798. Delegate to Continental Congress and Constitutional Convention.

Woodbury, Levi (1789–1851). New Hampshire. Democrat. Dartmouth, Tapping Reeve Law School. Nominated associate justice by James Polk; confirmed 1846 by voice vote; died in office 1851. New Hampshire state legislator, state court judge, governor, U.S. senator, secretary of the navy, secretary of the Treasury.

Woods, William B. (1824–1887). Georgia. Republican. Western Reserve College, Yale. Nominated associate justice by Rutherford B. Hayes; confirmed 1880 by 39–8 vote; died in office 1887. Ohio state legislator, Alabama chancellor, federal circuit court judge.

APPENDIX 3
Glossary

A fortiori: "With greater force or reason."

Abstention: A doctrine or policy of the federal courts to refrain from deciding a case so that the issues involved may first be definitively resolved by state courts.

Acquittal: A decision by a court that a person charged with a crime is not guilty.

Advisory opinion: An opinion issued by a court indicating how it would rule on a question of law should such a question come before it in an actual case. Federal courts do not hand down advisory opinions, but some state courts do.

Affidavit: A written statement of facts voluntarily made under oath or affirmation.

Affirm: To uphold a decision of a lower court.

Aggravating circumstances: Conditions that increase the seriousness of a crime but are not a part of its legal definition.

Amicus curiae: "Friend of the court." A person (or group), not a party to a case, who submits views (usually in the form of written briefs) on how the case should be decided.

Ante: "Prior to."

Appeal: The procedure by which a case is taken to a superior court for a review of the lower court's decision.

Appellant: The party dissatisfied with a lower court ruling who appeals the case to a superior court for review.

Appellate jurisdiction: The legal authority of a superior court to review and render judgment on a decision by a lower court.

Appellee: The party usually satisfied with a lower court ruling against whom an appeal is taken.

Arbitrary: Unreasonable; capricious; not done in accordance with established principles.

Arguendo: "In the course of argument."

Arraignment: A formal stage of the criminal process in which the defendant is brought before a judge, is confronted with the charges against him or her, and then enters a plea to those charges.

Arrest: The act of physically taking into custody or otherwise depriving the freedom of a person suspected of violating the law.

Attainder, bill of: A legislative act declaring a person or easily identified group of people guilty of a crime and imposing punishments without the benefit of a trial. Such legislative acts are prohibited by the U.S. Constitution.

Attest: To swear to; to be a witness.

Bail: A security deposit, usually in the form of cash or bond, that allows a person accused of a crime to be released from jail and guarantees the accused's appearance at trial.

Balancing test: A process of judicial decision making in which the court weighs the relative merits of the rights of the individual against the interests of the government.

Bench trial: A trial, without a jury, conducted before a judge.

Bicameral: Having two houses within a legislative body, as does the U.S. Congress.

Bona fide: "Good faith."

Brandeis brief: A legal argument that stresses economic and sociological evidence along with traditional legal authorities. Named for Louis Brandeis, who pioneered the use of such briefs.

Brief: A written argument of law and fact submitted to the court by an attorney representing a party having an interest in a lawsuit.

Case: A legal dispute or controversy brought to a court for resolution.

Case in chief: The primary evidence offered by a party in a court case.

Case law: Law that has evolved from past court decisions, as opposed to law created by legislative acts.

Case or controversy rule: The constitutional requirement that courts may hear only real disputes brought by adverse parties.

Casus faederis: "The case of a treaty." In international law, the particular event contemplated by the treaty or stipulated for, or that comes within the treaty's terms.

Certification: A procedure whereby a lower court requests that a superior court rule on specified legal questions so that the lower court may correctly apply the law.

Certiorari, writ of: The primary method by which the U.S. Supreme Court exercises its discretionary jurisdiction to accept appeals for a full hearing.

Civil law: Law that deals with the private rights of individuals (e.g., property, contracts, negligence), as contrasted with criminal law.

Class action: A lawsuit brought by one or more persons on behalf of themselves and all others similarly situated.

Collateral estoppel: A rule of law that prohibits an already settled issue from being relitigated in another form.

Comity: The principle by which the courts of one jurisdiction give respect and deference to the laws and legal decisions of another jurisdiction.

Common law: Law that has evolved from usage and custom as reflected in the decisions of courts.

Compensatory damages: A monetary award, equivalent to the loss sustained, to be paid to the injured party by the party at fault.

Concurrent powers: Authority that may be exercised by both the state and federal governments.

Concurring opinion: An opinion that agrees with the result reached by the majority but disagrees as to the appropriate rationale for reaching that result.

Confrontation: The right of a criminal defendant to see the testimony of prosecution witnesses and subject such witnesses to cross-examination.

Consent decree: A court-ratified agreement voluntarily reached by parties to settle a lawsuit.

Constitutional court: A court created under authority of Article III of the Constitution. Judges serve for terms of good behavior and are protected against having their salaries reduced by the legislature.

Contempt: A purposeful failure to carry out an order of a court (civil contempt) or a willful display of disrespect for the court (criminal contempt).

Contraband: Articles that are illegal to possess.

Courts of appeals (federal): The intermediate-level appellate courts in the federal system, each of which has jurisdiction over a particular region known as a circuit.

Criminal law: Law governing the relationship between individuals and society. Deals with the enforcement of laws and the punishment of those who, by breaking laws, commit crimes.

Curtilage: The land and outbuildings immediately adjacent to a home and regularly used by its occupants.

De facto: "In fact, actual."

De jure: "By law." As a result of law or official government action.

De minimis: "Small or unimportant." A de minimis issue is an issue too trivial for a court to consider.

De novo: "New, from the beginning."

Declaratory judgment: A court ruling determining a legal right or interpretation of the law, but not imposing any relief or remedy.

Defendant: A party at the trial level being sued in a civil case or charged with a crime in a criminal case.

Demurrer: A motion to dismiss a lawsuit in which the defendant admits to the facts alleged by the plaintiff but contends that those facts are insufficient to justify a legal cause of action.

Deposition: Sworn testimony taken out of court.

Dicta; obiter dicta: Those portions of a judge's opinion that are not essential to deciding the case.

Directed verdict: An action by a judge ordering a jury to return a specified verdict.

Discovery: A pretrial procedure whereby one party to a lawsuit gains access to information or evidence held by the opposing party.

Dissenting opinion: A formal written expression by a judge who disagrees with the result reached by the majority.

Distinguish: A court's explanation of why a particular precedent is inapplicable to the case under consideration.

District courts: The trial courts of general jurisdiction in the federal system.

Diversity jurisdiction: The authority of federal courts to hear cases in which a party from one state is suing a party from another state.

Docket: The schedule of cases to be heard by a court.

Double jeopardy: The trying of a defendant a second time for the same offense. Prohibited by the Fifth Amendment to the Constitution.

Due process: Government procedures that follow principles of essential fairness.

Eminent domain: The authority of the government to take private property for public purpose.

En banc: An appellate court hearing with all the judges of the court participating.

Enjoin: An order from a court requiring a party to do or refrain from doing certain acts.

Entrapment: A situation in which law enforcement officials induce an otherwise innocent person into the commission of a criminal act.

Equity: Law based on principles of fairness rather than strictly applied statutes.

Error, writ of: An order issued by an appeals court commanding a lower court to send up the full record of a case for review.

Exclusionary rule: A principle of law that illegally gathered evidence may not be admitted in court.

Exclusive powers: Powers reserved for either the federal government or the state governments, but not exercised by both.

Ex parte: "By or for one party." A hearing in which only one party to a dispute is present.

Ex post facto law: A criminal law passed by the legislature and made applicable to acts committed prior to passage of the law. Prohibited by the U.S. Constitution.

Ex rel.: "Upon information from." Used to designate a court case instituted by the government but instigated by a private party.

Ex vi termini: "From the force or very meaning of the term or expression."

Federal question: A legal issue based on the U.S. Constitution, laws, or treaties.

Felony: A serious criminal offense, usually punishable by incarceration of one year or more.

Gerrymander: To construct political boundaries for the purpose of giving advantage to a particular political party or interest.

Grand jury: A panel of twelve to twenty-three citizens who review prosecutorial evidence to determine if there are sufficient grounds to issue an indictment binding an individual over for trial on criminal charges.

Guilty verdict: A determination that a person accused of a criminal offense is legally responsible as charged.

Habeas corpus: "You have the body." A writ issued to determine if a person held in custody is being unlawfully detained or imprisoned.

Harmless error: An error occurring in a court proceeding that is insufficient in magnitude to justify the overturning of the court's final determination.

Hearsay: Testimony based not on the personal knowledge of the witness but on what the witness has heard others say.

Immunity: An exemption from prosecution granted in exchange for testimony.

In camera: "In chambers." A legal hearing held in the judge's chambers or otherwise in private.

In forma pauperis: "In the form of a pauper." A special status granted to indigents that allows them to proceed without payment of court fees and to be exempt from certain procedural requirements.

In re: "In the matter of." The designation used in a judicial proceeding in which there are no formal adversaries.

In rem: "Against the thing." A legal action directed against a thing rather than against a person.

Incorporation: The process whereby provisions of the Bill of Rights are declared to be included in the due process guarantee of the Fourteenth Amendment and made applicable to state and local governments.

Indictment: A document issued by a grand jury officially charging an individual with criminal violations and binding the accused over for trial.

Information: A document serving the same purpose as an indictment but issued directly by the prosecutor.

Infra: "Below."

Injunction: A writ prohibiting the person to whom it is directed from committing certain specified acts.

Inter alia: "Among other things."

Interlocutory decree: A provisional action that temporarily settles a legal question pending the final determination of a dispute.

Ipse dixit: "He himself said it." A statement, not supported by proof, that depends for its persuasiveness on the authority of the one who said it.

Judgment of the court: The final ruling of a court, independent of the legal reasoning supporting it.

Judicial activism: A philosophy that courts should not be reluctant to review and, if necessary, strike down legislative and executive actions.

Judicial notice: The recognition by a court of the truth of certain facts without requiring one of the parties to put them into evidence.

Judicial restraint: A philosophy that courts should defer to the legislative and executive branches whenever possible.

Judicial review: The authority of a court to determine the constitutionality of acts committed by the legislative and executive branches and to strike down acts judged to be in violation of the Constitution.

Jurisdiction: The authority of a court to hear and decide legal disputes and to enforce its rulings.

Justiciable: Capable of being heard and decided by a court.

Legislative court: A court created by Congress under authority of Article I of the Constitution to assist in carrying out the powers of the legislature.

Litigant: A party to a lawsuit.

Magistrate: A low-level judge with limited authority.

Mandamus: "We command." A writ issued by a court commanding a public official to carry out a particular act or duty.

Mandatory jurisdiction: A case that a court is required to hear.

Marque and reprisal: An order from the government of one country requesting and legitimating the seizure of persons and property of another country.

Merits: The central issues of a case.

Misdemeanor: A minor criminal act, usually punishable by less than one year of incarceration.

Mistrial: A trial that is prematurely ended by a judge because of procedural irregularities.

Mitigating circumstances: Conditions that lower the moral blame of a person who commits a criminal act but do not justify or excuse the act.

Moot: A question presented in a lawsuit that cannot be answered by a court either because the issue has resolved itself or because conditions have so changed that the court is unable to grant the requested relief.

Motion: A request made to a court for a certain ruling or action.

Natural law: Law considered applicable to all persons in all nations because it is thought to be basic to human nature.

Nolle prosequi: "We will no longer prosecute." The decision of a prosecutor to drop criminal charges against an accused.

Nolo contendere: "I will not contest it." A plea entered by a criminal defendant in which the accused does not admit guilt but submits to sentencing and punishment as if guilty.

Opinion of the court: An opinion announcing the judgment and reasoning of a court endorsed by a majority of the judges participating.

Order: A written command issued by a judge.

Original jurisdiction: The authority of a court to try a case and to decide it, as opposed to appellate jurisdiction.

Per curiam: "By the court." An unsigned or collectively written opinion issued by a court.

Per se: "In and of itself."

Peremptory challenge: An action taken by an attorney to excuse a prospective juror without explaining the reasons for doing so.

Petit jury: A trial court jury to decide criminal or civil cases.

Petitioner: A party seeking relief in court.

Plaintiff: The party who brings a legal action to court for resolution or remedy.

Plea bargain: An arrangement in a criminal case in which the defendant agrees to plead guilty in return for the prosecutor reducing the criminal charges or recommending a lenient sentence.

Plurality opinion: An opinion announcing the judgment of a court with supporting reasoning that is not endorsed by a majority of the justices participating.

Police powers: The power of the state to regulate for the health, safety, morals, and general welfare of its citizens.

Political question: An issue more appropriate for determination by the legislative or executive branch than by the judiciary.

Precedent: A previously decided case that serves as a guide for deciding a current case.

Preemption: A doctrine under which an area of authority previously left to the states is, by act of Congress, brought into the exclusive jurisdiction of the federal government.

Prima facie: "At first sight." A case that is sufficient to prevail unless effectively countered by the opposing side.

Pro bono publico: "For the public good." Usually refers to legal representation done without fee for some charitable or public purpose.

Pro se: "For himself or herself." A person who appears in court without an attorney.

Punitive damages: A monetary award (separate from compensatory damages) imposed by a court for punishment purposes to be paid by the party at fault to the injured party.

Quash: To annul, vacate, or totally do away with.

Ratio decidendi: "The rationale for the decision." A court's primary reasoning for deciding a case the way it did.

Recuse: The action taken by a judge who decides not to participate in a case because of conflict of interest or other disqualifying condition.

Remand: To send a case back to an inferior court for additional action.

Res judicata: "A matter already judged." A legal issue that has been finally settled by a court judgment.

Respondent: The party against whom a legal action is filed.

Reverse: An action by an appellate court setting aside or changing a decision of a lower court.

Ripeness: A condition in which a legal dispute has evolved to the point where the issues it presents can be effectively resolved by a court.

Selective incorporation: The policy of the Supreme Court to decide incorporation issues on a case-by-case, right-by-right basis.

Show cause: A judicial order commanding a party to appear in court and explain why the court should not take a proposed action.

Solicitor general: Justice Department official whose office represents the federal government in all litigation before the U.S. Supreme Court.

Standing; standing to sue: The right of parties to bring legal actions because they are directly affected by the legal issues raised.

Stare decisis: "Let the decision stand." The doctrine that once a legal issue has been settled, it should be followed as precedent in future cases presenting the same question.

State action: An action taken by an agency or official of a state or local government.

Stay: To stop or suspend.

Strict construction: Narrow interpretation of the provisions of laws.

Sub silentio: "Under silence." A court action taken without explicit notice or indication.

Subpoena ad testificandum: An order compelling a person to testify before a court, legislative hearing, or grand jury.

Subpoena duces tecum: An order compelling a person to produce a document or other piece of physical evidence that is relevant to issues pending before a court, legislative hearing, or grand jury.

Summary judgment: A decision by a court made without a full hearing.

Supra: "Above."

Temporary restraining order: A judicial order prohibiting certain challenged actions from being taken prior to a full hearing on the question.

Test: A criterion or set of criteria used by courts to determine if certain legal thresholds have been met or constitutional provisions violated.

Three-judge court: A special federal court made up of appellate and trial court judges, created to expedite the processing of certain issues made eligible for such priority treatment by congressional statute.

Ultra vires: "Beyond the powers." Actions taken that exceed the legal authority of the person or agency performing them.

Usus loquendi: The common usage of ordinary language.

Vacate: To void or rescind.

Vel non: "Or not."

Venireman: A juror.

Venue: The geographical jurisdiction in which a case is heard.

Voir dire: "To speak the truth." The stage of a trial in which potential jurors are questioned to determine their competence to sit in judgment of a case.

Warrant: A judicial order authorizing an arrest or search and seizure.

Writ: A written order of a court commanding the recipient to perform or not to perform certain specified acts.

APPENDIX 4
Online Case Archive List

Space limitations prevent us from including in this volume excerpts of every important Supreme Court decision dealing with the constitutional powers of government and the rights of the people. To make a larger number of decisions available to instructors and students, we have created an online archive of additional case excerpts (*see list below*). In the text, boldface case names indicate that they are in the archive. As the Court hands down new rulings of significance, we will add them to the archive to ensure that the materials available to our readers will always be current. Access the archive at http://edge.sagepub.com/conlaw.

Abrams v. United States (1919)

Adarand Constructors, Inc. v. Peña (1995)

Akron v. Akron Center for Reproductive Health (1983)

A. L. A. Schechter Poultry Corp. v. United States (1935)

Alabama v. Shelton (2002)

Alden v. Maine (1999)

Allegheny, County of v. ACLU (1989)

Allgeyer v. Louisiana (1897)

Allied Structural Steel Co. v. Spannaus (1978)

American Communications Association v. Douds (1950)

Argersinger v. Hamlin (1972)

Arizona Christian School Tuition Organization v. Winn (2011)

Ashcroft v. American Civil Liberties Union [I] (2002)

Ashcroft v. American Civil Liberties Union [II] (2004)

Ashcroft v. Free Speech Coalition (2002)

Ashe v. Swenson (1970)

Associated Press v. Walker (1967)

Bailey v. Drexel Furniture Co. (1922)

Baker v. Carr (1962)

Barenblatt v. United States (1959)

Barron v. Baltimore (1833)

Batson v. Kentucky (1986)

Baze v. Rees (2008)

Berman v. Parker (1954)

Betts v. Brady (1942)

BMW of North America v. Gore (1996)

Board of Education v. Allen (1968)

Board of Regents of the University of Wisconsin System v. Southworth (2000)

Boerne, City of v. Flores (1997)

Bolling v. Sharpe (1954)

Boumediene v. Bush (2008)

Bowers v. Hardwick (1986)

Bowsher v. Synar (1986)

Bradfield v. Roberts (1899)

Bradwell v. Illinois (1873)

Brauneld v. Brown (1961)

Brown v. Board of Education [II] (1955)

Buckley v. Valeo (1976)

Bunting v. Oregon (1917)

Burwell v. Hobby Lobby (2014)

Butler; United States v. (1936)

Butler v. Michigan (1957)

Cantwell v. Connecticut (1940)

Caperton v. A. T. Massey Coal Co. (2009)

Carolene Products Co.; United States v. (1938)

Carter v. Carter Coal Co. (1936)

Causby; United States v. (1946)

Champion v. Ames (1903)

Chandler v. Miller (1997)

Chicago, Burlington & Quincy Railroad v. Chicago (1897)

Chicago, Milwaukee & St. Paul Railway v. Minnesota (1890)

Chisholm v. Georgia (1793)

City of. *See name of city.*

Civil Rights Cases (1883)

Cohens v. Virginia (1821)

Colegrove v. Green (1946)

Coleman v. Miller (1939)

Collector v. Day (1871)

Comstock; United States v. (2010)

Cooper v. Aaron (1958)

County of. *See name of county.*

Crawford v. Washington (2004)

Curtis Publishing Company v. Butts (1967)

Curtiss-Wright Export Corp.; United States v. (1936)

Cutter v. Wilkinson (2005)

Daniel v. Paul (1969)

Davis v. Michigan Department of Treasury (1989)

Davis v. Washington (2006)

De Jonge v. Oregon (1937)

Dennis v. United States (1951)

Dickerson v. United States (2000)

Dolan v. City of Tigard (1994)

Douglas v. California (1963)

Dunn v. Blumstein (1972)

E. C. Knight Co.; United States v. (1895)

Edwards v. Aguillard (1987)

Energy Reserves Group, Inc. v. Kansas Power and Light Co. (1983)

Engel v. Vitale (1962)

Epperson v. Arkansas (1968)

Escobedo v. Illinois (1964)

Ewing v. California (2003)

Ex parte. *See name of party.*

Ferguson v. City of Charleston (2001)

Fisher v. University of Texas (2013)

Flast v. Cohen (1968)

Fletcher v. Peck (1810)

Flowers v. Mississippi (2019)

Frothingham v. Mellon (1923)

Fullilove v. Klutznick (1980)

Furman v. Georgia (1972)

Gamble v. United States (2019)

Gertz v. Welch, Inc. (1974)

Gitlow v. New York (1925)

Goldman v. United States (1942)

Goldman v. Weinberger (1986)

Gomillion v. Lightfoot (1960)

Gonzales v. Carhart (2007)

Gonzales v. O Centro Espirita Beneficente Uniao do Vegetal (2006)

Gonzales v. Oregon (2006)

Graham v. Florida (2010)

Gratz v. Bollinger (2003)

Gravel v. United States (1972)

Graves v. New York ex rel. O'Keefe (1939)

Green v. School Board of New Kent County (1968)

Griffin v. Prince Edward County School Board (1964)

Grutter v. Bollinger (2003)

Hamdan v. Rumsfeld (2006)

Hampton & Co. v. United States (1928)

Harper v. Virginia State Board of Elections (1966)

Harris v. McCrae (1980)

Hawaii Housing Authority v. Midkiff (1984)

Hein v. Freedom from Religion Foundation (2007)

Hirabayashi v. United States (1943)

Holden v. Hardy (1898)

Hollingsworth v. Perry (2013)

Horne v. Department of Agriculture (2015)

Houchins v. KQED, Inc. (1978)

Houston, E. & W. Texas Railway Co. v. United States (1914)

Humphrey's Executor v. United States (1935)

Hurley v. Irish-American Gay, Lesbian and Bisexual Group of Boston (1995)

Hylton v. United States (1796)

Illinois v. Allen (1970)

In re. *See name of party.*

Jacobellis v. Ohio (1964)

Katz v. United States (1967)

Keystone Bituminous Coal Association v. DeBenedictis (1987)

Kidd v. Pearson (1888)

Kilbourn v. Thompson (1881)

Kramer v. Union Free School District (1969)

Lamb's Chapel v. Center Moriches Union Free School District (1993)

Lee; United States v. (1982)

Lee v. Weisman (1992)

Louisiana v. United States (1965)

Lujan v. Defenders of Wildlife (1992)

Luther v. Borden (1849)

Lynch v. Donnelly (1984)

Martin v. Hunter's Lessee (1816)

Maryland v. Craig (1990)

McCleskey v. Kemp (1987)

McConnell v. Federal Election Commission (2003)

McCray v. United States (1904)

McCreary County, Kentucky v. American Civil Liberties Union of Kentucky (2005)

McCutcheon v. Federal Election Commission (2014)

McDonald v. City of Chicago, Illinois (2010)

McGrain v. Daugherty (1927)

McLaurin v. Oklahoma State Regents for Higher Education (1950)

Melendez-Diaz v. Massachusetts (2009)

Memoirs v. Massachusetts (1966)

Metro Broadcasting v. Federal Communications Commission (1990)

Meyer v. Nebraska (1923)

Michael M. v. Superior Court of Sonoma County (1981)

Michigan v. Bryant (2011)

Miller; United States v. (1939)

Milligan, Ex parte (1866)

Minersville School District v. Gobitis (1940)

Mississippi v. Johnson (1867)

Mississippi University for Women v. Hogan (1982)

Missouri ex rel. Gaines v. Canada (1938)

Mistretta v. United States (1989)

Morehead v. New York ex rel. Tipaldo (1936)

Morrison; United States v. (2000)

Morrison v. Olson (1988)

Mugler v. Kansas (1887)

Muller v. Oregon (1908)

Munn v. Illinois (1877)

Myers v. United States (1926)

National Labor Relations Board v. Noel Canning (2014)

National League of Cities v. Usery (1976)

National Treasury Union v. Von Raab (1989)

Neagle, In re (1890)

Nebbia v. New York (1934)

Nevada Department of Human Resources v. Hibbs (2003)

New York v. United States (1992)

New York Times v. United States (1971)

Nixon v. Fitzgerald (1982)

Nollan v. California Coastal Commission (1987)

Northern Securities Co. v. United States (1904)

Northwestern Fertilizing Co. v. Hyde Park (1878)

NOW v. Idaho (1982)

O'Brien; United States v. (1968)

Olmstead v. United States (1928)

Oregon v. Mitchell (1970)

Orr v. Orr (1979)

Palmore v. Sidoti (1984)

Panama Refining Co. v. Ryan (1935)

Paris Adult Theatre I v. Slaton (1973)

Patchak v. Zinke (2018)

Pennell v. City of San Jose (1988)

Pennsylvania Coal Co. v. Mahon (1922)

Planned Parenthood of Central Missouri v. Danforth (1976)

Poe v. Ullman (1961)

Powell v. Alabama (1932)

Powell v. McCormack (1969)

Prince v. Massachusetts (1940)

Prize Cases (1863)

Quirin, Ex parte (1942)

Ramos v. Louisiana (2020)

Randall v. Sorrell (2006)

R.A.V. v. City of St. Paul (1992)

Regents of the University of California v. Bakke (1978)

Reynolds v. United States (1879)

Richmond, City of v. J. A. Croson Co. (1989)

Roberts v. United States Jaycees (1984)

Rosenberger v. University of Virginia (1995)

Ross v. Moffitt (1974)

Rostker v. Goldberg (1981)

Roth v. United States (1957)

Rucho v. Common Cause (2019)

Rumsfeld v. Forum for Academic and Institutional Rights (2006)

Saenz v. Roe (1999)

Salinas v. Texas (2013)

Santa Fe Independent School District v. Doe (2000)

Schneider v. State of New Jersey (Town of Irvington) (1939)

Schuette v. Coalition to Defend Affirmative Action, Integration and Immigration Rights and Fight for Equality by Any Means Necessary (2014)

Scott v. Illinois (1979)

Scott v. Sandford (1857)

Seminole Tribe of Florida v. Florida (1996)

Shapiro v. Thompson (1969)

Shaw v. Reno (1993)

Sheppard v. Maxwell (1966)

Slaughterhouse Cases (1873)

Solem v. Helm (1983)

Solid Waste Agency of Northern Cook County v. United States Army Corps of Engineers (2001)

South Carolina v. Baker (1988)

South Carolina v. Katzenbach (1966)

Springer v. United States (1881)

Stafford v. Wallace (1922)

Stanley v. Georgia (1969)

Stenberg v. Carhart (2000)

Stevens; United States v. (2010)

Stone v. Mississippi (1880)

Stromberg v. California (1931)

Swann v. Charlotte-Mecklenburg County Board of Education (1971)

Sweatt v. Painter (1950)

Swift & Company v. United States (1905)

Tahoe-Sierra Preservation Council v. Tahoe Regional Planning Agency (2002)

Terry v. Ohio (1968)

Thomas v. Collins (1945)

Thomas v. Review Board of Indiana Employment Security Division (1981)

Time, Inc. v. Firestone (1976)

Tinker v. Des Moines (1969)

Train v. City of New York (1975)

Trump v. Hawaii (2018)

Trustees of Dartmouth College v. Woodward (1819)

United Jewish Organizations of Williamsburgh v. Carey (1977)

United States v. *See name of opposing party*.

United States Shoe Corp.; United States v. (1998)

United States Trust Co. v. New Jersey (1977)

Vacco v. Quill (1997)

Vermont v. Brillon (2009)

Vernonia School District 47J v. Acton (1995)

Virginia; United States v. (1996)

Wallace v. Jaffree (1985)

Walz v. Tax Commission of the City of New York (1970)

Ward v. Rock Against Racism (1989)

Washington v. Davis (1976)

Washington v. Glucksberg (1997)

Watkins v. United States (1957)

Wayman v. Southard (1825)

Webster v. Reproductive Health Services (1989)

Weeks v. United States (1914)

Wesberry v. Sanders (1964)

Whitney v. California (1927)

Whole Woman's Health v. Hellerstedt (2016)

Williamson v. Lee Optical Co. (1955)

Windsor; United States v. (2013)

Wisconsin v. Mitchell (1993)

Wisconsin v. Yoder (1972)

Wolf v. Colorado (1949)

Wooley v. Maynard (1977)

Yick Wo v. Hopkins (1886)

Zivotofsky v. Clinton (2012)

Zivotofsky v. Kerry (2015)

Zurcher v. Stanford Daily (1978)

CASE INDEX

CPEARL v. Nyquist, 413 U.S. 756 (1973), 394*n*

Craig v. Boren, 429 U.S. 190 (1976), 615*n*, **651–653**, 654

Crawford v. Marion County Election Board, 553 U.S. 181 (2008), **678–682**

Crawford v. Washington, 541 U.S. 36 (2004), 594–595

Crist v. Bretz, 437 U.S. 28 (1978), 18*t*

Cruikshank, United States v., 92 U.S. 542 (1876), 670

Cruzan v. Director, Missouri Department of Health, 497 U.S. 261 (1990), **539–542**

Curtis Publishing Company v. Butts, 388 U.S. 139 (1967), 472–473

Curtiss-Wright Export Corp., United States v., 299 U.S. 304 (1936), **113–115**, 172

Cutter v. Wilkinson, 544 U.S. 709 (2005), 380

Dames & Moore v. Regan, 453 U.S. 654 (1981), 170*n*

Daniel v. Paul, 395 U.S. 298 (1969), 241*n*

Darby, United States v., 312 U.S. 100 (1941), 78, 200, **234–236**, 238, 241, 243, 244, 245, 249, 258

Davis v. Bandemer, 478 U.S. 109 (1986), 700

Davis v. Federal Election Commission, 554 U.S. 724 (2008), 684

Davis v. Michigan Department of Treasury, 489 U.S. 803 (1989), 274

Davis v. Passman, 442 U.S. 228 (1979), 98*t*

Davis v. United States, 512U.S. 452 (1994), 580*t*

Davis v. Washington, 547 U.S. 813 (2006), 594

Debs v. United States, 249 U.S. 211 (1919), 417*n*

DeFunis v. Odegaard, 416 U.S. 312 (1974), 78

De Jonge v. Oregon, 18*t*

Dennis v. United States, 341 U.S. 494 (1951), 413*n*, 420, 421, 422

Department of Agriculture v. Moreno, 413 U.S. 528 (1973), 617*n*

Diamond v. Charles (1986), 409

Dickerson v. United States, 530 U.S. 428 (2000), 121, 579*n*, 582

District of Columbia v. Heller, 554 U.S. 570 (2008), 32, **493–498**

Dobbins v. Commissioners of Erie County, 16 Pet. 435 (1842), 273*n*, 274

Doe v. Bolton, 410 U.S. 179 (1971), 510, 512, 515, 516, 518

Doe v. McMillan, 412 U.S. 306 (1973), 98*t*

Dolan v. City of Tigard, 512 U.S. 687 (1994), 343

Donovan v. San Antonio Metropolitan Authority, 469 U.S. 528 (1985), 201

Doran v. Salem Inn, Inc., 422 U.S. 922 (1975), 686

Doremus, United States v., 249 U.S. 86 (1919), 276

Douglas v. California, 372 U.S. 353 (1963), 591

Dow Chemical v. United States (1986), 557

Duncan v. Louisiana, 391 U.S. 145 (1968), 18*t*

Dunn v. Blumstein, 405 U.S. 330 (1972), 616, 671

Earley v. DiCenso, 403 U.S. 602 (1971), 391–393

Eastland v. U.S. Servicemen's Fund, 421 U.S. 491 (1975), 98*t*

E. C. Knight Co., United States v., 156 U.S. 1 (1895), 222, 226–227, 233, 249

Eddings v. Oklahoma, 455 U.S. 104 (1982), 598*n*, 608

Edmondson v. Leesville Concrete Co.500 U.S. 614 (1991), 699

Edmond v. United States, 520 U.S. 651 (1997), 139–140

Edwards v. Aguillard, 482 U.S. 578 (1987), 377, 401, 410

Eichman, United States v., 496 U.S. 310 (1990), 455

Eisenstadt v. Baird, 405 U.S. 438 (1972), 510

Elfbrandt v. Russell, 384 U.S. 11 (1966), 422*n*

Elk Grove Unified School District v. Newdow, 542 U.S. 1 (2004), 402

Employment Division, Department of Human Resources of Oregon v. Smith, 494 U.S. 872 (1990), 121, **370–379**

Energy Reserves Group, Inc. v. Kansas Power and Light Co., 459 U.S. 400 (1983), 308

Engel v. Vitale, 370 U.S. 421 (1962), 15, 385–386, 387, 388, 389, 401, 410

Enmund v. Florida, 458 U.S. 782 (1982), 605, 607, 608

Epperson v. Arkansas, 393 U.S. 97 (1968), 410

Escobedo v. Illinois, 378 U.S. 478 (1964), 574–576, 578

Estes v. Texas, 381 U.S. 532 (1965), 593

Eu v. San Francisco County Democratic Central Comm., 489 U.S. 214 (1989), 685

Everson v. Board of Education, 330 U.S. 1 (1947), 18*t*, 382–385, 387, 393, 398

Ewing v. California, 538 U.S. 11 (2003), 596–597

Ex parte Clark, 100 U.S. 399 (1880), 596

Ex parte Jackson, 96 U.S. 727 (1878), 473

Ex parte McCardle, 74 U.S. (7 Wall) 506 (1869), 74–76, 177*n*

Ex parte Milligan, 4 Wall. 2 (1866), 75*n*, 171, 173, 175, 177

Ex parte Quirin, 317 U.S. 1 (1942), 158, 171, 172, 177

Ex parte Siebold, 100 U.S. 371 (1880), 670

Ex parte Yarbrough, 110 U.S. 651 (1994), 670

Ex parte Yerger, 8 Wall. 85 (1869), 76*n*

FCC v. League of Women Voters of California (1984), 425, 447

Federal Communications Commission v. Pacifica Foundation, 438 U.S. 726 (1978), 428*n*, 487

Federal Election Commission v. Massachusetts Citizens for Life, Inc., 479 U.S. 238 (1986), 687

Federal Election Commission v. Wisconsin Right to Life, Inc., 551 U.S. 449 (2007), 685, 686

Feiner v. New York (1951), 424

Ferguson v. Skrupa, 372 U.S. 76 (1963), 503*n*

First English Evangelical Lutheran Church of Glendale v. County of Los Angeles, 482 U.S. 304 (1987), 339

Budget deficit, 134
Buffalo News, 390
Burger Court
    civil liberties-based opinions, 360
    criminal rights interpretations, 552
    death penalty cases, 596–597
    dual versus cooperative federalism, 190*t*
    establishment of religion clause interpretations, 389, 391
    free exercise clause interpretations, 369
    gender discrimination cases, 649–655
    ideological viewpoints, 45, 360
    legislation invalidation, 45
    obscenity standards, 478*t*
    overruled precedents, 39*t*
    right to counsel protections, 591
    school desegregation, 631
Burger, Warren
    appointment as chief justice, 200, 308
    Bakke case, 639
    biographical data, 723
    Bowers opinion, 657*t*
    central holding support, 527*t*
    Chadha opinion, 38, 123–124
    death penalty cases, 597
    on establishment clause jurisprudence, 411–412
    Houchins opinion, 465
    ideological viewpoints, 27, 43, 43*f*, 360, 552, 569
    Lemon/DiCenso opinion, 391–393
    Lynch opinion, 399
    Miller opinion, 476–477
    Nixon opinion, 144–146
    presidential relationships, 49
    prior restraint jurisprudence, 462
    Reed v. Reed opinion, 650
    Roe v. Wade case, 511, 516
    Thomas opinion, 369
    Walz opinion, 389
    Yoder opinion, 368
Burr, Aaron, 66, 129, 141, 150
Burton, Harold, 724
Bush, George H. W.
    civil rights legislation, 619
    Court relationships, 49
    flag desecration ruling, 455
    ideological viewpoints, 360
    judicial appointments, 204, 208, 642
    military actions, 154
    minority-based political representation, 695
    presidential line of succession, 132
Bush, George W.
    election of 2000, 702–707
    executive privilege, 142
    faith-based initiatives, 82

    judicial appointments, 43, 360, 553
    military actions, 154, 171
    use of military tribunals, 176
    war on terrorism, 170–171
Bush, Jeb, 707
Butchers' Benevolent Association, 313
Butler, Pierce
    background, 226
    biographical data, 724
    death, 233
    ideological viewpoints, 223, 325
    Morehead opinion, 326
    New Deal program decisions, 227
    New Deal program opposition, 225
    on states' rights, 63
Butler, William M., 276, *277*
Butterfield, Alexander, 142
Buxton, C. Lee, *503*, 504, 508
Byrnes, James, 49, 724

Calhoun, John C., 194
California Coastal Commission, 339
California Communist Labor Party, 418
California Democratic Party, 684
Campaign contributions and expenditure regulations, 682–689
Campbell, John A., 313, 724
Capital punishment
    Atkins case, 603–609
    constitutionality challenges, 596–602
    fair trial challenges, 603
    framers' intent, 596, 599
    functional role, 603
    Furman case, 597
    Gregg aftermath, 603, 604
    Gregg case, 597–603
    intellectually disabled offenders, 603–609
    judicial ideological impacts, 43
    South African ruling, 41
Capitation tax, 264, 265, 267, 282
Cardozo, Benjamin
    biographical data, 724
    Carter dissent, 243
    death, 233
    Defore opinion, 565, 567, 568
    ideological viewpoints, 223
    New Deal program decisions, 225, 227, 230
    Palko opinion, 421
    on public opinion impact, 48
Carpenter, Dale, 533
Carta, Magna, 311
Carter, Jimmy, 122, 123, 170*n*, 204
Case citations, 51
Casper, Jonathan, 48

Exceptions clause, 76

Excessive bail and monetary fines, 549, 550f, 595, 605

Excise taxes, 263, 265, 269, 272t, 275–276, 492–493

Exclusionary rule
    basic concepts, 564
    cost-benefit analyses, 40, 572
    exceptions, 40, 573t
    Fourteenth Amendment interpretations, 18t
    illegal searches and seizures, 564–565
    Leon case, 570–572
    Mapp case, 18t, 40, 566–568, 569
    self-incrimination protections, 568
    Wolf case, 565

Executive branch
    congressional authority, 121–122
    constitutional amendments, 14
    constitutional powers, 7, 8f, 57, 58, 59–60, 62, 131–133, 169
    constitutional war-making powers, 153
    Court relationships, 49
    delegation of powers principle, 225
    domestic policies, 133–135
    enforcement of the law, 133
    foreign policy, 169–170
    formal powers, 131, 169
    Roosevelt administration, 224
    see also Presidency

Executive Committee of Southern Cotton Manufacturers, 220, 222

Executive privilege, 141–146

Expressive association
    constitutional protections, 439
    membership restrictions, 438–444
    Warren Court era, 422

Extraconstitutional powers, 89, 116

Fair Labor Standards Act (1938, FLSA), 189, 200, 201, 202, 203, 210, 234, 244, 618

Fair market value, 335

Fairness guarantees, 616–617

Fair trials, 589, 591–593

Fanny Hill (Cleland), 475

Farmers' Loan & Trust Company, 268

FBI agents
    GPS tracking device, 559

Federal budget deficit, 134

Federal Child Labor Act (1916), 220

Federal Communications Commission (FCC), 224

Federal Election Campaign Act (1971), 682

Federal Election Campaign Act (1974), 682

Federal Election Commission (FEC), 684, 689

Federal fiscal/taxation authority, 263–264, 265–267

Federal Government, 430

Federalism
    allocation of government powers, 183–187, 185t
    balance of power controversy, 185–187
    basic concepts, 183–184
    commercial regulation, 214–222
    constitutional powers, 7–9, 121
    doctrinal cycles, 191t, 190
    dual versus cooperative federalism, 189–190, 190t, 197–210
    framers' vision, 184–185
    post-Civil War era, 197–200
    taxation and expenditures, 191–193, 665

Federalist Papers, 12
    No. 3, 261
    No. 7, 294
    No. 15, 206
    No. 21, 265
    No. 22, 214
    No. 27, 206
    No. 33, 207
    No. 36, 206
    No. 39, 186, 202, 206
    No. 42, 214
    No. 44, 294, 306
    No. 45, 112, 185, 206, 219
    No. 51, 133, 207
    No. 70, 207
    No. 77, 140
    No. 78, 50, 62, 203, 536
    No. 81, 209

Federalist Party, 414

Federalists
    bill of rights debate, 13
    congressional powers, 98, 99
    constitutional ratification, 12, 13
    federal court system, 64–65
    presidential election of 1800, 66–67
    taxation authority, 265–267

Federal judiciary system
    congressional authority, 121–122
    constitutional powers, 7, 8f, 57, 58, 59–60, 61, 82
    constitutional war-making role, 155
    establishment, 61–66
    jurisdiction, 63, 63–64, 74
    justiciability, 76–79
    organizational structure, 23f
    power constraints, 8f, 57, 73–82
    reorganization proposal, 228, 232, 276
    selection process, 59, 62
    standing to sue, 80–82, 136
    vesting clauses, 58
    see also Article III; Judiciary Act (1789)

Federal Reserve System, 99, 106

Federal supremacy
  see National supremacy
Federal Trade Commission (FTC), 225
Federal Water Pollution Control Act Amendments
    (1972), 133
Feder, Jody, 619
Feiner, Irving, 424
Field, Stephen J., 133, 157, 269, 314, 315, 418, 648, 724
Fifteenth Amendment (U.S. Constitution), 719
  basic principles, 620, 622
  congressional enforcement, 672
  redistricting effects, 695
  voting rights, 112, 197, 624, 669–671, 676
Fifth Amendment (U.S. Constitution), 717
  affirmative action programs, 636–647
  constitutional provisions, 18t, 599
  double jeopardy clause, 549, 609
  fairness guarantees, 616–617
  invidious discriminatory practices, 239, 617
  property rights protection, 292, 333–350, 351, 352, 354
  right to privacy protections, 507t
  same-sex marriage protections, 532
  self-incrimination protections, 18t, 464, 501, 549, 550f,
      568, 572–583
  state regulatory statutes, 309
  substantive due process doctrine, 311, 314,
      323–325, 501
  takings clause, 333–334, 337
Filburn, Roscoe, 236, *237*, 238, 245
Financial Times, 351
FindLaw, 52
Firearm possession, 244–246, 276, 491–499
  see also Handgun possession; Second Amendment
    (U.S. Constitution)
First Amendment (U.S. Constitution), 717
  campaign finance reform, 684–689
  civil liberties-based opinions, 360
  constitutional provisions, 18t
  discrimination, essence of viewpoint, 431
  establishment clause, 82, 381–412
  Free Speech Clause, 430
  Fourteenth Amendment interpretations, 383, 395, 397
  framers' intent, 34, 186, 362, 381, 413, 457
  freedom of expression, 413, 418, 469–471, 475–478
  freedom of the press, 458–488
  free exercise clause, 81, 121, 362–381
  interpretive challenges, 61, 81, 359
  judicial attitude impacts, 42
  literalist perspective, 36–37
  neutrality principle, 432
  preferred freedoms doctrine, 419–421
  right to privacy protections, 504–507, 507t
  separation of church and state, 381–382, 383–388,
      389–412

symbolic speech protections, 450–455
unprotected expression, 34, 466–480
vote shifts, 46–47
Walker Court, 431
First Amendment protection, 37, 362, 442, 447, 449,
    451, 461, 463, 466, 467, 473, 475, 477, 478, 479, 480,
    481, 484, 485
Fisher, Abigail Noel, 643, *644*
Fitzgerald, A. Ernest, 147
Fitzsimmons, Morris, 87
Flag desecration
  proposed constitutional amendments, 15, 455
  symbolic speech protections, 450–455
Flag Protection Act (1989), 455
Flag salute cases, 365
Florida Supreme Court, 702–707
Footnote Four, 420, 421, 632, 633
Ford, Gerald R., 131, 150, 360
Fordney-McCumber Act (1922), 117
Foreign affairs authority, 115
Foreign commerce regulation, 214, 216–218
Foreign policy, 152–153, 155, 169–170
Foreign Relations Authorization Act (2002), 170
Formal declaration of war, 154
Fortas, Abe, 49, 385, 552, 588, 725
Forte, David F., 72
Fort Laramie Treaty (1868), 335n
Four Horsemen of the Apocalypse, 225, 228, 233, 325
Fourteenth Amendment (U.S. Constitution), 718–719
  affirmative action programs, 636–647
  anti-miscegenation laws, 635, 636
  basic principles, 614–617
  Carpenter case, 558–562
  citizenship ruling, 197, 613–614
  congressional enforcement, 112, 209, 239,
      617–619, 670
  congressional membership qualifications, 88–89
  constitutional provisions, 599, 614, 623
  educational systems, 626–630, 638–640
  establishment of religion clause interpretations, 383,
      384, 392, 395, 397
  First Amendment principles, 18t, 383, 395, 397
  free exercise clause interpretations, 363
  historical perspective, 622
  invalidation of *Scott v. Sandford* (1857), 16t, 197
  invidious discriminatory practices, 614–617, 649–650,
      662–663
  Plessy case, 623–625
  population-based legislative apportionment, 693–694
  private discriminatory behavior regulation, 239, 616,
      617, 622
  private sexual behavior protections, 527, 529, 531,
      657t, 658
  privileges or immunities clause, 313, 613–614, 622, 623

Lemon test, 391–394, 399, 401, 405, 411
Lesbian rights
  see Gay rights; Sexual orientation
Levy, Robert, 494
Lewinsky, Monica, 151
LexisNexis, 52
Libel
  First Amendment protections, 466–467, 503
  Hutchinson v. Proxmire case, 97, 98*t*
  McCardle case, 74
  Near v. Minnesota case, 458–460
  seditious libel, 419, 467, 471
  Sullivan case, 467–471
Liberal judicial attitudes, 42–46, 43*f*, 48
  see also specific Court; specific justice
Liberty, 501
Life Legal Defense Foundation, 50
Limited jurisdiction courts, 23*f*
Lincoln, Abraham, 75, 130*n*, 155, 195*t*, 197, 362, 414
Line-item veto, 135–138
Line Item Veto Act (1996), 135–137
Line of succession, 130–131
Liptak, Adam, 533
Literalism, 37
Lithwick, Dahlia, 533
Livingston-Fulton steamship transportation
    monopoly, 215
Livingston, Henry B., 726
Locke, John, 13
Los Angeles Times, 151, 351, 517, 569
Loss of liberty rule, 589
Lotteries, 303–304, 306
Lottery ticket commerce, 219, 282, 564
Louisville Courier-Journal, 463, 466
Loving, Richard and Mildred, 635, 637
Lower federal courts, 62–64, 74
Low-Level Radioactive Waste Policy Act (1980), 204
Loyalty oaths, 89
Lurton, Horace H., 198–199, 726
Lyon, Matthew, 414

Madison, James
  on advisory opinions, 76
  bill of rights debate, 13, 556
  on commercial regulation, 214
  on the constitutional contract, 184
  constitutional conventions, 5, 36
  on contractual agreements, 294
  convention note-taking, 36
  council of revision proposal, 63
  on delegated powers, 112, 185, 219
  on executive powers, 133
  Federalist Papers, 12
  on federal spending power, 264

  on governmental power, 58
  on individual rights, 291
  law violate the Constitution, 414
  on presidential appointment and removal authority, 140
  property rights protection, 333
  as secretary of state, 67, 72
  Sedition Act, critical of, 414
  on state sovereignty, 202, 206
  support of congressional veto authority, 87
  on taxation authority, 276
Magna Carta, 13
Magrath, C. Peter, 297
Majority-minority districts, 695–700, 701
Malapportioned congressional districts, 690–700
Malbin, Michael J., *701*
Mann Act (1910), 220
Mann, Thomas E., *701*
Manufacturing industry regulation, 222, 249
Mapp, Dollree, 565, *567*, 569
Marbury, William, 67, *67*, 72
Marshall Court
  contract clause interpretations, 295–298
  dual versus cooperative federalism, 190*t*
  nation-state relations, 191–194, 197
  use of the contract clause, 292
Marshall, John
  Barron opinion, 334
  biographical data, 726
  as chief justice, 67, 72
  Cohens opinion, 209
  contract clause decisions, 296, 298
  death, 298
  economic viewpoints, 295
  on executive immunity, 150
  Fletcher opinion, 296
  Gibbons opinion, 215–218, 238, 240, 244, 249
  implied powers doctrine, 98
  intergovernmental tax immunity doctrine, 273
  judiciary veto power, 63
  Marbury opinion, 66–73, 79
  McCulloch opinion, 98, 102–105, 106, 191–193, 255, 273
  on nation-state relations, 191–193
  on political questions and nonjusticiability, 79
  single opinion use, 267*n*
  structuralist perspective, 38
  on the takings clause, 334
  on taxation authority, 273, 275
  United States case, 352–354
  Wayman opinion, 116
Marshall, Thurgood
  biographical data, 726
  central holding support, 527*t*
  on constitutional limitations, 6, 35–36, 621
  death penalty cases, 597

desegregation litigation, 625–626, 627
on equal protection clause tests, 616
Gregg dissent, 602
ideological viewpoints, 204
interest group relationships, 51
leadership of Legal Defense Fund, 625–626
obscene expression jurisprudence, 478
prior restraint jurisprudence, 461–462
retirement, 339, 642
Rodriguez dissent, 665–666
Martial law, 156, 162
Martin, Douglas, 533
Maryland law, 429
Mason, George, 9
Massachusetts Act, 447
Massachusetts Reproductive Health Care Facilities Act, 449
Matthews, Stanley, 726
McCarthy, Joseph, 110, 420, 422
McConnell, Mitch, 684
McCord, James, Jr., 142
McCorvey, Norma, 78, 510, 516, 517
McCullen, Eleanor, *448*
sidewalk abortion counsellor, 447
McCulloch, James, 102, 105, 106, 191
McHenry, James, 87
McKenna, Joseph, 241, 726
McKinley, John, 726
McKinley, William, 130*n*
McKinney, Cynthia, 696
McLean, John, 241, 726
McReynolds, James C.
background, 226
biographical data, 726
ideological viewpoints, 223, 325
Miller opinion, 493
New Deal program opposition, 225, 227*t*
NLRB v. Jones & Laughlin Steel dissent, 232
retirement, 233
Medicaid expansion and funding, 208, 254, 280–287, 518*n*, 518–519
Medical marijuana use, 248, 250–254
Meese, Edwin, 35
Membership restrictions, 439–444
Memoirs of a Woman of Pleasure/Fanny Hill (Cleland), 475
Mencken, H. L., 473, *474*
Merchant, Nomaan, 444
Mere designation of office theory, 132, 169
Mexican War, 154
Middle East policy, 169–170
Midnight appointments, 66
Military Commissions Act (2006), 177
Military draft, 415, 450–451, 655
Military tribunals, 157–158, 173, 176
Milk Control Board, 326

Mill, John Stuart, 414
Miller, Samuel, 157, 313, 315, 726
Miller test, 478, 479
Milligan, Lambdin P., 156–157, 158
Minimum voting age, 670
Minimum wage enforcement
Adkins case, 323–325
constitutional challenges, 292
Darby case, 200, 234–236
Garcia case, 201–203
Morehead case, 326
West Coast Hotel case, 326–329
Ministerial versus executive actions, 147
Minnesota Mortgage Moratorium Act, 305, 307
Minority groups
affirmative action programs, 636–647
congressional representation, 701
political representation, 695–700, 701
Minority set-aside programs, 638, 641
Minton, Sherman, 169, 726
Miranda, Ernesto, 575, *576*, 579
Miranda warnings, 579, 580*t*, 581–583
Miscegenation laws, 635, 637
Mississippi Agricultural, Educational, and Manufacturing Aid Society, 304
Missouri Compromise (1820), 196–197, 537
Missouri Supreme Court, 196
Mobbs Declaration, 172
Mondale, Walter, 588
Money, 351
Monroe, James, 150
Monson, Diane, *248*, 250–251, 253
Montesquieu, Charles de, 8, 57
Moody, William H., 726–727
Moore, Alfred, 727
Mootness, 78
Morality legislation, 219, 241, 303–304, 306
Mormon Church, 362
Morrill Anti-Bigamy Act (1862), 362
Mortgage contract protections, 304–308
Municipal Bankruptcy Act (1934), 227
Murphy, William F. (Frank)
biographical data, 727
Korematsu dissent, 159, 161–162
Murray, Madalyn
see O'Hair, Madalyn Murray
Murray, William J., III, 387, 390
Muskrat, David, 77

NARAL Pro-Choice America, 509–510
National Abortion Rights Action League, 509
National Association for the Advancement of Colored People (NAACP) Legal Defense Fund, 50, 597, 625, 627, *628*

Obama, Barack
    election campaign reform, 689
    enemy combatant, 177
    executive privilege, 142
    judicial appointments, 43, 360, 553
Obiter dicta, 39
O'Brien, David, 450, *451*
Obscenity, 37, 61, 473–480, 478*t*, 481
O'Connor, Sandra Day
    Akron dissent, 519–520, 525
    biographical data, 727
    campaign finance reform cases, 684
    Casey opinion, 521–524
    central holding support, 527*t*
    Clinton v. New York case, 137–138
    Craig opinion, 593
    Cruzan opinion, 541–542
    endorsement standard, 411
    Ewing opinion, 596
    Garcia dissent, 203–204
    Goldman dissent, 370
    Gonzales dissent, 252–253
    Hamdi opinion, 172–174
    ideological viewpoints, 519, 642
    Kelo dissent, 349–350
    Lawrence opinion, 530
    legislative redistricting jurisprudence, 700
    New York opinion, 204–205
    Seibert dissent, 583
    Smith opinion, 373–374
    South Carolina v. Baker dissent, 274
    South Dakota dissent, 279
    on use of racial preference, 642
    Zelman opinion, 397–398
Offensive speech, 427–433
Office of Faith-Based and Community Initiatives, 82
Ogden, Aaron, 215, *215*
O'Hair, Madalyn Murray, 387, 390
Ohio act, 422
Ohio Criminal Syndicalism Statute, 422
Oil industry regulation, 225
Olson, Floyd B., *459*
Olson, Theodore B., 139, 707
Omaha World-Herald, 151, 517
One-shotters, 51
"On Liberty" (Mill), 414
On-the-scene statements, 594
Opinion assignment and circulation, 30–31
Opinion revisions, 47
Oral arguments, 29–30
Organic Act (1801), 66–67
Organized labor, 219, 230, 683
Originalism, 32–36, 33*t*
Original jurisdiction, 23, 64, 74

Ornstein, Norman J., 701
Out-of-court testimony, 594
Overbreadth, 427
Overruled precedents, 39, 39*t*
The Oxford Companion to the Supreme Court of the United States, 53
Oyez Project, xviii, 53

Paris Adult Theatre, 478
Parmenter, James, 473
Parochial schools
    see Educational policies and services
Partisan gerrymandering, 700
Partisan politics, 48–49
Patent and Trademark Office (PTO), 430, 432
Patently offensive display provision, 485–486, 487
Paterson, William, 267, 727
Patient Protection and Affordable Care Act (2010), 29, 50, 208, 254–261, 281–287, 380
Patriotism, 415, 418–419
PBS Newshour, 637
Peckham, Rufus, 316, 318–320, 727
Penn Central Transportation Company, 336, 338
Pentagon Papers, 96, 460, 462
Per curiam opinion, 422–423, 703–705
Peremptory challenges, 592
Perlman, Philip B., *164*
Perry, Rick, 400
Persian Gulf War, 154
Personal privacy rights
    abortion and reproductive rights, 330, 501, 503, 509–526
    constitutional protections, 501, 504–506, 508
    Griswold case, 18*t*, 47, 330, 501, 504–507, 508, 510, 526
    right-to-die, 539–544
    same-sex marriage, 531–539
    search and seizure rights, 557, 566–568
    sexual activity, 526–531, 533, 656, 657*t*
    substantive due process, 330, 501, 502
Personal property protections, 343
    see also Takings clause
Peyote use, 370–371, 374
Physical evidence, 555
Physical penetration rule, 557
Pinckney, Charles, 9
Pinkney, William, 102
Pitney, Mahlon, 727
Plain view searches, 563*t*
Planned Parenthood, 50, 446–448, 504, 508, 518, 521
Plea bargaining, 549, 570, 591
Pledge of Allegiance, 364
Plessy, Homer Adolph, 623
Pocket veto, 135

on taxpayer standing for litigation, 80
West Coast Hotel dissent, 328–329
Swayne, Noah H., 157, 303, 648, 728
Sweeping clause, 97
Symbolic speech, 450–452
Syndicalism laws, 418–419, 422

Taft-Hartley Act (1947), 164
Taft, William Howard
    Adkins dissent, 324
    biographical data, 728
    on executive powers, 132
    Hampton opinion, 117, 118
    ideological viewpoints, 223
    judicial appointments, 226
    Myers opinion, 141
    on regulatory taxation, 275
Take care clause, 169
Takings clause
    basic concepts, 335–336, 339
    Court interpretations, 335–350, 351
    historical perspective, 333–335
    property rights protection, 291, 334–350, 351
    public use requirement, 344–350, 351
    state regulatory statutes, 309
Taliban, 171, 172–173
Taney Court
    contract clause interpretations, 292, 298–303
    dual versus cooperative federalism, 190t, 197–198, 200
    ideological viewpoints, 298, 300
    Scott v. Sandford case, 196–198
    use of the contract clause, 292
Taney, Roger B.
    biographical data, 728
    on black inferiority, 622
    Charles River Bridge opinion, 300–302
    ideological viewpoints, 194–195, 199, 298
    on political questions, 79
    Scott opinion, 196–197, 622
Targeted Regulation of Abortion Providers (TRAP) laws, 525, 526
Tariff powers, 117, 194, 268, 272
Taxation and spending powers
    direct taxation, 264, 265–271, 282
    enumerated powers, 263
    federal fiscal/taxation authority, 263–264, 265–269
    firearm registration, 492
    general welfare, 276–287
    geographical uniformity, 265, 266
    historical perspective, 263
    income taxes, 77, 267–271, 272t
    individual mandate requirement, 254–261, 281–287
    intergovernmental immunity, 273–275
    laissez-faire courts, 312t

nation-state relations, 191–194, 664
    population-based apportionment, 265–271, 282
    as a regulatory power, 275–276, 282
    state fiscal/taxation authority, 264–265, 269, 273–275, 277–280, 283
Taxation/fiscal authority, 87, 190–194, 263–265
Taxpayer lawsuits, 80–82
Taxpayer Relief Act (1997), 136
Teapot Dome scandal, 108, 109
Telecommunications industry regulation legislation
    see Internet
Ten Commandments display, 400–406, *402*
Tennessee Valley Authority (TVA), 225
Tenth Amendment (U.S. Constitution), 718
    basic principles, 185–187
    child labor regulation, 233
    commerce regulation, 217, 218, 222, 230, 236
    congressional qualifications, 92, 95
    constitutional violations, 243n, 247
    dual versus cooperative federalism, 189, 190t, 190, 200–201, 213
    election regulation, 674
    exercise of delegated powers, 208, 218
    Garcia case, 201–204
    Hammer case, 220–222, 312t
    laissez-faire courts, 312t
    Marshall's interpretation, 191–194, 218
    McCulloch case, 191–194
    Medicaid expansion and funding, 208
    New Deal program decisions, 227
    state-delegated powers, 112, 115, 185–187, 206–208, 232, 236, 260, 507
    state election regulations, 674
    Stewart's interpretation, 200
    Stone's interpretation, 200, 236, 239
    Taney's interpretation, 195, 196
    see also State powers; States' rights; Term limits
Tenure of Office Act (1867), 140
Term limits
    constitutional provisions, 59, 91–92
    Court decision, 91–95
    presidency, 130
Terrorism, 170–178
Testimonial evidence, 555, 572–583, 593–595
Test Oath Law (1862), 89
Textualism, 33t, 36–38
Third Amendment (U.S. Constitution), 504, 507t, 717
Thirteenth Amendment (U.S. Constitution), 16t, 197, 416, 613, 617, 622, 624, 718
Thomas, Clarence
    Ashcroft I opinion, 488
    biographical data, 720
    Brown dissent, 483, 485
    Casey opinion and dissent, 524–525

Flast opinion, 81
ideological viewpoints, 27, 42, 43f, 360
on justiciability, 76
Loving opinion, 635–636
Miranda opinion, 576–578
O'Brien opinion, 450
on oral arguments, 29
Powell opinion, 90
on reapportionment decisions, 695
retirement, 308
Reynolds opinion, 692–694
right to privacy protections, 507t, 507
on taxpayer standing for litigation, 81
voting rights cases, 672
Washington, Bushrod, 729
Washington, George, 14, 76–77, 99, 128, 130, 141
Washington Post, 390, 460, 569, 575, 604, 637, 641
Watergate scandal, 142, 146, 458
Water Resources Development Act (1986), 264
Wayman, 116
Wayne, James, 157, 196, 729
Webster, Daniel, 102, 216, 218, 298, 299, 300
Webster's Third New International Dictionary, 252
Weddington, Sarah, 29, 511
Westboro Baptist Church, 428, *428*
Westlaw, 52
White, Byron R.
    biographical data, 729
    Bowers opinion, 526
    Branzburg opinion, 464–465
    Casey opinion and dissent, 524–525
    central holding support, 527t
    Chadha dissent, 38, 124–125
    death penalty cases, 597
    on equal protection clause tests, 616
    on the exclusionary rule, 40, 570–571
    Gravel opinion, 96
    Gregg opinion, 601–602
    ideological viewpoints, 204
    Leon opinion, 40, 570–571
    Miranda dissent, 578
    opinion assignment, 31
    oral argument process, 29
    prior restraint jurisprudence, 462
    right to privacy protections, 507t, 507
    Roe v. Wade dissent, 515, 516

United Jewish Organizations opinion, 695
Washington v. Davis opinion, 636
White, Edward D., 275, 415, 729
White House Office of Faith-Based and Community Initiatives, 82
Whitener, Carolyn, *651*, *652*, 655
Whitney, Charlotte, 418–419, *419*
Whittaker, Charles, 111, 729
Whittemore, Benjamin F., 89t
Williams, George, 106
Wilson-Gorman Tariff Act (1894), 268
Wilson, James, 267n, 660, 729
Wilson, Woodrow, 108, 141, 226, 323, 417
Wimpy, John A., 89t
Windsor, Edith, 28
Wiretapping jurisprudence, 501, 556–557
Wirt, William, 216
Witnesses
    adverse witnesses, 18t
    compulsory processes, 18t
    right to confront witnesses, 18t, 550f, 593–595
Witness rights and protection, 108–111
Women's rights movement, 649, 650
    see also Gender discrimination
Women's Rights Project, 50
Woodbury, Levi, 729
Woods, William B., 729
Woodward, William, 298
Worker exploitation, 220, 228, 317–320, 502–503
World War I, 154, 415, 418–419
World War II, 154
    presidential powers, 157–164
Wright, Susan Webber, 151
Writ of certiorari, 24–25, 26
Writ of habeas corpus, 74–75, 156, 157, 158, 173, 174, 176–177
Writs of assistance, 555
Writs of certification, 24
Writs of mandamus, 64, 67
Written arguments (briefs), 27

Yazoo River land fraud case, 295–296, 297
Young, Clement C., 419
Young, John D., 89t

Zalman, Marvin, 583
Zoning laws, 255, 335, 337–338

ABOUT THE AUTHORS

Lee Epstein (PhD, Emory University) is the Ethan A. H. Shepley Distinguished University Professor at Washington University in St. Louis. She is a fellow of the American Academy of Arts and Sciences and the American Academy of Political and Social Science. She is author, coauthor, and/or editor of eighteen books, including *The Supreme Court Compendium: Data, Decisions, and Developments*, 6th Edition, with Jeffrey A. Segal, Harold J. Spaeth, and Thomas G. Walker and *The Choices Justices Make* with Jack Knight, which won the C. Herman Pritchett Award for the best book on law and courts. Her most recent books are *The Behavior of Federal Judges* with William M. Landes and Richard A. Posner, *An Introduction to Empirical Legal Research* with Andrew D. Martin, and *The Oxford Handbook on U.S. Judicial Behavior* with Stefanie A. Lindquist.

Kevin T. McGuire (PhD, The Ohio State University) is Professor of Political Science at the University of North Carolina at Chapel Hill. A former Fulbright Scholar at Trinity College, Dublin, he is the author of *Understanding the U.S. Supreme Court: Cases and Controversies* and *The Supreme Court Bar: Legal Elites in the Washington Community*. He is the editor of *New Directions in Judicial Politics*, and coeditor, with Kermit L. Hall, of *Institutions of American Democracy: The Judiciary*.

Thomas G. Walker (PhD, University of Kentucky) is the Goodrich C. White Professor Emeritus at Emory University, where he won several teaching awards for his courses on constitutional law and the judicial process. His book *A Court Divided*, written with Deborah J. Barrow, won the prestigious V. O. Key Award for the best book on Southern politics. He is the author of *Eligible for Execution* and coauthor of *The Supreme Court Compendium: Data, Decisions, and Developments*, 6th Edition, with Lee Epstein, Jeffrey A. Segal, and Harold J. Spaeth.